**CourseMate** **Engaging. Trackable. Affordable.**

CourseMate brings course concepts to life with interactive learning, study, and exam preparation tools that support CMPTR.

INCLUDES:
Integrated eBook, **interactive teaching and learning tools,** and **Engagement Tracker**, a first-of-its-kind tool that monitors student engagement in the course.

ON THE WEB

CMPTR
Are you in?

ONLINE RESOURCES INCLUDED!

FOR INSTRUCTORS:
- First Day Class Instructions
- Custom Options through 4LTR+ Program
- Annotated Solution Files
- Instructor's Manual
- Test Bank
- PowerPoint® Slides
- Instructor Prep Cards
- Engagement Tracker
- Easy Access to SAM Central

FOR STUDENTS:
- Interactive eBook
- Auto-Graded Quizzes
- Printable and Audio Flashcards
- Games: Memory & Beat the Clock
- Additional Assignments
- Videos
- Interactive Infographics

Students sign in at **login.cengagebrain.com**

COURSE TECHNOLOGY
CENGAGE Learning™

CMPTR

Vice President, Publisher: Nicole Jones Pinard

Executive Editor: Marie L. Lee

Acquisitions Editor: Brandi Shailer

Senior Product Manager: Kathy Finnegan

Product Manager: Leigh Hefferon

Associate Product Manager: Julia Leroux-Lindsey

Editorial Assistant: Jacqueline Lacaire

Vice President, Marketing: Cheryl Costantini

Senior Marketing Manager: Ryan DeGrote

Marketing Coordinator: Kristen Panciocco

Developmental Editors: Katherine T. Pinard and
Robin M. Romer

Senior Content Project Manager:
Jennifer Goguen McGrail

Composition: MPS Content Services

Art Director: Marissa Falco

Cover Designer: Studio Montage

Cover Art: © Image Source/Getty Images

Proofreader: Suzanne Huizenga

Indexer: Rich Carlson

For product information and technology assistance, contact us at
Cengage Learning Customer & Sales Support, 1-800-354-9706.

For permission to use material from this text or product,
submit all requests online at **www.cengage.com/permissions**.
Further permissions questions can be e-mailed to
permissionrequest@cengage.com

Some of the product names and company names used in this book have been used for identification purposes only and may be trademarks or registered trademarks of their respective manufacturers and sellers.

Microsoft and the Office logo are either registered trademarks or trademarks of Microsoft Corporation in the United States and/or other countries. Course Technology, Cengage Learning is an independent entity from the Microsoft Corporation, and not affiliated with Microsoft in any manner.

Disclaimer: Any fictional data related to persons or companies or URLs used throughout this book is intended for instructional purposes only. At the time this book was printed, any such data was fictional and not belonging to any real persons or companies.

Library of Congress Control Number: 2011920507

ISBN-13: 978-1-111-52799-0
ISBN-10: 1-111-52799-7

Course Technology
20 Channel Center Street
Boston, MA 02210
USA

Cengage Learning is a leading provider of customized learning solutions with office locations around the globe, including Singapore, the United Kingdom, Australia, Mexico, Brazil, and Japan. Locate your local office at:
international.cengage.com/global

Cengage Learning products are represented in Canada by Nelson Education, Ltd.

To learn more about Course Technology, visit **www.cengage.com/course technology**

To learn more about Cengage Learning, visit **www.cengage.com**

Purchase any of our products at your local college store or at our preferred online store **www.cengagebrain.com**

Printed in the United States of America
2 3 4 5 6 7 8 9 15 14 13 12 11

Brief Contents

CONCEPTS

absolute-india/shutterstock.com

NETWORKS AND THE INTERNET

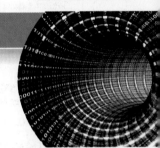

Lukiyanova Natalia/frenta/shutterstock.com

WINDOWS 7

Leigh Prather/shutterstock.com

OFFICE 2010

Harper/shutterstock.com

WORD 2010

Carlos Caetano/shutterstock.com

EXCEL 2010

newyear2008/shutterstock.c

ACCESS 2010

Maxim Tupikov/shutterstock.c

POWERPOINT 2010

New Image/shutterstock.c

INTEGRATION

Sychugina/shutterstock.c

INDEX 772

Table of Contents

Jozsef Bagota/shutterstock.com

NETWORKS AND THE INTERNET

4 Computer Networks 108

5 Introducing the Internet and Email 140

6 Network and Internet Security and Privacy 188

ARENA Creative /shutterstock.com

ArchMan/shutterstock.com

N-trash/shutterstock.com

bioraven/Shutterstock.com

Andreas G. Karelias/Shutterstock.com

ACCESS 2010

17 Creating a Database 566

3DProfit/Shutterstock.com

Introduction to Computers and the Internet

Introduction

Learning Objectives

After studying the material in this chapter, you will be able to:

LO1.1 Explain what computers do

LO1.2 Identify types of computers

LO1.3 Describe computer networks and the Internet

LO1.4 Understand how computers impact society

Computers and other forms of technology impact your daily life in many ways. You encounter computers in stores, restaurants, and other retail establishments. You probably use computers and the Internet regularly to obtain information, find entertainment, buy products and services, and communicate with others. You might carry a mobile phone or other mobile device at all times so you can remain in touch with others and access Internet information as you need it. You might even use these portable devices to pay for purchases, play online games with others, watch TV and movies, and much, much more.

Businesses also use computers extensively, such as to maintain employee and customer records, manage inventories, maintain online stores and other Web sites, process sales, control robots and other machines in factories, and provide executives with the up-to-date information they need to make decisions. The government uses computers to support the nation's defense systems, for space exploration, for storing and organizing vital information about citizens, for law enforcement and military purposes, and other important tasks. In short, computers and computing technology are used in an endless number of ways.

LO1.1 What Is a Computer?

A **computer** is a programmable, electronic device that accepts data, performs operations on that data, presents the results, and stores the data or results as needed. The fact that a computer is programmable means that a computer will do whatever the instructions tell it to do. The programs used with a computer determine the tasks the computer is able to perform.

computer A programmable, electronic device that accepts data input, performs processing operations on that data, and outputs and stores the results.

The primary four operations of a computer are referred to as input, processing, output, and storage. These operations can be defined as follows:

istockphoto.com/track5

People use computers in virtually every aspect of their lives—at home, at school, on the job, and while on the go as they work, learn, and play.

CONCEPTS

▶ **Input**—entering data into the computer

▶ **Processing**—performing operations on the data

▶ **Output**—presenting the results

▶ **Storage**—saving data, programs, or output for future use

input The process of entering data into a computer; can also refer to the data itself.

processing Performing operations on data that has been input into a computer to convert that input to output.

output The process of presenting the results of processing; can also refer to the results themselves.

storage The operation of saving data, programs, or output for future use.

Exhibit 1-1 Information processing cycle

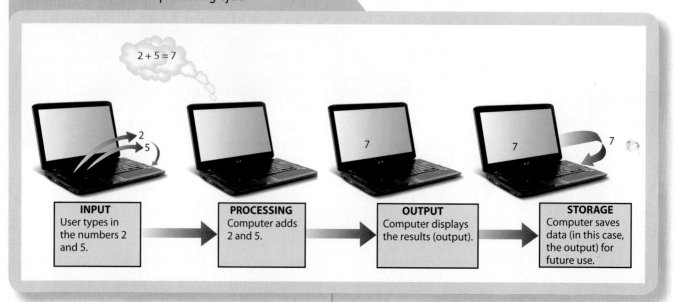

INPUT	PROCESSING	OUTPUT	STORAGE
User types in the numbers 2 and 5.	Computer adds 2 and 5.	Computer displays the results (output).	Computer saves data (in this case, the output) for future use.

For a computer that has been programmed to add two numbers, as shown in Exhibit 1-1, input occurs when data (in this example, the numbers 2 and 5) is entered into the computer, processing takes place when the computer program adds those two numbers, and output happens when the sum of 7 is displayed on the computer screen. The storage operation occurs any time the data, a change to a program, or some output is saved for future use.

Another example of a computer is a supermarket barcode reader. First, the grocery item being purchased is passed over the barcode reader—input. Next, the description and price of the item are looked up—processing. Then, the item description and price are displayed on the cash register and printed on the receipt—output. Finally, the inventory, ordering, and sales records are updated—storage.

Today's computers also typically perform **communications** functions, such as sending or retrieving data via the Internet, accessing information located in a shared company database, or exchanging email messages. Therefore, communications—technically an input or output operation, depending on which direction the information is going—is increasingly considered the fifth primary computer operation.

Data vs. Information

A user inputs **data** into a computer, and then the computer processes it. When data is modified, or **processed**, into a meaningful form, it becomes **information**. Information is frequently generated to answer some type of question, such as how many of a restaurant's employees work fewer than 20 hours per week, how many seats are available on a particular flight from Los Angeles to San Francisco, or what is Hank Aaron's lifetime home run total.

Of course, you don't need a computer system to process data into information. For example, anyone can go through time cards or employee files and make a list of people who work a certain number of hours. This work could take a lot of time when done by hand, especially for a company with many employees. Computers, however, can perform such tasks almost instantly, with

communications The transmission of data from one device to another.

data Raw, unorganized facts.

process To modify data.

information Data that has been processed into a meaningful form.

The progression of input, processing, output, and storage is sometimes called the IPOS cycle or the information processing cycle.

Data

Any fact or set of facts can become computer data, such as the words in a letter to a friend, the numbers in a monthly budget, the images in a photograph, the notes in a song, or the facts stored in an employee record.

accurate results. Information processing (the conversion of data into information) is a vital activity today for all computer users, as well as for businesses and other organizations.

Hardware and Software

The physical parts of a computer (the parts you can touch) are called **hardware**. Hardware components can be internal (located inside the computer) or external (located outside the computer and connected to the computer via a wired or wireless connection). Exhibit 1-2 illustrates typical computer hardware.

The term **software** refers to the programs or instructions used to tell the computer hardware what to do and to allow people to use a computer to perform specific tasks, such as creating letters, preparing budgets, managing inventory and customer databases, playing games, watching videos, listening to music, scheduling appointments, editing digital photographs, designing homes, viewing Web pages, burning DVDs, and exchanging email. In Exhibit 1-2, the software being used allows you to look at information on the Internet.

Computer Users and Professionals

Computer users, often called **end users**, are the people who use computers to perform tasks or obtain information. This includes an accountant electronically preparing a client's taxes, an office worker using a word processing program to create a letter, a supervisor using a computer to check and see whether or not manufacturing workers have met the day's quotas, a parent emailing his or her child's teacher, a college student analyzing science lab data, a child playing a computer game, and a person bidding at an online auction over the Internet.

Programmers, on the other hand, are computer professionals who write the programs that computers use. Other computer professionals include systems analysts, who design computer systems to be used within their companies, computer operations personnel, who are responsible for the day-to-day computer operations at a company, such as maintaining systems or troubleshooting user-related problems, and security specialists, who are responsible for securing the company computers and networks against hackers and other intruders.

hardware The physical parts of a computer.

software Programs or instructions used to tell the computer what to do to accomplish tasks.

end user A person who uses a computer to perform tasks or obtain information.

Exhibit 1-2 Typical computer hardware and software

Cloud Computing

In general, **cloud computing** refers to data, applications, and even resources stored on computers accessed over the Internet—in a "cloud" of computers—rather than on users' computers, and you access only what you need when you need it. This type of network has been used for several years to create the supercomputer-level power needed for research and other power-hungry applications, but it was more typically referred to as *grid computing* in this context. Today, cloud computing typically refers to accessing Web-based applications and data using a personal computer, mobile phone, or any other Internet-enabled device (see the accompanying illustration). Although many of today's cloud applications (such as Google Apps, Windows Live, Facebook, and YouTube) are consumer-oriented, business applications are also available and are expected to grow in the near future. Consequently, the term is also used to refer to businesses purchasing computing capabilities as they need them from companies that provide Web-based applications, computing power, storage, and other services.

Advantages of cloud computing include easy scalability, lower capital expenditure, and access to data from anywhere. It is also beneficial to business travelers and other individuals whose computers, mobile phones, or other devices may be lost or otherwise compromised while the individual is on the go—if no personal or business data is stored on the device, none can be compromised. Disadvantages include a possible reduction in performance of applications if they run more slowly via

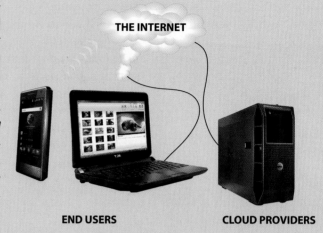

THE INTERNET

END USERS

CLOUD PROVIDERS

From left: Courtesy of HTC, Acer America Corporation, Microsoft Corporation and Dell Inc.

the cloud than they would run if installed locally, and the potentially high expense related to data transfer for companies with high bandwidth applications. In addition, numerous security concerns exist, such as how the data is protected against unauthorized access and data loss.

Despite the potential risks, many believe that cloud computing is the wave of the future and will consist of millions of computers located in data centers around the world that are connected together via the Internet. They also view cloud computing as a way to enable all of an individual's devices to stay synchronized, allowing an individual to work with his or her data and applications on a continual basis.

LO1.2 Types of Computers

The types of computers available today vary widely—from the tiny computers embedded in consumer devices and appliances, to the pocket-sized computers and mobile phones that do a limited number of computing tasks, to the powerful and versatile computers found in homes and businesses, to the super- powerful computers used to control the country's defense systems. Computers are generally classified by category, based on size, capability, and price.

Embedded Computers

An **embedded computer** is a tiny computer embedded into a product designed to perform specific tasks or functions for that product. For example, computers are often embedded into household appliances, such as dishwashers, microwaves, ovens, and coffee makers, as well as into other everyday objects, such as thermostats, answering machines, treadmills, sewing machines, DVD players, and televisions, to help those appliances and objects perform their designated tasks. Cars also use many embedded computers to assist with diagnostics, to notify

cloud computing To use data, applications, and resources stored on computers accessed over the Internet rather than on users' computers.

embedded computer A tiny computer embedded in a product and designed to perform specific tasks or functions for that product.

the user of important conditions (such as an underin-flated tire or an oil filter that needs changing), to facilitate the car's navigational or entertainment systems, to help the driver perform tasks, and to control the use of the airbag and other safety devices, such as cameras that alert a driver that a vehicle is in his or her blind spot as shown in Exhibit 1-3. Because embedded computers are designed for specific tasks and specific products, they cannot be used as general-purpose computers.

Exhibit 1-3 Embedded computer in a car

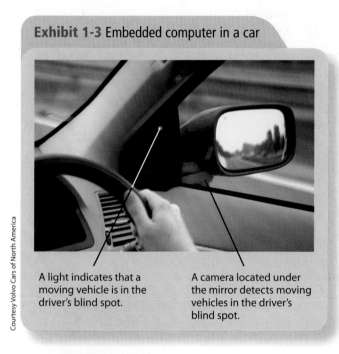

A light indicates that a moving vehicle is in the driver's blind spot.

A camera located under the mirror detects moving vehicles in the driver's blind spot.

Mobile Devices

A **mobile device** is loosely defined as a very small communications device, such as a mobile phone, that has built-in computing or Internet capability. Mobile devices are commonly used to make telephone calls, send text messages, view Web pages, take digital photos, play games, download and play music, watch TV shows, and access calendars and other personal productivity features. Most (but not all) mobile phones today include computing and Internet capabilities; these phones, such as the one in Exhibit 1-4, are sometimes called smart-

An older term for a smartphone is PDA (personal digital assistant), though PDAs may not include telephone capabilities.

Exhibit 1-4 Smartphone

phones. Handheld gaming devices, such as the Sony PSP and the Nintendo DSi, and portable digital media players, such as the iPod touch and Zune, that include Internet capabilities can also be referred to as mobile devices, though they have fewer overall capabilities than conventional mobile devices.

Today's mobile devices tend to have small screens and keyboards. Because of this, mobile devices are more appropriate for individuals wanting continual access to email; timely Web content such as breaking news, weather forecasts, driving directions, and updates from Web sites like Facebook; and music collections than for those individuals wanting general Web browsing and computing capabilities. This is beginning to change, however, as mobile devices continue to grow in capabilities, as wireless communications continue to become faster, and as mobile input options, such as voice input, continue to improve. For instance, some mobile devices can perform Internet searches and other tasks via voice commands, some can be used to pay for purchases while you are on the go, and many can view and edit documents stored in a common format, such as Microsoft Office documents.

mobile device A very small communications device with built-in computing or Internet capability.

Computers Then and Now

The history of computers is often referred to in terms of generations, with each new generation characterized by a major technological development.

Precomputers and Early Computers (before approximately 1946)

Courtesy IBM Corporate Archives

Early computing devices include the abacus, the slide rule, the mechanical calculator, and Dr. Herman Hollerith's Punch Card Tabulating Machine and Sorter (shown here). This was the first electromechanical machine that could read punch cards. It was used to process the 1890 U.S. Census data. Hollerith's company eventually became International Business Machines (IBM).

First-Generation Computers (approximately 1946–1957)

Courtesy U.S. Army

The first computers were enormous, often taking up entire rooms. First-generation computers could solve only one problem at a time because they needed to be physically rewired with cables to be reprogrammed. Paper punch cards and tape were used for input, and output was printed on paper. Completed in 1946, ENIAC (shown here) was the world's first large-scale, general-purpose computer. UNIVAC, released in 1951, was initially built for the U.S. Census Bureau and was used to analyze votes in the 1952 U.S. presidential election. UNIVAC became the first computer to be mass produced for general commercial use.

Second-Generation Computers (approximately 1958–1963)

Courtesy IBM Corporate Archives

The second generation of computers, such as the IBM 1401 mainframe (shown here) were physically smaller, less expensive, more powerful, more energy-efficient, and more reliable than first-generation computers. Pro-grams and data were input on punch cards and magnetic tape, output was on punch cards and paper printouts, and magnetic tape was used for storage. Magnetic hard drives and programming languages, such as FORTRAN and COBOL, were developed and implemented during this generation.

Third-Generation Computers (approximately 1964–1970)

Courtesy IBM Corporate Archives

Integrated circuits (ICs) marked the beginning of the third generation of computers, such as the IBM System/360 mainframe (shown here). Integrated circuits incorporate many transistors and electronic circuits on a single tiny silicon chip, making computers even smaller and more reliable than the earlier computers.

Fourth-Generation Computers (approximately 1971–present)

Courtesy IBM Corporate Archives

The invention of the microprocessor in 1971 ushered in the fourth generation of computers. In essence, a microprocessor contains the core processing capabilities of an entire computer on one single chip. The original IBM PC (shown here) and Apple Macintosh computers, and most of today's modern computers, fall into this category.

Fifth-Generation Computers (Now and the Future)

Fifth-generation computers have no precise classification because experts disagree about its definition. One common opinion is that fifth-generation computers will be based on artificial intelligence, allowing them to think, reason, and learn. Voice and touch are expected to be a primary means of input, and computers may be constructed in the form of optical computers that process data using light instead of electrons, tiny computers that utilize nanotechnology, or as entire general-purpose computers built into desks, home appliances, and other everyday devices.

Personal Computers (PCs)

A **personal computer** (**PC**) is a small computer designed to be used by one person at a time. Personal computers are widely used by individuals and businesses today.

Conventional personal computers that are designed to fit on or next to a desk, as shown in Exhibit 1-5, are often referred to as **desktop computers**. The most common style of desktop computer today uses a tower case, which is a system unit designed to sit vertically, typically on the floor. Desktop computers can also have a desktop case, which is designed to be placed horizontally on a desk's surface, or an all-in-one case, which incorporates the monitor and system unit into a single piece of hardware.

The term PC usually refers to personal computers that use Microsoft Windows. Personal computers sold only by Apple, Inc. are referred to as Macs (short for Macintosh).

puters, such as those made by Dell, Hewlett-Packard, NEC, Acer, Lenovo, Fujitsu, and Gateway. These computers typically run the Microsoft Windows operating system. Macintosh computers are made by Apple, use the Mac OS operating system, and often use different hardware and software than PC-compatible computers. Macintosh computers are traditionally the computer of choice for artists, designers, and others who require advanced graphics capabilities.

Portable computers are computers that are designed to be carried around easily, such as in a briefcase or pocket, depending on their size. Portable computers now outsell desktop computers and are often the computer of choice for students and home users, as well as for many businesses. In fact, portable computers are essential for many workers, such as salespeople who make presentations or take orders from clients offsite, agents who collect data at remote locations, and managers who need computing and communications

Exhibit 1-5 Desktop computers

TOWER CASE

ALL-IN-ONE CASE

From left: Courtesy, Hewlett-Packard Company and Dell Inc.

Desktop computers usually conform to one of two standards or platforms: PC-compatible or Macintosh. PC-compatible computers evolved from the original IBM PC—the first personal computer that was widely accepted for business use—and are the most common type of personal computer used today. In general, PC-compatible hardware and software are compatible with all brands of PC-compatible com-

Extra powerful desktop computers designed for high-end graphics, music, film, architecture, science, and other powerful applications are sometimes called workstations.

personal computer (PC) A type of computer based on a microprocessor and designed to be used by one person at a time.

desktop computer A personal computer designed to fit on or next to a desk.

portable computer A small personal computer designed to be carried around easily.

Exhibit 1-6 Portable computers

NOTEBOOK

SLATE TABLET

NETBOOK

ULTRA-MOBILE PC

resources as they travel. Portable computers (see Exhibit 1-6) are available in the following configurations:

▸ **Notebook computers (laptop computers)**—computers that are about the size of a paper notebook and open to reveal a screen on the top half of the computer and a keyboard on the bottom. They are comparable to desktop computers in features and capabilities.

▸ **Tablet computer**—notebook-sized computers that are designed to be used with a digital pen or stylus. They can be either slate tablets (one-piece computers with a screen on top and no keyboard, such

as the one shown in Exhibit 1-6) or convertible tablets, which use the same clamshell design as notebook computers but whose top half can be rotated and folded shut so it can also be used as a slate tablet.

▸ **Netbooks**—also called mini-notebooks, mini-laptops, and ultraportable computers; notebook computers that are smaller (a 10-inch-wide screen is common), lighter (typically less than three pounds), and less expensive than conventional notebooks, so they are especially appropriate for students and business travelers. They typically don't include a CD or DVD drive and they have a smaller keyboard than a notebook computer. The market for netbooks is growing rapidly and it is expected to reach 50 million by 2012, according to the research firm Gartner.

▸ **Ultra-mobile PCs (UMPCs)**—sometimes called handheld computers; computers that are small enough to fit in one hand. UMPCs are smaller (screen size is often seven inches or smaller) and lighter (usually less than two pounds) than netbooks. They can support keyboard, touch, and/or pen input, depending on the particular design being used.

Most personal computers today are sold as stand-alone, self-sufficient units that are equipped with all the hardware and software needed to operate independently. In other words, they can perform input, processing, output, and storage without being connected to a network, although they can be networked if desired. In contrast, a device that must be connected to a network to perform processing or storage tasks is referred to as a **dumb terminal**. Two types of personal computers that may be able to perform a limited amount of independent processing (like a desktop or notebook computer) but are designed to be used with a network (like a dumb terminal) are thin clients and Internet appliances.

A **thin client**—also called a network computer (NC)—is a device that is designed to be used in conjunction with a company network. Instead of using local hard drives for storage, programs are accessed from and data is stored on a network server. The main advantage of thin clients over desktop computers is lower

notebook computer (laptop computer) A small personal computer designed to be carried around easily.

tablet computer A portable computer about the size of a notebook that is designed to be used with an electronic pen.

netbook A very small notebook computer.

ultra-mobile PC (UMPC) A portable personal computer that is small enough to fit in one hand.

dumb terminal A computer that must be connected to a network to perform processing or storage tasks.

thin client A personal computer designed to access a network for processing and data storage instead of performing those tasks locally.

> Thin clients are a good choice for companies that manipulate highly secure data that needs to be prevented from leaving the facility.

Exhibit 1-8 Nintendo Wii gaming console

cost (such as for overall hardware and software, computer maintenance, and power and cooling costs), increased security because data is not stored locally, and easier maintenance because all software is located on a central server. Disadvantages include having limited or no local storage and not being able to function as a stand-alone computer when the network is not working. Thin clients are used by businesses to provide employees with access to network applications; they are also sometimes used to provide Internet access to the public. For instance, a thin client might be installed in a hotel lobby to provide guests with Internet access, hotel and conference information, room-to-room calling, and free phone calls via the Internet.

Network computers or other devices designed primarily for accessing Web pages and/or exchanging email are called **Internet appliances** (sometimes referred to as Internet devices). Internet appliances are designed to be located in the home and can be built into another product, such as a refrigerator or telephone console, or can be stand-alone Internet devices, such as the chumby device shown in Exhibit 1-7, that is designed to deliver

news, sports scores, weather, and other personalized Web-based information. Gaming consoles, such as the Nintendo Wii shown in Exhibit 1-8 and the Sony PlayStation 3, that can be used to view Internet content, in addition to their gaming abilities, can be classified as Internet appliances when they are used to access the Internet. Internet capabilities are also beginning to be built into television sets, which make them Internet appliances, as well.

Midrange Servers

A **midrange server** (sometimes called a **minicomputer**) is a medium-sized computer used to host programs and data for a small network. Typically larger, more powerful, and more expensive than a desktop computer, a midrange server is usually located in a closet or other out-of-the-way place and can serve many users at one time. Users connect to the server through a network, using their desktop computer, portable computer, thin client, or a dumb terminal consisting of just a monitor and keyboard (see Exhibit 1-9). Midrange servers are often used in small- to medium-sized businesses such as medical or dental offices, as well as in school computer labs. There are also special home servers designed for home

Exhibit 1-7 The chumby stand-alone Internet device

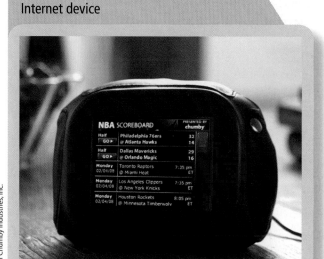

> **Internet appliance** A specialized network computer designed primarily for Internet access and/or email exchange.
>
> **midrange server** (**minicomputer**) A medium-sized computer used to host programs and data for a small network.

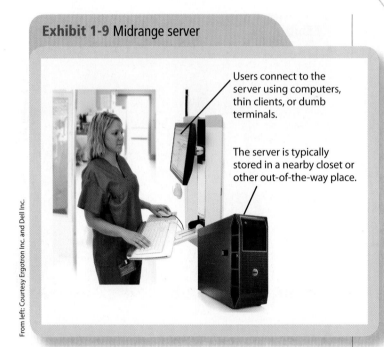

Users connect to the server using computers, thin clients, or dumb terminals.

The server is typically stored in a nearby closet or other out-of-the-way place.

From left: Courtesy Ergotron Inc. and Dell Inc.

use, which are often used to back up (make duplicate copies of) the content located on all the computers in the home and to host music, photos, movies, and other media to be shared via a home network.

One trend involving midrange servers as well as mainframe computers is **virtualization**—the creation of virtual (rather than actual) versions of a computing resource; in this case, separate server environments that are physically located on the same computer, but function as separate servers and do not interact with each other. For instance, all applications for an organization can be installed in virtual environments on a single physical server instead of using a separate server for each application. Using a separate server for each application wastes resources because the servers are often not used to full capacity—one estimate is that about only 10 percent of server capability is frequently utilized. With virtualization, companies can fulfill their computing needs with fewer servers, which translates into reduced costs for hardware and server management, as well as lower power and cooling costs. Consequently, one of the most significant appeals of server virtualization today is increased efficiency.

virtualization The creation of virtual versions of a computing resource.

mainframe computer A computer used in large organizations that manage large amounts of centralized data and run multiple programs simultaneously.

Virtualization concepts are beginning to be applied to other computing areas, such as networking and storage.

Mainframe Computers

A **mainframe computer** is a powerful computer used in many large organizations that need to manage large amounts of centralized data. Larger, more expensive, and more powerful than midrange servers, mainframes can serve thousands of users connected to the mainframe via personal computers, thin clients, or dumb terminals in a manner similar to the way users connect to midrange servers. Mainframe computers, such as the one shown in Exhibit 1-10, are typically located in climate-controlled data centers and connect to the rest of the company computers via a computer network. During regular business hours, a mainframe typically runs the programs needed to meet the different needs of its wide variety of users. At night, it commonly performs large processing tasks, such as payroll and billing. Today's mainframes are sometimes referred to as high-end servers or enterprise-class servers.

Courtesy of IBM

Business Concerns about Energy Efficiency

One issue facing businesses today is the high cost of electricity to power and cool the mainframes, servers, and personal computers used in an organization. Consequently, making the computers located in a business—particularly mainframes and servers—more energy efficient is a high priority today. For example, IBM recently consolidated approximately 4,000 servers located in its data centers into just 30 mainframes (like the one shown in Exhibit 1-10). This new environment is expected to consume approximately 80% less energy and result in significant savings in energy, software, and system support costs.

Exhibit 1-11 Supercomputer

Courtesy of IBM

Converging Technologies

In practice, classifying a computer into one of the six categories described in this section is not always easy or straightforward. For example, some high-end personal computers are as powerful as midrange servers, and some personal computers are nearly as small as a mobile phone. In addition, technology changes too fast to have precisely defined categories. The computer of the future may not look anything like today's computers. In fact, future predictions envision personal computers built into a variety of useful objects to best fit a person's lifestyle, such as a ring or watch for an older person, eyeglasses for a technical worker, and a flexible mobile device that can physically change its shape as needed for general consumer use. Future devices are also expected to use voice, touch, or gesture input instead of a keyboard and mouse, and to project output on any appropriate surface instead of using a monitor. Nevertheless, these six categories are commonly used today to refer to groups of computers designed for similar purposes.

Supercomputers

Some applications require extraordinary speed, accuracy, and processing capabilities—for example, sending astronauts into space, controlling missile guidance systems and satellites, forecasting the weather, exploring for oil, and assisting with some kinds of scientific research. **Supercomputers**—the most powerful and most expensive type of computer available—were developed to fill this need. Some relatively new supercomputing applications include hosting extremely complex Web sites and decision support systems for corporate executives, as well as three-dimensional applications, such as 3D medical imaging, 3D image projections, and 3D architectural modeling. Unlike mainframe computers, which typically run multiple applications simultaneously to serve a wide variety of users, supercomputers generally run one program at a time as fast as possible.

Conventional supercomputers can cost several million dollars each. To reduce the cost, supercomputers are often built by connecting hundreds of smaller and less expensive computers (increasingly midrange servers) into a **supercomputing cluster** that acts as a single supercomputer. The computers in the cluster usually contain multiple CPUs each and are dedicated to processing cluster applications. For example, IBM's Roadrunner supercomputer, which is shown in Exhibit 1-11,

supercomputer The fastest, most expensive, and most powerful type of computer.

supercomputing cluster A supercomputer composed of numerous smaller computers connected together to act as a single computer.

contains approximately 19,000 CPUs and is one of the fastest computers in the world. This supercomputing cluster, built for the U.S. Department of Energy, is installed at Los Alamos National Lab in California, and is used primarily to ensure the safety and reliability of the nation's nuclear weapons stockpile. Roadrunner, which cost about $100 million and occupies about 5,200 square feet, is the first supercomputer to reach petaflop (quadrillions of floating point operations per second) speeds. This supercomputer is also one of the most energy-efficient computers in the TOP500 list of the 500 fastest computers in the world. A new IBM supercomputer named Sequoia that is currently under development for the Lawrence Livermore National Laboratory is expected to use approximately 1.6 million CPUs and perform at 20 petaflops.

LO1.3 Computer Networks and the Internet

A **network** is a collection of computers and other devices that are connected to enable users to share hardware, software, and data, as well as to communicate electronically. Computer networks exist in many sizes and types. For instance, home networks are commonly used to allow home computers to share a single printer and Internet connection, as well as to exchange files. Small office networks enable workers to access company records stored on a network server, communicate with other employees, share a high-speed printer, and access the Internet, as shown in Exhibit 1-12. School networks

Exhibit 1-12 Example of a computer network

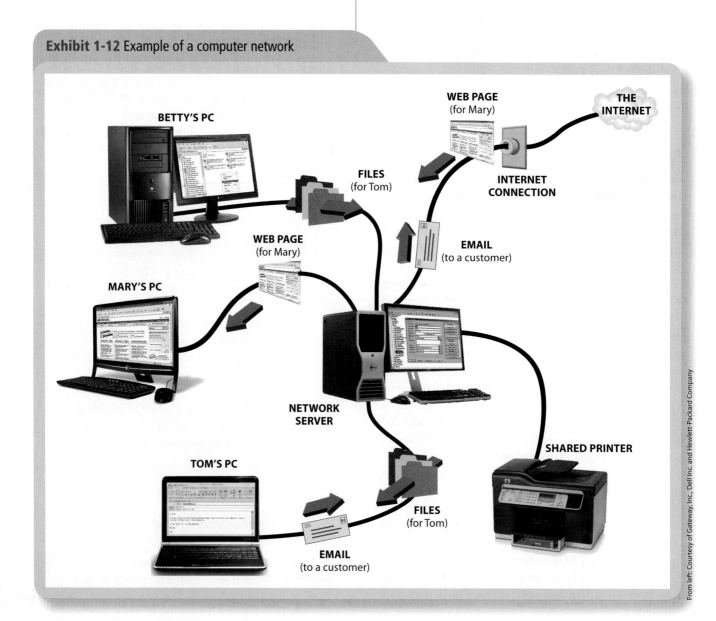

allow students and teachers to access the Internet and school resources, and large corporate networks often connect all of the offices or retail stores in the corporation, creating a network that spans several cities or states. Public wireless networks, such as those available at some coffeehouses, restaurants, public libraries, and parks, provide Internet access to individuals via their portable computers and mobile devices.

The Internet and the World Wide Web

The **Internet** is the largest and most well-known computer network in the world. It is technically a network of networks, because it consists of thousands of networks that can all access each other via the main backbone infrastructure of the Internet. Individual users connect to the Internet by connecting their computers to servers belonging to an **Internet service provider** (**ISP**)—a company that provides Internet access, usually for a fee. ISPs—which include conventional and mobile telephone companies like AT&T, Verizon, and Sprint; cable providers like Comcast and Time Warner; and standalone ISPs like NetZero and EarthLink—function as gateways or onramps to the Internet, providing Internet access to their subscribers. ISP servers are continually connected to a larger network, called a regional network, which, in turn, is connected to one of the major high-speed networks within a country, called a backbone network. Backbone networks within a country are connected to each other and to backbone networks in other countries. Together they form one enormous network of networks—the Internet.

While the term *Internet* refers to the physical structure of that network, the **World Wide Web** (**Web** or **WWW**) refers to one resource—a collection of documents called **Web pages**—available through the Internet. A group of Web pages belonging to one individual or company is called a **Web site**. Web pages are stored on computers called **Web servers** that are continually connected to the Internet; they can be accessed at any time by anyone with a computer or other Web-enabled device and an Internet connection. A wide variety of information is available via Web pages, such as company and product information, government forms and publications, maps, telephone directories, news, weather, sports results, airline schedules, and much, much more. You can also use Web pages to shop, bank, trade stock, and perform other types of online financial transactions; access social networks like Facebook and MySpace; and listen to music, play games, watch television shows, and perform other entertainment-oriented activities

(see Exhibit 1-13). Web pages are viewed using a **Web browser**, such as Internet Explorer (IE), Chrome, Safari, Opera, or Firefox.

Accessing a Network or the Internet

To access a local computer network, you need to use a network adapter, either built into your computer or attached to it, to connect your computer to the network. With some computer networks you need to supply information, such as a username and a password, to connect to the network. After you are connected to the network, you can access network resources, including the network's Internet connection. If you are connecting to the Internet without going through a computer network, your computer needs to use a modem to connect to the communications media, such as a telephone line or cable connection, used by your ISP.

To request a Web page or other resource located on the Internet, its **Internet address**—a unique numeric or text-based address—is used. The most common types of Internet addresses are IP addresses and domain names (to identify computers), URLs (to identify Web pages), and email addresses (to identify people).

IP addresses and their corresponding **domain names** are used to identify computers available through

---

network Computers and other devices that are connected to share hardware, software, and data.

Internet The largest and most well-known computer network, linking millions of computers all over the world.

Internet service provider (**ISP**) A business or other organization that provides Internet access to others, typically for a fee.

World Wide Web (**Web** or **WWW**) The collection of Web pages available through the Internet.

Web page A document located on a Web server.

Web site A collection of related Web pages.

Web server A computer continually connected to the Internet that stores Web pages accessible through the Internet.

Web browser A program used to view Web pages.

Internet address An address that identifies a computer, person, or Web page on the Internet, such as an IP address, domain name, or email address.

IP address A numeric Internet address used to uniquely identify a computer on the Internet.

domain name A text-based Internet address used to uniquely identify a computer on the Internet.

Exhibit 1-13 Examples of common Web activities

ACCESSING PRODUCT INFORMATION

LOOKING UP REFERENCE INFORMATION

READING NEWS

SHOPPING

ACCESSING SOCIAL NETWORKS

WATCHING TV SHOWS AND MOVIES

the Internet. IP (short for Internet Protocol) addresses are numeric, such as 207.46.197.32, and are commonly used by computers to refer to other computers. A computer that hosts information available through the Internet, such as a Web server hosting Web pages, usually has a unique text-based domain name, such as microsoft.com, that corresponds to that computer's IP address to make it easier for people to request Web pages located on that computer. IP addresses and domain names are unique; that is, no two computers on the Internet use the exact same IP address or the exact same domain name. To ensure this, specific IP addresses are allocated to each network, such as a company network or an ISP, to be used with the computers on that network. There is a worldwide registration system for domain name registration. When a domain name is registered, the IP address of the computer that will be hosting the Web site associated with that domain name is also registered. The Web site can be accessed using either its domain name or corresponding IP address. When a Web site is requested by its domain name, the corresponding IP address is looked up using one of the Internet's domain name system (DNS) servers, and then the appropriate Web page is displayed.

Domain names typically reflect the name of the individual or organization associated with that Web site. The different parts of a domain name are separated by a period. The far right part of the domain name (beginning with the rightmost period) is called the top-level domain (TLD) and traditionally identifies the type of organization or its location, such as *.com* for businesses, *.edu* for educational institutions, *.jp* for Web sites located in Japan, or *.fr* for Web sites located in France. There were seven original TLDs used in the United States; additional TLDs and numerous two-letter country code TLDs have since been created. See Exhibit 1-14 for some examples.

Exhibit 1-14 Sample top-level domains (TLDs)

Original TLDs	Intended use
.com	Commercial businesses
.edu	Educational institutions
.gov	Government organizations
.int	International treaty organizations
.mil	Military organizations
.net	Network providers and ISPs
.org	Noncommercial organizations

Newer TLDs	Intended use
.aero	Aviation industry
.biz	Businesses
.fr	French businesses
.info	Resource sites
.jobs	Employment sites
.mobi	Sites optimized for mobile devices
.name	Individuals
.pro	Licensed professionals
.uk	United Kingdom businesses

Similar to the way an IP address or domain name uniquely identifies a computer on the Internet, a **uniform resource locator** (**URL**) uniquely identifies a specific Web page by specifying the protocol—or standard—being used to display the Web page, the Web server hosting the Web page, the name of any folders on the Web server in which the Web page file is stored, and finally, the Web page's filename if needed.

The most common Web page protocols are Hypertext Transfer Protocol (http://) for regular Web pages or Hypertext Transfer Protocol Secure (https://) for secure Web pages that can safely be used to transmit sensitive information, such as credit card numbers. File Transfer Protocol

Custom TLDs

A new proposal allows for the creation of new TLDs that can be virtually any combination of up to 64 characters and that can use non-Latin characters. Although custom TLDs are possible (such as to better represent a company name or personal name), they are also expected to be expensive to register (one estimate is about $100,000 each). Consequently, the initial interest in custom TLDs is by countries such as Russia whose native languages use non-Latin characters, groups of businesses and organizations that are interested in new activity-oriented TLDs like *.sports* and *.shop*, and community organizations interested in city-based TLDs like *.nyc* and *.paris* for New York City and Paris businesses, respectively.

(ftp://) is sometimes used to upload and download files. The file extension used for the Web page file, such as .html or .htm, indicates the type of Web page that will be displayed. For example, looking at the URL for the Web page shown in Exhibit 1-15 from right to left, you can see that the Web page called *index.html* is stored in a folder called *jobs* on the Web server associated with the *twitter.com* domain, and is a regular (nonsecure) Web page because the standard *http://* protocol is being used.

To contact people using the Internet, you most often use their **email addresses**. An email address consists of a **username** (an identifying name), followed by the @ symbol, followed by the domain name for the computer that will be handling that person's email (called a mail server). For example,

jsmith@cengage.com
maria_s@cengage.com
sam.peterson@cengage.com

uniform resource locator (**URL**) An Internet address that uniquely identifies a Web page.

email address An Internet address consisting of a username and computer domain name that uniquely identifies a person on the Internet.

username A name that uniquely identifies a user on a specific computer network.

Exhibit 1-15 URL for a Web page

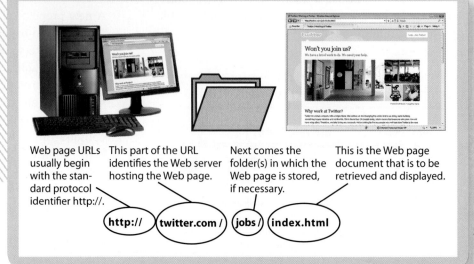

Web page URLs usually begin with the standard protocol identifier http://.

This part of the URL identifies the Web server hosting the Web page.

Next comes the folder(s) in which the Web page is stored, if necessary.

This is the Web page document that is to be retrieved and displayed.

http:// | twitter.com / | jobs / | index.html

Courtesy of Gateway, Inc.

Pronouncing Internet Addresses

Because Internet addresses are frequently given verbally, it is important to know how to pronounce them. Keep in mind the following tips when you say an Internet address:

- If a portion of the address forms a recognizable word or name, it is spoken; otherwise, it is spelled out.
- The @ sign is pronounced *at*.
- The period (.) is pronounced *dot*.
- The forward slash (/) is pronounced *slash*.

Type of address	Sample address	Pronunciation
Domain name	berkeley.edu	berkeley dot e d u
URL	microsoft.com/windows/ie/default.asp	microsoft dot com slash windows slash i e slash default dot a s p
Email address	president@whitehouse.gov	president at white house dot gov

jsmith@cengage.com and a *jsmith* at Stanford University using the email address *jsmith@stanford.edu*, the two email addresses are unique. It is up to each organization with a registered domain name to ensure that one—and only one— exact same username is assigned to its domain.

Surfing the Web

Once you have an Internet connection, you are ready to begin **surfing the Web**—that is, using a Web browser to view Web pages. The first page that your Web browser displays when it is opened is your browser's starting page or home page. From your browser's home page, you can move to other Web pages.

To navigate to a new Web page for which you know the URL, type that URL in the appropriate location for your Web browser (such as Internet Explorer's Address bar, as shown in Exhibit 1-16) and press the Enter key. After that page is displayed, you can use the hyperlinks—graphics or text linked to other Web pages—on that page to display other Web pages.

are the email addresses assigned respectively to jsmith (John Smith), maria_s (Maria Sanchez), and sam.peterson (Sam Peterson), three hypothetical employees at Cengage Learning, the publisher of this textbook. To ensure a unique email address for everyone in the world, usernames must be unique within each domain name. So, even though there could be a *jsmith* at Cengage Learning who is using the email address

surf the Web To use a Web browser to view Web pages.

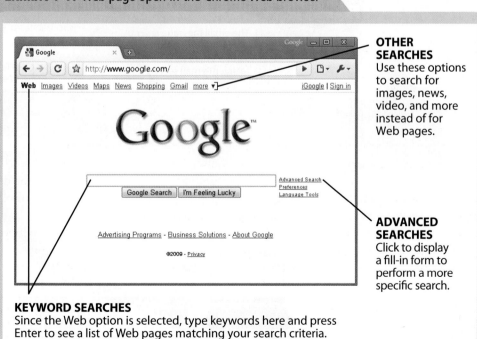

Exhibit 1-16 IE8 Web browser displaying a Web page

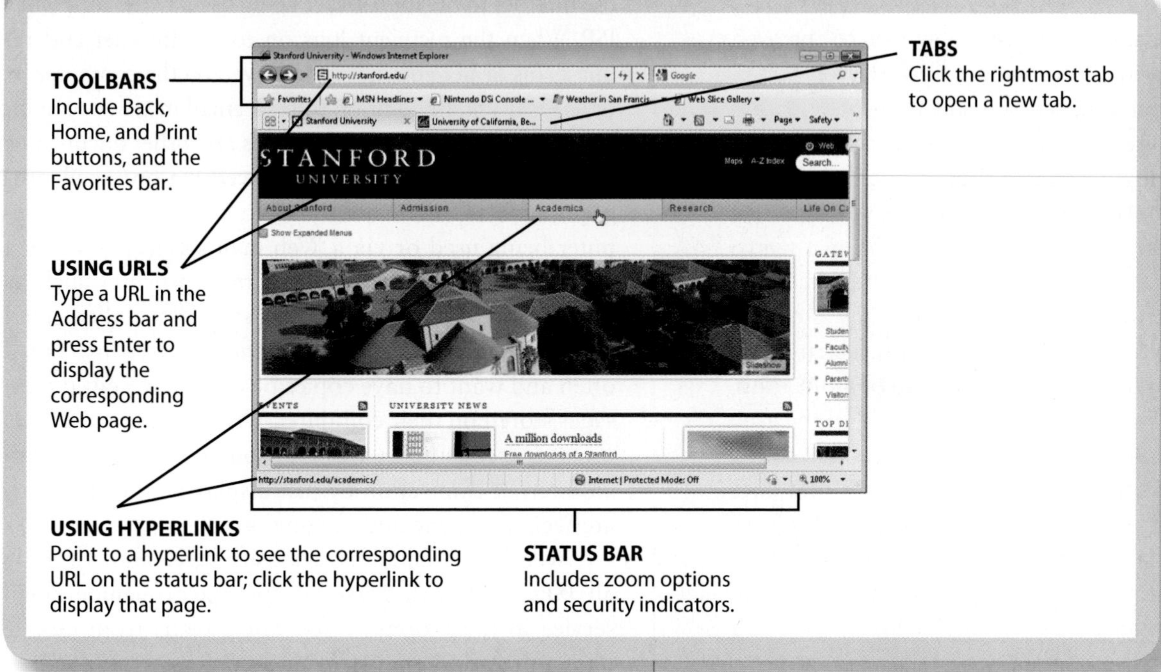

TOOLBARS
Include Back, Home, and Print buttons, and the Favorites bar.
USING URLS
Type a URL in the Address bar and press Enter to display the corresponding Web page.
USING HYPERLINKS
Point to a hyperlink to see the corresponding URL on the status bar; click the hyperlink to display that page.
STATUS BAR
Includes zoom options and security indicators.
TABS
Click the rightmost tab to open a new tab.
STANFORD
UNIVERSITY

Courtesy of Stanford University

The most commonly used Web browsers include Internet Explorer (shown in Exhibit 1-16), Chrome (shown in Exhibit 1-17), and Firefox. The newest versions of these browsers include tabbed browsing (so you can open multiple Web pages at the same time), improved crash recovery and security, and improved ability to search for and bookmark Web pages.

All Web browsers have a feature (usually called Favorites or Bookmarks that is accessed via a Favorites or Bookmarks menu or button) that you can use to save Web page URLs. Once a Web page is saved as a favorite or a bookmark, you can redisplay that page without typing its URL—you simply select its link from the Favorites or Bookmarks list. Web browsers also maintain a History list, which is a record of all Web pages visited during a period of time specified in the browser settings; you can revisit a Web page located on the History list by displaying the History list and selecting that page.

Exhibit 1-17 Web page open in the Chrome Web browser

OTHER SEARCHES
Use these options to search for images, news, video, and more instead of for Web pages.
ADVANCED SEARCHES
Click to display a fill-in form to perform a more specific search.
KEYWORD SEARCHES
Since the Web option is selected, type keywords here and press Enter to see a list of Web pages matching your search criteria.
http://www.google.com/
Web Images Videos Maps News Shopping Gmail more
iGoogle | Sign in
Google
Google Search
I'm Feeling Lucky
Advanced Search
Preferences
Language Tools
Advertising Programs - Business Solutions - About Google
©2009 - Privacy

Google Chrome screenshot © Google Inc. and used with permission.

Searching the Web

You, like many people, probably turn to the Web to find specific information. Special Web pages, called search sites, are available to help you locate what you are looking for on the Internet. One of the most popular search sites—Google—is shown in Exhibit 1-17. To conduct a search, you type one or more keywords into the search box on a search site, and a list of links to Web pages matching your search criteria is displayed. Many browsers also perform an Internet search on search terms you type in the Address bar instead of a URL. Also, numerous reference sites are available on the Web to look up addresses, phone numbers, ZIP codes, maps, and other information. To find a reference site, type the information you are looking for (such as "ZIP code lookup" or "topographical maps") in a search site's search box to see links to sites with that information.

Email

Email is the process of exchanging messages between computers over a network—usually the Internet. Email is one of the most widely used Internet applications—Americans alone send billions of email messages daily and worldwide email traffic is expected to exceed one-half trillion messages per day by 2013, according to the Radicati Group. You can send an email message from any Internet-enabled device, such as a desktop computer, portable computer, or mobile device, to anyone who has an Internet email address. As illustrated

email
Messages sent from one user to another over the Internet or other network.

in Exhibit 1-18, email messages travel from the sender's computer to his or her ISP's mail server, and then through the Internet to the mail server being used by the recipient's ISP. When the recipient logs on to the Internet and requests his or her email, it is displayed on the computer he or she is using. In addition to text, email messages can include attached files, such as photos and other documents.

Email can be sent and received via an email program, such as Microsoft Outlook, installed on the computer being used or via a Web mail service, which is a Web page belonging to a Web mail provider such as Gmail or Windows Live Mail. Using an installed email program is convenient for individuals who use email often and want to have copies of sent and received messages stored on their computer. Web-based email allows users to access their messages from any computer with an Internet connection by just displaying the appropriate Web mail page and logging on.

Web-based email is typically free, and virtually all ISPs used with personal computers include email service in their monthly fee. Some plans from mobile phone providers that provide Internet service for mo-

Exhibit 1-18 How email works

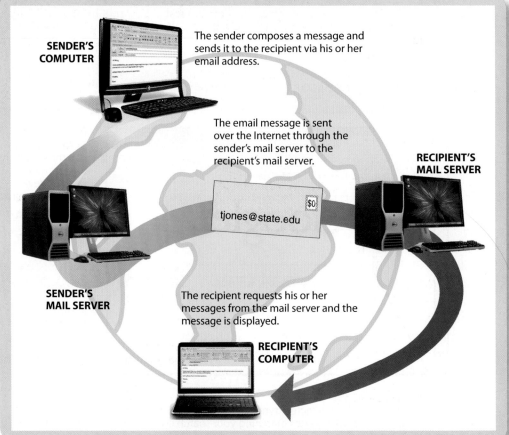

SENDER'S COMPUTER

The sender composes a message and sends it to the recipient via his or her email address.

The email message is sent over the Internet through the sender's mail server to the recipient's mail server.

RECIPIENT'S MAIL SERVER

tjones@state.edu

$0

SENDER'S MAIL SERVER

The recipient requests his or her messages from the mail server and the message is displayed.

RECIPIENT'S COMPUTER

bile phones include a limit on the number and/or size of email messages that can be sent or received during a billing period; messages after that point result in additional fees. Other types of mobile communications, such as text messages, may also incur a fee.

LO1.4 Computers and Society

The vast improvements in technology over the past decade have had a distinct impact on daily life. Computers have become indispensable tools at home and work. Related technological advancements have changed the way everyday items—cars, microwaves, coffee pots, toys, exercise bikes, telephones, televisions, and more—look and function. As computers and everyday devices become smarter, they work faster, better, and more reliably than before, as well as take on additional capabilities. Computerization and technological advances have also changed society as a whole. Without computers, banks would be overwhelmed by the job of tracking all the transactions they process, moon exploration and the space shuttle would still belong to science fiction, and scientific advances such as DNA analysis and gene mapping would be nonexistent. Everyday activities, such as shopping and banking, are increasingly automated, and fast and easy access to information via the Internet and communications via email and instant messaging is expected. In fact, the Internet and its resources have quickly become an integral part of our society.

Benefits and Risks of a Computer-Oriented Society

The benefits of having such a computer-oriented society are numerous. The capability to virtually design, build, and test new buildings, cars, and airplanes before the actual construction begins helps professionals create safer products. Technological advances in medicine allow for earlier diagnosis and more effective treatment of diseases than ever before. The ability to shop, pay bills, research products, participate in online courses, and look up vast amounts of information 24 hours a day, 7 days a week, 365 days a year via the Internet is a huge convenience. In addition, a computer-oriented society generates new opportunities. For example, technologies, such as speech recognition software and Braille input and output devices, enable physically- or visually-challenged individuals to perform necessary job tasks and to communicate with others more easily.

Technology has also made a huge number of tasks in our lives go much faster. Instead of experiencing a long delay for a credit check, an applicant can get approved for a purchase, loan, or credit card almost immediately. Documents and photographs can be emailed or faxed in moments, instead of taking at least a day to be mailed physically. Viewers can watch favorite TV shows online and access up-to-the-minute news at their convenience. And we can download information, programs, music files, movies, and more on demand when we want or need them, instead of having to order them and then wait for delivery or go to a physical store to purchase the items.

Although there are a great number of benefits from having a computer-oriented society, there are risks as well. A variety of problems have emerged from our extensive computer use, ranging from stress and health concerns, to the proliferation of unsolicited emails and harmful programs that can be installed on our computers without our knowledge, to security and privacy issues, to legal and ethical dilemmas. Many security and privacy concerns stem from the fact that so much personal business takes place online—or at least ends up as data in a computer database somewhere—and the potential for misuse of this data is enormous.

Another concern is the repercussions of collecting such vast amounts of information electronically. Some people worry about creating a "Big Brother" situation, in which the government or another organization is watching everything that we do. And some Internet behavior, such as downloading music or movies from an unauthorized source or viewing pornography on an office computer, can get you arrested or fired.

Some people view the potential risk to personal privacy as one of the most important societal issues. As more and more data about our everyday activities is collected and stored on computers accessible via the Internet, our privacy is at risk because the potential for privacy violations increases. Today, data is collected about practically anything we buy online or offline, although offline purchases may not be associated with our identity unless we use a credit card or a membership or loyalty card. The issue is not that data is collected—with virtually all organizations using computers for recordkeeping, that is unavoidable—but how the collected data is used and how secure it is. Data collected by businesses may be used only by that company or shared with others. Data shared with others often results in spam—unsolicited emails. Spam is an enormous problem for individuals and businesses today, and it is considered by many to be a violation of personal privacy.

Protecting Your Computer

To help protect your computer, never open an email attachment from someone you do not know or that has an executable file extension (the last three letters in the filename preceded by a period), such as *.exe*, *.com*, or *.vbs*, without checking with the sender first to make sure the attachment is legitimate. You should never click a link in an email message. You should also be careful about what files you download from the Internet. In addition, it is crucial to install security software on your computer and to set up the program to monitor your computer on a continual basis, and detect or block any harmful programs.

Understanding Intellectual Property Rights

All computer users should be aware of **intellectual property rights**, which are the legal rights to which the creators of intellectual property—original creative works—are entitled. Examples of intellectual property include music and movies; paintings, computer graphics, and other works of art; poetry, books, and other types of written

intellectual property rights The legal rights to which creators of original creative works are entitled.

copyright The legal right to sell, publish, or distribute an original artistic or literary work; it is held by the creator of a work as soon as it exists in physical form.

fair use Permits limited duplication and use of a portion of copyrighted material for specific purposes, such as criticism, commentary, news reporting, teaching, and research.

digital watermark A subtle alteration of digital content that identifies the copyright holder.

digital rights management (DRM) software Software used to protect and manage the rights of creators of digital content.

trademark A word, phrase, symbol, or design that identifies goods or services.

plagiarism Presenting someone else's work as your own.

works; symbols, names, and designs used in conjunction with a business; architectural drawings; and inventions. The three main types of intellectual property rights are copyrights, trademarks, and patents.

A **copyright** is a form of protection available to the creator of an original artistic, musical, or literary work, such as a book, movie, software program, musical composition, or painting. It gives the copyright holder the exclusive right to publish, reproduce, distribute, perform, or display the work. Immediately after creating a work, the creator automatically owns the copyright of that work. Copyrights apply to both published and unpublished works and remain in effect until 70 years after the creator's death. Copyrights for works registered by an organization or as anonymous works last 95 years from the date of publication or 120 years from the date of creation, whichever is shorter. Although works created in the United States after March 1, 1989 are not required to display a copyright notice to retain their copyright protection, displaying a copyright statement on a published work, such as the ones shown in Exhibit 1-19, reminds others that the work is protected by copyright law and that any use must comply with copyright law.

Exhibit 1-19 Copyright statements

© 2012 Course Technology, Cengage Learning

ALL RIGHTS RESERVED. No part of this work covered by the copyright herein may be reproduced, transmitted, stored or used in any form or by any means graphic, electronic, or mechanical, including but not limited to photocopying, recording, scanning, digitizing, taping, Web distribution, information networks, or information storage and retrieval systems, except as permitted under Section 107 or 108 of the 1976 United States Copyright Act, without the prior written permission of the publisher.

BOOK COPYRIGHT NOTICE

© Red Lobster. All rights reserved.

WEB SITE COPYRIGHT NOTICE

Anyone wishing to use copyrighted materials must first obtain permission from the copyright holder and pay any required fee. One exception is the legal concept of **fair use**, which permits limited duplication and use of a portion of copyrighted material for specific purposes, such as criticism, commentary, news reporting, teaching, and research. For example, a teacher may legally read a copyrighted poem for discussion in a poetry class, and a news crew may videotape a small portion of a song at a concert to include in a news report of that concert.

Protecting Digital Content

To protect their rights, some creators of digital content (such as art, music, photographs, and movies) use **digital watermarks**—a subtle alteration of digital content that is not noticeable when the work is viewed or played but that identifies the copyright holder. For instance, the digital watermark for an image might consist of slight changes to the brightness of a specific pattern of pixels that are imperceptible to people but are easily read by software. Digital watermarks can be added to images, music, video, TV shows, and other digital content. The purpose of digital watermarking is to give digital content a unique identity that remains intact even if the work is copied, edited, compressed, or otherwise manipulated.

Another rights-protection tool used with digital content is **digital rights management (DRM) software**, which is used to control the use of a work. For instance, DRM used in conjunction with business documents (called enterprise rights management) can protect a sensitive business document by controlling usage of that document, such as by limiting who can view, print, or copy it. DRM used with digital content, such as movies and music, downloaded via the Internet can control whether the downloaded file can be copied to another device, as well as make a video-on-demand movie unviewable after the rental period expires.

A **trademark** is a word, phrase, symbol, or design (or a combination of words, phrases, symbols, or designs) that identifies one product or service from another. Trademarks that are claimed but not registered with the U. S. Patent and Trademark Office (USPTO) can use the mark ™. The symbol ® is reserved for registered trademarks. Trademarked words and phrases—such as iPod®, Chicken McNuggets®, and Windows Vista™—are widely used today. Trademarked logos are also common.

Businesses and individuals should be very careful when copying, sharing, or otherwise using copyrighted material to ensure that the material is used in both a legal and an ethical manner. Students, researchers, authors, and other writers need to be especially careful when using literary material as a resource for papers, articles, books, and so forth, to ensure the material is used appropriately and is properly credited to the original author. To present someone else's work as your own is **plagiarism**, which is a violation of copyright law and an unethical act. It can also get you fired, as some reporters have found out after faking quotes or plagiarizing content from other newspapers. Examples of acts that would normally be considered or not considered plagiaristic are shown in Exhibit 1-20.

Exhibit 1-20 Examples of what is and what is not plagiarism

Plagiarism	Not plagiarism
A student including a few sentences or a few paragraphs written by another author in his term paper without crediting the original author.	A student including a few sentences or a few paragraphs written by another author in his term paper, either indenting the quotation or placing it inside quotation marks, and crediting the original author with a citation in the text or with a footnote or endnote.
A newspaper reporter changing a few words in a sentence or paragraph written by another author and including the revised text in an article without crediting the original author.	A newspaper reporter paraphrasing a few sentences or paragraphs written by another author without changing the meaning of the text, including the revised text in an article, and crediting the original author with a proper citation.
A student copying and pasting information from various online documents to create her research paper without crediting the original authors.	A student copying and pasting information from various online documents and using those quotes in her research paper either indented or enclosed in quotation marks with the proper citations for each author.
A teacher sharing a poem with a class, leading the class to believe the poem was his original work.	A teacher sharing a poem with a class, clearly identifying the poet.

Ethics

The term **ethics** refers to standards of moral conduct. For example, telling the truth is a matter of ethics. An unethical act is not always illegal, but an illegal act is usually viewed as unethical by most people. For example, purposely lying to a friend is unethical but usually not illegal; whereas perjuring oneself in a courtroom as a witness is both illegal and unethical.

Ethical beliefs can vary widely from one individual to another. Ethical beliefs may also vary based on religion, country, race, or culture. In addition, different ethical standards can apply to different areas of one's life. For example, personal ethics guide an individual's personal behavior and business ethics guide an individual's workplace behavior.

Ethics with respect to the use of computers are referred to as **computer ethics**. Computer ethics have taken on more significance in recent years because the proliferation of computers in the home and the workplace provides more opportunities for unethical acts than in the past. The Internet also makes it easy to distribute information such as computer viruses, spam, and spyware that many people would view as unethical, as well as to distribute copies of software, movies, music, and other digital content in an illegal and, therefore, unethical manner.

Whether at home, at work, or at school, ethical issues crop up every day. For example, you may need to make ethical decisions such as whether to accept a relative's offer of a free copy of a downloaded song or movie, whether to have a friend help you take an online exam, whether to upload a photo of your friend to Facebook without asking permission, or whether to post a rumor on a campus gossip site.

Employees may need to decide whether to print their birthday party invitations on the office color printer, whether to correct the boss for giving them credit for another employee's idea, or whether to sneak a look at information that they can access but have no legitimate reason to view. IT employees, in particular, often face this latter ethical dilemma because they typically have both access and the technical ability to retrieve a wide variety of personal and professional information about other employees, such as their salary information, Web surfing history, and personal email.

Businesses also deal with a variety of ethical issues in the course of normal business activities—from determining how many computers on which a particular software program should be installed, to identifying how customer and employee information should be used, to deciding business practices. **Business ethics** are the standards of conduct that guide a business's policies, decisions, and actions.

With the widespread availability of online articles and fee-based online term paper services, some students might be tempted to create their papers by copying and pasting excerpts of online content into their documents to pass off as their original work. But these students should realize that this is plagiarism, and instructors can usually tell when a paper is created in this manner. There are also online sources instructors can use to test the originality of student papers. Most colleges and universities have strict consequences for plagiarism, such as automatically failing the assignment or course, or being expelled from the institution. As Internet-based plagiarism continues to expand to younger and younger students, many middle schools and high schools are developing strict plagiarism policies as well.

Computers and Health

Common physical conditions caused by computer use include eyestrain, blurred vision, fatigue, headaches, backaches, and wrist and finger pain. Some conditions are classified as **repetitive stress injuries (RSIs)**, in which hand, wrist, shoulder, or neck pain is caused by per-

ethics Overall standards of moral conduct.

computer ethics Standards of moral conduct as they relate to computer use.

business ethics Standards of moral conduct that guide a business's policies, decisions, and actions.

repetitive stress injury (RSI) A type of injury, such as carpal tunnel syndrome, that is caused by performing the same physical movements over and over again.

> Repetitive stress as well as other injuries related to the work environment are estimated to account for one-third of all serious workplace injuries.

forming the same physical movements over and over again. For instance, extensive keyboard and mouse use has been associated with RSIs, although RSIs can be caused by non-computer-related activities as well. One RSI related to the repetitive finger movements made when using a keyboard is **carpal tunnel syndrome** (**CTS**)—a painful and crippling condition affecting the hands and wrists. CTS occurs when the nerve in the *carpal tunnel* located on the underside of the wrist is compressed. An RSI associated with typing on the tiny keyboards and thumbpads commonly found on mobile phones and mobile devices is **DeQuervain's tendonitis**— a condition in which the tendons on the thumb side of the wrists are swollen and irritated. Computer vision syndrome (CVS) is a collection of eye and vision problems, including eyestrain or eye fatigue, dry eyes, burning eyes, light sensitivity, and blurred vision. Extensive computer use can also lead to headaches and pain in the shoulders, neck, or back.

Some recent physical health concerns center on heat. For instance, one study measured the peak temperature on the underside of a typical notebook computer at over 139° Fahrenheit. Consequently, many portable computer manufacturers now warn against letting any part of the computer touch your body, and a variety of notebook cooling stands are available to place between the computer and your lap for those occasions when a better work surface is not available.

Environmental Concerns

The increasing use of computers in our society has created a variety of environmental concerns. The term **green computing** refers to the use of computers in an environmentally friendly manner. Minimizing the use of natural resources, such as energy and paper, is one aspect of green computing. To encourage the development of energy-saving devices, the U.S. Department of Energy and the Environmental Protection Agency (EPA) developed the ENERGY STAR pro-

gram. Hardware that is ENERGY STAR–compliant exceeds the minimum federal standards for reduced energy consumption and can display the ENERGY STAR label. **Eco-labels**—environmental performance certifications—are used in other countries as well.

The high cost of electricity and the recent increase in data center energy usage has made power consumption and heat generation by computers key concerns for businesses and individuals. A recent EPA study showed that servers and data centers use more than 1.5 percent of all electricity generated in the U.S., and that number is expected to double in the next five years. The average U.S. household spends an estimated $100 per year powering devices that are turned off or in standby mode. Devices like computers, home electronics, and appliances that draw power when they are turned off are sometimes called energy vampires. Although computers have become more energy efficient, they can still draw quite a bit of power in standby and sleep modes—particularly with a screen saver enabled.

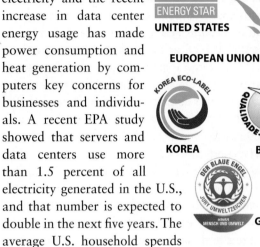

UNITED STATES
EUROPEAN UNION
KOREA
BRAZIL
GERMANY

Courtesy of U.S. Environmental Protection Agency; European Commission, Environment Directorate-General; Korea Environmental Labeling Association (KELA); ABNT - ASSOCIAÇÃO BRASILEIRA DE NORMAS TÉCNICAS; The Blue Angel is the Environmental Label for Germany.

Image copyright Carsten Reisinger, 2010. Used under license from Shutterstock.com.

> To save on vampire power costs, unplug your devices whenenver you are not using them.

carpal tunnel syndrome (CTS) A painful and crippling condition affecting the hands and wrists that can be caused by computer use.

DeQuervain's tendonitis A condition in which the tendons on the thumb side of the wrist are swollen and irritated.

green computing The use of computers in an environmentally friendly manner.

eco-label A certification, usually issued by a government agency, that identifies a device as meeting minimal environmental performance specifications.

Workspace Design

Ergonomics is the science of fitting a work environment to the people who work there. With respect to computer use, it involves designing a safe and effective workspace, which includes properly adjusting furniture and hardware and using ergonomic hardware when needed. A proper work environment—used in conjunction with good user habits and procedures—can prevent many physical problems caused by computer use. Proper placement and adjustment of furniture is a good place to start when evaluating a workspace from an ergonomic perspective.

The desk should be placed where the sun and other sources of light cannot shine directly onto the screen or into the user's eyes. The monitor should be placed directly in front of the user about an arm's length away, and the top of the screen should be no more than 3 inches above the user's eyes once the user's chair is adjusted. The desk chair should be adjusted so that the keyboard is at, or slightly below, the height at which the user's forearms are horizontal to the floor (there are also special ergonomic chairs that can be used). A footrest should be used, if needed, to keep the user's feet flat on the floor after the chair height has been set. The monitor settings should be adjusted to make the screen brightness match the brightness of the room and to have a high amount of contrast; the screen should also be periodically wiped clean of dust. Some setups allow the user to raise the workspace in order to work while standing, when desired.

A notebook stand can also be used to connect peripheral devices to a portable computer, but is designed primarily to elevate the display screen of a notebook or tablet computer to the proper height.

In addition to workspace devices, a variety of ergonomic hardware can be used to help users avoid or alleviate physical problems associated with computer use. These include:

- Ergonomic keyboards designed to lessen the strain on the hands and wrist.

- Trackballs that are essentially upside-down mice that can be more comfortable to use than a mouse.

- Document holders to allow the user to see both the document and the monitor without turning his or her head.

- Antiglare screens that cover the monitor and lessen glare and resulting eyestrain.

- Keyboard drawers that lower the keyboard and enable the user to keep his or her forearms parallel to the floor.

- Wrist supports to keep wrists straight while using the mouse or keyboard and to support the wrists and forearms when not using those devices.

- Computer gloves designed to prevent and relieve RSIs by supporting the wrist and thumb while allowing the full use of hands.

These devices can help users to avoid and reduce discomfort while working on a computer. In addition, computer users should take frequent breaks in typing, use good posture, stretch from time to time, and periodically refocus their eyes on a distant object for a minute or so.

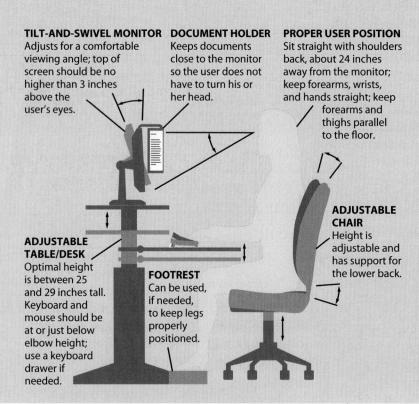

TILT-AND-SWIVEL MONITOR
Adjusts for a comfortable viewing angle; top of screen should be no higher than 3 inches above the user's eyes.

DOCUMENT HOLDER
Keeps documents close to the monitor so the user does not have to turn his or her head.

PROPER USER POSITION
Sit straight with shoulders back, about 24 inches away from the monitor; keep forearms, wrists, and hands straight; keep forearms and thighs parallel to the floor.

ADJUSTABLE CHAIR
Height is adjustable and has support for the lower back.

ADJUSTABLE TABLE/DESK
Optimal height is between 25 and 29 inches tall. Keyboard and mouse should be at or just below elbow height; use a keyboard drawer if needed.

FOOTREST
Can be used, if needed, to keep legs properly positioned.

ergonomics The science of fitting a work environment to the people who work there.

In addition to more energy-efficient hardware, alternate power sources are being developed for greener computing. For instance, solar power is a growing alternative for powering electronic devices, including computers and mobile phones. With solar power, solar panels converts sunlight into electricity, which is then stored in a battery. Improvements in solar technology are making its use increasingly more feasible and economical.

Another environmental concern is the amount of trash—and sometimes toxic trash—generated by computer use. Most obvious is the extensive use of paper for printing. In addition to paper-based trash, computing refuse includes used toner cartridges, obsolete or broken hardware, and discarded CDs, DVDs, and other storage media. Much of this **e-trash** (also called e-waste) ends up in landfills.

Compounding the problem of the amount of e-trash generated is that computers, mobile phones, and related hardware contain a variety of toxic and hazardous materials. For instance, the average CRT monitor alone contains about eight pounds of lead, and a desktop computer may contain up to 700 different chemical elements and compounds, many of which (such as arsenic, lead, mercury, and cadmium) are hazardous and expensive to dispose of properly.

A global concern regarding e-trash is where it all eventually ends up. According to most estimates, at least 70% of all discarded computer equipment ends

> The estimated number of pages generated by computer printers worldwide is almost one-half billion a year—an amount that would stack more than 25,000 miles high.

up in landfills and in countries such as China, India, and Nigeria that have lower recycling costs, cheaper labor, and more lax environmental standards than the United States. Much of the e-trash exported to these countries is simply dumped into fields and other informal dumping areas. Unaware of the potential danger of these components, rural villagers often sort through and dismantle discarded electronics parts looking for precious metals and other sources of revenue—potentially endangering their health as well as polluting nearby rivers, ponds, and other water sources. Compounding the problem, the remaining waste is often burned, generating huge clouds of potentially toxic smoke.

© Basel Action Network 2006

Recycling computer equipment is difficult because of the materials being used. However, proper disposal is essential to avoid pollution and health hazards. Some recycling centers will accept computer equipment, but many charge a fee for this service. Many computer manufacturers have recycling programs that will accept obsolete or broken computer equipment from consumers. Expired toner cartridges and ink cartridges can sometimes be returned to the manufacturer or exchanged when ordering new cartridges; the cartridges are then refilled and resold. Cartridges that cannot be refilled can

Going Green

In addition to being more energy efficient, computers today are being built to run quieter and cooler, and they are using more recyclable hardware and packaging. Many computer manufacturers are also reducing the amount of toxic chemicals such as cadmium, mercury, and lead, being used in personal computers. In the United States, computer manufacturers are beginning to produce more environmentally friendly components, such as system units made from recyclable plastic, nontoxic flame-retardant coatings, and lead-free solder on the motherboard. Recycling programs to reuse and salvage components are becoming more available.

e-trash Electronic trash or waste, such as discarded computer components.

> Completely remove data stored on computing equipment before disposal so someone else cannot recover it from that device.

be sent to a recycling facility. In addition to helping to reduce e-trash in landfills, using refilled or recycled printer cartridges saves the consumer money because they are less expensive than new cartridges. Other computer components—such as CDs, DVDs, USB flash drives, and hard drives—can also be recycled through some organizations, such as GreenDisk, that reuse salvageable items and recycle the rest.

In lieu of recycling, older equipment that is still functioning can be used for alternate purposes, such as for a child's computer, a personal Web server, or a DVR. Or it can be donated to schools and nonprofit groups. Some organizations accept and repair donated equipment and then distribute it to disadvantaged groups or other individuals in need of the hardware.

Quiz Yourself

1. Define *computer*.
2. What are the four primary operations of a computer?
3. Describe the difference between data and information.
4. What is the difference between hardware and software?
5. Explain *cloud computing*.
6. List the six general types of computers.
7. What is the difference between a desktop computer and a portable computer?
8. Describe *virtualization*.
9. What are supercomputers?
10. What is a network?
11. What is the largest and most well-known computer network in the world?
12. Explain the difference between the Internet and the World Wide Web.
13. Describe the three most common types of Internet addresses.
14. What are the three parts of an email address?
15. What are intellectual property rights?
16. Define *computer ethics*.
17. Why are repetitive stress injuries associated with computer use?
18. How does ergonomics relate to computer use?

Practice It

Practice It 1-1

A computer along with the Internet and World Wide Web are handy tools that you can use to research topics covered in this book, complete projects, and perform the online activities available at the book's Web site that are designed to enhance your learning and understanding of the content covered in this book. Use an Internet-enabled computer to access the CMPTR Web site located at login.cengagebrain.com.

1. What types of information and activities are available on the CMPTR Web site?
2. Select an activity and use your mouse to click its link, and then explore the activity. Repeat the process to explore at least two more activities.
3. Evaluate the usefulness of the available resources in enhancing your learning experience.
4. Evaluate your experience using the CMPTR Web site.
5. Prepare a one-page summary that answers these questions, and then submit it to your instructor.

Practice It 1-2

A great deal of obsolete computer equipment eventually ends up in a landfill, even though there may be alternative actions that could be taken instead.

1. Research what options are available to discard the following:
   a. a 10-year-old computer that is no longer functioning
   b. a four-year-old computer that still works, but is too slow to meet your needs
   c. a used-up toner cartridge for a laser printer

2. Which local schools and charitable organizations, if any, would accept any of these items?

3. Check with at least one computer manufacturer and one recycling company to see if they would accept the computers. If so, what would the procedure and cost be?

4. Check with at least one vendor selling refilled toner cartridges to see if it buys old cartridges or requires a trade-in with an order. If the vendor purchases old cartridges, how much will it pay per cartridge?

5. Prepare a one-page summary that describes your findings, answers these questions, and presents your recommendations, and then submit it to your instructor.

On Your Own

On Your Own 1-1

Some aspects of an ergonomic workspace, such as a comfortable chair and nonglaring light, may feel good right from the beginning. Others, such as using an ergonomic keyboard or a wrist rest, may take a little getting used to.

1. Go to a local store that has some ergonomic equipment—such as adjustable office chairs, desks with keyboard drawers, ergonomic keyboards, or notebook stands—on display that you can try out.

2. Test each piece, adjusting it as needed, and evaluate how comfortable it seems.

3. Evaluate your usual computer workspace. Are there any adjustments you should make? Is there any new equipment you would need to acquire to make your workspace setup more comfortable?

4. Create a list of any changes you could make for free, as well as a list of items you would need to purchase and the estimated cost. Which changes and items do you think would most increase your comfort?

5. Prepare a one-page summary that describes your findings and answers these questions, and then submit it to your instructor.

ADDITIONAL STUDY TOOLS

Chapter 1

IN THE BOOK

▶ Complete end-of-chapter exercises

▶ Study tear-out Chapter Review Card

ONLINE

▶ Complete additional end-of-chapter exercises

▶ Take practice quiz to prepare for tests

▶ Review key term flash cards (online, printable, and audio)

▶ Play "Beat the Clock" and "Memory" to quiz yourself

▶ Watch the videos "Searching the Web on Your iPhone" and "Climate Savers Computing Initiative"

Computer Hardware

Introduction

When most people think of computers, images of hardware usually fill their minds. Hardware includes the system unit, keyboard, mouse, monitor, and all the other pieces of equipment that make up a computer system. This chapter describes the hardware located inside the system unit, which is the main box of the computer and where most of the work of a computer is performed. It discusses the different types of devices that can be used for data storage. It also covers the wide variety of hardware that can be used for input and output. Keep in mind that hardware needs instructions from software in order to function. Hardware without software is like a car without a driver or a canvas and paintbrush without an artist. Software is discussed in the next chapter.

LO2.1 Digital Data Representation

Virtually all computers today are digital computers. Most digital computers are binary computers, which can understand only two states, represented by the digits 0 and 1, and usually thought of as off and on. Consequently, all data processed by a binary computer must be in binary form. The 0s and 1s used to represent data can be represented in a variety of ways, such as with an open or closed circuit, the absence or presence of electronic current, two different types of magnetic alignment on a storage medium, and so on, as shown in Exhibit 2-1.

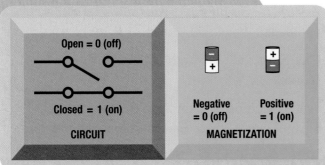

Exhibit 2-1 Ways of representing 0 and 1

Open = 0 (off)
Closed = 1 (on)
CIRCUIT

Negative = 0 (off)   Positive = 1 (on)
MAGNETIZATION

Hardware surrounds us in all areas of our lives—from computers and cell phones to cameras, digital music/media players, and gaming devices to barcode readers, ATMs, and toll booths.

© Fancy Collection/SuperStock

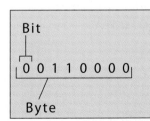

Regardless of their physical representations, these 0s and 1s are commonly referred to as bits, a computing term derived from the phrase *binary digits*. A **bit** is the smallest unit of data that a binary computer can recognize. The input you enter via a keyboard, the software program you use to play your music collection, the term paper stored on your computer, and the digital photos located on your mobile phone are all just groups of bits. A bit by itself typically represents only a fraction of a piece of data. Eight bits grouped together are collectively referred to as a **byte**. A named collection of bytes that represent something such as a written document, a computer program, a digital photo, a song, or virtually any other type of data is called a **file**. Because

bit The smallest unit of data that a binary computer can recognize.

byte Eight bits grouped together.

file A named collection of bytes that represent virtually any type of data.

The computer translates data into binary 0s and 1s, processes it, and then translates it back to output the results in a form we can understand.

the numbers of bytes needed to represent a file can be in the thousands or millions of bytes, prefixes are commonly used with the term *byte* to represent larger amounts of data.

A Bit about Bytes

The following terms show how prefixes are combined with the term *byte* to describe data that is large than a byte:

▶ 1 **kilobyte (KB)** is equal to 1,024 bytes, but is usually thought of as approximately 1,000 bytes.

▶ 1 **megabyte (MB)** is about 1 million bytes.

▶ 1 **gigabyte (GB)** is about 1 billion bytes.

▶ 1 **terabyte (TB)** is about 1 trillion bytes.

▶ 1 **petabyte (PB)** is about 1,000 terabytes (2^{50} bytes).

▶ 1 **exabyte (EB)** is about 1,000 petabytes (2^{60} bytes).

▶ 1 **zettabyte (ZB)** is about 1,000 exabytes (2^{70} bytes).

▶ 1 **yottabyte (YB)** is about 1,000 zettabytes (2^{80} bytes).

system unit The main case of a computer.

circuit board A thin board containing computer chips and other electronic components.

computer chip A very small piece of silicon or other semi-conducting material that contains integrated circuits (ICs) and transistors.

motherboard The main circuit board inside the system unit.

port A connector on the exterior of the system unit case that is used to connect an external hardware device.

The **system unit** is the main case of a computer. It houses the processing hardware for that computer, as well as a few other devices, such as storage devices, the power supply, and cooling fans. The system unit for a desktop computer is often a rectangular box, although other shapes and sizes are available. The inside of a system unit for a typical desktop computer system is shown in Exhibit 2-2.

The Motherboard

A **circuit board** is a thin board containing computer chips and other electronic components. **Computer chips** are very small pieces of silicon or other semiconducting material that contain integrated circuits (ICs), which are collections of electronic circuits containing microscopic pathways along which electrical current can travel, and transistors, which are switches controlling the flow of electrons along the pathways. The main circuit board inside the system unit is called the **motherboard**.

All devices used with a computer need to be connected via a wired or wireless connection to the motherboard. Typically, external devices such as monitors, keyboards, mice, and printers connect to the motherboard by plugging into a port. A **port** is a special connector accessible through the exterior of the system unit case that is used to connect an external hardware device. The port is either built into the motherboard or created with an expansion card inserted into an expansion slot on the motherboard. Wireless external devices typically use a transceiver that plugs into a port on the computer to transmit data between the wireless device and the motherboard or they use wireless networking technology, such as Bluetooth, built into the motherboard.

The system unit for portable computers and mobile devices is usually combined with the screen to form a single piece of hardware.

Exhibit 2-2 Inside a typical system unit

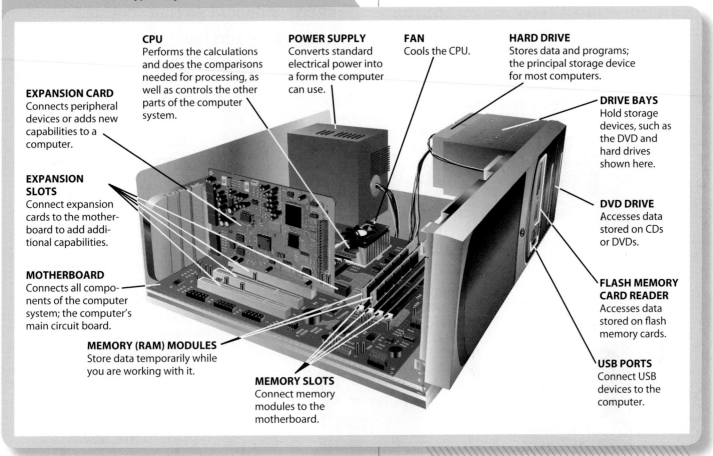

CPU
Performs the calculations and does the comparisons needed for processing, as well as controls the other parts of the computer system.

POWER SUPPLY
Converts standard electrical power into a form the computer can use.

FAN
Cools the CPU.

HARD DRIVE
Stores data and programs; the principal storage device for most computers.

EXPANSION CARD
Connects peripheral devices or adds new capabilities to a computer.

EXPANSION SLOTS
Connect expansion cards to the motherboard to add additional capabilities.

MOTHERBOARD
Connects all components of the computer system; the computer's main circuit board.

MEMORY (RAM) MODULES
Store data temporarily while you are working with it.

MEMORY SLOTS
Connect memory modules to the motherboard.

DRIVE BAYS
Hold storage devices, such as the DVD and hard drives shown here.

DVD DRIVE
Accesses data stored on CDs or DVDs.

FLASH MEMORY CARD READER
Accesses data stored on flash memory cards.

USB PORTS
Connect USB devices to the computer.

The Power Supply

The power supply inside a desktop computer connects to the motherboard to deliver electricity to the computer. Portable computers almost always contain a rechargeable battery pack to power the computer when it is not connected to a power outlet, as well as an external power supply adapter that connects the computer to a power outlet to recharge the battery when needed.

Nonremovable Batteries

One issue with newer portable computers and mobile devices is the growing use of nonremovable batteries. These batteries make the devices lighter and are supposed to last for the typical life of the device. However, they are more difficult and expensive to replace if they fail. And, often it is not worth the trouble and expense to replace them in mobile devices such as mobile phones and portable digital media players.

A growing amount of e-trash is being generated worldwide from discarded mobile phones and other electronics.

The CPU

The **central processing unit** (**CPU** or **processor**) is a computer chip that performs the calculations and comparisons needed for processing; it also controls the computer's operations. The CPU is the main processing device for a computer and is often considered the "brain" of the computer. The CPU consists of a variety of circuitry and components that are packaged together and are

central processing unit (**CPU** or **processor**)
The chip located on the motherboard of a computer that performs the processing for a computer.

connected directly to the motherboard. Most personal computers today use CPUs manufactured by Intel or Advanced Micro Devices (AMD). Some examples of their processors are shown in Exhibit 2-3.

Exhibit 2-3 Examples of CPUs

Four cores

Shared Level 3 cache memory

DESKTOP PROCESSORS
Typically have 2 to 4 cores and are designed for performance.

SERVER AND WORKSTATION PROCESSORS
Typically have at least 4 cores and are designed for very high performance.

NOTEBOOK PROCESSORS
Typically have 2 to 4 cores and are designed for performance and increased battery life.

NETBOOK PROCESSORS
Typically have 1 to 2 cores, are small in size, and are designed for extended battery life.

CPUs are becoming more energy-efficient so that they use less power and have a longer battery life.

Many CPUs today are **multi-core CPUs**; that is, CPUs that contain the processing components or cores of multiple independent processors in a single CPU. For example, dual-core CPUs contain two cores and quad-core CPUs contain four cores. Multi-core CPUs allow computers to work simultaneously on more than one task at a time, such as burning a DVD while surfing the Web, as well as to work faster within a single application if the software is designed to take advantage of multiple cores.

One measurement of the processing speed of a CPU is the CPU **clock speed**, which measures of the number of instructions that can be processed per second. Clock speed is typically rated in megahertz (MHz) or gigahertz (GHz). A higher CPU

The CPU is also called the microprocessor when talking about personal computers, and just the processor when speaking in general terms for any computer.

multi-core CPU A CPU that contains the processing components or cores of multiple independent processors in a single CPU.

clock speed A measurement of the number of instructions that a CPU can process per second.

Measuring Computer Speed

Although CPU clock speed is important to computer performance, other factors (such as the number of cores, the amount of RAM and cache memory, the speed of external storage devices, and the bus width and bus speed) greatly affect the overall processing speed of the computer. As a result, computers today are beginning to be classified less by CPU clock speed and more by the computer's overall processing speed or performance.

Cooling Components

One byproduct of packing an increasing amount of technology in a smaller system unit is heat, an ongoing problem for CPU and computer manufacturers. Because heat can damage components and cooler chips can run faster, virtually all computers today employ fans, heat sinks (small components typically made out of aluminum with fins that help to dissipate heat), or other methods to cool the CPU and system unit, including liquid-filled tubes that draw heat away from processors. Notebook computer users can use a notebook cooling stand if the built-in fan is not sufficient to cool the PC.

Fans on the back of the system unit

Fan on top of the CPU

Water cooling tubes

FANS AND WATER COOLING SYSTEMS
These cooling methods and heat sinks are used with computers today to cool the inside of the computer.

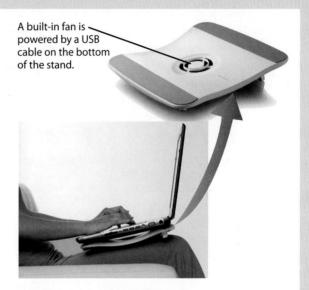

A built-in fan is powered by a USB cable on the bottom of the stand.

NOTEBOOK COOLING STANDS
These stands cool the underside of a notebook computer by allowing for better air circulation; some stands also include a fan.

clock speed means that more instructions can be processed per second than the same CPU with a lower CPU clock speed.

A computer **word** is the amount of data (measured in bits or bytes) that a CPU can manipulate at one time. While CPUs just a few years ago used 32-bit words (referred to as 32-bit processors), most CPUs today are 64-bit processors (that is, they are capable of using 64-bit words, in addition to 32-bit words). Usually, a larger word size allows for faster processing, provided the software being used is written to take advantage of 64-bit processing.

Cache memory is a special group of very fast memory circuitry located on or close to the CPU that is used to speed up processing by storing the data and instructions that may be needed next by the CPU in handy locations. When cache memory is full and the CPU calls for additional data or a new instruction, the system overwrites as much data in cache memory as needed to make room for the new data or instruction. This allows the data and instructions that are most likely still needed to remain in cache memory.

> CPUs for the earliest personal computers ran at less than 5 MHz; the fastest CPUs have today a clock speed of more than 3 GHz.

word The amount of data (measured in bits or bytes) that a CPU can manipulate at one time.

cache memory A group of very fast memory circuitry located on or close to the CPU to speed up processing.

Cache Memory Level Numbers

Cache memory level numbers indicate the order in which the various caches are accessed by the CPU when it requires new data or instructions. Level 1 (L1) cache (which is the fastest type of cache but typically holds less data than other levels of cache) is checked first, followed by Level 2 (L2) cache, followed by Level 3 (L3) cache if it exists. Typically, more cache memory results in faster processing. Most multi-core CPUs today have some cache memory (such as an L1 and L2 cache) dedicated to each core. They might also use a larger shared cache memory (such as L3 cache) that can be accessed by any core as needed.

Memory

In a computer, **memory** is chips located inside the system unit that the computer uses to store data and instructions while it is working with them. **RAM** (**random access memory**) is used to store the essential parts of the operating system while the computer is running, as well as the programs and data that the computer is currently using. The term *memory* in reference to computers usually means RAM. Because RAM is volatile, its content is erased when the computer is shut off. Data in RAM is also deleted when it is no longer needed, such as when the program using that data is closed.

Like the CPU, RAM consists of electronic circuits etched onto chips. As shown in Exhibit 2-4, these chips are arranged onto circuit boards called memory modules, which, in turn, are plugged into the motherboard. Most personal computers sold today have slots for two to four memory modules, and at least one slot will be filled. For example, the motherboard shown in Exhibit 2-2 has two memory modules installed and room to add two more modules. If you want to add more RAM to a computer and no empty slots are available, you must replace at least one of the existing memory modules with higher capacity modules.

memory Chips located inside the system unit used to store data and instructions while it is working with them.

RAM (**random access memory**) Memory used to store data and instructions while the computer is running.

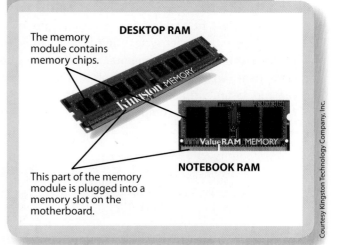

Exhibit 2-4 RAM memory modules

The memory module contains memory chips.

DESKTOP RAM

NOTEBOOK RAM

This part of the memory module is plugged into a memory slot on the motherboard.

Courtesy Kingston Technology Company, Inc.

RAM capacity is measured in bytes. The amount of RAM that can be installed in a computer system depends on the CPU in that computer and the operating system being used. For instance, while computers using 64-bit CPUs today can utilize a virtually unlimited amount of RAM (older 32-bit CPUs can use up to only 4 GB of RAM), a 64-bit operating system is needed in order to use more than 4 GB of RAM. In addition, different versions of a 64-bit operating system may support different amounts of RAM. For instance, the 64-bit versions of Windows Vista can use up to 8 GB, up to 16 GB, or more than 128 GB of RAM, depending on the edition of Windows Vista being used. Consequently, when adding RAM to a computer, it is important to determine that the computer can support it. Having more RAM allows more applications to run at one time and the computer to respond more quickly when a user switches from task to task.

It is also important to select the proper type and speed of RAM when adding new memory. Most personal computers today use SDRAM (synchronous dynamic RAM). SDRAM is commonly available in DDR (double-data rate), DDR2, and DDR3 versions. DDR memory sends data twice as often as ordinary SDRAM to increase

Most personal computers sold today have at least 1 GB of RAM, and 2 to 8 GB of RAM is generally considered a normal amount for home computers.

> For optimal performance, you should use the type and speed of RAM that was designed to work with your computer.

throughput, DDR2 transmits twice as much data in the same time period as DDR, and DDR3 is about twice as fast as the highest-speed DDR2 memory available today. Each type of SDRAM is typically available in a variety of speeds (measured in MHz).

To further improve memory performance, memory today typically uses a dual-channel memory architecture, which has two paths that go to and from memory and so it can transfer twice as much data at one time as single-channel memory architecture of the same speed. Tri-channel (three paths) and quad-channel (four paths) memory architecture are also beginning to be used for higher performance. Multi-channel RAM typically needs to be installed in matched sets, such as two 1 GB dual-channel memory modules instead of a single 2 GB dual-channel memory module.

A **register** is high-speed memory built into the CPU that temporarily stores data during processing. Registers are used by the CPU to store data and intermediary results temporarily during processing. Registers are the fastest type of memory used by the CPU, even faster than Level 1 cache. Generally, more registers and larger registers result in increased CPU performance. Most CPUs contain multiple registers that are used for specific purposes.

ROM (**read-only memory**) consists of nonvolatile chips that permanently store data or programs. Like RAM, these chips are attached to the motherboard inside the system unit, and the data or programs are retrieved by the computer when they are needed. An important difference, however, is that you can neither write over the data or programs in ROM chips (which is the reason ROM chips are called read-only), nor erase their content when you shut off the computer's power. ROM is used for storing permanent instructions used by a computer (referred to as firmware).

Flash memory consists of nonvolatile memory chips that can be used for storage by the computer or the user. Flash memory chips have begun to replace ROM for storing system information. By storing this information in flash memory instead of ROM, the BIOS information can be updated as needed. For instance, firmware for personal computers and other devices, such

Memory Addresses

Regardless of the type of RAM used, the CPU must be able to find data and programs located in memory when they are needed. To accomplish this, each location in memory has an address. Each address typically holds only one byte. When the computer has finished using a program or set of data, it frees up that memory space to hold other programs and data. Therefore, the content of each memory location constantly changes. This process can be roughly compared with the handling of the mailboxes in your local post office: the number on each P.O. box (memory location) remains the same, but the mail (data) stored inside changes as patrons remove their mail and as new mail arrives.

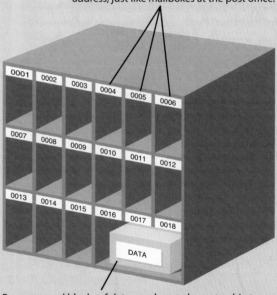

Each location in memory has a unique address, just like mailboxes at the post office.

Programs and blocks of data are almost always too big to fit in a single address. A directory keeps track of the first address used to store each program and data block, and the number of addresses each block spans.

register High-speed memory built into the CPU.

ROM (**read-only memory**) Nonvolatile chips on the motherboard that permanently store data or programs.

flash memory Nonvolatile memory chips that can be used for storage by the computer or the user.

> Cache memory and registers are volatile like RAM, which means that their content is erased when power to the memory ceases.

as mobile phones and networking hardware, is now typically stored in flash memory that is embedded in the device so the firmware can be updated over the life of the product.

Flash Memory Uses

Flash memory chips have begun to replace ROM for storing system information, such as a computer's **BIOS** or basic input/output system—the sequence of instructions the computer follows during the boot process. For instance, one of the computer's first activities when you turn on the power is to perform a power-on self-test or POST. The POST takes an inventory of system components, checks each component for proper functioning, and initializes system settings, which produces the beeps you may hear as your computer boots. Traditionally, the instructions for the POST have been stored in ROM. By storing this information in flash memory instead of ROM, however, the BIOS information can be updated as needed.

Expansion Slots, Expansion Cards, and ExpressCard Modules

Expansion slots are locations on the motherboard into which expansion cards can be inserted to connect those cards to the motherboard. **Expansion cards** (also called

BIOS (basic input/output system) The sequence of instructions the computer follows during the boot process.

expansion slot A location on the motherboard into which an expansion card is inserted to connect it to the motherboard.

expansion card (interface card) A circuit board used to give desktop computers additional capabilities.

bus An electronic path over which data travels.

throughput (bandwidth) The amount of data that can be transferred via the bus in a given time period.

interface cards) are used to give desktop computers additional capabilities, such as to connect the computer to a network, to add a TV tuner to allow television shows to be watched and recorded on the computer, or to connect a monitor to the computer. Most desktop computers come with a few empty expansion slots so new expansion cards can be added as needed. Traditionally, PC Cards were used for notebook expansion, but today most notebook and netbook computers use the newer ExpressCard modules. ExpressCard modules are inserted into the computer's ExpressCard slot; they can also be used with any desktop computer that has an ExpressCard slot. Exhibit 2-5 shows a typical expansion card and ExpressCard module.

Exhibit 2-5 Expansion card and ExpressCard module

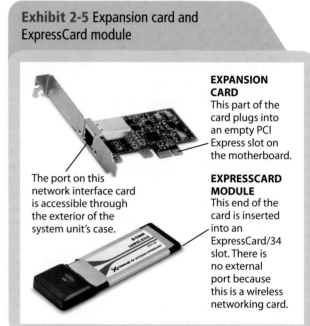

EXPANSION CARD
This part of the card plugs into an empty PCI Express slot on the motherboard.

The port on this network interface card is accessible through the exterior of the system unit's case.

EXPRESSCARD MODULE
This end of the card is inserted into an ExpressCard/34 slot. There is no external port because this is a wireless networking card.

Courtesy D-Link Systems, Inc.

Buses

A **bus** is an electronic path over which data can travel. Buses are located within the CPU to move data between CPU components; a variety of buses are also etched onto the motherboard to tie the CPU to memory and to peripheral devices.

You can picture a bus as a highway with several lanes; each wire in the bus acts as a separate lane, transmitting one bit at a time. The number of bits being transmitted at one time depends on the bus width, which is the number of wires in the bus over which data can travel (see Exhibit 2-6). The bus speed is also a very important factor because the bus width and bus speed together determine the bus's **throughput** or **bandwidth**; that is, the amount of data that can be transferred via the bus in a given time period.

Exhibit 2-6 Bus width

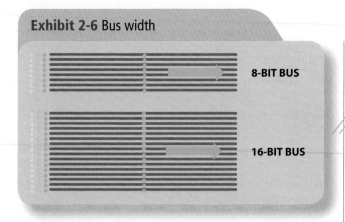

8-BIT BUS

16-BIT BUS

The buses that connect peripheral (typically input and output) devices to the motherboard are often called **expansion buses**. Expansion buses connect directly to ports on the system unit case or to expansion slots on the motherboard. Some of the most common expansion buses and expansion slots are illustrated in Exhibit 2-7.

Each type of expansion slot is designed for a specific type of expansion card.

One of the more versatile bus architectures is the **Universal Serial Bus** (**USB**). The USB standard allows 127 different devices to connect to a computer via a single USB port on the computer's system unit. At 12 Mbps (millions of bits per second), the original USB 1.0 standard is slow. However, the newer USB 2.0 standard supports data transfer rates of 480 Mbps, and the emerging 4.8 Gbps USB 3.0 standard (also called SuperSpeed USB) is about 10 times faster than USB 2.0. The convenience and universal support of USB have made it one of the most widely used standards for connecting peripherals today.

FireWire (also known as **IEEE 1394**) is a high-speed bus standard developed by Apple for connecting devices—particularly multimedia devices like digital video cameras—to a computer. Like USB, FireWire can connect multiple external devices via a single port. FireWire is relatively fast—the original FireWire standard supports data transfer rates of up to 320 Mbps, the newer FireWire standard (called FireWire 800) supports data transfer rates up to 800 Mbps, and the emerging FireWire 3200 standard offers 3.2 Gbps transfer rates.

Exhibit 2-7 Buses and expansion slots

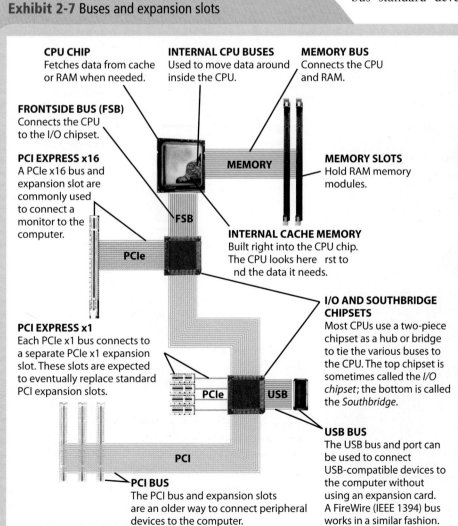

CPU CHIP
Fetches data from cache or RAM when needed.

INTERNAL CPU BUSES
Used to move data around inside the CPU.

MEMORY BUS
Connects the CPU and RAM.

FRONTSIDE BUS (FSB)
Connects the CPU to the I/O chipset.

PCI EXPRESS x16
A PCIe x16 bus and expansion slot are commonly used to connect a monitor to the computer.

MEMORY SLOTS
Hold RAM memory modules.

INTERNAL CACHE MEMORY
Built right into the CPU chip. The CPU looks here rst to nd the data it needs.

PCI EXPRESS x1
Each PCIe x1 bus connects to a separate PCIe x1 expansion slot. These slots are expected to eventually replace standard PCI expansion slots.

I/O AND SOUTHBRIDGE CHIPSETS
Most CPUs use a two-piece chipset as a hub or bridge to tie the various buses to the CPU. The top chipset is sometimes called the *I/O chipset*; the bottom is called the *Southbridge*.

USB BUS
The USB bus and port can be used to connect USB-compatible devices to the computer without using an expansion card. A FireWire (IEEE 1394) bus works in a similar fashion.

PCI BUS
The PCI bus and expansion slots are an older way to connect peripheral devices to the computer.

MEMORY

FSB

PCIe

PCIe

USB

PCI

expansion bus A bus on the motherboard used to connect peripheral devices.

Universal Serial Bus (**USB**) A versatile bus architecture widely used for connecting peripherals.

FireWire (**IEEE 1394**) A high-speed bus standard used to connect devices—particularly multimedia devices like digital video cameras—to a computer.

Ports and Connectors

As already mentioned, ports are the connectors located on the exterior of the system unit that are used to connect external hardware devices. Each port is attached to the appropriate bus on the motherboard so that when a device is plugged into a port, the device can communicate with the CPU and other computer components. Typical ports for a desktop computer and the connectors used with those ports are shown in Exhibit 2-8.

Notebook and netbook computers have ports similar to desktop computers, but sometimes have fewer of them. UMPCs and mobile devices have a more limited amount of expandability. However, these devices usually come with at least one built-in expansion slot—typically a USB port or an SD slot, which can be used with both the postage-stamp-sized Secure Digital (SD) flash memory cards and with peripheral devices adhering to the Secure Digital Input/Output (SDIO) standard.

Plug and Play

Most computers today support the Plug and Play standard, which means the computer automatically configures new devices as soon as they are installed and the computer is powered up. If you want to add a new device to your desktop computer and a port is available for the device you want to add, then you just need to plug it in. However, you should shut down the computer first unless the device uses a USB or FireWire port. USB and FireWire devices are hot-swappable, meaning they can be plugged into their respective ports while the computer is powered up. Before plugging in other devices, shut the computer down first, and the new devices will be recognized by the computer when the computer is powered up after the device has been added.

Exhibit 2-8 Typical ports and connectors for desktop computers

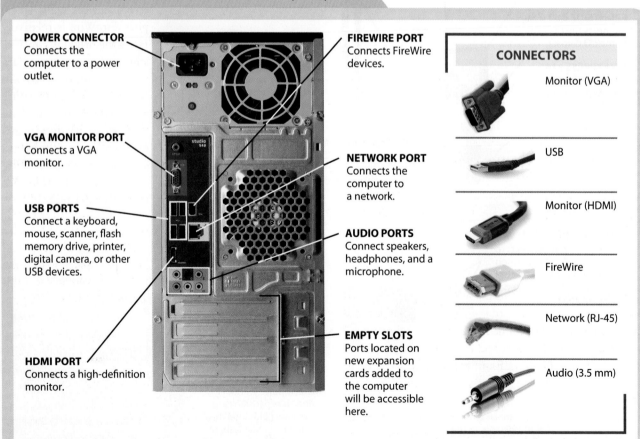

POWER CONNECTOR Connects the computer to a power outlet.

VGA MONITOR PORT Connects a VGA monitor.

USB PORTS Connect a keyboard, mouse, scanner, flash memory drive, printer, digital camera, or other USB devices.

HDMI PORT Connects a high-definition monitor.

FIREWIRE PORT Connects FireWire devices.

NETWORK PORT Connects the computer to a network.

AUDIO PORTS Connect speakers, headphones, and a microphone.

EMPTY SLOTS Ports located on new expansion cards added to the computer will be accessible here.

CONNECTORS

Monitor (VGA)

USB

Monitor (HDMI)

FireWire

Network (RJ-45)

Audio (3.5 mm)

Exhibit 2-9 CPU components

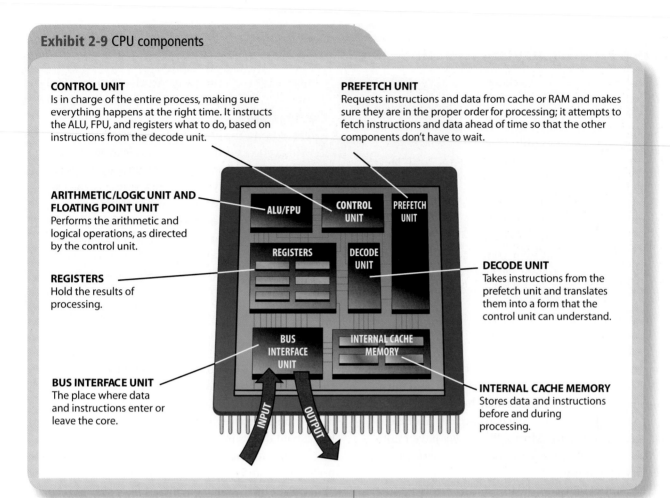

CONTROL UNIT
Is in charge of the entire process, making sure everything happens at the right time. It instructs the ALU, FPU, and registers what to do, based on instructions from the decode unit.

PREFETCH UNIT
Requests instructions and data from cache or RAM and makes sure they are in the proper order for processing; it attempts to fetch instructions and data ahead of time so that the other components don't have to wait.

ARITHMETIC/LOGIC UNIT AND FLOATING POINT UNIT
Performs the arithmetic and logical operations, as directed by the control unit.

REGISTERS
Hold the results of processing.

BUS INTERFACE UNIT
The place where data and instructions enter or leave the core.

DECODE UNIT
Takes instructions from the prefetch unit and translates them into a form that the control unit can understand.

INTERNAL CACHE MEMORY
Stores data and instructions before and during processing.

ALU/FPU · CONTROL UNIT · PREFETCH UNIT · REGISTERS · DECODE UNIT · BUS INTERFACE UNIT · INTERNAL CACHE MEMORY · INPUT · OUTPUT

LO2.3 How the CPU Works

A CPU consists of a variety of circuitry and components packaged together into a single component. The key element of the CPU is the **transistor**—a device made of semiconductor material that controls the flow of electrons inside a chip. Today's CPUs contain hundreds of millions of transistors.

Typical CPU Components

To begin to understand how a CPU works, you need to know how the CPU is organized and what components it includes. A simplified example of the principal components that might be included in a single core of a typical CPU is shown in Exhibit 2-9. Additional components are also typically located inside the CPU, but not within each core. For instance, there are buses to connect the CPU cores to each other, buses to connect each core to the CPU's memory controller (which controls the communication between the CPU cores and RAM), and buses to connect each core to any cache memory that is shared between the cores.

The **arithmetic/logic unit** (**ALU**) is the section of a CPU core that performs arithmetic (addition, subtraction, multiplication, and division) involving integers and logical operations (such as comparing two pieces of data to see if they are equal or determining if a specific condition is true or false). Arithmetic requiring decimals is usually performed by the **floating point unit** (**FPU**). Arithmetic operations are performed when mathematical calculations are requested by the user, as well as when many other common computing tasks are performed. For example, editing a digital

transistor A device made of semiconductor material that controls the flow of electrons inside a chip.

arithmetic/logic unit (**ALU**) The part of a CPU core that performs logical operations and integer arithmetic.

floating point unit (**FPU**) The part of a CPU core that performs decimal arithmetic.

High-Tech Investigators

With the high value of technology, claims of stolen technology and patent infringements are happening all the time. Increasingly, companies in the computer industry turn to reverse engineering companies, such as TAEUS International, which tear products apart to hunt for patented technologies that should not be there. Just as with criminal investigations, patent infringement claims require physical proof. Engineers inspect and photograph criti-

A TAEUS engineer at work

cal elements of a product (see the accompanying photo) to compare that product to existing patents. Other companies in the area of computer forensics specialize in finding different types of digital evidence needed for legal proceedings, such as recovering files deleted from a computer or storage medium, determining activities previously performed on a computer, and unlocking encrypted files.

photograph in an image editing program, running the spell checker in a word processing program, and burning a music CD are all performed by the ALU, with help from the FPU when needed, using only arithmetic and logical operations. Most CPUs today have multiple ALUs and FPUs that work together to perform the necessary operations.

The **control unit** coordinates and controls the operations and activities taking place within a CPU core, such as retrieving data and instructions and passing them on to the ALU or FPU for execution. In other words, it directs the flow of electronic traffic within the core, much like a traffic cop controls the flow of vehicles on a roadway. Essentially, the control unit tells the ALU and FPU what to do and makes sure that everything happens at the right time in order for the appropriate processing to take place.

The **prefetch unit** orders data and instructions from cache or RAM based on the current task. The prefetch unit tries to predict what data and instructions will be needed and retrieves them ahead of time, in order to help avoid delays in processing.

The **decode unit** takes the instructions fetched by the prefetch unit and translates them into a form that can be understood by the control unit, ALU, and FPU. The decoded instructions go to the control unit for processing.

The **bus interface unit** allows the core to communicate with other CPU components, such as the memory controller and other cores. As previously mentioned, the memory controller controls the flow of instructions and data going between the CPU cores and RAM.

The System Clock and the Machine Cycle

In order to synchronize all of a computer's operations, a **system clock**—a small quartz crystal located on the motherboard—is used. The system clock sends out a signal on a regular basis to all other computer components, similar to a musician's metronome or a person's heartbeat. Each signal is referred to as a cycle. The number of cycles per second is measured in hertz (Hz). One megahertz (MHz) is equal to one million ticks of the system clock. Many personal computers today have system clocks that run at 200 MHz, and all devices (such as CPUs) that are synchronized with these system clocks run at either the system clock speed or at a multiple of or a fraction of the system clock speed. During each CPU clock tick, the CPU can execute one or more pieces of microcode.

control unit The part of a CPU core that coordinates its operations.

prefetch unit The part of a CPU core that attempts to retrieve data and instructions before they are needed for processing in order to avoid delays.

decode unit The part of a CPU core that translates instructions into a form that can be processed by the ALU and FPU.

bus interface unit The section of a CPU core that allows the core to communicate with other CPU components.

system clock A small quartz crystal located on the motherboard that synchronizes the computer's operations.

Exhibit 2-10 Machine cycle

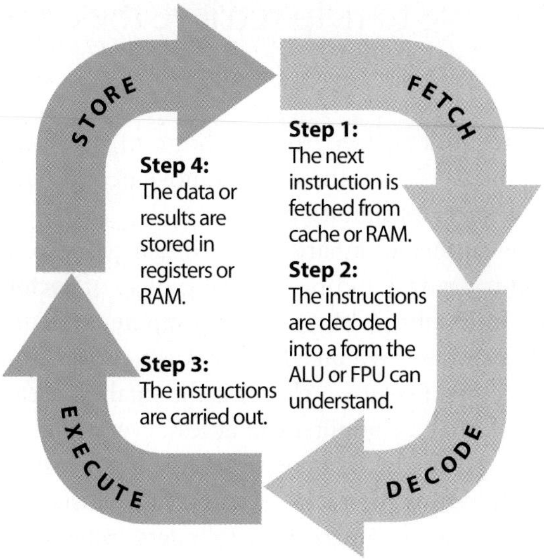

Step 1: The next instruction is fetched from cache or RAM.

Step 2: The instructions are decoded into a form the ALU or FPU can understand.

Step 3: The instructions are carried out.

Step 4: The data or results are stored in registers or RAM.

STORE · FETCH · DECODE · EXECUTE

Whenever the CPU processes a single piece of microcode, it is referred to as a **machine cycle**. Each machine cycle consists of four general operations as shown in Exhibit 2-10.

LO2.4 Storage Systems

When you first create a document on your computer, both the program you are using to create the document and the document itself are temporarily stored in RAM. But when the program is closed, the computer no longer needs to work with the program or the document, and so they are both erased from RAM. Consequently, anything that needs to be preserved for future use, such as a word processing document, must be stored on a more permanent medium.

Storage systems make it possible to save programs, data, and processing results for later use. They provide nonvolatile storage, so that when the power is shut off, the data stored on the storage medium remains intact. All storage systems involve two physical parts: A **storage medium** is the hardware where data is actually stored; a storage medium is inserted into its corresponding **storage device** in order to be read from or written to.

Letters of the alphabet and/or names are typically assigned to each storage device so that the user can identify a device easily when it needs to be used (see Exhibit 2-11). Some drive letters, such as the letter C typically used with the primary hard drive, are usually consistent from computer to computer and do not change even if more storage devices are added to a computer. The rest of the drive letters on a computer might change as new devices are added. When a new storage device is detected, the computer just assigns and reassigns drive letters, as needed.

Hard Drives

With the exception of computers designed to use only network storage devices (such as network computers and some Internet appliances), virtually all personal computers come with a **hard drive** that is used to store most programs and data. Internal hard drives (those located inside the system unit) are not designed to be removed, unless they need to be repaired or replaced.

Exhibit 2-11 Storage device identifiers

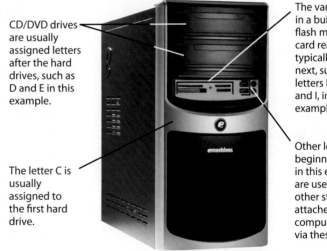

CD/DVD drives are usually assigned letters after the hard drives, such as D and E in this example.

The letter C is usually assigned to the first hard drive.

The various slots in a built-in flash memory card reader are typically assigned next, such as the letters F, G, H and I, in this example.

Other letters, beginning with J in this example, are used for any other storage devices attached to the computer, such as via these USB ports.

Courtesy of Gateway, Inc.

machine cycle The series of steps performed by the computer when the CPU processes a single piece of microcode.

storage medium The hardware where data is actually stored.

storage device The hardware where a storage medium is read from or written to.

hard drive Hardware used to store most programs and data on a computer.

External hard drives typically connect to a computer via a USB or FireWire port and are frequently used for additional storage (such as for digital photos, videos, and other large multimedia files), to move files between computers, and for backup purposes.

Most hard drives are magnetic. **Magnetic hard drives** contain one or more round pieces of metal (called hard disks or platters) that are coated with a magnetizable substance. These hard disks are permanently sealed inside the hard drive case, along with the read/write heads used to store (write) and retrieve (read) data and an access mechanism used to move the read/write heads in and out over the surface of the hard disks (see Exhibit 2-12). One hard drive usually contains a stack of several hard disks. If so, there is a read/write head for

Exhibit 2-12 How data is stored on magnetic disks

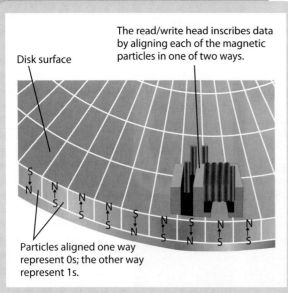

The read/write head inscribes data by aligning each of the magnetic particles in one of two ways.

Disk surface

Particles aligned one way represent 0s; the other way represent 1s.

magnetic hard drive A hard drive consisting of one or more metal magnetic disks permanently sealed, with an access mechanism and read/write heads, inside its drive.

track A concentric ring on the surface of a hard disk where data is recorded.

sector A pie-shaped section on the surface of a hard disk.

cluster The smallest storage area on a hard disk formed by one or more sectors.

cylinder The collection of tracks located in the same location on a set of hard disk surfaces.

> When hard drives become damaged, data recovery firms may be able to help retrieve the data.

each hard disk surface (top and bottom), as illustrated in Exhibit 2-13, and these heads move in and out over the disk surfaces simultaneously.

The surface of a hard disk is organized into **tracks** (concentric rings) and pie-shaped groups of **sectors**, as shown in Exhibit 2-14. On most computer systems, the smallest storage area on a hard disk is a **cluster**—one or more sectors. Because a cluster is the smallest area on a hard disk that a computer can access, everything stored on a hard disk always takes up at least one cluster.

In addition to tracks, sectors, and clusters, hard disks are also organized into **cylinders** (refer again to Exhibit 2-14). A cylinder is the collection of one particular track, such as the first track or the tenth track, on each hard disk surface.

It is important to realize that a magnetic hard drive's read/write heads never touch the surface of the hard disks at any time, even during reading and writing. If the read/write heads do touch the surface—for example, if a desktop computer is bumped while the hard drive is spinning or if a foreign object gets onto the surface of a hard disk—a head crash occurs, which may permanently damage the hard drive. Because the read/write heads are located extremely close to the surface of the hard disks (less than one-half millionth of an inch above the surface), the presence of a foreign object the width of a human hair or even a smoke particle on the surface of a hard disk is like placing a huge boulder on a road and then trying to drive over it with your car.

Back Up Data

Because you never know when a head crash or other hard drive failure will occur—there may be no warning whatsoever—be sure to back up the data on your hard drive on a regular basis. Backing up data—that is, creating a second copy of important files—is critical not only for businesses but also for individuals.

Exhibit 2-13 Magnetic hard drives

MOUNTING SHAFT
The mounting shaft spins the hard disks at a speed of several thousand revolutions per minute while the computer is turned on.

SEALED DRIVE
The hard disks and the drive mechanism are hermetically sealed inside a case to keep them free from contamination.

2.5-INCH HARD DRIVE LOCATED INSIDE A NOTEBOOK COMPUTER

READ/WRITE HEADS
There is a read/write head for each hard disk surface, and they move in and out over the disks together.

HARD DISKS
There are usually several hard disk surfaces on which to store data. Most hard drives store data on both sides of each disk.

ACCESS MECHANISM
The access mechanism moves the read/write heads in and out together between the hard disk surfaces to access required data.

INSIDE A 3.5-INCH HARD DRIVE

Exhibit 2-14 Organization of a magnetic hard disk

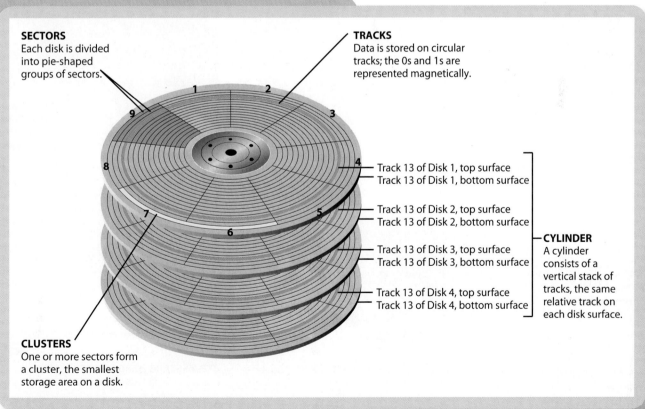

SECTORS
Each disk is divided into pie-shaped groups of sectors.

TRACKS
Data is stored on circular tracks; the 0s and 1s are represented magnetically.

Track 13 of Disk 1, top surface
Track 13 of Disk 1, bottom surface

Track 13 of Disk 2, top surface
Track 13 of Disk 2, bottom surface

Track 13 of Disk 3, top surface
Track 13 of Disk 3, bottom surface

Track 13 of Disk 4, top surface
Track 13 of Disk 4, bottom surface

CYLINDER
A cylinder consists of a vertical stack of tracks, the same relative track on each disk surface.

CLUSTERS
One or more sectors form a cluster, the smallest storage area on a disk.

A newer type of hard drive is the **solid-state drive** (**SSD**, also called a **flash memory hard drive**), which is a hard drive that uses flash memory technology instead of spinning hard disk platters and magnetic technology. Consequently, data is stored as electrical charges on flash memory media and SSDs have no moving parts. See Exhibit 2-15. These characteristics mean that SSDs are not subject to mechanical failures like magnetic hard drives, and are, therefore, more resistant to shock and vibration. They also consume less power, make no noise, and boot faster. Although previously too expensive for all but specialty applications, prices of SSDs have fallen significantly over the past few years and they are becoming the norm for netbooks and other very portable computers.

Hard drives can be internal or external. Internal hard drives are permanently located inside a computer's system unit and typically are not removed unless a problem occurs with them. Virtually all computers have at least one internal hard drive that is used to store programs and data. In addition, a variety of external hard drives are available (see Exhibit 2-16). External hard drives are commonly used to transport a large amount of data from one computer to another, for backup purposes, and for additional storage.

Exhibit 2-15 Solid-state drives (SSDs)

Data is stored in flash memory chips located inside the drive; there are no moving parts like in magnetic hard drives.

The total time that it takes for a hard drive to read or write data is called the **disk access time** and requires the following:

External hard drives are typically magnetic hard drives and hold between 500 GB and 4 TB.

Exhibit 2-16 External hard drives

FULL-SIZED EXTERNAL HARD DRIVES
Are about the size of a 5 by 7-inch picture frame, but thicker; this drive holds 1.5 TB.

PORTABLE HARD DRIVES (MAGNETIC)
Are about the size of a 3 by 5-inch index card, but thicker; this drive holds 500 GB.

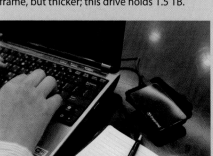

PORTABLE HARD DRIVES (SSD)
Are about the size of a credit card, but thicker; this drive holds 18 MB.

EXPRESSCARD HARD DRIVES
Fit into an ExpressCard slot; this drive holds 32 GB.

solid state drive (**SSD** or **flash memory hard drive**) A hard drive that uses flash memory media.

disk access time The total time that it takes for a hard drive to read or write data.

1. **Seek time**—The read/write heads move to the cylinder that contains (or will contain) the desired data.

2. **Rotational delay**—The hard disks rotate into the proper position so that the read/write heads are located over the part of the cylinder to be used.

3. **Data movement time**—The data moves, such as reading the data from the hard disk and transferring it to memory, or transfers from memory and is stored on the hard disk.

A typical disk access time is around 8.5 milliseconds (ms). To minimize disk access time, magnetic hard drives usually store related data on the same cylinder. This strategy reduces seek time and, therefore, improves the overall access time.

Because SSDs do not have to move any parts to store or retrieve data, they don't require seek time or rotational delay and their access time is much faster than magnetic hard drives—essentially instantaneous at about 0.1 ms on some benchmark tests. To speed up magnetic hard drive performance, disk caching is often used. A **disk cache** stores copies of data or programs that are located on the hard drive and that might be needed soon in memory chips to avoid having to retrieve the data or programs from the hard drive when they are requested. Because the hard disks do not have to be accessed if the requested data is located in the disk cache, and because retrieving data from memory is much faster than from a magnetic hard disk, disk caching can speed up performance. Disk caching also saves wear and tear on the hard drive and, in portable computers, can also extend battery life. Memory used for disk caching typically consists of memory chips located on a circuit board inside the hard drive case. It can also be a designated portion of RAM.

Most conventional magnetic hard drives today include a flash memory-based disk cache ranging in size from 2 MB to 16 MB built into the hard drive case. However, **hybrid hard drives**—essentially a combination flash memory/magnetic hard drive (see Exhibit 2-17)—use a much larger amount of flash memory (up to 1 GB today). In addition to using the flash memory to reduce the number of times the hard disks in a hybrid hard drive need to be read, hybrid hard drives can also use the flash memory to temporarily store (cache) data to be written to the hard disks, which can further extend the battery life of portable computers and mobile devices. The additional flash memory in a hybrid hard drive can also allow encryption or other security measures to be built into the drive.

Exhibit 2-17 Hybrid hard drive

MAGNETIC HARD DRIVE
This drive contains 2 hard disks and 4 read/write heads that operate in a manner similar to a conventional hard drive.

FLASH MEMORY DISK CACHE
This drive uses 256 MB of flash memory disk cache to duplicate data as it is stored on the hard disks so the data can be accessed when hard disks are not spinning.

Optical Discs

Optical discs are thin circular discs made out of polycarbonate substrate—essentially a type of very strong plastic—that are topped with layers of other materials and coatings used to store data and protect the disc. Data on optical discs is stored and read optically using laser beams. Data can be stored on one or both sides of an optical disc, depending on the disc design, and some types of discs use multiple recording layers on each side of the disc to increase capacity. An optical disc contains a single spiral track (instead of multiple tracks like magnetic disks), and the track is divided into sectors to keep data organized. As shown in Exhibit 2-18, this track (sometimes referred to as a *groove* in order to avoid confusion with the term *tracks* that refers to songs on an audio CD) begins at the center of the disc and spirals out to the edge of the disc.

Advantages of optical discs include relatively large capacity for their size and durability (they are more

> **disk cache** Memory used in conjunction with a magnetic hard drive to improve system performance.
>
> **hybrid hard drive** A combination flash memory/magnetic hard drive.
>
> **optical disc** A storage medium in the shape of a thin circular disc made out of polycarbonate substrate read from and written to using a laser beam.

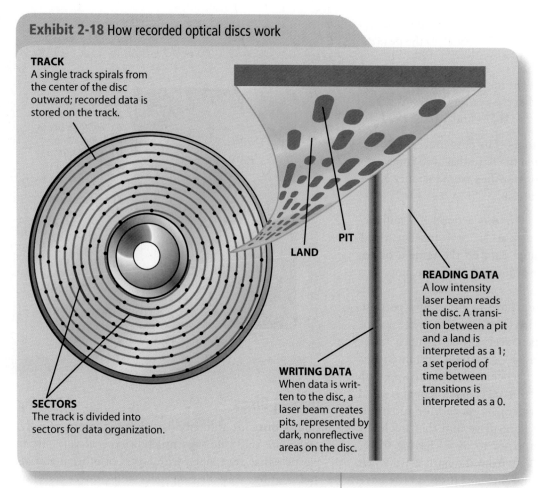

Exhibit 2-18 How recorded optical discs work

TRACK
A single track spirals from the center of the disc outward; recorded data is stored on the track.

SECTORS
The track is divided into sectors for data organization.

LAND

PIT

READING DATA
A low intensity laser beam reads the disc. A transition between a pit and a land is interpreted as a 1; a set period of time between transitions is interpreted as a 0.

WRITING DATA
When data is written to the disc, a laser beam creates pits, represented by dark, nonreflective areas on the disc.

durable than magnetic media and don't degrade with use, as some magnetic media does). However, the discs should be handled carefully and stored in their cases when not in use to protect the recorded surfaces of the discs from scratches, fingerprints, and other marks that can interfere with the usability of the discs. Optical discs are the standard today for software delivery. They are also commonly used for backup purposes, and for storing and/or transporting music, photo, video, and other large files.

Data is written to an optical disc in one of two ways. With read-only optical discs like movie, music, and software CDs and DVDs, the surface of the disc is molded or stamped appropriately to represent the data. To accomplish this with molded or stamped optical discs, tiny depressions (when viewed from the top side of the disc) or bumps (when viewed from the bottom) are created on the disc's surface. These bumps are called *pits*; the areas on the disc that are not changed are called *lands*. With recordable or rewritable optical discs that can be written to using an optical drive such as a CD drive or DVD drive, the reflectivity of the disc is changed using a laser to represent the data. In either case, the

disc is read with a laser and the computer interprets the reflection of the laser off the disc surface as 1s and 0s. With a CD or DVD that is recorded using a CD or DVD drive, the recording laser beam changes the reflectivity of the appropriate areas on the disc to represent the data stored there—dark, nonreflective areas are pits; reflective areas are lands, as illustrated in Exhibit 2-18.

Instead of having physically molded pits, most recordable optical discs have a recording layer containing organic light-sensitive dye embedded between the disc's plastic and reflective layers. One exception to this is the BD-R disc, which has a recording layer consisting of inorganic material. When data is written to a recordable disc, the recording laser inside the recordable optical drive burns the dye (for CD and DVD discs) or melts and combines the inorganic material (for BD-R discs), creating nonreflective areas that function as pits. In either case, the marks are permanent, so data on the disc cannot be erased or rewritten.

To write to, erase, or overwrite rewritable optical discs, phase change technology is used. With this technology, the rewritable CD or DVD disc is coated with layers of a special metal alloy compound that can have two different appearances after it has been heated

> When the optical drive detects a transition between a pit and a land, it is interpreted as a 1; a specific period of time with no transition indicates a 0.

and then cooled, depending on the heating and cooling process used. With one process, the material crystallizes and that area of the disc is reflective. With another process, the area cools to a nonreflective amorphous state. Before any data is written to a rewritable optical disc, the disc is completely reflective. To write data to the disc, the recording laser heats the metal alloy in the appropriate locations on the spiral track and then uses the appropriate cooling process to create either the nonreflective areas (pits) or the reflective areas (lands). To erase the disc, the appropriate heating and cooling process is used to change the areas to be erased back to their original reflective state.

Types of Laser Beams

Different types of optical discs use different types of laser beams. Conventional CD discs use infrared lasers; conventional DVD discs use red lasers, which allow data to be stored more compactly on the same size disc; and high-definition Blu-ray Discs (BD) use blue-violet lasers, which can store data even more compactly on a disc.

Optical discs in each of the three categories (CD, DVD, and BD) can be read-only, recordable, or rewritable; they can use the + or – standard; and they can be either single-layer or dual-layer (DL) discs. See Exhibit 2-19. Optical discs are designed to be read by **optical drives**, such as CD, DVD, and BD drives, and the type of optical drive being used must support the type of optical disc being used. Most optical drives today support multiple types of optical discs—some support all possible types. Optical drives are almost always downward-compatible, meaning they can be used with lower (older) types of discs but not higher (newer) ones. So, while a DVD drive would likely support all types of CD and DVD discs, it cannot be used with BD discs; but most BD drives today support all types of CD, DVD, and Blu-ray Discs.

The process of recording data onto an optical disc is called burning. To burn an optical disc (such as a CD-R or a DVD-R disc), the optical drive being used must support burning and the type of disc being used. In addition, CD-burning or DVD-burning software is required. Many burning programs are available commercially, and recent versions of operating systems (including Windows and Mac OS) include CD and DVD burning capabilities. In addition, most CD and DVD drives come bundled with burning software.

Exhibit 2-19 Recordable CDs and DVDs

CD-R DISCS
Hold 700 MB.

DVD+R DL DISCS
Hold 8.5 GB.

BD-R DL DISCS
Hold 50 GB.

Courtesy Verbatim America LLC; Memorex Products, Inc.; and Sony Electronics Inc.

optical drive A drive designed to read optical discs.

Nonstandard Shapes for Optical Discs

Optical discs can be made into a variety of sizes and shapes—such as a heart, triangle, irregular shape, or the hockey-rink shape commonly used with business card CDs—because the track starts at the center of the disc and the track stops when it reaches an outer edge of the disc. Standard shapes are molded and less expensive; custom shapes—such as those that match a service or product being sold (a soda can, musical instrument, saw blade, candy bar, or house)—are custom cut and more costly.

For marketing purposes, flexible DVDs and scented discs are also available. Flexible DVDs can be bent or rolled so they can be attached to the cover of a magazine or wrapped around a product, for example. Scented discs have a specific aroma, such as a particular perfume, popcorn, pine trees, or a specific fruit, added to the label side of the disc; the scent is released when the surface of the disc is rubbed.

One of the biggest advantages of optical discs is their large capacity. To further increase capacity, many discs are available as dual-layer or double-layer discs that store data in two layers on a single side of the disc, so the capacity is approximately doubled. For an even larger capacity, discs with more than two layers are in development. Discs can also be double sided, which doubles the capacity; however, the disc must be turned over to access the second side. Double-sided discs are most often used with movies and other prerecorded content, such as to store a widescreen version of a movie on one side of a DVD disc and a standard version on the other side. Small optical discs have a smaller storage capacity than their larger counterparts.

Flash Memory

As previously discussed, flash memory is a chip-based storage medium that represents data using electrons. It is used in a variety of storage systems, such as the SSDs and hybrid hard drives already discussed and the additional storage systems shown in Exhibit 2-20. Because flash memory media is physically very small, it is increasingly being embedded directly into a variety of consumer products—such as portable digital media players, digital cameras, handheld gaming devices, GPS devices, mobile phones, and even sunglasses and wristwatches—to provide built-in data storage. In addition, a variety of types of flash memory cards and USB flash drives are available to use with computers and other devices for data storage and data transfer, as discussed next.

Exhibit 2-20 Flash memory systems

Flash memory card

EMBEDDED FLASH MEMORY
Flash memory is often embedded into consumer products, such as this digital media player, for storage purposes.

FLASH MEMORY CARDS AND READERS
Flash memory cards are often used to store data for digital cameras and other devices; the data can be transferred to a computer via a flash memory card reader, as needed.

USB FLASH DRIVES
USB flash drives are often used to store data and transfer files from one computer to another.

One of the most common types of flash memory media is the **flash memory card**—a small card containing one or more flash memory chips, a controller chip, other electrical components, and metal contacts to connect the card to the device or reader with which it is being used. Flash memory cards are available in a variety of formats, as shown in Exhibit 2-21. These formats are

Exhibit 2-21 Flash memory cards

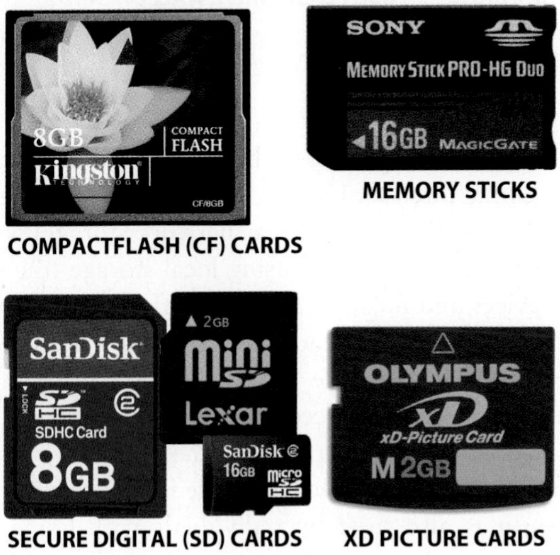

COMPACTFLASH (CF) CARDS

MEMORY STICKS

SECURE DIGITAL (SD) CARDS

XD PICTURE CARDS

not interchangeable, so the type of flash memory card used with a device is determined by the type of flash media card that device can accept. Flash memory cards are the most common type of storage media for digital cameras, portable digital media players, mobile phones, and other portable devices. They can also be used to store data for a personal computer, as needed, as well as to transfer data from a portable device to a computer. Consequently, most desktop and notebook computers today come with a flash memory card reader capable of reading flash memory cards; an external flash memory card reader (that typically connects via a USB port) can be used if a built-in reader is not available. The capacity of flash memory cards is continually growing and is up to about 4 GB for standard cards and 32 GB for high-capacity cards; extended capacity cards are just beginning to become available and are expected to reach capacities of 2 TB by 2014.

USB flash drives (sometimes called **USB flash memory drives**, **thumb drives**, or **jump drives**) consist of flash memory media integrated into a self-contained unit that connects to a computer or other device via a stan-

USB flash drives are available in a range of sizes, colors, and appearances.

Thumb Drive PCs

USB flash drives are a great way to transport documents from one location to another. But what about using one to take a personalized computer with you wherever you go? It's possible and easy to do with the use of portable applications (also called portable apps)—computer programs that are designed to be used with portable devices like USB flash drives. When the device is plugged into the USB port of any computer, you have access to the software and personal data (including your browser bookmarks, calendar, email and instant messaging contacts, and more) stored on that device, just as you would on your own computer. And when you unplug the device, none of your personal data is left behind because all programs are run directly from the USB flash drive. Many portable applications, such as the Portable-Apps suite, are free and include all the basics you might want in a single package. For instance, PortableApps includes a menu structure, antivirus program, Web browser, email program, calendar program, the OpenOffice.org office suite, and more.

dard USB port and is powered via the USB port. See Exhibit 2-22. USB flash drives are designed to be very small and very portable. Because they are becoming so widely used, additional hardware related to USB flash drives is becoming available, such as USB duplicator systems used by educators to copy assignments or other materials to and from a large collection of USB flash drives at one time.

flash memory card A small rectangular flash memory medium.

USB flash drive Flash memory media integrated into a self-contained unit that plugs into a USB port.

Exhibit 2-22 USB flash drives

CONVENTIONAL USB FLASH DRIVES **USB FLASH DRIVE WRISTBANDS** **USB FLASH DRIVE WALLET CARDS**

To read from or write to a USB flash drive, you just plug it into a USB port. If the USB flash drive is being used with a computer, it is assigned a drive letter by the computer, just like any other type of attached drive, and files can be read from or written to the USB flash drive until it is unplugged from the USB port. The capacity of most USB flash drives today ranges from 1 GB to 64 GB.

Network Storage and Online/Cloud Storage Systems

Remote storage refers to using a storage device that is not connected directly to the user's computer; in-stead, the device is accessed through a local network or through the Internet. Using a remote storage device via a local network (referred to as network storage) works in much the same way as using local storage (the storage devices and media that are directly attached to the user's computer). To read data from or write data to a remote storage device (such as a hard drive in another computer being accessed via a network), the user just selects it and then performs the necessary tasks in the usual fashion. Network storage is common in businesses; it is also used by individuals with home networks for backup purposes or to share files with another computer in the home.

Because of the vast amount of data shared and made available over networks today, network storage has become increasingly important. There are two common types of network storage. **Network attached storage (NAS)** consists of high-performance storage servers that are connected individually to a network to provide storage for the computers connected to that network. They can be large storage servers designed for a large business, or smaller NAS devices designed for a home or small business. A growing trend, in fact, is home NAS devices designed to store multimedia data to be distributed over a home entertainment network. A **storage area network (SAN)** also provides storage for a network, but it consists of a separate network of hard drives or other storage devices, which is attached to the main network.

The primary difference between network attached storage and a storage area network is how the storage devices interface with the network—that is, whether the storage devices act as individual network nodes, just like computers, printers, and other devices on the network (NAS), or whether they are located in a completely separate network of storage devices that is accessible to the main network (SAN). However, in terms of functionality,

> USB flash drives can include biometric features—such as a built-in fingerprint reader—to allow only authorized individuals access to the data stored on them.

remote storage A storage device that is not connected directly to the user's computer.

network attached storage (NAS) A high-performance storage server connected individually to a network to provide storage for computers on that network.

storage area network (SAN) A network of hard drives or other storage devices that provide storage for another network.

the distinction between NAS and SANs is blurring because they both provide storage services to the network. Typically, both NAS and SAN systems are scalable, so new devices can be added as more storage is needed, and devices can be added or removed without disrupting the network.

Remote storage devices accessed via the Internet are often referred to as **online storage** or **cloud storage**. Although these terms are often used interchangeably, some view cloud storage as a specific type of online storage that can be accessed on demand by various Web applications. Most online applications, such as Google Docs, the Flickr photo sharing service, and social networking sites like Facebook, provide online storage for these services. There are also sites whose primary objective is to allow users to store documents online, such as Box.net or Windows Live SkyDrive. Typically, online/cloud storage sites are password-protected and allow users to specify uploaded files as private files or as shared files that designated individuals can access.

© Image copyright devi. Used under license from Shutterstock.com

Storing Documents in the Cloud

The ability to store documents online (or "in the cloud") is growing in importance as more and more applications are becoming Web based and as individuals increasingly want access to their files from anywhere with any Internet-enabled device, such as a portable computer or mobile phone. Online storage is also increasingly being used for backup purposes—some online storage sites have an automatic backup option that uploads the files in designated folders on your computer to your online account at regular specified intervals, as long as your computer is connected to the Internet. Many Web sites providing online storage to individuals offer the service for free (for instance, SkyDrive gives each individual 25 GB of free storage space); others charge a small fee, such as $10 per month for 50 GB of storage space.

Smart Cards

A **smart card** is a credit card–sized piece of plastic that contains computer circuitry and components—typically a processor, memory, and storage. Smart cards today store a relatively small amount of data (typically 64 KB or less). Smart cards are commonly used for national and student ID cards, credit and debit cards, and cards that store identification data for accessing facilities or computer networks.

To use a smart card, it must either be inserted into a smart card reader (if it is the type of card that requires contact) or placed close to a smart card reader (if it is a contactless card) built into or attached to a computer, keyboard, vending machine, or other device (see Exhibit 2-23). Once a smart card has been verified by the card reader, the transaction—such as making a purchase or unlocking a door—can be completed. For an even higher level of security, some smart cards today store biometric data in the card and use that data to ensure the authenticity of the card's user before authorizing the smart card transaction.

A smart card can store a prepaid amount of digital cash.

online storage (**cloud storage**) Remote storage devices accessed via the Internet.

smart card A credit card–sized piece of plastic that contains a chip and computer circuitry that can store data.

Exhibit 2-23 Smart card uses

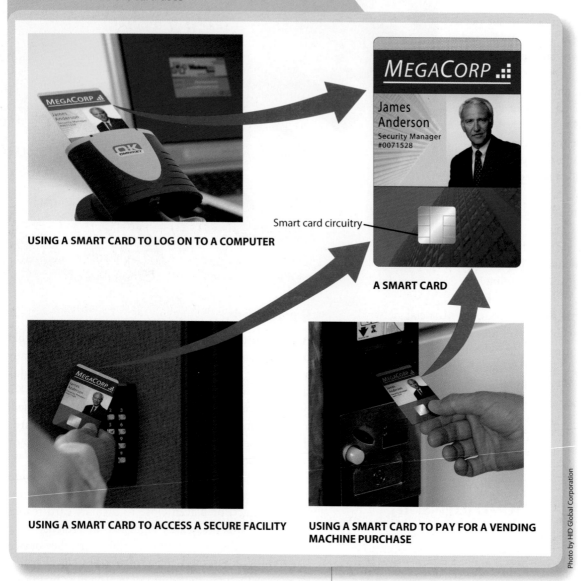

USING A SMART CARD TO LOG ON TO A COMPUTER

Smart card circuitry

A SMART CARD

USING A SMART CARD TO ACCESS A SECURE FACILITY

USING A SMART CARD TO PAY FOR A VENDING MACHINE PURCHASE

Photo by HID Global Corporation

MEGACORP

James Anderson
Security Manager
#0071528

Storage Systems for Large Computer Systems

Businesses and other organizations have tremendous storage needs and the documents must be stored in a manner in which they can be readily retrieved as needed.

For large computer systems, instead of finding a single hard drive installed within the system unit, you are most likely to find a **storage server**—a separate piece of hardware containing multiple high-speed hard drives—connected to the computer system or network.

storage server A storage device containing multiple high-speed hard drives connected to the computer system or network.

Large storage servers typically contain racks (also called chassis) of hard drives for a large total capacity. For instance, the storage system shown in Exhibit 2-24 can include up to 1,280 hard drives for a total capacity of 600 TB.

A federal mandate requires businesses to locate and provide to the courts in a timely manner any document stored electronically that is needed for evidence in civil litigation.

Exhibit 2-24 Storage servers

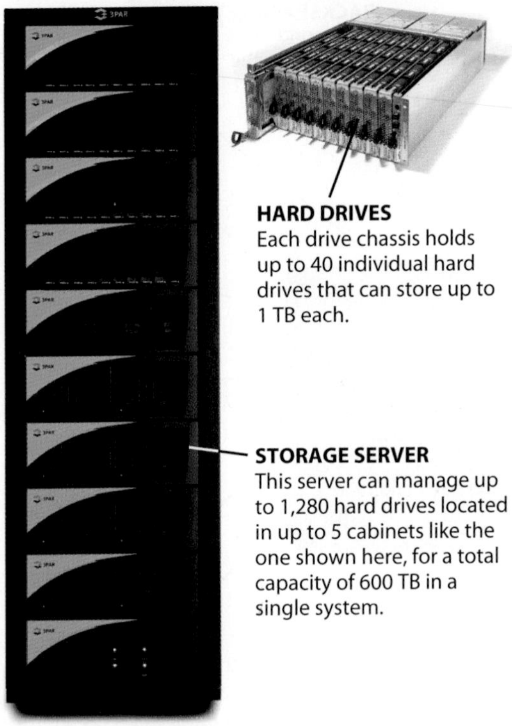

HARD DRIVES
Each drive chassis holds up to 40 individual hard drives that can store up to 1 TB each.

STORAGE SERVER
This server can manage up to 1,280 hard drives located in up to 5 cabinets like the one shown here, for a total capacity of 600 TB in a single system.

In addition to being used as stand-alone storage for large computer systems, storage servers may also be used in network attached storage (NAS), storage area network (SAN), and RAID (redundant array of independent disks) storage systems. **RAID (redundant array of independent disks)** is a method of storing data on two or more hard drives that work together. Although RAID can be used to increase performance, it is most often used to protect critical data on a storage server. Because RAID usually involves recording redundant (duplicate) copies of stored data, the copies can be used, when necessary, to reconstruct lost data. This helps to increase the fault tolerance—the ability to recover from an unexpected hardware or software failure, such as a system crash—of a storage system.

Most storage servers are based on magnetic hard disks, although magnetic tape storage systems are also possible. **Magnetic tape** consists of plastic tape coated with a magnetizable substance that represents the bits and bytes of digital data, similar to magnetic hard disks. Although magnetic tape is no longer used for everyday storage applications because of its sequential-access property, it is still used today for business data archiving and backup. One advantage of magnetic tape is its low cost per megabyte.

Which Type of Storage Do You Need?

With so many storage alternatives available, which devices and media are most appropriate for your personal situation? In general, you'll need a hard drive (for storing programs and data), some type of recordable or rewritable optical drive (for installing programs, backing up files, and sharing files with others), and a flash memory card reader (for transferring photos, music, and other content between portable devices and the computer). If you plan to transfer music, digital photos, and other multimedia data on a regular basis between devices—such as a computer, digital camera, mobile phone, and printer—you'll want to select and use the flash memory media that are compatible with the devices you are using. You will also need to obtain the necessary adapter for your computer if it does not include a compatible built-in flash memory reader. You will also need at least one convenient free USB port to use to connect external hard drives, USB flash drives, and other USB-based storage hardware, as well as USB devices that contain storage media, such as digital cameras and portable digital media players.

LO2.5 Input Devices

An **input device** is any piece of equipment that is used to enter data into the computer. The most common input devices used with personal computers are keyboards and pointing devices, such as a mouse or pen. There are also input devices designed for capturing data in electronic form, such as scanners, barcode readers, and digital cameras, and devices that are used to input audio data.

> **RAID (redundant array of independent disks)** A method of storing data on two or more hard drives that work together.
>
> **magnetic tape** Storage media consisting of plastic tape coated with a magnetizable substance.
>
> **input device** Any piece of equipment that is used to enter data into the computer.

Exhibit 2-25 Typical desktop keyboard

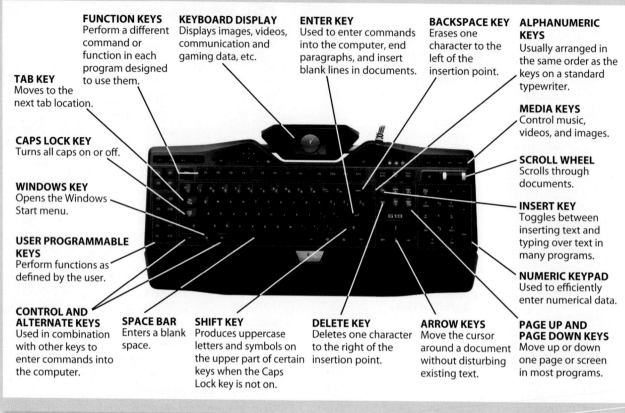

FUNCTION KEYS
Perform a different command or function in each program designed to use them.

KEYBOARD DISPLAY
Displays images, videos, communication and gaming data, etc.

ENTER KEY
Used to enter commands into the computer, end paragraphs, and insert blank lines in documents.

BACKSPACE KEY
Erases one character to the left of the insertion point.

ALPHANUMERIC KEYS
Usually arranged in the same order as the keys on a standard typewriter.

TAB KEY
Moves to the next tab location.

CAPS LOCK KEY
Turns all caps on or off.

WINDOWS KEY
Opens the Windows Start menu.

USER PROGRAMMABLE KEYS
Perform functions as defined by the user.

MEDIA KEYS
Control music, videos, and images.

SCROLL WHEEL
Scrolls through documents.

INSERT KEY
Toggles between inserting text and typing over text in many programs.

NUMERIC KEYPAD
Used to efficiently enter numerical data.

CONTROL AND ALTERNATE KEYS
Used in combination with other keys to enter commands into the computer.

SPACE BAR
Enters a blank space.

SHIFT KEY
Produces uppercase letters and symbols on the upper part of certain keys when the Caps Lock key is not on.

DELETE KEY
Deletes one character to the right of the insertion point.

ARROW KEYS
Move the cursor around a document without disturbing existing text.

PAGE UP AND PAGE DOWN KEYS
Move up or down one page or screen in most programs.

Keyboards

Most computers today are designed to be used with a **keyboard**—a device containing keys used to enter characters on the screen. Keyboards can be built into a device, attached using a wired cable, such as via a USB or keyboard port, or connected via a wireless connection. A typical desktop computer keyboard is shown in Exhibit 2-25. Like most keyboards, this keyboard contains standard alphanumeric keys to input text and numbers, as well as additional keys used for various purposes. To allow individuals to work under a variety of lighting conditions, such as in a dark living room or in an airplane, keyboards (such as the one in Exhibit 2-25) are increasingly using illuminated keys to light up the characters on the keyboard.

keyboard An input device containing keys used to enter characters on the screen.

Keyboards on Clothing

One possibility for the future is printing keyboards directly on clothing and other products that can connect wirelessly to the devices being used. For example, keyboards might be printed on jackets to allow consumers to wirelessly input data or otherwise control their mobile phones while on the go, or keyboards might be printed on soldiers' uniforms to be used with UMPCs or other small computers while in the field.

Some keyboards also contain special keys that are used for a specific purpose, such as to control the speaker volume or to launch an email program.

Pointing Devices

In addition to a keyboard, most computers today are used in conjunction with some type of pointing device. **Pointing devices** are used to select and manipulate objects, to input certain types of data, such as handwritten data, and to issue commands to the computer. The **mouse** (see Exhibit 2-26) is the most common pointing device for a desktop computer. It typically rests on the desk or other flat surface close to the user's computer, and it is moved across the surface with the

Exhibit 2-26 Examples of mice

A LASER MOUSE   A 3D MOUSE

3D Mice

For use with virtual worlds, animation programs, and other 3D applications, 3D mice are available that are designed to make navigation through a 3D environment easier. For example, the 3Dconnexion SpaceNavigator 3D mouse shown in Exhibit 2-26 has a controller cap, which can be lifted up to move an object up, rotated to "fly" around objects, or tilted to "look" up. In addition to being used with desktop computers, mice can also be used with portable computers (such as notebook and netbook computers) as long as an appropriate port (such as a USB port) is available. Also, special cordless presenter mice can be used to control on-screen slide shows.

user's hand in the appropriate direction to point to and select objects on the screen. As it moves, an on-screen mouse pointer—usually an arrow—moves accordingly. Once the mouse pointer is pointing to the desired object on the screen, the buttons on the mouse are used to perform actions on that object (such as to open a hyperlink or to resize an image). Similar to keyboards, mice typically connect via a USB or mouse port, or via a wireless connection. Older mechanical mice have a ball exposed on the bottom surface of the mouse to control the pointer movement. Most mice today are optical mice or laser mice that track movements with light.

Similar to an upside-down mechanical mouse, a **trackball** has the ball mechanism on top, instead of on the bottom. The ball is rotated with the thumb, hand, or finger to move the on-screen pointer. Because the device itself does not need to be moved, trackballs take up less space on the desktop than mice. They also are easier to use for individuals with limited hand or finger mobility.

Many devices, including some desktop computers and many tablet computers and mobile devices, can accept pen input; that is, input by writing, drawing, or tapping on the screen with a pen-like device called a **stylus**. Sometimes, the stylus (also called a digital pen, electronic pen, or tablet pen) is simply a plastic device with no additional functionality; more commonly, it is a pressure-sensitive device that transmits the pressure applied by the user to the device that the stylus is being used with in order to allow more precise input. These more sophisticated styluses also are typically powered by the device that

pointing device An input device that moves an on-screen pointer used to select and manipulate objects and to issue commands to the computer.

mouse A common pointing device that the user slides along a flat surface to move the pointer on the screen.

trackball A pointing device similar to an upside-down mechanical mouse with the ball mechanism on top.

stylus A pen-like device used for input by writing, drawing, or tapping on the screen.

they are being used with, have a smooth rounded tip so they don't scratch the screen, and contain buttons or switches to perform actions such as erasing content or right-clicking.

A variety of gaming devices today, such as the joystick, gamepad, and steering wheels shown in Exhibit 2-27, can be used as controllers to supply input

proprietary controllers such as the Wii Remote used with the Nintendo Wii gaming system.

Many consumer devices, such as portable digital media players, GPS devices, and handheld gaming devices, use special buttons and wheels to select items and issue commands to the device. For instance, the portable digital media player shown in Exhibit 2-27 contains a thumb wheel that is rotated to navigate through menus and a select button to access music and other content stored on the device.

Exhibit 2-27 Other common pointing devices

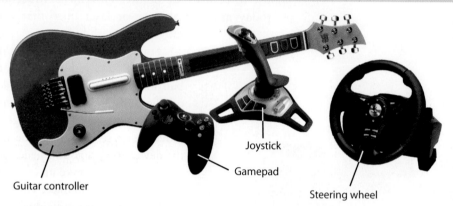

Guitar controller

Joystick

Gamepad

Steering wheel

GAMING DEVICES
Most often used for gaming applications.

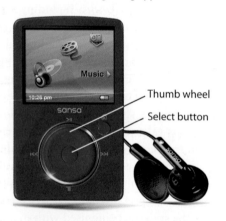

Thumb wheel

Select button

BUTTONS AND WHEELS
Commonly found on portable digital media players and other consumer devices.

TOUCH PADS
Commonly found on notebook and netbook computers.

to a computer. Other input devices are intended to be used with gaming consoles, including guitars, drums, and other musical instruments; dance pads and balance boards, and other motion-sensitive controllers; and

touch screen An input device that is touched with the finger to select commands or otherwise provide input to the computer.

Touch Devices

Touch screens allow the user to touch the screen with his or her finger to select commands or otherwise provide input to the computer associated with the touch screen. Their use is becoming common with devices such as personal computers, mobile phones, mobile devices, and consumer kiosks (see Exhibit 2-28) in order to provide easy input. Some touch screens, such as the one used on the Apple iPhone 3G, are multi-touch; that is, they can recognize input from more than one finger at a time. Similar multi-touch products are used for large wall displays, such as for use in museums, government command centers, and newsrooms. Touch screens are also used in consumer kiosks and other point-of-sale (POS) systems, and they are useful for on-the-job applications (such as factory work) where it might be impractical to use a keyboard or mouse. A growing trend is to use touch screens that provide tactile feedback—a slight movement or other physical sensation in response to the users' touch so they know their input has been received by the computer.

Exhibit 2-28 Touch screens

DESKTOP COMPUTERS

MOBILE DEVICES

SURFACE COMPUTING DEVICES

CONSUMER KIOSKS

One concern is that touch devices and their applications are not accessible to individuals who are blind, have limited mobility, or have some other disability.

A **touch pad** is a rectangular pad across which a fingertip or thumb slides to move the on-screen pointer; tapping the touch pad typically performs clicks and other mouse actions. Although most often found on notebook and netbook computers (see Exhibit 2-27), touch pads are also available as stand-alone devices to be used with desktop computers and are built into some keyboards.

Surface Computing

One new trend in touch screens is referred to as surface computing—using a combination of multi-touch input from multiple users and object recognition to interact with computers that are typically built into tabletops and other surfaces. One example is Microsoft Surface. This product (shown in Exhibit 2-28) uses touch and gestures performed via the screen, as well as objects placed on the screen, as input. It can recognize input from multiple users and multiple objects placed on the table simultaneously.

Scanners and Readers

A variety of input devices are designed to capture data in digital form so a computer can manipulate it. A **scanner**, more officially called an optical scanner, captures an image of an object—usually a flat object, such as a printed document, photograph, or drawing—in digital form, and then transfers that data to a computer. Typically, the entire document is input as a single graphical image that can be resized, inserted into other documents, posted on a Web page, emailed to someone, printed, or otherwise treated like any other graphical image. The text in the scanned image, however, cannot be edited unless optical character recognition (OCR) software is used in conjunction with the scanner to input the scanned text as individual text characters.

The quality of scanned images is indicated by optical resolution, usually measured in the number of **dots per inch** (**dpi**). When a document is scanned (typically

touch pad A rectangular pad across which a fingertip or thumb slides or taps to control the pointer.

scanner An input device that reads printed text or captures an image of an object, and then transfers that data to a computer.

dots per inch (**dpi**) A measurement of resolution that indicates the quality of an image or output.

using scanning software, though some application programs allow you to scan images directly into that program), the resolution of the scanned image can often be specified. Scanners today usually scan at between 2,400×2,400 dpi and 4,800×9,600 dpi. A higher resolution results in a better image as well as a larger file size, as illustrated in Exhibit 2-29. A higher resolution

Exhibit 2-29 Same photo at different resolutions

96 dpi
(833 KB)

300 dpi
(1,818 KB)

600 dpi
(5,374 KB)

is needed, however, if the image will be enlarged significantly or if only one part of the image will be extracted and enlarged. The file size of a scanned image is also determined in part by the physical size of the image. After an image has been scanned, it can usually be resized and then saved in the appropriate file format and resolution for the application with which the image is to be used.

A variety of readers are available to read different types of codes and marks. A **barcode** is an optical code that represents data with bars of varying widths or heights. Two of the most familiar barcodes are UPC (Universal Product Code), the barcode found on packaged goods in supermarkets and other retail stores, and

barcode Machine-readable code that represents data as a set of bars.

barcode reader An input device that reads barcodes.

Consumers are beginning to use mobile phones for activities such as downloading a coupon or ticket by capturing the barcode with the phone's camera.

ISBN (International Standard Book Number), the barcode used with printed books (see Exhibit 2-30). Businesses and organizations can also create and use custom barcodes to fulfill their unique needs. For instance, shipping organizations (such as FedEx and UPS) use custom barcodes to mark and track packages, retailers (such as Target and Wal-Mart) use custom barcodes added to customer receipts to facilitate returns, hospitals use custom barcodes to match patients with their charts and medicines, libraries and video stores use custom barcodes for checking out and checking in books and movies, and law enforcement agencies use custom barcodes to mark evidence.

Exhibit 2-30 Common types of barcodes

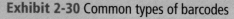

ISBN CODES

UPC (UNIVERSAL PRODUCT CODE) CODES

DATABAR CODES

INTELLIGENT MAIL CODES

CODE 39 CODES

QR CODES

Courtesy of Motorola

Barcodes are read with **barcode readers**. Barcode readers use either light reflected from the barcode or imaging technology to interpret the bars contained in the barcode as the numbers or letters they represent. Then, data associated with that barcode—typically identifying data, such as data used to uniquely identify a product, shipped package, or other item—can be retrieved.

Exhibit 2-31 Barcode readers

FIXED BARCODE READERS
Used most often in retail point-of-sale applications.

PORTABLE BARCODE READERS
Used when portability is needed.

INTEGRATED BARCODE READERS
Used most often for consumer applications.

Fixed barcode readers are frequently used in point-of-sale (POS) systems (see Exhibit 2-31). Portable barcode readers are also available for people who need to scan barcodes while on the go, such as while walking through a warehouse, retail store, hospital, or other facility.

Radio frequency identification (**RFID**) is a technology that can store, read, and transmit data located in RFID tags. **RFID tags** contain tiny chips and radio antennas (see Exhibit 2-32); they can be attached to objects, such as products, price tags, shipping labels, ID cards, assets (such as livestock, vehicles, computers, and other ex-

pensive equipment), and more. The data in RFID tags is read by **RFID readers**. Whenever an RFID-tagged item is within range of an RFID reader (from two inches to up to 300 feet or more, depending on the type of tag and the frequency being used), the tag's built-in antenna allows the information located within the RFID tag to be sent to the reader. Because RFID technology

Exhibit 2-32 RFID tag

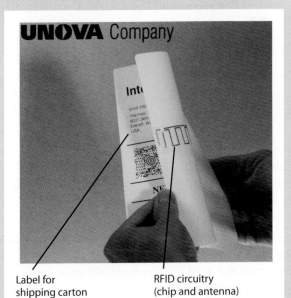

Label for shipping carton

RFID circuitry (chip and antenna)

RFID and Privacy

Keep your enhanced driver's license and passport in the supplied protective sleeve when not in use to protect against unauthorized reading or tracking. While currently no personal data is stored in the RFID chips used in these documents, hackers have demonstrated the ability to read these documents if they are not properly shielded. Because of this, privacy advocates recommend taking this precaution with any RFID-enabled identity document.

radio frequency identification (**RFID**) A technology that can store, read, and transmit data in RFID tags.

RFID tag A tiny chip and radio antenna attached to an object so it can be identified using RFID technology.

RFID reader A device that reads the data in an RFID tag.

can read numerous items at one time, it is also possible that, someday, RFID will allow a consumer to perform self-checkout at a retail store by just pushing a shopping cart past an RFID reader, which will ring up all items in the cart at one time. RFID is used today for many different applications (Exhibit 2-33 shows some examples).

Despite all its advantages, a number of privacy and security issues need to be resolved before RFID gains widespread use at the consumer level. Precautions against fraudulent use—such as using high-frequency tags that need to be within a few inches of the reader, and requiring a PIN code, a signature, or another type of authorization when an RFID payment system is used—are being developed. Currently, a price limit (such as $25) for completely automated purchases (without a signature or other authorization) is being debated as a compromise between convenience and security. Privacy advocates are concerned about linking RFID tag data with personally identifiable data contained in corporate databases, such as to track consumer movements or shopping habits. As of now, no long-term solution to this issue has been reached.

Courtesy Intermec Technologies, teamaxess.com, MasterCard Worldwide, and AP Images/Denis Poroy

Exhibit 2-33 RFID applications

INVENTORY TRACKING
This portal RFID reader reads all of the RFID tags attached to all of the items on the pallet at one time.

TICKETING APPLICATIONS
This stationary RFID reader is used to automatically open ski lift entry gates for valid lift ticket holders at a ski resort in Utah.

MOBILE PAYMENTS
This stationary RFID reader is used at checkout locations to quickly process payments via RFID-enabled credit cards or mobile phones.

BORDER SECURITY
This stationary RFID reader is used at the U.S.-Mexico border crossing located in San Diego to reduce wait time.

optical mark reader (OMR) A device that inputs data from special forms to score or tally the data on those forms.

optical character recognition (OCR) The ability of a computer to recognize scanned text characters.

Optical mark readers (**OMRs**) input data from special forms to score or tally exams, questionnaires, ballots, and so forth. Typically, you use a pencil to fill in small circles or other shapes on the form to indicate your selections, and then the form is inserted into an optical mark reader (such as shown in Exhibit 2-34) to be scored or tallied. The results can be input into a computer system if the optical mark reader is connected to a computer.

Optical character recognition (**OCR**) refers to the ability of a computer to recognize text characters. The characters are read by a compatible scanning device, such as a flatbed scanner, barcode reader, or dedicated OCR reader, and then OCR software is used to identify

Exhibit 2-34 Optical mark readers (OMRs)

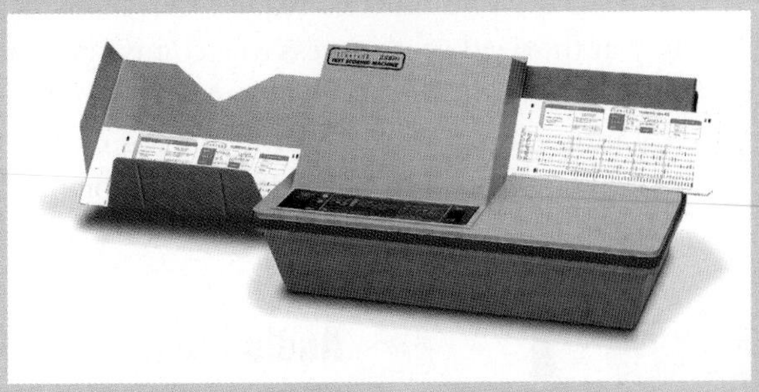

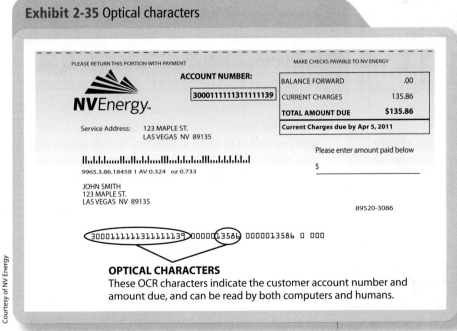

each character and convert it to editable text. While OCR systems can recognize many typed fonts, optical characters—which are characters specifically designed to be identifiable by humans as well as by an OCR device—are often used on documents intended to be processed by an OCR system. For example, optical characters are widely used in processing turnaround documents, such as the monthly bills for credit card and utility companies (see Exhibit 2-35). These documents contain optical characters in certain places on the bill to aid processing when consumers send it back with payment—or "turn it around."

Magnetic ink character recognition (MICR) is a technology used primarily by the banking industry to facilitate check processing. MICR characters, such as those located on the bottom of a check that represent the bank routing number, check number, and account number, are inscribed on checks with magnetic

MICR readers are used by businesses to deposit paper checks electronically.

ink when the checks are first printed. These characters can be read and new characters, such as to reflect the check's amount, can be added by an MICR reader (also called a check scanner) when needed. High-volume MICR readers are used by banks to process checks deposited at the bank. Smaller units, such as the one shown in Exhibit 2-36, are used by many businesses to

Exhibit 2-36 Magnetic ink character recognition (MICR) readers

Courtesy of NCR Corporation

deposit paper checks remotely. MICR readers are also incorporated in most new ATMs to enable the MICR information located on checks inserted into the ATM to be read at the time of the deposit.

Biometrics is the science of identifying individuals based on measurable biological characteristics. **Biometric readers** are used to read biometric data about a person so that the individual's

Exhibit 2-35 Optical characters

PLEASE RETURN THIS PORTION WITH PAYMENT   MAKE CHECKS PAYABLE TO NV ENERGY

NVEnergy™

ACCOUNT NUMBER:
3000111111311111139

BALANCE FORWARD	.00
CURRENT CHARGES	135.86
TOTAL AMOUNT DUE	**$135.86**

Current Charges due by Apr 5, 2011

Service Address: 123 MAPLE ST.
LAS VEGAS NV 89135

Please enter amount paid below

$ _____

9965.3.86.18458 1 AV 0.324 oz 0.733

JOHN SMITH
123 MAPLE ST.
LAS VEGAS NV 89135

89520-3086

3000111111311111139 000000l358b 0000013586 0 000

OPTICAL CHARACTERS
These OCR characters indicate the customer account number and amount due, and can be read by both computers and humans.

Courtesy of NV Energy

biometric reader A device used to input biometric data, such as an individual's fingerprint or voice.

identity can be verified based on a particular unique physiological characteristic, such as a fingerprint or a face, or personal trait, such as a voice or a signature. As shown in Exhibit 2-37, a biometric reader can be stand-alone or built into another piece of hardware, such as a keyboard, a portable computer, an external hard drive, or a USB flash drive. Biometric readers can be used to allow only authorized users access to a computer or facility or to the data stored on a storage device, as well as to authorize electronic payments, log on to secure Web sites, or punch into and out of work.

Exhibit 2-37 Biometric readers

STAND-ALONE FINGERPRINT READERS
Often used to control access to facilities or computer systems, such as to the notebook computer shown here.

BUILT-IN FINGERPRINT READERS
Typically used to control access to the device into which the reader is built, such as to the external hard drive shown here.

Digital Cameras

Digital cameras record images on a digital storage medium, such as a flash memory card, digital tape cartridge, built-in hard drive, or DVD disc. Digital cameras are usually designated either as still cameras (which take individual still photos) or video cameras (which capture moving video images), although many cameras today take both still images and video. In addition to stand-alone still and video cameras, digital camera capabilities are integrated into many portable computers and mobile phones today. Video cameras used with personal computers—commonly called Web cams—are typically used to transmit still or video images over the Internet or to broadcast images continually to a Web page.

speech recognition system Hardware and software that enable a computer to recognize voice input.

Audio Input

Audio input is the process of entering audio data into the computer. The most common types of audio input are voice and music. Voice input—inputting spoken words and converting them to digital form—is typically performed via a microphone or headset (a set of headphones with a built-in microphone). It can be used in conjunction with sound recorder software to store the voice in an audio file as well as with Voice over IP systems that allow individuals to place telephone calls from a computer over the Internet. It can also be used in conjunction with speech recognition software to provide spoken instructions to a computer. **Speech recognition systems** enable the computer to recognize voice input as spoken words and require appropriate software, such as Dragon NaturallySpeaking or Windows Speech Recognition. See Exhibit 2-38. To enable hands-free operation, speech recognition capabilities are increasingly incorporated into mobile phones, GPS systems, and other mobile devices. They are also commonly built into cars to enable hands-free control of navigation systems and sound systems, as well as to allow hands-free mobile phone calls to take place via the car's voice interface. Specialty speech recognition systems are frequently used to control machines, robots, and other electronic equipment, such as by surgeons during surgical procedures.

Voice input systems are used by individuals who cannot use a keyboard.

Exhibit 2-38 Speech recognition systems

2. An analog-to-digital converter on the sound card located inside the computer converts the spoken words to phonemes, the fundamental sounds in the language being used, and digitizes them.

The patient exhibits signs of...

The patient exhibits signs of

1. The user speaks into a microphone that cancels out background noise and inputs the speech into the computer.

4. The spoken words appear on the screen in the application program (such as a word processor or an email program) being used.

3. Voice recognition software determines the words that were spoken.

Music input systems are used to input music into a computer, such as to create an original music composition or arrangement, or to create a custom music CD. Existing music can be input into a computer via a music CD or a Web download. For original compositions, microphones and keyboard controllers—essentially piano keyboards connected to a computer—can be used (see Exhibit 2-39). Original music compositions can also be created using a conventional computer keyboard with appropriate software or a special device (such as a microphone or digital pen) designed to input music and convert it to a printed musical score. Once the music is input into the computer, it can be saved, modified, played, inserted into other programs, or burned to a CD or DVD.

Exhibit 2-39 Music input systems

LO2.6 **Output Devices**

An **output device** accepts processed data from the computer and presents the results to the user, most of the time on the computer screen, on paper, or through a speaker.

Display Devices

A **display device**—the most common form of output device—presents output visually on some type of screen.

> **output device** A device that accepts processed data from the computer and presents the results to the user.
>
> **display device** An output device that contains a viewing screen.

Exhibit 2-40 Uses for display devices

PORTABLE COMPUTERS

HANDHELD GAMING DEVICES

DIGITAL PHOTO FRAMES

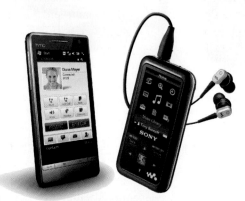

MOBILE DEVICES

DIGITAL SIGNAGE SYSTEMS

The display device for a desktop computer is more formally called a **monitor**. The display device for a notebook computer, netbook computer, UMPC, mobile phone, or other device for which the screen is built into the device is typically called a **display screen**. In addition to being used with computers and mobile devices, display screens are also built into handheld gaming devices, home entertainment devices, such as remote controls, televisions, and portable DVD players, and kitchen appliances. They are also an important component in digital photo frames, e-book readers, portable digital media players, and other consumer products (see Exhibit 2-40).

monitor A display device for a desktop computer.

display screen A display device built into a notebook computer, netbook, UMPC, or other device.

CRT monitor A display device that uses cathode-ray tube technology.

flat-panel display A slim display device that that uses electronically charged chemicals or gases to display images.

The **CRT monitor** used to be the norm for desktop computers. CRT monitors use the same cathode-ray tube technology used in conventional televisions in which an electron gun sealed inside a large glass tube projects an electron beam at a screen coated with red, green, and blue phosphor dots; the beam lights up the appropriate colors in each pixel to display the necessary image. As a result, CRTs are large, bulky, and heavy.

Most computers today (as well as most television sets) use the thinner and lighter **flat-panel displays**. Flat-panel display technology is also used in the display screens integrated into mobile phones and consumer electronics. Flat-panel displays form images by manipulating electronically charged chemicals or gases sandwiched between thin panes of glass or other transparent material. Flat-panel displays take up less desk space, which makes it possible to use multiple monitors working together to increase the amount of data the user can view at one time (see Exhibit 2-41), increasing productivity. Flat-panel displays also consume less power than CRTs and most use digital signals to

Exhibit 2-41 Flat-panel displays

Four flat-panel monitors

display images (instead of the analog signals used with CRT monitors), which allows for sharper images. To use multiple monitors, you must have the necessary hardware to support them, such as a monitor port on a notebook computer or an appropriate video adapter, as discussed shortly. One disadvantage to a flat-panel display is that the images sometimes cannot be seen clearly when viewed from certain angles.

One of the most common flat-panel technologies is **liquid crystal display** (**LCD**), which uses charged liquid crystals located between two sheets of clear material (usually glass or plastic) to light up the appropriate pixels to form the image on the screen. Several layers of liquid crystals are used, and, in their normal state, the liquid crystals are aligned so that light passes through the display. When an electrical charge is applied to the liquid crystals (via an electrode grid layer contained within the LCD panel), the liquid crystals change their orientation or "twist" so that light cannot pass through the display, and the liquid crystals at the charged intersections of the electrode grid appear dark. Color LCD displays use a color filter that consists of a pattern of red, green, and blue subpixels for each pixel. The voltage used controls the orientation (twisting) of the liquid crystals and the amount of light that gets through, affecting the color and shade of that pixel—the three different colors blend to make the pixel the appropriate color.

LCD displays can be viewed only with reflective light, unless light is built into the display. Consequently, LCD panels used with computer monitors typically include a light inside the panel, usually at the rear of the display—a technique referred to as backlighting. LCDs are currently the most common type of flat-panel technology used for small- to medium-sized computer monitors. The monitors shown in Exhibit 2-41 are LCD monitors.

Another common flat-panel technology is **LED** (**light emitting diode**), which is also commonly used with consumer products, such as alarm clocks, Christmas lights, car headlights, and more. LEDs are also beginning to be used to backlight LCD panels, although **organic light emitting diode** (**OLED**) might eventually replace LCD technology entirely. OLED displays use layers of organic material, which emit a visible light when electric current is applied. Because they emit a visible light, OLED displays do not use backlighting. This characteristic makes OLEDs more energy efficient than LCDs and lengthens the battery life of portable devices using OLED displays. Other advantages of OLEDs are that OLEDs are thinner than LCDs, they have a wider viewing angle than LCDs and so displayed content is visible from virtually all directions, and their images are brighter and sharper than LCDs. OLED displays are incorporated into many digital cameras, mobile phones,

Special OLEDs

A flexible OLED (FOLED) is an OLED display built on a flexible surface. A transparent OLED (TOLED) is a display built on a transparent surface that emits light toward the top and bottom of the display surface. Finally, a Phosphorescent OLED (PHOLED) is a display that uses phosphorescence, a process that results in much more conversion of electrical energy into light instead of heat, creating a more efficient OLED.

FOLEDS   **TOLEDS**

liquid crystal display (**LCD**) A type of flat-panel display that uses charged liquid crystals to display images.

LED (**light emitting diode**) A common flat-panel technology.

organic light emitting diode (**OLED**) A type of flat-panel display that uses emissive organic material to display brighter and sharper images.

portable digital media players, and other consumer devices (see Exhibit 2-42). They are also beginning to appear in television and computer displays.

Plasma displays use a layered technology like LCDs and OLEDs and look similar to LCD displays, but they use a layer of gas between two plates of glass instead of liquid crystals or organic material. A phosphor-coated screen (with red, green, and blue phosphors for each pixel) is used, and an electron grid layer and electronic charges are used to make the gas atoms light up the appropriate phosphors to create the image on the screen. The very large displays used by businesses, as well as many large screen televisions, are typically plasma displays.

Display devices form images by lighting up the proper configurations of **pixels**, which are the smallest colorable areas on a display device—essentially tiny dots on a display screen. A variety of technologies can be used to lighten up the pixels needed to display a particular image. Display devices can be monochrome displays, in which each pixel can only be one of two colors, such as black or white, or color displays, in which each pixel can display a combination of three colors—red, green, and blue—in order to display a large range of colors. Most monitors and display devices today are color displays.

The number of pixels used on a display screen determines the screen resolution, which affects the amount

Exhibit 2-42 How OLED displays work

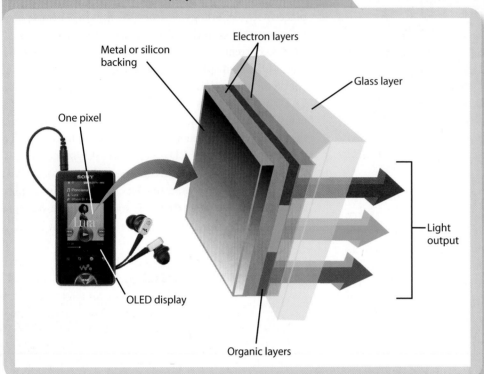

Electron layers

Metal or silicon backing

Glass layer

One pixel

SONY

OLED display

Light output

Organic layers

Another emerging flat-panel display technology is **interferometric modulator (IMOD) displays**. Designed initially for mobile phones and other portable devices, an IMOD display is essentially a complex mirror that uses external light—such as from the sun or artificial light inside a building—to display images. Because IMOD displays are utilizing light instead of fighting it the way LCD displays do, images are bright and clear even in direct sunlight. And, because backlighting isn't used, power consumption is much less than what is needed for LCD displays.

interferometric modulator (IMOD) display A flat-panel display technology that uses external light to display images.

plasma display A flat-panel display technology that uses a layer of gas between two plates of glass instead of liquid crystals or organic material.

pixel The smallest colorable areas on a display device.

surface-conduction electron-emitter display (SED) A high-definition display technology that is in development.

High-Definition Displays in Development

Surface-conduction electron-emitter display (SED) is being developed by Toshiba and Canon. It uses millions of tiny electron guns (similar to those used in CRTs but much smaller and millions of them instead of one) to power the pixels on a flat-panel display. SED displays are thin and bright, and they have less flicker than LCD and plasma screens. Televisions based on SED technology are beginning to become available.

of information that can be displayed on the screen at one time. When a higher resolution is selected, such as 1,280 pixels horizontally by 1,024 pixels vertically for a standard computer monitor (written as 1,280×1,024 and read as *1280 by 1024*), more information can fit on the screen, but everything will be displayed smaller than with a lower resolution, such as 1,024×768. The screen resolution on many computers can be changed by users to match their preferences and the software being used.

Display device size is measured diagonally from corner to corner. Most desktop computer monitors today are between 17 inches and 27 inches (though larger screens—up to 60 inches and more—are becoming increasingly common); notebook and tablet displays are usually between 15 inches and 20 inches; and netbooks typically have displays 10 inches or smaller. To better view DVDs and other multimedia content, many monitors today are widescreen, which conform to the 16:9 aspect ratio of widescreen televisions, instead of the conventional 4:3 aspect ratio.

The video card installed inside a computer or the integrated graphics component built directly into the motherboard of the computer houses the graphics processing unit (GPU)—the chip devoted to rendering images on a display device. The video card or the integrated graphics component determines the graphics capabilities of the computer, including the screen resolutions available, the number of bits used to store color information about each pixel (called the bit depth), the total number of colors that can be used to display im-

ages, the number of monitors that can be connected to the computer via that video card or component, and the types of connectors that can be used to connect a monitor to the computer. Video cards typically contain a fan and other cooling components to cool the card. Most video cards also contain memory chips (typically called video RAM or VRAM) to support graphics display, although some do not and are designed to use a portion of the computer's regular RAM as video RAM instead. Most video cards today contain between 256 MB and 1 GB of video RAM. A typical video card is shown in Exhibit 2-43.

The three most common types of interfaces used to connect a monitor to a computer are VGA (Video Graphics Array), DVI (Digital Visual Interface), and HDMI (High-Definition Multimedia Interface). VGA uses a 15-pin D-shaped connector and it is commonly used with CRT monitors and many flat-panel monitors to transfer analog images to the monitor. DVI uses a more rectangular connector and it is frequently used with flat-panel displays to allow the monitor to receive clearer, more reliable digital signals than is possible with a VGA interface. HDMI uses a smaller connector and can be used with display devices that support high-definition content. A newer type of connector is Display-Port, which is designed to eventually replace VGA and DVI ports on computers, video cards, and monitors. In fact, Apple already includes a smaller version—referred to as a Mini DisplayPort—on its newest MacBooks. The ports used with each of these possible connections are illustrated in Exhibit 2-43.

Exhibit 2-43 Video card

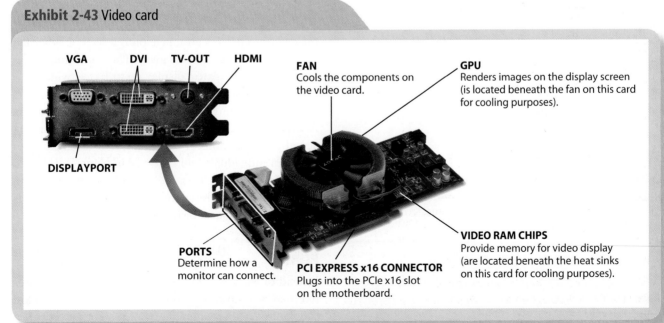

VGA **DVI** **TV-OUT** **HDMI**

DISPLAYPORT

FAN
Cools the components on the video card.

GPU
Renders images on the display screen (is located beneath the fan on this card for cooling purposes).

PORTS
Determine how a monitor can connect.

PCI EXPRESS x16 CONNECTOR
Plugs into the PCIe x16 slot on the motherboard.

VIDEO RAM CHIPS
Provide memory for video display (are located beneath the heat sinks on this card for cooling purposes).

Courtesy ZOTAC

3D Flat-Panel Displays

Recent improvements in flat-panel display technology and graphics processing have led to several emerging 3D output devices. The newest 3D products use filters, prisms, multiple lenses, and other technologies built into the display screen to create the 3D effect and, as a result, do not require 3D glasses. Some 3D displays resemble conventional monitors; others are shaped differently, such as the dome-shaped Perspecta 3D display. Other 3D displays are designed to be wearable, such as the eyeglasses-based display shown in the photo. This device projects the image from a mobile device (typically a mobile phone or portable digital media player) to a display screen built into the glasses. The technology allows the user to see the image as if it is on a distant large screen display, and many 3D wearable displays overlay the projected image on top of what the user is seeing in real time to provide situational awareness while the display is being used. Wearable 3D displays are also designed for soldiers and other mobile workers.

The display is built into eyeglasses, which connect to a mobile device.

Images from the source device (an email message in this example) are displayed on top of the user's normal vision.

Courtesy Lumus Ltd.

A video card or integrated video component in a desktop computer will have at least one port exposed through the system unit case to connect a monitor. Notebook computers and other computers with a built-in display typically contain a monitor port to connect a second monitor to the computer. An emerging option is connecting monitors to a computer via a USB port. USB monitors (monitors designed to connect via a USB port) can be added to a computer without requiring a video card that supports multiple monitors.

Most computer monitors today are physically connected to the system unit via a cable. Some display devices, such as digital photo frames, e-book readers, and some computer monitors and television sets, however, are designed to be wireless.

Data and Multimedia Projectors

A **data projector** is used to display output from a computer to a wall or projection screen. Conventional data projectors are often found in classrooms, conference rooms, and similar locations and can be freestanding units or permanently mounted onto the ceiling. While most data projectors connect via cable to a computer, wireless projectors are available. Some projectors also include an iPod dock to connect a video iPod in order to project videos stored on that device.

Another type of data projector is the integrated projector—tiny projectors that are beginning to be built into mobile phones, portable computers, portable digital media players, and other portable devices to enable the device to project an image onto a wall or other flat surface from up to 12 feet away. These integrated projectors typically create a display up to 10 feet wide in order to easily share information on the device with others on the go without having to crowd around a tiny screen. Another type of data projector is designed to project actual 3D projections or holograms. For instance, holograms of individuals and objects can be projected onto a stage for a presentation. Hologram display devices can be used in retail stores, exhibitions, and other locations to showcase products or other items in 3D.

Printers

Instead of the temporary, ever-changing soft copy output that a monitor produces, printers produce **hard copy**; that is, a permanent copy of the output on paper.

data projector A display device that projects computer output to a wall or projection screen.

hard copy A permanent copy of output on paper.

Most desktop computers are connected to a printer; portable computers can use printers as well.

Printers produce images through either impact or nonimpact technologies. Impact printers, like old ribbon typewriters, have a print mechanism that actually strikes the paper to transfer ink to the paper. For example, a dot-matrix printer such as the one shown in Exhibit 2-44 uses a print head consisting of pins that strike an inked ribbon to transfer the ink to the paper—the appropriate pins are extended (and, consequently, strike the ribbon) as the print head moves across the paper in order to form the appropriate words or images. Impact printers are used today primarily for producing multipart forms, such as invoices, packing slips, and credit card receipts.

Exhibit 2-44 Dot-matrix printer

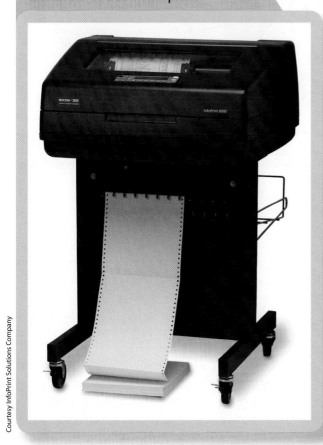

Courtesy InfoPrint Solutions Company

Most printers today are nonimpact printers, meaning they form images without the print mechanism actually touching the paper. Nonimpact printers usually produce higher-quality images and are much quieter than impact printers. The two most common types of printers today—laser printers and ink-jet printers—are both nonimpact printers. Both impact and nonimpact

Multifunction Devices

Some printers today offer more than just printing capabilities. These units—referred to as **multifunction devices (MFDs)** or *all-in-ones*—typically copy, scan, fax, and print documents. MFDs can be

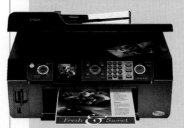

based on ink-jet printer or laser printer technology, and they are available as both color and black-and-white devices. Although multifunction devices have traditionally been desktop units used in small offices and home offices, larger workgroup multifunction devices are now available that are designed for multiple users, either as stand-alone stations or as networked units.

Courtesy Epson America

printers form images with dots, in a manner similar to the way monitors display images with pixels. Because of this, printers are very versatile and can print text in virtually any size, as well as print photos and other graphical images. In addition to paper, both impact and nonimpact printers can print on transparencies, envelopes, mailing labels, and more.

Most printing technologies today form images with dots of liquid ink or flecks of toner powder. The print resolution is measured in dots per inch (dpi). Guidelines for acceptable print resolution are typically 300 dpi for general purpose printouts, 600 dpi for higher-quality documents, 1,200 dpi for photographs, and 2,400 dpi for professional applications.

Print speed is typically measured in **pages per minute (ppm)**. How long it takes a document to print depends on the actual printer being used, the selected print resolution, and the content being printed. For instance, pages containing photographs or other images typically take longer to print than pages containing only text, and full-color pages take longer to print than black-and-white pages. Common speeds for personal printers range from about 15 to 35 ppm; network printers typically print from 40 to 100 ppm.

> **pages per minute (ppm)** The typical measurement of print speed.
>
> **multifunction device (MFD)** An output device that can copy, scan, fax, and print documents.

Exhibit 2-45 How black-and-white laser printers work

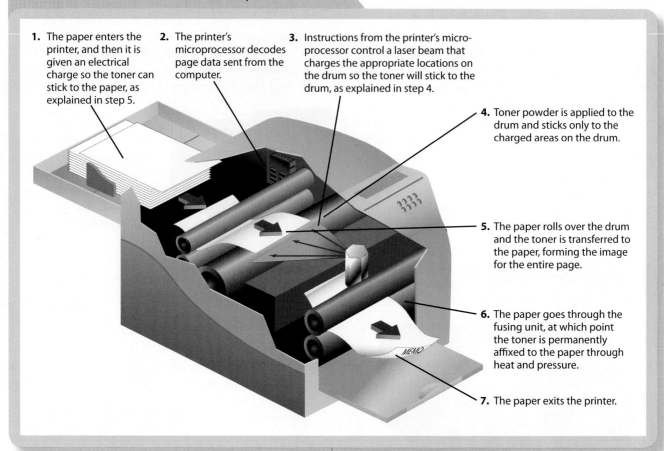

1. The paper enters the printer, and then it is given an electrical charge so the toner can stick to the paper, as explained in step 5.

2. The printer's microprocessor decodes page data sent from the computer.

3. Instructions from the printer's microprocessor control a laser beam that charges the appropriate locations on the drum so the toner will stick to the drum, as explained in step 4.

4. Toner powder is applied to the drum and sticks only to the charged areas on the drum.

5. The paper rolls over the drum and the toner is transferred to the paper, forming the image for the entire page.

6. The paper goes through the fusing unit, at which point the toner is permanently affixed to the paper through heat and pressure.

7. The paper exits the printer.

Most personal printers today connect to a computer via a USB connection; some have the option of connecting wirelessly. In addition, many personal printers can receive data to print via a flash memory card, a cable connected to a digital camera, or a camera docking station (a device connected to a printer into which a digital camera is placed so images stored in the camera can be printed).

Laser printers form images with toner powder (essentially ink powder) and are the standard for business documents. To print a document, the laser printer uses a laser beam to charge the appropriate locations on a drum to form the page's image, and then toner powder is released from a toner cartridge and sticks to the drum. The toner is transferred to a piece of paper when the paper is rolled over the drum, and a heating unit fuses the toner powder to the paper to permanently form the image, as illustrated in Exhibit 2-45. Common print resolutions for laser printers are between 600 and 2,400 dpi; speeds for personal laser printers range from about 15 to 30 ppm.

Ink-jet printers form images by spraying tiny drops of liquid ink from one or more ink cartridges onto the page, one line at a time, as illustrated in Exhibit 2-46. Some printers print with one single-sized ink droplet; others print using different-sized ink droplets and using multiple nozzles or varying electrical charges for more precise printing. The printhead for an ink-jet printer typically travels back and forth across the page, which is one reason why ink-jet printers are slower than laser printers. However, an emerging type of ink-jet printer uses a printhead that is the full width of the paper, which allows the printhead to remain stationary while the paper feeds past it. These printers are very fast, printing up to 60 ppm for letter-sized paper.

Because they are relatively inexpensive, have good-quality output, and can print in color, ink-jet printers

laser printer An output device that forms images with toner powder (essentially ink powder).

ink-jet printer An output device that forms images by spraying tiny drops of liquid ink from one or more ink cartridges onto paper.

Exhibit 2-46 How ink-jet printers work

Each ink cartridge is made up of multiple tiny ink-filled firing chambers; to print images, the appropriate color ink is ejected through the appropriate firing chamber.

Ink-jet printer

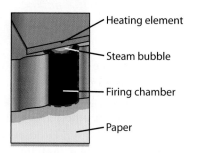

- Heating element
- Steam bubble
- Firing chamber
- Paper

1. A heating element makes the ink boil, which causes a steam bubble to form.

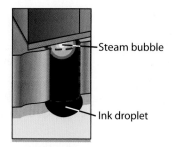

- Steam bubble
- Ink droplet

2. As the steam bubble expands, it pushes ink through the firing chamber.

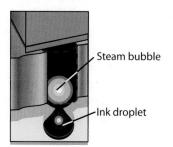

- Steam bubble
- Ink droplet

3. The ink droplet is ejected onto the paper and the steam bubble collapses, pulling more ink into the firing chamber.

are usually the printer of choice for home use. With the use of special photo paper, photo-quality ink-jet printers can also print photograph-quality digital photos. Starting at less than $50 for a simple home printer, ink-jet printers are affordable, although the cost of the replaceable ink cartridges can add up, especially if you do a lot of color printing.

Barcode printers enable businesses and other organizations to print custom barcodes on price tags, shipping labels, and other documents for identification or pricing purposes. Most barcode printers can print labels in a variety of barcode standards; some can also encode RFID tags embedded in labels.

Portable printers are small, lightweight printers that can be used on the go, such as with a notebook computer or mobile device, and connect via either a wired or wireless connection. Portable printers that can print on letter-sized (8.5 by 11-inch) paper are used by businesspeople while traveling. Portable receipt and barcode printers are used in some service professions. Printers can also be integrated into other devices. For instance, some digital cameras contain an integrated printer that is based on a new technology developed by ZINK (for "zero ink") Imaging. This printer uses no ink; instead, it uses special paper that is coated with special color dye crystals. Before printing, the embedded dye crystals are clear, so ZINK Paper looks like regular white photo paper. The ZINK printer uses heat

Ink-jet technology may eventually be used for dispensing liquid metals, aromas, computer chips, and other circuitry.

barcode printer A printer used to print barcodes.

portable printer A small, lightweight printer that can be used on the go, such as with a notebook computer or mobile device.

to activate and colorize these dye crystals when a photo is printed, creating a full-color image. In addition to being integrated into a variety of consumer electronics devices, including digital cameras and digital picture frames, stand-alone ZINK printers are also available.

To print charts, drawings, maps, blueprints, posters, signs, advertising banners, and other large documents in one piece, a larger printer is needed. Today, most large format printers (sometimes called plotters) are wide-format ink-jet printers, which are designed to print documents from around 24 inches to 60 inches in width. Although typically used to print on paper, some wide-format ink-jet printers can print directly on fabric and other types of materials.

When 3D output is required, such as to print a 3D model of a new building or prototype of a new product, **3D printers** can be used. Instead of printing on paper, these printers typically form output in layers using molten plastic during a series of passes to build a 3D version of the desired output—a process called fused deposition modeling (FDM). Some printers can produce multicolor output; others print in only one color and need to be painted by hand, if color output is desired.

Audio Output

Audio output includes voice, music, and other audible sounds. Computer speakers, the most common type of audio output device, connect to a computer and provide audio output for computer games, music, video clips and TV shows, Web conferencing, and other applications. Computer speaker systems resemble their stereo system counterparts and are available in a wide range of prices. Some speaker systems (such as the one shown in Exhibit 2-47) consist of only a pair of speakers. Others include additional speakers and a subwoofer to create better sound (such as surround sound) for multimedia content. Instead of being stand-alone units, the speakers for some desktop computers are built directly into, or are permanently attached to, the monitor. Portable computers and mobile devices typically have speakers integrated into the device; mobile devices can also be connected to a stereo system or other consumer device that contains an iPod/MP3 dock and integrated speakers designed to be used to play music stored on a portable digital media player. In addition, many cars can connect a portable digital media player to the car's

> **3D printer** A printer that uses molten plastic during a series of passes to build a 3D version of the desired output.

Exhibit 2-47 Audio output device

stereo system; typically devices are connected via the device's headphone jack or USB port.

Headphones can be used instead of speakers so the audio output does not disturb others (such as in a school computer lab or public library). Headsets are headphones with a built-in microphone, and are often used when dictating to a computer and when making telephone calls or participating in Web conferences using a computer; wireless headsets are commonly used in conjunction with mobile phones. Even smaller than headphones are the earphones and earbuds often used with portable digital media players, handheld gaming devices, and other mobile devices.

Quiz Yourself

1. How is data represented in a computer?

2. What is a bit?

3. What is a byte?

4. What is the main circuit board inside the system unit called?

5. What is the main processing device for a computer called?

6. Explain the difference between RAM and ROM.

7. What is an expansion card?

8. What is Plug and Play?

9. What does the ALU do?

10. Describe the difference between a storage medium and a storage device.

11. How is the surface of a hard disk organized?

12. How does a disk cache speed up performance?

13. List three types of optical discs.

14. What is cloud storage?

15. Define *input device* and *output device*.

16. What is the most common pointing device?

17. How is the quality of scanned images and printed output measured?

18. What is one of the most common types of flat-panel technologies in use today?

Practice It

Practice It 2-1

Adding additional RAM to a computer is one of the most common computer upgrades. Before purchasing additional memory, however, it is important to make sure that the memory about to be purchased is compatible with the computer.

1. Select a computer (such as your own computer, a school computer, or a computer at a local store) and then determine (by looking at the computer or asking an appropriate individual—such as a lab aide in the school computer lab or a salesperson at the local store) the manufacturer and model number, CPU, current amount of memory, total number of memory slots, and the number of available memory slots. (If you look inside the computer, be sure to unplug the power cord first and do not touch any components inside the system unit.)

2. Use the information you learned and a memory supplier's Web site to determine the appropriate type of memory needed for your selected computer.

3. What choices do you have in terms of capacity and configuration?

4. Can you add just one memory module, or do you have to add memory in pairs?

5. Can you keep the old memory modules, or do they have to be removed?

6. Prepare a one-page summary of your findings and recommendations and submit it to your instructor.

Practice It 2-2

USB flash drives can be used to bring your personal software and settings with you to any computer with which you use that drive. In addition, USB flash drives can be used to securely store files, grant access to a computer, and more.

1. Research two features that USB flash drives can provide in addition to data storage.

2. For your selected features, determine what the feature does, how it works, and what benefits it provides.

3. What are some examples of USB flash drives that are currently being sold that include that feature?

4. Is there an additional cost for drives that contain this feature? If so, do you think it is worth the extra cost?

5. Do you think the feature is beneficial? Why or why not?

6. Prepare a one- to two-page summary of your findings and opinions, and submit it to your instructor.

On Your Own

On Your Own 2-1

The choice of an appropriate input device for a product is often based on both the type of device being used and the target market for that device. For instance, a device targeted to college students and one targeted to older individuals may use different input methods. Suppose that you are developing a device to be used primarily for Internet access that will be marketed to senior citizens.

1. What type of hardware would you select as the primary input device? Why?

2. What are the advantages of your selected input device?

3. What are the disadvantages of your selected input device?

4. How could the disadvantages be minimized?

5. Prepare a one-page summary of your opinions and submit it to your instructor.

Computer Software

Introduction

All computers require software to operate and perform basic tasks. System software is the software used to run a computer. It runs in the background at all times, making it possible for you to use your computer. System software enables the hardware of a computer system to operate and to run application software. Application software is the software that performs the specific tasks users want to accomplish using a computer. Different application software is available to meet virtually any user need, and individuals and businesses use software to perform hundreds of tasks. Some of the most common types of application software used today are word processing, spreadsheet, database, presentation graphics, and multimedia software.

In this chapter, you'll learn about system software, including the operating systems that are the primary component of system software and utility programs that perform support functions for the operating system. You'll also learn about the various types of application software you may encounter in your personal and professional life.

Learning Objectives

After studying the material in this chapter, you will be able to:

LO3.1 Explain system software and operating systems

LO3.2 Identify operating systems for desktop PCs

LO3.3 Identify operating systems for handheld PCs and larger computers

LO3.4 Describe common types of application software

LO3.5 Describe application software used for business

LO3.6 Describe application software used for working with multimedia

LO3.7 Describe other types of application software

LO3.1 Introduction to System Software and Operating Systems

System software consists of the operating system and utility programs that control a computer system and allow you to use a computer. These programs enable the computer to boot, to launch application programs, and to facilitate important jobs, such as transferring files from one storage medium to another, configuring the computer to work with the hardware connected to it, managing files on the hard drive, and protecting the computer system from unauthorized use.

system software Programs such as the operating system and utility programs that control a computer and its devices, and enable application software to run on the computer.

All computers require software in order to operate and perform basic tasks. Without system software and application software, a computer is just a pile of hardware.

A computer's **operating system** is a collection of programs that manage and coordinate the activities taking place within the computer, and it is the most critical piece of software installed on the computer. The operating system is loaded into memory during the **boot process**, which is the first thing that occurs when you turn on a computer. The operating system then completes the boot process, provides access to application software, and ensures that all actions requested by a user are valid and processed in an orderly fashion. For example, when you issue the command for

operating system A collection of programs that manage and coordinate the activities taking place within the computer.

boot process The actions taken by programs built into the computer's hardware to start the operating system.

your computer to store a document on your hard drive, the operating system must perform the following steps:

1. Make sure that the specified hard drive exists.

2. Verify that there is adequate space on the hard drive to store the document, and then store the document in that location.

3. Update the hard drive's directory with the file name and disk location for that file so that the document can be retrieved when needed.

In addition to managing all of the resources associated with your computer, the operating system also facilitates connections to the Internet and other networks.

Functions of an Operating System

In general, the operating system serves as an intermediary between the user and the computer, as well as between application programs and the computer system's hardware, as shown in Exhibit 3-1. Without an operating system, no other program can run, and the computer cannot function. Many tasks performed by the operating system, however, go unnoticed by the user because the operating system works in the background much of the time.

As Exhibit 3-1 illustrates, one principal role of every operating system is to translate user instructions into a form the computer can understand. It also translates any feedback from hardware—such as a signal that the

user interface The means by which an operating system or other program interacts with the user.

kernel The essential portion, or core, of the operating system.

Current Software

Writing about software is like writing about clouds. By the time you have finished writing, the software version or cloud formation has changed. This chapter provides an overview about the types of computer software available. It is intended to be a starting point. Although sometimes specific software versions are mentioned, they are not necessarily the most current versions (though they were as this chapter was being written). If you want or need information about the latest software available, you should research the specific software in which you are interested.

printer has run out of paper or that a new hardware device has been connected to the computer—into a form that the user can understand. The means by which an operating system or any other program interacts with the user is called the **user interface**.

During the boot process, the essential portion, or core, of the operating system (called the **kernel**) is loaded into memory. The kernel remains in memory

Exhibit 3-1 Intermediary role of the operating system

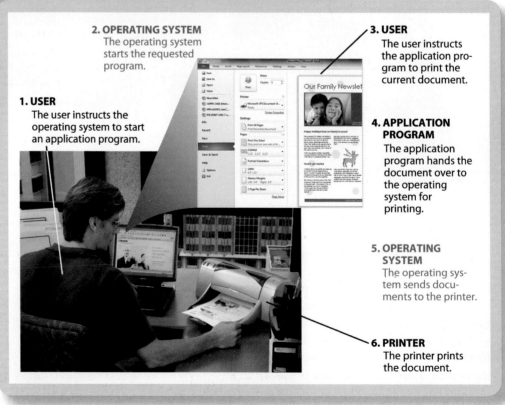

2. OPERATING SYSTEM
The operating system starts the requested program.

1. USER
The user instructs the operating system to start an application program.

3. USER
The user instructs the application program to print the current document.

4. APPLICATION PROGRAM
The application program hands the document over to the operating system for printing.

5. OPERATING SYSTEM
The operating system sends documents to the printer.

6. PRINTER
The printer prints the document.

Courtesy Bluetooth SIG

> In Windows, users can see some of the programs that are running in the background by looking at the icons in the system tray.

the entire time the computer is on so that it is always available, and other parts of the operating system are retrieved from the hard drive and loaded into memory when they are needed. Before the boot process ends, the operating system determines the hardware devices that are connected to the computer and configured properly, and it reads an opening batch of instructions. These startup instructions assign tasks for the operating system to carry out each time the computer boots, such as prompting the user to sign in to an instant messaging program or launching a security program to run continually in the background to detect possible threats.

Typically, many programs are running in the background at any one time, even before the user launches any application software. Exhibit 3-2 lists all the programs running on one computer immediately after it boots. These programs are launched automatically by

the operating system, consuming memory and processing power.

The operating system also configures all devices connected to a computer. Small programs called **device drivers** (or simply **drivers**) are used to communicate with peripheral devices, such as monitors, printers, and keyboards. Most operating systems include the drivers needed for the most common peripheral devices. In addition, drivers often come on a CD packaged with the peripheral device, or they can be downloaded from the manufacturer's Web site. Most operating systems look for and recognize new devices each time the computer boots. If a new device is found, the operating system tries to install the appropriate driver automatically to get the new hardware ready to use—a feature called Plug and Play. Exhibit 3-3 shows the message displayed when a new device is identified by the Windows 7 operating system.

Exhibit 3-3 Message that Windows found new hardware

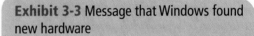

As you work on your computer, the operating system continuously manages the computer's resources (such as software, disk space, and memory) and makes them available to devices and programs when they are needed. If a problem occurs—such as a program stops functioning or too many programs are open for the amount of memory installed in the computer—the operating system notifies the user and tries to correct the problem, often by closing the offending program. If the problem cannot be corrected by the operating system, then the user typically needs to reboot the computer.

Another important task that the operating system performs is **file management**, which involves keeping track of the files stored on a computer so that they can be retrieved when needed.

Exhibit 3-2 Programs launched by the operating system when the computer boots

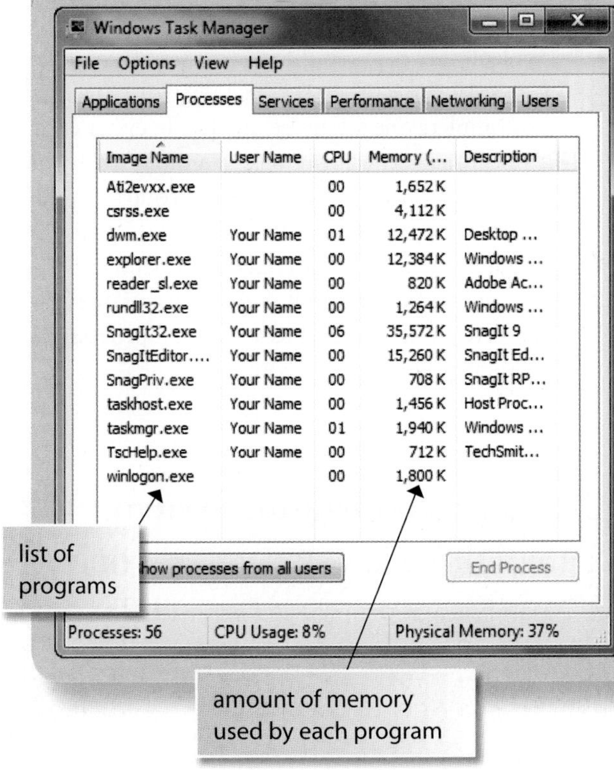

Windows Task Manager

File   Options   View   Help

| Applications | Processes | Services | Performance | Networking | Users |

Image Name	User Name	CPU	Memory (...	Description
Ati2evxx.exe		00	1,652 K	
csrss.exe		00	4,112 K	
dwm.exe	Your Name	01	12,472 K	Desktop ...
explorer.exe	Your Name	00	12,384 K	Windows ...
reader_sl.exe	Your Name	00	820 K	Adobe Ac...
rundll32.exe	Your Name	00	1,264 K	Windows ...
SnagIt32.exe	Your Name	06	35,572 K	SnagIt 9
SnagItEditor....	Your Name	00	15,260 K	SnagIt Ed...
SnagPriv.exe	Your Name	00	708 K	SnagIt RP...
taskhost.exe	Your Name	00	1,456 K	Host Proc...
taskmgr.exe	Your Name	01	1,940 K	Windows ...
TscHelp.exe	Your Name	00	712 K	TechSmit...
winlogon.exe		00	1,800 K	

list of programs

how processes from all users   End Process

Processes: 56   CPU Usage: 8%   Physical Memory: 37%

amount of memory used by each program

device driver (**driver**) A small program used to communicate with a peripheral device, such as a monitor, printer, or keyboard.

file management To keep track of the files stored on a computer so they can be retrieved when needed.

Detecting Problems and Installing Updates

Once a device and its driver have been installed properly, they usually work fine. If the device driver file is deleted, becomes corrupted, or has a conflict with another piece of software, then the device will no longer work. Usually, the operating system detects problems like this during the boot process and notifies the user, and then tries to reinstall the driver automatically. If the operating system is unable to correct the problem, the user can reinstall the driver manually. You may also need to update or reinstall some device drivers if you upgrade your operating system to a newer version. To keep your system up to date, many operating systems have an option to check for operating system updates automatically—including updated driver files—on a regular basis. Enabling these automatic updates is a good idea to keep your system running smoothly and protected from new threats (such as computer viruses).

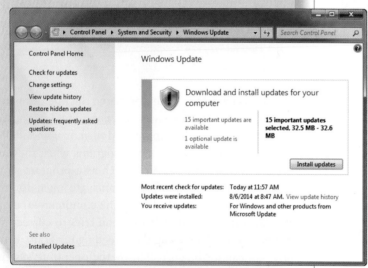

multitasking The ability of an operating system to have more than one program (also called a task) open at one time.

thread A sequence of instructions within a program that is independent of other threads.

multiprocessing A processing technique in which multiple processors or multiple processing cores in a single computer each work on a different job.

parallel processing A processing technique that uses multiple processors or multiple processing cores simultaneously, usually to process a single job as fast as possible.

Processing Techniques for Increased Efficiency

Operating systems often utilize various processing techniques in order to operate more efficiently and increase the amount of processing the computer system can perform in any given time period. One way computers operate more efficiently is to multitask. **Multitasking** refers to the ability of an operating system to have more than one program (also called a task) open at one time. For example, multitasking allows a user to edit a spreadsheet file in one window while loading a Web page in another window, or to retrieve new email messages in one window while a word processing document is open in another window.

A **thread** is a sequence of instructions within a program that is independent of other threads. Examples include spell checking, printing, and opening documents in a word processing program. Operating systems that support multithreading have the ability to rotate between multiple threads (similar to the way multitasking can rotate between multiple programs) so that processing is completed faster and more efficiently, even though only one thread is executed by a single core at one time.

If a computer has two or more CPUs, techniques that perform operations simultaneously are possible. **Multiprocessing** is a technique in which each processor or core works on a different job; **parallel processing** is a technique in which multiple processors or cores work together to make one single job finish sooner. The primary difference between these two techniques is that with multiprocessing, each CPU typically works on a different job; with parallel processing, the processors usually work together to complete one job more quickly. In either case, the CPUs can perform tasks simultaneously (at the exactly the same time), in contrast with multitasking and multithreading, which use a single CPU and process tasks sequentially (by rotating through tasks). Exhibit 3-4 illustrates the difference between simultaneous and sequential processing, using tasks typical of a desktop computer.

Because an operating system can multitask, you can keep one or more programs open while opening other programs.

Exhibit 3-4 Simultaneous vs. sequential processing

SEQUENTIAL PROCESSING Tasks are performed one right after the other.	Begin word processing document spell check	Begin Web page loading		Check email	Perform spreadsheet calculation	Continue word processing document spell check	Finish Web page loading	SINGLE CPU

(multitasking and multithreading)

SIMULTANEOUS PROCESSING Multiple tasks are performed at the exact same time.

Begin word processing document spell check	Perform spreadsheet calculation	Continue word processing document spell check	CPU 1
Begin Web page loading	Check email	Finish Web page loading	CPU 2

Load Web page	Spell check document	Check email	Perform spreadsheet calculation	CPU 1
				CPU 2

(multiprocessing)   (parallel processing)

Multiprocessing is supported by most operating systems and is used with personal computers that have multi-core CPUs, as well as with servers and mainframe computers that have multi-core CPUs and/or multiple CPUs. Parallel processing is used most often with supercomputers and supercomputing clusters.

Another key function of the operating system is memory management, which involves optimizing the use of main memory (RAM). The operating system allocates RAM to programs as needed and then reclaims that memory when the program is closed. Each additional running program or open window consumes memory. One memory management technique frequently used by operating systems is **virtual memory**, which uses a portion of the computer's hard drive as additional RAM. When the amount of RAM required exceeds the amount of RAM available, the operating system moves pages from RAM to the virtual memory area of the hard drive, which is called the **page file** or **swap file**. See Exhibit 3-5. Consequently, as a program is executed, some of the program may be stored in RAM and some in virtual memory. This paging or swapping process continues until the program finishes executing.

Exhibit 3-5 How virtual memory works

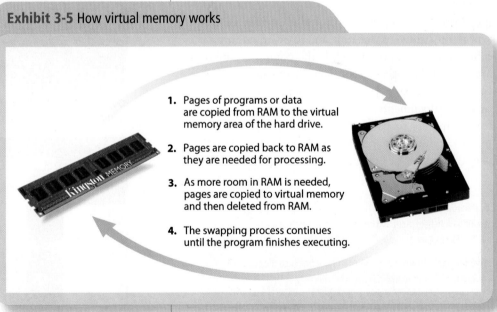

1. Pages of programs or data are copied from RAM to the virtual memory area of the hard drive.

2. Pages are copied back to RAM as they are needed for processing.

3. As more room in RAM is needed, pages are copied to virtual memory and then deleted from RAM.

4. The swapping process continues until the program finishes executing.

Courtesy Kingston Technology Company, Inc., and Western Digital

virtual memory A memory management technique frequently used by operating systems that uses a portion of the computer's hard drive as additional RAM.

page file (swap file) The virtual memory area of a hard drive.

If you are using the Windows 7 operating system, you can use flash memory media (such as a USB flash drive) along with the ReadyBoost feature for additional memory.

Virtual memory allows you to use more memory than is physically available on your computer, but using virtual memory is slower than just using RAM.

Some input and output devices are exceedingly slow, compared to today's CPUs. If the CPU had to wait for these slower devices to finish their work, the computer system would experience a horrendous bottleneck. To avoid this problem, most operating systems use buffering and spooling. A **buffer** is an area in RAM or on the hard drive designated to hold input and output on their way into or out of the system. For instance, a keyboard buffer stores characters as they are entered via the keyboard, and a print buffer stores documents that are waiting to be printed. The process of placing items in a buffer so they can be retrieved by the appropriate device when needed is called **spooling**. The most common use of buffering and spooling is print spooling. Print spooling allows multiple documents to be sent to the printer at one time and to print, one after the other, in the background while the computer and user are performing other tasks. The documents waiting to be printed are in a print queue, which designates the order the documents will be printed. It is also common for computers to use buffers to assist in redisplaying images on the screen and to temporarily store data that is in the process of being burned onto a CD or DVD.

buffer An area in RAM or on the hard drive designated to hold input and output on their way into or out of the system.

spooling The process of placing items in a buffer so they can be retrieved by the appropriate device when needed.

graphical user interface (**GUI**) A graphically based interface that allows a user to communicate instructions by clicking icons or commands.

command line interface A text-based user interface that requires the user to communicate instructions to the computer via typed commands.

Differences Among Operating Systems

Different types of operating systems are available to meet different needs. Some of the major distinctions among operating systems include the type of user interface utilized, whether the operating system is targeted for personal or network use, and what type of processing the operating system is designed for.

Most operating systems today use a **graphical user interface** (**GUI**), in which users can click icons or commands on the screen to issue instructions to the computer. The older DOS operating system and some versions of the UNIX and Linux operating systems use a **command line interface**, which requires users to type commands to issue instructions to the computer. See Exhibit 3-6.

Exhibit 3-6 Command line interface vs. graphical user interface

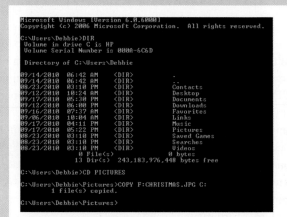

COMMAND LINE INTERFACE
Commands are entered using the keyboard.

GRAPHICAL USER INTERFACE
Icons, buttons, menus, and other objects are selected with the mouse to issue commands to the computer.

Exhibit 3-7 How operating systems are used in a network environment

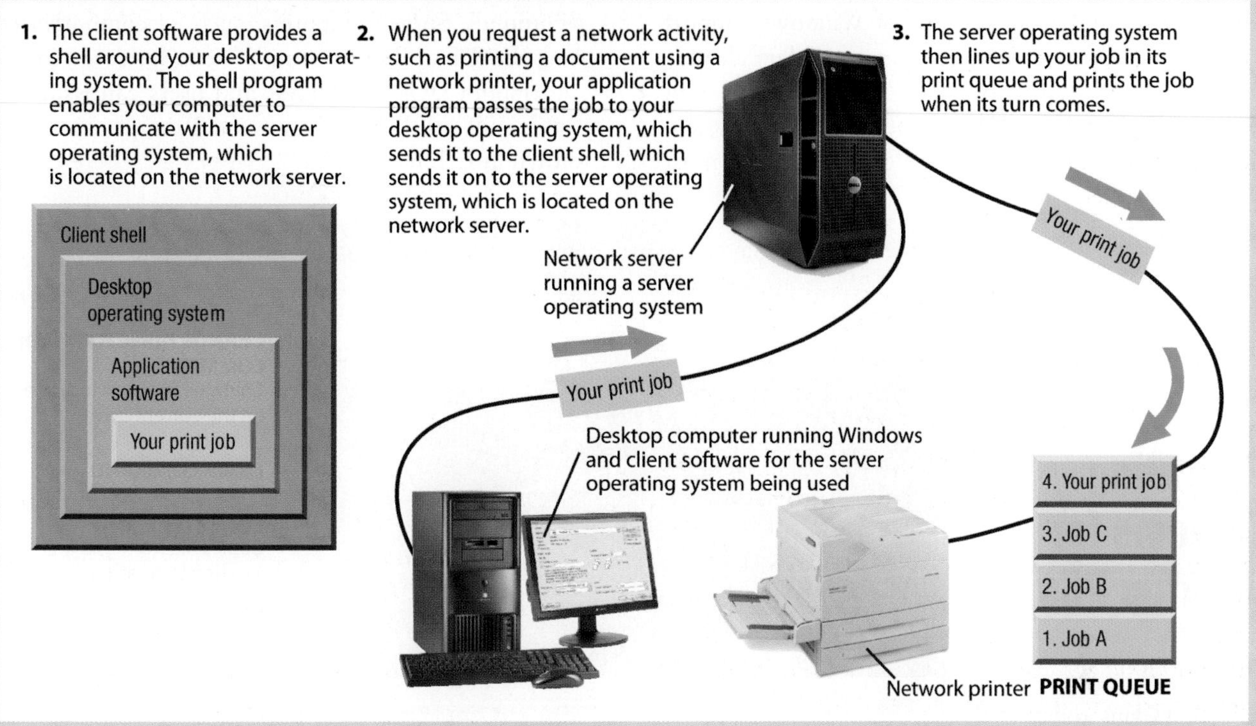

1. The client software provides a shell around your desktop operating system. The shell program enables your computer to communicate with the server operating system, which is located on the network server.

2. When you request a network activity, such as printing a document using a network printer, your application program passes the job to your desktop operating system, which sends it to the client shell, which sends it on to the server operating system, which is located on the network server.

3. The server operating system then lines up your job in its print queue and prints the job when its turn comes.

Client shell

Desktop operating system

Application software

Your print job

Network server running a server operating system

Your print job

Your print job

Desktop computer running Windows and client software for the server operating system being used

4. Your print job
3. Job C
2. Job B
1. Job A

Network printer **PRINT QUEUE**

Courtesy Dell Inc.; Gateway, Inc.; and InfoPrint Solutions Company

Operating systems used with personal computers are typically referred to as **personal operating systems** (also called **desktop operating systems**) and they are designed to be installed on a single computer. In contrast, **server operating systems** (also called **network operating systems**) are designed to be installed on a network server to grant multiple users access to a network and its resources. Each computer on a network has its own personal operating system installed (just as with a stand-alone computer) and that operating system controls the activity on that computer, while the server operating system controls access to network resources. Computers on a network may also need special client software to access the network and issue requests to the server. An overview of how a typical personal operating system and a server operating system interact on a computer network is illustrated in Exhibit 3-7.

In addition to personal operating systems and server operating systems, **mobile operating systems** are designed to be used with mobile phones and other mobile devices, and **embedded operating systems** are built into consumer kiosks, cash registers, some consumer electronics, and other devices.

As new technologies or trends (such as new types of buses, virtualization, power consumption concerns, touch and gesture input, and Web-based software, for example) emerge, operating systems must be updated to support them. On the other hand, as technologies

Graphical versions of the UNIX and Linux operating systems are also available.

personal operating system (desktop operating system) An operating system designed to be installed on a single computer.

server operating system (network operating systems) An operating system designed to be installed on a network server to grant multiple users access to a network and its resources.

mobile operating system An operating system designed to be used with mobile phones and other mobile devices.

embedded operating system An operating system that is built into devices such as consumer kiosks, cash registers, and consumer electronics.

become obsolete, operating system manufacturers need to decide when to end support for those technologies. Likewise, hardware manufacturers also need to respond to new technologies introduced by operating systems. For instance, the latest versions of Windows support a SideShow feature that requires a secondary display device built into hardware, such as into the cover of a notebook computer. When a new operating system feature is introduced, hardware manufacturers must decide whether to adapt their hardware to support the new feature.

Corporation, but neither version is updated any longer. DOS is not widely used with personal computers today because it does not utilize a graphical user interface and does not support modern processors and processing techniques. Some computers, such as computers running the Windows operating system, however, can still understand DOS commands and users can issue these commands using the Command Prompt window, as shown in Exhibit 3-8.

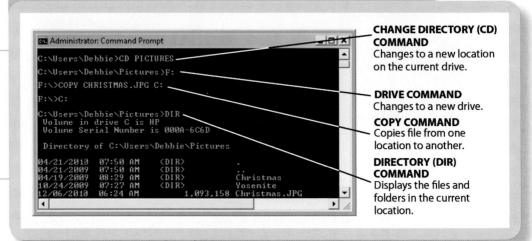

Exhibit 3-8 DOS commands issued via the Command Prompt window

CHANGE DIRECTORY (CD) COMMAND
Changes to a new location on the current drive.

DRIVE COMMAND
Changes to a new drive.

COPY COMMAND
Copies file from one location to another.

DIRECTORY (DIR) COMMAND
Displays the files and folders in the current location.

LO3.2

Operating Systems for Desktop PCs

Many operating systems today are designed either for personal computers (such as desktop and notebook computers) or for network servers. The most widely used personal and server operating systems are discussed next.

DOS

During the 1980s and early 1990s, **DOS** (**Disk Operating System**) was the dominant operating system for microcomputers. DOS traditionally used a command line interface, although newer versions of DOS support a menu-driven interface. The two primary forms of DOS are PC-DOS and MS-DOS. PC-DOS was created originally for IBM PCs (and is owned by IBM), whereas MS-DOS was created for use with IBM-compatible PCs. Both versions were originally developed by Microsoft

Windows

Microsoft created the original version of **Windows**—Windows 1.0—in 1985 in an effort to meet the needs of users frustrated by having to learn and use DOS commands. Windows 1.0 through Windows 3.x (where x stands for the version number of the software, such as Windows 3.0, 3.1, or 3.11) were not, however, full-fledged operating systems. Instead, they were operating environments for the DOS operating system—that is, they were graphical shells that operated around the DOS operating system—which were designed to make DOS easier to use.

Windows 95 (released in 1995) and Windows 98 (released in 1998) both used a GUI similar to the one

DOS (**Disk Operating System**) The dominant operating system for microcomputers during the 1980s and early 1990s.

Windows The operating system created by Microsoft in 1985 with a graphical user interface.

Microsoft Windows has been the predominant personal operating system for many years and holds about 90 percent of the market.

used with Windows 3.x but were easier to use than earlier versions of Windows. Both Windows 95 and Windows 98 supported multitasking, long file names, a higher degree of Internet integration, more options for customizing the desktop user interface, larger hard drives, DVD drives, and USB devices.

Windows NT (New Technology) was the first 32-bit version of Windows designed for high-end workstations and servers. Windows NT was built from the ground up using a different kernel than the other versions of Windows.

Windows Me (Millennium Edition) replaced Windows 98. Designed for home computers, Windows Me supported improved home networking and a shared Internet connection. It also featured improved multimedia capabilities, better system protection, a faster boot process, and more Internet-ready activities and games.

Windows 2000, released in 2000 to replace Windows NT, was geared toward high-end business workstations and servers, and it included support for wireless devices and other types of new hardware.

Windows XP replaced both Windows 2000 (for business use) and Windows Me (for home use). It included improved photo, video, and music editing and sharing; improved networking capabilities; and support for handwriting and voice input. Although Microsoft is phasing out Windows XP and only netbooks can be purchased with that version of Windows today, there is still a large installed base of Windows XP users. Microsoft plans to support Windows XP until 2014.

Windows Vista replaced Windows XP and was the current version of Windows until Windows 7 was released in late 2009. However, Windows Vista is still widely used today. It comes in four basic editions (Home Basic, Home Premium, Business, and Ultimate) and in both 32-bit and 64-bit versions. One of the most obvious changes in Windows Vista is the Aero interface, which is a visual graphical user interface that uses glass-like transparency, vibrant colors, and dynamic elements such as Live Thumbnails of taskbar buttons. Windows Vista also introduced the Sidebar feature that contains gadgets—small applications that are used to perform a variety of tasks, such as displaying weather information, a clock, a calendar, a calculator, sticky notes, news headlines, personal photos, email messages, and stock tickers. The Vista Start menu contains an Instant Search feature to allow users to easily search for and open programs and documents stored on their computers. Vista also contains several built-in security features

Windows 7 runs on netbooks, which are one of the fastest growing areas of the personal computer market.

and much improved networking, collaboration, and synchronization tools.

Windows 7, released in late 2009, is the newest version of Windows. Windows 7 is available in both 32-bit and 64-bit versions and in four main editions, including Home Premium (the primary version for home users) and Professional (the primary version for businesses). Although the minimum suggested system requirements for Windows 7 are essentially the same as for Vista, Windows 7 is designed to start up and respond faster than Vista. In addition, Microsoft states that all versions of Windows 7 will run well on netbooks—something Vista could not do.

Windows 7 Features

The appearance of Windows 7 is similar to Windows Vista—many of the improvements in Windows 7 focus on making it faster and easier to use. For instance, you can drag taskbar buttons to rearrange them in the order you prefer. To quickly arrange two windows side by side, you can drag a window to the left or right edge of the desktop to have it automatically resize and snap into place to fill half of the screen. Gadgets have moved from the Sidebar (as in Windows Vista) to free up space on the screen. To make it easier to use and manage all of your connected devices (such as printers, portable digital media players, and USB flash drives), Windows 7 includes a Device Stage. To easily stream media content stored on your computer to any networked device (such as another computer, a stereo, or an Xbox 360), Windows 7 includes a Play To option. In addition, Windows 7 includes a HomeGroup feature for improved home networking, one-click Wi-Fi connections, support for both touch and pen input, and improved accessory programs (such as a more versatile Calculator and a Paint program that uses the Ribbon interface found in recent versions of Microsoft Office).

Windows Server and Windows Home Server

Windows Server is the version of Windows designed for server use. Windows Server 2008 includes Internet Information Services 7.0, which is a powerful Web platform for Web applications and Web services; built-in virtualization technologies; a variety of new security tools and enhancements; and streamlined configuration and management tools. The latest version of Windows Server 2008 is called Windows Server 2008 R2 and includes features that are designed specifically to work with client computers running Windows 7.

A related operating system designed for home use is Windows Home Server, which is preinstalled on home server devices and designed to provide services for a home network. For instance, a home server can serve as a central storage location for all devices in the home, such as computers, gaming consoles, and portable digital media players. Home servers also can be set up to back up all devices in the home on a regular basis, as well as to give users access to the data on the home server and to control the home network from any computer via the Internet.

Mac OS and Mac OS X Server

Mac OS is the proprietary operating system for computers made by Apple Inc. It is based on the UNIX operating system and set the original standard for graphical user interfaces. Many of today's operating systems

follow the trend that Mac OS started and, in fact, use GUIs that highly resemble the one used with Mac OS.

The latest versions of Mac OS, such as Mac OS X Leopard (shown in Exhibit 3-9) and Mac OS X Snow Leopard, are part of the Mac OS X family. Mac OS X allows multithreading

Exhibit 3-9 Mac OS X Leopard

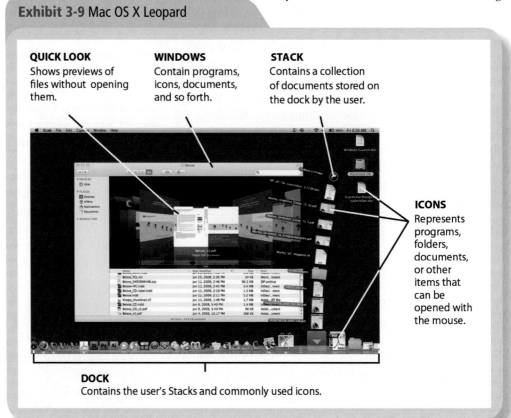

QUICK LOOK
Shows previews of files without opening them.

WINDOWS
Contain programs, icons, documents, and so forth.

STACK
Contains a collection of documents stored on the dock by the user.

ICONS
Represents programs, folders, documents, or other items that can be opened with the mouse.

DOCK
Contains the user's Stacks and commonly used icons.

and multitasking, supports dual 64-bit processors, and has a high level of multimedia functions and connectivity. In addition, it includes the Safari Web browser, a Spaces feature that allows you to organize groups of applications and windows into Spaces that can be displayed or hidden as desired, a Stacks feature that allows you to store files (documents, programs, and so on) in a Stack on the Dock, and a Quick Look feature that shows you previews of files without opening them. The main improvement provided by the most recent version of Mac OS X (Snow Leopard) over the previous version (Leopard) is responsiveness. For instance, the

Windows Server The version of Windows designed for server use.

Mac OS The proprietary operating system for computers made by Apple Inc.

An upgrade that installs over your existing operating system or application program is less expensive than buying a new full version.

Time Machine automatic backup and restore system is 50 percent faster, Mail loads messages 85 percent faster and conducts searches up to 90 percent faster, and the new 64-bit Safari browser is faster and more resistant to crashes. Snow Leopard is also more efficient, requiring only about one-half the hard drive space as previous versions.

Mac OS X Server is the server version of Mac OS X. The latest version—Mac OS X Server Snow Leopard—is a full 64-bit operating system that is up to twice as fast as earlier server versions. New capabilities built into Snow Leopard Server include Podcast Producer 2 for creating and publishing podcasts, and Mobile Access Server for providing authorized users secure remote access to firewall protected servers via Macs, iPhones, and other Apple devices.

UNIX

UNIX was developed in the late 1960s at AT&T Bell Laboratories as an operating system for midrange servers. UNIX is a multiuser, multitasking operating system. Computer systems ranging from microcomputers to mainframes can run UNIX, and it can support a variety of devices from different manufacturers. This flexibility gives UNIX an advantage over competing operating systems in some situations. However, UNIX is more expensive, requires a higher level of technical knowledge, and tends to be harder to install, maintain, and upgrade than most other commonly used operating systems.

Many versions of UNIX are available, as are many operating systems based on UNIX. These operating systems—such as Mac OS—are sometimes referred to as UNIX flavors. In fact, the term *UNIX*, which initially referred to the original UNIX operating system, has evolved to refer to a group of similar operating systems based on UNIX. Many UNIX flavors are incompatible, which creates some problems when a program written for one UNIX computer system is moved to another computer system running a different flavor of UNIX. To avoid this incompatibility problem, the Open Group open source consortium is dedicated to the development and evolution of the Single UNIX Specification—a standardized programming environment for UNIX applications. Both personal and server versions of UNIX-based operating systems are available.

Linux

Linux is an operating system developed by Linus Torvalds in 1991 when he was a student at the University of Helsinki in Finland. Though the operating system resembles UNIX, Linux was developed independently from it. Linux was released to the public as open source software; that is, a program whose source code is available to the public and can be modified to improve it or to customize it to a particular application. Over the years, the number of Linux users has grown, and volunteer programmers from all over the world have collaborated to improve it, sharing their modified code with others over the Internet. Although Linux originally used a command line interface, most recent versions of Linux programs use a graphical user interface, as shown in Exhibit 3-10. Linux is widely available as a

Exhibit 3-10 Linux with a 3D graphical user interface

Courtesy Novell, Inc.

Mac OS X Server The server version of Mac OS X.

UNIX A multiuser, multitasking operating system developed in the late 1960s at AT&T Bell Laboratories as an operating system for midrange servers.

Linux An open source operating system developed by Linus Torvalds in 1991 when he was a student.

free download via the Internet. Companies are also permitted to customize Linux and sell it as a retail product. Commercial Linux distributions, such as those available from Red Hat and Novell, come with maintenance and support materials (something that many of the free versions do not offer), making the commercial versions more attractive for corporate users.

Over the years, Linux has grown from an operating system used primarily by computer techies who disliked Microsoft to a widely accepted operating system with strong support from mainstream companies such as IBM, HP, Dell, and Novell. Linux is available in both personal and server versions. It is also widely used with mobile phones. The use of Linux with inexpensive personal computers is growing. In fact, one Linux-based operating system (Android) developed for mobile phones may soon be extended to netbooks and other very portable personal computers.

One reason individuals and organizations are switching to Linux and other open source software is cost. Using the Linux operating system and a free or low-cost office suite, Web browser program, and email program can save hundreds of dollars per computer.

LO3.3 Operating Systems for Handheld PCs and Larger Computers

Although notebook, netbook, UMPCs, and other portable personal computers typically use the same operating systems as desktop computers, mobile phones and other mobile devices usually use mobile operating systems—either mobile versions of personal operating systems (such as Windows or Linux) or special operating systems (such as Apple iPhone OS or Black-Berry OS) that are designed solely for mobile devices. There are also embedded operating systems designed to be used with everyday objects, such as home appliances, gaming consoles, digital cameras, toys, watches, GPS systems, home medical devices, voting terminals, and cars. Most users select a mobile phone by considering the mobile provider, hardware, and features associated with the phone, instead of considering the operating system used. However, the operating system

Windows Mobile The version of Windows designed for mobile phones.

used with a phone or other device determines some of the phone's capabilities (such as whether it can accept touch input or its display can rotate automatically as the phone changes orientation), the interface used, and the applications that can run on that device.

Mobile and Embedded Versions of Windows

Windows Mobile is the version of Windows designed for mobile phones. It has some of the look and feel of the larger desktop versions of Windows (see the Start button in the upper-left corner of the Windows Mobile device shown in Exhibit 3-11), but it also has features useful to mobile users. For instance, Windows Mobile supports multitasking; includes an improved mobile Web browser; supports a free My Phone service that

Exhibit 3-11 Examples of operating systems for mobile devices

WINDOWS MOBILE

ANDROID

IPHONE OS

BLACKBERRY OS

automatically syncs and backs up contacts, text messages, and other information to the Web; and supports a variety of software, including Facebook applications, mobile versions of Microsoft Word, Excel, and PowerPoint; and more. Windows Mobile 6.5, also called Microsoft Phone, features a honeycomb Home screen interface that allows users to view the information most important to them at a glance and accurately select the desired item by touch, and a Windows Marketplace for Mobile application store to help users locate and purchase additional mobile applications.

Windows Embedded is a family of operating systems based on Windows that is designed primarily for consumer and industrial devices that are not personal computers, such as cash registers, digital photo frames, GPS devices, ATMs, medical devices, and robots. There are multiple versions of Windows Embedded based on different versions of Windows (including Windows XP, Windows Vista, and Windows Mobile) to match the type of device the operating system is to be used with and the computers with which the devices may need to interact. There are also versions of Windows specifically designed to be embedded into cars, such as Microsoft Auto—an embedded version of Windows that is designed specifically for integrated in-vehicle communication, entertainment, and navigation systems. For instance, Microsoft Auto powers the Ford SYNC system, which enables calls from mobile phones and music from portable digital media players to be controlled by voice or with buttons on the steering wheel.

Mobile Phone Operating Systems

Android (shown in Exhibit 3-11) is a Linux-based operating system developed by the Open Handset Alliance, a group that includes Google and more than 30 technology and mobile companies. Android supports multitasking and, as a relatively new operating system, it was built from the ground up with current mobile device capabilities in mind, which enables developers to create mobile applications that take full advantage of all the features a mobile device has to offer. It is an open platform, so users can connect to any mobile network and mobile phone provider they choose and they can customize their mobile phones (including the home screen, dialer, and applications used) as much as desired.

The mobile operating system designed for Apple mobile phones and mobile devices, such as the iPhone 3G, is **iPhone OS** (see Exhibit 3-11). This operating system is based on Apple's Mac OS X operating system, supports multi-touch input, and has thousands of applications available via the App Store. Although earlier versions of iPhone OS do not allow multitasking of third-party software (reportedly to increase battery life and stability), the latest versions support multitasking and include an improved version of the Safari Web browser; a new media player; the ability to copy, cut, and paste text; the ability to send photos via text messaging; and better search capabilities.

BlackBerry OS is the operating system designed for BlackBerry devices (see Exhibit 3-11). It supports multitasking and, like other mobile operating systems, it includes email and Web browsing support, music management, video recording, calendar tools, and more. In addition, BlackBerry OS includes a voice note feature that allows you to send a voice note via email or text message and has an integrated maps feature.

Palm OS is the original operating system designed for Palm devices. In 2009, Palm released **Palm webOS**—a new Linux-based mobile operating system developed for next-generation Palm mobile phones, such as the Palm Pre. Unlike Palm OS, Palm webOS supports full multitasking; it also includes Palm Synergy to synchronize contacts and calendars from multiple locations, an improved Web browser, and a Web-based application suite.

Symbian OS, used on most Nokia mobile phones, is a mobile operating system that supports multithreading

---

Windows Embedded A family of operating systems based on Windows that is designed primarily for consumer and industrial devices that are not personal computers.

Android A Linux-based operating system developed by the Open Handset Alliance that supports multitasking.

iPhone OS The mobile operating system designed for Apple mobile phones and mobile devices.

BlackBerry OS The operating system designed for BlackBerry devices.

Palm OS The original operating system designed for Palm devices.

Palm webOS A new Linux-based mobile operating system developed for next-generation Palm mobile phones released in 2009.

Symbian OS A mobile operating system that supports multithreading and multitasking.

Utility Programs

A **utility program** is a software program that performs a specific task, usually related to managing or maintaining the computer system. Many utility programs—such as programs for finding files, diagnosing and repairing system problems, cleaning up a hard drive, viewing images, playing multimedia files, and backing up files—are built into operating systems. There are also many stand-alone utility programs available as an alternative to the operating system's utility programs (such as a search or a backup program) or to provide additional utility features not usually built into operating systems (such as an antivirus or a file compression program). Stand-alone utility programs are often available in a suite of related programs (such as a collection of maintenance programs or security programs). Some of the most commonly used integrated and stand-alone utility programs include:

▶ **File management programs**—Perform file management tasks so you can see the folders and files are stored on a drive as well as copy, move, rename, and delete them.

▶ **Search tools**—Search for documents and other files on a storage medium that meet specific criteria.

▶ **Diagnostic programs**—Evaluate your computer system, looking for problems and making recommendations for fixing any errors that are discovered.

▶ **Disk management programs**—Diagnose and repair problems related to your hard drive.

▶ **Uninstall programs**—Remove the programs along with related extraneous data, such as references to those programs in your system files.

▶ **Cleanup utilities**—Delete temporary files (such as deleted files still in the Recycle Bin, temporary Internet files, and temporary installation files) to free up disk space, and sometimes locate unnecessary information in the Windows registry and other system files (such as from uninstalled programs) and delete it.

Courtesy of Symantec

▶ **File compression programs**—Reduce the size of files so they take up less storage space; also used to decompress or restore the files to their original size.

▶ **Backup and recovery programs**—Make a copy of important files, and then restore them in case of a power outage, hardware failure, or accidental deletion or overwriting of files.

▶ **Security programs**—protect against malicious software being installed on your computer and against someone accessing your computer via the Internet or a wireless connection.

and multitasking. It also includes support for Web browsing, email, handwriting recognition, synchronization, and a range of other applications designed for mobile communications and computing. It has a flexible user interface framework that enables mobile phone manufacturers to develop and customize user interfaces to meet the needs of their customers.

Embedded Linux is another operating system alternative for mobile phones, GPS devices, portable digital

media players, and other mobile devices. Just as with desktop and server versions of Linux, embedded Linux is available in a variety of flavors from different companies. Linux is also the basis for several other mobile operating systems, such as Android, iPhone OS, and Palm webOS.

Operating Systems for Larger Computers

Larger computer systems—such as high-end servers, mainframes, and supercomputers—sometimes use operating systems designed solely for that type of system. For instance, IBM's i5/OS and z/OS are designed for IBM servers and mainframes, respectively. In addition, many servers and mainframes today run conventional operating systems, such as Windows, UNIX, and Linux. Linux in particular is increasingly being used with both

embedded Linux An operating system alternative for mobile phones, GPS devices, portable digital media players, and other mobile devices.

utility program A software program that performs a specific task, usually related to managing or maintaining the computer system.

The file management program that is incorporated into the Windows operating systems is Windows Explorer.

mainframes and supercomputers; often a group of Linux computers are linked together to form a Linux supercomputing cluster. Larger computer systems may also use a customized operating system based on a conventional operating system. For instance, many IBM mainframes and Cray supercomputers use versions of UNIX developed specifically for those computers (AIX and UNICOS, respectively).

LO3.4 Introduction to Application Software

Application software includes all the programs that allow you to perform specific tasks on a computer, such as writing a letter, preparing an invoice, viewing a Web page, listening to a music file, checking the inventory of a particular product, playing a game, preparing financial statements, and designing a home.

Software Categories

The four basic categories of software are commercial software, shareware, freeware, and public domain software, which are described in Exhibit 3-12. Each type of software has different ownership rights. In addition, software that falls into any of these four categories can also be **open source software**—programs whose source code is available to the public. An open source program can be copyrighted, but individuals and businesses are allowed to modify the program and redistribute it—the only restrictions are that changes must be shared with

System Software or Application Software?

The difference between system and application software is not always straightforward. Some programs, such as those used to burn DVDs, were originally viewed as utility programs. Today, these programs typically contain a variety of additional features, such as the ability to organize and play music and other media files, transfer videos and digital photos to a computer, edit videos and photos, create DVD movies, copy CDs and DVDs, and create slide shows. Consequently, these programs now fit the definition of application programs more closely. On the other hand, system software now typically contains several application software components. For example, the Microsoft Windows operating system includes a variety of application programs, including a Web browser, a calculator, a calendar program, a painting program, a media player, a movie making program, an instant messaging program, and a text editing program. A program's classification as system or application software usually depends on the principal function of the program, and the distinction between the two categories is not always clear cut.

the open source community and the original copyright notice must remain intact.

Commercial software includes any software program that is developed and sold for a profit. When you buy a commercial software program (such as Microsoft Office, TurboTax, or GarageBand), it typically comes with a single-user license, which means you cannot legally make copies of the installation CD to give to your friends and you cannot legally install the software on their computers using your CD. You cannot even install the software on a second computer that you own, unless allowed by the license. For example, some software licenses state that the program can be installed on one desktop

application software The programs that allow you to perform specific tasks on a computer.

open source software Programs whose source code is available to the public.

commercial software A software program that is developed and sold for a profit.

The most common format used for compressed files in the Windows environment is the .zip format.

Exhibit 3-12 Types of software

Category	Description	Examples
Commercial software	A software program that is developed and sold for a profit.	Microsoft Office (office suite) Norton AntiVirus (antivirus program) Adobe Photoshop (image editing program) World of Warcraft (game)
Shareware	A software program that is distributed on the honor system; typically available free of charge but may require a small registration fee.	WinZip (file compression program) Ulead Video ToolBox (video editing/conversion program) Image Shrinker (image optimizer) Deluxe Ski Jump 3 (game)
Freeware	A software program that is given away by the author for others to use free of charge.	Internet Explorer (Web browser) OpenOffice.org (office suite) QuickTime Player (media player) Yahoo! Messenger (instant messaging program)
Public domain software	A software program that is not copyrighted.	Lynx (text-based Web browser) Pine (email program)

computer and one portable computer belonging to the same individual. To determine which activities are allowable for a particular commercial software program, refer to its software license. Schools or businesses that need to install software on a large number of computers or need to have the software available to multiple users over a network can usually obtain a site license or network license for the number of users needed.

Open Source Software

The use of open source software has grown over the past few years, primarily for cost reasons. One of the first widely known open source programs was the Linux operating system. However, low-cost or no-cost open source alternatives are also available for a wide selection of application programs today. For instance, the free OpenOffice.org office suite can be used as an alternative to Microsoft Office, and the free GIMP program can be used to retouch photos instead of Adobe Photoshop or another pricey image editing program. In addition to saving money, these alternative programs often require less disk space and memory than their commercial software counterparts require. Other possible benefits of using open source software include increased stability and security (because they are tested and improved by a wide variety of programmers and users), and the ability to modify the application's source code. Perceived risks of using open source software include lack of support and compatibility issues. An emerging trend is applying open source principles to hardware—some hardware designers are releasing designs for new hardware to the public in hopes that manufacturing companies will use the designs in new products and credit them as the original designer.

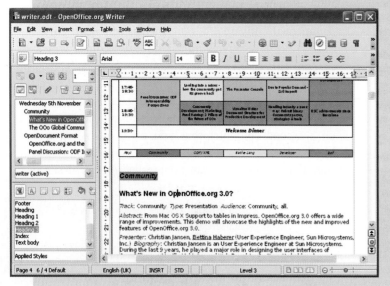

The OpenOffice.org Writer word processing program.

Courtesy OpenOffice.org

In addition to their full versions, some commercial software is available in a demo or trial version. Typically, these versions can be used free of charge and distributed to others, but often they are missing some key features (such as the ability to save or print a document) or they will not run after the trial period expires. Because these programs are not designed as replacements for the fee-based version, it is ethical to use them only to determine whether you want to buy the full program. If the decision is made against purchasing the product, you should uninstall the demo or trial version from your computer.

Recent trends in computing—such as multiprocessing, virtualization, and cloud computing—are leading to new software licensing issues for commercial software companies. For example, software companies must decide whether the number of installations allowed by the license is counted by the number of computers on which the software is installed or by the total number of processors or CPU cores used by those computers, as well as decide how to determine the number of users in a virtualized environment. Software vendors are expected to develop and implement new licensing models to address these and other trends in the future.

Shareware programs are software programs that are distributed on the honor system. Most shareware programs are available to try free of charge, but typically require a small fee if you choose to use the program regularly. By paying the requested registration fee, you can use the program for as long as you want to use it and may be entitled to product support, updates, and other benefits. You can legally and ethically copy shareware programs to pass along to friends and colleagues for evaluation purposes, but those individuals are expected to pay the shareware fee if they decide to keep the product.

Many shareware programs have a specified trial period, such as one month. Although it is not illegal to use shareware past the specified trial period, it is unethical to do so. Shareware is typically much less expensive than commercial versions of similar software because it is often developed by a single programmer and because it uses the shareware marketing system to sell directly to consumers (usually via a variety of software download sites, such as the one shown in Exhibit 3-13) with little or no packaging or advertising expenses. Shareware authors stress that the ethical use of shareware helps

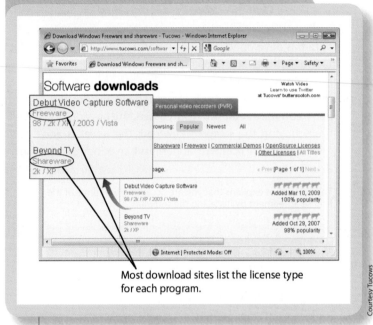

Exhibit 3-13 Shareware and freeware programs are typically downloaded via the Web

Most download sites list the license type for each program.

Courtesy Tucows

to cultivate this type of software distribution. Legally, shareware and demo versions of commercial software are similar, but shareware is typically not missing key features.

Freeware programs are software programs that are given away by the author for others to use free of charge. Although freeware is available without charge and can be shared with others, the author retains the ownership rights to the program, so you cannot do anything with it—such as sell it or modify it—that is not expressly allowed by the author. Freeware programs are frequently developed by individuals. Commercial software companies sometimes release freeware as well, such as Microsoft's Internet Explorer and RealNetworks' RealPlayer. Like shareware programs, freeware programs are widely available over the Internet.

Public domain software is not copyrighted; instead, the ownership rights to the program have been donated

> **shareware program** A software program that is distributed on the honor system; typically available free of charge but may require a small registration fee.
>
> **freeware program** A software program that is given away by the author for others to use free of charge.
>
> **public domain software** A software program that is not copyrighted.

Software Ownership Rights

The ownership rights of a software program specify the allowable use of that program. After a software program is developed, the developer (typically an individual or an organization) holds the ownership rights for that program and decides whether the program can be sold, shared with others, or otherwise distributed. When a software program is purchased, the buyer is not actually buying the software. Instead, the buyer is acquiring a **software license** that permits him or her to use the software. This license specifies the conditions under which a buyer can use the software, such as the number of computers on which it may be installed (many software licenses permit the software to be installed on just one computer). In addition to being included in printed form inside the packaging of most software programs, the licensing agreement is usually displayed and must be agreed to by the end user at the beginning of the software installation process.

This statement explains that you are accepting the terms of the license agreement by installing the software.

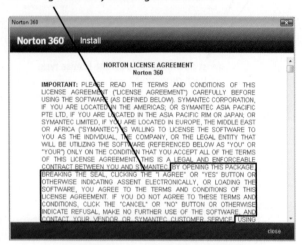

COMMERCIAL SOFTWARE PROGRAM

This statement explains that the program can be tried for 14 days and then it needs to be either registered or uninstalled.

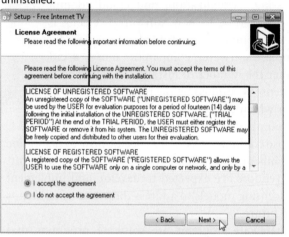

SHAREWARE PROGRAM

Courtesy Symantec Corp. and Holtsoft

to the public domain. Consequently, it is free and can be used, copied, modified, and distributed to others without restrictions.

Desktop vs. Mobile Software

Notebook computers, tablet computers, UMPCs, and other portable computers typically run the same application software as desktop computers. However, mobile phones and other mobile devices usually require mobile software; that is, software designed for a specific type of mobile phone or other mobile device. See Exhibit 3-14.

In addition to having a more compact, efficient appearance, many mobile applications include features for easier data input, such as an on-screen keyboard, a phrase list, or handwriting recognition capabilities.

software license A permit that specifies the conditions under which a buyer can use the software.

installed software A software program that must be installed on a computer before it is run.

Web-based software A software program that is run directly from the Internet; also referred to as Software as a Service (SaaS) and cloudware.

The number of mobile applications is growing all the time, and many are available free of charge.

Courtesy DataViz, Inc., Microsoft Corporation, Ilium Software, and T-Mobile USA

Exhibit 3-14 Mobile software

Some mobile software programs are designed to be compatible with popular desktop software, such as Microsoft Office, to facilitate sharing documents between the two platforms.

Installed vs. Web-Based Software

Software also differs in how it is accessed by the end user. It can be installed on and run from the end user's computer (or installed on and run from a network server in a network setting), or it can be Web-based and accessed by the end user over the Internet.

Installed software must be installed on a computer before it is run. Desktop software can be purchased in physical form (such as on a CD or DVD) or downloaded from the Internet (see Exhibit 3-15); mobile software is almost always downloaded. Many mobile phone manufacturers have download sites to facilitate this, such as Apple's App Store, BlackBrry's App World, and the Android Market. In either case, the program is installed using its installation program (which typically runs automatically when the software CD or DVD is inserted into the drive or when the downloaded program is opened). After the software is installed, it is ready to use. Whether installed software requires a fee depends on whether the program is a commercial, demo/trial, shareware, freeware, or public domain program.

Instead of being available in an installed format, some software is run directly from the Internet as **Web-based software**.

Exhibit 3-15 Installed software

Downloaded version will be downloaded to the buyer's computer.

Packaged version will be shipped to the buyer.

Courtesy Symantec Corp.

Exhibit 3-16 Web-based software

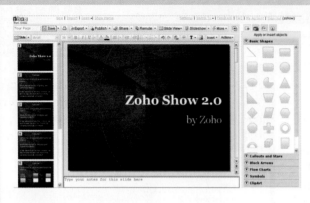

ONLINE APPLICATIONS
This program allows you to create presentations online.

BUSINESS SAAS APPLICATIONS
This program allows you to share documents and collaborate on projects online.

WEB DATABASE APPLICATIONS
This application allows you to retrieve property information, such as home values and homes for sale.

See Exhibit 3-16. A Web-based software program is delivered on demand via the Web to wherever the user is at the moment, provided he or she has an Internet connection (and has paid to use the software if a payment is required). Also referred to as Software as a Service (SaaS) and cloudware, the use of Web-based software is growing rapidly. In fact, research firm Gartner predicts that 25 percent of new business software will be delivered via the Web by 2011, up from 5 percent of new software purchases in 2006. Typically, documents created using Web-based software are stored online.

software suite Related software programs (such as a group of graphics programs, utility programs, or office-related software) that are sold bundled together.

LO3.5 Application Software for Business

Sometimes, related software programs (such as a group of graphics programs, utility programs, or office-related software) are sold bundled together as a **software suite**. Businesses and individuals often use office suites, sometimes called productivity software suites, to produce written documents. Typically, office suites contain the following programs, and many also contain additional productivity tools—such as a calendar, a messaging program, or collaboration tools:

▶ **Word processing software**—allows users to create and edit complex text-based documents that can also include images and other content.

Using software instead of paper and pencil to create a document means that you do not have to recreate the entire document when you want to make changes to it.

▶ **Spreadsheet software**—provides users with a convenient means of creating documents containing complex mathematical calculations.

▶ **Database software**—allows users to store and organize vast amounts of data and retrieve specific information when needed.

▶ **Presentation graphics software**—allows users to create visual presentations to convey information more easily to others.

One of the most widely used office software suites is Microsoft Office. The latest version is Microsoft Office 2010. Similar suites are available from Corel (WordPerfect Office) and Apple (iWork); a free alternative office suite is OpenOffice.org. Many office suites are available in a variety of versions, such as a home or student version that contains fewer programs than a professional version. Not all software suites are available for all operating systems, however. For example, Microsoft Office is available for both Windows and Mac OS computers; iWork is available only for Mac OS computers; and OpenOffice.org is available for Windows, Linux, and Mac OS computers. OpenOffice.org is also available in more than 30 different languages.

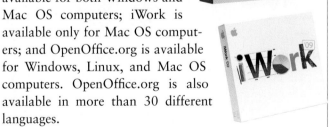

Courtesy Microsoft Corporation; Box shot reprinted with permission of Corel Corporation; Courtesy of Apple Inc.

Word Processing Concepts

Virtually all formal writing today is performed using a word processing program. **Word processing** refers to using a computer and word processing software to create, edit, save, and print written documents, such as letters, contracts, manuscripts, newsletters, invoices, marketing ma-

terial, and reports. At its most basic level, word processing is used to do what was done on a typewriter before computers were commonplace. Many documents created with word processing software also include content that was not possible to create using a typewriter, such as photos, drawn objects, clip art images, hyperlinks, video clips, and text in a variety of sizes and appearances. Like any document created with software instead of paper and pencil, word processing documents can be retrieved, modified, and printed as many times as needed. The most frequently used word processing programs are Microsoft Word, Corel WordPerfect, and Apple Pages.

Word processing programs typically include improved collaboration, security, and rights-management tools (tools used to protect original content from misuse by others). Word processing programs also typically include a variety of Web-related tools, as well as support for speech and pen input. Web-related features include the ability to send a document as an email message via the word processing program, the inclusion of hyperlinks in documents, and the ability to create or modify Web pages or blogs. The latest versions of Office also include the ability to collaborate with others online.

Spreadsheet Concepts

Another widely used application program is spreadsheet software. **Spreadsheet software** is the type of application software used to create computerized spreadsheets. A **spreadsheet** is a group of values and other data organized into rows and columns, similar to the ruled paper worksheets traditionally used by bookkeepers and accountants. Most spreadsheets include formulas that are used to compute calculations based on data entered into the spreadsheet.

In spreadsheets created with spreadsheet software, all formula results are updated automatically whenever any changes are made to the data. Consequently, no manual computations are required, which increases accuracy. In addition, the automatic recalculation of formulas allows individuals to modify spreadsheet data as

> **word processing** The use of a computer and word processing software to create, edit, save, and print written documents.
>
> **spreadsheet software** The type of application software used to create computerized spreadsheets.
>
> **spreadsheet** A group of values and other data organized into rows and columns, similar to the ruled paper worksheets traditionally used by bookkeepers and accountants.

often as necessary either to create new spreadsheets or to experiment with various possible scenarios (called what-if analysis) to help make business decisions. Spreadsheet software typically includes a variety of data analysis tools, as well as the ability to generate charts. The most widely used spreadsheet programs today are Microsoft Excel, Corel Quattro Pro, and Apple Numbers—again, all are part of their respective software suites. Spreadsheet software is commonly used by a variety of businesses and employees, including CEOs, managers, assistants, analysts, and sales representatives.

Most spreadsheet programs have built-in Web capabilities. Although they are used less commonly to create Web pages, many spreadsheet programs include the option to save the current worksheet as a Web page, and insert hyperlinks into worksheet cells. Microsoft Excel includes the ability to collaborate online, as well as to copy ranges of cells to a Web publishing or word processing program to insert spreadsheet data into a document as a table.

Database Concepts

People often need to retrieve specific data rapidly while on the job. For example, a customer service representative may need to locate a customer's order status quickly while the customer is on the telephone. The type of software used for such tasks is a database management system. A **database** is a collection of related data that is stored on a computer and organized in a manner that enables information to be retrieved as needed. A database management system (DBMS)—also called **database software**—is the type

of program used to create, maintain, and organize data in a database, as well as to retrieve information from the database. The most commonly used relational database management systems include Microsoft Access, Oracle Database, and IBM DB2.

Databases are often used on the Web. For instance, many Web sites use one or more databases to keep track of inventory; to allow searching for people, documents, or other information; and to place real-time orders. In fact, any time you type keywords in a search box on a search site or hunt for a product on a retail store's Web site using its search feature, you are using a Web database.

Presentation Graphics Concepts

If you try to explain to others what you look like, it may take several minutes. Show them a color photograph, on the other hand, and you can convey the same information within seconds. The saying "a picture is worth a thousand words" is the cornerstone of presentation graphics. A **presentation graphic** (see Exhibit 3-17) is an image designed to visually enhance a presentation (such as an electronic slide show or a printed report), typically to convey information more easily to people. A variety of software (including spreadsheet programs, image editing programs, and presentation graphics software) can be used to create presentation graphics.

database A collection of related data that is stored on a computer and organized in a manner that enables information to be retrieved as needed.

database software The type of program used to create, maintain, and organize data in a database, as well as to retrieve information from it; also called a database management system (DBMS).

presentation graphic An image designed to visually enhance a presentation (such as an electronic slide show or a printed report).

Exhibit 3-17 Examples of presentation graphics

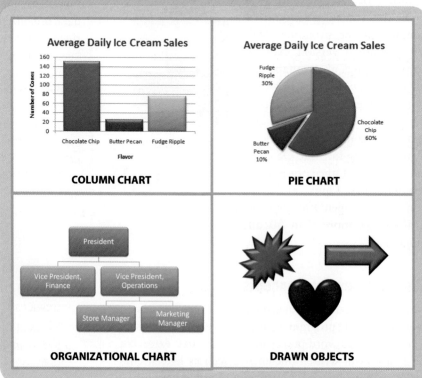

COLUMN CHART

PIE CHART

ORGANIZATIONAL CHART

DRAWN OBJECTS

Exhibit 3-18 Graphics software

PAINTING PROGRAMS
Typically create images pixel by pixel so images cannot be layered or resized.

DRAWING PROGRAMS
Typically create images using mathematical formulas so images can consist of multiple objects that can be layered, and the images can be resized without distortion.

PHOTO EDITING PROGRAMS
Allow users to edit digital photos.

Presentation graphics often take the form of electronic slides containing images, text, video, and more that are displayed one after the other in an electronic slide show. Electronic slide shows are created with **presentation graphics software** and can be run on individual computers or presented to a large group using a computer projector; for instance, they are frequently used for business and educational presentations. Some of the most common presentation graphics programs are Microsoft PowerPoint, Corel Presentations, and Apple Keynote—again, all part of their respective software suites.

Presentation graphics programs can be used to generate Web pages or Web page content, and slides can include hyperlinks.

LO3.6 Application Software for Working with Multimedia

Graphics are images, such as digital photographs, clip art, scanned drawings, and original images created using a software program. **Multimedia** technically refers to any application that contains more than one type of media, but is often used to refer to audio and video content. There are a variety of software programs

designed to help individuals create or modify graphics, edit digital audio or video files, play media files, burn CDs and DVDs, and so forth, as discussed next. Some programs focus on just one task; others are designed to perform multiple tasks, such as to import and edit images, audio, and video, and then create a finished DVD.

Graphics Software

Graphics software—also called digital imaging software—is used to create or modify images. Graphics software programs are commonly distinguished by whether they are primarily oriented toward painting, drawing, or image editing, although these are general categories, not strict classifications. See Exhibit 3-18.

presentation graphics software The type of program used to create electronic slide shows that can be run on individual computers or presented to a large group using a computer projector.

graphic An image, such as a digital photograph, clip art, a scanned drawing, or an original image created using a software program.

multimedia Any application that contains more than one type of media; often used to refer to audio and video content.

graphics software A program used to create or modify images; also called digital imaging software.

Painting programs traditionally create **bitmap images**, which are created by coloring the individual pixels in an image. One of the most common painting programs is Microsoft Paint. Painting programs are often used to create and modify simple images, but, unless the painting program supports layers and other tools discussed shortly, use for these programs is relatively limited. This is because when something is drawn or placed on top of a bitmap image, the pixels in the image are recolored to reflect the new content, and whatever was beneath the new content is lost. In addition, bitmapped images cannot be enlarged and still maintain their quality, because the pixels in the images just get larger, which makes the edges of the images look jagged. Some painting programs (such as Corel Painter) do support layers and so are more versatile. Painting tools are also increasingly included in other types of software, such as in office suites and drawing programs.

Drawing programs (also referred to as illustration programs) typically create **vector graphics**, which use mathematical formulas to represent image content instead of pixels. Unlike bitmap images, vector images can be resized and otherwise manipulated without loss of quality. Objects in drawing programs can also typically be layered. So, if you place one object on top of another, you can later separate the two images if desired. Drawing programs are often used by individuals and small business owners to create original art, logos, business cards, and more. They are also used by professionals to create corporate images, Web site graphics, and so forth. Popular drawing programs include Adobe Illustrator and CorelDRAW.

Image editing or photo editing programs are drawing or painting programs that are specifically designed for touching up or modifying images, such as original digital images and digital photos. Some widely used consumer image editing and photo editing programs are

Adobe Photoshop Elements, Ulead Photo Express, Apple iPhoto, Corel Paint Shop Pro Photo X2, Microsoft Office Picture Manager, and the free Picasa 3 program. For professional image editing, Adobe Photoshop is the leading program.

Audio Capture and Editing Software

For creating and editing audio files, audio capture and audio editing software is used. To capture sound from a microphone, sound recorder software is used; to capture sound from a CD, ripping software is used. In either case, after the audio is captured, it can then be modified, as needed. For instance, background noise or pauses can be removed, portions of the selection can be edited out, multiple segments can be spliced together, and special effects such as fade-ins and fade-outs can be applied. See Exhibit 3-19. Also available are specialized

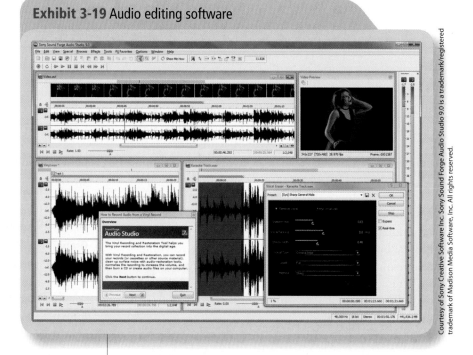

Exhibit 3-19 Audio editing software

audio capture and editing programs designed for specific applications, such as creating podcasts or musical compositions. Professional audio capture and editing software (such as Sony Creative Software Sound Forge 9 and Adobe Audition 3) is used to create professional audio for end products, Web pages, commercial podcasts, presentations, and so forth. Common consumer audio capture and editing programs include Windows Sound Recorder, Apple GarageBand, and Sony Creative Software Sound Forge Audio Studio software.

> **bitmap image** A graphic created by coloring the individual pixels in an image.
>
> **vector graphic** A graphic that uses mathematical formulas to represent image content instead of pixels.

Exhibit 3-20 Video creation software

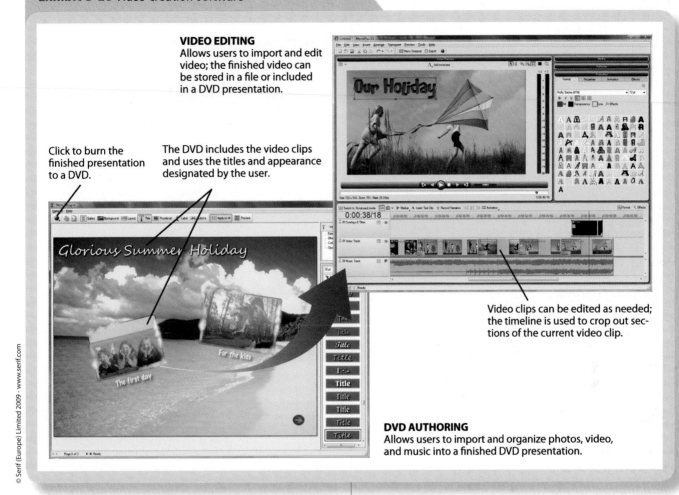

VIDEO EDITING
Allows users to import and edit video; the finished video can be stored in a file or included in a DVD presentation.

Click to burn the finished presentation to a DVD.

The DVD includes the video clips and uses the titles and appearance designated by the user.

Video clips can be edited as needed; the timeline is used to crop out sections of the current video clip.

DVD AUTHORING
Allows users to import and organize photos, video, and music into a finished DVD presentation.

Video Editing and DVD Authoring Software

Digital video can be imported directly into a video editing program by connecting the camera to the computer or by inserting the storage media containing the video (such as a DVD) into the computer. After the video has been imported, video editing (such as deleting or rearranging scenes, adding voice-overs, and adding other special effects) can be performed, as shown in Exhibit 3-20. Some video editing software today can edit video in high definition format.

DVD authoring refers to organizing content to be transferred to DVD, such as importing video clips and then creating the desired menu structure for the DVD to control the playback of those videos. DVD burning refers to recording data (such as a collection of songs or a finished video) on a recordable or rewritable DVD. DVD authoring and burning capabilities are commonly included with video editing capabilities in video creation software; there are also stand-alone DVD authoring programs, and DVD burning capabilities are preinstalled on computers containing a recordable or rewritable optical drive. Many file management programs (such as Windows Explorer) include CD and DVD burning capabilities, as well.

Media Players

Media players are programs designed to play audio and video files available via your computer—such as music

Individuals use video editing software to edit home videos or to create videos to upload to YouTube.

media player A program designed to play audio and video files available via your computer.

Exhibit 3-21 Typical media player program

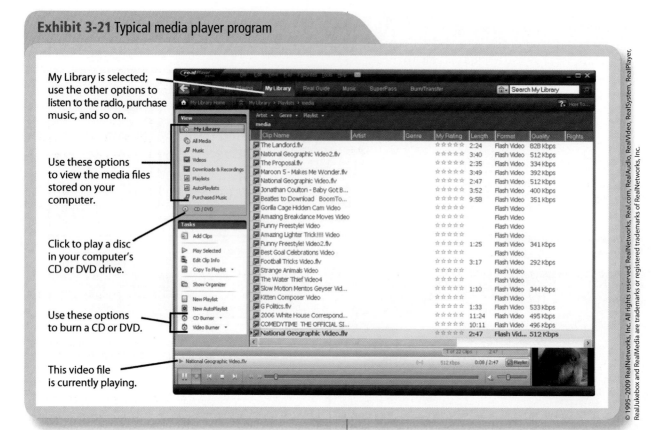

My Library is selected; use the other options to listen to the radio, purchase music, and so on.

Use these options to view the media files stored on your computer.

Click to play a disc in your computer's CD or DVD drive.

Use these options to burn a CD or DVD.

This video file is currently playing.

CDs, downloaded music, or video streamed from the Internet. Many media players are available for free, such as RealPlayer (see Exhibit 3-21), Windows Media Player, and QuickTime Player. Media players typically allow you to arrange your stored music and videos into playlists, and then transfer them to CDs or portable digital music players. Some also include the ability to download video from the Web and/or purchase and download music via an associated music store.

Graphics, Multimedia, and the Web

Graphics and multimedia software is often used by individuals and businesses alike to create Web sites or content to be shared or distributed via the Web. In addition, games, tutorials, videos, demonstrations, and other multimedia content available on the Web are often created with multimedia software.

Music and Copyright Law

It is important when using digital music to adhere to copyright laws, such as only transferring music from CDs that you have purchased and only downloading digital music files from sites that compensate the artists and record labels. While most music download sites today are legal and charge around $1 per title, illegal peer-to-peer (P2P) MP3 file exchanges do exist.

LO3.7 Other Types of Application Software

There are many other types of application software available today. Some are geared for business or personal productivity; others are designed for entertainment or educational purposes. Still others are intended to help users with a particular specialized application, such as preparing financial reports, issuing prescriptions electronically, designing buildings, controlling machinery, and so forth.

Desktop and Personal Publishing Software

Desktop publishing refers to using a personal computer to combine and manipulate text and images to create attractive documents that look as if they were created by a professional printer (see Exhibit 3-22). Although

Exhibit 3-22 Desktop publishing software

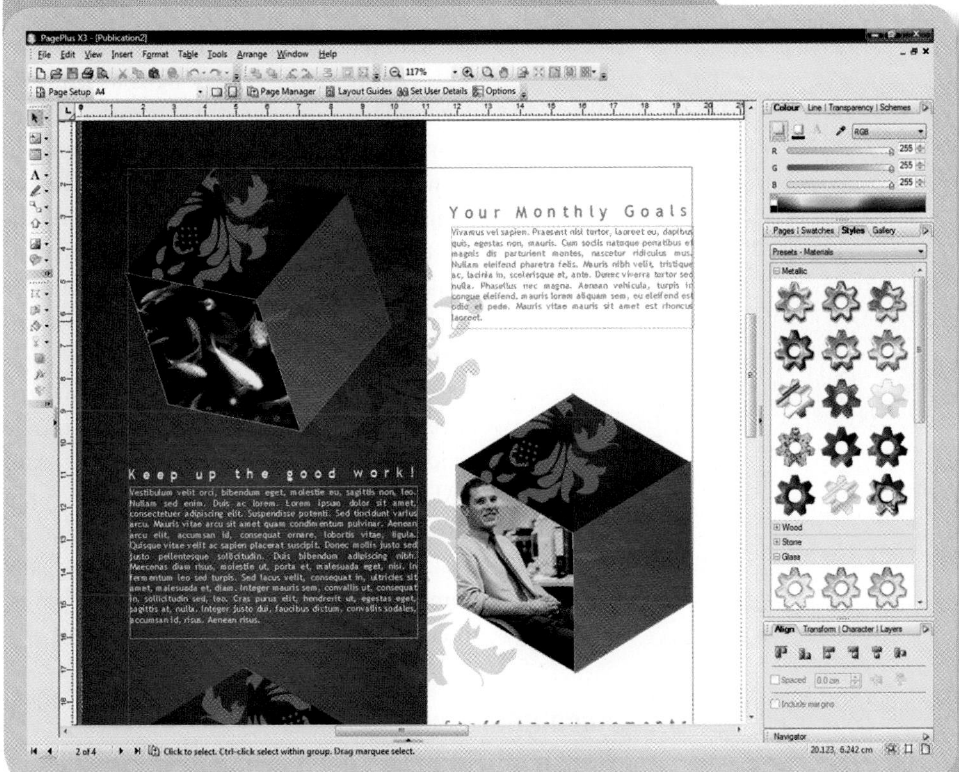

© Serif (Europe) Limited 2009 - www.serif.com

many desktop publishing effects can be produced using a word processing program, users who frequently create publication-style documents usually find a desktop publishing program a more efficient means of creating those types of documents. Some popular desktop publishing programs are Adobe InDesign, Microsoft Publisher, and Serif PagePlus X3. Personal publishing refers to creating desktop publishing–type documents—such as greeting cards, invitations, flyers, calendars, certificates, and so forth—for personal use. Specialized personal publishing programs are available for particular purposes, such as to create scrapbook pages, cross stitch patterns, and CD and DVD labels.

Educational, Entertainment, and Reference Software

A wide variety of educational and entertainment application programs are available. **Educational software** is designed to teach one or more skills, such as reading, math, spelling, a foreign language, and world geography, or to help prepare for standardized tests. **Entertainment software** includes games, simulations, and other programs that provide amusement. A hybrid of these two categories is called edutainment—educational software that also entertains. **Reference software** includes encyclopedias, dictionaries, atlases, mapping/travel programs, cookbook programs, and other software designed to provide valuable information. Although still available as stand-alone software packages, reference information today is also obtained frequently via the Internet.

Note Taking Software and Web Notebooks

Note taking software is used by both students and businesspeople to take notes during class lectures, meetings, and similar settings. It is used most often with tablet computers and other devices designed to accept pen input. Typically, note taking software, such as Microsoft OneNote or Circus Ponies NoteBook 3.0, supports both typed and handwritten input; handwritten input can usually be saved in its handwritten form

desktop publishing The use of a personal computer to combine and manipulate text and images to create attractive documents that look as if they were created by a professional printer.

educational software An application program designed to teach one or more skills.

entertainment software An application program that provides amusement, such as a game or simulation.

reference software An application program such as an encyclopedia, dictionary, or atlas designed to provide information.

note taking software An application program used by both students and business people to take notes during class lectures, meetings, and similar settings.

Exhibit 3-23 Note taking software

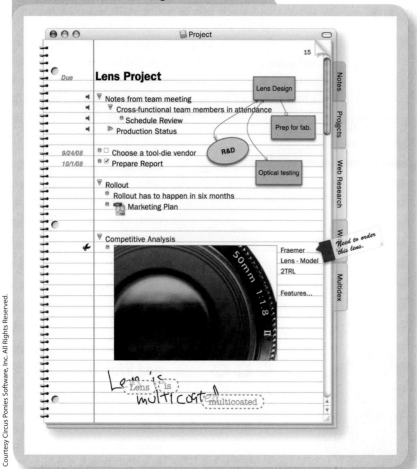

images, Web links, search results, and other content located on Web pages.

CAD and Other Types of Design Software

Computer-aided design (CAD) software enables users to design objects on the computer. For example, engineers or architects can create designs of buildings or other objects and modify the designs as often as needed. Increasingly, CAD programs are including capabilities to analyze designs in terms of how well they meet a number of design criteria, such as testing how a building design will hold up during an earthquake or how a car will perform under certain conditions. Besides playing an important role in the design of finished products, CAD is useful in fields such as art, advertising, law, architecture, and movie production. In addition to the powerful CAD programs used in business, design programs are available for home and small business use, such as for designing new homes and for making remodeling plans, interior designs, and landscape designs.

as an image or converted to typed text. See Exhibit 3-23. Note taking software contains features designed specifically to make note taking—and, particularly, retrieving information from the notes—easier. Like a paper notebook, tabbed sections can be created (such as one tab per course) and files, notes, Web links, and any other data are stored under the appropriate tabs. The built-in search tools allow you to find the information that you need quickly and easily. Online versions of these programs, such as Google Notebook and Zoho Notebook, are referred to as **Web notebooks** and are designed to help organize your online research, including text,

Web notebook An online version of a note taking software program.

computer-aided design (CAD) software An application program that enables users to design objects on the computer.

accounting software An application program that is used to automate some accounting activities.

personal finance software Accounting software that is commonly used at home by individuals.

Accounting and Personal Finance Software

Accounting software is used to automate common accounting activities, such as managing inventory, creating payroll documents and checks, preparing financial statements, and keeping track of business expenses (see Exhibit 3-24). **Personal finance software** is commonly used at home by individuals to write checks and balance checking accounts, track personal expenses, manage stock portfolios, and prepare income taxes. Increasingly, personal finance activities are becoming Web-based, such as the online banking and online

Exhibit 3-24
Accounting software

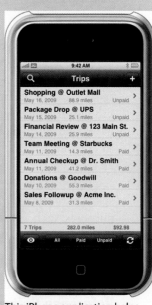

This iPhone application helps individuals track business expenses.

Exhibit 3-25 File sending application

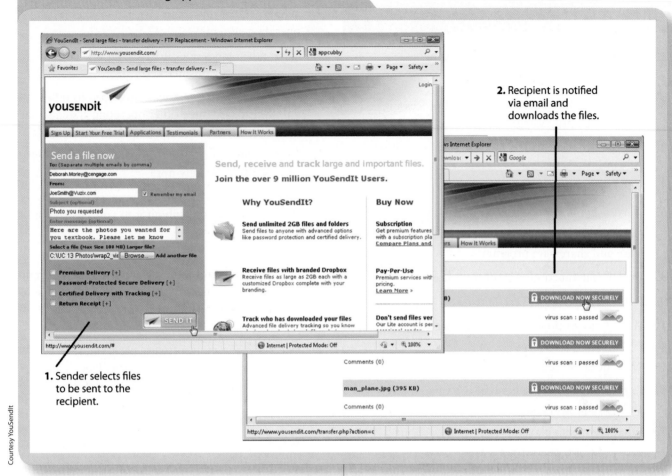

2. Recipient is notified via email and downloads the files.

1. Sender selects files to be sent to the recipient.

portfolio management services available through many banks and brokerage firms.

Project Management, Collaboration, and Remote Access Software

Project management software is used to plan, schedule, track, and analyze the tasks involved in a project, such as the construction of a building or the schedule for preparing a large advertising campaign for a client. Project management capabilities are often included in **collaboration software**—software that enables a group of individuals to work together on a project—and are increasingly available as Web-based software programs.

Remote access software enables individuals to access content on another computer they are authorized to access, via the Internet. Some programs allow you to control the remote computer directly; others allow you to access your media files (such as recorded TV shows or music) from any Web-enabled device while you are away from home. For instance, the Slingbox product gives you access to and control over your cable box and DVR via the Internet, and Orb software allows you to

access the files on your computer (documents, as well as recorded TV shows and music) from any Web-enabled device while you are away from home. Other remote access software automatically backs up all data files on your main computer to a secure Web server so they can be accessed from any Web-enabled device (such as a portable computer or mobile phone, in some cases), as well as shared with others for collaboration purposes. To make it easier to share single large files with others, you can use Web-based **file sending applications**, such as YouSendIt, which is shown in Exhibit 3-25.

project management software An application program used to plan, schedule, track, and analyze the tasks involved in a project.

collaboration software Software that enables a group of individuals to work together on a project.

remote access software Software that enables individuals to access content on another computer they are authorized to access, via the Internet.

file sending application A Web-based program used to share single large files with others.

Quiz Yourself

1. What is the purpose of system software?

2. Explain multitasking.

3. What is the difference between multiprocessing and parallel processing?

4. List the five most widely used personal operating systems.

5. What is a utility program?

6. What is application software?

7. Explain the difference between commercial software and shareware programs.

8. Explain the function of a software license.

9. Describe what a software suite is.

10. What types of programs do office suites typically contain?

11. What does multimedia refer to?

12. Explain the difference between a bitmap image and a vector graphic.

13. What are media players?

14. Explain desktop publishing.

15. Why would an individual use personal finance software?

16. What type of software enables a group of people to work together on a project?

Practice It

Practice It 3-1

A number of new operating systems have been developed in the past few years, such as Android, Palm webOS, and the Google Chrome OS.

1. Select one new or emerging operating system and research it.

2. What is the purpose and targeted market for this operating system?

3. What advantages does it have over any current competition for this market?

4. If the operating system was developed to fulfill a new need, are there other operating systems that are being adapted or being developed as a result?

5. Do you think your selected operating system will succeed? Why or why not?

6. Prepare a one- or two-page summary that answers these questions, and submit it to your instructor.

Practice It 3-2

Many online tours and tutorials are available for application programs. Some are available through the software company's Web site; others are located on third-party Web sites.

1. Select one common software program, such as Word, Excel, PowerPoint, Chrome, Google Docs, or Paint. Locate a free online tour or tutorial for the program you selected, and then work your way through one tour or tutorial.

2. What features of the application program do you think are most interesting?

3. How helpful is the tour or tutorial? Is the tour or tutorial easy to use and understand?

4. Did you encounter any errors or other problems as you worked through the tour or tutorial?

5. Would you recommend this tour or tutorial to others? Why or why not?

6. Prepare a one-page summary that answers these questions, and submit it to your instructor.

On Your Own

On Your Own 3-1

No matter which operating system you have, it's likely you will eventually need to get some help resolving a problem. Support options typically include the following: searchable knowledge bases, technical support phone numbers and email addresses, online chat, FAQs, and user discussion groups.

1. Research the different types of support options that are typically available (listed above).

2. Select one operating system and go to the manufacturer's Web site. Which of the support options listed in the previous paragraph are available?

3. Select one support option. How it is used? What type of information can be obtained?

4. Which support option would you prefer if you encountered a problem with your operating system? Why?

5. Prepare a one-page summary that answers these questions, and submit it to your instructor.

ADDITIONAL STUDY TOOLS

Chapter 3

IN THE BOOK

▶ Complete end-of-chapter exercises

▶ Study tear-out Chapter Review Card

ONLINE

▶ Complete additional end-of-chapter exercises

▶ Take practice quiz to prepare for tests

▶ Review key term flash cards (online, printable, and audio)

▶ Play "Beat the Clock" and "Memory"

▶ Watch the videos "How to Back Up Your Files Automatically," "How to Find Out What's Running on Your PC," and "How to Use Free Web App Alternatives to Expensive Software"

Computer Networks

Introduction

From telephone calls to home and business networks to Web surfing and online shopping, networking and the Internet are deeply embedded in our society. Because of this, it is important to be familiar with basic networking concepts and terminology, as well as with the variety of activities that take place today via networks—including the Internet, the world's largest network. It is also important to be aware of the potential problems and risks associated with networks and our networked society.

This chapter introduces basic networking principles, including what a computer network is, how it works, and what it can be used for.

Learning Objectives

After studying the material in this chapter, you will be able to:

LO4.1 Explain what networks are

LO4.2 Identify network characteristics

LO4.3 Understand how data is transmitted over a network

LO4.4 Describe common types of network media

LO4.5 Identify protocols and networking standards

LO4.6 Describe networking hardware

LO4.1 What Is a Network?

Recall that a **computer network** is a collection of computers and other hardware devices that are connected so users can share hardware, software, and data, as well as communicate with each other electronically. Today, computer networks are converging with telephone networks and other communications networks, with both data and voice being sent over these networks. Computer networks range from small private networks to the Internet and are widely used by individuals and businesses. Common uses include:

- Sharing an Internet connection among several users

- Sharing application software, printers, and other resources

- Facilitating Voice over IP (VoIP), email, videoconferencing, IM, and other communications applications

- Working collaboratively, such as sharing a company database or using collaboration tools to create or review documents

- Exchanging files among network users and over the Internet

computer network Computers and other hardware devices that are connected to share hardware, software, and data.

Computer networks are used extensively throughout society—people around the world use them every day in business, at school, at home, and on the go.

- Connecting the computers and the entertainment devices, such as TVs, gaming consoles, and stereo systems, located within a home

In most businesses, computer networks are essential. They enable employees to share expensive resources, access the Internet, and communicate with each other as well as with business partners and customers. They facilitate the exchange and collaboration of documents, and they are often a key component of the ordering, inventory, and fulfillment systems used to process customer orders. In homes, computer networks enable individuals to share resources, access the Internet, and communicate with others. In addition, they allow people to access a wide variety of information, services, and entertainment, as well as share data, such as digital photos, downloaded movies, and music, among the networked devices in a home. On the go, networks enable individuals to work from remote locations, locate information whenever and wherever it is needed, and stay in touch with others.

Networking Applications

Businesses and individuals use a wide variety of networking applications for communications, information retrieval, and other applications. Some of the most common are:

▶ **Internet**—The **Internet** is the largest computer network in the world. Many networking applications today, such as information retrieval, shopping, entertainment, and email, take place via the Internet.

▶ **Telephone**—One of the first communications networks is the original telephone network. **Mobile phones** (also called **wireless phones**) use a wireless network for communications instead of the regular telephone network. The most common type of mobile phone is the **cellular** (**cell**) **phone**, which communicates via cellular technology. Another, but less common, type of mobile phone is the **satellite phone**, which communicates via satellite technology.

Courtesy of Motorola

▶ **Television and Radio Broadcasting**—Two other original communications networks are broadcast television networks and radio networks. Other networks involved with television content delivery are cable TV networks, satellite TV networks, and the private closed-circuit television (CCTV) systems used by businesses for surveillance and security purposes.

▶ **Global Positioning System (GPS) Applications**—The **global positioning system** (**GPS**) network consists of 24 Department of Defense GPS satellites (in orbit approximately 12,000 miles above the earth). A GPS receiver measures the distance between the receiver and four GPS satellites simultaneously to determine the receiver's exact geographic location.

▶ **Monitoring Systems**—Monitoring systems use networking technology to determine the current location or status of an object, such as where a vehicle was driven and how fast it was driven, the vital signs of elderly or infirm individuals, and the temperature and relative humidity in pharmaceutical plants during the drug development process. Monitoring systems are also in homes to manage and control smart devices such as smart appliances and home automation systems.

▶ **Multimedia Networking**—A growing use of home networks is to deliver digital multimedia content, such as digital photos, digital music, home movies, downloaded movies, and recorded TV shows, to devices such as computers, televisions, and home entertainment systems on that network.

▶ **Collaborative Computing**—Workgroup or collaborative computing uses networking technology with collaborative software tools to enable individuals to work together on documents and other project components.

▶ **Telecommuting**—With **telecommuting**, individuals work from a remote location (typically their homes) and communicate with their places of business and clients via networking technologies.

▶ **Videoconferencing**—Videoconferencing is the use of networking technology to conduct real-time, face-to-face meetings between individuals physically located in different places.

Courtesy Cisco Systems, Inc.

▶ **Telemedicine**—Telemedicine uses networking technology to provide medical information and services. It is most often used to provide care to individuals who may not otherwise have access to that care, such as allowing people living in remote areas to consult with a specialist. Telesurgery is a form of robot-assisted surgery in which at least one of the surgeons performs the operation by controlling the robot remotely over the Internet or another network.

LO4.2 Network Characteristics

Networks can be identified by a variety of characteristics, including whether they are designed for wired or wireless access, their topology, their architecture, and their size or coverage area.

A new wireless power technology is being developed that will charge systems without any direct physical contact.

Wired vs. Wireless Networks

Networks can be designed for access via wired and/or wireless connections. With a **wired network** connection, the computers and other devices on the network are physically connected via cabling to the network. With a **wireless network** connection, wireless (usually radio) signals are used to send data through the air between devices, instead of using physical cables. Wired networks include the conventional telephone network, cable TV networks, and the wired networks commonly found in schools, businesses, and government facilities. Wireless networks include conventional television and radio networks, cellular telephone networks, satellite TV networks, and the wireless networks commonly found in homes, schools, and businesses. Wireless networks are also found in many public locations, such as coffeehouses, businesses, airports, hotels, and libraries, to provide Internet access to users while they are on the go via public wireless **hotspots**.

Many networks today are accessible via both wired and wireless connections. For instance, a business may have a wired main company network to which the computers in employee offices are always connected, as well as provide wireless access to the network for visitors and employees to use while in waiting rooms, conference rooms, and other locations. A home network may have a wired connection between one computer and the devices needed to connect that computer to the Internet, plus wireless access for other devices that may need to access the home network wirelessly.

Wired networks tend to be faster and more secure than wireless networks. Wireless networks have the advantage of allowing easy connections in locations where physical wiring is impractical or inconvenient, as well as giving users much more freedom about where they can use their computers. With wireless networking, for example, you can surf the Web on your notebook computer from anywhere in your house, access the Internet with your portable computer or mobile phone while on the go, and create a home network without having to run wires among the rooms in your house.

Network Topologies

The physical topology of a computer network indicates how the devices in the network are arranged. The three most common physical topologies are star, bus, and mesh, as shown in Exhibit 4-1.

▶ **Star network**—A network in which all the networked devices connect to a central device through which all network transmissions are sent. If the central device fails, the network cannot function.

▶ **Bus network**—A network that uses a central cable to which all network devices connect. All data is transmitted down the bus line from one device to another so, if the bus line fails, then the network cannot function.

▶ **Mesh network**—A network that uses a number of different connections between network devices so that data can take any of several possible paths from source to destination. Consequently, if one device on a mesh network fails, the network can still function, assuming there is an alternate path available. Mesh networks are used most often with wireless networks.

telecommute The use of computers and networking technology to enable an individual to work from a remote location.

wired network A network in which computers and other devices are connected to the network via physical cables.

wireless network A network in which computers and other devices are connected to the network without physical cables.

hotspot A location that provides wireless Internet access to the public.

star network A network that uses a host device connected directly to several other devices.

bus network A network that uses a central cable to which all network devices are attached.

mesh network A network that uses multiple connections between network devices.

Exhibit 4-1 Common network topologies

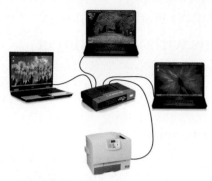

STAR NETWORKS
Use a central device to connect each device
directly to the network.

BUS NETWORKS
Use a single central cable to connect
each device in a linear fashion.

MESH NETWORKS
Each computer or device is connected to multiple
(sometimes all of the other) devices on the network.

architecture The way computers are designed to
communicate.

client-server network A network that includes both clients and
servers.

client A computer or other device on a network that requests and uses
network resources.

Many networks, however, don't conform to a standard topology. Some networks combine topologies and connect multiple smaller networks, in effect turning several smaller networks into one larger one. For example, two star networks may be joined together using a bus cable.

Network Architectures

Networks also vary by their **architecture**; that is, the way they are designed to communicate. The two most common network architectures are client-server and peer-to-peer.

Client-server networks include both **clients**, which are computers and other devices on the network that request and use network resources, and **servers**, which are computers that are dedicated to processing client requests. Network servers are typically powerful computers with lots of memory and a very large hard drive. They provide access to software, files, and other resources that are being shared via the network. Servers typically perform a variety of tasks. For example, a single server can act as a network server to manage network traffic, a file server to manage shared files, a print server to handle printing-related activities, and/or a mail server or Web server to manage email and Web page requests, respectively. Only one server appears in the network illustrated in Exhibit 4-2, and it is capable of performing all server tasks for that network. When a client retrieves files from a server, it is called **downloading**; transferring data from a client to a server is called **uploading**.

With a **peer-to-peer** (**P2P**) **network**, a central server is not used. As shown in Exhibit 4-3, all the computers on the network work at the same functional level, and users have direct access to the computers and other devices attached to the network. For instance, users can access files stored on a peer computer's hard drive and print using a peer computer's printer, provided those devices have been designated as shared devices. Peer-to-peer networks are less expensive and less complicated to implement than client-server networks because there are no dedicated servers, but they may not have the same performance as client-server networks under heavy use. Peer-to-peer capabilities are built into many personal operating systems and are often used in conjunction with small office or home networks.

Another type of peer-to-peer networking—sometimes called Internet peer-to-peer (Internet P2P) computing—is performed via the Internet. Instead of

Connecting to a Wi-Fi Hotspot

To connect to a Wi-Fi hotspot, all you need is a device, such as a mobile phone or a notebook computer, with a Wi-Fi adapter installed and enabled. On a Windows computer that has a Wi-Fi adapter installed, an icon should appear in the system tray representing your wireless network connection. When you are within range of a Wi-Fi hotspot, a small yellow circle appears on the icon indicating that wireless networks were found. Click this icon to see all of the Wi-Fi access points in the area. If more than one hotspot is listed, click the network to which you want to connect. If the network does not require a passphrase, it is an unsecured network and this information appears below the network name in the list. To connect to the selected network, click the Connect button. For free hotspots, you should be connected shortly. For some free hotspots, you need to start your browser, and then click a button to indicate that you agree with the network usage terms.

Then you can use your browser and email program as usual. For secured networks, you will need to supply the appropriate passphrase before you can connect to the Internet via that hotspot. For most fee-based hotspots, a logon screen appears. You need to enter a username and password, and then agree with the network usage terms before being connected.

3. Click Connect.

2. Select a network in the list.

This message appears when you select an unsecure network in the list.

1. Click the wireless network icon.

placing content on a Web server for others to view via the Internet, content is exchanged over the Internet directly between individual users via a peer-to-peer network. For instance, one user can copy a file from another user's hard drive to his or her own computer via the Internet. Internet P2P networking is commonly used for exchanging music and video files with others over the Internet—an illegal act if the content is copyright-protected and the exchange is unauthorized, although legal Internet P2P networks exist.

server A computer that is dedicated to processing client requests.

download To retrieve files from a server to a client.

upload To transfer files from a client to a server.

peer-to-peer (P2P) network A network in which the computers on the network work at the same functional level, and users have direct access to the network devices.

Exhibit 4-2 Client-server network with one server

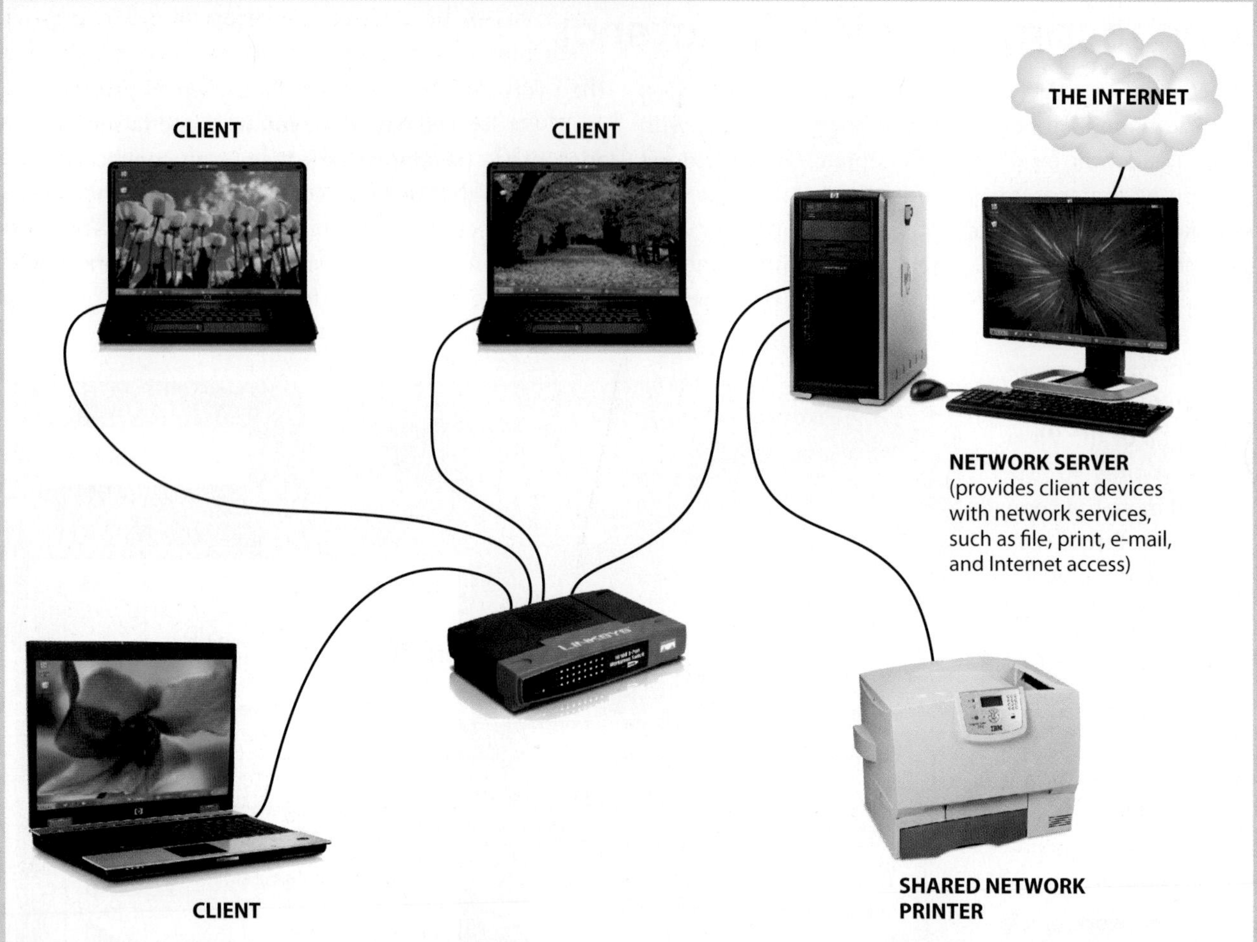

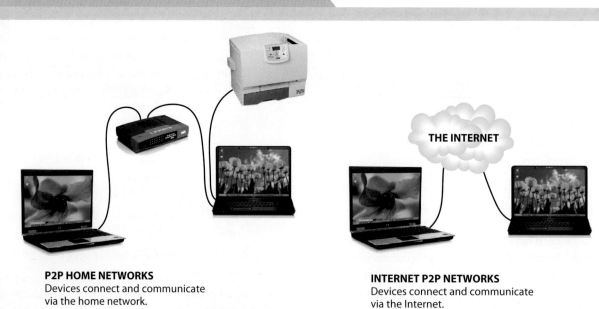

CLIENT

CLIENT

THE INTERNET

CLIENT

NETWORK SERVER
(provides client devices
with network services,
such as file, print, e-mail,
and Internet access)

**SHARED NETWORK
PRINTER**

Courtesy Hewlett-Packard Company, Cisco Systems Inc., and InfoPrint Solutions Company

Exhibit 4-3 Peer-to-peer networks

THE INTERNET

P2P HOME NETWORKS
Devices connect and communicate
via the home network.

INTERNET P2P NETWORKS
Devices connect and communicate
via the Internet.

Courtesy Hewlett-Packard Company, Cisco Systems Inc., and InfoPrint Solutions Company

Sharing Folders on a Network

Do not enable sharing for folders that you want to keep private from others on your network. When you enable sharing for a folder, other people on your network can see it. If you choose to use a P2P network, be sure to designate the files in your shared folder as read-only to prevent your original files from being overwritten by another P2P user.

Image copyright Mike Flippo, 2009. Used under license from Shutterstock.com

Network Size and Coverage Area

Networks are also classified by their size and their coverage area. This impacts the types of users the network is designed to service. The most common categories of networks can use both wired and wireless connections.

A **personal area network** (**PAN**) is a network of personal devices for one individual (such as his or her portable computer, mobile phone, headset, digital camera, portable digital media player, and printer) that is designed to enable those devices to communicate and share data. PANs can be set up to work together automatically as soon as the devices get within a certain physical distance of each other. For instance, a PAN can be used to synchronize portable devices automatically with a desktop computer as soon as the individual returns home or to the office. The range of a PAN is very limited, so devices in a PAN must be physically located close together.

A **local area network** (**LAN**) is a network that covers a relatively small geographical area, such as a home, an office building, or a school. LANs allow users on the network to exchange files and email, share printers and other hardware, and access the Internet. The client-server network shown in Exhibit 4-2 is an example of a LAN.

A **metropolitan area network** (**MAN**) is a network designed to service a metropolitan area, typically a

city or county. Most MANs are owned and operated by a city or by a network provider in order to provide individuals in that location access to the MAN. Some wireless MANs are created by cities or large organizations (including Microsoft and Google) to provide free or low-cost Internet access to area residents. These projects are typically supported by local taxes and are sometimes referred to as municipal Wi-Fi projects. Exhibit 4-4 shows a sign identifying a wireless MAN in

Exhibit 4-4 Sign describing a MAN in Riverside, California

Courtesy City of Riverside

downtown Riverside, California. In addition, some Internet service providers are experimenting with setting up free wireless MANs in select metropolitan areas for their subscribers to use when they are on the go.

A **wide area network** (**WAN**) is a network that covers a large geographical area. Typically, a WAN consists of two or more LANs that are connected together using communications technology. The Internet, by this definition, is the world's largest WAN. WANs may be

Wirelss PANs (WPANs) are more common today than wired PANs.

> **personal area network** (**PAN**) A network that connects an individual's personal devices that are located close together.
>
> **local area network** (**LAN**) A network that connects devices located in a small geographical area.
>
> **metropolitan area network** (**MAN**) A network designed to service a metropolitan area.
>
> **wide area network** (**WAN**) A network that connects devices located in a large geographical area.

publicly accessible, like the Internet, or they may be privately owned and operated. For instance, a company may have a private WAN to transfer data from one location to another, such as from each retail store to the corporate headquarters. Large WANs, like the Internet, typically use a mesh topology.

An **intranet** is a private network, such as a company LAN, that is designed to be used by an organization's employees and is set up like the Internet with data posted on Web pages that are accessed with a Web browser. Consequently, little or no employee training is required to use an intranet, and intranet content can be accessed using a variety of devices. Intranets today are used for many purposes, such as coordinating internal email and communications, making company publications available to employees, facilitating collaborative computing, and providing access to shared calendars and schedules.

A company network that is accessible to authorized outsiders is called an **extranet**. Extranets are usually accessed via the Internet, and they can be used to provide customers and business partners with access to the data they need. Access to intranets and extranets is typically restricted to employees and other authorized users, similar to other company networks.

> VPNs allow an organization to provide secure, remote access to the company network without the cost of physically extending the private network.

intranet A private network that is set up similarly to the Internet and is accessed via a Web browser.

extranet An intranet that is at least partially accessible to authorized outsiders.

virtual private network (**VPN**) A private, secure path over the Internet used for accessing a private network.

bandwidth (**throughput**) The amount of data that can be transferred in a given time period.

digital signal A type of signal where the data is represented by 0s and 1s.

analog signal A type of signal where the data is represented by continuous waves.

A **virtual private network** (**VPN**) is a private, secure path across a public network (usually the Internet) that is set up to allow authorized users private, secure access to the company network. For instance, a VPN can allow a traveling employee, a business partner, or an employee located at a satellite office or public wireless hotspot to connect securely to the company network via the Internet. A process called tunneling is typically used to carry the data over the Internet; special encryption technology is used to protect the data so it cannot be understood if it is intercepted during transit.

LO4.3 Data Transmission

Data transmitted over a network has specific characteristics, and it can travel over a network in various ways. The amount of data that can transfer during a given time period, how the data is transmitted, how it is timed, and how it is delivered all factor into the transmission.

Bandwidth

Bandwidth (also called **throughput**) is to the amount of data that can be transferred in a given time period. Just as a wide fire hose allows more water to pass through it per unit of time than a narrow garden hose allows, a networking medium with a high bandwidth allows more data to pass through it per unit of time than one with a low bandwidth. Text data requires the least amount of bandwidth; video data requires the most.

Analog vs. Digital Signals

Data can be represented as either analog or digital signals. Voice and music data in its natural form, for instance, is analog. Data stored on a computer is digital. Most networking media send data using **digital signals**, in which data is represented by only two discrete states: 0s and 1s. **Analog signals**, such as those used by the conventional telephone system, represent data with continuous waves. The data to be transmitted over a networking medium must match the type of

DIGITAL SIGNALS

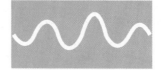

ANALOG SIGNALS

Bandwidth is usually measured in the number of bps (bits per second), Kbps (thousands of bits per second), Mbps (millions of bits per second), or Gbps (billions of bits per second).

signal—analog or digital—that the medium supports. If it doesn't, then the data must be converted before it is transmitted. For instance, analog data that is to be sent using digital signals, such as analog music broadcast by a digital radio station, must first be converted into digital form. Likewise, digital data to be sent using analog signals, such as computer data sent over a conventional analog telephone network, must first be converted into analog form. The conversion of data between analog and digital form is performed by networking hardware.

Transmission Type and Timing

Networking media can also use either serial transmission or parallel transmission. With **serial transmission**, data is sent one bit at a time, one after the other along a single path. When **parallel transmission** is used, the message is sent at least one byte at a time, with each bit in the byte taking a separate path. See Exhibit 4-5. Although parallel transmission is frequently used within computer components, such as for buses, and is used

for some wireless networking applications, networking media typically use serial transmission.

When data is sent using serial transmission, one of the following three techniques is used to organize the bits being transferred so the data can be reconstructed after it is received:

▶ **Synchronous transmission**—Data is organized into groups or blocks of data, which are transferred at regular, specified intervals. Because the transmissions are synchronized, both devices know when data can be sent and when it should arrive. Most data transmissions within a computer and over a network are synchronous transmissions.

▶ **Asynchronous transmission**—Data is sent when it is ready to be sent, without being synchronized. To identify the bits that belong in each byte, a start bit and stop bit are used at the beginning and end of the byte, respectively. This overhead makes asynchronous transmission less efficient than synchronous transmission, and so it is not as widely used as synchronous transmission.

▶ **Isochronous transmission**—Data is sent at the same time as other related data to support types of real-time applications that require the different types of data to be delivered at the proper speed for that application. For example, when transmitting a video file, the audio data must be received at the proper time in order for it to be played with its corresponding video data. To accomplish this with isochronous transmission, the sending and receiving devices first communicate to determine the bandwidth and other factors needed for the transmission, and then the necessary bandwidth is reserved just for that transmission.

Exhibit 4-5 Serial vs. parallel transmissions

01000001 →

SERIAL TRANSMISSIONS
All the bits in one byte follow one another over a single path.

0 →
1 →
0 →
0 →
0 →
0 →
0 →
1 →

PARALLEL TRANSMISSIONS
The eight bits in each byte are transmitted over separate paths at the same time.

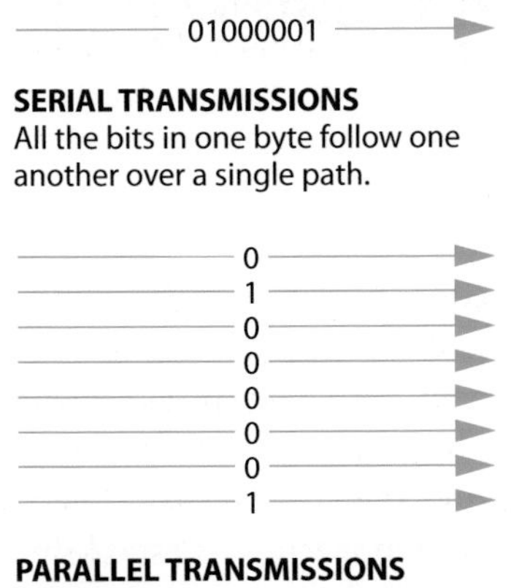

serial transmission A type of data transmission in which the bits in a byte travel down the same path one after the other.

parallel transmission A type of data transmission in which bytes of data are transmitted at one time with the bits in each byte taking a separate path.

synchronous transmission A type of serial data transmission in which data is organized into groups or blocks of data that are transferred at regular, specified intervals.

asynchronous transmission A type of serial data transmission in which data is sent when it is ready to be sent without being synchronized.

isochronous transmission A type of serial data transmission in which data is sent at the same time as other related data.

Exhibit 4-6 Transmission timing

SYNCHRONOUS TRANSMISSIONS
Data is sent in blocks and the blocks are timed so that the receiving device knows when they will arrive.

Dear Mary, Today we did quite a | bit in class. The professor intr | oduced a speaker, who talked abo

Data is sent in blocks.

RECEIVING DEVICE　　　　　　　　　**SENDING DEVICE**

ASYNCHRONOUS TRANSMISSIONS
Data is sent one byte at a time, along with a start bit and a stop bit.

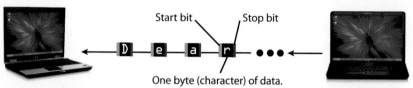

Start bit　　　Stop bit

D e a r

One byte (character) of data.

RECEIVING DEVICE　　　　　　　　　**SENDING DEVICE**

ISOCHRONOUS TRANSMISSIONS
The entire transmission is sent together after requesting and being assigned the bandwidth necessary for all the data to arrive at the correct time.

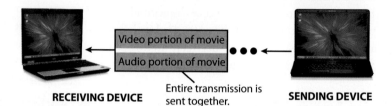

Video portion of movie
Audio portion of movie

Entire transmission is sent together.

RECEIVING DEVICE　　　　　　　　　**SENDING DEVICE**

Courtesy Hewlett-Packard Company

Although all three of these methods send data one bit at a time, the three methods vary with respect to how the bits are organized for transfer, as shown in Exhibit 4-6.

Another distinction between the different types of transmissions is the direction in which transmitted data can move.

▶ **Simplex transmission**—Data travels in a single direction only (like a doorbell). Simplex transmission is relatively uncommon in data transmissions because most devices that are mainly one-directional, such as a printer, can still transmit error messages and other data back to the computer.

simplex transmission A type of data transmission in which data travels in a single direction only.

half-duplex transmission A type of data transmission in which data can travel in either direction, but only in one direction at a time.

full-duplex transmission A type of data transmission in which data can move in both directions at the same time.

▶ **Half-duplex transmission**—Data can travel in either direction, but only in one direction at a time (like a walkie-talkie where only one person can talk at a time). Some network transmissions are half-duplex.

▶ **Full-duplex transmission**—Data can move in both directions at the same time (like a telephone). Many network and most Internet connections are full-duplex; sometimes two connections between the sending device and receiving device are needed to support full-duplex transmissions.

Delivery Method

When data needs to travel across a large network, typically one of the three methods shown in Exhibit 4-7 is used. With circuit switching, a dedicated path over a network is established between the sender and receiver and all data follows that path from the sender to the receiver. Once the connection is established, the physical path or circuit is dedicated to that connection and cannot be used by any other device until the transmission is finished. The most common example of a circuit-switched network is the conventional telephone system.

Exhibit 4-7 Circuit-switched, packet-switched, and broadcast networks

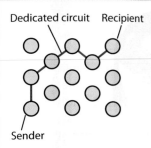

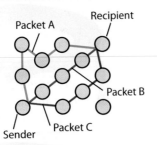

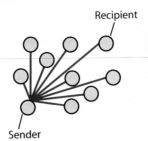

CIRCUIT-SWITCHED NETWORKS
Data uses a dedicated path from the sender to the recipient.

PACKET-SWITCHED NETWORKS
Data is sent as individual packets, which are assembled at the recipient's destination.

BROADCAST NETWORKS
Data is broadcast to all nodes within range; the designated recipient retrieves the data.

The technique used for data sent over the Internet is packet switching. With **packet switching**, messages are separated into small units called packets. Packets contain information about the sender and the receiver, the actual data being sent, and information about how to reassemble the packets to reconstruct the original message. Packets travel along the network separately, based on their final destination, network traffic, and other network conditions. When the packets reach their destination, they are reassembled in the proper order. Another alternative is **broadcasting**, in which data is sent out, typically in packets, to all nodes on a network and is retrieved only by the intended recipient. Broadcasting is used primarily with LANs.

LO4.4 Networking Media

To connect the devices in a network, either wired media (physical cables) or wireless media (typically radio signals) can be used. The most common wired and wireless networking media are discussed next.

Wired Networking Media

The most common types of wired networking media are twisted-pair, coaxial, and fiber-optic cable, which are shown in Exhibit 4-8.

A **twisted-pair cable** is made up of pairs of thin strands of insulated wire twisted together. Twisted-pair is the least expensive type of networking cable and has been in use the longest. In fact, it is the same type of cabling used inside most homes for telephone communications. Twisted-pair cabling can be used with both analog and digital data transmission and is commonly used for LANs. Twisted-pair cable is rated by category, which indicates the type of data, speed, distance, and other factors that the cable supports. Category 3 (Cat 3) twisted-pair cabling is regular telephone cable; higher speed and quality cabling—such as Category 5 (Cat 5), Category 6 (Cat 6), and Category 7 (Cat 7)—is frequently used for home or business networks. The pairs of wires in twisted-pair wire are twisted together to reduce interference and improve performance. To further improve performance, it can be shielded with a metal lining. Twisted-pair cables used for networks have different connectors than those used for telephones.

Coaxial cable (also known as **coax**) was originally developed to carry a large number of high-speed video transmissions at one time, such as to deliver cable TV service. A coaxial cable consists of a relatively thick center wire surrounded by insulation and then covered with a shield of braided wire to block electromagnetic signals from entering the cable. Coaxial cable is commonly used today in computer networks, for short-run telephone transmissions outside of the home, and for cable television delivery. Although more expensive than twisted-pair cabling, it is much less susceptible to interference and can carry more data more quickly.

packet switching A method of transmitting data in which messages are separated into packets that travel along the network separately, and then are reassembled in the proper order at the destination.

broadcasting A method of transmitting data in which data is sent out to all nodes on a network and is retrieved only by the intended recipient.

twisted-pair cable A networking cable consisting of insulated wire strands twisted in sets of two and bound into a cable.

coaxial cable (coax) A networking cable consisting of a center wire inside a grounded, cylindrical shield, capable of sending data at high speeds.

Exhibit 4-8 Wired network transmission media

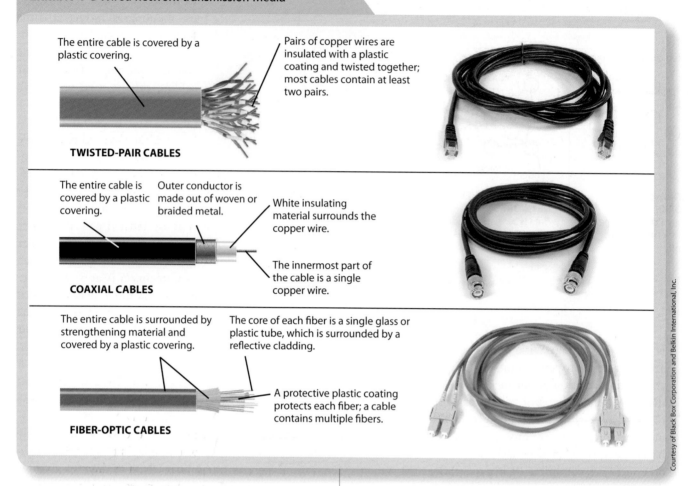

The entire cable is covered by a plastic covering.

Pairs of copper wires are insulated with a plastic coating and twisted together; most cables contain at least two pairs.

TWISTED-PAIR CABLES

The entire cable is covered by a plastic covering.

Outer conductor is made out of woven or braided metal.

White insulating material surrounds the copper wire.

The innermost part of the cable is a single copper wire.

COAXIAL CABLES

The entire cable is surrounded by strengthening material and covered by a plastic covering.

The core of each fiber is a single glass or plastic tube, which is surrounded by a reflective cladding.

A protective plastic coating protects each fiber; a cable contains multiple fibers.

FIBER-OPTIC CABLES

Although not used extensively for networking home computers at the moment, that may change with the relatively new option of networking via the existing coax in a home. Coax is also growing in popularity for home multimedia networks.

Fiber-optic cable is the newest and fastest of these three types of wired transmission media. It contains multiple—sometimes several hundred—clear glass or plastic fiber strands, each about the thickness of a human hair. Fiber-optic cable transfers data represented by light pulses at speeds of billions of bits per second. Each strand has the capacity to carry data for several television stations or thousands of voice conversations. However, each strand can send data in only one direction, so two strands are needed for full-duplex data transmissions.

fiber-optic cable A networking cable that contains hundreds of thin transparent fibers over which lasers transmit data as light.

Fiber-optic cable is commonly used for the high-speed backbone lines of a network, such as to connect networks housed in separate buildings or for the Internet infrastructure. It is also used for telephone backbone lines and, increasingly, is being installed by telephone companies all the way to the home or business to provide super-fast connections directly to the end user. The biggest advantage of fiber-optic cabling is speed; the main disadvantage of fiber-optic cabling is the initial expense of both the cable and the installation.

Wireless Networking Media

Wireless networks usually use radio signals to send data through the airwaves. All wireless applications in the United States—such as wireless networks, mobile phones, radio and TV broadcasts, sonar and radar applications, and GPS systems—use specific frequencies as assigned by the Federal Communications Commission

(FCC). Frequencies are measured in hertz (Hz). The frequencies that comprise the electromagnetic spectrum—the range of common electromagnetic radiation—are shown in Exhibit 4-9. Different parts of the spectrum have different properties, such as the distance a signal can travel, the amount of data a signal can transmit in a given period of time, and the types of objects a signal can pass through. These properties make certain frequencies more appropriate for certain applications. Each type of communication is assigned specific frequencies within which to operate. As illustrated in Exhibit 4-9, most wireless networking applications use

The 2009 switch from analog to digital television broadcasts freed up some of the VHF and UHF frequencies for other applications.

own frequency. Most radio frequencies in the United States are licensed by the FCC and can only be used for that specific application by the licensed individuals in their specified geographic areas. However, the 900 MHz, 2.4 GHz, 5 GHz, and 5.8 GHz frequencies used by many cordless landline phones, garage door openers, and other consumer devices—as well as for Wi-Fi, WiMAX, and Bluetooth wireless networking—fall within an unlicensed part of the spectrum and, therefore, can be used by any product or individual. A frequency range can be further broken down into multiple channels, each of which can be used simultaneously by different users. There are also ways to combine multiple signals to send them over a transmission medium at one time to allow more users than would otherwise be possible.

Because the number of wireless applications is growing all the time and the parts of the spectrum appropriate for today's wireless networking applications are limited, the wireless spectrum is relatively crowded and frequencies are in high demand.

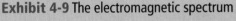

Exhibit 4-9 The electromagnetic spectrum

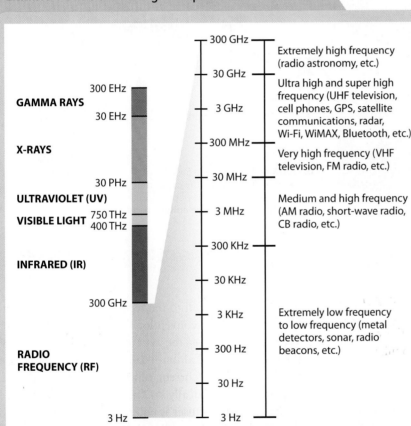

frequencies located in the radio frequency (RF) band at the low end of the electromagnetic spectrum. This range—up to 300 GHz—is sometimes referred to as the wireless spectrum.

The frequencies assigned to an application, such as FM radio or cell phone service, typically consist of a range of frequencies to be used as needed for that application. For instance, FM radio stations broadcast on frequencies from 88 MHz to 108 MHz and each radio station in a particular geographic area is assigned its

Radio Signals

Radio signals can be short range (such as to connect a wireless keyboard or mouse to a computer), medium range (such as to connect a computer to a wireless LAN or public hotspot), or long range (such as to provide Internet access to a large geographic area or to broadcast a TV show).

Exhibit 4-10 How cellular phones work

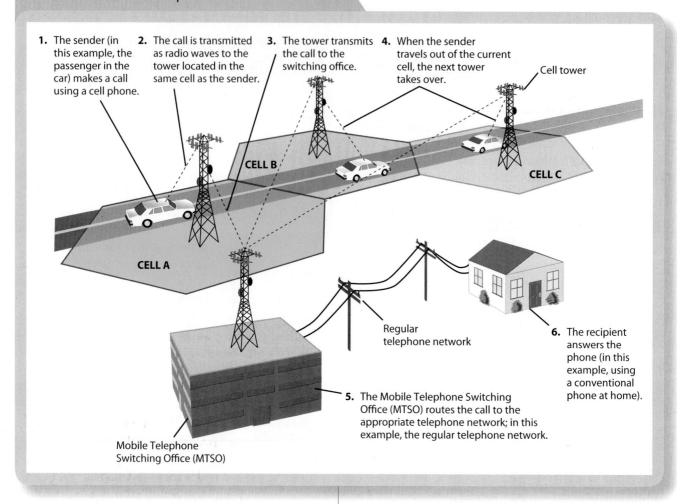

1. The sender (in this example, the passenger in the car) makes a call using a cell phone.

2. The call is transmitted as radio waves to the tower located in the same cell as the sender.

3. The tower transmits the call to the switching office.

4. When the sender travels out of the current cell, the next tower takes over.

Cell tower

CELL B

CELL C

CELL A

Regular telephone network

5. The Mobile Telephone Switching Office (MTSO) routes the call to the appropriate telephone network; in this example, the regular telephone network.

6. The recipient answers the phone (in this example, using a conventional phone at home).

Mobile Telephone Switching Office (MTSO)

Cellular radio transmissions are used with cell phones and are sent and received via cellular (cell) towers—tall metal poles with antennas on top. Cellular service areas are divided into honeycomb-shaped zones called cells; each cell contains one cell tower. When a cell phone user begins to make a call, it is picked up by the cell tower located in the cell in which the cell phone is located and that belongs to the user's mobile phone provider. That cell tower then forwards the call to the mobile phone company's Mobile Telephone Switching Office (MTSO),

which routes the call to the recipient's telephone via his or her mobile or conventional telephone service provider, depending on the type of phone being used by the recipient. See Exhibit 4-10. When a cell phone user moves out of the current cell into a new cell, the call is passed automatically to the appropriate cell tower in the cell that the user is entering. The transmission of data, such as email and Web page requests, sent via cell phones works in a similar manner. The speed of cellular radio transmissions depends on the type of cellular standard being used.

Microwaves are high-frequency radio signals that can send large quantities of data at high speeds over long distances. Microwave signals can be sent or received using microwave stations or communications satellites, but must travel in a straight line from one station or satellite to another without encountering any obstacles, since microwave signals are line of sight. **Microwave stations** are earth-based stations that can transmit microwave signals directly to each other over

cellular radio transmission A type of data transmission used with cell phones in which the data is sent and received via cell towers.

microwaves High-frequency radio signals that can send large quantities of data at high speeds over long distances.

microwave station A device that sends and receives high-frequency, high-speed radio signals.

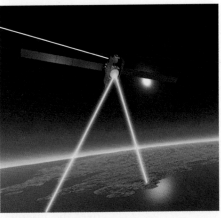

Exhibit 4-11 How satellite Internet works

3. An orbiting satellite receives the request and beams it down to the satellite dish at the ISP's operations center.

2. The request is sent up to a satellite from the individual's satellite dish.

HughesNet

1. Data, such as a Web page request, is sent from the individual's computer to the satellite dish via a satellite modem.

4. The ISP's operations center receives the request (via its satellite dish) and transfers it to the Internet.

THE INTERNET

5. The request travels over the Internet as usual. The requested information takes a reverse route back to the individual.

distances of up to about 30 miles. To avoid buildings, mountains, and the curvature of the earth obstructing the signal, microwave stations are usually placed on tall buildings, towers, and mountaintops. Microwave stations typically contain both a dish-shaped microwave antenna and a transceiver. When one station receives a transmission from another, it amplifies it and passes it on to the next station. Microwave stations can exchange data transmissions with communications satellites, as well as with other microwave stations.

Communications satellites are space-based devices launched into orbit around the earth to receive and transmit microwave signals to and from earth (see the satellite Internet example in Exhibit 4-11). Communications satellites were originally used to facilitate microwave transmission when microwave stations were not economically viable, such as over large, sparsely populated areas, or were physically impractical, such as over large bodies of water. Today, communications satellites are used to send and receive transmissions to and from a variety of other devices, such as personal satellite dishes used for satellite television and Internet

service, GPS receivers, satellite radio receivers, and satellite phones.

Traditional communications satellites maintain a geosynchronous orbit 22,300 miles above the earth. Because these satellites are so far above the surface of the earth, there is a slight delay while the signals travel from earth, to the satellite, and back to earth again. This delay—less than one half-second—is not normally noticed by most users, such as individuals who receive Internet or TV service via satellite, but it does make geosynchronous satellite transmissions less practical for voice, gaming, and other real-time communications. Because of this delay factor, low earth orbit (LEO) satellite systems were developed for use with satellite telephone systems. LEO satellites typically are located anywhere from 100 to 1,000 miles above the earth and, consequently, provide faster transmission than traditional satellites. Medium earth orbit (MEO) systems typically use satellites located about 1,000 to 12,000 miles above the earth and are used most often for GPS.

One type of wireless networking that does not use signals in the RF band of the electromagnetic spectrum is **infrared (IR) transmission**, which sends data as infrared light rays over relatively short distances. Like an infrared television remote control, infrared technology requires

Microwave stations designed specifically to communicate with satellites, such as for satellite TV and Internet services, are typically called satellite dishes.

communications satellite A device that orbits the earth and relays communications signals over long distances.

infrared (IR) transmission A wireless networking medium that sends data as infrared light rays.

Because satellites travel at a speed and direction that keeps pace with the earth's rotation, they appear to remain stationary over any given spot.

line-of-sight transmission. Because of this limitation, many formerly infrared devices, such as wireless mice and keyboards, now use RF radio signals instead. Infrared transmissions are still used with remote controls, such as for computers that contain TV tuners. They are also used to beam data between some mobile devices, as well as between some game consoles, handheld gaming devices, and other home entertainment devices.

LO4.5 Communications Protocols and Networking Standards

A **protocol** is a set of rules to be followed in a specific situation. In networking, for instance, communications protocols determine how devices on a network communicate. The term *standard* refers to a set of criteria or requirements that has been approved by a recognized standards organization, such as the American National Standards Institute (ANSI), which helps to develop standards used in business and industry, or IEEE, which develops networking standards, or is accepted as a de facto standard by the industry.

Standards help manufacturers ensure their hardware and software products work with other computing products.

protocol A set of rules to be followed in a specific situation.

TCP/IP A networking protocol that uses packet switching to facilitate the transmission of messages; the protocol used with the Internet.

Networking standards typically address both how the devices in a network physically connect, such as the types of cabling that can be used, and how the devices communicate, such as the communications protocols that can be used.

TCP/IP and Other Communications Protocols

The most widely used communications protocol today is TCP/IP. **TCP/IP** is the protocol used for transferring data over the Internet and actually consists of two protocols: Transmission Control Protocol (TCP), which is responsible for the delivery of data, and Internet Protocol (IP), which provides addresses and routing information. TCP/IP uses packet switching to transmit data over the Internet; when the packets reach their destination, they are reassembled in the proper order (see Exhibit 4-12). Support for TCP/IP is built into virtually all operating systems, and IP addresses are commonly used to identify the various computers and devices on networks such as LANs.

The first widely used version of IP—Internet Protocol Version 4 (IPv4)—was standardized in the early 1980s. IPv4 uses 32-bit addresses, which allows for 2^{32} possible unique addresses. Although still widely used today, IPv4 was never designed to be used with the billions of devices that access the Internet today and, consequently, a newer version of IP (IPv6) was developed. IPv6 uses 128-bit addresses, which allows for 2^{128} possible unique addresses, and adds many improvements to IPv4 in areas such as routing, data security, and network autoconfiguration. While IPv4 and IPv6 are expected to coexist for several years until IPv6 eventually replaces IPv4, the U.S. government has mandated that all federal agencies be capable of switching to IPv6.

While TCP/IP is used to connect to and communicate with the Internet, other protocols are used for specific Internet applications. Some examples are:

▶ **HTTP** (Hypertext Transfer Protocol)—used to display Web pages

▶ **HTTPS** (Secure Hypertext Transfer Protocol)—used to display Web pages

▶ **FTP** (File Transfer Protocol)—used to transfer files over the Internet

▶ **SMTP** (Simple Mail Transfer Protocol)—used to deliver e-mail over the Internet

▶ **POP3** (Post Office Protocol)—used to deliver email over the Internet

Exhibit 4-12 How TCP/IP works

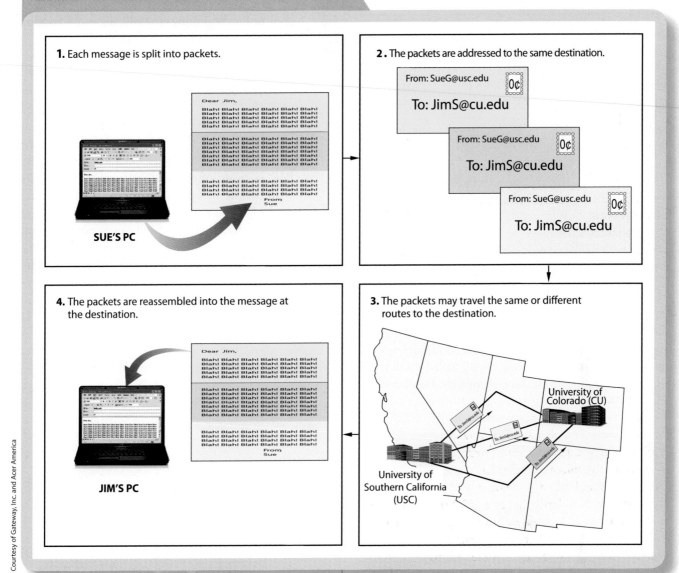

1. Each message is split into packets.

SUE'S PC

2. The packets are addressed to the same destination.

From: SueG@usc.edu 0¢
To: JimS@cu.edu

From: SueG@usc.edu 0¢
To: JimS@cu.edu

From: SueG@usc.edu 0¢
To: JimS@cu.edu

4. The packets are reassembled into the message at the destination.

JIM'S PC

3. The packets may travel the same or different routes to the destination.

University of Colorado (CU)

University of Southern California (USC)

Courtesy of Gateway, Inc. and Acer America

Ethernet (802.3)

Ethernet (**802.3**) is the most widely used standard for wired networks. It is typically used with LANs that have a star topology, though it can also be used with WANs and MANs, and can be used in conjunction with twisted-pair, coaxial, or fiber-optic cabling.

About every three years, the new approved amendments are incorporated into the existing IEEE 802.3 Ethernet standard to keep it up to date. Exhibit 4-13 summarizes the various Ethernet standards. Of these, the most common are Fast Ethernet, Gigabit Ethernet, and 10 Gigabit Ethernet. The even faster standards listed in Exhibit 4-13 are currently under development and are expected to be used for connections between

> Experts suggest that businesses perform a network audit to determine what hardware and software changes will be needed to switch to IPv6.

Ethernet The most widely used standard for wired networks.

Exhibit 4-13 Ethernet standards

Standard	Maximum Speed
10BASE-T	10 Mbps
Fast Ethernet (100BASE-T or 100BASE-TX)	100 Mbps
Gigabit Ethernet (1000BASE-T)	1,000 Mbps (1 Gbps)
10 Gigabit Ethernet (10GBASE-T)	10 Gbps
40 Gigabit Ethernet*	40 Gbps
100 Gigabit Ethernet*	100 Gbps
Terabit Ethernet**	1,000 Gbps (1 Tbps)

* Expected by 2010

** Expected by 2015

servers, as well as for delivering video, digital X-rays and other digital medical images, and other high-speed, bandwidth-intensive, networking applications.

Early Ethernet networks were half-duplex and used a set of procedures collectively called CSMA/CD (Carrier Sense Multiple Access/Collision Detection) to avoid multiple messages from being sent at one time and to detect any collisions of messages as they occur. Beginning in 1997, Ethernet became full-duplex, so collisions no longer occur.

A recent Ethernet development is Power over Ethernet (PoE), which allows electrical power to be sent along the cables in an Ethernet network along with data. These cables are often referred to as Ethernet cables. Consequently, in addition to sending data, the Ethernet cable can be used to supply power to the devices on the network. PoE is most often used in business networks with remote wired devices, such as outdoor networking hardware, security cameras, and other devices, that are not located near a power outlet. It can also be used to place networked devices near ceilings or other locations where a nearby power outlet may not be available. Using PoE requires special hardware and devices designed for PoE but it eliminates the need for access to power outlets for that portion of the network. Regular Ethernet-enabled devices can be powered via PoE if a special PoE adapter, such as the one shown in Exhibit 4-14, is used.

Exhibit 4-14 Ethernet-enabled devices powered via PoE

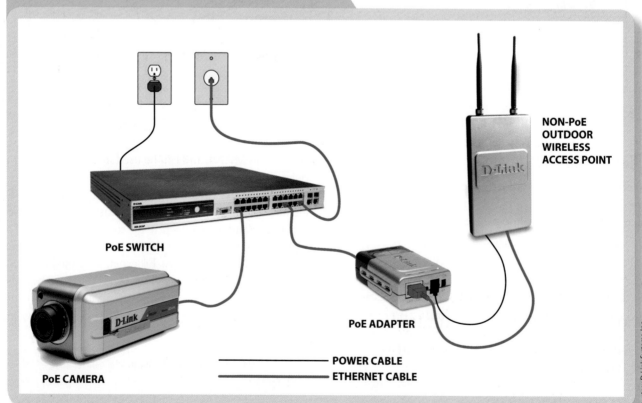

NON-PoE OUTDOOR WIRELESS ACCESS POINT

PoE SWITCH

PoE ADAPTER

PoE CAMERA

POWER CABLE
ETHERNET CABLE

Courtesy D-Link Systems, Inc.

> Ethernet has continued to evolve since it was invented in the mid-1970s.

Phoneline, Powerline, G.hn, and Broadband over Powerline (BPL)

Two alternatives to the Ethernet standard for wired home networks are the Phoneline and Powerline standards. Phoneline (also called the HomePNA Alliance or HomePNA standard) allows computers to be networked through ordinary telephone wiring and telephone jacks without interfering with voice telephone calls, as well as over existing home coaxial cable wiring. The newest version of this standard—HomePNA 3.0—supports speeds up to 320 Mbps and is designed to network both the computers and the home entertainment devices within a home. The Powerline (also called HomePlug) standard allows computers to be networked over existing power lines using conventional electrical outlets. Similar to Phoneline networks, Powerline networks are quick and easy to set up and are relatively fast (up to 200 Mbps). In addition, they have the advantage that houses usually have many more power outlets than phone outlets. Similar to the newest Phoneline standard, the newest Powerline standard—named HomePlug AV—can be used to network home entertainment devices in addition to computers.

The G.hn standard is an emerging standard designed as a unified worldwide standard for creating home networks over phone lines, power lines, and coaxial cable. It is being promoted by the HomeGrid Forum and is supported by the HomePNA Alliance. Once the standard is finalized, products that support all three types of home networking connections discussed in this section can be developed.

An emerging technology based on the Powerline standard that is under development and that is designed to deliver broadband Internet to homes via the existing outdoor power lines (with the addition of some new hardware at the power poles) is broadband over Powerline (BPL). Currently, BPL service is available only in limited areas through the area's power company, but BPL has great potential for delivering broadband Internet access to virtually any home or business that has access to electricity.

Wi-Fi (802.11)

One of the most common networking standards used with wireless LANs is **Wi-Fi (802.11)**, which is a family of wireless networking standards that use the IEEE 802.11 standard. Wi-Fi is the current standard for wireless networks in the home or office, as well as for public Wi-Fi hotspots. It is sometimes called wireless Ethernet because it is designed to easily connect to a wired Ethernet network. Wi-Fi hardware is built into virtually all portable computers sold today. It is also built into many mobile phones to allow faster Web browsing via Wi-Fi when the user is within range of a Wi-Fi network. In addition to portable computers and mobile phones, Wi-Fi capabilities are becoming increasingly integrated into everyday products, such as printers, digital cameras, portable digital media players, handheld gaming devices, and gaming consoles (see Exhibit 4-15), to allow those devices to wirelessly network with other devices or to access the Internet.

Exhibit 4-15 Wi-Fi enabled products

PORTABLE COMPUTERS

MOBILE PHONES

DIGITAL CAMERAS

PORTABLE DIGITAL MEDIA PLAYERS

GAMING CONSOLES

Courtesy Dell Inc., Verizon Wireless, Sony Electronics Inc., ARCHOS, and Nintendo

Wi-Fi (802.11) A widely used networking standard for medium-range wireless networks.

The speed of a Wi-Fi network and the area it can cover depend on a variety of factors, including the Wi-Fi standard and hardware being used, the number of solid objects, such as walls, trees, or buildings, between the access point and the computer or other device being used, and the amount of interference from cordless phones, baby monitors, microwave ovens, and other devices that also operate on the same radio frequency as Wi-Fi (usually 2.4 GHz). In general, Wi-Fi is designed for medium-range data transfers—typically between 100 and 300 feet indoors and 300 to 900 feet outdoors. Usually both speed and distance degrade with interference. The distance of a Wi-Fi network can be extended using additional antennas and other hardware designed for that purpose.

A summary of the different Wi-Fi standards in use and under development is shown in Exhibit 4-16. The most widely used of these are 802.11g and 802.11n.

Exhibit 4-16 Wi-Fi standards

Wi-Fi Standard	Description
802.11b	An early Wi-Fi standard; supports data transfer rates of 11 Mbps.
802.11a	Supports data transfer rates of 54 Mbps, but uses a different radio frequency (5 GHz) than 802.11g/b (2.4 GHz), making the standards incompatible.
802.11g	A current Wi-Fi standard; supports data transfer rates of 54 Mbps and uses the same 2.4 GHz frequency as 802.11b, so their products are compatible.
802.11n	The newest Wi-Fi standard; supports speeds up to about 300 Mbps and has twice the range of 802.11g. It can use either the 2.4 GHz or 5 GHz frequency.
802.11s*	Designed for Wi-Fi mesh networks.
802.11u*	Includes additional security features.
802.11Z*	Designed for direct (ad hoc) networking between devices.
802.11ac and 802.11ad**	Designed to increase throughput.

  * Expected by 2010

** Expected no earlier than 2012

The 802.11n standard is currently the fastest Wi-Fi standard today. Its use of MIMO (multiple in, multiple out) antennas to transfer multiple streams of data at one time, in addition to other improvements, allows for data transmissions typically about five times as fast as 802.11g.

WiMAX (802.16a) An emerging wireless networking standard that is faster and has a greater range than Wi-Fi.

802.11g and 802.11n products can be used on the same network, but computers using older 802.11g hardware to connect to 802.11n networks will only connect at 802.11g speeds.

and about twice the range. To ensure that hardware from various vendors will work together, consumers can look for products that are certified by the Wi-Fi Alliance.

Courtesy Wi-Fi Alliance. The Wi-Fi CERTIFIED logo is registered trademark of the Wi-Fi Alliance

While Wi-Fi is very widely used today, it does have some limitations—particularly its relatively limited range. For instance, an individual using a Wi-Fi hotspot inside a coffeehouse will lose that Internet connection when he or she moves out of range of that network and will need to locate another hotspot at his or her next location. In addition, many businesses may be physically too large for a Wi-Fi network to span the entire organization. While hardware can be used to extend a Wi-Fi network, an emerging possibility for creating larger wireless networks is WiMAX.

WiMAX and Mobile WiMAX

WiMAX (Worldwide Interoperability for Microwave Access) is a series of standards designed for longer range wireless networking connections. Similar to Wi-Fi, WiMAX (also known as **802.16a**) is designed to provide Internet access to fixed locations, sometimes called hotzones. However, WiMAX hotzones can provide service to anyone in the hotzone, including mobile users, while the range of Wi-Fi hotspots is fairly limited. The coverage of a hotzone is significantly larger; a typical hotzone radius is close to 2 miles, though WiMAX can transmit data as far as 6 miles or so without line of sight. With WiMAX, it is feasible to provide coverage to an entire city or other geographical area by using

Wi-Fi SD Cards

One interesting new Wi-Fi product that became available recently is the Wi-Fi SD card. These cards are designed to upload photos wirelessly and automatically from your camera to your computer via a Wi-Fi network. Some cards can also tag your photos with location information based on geographic coordinates as you take them (called geotags); others can automatically upload your photos to photo sharing Web sites like Flickr, Facebook, or Picasa.

For instance, all three Eye-Fi cards in the accompanying photo wirelessly transfer the photos from your digital camera to your home computer as soon as the camera is within range of your home Wi-Fi network. The Eye-Fi Share and the Eye-Fi Pro cards can also wirelessly upload photos to your favorite photo sharing Web site, and the Eye-Fi Pro card automatically geotags your photos. In addition, the Eye-Fi Pro card can upload videos and uncompressed RAW files in addition to photos, send images to photo sharing Web sites and your home computer via a wireless hotspot when you are away from home, and upload photos

Courtesy Eye-Fi

directly to your computer while on the go whenever the camera is in range of your computer.

In addition to allowing you to share your photos immediately with others, using a Wi-Fi SD card for your digital photos can also give you the peace of mind that your photos are backed up on your home computer and/or online. This is especially beneficial if your camera is stolen or the card becomes damaged. In fact, using an Eye-Fi card enabled one woman to catch the individual who stole her camera gear while she was on vacation—her photos, along with images of the thief with the camera gear, were uploaded to her home computer and the police were able to apprehend the thief and recover the stolen gear.

multiple WiMAX towers, similar to the way cell phone cells overlap to provide continuous cell phone service. See Exhibit 4-17. WiMAX can use licensed radio frequencies, in addition to unlicensed frequencies like Wi-Fi, to avoid interference issues.

Mobile WiMAX (**802.16e**) is the mobile version of the WiMAX wireless networking standard. It is designed

to deliver broadband wireless networking to mobile users via a mobile phone, portable computer, or other WiMAX-enabled device. WiMAX capabilities are beginning to be built into portable computers and other devices, and WiMAX is currently being used to provide Internet access to selected geographical areas by a number of companies in over 135 countries. In the United States, for instance, Sprint Nextel's WiMAX division and WiMAX leader Clearwire have merged and are in the process of building a new WiMAX-based nationwide high-speed network designed to deliver both fixed and mobile WiMAX-based Internet service to businesses and individuals.

Exhibit 4-17 WiMAX vs. Wi-Fi

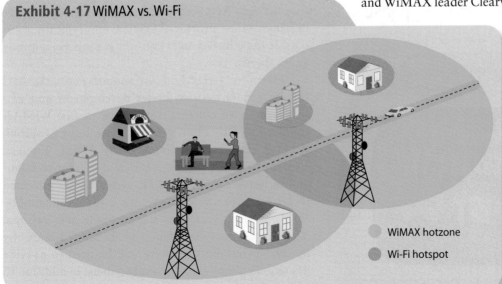

- WiMAX hotzone
- Wi-Fi hotspot

mobile WiMAX (**802.16e**) A version of WiMAX designed to be used with mobile phones.

Cellular Standards

Cellular standards have evolved over the years to better fulfill the demand for mobile Internet, mobile multimedia delivery, and other relatively recent mobile trends. The original first-generation phones were analog and designed for voice only. Newer cell phones, starting with second-generation (2G) phones, are digital, support both data and voice, and are faster. Common 2G wireless standards include GSM (Global System for Mobile communications) and CDMA (Code Division Multiple Access). Both of these standards are designed for voice traffic and both support speeds up to 14.4 Kbps, though some wireless providers have developed technologies such as EDGE (Enhanced Data Rates for GSM Evolution) that can be used with 2G networks to provide faster service; for instance, EDGE supports speeds up to 135 Kbps. These interim developments are sometimes referred to as 2.5G cellular standards. Both GSM and CDMA are used in the United States, although they are not compatible with each other. (Some phones that can be used with both standards are available.) GSM is also widely used overseas, though with different frequencies so international travelers will need to ensure their 2G phone supports the frequencies used in their destination location—some 2G phones support multiple frequencies to permit international roaming.

The current standard for cellular networks today in the United States and many other countries is 3G (third generation). 3G cellular standards use packet switching instead of circuit switching and are designed to support both data and voice. Users of 3G mobile phones and other 3G mobile devices can access broadband Internet content (such as online maps, music, games, TV, videos, and more—see Exhibit 4-18) at relatively fast speeds—up to about 1.7 Mbps at the present time, with speeds expected to reach 3 Mbps in the near future. These speeds are equivalent to the speeds many home broadband Internet users experience. Consequently, Internet access via a 3G network is often referred to as mobile broadband. In addition to mobile phones, computers can access the Internet via a 3G network with appropriate hardware.

Locked vs. Unlocked Phones

Although many mobile phones are locked to a particular cellular provider, buying an unlocked mobile phone allows you to switch providers and keep your same phone, as well as carry your contacts and other data with you to a new unlocked phone just by moving the SIM card containing that data to the new phone.

Virtually all mobile phone providers today have, or are in the process of building, a 3G network. The 3G standard used with a network depends on the type of cellular network. For instance, GSM mobile networks, such as AT&T Wireless and T-Mobile, typically use the HSDPA (High Speed Downlink Packet Access)/UMTS (Universal Mobile Telecommunications System) 3G standards for their 3G networks; CDMA networks, such as Verizon Wireless and Cricket Wireless, typically use the EV-DO (Evolution Data Optimized) 3G standard instead. To get 3G speeds, mobile users need to be in range of their providers' 3G network; typically, users outside the coverage area can still get service, but only at 2G speeds.

The next generation for mobile networks—4G (fourth generation)—is under development and two standards have emerged so far: the mobile WiMAX standard already discussed and Long Term Evolution (LTE). LTE, which is supported by AT&T Wireless, Verizon Wireless, and T-Mobile, is a cellular standard and is based on UMTS. LTE networks are expected to arrive in the United States. by 2011. While mobile WiMAX is not a cellular standard, the new national WiMAX network being built in the United States by Sprint Nextel and Clearwire will be used to provide 4G mobile phone service to subscribers, in addition to Internet service.

Exhibit 4-18 Mobile broadband

Courtesy Sprint Nextel

Personal Mobile Hotspots

You know you can access Wi-Fi hotspots in many locations, but how about creating your own hotspot whenever you need it? That's now possible with several emerging products designed to create personal mobile hotspots that can be used with any Wi-Fi device, such as notebook computers, mobile phones, and portable gaming devices. One such product is Verizon Wireless's MiFi Intelligent Mobile Hotspot, shown in the accompanying illustration. The MiFi is about the size of several stacked credit cards. After its initial setup, it creates a mobile hotspot by just powering up the device. The MiFi device connects to Verizon Wireless's 3G mobile network and provides access to that network for up to five Wi-Fi devices. To those devices, the MiFi hotspot appears as any other Wi-Fi hotspot, so users connect as they normally would. While the cost per MB is relatively expensive and there is currently no unlimited data plan, this device is useful for many situations—such as iPhone users who need to quickly download files larger than the limit allowed via a cellular connection and so need to use a Wi-Fi connection instead, and families who want to all access the Internet while traveling in a car. With a recent poll indicating that 90% of consumers surveyed prefer Internet access to DVD video players in their cars, it appears that mobile personal hotspots are hot.

Bluetooth, Ultra Wideband (UWB), and Other Short-Range Wireless Standards

Several wireless networking standards are in existence or being developed that are designed for short-range wireless networking connections. Most of these are used to facilitate PANs or very small, special-purpose home networks, such as connecting home entertainment devices or appliances within a home.

Bluetooth is a wireless standard that is designed for very short-range (10 meters—approximately 33 feet—

Bluetooth can automatically synchronize a portable computer or mobile phone with a desktop computer, or connect a wireless keyboard as soon as the computer is powered up.

or less) connections. It is designed to replace cables between devices, such as to connect a wireless keyboard or mouse to a desktop computer, to send print jobs wirelessly from a portable computer to a printer, or to connect a mobile phone to a wireless headset. Bluetooth devices automatically recognize and network with each other when they get within transmission range. Bluetooth signals can transmit through clothing and other nonmetallic objects, so a mobile phone or other device in a pocket or briefcase can connect with Bluetooth hardware, such as a headset, without having to be removed from the pocket or briefcase. In addition, some industry experts predict that major household appliances will be Bluetooth-enabled in the future, resulting in an automatic, always connected, smart home.

Bluetooth works using radio signals in the frequency band of 2.4 GHz, the same as Wi-Fi. It traditionally supports data transfer rates up to 3 Mbps, though the newest Bluetooth 3.0 standard incorporates 802.11 technology to support transfers up to 24 Mbps. When two Bluetooth-enabled devices come within range of each other, their software identifies each other using their unique identification numbers and establishes a link. Because there may be many Bluetooth devices within range, up to 10 individual Bluetooth networks (called **piconets**) can be in place within the same physical area at one time. Each piconet can connect up to eight devices, for a maximum of 80 devices within any 10-meter radius. See Exhibit 4-19. To facilitate this, Bluetooth divides its allocated radio spectrum into multiple channels of 1 MHz each. Each Bluetooth device can use the entire range of frequencies, jumping randomly (in unison with the other devices in that piconet) on a regular basis to minimize

Bluetooth A networking standard for very short-range wireless connections.

piconet A Bluetooth network.

Exhibit 4-19 Piconets

The desktop computer, keyboard, printer, and mouse form a piconet to communicate with each other. The headset and cell phone (not shown in this photo) belong to another piconet.

The headset and cell phone form a piconet when they are within range to communicate with each other.

Courtesy Bluetooth SIG

Because Bluetooth transmitters change frequencies 1,600 times every second, two transmitting devices are unlikely to be on the same frequency at the same time.

interference between piconets, as well as from other devices, such as garage-door openers, Wi-Fi networks, and some cordless phones and baby monitors, that use the same frequencies.

As the use of Bluetooth grows, the standard is evolving to meet new needs. For instance, Bluetooth 2.1 includes support for Near Field Communications (NFC), a standard for making payments via mobile phone, and the newest Bluetooth 3.0 standard is fast enough to support multimedia applications, such as transferring music, photos, and videos between computers, mobile phones, and other devices. One interesting emerging Bluetooth application is intended to protect teenagers from texting or talking on their mobile phones while driving—a special Bluetooth-enabled car key prevents the driver's mobile phone from being used while the car is on.

wireless USB A wireless version of USB designed to connect peripheral devices.

Ultra Wideband (UWB) A networking standard for very short-range wireless connections among multimedia devices.

WirelessHD (WiHD) An emerging wireless networking specification designed for connecting home consumer devices.

TransferJet A networking standard for wireless connections between devices that are touching.

A new standard that is designed to connect peripheral devices, similar to Bluetooth, but that transfers data more quickly is **wireless USB**. The speed of wireless USB depends on the distance between the devices being used, but is approximately 100 Mbps at 10 meters (about 33 feet) or 480 Mbps at 2 meters (about 6.5 feet).

Bluetooth and Wireless USB

Although Bluetooth and wireless USB can be used for similar applications, it is possible they might coexist. For example, wireless USB might be used to connect computer hardware in more permanent setups, whereas Bluetooth might be used in short-range mobile situations with portable computers and mobile devices.

There are several wireless technologies being developed to transfer multimedia content quickly between nearby devices. One example is **Ultra Wideband (UWB)**. Similar to wireless USB (because wireless USB is based on UWB), UWB speeds vary from 100 Mbps at 10 meters (about 33 feet) to 480 Mbps at 2 meters (about 6.5 feet).

Another possibility is **WirelessHD (WiHD)**. Similar to UWB, WiHD is designed for fast transfers of high-definition video between home consumer electronic devices, such as high-definition TVs, set-top boxes, gaming consoles, and DVD players, but it is faster. Backed by seven major electronics companies, WiHD is designed to transfer full-quality uncompressed high-definition audio, video, and data within a single room at speeds up to 25 Gbps, though those speeds have not been obtained yet. WiHD operates at 60 GHz and incorporates a smart antenna system that allows the system to steer the transmission, allowing for non-line-of-sight communications. WiHD aims to help users create an easy-to-manage wireless video network. Devices that include WiHD capabilities began to become available in 2009.

A new wireless standard designed for very fast transfers between devices that are extremely close together (essentially touching each other) is **TransferJet**. Developed by Sony, TransferJet is designed to quickly transfer large files, such as digital photos, music, and video, between devices as soon as they come in contact with each other. For example, you can use TransferJet to transfer data between mobile phones or between digital cameras, to download music or video from a consumer kiosk or digital signage system to a mobile phone or other mobile device, or to transfer images or video from a digital camera to a TV set or printer. At a maximum speed of 560 Mbps, TransferJet is fast enough to support the transfer of video files.

An emerging networking standard designed for inexpensive and simple short-range networking (particularly sensor networks) is ZigBee (802.15). ZigBee is intended for applications that require low data transfer rates and several years of battery life. For instance, Zig-

> UWB is especially appropriate for applications that require high-speed transfers over short distances, such as wirelessly delivering multimedia content.

Bee can be used for home and commercial automation systems to connect a wide variety of devices (such as appliances and lighting, heating, cooling, water, filtration, and security systems), and allows for their control from anywhere in the world. ZigBee is also used in industrial plant manufacturing, personal home healthcare, device tracking, telecommunications, and wireless sensor networks.

ZigBee is designed to accommodate more than 65,000 devices on a single network and supports speeds from 20 Kbps to 250 Kbps, depending on the frequency being used (several different frequencies are available for ZigBee networks). ZigBee has a range of 10 to 100 meters (about 33 to 328 feet) between devices, depending on power output and environmental characteristics. A wireless mesh configuration can be used to greatly extend the range of the network.

For a summary of the wireless networking standards just discussed, see Exhibit 4-20.

Exhibit 4-20 Summary of common wireless networking standards

Category	Examples	Intended Purpose	Approximate Range
Short range	Bluetooth Wireless USB	To connect peripheral devices to a mobile phone or computer.	33 feet
	Ultra Wideband (UWB) WirelessHD (WiHD) TransferJet	To connect and transfer multimedia content between home consumer electronic devices (computers, TVs, DVD players, etc.).	1 inch–33 feet
	ZigBee	To connect a variety of home, personal, and commercial automation devices.	33 feet–328 feet
Medium range	Wi-Fi (802.11)	To connect computers and other devices to a local area network.	100–300 feet indoors; 300–900 feet outdoors
Long range	WiMAX Mobile WiMAX	To provide Internet access to a large geographic area for fixed and/or mobile users.	6 miles non-line of sight; 30 miles line of sight
	Cellular standards (2G and 3G)	To connect mobile phones and mobile devices to a cellular network for telephone and Internet service.	10 miles

LO4.6 Networking Hardware

Various types of hardware are necessary to create a computer network, to connect multiple networks together, or to connect a computer or network to the Internet. The following sections discuss the most common types of networking hardware used in home and small office networks.

Network Adapters and Modems

A **network adapter**, also called a **network interface card** (**NIC**) when it is in the form of an expansion card, is used to connect a computer to a network (such as a home or business network). A **modem** (derived from the terms *modulate* and *demodulate*) is used to connect a computer to a network over telephone lines. Technically, to be called a modem, a device must convert digital signals (such as those used by a computer) to modulated analog signals (such as those used by conventional telephone lines) and vice versa. However, in everyday use, the term *modem* is also used to refer to any device that connects a computer to a broadband Internet connection, such as a cable modem used for cable Internet service. In addition, the term *modem* is often used interchangeably with *network adapter* when

Slow Internet connection? Try power cycling: Unplug your modem and router for 30 seconds, then plug in your modem and wait 30 seconds, then plug in your router.

network adapter A device used to connect a computer to a network.

network interface card (**NIC**) A network adapter in the form of an expansion card.

modem A device that is used to connect a computer to a network over telephone lines.

switch A device that connects multiple devices on a wired network and forwards data only to the intended recipient.

describing devices used to obtain Internet access via certain networks, such as cellular or WiMAX networks.

When selecting a network adapter or modem, the type of device being used and the expansion slots and ports available on that device need to be considered as well. For example, network adapters and modems for desktop computers typically come in PCI, PCI Express (PCIe), or USB format, and network adapters and modems for portable computers usually connect via USB or an ExpressCard slot. In addition, the network adapter or modem needs to support the type of networking media (such as twisted-pair cabling, coaxial cabling, or wireless signal) being used. Some examples of network adapters and modems are shown in Exhibit 4-21.

Switches, Routers, and Other Hardware for Connecting Devices and Networks

A variety of networking hardware is used to connect the devices on a network, as well as to connect multiple networks together. For instance, as mentioned earlier in this chapter, networks using the star topology need a central device to connect all of the devices on the network. In a wired network, this device was originally a hub. A hub transmits all data received to all network devices connected to the hub, regardless of which device the data is being sent to, so the bandwidth of the network is shared and the network is not extremely efficient. Today, the central device in a wired network is usually a **switch**. A switch contains ports to which the devices on the network connect (typically via networking cables) and facilitates communications between the devices, similar to a hub. But, unlike hubs, switches identify which device connected to the switch is the one the data is intended for and send the data only to that device, rather than sending data out to all connected devices. Consequently, switches are more efficient than hubs.

Updating Firmware

You can often update the firmware—embedded instructions—for a router and other networking hardware to improve performance or obtain new capabilities. Firmware updates are usually downloaded from the manufacturer's site; often router updates need to be installed with a computer connected to the device via a wired, not wireless, connection.

Exhibit 4-21 Network adapters and modems

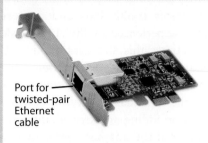

Port for twisted-pair Ethernet cable

PCI EXPRESS GIGABIT ETHERNET ADAPTERS FOR DESKTOP COMPUTERS

Connects to USB port

USB WI-FI ADAPTERS FOR DESKTOP OR NOTEBOOK COMPUTERS

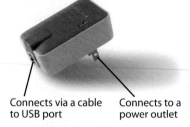

Connects via a cable to USB port

Connects to a power outlet

USB POWERLINE ADAPTERS FOR DESKTOP OR NOTEBOOK COMPUTERS

Slides into ExpressCard slot

EXPRESSCARD WI-FI ADAPTERS FOR NOTEBOOK COMPUTERS

Connects to USB port

USB 3G EV-DO MODEMS FOR DESKTOP OR NOTEBOOK COMPUTERS

Incoming coaxial cable from cable provider and either a USB or Ethernet cable coming from the computer or router connect to the back of the modem.

USB/ETHERNET CABLE MODEMS

To connect multiple networks (such as two LANs, two WANs, or a LAN and the Internet), a **router** is used. Routers pass data on to the intended recipient only and can plan a path through the network to ensure the data reaches its destination in the most efficient manner possible, and are used to route traffic over the Internet.

A **wireless access point** is a device used to grant network access to wireless client devices. In home and small business networks, typically the capabilities of a switch, router, and wireless access point are integrated into a single **wireless router** device. A wireless router (such as the one shown in Exhibit 4-22) is

Exhibit 4-22 Wireless routers

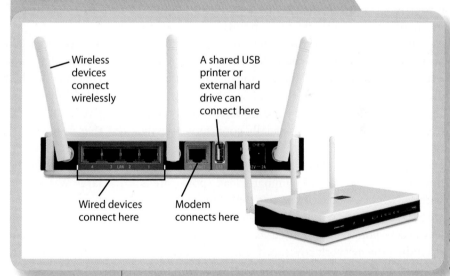

Wireless devices connect wirelessly

A shared USB printer or external hard drive can connect here

Wired devices connect here

Modem connects here

router A device that connects multiple networks together and passes data to the intended recipient using the most efficient route.

wireless access point A device on a wireless network that connects wireless devices to that network.

wireless router A router with a built-in wireless access point.

Most computers and mobile devices come with a network adapter and/or a modem built in.

commonly used to connect both wireless (via Wi-Fi) and wired (via Ethernet cables) devices to a network and to connect that network to an Internet connection. Some broadband modems today include wireless router capabilities to create a wireless network and to provide Internet access using a single piece of hardware. To connect just two LANs together, a **bridge** can be used. The most common use for a bridge in a home network is to wirelessly connect a wired device (such as a home audio/video system, DVR, or gaming console) to a home network via a wireless connection.

Also, routers and other devices are used to connect multiple devices to a cellular network. For instance, 3G mobile broadband routers are used to share a 3G mobile wireless Internet connection with multiple devices (such as your cell phone, personal computer, and handheld gaming device)—essentially creating a Wi-Fi hotspot that connects to your 3G Internet connection. Other devices can be used to route cell phone calls over a broadband network in order to provide better cellular coverage while indoors.

Other Networking Hardware

Additional networking hardware is often needed to extend the range of a network and to share networking media.

Repeaters are devices that amplify signals along a network. They are necessary whenever signals have to travel farther than would be otherwise possible over the networking medium being used. Repeaters are available for both wired and wireless networks; repeaters for a wireless network are often called **range extenders**. Range extenders usually connect wirelessly to the network and repeat the wireless signal to extend coverage of that network outside or to an additional floor of a building, or to eliminate dead spots—areas within the normal network range that don't have coverage. Some WDS (Wireless Distribution System) wireless access points can be used as range extenders by extending the network coverage from one access point to another.

bridge A device used to connect two LANs.

repeater A device on a network that amplifies signals.

range extender A repeater for a wireless network.

antenna A device used for receiving or sending radio signals and often used to increase the range of a network.

Another alternative for increasing the range of a Wi-Fi network is using a higher-gain (stronger) **antenna**. The MIMO antennas used by many 802.11n routers allow for faster connections and a greater range than typically experienced by 802.11g wireless networks, but sometimes this still isn't enough. Using a network adapter designed for the router being used typically helps the network range to some extent; so does replacing the antenna on the router with a higher-gain antenna or adding an external antenna to a networking adapter, if the adapter contains an antenna connector.

Antennas

When buying an external antenna for a device, be sure they are compatible. For instance, 802.11n MIMO routers with three antennas cannot use a single antenna designed for 802.11g devices. There are also range extenders and antennas designed to extend the range of a cellular network, such as to boost reception inside a home in order to use a cell phone as a primary home telephone.

Antennas come in a variety of formats and are classified as either directional antennas (antennas that concentrate the signal in a particular area) or omnidirectional antennas (antennas that are equally effective in all directions). Directional antennas have a farther range than omnidirectional antennas, but a more limited delivery area. The strength of an antenna is measured in decibels (dB). For applications where a large Wi-Fi coverage area is needed (such as in a large business or a hotel), high-gain outdoor antennas can be used (in conjunction with outdoor range extenders and access points, if needed) to enable the network to span a larger area than the hardware would normally allow.

High-speed communications lines are expensive and almost always have far greater capacity than a single device can use. Because of this, signals from multiple devices are often combined and sent together to share a single communications medium. A multiplexer combines the transmissions from several different devices and sends them as one message. Regardless of how the signals are sent, when the combined signal reaches its destination, the individual

Devices in a Network

This is an example of how the devices discussed in this chapter might be used in a network. As shown, many different types of hardware are used to connect networking devices.

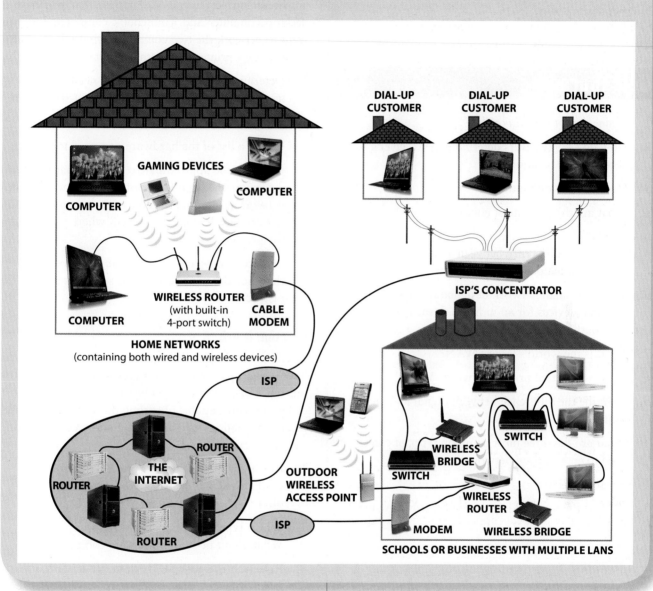

Multiple analog signals can be sent at one time by using multiple frequencies, and multiple optical signals can be sent at one time by using multiple wavelengths.

messages are separated from one another. Multiplexing is frequently used with fiber-optic cables and other high-capacity media to increase data throughput. For instance, if eight signals are multiplexed and sent together over each fiber in one fiber-optic cable, then the throughput of that cable is increased by a factor of eight.

A concentrator is a type of multiplexer that combines multiple messages and sends them via a single transmission medium in such a way that all the individual messages are simultaneously active, instead of being sent as a single combined message. For example, ISPs often use concentrators to combine the signals from their conventional dial-up modem customers to be sent over faster communications connections to their Internet destinations.

Quiz Yourself

1. Define *computer network*.

2. How do GPS receivers determine the receiver's geographical location?

3. Describe telecommuting.

4. What are the three most common network topologies?

5. What is the difference between a client-server network and a peer-to-peer network?

6. What is a small network designed to connect the personal devices for an individual (such as via Bluetooth) called?

7. What is the world's largest WAN?

8. What is a virtual private network (VPN)?

9. Describe the difference between digital and analog signals.

10. What are the three most common types of cables used to create wired networks?

11. What is TCP/IP?

12. What is the most widely used standard for wired networks?

13. What is the current standard for wireless networks?

14. What is an emerging wireless networking standard that is faster and has a greater range than Wi-Fi?

15. What is Bluetooth?

16. What is a switch?

17. What does a router do?

18. What is a repeater?

Practice It

Practice It 4-1

Home networks—particularly wireless home networks—are becoming very common. Suppose that you have a desktop computer and a notebook computer, and you want to network the two computers wirelessly. You also want to use a printer with both computers.

1. Determine the hardware you will need to wirelessly network the two computers and the printer.

2. Create a labeled sketch of the network.

3. Create a list of the hardware you need to acquire.

4. Research the approximate cost of the hardware to determine the overall cost of creating the wireless network (excluding the cost of the computers and the printer). Record the sources where you found the prices.

5. Prepare a one-page summary of your findings that includes your sketch, and submit it to your instructor.

Practice It 4-2

As computers get smaller and devices such as cell phones have more capabilities, the differences between the various types of computers are blurring. For example, most cell phones are capable of surfing the Web, sending and receiving email, as well as making and receiving phone calls and text messages.

1. Research Wi-Fi, WiMAX, and 3G and 4G networks. Which type of networks are used most often by cell phone users? Why?

2. Which type of network do most laptops use? What about netbooks and slate computers?

3. Research the cost of 3G data plans with at least three cell phone companies. What is the average cost? Find at least one company that offers a 4G data plan. How does the average cost of the 3G data plans compare to the cost of the 4G data plan?

4. If you need to transfer a large file from your cell phone or slate computer to another computer, which type of network would be the fastest? How much faster? What conditions might affect download time?

5. Prepare a one-page summary that answers these questions, and submit it to your instructor.

On Your Own

On Your Own 4-1

Internet peer-to-peer (P2P) networking involves sharing files and other resources directly with other computers via the Internet. While some content is legally exchanged via an Internet P2P network, some content (such as movies and music) is exchanged illegally.

1. Should Internet P2P networks be regulated to ensure they are used for only legal activities? Why or why not?

2. If a P2P network set up for legitimate use is used for illegal purposes, should the organization or person who set up the P2P network be responsible? Explain your answer.

3. Would you want to use an Internet P2P network? Why or why not?

4. Use the Web to research more about BitTorrent and Gnutella's LimeWire. Do you think these are legitimate P2P networks? Why or why not?

5. Prepare a one-page summary that answers these questions, and submit it to your instructor.

ADDITIONAL STUDY TOOLS

Chapter 4

IN THE BOOK

▶ Complete end-of-chapter exercises

▶ Study tear-out Chapter Review Card

ONLINE

▶ Complete additional end-of-chapter exercises

▶ Take practice quiz to prepare for tests

▶ Review key term flash cards (online, printable, and audio)

▶ Play "Beat the Clock" and "Memory" to quiz yourself

▶ Watch the videos "How to Select a Wireless Router," "How to Set Up a Wireless Network," "How to Share a Printer over a Network," and "WiMAX vs. Wi-Fi"

100101010

Introducing the Internet and Email

Introduction

With the prominence of the Internet in our personal and professional lives today, it is hard to believe that there was a time not too long ago when few people had even heard of the Internet, let alone used it. But technology is continually evolving. In fact, it is only relatively recently that technology has evolved enough to allow the use of multi-media applications—such as downloading music and movies, watching TV and videos, and playing multimedia interactive games—over the Internet to become everyday activities. Today, *Internet* and *World Wide Web* are household words, and, in many ways, they have redefined how people think about computers, communications, and the availability of news and information.

Despite the popularity of the Internet, however, many users cannot answer some important basic questions about it. What makes up the Internet? Is it the same thing as the World Wide Web? How did the Internet begin, and where is it heading? How can the Internet be used to find specific information? This chapter addresses these types of questions and more.

Learning Objectives

After studying the material in this chapter, you will be able to:

LO5.1 Understand how the Internet evolved

LO5.2 Describe common Internet communication methods and activities

LO5.3 Set up your computer to use the Internet

LO5.4 Use Microsoft Internet Explorer

LO5.5 Use Windows Mail

LO5.1 Evolution of the Internet

The Internet is a worldwide collection of separate, but interconnected, networks accessed daily by millions of people using a variety of devices to obtain information, disseminate information, access entertainment, or communicate with others. Although *Internet* has become a household word only during the past two decades or so, it has actually operated in one form or another for much longer than that.

ARPANET The predecessor of the Internet, named after the Advanced Research Projects Agency (ARPA), which sponsored its development.

From ARPANET to Internet2

The U.S. Department of Defense Advanced Research Projects Agency (ARPA) created **ARPANET** in 1969. One objective of the ARPANET project

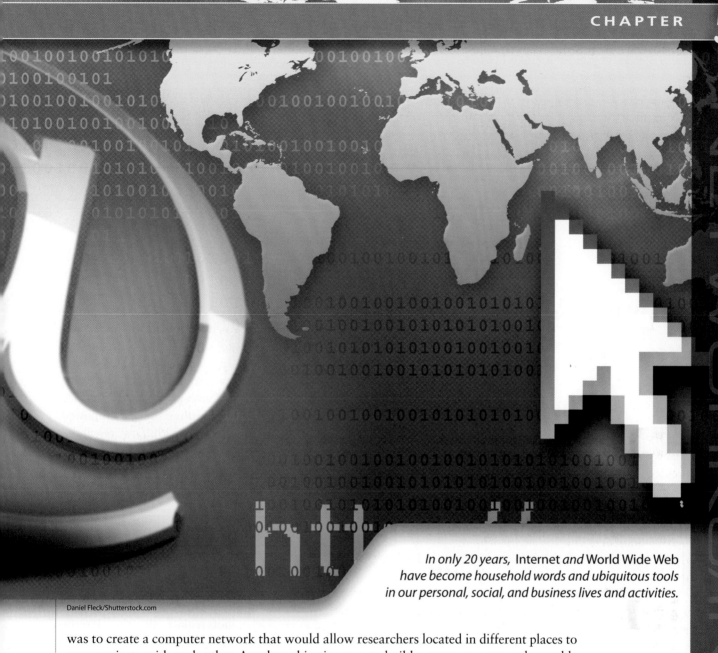

Daniel Fleck/Shutterstock.com

In only 20 years, Internet and World Wide Web have become household words and ubiquitous tools in our personal, social, and business lives and activities.

was to create a computer network that would allow researchers located in different places to communicate with each other. Another objective was to build a computer network capable of sending or receiving data over a variety of paths to ensure that network communications could continue even if part of the network was destroyed, such as in a nuclear attack or by a natural disaster.

Initially, ARPANET connected four supercomputers and enabled researchers at a few dozen academic institutions to communicate with each other and with government agencies. Exhibit 5-1 is a sketch of ARPANET that was drawn in 1969. As the project grew during the next decade, students were granted access to ARPANET as hundreds of college and university networks were connected to it. These networks consisted of a mixture of different computers so, over the years, protocols were developed for tying this mix of computers and networks together, for transferring data over the network, and for ensuring that data was transferred intact. Additional networks soon connected to ARPANET, and this internet—or network of networks—eventually evolved into the present-day Internet.

The roots of the Internet began with an experimental project called ARPANET.

Exhibit 5-1 Hand-drawn sketch of ARPANET from 1969

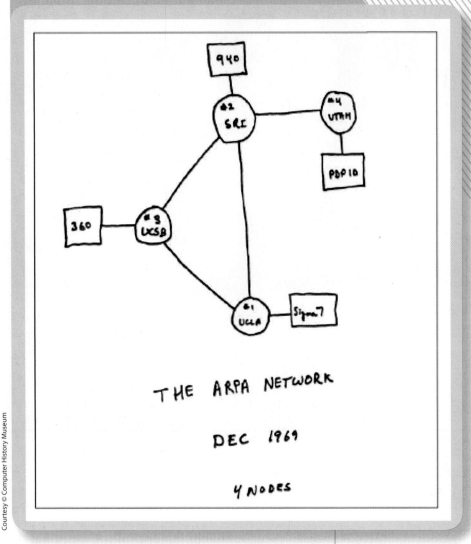

THE ARPA NETWORK

DEC 1969

4 NODES

The Internet we know today is the result of the evolution of ARPANET and the creation of the World Wide Web (WWW).

decades because (1) it required a computer and (2) it was hard to use (see the left image in Exhibit 5-2). As always, however, computer and networking technology improved and new applications quickly followed. Then, in 1989, a researcher named Tim Berners-Lee proposed the idea of the World Wide Web (WWW). He envisioned the World Wide Web as a way to organize information in the form of pages linked together through selectable text or images (today's hyperlinks) on the screen. Although the introduction of Web pages did not replace all other Internet resources, such as email and collections of downloadable files, it became a popular way for researchers to provide written information to others.

In 1993, a group of professors and students at the University of Illinois National Center for Supercomputing Applications (NCSA) released the Mosaic Web browser. Soon after, use of the World Wide Web began to increase dramatically because Mosaic's graphical user interface and its ability to display images on Web pages made using the World Wide Web both easier and more fun than in the past. Today's Web pages are a true multimedia, interactive experience, as shown in the right image in Exhibit 5-2. They can contain text, graphics, animation, sound, video, and three-dimensional virtual reality objects.

A growing number of today's Web-based applications and services are referred to as Web 2.0 applications.

The Internet infrastructure can be used for a variety of purposes, such as researching topics of interest; exchanging email and instant messages; participating in videoconferences and making telephone calls; downloading software, music, and movies; purchasing goods and services; watching TV and video online; accessing computers remotely; and sharing files with others. Most of these activities are available through the primary Internet resource—the World Wide Web.

The World Wide Web

In its early years, the Internet was used primarily by the government, scientists, and educational institutions. Despite its popularity in academia and with government researchers, the Internet went virtually unnoticed by the public and the business community for over two

Exhibit 5-2 The Internet: Then and Now

EARLY 1990S

TODAY

Although there is no precise definition, Web 2.0 generally refers to applications and services that use the Web as a platform to deliver rich applications that enable people to collaborate, socialize, and share information online. Some Web 2.0 applications include cloud computing, social networking sites, podcasts, blogs, and wikis.

The Web is only part of the Internet, but it is by far the most widely used part. Today, most companies regard their use of the Internet and their World Wide Web presence as indispensable competitive business tools, and many individuals view the Internet—and especially the Web—as a vital research, communications, and entertainment medium.

The Internet Is Not the World Wide Web

Even though many people use the terms *Internet* and *Web* interchangeably, they are not the same thing. Technically, the Internet is the physical network, and the Web is the collection of Web pages accessible over that network. A majority of Internet activities today take place via Web pages, but Internet resources other than the Web are not accessed via a Web browser. For instance, files can be uploaded and downloaded using an FTP (File Transfer Protocol) program and conventional email can be accessed using an email program.

Internet2

Internet2 is a consortium of researchers, educators, and technology leaders from industry, government, and the international community that is dedicated to the development of revolutionary Internet technologies. Internet2 uses high-performance networks linking over 200 member institutions to deploy and test new network applications and capabilities. However, the Internet2 network is not a new network designed to eventually replace the Internet—it is simply a research and development tool to help create technologies that ensure the Internet in the future can handle tomorrow's applications. Much of Internet2 research is focused on speed. For instance, the Internet2 Land Speed Record is an ongoing contest for the highest-bandwidth end-to-end network. The current record is an average speed of 9.08 Gbps while transferring 20.42 TB of data across about 30,000 miles of network.

The Internet Community Today

The Internet community today consists of individuals, businesses, and a variety of organizations located throughout the world. Virtually anyone with a computer or other Web-enabled device can be part of the Internet, either as a user or as a supplier of information or services. Most members of the Internet community fall into one or more of the following groups:

▶ **Users**—People who use the Internet to retrieve content or perform online activities, such as to look up a telephone number, read the day's news

The Internet, according to the Pew Internet & American Life Project, is used by approximately 75 percent of the U.S. population.

headlines or top stories, browse through an online catalog, make an online purchase, download a music file, watch an online video, make a phone call, or send an email message.

▶ **Internet service providers (ISPs)**—Businesses or other organizations, including telephone, cable, and satellite companies, that provide Internet access to others, typically for a fee. Exhibit 5-3 shows the logos of some of these companies. Regardless of their delivery method and geographical coverage, ISPs are the onramp to the Internet, providing their subscribers with access to the World Wide Web, email, and other Internet resources. Some ISPs also provide proprietary online services available only to their subscribers.

Exhibit 5-3 ISP logos

Use of the AT&T logo is granted under permission by AT&T Intellectual Property.; Courtesy of Verizon Communications; Comcast; Hughes Network Systems, LLC; EarthLink, Inc.; and Clearwire

▶ **Internet content providers**—The suppliers of the information that is available through the Internet. Internet content providers can be commercial businesses, nonprofit organizations, educational institutions, individuals, and more.

Internet service provider (ISP) A business or other organization that provides Internet access to others, typically for a fee.

Internet content provider A person or an organization that provides Internet content.

application service provider (ASP) A company that manages and distributes software-based services over the Internet.

▶ **Application service providers (ASPs)**—The companies that manage and distribute Web-based software services to customers over the Internet. Instead of providing access to the Internet like ISPs do, ASPs provide access to software applications via the Internet. Common ASP applications for businesses include office suites, collaboration and communications software, accounting programs, and e-commerce software.

▶ **Infrastructure companies**—The enterprises that own or operate the paths or "roadways" along which Internet data travels, such as the Internet backbone and the communications networks connected to it. Examples of infrastructure companies include conventional and mobile phone companies, cable companies, and satellite Internet providers.

▶ **Hardware and software companies**—The organizations that make and distribute the products used with the Internet and Internet activities. For example, companies that create or sell the software used in conjunction with the Internet, such as Web browsers, email programs, e-commerce and multimedia software, and Web development tools, fall into this category. So, too, do the companies that make the hardware, such as network adapters, modems, cables, routers, servers, computers, and mobile phones, for instance, that is used with the Internet.

▶ **Governments**—The ruling bodies of countries that can pass laws limiting both the information made available via Web servers located in a particular country and the access individuals residing in that country have to the Internet. For example, in France, it is illegal to sell items or post online content related to racist groups or activities. In China, tight controls are imposed on what information is published on Web servers located in China, as well as on the information available to its citizens. And in the United States, anything illegal offline is illegal online.

▶ **Key Internet organizations**—Other organizations that are responsible for many aspects of the Internet. For example, the Internet Society (ISOC) provides leadership in addressing issues that may impact the future of the Internet. It also oversees the groups responsible for Internet infrastructure standards, such as determining the protocols that can be used and how Internet addresses are constructed. ICANN (Internet Corporation for Assigned Names and Numbers) coordinates

Who's in Charge of the Internet and the World Wide Web?

One remarkable characteristic of both the Internet and World Wide Web is that they are not owned by any person or business, and no single person, business, or organization is in charge. Each network connected to the Internet is privately owned and managed individually by that network's administrator, and the primary infrastructure that makes up the Internet backbone is typically owned by communications companies, such as telephone and cable companies. The closest the Internet comes to having a governing body is a group of organizations, including the ISOC, ICANN, and W3C, that are involved with issues such as establishing the protocols used on the Internet, making recommendations for changes, and encouraging cooperation between and coordinating communications among the networks connected to the Internet. Governments in each country have the power to regulate the content and use of the Internet within their borders, as allowed by their laws. However, legislators often face serious obstacles getting legislation passed into law—let alone getting it enforced. Making governmental control even harder is the "bombproof" design of the Internet itself. If a government tries to block access to or from a specific country or Web site, for example, users can use a third party, such as an individual located in another country or a different Web site, to circumvent the block.

activities related to the Internet's naming system, such as IP address allocation and domain name management. The World Wide Web Consortium (W3C) is a group of over 450 organizations dedicated to developing new protocols and specifications to promote the evolution of the Web and to ensure its interoperability. In addition, many colleges and universities support Internet research and manage blocks of the Internet's resources.

LO5.2 Beyond Browsing and Email

In addition to basic browsing and email, many other activities can take place via the Internet. Although originally the programs that supported these various types of online communications were dedicated to a single task, today's programs often can be used for a variety of types of online communications.

Other Types of Online Communications

Instant messaging (**IM**) allows you to exchange real-time typed messages with people on your buddy list—a list of individuals such as family, friends, and business associates whom you specify. Instant messages (IMs) can be sent via computers and mobile phones using installed messaging programs such as AIM, Windows Live Messenger, Yahoo! Messenger, or Google Talk; Web-based messaging services such as Meebo.com or Web versions of AIM, Yahoo! Messenger, or Google Talk; or other online communications programs that support instant messaging. Originally a popular communications method among friends, IM has also become a valuable business tool. Instant messaging capabilities are also sometimes integrated into Web pages, such as to ask questions of a customer service representative or to start a conversation with one of your friends via a social networking site; this type of messaging is sometimes referred to as chat.

Text messaging is a form of messaging frequently used by mobile phone users. Also called Short Message Service or SMS, text messaging is used to send short

> Instant messaging (IM) uses presence technology, which allows one computing device to identify the status of another.

instant messaging (**IM**) A way of exchanging real-time typed messages with other individuals.

text messaging A way of exchanging real-time typed messages with other individuals via a cellular network and, typically, cell phones.

(less than 160 characters) text-based messages via a cellular network. The messages are typically sent to the recipient via his or her mobile phone number.

Tweeting, sometimes referred to as microblogging, is a free service that allows members (both individuals and businesses) to post short (up to 140 characters) updates—called tweets—about what they are doing at any moment. The updates can be sent via text message, IM, email, or even Xbox (see Exhibit 5-4), and are posted to the member's Twitter.com page. Tweet updates can also be sent to your friends' mobile phones if they have set up their accounts to follow you via text. Members can also search the Twitter Web site to find tweets of interest.

Exhibit 5-4 Twitter

Courtesy Yahoo! and Microsoft Corporation

Internet telephony is the original industry term for the process of placing telephone calls over the Internet. Today, the standard term for placing telephone calls over the Internet or any other type of data network is **Voice over Internet Protocol** (**VoIP**) and it can take many forms. At its simplest level, VoIP calls can take place from computer to computer, such as by starting a voice conversation with an online buddy using an IM program and a headset or microphone connected to the computer. Computer-to-computer calls, such as via the popular Skype service, as well as via messaging programs that support voice calls, are generally free. Often calls can be received from or made to conventional or mobile phones for a small fee, such as two cents per minute for domestic calls.

More permanent VoIP setups—sometimes referred to as digital voice, broadband phone, or Internet phone service—are designed to replace conventional landline phones in homes and businesses. VoIP is offered through some ISPs, such as cable, telephone, and mobile phone companies; it is also offered through dedicated VoIP providers, such as Vonage. Permanent VoIP setups require a broadband Internet connection and a VoIP phone adapter, also called an Internet phone adapter, that goes between a conventional phone and a broadband router, as shown in Exhibit 5-5. Once your phone calls are routed through your phone adapter and router to the Internet, they travel to the recipient's phone, which can be another VoIP phone, a mobile phone, or a landline phone. VoIP phone adapters are typically designed for a specific VoIP provider. With these more permanent VoIP setups, most users switching from landline phone service can keep their existing telephone number.

The biggest advantage of VoIP is cost savings, such as unlimited local and long-distance calls for as little as $25 per month, or cable and VoIP services bundled together for about $50 per month. One of the biggest disadvantages of VoIP at the present time is that it does not function during a power outage or if your Internet connection goes down.

Web conferences typically take place via a personal computer or mobile phone and are used by businesses

tweeting Sending short status updates about your current activities via the Twitter service.

Voice over Internet Protocol (**VoIP**) The process of placing telephone calls via the Internet.

Web conference A face-to-face meeting taking place via the Web.

Exhibit 5-5 How VoIP works

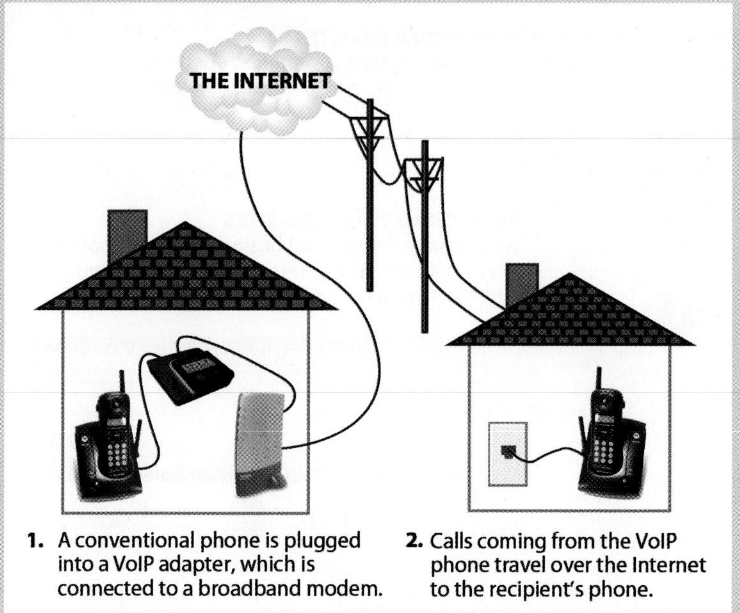
THE INTERNET
1. A conventional phone is plugged into a VoIP adapter, which is connected to a broadband modem.
2. Calls coming from the VoIP phone travel over the Internet to the recipient's phone.

Courtesy Vonage and D-Link Systems, Inc.

You can limit access to your Facebook page to the individuals you identify.

and individuals. Basic Web conferences, such as a video call between individuals as in Exhibit 5-6, can be performed via any online communications program, such as an instant messaging program, that supports video phone calls. Business Web conferences that require multiple participants or other communication tools, such as a shared whiteboard or the ability for attendees to share the content on their computer screens, may need to use Web conferencing software or services instead. Business Web conferencing is often used for meetings between individuals located in different geographical locations, as well as for employee training, sales presentations, customer support, and other business applications.

Webinars (Web seminars) are similar to Web conferences, but typically have a designated presenter and an audience. Although interaction with the audience is usually included, a Webinar is typically more one-way communication than a Web conference.

A **social networking site** can be loosely defined as any site that creates a community of individuals who can communicate with and/or share information with one another. Some examples are MySpace and Facebook, which allow users to post information about themselves for others to read; Meetup.com, which connects people with common hobbies and interests; video sharing sites like YouTube; and photo sharing sites like Flickr and Fotki. Social networking can be performed via personal computers, though the use of mobile social networking—social networks accessed with a mobile phone or other mobile device—is growing rapidly. In fact, Jupiter Research predicts the number of active mobile social networking users will rise from 54 million today to 730 million in five years, and MySpace expects half of its traffic to come from mobile devices within a few years. Some reasons for this include that most individuals carry a mobile phone with them all the time, many individuals like to communicate with others via the Web while they are on the go, and the use of a mobile phone enables location applications to be integrated into the social networking experience.

Social networking sites are used most often to communicate with existing friends. Facebook, for instance (shown in Exhibit 5-7), allows you to post photos, videos, music, and other content. You can also chat with

Exhibit 5-6 Web conferencing

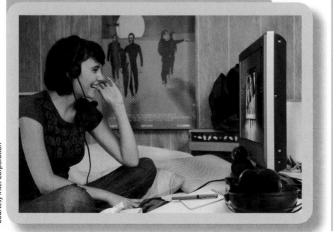

Courtesy Intel Corporation

Webinar A seminar presented via the Web.

social networking site A site that enables a community of individuals to communicate and share information.

Exhibit 5-7 Social networking sites

PERSONAL PROFILING SITES
Allow individuals to post information about themselves, link pages with friends, exchange messages, and so forth.

BUSINESS NETWORKING SITES
Help businesspeople find business contacts, potential new employees and clients, dinner and traveling partners during business trips, and so forth.

Courtesy Facebook, Inc. and LinkedIn

Facebook friends who are currently online, and publish notes and status updates on your Facebook wall, as well as the walls of your friends' Facebook pages.

In addition to being used for personal activities, social networking sites today are also viewed as a business marketing tool. For instance, MySpace, Facebook, and YouTube are often used by businesses, political candidates, emerging musicians, and other professionals or professional organizations to increase their online presence. There are also business social networking sites designed for business networking. These sites (such as LinkedIn shown in Exhibit 5-7) are used for recruiting new employees, finding new jobs, building professional contacts, and other business activities. Other specialized social networking sites include sites designed for children and families, such as to exchange messages, view online tasks lists, and access a shared family calendar.

Blogs, Wikis, and Other Types of Online Writing

A **blog**—also called a Web log—is a Web page that contains short, frequently updated entries in chronological order, typically as a means of expression or communication (see Exhibit 5-8). In essence, a blog is an online personal journal accessible to the public that is usually created and updated by one individual. Blogs are written by a wide variety of individuals—including ordinary people, as well as celebrities, writers, students, and experts on particular subjects—and can be used to post personal commentary, research updates, comments on current events, political opinions, celebrity gossip, travel diaries, television show recaps, and more.

blog A Web page that contains short, frequently updated entries in chronological order, typically by just one individual.

Understanding E-Commerce

Online shopping and online investing are examples of **e-commerce**—online financial transactions. It is very common today to order products, buy and sell stock, pay bills, and manage financial accounts online. However, since online fraud, credit card fraud, and identity theft (a situation in which someone gains enough personal information to pose as another person) are continuing to grow at a rapid pace, it is important to be cautious when participating in online financial activities. To protect yourself, use a credit card or online payment service such as PayPal whenever possible when purchasing goods or services online so that any fraudulent activities can be disputed. Also, be sure to enter your payment information only on a secure Web page (look for a URL that begins with *https* instead of *http*). Online financial accounts should also be protected with strong user passwords that are changed frequently.

Online shopping is commonly used to purchase both physical products, such as clothing, books, DVDs, shoes, furniture, and more, and downloadable products, such as software, movies, music, and e-books, via Web pages. Forrester Research predicts that U.S. online sales will reach approximately $335 billion by 2012.

Online auctions are the most common way to purchase items online from other individuals. Sellers list items for sale on an auction site, such as eBay or Yahoo! Auctions, and pay a small listing fee and a commission to the auction site if the item is sold. Individuals can visit the auction site and enter bids on auction items until the end of the auction. Another common way to purchase items from other individuals is via online classified ads, such as those posted on the popular craigslist site.

Many banks today offer online banking as a free service to their customers to enable customers to check balances on all their accounts, view cashed checks and other transactions, transfer funds between accounts, pay bills electronically, and perform other activities related to their bank accounts. Online banking is continually growing—according to the Pew Internet & American Life Project, close to one-half of all U.S. adults now bank online.

Buying and selling stocks, bonds, mutual funds, and other types of securities is referred to as online investing. Although it is common to see stock quote capabilities on many search and news sites, trading stocks and other securities requires an online broker. Common online investing services include the ability to order sales and purchases; access performance histories, corporate news, and other useful investment information; and set up an online portfolio that displays the status of the stocks you specify.

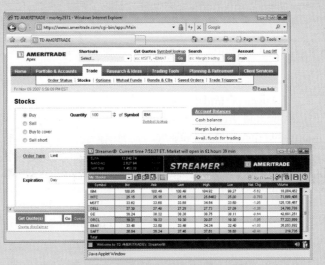

e-commerce Online financial transactions.

Exhibit 5-8 An example of a blog

Blogging software, available via blogging sites such as Blogger.com, is usually used to easily create and publish blogs and blog updates to the Web. Blogs are also frequently published on school, business, and personal Web sites. Blogs are usually updated frequently, and entries can be posted via computers, email, and mobile phones. Blogs often contain text, photos, and video clips.

With their growing use and audiences, bloggers are beginning to have increasing influence on businesses, politicians, and individuals today. One new ethical issue surrounding blogging relates to bloggers who are paid to blog about certain products. Although some Web sites that match up bloggers with advertisers require that the blogger reveal that he or she receives payment for "sponsored" posts, some believe that commercializing blogging will corrupt the blogosphere. Others, however, view it as a natural evolution of word-of-mouth advertising.

Another form of online writing sometimes used for educational purposes is the wiki. **Wikis**, named for the Hawaiian phrase *wiki wiki* meaning quick, are a way of creating and editing collaborative Web pages quickly and easily. Similar to a blog, the content on a wiki page can be edited and republished to the Web just by pressing a Save or Submit button. However, wikis are intended to be modified by others and so are especially appropriate for collaboration, such as for class Web pages or group projects. To protect the content of a wiki from sabotage, the entire wiki or editing privileges for a wiki can be password protected.

You can also use Microsoft Word to create blog posts.

wiki A collaborative Web page that is designed to be edited and republished by a variety of individuals.

Exhibit 5-9 Wikipedia

Product, Corporate, Government, and Other Information

The Web is a very useful tool for locating product and corporate information. Manufacturer and retailer Web sites often include product specifications, instruction manuals, and other information that is useful to consumers before or after they purchase a product. There are also numerous consumer review sites, such as Epinions.com, to help purchasers evaluate their options before buying a product online or in a physical store. For investors and consumers, a variety of corporate information is available online, from both company Web sites and sites, such as hoovers.com, that offer free or fee-based corporate information.

One of the largest wikis is Wikipedia (shown in Exhibit 5-9), a free online encyclopedia that contains over eight million articles written in 250 languages, is updated by more than 75,000 active contributors, and is visited by hundreds of thousands of individuals each day. While most Wikipedia contributors edit articles in a responsible manner, there are instances of erroneous information being added to Wikipedia pages intentionally. As with any resource, visitors should carefully evaluate the content of a Wikipedia article before referencing it in a report, Web page, or other document.

An **e-portfolio**, also called an electronic portfolio or digital portfolio, is a collection of an individual's work accessible through a Web site. Today's e-portfolios are typically linked to a collection of student-related information, such as résumés, papers, projects, and

> **e-portfolio** A collection of an individual's work accessible via the Web.

other original works. Some e-portfolios are used for a single course; others are designed to be used and updated throughout a student's educational career, culminating in a comprehensive collection of information that can be used as a job-hunting tool.

Cookies

Many Web pages today use **cookies**—small text files that are stored on your hard drive by a Web server—to identify return visitors and their preferences. Although some individuals view all cookies as a potential invasion of privacy, Web sites can read only their own cookie files and the use of cookies can provide some benefits to consumers. For example, cookies can enable a Web site to remember preferences for customized Web site content, as well as to retrieve a shopping cart containing items selected during a previous session. Some Web sites also use cookies to keep track of which pages on their Web sites each person has visited, in order to recommend products on return visits that match that person's interests. A use of cookies that is more objectionable to some is the use of **third-party cookies**, which are cookies placed on your hard drive by a company other than the one associated with the Web page that you are viewing—typically a Web advertising company. Third-party cookies target advertisements to Web site visitors based on their activities on the site, such as products viewed or advertisements clicked.

The information stored in a cookie file typically includes the name of the cookie, its expiration date, and the domain that the cookie belongs to. In addition, a cookie contains either personal information that you entered while visiting the Web site or an ID number assigned by the Web site that allows the Web site's server to retrieve your personal information from its database.

You can look at cookies stored on your computer's hard drive, although sometimes deciphering the information contained in a cookie file is difficult. Internet Explorer users can view and delete cookies and other temporary files by using Internet Explorer's Tools menu to open the Internet Options dialog box and selecting the appropriate options in the Browsing history section on the General tab. The Privacy tab in this dialog box (shown in Exhibit 5-10) can be used to specify which types of cookies (if any) are allowed to be used, such as permitting the use of regular cookies but not third-party cookies or cookies using personally identifiable information. Be aware that turning off cookies entirely might make some features—such as a shopping cart—on some Web sites inoperable.

cookie A small file stored on a user's hard drive by a Web server; commonly used to identify personal preferences and settings for that user.

third-party cookie A cookie placed on your hard drive by a company other than the one associated with the Web page that you are viewing.

Exhibit 5-10 Managing cookies

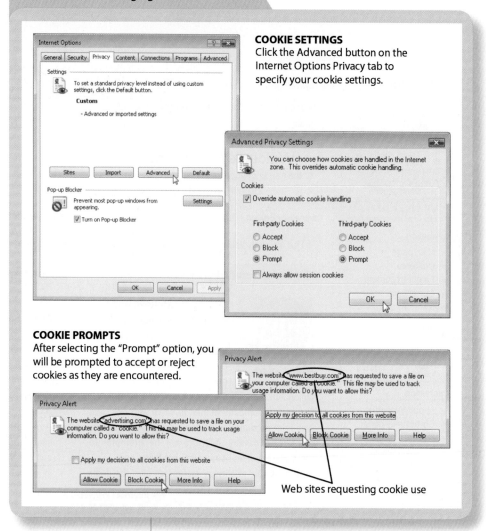

COOKIE SETTINGS
Click the Advanced button on the Internet Options Privacy tab to specify your cookie settings.

COOKIE PROMPTS
After selecting the "Prompt" option, you will be prompted to accept or reject cookies as they are encountered.

Web sites requesting cookie use

Tracking Cookies

Cookies that attempt to track your activities across a Web site or the Web sites belonging to an advertising network are referred to as tracking cookies. If your security software includes tracking cookie protection, be sure it is enabled to avoid these cookies from being stored on your computer. Setting your browser's privacy settings to block third-party cookies can offer you some additional protection against tracking cookies.

Users who want more control over their cookies can choose to accept or decline cookies as they are encountered in most browsers. Although this option interrupts your Web surfing frequently, it is interesting to see the cookies generated from each individual Web site. Another alternative is the private browsing option available with many Web browsers, including Internet Explorer, Chrome, and Safari. This option allows you to browse the Web without leaving any history, including browsing history, form data, cookies, usernames, and passwords, on the computer you are using. Private browsing is useful for individuals using school, library, or other public computers to visit password-protected sites, research medical information, or perform other tasks that the user may prefer to keep private. Indi-

Most users who have access to a personal computer such as a desktop or notebook computer at home, work, or school will use it to access the Internet.

viduals using a computer to shop for presents or other surprises for family members who share the same computer may find the feature useful, as well.

LO5.3 Getting Set Up to Use the Internet

Getting set up to use the Internet typically involves three decisions—determining the type of device you will use to access the Internet, deciding which type of connection you want, and selecting the Internet service provider to use. Once you have made these determinations, you can set up your computer to access the Internet.

Selecting the Type of Device

The Internet can be accessed using a variety of devices. The type of device used depends on a combination of factors, such as the devices available to you, if you need access just at home or while on the go, and what types of Internet content you want to access. Some possible devices are shown in Exhibit 5-11.

Exhibit 5-11 Devices used to access the Internet

PERSONAL COMPUTERS   **MOBILE PHONES**   **TELEVISIONS**

One advantage of using personal computers for Internet access is that they have relatively large screens for viewing Internet content, and they typically have a full keyboard for easier data entry. They can also be used to view or otherwise access virtually any Web page content, such as graphics, animation, music files, games, and video clips. In addition, they typically have a large hard drive and are connected to a printer so Web pages, email messages, and downloaded files can be saved and/or printed easily.

Mobile phones are increasingly being used to view Web page content, exchange email and text messages, and download music and other online content. In fact, mobile Web use—or wireless Web, as it is sometimes called—is one of the fastest growing uses of the Internet. Although mobile phones are convenient to use on the go, they typically have a relatively small display screen. Some devices include a built-in or sliding keyboard for easier data entry; others utilize pen or touch input instead.

Another option is using a gaming console or handheld gaming device to access Web content, in addition to using that device to play games. For instance, the Sony PlayStation 3, Sony PSP, Nintendo Wii, and Nintendo DSi all have Web browsers that can be used to access Web content. In addition to gaming consoles that can connect to television sets to display Internet content, an emerging option is broadband-enabled TVs that have Internet capabilities built-in in order to display Web pages and other Web content, such as the weather, stock quotes, and other information displayed at the bottom of the TV screen shown in Exhibit 5-11, without any additional hardware.

Choosing the Type of Connection and Internet Access

Your computer needs to be connected to the Internet to use it. Typically, this occurs by connecting your computer or other device you are using to a computer or a network, usually belonging to your ISP, school, or employer, that is connected continually to the Internet. Keep in mind that there are a variety of wired and wireless ways to connect to another device. Most types of connections today are broadband or high-speed connections. In fact, more than 60 percent of all home Internet connections in the United States are broadband connections, and that percentage is expected to climb

The Internet Is Not Free

The myth that the Internet is free stems from the fact that traditionally no cost has been associated with accessing online content—such as news and product information—or with email exchange, other than what Internet users pay ISPs for Internet access. But, someone somewhere has to pay to keep the Internet up and running.

Businesses, schools, public libraries, and most home users pay ISPs flat monthly fees to connect to the Internet. In addition, businesses, schools, libraries, and other large organizations might have to lease high-capacity communications lines, such as from a telephone company, to support their high level of Internet traffic. Mobile users who want Internet access while on the go typically pay hotspot providers or mobile phone providers for this access. ISPs, phone companies, cable companies, and other organizations that own part of the Internet infrastructure pay to keep their parts of the Internet running smoothly. ISPs also pay software and hardware companies for the resources they need to support their subscribers. Eventually, most of these costs are passed along to end users through ISP fees.

ISPs that offer free Internet access typically obtain revenue by selling on-screen ads that display on the screen when the service is being used. Also, the growing trend of subscription or per-use fees to access Web-based resources negates the myth that the Internet is free. For instance, downloadable music and movies are very common, and some journal or newspaper articles require a fee to view them online. In fact, some newspapers and magazines have moved entirely online and most charge a subscription fee to view the level of content that was previously published in a print version. In lieu of a mandatory fee, some Web sites request a donation for use of the site. Many experts expect the use of fee-based Internet content to continue to grow at a rapid pace.

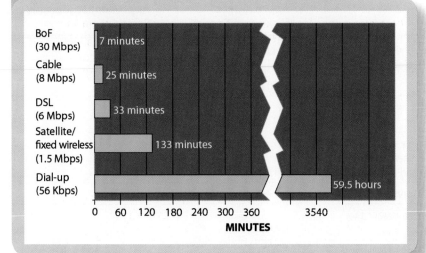

Exhibit 5-12 Length of time to download a 1.5 GB movie using different connection options

BoF (30 Mbps)	7 minutes
Cable (8 Mbps)	25 minutes
DSL (6 Mbps)	33 minutes
Satellite/fixed wireless (1.5 Mbps)	133 minutes
Dial-up (56 Kbps)	59.5 hours

MINUTES: 0 60 120 180 240 300 360 3540

to 77 percent by 2012, according to a recent Gartner study. As applications requiring high-speed connections continue to grow in popularity, access to broadband Internet speeds are needed in order to take full advantage of these applications. For instance, high-definition television, video-on-demand (VOD), and other multimedia applications all benefit from fast broadband connections, as shown in Exhibit 5-12.

Some Internet connections are dial-up connections, in which your computer dials up and connects to your ISP's computer only when needed. Dial-up connections usually work over standard telephone lines. To connect to the Internet, your computer dials its modem and then connects to a modem attached to a computer belonging to your ISP via the telephone lines. While connected to your ISP, your computer can access Internet resources. To end that Internet session, you disconnect from your ISP. One advantage of a dial-up connection is security. Because you are not continually connected to the Internet, it is much less likely that anyone will gain access to your computer via the Internet, either to access the data on your computer or, more commonly, to use your computer in some illegal or unethical manner.

Broadband over power lines (BPL), a new way to connect to the Internet through power outlets, will likely be available in the future.

However, dial-up connections are much slower than other types of connections. They are also inconvenient, because you have to instruct your computer to dial up your ISP every time you want to connect to the Internet. Also, that telephone line will be tied up while you are accessing the Internet.

Most Internet connections today are direct (or always-on) connections, in which you have a continuous connection to your ISP. Direct connections keep you continually connected to your ISP and, therefore, continually connected to the Internet. With a direct connection, such as cable, DSL, satellite, or fixed wireless, you access the Internet simply by opening a Web browser, such as Internet Explorer, Chrome, or Firefox. Direct Internet connections are typically broadband connections, are commonly used in homes and businesses, and are often connected to a LAN to share the Internet connection with multiple devices within the home or business.

The most common types of Internet connections for personal use today are summarized in Exhibit 5-13 and are described below.

Conventional dial-up Internet access uses a conventional dial-up modem connected to a standard telephone jack with regular twisted-pair telephone cabling. Conventional dial-up Internet service is most often used with home computers for users who don't need, or do not want to pay for, broadband Internet service. Advantages include inexpensive hardware, ease of setup and use, and widespread availability. The primary disadvantage is slow connection speed, since conventional dial-up modems connect to the Internet at a maximum of 56 Kbps.

Cable Internet access uses a direct connection and is the most widely used type of home broadband connection, with over half of the home broadband market. Cable connections are very fast, typically between 5 and 20 Mbps, though some faster services are available for a premium fee, and are available wherever cable TV access is offered as long as the local cable provider supports Internet access. Consequently, cable Internet is

conventional dial-up Internet access Dial-up Internet access via standard telephone lines.

cable Internet access Fast, direct Internet access via cable TV lines.

Exhibit 5-13 Typical home Internet connection options

Type of Internet Connection	Availability	Approximate Maximum Speed*	Approximate Monthly Price
Conventional dial-up	Anywhere there is telephone service	56 Kbps	Free–$20
Cable	Virtually anywhere cable TV service is available	5–20 Mbps	$40–60
DSL	Within three miles of a switching station that supports DSL	1–7 Mbps	$20–40
Satellite	Anywhere there is a clear view to the southern sky and where a satellite dish can be mounted and receive a signal	1–1.5 Mbps	$60–80
Fixed wireless	Selected areas where service is available	1–2 Mbps	$40–60
Broadband over fiber (BoF)	Anywhere fiber has been installed to the building	10–50 Mbps	$50–145
Mobile wireless (3G)	Virtually anywhere cellular phone service is available	700 Kbps–1.7 Mbps	Varies greatly; often bundled with mobile phone service

* Download speed; most connections have slower upload speeds.

not widely available in rural areas. Cable Internet service requires a cable modem.

DSL (**Digital Subscriber Line**) **Internet access** is a direct connection that transmits via standard telephone lines, but it does not tie up your telephone line. DSL requires a DSL modem and is available only to users who are relatively close (within three miles) to a telephone switching station and who have telephone lines capable of handling DSL. DSL speeds are about one-half of cable speeds, and the speed of the connection degrades as the distance between the modem and the switching station gets closer and closer to the three-mile limit. Consequently, DSL is usually only available in urban areas. Download speeds are typically between 1 and 7 Mbps.

Satellite Internet access uses a direct connection, but is slower and more expensive than cable or DSL access—

typically up to around 1.5 Mbps. However, it is often the only broadband option for rural areas. In addition to a satellite modem, it requires a transceiver satellite dish mounted outside the home or building to receive and transmit data to and from the satellites being used. Installation requires an unobstructed view of the southern sky to have a clear line of sight between the transceiver and appropriate satellite. Performance might degrade or stop altogether during very heavy rain or snowstorms.

Fixed wireless Internet access uses a direct connection and is similar to satellite Internet in that it uses wireless signals, but it uses radio transmission towers—either stand-alone towers like the one shown in Exhibit 5-14 or transmitters placed on existing cell phone towers—instead of satellites. Fixed wireless Internet access requires a modem and, sometimes, an outside-mounted transceiver. Fixed wireless companies typically use Wi-Fi and/or WiMAX technology to broadcast the wireless signals to customers. Speeds are typically up to about 2 Mbps, though the speed depends somewhat on the distance between the tower and the customer, the type and number of obstacles in the path, and the type and speed of the connection between the wireless transmitter and the Internet.

In areas where fiber-optic cabling runs all the way to the building, a new type of direct connection is available to homes and businesses that is generically called **broadband over fiber** (**BoF**) or **fiber-to-the-premises** (**FTTP**) **Internet access**, with other names being used by

DSL (**Digital Subscriber Line**) **Internet access**
Fast, direct Internet access via standard telephone lines.

satellite Internet access Fast, direct Internet access via the airwaves and a satellite dish.

fixed wireless Internet access Fast, direct Internet access available in some areas via the airwaves.

broadband over fiber (**BoF**) or **fiber-to-the-premises** (**FTTP**) **Internet access** Very fast, direct Internet access via fiber-optic networks.

ISP Bandwidth Limits

Internet traffic has increased tremendously recently as people are watching TV and videos online, downloading music and movies, playing online multiplayer games, using online backup services, and otherwise performing high-bandwidth activities. This has created the issue of ISPs potentially running out of bandwidth available for customers, resulting in outages or delays. In response, some ISPs have, at times, blocked selected traffic to and from their customers, such as cable giant Comcast blocking the use of P2P sites like BitTorrent, which is often used to download movies, music, and other large files. Other ISPs are slowing down traffic to and from heavy users during peak Internet usage periods or experimenting with bandwidth caps as Internet usage management tools. For instance, Comcast is currently testing slowing down traffic to and from heavy users during peak periods, Time Warner Cable is testing tiered pricing based on usage in certain areas, and AT&T is testing bandwidth caps for new customers in certain areas. With a bandwidth cap, customers either temporarily lose Internet access or are charged an additional fee if they exceed their download limit (often 5 GB to 150 GB per month).

Comcast, like most ISPs, includes a statement in its terms of service agreement that allows it to "efficiently manage its networks" in order to prevent customers from using a higher than normal level of bandwidth. However, many considered Comcast's blocking of P2P content to be a blatant net neutrality issue because Comcast was blocking access to multimedia from a source other than its own cable source, and the Internet is designed for all content to be treated equally. There are also concerns about bandwidth caps and that overcharges will grow to an unreasonable level—particularly by cable companies and other providers that may want to stifle Internet multimedia to protect their TV advertising revenues. To protect against this, the Broadband Internet Fairness Act has been introduced in the United States to require broadband providers to submit tiered pricing plans to the FTC to ensure they are not unreasonable or discriminatory. It is unclear at this time as to the bill's outcome, as well as whether or not bandwidth caps will be part of the future of home Internet service. However, it is clear that, as Internet usage by the average consumer continues to grow, the issue of a finite amount of Internet bandwidth versus an increasing demand for online multimedia content will remain.

individual providers, such as Verizon's fiber-optic service (FiOS). These fiber-optic networks are most often installed by telephone companies in order to upgrade their overall infrastructures and, where installed, are used to deliver telephone and TV service in addition to Internet service. However, some cities are creating fiber-optic MANs that include connections to businesses and homes to provide very fast broadband Internet services. Where available, download speeds for BoF service typically range between 10 Mbps and 50 Mbps and the cost varies accordingly. BoF requires a special networking terminal installed at the building to convert the optical signals into electrical signals that can be sent to a computer or over a LAN.

Mobile wireless Internet access is the direct connection most commonly used with mobile phones and other mobile devices to keep them

Exhibit 5-14 WiMAX tower at the peak of Whistler Mountain in British Columbia

mobile wireless Internet access Internet access via a mobile phone network.

connected to the Internet via a mobile phone network, even as they are carried from place to place. Some mobile wireless services can be used with notebook computers and other computers as well. For instance, AT&T's DataConnect service allows access to the Internet on a notebook or netbook computer via the AT&T wireless network, and some mobile phones can be connected to a notebook computer to act as a modem to connect that computer to the mobile phone's wireless network. The speed of mobile wireless depends on the cellular standard being used—3G networks typically have speeds between 1 and 1.7 Mbps. Costs for mobile wireless Internet access vary widely, with some packages including unlimited Internet, some charging by the number of minutes of Internet use, and some charging by the amount of data transferred.

A **Wi-Fi hotspot** is a location with a direct Internet connection and a wireless access point that allows users to connect wirelessly (via Wi-Fi) to the hotspot to use its Internet connection; see Exhibit 5-15. A Wi-Fi hotspot is not commonly used for home Internet access. Public Wi-Fi hotspots are widely available today, such as at many coffeehouses and restaurants; at hotels, airports, and other locations frequented by business travelers; and in or nearby public areas such as libraries, subway stations, and parks. Some public Wi-Fi hotspots are free; others charge per hour, per day, or on a subscription basis. College campuses also typically have Wi-Fi hotspots to provide Internet access to students. Many businesses and other organizations have Wi-Fi hotspots for use by employees in

Wi-Fi hotspot A location that provides wireless Internet access to the public.

Exhibit 5-15 Typical Wi-Fi hotspots

COFFEEHOUSES AND OTHER PUBLIC LOCATIONS
Often free, but some charge a fee.

HOSPITALS, BUSINESSES, AND OTHER ORGANIZATIONS
Usually designed for employees but are sometimes also available free to visitors.

COLLEGE CAMPUSES
Usually designed for students and faculty; sometimes used directly in class for student assignments, as shown here.

Courtesy/iStockphoto © Sean Locke, Fujitsu America, and Abilene Christian University

their offices, as well as by employees and guests in conference rooms, waiting rooms, lunchrooms, and other onsite locations.

Selecting an ISP

The type of device used (such as a personal computer or mobile phone), the type of Internet connection and service desired (such as cable Internet or mobile wireless), and your geographical location (such as metropolitan or rural) will likely determine your ISP options. The pricing and services available through any two ISPs will probably differ somewhat, based on the speed of the service, as well as other services available. The questions listed in Exhibit 5-16 can help you narrow your ISP choices and determine the questions you want answered before you decide on an ISP. A growing trend is for ISPs to offer a number of tiers; that is, different levels (speeds) of service for different prices so users requiring faster service can get it, but at a higher price.

Exhibit 5-16 Questions to ask before choosing an ISP

Area	Questions to Ask
Services	Is the service compatible with my device?
	Is there a monthly bandwidth limit?
	How many email addresses can I have?
	What is the size limit on incoming and outgoing email messages and attachments?
	Do I have a choice between conventional and Web-based email?
	Is there dial-up service that I can use when I'm away from home?
	Are there any special member features or benefits?
	Does the service include Web site hosting?
Speed	How fast are the maximum and usual downstream (ISP to my PC) speeds?
	How fast are the maximum and usual upstream (my PC to ISP) speeds?
	How much does the service slow down under adverse conditions, such as high traffic or poor weather?
Support	Is 24/7 telephone technical support available?
	Is Web-based technical support (such as via email) available?
	Is there ever a charge for technical support?
Cost	What is the monthly cost for the service? Is it lower if I prepay a few months in advance? Are different tiers available?
	Is there a setup fee? If so, can it be waived with a 6-month or 12-month agreement?
	What is the cost of any additional hardware needed, such as modem or transceiver? Can the fee be waived with a long-term service agreement?
	Are there any other services (telephone service, or cable or satellite TV, for instance) available from this provider that I have or want and that can be combined with Internet access for a lower total cost?

Setting Up Your Computer

The specific steps for setting up your computer to use your selected type of Internet connection depend on the type of device, the type of connection, and the ISP you have chosen to use. Some types of Internet connections, such as satellite and broadband over fiber, require professional installation, after which you will be online. With other types, you can install the necessary hardware—typically a modem that connects to your computer or wireless router via an Ethernet cable—yourself. You will usually need to select a username and your desired payment method at some point during the ordering or setup process. This username is needed to log on to some types of Internet connections; it is also used in your email address that will be associated with that Internet service.

After one computer is successfully connected to the Internet, you may need to add additional hardware to connect other computers and devices that you want to be able to access the Internet. For instance, to share a broadband connection, you can connect other computers directly to the modem via an Ethernet cable or Wi-Fi connection if the modem contains a built-in switch or wireless router. If the modem does not include switching or wireless routing capabilities, you will need to connect a switch or wireless router to the modem, typically via an Ethernet cable, and then connect your devices to the switch or router, in order to share the Internet connection with those devices.

LO5.4 Using Microsoft Internet Explorer

Internet Explorer 8, the current version of Microsoft's Web browser, provides all the tools you need to communicate, access, and share information on the Web.

Internet Explorer is the most popular browser in the world.

home page (start page) The page that appears when you start a browser.

Starting Internet Explorer

When you start Internet Explorer, the page that appears is called the **home page** or the **start page**.

 **ACTIVITY**

Start Internet Explorer.

1 On the taskbar, click the **Internet Explorer button** .

> ⚠ **Problem?** If the Internet Explorer button does not appear on the taskbar, click the **Start button**, click **All Programs**, and then click **Internet Explorer**.

2 If the program window does not fill the screen entirely, click the **Maximize button** on the title bar. The home page appears in your browser window. The default home page for Internet Explorer is MSN.com. See Exhibit 5-17. The home page on your screen might be different.

Entering a URL in the Address Bar and Using Links

To navigate to different Web pages, you can click the links on a Web page. As you click different links, the URL in the Address bar changes. Recall from Chapter 1 that the URL is the address of a Web page. To display a specific Web page, you can enter its URL in the Address bar. In most cases, URLs are not case-sensitive. However, if you are entering a URL that includes mixed cases, it is safer to use the mixed-case format of the URL.

When a Web page appears, or **loads**, in a browser window, it is copied from the Web server to your computer. The main page on a Web site is also called the **home page**. The home page appears when you type the domain name and top-level domain of a Web site.

Exhibit 5-17 MSN.com, the default start page for Internet Explorer

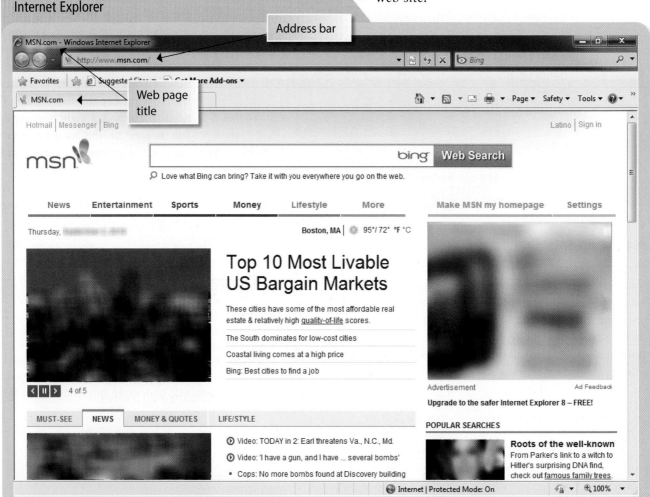

Exhibit 5-18 NASA home page

ACTIVITY

Go to a specific Web page and use a link.

1 Click anywhere in the **Address bar**. The current URL is selected. Anything you type will replace the selected URL.

2 Type **www.nasa.gov**.

3 Press the **Enter key**. Internet Explorer adds *http://* to the URL, and then displays the page in the browser window. The home page for the NASA Web site appears, and the name of the Web page appears on the tab and in the title bar.

> ▶ **Tip:** You can also click the Go to button ➡ on the Address bar to display the page indicated by the URL.

The Dynamic Web

The Web is a dynamic medium, so the screenshots of Web pages shown in this book will most likely differ from the pages you see when the Web pages appear in your browser window. You should still be able to identify the elements called out in the figures.

(Another page might open instead of the NASA home page, but the home page should appear momentarily.) See Exhibit 5-18.

4 Near the top of the window, point to **ABOUT NASA** so that the pointer changes to ⌐ᕼ, and then click **ABOUT NASA**. The About NASA Web page appears in the browser window, and the URL in the Address bar changes to the address for that page.

Visiting Previously Viewed Web Pages

After you visit a Web page during a browser session, you can use the Back and Forward buttons to the left of the Address bar to move to the most recently viewed Web pages. You can also quickly go to the start page for your browser by clicking the Home button on the Command bar.

Once you have visited a Web page by typing its URL in the Address bar, you can start typing the URL, and a list of Web sites you previously visited that contain the string of characters you are typing appears in a drop-down list below the Address bar.

load To copy a Web page from a server to a computer.

home page The main page on a Web site.

ACTIVITY

Go to previously viewed Web pages.

1 To the left of the Address bar, click the **Back button** ⬅. The previously viewed Web page—the NASA Web site home page—appears in the browser window. Now the Forward button is available.

2 To the left of the Address bar, click the **Forward button** ➡. The About NASA page loads again. The Forward button is again unavailable (dimmed) because there are no more pages after the current page in the history list.

3 On the Command bar, click the **Home button** 🏠. Your browser's start page appears in the browser window.

4 Click in the **Address bar**, and then type **n**. A list of URLs beginning with *n* that were visited using the browser appears below the Address bar. See Exhibit 5-19.

5 In the list, click **http://www.nasa.gov/**. The NASA Web site home page appears again.

You can click the Quick Tabs button to view thumbnails of all open tabs.

a New Tab. When you open a new tab by right-clicking a link, the current tab and the new tab create a **tab group**, which is a collection of related tabs. When multiple tabs are open, the tab that appears to be on top is the **active tab**. To make another tab the active tab and display the Web page on that tab in the browser window, click the tab. Finally, you can close a tab for a Web page that no longer interests you.

ACTIVITY

Use tabs.

1 To the right of the NASA – Home tab, point to the **New Tab button**. The NewTab button 🗋 appears on it.

2 Click the **New Tab button** 🗋. A new tab appears in the browser window. In the Address bar, the text "about: Tabs" appears. This text appears in the Address bar whenever a new, blank tab is created.

Exhibit 5-19 List of previously visited Web pages

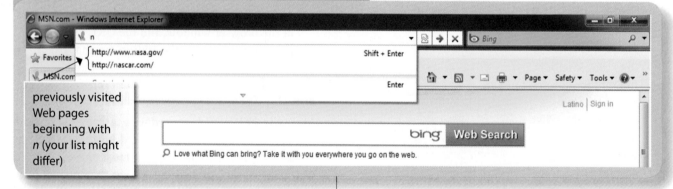

previously visited Web pages beginning with *n* (your list might differ)

Using Tabs

Tabs allow you to display multiple Web pages in the same browser window. With tabbed browsing, you can create a tab for each Web page you visit that you might want to return to quickly. To open a new tab, you click the New Tab button to the right of the current tabs, or right-click a link on a Web page, and then click Open in

tab group A collection of related tabs.

active tab The tab that appears to be on top in a browser window.

The text in the Address bar is selected. See Exhibit 5-20.

3 Type **www.usa.gov** and then press the **Enter key**. The home page for the USA.gov Web site appears in the new tab.

4 Scroll down to the bottom of the page. Right-click the **Contact Us link**, and then on the shortcut menu, click **Open in**

▶ **Tip:** You can also press and hold the Ctrl key while you click a link to open the linked page in a new tab.

Exhibit 5-20 New, blank tab in Internet Explorer window

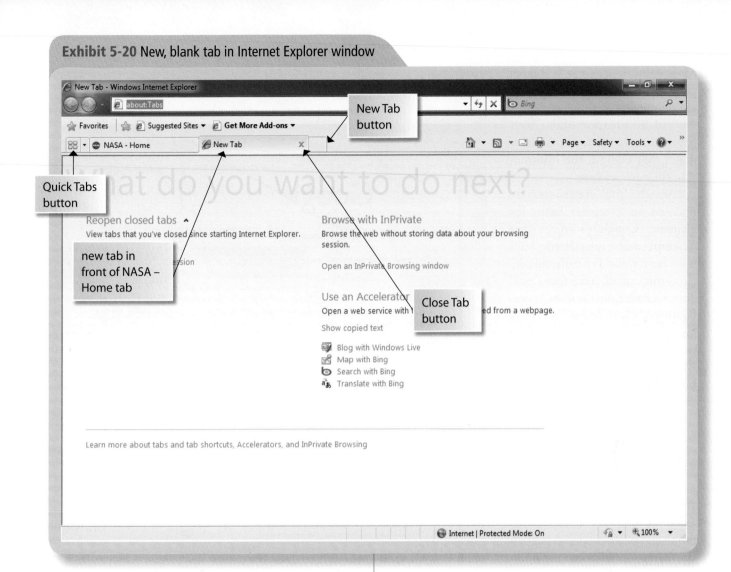

New Tab. A new tab opens to the right of the current tab displaying Contact Us: USA.gov as the Web page title on the tab. The USA.gov tab and the Contact Us: USA.gov tabs are the same color to indicate they are in the same tab group.

5 Click the **Contact Us: USA.gov tab**. The Contact Us page becomes the active tab in the window.

6 On the Contact Us: USA.gov tab, point to the **Close Tab button** ☒. The button changes to ☒.

> **Tip:** You can click the Quick Tabs button ▦ to the left of the first tab to see thumbnail images of open tabs, and then you can click a thumbnail to switch to that tab.

7 Click the **Close Tab button** ☒. The Contact Us: USA.gov tab closes. Because there is only one tab left in the tab group that had been colored green, the USA.gov tab is no longer colored.

8 Right-click the **NASA – Home tab**, and then on the shortcut menu, click **Close Other Tabs**. The USA.gov tab closes, and the NASA – Home tab becomes the current tab.

Using Search Sites

Finding information on the Internet is made easier through the power of search engines, available through search sites. **Search sites** are Web sites designed specifically to help you find information on the Web. Some popular search engines are Google, Bing (the default search engine for Internet Explorer 8), and Yahoo!, which is now powered by Microsoft Bing technology.

> **search site** A Web site designed to help users search for Web pages that match specified keywords or selected categories.

Most search sites use a **search engine**—a software program—in conjunction with a huge database of information about Web pages to help visitors find Web pages that contain the information they are seeking.

Search site databases are updated on a regular basis; for example, Google estimates that its entire index is updated about once per month. Typically, this occurs using small, automated programs (often called spiders or webcrawlers) that use the hyperlinks located on Web pages to jump continually from page to page. At each Web page, the spider program records important data about the page into the search site's database, such as the page's URL, its title, the keywords that appear frequently on the page, and the keywords and descriptive information added to the page's code by the Web page author when the page was created. In addition to spider programs, search site databases also obtain information from Web page authors who submit Web page URLs and keywords associated with their Web sites to the search site.

To conduct a search, type appropriate **keywords**—one or more words describing what you are looking for—into a search box on a search site. Multiple keywords are sometimes called a **search phrase**. The site's search engine then uses those keywords to return a list of links to Web pages (called **hits**) that match your search criteria (see Exhibit 5-21). Search sites differ in determining how close a

Exhibit 5-21 Using a search site

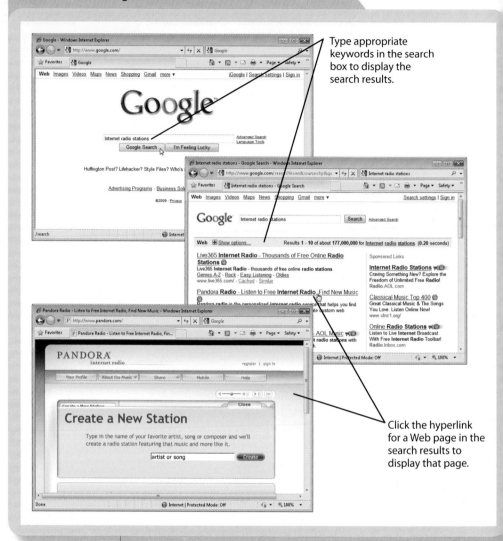

Type appropriate keywords in the search box to display the search results.

Click the hyperlink for a Web page in the search results to display that page.

search engine A software program used by a search site to retrieve matching Web pages from a search database.

keyword A word typed in a search box on a search site or other Web page to locate information related to that keyword.

search phrase Multiple keywords.

hit A link that matches search criteria in a search site.

Evaluating Web Sites

When you gather information from Web pages, you need to determine if the information can be trusted. You should evaluate both the author and the source to decide if the information can be considered reliable and whether it is biased. Be sure to also check for a date to see how up to date the information is—many online articles are years old. If you will be using the information in a report, paper, or other document in which accuracy is important, try to verify the information with a second source.

Setting a Search Engine in Internet Explorer

You can change the search engine used with the Search box in Internet Explorer. To do this, click the Search box arrow, and then click Find More Providers. The Internet Explorer Add-ons Gallery Web page appears listing search engines you can add. Click the search engine you want to use, and then click Add to Internet Explorer. This opens the Add Search Provider dialog box. If you want the search engine you selected to be the default search engine, click the Make this my default search provider check box to select it. Click Add to close the dialog box and add the search engine to the Search box.

match must be between the specified search criteria and a Web page before a link to that page is displayed, so the number of hits from one search site to another may vary.

You can also use the Search box in Internet Explorer to access a search site. The Search box is located to the right of the Address bar. To conduct a search using the Search box, you type keywords in the Search box, and then click the Search button 🔍 or press the Enter key to begin the search. The hits are displayed on the search site you used.

Often, a search phrase returns millions of hits. To narrow the search, you can add words to the search phrase. For example, if you type *cooking* as the search phrase, the list of results will include recipe sites, sites with definitions of cooking, links to books about cooking, and so on. To restrict the list of results to only Web sites that contain recipes for cooking in the fusion style with fish, you can add *fusion*, *fish*, and *recipes* to the search phrase.

Spider programs can be tremendously fast, visiting millions of pages per day.

ACTIVITY

Search the Internet using a search engine.

Tip: If the search phrase you want to use appears in the list, you can click it to select it and execute the search.

1. To the right of the Address bar, click in the **Search box**, and then type **live green**. A list of suggestions for completing the search phrase appears. See Exhibit 5-22.

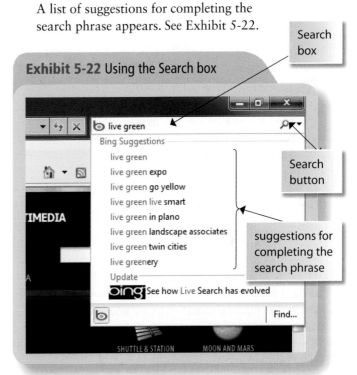

Exhibit 5-22 Using the Search box

Search box

Search button

suggestions for completing the search phrase

2. To the right of the Search box, click the **Search button** 🔍. A list of hits for the search phrase *live green* appears in your default search site in the current tab. Usually, the first 10 hits appear on the page and links to additional pages of results are listed at the bottom of the page.

3. Scroll down the page to examine the top 10 hits.

4. Scroll back up to the top of the page, click in the **Search box** at the top of the search site page after the keyword *green*. Press the **Spacebar**, type **on a budget** and then press the **Enter key**. The list of results changes to include only Web sites that discuss living green on a budget.

5. Scroll down the list on the first page of results and click one that interests you. The Web page you clicked loads in the current tab, replacing the list of results. Examine the Web page you selected.

6. To the left of the Address bar, click the **Back button** ⬅. The list of results appears in the tab again.

After you close your browser, the pages you visited are not available via the tabs or Back and Forward buttons.

Notice that in the list of results, the link you clicked has changed from blue to purple to indicate that you have visited that Web page.

7 To the left of the Address bar, click the **Back button** ⊙ twice. The home page on the NASA Web site appears in the browser window again.

Using Favorites

Web addresses can be very long and, as a result, difficult to remember, so you can save the URL of a Web page as a favorite. A **favorite** is a shortcut to a Web page saved in a list. You can use favorites to store and organize a list of Web pages you want to revisit. When you add a Web page as a favorite, you can choose to add it to the list in the Favorites Center, or you can add it to the Favorites bar, which is directly below the Address bar. To add a Web page as a favorite, you first need to open the Favorites Center by clicking the Favorites button in the Favorites bar. The Favorites Center contains three tabs: Favorites, Feeds, and History. Favorites are listed on the Favorites tab. See Exhibit 5-23. To add a favorite, click Add to Favorites; to add all the open tabs as favorites in a folder in the Favorites list, click the Add to Favorites arrow, and then click Add Current Tabs to Favorites. To help keep your favorites organized, you can create folders. You can also add a favorite to the Favorites bar.

 **ACTIVITY**

Add Web pages as favorites and pin the Favorites Center.

1 On the Favorites bar, click the **Favorites button**. The Favorites Center opens on top of the browser window.

favorite A shortcut to a Web page saved in a list.

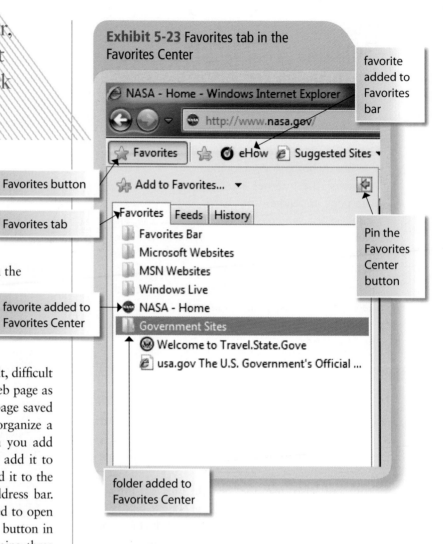

Exhibit 5-23 Favorites tab in the Favorites Center

favorite added to Favorites bar

Favorites button

Favorites tab

favorite added to Favorites Center

Pin the Favorites Center button

folder added to Favorites Center

2 If the Favorites tab is not selected, click the **Favorites tab**. The list of favorites stored on the computer appears. Refer to Exhibit 5-23.

3 At the top of the Favorites Center, click the **Add to Favorites button**. The Add a Favorite dialog box opens. See Exhibit 5-24. The text in the Name box is the name of the currently displayed Web page, as it appears on the Internet Explorer title bar. You can edit this to change the name of the favorite, if you want. The Create in box also displays the name of the folder in which the favorite will be stored—the default Favorites folder means that the favorite will be stored in the main Favorites list.

Tip: You can select a different folder by clicking the Create in arrow and choosing another folder, or creating a new folder by clicking New Folder.

Exhibit 5-24 Add a Favorite dialog box

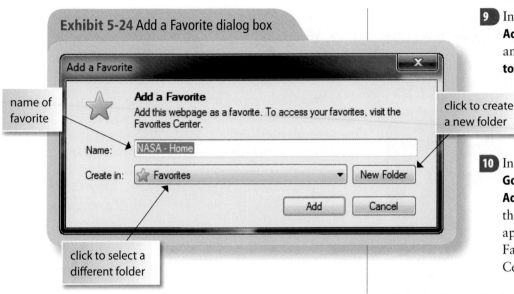

name of favorite

Add a Favorite
Add this webpage as a favorite. To access your favorites, visit the Favorites Center.

Name: NASA - Home

Create in: ⭐ Favorites   New Folder

Add   Cancel

click to create a new folder

click to select a different folder

4 In the dialog box, click **Add**. The Add a Favorite dialog box closes and the Web page is saved as a favorite.

5 On the Favorites bar, click the **Favorites button**. The NASA – Home Web page is listed as the last favorite in the Favorites list.

6 In the upper-right corner of the Favorites Center, click the **Pin the Favorites Center button** 🔲. The Favorites Center changes to a pane that remains open to the left of the browser window, and the Close the Favorites Center button ❎ appears in place of the Pin the Favorites Center button.

7 Click in the **Address bar**, type **usa.gov** and then press the **Enter key**. The USA.gov home page appears in the current tab.

8 Create a new tab, type **travel.state.gov** in the Address bar, and then press the **Enter key**.

Using the Favorites Bar

If you know you will revisit a favorite often, you can make it more accessible by saving it to the Favorites bar. When you add a favorite to the Favorites bar, it appears to the right of the Favorites button and to the left of any other favorites currently stored on the Favorites bar. To visit a favorite stored on the Favorites bar, simply click it.

9 In the Favorites Center, click the **Add to Favorites button arrow**, and then click **Add Current Tabs to Favorites**. The Add Tabs to Favorites dialog box opens. Instead of the Name box, the top box is the Folder Name box.

10 In the Folder Name box, type **Government Sites** and then click **Add**. The dialog box closes and the folder Government Sites appears as the last item in the Favorites list in the Favorites Center.

After you have added a Web page as a favorite, you can click its link in the Favorites Center, and that page will load in the current tab. To help keep your favorites organized, you can also delete a favorite if you no longer need it.

ACTIVITY

Go to a favorite and delete favorites.

1 In the Favorites Center, click the **NASA – Home favorite**. The NASA home page loads in the current tab.

> **Tip:** To open all the favorites stored in a folder, right-click the folder in the Favorites Center, and then on the shortcut menu, click Open in Tab group.

2 In the Favorites Center, right-click the **NASA – Home favorite**, and then on the shortcut menu, click **Delete**. A dialog box appears asking if you are sure you want to move the shortcut to the Recycle Bin.

3 Click **Yes**. The dialog box closes and the favorite is deleted.

4 On the Favorites bar, click the **Favorites button**.

5 In the Favorites list, right-click the **Government Sites folder**, and then on the shortcut menu click **Delete**.

6 In the dialog box, click **Yes**. The folder in the Favorites list and its contents are deleted.

Subscribing to RSS Feeds and Web Slices

A **feed** is frequently updated Web site content, such as news or blogs, delivered directly to your browser, usually from a news site. Feeds are sometimes called RSS Feeds because the RSS file format is often used to make feeds available. If a Web page provides a feed, the Feeds button on the Command bar is orange. To subscribe to the feed, click the Feeds button, and then on the page that appears, click the Subscribe to this feed link. The feed is added to the Feeds tab in the Favorites Center. When the feed is up-

dated, the feed name on the Feeds tab is bold. Click it to see the list of updated stories from the Web page.

A **Web Slice** is a portion of a Web page that is frequently updated. If a Web page provides a Web Slice, the Feeds button on the Command bar is green. To subscribe to a Web Slice, click the green Feeds button, and then in the dialog box that opens, click Add to Favorites Bar. As with a feed, when the Web Slice is updated, the button on the Favorites bar is bold, and you can click it to view the updated content.

Using the History List

The **History list** tracks the Web pages you visit over a certain time period, not just during a browsing session. The History list contains the URLs for the Web sites and pages that you have visited. To display the History list, you open a panel called the Favorites Center, and then click the History button. To return to a page in the History list, click the Web site's entry in the list for a particular day, and then click the URL to revisit a specific page on that site. By default, the entries in the History list are organized into date folders (Today, Yesterday, Two Weeks ago, and so on). Within each date folder, there is a folder for every Web site you visited. Within each site folder, the Web pages you visited appear in alphabetical order.

ACTIVITY

Use the History list and unpin the Favorites Center.

1 In the Favorites Center, click the **History tab**. The History list appears in the Favorites Center.

feed Frequently updated Web site content, such as news or blogs, delivered directly to your browser.

Web Slice A portion of a Web page that is frequently updated and delivered to your browser.

History list A list that tracks the Web pages you visit over a certain time period.

2 Click the **Today link** to expand that folder. A list of Web sites you visited today appears in alphabetical order, with a separate folder for each site. See Exhibit 5-25.

3 In the list, click the **usa (www.usa.gov) folder link**, and then click the **Contact Us: USA.gov link**. The

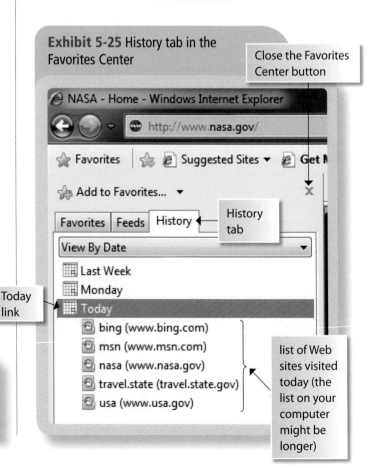

Exhibit 5-25 History tab in the Favorites Center

Close the Favorites Center button

History tab

Today link

list of Web sites visited today (the list on your computer might be longer)

Copyright Law and the Internet

Recall that copyright is the legal right to sell, publish, or distribute an original artistic or literary work; it is held by the creator of a work as soon as it exists in physical form. Before you download or copy graphics, maps, images, sounds, or information from Web sites that you visit, you need to find out if and how you can use the materials and then, if necessary, get permission from the owner of the content. Some Web sites include their copyright and permission request information on their home pages. Some Web sites indicate that the material is free, but almost everything on the Internet is copyrighted. Under the fair use policy, you can use copyrighted material for educational or nonprofit purposes, as opposed to commercial profit. Information that is considered factual and materials that are so old that copyright protection no longer exists also fall under the category of fair use. You should still give credit to any Web site that you use in your research. By carefully checking the copyright and permission policies of the Web sites you visit, you can ensure that you make the right decision regarding if and how you can use the content you find and avoid violating any copyright laws.

The guidelines for citing Web page content are similar to those for written sources. In general, the author, date of publication, and article or Web page title are listed along with a "Retrieved" statement listing the date the article was retrieved from the Internet and the URL of the Web page used to retrieve the article. If in doubt when preparing a research paper, check with your instructor as to the style manual, such as APA, Modern Language Association (MLA), or Chicago Manual of Style, he or she prefers you to follow and refer to that guide for direction.

Favorites Center closes and the Contact Us page on the USA.gov Web site loads in the current tab.

4 In the upper-right corner of the Favorites Center, point to the **Close the Favorites Center button** ☒, and then click the **Close the Favorites Center button** ☒. The Favorites Center closes, and the browser window resizes as large as possible on the screen.

> ➤ **Tip:** To delete your browsing history, click the Safety button on the Command bar, and then click Delete Browsing History. Select the items you want to delete, and then click Delete.

Purchasing a copyrighted item does not change the creator's copyright protection; you cannot legally duplicate it or portray the item as your own creation.

Printing a Web Page

It is not always easy to read a Web page on a computer monitor, especially if the page presents a large amount of information. Printing the page might seem like the best option. However, Web pages are not usually designed with printing in mind. The default letter-size paper is 8½ × 11. A Web page could be wider than your paper, especially if it is designed for a large, high-resolution screen. In this case, text might wrap to another page; however, large graphics and tables might not wrap correctly, causing problems when you print. Because of this, before you print a Web page, it's a good idea to preview it. Changing the orientation from portrait to landscape might help to better accommodate the text and graphics on the page. Then, if necessary, open the Page Setup dialog box and change other settings to adjust the Web page to fit better on the paper. You can also adjust the margins. When you open the Print dialog box, you can select a printer, change the number of pages to print, or change the number of copies to print.

Many Web pages provide a link to a separate printer-friendly version of the page. This option controls what is printed, including only essential information and ensuring that it will print in an appropriate format.

ACTIVITY

Print a Web page.

1 On the Command bar, click the **Print button arrow** [icon], and then click **Print Preview**. The Print Preview window opens on top of the Web browser window. See Exhibit 5-26. The title of the Web page and the page number appear in the header, and the URL and the current date appear in the footer.

2 On the toolbar, click the **Landscape button** [icon]. The orientation of the page in the preview changes to landscape.

3 On the toolbar, click the **Page Setup button** [icon]. The Page Setup dialog box opens. See Exhibit 5-27. Notice

> ➤ **Tip:** You can also click Page Setup on the Print button menu to open the Page Setup dialog box.

that in addition to the commands that appear on the toolbar, you can also customize the header and footer.

4 In the Headers and Footers section, under Header, click the **–Empty– arrow**, and then click Custom. The Custom dialog box opens with the insertion point in the empty box.

5 Type your name, and then click **OK**. The dialog box closes.

6 In the Page Setup dialog box, click **OK**. The Page Setup dialog box closes, and your name appears in the center of the header.

7 On the toolbar in the Print Preview window, click the **Print button** [icon]. The Print dialog box opens. See Exhibit 5-28.

8 In the Page Range section, click the **Pages option button**. In the box next to Pages, 1 is selected.

Exhibit 5-26 Print Preview window in Internet Explorer

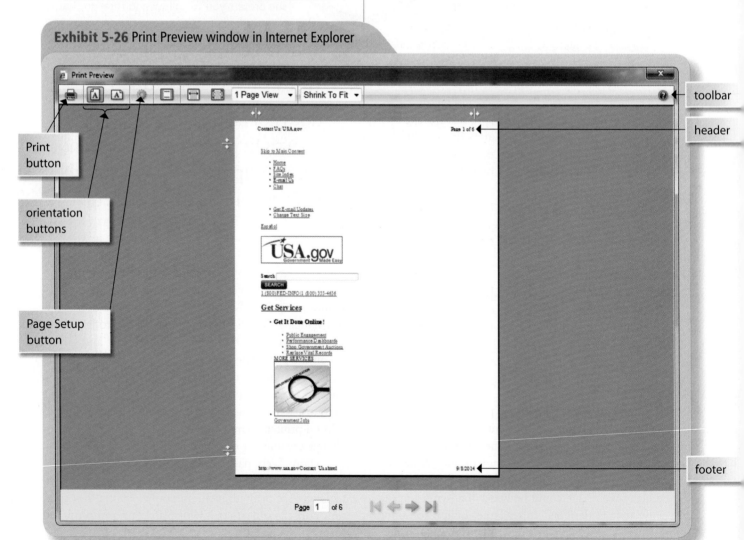

Print button

orientation buttons

Page Setup button

toolbar

header

footer

Exhibit 5-27 Page Setup dialog box in Internet Explorer

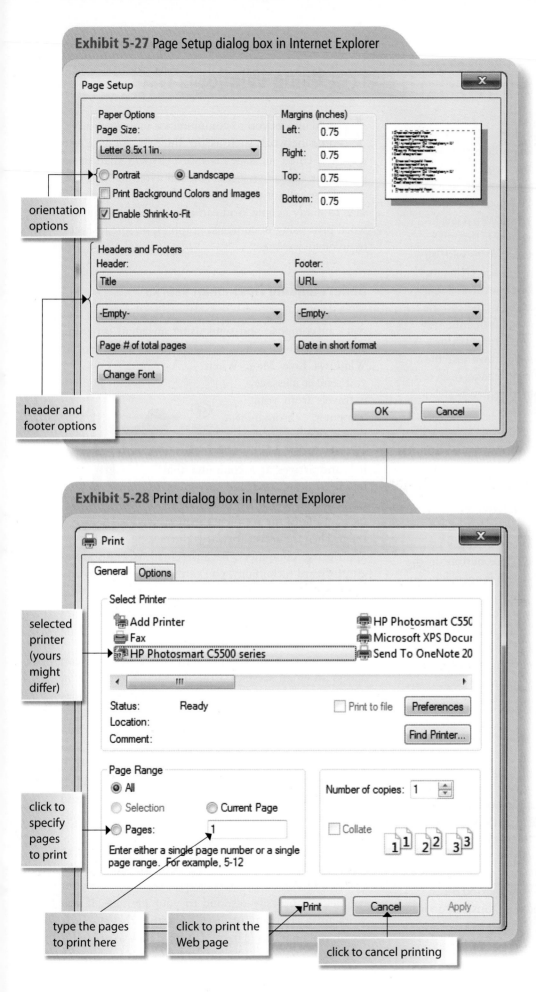

orientation options

header and footer options

Exhibit 5-28 Print dialog box in Internet Explorer

selected printer (yours might differ)

click to specify pages to print

type the pages to print here

click to print the Web page

click to cancel printing

9 Type **3**. Now only the third page will print.

10 If you are instructed to print, click **Print**. If your instructor does not want you to print, click **Cancel**. If you clicked Print, the dialog box and the Print Preview window close, the Contact Us page on the USA.gov Web site appears in the normal Internet Explorer window, and page 3 prints. If you clicked Cancel, the dialog box closes and the Print Preview window is still open.

11 If the Print Preview window is still open, in the upper-right corner of the Print Preview window, click the **Close button**. The Print Preview window closes and the Contact Us page on the USA.gov Web site appears in the normal Internet Explorer window. The changes you made to the header in the Page Setup dialog box are saved, so you will change the middle part of the header back to Empty.

12 On the Command bar, click the **Print button arrow**, and then click **Page Setup**. The Page Setup dialog box opens again.

13 In the Headers and Footers section, under Header, click the **Custom arrow**, and then click **-Empty-**.

14 Click **OK**. The Page Setup dialog box closes.

Saving a Web Page

If you want to save a Web page, click the Page button on the Command bar, and then click Save As to open the Save Webpage dialog box. Depending on what portion of the Web page you want to save, you can click the Save as type arrow and choose from four options. The Webpage, complete (*htm,*.html) option saves the entire Web page, including its graphics and other elements that make up the page. This option creates a folder with all of the site's related files, including page elements, such as images and sounds. The Web Archive, single file (*.mht) option saves a "picture" of the current Web page, without any of the page elements. The two other options—Webpage, HTML only (*htm,*. html) and Text File (*.txt)—let you save just the HTML code or the text from the Web page, respectively, without saving the graphics, frames, or styles on the Web page.

Exiting Internet Explorer

When you are done using Internet Explorer, you can end the Internet Explorer session. If you have only one tab open, you close Internet Explorer the same way you do any other program, using the Close button on the title bar. However, if more than one tab is open, you can choose to close one tab to leave a Web page instead of closing Internet Explorer entirely. To close the tab for the current Web page, click its Close Tab button. If you have more than one tab open and you close Internet Explorer, a dialog box will open asking if you want to close all tabs before exiting the program.

Exit Internet Explorer.

1 In the upper-right corner of the title bar, click the **Close button** ▬ **X** ▬.
A dialog box opens, asking if you want to close all tabs or the current tab.

2 Click **Close all tabs** to close all the tabs and exit Internet Explorer.

▲ **Tip:** To automatically close all tabs when you exit Internet Explorer, click the Always close all tabs check box before clicking the Close all tabs button in the dialog box.

LO5.5 Using Windows Mail

Email allows you to communicate with other users on a network such as the Internet. Sending and receiving email messages is more efficient than using ground or airmail services. You can avoid making several phone calls or printing memos by sending one message to many people. You can also attach files, such as word processing documents, graphics, or spreadsheets, to an email message.

Understanding How Email Works

An email message is a simple text document that you can compose and send using an email program, also called email client software, such as Microsoft Windows Live Mail. When you send a message, it travels from your computer, through the network, such as a LAN or the Internet, and arrives at a computer that has been designated and set up as an email server, which stores the email messages until the recipients request them. Then the server forwards the messages to the appropriate computers. Because email uses this store-and-forward technology, you can send messages to any users on the network, even if they do not have their computers turned on. When it's convenient, your recipients log on to the network and use their email programs to receive and read their messages.

If your computer is not part of a LAN, you can access an email server via the Internet. To do so, you open an email account with a service that provides Internet access. For example, email accounts are included as part of the subscription fee for America Online (AOL) and most ISPs. Email accounts are also provided free of charge by advertiser-supported Web sites, such as Yahoo! and Hotmail. After you establish an email account, you can connect to the Internet and go to the service provider's Web site to access your email account.

The email address you use directs the message to its destination. Your email address is included as the return address in any message you send, so that your recipients can easily respond to your message. If you work for a company or attend a school that provides email, you might have been instructed how to apply for

Tom Wang /Shutterstock.com

Writing Effective and Appropriate Email Messages

When you communicate using email, the information you send might be read by users other than the intended recipient(s), especially if you work for a corporation or private institution, so be aware that email is not private. Keep the following guidelines in mind as you compose email messages:

▶ Use appropriate language—that is, do not use slang, abbreviations that others might not understand, or profanity. Humor and sarcasm can also be misinterpreted in an email.

▶ Provide meaningful information in the subject line to clearly indicate the contents of the message. Even after people read your message, the subject helps them quickly locate information they might need later.

▶ Keep the content of the message short and related to the topic in the subject line.

▶ State any action that you expect the recipient to take, indicating the timeframe, if appropriate.

▶ Limit the file size of attachments so downloading your message doesn't take too long. Note that most email servers limit the size of the files you can send or receive as attachments.

▶ Check the spelling in the message, and proofread it before you send it.

An email message, like any written document, reflects your ability to communicate clearly and effectively—an important skill in any personal, academic, or professional endeavor. By following these guidelines, you can ensure that recipients of your email messages are not distracted by inappropriate language or tone, or confused by typing or grammatical errors.

---

an email account or you might have been assigned one by a system administrator. In other situations, you create your own email address, though it must follow a particular format.

The email address *john_wynn@wynnco.biz* is a typical email address. It begins with a username, or login ID; in this case, *john_wynn*. This is the name that you enter or are assigned when your email account is set up. The @ symbol signifies that the email server name will be provided next—which, in this case, is *wynnco.biz*.

Downloading Windows Live Mail

Windows Live Mail is a free email program that allows you to send, receive, and manage email. You can send email to and receive email from anyone in the world who has an email address, regardless of the operating system or type of computer the person is using.

If your email address changes, you can subscribe to an email forwarding service so you don't miss any mail that might be sent to your old address.

You must download and install Windows Live Mail before you can use it. Once Windows Live Mail is installed, you sign in to it with your email username and a password.

 **ACTIVITY**

Check to see if Windows Live Mail is installed.

1 On the taskbar, click the **Start button** ⊞. The insertion point is blinking in the Search programs and files box at the bottom of the Start menu.

2 Type **Windows Live Mail**. The Start menu changes to display items that match those keywords. If Windows Live Mail appears at the top of the list under Programs, then it is installed on your computer. If Windows Live Mail did not appear under Programs when you conducted your search, it is not installed, and you need to download and install it before you can use it.

3 Click a blank area of the desktop to close the Start menu without selecting anything.

If Windows Live Mail is not installed on your computer, complete the next Activity. If it is installed, skip the next Activity and go to the section titled "Sending and Receiving Email Using Windows Live Mail."

**Download and install
Windows Live Mail.**

1 Start **Internet Explorer**.
Click in the **Address bar**,
type **explore.live.com** and
then press the **Enter key**.
A Web page listing the
Windows Live programs
appears.

⚠ **Problem?** If the URL
isn't valid, click in the
Search box to the right
of the Address bar,
type **Windows Live
Essentials** and then
click the result link that
lists Windows Live Mail.

2 Click the **Essentials link**.
Windows Live Mail is one
of several programs you
can download.

3 Click the **Download now link**. The File Download –
Security Warning dialog box opens.

4 Click **Run**. The dialog box closes, the program
downloads, and then the User Account Control
dialog box opens asking if you want to allow the
program to make changes to the computer.

5 Click **Yes**. The dialog box closes, and then Windows Live installer starts. After a moment, it lists
the programs available with Windows Live. See
Exhibit 5-29.

6 Click the check
boxes next to all
the programs except
Mail to deselect
them.

⚠ **Problem?** If Mail has
a green check mark
next to it instead of a
check box, it is already
installed. Click **Cancel**
and skip the rest of
the steps in this set of
steps.

7 Click **Install**. The
dialog box changes
to tell you that some
programs, including
Internet Explorer, need to be closed before you
install the programs. The Close these programs for
me option button is selected.

Exhibit 5-29 List of Windows Live Essentials programs

8 Click **Continue**. Internet Explorer closes, and the
dialog box changes to show the progress of the
installation. After the program is installed, the
dialog box changes to tell you that you're almost
done, and asks you to select your settings to set
your search provider, your home page, and to
improve Windows Live. The first two check boxes
set options in Internet Explorer, and the last one
collects information about your system and periodically sends it to Microsoft.

9 Click the **Set your search provider check box** to
deselect it. Click the **Set your home page check box**
to deselect it. If you want, click the **Help improve
Windows Live check box** to select it.

10 Click **Continue**. Internet Explorer starts again.

11 On the title bar, click the **Close button** [X]
to close the Internet Explorer window. The
Windows Live installation dialog box says
"Welcome to Windows Live" and asks if you
have a Windows Live ID. You will not sign up
for one at this time.

12 Click **Close**. The installation is complete.

Sending and Receiving Email Using Windows Live Mail

To use Windows Live Mail, you need an Internet connection, an email address, and a password. The first thing you need to do is start the program.

Start Windows Live Mail.

1 On the taskbar, click the **Start button** , point to **All Programs**, scroll to the bottom of the list, and then click the **Windows Live folder**. The list of Windows Live programs installed on your computer appears.

2 Click **Windows Live Mail**. The Start menu closes and Windows Live Mail starts.

3 If the window does not already fill your screen, on the title bar, click the **Maximize button** .

Now you need to create an account. To do this, you need to have a valid email address and a password from an ISP.

Create an email account.

1 If the Add your email account dialog box is not already open, click the **Accouts tab** and then click the **Email button**. The Add an E-mail Account dialog box opens. See Exhibit 5-30.

2 Type your email address, click in the **Password box**, and then type your password. If you are working on a public computer, click the **Remember password check box** to deselect it.

3 Click in the **Display Name box**, and then type your first and last name.

4 Click **Next**. The dialog box changes to display a message asking you if you want to sign in using your email address.

5 Click **Yes**. Enter your email address and password and then click **Sign in**. A dialog box opens saying your email account was added.

Exhibit 5-30 Add an E-mail Account dialog box

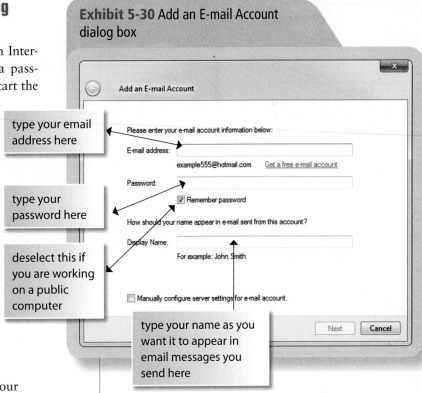

type your email address here

type your password here

deselect this if you are working on a public computer

type your name as you want it to appear in email messages you send here

6 Click **Finish**. The dialog box closes and the account and its folders appear in the pane on the left. Exhibit 5-31 shows the Windows Live Mail window with two emails in the Inbox. The various elements in the Mail window are labeled in the exhibit.

⚠ **Problem?** If you don't see folders below your account name in the pane on the left, point to your account name, and then click the **Expand arrow** ▷.

An email message looks similar to a memo, with header lines for Date, To, From, Cc, and Subject, followed by the body of the message. The Date line shows the date on which you send the message and the From line lists your name or email address; these lines are not visible in the window in which you create your email message. You complete the other lines. The To line lists the email addresses of one or more recipients. The Cc line lists the email addresses of anyone who will receive a courtesy copy of the message, and the Bcc line lists the email addresses of anyone who will receive a blind courtesy copy of the message. Bcc recipients are not visible to each other or to the To and Cc recipients. The Subject line provides a quick overview of the message topic,

Exhibit 5-31 Windows Live Mail window listing the messages in the Inbox

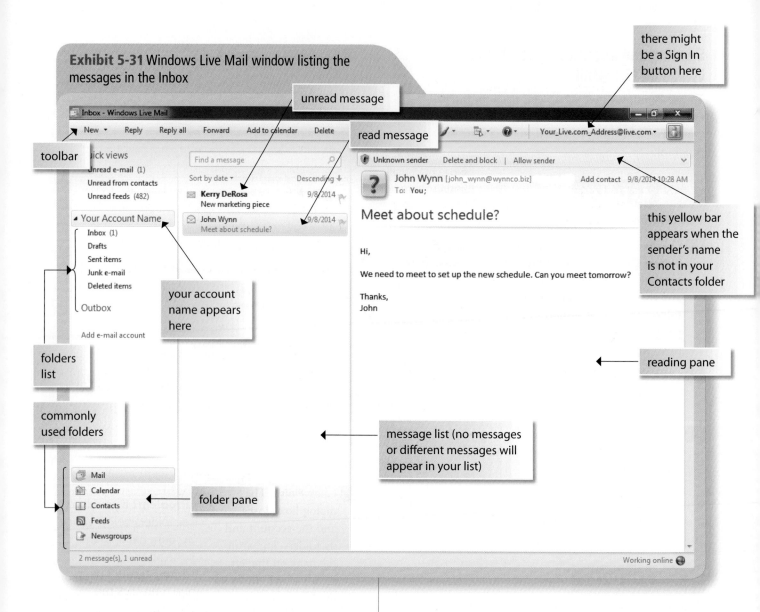

there might be a Sign In button here

unread message

read message

toolbar

this yellow bar appears when the sender's name is not in your Contacts folder

your account name appears here

reading pane

folders list

commonly used folders

message list (no messages or different messages will appear in your list)

folder pane

---

similar to a headline. The main part of the email is the message body.

When you click the Sync button, Windows Live Mail moves the message from your computer to your email server, which routes it to the recipient. It also keeps a copy of the message in the Sent items folder, which you can open to see all the messages you have sent or replied to.

Setting Up a Hotmail Account in Windows Mail

If you have a Windows Live ID, you can set up your Hotmail account in Windows Live Mail so that you can check your Hotmail account from Windows Mail. (If you have a Hotmail account, then you already have a Windows Live ID. If you need a Windows Live ID, you can create one by going to the Windows Live home page at home.live.com.) To do this, in the Add an E-mail Account dialog box that opens when you click the Add e-mail account link, type your live.com or hotmail.com email address in the E-mail address box and the corresponding password in the Password box. After you create the account, a bar appears at the top of the Windows Live Mail window asking you to click Download to download the folders associated with that account. Click Download, and the folders and messages stored on your Hotmail account will download to your computer.

Create and send an email message.

1 On the toolbar, click the **New button**. A New Message window opens.

2 To the right of the Subject box, click the **Show Cc & Bcc link**. The Cc and Bcc boxes appear below the To box and above the Subject box. See Exhibit 5-32.

> ⚠ **Problem?** If the link to the right of the Subject box is Hide Cc & Bcc, the Cc and Bcc boxes are already displayed. Skip Step 2.

3 Click in the **To box**, and then type your email address.

4 Click in the **Subject box**, and then type **Test Message**. On the title bar, the name of the window changes to Test Message.

5 Click in the large box in the bottom half of the Test Message window, type **This is a test message.**, press the **Enter key** twice, and then type your name.

6 In the Test Message window, on the toolbar, click the **Send button**. The message is moved to the Outbox folder before it is routed to the email server. Unless a problem occurs, you probably won't notice this transmission; it occurs quickly.

7 In the folders list, click the **Sent items folder**. The message list changes to display the list of messages that you have sent.

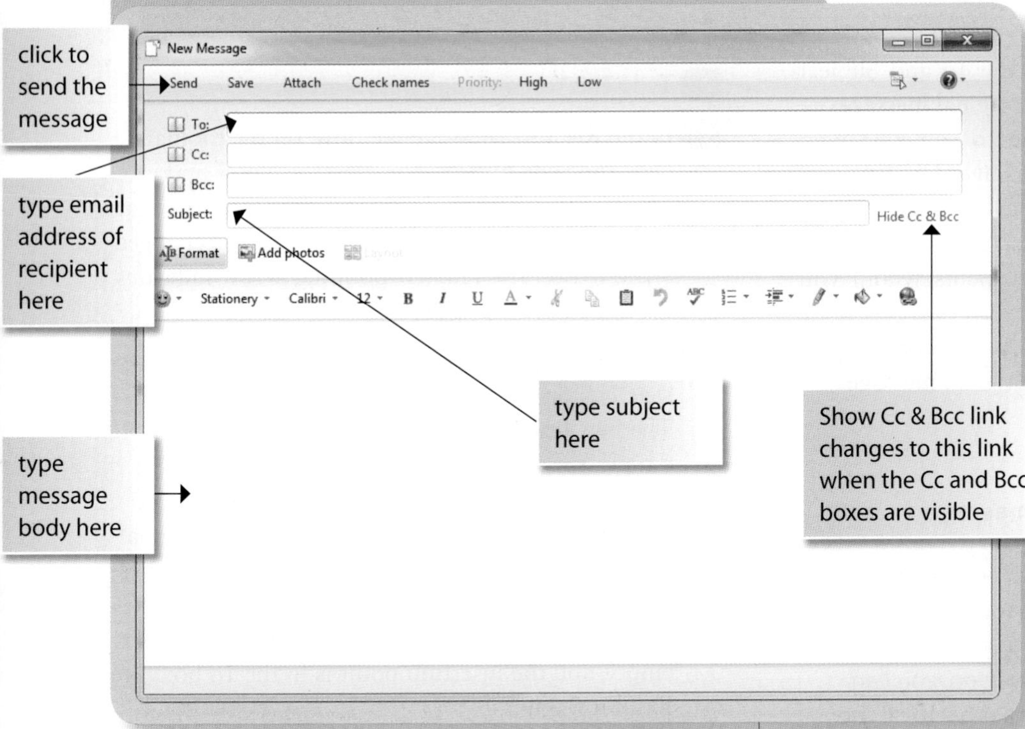

Windows Live Mail transfers, or downloads, messages addressed to you from your email server to your Inbox. After messages have been downloaded to your Inbox, they appear in a list with the name of the sender and the subject displayed; unread messages appear in bold, with an unread mail icon. The number of unread messages appears in parentheses to the right of the Inbox folder. To preview a message, you click the message in the list to display its contents in the reading pane, or you can double-click the message to open it in a separate window. You can also print the messages that you receive.

Exhibit 5-32 New Message window

click to send the message

type email address of recipient here

type message body here

type subject here

Show Cc & Bcc link changes to this link when the Cc and Bcc boxes are visible

Focusing on only one topic per email keeps each conversation thread distinct and makes it simpler to find all the messages related to that topic.

Receive and read an email message.

1 In the folders list, click the **Inbox folder**. The message list changes to show the list of messages in your Inbox.

2 On the toolbar, click the **Sync button**. Windows Live Mail downloads your email messages from the email server, and Test Message appears in the message list.

3 In the message list, click **Test Message**. The content of the selected message appears in the reading pane and, to indicate that you have read the message, the read mail icon  appears next to the name of the sender in the Inbox.

Replying to and Forwarding Email Messages

Some of the email you receive will ask you to provide information, answer questions, or confirm decisions. Instead of creating a new email message, you can reply directly to a message that you received. As part of the reply, Windows Live Mail fills in the To and Subject boxes, and includes the text of the original message.

You can also send a message to someone who wasn't included on the original message. The Forward feature creates a copy of the original message subject and body, but leaves the To, Cc, and Bcc boxes blank. You can enter the recipient or recipients whom you want to receive a copy of the message.

With both the reply to and forward features, you can add a new message above the original message.

ACTIVITY

Reply to and forward an email message.

1 Make sure Test Message is selected in the message list, and then on the toolbar, click the **Reply button**. The Re: Test Message window opens. Your name or email address appears in the To box, and Re: Test Message appears in the Subject box. The original message appears in the bottom portion of the message body, and the insertion point is in the message body above the original message. See Exhibit 5-33.

Tip: If copies of the message have been sent to more than one person, you can send a reply to all the recipients at once by clicking the Reply all button.

Exhibit 5-33 Message window with a reply

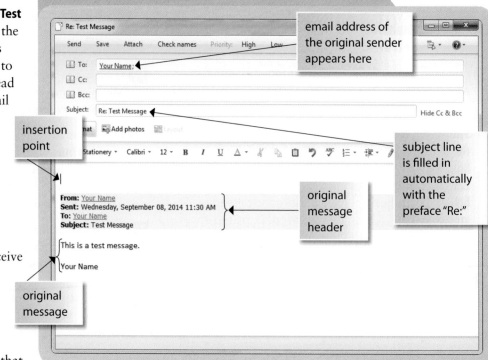

2 Type **This test message was received.**

3 In the Re: Test Message window, on the toolbar, click the **Send button**. The message closes and is sent to your Outbox. In the message list, note that the icon for the original Test Message has changed again to [icon]. The red, left-pointing arrow indicates that you have replied to this message.

4 With the original Test Message selected in the message list, on the toolbar, click the **Forward button**. The Fw: Test Message window opens. As with a reply, the subject line is filled in automatically, although with Fw: prefacing the original subject to indicate it is a forwarded message. The original message appears in the bottom portion of the message body. With forwarded messages, the To box is not filled in automatically. Instead, the To box is empty, and the insertion point is in the To box. See Exhibit 5-34.

5 In the To box, type your email address.

6 Click in the blank area of the message body above the copied original message, type **This is an example of a forwarded message.**, and then on the toolbar, click the **Send button**. The message closes and is sent to your Outbox. In the message list, the icon for the original Test Message is now [icon]. The green, right-pointing arrow indicates that this message has been forwarded.

Exhibit 5-34 Message window with a forwarded message

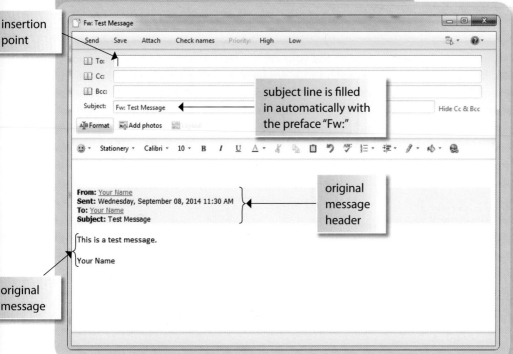

insertion point

subject line is filled in automatically with the preface "Fw:"

original message header

original message

Fw: Test Message

Send   Save   Attach   Check names   Priority: High   Low

To:
Cc:
Bcc:
Subject: Fw: Test Message   Hide Cc & Bcc

Format   Add photos   Layout

Stationery   Calibri   10   B   I   U   A   ✂   🔲   📋   ↺   💬   ☰   ⊞   ✎   🔊   😊

From: Your Name
Sent: Wednesday, September 08, 2014 11:30 AM
To: Your Name
Subject: Test Message

This is a test message.

Your Name

Reply All and Forwarding

It's important to use the Reply and Reply All features appropriately. If not all message recipients need to read your reply, use the Reply feature so that you do not clutter others' Inboxes unnecessarily, and so that you don't inadvertently send a reply to many people when you meant to send it to one person. Likewise, if it's important that everyone who received the original email remain in the "conversation" created by the email chain, be sure to use the Reply All feature so that no one is left out by mistake. When you forward a message, be aware that you might be forwarding private email addresses contained in the header in the original message. Finally, be aware that there is nothing to stop anyone to whom you send, reply, or forward a message from forwarding it on to others, including people you don't know.

CAUTION

Mike Flippo/Shutterstock.com

7 If the reply and forwarded messages are not in your Inbox, on the toolbar, click the **Sync button**.

Deleting Email Messages

After you read and respond to your messages, you can delete any message that you no longer need. When you delete a message from the Inbox, it moves to the Deleted items folder. Just as your Inbox will accumulate lots of messages, your Deleted items folder will too; therefore, you should empty the contents of this folder periodically. Doing so permanently removes those items from your computer. To empty the Deleted items folder, right-click it in the Folders list, click Empty 'Deleted items' folder on the shortcut menu, and then click Yes in the confirmation box to confirm the deletion. You can move a deleted message from the Deleted items folder to another folder if you don't want the message permanently deleted; however, once the Deleted items folder is emptied, the message no longer exists on your computer.

ACTIVITY

Delete email messages.

1 In the message list, click **Test Message** to select it, if it is not already selected.

2 On the toolbar, click the **Delete button**. The selected message is moved to the Deleted items folder.

3 In the message list, click **Re: Test Message** to select it, press and hold the **Ctrl key**, and then click **Fw: Test Message**. Both messages are selected.

4 On the toolbar, click the **Delete button**. The selected messages are moved to the Deleted items folder.

5 In the folders list, click the **Sent items folder**.

Email Privacy

Many people mistakenly believe that the email they send and receive is private and will never be read by anyone other than the intended recipient. Because email is transmitted over public media, however, only encrypted (electronically scrambled) email can be transmitted safely. Although unlikely to happen to your personal email, nonencrypted email can be intercepted and read by someone else. Consequently, from a privacy standpoint, a nonencrypted email message should be viewed more like a postcard than a letter.

It is also important to realize that your em-ployer and your ISP have access to the email you send through those organizations. Businesses and ISPs typically archive (keep copies of) email messages that travel through their servers and are required to comply with subpoenas from law enforcement agencies for archived email messages.

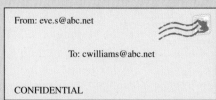

Chris,

The meeting is Monday at 2 pm. Please bring all related personnel files detailing the anticipated firing of Joe D.

Eve

To: cwilliams@abc.net
From: eve.s@abc.net

From: eve.s@abc.net

To: cwilliams@abc.net

CONFIDENTIAL

REGULAR (NONENCRYPTED EMAIL) = POSTCARD   **ENCRYPTED EMAIL = SEALED LETTER**

---

6 In the message list, select the **Test Message**, **Re: Test Message**, and **Fw: Test Message messages**, and then move them to the **Deleted items folder**.

> **Tip:** You can also right-click the Deleted items folder, and then click Empty 'Deleted Items' folder.

7 In the folders list, click the **Deleted items folder**. The messages you deleted appear in the message list, and the Empty this folder button ⊠ appears to the right of Deleted items.

8 Next to the Deleted items folder, click the **Empty this folder button** ⊠. A dialog box opens asking if you are sure you want to permanently delete the contents of the 'Deleted Items' folder.

9 Click **Yes**. The dialog box closes and the messages in the Deleted items folder are permanently deleted.

10 In the folders list, click the **Inbox folder**. Any messages that are still in your Inbox appear in the message list.

> **contact** Each person or organization with whom you communicate and about whom you store information.

Adding Contacts to the Contacts Folder

The Contacts folder is an address book where you store information about the people and businesses with whom you communicate. Each person or organization is called a **contact**. You can store business-related information about each contact, including job title, phone and fax numbers, postal and Web addresses, and email addresses, as well as more personal information, such as birthdays, anniversaries, and spouse and children's names.

ACTIVITY

Add contacts to the Contacts folder.

1 At the bottom of the folder pane, click the **Contacts button**. The Windows Live Contacts window opens. See Exhibit 5-35.

2 On the toolbar, click the **New button**. The Add a Contact dialog box opens. Quick add is selected in the list of forms on the left. See Exhibit 5-36. The form that appears by default is the Quick add form in which you can enter basic contact information.

3 In the list of forms, click **Contact**. The dialog box changes to show the fields available in the Contact form. The insertion point is in the First name box.

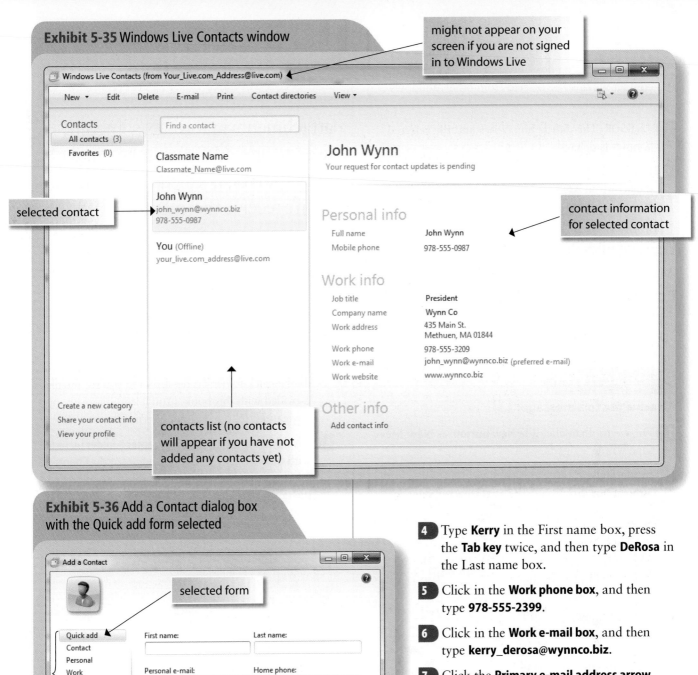

Exhibit 5-35 Windows Live Contacts window

might not appear on your screen if you are not signed in to Windows Live

Windows Live Contacts (from Your_Live.com_Address@live.com)

New ▾   Edit   Delete   E-mail   Print   Contact directories   View ▾

Contacts
All contacts (3)
Favorites (0)

Find a contact

Classmate Name
Classmate_Name@live.com

selected contact

John Wynn
john_wynn@wynnco.biz
978-555-0987

You (Offline)
your_live.com_address@live.com

Create a new category
Share your contact info
View your profile

contacts list (no contacts will appear if you have not added any contacts yet)

John Wynn
Your request for contact updates is pending

contact information for selected contact

Personal info
Full name   John Wynn
Mobile phone   978-555-0987

Work info
Job title   **President**
Company name   **Wynn Co**
Work address   435 Main St.
                     Methuen, MA 01844
Work phone   978-555-3209
Work e-mail   john_wynn@wynnco.biz (preferred e-mail)
Work website   www.wynnco.biz

Other info
Add contact info

Exhibit 5-36 Add a Contact dialog box with the Quick add form selected

Add a Contact

selected form

Quick add
Contact
Personal
Work
IM
Notes
IDs

First name: Last name:

Personal e-mail: Home phone:

Company:

list of forms

Add contact   Cancel

4 Type **Kerry** in the First name box, press the **Tab key** twice, and then type **DeRosa** in the Last name box.

5 Click in the **Work phone box**, and then type **978-555-2399**.

6 Click in the **Work e-mail box**, and then type **kerry_derosa@wynnco.biz**.

7 Click the **Primary e-mail address arrow**, and then click **Work**. This sets Kerry's work email address as the default email address.

8 At the bottom of the dialog box, click **Add contact**. The dialog box closes, and Kerry DeRosa appears in the contacts list.

9 Add your own information as a contact. You can delete contacts if you no longer need them.

> **Tip:** To print a list of contacts, click the Print button on the toolbar.

10 In the contacts list, click **Kerry DeRosa**, and then on the toolbar, click the **Delete button**.

A warning dialog box appears telling you that the contact will also be deleted from other Windows Live locations.

11 Click **OK**. The dialog box closes and the selected contact is deleted.

12 In the Windows Live Contacts window, click the **Close button** ❌. The window closes and the Windows Live Mail window appears.

Working with Attachments

An **attachment** is a file that you send with an email message. The file content does not appear within the message body, and the recipients can save the file to their computer, and then open, edit, and print it just as they can a file they created.

 **ACTIVITY**

Attach a file to a message.

1 On the toolbar, click the **New button**. A New Message window opens.

2 In the To box, type your email address, click in the **Subject box**, and then type **First Quarter Sales**.

> ▶ **Tip:** If the name you are entering as a recipient is listed in your contacts list, the name appears just below the box as you are typing it, and you can click it to add the name as a recipient.

3 Click in the message body box, type **Hi,** (including the comma), press the **Enter key** twice, type **The attached workbook contains the sales numbers from the first quarter. Let me know if you have any questions.**, press the **Enter key** twice, and then type your name.

attachment A file that you send with an email message.

If an ISP does not accept messages with large attachments or attachments in formats sometimes used to spread viruses, the sender might not be notified that a recipient didn't receive the message.

4 In the First Quarter Sales window, on the toolbar, click the **Attach button**. The Open dialog box appears.

5 In the pane on the left, click the drive or folder containing the files you need as you work through the steps in this book. In the right side of the dialog box, double-click folders as needed until you see the files provided with this book. (You'll learn more about navigating to drives and folders in Chapter 7.)

6 Display the contents of the **Chapter 5 folder** included with this book, display the contents of the **Chapter folder**, click the data file **Quarterly Sales**, and then at the bottom of the dialog box, click **Open**. The dialog box closes, and the file is listed as an attachment below the subject, as shown in Exhibit 5-37.

Exhibit 5-37 Message window with an attachment

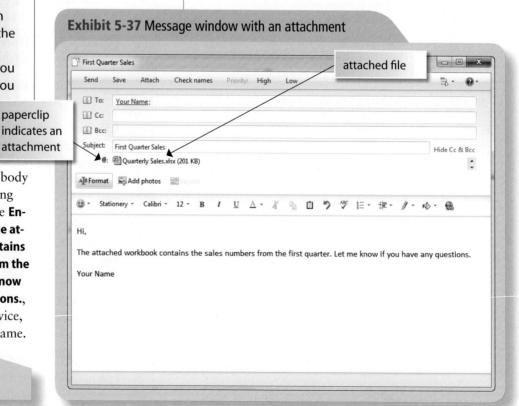

paperclip indicates an attachment

attached file

Exhibit 5-38 Message with an attachment selected in the message list

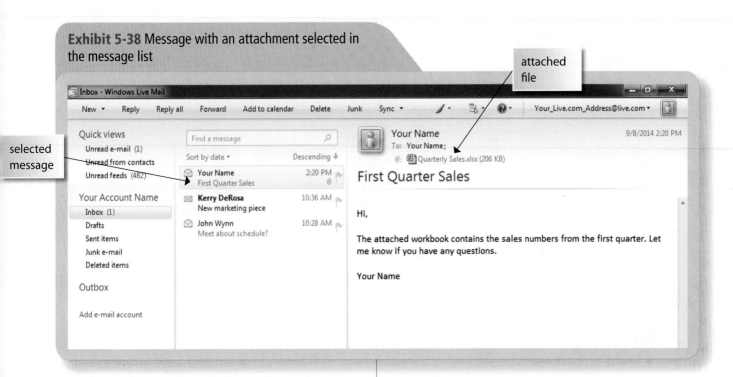

selected message

attached file

---

7. On the toolbar, click the **Send button**. The message window closes and is sent, along with the attached file.

Large Attachments

If you attach a large file to an email message, it might take a long time for your recipient to download your message. Most email servers limit the size of the files you can attach; some allow files no larger than 1 MB. Check with your correspondents before sending large file attachments to find out about size restrictions and to set up a convenient time to send the attachment.

When you receive a message that contains an attachment, you can choose to open or save the attachment. To open the attachment, you need to make sure the program used to create the attachment is installed on your computer. If the program is not installed, sometimes you can use a text editor, such as WordPad or Notepad, to open and read the attached file.

 **ACTIVITY**

Open a message attachment.

1. If the First Quarter Sales message is not in your Inbox, on the toolbar, click the **Sync button**. The First Quarter Sales message appears in the message list. A paperclip appears below the time that the message was received in the message list to indicate that an attachment is included in the message.

2. In the message list, click the **First Quarter Sales message**. The message appears in the reading pane, and the attachment is listed in the message header. See Exhibit 5-38.

3. In the reading pane, double-click **Quarterly Sales.xlsx**. The Mail Attachment dialog box opens asking if you want to open the file.

   ⚠ **Problem?** If the Mail Attachment dialog box did not open, someone deselected the Always ask before opening this type of file check box in that dialog box. Skip Step 4.

4. Click **Open**. The Microsoft Excel program starts and the file opens in the Excel window.

5. On the right end of the title bar, click the **Close button** ❌. The Excel window closes.

6. Delete the **First Quarter Sales message** from the Inbox and Sent items folders, and then empty the Deleted items folder.

7 On the title bar of the Windows Live Mail window, click the Close button ![x]. The Windows Live Mail window closes and the program exits.

> ▲ **Tip:** If you want to save the attachment, right-click the attachment, and then on the shortcut menu, click Save as.

Sending Photos

Windows Live Mail lets you avoid using attachments when you send photographs. Instead of attaching photos, which usually are large files, you can click the Add photos button in a New Message window to send thumbnails, which are smaller versions of your photos. Recipients can then click the thumbnails to display larger versions of the photos.

Quiz Yourself

1. What is an Internet service provider?
2. What is a Webinar?
3. Which is more appropriate for collaborating with others—a blog or a wiki?
4. Why do some people object to third-party cookies?
5. What are the two definitions of *home page*?
6. What is a tab group?
7. How are search site databases typically updated?
8. How do you use a search engine to conduct a search?
9. Is the number of hits returned for a particular search phrase always the same from one search site to another? Why or why not?
10. If you want to be able to quickly revisit a Web page, how do you save the URL?
11. What is the History list?
12. What does a printer-friendly version of a Web page provide?
13. What is included in an email message header?
14. What is the difference between replying to an email message and forwarding it?
15. What happens when you delete an email message?
16. What is an attachment?

Practice It

Practice It 5-1

1. Start Internet Explorer, type **www.computerhistory.org** in the Address bar, and then press the Enter key.
2. Click the Exhibits link, and then click the Internet History 1962 to 1992 link. Examine this Web page.
3. Use the Back button to return to the home page on the Computer History Museum Web site.
4. Open a new tab, and then go to **www.archive.org**, the Internet Archive Web site.
5. Open any link on the current Web page in a new tab.
6. Open a new tab, and then conduct a search using **computer history** as the search phrase. In the list of results, click the link to the Computer History page on the Web site computersciencelab.com.
7. Add the home page of the Computer History Museum as a favorite.
8. Close the tabs displaying the home pages of the Computer History Museum and the Computer Science Lab. Add the two Web pages on the Internet Archive Web site as favorites in a folder named **Archive**.
9. In the current tab, use the Favorites list to go to the home page of the Computer History Museum.
10. In a new tab, use the History list to go to the Computer History page on the Computer Science Lab Web site.
11. Display the home page of the Computer History Museum in the Print Preview window, switch the orientation to landscape, and then add your name to the middle portion of the header. If instructed, print page 1.

12. Reset the the middle portion of the header to -Empty-, delete the favorites and the favorites folder you added, and then exit Internet Explorer.

13. Start Windows Live Mail.

14. Create a new email message. Address it to yourself.

15. Type **Web Sites about Computer History** as the subject.

16. Type the following as the message body:

Hi,

The Computer History Museum Web site has several interesting exhibits illustrating the history of computers.

Your Name

17. Send the email, and then download messages from your server to your Inbox.

18. Reply to the Web Sites about Computer History message, typing the following as the message:

Thanks for the information.

19. Forward the Re: Web Sites about Computer History message to yourself. Type the following as the message:

The Internet Archive Web site stores historical, digital collections.

20. Add the following person as a contact, and then select the work email address as the primary email address:

First name: John

Last name: Wynn

Work phone: 978-555-3209

Work e-mail: john_wynn@wynnco.biz

21. Reply to the Fw: Web Sites about Computer History message. Attach the data file **Computer History Sites** located in the Chapter 5/Practice It folder included with this book. Type the following as the message body:

Please see the attached list.

22. When the message with the attachment arrives in your Inbox, open the attachment in Microsoft Word. Exit Word after reading the document.

23. Move the four messages you received from your Inbox to the Deleted items folder. Move the four

messages you sent to the Deleted items folder. Empty the Deleted items folder.

24. Delete the contact John Wynn. Exit Windows Mail.

Practice It 5-2

1. Start Internet Explorer, and then go to **www.yelp.com**. If the URL doesn't change to include a large city near your location at the end of it, click in the Search box on the Yelp.com page, type your city and state, and then click Search.

2. Display the Restaurants category in a new tab, and then click a link for a popular restaurant in that category to read reviews of that restaurant.

3. Open a new tab, and then go to **www.citysearch.com** in the new tab. If the site doesn't automatically display the Citysearch page for a large city near you, click in the Search box on the Citysearch page, type your city and state, and then click GO!

4. Display the Restaurants category in the current tab, and then click links to find reviews of the same restaurant you read about on Yelp.com. (*Hint*: If you can't find the same restaurant by clicking links, click in the Search box on the Citysearch page, type the restaurant name, and then click GO!)

5. Add the pages with reviews on each site as favorites.

6. Print one review of the restaurant you chose.

7. Start Windows Live Mail.

8. Add a friend, classmate, or your instructor as a contact.

9. Create a new email message addressed to the person you added as a contact. Type your email address in the Cc box.

10. Type **Restaurant Suggestion** as the subject. Type the following as the message body, replacing the italicized text with the name of the restaurant about which you read reviews and with your name:

Hi,

I read a review of *Restaurant,* and I think we should plan on going to lunch there.

Your Name

11. If a friend or classmate sent you the message, reply to it; otherwise, reply to the copy that you sent to yourself. Type **Please see the attached file.** as the message body, and then attach the data file **Restaurant Review Sites** located in the Chapter 5/Practice It folder included with this book.

12. Delete the favorites you added, and then exit Internet Explorer. Delete the messages you sent and received, delete the contact you added, and then exit Windows Live Mail.

On Your Own

On Your Own 5-1

1. Start Internet Explorer, and then search for information on Internet hoaxes.

2. Display a result in the current tab, examine the site, and then return to the list of results. Display three more sites in the same manner, returning to the list of results after examining each site.

3. Use the History list to display the home pages of two of the sites you examined in separate tabs. Add these tabs as favorites in a folder named **Hoax Sites**.

4. Close all but one tab, and then search for sites that contain information about Internet scams. Display three results from the results list in new tabs. (Do not display the pages of any Web sites you already visited.) Add these three Web pages as favorites (do not create a folder).

5. Open the Favorites Center, and then open the Organize Favorites dialog box by clicking the Add to Favorites button arrow, and then clicking Organize Favorites. Use the New Folder command in this dialog box to create a new folder named **Scam Sites**. One at a time, select the three favorites that contain information about Internet scams, and then use the Move command in this

dialog box to move these commands into the new folder. Close the dialog box when you are finished.

6. Start Windows Live Mail, and then create a new message.

7. Address the message to your instructor, and add your email address to the Cc box.

8. Type **Helpful Sites** as the subject, and then type the following as the message body, replacing the italicized text with the name of the Web site with information about Internet hoaxes that you liked the best:

Hi,

I think the Web site *Hoax Site* contains useful information about avoiding Internet hoaxes.

Your Name

9. Send the email message.

10. When the message arrives in your Inbox, forward it to your instructor, again Ccing yourself. Add a sentence identifying the site with the most useful information about Internet scams.

11. Delete the message you sent and received, and then exit Windows Mail.

12. In Internet Explorer, close all but one tab, and then go to the site that you identified as containing useful information about Internet hoaxes.

13. Display the Web page in Print Preview, and then examine the page in landscape orientation.

14. Change the page setup so that your name appears in the middle of the footer.

15. Print the page if instructed, and then reset the middle area in the footer to -Empty-.

16. Delete the favorites and favorites folder that you created.

17. Delete your browsing history. To do this, start by clicking the Safety button on the Command bar.

18. Exit Internet Explorer.

ADDITIONAL STUDY TOOLS

Chapter 5

IN THE BOOK

▶ Complete end-of-chapter exercises

▶ Study tear-out Chapter Review Card

ONLINE

▶ Complete additional end-of-chapter exercises

▶ Take practice quiz to prepare for tests

▶ Review key term flash cards (online, printable, and audio)

▶ Play "Beat the Clock" and "Memory" to quiz yourself

▶ Watch the videos "Google 15-Second Search Tips" and "Google Search Plain and Simple"

Network and Internet Security and Privacy

Introduction

Learning Objectives

After studying the material in this chapter, you will be able to:

LO6.1 Explain network and Internet security concerns

LO6.2 Identify online threats

LO6.3 Describe cyberstalking and other personal safety concerns

LO6.4 Assess personal computer security

LO6.5 Identify privacy concerns

LO6.6 Discuss current network and Internet security legislation

Networks and the Internet help many of us be more efficient and effective workers, as well as add convenience and enjoyment to our personal lives. However, the widespread use of home and business networks and the Internet increases the risk of unauthorized computer access, theft, fraud, and other types of computer crime, and the vast amount of business and personal data stored on computers accessible via company networks and the Internet increases the chances of data loss due to crime or employee errors. In addition, our networked society has raised a number of privacy concerns. Although sometimes selected people or organizations have a legitimate need for some types of personal information, there is always the danger that information provided to others will be misused.

This chapter looks at a variety of security and privacy concerns stemming from the use of computer networks and the Internet in our society, and introduces safeguards for each concern, along with an explanation of precautions you can take to reduce the chance that these security problems will happen to you. The chapter also looks at legislation related to network and Internet security.

LO6.1 Understanding Security Concerns

Why should you be concerned about network and Internet security? From a computer virus making your computer function abnormally, to a hacker using your personal information to make fraudulent purchases, to someone harassing you online in a discussion group, a variety of security concerns related to computer networks and the Internet exist.

Many Internet security concerns today can be categorized as computer crimes. **Computer crime**—sometimes referred to as **cybercrime**—includes any illegal act involving a computer. Cybercrime is an important security concern today. It is a multibillion-dollar business that is often conducted by seasoned criminals. In fact, according to the FBI, organized crime organizations in many

computer crime (cybercrime)
Any illegal act involving a computer.

With the growing use of wireless networks, social networking sites, and remote network access, network and Internet security has never been more essential to all computer users.

countries are increasingly turning to computer crime to target millions of potential victims easily, and phishing attacks and other Internet scams are expected to increase in reaction to the recent troubled economy. Other types of computer crime do not include the Internet, such as using a computer to create counterfeit currency or make illegal copies of a DVD.

With some security concerns, such as when a spyware program changes your browser's home page, the consequence may be just an annoyance. In other cases, such as when someone steals your identity and purchases items using your name and credit card number, the consequences are much more serious. In addition, with the growing use of wireless networks, applications such as social networking sites, and individuals accessing company networks remotely, paired with an increasing number of security and privacy regulations that businesses need to comply with, network and Internet security has never been more important. Consequently, all computer users should be aware of the security concerns surrounding computer network and Internet use, and they should take appropriate precautions.

Unauthorized Access and Unauthorized Use

Unauthorized access occurs whenever an individual gains access to a computer, network, file, or other resource without permission—typically by hacking into the resource. **Unauthorized use** involves using a computer resource for unauthorized activities. Often, they happen at the same time, but unauthorized use can occur when a user is authorized to access a particular computer or network but is not authorized for the particular activity the user performs. For instance, students may be authorized to access the Internet via a campus computer lab, but some use, such as viewing pornography, would likely be deemed off-limits. For employees, checking personal email or visiting personal Facebook pages at work might be classified as unauthorized use.

Unauthorized access and many types of unauthorized use are criminal offenses in the United States and many other countries. They can be committed by both insiders—people who work for the company whose computers are being accessed—and outsiders. Whether a specific act constitutes unauthorized use or is illegal depends on the circumstances, as well as the specific company or institution involved. To explain acceptable computer use to their employees, students, or other users, many organizations and educational institutions publish guidelines for behavior, often called **codes of conduct** (see Exhibit 6-1).

> **unauthorized access** When an individual gains access to a computer, network, file, or other resource without permission.
>
> **unauthorized use** When someone uses a computer resource for unauthorized activities.
>
> **codes of conduct** Guidelines for behavior that explain acceptable computer use.
>
> **hack** To break into a computer or network.
>
> **cyberterrorism** An attack launched by terrorists via the Internet.

Exhibit 6-1 Sample code of conduct

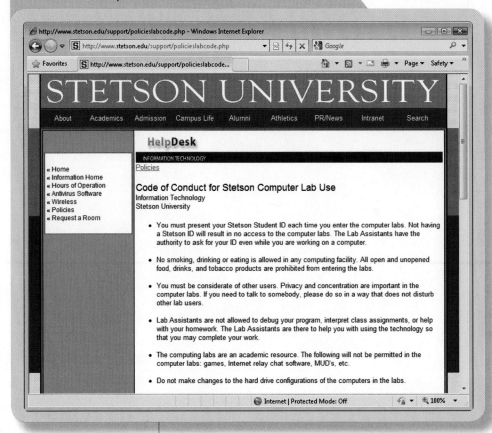

Hacking

Hacking refers to the act of breaking into a computer or network. It can be performed in person if the hacker has physical access to the computer, but it is more often performed via the Internet or another network. Hacking in the United States and many other countries is a crime.

Typically, the motivation for hacking is to steal data, sabotage a computer system, or perform some other type of illegal act. In particular, the theft of consumer data, such as credit card numbers and cardholder information, has increased dramatically over the past several years. Another growing trend is to hack into a computer and "hijack" it for use in an illegal or unethical act, such as generating spam or hosting pornographic Web sites.

In addition to being a threat to individuals and businesses, hacking is also considered a very serious threat to national security in the United States. The increased number of systems that are controlled by computers and are connected to the Internet, along with the continually improving abilities of hackers and the increasing availability of sets of tools that allow hackers to access a system, has led to an increased risk of **cyberterrorism**—where terrorists launch attacks via the Internet. Current concerns include attacks against the

War Driving and Wi-Fi Piggybacking: Legal and Ethical?

Both war driving and Wi-Fi piggybacking are ethically—if not legally—questionable acts. Both the hacker and the owner of the Wi-Fi network risk the introduction of computer viruses (either intentionally or unintentionally) and unauthorized access of the data located on their computers. In addition, the network owner may experience reduced performance or even cancelled Internet service if the ISP limits bandwidth or the number of computers allowed to use a single Internet connection. Although products and services are available to help mobile users locate legitimate public Wi-Fi hotspots, laws in some countries, such as the U.K., are clear that unauthorized access of a Wi-Fi connection is illegal. In the United States, federal law is not as clear, although some states have made using a Wi-Fi connection without permission illegal. Advocates of war driving and Wi-Fi piggybacking state that, unless individuals or businesses protect their access points, they are welcoming others to use them. Critics compare that logic to that of an unlocked front door—you cannot legally enter a home just because the front door is unlocked. Some wireless network owners do leave their access points unsecured

Wi-Fi finder lists hotspots for specific area

Courtesy JiWire, Inc.

on purpose and some communities are creating a collection of wireless access points to provide wireless Internet access to everyone in that community. However, it is difficult—if not impossible—to tell if an unsecured network is that way intentionally, unless connecting to the wireless network displays a welcome screen stating that it is a free public Wi-Fi hotspot.

computers controlling vital systems, such as the nation's power grids, banks, and water filtration facilities, as well as computers related to national defense, the airlines, and the stock market.

Today, hackers often gain access via a wireless network. This is because wireless networks are becoming increasingly common and it is easier to hack into a wireless network than a wired network. In fact, it is possible to gain access to a wireless network just by being within range of a wireless access point, unless the access point is sufficiently protected. Although security features are

built into wireless routers and other networking hardware, they are typically not enabled by default.

War Driving and Wi-Fi Piggybacking

Unauthorized use of a Wi-Fi network is called war driving or Wi-Fi piggybacking, depending on the location of the hacker at the time. **War driving** typically involves driving in a car with a portable computer looking for unsecured Wi-Fi networks to connect to. **Wi-Fi piggybacking** refers to accessing someone else's unsecured Wi-Fi network from the hacker's current location, such as inside his or her home or outside a Wi-Fi hotspot location.

According to some estimates, as many as 70 percent of all Wi-Fi networks—belonging to businesses and individuals—are left unsecured.

> **war driving** Driving around an area with a Wi-Fi-enabled computer or mobile device to find a Wi-Fi network to access and use without authorization.
>
> **Wi-Fi piggybacking** Accessing an unsecured Wi-Fi network from your current location without authorization.

Interception of Communications

Instead of accessing data stored on a computer via hacking, some criminals gain unauthorized access to data, files, email messages, VoIP calls, and other content as it is being sent over the Internet. For instance, unencrypted messages, files, logon information, and more sent over an unsecured wireless network can be captured and read by anyone within range using software designed for that purpose.

Although it is unlikely that anyone would be interested in intercepting personal email sent to friends and relatives, proprietary corporate information and sensitive personal information is at risk if it is sent unsecured over the Internet or over a wireless home or corporate network. The widespread use of wireless networks, as well as the increased use of wireless connections to transmit data via mobile phones and other portable devices, has opened up new opportunities for data interception. For instance, the data on mobile devices with Bluetooth capabilities enabled can be accessed by other Bluetooth devices that are within range.

A new trend is criminals intercepting credit and debit card information during the card verification process; that is, intercepting the data from a card in real time as a purchase is being authorized. In several recent cases, this occurred via packet-sniffing software installed  at payment terminals, such as restaurant cash registers or gas station credit/debit card readers, by hackers. The packet-sniffing software gathered the data during transactions and then sent it to the hackers. The increased occurrence of real-time attacks may be partly because of the new Payment Card Industry Data Security Standard (PCI DSS) rules that require companies to limit the credit card data stored on company servers and to encrypt the data that is allowed to be stored. Consequently, hackers may be moving away from targeting data stored on company servers and focusing on stealing data in real time during credit card and debit card transactions.

LO6.2 Online Threats

Computer sabotage—acts of malicious destruction to a computer or computer resource—is another common type of computer crime today. Computer sabotage can take several forms, including launching a computer virus, altering the content of a Web site, or changing data or programs located on a computer. Computer sabotage is illegal in the United States, and acts of sabotage are estimated to cost individuals and organizations billions of dollars per year, primarily for labor costs related to correcting the problems caused by the sabotage, lost productivity, and lost sales.

Botnets

A common tool used to perform computer sabotage is a botnet. A computer that is controlled by a hacker or other computer criminal is referred to as a **bot** or **zombie computer**; a group of bots that are controlled by one individual and can work together in a coordinated fashion is called a **botnet**. According to the FBI, an estimated one million U.S. computers are currently part of a botnet.

Computer Viruses and Other Types of Malware

Malware is a generic term that refers to any type of malicious software. Malware programs are intentionally written to perform destructive acts, such as damaging programs, deleting files, erasing a hard drive, or slowing down the performance of a computer. This damage can take place immediately after a computer is infected or it can begin when a particular condition is met. A malware program that activates when it detects

Christophe Testi/Shutterstock.com

---

computer sabotage An act of malicious destruction to a computer or computer resource.

bot (**zombie computer**) A computer that is controlled by a hacker or other computer criminal.

botnet A group of bots that are controlled by one individual.

malware Any type of malicious software.

Spyware is one type of malware often used by computer criminals to send sensitive data secretly from infected computers to the criminal.

Exhibit 6-2 How a computer virus might spread

1. A computer virus originates when an unscrupulous programmer intentionally creates it and embeds it in a file. The infected file is then posted to a Web page where it will be downloaded via the Internet or is sent as an email attachment to a large group of people.

THE INTERNET

COMPANY NETWORK

3. A virus can spread very quickly because every computer that comes in contact with the virus—whether through an infected removable storage medium, infected downloaded file, or infected email attachment—becomes infected, unless virus-protection software is used to prevent it.

2. When the infected file is opened on a computer, the virus copies itself to that computer's hard drive and the computer becomes infected. The virus may then email itself to people in the newly infected computer's email address book or copy itself to any removable storage medium inserted into that computer.

a certain condition, such as when a particular keystroke is pressed or an employee's name is deleted from an employee file, is called a logic bomb. A logic bomb that is triggered by a particular date or time is called a time bomb.

Writing a computer virus or other type of malware or even posting the malware code on the Internet is not illegal, but it is considered highly unethical and irresponsible behavior. Distributing malware, on the other hand, is illegal, and virus writers who release their malware are being vigorously prosecuted.

One type of malware is the **virus**—a software program that is installed without the permission or knowledge of the computer user, that is designed to alter the way a computer operates, and that can replicate itself to infect any new media it has access to. Computer viruses are often embedded into program or data files, such as games, videos, and music files downloaded from Web pages or shared via a P2P service. They are spread when an infected file is downloaded, transferred to a new computer via an infected removable storage medium, or emailed to another computer (see Exhibit 6-2). Viruses can also be installed when a recipient clicks a link in an

Costs of Malware

Malware can be very costly in terms of the labor costs associated with removing the viruses and correcting any resulting damage, as well as the cost of lost productivity of employees.

virus A software program installed without the user's knowledge and designed to alter the way a computer operates or to cause harm to the computer system.

> *The Mydoom worm, released in 2004, spread so rapidly that, at one point, one out of every ten emails contained the worm.*

email message or an instant message, such as an electronic greeting card email that contains a link to view the card. Once a copy of the infected file reaches a new computer, it typically embeds itself into program, data, or system files on the new computer and remains there, affecting that computer according to its programmed instructions until it is discovered and removed.

Another common form of malware is the worm. Like a computer virus, a computer **worm** is a malicious program that is typically designed to cause damage. Unlike a computer virus, however, a computer worm does not infect other computer files on the infected computer to replicate itself; instead, it spreads by creating copies of its code and sending those copies to other computers via a network. Often, the worm is sent to other computers as an email attachment. Usually after the infected email attachment is opened by an individual, the worm inflicts its damage and then automatically sends copies of itself to other computers via the Internet or a private network, typically using addresses in the email address book located on the newly infected computer.

Some newer worms do not require any user action to infect the user's computer. Instead, the worm scans the Internet looking for computers that are vulnerable to that particular worm and sends a copy of itself to those computers to infect them. Other worms just require the user to view an infected email message or insert an infected removable storage medium into the computer

to infect the computer. Still other worms are specifically written to take advantage of newly discovered security holes in operating systems and email programs.

A **Trojan horse** is a type of malware that masquerades as something else—usually an application program. When the seemingly legitimate program is downloaded or installed, the malware part of the Trojan horse infects the computer. Many recent Trojan horses masquerade as normal ongoing activities when they are installed, such as the Windows Update service or an antivirus or antispyware program telling the user to download a file containing program updates, to try to trick unsuspecting users into downloading another malware program or buying a useless program. For instance, after a rogue antivirus program like the one shown in Exhibit 6-3 is installed (usually without the user's direct knowledge or permission), the malware takes over the computer displaying warning messages or scan results indicating the computer is infected with malware. In addition, the rogue antivirus program typically prevents access to any Web sites other than its own and prompts the user to buy a fake anti-malware program to get rid of the "malware."

Unlike viruses and worms, Trojan horses cannot replicate themselves. Trojan horses are usually spread by being downloaded from the Internet, though they may also be sent as an email attachment, either from the Trojan horse author or from individuals who forward

worm A malicious program designed to spread rapidly to a large number of computers by sending copies of itself to other computers.

Trojan horse A malicious program that masquerades as something else.

Exhibit 6-3 Rogue antivirus program

Exhibit 6-4 How a DoS attack might work

1. The hacker's computer sends several simultaneous requests; each request asks to establish a connection to the server but supplies false return information. In a distributed DoS attack, multiple computers send multiple requests at one time.

Hello? I'd like some info...

Hello? I'd like some info...

2. The server tries to respond to each request but can't locate the computer because false return information was provided. The server waits for a short period of time before closing the connection, which ties up the server and keeps others from connecting.

I'm busy, I can't help you right now.

I can't find you, I'll wait and try again...

LEGITIMATE COMPUTER

3. The hacker's computer continues to send new requests, so as a connection is closed by the server, a new request is waiting. This cycle continues, which ties up the server indefinitely.

4. The server becomes so overwhelmed that legitimate requests cannot get through and, eventually, the server usually crashes.

Hello? I'd like some info...

HACKER'S COMPUTER

WEB SERVER

Courtesy Hewlett-Packard Company and Dell Inc.

---

it, not realizing the program is a Trojan horse. Some Trojan horses today act as spyware and are designed to find private information located on infected computers and then send that information to the malware creator to be used in illegal activities. Another type of Trojan horse records every keystroke made on the infected computer, and then sends the sensitive information it recorded to criminals.

Denial of Service (DoS) Attacks

A **denial of service (DoS) attack** is an act of sabotage that attempts to flood a network server or Web server with so many requests for action that it shuts down or simply cannot handle legitimate requests any longer, causing legitimate users to be denied service. For example, a hacker might set up one or more computers to contact a server continually with a request to send a responding ping back to a false return address, or to request nonexistent information continually. If enough useless traffic is generated, the server has no resources left to deal with legitimate requests (see Exhibit 6-4). An emerging trend is DoS attacks aimed at mobile wireless networks. These attacks typically involve repeatedly establishing and releasing connections with the goal of overloading the network to disrupt service.

DoS attacks today are often directed toward popular sites and typically are carried out via multiple computers. This is known as a **distributed denial of service (DDoS) attack**. DDoS attacks are typically performed by botnets created by hackers; the computers in the botnet participate in the attacks without the owners' knowledge. Because home computers are increasingly using direct Internet connections but tend to be less protected than school and business computers, hackers are increasingly targeting home computers for botnets used in DDoS attacks and other forms of computer sabotage.

It is common for all types of malware to be referred to as "viruses," even though some might not technically be computer viruses.

denial of service (DoS) attack An act of sabotage that attempts to flood a network server or a Web server with so much activity that it is unable to function.

distributed denial of service (DDoS) attack A DoS attack carried out by multiple computers.

Security company Websense reports that over half of the Web sites classified as malicious are actually legitimate Web sites that have been compromised.

Data, Program, or Web Site Alteration

Another type of computer sabotage occurs when a hacker breaches a computer system to delete data, change data, modify programs, or otherwise alter the data and programs located there. For example, a student might try to hack into the school database to change his or her grade, or a hacker might change a program located on a company server to steal money or information.

Data on Web sites can also be altered by hackers. For instance, individuals sometimes hack into and alter other people's social networking accounts. In early 2009, for instance, the Twitter accounts of over 30 high-profile individuals, including then President-elect Obama, were accessed by an unauthorized individual who sent out fake and sometimes embarrassing tweets posing as those individuals. It is also becoming more common for hackers to compromise legitimate Web sites and then use those sites to perform malware attacks. Typically, a hacker alters a legitimate site to display an official-looking message that informs the user that a particular software program must be downloaded, or the hacker posts a rogue banner ad on a legitimate site that redirects the user to a malware site instead of the site for the product featured in the banner ad.

Online Theft, Online Fraud, and Other Dot Cons

A booming area of computer crime involves online fraud, theft, scams, and related activities designed to steal money or other resources from individuals or businesses—these are collectively referred to as **dot cons**.

dot con A fraud or scam carried out through the Internet.

data theft (information theft) The theft of data or information located on or being sent from a computer.

The best protection against many dot cons is protecting your identity—that is, protecting any identifying information about you that could be used in fraudulent activities. With any dot con, it is important to act quickly if you think you have been a victim. For instance, you should work with your local law enforcement agency, credit card companies, and the three major consumer credit bureaus—Equifax, Experian, and TransUnion—to close any accessed or fraudulent accounts, place fraud alerts on your credit report, and take other actions to prevent additional fraudulent activity while the fraud is being investigated.

Theft of Data, Information, and Other Resources

Data theft or **information theft** is the theft of data or information located on or being sent from a computer. It can be committed by stealing an actual computer, or it can take place over the Internet or a network by an individual gaining unauthorized access to that data by hacking into the computer or by intercepting the data in transit.

Money is another resource that can be stolen via a computer. Company insiders sometimes steal money by altering company programs to transfer small amounts of money—for example, a few cents' worth of bank account interest—from a very large number of transactions to an account controlled by the thieves. Added together, the amounts can be substantial. Another example of monetary theft performed via computers involves hackers electronically transferring money illegally from online bank accounts, traditional bank accounts, credit card accounts, or accounts at online payment services such as PayPal.

You should be vigilant about protecting private information by sending sensitive information via secure Web servers only and not disclosing personal information—especially a Social Security number or your mother's maiden name—unless it is absolutely necessary and you know how the information will be used and that it will not be shared with others. In addition, never give out sensitive personal information to anyone who requests it over the phone or by email; businesses that legitimately need bank account information, passwords, or credit card numbers will not request that information via phone or email. Encrypting computers and other hardware containing sensitive information so it will not be readable if the hardware is lost or stolen is another important precaution discussed later in this chapter.

Exhibit 6-5 How identity theft works

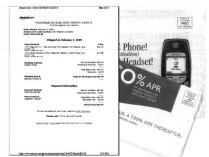

1. The thief obtains information about an individual from discarded mail, employee records, credit card transactions, Web server files, or some other method.

2. The thief uses the information to make purchases, open new credit card accounts, and more in the victim's name. Often, the thief changes the address on the account to delay the victim's discovery of the theft.

3. The victim usually finds out by being denied credit or by being contacted about overdue bills generated by the thief. Clearing one's name after identity theft is time-consuming and can be very difficult and frustrating for the victim.

Identity Theft, Phishing, and Pharming

A growing dot con trend is obtaining enough information about an individual to perform fraudulent financial transactions. Often, this is carried out in conjunction with identity theft. **Identity theft** occurs when someone obtains enough information about a person to be able to masquerade as that person—usually to buy products or services in that person's name, as illustrated in Exhibit 6-5. Typically, identity theft begins with obtaining a person's name, address, and Social Security number, often from a discarded or stolen document, such as a preapproved credit card application that was sent in the mail; from information obtained via the Internet, such as a résumé posted online; from information located on a computer, such as on a stolen computer or hacked server; or from information sent from a computer via a computer virus or spyware program installed on that computer. The thief may then order a copy of the individual's birth certificate, obtain a "replacement" driver's license, make purchases and charge them to the victim, and/or open credit or bank accounts in the victim's name. Identity theft is illegal and, in 1998, the federal government passed the Identity Theft and Assumption Deterrence Act, which made identity theft a federal crime.

Other commonly used techniques are skimming and social engineering. Skimming involves stealing

Dmitry Kalinovsky/Shutterstock.com

> Although information used in identity theft is often gathered via computer, it can also be obtained from mailboxes, trash dumpsters, and other locations.

credit card or debit card numbers by using an illegal device attached to an ATM or credit card reader that reads and stores the card numbers to be retrieved by the thief at a later time. Social engineering involves pretending—typically via phone or email—to be a bank officer, potential employer, or other trusted individual in order to get the potential victim to supply personal information.

Phishing (pronounced "fishing") is the use of a spoofed email message—an email that appears to come from a legitimate organization such as eBay, PayPal, or a bank, but is actually sent from a phisher—to trick

identity theft Using someone else's identity to purchase goods or services, obtain new credit cards or bank loans, or otherwise illegally masquerade as that individual.

phishing The use of spoofed email messages to gain credit card numbers and other personal data to be used for fraudulent purposes.

Identity theft can be extremely distressing for victims, can take years to straighten out, and can be very expensive. For example, for a year and a half, a thief used the identity of victim Michelle Brown to obtain over $50,000 in goods and services, to rent properties—even to engage in drug trafficking. Although the culprit was eventually arrested and convicted for other criminal acts, she continued to use Brown's identity and was even booked into jail using Brown's stolen identity. As a final insult after the culprit was in prison, U.S. Customs agents detained the real Michelle Brown when she was returning from a trip to Mexico because of the criminal record of the identity thief. Brown states that she has not traveled out of the country since, fearing an arrest or some other serious problem resulting from the theft of her identity, and estimates she has spent over 500 hours trying to correct all the problems related to the identity theft.

the recipient into revealing sensitive personal information, such as Web site logon information or credit card numbers. Once obtained, this information is used in identity theft and other fraudulent activities. A phishing email typically looks legitimate and it contains links in the email that appear to go to the Web site of the legitimate business, but these links go to the phisher's Web site that is set up to look like the legitimate site instead—an act called Web site spoofing. Phishing emails are typically sent to a wide group of individuals and

spear phishing A personalized phishing scheme targeted at an individual.

pharming The use of spoofed domain names to obtain personal information to be used in fraudulent activities.

> Spear phishing schemes may might include personalized information. Don't be fooled—the email is not legitimate.

usually include an urgent message stating that the individual's credit card or account information needs to be updated and instructing the recipient of the email to click the link provided in the email in order to keep the account active, as shown in Exhibit 6-6. If the victim clicks the link and supplies the requested information via the spoofed site, the criminal gains access to all information provided by the victim. Phishing attempts can also occur via instant messages, text messages, fake messages sent via eBay or MySpace, Twitter tweets, and pop-up security alert windows. Phishers also frequently utilize spyware; typically, clicking the link in the phishing email installs the spyware on the victim's computer, and it will remain there, transmitting passwords and other sensitive data to the phisher, until it is detected and removed.

Another recent trend is the use of more targeted, personalized phishing schemes, known as **spear phishing**. Spear phishing emails are directly targeted to a specific individual and typically appear to come from an organization or person that the targeted individual has an association with. They also often include personalized information, such as the potential victim's name, to make the spear phishing emails seem even more legitimate. Spear phishers also target employees of selected organizations by posing as someone within the company, such as a human resources or technical support employee. These spear phishing emails often request confidential information or direct the employee to click a link to supposedly reset his or her password. The goal of corporate spear phishing attacks is usually to steal intellectual property, such as software source code, design documents, or schematics.

Pharming is another type of scam that uses spoofed domain names to obtain personal information for use in fraudulent activities. With pharming, the criminal reroutes traffic intended for a commonly used Web site to a spoofed Web site set up by the pharmer. Sometimes pharming takes place via malicious code sent to a computer via an email message or other distribution method. More often, it takes place via changes made to a DNS server—a computer that translates URLs into the appropriate IP addresses needed to display the Web page

Exhibit 6-6 Phishing email

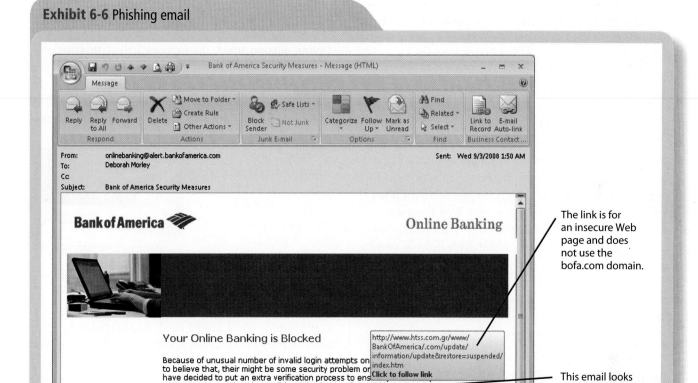

The link is for an insecure Web page and does not use the bofa.com domain.

This email looks legitimate, but the link goes to a spoofed Web page.

corresponding to a URL. After hacking into a company DNS server, the pharmer changes the IP addresses used in conjunction with a particular company URL (called DNS poisoning) so any Web page requests made via the legitimate company URL are routed via the company's poisoned DNS server to a phony spoofed Web page located on the pharmer's Web server. So, even though a user types the proper URL to display the legitimate company Web page in his or her browser, the spoofed page is displayed instead. Because spoofed sites are set up to look like the legitimate sites, the user typically does not notice any difference, and any information sent via that site is captured by the pharmer.

Protecting Against Identity Theft

In addition to disclosing personal information only when it is necessary and only via secure Web pages, you should use security software and keep it up to date to guard against computer viruses, spyware, and other malware that can be used to send information from your computer or about your activities to a criminal. In addition, shred the preapproved credit card offers and other documents containing personal information that frequently arrive in the mail before recycling them. To prevent the theft of outgoing mail containing sensitive information, don't place it in your mailbox—mail it at the post office or in a USPS drop box.

To avoid phishing schemes, never click a link in an email message to go to a secure Web site—always type the URL for that site in your browser (not necessarily the URL shown in the email message) instead. If you think an unsolicited email message requesting information from you may be legitimate, type the URL for that site in your browser to load the legitimate site and then update your account information.

To prevent identity theft, protect your Social Security number and give it out only when necessary. Keep a close eye on your credit card bills and credit history to make sure you catch any fraudulent charges or accounts opened by an identity thief as soon as possible. Make sure your bills arrive every month—some thieves will change your mailing address to delay detection—and read credit card statements carefully to look for unauthorized charges. Be sure to follow up on any calls you get from creditors, instead of assuming it is just a mistake. Most security experts also recommend ordering a full credit history on yourself a few times a year to check for accounts listed in your name that you did not open and any other problems.

You can also use browser-based antiphishing tools and digital certificates to help guard against identity theft and the phishing and pharming schemes used in conjunction with identity theft. Antiphishing tools are built into many email programs and Web browsers to help notify users of possible phishing Web sites. For instance, some email programs will disable links in email messages identified as questionable, unless the user overrides it; many browsers warn users when a Web page associated with a possible phishing URL is requested (see Exhibit 6-7); and antiphishing capabilities are included in many recent security suites.

Online Auction Fraud and Other Internet Scams

Online auction fraud (sometimes called **Internet auction fraud**) occurs when an online auction buyer pays for merchandise that is never delivered, or that is delivered but it is not as represented. A wide range of other scams can occur via Web sites or unsolicited emails. Common types of scams include loan scams, work-at-home cons, pyramid schemes, bogus credit card offers and prize promotions, and fraudulent business opportunities and franchises. These offers typically try to sell potential victims nonexistent services or worthless information, or they try to convince potential victims to voluntarily supply their credit card details and other personal information, which are then used for fraudulent purposes.

One ongoing Internet scam is the Nigerian letter fraud scheme. This scheme involves an email message that appears to come from the Nigerian government and that promises the potential victim a share of a substantial amount of money in exchange for the use of the victim's bank account. Supposedly the victim's bank account information is needed to facilitate a wire transfer but the victim's account is emptied instead, or up-front cash is needed to pay for nonexistent fees, which the con artist keeps while giving nothing in return. See Exhibit 6-8. The theme of these scams often changes to fit current events.

The best protection against many dot cons is common sense. Be extremely cautious of any unsolicited email messages you receive and realize that if an offer sounds too good to be true, it probably is. Before bidding on an auction item, check out the feedback rating

Exhibit 6-7 Unsafe Web site alert

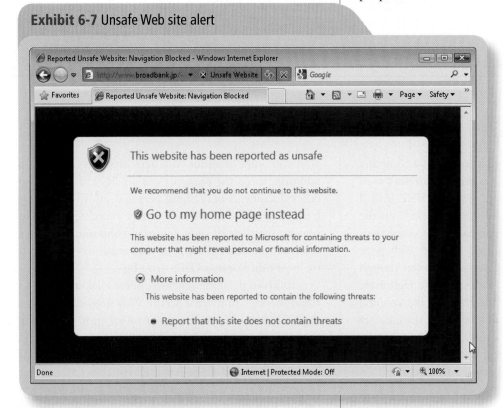

online auction fraud (Internet auction fraud) When an item purchased through an online auction is never delivered after payment, or the item is not as specified by the seller.

Digital Certificates and Digital Signatures

The purpose of a **digital certificate** is to authenticate the identity of an individual or organization. Digital certificates are granted by Certificate Authorities and typically contain the name of the person, organization, or Web site being certified along with a certificate serial number and an expiration date. Digital certificates also include a public/private key pair. In addition to being used by the certificate holder to encrypt files and email messages, these keys and the digital certificate are used with secure Web pages to guarantee the Web pages are secure and actually belong to the stated organization.

The keys included in a digital certificate can also be used to authenticate the identity of a person sending an email message or other document via a **digital signature**. To digitally sign an email message or other document, the sender's private key is used and that key, along with the contents of the document, generates a unique digital signature; consequently, a digital signature is different with each signed document. When a digitally signed document is received, the recipient's computer uses the sender's public key to verify the digital signature. Because the document is signed with the sender's private key and the digital signature will be deemed invalid if even one character of the document is changed after it is signed, digital signatures guarantee that the document was sent by a specific individual and that it was not tampered with after it was signed.

of the seller to see comments written by other auction sellers and buyers. Always pay for auctions and other online purchases using a credit card or an online payment service such as PayPal that accepts credit card payments so you can dispute the transaction through your credit card company, if needed. For expensive items, consider using an escrow service, which allows you to ensure that the merchandise is as specified before your payment is released to the seller.

LO6.3 Cyberstalking and Other Personal Safety Concerns

In addition to being expensive and inconvenient, cybercrime can also be physically dangerous. Although most of us may not ordinarily view using the Internet as a potentially dangerous activity, cases of physical harm due to Internet activity do happen. For example, children and teenagers have become the victims of pedophiles who arranged face-to-face meetings by using information gathered via email, message boards, social networking sites, or

digital certificate Electronic data that can be used to verify the identity of a person or an organization; includes a key pair that can be used for encryption and digital signatures.

digital signature A unique digital code that can be attached to a file or an email message to verify the identity of the sender and guarantee the file or message has not been changed since it was signed.

Exhibit 6-8 Nigerian letter fraud email

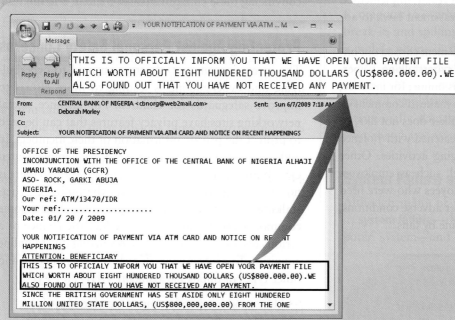

The most common security risks and computer crimes that take place via networks and the Internet are hacking, computer viruses, identity theft, and cyberbullying.

other online sources. Also, a growing number of incidents have occurred in which children are threatened by classmates via email, Web site posts, or text messages. Adults may fall victim to unscrupulous or dangerous individuals who misrepresent themselves online, and the availability of personal information online has made it more difficult for individuals to hide from people who may want to do them harm, such as abused women trying to hide from their abusive husbands.

Cyberbullying and Cyberstalking

Two of the most common ways individuals are harassed online are cyberbullying and cyberstalking. Children and teenagers bullying other children or teenagers via the Internet, such as through email, text messaging, a social networking site, or other online communications method, is referred to as **cyberbullying**. Unfortunately, cyberbullying is common today. By some estimates, it affects as many as one-half of all U.S. teenagers. Many states and schools have reviewed their harassment statutes and bullying policies and, as a result, implemented new laws or amended existing harassment laws to address cyberbullying.

Repeated threats or other harassment carried out online between adults is referred to as **cyberstalking**. Cyberstalkers sometimes find their victims online; for instance, someone in a discussion group who makes a comment or has a screen name that the cyberstalker does not like, or bloggers who are harassed and threatened with violence or murder because of their blogging activities. Other times, the attack is more personal, such as employers who are stalked online by ex-employees who were fired or otherwise left their position under adverse conditions, and celebrities who are stalked online by fans.

cyberbullying Children or teenagers bullying other children or teenagers via the Internet.

cyberstalking Repeated threats or harassing behavior between adults carried out via email or another Internet communications method.

Cyberstalking typically begins with online harassment, such as sending harassing or threatening email messages to the victim, posing as the victim in order to sign the victim up for pornographic or otherwise offensive email newsletters, publicizing the victim's home address and telephone number, or hacking into the victim's social networking pages to alter the content. Cyberstalking can also lead to offline stalking and possibly physical harm—in at least one case, it led to the death of the victim.

Although there are as yet no specific federal laws against cyberstalking, all states have made it illegal, and some federal laws do apply if the online actions include computer fraud or another type of computer crime, suggest a threat of personal injury, or involve sending obscene email messages.

Online Pornography

A variety of controversial and potentially objectionable material is available on the Internet. Although there have been attempts to ban this type of material from the Internet, they have not been successful. Like its printed counterpart, online pornography involving minors is illegal. Because of the strong link experts believe exists between child pornography and child molestation, many experts are very concerned about the amount of child pornography that can be found and distributed via the Internet. They also believe that the Internet makes it easier for sexual predators to act out, such as by striking up "friendships" with children online and convincing these children to meet them in real life.

Protecting Against Personal Safety Concerns

The increasing amount of attention paid to cyberbullying and cyberstalking is leading to more efforts to improve safeguards for children. For instance, social networking sites have privacy features that can be used to protect the private information of their members. In addition, numerous states in the U.S. have implemented cyberbullying and cyberstalking laws. Although there is no surefire way to protect against cyberbullying, cyberstalking, and other online dangers completely, some common-sense precautions can reduce the chance of a serious personal safety problem occurring due to online activities. To protect yourself against cyberstalking and other types of online harassment:

- Use gender-neutral, nonprovocative identifying names, such as *jsmith*, instead of *janesmith* or *iamcute*.

- Be careful about the types of photos you post of yourself online and do not reveal personal information, such as your real name, address, or telephone number, to people you meet online.

- Do not respond to any insults or other harassing comments you may receive online.

- Consider requesting that your personal information be removed from online directories, especially those associated with your email address or other online identifiers.

LO6.4 Personal Computer Security

There are a number of security concerns surrounding computers and related technology that all individuals should be concerned about, including having your computer stolen, losing a term paper because the storage medium your paper was stored on becomes unreadable, losing your mobile phone containing your entire contact list and calendar, or buying pirated or digitally counterfeited products. Although concerns about hacking, computer viruses, identity theft, and cyberbullying are valid, there are additional computer security issues that are not related specifically to networks and the Internet.

Hardware Loss and Damage

Hardware loss can occur when a personal computer, USB flash drive, mobile device, or other piece of hardware is stolen or is lost by the owner. Hardware loss, as well as other security issues, can also result from hardware damage—both intentional and accidental—and system failure.

One of the most obvious types of hardware loss is **hardware theft**, which occurs when hardware is stolen from an individual or from a business, school, or other organization. Although security experts stress that the vast majority of hardware theft is stolen to obtain the value of the hardware itself, corporate executives and

One study revealed that 80 percent of users store information on their mobile phones that could be used for identity theft.

government employees may be targeted by computer thieves for the information contained on their computers. And even if the data on a device is not the primary reason for a theft, any unencrypted sensitive data stored on the stolen device is at risk of being exposed or used for fraudulent purposes, which is happening at unprecedented levels today.

Hardware loss also occurs when hardware is being transported in luggage or in a package that is lost by an airline or shipping company, or when an individual misplaces or otherwise loses a piece of hardware. If any sensitive data was contained on the lost hardware, individuals risk identity theft. Businesses hosting sensitive data that is breached have to deal with the numerous issues and potential consequences of that loss, such as notifying customers that their personal information was exposed, responding to potential lawsuits, and trying to repair damage to the company's reputation.

Computer hardware often consists of relatively delicate components that can be damaged easily by power fluctuations, heat, dust, static electricity, water, and abuse. For instance, fans clogged by dust can cause a computer to overheat; dropping a computer will often break it; and spilling a drink on a keyboard or leaving a mobile phone in the pocket of your jeans while they go through the wash will likely cause some damage. In addition to accidental damage, burglars, vandals, disgruntled employees, and other individuals sometimes intentionally damage the computers and other hardware they have access to.

System Failure and Other Disasters

Although many of us may prefer not to think about it, **system failure**—the complete malfunction of a computer system—and other types of computer-related

According to FBI statistics, the recovery rate of a lost or stolen computer is about 2 or 3 percent.

hardware theft The theft of computer hardware.

system failure The complete malfunction of a computer system.

A 5-character password can be cracked by a computer program in less than one minute. A 10-character password has 3,700 trillion possible character permutations.

Exhibit 6-9 Cable locks secure computers and other hardware

NOTEBOOK COMPUTERS
This combination cable lock connects via a security slot built into the notebook computer.

DESKTOP COMPUTERS AND MONITORS
This keyed cable lock connects via a cable anchor attached to the back of the monitor.

Courtesy Kensington

disasters do happen. From accidentally deleting a file to having your computer just stop working, computer problems can be a huge inconvenience, as well as cost a great deal of time and money. When the system contains your personal documents and data, it is a problem; when it contains the only copy of your company records or controls a vital system—such as a nuclear power plant—it can be a disaster. System failure can occur because of a hardware problem, software problem, or computer virus. It can also occur because of a natural disaster, sabotage, or a terrorist attack.

Protecting Against Hardware Loss, Hardware Damage, and System Failure

Locked doors and equipment can be simple deterrents to computer theft. To secure computers and other hardware to a table or other object that is difficult to move, you can use cable locks, such as the ones shown in Exhibit 6-9. As an additional precaution with portable computers, you can use laptop alarm software that emits a very loud alarm noise if the computer is unplugged, if USB devices are removed, or if the computer is shut down without the owner's permission.

full disk encryption (FDE) A technology that encrypts everything stored on a storage medium automatically, without any user interaction.

self-encrypting hard drive A hard drive that uses full disk encryption (FDE).

Encryption can be used to prevent a file from being readable if it is intercepted or viewed by an unauthorized individual. **Full disk encryption** (**FDE**) provides an easy way to protect the data on an entire computer in case it is lost or stolen. FDE systems encrypt everything stored on the drive (the operating system, application programs, data, temporary files, and so forth) automatically, so users don't have to remember to encrypt sensitive documents and the encryption is always enabled. A hard drive that uses FDE, which is often referred to as a **self-encrypting hard drive**, typically needs a username and password or biometric characteristic before the computer containing the drive will boot.

Encryption can also be used to protect the data stored on removable storage media; either a strong password or a biometric feature (such as a built-in fingerprint reader, as in the USB drive in Exhibit 6-10) is used to provide access to the data on the drive.

Some software tools are designed to aid in hardware recovery. One software tool that can be used to help increase the chances of a stolen or lost computer being recovered is computer tracking

Exhibit 6-10 Encrypted USB flash drive

Safeguarding Passwords

Passwords are secret words or character combinations associated with an individual. They are typically used in conjunction with a username. Username/password combinations are often used to restrict access to networks, computers, Web sites, routers, and other computing resources—the user is granted access to the requested resource only after supplying the correct information. Passwords typically appear as asterisks or dots as they are being entered so they cannot be viewed.

Create strong passwords that are at least eight characters long; use a combination of upper and lowercase letters, numbers, and symbols; and do not form words found in the dictionary or that match the username that the password is associated with. One way to create a strong password is to create a passphrase that you can remember and use corresponding letters and symbols, such as the first letter of each word, for your password. For instance, the passphrase "My son John is five years

older than my daughter Abby" could be used to remember the corresponding strong password "Msji5yotMd@". Or you can choose an abbreviation or unusual words you will remember, and then add a mix of numbers and special characters. Do not use your name, your kids' or pets' names, your address, your birthdate, or any other public information as your password.

To keep your passwords safe, do not keep a written copy of the password in your desk or taped to your monitor. If you need to keep a record of your passwords, create a password-protected file on your computer. Also, use a different password for your highly sensitive activities, such as online banking or stock trading, than for Web sites that remember your settings or profile, such as online news, auction, or shopping sites. If a hacker determines your password on a low-security site, he or she can use it on an account containing sensitive data if you use the same password on both accounts.

software. Computer tracking software can be used to help increase the chances of a stolen or lost computer being recovered by sending identifying information, such as ownership information and location information determined from nearby Wi-Fi networks, to the computer tracking company on a regular basis. When the computer is in the owner's possession, this information is sent infrequently—maybe once a day. When the computer is reported lost or stolen, however, the computer tracking software typically increases its contact with the computer tracking software company, such as sending new information every 15 minutes, so current location information can be provided to law enforcement agencies to help them recover the computer. Some software can even take video or photos with the

computer's video camera of the person using the stolen computer to help identify and prosecute the thief.

Often any sign that computer tracking software is running on the computer or is sending information via the Internet is hidden from the user, so the thief is usually not aware that a computer tracking system is installed on the computer. An alternative is tracking software that displays a message on the screen when the computer is lost or stolen, such as a plea to return the device for a reward or a simple statement of "THIS COMPUTER IS STOLEN" in a big bright banner on the desktop. Messages typically reappear every 30 seconds, no matter how many times they are closed by the thief.

Another antitheft tool is the use of asset tags on hardware and other expensive assets. These labels usually identify the owner of the asset and are designed to be permanently attached to the asset. Some tags are designed to be indestructible; others are tamper evident labels that change their appearance if someone tries to remove them.

> Protect your passwords; don't write your passwords down on sticky notes that you leave attached to your monitor.

password A secret word or character combination associated with an individual.

Self-Destructing Devices

When you are less concerned about recovering a stolen device than about ensuring the data located on the computer is not compromised, devices that self-destruct upon command are a viable option. Available as part of some computer tracking software programs, such as the one shown in the accompanying illustration, as well as stand-alone utilities, kill switch capabilities destroy the data on a device, typically by overwriting preselected files multiple times, rendering them unreadable, when instructed. Kill switches are activated upon customer request when the device is determined to be lost or stolen. Once the kill switch is activated, all data on the computer is erased whenever it next connects to the Internet or when another predesignated remote trigger is activated, such as a certain number of unsuccessful logon attempts.

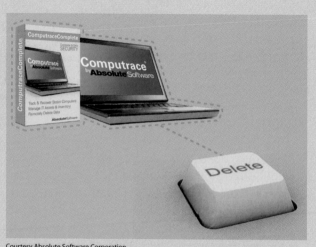

Courtesy Absolute Software Corporation

Keep in mind the following precautions when using portable computers and other mobile devices:

- Install and use encryption, antivirus, antispyware, and firewall software.

- Secure computers with boot passwords; set your mobile phone to autolock after a short period of time and require a passcode to unlock it.

- Use only secure Wi-Fi connections, and disable Wi-Fi and Bluetooth when they are not needed.

- Don't store usernames or passwords attached to a computer or inside its case.

- Use a plain case to make a portable computer less conspicuous.

- Keep an eye on your devices at all times, especially when traveling.

- Use a cable lock to secure devices to a desk or other object whenever you must leave them unattended.

- Regularly back up your data.

- Consider using tracking or kill switch software.

ruggedized device A device that is designed to withstand much more physical abuse than a conventional device.

Proper care of hardware can help prevent serious damage to a computer system. An obvious precaution is to not harm your hardware physically, such as by dropping a portable computer. To help protect portable devices against minor abuse, use protective cases, as shown in Exhibit 6-11. These cases are typically padded or made from protective material; they also often have a thin protective layer over the device's display to protect against scratches.

If you need more protection than a protective case can provide, **ruggedized devices** are designed to

Exhibit 6-11 Protective cases

MOBILE PHONE CASE   **NOTEBOOK CASE**

Courtesy OtterBox and Targus, Inc.

> To protect a portable computer from scratches and other damage, use a neoprene laptop sleeve when carrying it in a conventional briefcase or bag.

withstand much more physical abuse than conventional devices and range from semirugged to ultrarugged. Ruggedized devices are used most often by individuals who work outside of an office, such as field workers, construction workers, outdoor technicians, military personnel, police officers, and firefighters.

To protect hardware from damage due to power fluctuations, everyone should use a **surge suppressor** with a computer whenever it is plugged into a power outlet, as shown in Exhibit 6-12. The surge suppressor

prevents electrical power spikes from harming your system. For desktop computers, surge suppressors should be used with all of the powered components in the computer system. Surge suppressors designed for portable computers are typically smaller and designed to connect only one device.

Users who want their desktop computers to remain powered up when the electricity goes off should use an **uninterruptible power supply** (**UPS**), such as the one shown in Exhibit 6-12, which contains a built-in battery. The length of time that a UPS can power a system depends on the type and number of devices connected to the UPS, the power capacity of the UPS device, and the age of the battery. Most UPS devices also protect against power fluctuations. UPSs designed for use by individuals usually provide power for a few minutes to keep the system powered up during short power blips, as well as to allow the user to save open documents and shut down the computer properly in case the electricity remains off. Industrial-level UPSs typically run for a significantly longer amount of time (up to a few hours), but not long enough to power a facility during an extended power outage.

Dust, heat, static electricity, and moisture can also be dangerous to a computer, so be sure not to place your computer equipment in direct sunlight or in a dusty area. You can use a small handheld vacuum made for electrical equipment periodically to remove the dust from the keyboard and from inside the system unit, but be very careful when vacuuming inside the system unit. Also, be sure the system unit has plenty of ventilation, especially around the fan vents. To help reduce the amount of dust that is drawn into the fan vents, raise your desktop computer several inches off the floor. You should also avoid placing a portable computer on a soft surface, such as a couch or blanket, to help prevent overheating. Unless your computer is ruggedized, like the one shown in Exhibit 6-13, do not get it wet or otherwise expose it to adverse conditions.

Exhibit 6-12 Surge protectors and UPSs

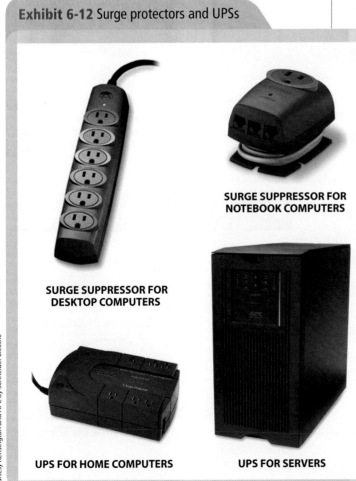

SURGE SUPPRESSOR FOR NOTEBOOK COMPUTERS

SURGE SUPPRESSOR FOR DESKTOP COMPUTERS

UPS FOR HOME COMPUTERS

UPS FOR SERVERS

Courtesy Kensington and APC by Schneider Electric

surge suppressor A device that protects a computer system from damage due to electrical fluctuations.

uninterruptible power supply (**UPS**) A device containing a built-in battery that provides continuous power to a computer and other connected components when the electricity goes out.

Over 50 percent of the phones received by one data recovery firm are water damaged.

To protect against becoming infected with a computer virus or other type of malware, all computers and other devices used to access the Internet or a company network should have security software installed. **Security software** typically includes a variety of security features, including a firewall, protection against spyware and bots, and protection against some types of online fraud. One of the most important components is **antivirus software**, which protects against computer viruses and other types of malware.

Antivirus software typically runs continuously whenever the computer is on to perform real-time monitoring of the computer and incoming email messages, instant messages, Web page content, and downloaded files to prevent malicious software from executing. Many antivirus programs also automatically scan any devices as soon as they are connected to a USB port in order to guard against infections from a USB flash drive, a portable digital media player, or other USB device. Antivirus software helps prevent malware from being installed on your computer because it deletes or quarantines any suspicious content as it arrives. Regular full system scans can detect and remove any viruses or worms that find their way onto your computer. See Exhibit 6-14.

Exhibit 6-13 A ruggedized computer

Courtesy General Dynamics Itronix

Exhibit 6-14 Security software

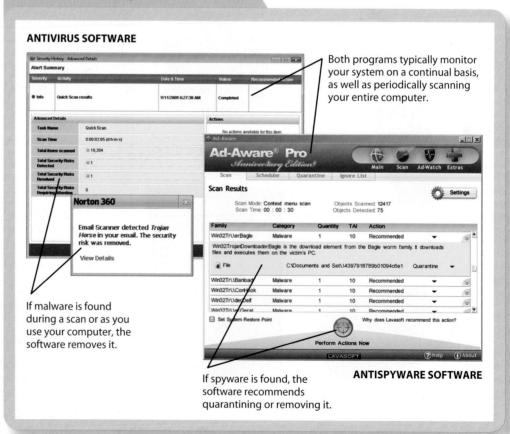

ANTIVIRUS SOFTWARE

Both programs typically monitor your system on a continual basis, as well as periodically scanning your entire computer.

If malware is found during a scan or as you use your computer, the software removes it.

If spyware is found, the software recommends quarantining or removing it.

ANTISPYWARE SOFTWARE

Courtesy Symantec and Lavasoft AB

security software Software, typically a suite of programs, used to protect your computer against a variety of threats.

antivirus software Software used to detect and eliminate computer viruses and other types of malware.

disaster recovery plan (business continuity plan) A written plan that describes the steps a company will take following the occurrence of a disaster.

hot site An alternate location equipped with the computers and other equipment necessary to keep a business's operations going.

firewall A collection of hardware and/or software that protects a computer or computer network from unauthorized access.

Disaster Recovery Plan

To supplement backup procedures, businesses and other organizations should have a **disaster recovery plan** (also called a **business continuity plan**)—a plan that spells out what the organization will do to prepare for and recover from a disruptive event, such as a fire, natural disaster, terrorist attack, power outage, or computer failure. Disaster recovery plans should include information about who will be in charge immediately after the disaster has occurred, what alternate facilities and equipment can be used, where backup media is located, the priority of getting each operation back online, disaster insurance coverage information, emergency communications methods, and so forth. If a **hot site**—an alternate location equipped with the computers, cabling, desks, and other equipment necessary to keep a business's operations going—is to be used following a major disaster, it should be set up ahead of time, and information about the hot site should be included in the disaster recovery plan. Businesses that cannot afford to be without email service should also consider making arrangements with an emergency mail system provider to act as a temporary mail server if the company mail server is not functioning. Copies of the disaster recovery plan should be located off-site.

Individuals and businesses can protect against some types of computer sabotage by controlling access to their computers and networks. Intrusion protection systems can help businesses detect and protect against denial of service (DoS) attacks. For extra protection against spyware, rogue antivirus programs, and other specialized malware, specialized security programs (such as the antispyware program shown in Exhibit 6-14) can be used. In addition, most Web browsers have security settings that can be used to help prevent programs from being installed on a computer without the user's permission. For example, the user can be prompted for permission whenever a download is initiated.

Firewalls, Encryption, and Virtual Private Networks (VPNs)

A **firewall** is a security system that essentially creates a barrier between a computer or network and the Internet in order to protect against unauthorized access.

Securing a Router

A home wireless network should be secured properly so it cannot be used by unauthorized individuals. Security settings are specified in the router's configuration screen, such as the one shown in the accompanying illustration. To open your router's configuration screen to check or modify the settings, type the IP address assigned to that device (such as 192.168.0.1—check for a sticker on the bottom of your router or your router's documentation for its default IP address and username) in your browser's Address bar. Use the default password listed in your router documentation to log on the first time, and then change the password using the configuration screen to prevent unauthorized individuals from changing your router settings. To secure the router, enter the network name (SSID) you want to have associated with the router, select the appropriate security mode, such as WEP, WPA, or WPA2, to be used, and then type a secure passphrase to be used in order to log on to the network.

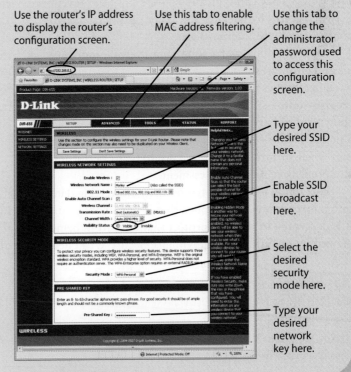

Use the router's IP address to display the router's configuration screen.

Use this tab to enable MAC address filtering.

Use this tab to change the administrator password used to access this configuration screen.

Type your desired SSID here.

Enable SSID broadcast here.

Select the desired security mode here.

Type your desired network key here.

Firewalls are typically two-way, so they check all incoming and outgoing traffic and allow only authorized traffic to pass through the firewall. Personal firewalls are typically software-based systems or they can be built into many operating systems, and they are geared toward protecting home computers from hackers attempting to access those computers through their Internet connections. All computers with direct Internet connections (DSL, cable, satellite, or fixed wireless Internet access) should use a firewall; computers using dial-up Internet access only are relatively safe from hackers. Many routers, modems, and other pieces of networking hardware also include built-in firewall capabilities to help secure the networks these devices are used with. Firewalls designed to protect business networks may be software-based, hardware-based, or a combination of the two. They can typically be used both to prevent network access by hackers and other outsiders, and to control employee Internet access.

After installing and setting up a firewall, individuals and businesses should test their systems to determine if vulnerabilities still exist. Individuals can use online security tests—such as the Symantec Security Check shown in Exhibit 6-15 or the tests at Gibson Research's ShieldsUP! site—to check their computers; businesses may wish to hire an outside consultant to perform a comprehensive security assessment.

Encryption is a way of temporarily converting data into a form, known as a cipher, that is unreadable until it is decrypted in order to protect that data from being viewed by unauthorized individuals. Secure Wi-Fi net-

Exhibit 6-15 Online security scans can check your system for vulnerabilities

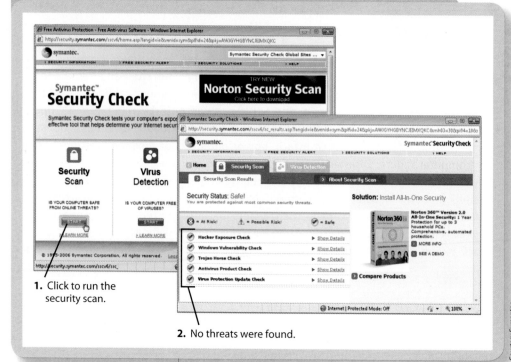

1. Click to run the security scan.

2. No threats were found.

works use encryption to secure data that is transferred over the network. **Secure Web pages** use encryption so that sensitive data sent via the Web page is protected as it travels over the Internet. The most common security protocols used with secure Web pages are Secure Sockets Layer (SSL) and Extended Validation Secure Sockets Layer (EV SSL). The URL for Web pages using either form of SSL begins with *https:* instead of *http:*.

Some Internet services, such as Skype VoIP calls and Hushmail Web-based emails, use built-in encryption. Encryption can also be added manually to a file or an email message before it is sent over the Internet to ensure that the content is unreadable if the file or message is intercepted during transit. In addition to securing files during transit, encryption can be used to protect the files stored on a hard drive so they will be unreadable if opened by an unauthorized person, such as if a hacker accesses a file containing sensitive data or if a computer containing sensitive files is lost or stolen. Increasingly, computers and hard drives, particularly those used with portable computers, are self-encrypting; that is, encrypting all data automatically and invis-

encryption A method of scrambling the contents of an email message or a file to make it unreadable if an unauthorized user intercepts it.

secure Web page A Web page that uses encryption to protect information transmitted via that Web page.

Sensitive information should be entered only on secure Web pages so that a criminal cannot intercept that data.

Exhibit 6-16 Using public key encryption to secure an email message

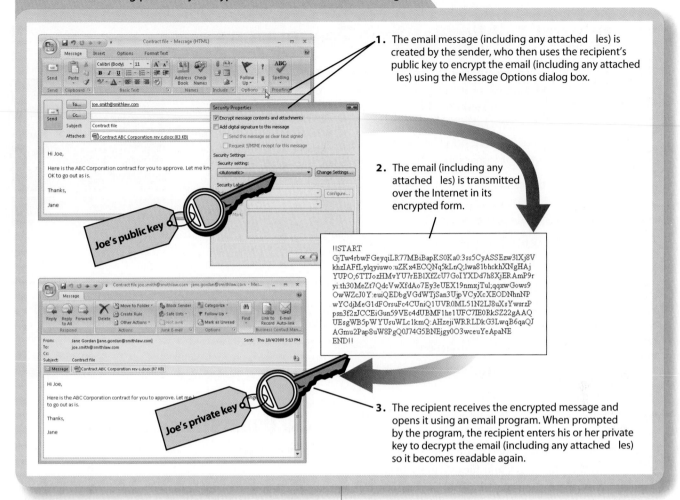

1. The email message (including any attached les) is created by the sender, who then uses the recipient's public key to encrypt the email (including any attached les) using the Message Options dialog box.

2. The email (including any attached les) is transmitted over the Internet in its encrypted form.

```
||START
GjTw4rbwFGeyqiLR77MBiBapKS0Ka0:3ss5CyASSEzw31Xj8V
khzIAFfLylqyiuwo:uZKx4ECQNq5kLnQ;Iwa81bhckhXNgHAj
YUPO;6TTJozHMvYU7rEBIXfZcU7GoIYXDd7h8XjERAmP9r
yi:th30MeZt7QdcVwXfdAo7Ey3eUEX19nmxjTul;qqxwGows9
OwWZcJ0Y:euiQEDbgVGdWTjSan3UjpVCyXcXEODNhnNP
wYCdjMeG1dFOrsuFc4CUniQ1UVR0ML51N2LJ8uXsYwsrzP
psn3f2zJCCEiGun59VEc4dUBMF1he1UFC7IE0RkSZ22gAAQ
UEsgWB5pWYUsuWLc1kmQ:AHzejiWRRLDkG3LwqB6qaQJ
AGmu2Pap8uW8PgQ0J74G5BNEjgy0O3wceuYeApaNE
END||
```

3. The recipient receives the encrypted message and opens it using an email program. When prompted by the program, the recipient enters his or her private key to decrypt the email (including any attached les) so it becomes readable again.

ibly to the user. Windows, Mac OS, and other current operating systems support encryption, and businesses are increasingly turning to encryption to prevent data loss if a data breach should occur.

The two most common types of encryption in use today are private key encryption and public key encryption. **Private key encryption**, also called symmetric key encryption, uses a single secret private key (essentially a password) to both encrypt and decrypt a file or message being sent over the Internet. It is often used to encrypt files stored on an individual's computer because the individual who selects the private key is likely the only one who will need to access those files. Private key encryption can also be used to send files securely to others, provided both the sender and recipient agree on the private key that will be used to access the file.

Public key encryption, also called asymmetric key encryption, utilizes two encryption keys to encrypt and decrypt documents. Specifically, public key encryption uses a private key and a public key that are related mathematically to each other and have been assigned to a particular individual. An individual's public key is not secret and is available for anyone to use, but the corresponding private key is used only by the individual to whom it was assigned. Documents or messages encrypted with a public key can only be decrypted with the matching private key. Exhibit 6-16 illustrates

An emerging encryption standard that may eventually replace SSL is Transport Layer Security (TLS).

private key encryption A type of encryption that uses a single key to encrypt and decrypt the file or message.

public key encryption A type of encryption that uses key pairs to encrypt and decrypt the file or message.

Additional Public Hotspot Precautions

Using firewall software, secure Web pages, VPNs, and encryption is a good start for protecting against unauthorized access and unauthorized use at a public Wi-Fi hotspot. However, you can use the additional precautions listed below to avoid data on your computers or data sent over the Internet from being compromised.

- Turn off automatic connections and pay attention to the list of available hotspots to try to make sure you connect to a legitimate access point.

- Only enter passwords, credit card numbers, and other data on secure Web pages using a VPN.

- If you're not using a VPN, encrypt all sensitive files before transferring or emailing them.

- If you're not using a VPN, avoid online shopping, banking, and other sensitive transactions.

- Turn off file sharing so others can't access the files on your hard drive.

- Turn off Bluetooth and Wi-Fi when you are not using them.

- Disable *ad hoc* capabilities to prevent another computer from connecting to your computer directly without using an access point.

Mike Flippo/Shutterstock.com

- Use antivirus software and make sure your operating system is up to date.

---

how public key encryption is used to secure an email message.

While email and file encryption can be used to transfer individual messages and files securely over the Internet, a **virtual private network** (**VPN**) is designed to be used when a continuous secure channel over the Internet is needed. A VPN provides a secure private tunnel from the user's computer through the Internet to another destination and is most often used to provide remote employees with secure access to a company network. VPNs use encryption and other security mechanisms to ensure that only authorized users can access the remote network and that the data cannot be intercepted during transit. Because it uses the Internet instead of an expensive private physical network, a VPN can provide a secure environment over a large geographical area at a manageable cost.

virtual private network (**VPN**) A private, secure path over the Internet that provides authorized users a secure means of accessing a private network via the Internet.

privacy The state of being concealed or free from unauthorized intrusion.

information privacy The rights of individuals and companies to control how information about them is collected and used.

LO6.5 Understanding Privacy Concerns

Privacy is usually defined as the state of being concealed or free from unauthorized intrusion. The term **information privacy** refers to the rights of individuals and companies to control how information about them is collected and used. The problem of how to protect personal privacy—that is, how to keep personal information private—existed long before computers entered the picture. For example, sealing wax and unique signet rings were used centuries ago to seal letters, wills, and other personal documents to guard against their content being revealed to unauthorized individuals, as well as to alert the recipient if such an intrusion occurred while the document was in transit. But computers, with their ability to store, duplicate, and

Whenever information is provided to others, there is always the danger that the information will be misused.

manipulate large quantities of data, combined with the fact that databases containing our personal information can be accessed and shared via the Internet, have added a new twist to the issue of personal privacy.

Many people are concerned about the privacy of their Web site activities and email messages. Recently, an unprecedented number of high-profile data breaches have occurred—some via hacking and other network intrusions; others due to lost or stolen hardware, or carelessness with papers or storage media containing Social Security numbers or other sensitive data. Because every data breach is a risk to information privacy, protecting the data stored in databases today is an important concern for everyone. Other privacy concerns are spam and other marketing activities, electronic surveillance, and electronic monitoring.

Databases, Electronic Profiling, Spam, and Other Marketing Activities

Information about individuals can be located in many different databases. For example, educational institutions have databases containing student information, organizations use a database to hold employee information, and most physicians and health insurance providers maintain databases containing individuals' medical information. If these databases are adequately protected from hackers and other unauthorized individuals, and if the data is not transported on a portable computer or other device that may be vulnerable to loss or theft, these databases do not pose a significant privacy concern to consumers because the information can rarely be shared without the individuals' permission. However, the data stored in these types of databases is not always sufficiently protected and has been breached quite often in the past. Consequently, these databases, along with marketing databases and government databases that are typically associated with a higher risk of personal privacy violations, are of growing concern to privacy advocates.

Marketing databases contain marketing and demographic data about people, such as where they live and what products they buy. This information is used for marketing purposes, such as sending advertisements that fit each individual's interests via regular mail or email, or trying to sign people up over the phone for some type of service. Almost any time you provide information about yourself online or offline—when you subscribe to a magazine, fill out a product registration card, or buy something using a credit card—there is a good chance that the information will find its way into a marketing database.

Marketing databases are also used in conjunction with Web activities, such as social network activity and searches performed via some personalized search services. For instance, the data stored on Facebook, MySpace, and other social networking sites can be gathered and used for advertising purposes by marketing companies, and the activities of users of personalized search services (where users log in to use the service) can be tracked and that data can be used for marketing purposes.

Information about individuals is also available in **government databases**. Some information, such as Social Security earnings and income tax returns, is confidential and can legally be seen only by authorized individuals. Other information, such as birth records, marriage certificates, and divorce information, as well as property purchases, assessments, liens, and tax values, is available to the public, including to the marketing companies that specialize in creating marketing databases.

In the past, the data about any one individual was stored in a variety of separate locations, such as at different government agencies, individual retail stores, the person's bank and credit card companies, and so forth. Because it would be extremely time consuming to locate all the information about one person from all these different places, there was a fairly high level of information privacy. Today, however, most of an individual's data is stored on computers that can communicate with each other via the Internet, which means accessing personal information about someone is much easier than it used to be. For example, a variety of public information about individuals is available free through the Internet, as demonstrated in Exhibit 6-17; there are also paid services that can perform online database searches for you.

Collecting in-depth information about an individual is known as **electronic profiling**. Electronic profiles are generally designed to provide specific information and can include an individual's name, current and previous

---

marketing database A collection of data about people that is stored in a large database and used for marketing purposes.

government database A collection of data about people that is collected and maintained by the government.

electronic profiling Using electronic means to collect a variety of in-depth information about an individual, such as name, address, income, and buying habits.

Exhibit 6-17 Searchable databases available via the Internet

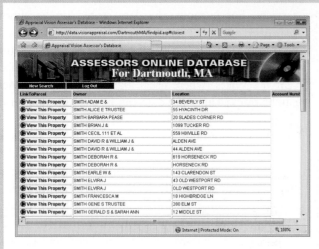

PROPERTY VALUE SEARCH

Some states permit searches for property located in that state, such as displaying the owner's name, address, and a link to additional information including property value for the supplied owner name.

VITAL RECORDS SEARCH

Some counties and states allow searches for documents related to marriages, divorces, births, legal judgments, deeds, liens, powers of attorney, and so forth.

ADDRESS NUMBER AND PHONE NUMBER SEARCH

Any information listed in a U.S. telephone book can be found using this site. You can search either by name or telephone number to view the available information.

addresses, telephone number, marital status, number and age of children, spending habits, and product preferences. The information retrieved from electronic profiles is then sold to companies upon request to be used for marketing purposes, as illustrated in Exhibit 6-18. For example, one company might request a list of all individuals in a particular state whose street addresses are considered to be in an affluent area and who buy baby products. Another company might request a list of all SUV owners in a particular city who have not purchased a car in five years.

Most businesses and Web sites that collect personal information have a **privacy policy** that discloses how the personal information you provide will be used (see Exhibit 6-19). As long as their actions do not violate their privacy policy, it is legal for businesses to sell the personal data that they collect. There are some problems with privacy policies, however, including that they are sometimes difficult to decipher and that most people do

> **privacy policy** A policy, commonly posted on a company's Web site, that explains how personal information provided to that company will be used.
>
> **spam** Unsolicited, bulk email sent over the Internet.

Exhibit 6-18 How electronic profiling might work

When you make an electronic transaction, information about who you are and what you buy is recorded, usually in a database.

Databases containing the identities of people and what they buy are sold to marketing companies.

The marketing companies add the new data to their marketing databases; they can then reorganize the data in ways that might be valuable to other companies.

The marketing companies create lists of individuals matching the specific needs of companies; the companies buy the lists for their own marketing purposes.

not take the time to read them before using a site. In addition, many businesses periodically change their privacy policies without warning, requiring consumers to reread privacy policies frequently or risk their personal information being used in a manner that they did not agree to when the information was initially provided.

Spam refers to unsolicited email sent to a large group of individuals at one time. The electronic equivalent of junk mail (see Exhibit 6-20), spam is most often used to sell products or services to individuals. Spam is also used in phishing schemes and other dot cons and is sent frequently via botnets. The text message spam shown in Exhibit 6-20 is an example of a phishing spam message. A great deal of spam involves health-related products, such as medicine or weight loss systems, counterfeit products, pornography, as well as new and often fraudulent business

Exhibit 6-19 Web site privacy policy

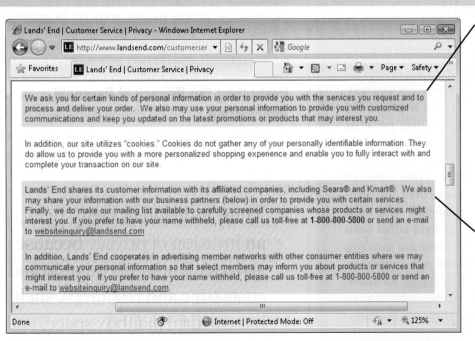

This indicates that your personal information may be used to keep you updated on products that might interest you.

This indicates that your personal information may be disclosed to third parties, unless you opt out.

Exhibit 6-22 Computer network and Internet security legislation

Date	Law and Description
2004	**Identity Theft Penalty Enhancement Act** Adds extra years to prison sentences for criminals who use identity theft (including the use of stolen credit card numbers) to commit other crimes, including credit card fraud and terrorism.
2003	**CAN-SPAM Act** Implements regulations for unsolicited email messages.
2003	**Fair and Accurate Credit Transactions Act (FACTA)** Amends the Fair Credit Reporting Act (FCRA) to require, among other things, that the three nationwide consumer reporting agencies (Equifax, Experian, and TransUnion) provide to consumers, upon request, a free copy of their credit report once every 12 months.
2003	**PROTECT Act** Includes provisions to prohibit virtual child pornography.
2003	**Health Insurance Portability and Accountability Act (HIPAA)** Includes a Security Rule that sets minimum security standards to protect health information stored electronically.
2002	**Homeland Security Act** Includes provisions to combat cyberterrorism, including protecting ISPs against lawsuits from customers for revealing private information to law enforcement agencies.
2002	**Sarbanes-Oxley Act** Requires archiving a variety of electronic records and protecting the integrity of corporate financial data.
2001	**USA PATRIOT Act** Grants federal authorities expanded surveillance and intelligence-gathering powers, such as broadening the ability of federal agents to obtain the real identity of Internet users, intercept email and other types of Internet communications, follow online activity of suspects, expand their wiretapping authority, and more.
1998	**Identity Theft and Assumption Deterrence Act of 1998** Makes it a federal crime to knowingly use someone else's means of identification, such as name, Social Security number, or credit card, to commit any unlawful activity.
1997	**No Electronic Theft (NET) Act** Expands computer piracy laws to include distribution of copyrighted materials over the Internet.
1996	**National Information Infrastructure Protection Act** Amends the Computer Fraud and Abuse Act of 1984 to punish information theft crossing state lines and to crack down on network trespassing.
1994	**Computer Abuse Amendments Act** Amends the Computer Fraud and Abuse Act of 1984 to include computer viruses and other harmful code.
1986	**Computer Fraud and Abuse Act of 1986** Amends the 1984 law to include federally regulated financial institutions.
1984	**Computer Fraud and Abuse Act of 1984** Makes it a crime to break into computers owned by the federal government. This act has been regularly amended over the years as technology has changed.

Another issue is weighing the need to implement legislation versus the use of voluntary methods to protect computer security and personal privacy. For instance, the Child Online Protection Act (COPA) has been highly controversial since it was passed in 1998, and, in fact, it has never been implemented. This legislation prohibited making pornography or any other content deemed harmful to minors available to minors via the Internet and carried a $50,000 fine. This law was blocked by the U.S. Supreme Court several times, based on the likelihood that it violates the First Amendment and the possibility that less restrictive alternatives such as Internet filtering can be used instead to prevent the access of inappropriate materials by minors. A list of selected federal laws related to computer security and privacy are shown in Exhibit 6-23.

Exhibit 6-18 How electronic profiling might work

When you make an electronic transaction, information about who you are and what you buy is recorded, usually in a database.

Databases containing the identities of people and what they buy are sold to marketing companies.

The marketing companies add the new data to their marketing databases; they can then reorganize the data in ways that might be valuable to other companies.

The marketing companies create lists of individuals matching the specific needs of companies; the companies buy the lists for their own marketing purposes.

not take the time to read them before using a site. In addition, many businesses periodically change their privacy policies without warning, requiring consumers to reread privacy policies frequently or risk their personal information being used in a manner that they did not agree to when the information was initially provided.

Spam refers to unsolicited email sent to a large group of individuals at one time. The electronic equivalent of junk mail (see Exhibit 6-20), spam is most often used to sell products or services to individuals. Spam is also used in phishing schemes and other dot cons and is sent frequently via botnets. The text message spam shown in Exhibit 6-20 is an example of a phishing spam message. A great deal of spam involves health-related products, such as medicine or weight loss systems, counterfeit products, pornography, as well as new and often fraudulent business

Exhibit 6-19 Web site privacy policy

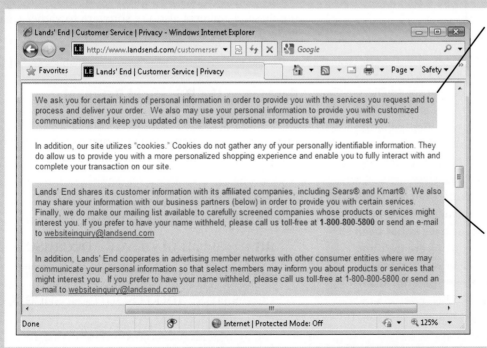

This indicates that your personal information may be used to keep you updated on products that might interest you.

We ask you for certain kinds of personal information in order to provide you with the services you request and to process and deliver your order. We also may use your personal information to provide you with customized communications and keep you updated on the latest promotions or products that may interest you.

In addition, our site utilizes "cookies." Cookies do not gather any of your personally identifiable information. They do allow us to provide you with a more personalized shopping experience and enable you to fully interact with and complete your transaction on our site.

Lands' End shares its customer information with its affiliated companies, including Sears® and Kmart®. We also may share your information with our business partners (below) in order to provide you with certain services. Finally, we do make our mailing list available to carefully screened companies whose products or services might interest you. If you prefer to have your name withheld, please call us toll-free at 1-800-800-5800 or send an e-mail to websiteinquiry@landsend.com

In addition, Lands' End cooperates in advertising member networks with other consumer entities where we may communicate your personal information so that select members may inform you about products or services that might interest you. If you prefer to have your name withheld, please call us toll-free at 1-800-800-5800 or send an e-mail to websiteinquiry@landsend.com

This indicates that your personal information may be disclosed to third parties, unless you opt out.

Exhibit 6-20 Examples of spam

EMAIL SPAM

TEXT MESSAGE SPAM

The sheer volume of spam is staggering. For instance, Symantec's MessageLabs recently estimated that more than 90 percent of all email messages is now spam. At best, large volumes of spam are an annoyance to recipients and can slow down a mail server's delivery of important messages. At worst, spam can disable a mail network completely, or it can cause recipients to miss or lose important email messages because those messages have been caught in a spam filter or were accidentally deleted by the recipient while he or she was deleting a large number of spam email messages. Most Internet users spend several minutes each day dealing with spam, making spam very expensive for businesses in terms of lost productivity, consumption of communications bandwidth, and drain of technical support. Spam sent to a mobile phone, either via text message or email, is also expensive for end users who have a limited data or text message allowance.

opportunities and stock deals. Spam can also be generated by individuals forwarding email messages they receive, such as jokes, recipes, or notices of possible new privacy or health concerns, to everyone in their address books. Spam can also be sent via instant messages, fax messages, mobile phones, Facebook or MySpace accounts, Twitter pages, and via other social networking communications methods.

One of the most common ways of getting on a spam mailing list is by having your email address entered into a marketing database, which can happen when you sign up for a free online service or use your email address to register a product or make an online purchase. Spammers also use software to gather email addresses from Web pages, message board posts, and social networking sites.

Protecting the Privacy of Personal Information

Protecting your email address is one of the best ways to avoid spam. One way to accomplish this is to use

Is Spam Legal?

Most spam is legal, but there are requirements that must be adhered to in order for it to be legal. For instance, the CAN-SPAM Act of 2003 established requirements for commercial emailers, such as using truthful subject lines and honoring remove requests, as well as specified penalties for companies and individuals that break the law. Although the CAN-SPAM Act has not reduced the amount of spam circulated today, it has increased the number of spammers prosecuted for sending spam. In fact, several spammers have been convicted in recent years. They have either been fined or sent to prison, and more are awaiting trial. For instance, one spammer was recently ordered to pay $230 million to MySpace for spamming MySpace users and another was ordered to pay Facebook a record $873 million for spamming its members.

Many individuals view spam as an invasion of privacy because it arrives without permission and costs time and resources, such as bandwidth, mailbox space, and hard drive space.

one private email address for family, friends, colleagues, and other trusted sources. For online shopping, signing up for free offers, message boards, product registration, and other activities that typically lead to junk email, use a disposable or **throw-away email address** (a second address obtained from your ISP or a free email address from Windows Live Hotmail or Google's Gmail).

Another advantage of using a throw-away email address for only noncritical applications is that you can quit using it and obtain a new one if spam begins to get overwhelming or too annoying.

Unsubscribe or Ignore Spam Emails?

To comply with truth-in-advertising laws, an unsubscribe email address included in an unsolicited email must be a working address. If you receive a marketing email from a reputable source, you may be able to unsubscribe by clicking the supplied link or otherwise following the unsubscribe instructions. Because spam from less-legitimate sources often has unsubscribe links that do not work or that are present only to verify that your email address is genuine—a very valuable piece of information for future use—many privacy experts recommend never replying to or trying to unsubscribe from any spam.

Protecting your personal information is a critical step toward safeguarding your privacy. Consequently, it makes sense to be cautious about revealing your private information to anyone. Privacy tips for safeguarding personal information include the following:

- Read a Web site's privacy policy, if one exists, before providing any personal information. Look for a phrase saying that the company will not share your information with other companies under any circumstances. If the Web site reserves the right to share your information if the company is sold or unless you specifically notify them otherwise, it is best to assume that any information you provide will eventually be shared with others.

- Avoid putting too many personal details about yourself on your Web site or on a social networking site. If you would like to post photographs or other personal documents on a Web site for faraway

friends and family members to see, consider using a photo sharing site that allows you to restrict access to your photos, such as Flickr, Snapfish, or Fotki.

- Beware of Web sites offering prizes or the chance to earn free merchandise in exchange for your personal information. Chances are good that the information will be sold to direct marketers, which will likely result in additional spam.

- Consider using privacy software, such as Anonymous Surfing or Privacy Guardian, to hide your personal information as you browse the Web so it is not revealed and your activities cannot be tracked by marketers.

Courtesy Anonymizer, Inc.

- Just because a Web site or registration form asks for personal information, that does not mean you have to give it. Supply only the required information. Required fields are often marked with an asterisk or are colored differently than nonrequired fields—if not, you can try leaving fields blank and see if the form will still be accepted.

- If you are using a public computer, be sure to remove any personal information and settings stored on the computer during your session. You can use browser options to delete this data manually from the computer before you leave. To prevent the deleted data from being recovered, run the Windows Disk Cleanup program on the hard drive, making sure that the options for Temporary Internet Files and the Recycle Bin are selected during the Disk Cleanup process. An easier option is using the private browsing mode offered by some browsers (see Exhibit 6-21) that allow you to browse the Web without leaving any history on the computer you are using. In either case, be sure to log out of any Web sites you were using before leaving the computer.

throw-away email address An email address used only for nonessential purposes and activities that may result in spam; the address can be disposed of and replaced if spam becomes a problem.

Exhibit 6-21 Private browsing can protect your privacy at public computers

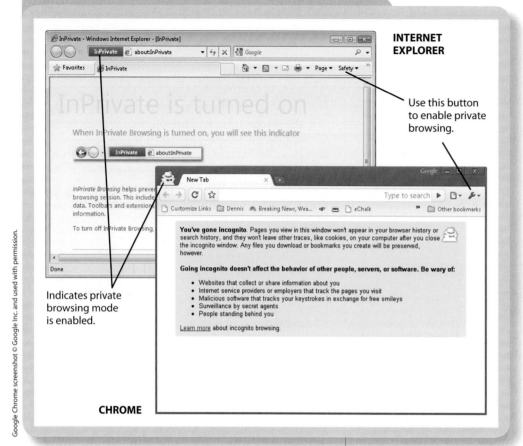

INTERNET EXPLORER

Use this button to enable private browsing.

InPrivate is turned on

When InPrivate Browsing is turned on, you will see this indicator

InPrivate   about:InPrivate

InPrivate Browsing helps preven browsing session. This include data. Toolbars and extension information.

To turn off InPrivate Browsing,

Indicates private browsing mode is enabled.

You've gone incognito. Pages you view in this window won't appear in your browser history or search history, and they won't leave other traces, like cookies, on your computer after you close the incognito window. Any files you download or bookmarks you create will be preserved, however.

Going incognito doesn't affect the behavior of other people, servers, or software. Be wary of:

- Websites that collect or share information about you
- Internet service providers or employers that track the pages you visit
- Malicious software that tracks your keystrokes in exchange for free smileys
- Surveillance by secret agents
- People standing behind you

Learn more about incognito browsing.

CHROME

identify possible spam and either flag it or move it to a Spam or Junk Email folder.

Custom email filters are used to route messages automatically to particular folders based on stated criteria. For example, you can specify that email messages with keywords frequently used in spam subject lines, such as *free*, *porn*, *opportunity*, *last chance*, *weight*, *pharmacy*, be routed into a folder named Possible Spam, and you can specify that all email messages from your boss's email address be routed into an Urgent folder. Filtering can help you find important messages in your Inbox by preventing it from becoming cluttered with spam.

While keeping your personal information as private as possible can help to reduce spam and other direct marketing activities, filtering can also be helpful. Some ISPs automatically block all email messages originating from known or suspected spammers so those email messages never reach the individuals' mailboxes; other ISPs flag suspicious email messages as possible spam, based on their content or subject lines, to warn individuals that those messages may contain spam. To deal with spam that makes it to your computer, you can use an **email filter**—a tool for automatically sorting incoming email messages. Email filters used to capture spam are called **spam filters**, or sometimes **junk email filters**. Many email programs have built-in spam filters that

Another alternative for reducing the amount of spam you receive is to **opt out**. Opting out refers to following a predesignated procedure to remove yourself from marketing lists, or otherwise preventing your personal information from being obtained by or shared with others. By opting out, you instruct companies you do business with not to share your personal information with third parties. You can also opt out of being contacted by direct and online marketing companies.

Opting-out procedures are confusing and time-consuming, and they do not always work well. Consequently, some privacy groups are pushing to change to an opt-in process, in which individuals would need to **opt in**—request participation in—to a particular

email filter A tool that automatically sorts your incoming email messages based on specific criteria.

spam filter (junk email filter) An email filter used to redirect spam from a user's Inbox.

opt out To request that you be removed from marketing activities or that your information not be shared with other companies.

opt in To request that you be included in marketing activities or that your information be shared with other companies.

Check your Junk or Spam folder periodically to locate any email messages mistakenly filed there—especially before you permanently delete those messages.

marketing activity before companies can collect or share any personal data. This is already the case in the European Union. In fact, Wal-Mart recently changed its privacy policy to share information with third parties only if customers opt in. However, the general practice in the U.S. business community is to use your information as allowed for by each privacy policy unless you specifically opt out.

Any business that stores personal information about employees, customers, or other individuals must take adequate security measures to protect the privacy of that information. Secure servers and encryption can protect the data stored on a server; firewalls and access control systems can protect against unauthorized access. To prevent personal information from being sent intentionally or inadvertently via email, organizations can use email encryption systems that automatically encrypt email messages containing certain keywords. For instance, some hospitals use encryption systems that scan all outgoing email messages and attachments, and then automatically encrypt all messages that appear to contain patient-identifiable information. The recipient of an encrypted email message typically receives a link to a secure Web site to log in and view the encrypted email message.

A final consideration for protecting the privacy of personal information for both individuals and businesses is protecting the information located on paper documents and hardware that are to be disposed of. Papers, CDs, DVDs, and other media containing sensitive data should be shredded, and the hard drives of computers to be disposed of should be wiped—overwritten several times using special disk-wiping or disk-erasing software—before they are sold or recycled. Unlike the data on a drive that has merely been erased or even reformatted (which can still be recovered), data on a properly wiped drive is very difficult or impossible to recover.

Courtesy Fellowes, Inc.

Wiping is typically viewed as an acceptable precaution for deleting sensitive data like Web site passwords and tax returns from hard drives and other storage media. However, before disposing of storage media containing sensitive data, businesses should consider physically destroying the media, such as by shredding or melting the hardware. To help with this process, data destruction services can be used.

Electronic Surveillance and Monitoring

There are many ways electronic tools can be used to watch individuals, listen in on their conversations, or monitor their activities. Some of these tools, such as devices used by individuals to eavesdrop on wireless telephone conversations, are not legal. Other products and technologies, such as the GPS devices that are built into some cars so they can be located if they are stolen or the monitoring ankle bracelets used for offenders sentenced to house arrest, are used solely for law enforcement purposes. Still other electronic tools, such as computer

Chief Privacy Officer

Ensuring that the private data stored by a business is adequately protected is increasingly the responsibility of a chief privacy officer (CPO)—a rapidly growing position in business. Typically, CPOs are responsible for ensuring privacy laws are complied with, identifying the data in a company that needs to be protected, developing policies to protect that data, and responding to any incidents that occur. Another issue that must be dealt with by CPOs is the changing definition of what information is regarded as personal and, therefore, needs to be safeguarded.

monitoring software, video surveillance equipment, and presence technology, can often be used legally by individuals, by businesses in conjunction with employee monitoring, and by law enforcement agencies.

Computer monitoring software records keystrokes, logs the programs or Web sites accessed, or otherwise monitors someone's computer activity. These programs are typically marketed toward parents, spouses, law enforcement agencies, or employers. Although it is legal to use computer monitoring software on your own computer or on the computers of your employees, installing it on other computers without the owners' knowledge to monitor their computer activity is usually illegal.

Video surveillance is closed circuit security cameras used to monitor activities taking place at facilities for security purposes. It is routinely used at retail stores, banks, office buildings, and other privately owned facilities that are open to the public, as well as public locations such as streets, parks, airports, sporting arenas, and subway systems for law enforcement purposes.

Public video surveillance systems are often used in conjunction with face recognition technology to try to identify known terrorists and other criminals, to identify criminals when their crimes are caught on tape, and to prevent crimes from occurring. Many privacy advocates object to the use of video surveillance and face recognition technology in public locations; their concerns are primarily based on how the video captured by these systems will be used.

Kirill R/Shutterstock.com

computer monitoring software Software that can be used to record an individual's computer usage, such as recording the actual keystrokes used or creating a summary of Web sites and programs accessed.

video surveillance The use of video cameras to monitor activities of individuals for work-related or crime-prevention purposes.

employee monitoring Observing or reviewing employees' actions while they are on the job.

presence technology Technology that enables one computing device to locate and identify the current status of another device on the same network.

Privacy Expectations in Public Places

Legally speaking, people typically have few rights to privacy in public places, but many believe that new technology—such as camera phones—will require the law to reconsider and redefine what is considered to be a public place. In fact, some places have banned mobile phones entirely to protect individuals' privacy, such as in locker rooms, restrooms, and courthouses, and by many research and production facilities to prevent corporate espionage.

Courtesy Nokia

Employee monitoring is the act of recording or observing the actions of employees while on the job. Common employee monitoring activities include screening telephone calls, reviewing email, and tracking computer and Internet usage. Although many employees feel that being watched at work is an invasion of their personal privacy, it is legal and very common in the United States.

Presence technology is the ability of one computing device on a network to identify another device on the same network and determine its status. It can be used

The American Management Association (AMA) reports that the majority of all U.S. companies use some type of electronic surveillance with their employees.

to tell when someone on the network is using his or her computer or mobile phone, as well as the individual's availability for communications; that is, whether or not the individual is able and willing to take a call or respond to an IM at the present time.

Protecting Personal and Workplace Privacy

There are not many options for protecting yourself against computer monitoring by your employer or the government, or against video surveillance systems. However, businesses should take the necessary security measures to ensure that employee activities are not being monitored by a hacker or other unauthorized individual. Individuals should also secure their home computers to protect against keystroke logging or other computer monitoring software that may be inadvertently installed via an electronic greeting card, game, or other downloaded file, and that is designed to provide a hacker with account numbers, passwords, and other sensitive data that could be used in identity theft or other fraudulent activities. Antispyware software can be used to detect and remove some types of illegal computer monitoring and spyware software.

Courtesy Omniquad Ltd.

To protect the personal privacy of their employees and customers, businesses and organizations have a responsibility to keep private information about their employees, the company, and their customers safe. Strong security measures can help to protect against unauthorized access by hackers. Businesses and organizations should take precautions against both intentional and accidental breaches of privacy by employees. Finally, businesses and organizations have the responsibility to monitor their employees' activities to ensure workers are productive. In general, businesses must maintain a safe and productive workplace environment and protect the privacy of their customers and employees, while at the same time ensure the company is not vulnerable to lawsuits.

Employees have the responsibility to read a company's employee policy that specifies what personal activities are allowed during company time or on company equipment, as well as what activities, such as Web surfing, email, telephone calls, and downloading files, may

Because employers can legally monitor at-work activities, it is wise—from a privacy standpoint—to avoid personal activities at work.

be monitored when initially hired. They should review it periodically to ensure that they understand the policy and do not violate any company rules while working for that organization.

LO6.6 Network and Internet Security Legislation

Although new legislation is passed periodically to address new types of computer crimes, it is difficult for the legal system to keep pace with the rate at which technology changes. In addition, there are both domestic and international jurisdictional issues because many computer crimes affect businesses and individuals located in geographic areas other than the one in which the computer criminal is located, and hackers can make it appear that activity is coming from a different location than it really is. Nevertheless, computer crime legislation continues to be proposed and computer crimes are being prosecuted. A list of selected federal laws concerning network and Internet security is shown in Exhibit 6-22.

The high level of concern regarding computer security and personal privacy has led state and federal legislators to pass a variety of laws since the 1970s. Internet privacy is viewed as one of the top policy issues facing Congress today, and numerous bills have been proposed in the last several years regarding spam, telemarketing, spyware, online profiling, and other very important privacy issues. However, Congress has had difficulty passing new legislation. In addition to the reasons stated above, including the rate at which technology changes and the jurisdictional issues when computer crimes affect businesses and individuals in geographic areas other than the one in which the computer criminal is located, privacy is difficult to define and there is a struggle to balance freedom of speech with the right to privacy.

Exhibit 6-22 Computer network and Internet security legislation

Date	Law and Description
2004	Identity Theft Penalty Enhancement Act Adds extra years to prison sentences for criminals who use identity theft (including the use of stolen credit card numbers) to commit other crimes, including credit card fraud and terrorism.
2003	CAN-SPAM Act Implements regulations for unsolicited email messages.
2003	Fair and Accurate Credit Transactions Act (FACTA) Amends the Fair Credit Reporting Act (FCRA) to require, among other things, that the three nationwide consumer reporting agencies (Equifax, Experian, and TransUnion) provide to consumers, upon request, a free copy of their credit report once every 12 months.
2003	PROTECT Act Includes provisions to prohibit virtual child pornography.
2003	Health Insurance Portability and Accountability Act (HIPAA) Includes a Security Rule that sets minimum security standards to protect health information stored electronically.
2002	Homeland Security Act Includes provisions to combat cyberterrorism, including protecting ISPs against lawsuits from customers for revealing private information to law enforcement agencies.
2002	Sarbanes-Oxley Act Requires archiving a variety of electronic records and protecting the integrity of corporate financial data.
2001	USA PATRIOT Act Grants federal authorities expanded surveillance and intelligence-gathering powers, such as broadening the ability of federal agents to obtain the real identity of Internet users, intercept email and other types of Internet communications, follow online activity of suspects, expand their wiretapping authority, and more.
1998	Identity Theft and Assumption Deterrence Act of 1998 Makes it a federal crime to knowingly use someone else's means of identification, such as name, Social Security number, or credit card, to commit any unlawful activity.
1997	No Electronic Theft (NET) Act Expands computer piracy laws to include distribution of copyrighted materials over the Internet.
1996	National Information Infrastructure Protection Act Amends the Computer Fraud and Abuse Act of 1984 to punish information theft crossing state lines and to crack down on network trespassing.
1994	Computer Abuse Amendments Act Amends the Computer Fraud and Abuse Act of 1984 to include computer viruses and other harmful code.
1986	Computer Fraud and Abuse Act of 1986 Amends the 1984 law to include federally regulated financial institutions.
1984	Computer Fraud and Abuse Act of 1984 Makes it a crime to break into computers owned by the federal government. This act has been regularly amended over the years as technology has changed.

Another issue is weighing the need to implement legislation versus the use of voluntary methods to protect computer security and personal privacy. For instance, the Child Online Protection Act (COPA) has been highly controversial since it was passed in 1998, and, in fact, it has never been implemented. This legislation prohibited making pornography or any other content deemed harmful to minors available to minors via the Internet and carried a $50,000 fine. This law was blocked by the U.S. Supreme Court several times, based on the likelihood that it violates the First Amendment and the possibility that less restrictive alternatives such as Internet filtering can be used instead to prevent the access of inappropriate materials by minors. A list of selected federal laws related to computer security and privacy are shown in Exhibit 6-23.

Exhibit 6-23 Federal legislation related to computer security and privacy

Date	Law and Description
2006	**U.S. SAFE WEB Act of 2006** Grants additional authority to the FTC to help protect consumers from spam, spyware, and Internet fraud and deception.
2005	**Real ID Act** Establishes national standards for state-issued driver's licenses and identification cards; will be modified if the proposed Pass ID Act of 2009 is passed.
2005	**Junk Fax Prevention Act** Requires unsolicited faxes to have a highly-visible opt-out notice.
2003	**CAN-SPAM Act** Implements regulations for unsolicited email messages and lays the groundwork for a federal Do Not E-Mail Registry.
2003	**Do Not Call Implementation Act** Amends the Telephone Consumer Protection Act to implement the National Do Not Call Registry.
2003	**Health Insurance Portability and Accountability Act (HIPAA)** Includes a Security Rule that sets minimum security standards to protect health information stored electronically.
2002	**Sarbanes-Oxley Act** Requires archiving a variety of electronic records and protecting the integrity of corporate financial data.
2001	**USA PATRIOT Act** Grants federal authorities expanded surveillance and intelligence-gathering powers, such as broadening the ability of federal agents to obtain the real identity of Internet users and intercept email and other types of Internet communications.
1999	**Financial Modernization (Gramm-Leach-Bliley) Act** Extends the ability of banks, securities firms, and insurance companies to share consumers' non-public personal information, but requires them to notify consumers and give them the opportunity to opt out before disclosing any information.
1998	**Child Online Protection Act (COPA)** Prohibits online pornography and other content deemed harmful to minors; has been blocked by the Supreme Court.
1998	**Children's Online Privacy Protection Act (COPPA)** Regulates how Web sites can collect information from minors and communicate with them.
1998	**Telephone Anti-Spamming Amendments Act** Applies restrictions to unsolicited, bulk commercial email.
1992	**Cable Act** Extends the Cable Communications Policy Act to include companies that sell wireless services.
1991	**Telephone Consumer Protection Act** Requires telemarketing companies to respect the rights of people who do not want to be called.
1988	**Computer Matching and Privacy Protection Act** Limits the use of government data in determining federal-benefit recipients.
1988	**Video Privacy Protection Act** Limits disclosure of customer information by video-rental companies.
1986	**Electronic Communications Privacy Act** Extends traditional privacy protections governing postal delivery and telephone services to include email, cellular phones, and voice mail.
1984	**Cable Communications Policy Act** Limits disclosure of customer records by cable TV companies.
1974	**Education Privacy Act** Stipulates that, in both public and private schools that receive any federal funding, individuals have the right to keep the schools from releasing such information as grades and evaluations of behavior.
1974	**Privacy Act** Stipulates that the collection of data by federal agencies must have a legitimate purpose.
1970	**Fair Credit Reporting Act** Prevents private organizations from unfairly denying credit and provides individuals the right to inspect their credit records.
1970	**Freedom of Information Act** Gives individuals the right to inspect data concerning them that is stored by the federal government.

1. How do many organizations and educational institutions explain acceptable computer use to their employees, students, or other users?

2. What is the typical motivation for hacking?

3. Why might hackers be moving away from targeting data stored on company servers and focusing on stealing data in real time during credit card and debit card transactions?

4. Define *botnet*.

5. What is malware?

6. How does a DoS attack disable a server?

7. Define *phishing*.

8. What is online auction fraud?

9. What is the purpose of a digital certificate?

10. Why are many states and schools reviewing their harassment statutes and bullying policies?

11. What is a hard drive that uses full-disk encryption often called?

12. What does antivirus software do?

13. How does a firewall help protect a computer?

14. What is a marketing database?

15. What is a throw-away email address?

16. What is the difference between *opt-out* and *opt-in*?

17. What does computer monitoring software do?

18. Is it legal for companies to review the email of their employees?

Practice It

Practice It 6-1

Some college computer classes include instruction on writing computer viruses. Some believe that students need to know how viruses work in order to be able to develop antivirus software; however, the antivirus industry disagrees, and most antivirus professionals were never virus writers.

1. At one university, precautions for containing code created during this course include only allowing fourth year students to take the course, not having a network connection in the classroom, and prohibiting the removal of storage media from the classroom. Do you think these precautions are sufficient?

2. Should writing virus code be allowed as part of a computer degree curriculum?

3. Is it ethical for colleges to teach computer virus writing? Is it ethical for students to take such a course?

3. Does teaching illegal and unethical acts (such as writing virus code) in college classes help to legitimize the behavior in society?

4. Would you feel comfortable taking such a course? Why or why not?

5. Prepare a one- or two-page summary that answers these questions, and submit it to your instructor.

Practice It 6-2

Some people view using live surveillance cameras as a valid crime prevention tool; other people think it is an invasion of privacy.

1. Is it ethical for businesses to use video cameras to record customers' activities? If so, for what purposes?

2. Does the government have the responsibility to use every means possible to protect the country and its citizens, or do citizens have the right not to be watched in public?

3. One objection stated about these systems is "It's not the same as a cop on the corner. This is a cop on every corner." What if it were a live police officer at each public video camera location instead of a camera? Would that be more acceptable from a privacy standpoint?

4. If people do not plan to commit criminal acts in public, should they be concerned that law enforcement personnel may see them?

5. Does the risk of being recorded deter some illegal or unethical acts?

6. Prepare a one- or two-page summary that answers these questions, and submit it to your instructor.

On Your Own

On Your Own 6-1

Although a company's privacy policy may look acceptable when you read it before submitting personal information to that company, there is no guarantee that the policy will not be changed.

1. Locate three different privacy policies on Web sites, analyze them, and compare them.

2. Do the policies specify what personal information might be shared and with whom?

3. Do the organizations reserve the right to change their policies at a later time without notice? If so, will they try to notify consumers?

4. Do any of the policies allow for any sharing of data with third-party organizations? If so, is the data personally identifiable, and can customers opt out?

5. What type of impact do you think a change in a company's privacy policy would have on customer loyalty?

6. Prepare a one- or two-page summary that answers these questions, and submit it to your instructor.

CAPSTONE

Computer Concepts

Technology is changing our world at an explosive pace. Older technology becomes obsolete very quickly, and new technology is being introduced all the time. Think about some of the technological advances you have seen in the last several months as well as recent technologies that have become obsolete.

1. Discuss the impact of new technology regularly and quickly replacing existing technology. Be sure to consider the personal, business, societal, economic, global, and environmental impacts of the new technology.

2. What benefits does new technology provide? Be sure to consider individuals, businesses, local communities, the country, and the world.

3. What risks are involved or related to new technology? Who is affected by these risks? Can these risks be minimized? If so, how? If not, why not?

4. Do the benefits of new technology outweigh the risks? Who should have the ultimate decision about this—consumers? government? businesses? Explain your answer.

5. What ethical concerns are related to the introduction of new technology?

6. Prepare a two- or three -page summary that answers these questions, and then submit it to your instructor.

Exploring Microsoft Windows 7

Introduction

Many personal computers use the **Microsoft Windows 7** operating system—Windows 7 for short. *Windows* is the name of the operating system, and 7 indicates the version you are using. Recall that the operating system is software that manages and coordinates activities on the computer and helps the computer perform essential tasks, such as displaying information on the computer screen and saving data on disks.

Much of the software created for the Windows 7 operating system looks and works similarly. This similarity in design means that after you learn how to use one Windows 7 program, you are well on your way to understanding how to use others. With Windows 7, you can use more than one program at a time, making it easy to switch between your word processing program and your appointment book program, for example. It also makes it easy to access the Internet.

In this chapter, you learn the basics of working with Windows 7. This provides the foundation you need to use Microsoft Office applications and other programs to accomplish both personal and business tasks.

Learning Objectives

After studying the material in this chapter, you will be able to:

LO7.1 Identify the parts of the Windows 7 desktop

LO7.2 Use common Windows elements

LO7.3 Navigate Windows

LO7.4 Work with the Recycle Bin

LO7.5 Get Help

LO7.6 Shut down Windows

LO7.1 Exploring the Windows 7 Desktop

In Windows terminology, the **desktop** is a workspace for projects and the tools that you need to manipulate your projects. Essentially, the desktop is the screen you see when you first start Windows. To learn about the features of the desktop, you'll start Windows and explore the various elements.

Microsoft Windows 7 An operating system from Microsoft used by many personal computers.

desktop The first screen you see when you start Windows; used as a workspace for projects and the tools that you need to manipulate your projects.

Starting Windows and Examining the Desktop

To start Windows, you simply turn your computer on. After completing the boot process, a Welcome screen appears listing

Microsoft Windows is the most common operating system for both desktop and portable PCs, whether for business or personal use.

Image copyright © Andresr. Used under license from Shutterstock.com

all the users for the computer. Before you start working with Windows 7, you might need to click your user name and type a password. After you provide this information, the Windows 7 desktop appears.

 **ACTIVITY**

Start Windows 7.

1 Turn on your computer. After a moment, Windows 7 starts and the Welcome screen appears.

2 On the Welcome screen, click your account name. If a password box appears, type your password in the box, and then click the **Go button** ➡. The Windows 7 desktop appears. See Exhibit 7-1. (Your desktop might have a different background and icons.)

> ⚠ **Problem?** If an account name button does not appear, the Welcome screen disappears, and the Windows desktop shown in Exhibit 7-1 appears. Skip Step 2.

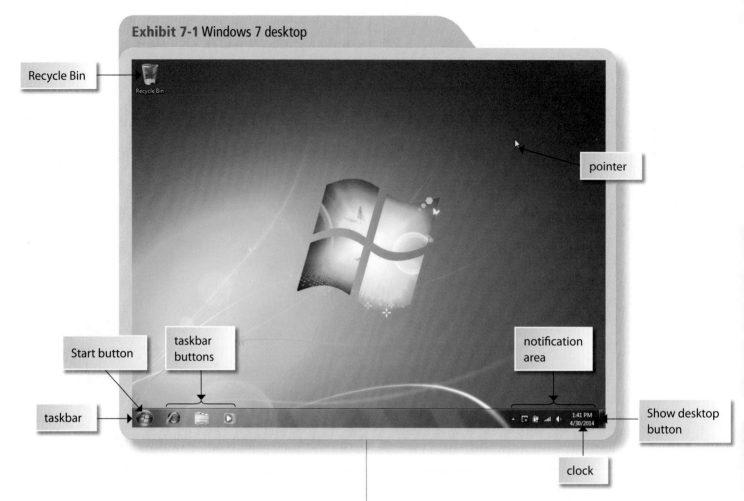

Exhibit 7-1 Windows 7 desktop

- Recycle Bin
- pointer
- Start button
- taskbar buttons
- notification area
- taskbar
- Show desktop button
- clock

The desktop is the whole workspace on the screen. The graphic in the middle and the colors used in the background are part of a **theme**, a set of desktop backgrounds, window colors, sounds, and screen savers. If you see a different background on your screen, someone personalized the desktop by changing the theme.

The **taskbar** is the horizontal bar at the bottom of the screen with buttons that provide quick access to common tools and running programs. The Start button appears on the left end of the taskbar. You use this to start programs, access documents, adjust settings on your computer, and other tasks. By default, three buttons appear next to the Start button. **Buttons** are graphical icons you click to start programs or perform commands. The **notification area** displays icons that provide information about the computer and some of the programs that are running, as well as display the current date and time. The Show desktop button at the right end of the taskbar hides everything on the desktop so that you can see the desktop.

The **Recycle Bin** stores deleted items until you remove them from the drive permanently. The Recycle Bin might be in a different position on your desktop compared to Exhibit 7-1.

theme A set of desktop backgrounds, window colors, sounds, and screen savers.

taskbar The horizontal bar at the bottom of the screen with buttons that provide quick access to common tools and running programs.

button A graphical icon you click to start a program or perform a command.

notification area The part of the taskbar that displays icons that provide information about the computer and programs that are running.

Recycle Bin Storage for deleted items until you remove them from the drive.

The desktop might be hidden by open windows, but the taskbar is almost always visible at the bottom of your screen.

Changing the Desktop Theme

The default desktop you see after you first install Windows 7 has a blue background with a four-color Windows logo. However, you can easily change the appearance of the desktop. To change the desktop theme, position the pointer on a blank area of the desktop, click the right mouse button, and then click Personalize to open the Personalization window. Click a theme in the box to select it. Then close the Personalization window. The desktop will be updated to show the theme you selected.

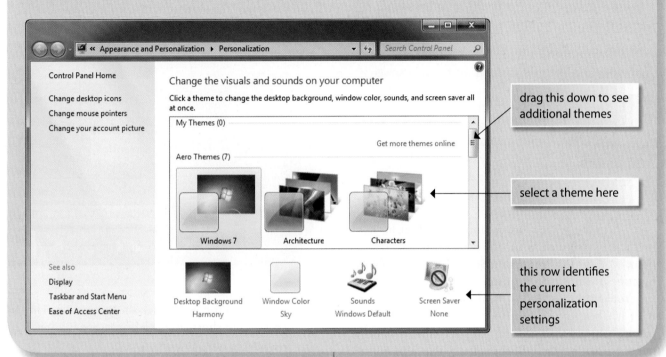

drag this down to see additional themes

select a theme here

this row identifies the current personalization settings

The **pointer** is a small object, such as an arrow, that moves on the screen when you move your mouse. The pointer is usually shaped like an arrow, although it changes shape depending on the pointer's location on the screen and the tasks you are performing.

Using the Mouse

To move the pointer on the screen, you use the pointing device connected to your computer. The most common type of pointing device is the mouse, so this book uses that term. If you are using a different pointing device, such as a trackball or touchpad, substitute that device whenever you see the term *mouse*. When you drag the mouse on a surface (or roll the trackball or slide your finger on a touch pad), the pointer on the screen moves in a corresponding direction. You use the mouse to perform specific actions:

▸ **Point**—Positioning the pointer directly on top of an item.

▸ **Click**—Pressing the left mouse button and immediately releasing it.

▸ **Right-click**—Clicking the right mouse button and immediately releasing it.

▸ **Double-click**—Clicking the left mouse button twice in quick succession.

▸ **Drag**—Positioning the pointer on top of an item, and then pressing and holding the left mouse button while moving the pointer.

> **pointer** A small object, such as an arrow, that moves on the screen when you move your mouse.
>
> **point** To position the pointer directly on top of an item.
>
> **click** To press the left mouse button and immediately release it.
>
> **right-click** To click the right mouse button and immediately release it.
>
> **double-click** To click the left mouse button twice in quick succession.
>
> **drag** To position the pointer on top of an item, and then press and hold the left mouse button while moving the pointer.

Clicking sends a signal to your computer that you want to perform an action on the object you click.

Screen Savers

If a blank screen or an animated design replaces the desktop, your computer is set to use a screen saver, which is a program that causes a monitor to go blank or to display an animated design after a specified amount of idle time. Press any key or move the mouse to display the desktop again.

When you want more information about an item on the desktop, such as an icon on the taskbar, you can point to that item to make a **ScreenTip** appear, which identifies the name or purpose of the item.

You need to select an item before you can work with it. To select an item with the mouse, you point to the item and then click it. The selected item is highlighted, usually by a different color, with a box around it, or by appearing pushed in.

When you right-click an item, a shortcut menu opens. A **menu** is a group or list of commands that you click to complete tasks. A **shortcut menu** lists actions you can take with the item you right-clicked. You can right-click practically anything on the desktop, including a blank area of the desktop, to view commands associated with that item.

ACTIVITY

Use the mouse.

1 On the desktop, point to the **Recycle Bin**. A light-colored box appears around the icon.

ScreenTip A box that appears with information such as the name or purpose of a selected item when you point to an item.

menu A group or list of commands that you click to complete tasks.

shortcut menu A menu that lists actions you can take with the item you right-clicked.

2 Point to the **desktop**. The box disappears from around the Recycle Bin.

3 Click the **Recycle Bin**, and then point to the desktop. The Recycle Bin is selected, as indicated by the box.

4 On the taskbar, in the notification area, point to the **clock**. Its ScreenTip appears showing the long version of the current date. See Exhibit 7-2.

Exhibit 7-2 ScreenTip for the clock

5 On the desktop, right-click the **Recycle Bin**. The Recycle Bin shortcut menu opens. See Exhibit 7-3. These are commands you can perform on the Recycle Bin.

Exhibit 7-3 Recycle Bin shortcut menu

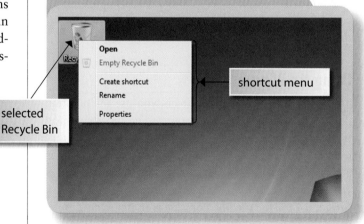

Shortcut menus provide the commands you need where you need them.

6 Click a blank area of the desktop. The shortcut menu closes without selecting a command.

7 Right-click a blank area of the desktop. The desktop shortcut menu opens. The commands differ from the commands that you saw on the Recycle Bin shortcut menu.

8 Press the **Esc key**. The shortcut menu closes without selecting a command.

Exploring the Start Menu

When you click the Start button, the Start menu opens. The **Start menu** provides access to programs, documents, and much more. The Start menu is organized into two **panes**, as shown in Exhibit 7-4, which are separate areas of a menu or window. Each pane lists items you can point to or click.

You can click a program on the All Programs list to start that program.

computer. The arrow ▶ next to the All Programs command on the Start menu indicates that you can view more options by opening a submenu.

Just below the All Programs command is the Search programs and files box, or simply the **search box**, which helps you quickly find anything stored on your computer, including programs, documents, pictures, music, videos, Web pages, and email messages. When you want to use the Search programs and files box, you open the Start menu, and then type one or more words related to what you want to find. For example, if you want to find and play the Happy Birthday song stored on your computer, you could type *birthday* in the Search programs and files box. Windows searches your computer for any program or file name that includes *birthday*, and displays the song and any other search results in the Start menu, where you can click the song to play it.

The right pane of the Start menu contains commands that open windows to access commonly used

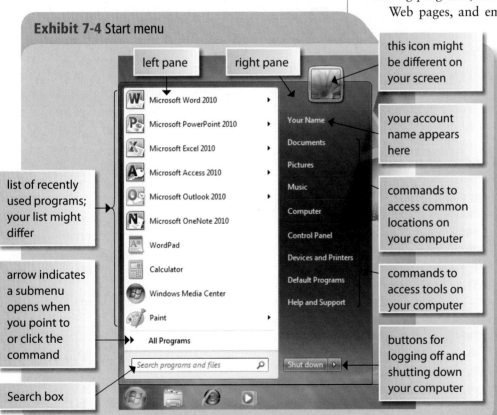

Exhibit 7-4 Start menu

- left pane
- right pane
- this icon might be different on your screen
- list of recently used programs; your list might differ
- arrow indicates a submenu opens when you point to or click the command
- Search box
- your account name appears here
- commands to access common locations on your computer
- commands to access tools on your computer
- buttons for logging off and shutting down your computer

The left pane contains the programs list and the search box. When you first click the Start button, you see a list of programs that were used recently on the computer. Near the bottom of the left pane is the All Programs command. You use this to display the All Programs list, which replaces the list of recently used programs with the list of all the programs installed on the

Start menu A menu that provides access to programs, documents, and much more.

pane A separate area of a menu or window.

search box A search feature that helps you quickly find anything stored on your computer.

Opening multiple windows gives you the flexibility and power to work simultaneously in two or more programs or files.

Program Organization on the Start Menu

The left pane organizes programs for easy access. When you first install Windows 7, the left pane contains a short list of programs on your computer. After you use a program, Windows 7 adds it to this list so you can quickly find it the next time you want to use it. The Start menu can list only a certain number of programs—after that, the programs you have not opened lately are replaced by the programs you used more recently.

locations on the computer or tools for managing Windows 7. A **window** is a rectangular work area that contains a program, text, files, or other data. For example, if you click Computer, the Computer window opens, which displays all the drives on your computer.

From the bottom section of the right pane, you can open windows that help you effectively work with Windows 7. For example, the **Control Panel** contains specialized tools to change the way Windows 7 looks and behaves, and Help and Support provides articles, video demonstrations, and steps for performing tasks in Windows 7.

Finally, you turn off your computer from the Start menu and log out from your user account. When you are finished working with your computer, you need to shut down the system. Shutting down the system before physically turning it off saves energy, preserves your data and settings, and ensures your computer starts quickly the next time you use it.

window A rectangular work area that contains a program, text, files, or other data.

Control Panel A window that contains specialized tools to change the way Windows 7 looks and behaves.

ACTIVITY

Use the Start menu.

1 On the taskbar, click the **Start button** . The Start menu opens.

2 Point to **All Programs**. The All Programs command is selected. After a short pause, the All Programs list appears on the Start menu, and the All Programs command changes to the Back command.

3 In the All Programs list, click **Accessories**. The list of accessory programs appears.

4 In the list, click **Calculator**. The Calculator program window opens. This window is an example of a window that contains a program. Notice that a corresponding button appeared on the taskbar.

5 Click the **Start button** , and then in the right pane, click **Computer**. The Computer window opens, and the Windows Explorer button on the taskbar becomes selected. See Exhibit 7-5.

> **Problem?** If the Computer window fills the entire screen and the Restore Down button is the middle sizing button, click it. If the Maximize button is the middle button, point to any border of the Computer window, and then drag it toward the center of the window to make the window smaller.

6 Click the **Start button** . In the right pane, click **Pictures**. The Pictures window opens, and two Windows Explorer buttons appear to be stacked one on top of the other.

When a program is started, it is said to be open or running. A button appears on the taskbar for each open program. A window is also considered to be open, and has a corresponding button on the taskbar. In this case, the Calculator program is open or running, and the Computer and Pictures windows are open.

A quick way to start a program is to double-click the corresponding program icon.

Calculator program window

Computer window

Windows Explorer button

Calculator program button

Shortcuts

Everything on the Start menu is actually a shortcut. A **shortcut** is a very small file that points to the location of the actual folder or file. When a file points to another folder or file, clicking it has the same effect as clicking the actual file. You can create shortcuts to any file or storage location on your computer. To create a shortcut, right-click an item, and then click Create shortcut on the shortcut menu. Icons associated with a shortcut has a small arrow at the lower-left. The shortcut shown here opens the Pictures window.

Pictures - Shortcut

LO7.2 Using Common Windows Elements

There are two types of windows: program windows and Windows Explorer windows. Program windows open when a program starts and display commands for working with the program and the program's workspace. Windows Explorer windows open to display the contents of the computer and its storage devices or commands for managing Windows 7. All windows, whether they contain a program, files, or

> **shortcut** A very small file that points to the location of the actual folder or file.

Exhibit 7-6 Window elements

other data, have the following elements in common (refer to Exhibit 7-6):

▶ **Title bar**—Displays the window title and contains the sizing buttons. In program windows, the window title appears directly in the title bar. In Windows Explorer windows, the title appears

in the window Address bar; if there are multiple words in the Address bar separated by triangles, the last (rightmost) name is the name of the window.

▶ **Sizing buttons**—Used to enlarge, shrink, or close a window.

▶ **Window title**—Identifies the program and document contained in the window.

▶ **Details pane/Status bar**—Displays information or messages about the task you are performing or the selected item.

Resizing and Moving Windows

After you open a window, you can manipulate it by changing its size and position. In most windows, three sizing buttons appear on the right end of the title bar. The first button is the Minimize button ▬, which

title bar A banner at the top of a window that displays the window title and contains the sizing buttons.

sizing buttons The buttons used to enlarge, shrink, or close a window.

Details pane A banner at the bottom of a window that displays information or messages about the selected item.

status bar A banner at the bottom of a window that displays information or messages about the task you are performing or the selected item.

If your computer seems to be responding slowly to keystrokes and mouse actions, you might have too many programs running.

shrinks a window to its button on the taskbar. A minimized window is still open; if the minimized window is a program window, the program is still running. You can redisplay a minimized window by clicking the window's button on the taskbar or by pointing to the button on the taskbar, and then clicking the **thumbnail** (small picture) that appears.

The middle sizing button changes depending on the state of the window. If the window is not as large as it can be on the screen, the middle button is the Maximize button ▣ . When you click the Maximize button, the window resizes to fill the screen. When the window is maximized, the button is the Restore Down button ▣ . Clicking the Restore Down button returns the window to the size it was before you maximized it.

The third button on the title bar is the Close button ⊠ . You click it to close the window. If the window is a program window, clicking the Close button can also stop the program from running. (This is called exiting or closing the program.)

You can also resize a window manually. When you point to a window border, the pointer changes to a two-headed arrow. Using the two-headed arrow pointer, you drag the window border until the window is the size you want. To move a window to a new position on the screen, you drag the window by its title bar. You cannot reposition a maximized window.

ACTIVITY

Resize, move, and close windows.

1 On the Pictures window title bar, click the **Minimize button** ▬ . The Pictures window shrinks to the Windows Explorer button on the taskbar.

2 Minimize the **Computer window**, and then minimize the **Calculator window**.

3 On the taskbar, point to the **Calculator button** ▦ . A thumbnail of the window appears.

4 Move the pointer on top of the **Calculator window thumbnail**. A small Close button ⊠ appears on the thumbnail, and the Calculator window reappears on the desktop.

5 Move the pointer off the **Calculator thumbnail**. The thumbnail and the Calculator window on the desktop disappear.

6 Click the **Calculator button** ▦ . The Calculator window reappears on the desktop.

7 On the taskbar, click the **Windows Explorer button** ▦ . Because two Windows Explorer windows are open, two thumbnails appear instead of either window being restored.

8 Click the **Computer window thumbnail**. The Computer window returns to its previous size and position.

9 On the Computer window title bar, click the **Maximize button** ▣ . The Computer window expands to fill the screen.

10 On the title bar, click the **Restore Down button** ▣ . The Computer window returns to its previous size.

11 Point to the **Computer window title bar**, press and hold down the left mouse button, and then drag in one direction. The window moves as you move the mouse.

12 Position the Computer window anywhere on the desktop, and then release the mouse button. The Computer window stays in its new location.

13 Point to the **left border** of the Computer window so that the pointer changes to ⟺, and then drag the border to the left about an inch. The window widens by the amount you dragged.

14 Drag the **left border** of the Computer window to the right about an inch to return the window to its previous size.

15 On the Computer window title bar, click the **Close button** ⊠ . The Computer window closes, and the Windows Explorer button on the taskbar is no longer selected.

> **Tip:** You can also click a taskbar button, and then click the Close button ⊠ in the upper-right corner of the thumbnail to close a window.

16 Drag the Calculator window by its **title bar** to reposition the window on the desktop.

thumbnail A small picture of an object.

A clean and organized desktop increases your productivity.

17 Close the **Calculator window**. The Calculator window button on the taskbar disappears.

18 On the taskbar, right-click the **Windows Explorer button** , and then on the shortcut menu, click **Close window**.

Switching Between Open Windows

When more than one window is open on the desktop, there can be only one **active window**, the window to which the next keystroke or command is applied. When more than one window is open, the active window is the window that appears to be on top.

Because only one window is active at a time, you must switch between windows if you want to work in another window. To make a window active, you can click in it or you can click its button on the taskbar. You can also use a shortcut key combination to switch from one open window to another. A **keyboard shortcut** is a key or combination of keys that perform a command. For example, you can use keyboard shortcuts to switch between open windows.

You can use a keyboard shortcut to activate **Aero Flip 3D** (often shortened to **Flip 3D**), which displays all your open windows in a three-dimensional stack of thumbnails. To activate Flip 3D, press and hold the Windows key, and then press and release the Tab key. Each time you press the Tab key, the next window moves to the top of the stack.

You can use another keyboard shortcut to activate **Windows Flip**, which displays a thumbnail of each open window in a box called the task switcher window. When you press and hold down the Alt key, and then press and release the Tab key without releasing the

active window The window to which the next keystroke or command is applied.

keyboard shortcut A key or combination of keys that perform a command.

Aero Flip 3D (Flip 3D) A Windows 7 feature that displays all open windows in a three-dimensional stack of thumbnails so you can switch between windows.

Windows Flip A Windows 7 feature that displays thumbnails of all open windows so you can switch between windows.

Windows 7 and the Aero Desktop Experience

Windows 7 provides themes, which are sets of desktop backgrounds, window colors, sounds, and screen savers that allow you to personalize the Aero desktop experience. The themes that take advantage of Aero's rich three-dimensional appearance are called Aero themes. You can use an Aero theme only if your computer hardware and version of Windows 7 support it. (The Microsoft Web site provides detailed information about the requirements for using Aero themes.) Otherwise, your computer is set by default to use a desktop theme called Windows 7 Basic, which provides most of the same elements as the enhanced experience, including windows and icons, but not the same graphic effects. In this book, the figures show the Windows 7 Aero theme. If you are using Windows 7 Basic or a high contrast theme, the images on your screen will vary slightly from the figures and some features will not be available. (These are noted throughout the chapter.)

Alt key, Windows Flip displays thumbnails of all your open windows. Continue holding down the Alt key as you press the Tab key to move from one thumbnail to the next. The window corresponding to the selected thumbnail appears on the desktop.

ACTIVITY

Switch between windows.

1 Right-click a blank area of the desktop, and then on the shortcut menu, click **Personalize**. The Personalization window opens.

2 On the taskbar, click the **Windows Explorer button** . The Libraries window opens.

3 On the taskbar, click the **Start button** , and then click **Computer** to open the Computer window.

4 Press and hold the **Windows key** (the key with the Microsoft Windows icon on it), and then press and release the **Tab key** without releasing the Windows key. The three open windows appear as a 3D stack of thumbnails along with a thumbnail of the desktop. See Exhibit 7-7.

Exhibit 7-7 Aero Flip 3D

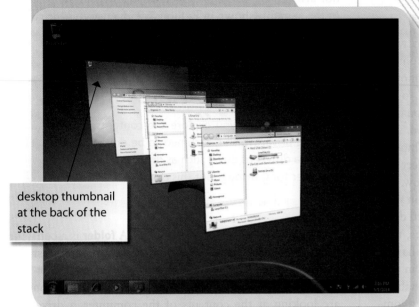

desktop thumbnail at the back of the stack

Having too many open windows can make it difficult to find specific information.

switcher window appears on top of the three open windows, the thumbnail in the task switcher window that corresponds to the Computer window is selected, and then after a few moments, all the windows except the Computer window become transparent except for a border. See Exhibit 7-8.

8 With the Alt key still pressed, press the **Tab key** two more times to select the desktop thumbnail in the task switcher window. All three windows are transparent.

9 Release the **Alt key**. The three windows are minimized to buttons on the taskbar.

10 Display the **Personalization window**, and then close it.

11 Display the **Computer window**, and then close it.

⚠ **Problem?** If nothing seems to happen or if parts of the Computer window become selected when you press the Windows+Tab keys, you are not using an Aero theme. Release the Windows+Tab keys, read but do not perform Steps 4 through 6. Continue with Step 7. You will not see the window corresponding to the selected thumbnail in Step 7.

5 With the Windows key still pressed, press the **Tab key** twice to flip the Personalization window to the front of the stack.

6 Release the **Windows key**. The Personalization window is the active window.

7 Press and hold the **Alt key**, and then press and release the **Tab key** without releasing the Alt key. The task

Exhibit 7-8 Windows Flip

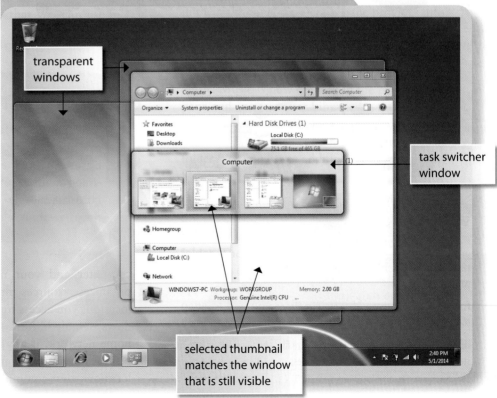

transparent windows

task switcher window

selected thumbnail matches the window that is still visible

Exhibit 7-14 Sort by options in a Windows Explorer window

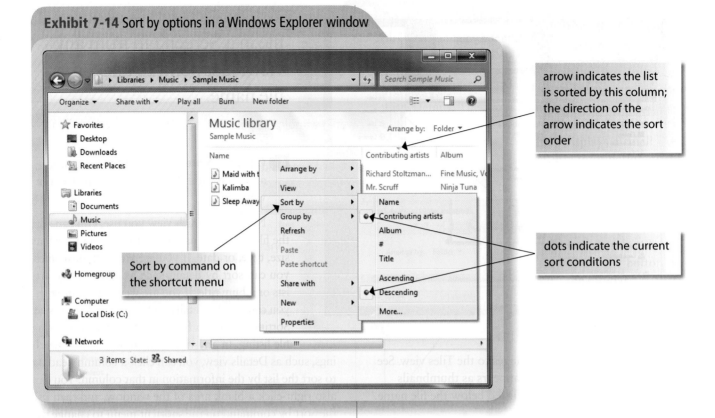

arrow indicates the list is sorted by this column; the direction of the arrow indicates the sort order

Sort by command on the shortcut menu

dots indicate the current sort conditions

To change the details shown in Details view for all Windows Explorer folders, right-click a column heading and then click a detail.

Using the Navigation Pane

As you have seen, you can click a folder in the Navigation pane to navigate directly to that folder and display its contents in the right pane. You can also use the Navigation pane to navigate to other locations on your computer and to subfolders. When you move the pointer into the Navigation pane, triangles appear next to some icons. Right-pointing, white triangles —called expand icons—indicate that a folder contains other folders that are not currently displayed in the Navigation pane. Downward-pointing black triangles —collapse icons—indicate the folder is expanded, and its subfolders are listed below the folder name.

ACTIVITY

Use the Navigation pane.

1 Move the pointer into the Navigation pane. Collapse arrows appear next to Favorites, Libraries, and Computer, and expand arrows appear next to the items listed under these elements. See Exhibit 7-15.

2 Next to Music, click the **expand icon** ▷ . The folders in the Music library appear below the list, and the icon next to Music changes to the collapse icon ◢ . This folder list includes the My Music and the Public Music folders.

3 In the Navigation pane, expand the **Public Music folder**. The Sample Music folder is listed under Public Music, and it is selected because the contents of this folder are displayed in the right pane.

4 In the Navigation pane, expand the **Documents folder**. The folder list in the Documents folder includes the My Documents and the Public Documents folders.

5 Close the **Sample Music window**.

Exhibit 7-7 Aero Flip 3D

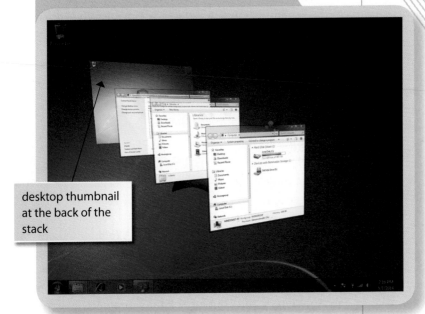

desktop thumbnail at the back of the stack

⚠ **Problem?** If nothing seems to happen or if parts of the Computer window become selected when you press the Windows+Tab keys, you are not using an Aero theme. Release the Windows+Tab keys, read but do not perform Steps 4 through 6. Continue with Step 7. You will not see the window corresponding to the selected thumbnail in Step 7.

5 With the Windows key still pressed, press the **Tab key** twice to flip the Personalization window to the front of the stack.

6 Release the **Windows key**. The Personalization window is the active window.

7 Press and hold the **Alt key**, and then press and release the **Tab key** without releasing the Alt key. The task

Having too many open windows can make it difficult to find specific information.

switcher window appears on top of the three open windows, the thumbnail in the task switcher window that corresponds to the Computer window is selected, and then after a few moments, all the windows except the Computer window become transparent except for a border. See Exhibit 7-8.

8 With the Alt key still pressed, press the **Tab key** two more times to select the desktop thumbnail in the task switcher window. All three windows are transparent.

9 Release the **Alt key**. The three windows are minimized to buttons on the taskbar.

10 Display the **Personalization window**, and then close it.

11 Display the **Computer window**, and then close it.

Exhibit 7-8 Windows Flip

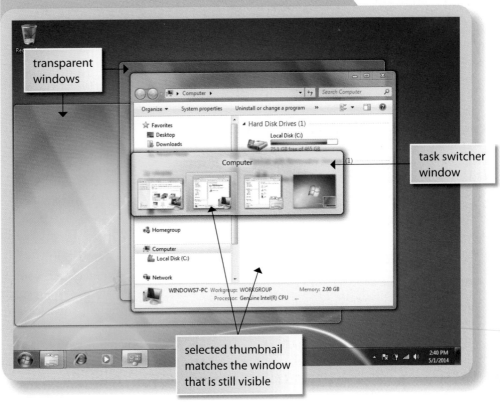

transparent windows

task switcher window

selected thumbnail matches the window that is still visible

LO7.3 Navigating Windows

You explore, or navigate, your computer to work with its contents and resources. In this context, **navigate** means to move from one location to another on your computer, such as from one window to another. To successfully navigate your computer, you need to understand a bit about how files are organized.

The Computer window represents your computer and its storage devices. The icon for each object appears in the right pane of the Computer window. See Exhibit 7-9. Each storage device you can access on your computer is associated with a letter. The first hard drive is usually drive C (if you add other hard drives, they are usually designated D, E, and so on). If you have a CD or DVD drive or a USB flash drive plugged in to a USB port, it usually has the next letter in the alphabetic sequence. If you can access hard drives on other computers in a network, those drives sometimes (although not always) have letters associated with them as well. In the example shown in Exhibit 7-9, the network drive has the drive letter E.

Hard Drive Reference

In this section, you explore the contents of your hard drive, which is assumed to be drive C. If you use a different drive, such as drive E, substitute its letter for C throughout this chapter.

Drives are organized into folders. A **folder** is a container that helps to organize files on a computer, just like a paper folder is used to organize files in a file cabinet. When you open a Windows Explorer window, you are looking at the contents of the computer, a drive, or a folder. In Windows 7, files and folders are also organized into libraries. A **library** is a central place to view and organize files and folders stored anywhere that the computer can access, such as those on your hard drive, removable drives, and network. For example, if you store some music files on your hard drive and others on an external drive, such as a digital music player attached to your computer, they all appear in the Music library.

The Libraries window is shown in Exhibit 7-10. The left pane in Windows Explorer windows is called the Navigation pane, and it lists locations on your computer and your network. The Navigation pane organizes resources into five categories: Favorites (for locations you access frequently), Libraries (for the Windows default libraries), Homegroup (for your shared home network, if any), Computer (for the drives and devices on your computer), and Network (for network locations your computer can access).

Exhibit 7-9 Relationship between your computer and the Computer window

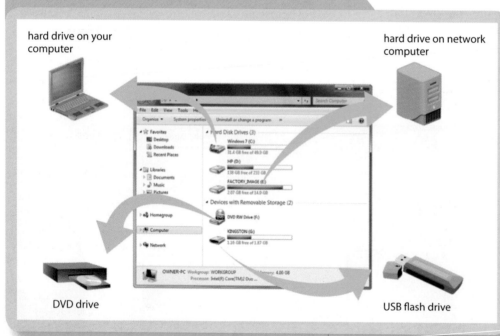

hard drive on your computer

hard drive on network computer

DVD drive

USB flash drive

navigate To move from one location to another on your computer.

folder A container that helps to organize files on a computer.

library A central place to view and organize files and folders stored anywhere that the computer can access.

Exhibit 7-10 Parts of a Windows Explorer window

search box

Address bar

toolbar

Libraries
Open a library to see your files and arrange them by folder, date, and other ...

Favorites
- Desktop
- Downloads
- Recent Places

Libraries
- Documents
- Music
- Pictures
- Videos

Homegroup

Computer
- Local Disk (C:)

Network

Navigation pane

Documents
Library

Music
Library

Pictures
Library

Videos
Library

Details pane

4 items

Search Libraries

Using Windows Explorer Windows

To display the contents of a drive or folder listed in a Windows Explorer window, you double-click it. If you double-click a file in a Windows Explorer window, the program that can display the contents of that file starts. If you click a location in the Navigation pane, the contents of that location is displayed in the window.

ACTIVITY

Navigate in Explorer windows.

1 On the taskbar, point to the **Windows Explorer button**, and then click the **Libraries window thumbnail**. The Libraries window becomes active. Notice that Libraries is selected in the Navigation pane, and because nothing is selected in the right pane, the Details pane provides information about the current folder; in this case, it contains four items.

2 In the Navigation pane, under Libraries, click **Music**. Music is now selected in the Navigation pane and appears after Libraries in the Address bar. The right pane displays the contents of the Music library, which contains the Sample Music folder (you might see additional folders or song files).

The Windows Explorer window also contains a toolbar with buttons to perform common tasks, and a Details pane that displays the characteristics of an object you select in the Computer window. As you open folders and navigate your computer, the contents of the toolbar change to include buttons that you can use in the current folder.

Windows Touch

If you have a multi-touch monitor, a Windows 7 feature called Windows Touch lets you perform tasks such as selecting icons, opening folders, and starting programs using your finger as a pointing device. To make it easier to select objects and identify which ones are selected, Windows Touch displays a check box next to objects such as files and icons on the desktop and in folder windows. If you are not using a multi-touch monitor, these check boxes do not appear in your folder windows or on the desktop.

3 In the right pane, double-click the **Sample Music folder**. The folder opens, its contents appear in the right pane of the window, and Sample Music appears in the Address bar after Music.

Tip: The search box next to the Address bar in a Windows Explorer window has the same function as the search box on the Start menu except the search is restricted to the current location.

4 In the right pane, click **Kalimba** (or another song file if Kalimba is not available). The Details pane changes to show information about the selected file. See Exhibit 7-11. You might see different music files.

Changing the View of Windows

You can change the appearance of folder windows to suit your preferences. Windows 7 provides a variety of ways to view the contents of a folder—Extra Large Icons, Large Icons, Medium Icons, Small Icons, List, Details, Tiles, and Content. Exhibit 7-11 shows a folder in Details view, which displays a small icon and lists information about each file. The icon provides a visual cue about the file type. You can change the view by using the Change your view button on the toolbar.

Exhibit 7-11 File selected in a Windows Explorer window

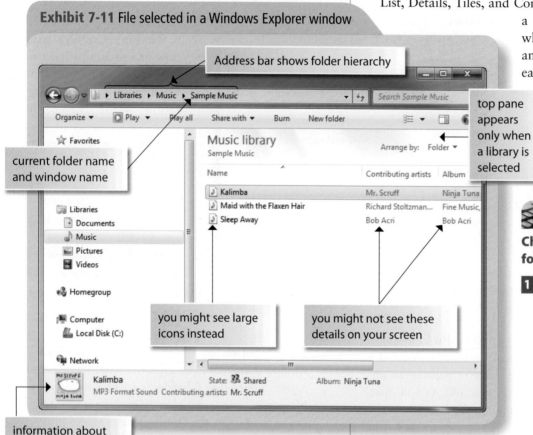

Address bar shows folder hierarchy

current folder name and window name

top pane appears only when a library is selected

you might see large icons instead

you might not see these details on your screen

information about the selected file

ACTIVITY

Change the view of folders.

1 On the toolbar in the Sample Music folder window, click the **More options button** (next to the Change your view button). The list of available views opens. See Exhibit 7-12.

Navigating Using the Address Bar

The Address bar displays your current location as a series of links separated by arrows. You can click a folder name in the Address bar to display the contents of that folder. You can also click an arrow to open a drop-down list with the names of each folder in that location. To display the contents of one of those folders, click the folder name in the list. You can also click the icon at the left end of the Address bar to change the hierarchy in the Address bar so each folder is separated by a backslash. You can then type a path directly in the Address bar to moe quickly to another folder.

Exhibit 7-12 Options for changing the folder view

column heading

Change your view button

indicates current view

Extra Large Icons
Large Icons
Medium Icons
Small Icons
List
Details
Tiles
Content

You can see details about a file in a ScreenTip from any view; just point to an icon or file name.

4 Click the **More options button** again, and then click **Details** to return to Details view.

No matter which view you use, you can sort the file list by file name or another detail, such as size, type, or date. If you are viewing music files, you can sort by details such as contributing artists or album title. If you are viewing picture files, you can sort by details such as date taken or size. Sorting helps you find a particular file in a long file listing. In any view that shows column headings, such as Details view, you can click a column heading to sort the list by the information in that column. You can also right-click a blank area of the window, and then use the Sort by command on the shortcut menu to change the sort order.

2 Click **Tiles**. The folder changes to the Tiles view. See Exhibit 7-13. The file list appears as thumbnails with the file type and size listed below the file name.

ACTIVITY

Sort a file list in a Windows Explorer window.

1 In the Windows Explorer window, click the **Contributing artists column heading**. The list is resorted in alphabetical order by the artist's name, as indicated by the small up arrow in the Contributing artists column heading.

Exhibit 7-13 Tiles view in a Windows Explorer window

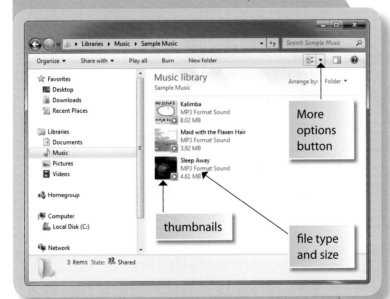

More options button

thumbnails

file type and size

2 Click the **Contributing artists column heading** again. The sort order is reversed, and the list is in descending alphabetic (Z–A) order, as indicated by the down arrow in the column heading.

3 Right-click a blank area of the right pane, and then on the shortcut menu, point to **Sort by**. A submenu of options by which you can sort the files opens. See Exhibit 7-14. These categories correspond to the column headings that are displayed in Details view.

3 On the toolbar, click the **More options button**, and then click **Large icons**. The folder now shows the file list as large icons with only the file name below each icon.

Tip: Click the Change your view button to cycle among the Large Icons, List, Details, Tiles, and Content views.

4 On the submenu, click **Name**. The list is resorted in alphabetical order by file name.

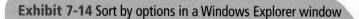

Exhibit 7-14 Sort by options in a Windows Explorer window

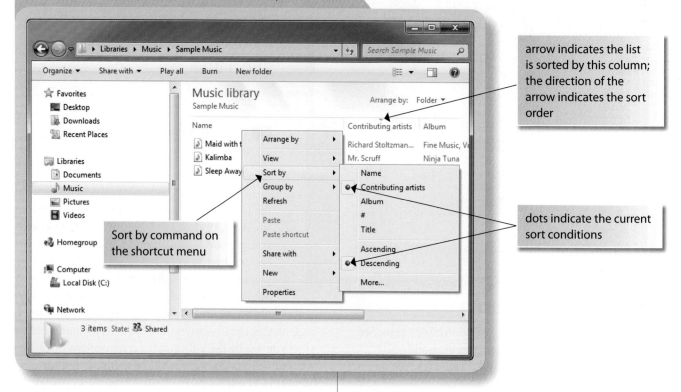

arrow indicates the list is sorted by this column; the direction of the arrow indicates the sort order

Sort by command on the shortcut menu

dots indicate the current sort conditions

To change the details shown in Details view for all Windows Explorer folders, right-click a column heading and then click a detail.

Using the Navigation Pane

As you have seen, you can click a folder in the Navigation pane to navigate directly to that folder and display its contents in the right pane. You can also use the Navigation pane to navigate to other locations on your computer and to subfolders. When you move the pointer into the Navigation pane, triangles appear next to some icons. Right-pointing, white triangles ⊳—called expand icons—indicate that a folder contains other folders that are not currently displayed in the Navigation pane. Downward-pointing black triangles ◢—collapse icons—indicate the folder is expanded, and its subfolders are listed below the folder name.

ACTIVITY

Use the Navigation pane.

1 Move the pointer into the Navigation pane. Collapse arrows appear next to Favorites, Libraries, and Computer, and expand arrows appear next to the items listed under these elements. See Exhibit 7-15.

2 Next to Music, click the **expand icon** ⊳. The folders in the Music library appear below the list, and the icon next to Music changes to the collapse icon ◢. This folder list includes the My Music and the Public Music folders.

3 In the Navigation pane, expand the **Public Music folder**. The Sample Music folder is listed under Public Music, and it is selected because the contents of this folder are displayed in the right pane.

4 In the Navigation pane, expand the **Documents folder**. The folder list in the Documents folder includes the My Documents and the Public Documents folders.

5 Close the **Sample Music window**.

Exhibit 7-15 Collapse and expand arrows in the Navigation pane

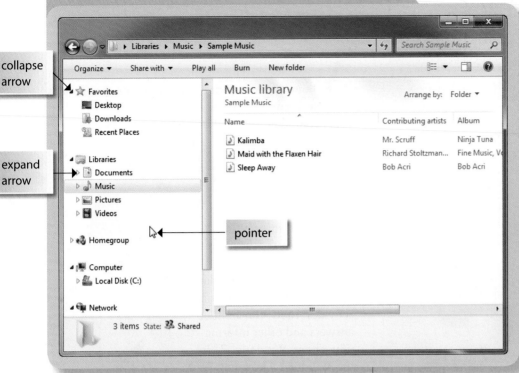

The My Documents folder is the default location for most files that you create on your computer.

LO7.4 **Working with the Recycle Bin**

When you delete a file from a hard drive, it is not removed from your computer. Instead, it is moved to the Recycle Bin. See Exhibit 7-16. The **Recycle**

Exhibit 7-16 Recycle Bin and Recycle Bin window

Bin holds deleted items until you remove them permanently. You can double-click the Recycle Bin to open the Recycle Bin window and see the files that are ready to be permanently deleted.

If you want to keep a file that is in the Recycle Bin instead of permanently deleting it, you can return the file to its previous location. To do so, right-click a file in the Recycle Bin window and then click Restore on the shortcut menu, or click the file to select it and then click the Restore this item button on the toolbar. Deleting a file from removable media, such as a USB or network drive, doesn't move the file to the Recycle Bin, but deletes it instantly.

When you no longer need the files in the Recycle Bin, you can permanently delete them. To do this, right-click the Recycle Bin and then click Empty Recycle Bin on the shortcut menu, or click the Empty the Recycle Bin button on the toolbar in the Recycle Bin window. Keep in mind that you cannot retrieve files that have been emptied from the Recycle Bin.

Recycle Bin A folder on your computer that holds deleted items until you remove them permanently.

A command on a menu or a button that is gray (sometimes called grayed out) is unavailable and clicking it has no effect.

Empty the Recycle Bin

Make it a practice to regularly empty the Recycle Bin. Storing many files in the Recycle Bin can slow down your computer's start up time. The unneeded files also take up space on your computer. Files you want to keep should be stored in other folders, not in the Recycle Bin. Remember, permanently deleted files can no longer be retrieved from the Recycle Bin.

 **ACTIVITY**

Work with the Recycle Bin.

1 Right-click the **Recycle Bin**. The Recycle Bin shortcut menu opens. If no files are currently in the Recycle Bin, the Empty Recycle Bin command will be gray (and unavailable).

2 Press the **Esc key** to close the shortcut menu.

3 Double-click the **Recycle Bin**. The Recycle Bin window opens. Any files or folders currently in the Recycle Bin are listed in this window.

4 Close the **Recycle Bin window**.

Windows Help and Support Help files stored on your computer as well as Help information stored on the Microsoft Web site.

LO7.5 Getting Help

As you work, you might need more information about Windows 7 or one of its programs. **Windows Help and Support** provides access to Help files stored on your computer as well as Help information stored on the Microsoft Web site. If you are not connected to the Web, you will have access to only the Help files stored on your computer.

The home page in Windows Help and Support provides tools for finding answers and other information about Windows 7. In the Windows Help and Support window, you can click a link in the Not sure where to start? section to display a list of topics. Each topic link opens an article providing detailed information about that topic or instructions for performing a task.

You can use the toolbar to navigate Windows Help and Support. For example, the Help and Support home button returns you to the home page. The Back and Forward buttons move you between the pages you have viewed.

khz/Shutterstock.com

 **ACTIVITY**

Use Windows Help and Support.

1 On the taskbar, click the **Start button** .

2 In the right pane of the Start menu, click **Help and Support**. The home page of Windows Help and Support opens, as shown in Exhibit 7-17. If you are not connected to the Web, the contents you see on the home page on your screen might differ.

> ▲ **Tip:** You can also start Windows Help and Support from a folder window by clicking the **Get help button** on the toolbar.

Exhibit 7-17 Windows Help and Support window

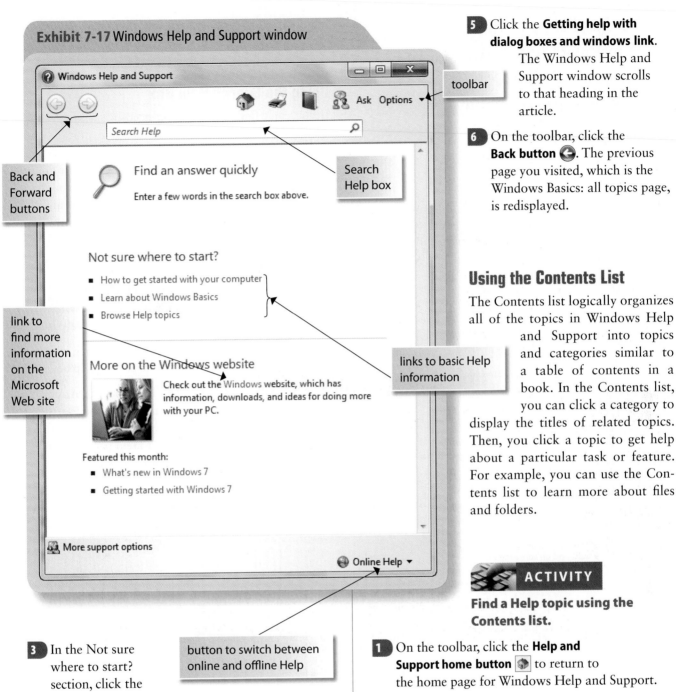

Back and Forward buttons

link to find more information on the Microsoft Web site

Search Help box

toolbar

links to basic Help information

button to switch between online and offline Help

5 Click the **Getting help with dialog boxes and windows link**. The Windows Help and Support window scrolls to that heading in the article.

6 On the toolbar, click the **Back button** . The previous page you visited, which is the Windows Basics: all topics page, is redisplayed.

Using the Contents List

The Contents list logically organizes all of the topics in Windows Help and Support into topics and categories similar to a table of contents in a book. In the Contents list, you can click a category to display the titles of related topics. Then, you click a topic to get help about a particular task or feature. For example, you can use the Contents list to learn more about files and folders.

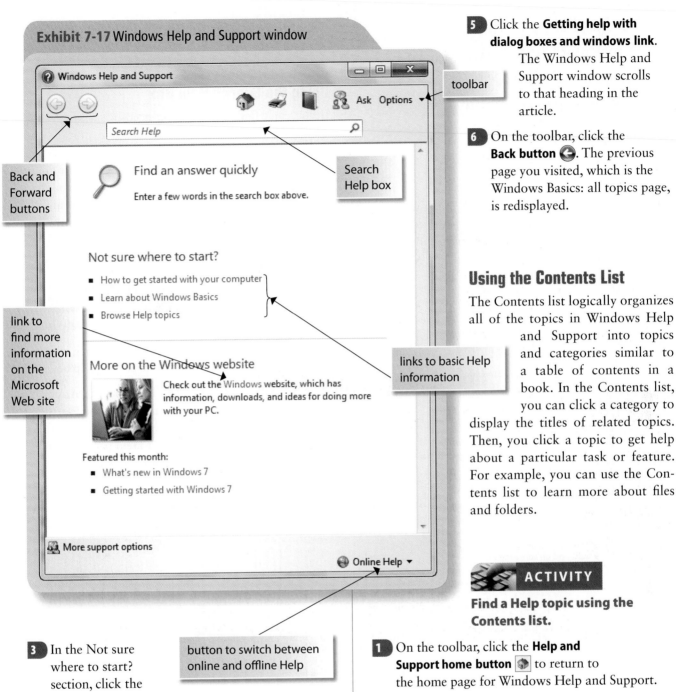

ACTIVITY

Find a Help topic using the Contents list.

1 On the toolbar, click the **Help and Support home button** to return to the home page for Windows Help and Support.

2 On the toolbar, click the **Browse Help button** . A list of categories appears in the Windows Help and Support window.

3 In the Contents list, click the **Files, folders, and libraries category**. A list of topics and other categories related to files, folders, and libraries appears in the window.

4 Click the **Working with files and folders topic**. The Windows Help and Support window displays information about that topic.

3 In the Not sure where to start? section, click the **Learn about Windows Basics link**. A list of topics related to using Windows 7 appears in the Windows Help and Support window.

4 Scroll down to the Help and support heading, and then click the **Getting help link**. An article explaining how to get help is displayed in the Windows Help and Support window. The "In this article" section on the right side of the window provides links to the headings in the article.

To quickly open the Windows Help and Support window, press the F1 key when the desktop is active.

5 In the first paragraph below the Working with files and folders heading, click the word **icons**, which is green by default. A ScreenTip shows the definition of *icons*. See Exhibit 7-18.

6 Click a blank area of the Windows Help and Support window to close the ScreenTip.

Using the Search Help Box

If you can't find the topic you need by clicking a link or using the toolbar, or if you want to quickly find Help pages related to a particular topic, you can use the Search Help box. You enter a word or phrase about the topic you want to find to see a list of Help pages containing those words. If none of the articles answer your question, you could click the Ask button on the toolbar to open a page listing other ways to get Help information.

ACTIVITY

Use the Search Help box.

1 On the toolbar, click in the **Search Help box**.

2 Type **shut down** and then click the **Search Help button**. A list of Help pages containing the words *shut down* appears in the Windows Help and Support window. See Exhibit 7-19 (your search results might differ).

3 Click the **Turning off your computer properly topic**. The article appears in the Windows Help and Support window.

⚠ **Problem?** If a Topic not found message appears in the Help window, click the **Back button** on the toolbar, and then click a different topic link.

4 Close the **Windows Help and Support window**.

Browse Help button

links to headings in the article

Exhibit 7-18 ScreenTip with definition

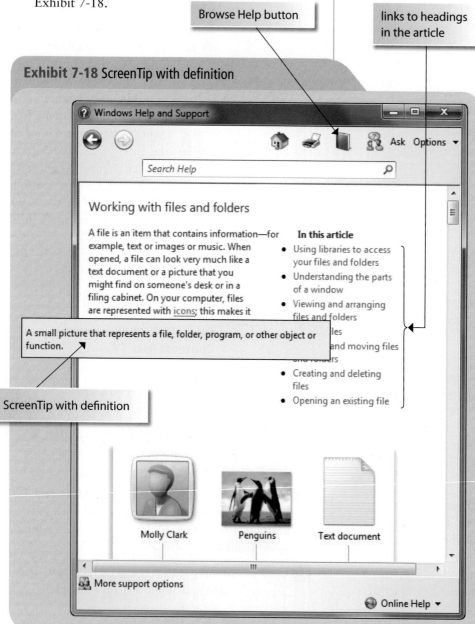

A small picture that represents a file, folder, program, or other object or function.

ScreenTip with definition

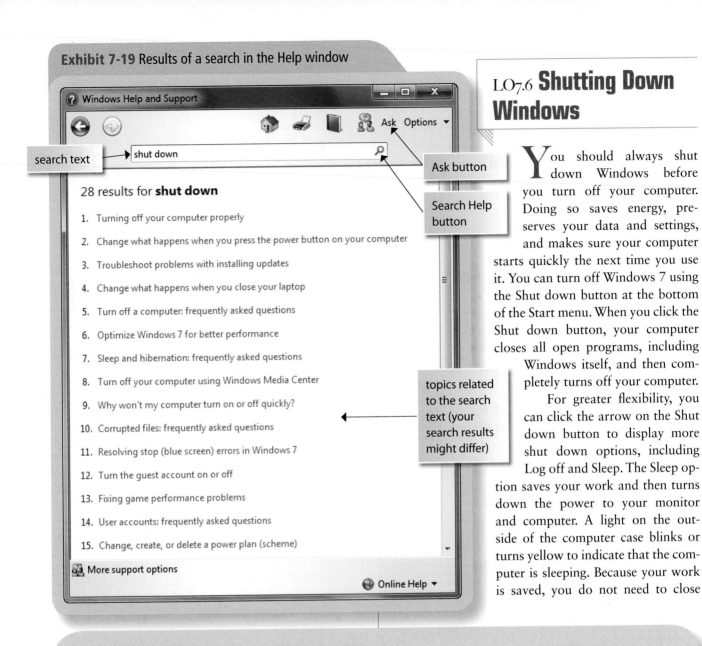

Exhibit 7-19 Results of a search in the Help window

search text

shut down

Ask button

Search Help button

Windows Help and Support

Ask Options ▼

28 results for **shut down**

1. Turning off your computer properly
2. Change what happens when you press the power button on your computer
3. Troubleshoot problems with installing updates
4. Change what happens when you close your laptop
5. Turn off a computer: frequently asked questions
6. Optimize Windows 7 for better performance
7. Sleep and hibernation: frequently asked questions
8. Turn off your computer using Windows Media Center
9. Why won't my computer turn on or off quickly?
10. Corrupted files: frequently asked questions
11. Resolving stop (blue screen) errors in Windows 7
12. Turn the guest account on or off
13. Fixing game performance problems
14. User accounts: frequently asked questions
15. Change, create, or delete a power plan (scheme)

topics related to the search text (your search results might differ)

More support options

Online Help ▼

LO7.6 Shutting Down Windows

You should always shut down Windows before you turn off your computer. Doing so saves energy, preserves your data and settings, and makes sure your computer starts quickly the next time you use it. You can turn off Windows 7 using the Shut down button at the bottom of the Start menu. When you click the Shut down button, your computer closes all open programs, including Windows itself, and then completely turns off your computer.

For greater flexibility, you can click the arrow on the Shut down button to display more shut down options, including Log off and Sleep. The Sleep option saves your work and then turns down the power to your monitor and computer. A light on the outside of the computer case blinks or turns yellow to indicate that the computer is sleeping. Because your work is saved, you do not need to close

Log Off, Sleep, or Shut Down

When you're finished working on the computer, you need to decide whether to log off the computer, put the computer to sleep, or shut down. If you are using a computer that belongs to someone else, follow that person's policy. Otherwise, the best approach depends on who uses the computer and how long it will be idle. Keep the following guidelines in mind as you make your decision:

▶ **Log off**—This command closes all programs and logs you off of Windows 7 but leaves the computer turned on. If another person might use the computer shortly, log off Windows to protect your data and prepare the computer for someone else to use.

▶ **Sleep**—By default, Windows 7 is set to sleep after 15 to 30 minutes of idle time, depending on whether you are using a notebook or desktop computer. If

you will be away from the computer for more than 15 minutes but less than a day, you can generally let the computer go to sleep on its own.

▶ **Shut down**—If your computer is plugged in to a power outlet and you don't plan to use the computer for more than a day, you save wear and tear on your electronic components and conserve energy by shutting down, which ends your Windows 7 session and turns off your computer. You should also turn off the computer when it is susceptible to electrical damage, such as during a lightning storm, and when you need to install new hardware or disconnect the computer from a power source. If your notebook computer is running on battery power only and you don't plan to use it for more than a few hours, you should also turn it off to save your battery charge.

your programs or files before putting your computer to sleep. To wake a desktop computer, you press any key or move the mouse. To wake a notebook computer, you might need to press the hardware power button on your computer case instead. After you wake a computer, the screen looks exactly as it did when you turned off your computer.

 **ACTIVITY**

Turn off Windows 7.

1 Click the **Start button** 🪟 on the taskbar.

2 Do one of the following:

- Click the **Shut down button**. Windows 7 displays a message that it is shutting down, and then turns off your computer.

- Next to the Shut down button, click the **More Options button** ▶, click **Log off**, and then follow your school's logoff procedure.

> ▲ **Tip:** Shutting down does *not* automatically save your work, so be sure to save your files before clicking the Shut down button.

Quiz Yourself

1. What happens when you point to the Start button? What happens when you click the Start button?

2. What happens when you right-click an item?

3. What is a library?

4. What is the left pane in a Windows Explorer window called?

5. How do you change the view in a Windows Explorer window?

6. How do you manually resize a window to a specific size that you want?

7. When more than one window is open, how many windows can be active at the same time?

8. In a Windows Explorer window, how do you display the contents of a folder in the window?

9. In the Navigation pane, how do you display the list of subfolders in a folder without displaying them in the right pane of the window?

10. How do you permanently delete files in the Recycle Bin from a drive?

11. How do you access Windows Help and Support?

12. Why should you shut down Windows before turning off your computer?

Practice It

Practice It 7-1

Write the steps you take as you complete this exercise.

1. Start Windows 7 and log on, if necessary.

2. Use ScreenTips to identify each of the icons on the taskbar.

3. Use the Start menu to open the program named Paint (in the Accessories folder). This program allows you to create simple drawings.

4. Use the Start menu to open the Music folder, and then use the Start menu to open the Documents folder.

5. Minimize the Documents window. Click the Paint window to make the Paint window active, and then minimize the Paint window. Maximize the Music window, and then restore it to its previous size.

6. Use Flip 3D to switch to the Documents window, and then resize the Documents window by making it approximately one inch taller.

7. Use Windows Flip to switch to the Paint window, and then close that window. Use the taskbar to close the Music window.

8. Resize the Documents window back to its original size (approximately one inch shorter).

9. In the open window, use the Navigation pane to display the contents of the Videos library. Display the contents of the Sample Videos folder in the right pane.

10. In the Navigation pane, expand the Documents library, and then expand the My Documents folder.

11. Change the view of the Sample Videos window to Large Icons.

12. In the Navigation pane, collapse the Documents library.

13. Change the view of the Sample Videos window back to Details.

14. Open the Recycle Bin window. If there is a file or folder in the Recycle Bin, select it, and then examine the details about the file in the Details pane.

15. Close the Recycle Bin window.

16. Open the Recycle Bin shortcut menu, and then click Properties. Examine the window that opens, and then click the Cancel button.

17. Open the Windows Help and Support window, and then display the Contents list. Click the Customizing your computer category, and then click the What is a theme? topic. Locate the green word *window*, and then display its definition in a ScreenTip.

18. Use the Search Help box to display a list of results for the word **libraries**. Click the Working with libraries topic, and then read the information in the window.

19. Close the Windows Help and Support window.

20. Turn off Windows 7 by using the Sleep command, shutting down, or logging off.

Practice It 7-2

Write the steps you take as you complete this exercise.

1. Start Windows 7 and log on, if necessary.

2. Open a Windows Explorer window using your log on name in the Start menu.

3. Open the Computer window. Identify the names of the drives on the computer.

4. In the Navigation pane, expand the Computer folder, and then expand the hard disk, such as Local Disk (C:). Expand the Users folder, expand the Public folder, and then expand the Public Music folder. Display the contents of the Sample Music folder in the window.

5. Use the Start menu to open the Pictures folder in a new window. Display the contents of the Sample Pictures folder in the window, and then change the view to Extra Large Icons.

6. Point to a file to display the ScreenTip, and note the date the photo was taken.

7. Use the Start menu to display the contents of the Accessories folder in the All Programs list, and then click Getting Started. In the list of topics, click Personalize Windows, and then in the top pane, click the Personalize Windows button.

8. Use the Start menu to open a program that you could use with DVDs.

9. Open Windows Help and Support, and then find a topic that explains how to use the program you started in a previous step. Read the information in the window.

10. Close all open windows.

On Your Own

On Your Own 7-1

Write the steps you take as you complete this project.

1. Open the All Programs list in the Start menu, and then use ScreenTips to locate the program that plays digital media. Start this program.

2. Display the Accessories folder in the Start menu, and then locate the program that allows you to create short notes. Start this program.

3. Use Windows Help and Support to research the program you started in the previous step.

4. Use the Search Help box in Windows Help and Support to list all the Help topics related to the program you researched in the previous step. Note whether all the results seem relevant.

5. Use ScreenTips to identify the two buttons on the note created on the desktop when you started the program in Step 2.

6. Use Flip 3D to make the program you started in Step 1 the active window.

7. Use Windows Flip to make the note created when you started the program in Step 2 active.

8. Use the taskbar to close the window associated with the program you started in Step 2.

9. Close all of the other open windows.

Managing Your Files

Introduction

Knowing how to save, locate, and organize computer files makes you more productive when you are working with a computer. A file, often referred to as a document, is a collection of data that has a name and is stored on a computer. You can open any file, edit its contents, print it, and save it again—usually with the same program used to create it. You organize files by storing them in folders. Having well organized files makes it easier and faster to find the files you want and to work efficiently.

In this chapter, you will learn strategies for organizing your files and folders, and then practice navigating the files and folders on your computer. You'll learn how to create, name, copy, move, and delete folders as well as name, copy, move, and delete files. You'll also work with compressed files.

LO8.1 Organizing Files and Folders

A computer can store folders and files on different types of disks, ranging from removable media—such as USB drives, CDs, and DVDs—to hard disks, which are permanently stored on a computer.

A computer distinguishes one drive from another by assigning each a drive letter. The hard disk is usually assigned to drive C. The remaining drives can have any other letters, but are usually assigned in the order that the drives were installed on the computer. So, your USB drive might be drive D or drive G.

The Windows 7 File System

Windows 7 stores thousands of files in many folders on the hard disk of your computer. These are system files that Windows 7 needs to display the desktop, use drives, and perform other operating system tasks. To ensure system stability and to find files quickly, Windows 7 organizes the folders and files in a hierarchy, or **file system**. At the top of the hierarchy, Windows 7 stores folders and files that

file system The hierarchy of how files and folders are organized.

Grafica/Shutterstock.com

Knowing how to save, locate, and organize computer files will make you more productive. To do this effectively, it is important to devise a strategy for managing files on your computer.

it needs when you turn on the computer. This location is called the **root directory**, and is usually drive C (the hard disk). The term *root* refers to a popular metaphor for visualizing a file system—an upside-down tree, which reflects the file hierarchy that Windows 7 uses. In Exhibit 8-1, the tree trunk corresponds to the root directory, the branches to the folders, and the leaves to the files.

Some folders contain other folders. An effectively organized computer contains a few folders in the root directory, and those folders contain other folders, also called **subfolders**.

The root directory, or top level, of the hard disk is only for system files and folders. You should not store your own work here because it could interfere with Windows or a program.

> **root directory** The top of the file system where Windows 7 stores folders and files that it needs when you turn on the computer.
>
> **subfolder** A folder contained within another folder.

Exhibit 8-1 Windows file hierarchy

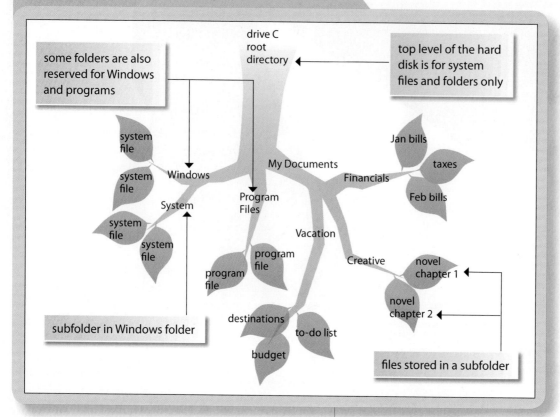

some folders are also reserved for Windows and programs

drive C root directory

top level of the hard disk is for system files and folders only

system file

system file · Windows

System

My Documents

Financials

Jan bills

taxes

Feb bills

system file

system file

Program Files

Vacation

Creative

novel chapter 1

novel chapter 2

subfolder in Windows folder

program file

program file

destinations

to-do list

budget

files stored in a subfolder

Don't Delete or Move System Files

Do not delete or move any files or folders from the root directory of the hard disk—doing so could disrupt the system so that you can't run or start the computer. In fact, you should not reorganize or change any folder that contains installed software because Windows expects to find the files for specific programs within certain folders. If you reorganize or change these folders, Windows cannot locate and start the programs stored in that folder. Likewise, you should not make changes to the folder (usually named Windows) that contains the Windows operating system.

Developing an Organizational Strategy

It is important to develop a strategy for organizing your folders and files. Exhibit 8-2 shows how you could organize your files on a hard disk if you were taking a full semester of distance-learning classes. To duplicate this organization, you would open the main folder for your documents, create four folders—one each for the Basic Accounting, Computer Concepts, Management Skills II, and Professional Writing courses—and then store the writing assignments you complete in the Professional Writing folder.

If you store your files on removable media, such as a USB drive or rewritable CD, you can use a simpler organization because you do not have to account for system files. In general, the larger the medium, the more

If you are working in a computer lab or on a public computer, you might not be allowed to access the root directory.

Syncing a Desktop and Laptop Computer

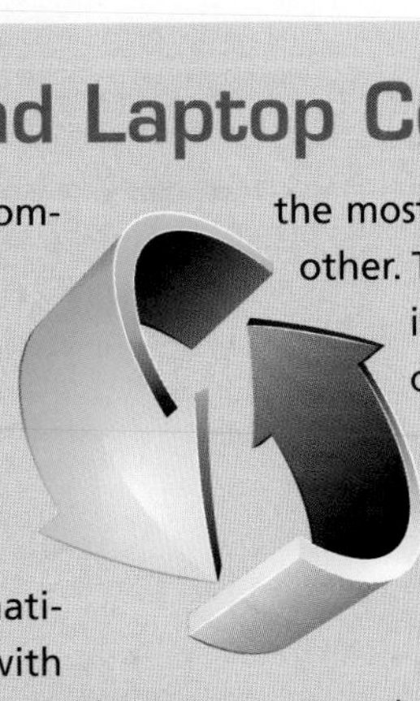

If you work on two computers, such as one computer at an office or school and another computer at home, or on a desktop and a laptop, you can copy the most recent version of your files from one computer to the other using a network connection or a portable storage device, such as a USB drive. Or, you can use a synchronization program to do this automatically to ensure that you are always working with the most recent version. **Synchronizing**—or **syncing**—folders and files between two computers means to copy the most updated version from one computer to the other. To do this, you can use the Sync Center, which is available in Windows 7 and Windows Vista, or programs specifically designed to do this, such as SyncToy, a free program available from Microsoft, or GoodSync from Siber Systems. You can also sync to the "cloud" by using Windows Live SkyDrive or a service such as Box.net or Dropbox. For more information about syncing, check the help information available from each program's manufacturer.

levels of folders you should use because large media can store more files, and, therefore, need better organization. For example, if you are organizing files on a USB drive, you could create folders in the top level of the USB drive for each general category of documents you store—one each for Courses, Creative, Financials, and Vacation. The Courses folder could then include one folder for each course, and each of those folders could contain the appropriate files.

When you open Windows Explorer, it shows the contents of the four Windows built-in libraries by default. Remember that a library is a central place to view and organize similar types of files and folders stored anywhere that your computer can access, such as your hard disk, removable drives, and a network. The four default libraries are the Documents, Music, Pictures, and Videos libraries. In contrast, a folder stores files in a specific location, such as in the Professional Writing subfolder of the My Documents folder on the Local Disk (C:) drive. To open the Report file stored in the Professional Writing folder, you must

Exhibit 8-2 Folders and files organized on a hard disk

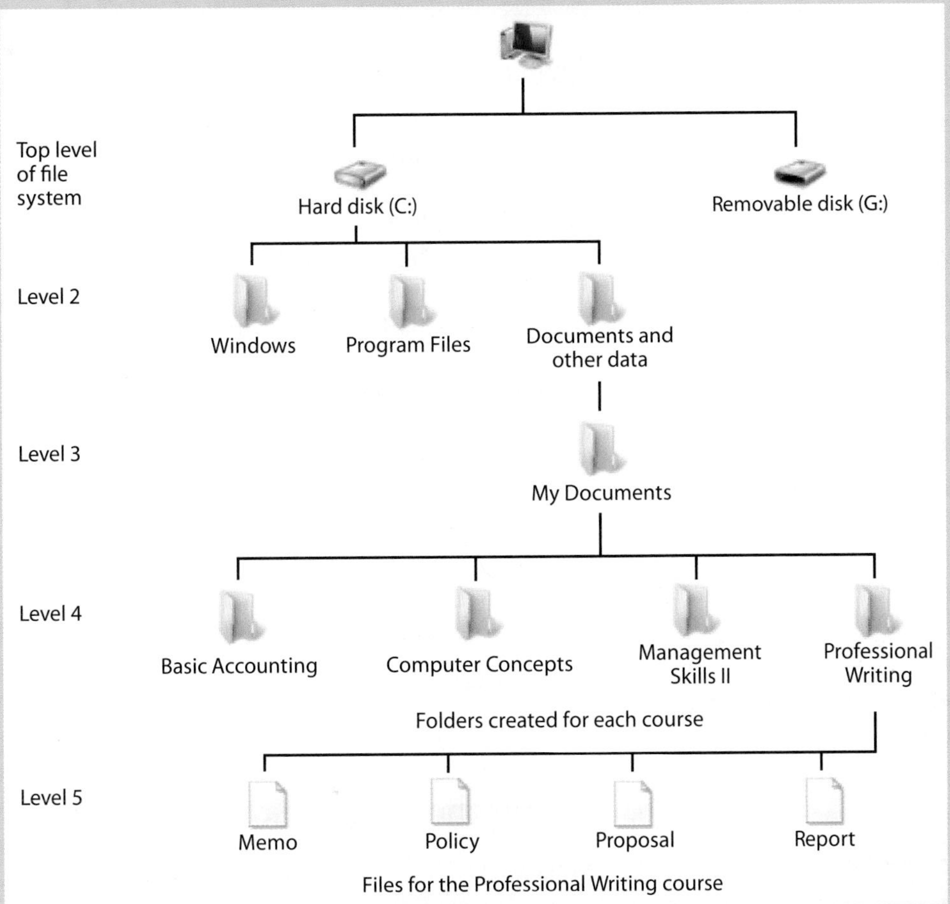

Top level of file system

Hard disk (C:)   Removable disk (G:)

Level 2

Windows   Program Files   Documents and other data

Level 3

My Documents

Level 4

Basic Accounting   Computer Concepts   Management Skills II   Professional Writing

Folders created for each course

Level 5

Memo   Policy   Proposal   Report

Files for the Professional Writing course

synchronize (sync) To copy the most updated version from one computer to another.

navigate to the Local Disk (C:) drive, then the My Documents folder, and finally the Professional Writing folder.

A library makes it easier to access similar types of files. For example, you might store some music files in the My Music folder and others in a folder named Albums on your hard disk. You might also store music files in a Tunes folder on a USB drive. If the USB drive is connected to your computer, the Music library can display all the music files in the My Music, Albums, and Tunes folders. You can then arrange the files to quickly find the ones you want to open and play.

Exhibit 8-3 Folders and files organized on a hard disk

Libraries folder selected in Navigation pane

expanded Documents folder in Navigation pane

ACTIVITY

Navigate to a library and a folder.

1 On the taskbar, click the **Windows Explorer button** . The Windows Explorer window opens, displaying the contents of the four default libraries—Documents, Music, Pictures, and Videos.

2 If the Windows Explorer window is maximized, click the **Restore Down button** .

3 In the Navigation pane, under Libraries, point to the **Documents folder** to display the Expand icon .

4 Click the **Expand icon** to expand the Documents folder. The folders in the Documents library appear in the Navigation pane. See Exhibit 8-3.

5 In the Navigation pane, click the **My Documents folder**. The contents of this folder appear in the right pane.

path A notation that indicates a file's location on your computer.

Navigating to Files

To navigate to the files you want, it helps to know the file path. The **path** shows the location of a file on a computer and leads you through the file and folder organization to the file. For example, the Customer List file is stored in the Chapter subfolder of the Chapter 8 folder included with your data files. If you are working on a USB drive, the path to this file might be:

G:\Chapter 8\Chapter\Customer List.accdb

This path has four parts, and each part is separated by a backslash (\):

▸ **G**—The drive name; for example, drive G might be the name for the USB drive

▸ **Chapter 8**—A top-level folder on drive G

▸ **Chapter**—A subfolder in the Chapter 8 folder

Using the Navigation pane helps you explore your computer and orients you to your current location.

▶ **Customer List.accdb**—The full file name, including the file extension

If someone tells you to find the file G:\Chapter 8\Chapter\Customer List.accdb, you must navigate to drive G, open the Chapter 8 folder, and then open the Chapter folder to find the Customer List file.

You can use any folder window to navigate to the data files you need for the rest of these chapters.

ACTIVITY

Navigate to a file.

1 In the Navigation pane, if the Computer folder is not expanded, click the **Computer folder Expand icon** ▷. The drives on your computer are listed below the Computer folder in the Navigation pane.

2 In the Navigation pane, click the **Computer folder**. The drives on your computer are now displayed in the right pane.

3 In the Computer window, double-click the drive containing your data files. For example, if your data files are on the hard drive, double-click **Local Disk (C:)**. If your Data Files are on a USB drive, double-click **Removable Disk (drive letter:)**, where *drive letter* is whatever letter your removable drive is, such as E, F, or G. If your data files are on a network drive, in the Navigation pane, click the **Network folder**, and then in the window, double-click the drive containing your data files.

4 In the folder window, double-click folders as needed until you see the Chapter 8 folder included with your data files.

5 Double-click the **Chapter 8 folder**. The contents of the Chapter 8 folder—the Chapter, On Your Own, and Practice It subfolders—appear in the window. The Address bar shows the path to the Chapter 8 folder.

6 In the Address bar, to the right of Chapter 8, click the **right-pointing arrow** ▶. The list of subfolders in the Chapter 8 folder appears.

7 In the list, click **Chapter**. The files in the Chapter folder appear in the Explorer window. The icon next to each file name indicates the type of file.

8 On the toolbar, click the **More options arrow** next to the **Change your view button** 📇 ▾. A menu appears.

9 On the menu, click **List**. The files appear in List view in the folder window. See Exhibit 8-4.

10 On the toolbar, click the **More options arrow** next to the **Change your view button** 📇 ▾, and then click **Large Icons**. The files appear in Large Icons view. Note that in any of the Icons views, you can see the contents of graphics files.

Exhibit 8-4 Files in the Chapter 8\Chapter folder in List view

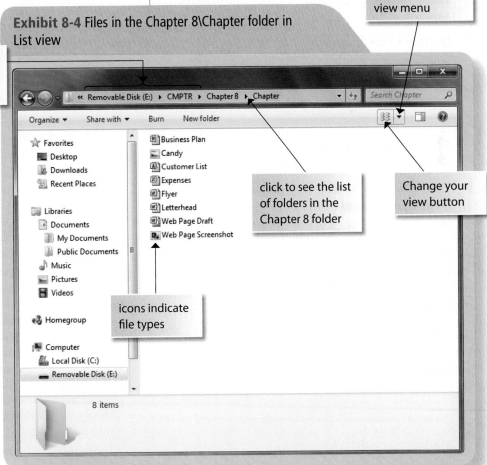

path on your screen might differ

click to open the Change your view menu

click to see the list of folders in the Chapter 8 folder

Change your view button

icons indicate file types

8 items

LO8.2 Managing Folders and Files

After you devise a plan for storing your files, you are ready to get organized by creating folders and subfolders that will hold your files and then moving the files into the appropriate folders.

Creating a Folder or Subfolder

First, determine which files seem to belong together. Then, develop an appropriate file structure. When you are working on your own computer, you usually create folders within the My Documents folder and other standard folders, such as My Music and My Pictures. When you create a folder, you give it a name, preferably one that describes its contents. A folder name can have up to 255 characters, but cannot include the / \ : * ? " < > or | characters.

For example, look again at the files in Exhibit 8-4. All of these files are related to a business named Cathy's Candy Shoppe.

▶ **Candy** and **Web Page Screenshot** are graphics files. Candy is a photograph of candy, and Web Page Screenshot is a graphic file in the file format PNG.

▶ **Business Plan** is a PowerPoint presentation that contains the beginning of a presentation to explain the store's business plan.

▶ **Customer List** is an Access file listing potential customer names and addresses.

▶ **Expenses** is an Excel file that lists projected expenses for the store.

▶ **Flyer** is a Word document that contains a flyer to announce the grand opening of the store.

▶ **Letterhead** is a Word document of (as the name implies) letterhead for the store.

▶ **Web Page Draft** is a Word document saved as an HTML document that can be published to a Web server and accessed as a Web page.

One way to organize these files is to create the following three folders—one for graphics, one for the finances, and one for marketing:

▶ **Graphics folder**—Candy and Web Page Screenshot

▶ **Finances folder**—Business Plan and Expenses

▶ **Marketing folder**—Customer List, Flyer, Letterhead, and Web Page Draft

Guidelines for Creating Folders

As you organize your files by creating folders, keep in mind the following guidelines to ensure that you and others who might later work with your files can quickly and easily find the files you need:

▶ **Keep folder names short and familiar.** Long names can be cut off in a folder window, so use names that are short but meaningful, such as project names or categories.

▶ **Develop standards for naming folders.** Use a consistent naming scheme that is logical to you and others. For example, you could use a project name as the name of the main folder, and include step numbers in each subfolder name, such as 01Plan, 02Approvals, 03Prelim, and so on.

▶ **Create subfolders to organize files.** If a file listing in a folder window is so long that you must scroll the window, consider organizing those files into subfolders.

ACTIVITY

Create folders.

1 On the toolbar in the Chapter 8\Chapter folder window, click the **New folder button**. A folder icon with the placeholder label *New folder* appears in the window. The folder name is highlighted, and a box appears around it. Text you type will replace the highlighted text. See Exhibit 8-5.

2 Type **Graphics** and then press the **Enter key**. *Graphics* replaces the placeholder name and the new Graphics folder is selected in the window.

3 Right-click a blank area of the window. A shortcut menu opens. See Exhibit 8-6.

4 On the shortcut menu, point to **New**, and then click **Folder**. A new folder is created.

⚠ **Problem?** If the New command is not on your shortcut menu or if the New command does not have an arrow next to it, click a blank area of the window to close that menu, and then repeat Step 3, being sure to click a *blank* area of the window.

Exhibit 8-5 New folder created in the current folder window

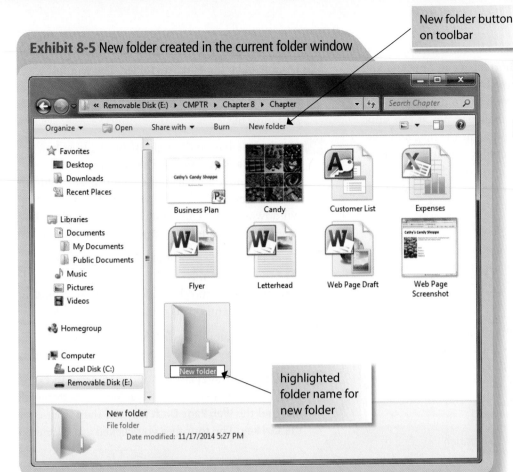

highlighted folder name for new folder

5 Type **Finances** and then press the **Enter key**. The new folder is renamed.

6 Create a new folder named **Marketing**. The Chapter 8\Chapter folder now contains three subfolders.

Moving or Copying Files and Folders

If you want to place a file into a folder from another location, you can move the file or copy it. Moving a file removes it from its current location and places it in a new location you specify. Copying also places the file in a new location that you specify, but does not remove it from its current location. You can move and copy folders in the same way that you move and copy files. When you do, you move or copy all the files contained in the folder.

The easiest way to move files or folders is to drag them, just as you dragged windows in Chapter 7. When you drag a file or folder from one location to another on the same drive, the file or folder is moved from its original location to the new location. When you drag a file or folder from one drive to another drive, the file or folder is copied instead of moved. You can override this default behavior by dragging a file using the right mouse button. When you drag a file or folder using

Exhibit 8-6 Shortcut menu in a folder window

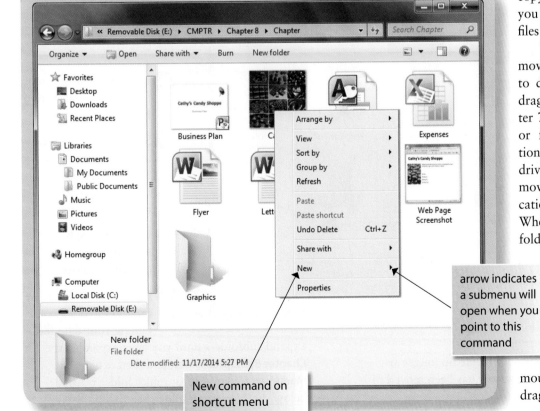

arrow indicates a submenu will open when you point to this command

New command on shortcut menu

the right mouse button, a shortcut menu appears, and you can choose the Move here or the Copy here command, depending on what you want to do.

To move or copy more than one file at the same time, you select all the files you want to copy, and then drag them as a group. To select files that are adjacent in a window, click the first file in the list, hold down the Shift key, click the last file in the list, and then release the Shift key. To select files that are not adjacent, click one file, hold down the Ctrl key, click the other files, and then release the Ctrl key.

ACTIVITY

Move files or folders.

1 Drag the **Business Plan file** on top of the **Finances folder**, but do not release the mouse button. A ScreenTip appears identifying the action as moving the file to the Finances folder. See Exhibit 8-7.

3 Double-click the **Finances folder**. The window changes to display the contents of the Finances folder, which now contains the Business Plan presentation file.

4 On the title bar, to the right of the Address bar, click the **Back button** ⊙. The contents of the Chapter folder appear in the window. The folders now appear first in the window because the window automatically resorts when you redisplay its contents, and folders appear first by default.

5 Right-click the **Expenses file**, but do not release the mouse button. Drag the **Expenses file** to the **Finances folder**, and then release the mouse button. A shortcut menu opens on the Finances folder.

6 On the shortcut menu, click **Move here**. The file is moved from the current folder to the Finances folder.

7 Click the **Customer List file**, and then press and hold the **Ctrl key**. Click the **Flyer file**, the **Letterhead file**, and the **Web Page Draft file**, and then release the **Ctrl key**. The four files you clicked are selected.

> **Tip:** Because the files are listed sequentially, you could also press the Shift key, click the first file in the list, click the last file in the list, and then release the Shift key to select all the files.

8 Drag the four selected files into the **Marketing folder**.

9 Select the **Candy file** and the **Web Page Screenshot file**, and then drag them into the **Graphics folder**.

10 Drag the **Graphics folder** into the **Marketing folder**.

11 In the Navigation pane, expand the drive containing your data files, expand subfolders until you have expanded the **Chapter 8\Chapter folder**, and then expand the **Marketing folder**. The Graphics folder is listed below the Marketing folder. See Exhibit 8-8.

Exhibit 8-7 Moving a file into a folder

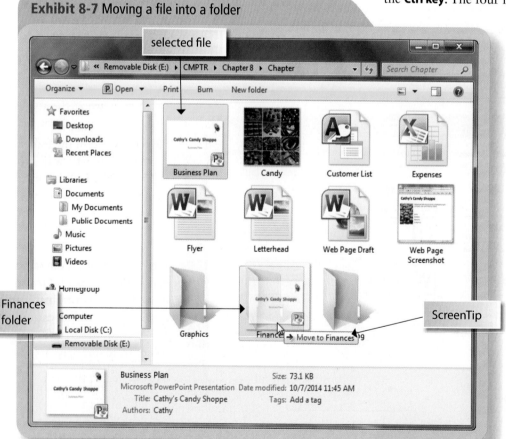

2 Release the mouse button. The file no longer appears in the window because it has been moved to the Finances folder.

Back button

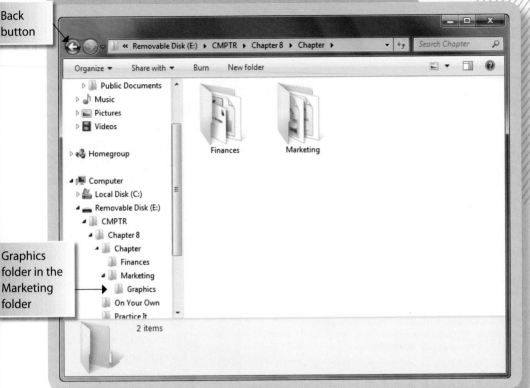

Graphics folder in the Marketing folder

TRINACRIA PHOTO/Shutterstock.com

Remember that the default result for dragging a file or folder from one drive to another is to copy the file or folder.

If you want to copy a file or folder from one location to another on the same drive, press and hold the Ctrl key while you drag. The ScreenTip that appears indicates that you are copying the item.

You can also copy a file or folder using the right mouse button to drag the file; click Copy here on the shortcut menu that appears when you release the mouse button instead of Move here. Remember when you copy a folder, its contents are also copied.

ACTIVITY

Copy files or folders.

1 In the Navigation pane, click the **Graphics folder**. The two files in the Graphics folder appear in the folder window.

2 Press and hold the **Ctrl key**, and then drag the **Web Page Screenshot file** to the **Finances folder** in the Navigation pane, but do not release the Ctrl key. The ScreenTip indicates that the file will be copied to the Finances folder. See Exhibit 8-9.

Using the Clipboard

Another way to move or copy files and folders is to use the **Clipboard**, a temporary storage area in Windows on which files, folders, text, or other objects are stored when you copy or move them. To use the Clipboard, right-click a file or folder, and then on the shortcut menu, click Cut to remove the file or folder from its current location and place it on the Clipboard, or click Copy to duplicate the file or folder on the Clipboard, leaving the original in its original location. To paste the contents of the Clipboard, right-click a blank area of the folder window in which you want to put the moved or copied file or folder, and then on the shortcut menu, click Paste.

Clipboard A temporary storage area in Windows on which objects are stored when you copy or move them.

Exhibit 8-9 Copying a file

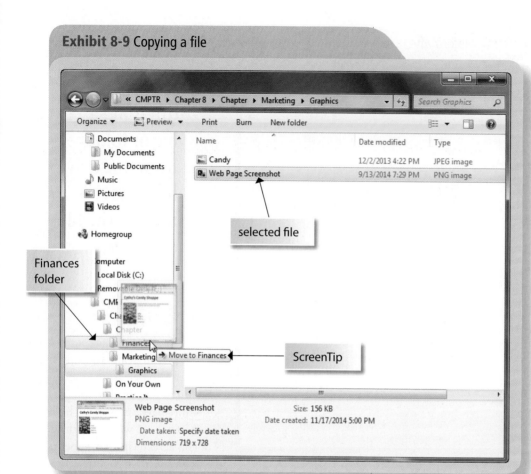

Organize ▾ | Preview ▾ | Print | Burn | New folder

« CMPTR ▸ Chapter 8 ▸ Chapter ▸ Marketing ▸ Graphics | ▾ | Search Graphics

Documents
  My Documents
  Public Documents
Music
Pictures
Videos

Homegroup

Computer
Local Disk (C:)
Removable Disk (E:)
CMf
Cha
Chapter
Finances
Marketing
  Graphics
On Your Own

Name	Date modified	Type
Candy	12/2/2013 4:22 PM	JPEG image
Web Page Screenshot	9/13/2014 7:29 PM	PNG image

Finances folder

selected file

Move to Finances ◀ **ScreenTip**

Web Page Screenshot
PNG image
Date taken: Specify date taken
Dimensions: 719 x 728
Size: 156 KB
Date created: 11/17/2014 5:00 PM

5 In the Address bar, after Chapter, click the **right-pointing arrow** ▶ , and then click **Marketing**. The contents of the Marketing folder appear in the folder window.

6 Right-click the **Web Page Draft file**, and then drag it to the **Finances folder** in the Navigation pane. The same shortcut menu you saw when you were moving files appears.

⚠ **Problem?** Even though you intend to copy the file, the ScreenTip *Move to Finances* appears. You can still choose the Copy here command on the shortcut menu when it appears.

3 Release the mouse button, and then release the **Ctrl key**. The file is copied to the Finances folder. Notice that the Web Page Screenshot file is still listed in the Graphics folder.

4 In the Navigation pane, click the **Finances folder**. The Web Page Screenshot file is listed in the folder window along with the other two files in the Finances folder.

7 On the shortcut menu, click **Copy here**. The file is copied to the Finances folder.

8 On the title bar, to the left of the Address bar, click the **Back button** ◀. The contents of the previously viewed folder, the Finances folder, appear in the window, including the Web Page Draft file.

Determining Where to Store Files

When you create and save files on your computer's hard disk, you should store them in subfolders. The top level of the hard disk is off-limits for your files because they could interfere with system files. If you are working on your own computer, store your files within the My Documents folder, which is where many programs save files by default. When you use a computer on the job, your employer might assign a main folder to you for storing your work. In either case, if you simply store all your files in one folder, you will soon have trouble finding the files you want. Instead, you should create subfolders within a main folder to separate files in a way that makes sense for you.

Even if you store most of your files on removable media, such as USB drives, you still need to organize those files into folders and subfolders. Before you start creating folders, whether on a hard disk or removable disk, be sure to plan the organization you will use.

9 Press and hold the **Ctrl key**. In the Navigation pane, drag the **Graphics folder** on top of the **Chapter folder**. Release the mouse button, and then release the **Ctrl key**. The Graphics folder is copied to the Chapter folder and appears after the Finances folder in the folders list.

10 In the Navigation pane, click the **Graphics folder** in the Chapter folder (not the original Graphics folder in the Marketing folder). The files in the original Graphics folder appear in the folder window because they were copied along with the folder.

Naming and Renaming Files

As you work with files, pay attention to file names—they provide important information about the file, including its contents and purpose. A file name such as Car Sales.docx has three parts:

▶ **Main part of the file name**—the name you provide when you create a file, and the name you associate with a file

▶ **Dot**—the period (.) that separates the main part of the file name from the file extension

▶ **File extension**—usually three or four characters that follow the dot in the file name

The main part of a file name can have up to 255 characters, which gives you plenty of space to name your file descriptively so that you will know its contents just by looking at the file name. You can use spaces and certain punctuation symbols in your file names. Like folder names, file names cannot contain the \ / ? : * " < > | symbols because these characters have special meaning in Windows 7.

Recall that the file extension—three or more characters following a dot after the file name—helps you identify files. For example, in the file name Car Sales.docx, the extension *docx* identifies the file as one created by Microsoft Office Word. You might also have a file called Car Sales.jpg—the *jpg* extension identifies the file as one created in a graphics program, such as Paint, or as a photograph. Though the main parts of these file names are identical, their extensions distinguish them as different files. You usually do not need to add extensions to file names because the program you use to create the file adds the file extension automatically. Also, although Windows 7 keeps track of extensions, not all computers are set to display them.

Guidelines for Naming Files

Be sure to give your files and folders meaningful names that help you remember their purpose and contents. You can easily rename a file or folder by using the Rename command on the file's shortcut menu. The following are a few suggestions for naming your files:

▶ **Use common names.** Avoid cryptic names that might make sense now, but could cause confusion later, such as nonstandard abbreviations or imprecise names like *Stuff2013*.

▶ **Don't change the file extension.** When renaming a file, don't change the file extension. If you do, Windows might not be able to find a program that can open it.

▶ **Find a balance between too short and too long.** Use file names that are long enough to be meaningful, but short enough to read easily on the screen.

 **ACTIVITY**

Rename files or folders.

1 Display the contents of the **Marketing folder** in the window.

2 Right-click the **Flyer file**. On the shortcut menu, click **Rename**. The shortcut menu closes, and the file name is highlighted in the same manner as it was when you created a new folder.

3 Type **Grand Opening Flyer** and then press the **Enter key**. The file name changes to the name you typed.

4 Click the **Letterhead file**, pause for a moment, and then click the **Letterhead file name**. The file name becomes highlighted.

⚠ **Problem?** If your computer is set to display file extensions, a dialog box might open asking if you are sure you want to change the file extension. Click **No**, right-click the **Flyer file**, on the shortcut menu, click **Rename**, type **Grand Opening Flyer**, and then press the **Enter key**.

5 Click immediately before the **L** in the file name, type **Company**, press the **Spacebar**, and then press the **Enter key**. The file is renamed.

Deleting Files and Folders

Recycle Bin

You should periodically delete unneeded files and folders so that your folders and drives don't get cluttered. When you delete a file or folder from the hard drive, the file or folder and all of its contents are moved to the Recycle Bin. After you empty the Recycle Bin, you can no longer recover the files it contained. When you delete a file or folder from removable media, such as a USB drive, or from a network drive, it is permanently deleted and cannot be recovered.

ACTIVITY

Delete files or folders.

1 Display the contents of the **Finances folder** in the folder window.

2 Drag the **Web Page Screenshot file** on top of the Recycle Bin on the desktop. If your data files are stored on the hard drive, the file is moved to the Recycle Bin. If your data files are stored on removable media or a network drive, a dialog box opens asking if you are sure you want to permanently delete the file.

⚠ **Problem?** If you can't see the Recycle Bin, drag the Finances folder window to a new location by its title bar.

3 If the Delete File dialog box is open, click **Yes**. The dialog box closes, and the file is deleted.

To retrieve a file or folder from the Recycle Bin, double-click the Recycle Bin to open its window, right-click the file or folder, and then click the Restore command.

compressed (zipped) folder A folder that stores files in a compact format.

4 In the folder window, right-click the **Web Page Draft file**. On the shortcut menu, click **Delete**. If your data files are stored on the hard drive, a dialog box opens asking if you are sure you want to move the file to the Recycle Bin. If your data files are stored on removable media or a network drive, a dialog box opens asking if you are sure you want to permanently delete the file.

5 Click **Yes**. The file is either moved to the Recycle Bin or permanently deleted.

6 If the Recycle Bin contains files, right-click the **Recycle Bin**. On the shortcut menu, click **Empty Recycle Bin**. A dialog box opens asking if you are sure you want to permanently delete the items.

7 Click **Yes**. The dialog box closes, and the files in the Recycle Bin are permanently deleted.

LO8.3 Working with Compressed Files

If you transfer files from one location to another, such as from your hard disk to a removable disk or vice versa, or from one computer to another via email, you can store the files in a compressed (zipped) folder. A **compressed (zipped) folder** stores files in a compact format so they take up less disk space. You can then transfer the files more quickly. When you create a compressed folder, Windows 7 displays a zipper on the folder icon.

You compress a folder so that the files it contains use less space on the disk. Compare two folders—a folder named Photos that contains about 8.6 MB of files, and a compressed folder containing the same files but requiring only 6.5 MB of disk space. In this case, the compressed files use about 25 percent less disk space than the uncompressed files.

Creating a Compressed Folder

You can create a compressed folder using the Send to Compressed (zipped) folder command on the shortcut menu of one or more selected files or folders. Then you can compress additional files or folders by dragging them into the compressed folder. You can open a file directly from a compressed folder, although you cannot modify the file. To edit and save a compressed file, you must extract it first.

If a different compression program, such as Win-Zip, has been installed on your computer, the Send to

Compressed (zipped) folder command might not appear on the shortcut menu. Instead, it might be replaced by the name of your compression program. In this case, refer to your compression program's Help system for instructions on working with compressed files.

 **ACTIVITY**

Compress folders and files.

1 Display the contents of the **Chapter folder** in the window.

2 Select the **Finances folder** and the **Marketing folder**.

3 Right-click either of the selected folders. On the shortcut menu, point to **Send to**, and then click **Compressed (zipped) folder** on the submenu. After a few moments, a new compressed folder with a zipper icon appears in the window with the file name selected. See Exhibit 8-10.

4 Type **Final Files** and then press the **Enter key** to rename the compressed folder.

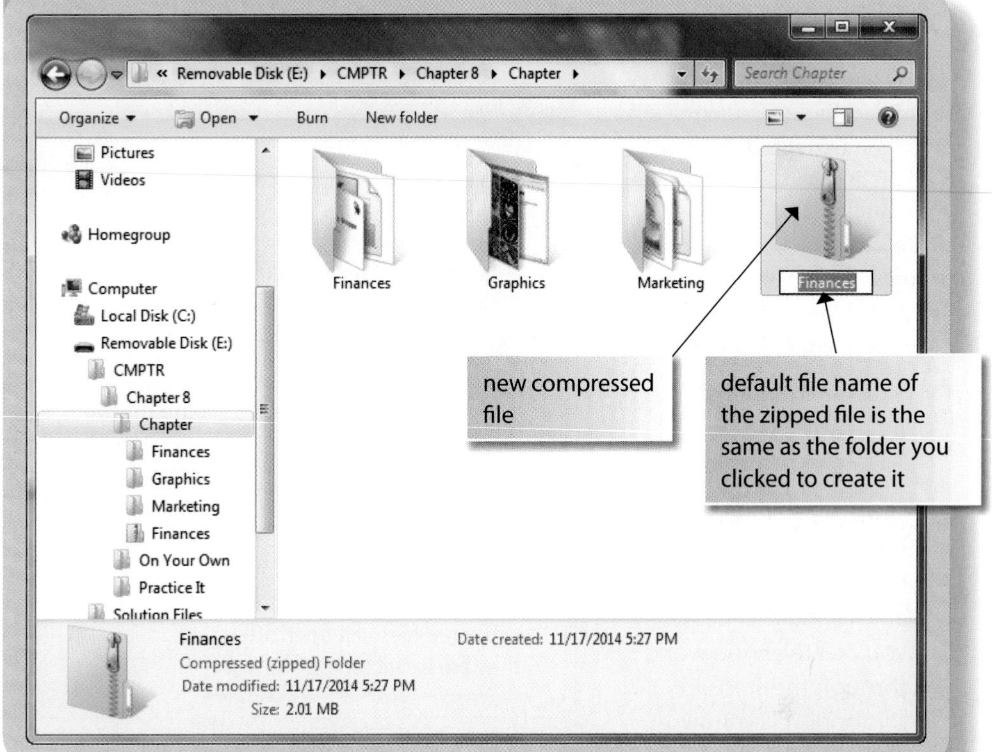

⚠ Problem? If the Compressed (zipped) folder command does not appear on the Send to submenu of the shortcut menu, a different compression program is probably installed on your computer. Click a blank area of the Chapter window to close the shortcut menu, and then read but do not perform the remaining steps.

Extracting a Compressed Folder

You open a compressed folder by double-clicking it. You can then move and copy files and folders in a compressed folder, although you cannot rename them.

Exhibit 8-10 New compressed folder

[Screenshot of file explorer window showing folders: Finances, Graphics, Marketing, and a new compressed Finances file]

Address bar: « Removable Disk (E:) ▸ CMPTR ▸ Chapter 8 ▸ Chapter ▸   Search Chapter

Organize ▾   Open ▾   Burn   New folder

Left pane:
- Pictures
- Videos
- Homegroup
- Computer
  - Local Disk (C:)
  - Removable Disk (E:)
    - CMPTR
      - Chapter 8
        - Chapter
          - Finances
          - Graphics
          - Marketing
          - Finances
        - On Your Own
        - Practice It
    - Solution Files

new compressed file

default file name of the zipped file is the same as the folder you clicked to create it

Finances
Compressed (zipped) Folder   Date created: 11/17/2014 5:27 PM
Date modified: 11/17/2014 5:27 PM
Size: 2.01 MB

When you **extract** a file, you create an uncompressed copy of the file in a folder you specify, preserving the files in their folders as appropriate. The original file remains in the compressed folder.

 **ACTIVITY**

Extract compressed files.

1 Right-click the **Final Files compressed folder**. On the shortcut menu, click **Extract All**. The Extract Compressed (Zipped) Folders dialog box opens.

Consider compressing files when sharing files electronically.

extract To create an uncompressed copy of a compressed file.

2 In the box with the selected path and file name, click to the right of the file name (Final Files), press the **Spacebar**, and then type **Extracted**. This is the name of the folder to which the files will be extracted. See Exhibit 8-11.

⚠️ **Problem?** If in the Extract Compressed (Zipped) Folders dialog box the path to the Final Files Extracted folder is not the location where you are storing the files you create as you work through the steps in this book, click **Browse**, click the **Expand arrows** as needed until you can select the folder in which you are storing solution files, and then click **OK**. In the Files will be extracted to this folder box, click at the end of the path, type \ (a backslash), and then type **Final Files Extracted**.

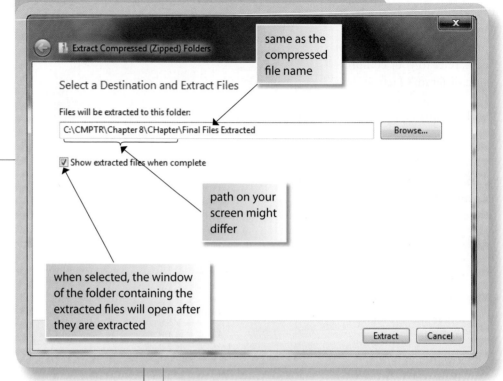

Exhibit 8-11 Extract Compressed (Zipped) Folders dialog box

Extract Compressed (Zipped) Folders

Select a Destination and Extract Files

Files will be extracted to this folder:

C:\CMPTR\Chapter 8\CHapter\Final Files Extracted   Browse...

same as the compressed file name

☑ Show extracted files when complete

path on your screen might differ

when selected, the window of the folder containing the extracted files will open after they are extracted

Extract   Cancel

3 Click **Extract**. A dialog box showing the progress of the extraction appears briefly, and then the Final Files Extracted folder window opens listing the Finances and Marketing folders.

Backing Up Your Data

You should back up your data regularly so that you can restore your files if something happens to your computer. Performing a backup can include backing up an entire computer (so it can be restored at a later date, if needed), backing up all data files (in order to restore them in case the computer is lost or damaged), or backing up only selected files (to make sure you have a clean copy of each file if the original is accidentally lost or destroyed). Depending on their size, backup data files can be placed on a recordable or rewritable CD or DVD disc, an external hard drive, a USB flash drive, or virtually any other storage medium. To protect against fires and other natural disasters, you should store backup media in a physical location other than where your computer is located or inside a fire-resistant safe. You can perform backups by manually copying files that change, but backup utility programs make the backup process easier. For convenience, many backup programs can be scheduled to back up specified files, folders, or drives on a regular basis (such as every night or once a week). You can also back up to the cloud using an online backup service, such as Carbonite or MozyHome. These services back up your files automatically to a secure Web server on a regular basis, provided you have a broadband Internet connection.

Tatiana Popova/Shutterstock.com

4 Double-click the **Marketing folder**. It contains all the files and the Graphics folder that you moved into the original Marketing folder.

5 In the Address bar, to the right of Final Files Extracted, click the **right-pointing arrow** ▸, and then click **Finances**. The contents of this folder match the contents of the Finances folder you compressed.

6 In the upper-right corner of the Finances folder window, click the **Close button** ⬛X⬛. The Finances folder window closes.

7 In the upper-right corner of the Chapter folder window, click the **Close button** ⬛X⬛.

Quiz Yourself

1. What is the root directory?

2. What is a folder contained within another folder called?

3. What are the four default libraries in Windows 7?

4. What is a path?

5. When you use the left mouse button to drag a file or folder from one location to another on a drive, what happens? What happens when you drag a file or folder from one drive to another drive?

6. Describe two ways to copy a file or folder from one location to another on the same drive without using the Clipboard.

7. How many characters can a file name have?

8. What happens to a file or folder you delete?

9. What happens to the files and folders in the Recycle Bin when you empty the Recycle Bin?

10. Why would you compress files?

11. How can you identify a compressed folder?

12. Is a file deleted from a compressed folder when you extract it?

Practice It

Practice It 8-1

1. Use a folder window as necessary to find the following information, and then record your answers:

   a. The path to the location where your data files for this book are stored.

   b. The path to the location where you will store the files you create as you work through the activities and projects in this book.

   c. The method you will use to navigate to these locations.

   d. Any guidelines or conventions you need to use when naming the files you save for this book. For example, should all the file names start with your course number or tutorial number? If so, describe the conventions.

2. Display the data files located in the Chapter 8\ Practice It folder in a folder window, and then display the files as Large Icons.

3. In the Chapter 8\Practice It folder window, create three folders: **Marketing Info**, **Sales Dept**, and **Sales Meeting**.

4. Move the Art1 for Brochure and Art2 for Brochure files from the Chapter 8\Practice It folder into the Marketing Info folder.

5. Move the Agenda, Evaluation Form, and Sales files from the Chapter 8\Practice It folder into the Sales Meeting folder.

6. Move the New Bonus Plan file from the Chapter 8\ Practice It folder into the Sales Dept folder.

7. Move the Sales Meeting folder from the Chapter 8\ Practice It folder into the Sales Dept folder.

8. Copy the New Bonus Plan file located in the Sales Dept folder into the Sales Meeting folder, and then copy the Sales file located in the Sales Meeting folder into the Sales Dept folder.

9. Rename the Sales Meeting folder as **Spring Sales Meeting**.

10. Delete the Sales file from the Spring Sales Meeting folder, and then empty the Recycle Bin, if necessary.

11. In the Chapter 8\Practice It\Sales Dept folder, create a compressed (zipped) folder named **Sales Meeting Zipped** that contains all of the files and folders in the Spring Sales Meeting folder, and then move the zipped folder into the Chapter 8\Practice It folder.

12. Extract the contents of the Sales Meeting Zipped folder to a new folder named **Sales Meeting Extracted** in the Chapter 8\Practice It folder.

13. Close all open windows.

Practice It 8-2

1. Display the data files located in the Chapter 8\Practice It folder in a folder window, and then display the files using List view.

2. Copy the Flyer file located in the Chapter 8\Practice It folder to the Chapter 8\Practice It folder. (*Hint*: Use the right mouse button to drag the file to a blank area of the folder window.) Rename the Flyer - Copy file as **Advertising Flyer**.

3. Copy the First Qtr Sales file located in the Chapter 8\Practice It folder to the Chapter 8\Practice It folder three times. Rename the files **Second Qtr Sales**, **Third Qtr Sales**, and **Fourth Qtr Sales**.

4. Create two folders in the Chapter 8\Practice It folder: **Auto Sales** and **Advertising**.

5. Move the Flyer and Advertising Flyer files into the Advertising folder, and then move the Advertising folder and the four "Qtr Sales" files into the Auto Sales folder.

6. Compress the Auto Sales folder to a folder named **Auto Sales Compressed**.

7. Extract the files from the Auto Sales Compressed folder to a folder named **Auto Sales Extracted**.

8. Delete the Flyer file from the Auto Sales Extracted\Auto Sales\Advertising folder.

9. Open the Recycle Bin folder window, and then restore the Flyer file to the Auto Sales Extracted\Auto Sales\Advertising folder. (*Hint:* Right-click the Flyer file in the Recycle Bin window, and then on the shortcut menu, click Restore.) Note that if you are working on a USB drive, you cannot complete this step.

10. Rename the Auto Sales Extracted folder as **Auto Sales Restored**.

11. Close all open windows.

On Your Own

On Your Own 8-1

1. Click the Start button, click Help and Support, and then use one of the following methods to locate topics on searching for files:

   - In the Windows Help and Support window, click the Learn about Windows Basics link. Click the Working with files and folders link.

   - In the Windows Help and Support window, click the Browse Help topics link. Click the Files, folders, and libraries link, and then click the Working with files and folders link.

   - In the Search Help box, type **searching for files** and then press the Enter key. In the search results, click the Working with files and folders link.

2. In the In this article section, click the Finding files link. Read the topic and click any *See also* or *For more information* links, if necessary, to provide the following information:

   a. Where is the Search box located?

   b. Do you need to type the entire file name to find a specific file?

   c. How do you create a filter?

3. Display the contents of the Chapter 8 folder, and then display the full path in the Address bar. (*Hint*: Click the icon in the Address bar.) What is the full path?

4. Write down the method you used to locate topics on searching for files and your answers to the remaining questions.

ADDITIONAL STUDY TOOLS

Chapter 8

IN THE BOOK

▶ Complete end-of-chapter exercises

▶ Study tear-out Chapter Review Card

ONLINE

▶ Complete additional end-of-chapter exercises

▶ Take practice quiz to prepare for tests

▶ Review key term flash cards (online, printable, and audio)

▶ Play "Beat the Clock" and "Memory" to quiz yourself

▶ Watch the videos "Navigate to a library and folder," "Navigate to Files," and more

Introducing Microsoft Office 2010

Introduction

Microsoft Office 2010, or **Office**, is a collection of Microsoft programs. The most commonly used programs include Word, Excel, Access, and PowerPoint. You use Word to enter, edit, and format text. With Excel, you enter, calculate, analyze, and present numerical data. Access enables you to enter, maintain, and retrieve related information (or data) in a format known as a database. PowerPoint is used to create a collection of slides that can contain text, charts, pictures, sound, movies, multimedia, and so on.

Office is available in many suites, each of which contains a different combination of these programs. For example, the Professional suite includes Word, Excel, PowerPoint, Access, Outlook, Publisher, and OneNote. Other suites are available and can include more or fewer programs. Each Office program contains valuable tools to help you accomplish many tasks, such as composing reports, analyzing data, preparing presentations, compiling information, sending email, planning schedules, and compiling notes.

Word is used to enter, edit, and format text. The files you create in Word are called documents, although many people use the term *document* to refer to any file created on a computer. Word, often called a word processing program, offers many special features that help you compose and update all types of documents, ranging from letters and newsletters to reports, brochures, faxes, and even books, in attractive and readable formats. You can also use Word to create, insert, and position figures, tables, and other graphics to enhance the look of your documents.

Excel is used to enter, calculate, analyze, and present numerical data. You can do some of this in Word with tables, but Excel provides many more tools for recording and formatting numbers as well as performing calculations. The graphics capabilities in Excel also enable you to display data visually. You might, for example, generate a pie chart or a bar chart to help people quickly see the significance of and the connections between information. The files you create in Excel are called workbooks (commonly referred to as spreadsheets), and Excel is often called a spreadsheet program.

Access is used to enter, maintain, and retrieve related information (or data) in a format known as a database. The files you create in Access are called

Learning Objectives

After studying the material in this chapter, you will be able to:

LO9.1 Start Office programs and explore common elements

LO9.2 Use the Ribbon

LO9.3 Work with files

LO9.4 Use the Clipboard

LO9.5 Get Help

LO9.6 Exit Office programs

Microsoft Office 2010 (Office)
A collection of Microsoft programs.

Business people commonly use Microsoft Office to collaborate with their colleagues.

databases, and Access is often referred to as a database or relational database program. With Access, you can create forms to make data entry easier, and you can create professional reports to improve the readability of your data.

PowerPoint is used to create a collection of slides that can contain text, charts, pictures, sound, movies, multimedia, and so on. The files you create in PowerPoint are called presentations, and PowerPoint is often called a presentation graphics program. You can show these presentations on your computer monitor, project them onto a screen as a slide show, print them, share them over the Internet, or display them on the Web. You can also use PowerPoint to generate presentation-related documents such as audience handouts, outlines, and speakers' notes.

In this chapter, you'll be introduced to Microsoft Office programs and learn about features common to all of the Office programs.

Integrating Office Programs

Most organizations rely heavily on teams to complete work tasks, and, consequently, team members rely on each other to complete their assigned projects successfully. For example, you might be responsible for providing data for others to analyze, or for collecting other team members' data and creating a report. When a team works together to complete a project, it is vital that each member of the team complete his or her piece of the project.

One of the main advantages of Office is **integration**, the ability to share information between programs. Integration ensures consistency and accuracy, and it saves time because you don't have to reenter the same information in several Office programs. It also means that team members can effortlessly share Office files. Team members can create files based on their skills and information that can be used by others as needed. Businesses can take advantage of the integration features of Office every day, as described in the following examples:

- An accounting department can use Excel to create a bar chart illustrating fourth-quarter results for the previous two years, and then insert it into a quarterly financial report created in Word. This report could include a hyperlink that employees can click to open the Excel workbook and view the original data.

- An operations department can include an Excel pie chart of sales percentages on a PowerPoint slide, which is part of a presentation to stockholders.

- A marketing department can combine a form letter created in Word with an Access database that stores the names and addresses of potential customers to produce a mailing to promote its company's product.

These few examples show how information from one Office program can be integrated with another to save time and effort.

© Image copyright Andresr, 2009. Used under license from Shutterstock.com.

integration The ability to share information between programs.

LO9.1 Starting Office Programs and Exploring Common Elements

All of the Office programs have common elements. To learn about some of the features the programs share, you will start a few Office programs and examine the program windows.

Starting Office Programs

You can start any Office program from the Start menu on the taskbar. As soon as the program starts, you can immediately begin to create new files or work with existing ones. You can have more than one Office program open at once. As you open each program, a button appears on the taskbar.

Exhibit 9-1 Start menu with Microsoft Office programs listed

Office programs

Start button

name of registered user appears here

click to start Word

ACTIVITY

Start Office programs.

1 Make sure your computer is on and the Windows desktop appears on your screen.

2 On the taskbar, click the **Start button**, and then click **All Programs**.

> ⚠ **Problem?** If you don't see Microsoft Office, point to **Microsoft Word 2010** on the All Programs list.

3 Click **Microsoft Office**, and then point to **Microsoft Word 2010**. See Exhibit 9-1. Depending on how your computer is set up, you might see different icons and commands on your desktop and menu.

4 Click **Microsoft Word 2010**. Word starts and a new, blank document opens. See Exhibit 9-2. The elements labeled in Exhibit 9-2 can be found in all of the Office programs.

> ⚠ **Problem?** If the window doesn't fill your screen as shown in Exhibits 9-2 and 9-3, click the **Maximize button** in the title bar.

5 On the taskbar, click the **Start button**, click **All Programs**, click **Microsoft Office**, and then click **Microsoft Excel 2010**. Excel starts and a new, blank workbook opens. See Exhibit 9-3.

6 On the taskbar, click the **Start button**, click **All Programs**, click **Microsoft Office**, and then click **Microsoft PowerPoint 2010**. PowerPoint starts and a new, blank presentation opens. You can see the same elements labeled in the Word and Excel windows in Exhibits 9-2 and 9-3 in the Power-Point window.

Although each Office program individually is a strong tool, their potential is even greater when used together.

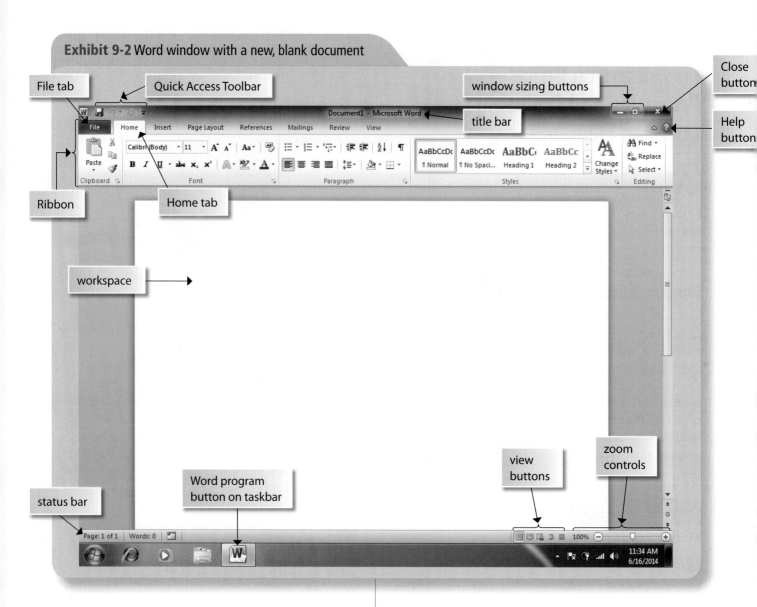

Exhibit 9-2 Word window with a new, blank document

File tab · Quick Access Toolbar · window sizing buttons · Close button · title bar · Help button · Ribbon · Home tab · workspace · view buttons · zoom controls · Word program button on taskbar · status bar

Examining Common Elements

As you can see in Exhibits 9-2 and 9-3, many of the elements in both the Word and Excel program windows are the same. In fact, all of the Office programs have these same elements, which are described in Exhibit 9-4. Because these elements are the same in each program, after you've learned one program, it's easy to learn the others.

Switching Between Open Programs and Files

Three programs are now running at the same time—Word, Excel, and PowerPoint. The taskbar contains buttons for all three programs. When two or more

programs are running or two files within the same program are open, you can use the program buttons on the taskbar to switch from one program or file to another. When you point to a program button, a **thumbnail** (small picture) of each open window in that program is displayed. To make a file active, you click its thumbnail.

 **ACTIVITY**

Switch between open files.

1 On the taskbar, point to the **Microsoft Word program button** [W]. A thumbnail of the open Word document appears. See Exhibit 9-5.

2 Click the **Document1 – Microsoft Word thumbnail**. The active program changes from PowerPoint to Word.

thumbnail A small picture of an object.

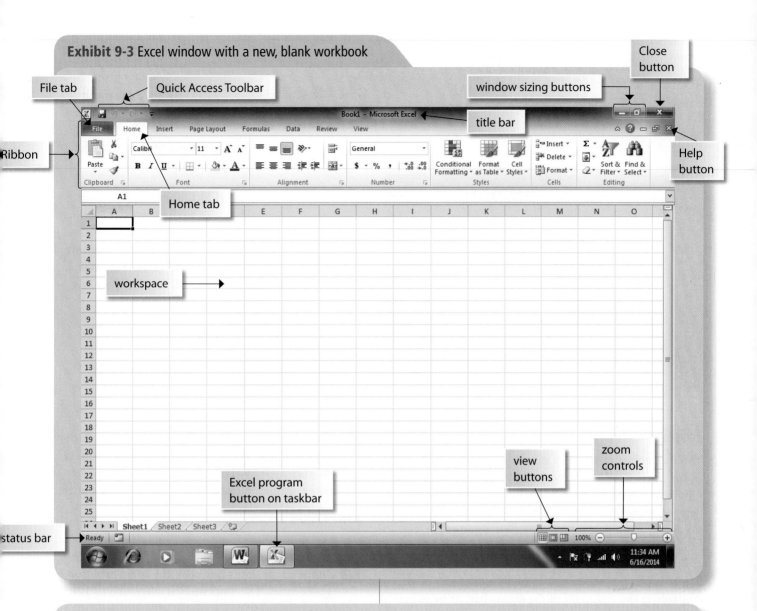

Exhibit 9-3 Excel window with a new, blank workbook

File tab · Quick Access Toolbar · Close button · window sizing buttons · title bar · Ribbon · Home tab · Help button · workspace · status bar · Excel program button on taskbar · view buttons · zoom controls

Exhibit 9-4 Elements common to all Office programs

Element	Description
Ribbon	Provides access to the main set of commands organized by task into tabs and groups
File tab	Provides access to document-level features and program settings
Quick Access Toolbar	Provides one-click access to commonly used commands, such as Save, Undo, and Repeat
Home tab	Contains buttons to access the most commonly used commands in each program
Title bar	Contains the name of the open file, the program name, the sizing buttons, and the Close button
Sizing buttons	Minimize and restore or maximize the program window
Close button	Closes the program window and the open file; if there is only one open file, also exits the program
Help button	Opens the Help window for that program
Workspace	Displays the file you are working on (Word document, Excel workbook, Access database, or PowerPoint slide)
Status bar	Provides information about the program, open file, or current task as well as the view buttons and zoom controls
View buttons	Change how a file is displayed in the workspace
Zoom controls	Magnify or shrink the content displayed in the workspace

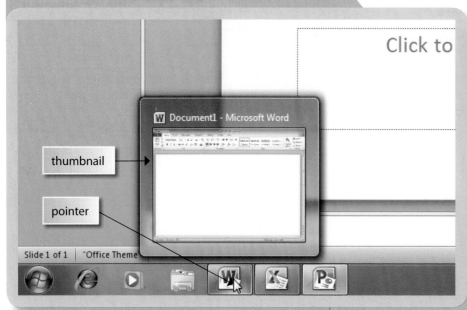

Exhibit 9-5 Thumbnail of the open Word document

thumbnail

pointer

Zooming

You can zoom in to get a closer look at the content of an open document, worksheet, slide, or database report. Likewise, you can zoom out to see more of the content at a smaller size. When you zoom, you can select a specific percentage or size to zoom to, or you can zoom to preset sizes, such as two pages displayed at once.

You change the zoom level by using the zoom controls at the right end of the status bar, or by using buttons in the Zoom group on the View tab on the Ribbon.

ACTIVITY

Zoom a program window.

1 On the Word status bar, drag the **Zoom slider** all the way to the left. The percentage on the Zoom level button is 10%, and the document is reduced to its smallest size. See Exhibit 9-6.

2 Click the **View tab**. In the Zoom group, click the **One Page button**. The zoom level changes so that the entire page appears in the window.

3 On the View tab, in the Zoom group, click the **Zoom button**. The Zoom dialog box opens. See Exhibit 9-7.

4 Click the **Page width option button**, and then click **OK**. The Word document is magnified to its page width.

5 On the taskbar, point to the **Microsoft Excel program button**, and then click the **Microsoft Excel – Book1 thumbnail**. Excel is the active program.

6 On the Excel status bar, click the **Zoom level button** `100%`. The Zoom dialog box opens. See Exhibit 9-8.

7 Click in the **Custom box** after *100*, press the **Backspace key** three times to delete the text in the box, and then type **60**. The Custom option button becomes selected instead of the 100% option button.

8 Click **OK**. The dialog box closes and the zoom level in the Excel window is changed to 60%.

9 On the Excel status bar, click the **Zoom In button** six times. The worksheet is magnified to 120% of its original size.

The zoom percentage ranges from 10 percent to 400 percent in Excel and PowerPoint and to 500 percent in Word.

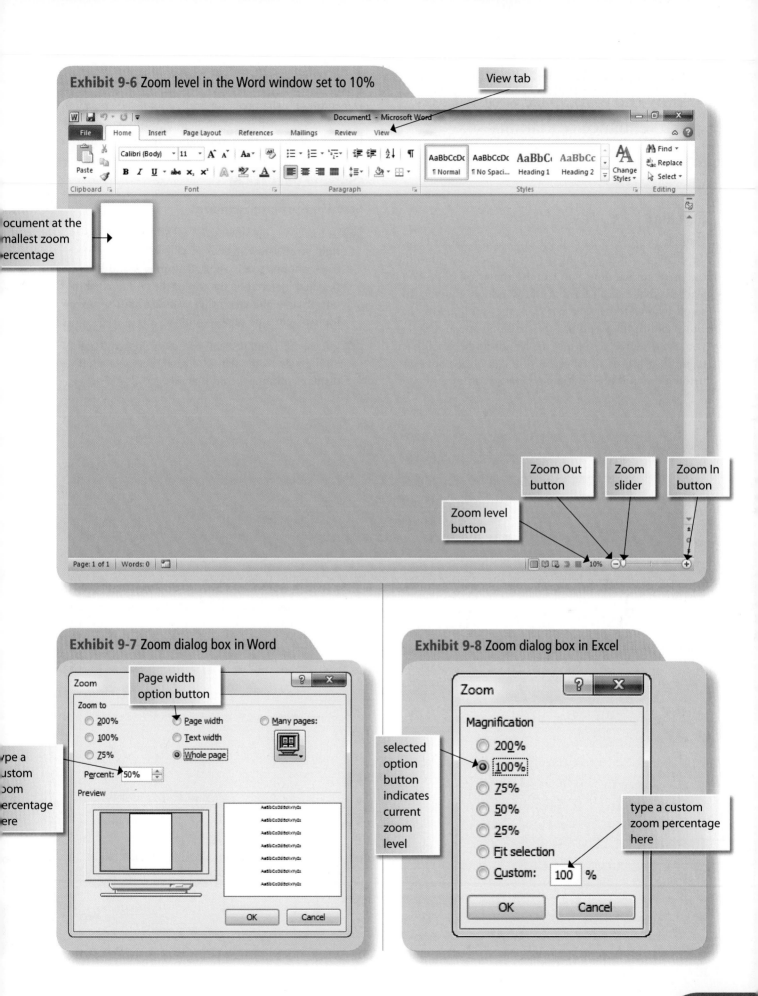

Exhibit 9-6 Zoom level in the Word window set to 10%

View tab

Document1 - Microsoft Word

File | Home | Insert | Page Layout | References | Mailings | Review | View

Document at the smallest zoom percentage

Zoom Out button

Zoom slider

Zoom In button

Zoom level button

Page: 1 of 1 | Words: 0 | 10%

Exhibit 9-7 Zoom dialog box in Word

Page width option button

Zoom

Zoom to
- 200%
- 100%
- 75%

- Page width
- Text width
- Whole page

Many pages:

Percent: 50%

type a custom zoom percentage here

Preview

OK | Cancel

Exhibit 9-8 Zoom dialog box in Excel

Zoom

Magnification
- 200%
- 100%
- 75%
- 50%
- 25%
- Fit selection
- Custom: 100 %

selected option button indicates current zoom level

type a custom zoom percentage here

OK | Cancel

The figures in this book show the workspace zoomed in to enhance readability.

Scrolling

Zooming can shift part of the workspace out of view. To change which area of the workspace is visible in the program window, you can use the scroll bars. You learned about scroll bars in the Windows chapter. To scroll in a window, you can click the scroll arrows at either end of the scroll bar to scroll one line at a time; you can drag the scroll box the length of the scroll bar to scroll a longer distance; or you can click above or below the scroll box to jump a screen at a time.

Scroll bars appear in Office program windows when the workspace is taller or wider than the window. Depending on the program and zoom level, you might see a vertical scroll bar, a horizontal scroll bar, or both. Exhibit 9-9 shows the scroll bars in the Excel window.

ACTIVITY

Scroll in a program window.

1 In Excel, on the horizontal scroll bar, click the **right scroll arrow** ▶ twice. The worksheet shifts two columns to the right. Columns A and B (labeled by letter at the top of the columns) shift out of view and two other columns shift into view on the right side of the window.

2 On the horizontal scroll bar, drag the **scroll box** all the way to the left. The worksheet shifts left to display columns A and B again.

Exhibit 9-9 Scroll bars in Excel

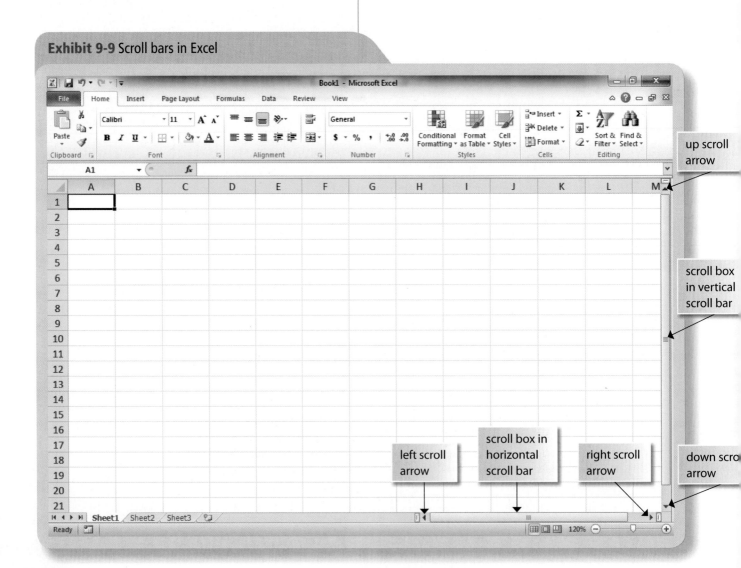

Exhibit 9-10 Ribbon in Word

buttons

tabs

Document1 - Microsoft Word

File | Home | Insert | Page Layout | References | Mailings | Review | View

Calibri (Body) | 11 | A⁺ A⁻ | Aa |
B I U | abc x₂ x² | A | A |

Paste

Clipboard | Font | Paragraph | Styles | Editing

AaBbCcDc ¶ Normal | AaBbCcDc ¶ No Spaci... | AaBbC Heading 1 | AaBbCc Heading 2 | Change Styles

Find | Replace | Select

groups

3 On the vertical scroll bar, click the **down scroll arrow** three times. Rows 1, 2, and 3 (labeled by number at the left of the rows) scroll up out of view and three new rows appear at the bottom of the window.

4 On the vertical scroll bar, drag the **scroll box** up to the top of the scroll bar. Rows 1, 2, and 3 scroll back into view.

LO9.2 Using the Ribbon

The Ribbon contains the buttons that you click to perform tasks. The Ribbon is organized into tabs. Each tab has buttons related to particular activities. For example, in Word, the Insert tab on the Ribbon provides access to all the commands for adding objects such as shapes, pages, tables, illustrations, text, and symbols to a document. Although the tabs differ from program to program, the Home tab in each program contains the commands for the most frequently performed activities, including cutting and pasting, changing fonts, and using editing tools. In addition, the Insert, Review, and View tabs appear on the Ribbon in all the Office programs except Access, although the commands they include might differ from program

to program. Other tabs are program specific, such as the Design tab in PowerPoint and the Datasheet tab in Access.

On each tab, the buttons are organized into groups. The group names appear at the bottom of the Ribbon below the buttons. Exhibit 9-10 shows the Home tab in Word.

The first tab on the Ribbon, the File tab, appears in all of the Office programs. Clicking the File tab doesn't change the commands on the Ribbon. Instead, it opens Backstage view. **Backstage view** provides access to file-level features, such as creating new files, opening existing files, saving files, printing files, and closing files, as well as the most common program options. In Backstage view, the left pane is called the **navigation bar** and contains commands and tabs. Like clicking a button on the Ribbon, clicking a command in the navigation bar in Backstage view performs an action or opens a dialog box in which you can choose options. Clicking a tab changes the information and options in the main part of the window in Backstage view. Exhibit 9-11 shows Backstage view in PowerPoint.

Switching Tabs

To display the commands on a Ribbon tab, you click the tab. The File tab is a little different from the other tabs. Click the File tab once to display Backstage view. Click it again to hide Backstage view and return to the document and the Ribbon tab that was previously active. You can also click another tab on the Ribbon to close Backstage view and display the commands on that tab.

Zooming changes the size of the content in the workspace; scrolling shifts the workspace that is visible in the program window.

Backstage view The view in Office programs that provides access to file-level features.

navigation bar The left pane in Backstage view.

Exhibit 9-11 Backstage view in PowerPoint with the Info tab selected

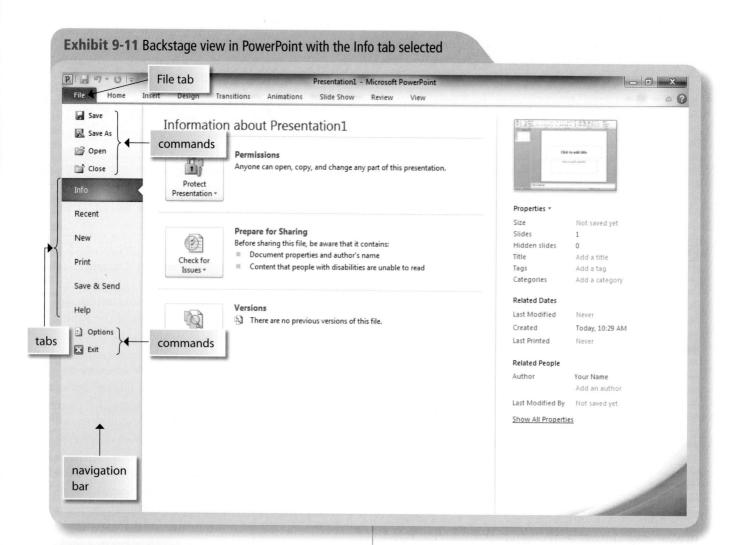

![ACTIVITY icon] **ACTIVITY**

Switch tabs on the Ribbon.

1 On the Ribbon in the Excel window, click the **Insert tab**. The commands on the Insert tab appear on the Ribbon. See Exhibit 9-12.

2 Click the **Formulas tab**. This tab appears only on the Excel Ribbon.

3 Make **PowerPoint** the active program.

4 On the Ribbon, click the **Slide Show tab**. This tab is unique to PowerPoint.

> **Tip:** To hide the commands on the Ribbon and display only the tab names, click the Minimize the Ribbon button ⌃ below the sizing buttons. Click the Expand the Ribbon button ♡ to redisplay the full Ribbon.

5 Click the **Insert tab**. The commands on the Insert tab on the PowerPoint Ribbon are similar, but not exactly the same as the commands on the Insert tab on the Excel Ribbon.

6 Click the **File tab**. Backstage view in PowerPoint appears, replacing the blank presentation in the workspace. In the navigation bar, either the Recent or the Info tab will be selected.

7 In the navigation bar, click the **Info tab**. Backstage view displays the Info tab, which contains information about the current file.

8 Click the **File tab** again. Backstage view closes, and the Insert tab is again the active tab on the Power-Point Ribbon.

9 Make **Word** the active program, and then click the **File tab**. Backstage view in Word appears.

10 On the Ribbon, click the **Home tab**. Backstage view closes, the blank document reappears, and the Home tab is the active tab on the Ribbon.

How Buttons and Groups Appear on the Ribbon

The buttons and groups on the Ribbon change based on your monitor size, your screen resolution, and the size of the program window. With smaller monitors, lower screen resolutions, and resized program windows, buttons can appear as icons without labels and some groups are condensed into a button that you click to display the commands in the group. The instructions and figures in this book were created using a screen resolution of 1024 × 768 and, unless otherwise specified, the program and workspace windows are maximized. If you are using a different screen resolution or window size, the buttons on the Ribbon might show more or fewer button names, and some groups might be reduced to a button. For example, at the lower resolutions, such as 800 × 600, the Editing group on the Word Home tab is collapsed into a button. If you are using a monitor set to a lower resolution, and you can't find a button referenced in the steps, you might need to click the group button first.

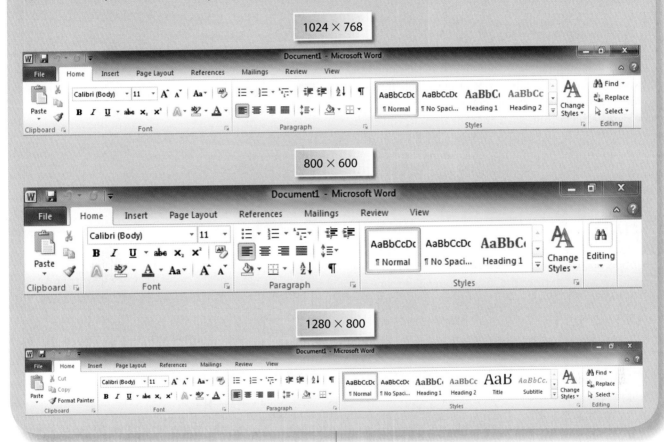

Exhibit 9-12 Insert tab on the Ribbon in Excel

Using Buttons

For the most part, when you click a button, something happens in the file. For example, the Clipboard group on the Home tab includes the Cut, Copy, Paste, and Format Painter buttons, which you can click to move or copy text, objects, and formatting.

Some buttons are **toggle buttons**: one click turns the feature on and the next click turns the feature off. While the feature is on, the button remains colored or highlighted to indicate that it is selected. For example, when you click the Bullets button in the Paragraph group on the Word Home tab to select it, the currently selected paragraphs are formatted as a bulleted list; clicking it again removes the bullets.

Some buttons have two parts: a button that executes the default command, and an arrow that opens a menu of all the commands or options available for that command. To use the default command, you click the icon part of the button. To change the default, you click the arrow part of the button and then click one of the commands or options that appears.

Clicking Two-Part Buttons

In this book, when you need to click the icon part of a two-part button, the instruction will be simply to *click the **button***. When you need to click the arrow part of a two-part button, the instruction will be to *click the button **arrow***. Sometimes, the arrow is to the right of the button.

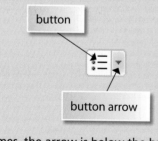

Other times, the arrow is below the button.

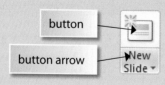

toggle button A button that you click once to turn a feature on and click again to turn it off.

Finally, some buttons have an arrow on them, but they are not two-part buttons. Clicking this type of button always opens a list of commands or options.

ACTIVITY

Use buttons on the Ribbon.

1 In the Word window, type **Landscaping Ideas** and then press the **Enter key**. The text appears in the first line of the document and the insertion point moves to the second line.

⚠ **Problem?** If you make a typing error, press the **Backspace key** to delete the incorrect letters and then retype the text.

2 On the Home tab, in the Font group, click the **Bold button** B. The button changes to orange to indicate that it is selected. See Exhibit 9-13.

Exhibit 9-13 Bold button toggled on in Word

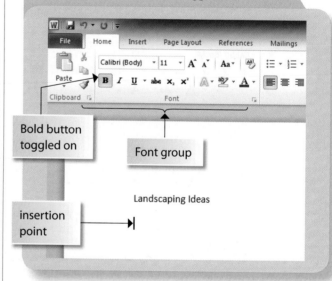

3 Type **Remodeling Ideas**. The text you typed is in bold.

4 Click the **Bold button** B. The button toggles off and changes back to its original color.

➤ **Tip:** Position the pointer on top of a button to see its name and keyboard shortcut (if it has one).

5 Press the **Enter key**, and then type **Organizing Ideas**. The text in the third line is not bold because you toggled the command off before you started typing.

6 On the Home tab, in the Paragraph group, point to the **Bullets button** 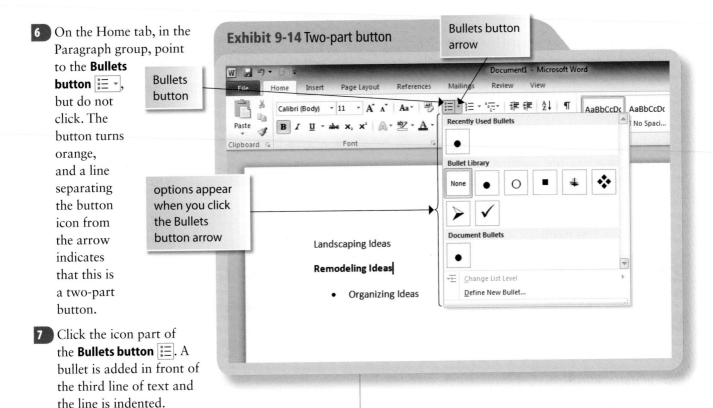, but do not click. The button turns orange, and a line separating the button icon from the arrow indicates that this is a two-part button.

7 Click the icon part of the **Bullets button**. A bullet is added in front of the third line of text and the line is indented.

8 Click in the second line of text, and then click the **arrow** part of the Bullets button. A list of types of bullets appears. See Exhibit 9-14.

Exhibit 9-14 Two-part button

Bullets button arrow

Bullets button

options appear when you click the Bullets button arrow

Recently Used Bullets

Bullet Library

None

Document Bullets

Landscaping Ideas

Remodeling Ideas

- Organizing Ideas

Change List Level
Define New Bullet...

Using Key Tips

You can use keyboard shortcuts to perform commands instead of clicking buttons on the Ribbon. To access the options on the Ribbon using the keyboard, press the Alt key. A label, called a Key Tip, appears over each tab and over each button on the Quick Access Toolbar. To select a tab, press the corresponding key. After you select a tab, new Key Tips appear over each button on that tab. Press the appropriate key or keys to select a button.

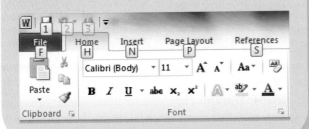

9 In the list, click the **check mark bullet style**. A check mark bullet is added in front of the second line of text and the line is indented.

10 On the Home tab, in the Paragraph group, point to the **Line and Paragraph Spacing button**. Although this button has an arrow next to its icon, there is no line dividing the button into two parts. The arrow indicates that a list of options will open when you click the button.

11 Click the **Line and Paragraph Spacing button**. A menu of options opens.

12 On the menu, click **3.0**. The spacing after the second line of text—the line the insertion point is currently in—changes to three lines.

Using Galleries and Live Preview

A **gallery** is a menu or grid that shows visual representations of the options available for a button. For example, when you clicked the Bullets button arrow in the previous set of steps, the Bullets gallery appeared. This gallery shows an icon of each bullet style you

gallery A menu or grid that shows visual representations of the options available for a button.

can select. Some galleries include a More button ⊽ that you click to expand the gallery to see all the options it contains. When you point to an option in a gallery, **Live Preview** shows the results that would occur in your file if you clicked that option. To continue the bullets example, when you point to a bullet style in the Bullets gallery, a button appears before the paragraph in which the insertion point is located. By moving the pointer from option to option, you can quickly see the text formatted with different bullet styles, making it easier to select the style you want.

ACTIVITY

Use galleries and Live Preview.

1 Double-click **Landscaping**. The entire word is highlighted with blue to indicate that it is selected.

2 On the Home tab, in the Font group, click the **Font Size button arrow** 11 ⊽. A gallery of font sizes (text sizes) opens.

3 In the gallery, point to **26**. Live Preview shows the selected text formatted in the larger size. See Exhibit 9-15.

> **Tip:** You can press the Esc key to close a menu or gallery without making a selection.

4 Click a blank area of the document to close the gallery without selecting anything.

5 Make **Excel** the active program.

6 Type **Budget** and then press the **Enter key**. Click the box containing the word you just typed.

7 On the Ribbon, click the **Home tab** to make it the active tab. In the Font group, click the **Font button arrow** Calibri ⊽ to display the Font gallery.

8 Point to several of the fonts to preview the effect on the text you just typed.

Live Preview Shows the results that would occur if you clicked the option to which you are pointing in a gallery.

dialog box A window in which you enter or choose settings for performing a task.

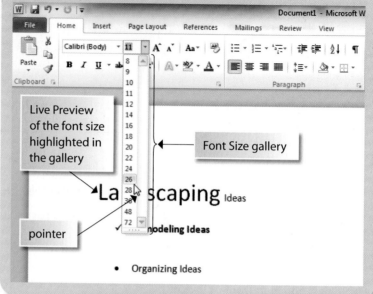

Exhibit 9-15 Live Preview using the Font Size gallery

9 In the gallery, click **Algerian**. The gallery closes and the text you typed is formatted with the Algerian font.

Using Dialog Boxes

Many of the groups on the Ribbon tabs have a small button in their right corners. This is a Dialog Box Launcher ▣; clicking this button opens a dialog box or task pane related to that group of buttons. A **dialog box** is a window that opens on top of the program window in which you enter or choose settings for performing a task. For example, the Page Setup dialog box in Word contains options to change how the document looks. Some dialog boxes organize related information into tabs, and related options and settings are organized into groups, just as they are on the Ribbon. You select settings in a dialog box using option buttons, check boxes, text and spin boxes, and lists to specify how you want to perform a task. Exhibit 9-16 shows the Page tab in the Excel Page Setup dialog box with the various controls labeled and described. The only control that does not appear in the dialog box shown in Exhibit 9-16 is a check box. Check boxes appear in groups. You can click one or more check boxes in a group to select them. A check mark in a check box indicates that it is selected.

Exhibit 9-16 Page tab in the Page Setup dialog box in Excel

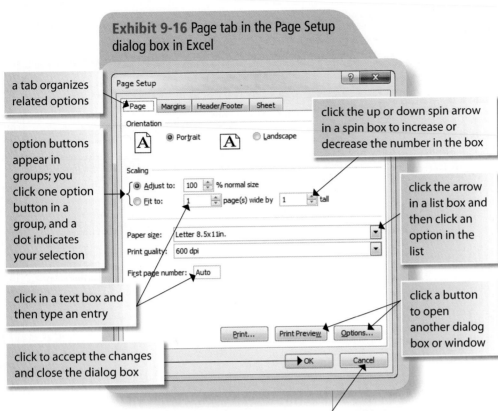

a tab organizes related options

option buttons appear in groups; you click one option button in a group, and a dot indicates your selection

click in a text box and then type an entry

click to accept the changes and close the dialog box

click the up or down spin arrow in a spin box to increase or decrease the number in the box

click the arrow in a list box and then click an option in the list

click a button to open another dialog box or window

click to close the dialog box without making changes

ACTIVITY

Open and use a dialog box.

1 On the Excel Ribbon, click the **Page Layout tab** to make it the active tab.

2 In the Page Setup group, click the **Dialog Box Launcher**. The Page Setup dialog box opens with the Page tab as the active tab in the dialog box.

3 In the Orientation section, click the **Landscape option button**. The blue dot moves from the Portrait option button to the Landscape option button, indicating that the Landscape option is now selected. Landscape means that when you print, the page will be wider than it is long.

4 Click the **Paper size arrow**. A list of paper sizes opens. The size that appeared in the box before you clicked the arrow (Letter 8.5×11in.) is selected. A scroll bar appears on the right side of the list because you need to scroll to see the additional choices in the list.

5 Drag the **scroll box** to the bottom of the scroll bar to see some of the additional choices, and then click a blank area of the dialog box to close the list without selecting anything.

6 Click the **Sheet tab** to make it the active tab in the dialog box.

7 In the Print section of the dialog box, click the **Black and white check box**. A check mark appears in the check box, indicating that it is selected. Unlike option buttons, you can select more than one check box in a section of a dialog box.

8 Click the **Draft quality check box**. A check mark appears in this check box as well.

9 Click the **Margins tab** to make it the active tab in the dialog box.

10 Click the **Top up arrow** three times. The value in the Top box changes from .75 to 1.5.

11 In the Bottom box, click after the **5**. The insertion point appears in the Bottom box after the 5.

12 Press the **Backspace key** four times, and then type **2**.

13 Click **Cancel**. The dialog box closes without changing the page setup in the Excel workbook.

Using Task Panes

A **task pane** is a narrow window that appears to the left or right of the document window to help you navigate through a complex task or feature. For example, you can use the Clipboard task pane to paste some or all of

task pane A narrow window that appears to the left or right of the document window to help you accomplish a set of tasks.

Exhibit 9-17 Research task pane in Excel

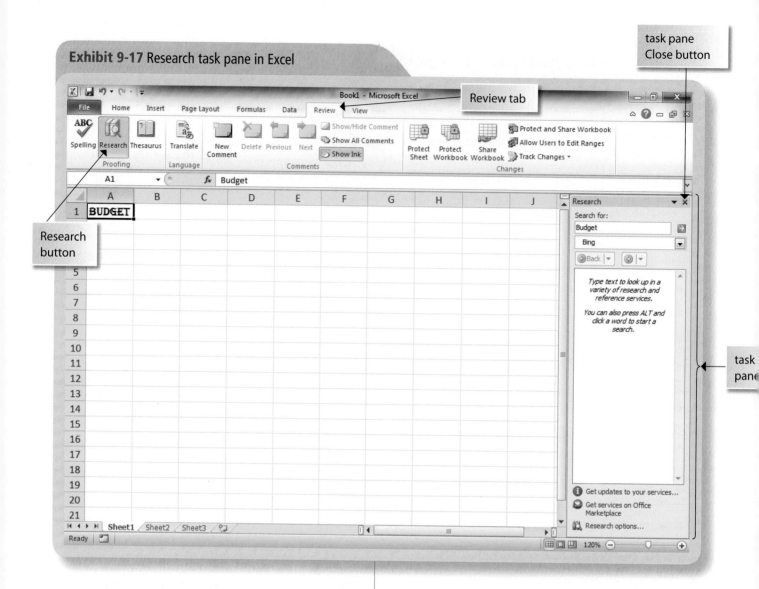

the items that were cut or copied from any Office program during the current work session.

The commands and options available in a task pane vary depending on the purpose of the task pane. You will learn how to use the specific task panes as you learn about those elements in the various Office programs.

Most task panes open when you click the button associated with the options in the task pane. For example, clicking the Research button in the Proofing group on the Review tab opens the Research task pane to the right of the window. When you are finished working with a task pane, you can click its Close button to close it.

contextual tab A tab on the Ribbon that contains commands related to a specific type of object or activity.

ACTIVITY

Open and close a task pane.

1. On the Excel Ribbon, click the **Review tab**.

2. In the Proofing group, click the **Research button**. The Research task pane opens to the right of the document window. See Exhibit 9-17. This task pane contains options for conducting research on the Internet.

3. In the Research task pane title bar, click the **Close button** .

Displaying Contextual Tabs

A **contextual tab** is a tab on the Ribbon that contains commands related to a specific type of object or activity.

Exhibit 9-18 Contextual Drawing Tools Format tab in PowerPoint

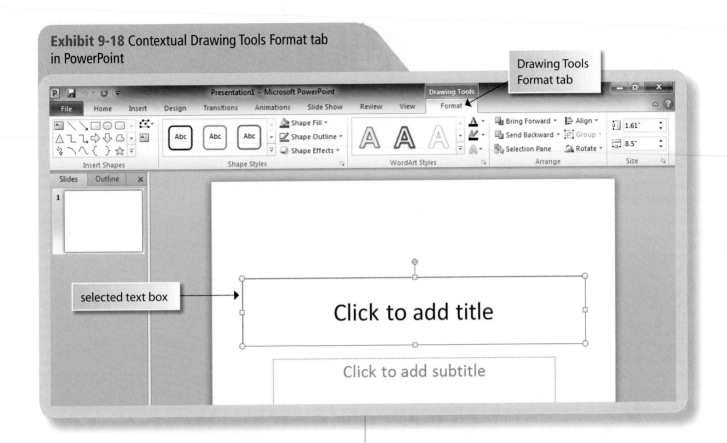

An **object** is anything in a document that can be manipulated as a whole, such as a table, a picture, a shape, a chart, or an equation. Any object that you can select in an Office document has a related contextual tab. The contextual tabs appear when the object is selected. Contextual tabs usually appear to the right of the standard Ribbon tabs just below a title label. For example, when you select a table in a Word document, two Table Tools contextual tabs appear to the right of the View tab. Although contextual tabs appear only when you select an object, they function in the same way as standard tabs on the Ribbon. Contextual tabs disappear when you click elsewhere on the screen, deselecting the object.

 **ACTIVITY**

Display and close a contextual tab.

1 Make **PowerPoint** the active program. The PowerPoint workspace contains two text boxes, which are boxes that contain text. A text box is an example of an object.

2 In the center of the window, position the pointer directly on top of the dotted line around *Click to add title* so that the pointer changes to ⁺ₖ.

3 With the pointer as ⁺ₖ, click the dotted line. A solid line appears on top of the dotted line because the text box object is now selected, and the Drawing Tools Format tab appears on the Ribbon.

4 Click the **Drawing Tools Format tab** to make it the active tab on the Ribbon. See Exhibit 9-18.

5 In the middle of the PowerPoint window, click anywhere on the white space outside of the selected text box object. The object is no longer selected, and the contextual tab disappears from the Ribbon. The Home tab is now the active tab because that was the active tab before you selected the contextual tab.

> **Tip:** Sometimes a contextual tab will become the active tab on the Ribbon automatically when you select an object.

object Anything in a document that can be manipulated as a whole.

Live Preview does not work with the Mini toolbar.

Using the Mini Toolbar

The **Mini toolbar**, which appears next to the pointer whenever you select text using the mouse or when you right-click, contains buttons for the most commonly used formatting commands, such as font, font size, styles, color, alignment, and indents. The exact buttons on the Mini toolbar differ in each Office program, and all of the commands on the Mini toolbar appear on the Ribbon for that program. When you use the mouse to select text by dragging over it, a transparent version of the Mini toolbar appears. To select text by dragging, you click before the first character you want to select, and then without releasing the mouse button, drag across the rest of the characters you want to select. When all of the characters that you want to select are highlighted, release the mouse button. After you cause the Mini toolbar to appear, you can move the pointer over the Mini toolbar to make it come into full view so you can click a button on it.

 **ACTIVITY**

Use the Mini toolbar.

1 Make **Word** the active program.

2 In the first line of text, double-click **Ideas**. The entire word is highlighted with blue to indicate that it is selected, and the Mini toolbar faintly appears

> ⚠ **Problem?** If the Mini toolbar disappears, you probably moved the pointer to another area of the worksheet. Repeat Step 2.

above and to the right of the selected text. See Exhibit 9-19.

3 Move the pointer toward the Mini toolbar until you can see it clearly.

> **Mini toolbar** A toolbar with buttons for commonly used formatting commands that appears next to the pointer when text is selected using the mouse or when you right-click.

Exhibit 9-19 Transparent Mini toolbar in Word

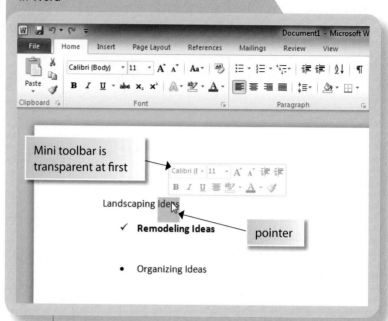

4 On the Mini toolbar, click the **Bold button** B. The Bold button on the Mini toolbar and the Bold button in the Font group on the Home tab are orange, and the selected text is formatted with bold.

5 Click a blank area of the document to deselect the text.

Using the Mini Toolbar

Although the Mini toolbar lets you quickly format text, it can disappear unexpectedly if you move the pointer away from the toolbar, press a key, or click in the workspace. Therefore, the steps in this book will instruct you to use the Ribbon. You may use the correct button on the Mini toolbar if you prefer.

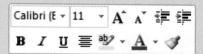

LO9.3 **Working with Files**

The most common tasks you perform in any Office program are to create, open, save, and close files. All of these tasks can be done from Backstage view, and the processes for these tasks are basically the same in all Office programs. To begin working in a program, you need to create a new file or open an existing file. When you start Word, Excel, or PowerPoint, the program opens along with a blank file—ready for you to begin working on a new document, workbook, or presentation. When you start Access, the New tab in Backstage view opens, displaying options for creating a new database or opening an existing one.

Saving a File

As you create and modify an Office file, your work is stored only in the computer's temporary memory, not on a hard drive. If you were to exit the program without saving, turn off your computer, or experience a power failure, your work would be lost. You can save files to the hard drive located inside your computer, an external hard drive, a network storage drive, or a portable storage drive such as a USB flash drive.

To save a file, you can click either the Save button on the Quick Access Toolbar or the Save command in Backstage view. If it is the first time you are saving a file, the Save As dialog box will open so that you can specify save options. You can also click the Save As command in Backstage view to open the Save As dialog box, in which you can name the file you are saving and specify a location to save it.

The first time you save a file, you need to name it. This **file name** includes a title you specify and a file extension assigned by Office to indicate the file type. You should specify a descriptive title that accurately reflects the content of the document, workbook, presentation, or database, such as *Budget Analysis* or *3rd Quarter Sales Memo*. Your descriptive title can include uppercase and lowercase letters, numbers, hyphens, and spaces in any combination, but not the special characters ? " / \ < > * | and :. Each file name ends with a **file extension**, which is a period followed by several characters that Office adds to your descriptive title to identify the program in which that file was created. The default file extensions for Office 2010 are .docx for Word, .xlsx for Excel, .accdb for Access, and .pptx for PowerPoint. File names (the descriptive title and extension) can include a maximum of 255 characters.

You also need to decide where to save the file—on which drive and in what folder. Store each file in a logical location that you will remember whenever you want to use the file again. The default storage location for Office files is the Documents folder; you can create additional storage folders within that folder or navigate to a new location.

Save a file for the first time.

1 On the Word Ribbon, click the **File tab**. Backstage view opens.

2 In the navigation bar, click **Save As**. Backstage view closes, and the Save As dialog box opens. See Exhibit 9-20. The text in the File name box is the suggested file name.

> ◤ **Tip:** The Save As dialog box looks similar to a Windows Explorer folder window, and you navigate through it in the same manner.

Exhibit 9-20 Save As dialog box in Word

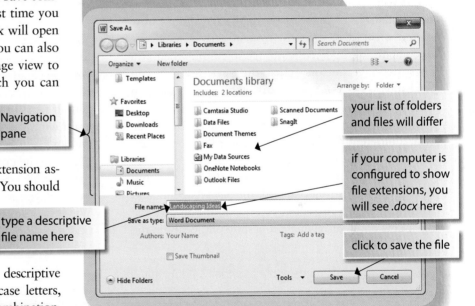

Navigation pane

type a descriptive file name here

your list of folders and files will differ

if your computer is configured to show file extensions, you will see .docx here

click to save the file

3 Use the techniques you learned in the Windows and File Management chapters to navigate to the drive and folder where you plan to store the files you create as you work through these steps.

> **file name** A title that describes the content of the file and a file extension assigned by Office.
>
> **file extension** A period followed by several characters that Office adds to the descriptive title part of a file name to identify the program in which that file was created.

The default Windows setup is to hide file extensions. The figures in these chapters do not show file extensions.

4 Click in the **File name box**. The default file name is selected.

5 Type **Bulleted List Example** in the File name box.

6 Click **Save**. The Save As dialog box closes, and the name of your file appears in the Word program window title bar. See Exhibit 9-21.

The saved file includes everything in the document at the time you last saved it. Any new edits or additions you make to the document exist only in the computer's memory and are not saved in the file on the drive.

If you make changes to the file, you need to save those changes to the version of the file that is now stored on a disk. Because you already named the document and selected a storage location, when you click the Save button or use the Save command in Backstage view, the Save As dialog box does not open again.

If you want to save a copy of the modified file with a different file name so that you still have the unchanged original version, or if you want to save the file to a different location, you can click the File tab, and then in the navigation bar, click the Save As command to open the Save As dialog box again. If you give the file a new name or navigate to a different location, the unchanged, original version of the file will still be stored in the location you specified.

ACTIVITY

Modify a file and save your changes.

1 In the third line of the document, click immediately after *Ideas*. The insertion point blinks at the location where you clicked.

2 Press the **Backspace key** five times to delete *Ideas*, and then type **Suggestions**.

3 On the Quick Access Toolbar, click the **Save button** 💾. The changes you made to the document are saved in the file stored on the drive.

> **Tip:** You can also press the Ctrl+S keys to save your changes.

Closing a File

Although you can keep multiple files open at one time, you should close any file you are no longer working on to conserve system resources as well as to ensure that you don't inadvertently make changes to the file. You can close a file by clicking the Close command in Backstage view. If that's the only file open in that program, the program window remains open and no file appears in the window. You can also close a file by clicking the Close button in the upper-right corner of the title bar. If that's the only file open in that program, the program exits. In Excel, you also have the option of clicking the Close Window button just above the Ribbon and below the title bar to close the file without exiting the program.

Exhibit 9-21 File name in the program window title bar

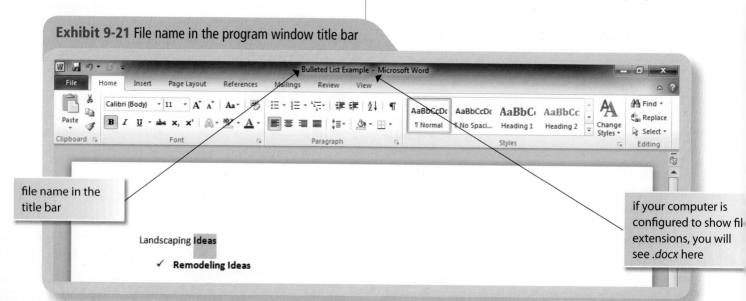

file name in the title bar

if your computer is configured to show file extensions, you will see *.docx* here

Exhibit 9-22 Protected View bar in Word

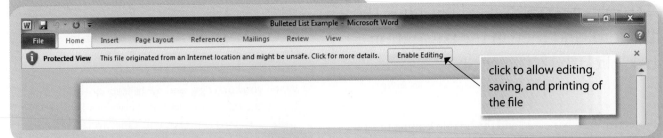

click to allow editing, saving, and printing of the file

ACTIVITY

Close a file.

1 On the Word Ribbon, click the **File tab** to open Backstage view.

2 In the navigation bar, click **Close**. Backstage view closes and the document closes, but the Word window stays open.

3 Make **PowerPoint** the active program.

4 In the title bar, click the **Close button** [X]. The file closes and the program exits. Word is the active program again.

Opening a File

When you want to open a blank document, workbook, presentation, or database, you create a new file. When you want to work on a previously created file, you must first open it. Opening a file transfers a copy of the file from the storage location (either a hard drive or a portable drive) to the computer's memory and displays it on your screen. The file is then in your computer's memory and on the drive.

ACTIVITY

Open a file.

1 On the Word Ribbon, click the **File tab** to open Backstage view.

Save frequently as you work so that the file is updated to reflect the latest content if the program or your computer shuts down unexpectedly.

Save Files Before Closing

As a standard practice, you should save files before closing them. If you try to close a file without saving your changes, a dialog box opens asking whether you want to save the file. Click Save to save the changes to the file before closing the file and program. Click Don't Save to close the file and program without saving changes. Click Cancel to return to the program window without saving changes or closing the file and program.

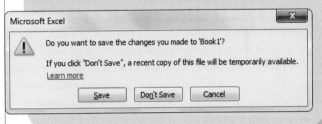

2 In the navigation bar, click **Open**. The Open dialog box, which looks very similar to the Save As dialog box, opens. The current folder should be the same folder in which you saved the file Bulleted List Example.

3 In the list of files, click **Bulleted List Example**, and then click **Open**. The file opens in the Word program window.

Any file you open that was downloaded from the Internet, accessed from a shared network, or received as an email attachment might open in Protected View. In **Protected View**, you can see the file contents, but you cannot edit, save, or print them until you enable editing. To do so, click the Enable Editing button on the Protected View bar, as shown in Exhibit 9-22. If the

> **Protected View** A view of a file in an Office program in which you can see the file contents, but you cannot edit, save, or print them until you enable editing.

To open a recently used file, click the File tab, and then in the navigation bar, click the Recent tab.

Protected View bar is red and the Enable Editing button does not appear on the bar, that means that a bigger potential security problem was detected and something in the file might harm your computer. If you decide that you want to edit the file anyway, you can click the File tab, and then click Edit Anyway.

LO9.4 Using the Clipboard

The **Clipboard** is a temporary storage area in Windows on which text or other objects are stored when you copy or cut them. To **copy** text or an object, you select it, and then use the Copy command to place a copy of it on the Clipboard so that you can paste it somewhere else. If you want to move text from one location and paste it somewhere else, you first need to **cut** it—that is, remove it from the original location and place it on the Clipboard using the Cut command. Once something is on the Clipboard, you can then **paste** it anywhere you want in the current document or in another Office document—that is, you insert a copy of the text or object on the Clipboard somewhere in the document. The text or object on the Clipboard stays on the Clipboard until you cut or copy something else or until you shut down your computer.

In all of the Office programs, you can click the Cut button in the Clipboard group on the Home tab to cut selected text or objects, click the Copy button in the same group to copy selected text or objects, and click the Paste button to paste the text or objects on the Clipboard. (Note that the Paste button is a two-part button,

Clipboard A temporary storage area in Windows on which text or other objects are stored when you copy or cut them.

copy To duplicate selected text or an object and place it on the Clipboard.

cut To remove selected text or an object from the original location and place it on the Clipboard.

paste To insert a copy of the text or object on the Clipboard in a document.

Keyboard Shortcuts for Cut, Copy, and Paste

When you cut, copy, and paste frequently, the keyboard shortcuts for the Cut, Copy, and Paste commands can save you time. To cut selected text or objects, press the Ctrl+X keys. To copy the selected text or objects, press the Ctrl+C keys. To paste the contents of the Clipboard, press the Ctrl+V keys.

deepspacedave and prism68/Shutterstock.com

and to paste the items on the Clipboard, you need to click the top part of the button.)

 **ACTIVITY**

Cut, copy, and paste with the Clipboard.

1 In the first line of text in the Word window, double-click **Ideas** to select it.

2 On the Home tab, in the Clipboard group, click the **Copy button**. The selected text remains in the document and is placed on the Clipboard.

3 In the third line of text, click in front of *Suggestions*. The text will be pasted at the insertion point.

4 On the Home tab, in the Clipboard group, click the **Paste button**. The copied text, *Ideas*, appears between *Organizing* and *Suggestions*. Another button appears below the pasted text; ignore this for now.

5 In the third line of text, double-click **Suggestions**.

6 In the Clipboard group, click the **Cut button**. The selected text is removed from the document and replaces the previously copied item on the Clipboard.

When you press the Delete or Backspace key, the deleted text or object is not placed on the Clipboard.

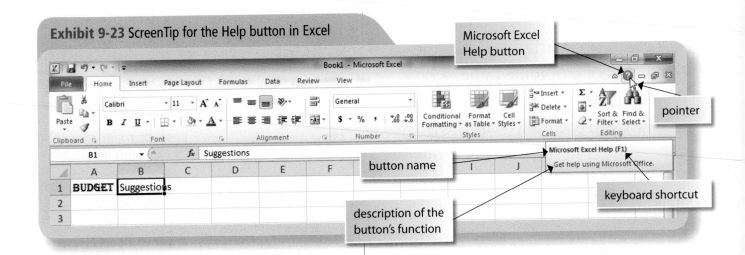

Exhibit 9-23 ScreenTip for the Help button in Excel

Microsoft Excel Help button

pointer

button name

Microsoft Excel Help (F1)
Get help using Microsoft Office.

keyboard shortcut

description of the button's function

7 Make **Excel** the active program, and then click the box to the right of the box containing *BUDGET*.

8 Click the **Home tab** on the Ribbon. In the Clipboard group, click the **Paste button**. The text you copied, *Suggestions*, appears in the current box.

LO9.5 Getting Help

Image copyright Yuri Arcurs, 2009. Used under license om Shutterstock.com.

If you don't know how to perform a task or want more information about a feature, you can turn to Office itself for information on how to use it. This information is referred to simply as **Help**. You can get Help in ScreenTips and from the Help window.

Viewing ScreenTips

ScreenTips are a fast and simple method you can use to get information about objects you see on the screen. A **ScreenTip** is a box with descriptive text about a button, an object, or another element on the screen. Just point to a button or an object to display its ScreenTip. In addition to the button's name, a ScreenTip might include the button's keyboard shortcut if it has one, a description of the command's function, and, in some cases, a link to more information so that you can press the F1 key while the ScreenTip is displayed to open the Help window with the relevant topic displayed.

ACTIVITY

View ScreenTips.

1 In the upper-right corner, just above the Ribbon, point to the **Microsoft Excel Help button**. The ScreenTip shows the button's name, keyboard shortcut, and a brief description of its function. See Exhibit 9-23.

2 Point to other buttons on the Ribbon and read their ScreenTips.

Using the Help Window

For more detailed information, you can use the **Help window** to access all the Help topics, templates, and training installed on your computer with Office and available on Office.com. **Office.com** is a Web site maintained by Microsoft that provides access to the latest information and additional Help resources. For example, you can access current Help topics and training for Office. To connect to Office.com, you need to be able to access the Internet from your computer. Otherwise, you see only topics that are stored on your computer.

Each program has its own Help window from which you can find information about all of the Office

ScreenTip A box that appears with descriptive text about an element on the screen when you point to it.

Help window A window in which you can access Help topics, templates, and training.

Office.com A Web site maintained by Microsoft that provides access to the latest information and additional Help resources.

You can use the Type words to search for box without displaying the Table of Contents pane. The results of your search will be displayed in the Help window.

commands and features as well as step-by-step instructions for using them.

There are two ways to find Help topics—the search function and the topic list. The search function enables you to search the Help system for a task or a topic you need help with. You can click a link to open a Help topic with explanations and step-by-step instructions for a specific procedure. The Table of Contents pane displays the Help system content organized by subjects and topics, similar to a book's table of contents. You click main subject links to display related topic links, and you click topic links to display that topic in the Help window.

ACTIVITY

Search Help.

1 Click the **Microsoft Excel Help button** [?]. The Excel Help window opens. Notice the toolbar at the top of the window.

2 If the Table of Contents pane is not open on the left side of the Help window, click the **Show Table of Contents button** on the toolbar to display the pane. See Exhibit 9-24.

3 In the Table of Contents pane, click the **Getting started with Excel link**. Subtopics under this main topic appear.

⚠ **Problem?** If the same list of topics appears in the right pane in the Help window as in the Table of Contents pane, you are not connected to the Internet. In this case, the Getting Started topic is the first topic in the Table of Contents pane.

Exhibit 9-24 Excel Help window with Table of Contents pane open

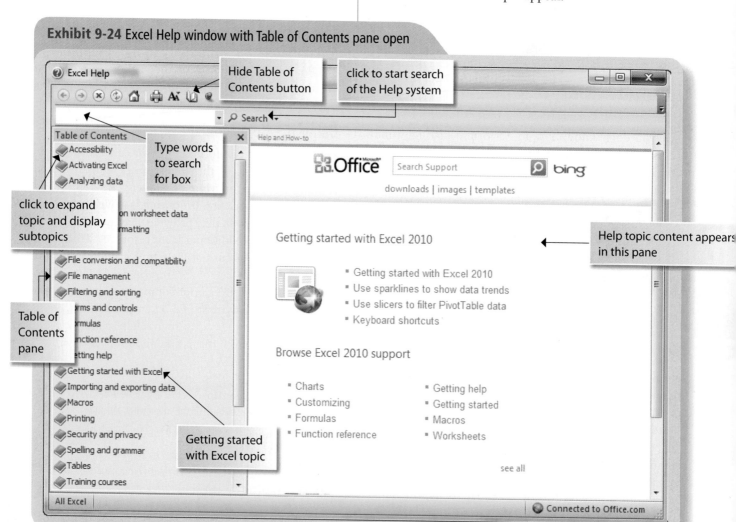

4 In the subtopic list, click the **Getting started with Excel 2010 link**. The right pane in the Help window displays the topic content.

5 Click in the **Type words to search for box**, and then type **enter data**.

6 Click the **Search button arrow**. The Search menu shows the online and local content available.

7 If your computer is connected to the Internet, click **All Excel** in the Content from Office.com list. If your computer is not connected to the Internet, click **Excel Help** in the Content from this computer list.

8 Click the **Search button**. The Help window displays a list of topics related to the keywords *enter data* in the right pane. You can use the vertical scroll bar in the Help window to view all of the topics.

9 Click **Quick start: Edit and enter data in a worksheet**. The topic content is displayed in the Help window.

> ⚠ **Problem?** If you are not connected to the Internet, click **Quick start: Enter data in a worksheet**.

10 On the Help window title bar, click the **Close button** ▬ X ▬ to close the Help window.

LO9.6 Exiting Office Programs

When you finish working with a program, you should exit it. As with many other aspects of Office, you can exit programs with a button or a command. As you have seen, when you click the Close button in the program window title bar and only one file is open in that program, the file closes and the program exits. You can also use the Exit command in Backstage view to exit a program and close an open file in one step. If you haven't saved the final version of the open file, a dialog box opens, asking whether you want to save your changes. Clicking the Save button in this dialog box saves the open file, closes the file, and then exits the program.

VikaSuh/Shutterstock.com

ACTIVITY

Exit Office programs.

1 On the Excel title bar, click the **Close button** ▬ X ▬. Because you haven't saved this file, a

Exiting programs after you are done using them keeps your Windows desktop uncluttered, frees up system resources, and prevents data from being lost.

dialog box opens asking whether you want to save the changes you made to the workbook. If you click Save, the Save As dialog box would open, and then Excel would exit after you finish saving the workbook.

2 Click **Don't Save**. The workbook closes without saving a copy, and the Excel program exits. The Word window is visible again.

3 On the Ribbon, click the **File tab** to open Backstage view.

4 In the navigation bar, click **Exit**. You are again asked if you want to save the changes you made.

5 Click **Save**. The changes you made since the last time you saved the document are saved, the document closes, and the Word program exits.

Quiz Yourself

1. Which Office program would you choose to develop a budget?

2. How do you start an Office program?

3. How is the Ribbon organized?

4. What is Backstage view?

5. What is Live Preview?

6. What is a contextual tab?

7. When does the Mini toolbar appear?

8. When you make changes to a file, and then attempt to close the file or exit the program without saving, what happens?

9. How do you close a file without exiting the program?

10. What is Protected View?

11. What is the Clipboard?

12. How long does text stay on the Clipboard?

13. What are ScreenTips?

14. How do you open the Help window?

Practice It

Practice It 9-1

1. Start Word, start Excel, and then start PowerPoint.

2. Make PowerPoint the active program, and then use the Zoom slider to zoom to 100%.

3. Use the Zoom Out button to zoom to 60%.

4. Make Word the active program, and then scroll down to the bottom of the page.

5. Make Excel the active program, and then make the Data tab the active tab.

6. Make PowerPoint the active program. Click in the box labeled *Click to add title*, type your first and last name. Double-click your first name. On the Home tab, in the Font group, click the Bold button.

7. In the Font group, open the Font Color gallery. (*Hint:* Use the ScreenTips to identify the Font Color button.)

8. Use Live Preview to preview several colors, and then change the color of the selected text to Red (under Standard Colors).

9. In the Font group, click the Dialog Box Launcher to open the Font dialog box. Use the Font style arrow to change the font style to Italic. Use the Size box to change the size to 32. In the Effects section, select the All Caps check box. Click Apply.

10. Click directly on the border of the box around *Click to add subtitle*. Make the Drawing Tools Format tab the active tab on the Ribbon. Make the Drawing Tools Format tab disappear from the Ribbon.

11. Make Word the active program. Type your name and address on three separate lines. Click in the line containing your name, and then use the Center button on the Mini toolbar to center the line of text containing your name.

12. Save the Word file to the drive and folder where you are storing your files using the file name **My Contact Info**.

13. Make PowerPoint the active program. Save the PowerPoint file using the file name **My Name**.

14. Close the My Name file without exiting Power-Point. Open the **My Name** file.

15. Double-click your last name, cut it, click in front of your first name, and then paste the text.

16. Make Word the active program. Double-click your street name, and then copy it to the Clipboard.

17. Make Excel the active program, and then paste the copied text.

18. Make PowerPoint the active program, and then open the PowerPoint Help window. Find information about WordArt. Close the Help window.

19. Exit PowerPoint, saving changes when asked.

20. Exit Excel and Word without saving changes.

Practice It 9-2

1. Start Excel. Open the data file named **Budget** located in the Chapter 9\Practice It folder.

2. Use a button in the Font group to make the text in the top box bold.

3. Use a button in the Font group to add an Ice Blue Fill Color to the top box.

4. Save the changed file as **Budget Totals** to the drive and folder where you are storing your files.

5. In the chart, click a blank area above the legend and to the right of the bars, and then copy it to the Clipboard.

6. Start Word. Open the data file named **Stockholder** located in the Chapter 9\Practice It folder.

7. Scroll down so you can see the large space between the body of the letter and the signature block, and then click in the middle of this space.

8. Paste the chart you copied. (*Hint:* It will be pasted with orange bars.)

9. Save the file as **Stockholder Letter** to the drive and folder where you are storing your files.

10. Make the Page Layout tab the active tab. In the Page Setup group, click the Margins button, and then click Wide to change the margins.

11. In the Page Setup group, click the Dialog Box Launcher to open the Page Setup dialog box. Make the Layout tab the active tab, and then use the Vertical alignment box in the Page section to change the vertical alignment to centered.

12. Close the Stockholder Letter file without exiting Word, saving changes when asked. Exit both open programs.

On Your Own

On Your Own 9-1

1. Open the PowerPoint data file named **Music** located in the Chapter 9\On Your Own folder.

2. Click anywhere on the bulleted list, and then click directly on top of the dotted line border.

3. Use the Font button in the Font group on the Home tab to change the font to Broadway.

4. Use the Text Shadow button in the Font group on the Home tab to add a shadow effect to the text.

5. Save the file as **Music Categories** to the drive and folder where you are storing your files.

6. Cut the selected text box from the file.

7. Open a new Word document, and paste the text you cut into the document.

8. Use the Bullets gallery to change the bullet symbols to check marks.

9. Use the appropriate button on the Page Layout tab to add a page border. In the dialog box that opens, click the 3-D button in the Setting list.

10. Save the file as **Music List** to the drive and folder where you are storing your files.

11. Exit Word.

12. Exit PowerPoint without saving changes.

CAPSTONE

Windows 7 and Office 2010: Organize Your Files

1. Develop an organization strategy for storing the files you create and work with. Consider various folder and subfolder structures and evaluate which one best fits your needs. Plan your approach for naming the files and folders so that you can easily remember their purposes.

2. Use Word to record your plan for organizing the files on your computer.
   a. List the types of files stored on your computer.
   b. Determine where to store the files: on your hard drive or on removable media.
   c. Sketch the folders and subfolders you will use to manage your files. If you choose a hard drive as your storage medium, plan to store your work files and folders in a subfolder of the Documents folder.
   d. Save the file with an appropriate file name, and then close it.

3. Implement your organization strategy:
   a. Create or rename the main and subfolders you want to use for your files.
   b. Move and copy files to the appropriate folders; rename and delete files as necessary.

4. Create a backup copy of your work files by creating a compressed file of the folders and files, and then copying the compressed file to a removable medium, such as a USB flash drive.

5. Use Windows Help and Support to learn about the Sync Center and how to use it.

6. Use Word to record information about what the Sync Center is and when you would use it. Save the file with an appropriate file name in the appropriate folder according to your plan.

7. Open the Sync Center, and then copy and paste an image of the Sync Center window to your document.
   a. Press and hold the Alt key as you press the Print Screen key to copy an image of the active window on your screen—in this case, the Sync Center window—to the Clipboard.
   b. Make the document about Sync Center the active window.
   c. With the insertion point on a blank line below the text you typed, paste the contents of the Clipboard.
   d. Save the file, and then close it.

Saving a File to Windows Live SkyDrive

Often the purpose of creating a file is to share it with other people—sending it attached to an email message for someone else to read or use, collaborating with others on the same document, or posting it as a blog for others to review. **Windows Live SkyDrive** is an online workspace provided by Microsoft. All you need to access your workspace on SkyDrive is a Windows Live ID.

When you are working in Word, Excel, and PowerPoint, you can click Save to Web on the Save & Send tab in Backstage view to save the current file directly to a folder on your SkyDrive. (You cannot save to SkyDrive from Backstage view in Access.) Exhibit 9-25 shows the Save to Web options on the Save & Send tab in Backstage view of Word before the user is signed in. Exhibit 9-26 shows the Save & Send tab in Backstage view in Excel after signing in to SkyDrive. You can also access your SkyDrive by opening a browser window, and then going to www.windowslive.com. After you sign in to your Windows Live account, click the Office link at the top of the window.

You can choose to share access to the folders on your SkyDrive. If you do, the people to whom you grant permission can open the folders you share, and then access, view, and download the files stored in those folders. To do this, you need to work in a browser. Exhibit 9-27 shows a SkyDrive account in a browser window with both a private and a shared folder.

Note: SkyDrive and Office Web Apps are dynamic Web pages and might change over time, including the way they are organized and how commands are performed. The steps and figures shown here were accurate at the time this book was published.

Exhibit 9-25 Save to Web options in the Save & Send tab in Word

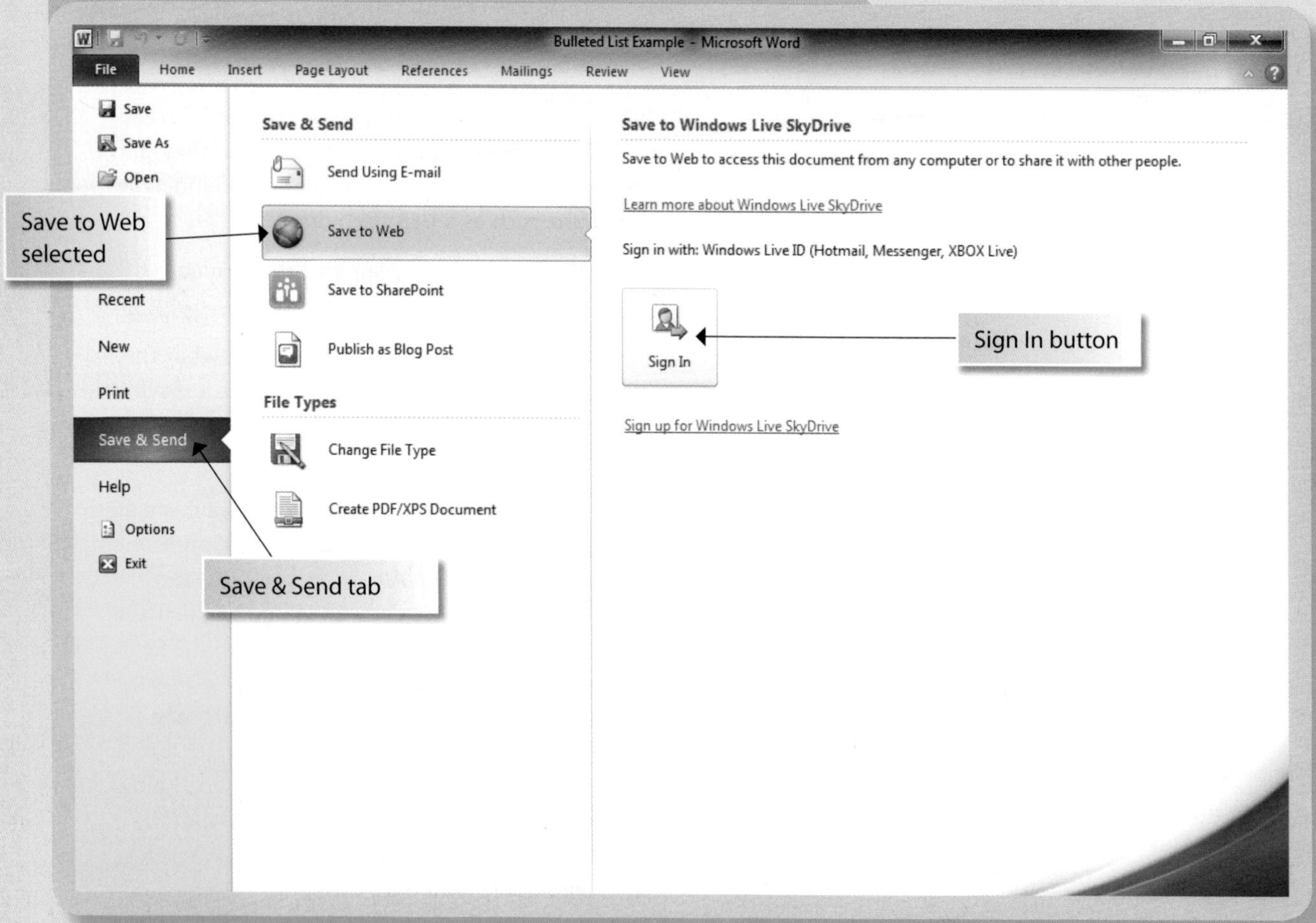

Exhibit 9-26 Save & Send tab in Excel after signing in to SkyDrive

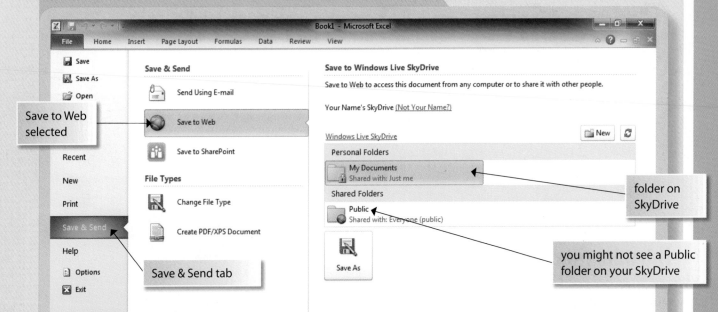

Save to Web selected

Save & Send tab

folder on SkyDrive

you might not see a Public folder on your SkyDrive

Exhibit 9-27 SkyDrive account in browser window

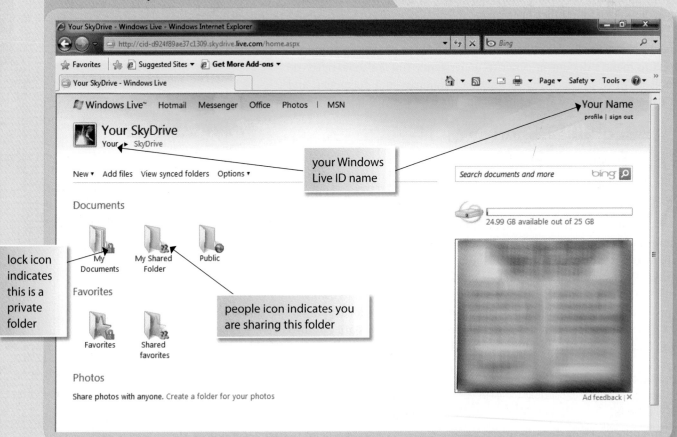

your Windows Live ID name

lock icon indicates this is a private folder

people icon indicates you are sharing this folder

Creating a Document

Introduction

Microsoft Word 2010 (or simply **Word**) is a word-processing program used to enter, edit, and change the appearance of text. Using Word, you can create all types of documents and make them attractive and easy to read. In addition to creating documents that include text, you can create and insert tables and charts in documents, and insert photos and drawings created in other programs.

In this chapter, you'll learn how to enter and edit text in documents. You will also learn how to change the way text and paragraphs look to make a document easier to understand. You'll also learn to use tools in Word to check the spelling and grammar in a document, and learn how to preview and print documents.

Learning Objectives

After studying the material in this chapter, you will be able to:

LO10.1 Enter text

LO10.2 Undo and redo actions

LO10.3 Create documents based on existing documents

LO10.4 Select text

LO10.5 Edit text

LO10.6 Format text

LO10.7 Format paragraphs

LO10.8 Copy formats

LO10.9 Find and replace text

LO10.10 Check spelling and grammar

LO10.11 Preview and print documents

LO10.1 Entering Text

When you work in Word, you can customize the workspace to suit your work style. One thing you can do is show or hide nonprinting characters in your documents. **Nonprinting characters** are characters that do not print and that control the way the document looks. For example, the ¶ character marks the end of a paragraph, and the • character marks the space between words. It is helpful to display nonprinting characters so you can see whether you have typed an extra space, ended a paragraph, and so on.

The first time you start Word, nonprinting characters are not displayed. To show them, you click the Show/Hide ¶ button in the Paragraph group on the Home tab. If you exit Word and nonprinting characters are displayed, they will appear again the next time you start Word. To hide nonprinting characters, click the Show/Hide ¶ button to toggle it off.

Another helpful tool in Word is the ruler. To display a horizontal ruler along the top of the workspace and a vertical ruler

Microsoft Word 2010 (Word)
Application software used to create and format documents.

nonprinting character A character that does not print and that controls the format of a document.

People use Microsoft Word to create all types of documents for both professional and personal use, including letters, résumés, newsletters, brochures, flyers, faxes, and more.

Monkey Business Images/Shutterstock.com

along the left side of the workspace, click the View Ruler button at the top of the vertical scroll bar or select the Ruler check box in the Show group on the View tab.

Finally, you can adjust the zoom level to make it easier to read text or see an entire page at once. As with any Office program, you can use the Zoom slider on the right end of the status bar. But Word also includes several preset zoom settings that you can click in the Zoom group on the View tab, including One Page, to display an entire page in the workspace, and Page Width, which widens the document to the width of the document window.

Figures in this book show the document window with nonprinting characters displayed, rulers visible, and the zoom level set to Page Width (unless specified otherwise).

Save Your Files

Remember to save your files to the drive and folder where you are storing the files you create as you complete the steps in this book. Also, be sure to save frequently as you go.

Start Word and set up the document window.

1 Start **Word**. Word starts and displays a blank document.

2 If the Word program window is not maximized, click the **Maximize button** 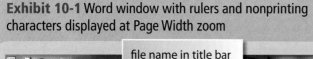.

3 If the rulers are not displayed along the top and left sides of the window, at the top of the vertical scroll bar, click the **View Ruler button**.

Tip: To create a new, blank document when Word is already running, click the File tab, in the navigation bar click New, and then, with Blank document selected on the New tab, click the Create button in the pane on the right.

4 On the Ribbon, click the **View tab**. In the Zoom group, click the **Page Width** button. The width of the page changes to match the width of the document window.

5 Click the **Home tab**. In the Paragraph group, click the **Show/Hide ¶ button** ¶ if it is not already selected. When it is selected, it toggles on and is orange (¶).

6 On the Quick Access Toolbar, click the **Save button** 📄. Because this is the first time this document has been saved, the Save As dialog box opens with the temporary file name selected in the File name box.

7 Type **Letter** to replace the temporary file name in the File name box.

8 Navigate to the drive and folder where you are saving the files you create as you complete the steps in this book.

9 Click **Save**. Compare your screen to Exhibit 10-1.

Exhibit 10-1 Word window with rulers and nonprinting characters displayed at Page Width zoom

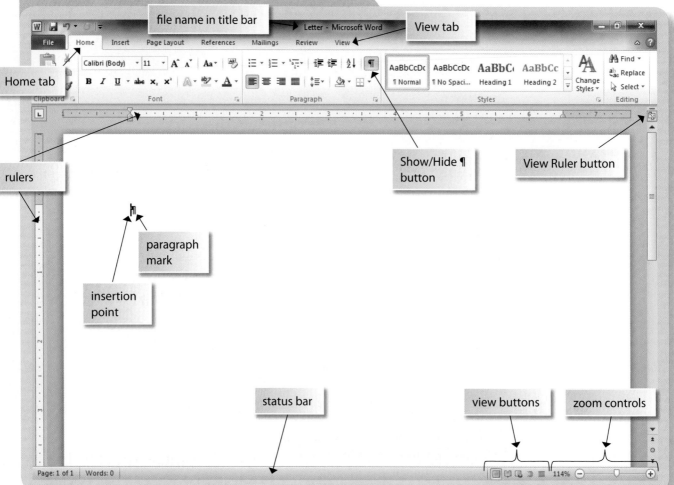

Entering Text

To enter text in a Word document, simply start typing. The characters you type appear at the insertion point. As you type, the text wraps to new lines as needed to accommodate the text. If you make errors as you type, you can press the Backspace key, which deletes the characters and spaces to the left of the insertion point one at a time. You can also press the Delete key, which deletes characters to the right of the insertion point one at a time.

When you press the Enter key, a new paragraph is created. A paragraph in Word can be several lines, one line, or even one word. For example, the heading for this section, *Entering Text*, would be a paragraph in a Word document.

ON THE JOB

Block Style Business Letters

One of the most common types of documents is a block style business letter. In the block style, each line of text is left-aligned—that is, it starts at the left margin. In other words, the inside address, the date, and the closing are all left-aligned, and the first line of paragraphs is not indented. To show when a new paragraph starts, a blank line is added between each paragraph. The block style is probably the easiest style to use when creating any Word document, and has become very common in many businesses. The accompanying figure shows the parts of a block style letter.

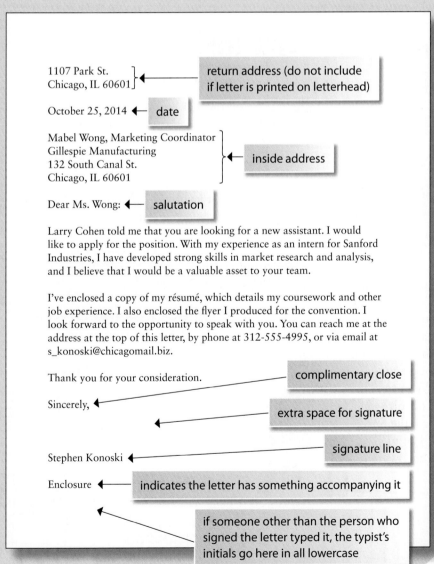

ACTIVITY

Enter text.

1. Move the **pointer** into the workspace. The pointer changes to I.

2. Type **1107 Parker Ave.** The text you typed appears on the screen, and the paragraph mark moves right as you type.

3. Press the **Backspace key** four times. The four characters to the left of the insertion point, *Ave.*, are deleted.

4. Type **St.** (including the period).

5. Press the **Left Arrow key** six times. The insertion point moves six characters to the left and is positioned between the *k* and the *e* in *Parker*.

6. Press the **Delete key** twice. The two characters to the right of the insertion point are deleted.

Some style guides recommend including additional space between the date and the inside address.

Inserting the Current Date

You can quickly insert the current date into a document in a variety of formats. Position the insertion point in the location where you want to insert the current date in the document. Click the Insert tab, and then in the Text group, click the Date & Time button to open the Date and Time dialog box. A variety of date formats are listed in the Available formats box. Click the format you want to use. If you want the current date to appear every time you open the document, select the Update automatically check box. If you want the date to remain unchanged, deselect the Update automatically check box. Click OK to close the dialog box and insert the current date in the format you specified.

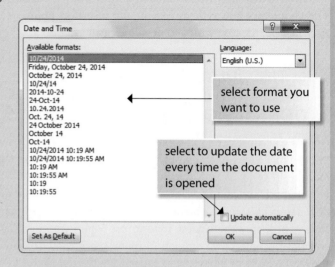

select format you want to use

select to update the date every time the document is opened

---

7 Click after **St.** The insertion point appears at the end of the line.

8 Press the **Enter key**. The insertion point moves to a new line, creating a new paragraph.

9 Type **Chicago, IL 60601** and then press the **Enter key**. A third paragraph is created.

Inserting a Date with AutoComplete

When you insert dates, you can take advantage of **AutoComplete**, a feature that automatically inserts dates and other regularly used items. To insert the date with AutoComplete, type the first four characters of all months except May, June, and July, and a ScreenTip appears telling you that you can press the Enter key to insert the month name into the document. If you want to type something other than the month name suggested in the ScreenTip, or if you don't want to use the AutoComplete feature, simply continue typing and the ScreenTip will disappear. If you type the current month—and it is not May, June, or July—then another ScreenTip appears after you press the Space-bar, instructing you to press the Enter key to insert the current date in the form *MMMM dd, yyyy* (for example, October 24, 2014).

AutoComplete A feature that automatically inserts dates and other regularly used items.

ACTIVITY

Insert the date with AutoComplete.

1 Type **Octo** (the first four letters of October). A ScreenTip appears above the letters, as shown in Exhibit 10-2, suggesting *October* as the complete word, and instructing you to press the Enter key to complete the word.

2 Press the **Enter key**. The rest of the word *October* is inserted in the document.

Exhibit 10-2 AutoComplete suggestion for a month name

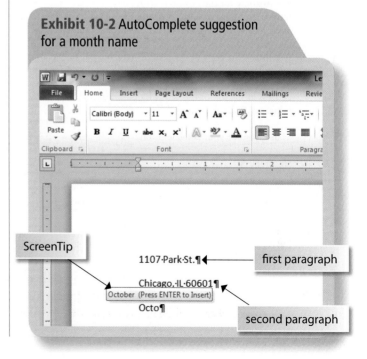

ScreenTip

first paragraph

second paragraph

3 Press the **Spacebar**. If the current month is October, another ScreenTip appears displaying the current date.

4 Type **25, 2014** and then press the **Enter key**.

Correcting Errors as You Type

The **AutoCorrect** feature automatically corrects certain misspelled words and typing errors. For example, if you type *teh* instead of *the*, as soon as you press the Spacebar or the Enter key, AutoCorrect changes it to *the*. AutoCorrect also fixes capitalization errors, including changing the first character in the first word of a sentence to an uppercase letter.

Additionally, printed publications usually include **typographic characters**, which are special characters not included on the standard keyboard and that appear in professionally prepared documents. The AutoCorrect feature automatically converts some standard characters into typographic characters as you type. For example, AutoCorrect changes (c) to the standard copyright symbol © as soon as you type the closing parenthesis. Exhibit 10-3 lists some of the other character combinations that AutoCorrect automatically converts to typographic characters.

Exhibit 10-3 Common typographic characters inserted with AutoCorrect

To insert this symbol or character	Type	AutoCorrect converts to
em dash	word--word	word—word
smiley	:) or :-)	☺
copyright symbol	(c)	©
trademark symbol	(tm)	TM
registered trademark symbol	(r)	®
ordinal numbers	1st, 2nd, 3rd, etc.	1st, 2nd, 3rd, etc.
fractions	1/2, 1/4	½, ¼
arrows	--> or <--	→ or ←

ACTIVITY

Use AutoCorrect.

1 Press the **Enter key** to insert a blank paragraph, and then type **DEar**. Make sure you type this word with the two uppercase letters as shown here.

2 Press the **Spacebar**. The incorrect capitalization is automatically corrected.

3 Type **Ms. Wong:** and then press the **Enter key**.

4 Type **from** and then press the **Spacebar**. The capitalization of the first word in the sentence is corrected.

5 Type **your Web site, i** and then press the **Spacebar**. The capitalization of the word *I* is corrected. In the next step, watch as AutoCorrect corrects the misspelled word *you* when you press the Spacebar.

6 Type **understand that yuo** and then press the **Spacebar**. The misspelled word automatically corrects to *you*. In the next step, watch as AutoCorrect corrects the misspelled word *assistant* when you type the period.

7 Type **are looking for a new assisstant.**

8 Press the **Spacebar**, and then type **i would like to apply for the position.**

9 Press the **Spacebar**, and then type **You can reach me at s_konoski@chicagomail.biz.** and then press the **Enter key**. AutoCorrect changes the email address you typed to blue and underlined, and changes it to a hyperlink. See Exhibit 10-4.

10 Right-click the **hyperlink**. On the shortcut menu, click **Remove Hyperlink**. The text is changed to ordinary black text and is no longer a hyperlink.

11 Click in the blank paragraph at the end of the document, and then type **I gained experience working at Sanford Industries.** (Do not type the period.) In the next step, watch as AutoCorrect changes characters to a symbol.

12 Type **(r)**. As soon as you type the closing parenthesis, the characters *(r)* changed to the registered trademark symbol ®, and the symbol is changed to a superscript.

13 Type **.** (a period). See Exhibit 10-5.

AutoCorrect A feature that automatically corrects certain misspelled words and typing errors.

typographic character A special character not included on the standard keyboard that appears in professionally prepared documents.

Exhibit 10-4 AutoCorrected text in document

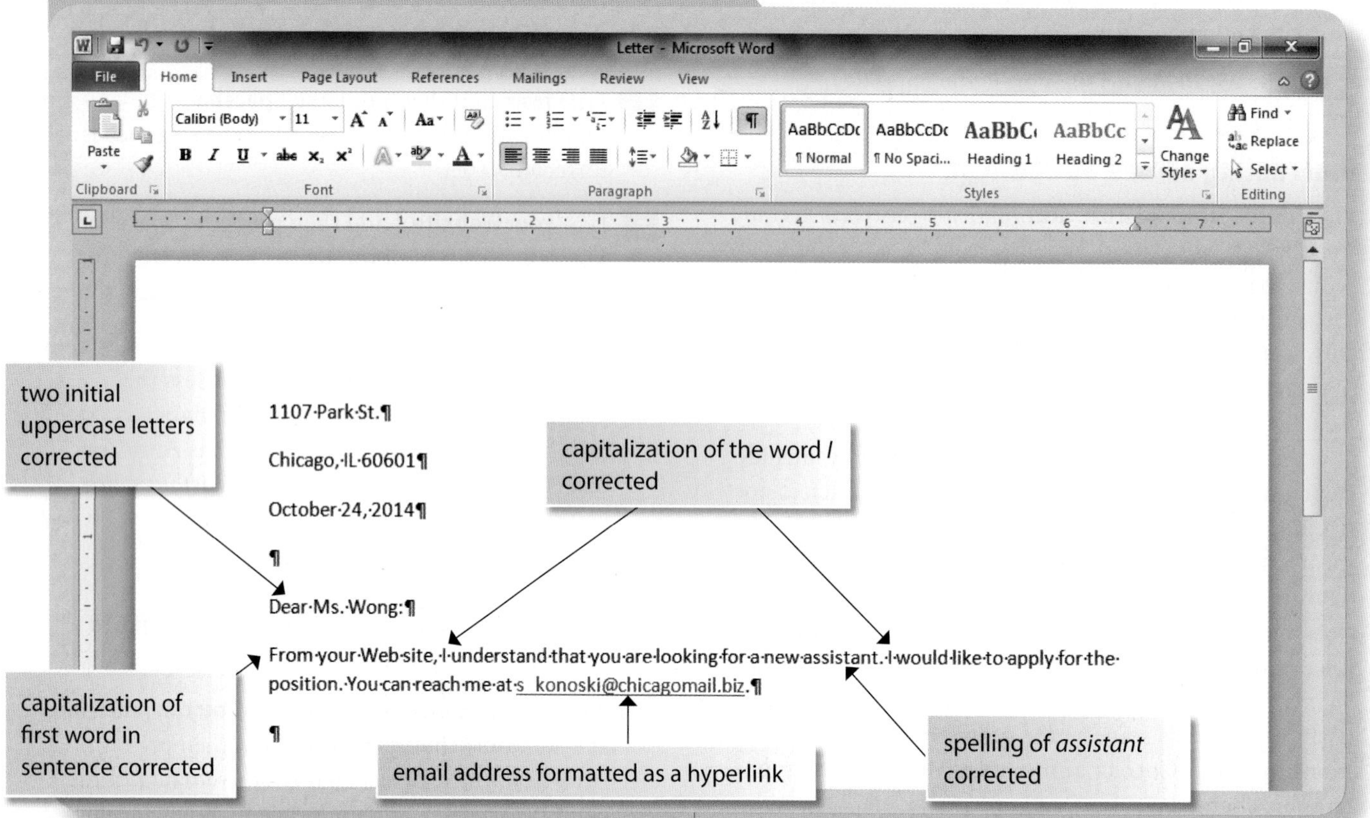

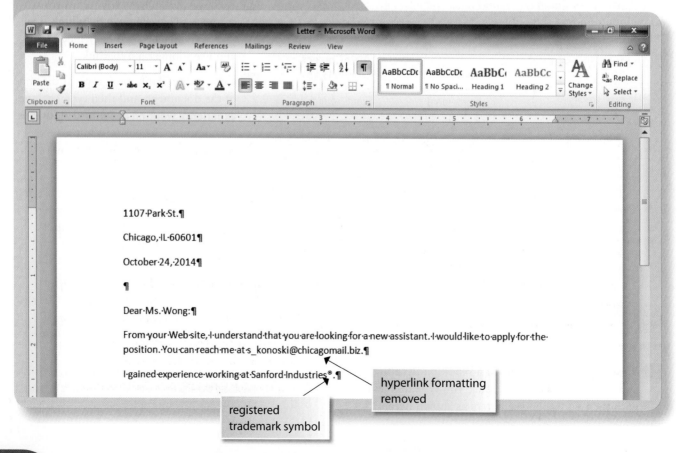

Letter - Microsoft Word
two initial uppercase letters corrected
capitalization of first word in sentence corrected
capitalization of the word *I* corrected
email address formatted as a hyperlink
spelling of *assistant* corrected
1107·Park·St.¶
Chicago,·IL·60601¶
October·24,·2014¶
¶
Dear·Ms.·Wong:¶
From·your·Web·site,·I·understand·that·you·are·looking·for·a·new·assistant.·I·would·like·to·apply·for·the·position.·You·can·reach·me·at·s_konoski@chicagomail.biz.¶
¶

Exhibit 10-5 Text entered in document

Letter - Microsoft Word
1107·Park·St.¶
Chicago,·IL·60601¶
October·24,·2014¶
¶
Dear·Ms.·Wong:¶
From·your·Web·site,·I·understand·that·you·are·looking·for·a·new·assistant.·I·would·like·to·apply·for·the·position.·You·can·reach·me·at·s_konoski@chicagomail.biz.¶
I·gained·experience·working·at·Sanford·Industries®.¶
hyperlink formatting removed
registered trademark symbol

Customizing AutoCorrect

When AutoCorrect changes a word, you can point to the corrected word to make the AutoCorrect symbol ▭ appear. When you point to the symbol, it changes to the AutoCorrect Options button ⅗▾, which you can then click to undo the AutoCorrection or instruct AutoCorrect to stop making that particular type of correction. For example, if Auto-Correct fixed the spelling of a word, the menu choices would be to change the text back to its original spelling or to stop automatically correcting that specific word. If you click Control AutoCorrect Options, the AutoCorrect dialog box opens with the AutoCorrect tab selected. You can deselect AutoCorrect options, review the list of misspelled words that will be automatically corrected, or add words that you frequently misspell to the list.

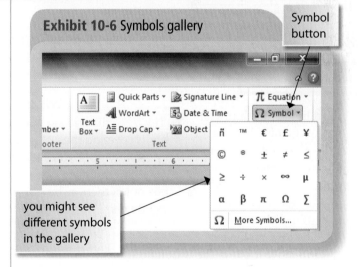

14 On the Quick Access Toolbar, click the **Save button** 🖫. The changes you made to the document are saved.

Inserting Symbols

Sometimes you will want to insert a typographic character not automatically entered with AutoCorrect. To do this, you can use the Symbol button in the Symbols group on the Insert tab. If the symbol you want to use appears in the Symbol gallery, simply click it to insert it. If the symbol doesn't appear there, click More Symbols to open the Symbol dialog box, scroll to find the symbol you want to use, click the symbol, click Insert, and then close the dialog box.

ACTIVITY

Insert symbols.

1 In the body of the letter, in the first paragraph, click after the period at the end of the second sentence (after *position.*), and then press the **Spacebar**.

2 Type **I've enclosed a copy of my r**. (Do not type the period.)

3 On the Ribbon, click the **Insert tab**. In the Symbols group, click the **Symbol button**. The Symbols gallery opens. See Exhibit 10-6.

Exhibit 10-6 Symbols gallery

Symbol button

you might see different symbols in the gallery

4 Below the gallery, click **More Symbols**. The Symbol dialog box opens.

5 Scroll through the list of symbols to see the types of symbols you can insert.

6 Click the **Font arrow**, scroll to the bottom of the list, and then click **Wingdings**. The symbols change to display the symbols in the Wingdings font.

7 Click the **Special Characters tab**. A list of special characters appears, including the paragraph symbol.

8 Click the **Symbols tab**, click the **Font arrow**, scroll to the top of the Font list, and then click **(normal text)**.

9 Click the **Subset arrow**, and then click **Latin-1 Supplement**. The list scrolls to display the first row in the Latin-1 Supplement subset.

10 Click the **down scroll arrow** ▼ three times to scroll the list three rows. Lowercase symbols appear in the bottom row. See Exhibit 10-7.

Exhibit 10-7 Symbol dialog box

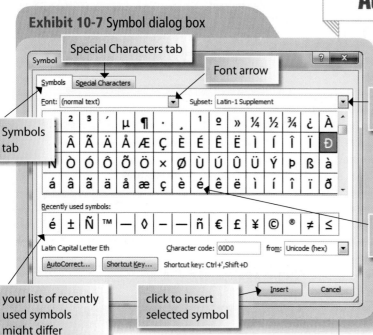

11 In the fourth row of symbols, click the **é symbol**, and then click **Insert**. The symbol is inserted in the document. (Drag the dialog box by its title bar to move it out of the way, if necessary.)

> **Tip:** If the dialog box is covering the inserted symbol, you can drag the dialog box out of the way by its title bar.

12 In the dialog box, click **Close**.

13 Type **sum**.

14 On the Insert tab, in the Symbols group, click the **Symbol button**. The é symbol appears in the gallery now.

15 In the gallery, click the **é symbol**. The gallery closes and the symbol is inserted in the document.

undo To reverse the last action completed in the document.

redo To restore the original change that was just undone.

16 Type a **period**.

17 Save the document.

LO10.2 Undoing and Redoing Actions

You can **undo** (or reverse) the last thing you did in a document. To do this, click the Undo button on the Quick Access Toolbar. To **redo**, or restore your original change, use the Redo button, which reverses the action of the Undo button (or redoes the undo). To undo more than your last action, you can continue to click the Undo button, or you can click the Undo button arrow on the Quick Access Toolbar. This opens a list of your recent actions in the order you completed them, with the most recent action at the top of the list. You can click any action in the list to undo it and all the actions above it in the list—in other words, every action you completed after the action you clicked.

The Redo button does not always appear. Sometimes, the Repeat button appears in its place. If the Repeat button appears and is not dimmed, you can click it to repeat the most recent action.

ACTIVITY
Undo and redo actions.

1 On the Quick Access Toolbar, point to the **Undo button** ↶. The ScreenTip *Undo Typing (Ctrl+Z)* appears. If you click the button, you will undo the most recent typing action. The button to the right of the Undo button is the Repeat button ↷. It is dimmed because you can't repeat the most recent action.

> ⚠ **Problem?** If the *Undo Typing (Ctrl+Z)* ScreenTip does not appear, select and then retype the last sentence in the Letter document that you created in this chapter. Then repeat Step 1.

2 Click the **Undo button** ↶. The period you typed after *résumé* is removed, and the Repeat button changes to the Redo button ↻.

To quickly undo the most recent action, press the Ctrl+Z keys; to quickly redo the most recently undone action, press the Ctrl+Y keys.

3 Point to the **Redo button** . The ScreenTip indicates that you can redo the typing that you just undid.

4 Point to the **Undo button** . The ScreenTip *Undo Symbol (Ctrl+Z)* appears. Inserting a symbol was the action performed immediately prior to typing the period.

5 Click the **Undo button** . The symbol that you inserted is removed from the document.

6 On the Quick Access Toolbar, point to the **Redo button** . The ScreenTip—Symbol—identifies the action you can redo.

7 Click the **Redo button** . The action you just undid—inserting the é symbol—is redone and the é symbol reappears.

8 On the Quick Access Toolbar, click the **Undo button arrow** . The list of actions you have completed appears. See Exhibit 10-8.

Exhibit 10-8 Undo button menu

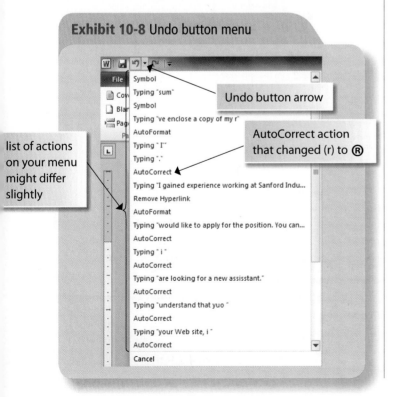

list of actions on your menu might differ slightly

Undo button arrow

AutoCorrect action that changed (r) to ®

9 In the list, click **AutoCorrect** immediately above *Typing "I gained experience working at Sanford Indu . . . "*. The list closes and the action you clicked—the AutoCorrect action that changed (r) to ®—as well as all the actions you performed after that action are undone. This means the sentence you typed about enclosing your résumé is deleted, and the period after the registration mark is removed.

10 Click at the end of the last sentence in the body of the letter, press the **Enter key**, and then type your name.

11 On the Quick Access Toolbar, click the **Save button** . The changes you made to the document are saved.

12 On the Ribbon, click the **File tab**. In the navigation pane, click **Close**. The document closes.

LO10.3 Creating Documents Based on Existing Documents

When you create a new document, you can start with a new blank document as you did when you started typing the letter, or you can start with an existing document. For example, if you saved and closed a document, you can re-open that document and continue working on it. If you simply open a document, make changes, and then save the document, the original document is modified. If you want the original document to remain unchanged, you can create a new document based on the original document.

Using the Save As Command

One way to create a new document based on an existing document is to use the Save As command. When you open a document and then save it with a new name, you create a copy of the original document. Any changes you make to the copy will not affect the original document.

 **ACTIVITY**

Use Save As to create a new document based on an existing document.

1 On the Ribbon, click the **File tab**. In the navigation bar, click **Open**. The Open dialog box appears.

You can change the location of the document you are saving.

2 Navigate to the drive and folder containing the **Chapter 10\Chapter folder** included with your data files.

3 Click **Resume**, and then click **Open**. The file Resume opens in the document window. The file name appears in the title bar.

4 On the Ribbon, click the **File tab**. In the navigation bar, click **Save As**. The Save As dialog box opens.

5 In the File name box, type **Resume Final**. If necessary, navigate to the folder in which you are saving your files.

6 Click **Save**. The file is saved with the new name.

Using the New from Existing Command

Another way to create a copy of a document is to use the New from existing command. Unlike using the Save As command, where you open the original document and then create a copy by saving it with a new name, the New from existing command opens a copy of the document as a new document. The name in the title bar of the copy is the temporary file name Word assigns to new documents—Document—followed by a number. This method is a little safer than using the Save As command because the original document remains closed and unchanged.

ACTIVITY

Create a new document based on an existing document.

1 On the Ribbon, click the **File tab**. In the navigation bar, click **New**. The New tab appears in Backstage view. See Exhibit 10-9.

> ▶ **Tip:** To open a recently used document, click the File tab, in the navigation bar click Recent, and then click a document in the list.

Exhibit 10-9 New tab in Backstage view

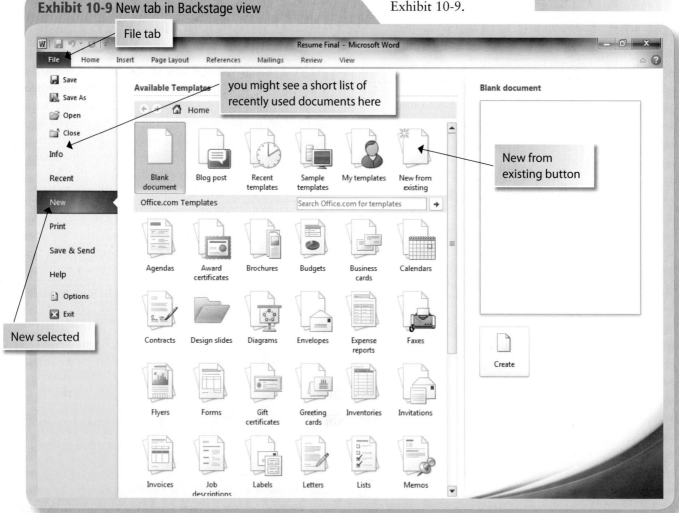

2 In the Available Templates section, click the **New from existing button**. The New from Existing Document dialog box opens. It is very similar to the Open dialog box. Notice that the command button next to Cancel is Open.

3 In the Chapter 10\Chapter folder, click the data file **Letter2**. The Open command button next to Cancel changes to Create New.

4 Click **Create New**. The dialog box closes and a copy of the Letter2 file is created. The temporary file name Document1 appears in the title bar of the new document.

⚠ **Problem?** The red, blue, and green wavy lines under some of the words indicate intentional errors in the document. Ignore them for now.

5 Save the document as **Cover Letter**.

Using Templates

A **template** is a file that contains instructions for changing the appearance of text and graphics, and often sample content, to guide you as you develop your own content. Word comes with templates that you can access by clicking the Sample templates button on the New tab in Backstage view. You can also use one of the many templates provided free of charge to Microsoft Office users on Office.com. To open one of these from Word, open the New tab in Backstage view, and then, in the Available Templates section, click a template category in the Office.com Templates to display the templates in that category. Click the template you want to use, and then click the Download button. Finally, you can create custom templates, such as company letterhead or memos, by saving a document as a template. To do this, in the Save As dialog box, click the Save as type arrow, and then click Word Template. When you open a template, you open a copy of the template as an unnamed document, not the template file itself (similar to the New from existing command).

You can use the New from existing command in Excel and PowerPoint as well.

LO10.4 Selecting Text

Selecting text is one of the most frequent actions you will perform as you work in Word, as well as the other Office programs. In fact, it's the first step in many tasks you can perform in a file. For example, you need to select text before you can move it to a new position in a document. You also need to select text before you can change its appearance.

There are many ways to select text in a document, as described in Exhibit 10-10. You can select text with the mouse or the keyboard. To select text with the mouse, you press and hold the mouse button, drag across a block of text, and then release the mouse button; you double- or triple-click it; or you position the pointer in the **selection bar**—the white space in the left margin—so that the pointer changes to ⩘, and then click or drag. To select text using the keyboard, you press and hold the Shift or Ctrl key, and then press one of the arrow keys to extend the selection in the direction of the arrow key. You can also use the mouse plus the Shift and Ctrl keys to select text.

When text is selected, it is highlighted in light blue. To deselect text, click anywhere in the document or press an arrow key.

ACTIVITY

Select text.

1 In the Cover Letter document, in the return address of the letter, in the first paragraph, double-click the word **Park**. The word and the space following it are selected, indicated by the blue highlight. See Exhibit 10-11.

2 Click anywhere in the document except on the word *Park*. The word is deselected.

➤ **Tip:** As you select text as you work through the steps in this book, refer back to Exhibit 10-10 for the different selection methods you can use.

3 In the body of the letter, in the first line, double-click

template A file that contains formatting and sometimes sample content.

selection bar The white space in the left margin of a document that you can use to select text.

Exhibit 10-10 Methods for selecting text

To select	Mouse	Keyboard	Mouse and keyboard
A character	Click before the character, and then drag over the character	Move the insertion point to the beginning of the word, press and hold the Shift key, and then press the Right Arrow key	
A word	Double-click the word	Move the insertion point to the beginning of the word, press and hold the Ctrl+Shift keys, and then press the Right Arrow key	
A line	Click ⅗ in the selection bar	Move the insertion point to the beginning of the line, press and hold the Shift key, and then press the Down Arrow key	
Multiple lines	Click ⅗ in the selection bar, and then drag up or down	Move the insertion point to the beginning of the first line, press and hold the Shift key, and then press the Down Arrow key until all the lines are selected	
A sentence	Click at the beginning of the sentence, and then drag until the sentence is selected		Press and hold the Ctrl key, then click any location within the sentence
A paragraph	Double-click ⅗ in the selection bar, or triple-click at any location within the paragraph	Move the insertion point to the beginning of the paragraph, press and hold the Ctrl+Shift keys, and then press the Down Arrow key	
Multiple paragraphs	Double-click ⅗ in the selection bar, and then drag up or down	Move the insertion point to the beginning of the first paragraph, press and hold the Ctrl+Shift keys, and then press the Down Arrow key until all the paragraphs are selected	
The entire document	Triple-click in the white space to the left of the document text, or click the Select button in the Editing group on the Home tab, and then click Select All	Press the Ctrl+A keys	Press and hold the Ctrl key, and click in the white space to the left of the document text
A block of text	Click at the beginning of the block, and then drag until the entire block is selected		Click at the beginning of the block, press and hold the Shift key, and then click at the end of the block
Nonadjacent blocks of text			Press and hold the Ctrl key, use any mouse method to select the first block, release the mouse button, and then use any mouse method to select another block

From, but do not release the mouse button. Drag to the right over the words **your Web site**, and then release the mouse button. The four words are selected.

4 Move the pointer into the selection bar so that it changes to ⅗.

5 Using ⅗, click to the left of the first line in the body of the letter. The entire line is selected.

6 With the line still selected, press and hold the **Ctrl key,** use any mouse method to select the first line in the second paragraph, and then release the **Ctrl key**.

Exhibit 10-11 Selected text

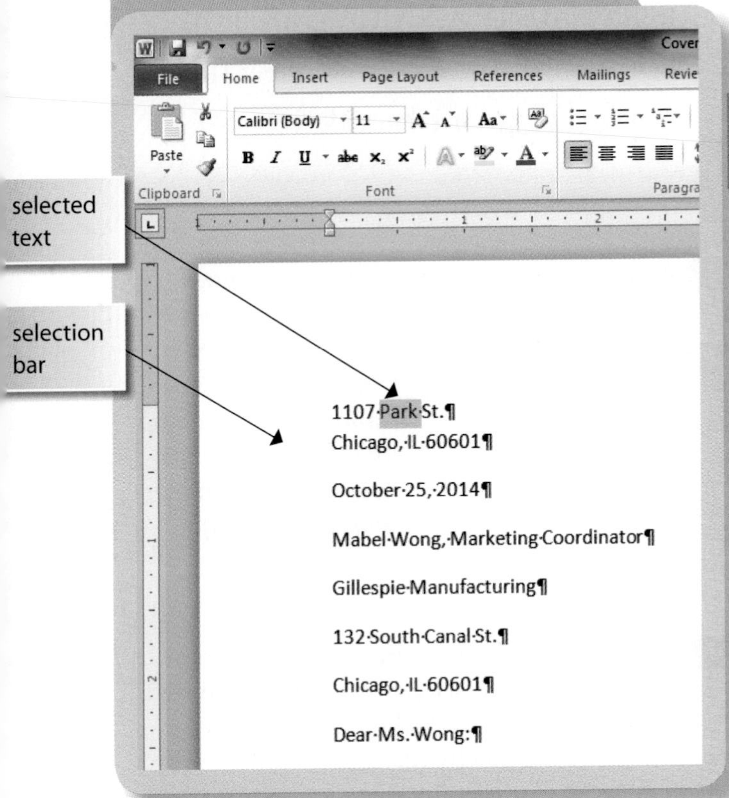

selected text
selection bar
Cover
File
Home
Insert
Page Layout
References
Mailings
Revie
Calibri (Body)
11
Paste
Clipboard
Font
Paragra
1107·Park·St.¶
Chicago,·IL·60601¶
October·25,·2014¶
Mabel·Wong,·Marketing·Coordinator¶
Gillespie·Manufacturing¶
132·South·Canal·St.¶
Chicago,·IL·60601¶
Dear·Ms.·Wong:¶

7 Continue to select text in the document using the different methods described in Exhibit 10-10. When you are done, deselect any selected text.

LO10.5 Editing Text

One of the fundamental features of a word processor is the ability to easily edit text without retyping an entire document. When you edit a document, you can type additional text in the document, delete existing text from the document, replace text already in the document, and copy or move text within the document.

Replacing Selected Text

To replace existing text, you select the text you no longer want, and then start typing. The text you type replaces the selected text, no matter how much text is selected. There is no need to press the Delete key to remove the selected text first.

Moving the Insertion Point

The insertion point indicates where text will be inserted in the document. You can click anywhere in a document to place the insertion point at the location where you clicked. You can also use the keyboard to move the insertion point in the document, which may be faster when your hands are already on the keyboard. Pressing the arrow keys moves the insertion point one character in the direction of the arrow key you pressed. If you combine other keys with the arrow keys, you can move the insertion point quickly to different locations. The table below summarizes the most common keystrokes for moving the insertion point in a document.

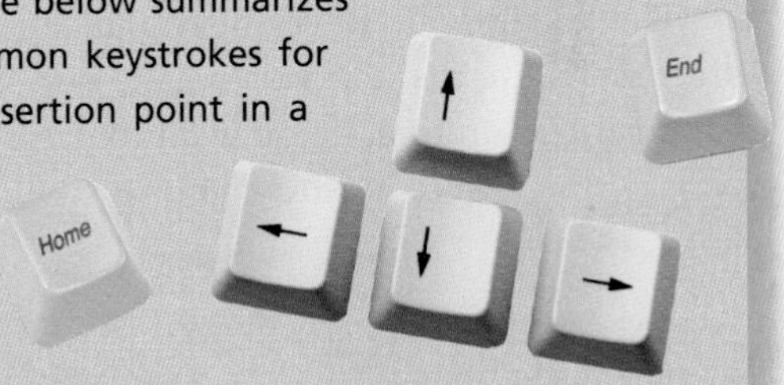

End
Home

Keystrokes for moving the insertion point

To move insertion point	Press
Left or right one character at a time	Left Arrow key or Right Arrow key
Up or down one line at a time	Up Arrow key or Down Arrow key
Left or right one word at a time	Ctrl+Left Arrow keys or Ctrl+Right Arrow keys
Up or down one paragraph at a time	Ctrl+Up Arrow keys or Ctrl+Down Arrow keys
To the beginning or to the end of the current line	Home key or End key
To the beginning or to the end of the document	Ctrl+Home keys or Ctrl+End keys
To the previous screen or to the next screen	Page Up key or Page Down key
To the top or to the bottom of the document window	Alt+Ctrl+Page Up keys or Alt+Ctrl+Page Down keys

Cameramannz; pzAxe/Shutterstock.com

ACTIVITY

Replace selected text.

1 In the Cover Letter document, in the body of the letter, in the first sentence in the first paragraph, select **From your Web site, I understand** and then release the mouse button. The text you dragged across is selected.

2 Type **L**. The selected text is replaced with the character you typed.

3 Type **arry Cohen told me**. The first sentence now reads *Larry Cohen told me that you are looking for a new assistant to the Marketing Coordinator.*

Using Drag and Drop

One technique for moving and copying text is **drag and drop**. To use drag and drop to move text, select the text you want to move, press and hold the mouse button, drag the selected text to a new location, and then release the mouse button. To copy text using drag and drop, select the text you want to copy, press and hold the Ctrl key, drag the text to the new location, and then release the mouse button and the Ctrl key. In either case, as you drag, the selected text remains in its original location and a dotted vertical line indicates exactly where the selected text will be dropped when you release the mouse button. When you release the mouse button, the text is pasted in the new location (and if you did not press the Ctrl key, removed from its original location).

Unlike the Cut or Copy commands, when you drag and drop, the text you drag is *not* placed on the Clipboard. Therefore, if you want to paste the text you dragged to another location, you need to drag it again or use the Cut or Copy command.

ACTIVITY

Use drag and drop to move and copy text.

1 In the body of the letter, in the first paragraph at the end of the first sentence, select **Marketing Coordinator**.

drag and drop A technique for moving or copying selected text or objects to a new location.

Office Clipboard A Clipboard available only to Office programs that can store up to 24 cut or copied blocks of text or other objects.

Remember that the Clipboard is a temporary storage area on your computer that holds cut or copied text or objects.

2 Point to the selected text so that the pointer changes to ⬚.

3 Press and hold the mouse button. After a moment, the pointer changes to ⬚ and a faint, dotted vertical line appears within the selected text.

⚠ **Problem?** If you cannot see the pointer or the dotted vertical line, move the pointer slightly left or right.

4 Drag up to the inside address until the vertical line shows that the selected text will be dropped following the comma and space after *Mabel Wong*. See Exhibit 10-12.

5 Release the mouse button. The selected text is moved from the first sentence to after *Mabel Wong*, in the inside address.

6 In the body of the letter, at the end of the first sentence in the first paragraph, select **to the**, and then press the **Delete key**. The selected words as well as the space before the word *to* are deleted. The first sentence now ends with *assistant*.

7 Scroll the document until the first paragraph in the body of the letter is at the top of the window.

8 In the body of the letter, select the second paragraph.

9 Drag the selected text down to the closing until the vertical line indicating the position of the text is positioned before the word *Sincerely*, and then release the mouse button. The paragraph is now the last paragraph in the body of the letter.

10 In the body of the letter, in the second sentence in the first paragraph, select **Sanford Industries**.

11 Point to the selected text, press and hold the **Ctrl key**, and then press and hold the mouse button.

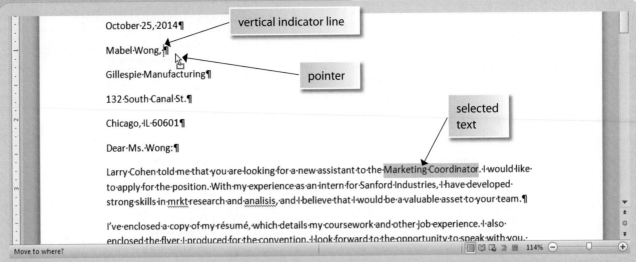

Exhibit 10-12 Text being moved using drag and drop

October·25,·2014¶

Mabel·Wong,·¶ → vertical indicator line

Gillespie·Manufacturing¶ → pointer

132·South·Canal·St.¶

Chicago,·IL·60601¶ → selected text

Dear·Ms.·Wong:¶

Larry·Cohen·told·me·that·you·are·looking·for·a·new·assistant·to·the·Marketing·Coordinator.·I·would·like·to·apply·for·the·position.·With·my·experience·as·an·intern·for·Sanford·Industries,·I·have·developed·strong·skills·in·mrkt·research·and·analisis,·and·I·believe·that·I·would·be·a·valuable·asset·to·your·team.¶

I've·enclosed·a·copy·of·my·résumé,·which·details·my·coursework·and·other·job·experience.·I·also·enclosed·the·flyer·I·produced·for·the·convention.·I·look·forward·to·the·opportunity·to·speak·with·you.·

Move to where?   114%

After a moment, the pointer changes to ⬚ to indicate that the text you are dragging is being copied instead of moved.

12 Drag the selected text down to the beginning of the second paragraph in the body of the letter until the vertical indicator line appears between the words *At* and *I.* Release the mouse button, and then release the **Ctrl key**. The text you copied, *Sanford Industries*, appears after the word *At.*

13 Save the document.

> ⚠️ **Problem?** If the selected text moves to the new location instead of being copied there, you released the Ctrl key before the mouse button. Undo your last action, and then repeat Step 12.

LO10.6 **Formatting Text**

Once you have entered the text of a document, you can change how it looks—that is, you can **format** the document. The purpose of formatting is to make the document attractive, emphasize certain points in the document, and make the organization and flow of the document clear to readers. You can format the document by changing the style of the text, adding color to text or as shading behind text, adding borders, and adding and removing space between lines and paragraphs.

The Office Clipboard

The system Clipboard is a feature of Windows and is available to every program running on the computer. So if you cut text in a Word document, and then switch to a Windows Explorer window and cut a file, the cut file replaces the Word text on the Clipboard. When you use Microsoft Office programs, however, you also have access to the Office Clipboard. The **Office Clipboard** collects up to 24 items cut or copied from Office programs, and you can paste these items in any order in a document created in Word, Excel, Access, or PowerPoint. To use the Office Clipboard, you need to open the Clipboard task pane by clicking the Dialog Box Launcher in the Clipboard group on the Home tab. If you do not open the Clipboard task pane, the Office Clipboard is not available and each block of text or other object cut or copied replaces the current block of text or other object currently on the Clipboard. When the Clipboard task pane is open, the system Clipboard continues to work normally, but you can also use the Office Clipboard to store 24 cut or copied items. The last item cut or copied to the Clipboard is the first item listed in the Clipboard task pane.

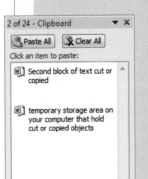

2 of 24 - Clipboard

Paste All   Clear All

Click an item to paste:

Second block of text cut or copied

temporary storage area on your computer that hold cut or copied objects

format To change the appearance of a file and its content.

To format text, you can either select text that is already entered and then change the format, or you can change the format and then type, and all the text from that point on will retain the new formatting.

Changing the Font and Font Size

An easy way to change the look of a document is to change the font. A **font** is the design of a set of characters. For example, the font used for the text you are reading right now is Sabon font, and the font used for the heading *Changing the Font and Font Size* is Eurostile font. Fonts are measured in **points**, which are units of measurement. One point equals 1/72 of an inch. Text in a book is typically printed in 10- or 12-point type. The font size of this text is 10 points, and the font size of the *Changing the Font and Font Size* heading is 14 points.

To change the font, select the text you want to change (or position the insertion point at the location where you will type new text), click the Font box arrow in the Font group on the Home tab, and then select a font. See Exhibit 10-13. The first font listed is the font Word suggests using for headings in the document. The second font listed is the font used for ordinary text in a document, or **body text**. The list of All Fonts is a complete alphabetical list of all available fonts. Each font name in the list is shown in the font that it names. For example, Arial appears in the Arial font, and Times New Roman appears in the Times New Roman font.

To change the font size, again select the text you want to change (or position the insertion point at the location where you will type new text), click the Font Size box arrow in the Font group on the Home tab, and then select a size.

Change the font and font size.

1 Switch to the **Resume Final document**, and then select all the text in the document.

font The design of a set of characters.

point The unit of measurement used for type; equal to 1/72 of an inch.

body text Ordinary text in a document.

Exhibit 10-13 Font menu

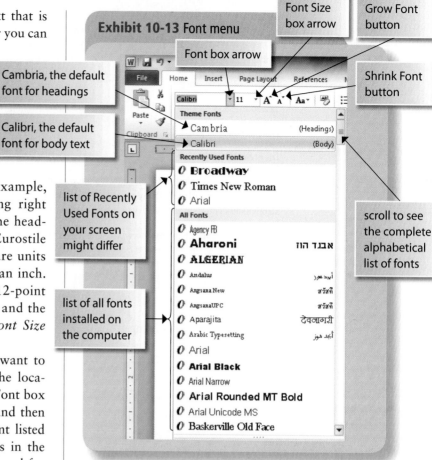

Font Size box arrow

Grow Font button

Font box arrow

Cambria, the default font for headings

Shrink Font button

Calibri, the default font for body text

list of Recently Used Fonts on your screen might differ

scroll to see the complete alphabetical list of fonts

list of all fonts installed on the computer

2 On the Home tab, in the Font group, click the **Font box arrow**. A list of available fonts appears. Calibri (Body) is highlighted in orange, indicating that this font is currently applied to the selected text.

3 Point to several fonts, watching the Live Preview in the selected text in the document.

4 Scroll down the list, and then click **Verdana**. The Font gallery closes, and the selected text is formatted in Verdana.

5 With all the text in the document still selected, on the Home tab, in the Font group, look at the Font Size box 11 to see that the font size of the selected text is 11 points.

6 On the Home tab, in the Font group, click the **Shrink Font button** A˅. The font size of the selected text changes from 11 points to 10 points.

7 Deselect the text, and then select the **Education heading** and the **paragraph mark** after it.

8 In the Font group, click the **Grow Font button** A˄ twice. The point size of the selected heading increases from 10 points to 12 points.

Exhibit 10-14 Nonadjacent text formatted as bold

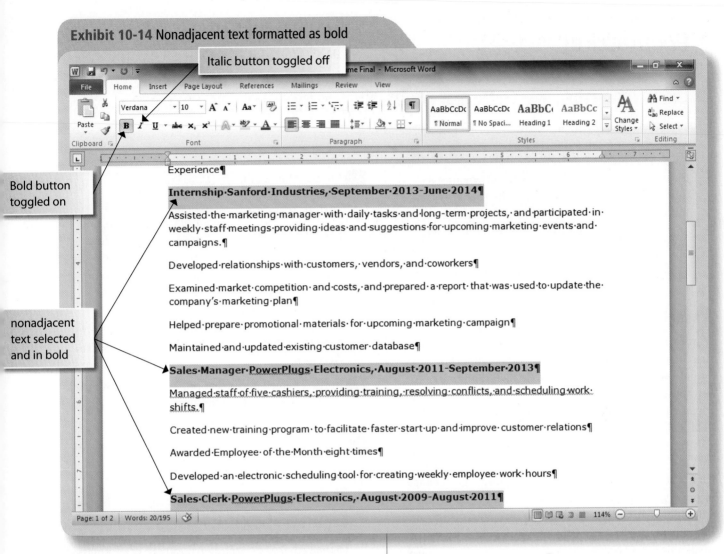

Italic button toggled off

Bold button toggled on

nonadjacent text selected and in bold

Experience¶

Internship·Sanford·Industries,·September·2013-June·2014¶

Assisted·the·marketing·manager·with·daily·tasks·and·long-term·projects,·and·participated·in·weekly·staff·meetings·providing·ideas·and·suggestions·for·upcoming·marketing·events·and·campaigns.¶

Developed·relationships·with·customers,·vendors,·and·coworkers¶

Examined·market·competition·and·costs,·and·prepared·a·report·that·was·used·to·update·the·company's·marketing·plan¶

Helped·prepare·promotional·materials·for·upcoming·marketing·campaign¶

Maintained·and·updated·existing·customer·database¶

Sales·Manager·PowerPlugs·Electronics,·August·2011-September·2013¶

Managed·staff·of·five·cashiers,·providing·training,·resolving·conflicts,·and·scheduling·work·shifts.¶

Created·new·training·program·to·facilitate·faster·start·up·and·improve·customer·relations¶

Awarded·Employee·of·the·Month·eight·times¶

Developed·an·electronic·scheduling·tool·for·creating·weekly·employee·work·hours¶

Sales·Clerk·PowerPlugs·Electronics,·August·2009-August·2011¶

Page: 1 of 2 | Words: 20/195 | 114%

9 At the top of the document, select **Stephen Konoski**.

10 On the Home tab, in the Font group, click the **Font Size box arrow** 10, and then click **20**. The size of the selected text changes to 20 points.

Changing Font Styles

To make text stand out, you can change the style of a font. **Font style** refers to format attributes applied to text, such as **bold** and *italics*. To change the font style, use the formatting commands in the Font group on the Home tab.

 **ACTIVITY**

Change the font style.

1 With *Stephen Konoski* still selected, press and hold the **Ctrl key**, drag across the **Education heading**, and then release the **Ctrl key**.

2 On the Home tab, in the Font group, click the **Bold button B**. The button toggles on and changes to **B**, and the selected text is formatted in bold.

3 Scroll down until the Experience heading is at the top of the document window, and then select the three lines beginning with **Internship**, **Sales Manager**, and **Sales Clerk**.

4 In the Font group, click the **Bold button B**. The three selected lines are in bold. See Exhibit 10-14.

5 Scroll up until the Education heading is at the top of the document window. In the second line below that heading, select **cum laude**.

6 In the Font group, click the **Italic button I**. The button toggles on, and the selected text is italicized.

font style Formatting attributes applied to text.

Formatting Professional Documents

In professional documents, use color and special fonts sparingly. The goal of letters, reports, and other documents is to convey important information, not to dazzle the reader with fancy fonts and colors. Overuse of such elements only serves to distract the reader from the main point.

Changing Text Color

Another way to emphasize text is to use color. Judicious use of color makes headings or other important text stand out. To apply color to text, click the Font Color button arrow in the Font group on the Home tab to open the document's color palette. See Exhibit 10-15. The color palette contains a top row of colors labeled Theme Colors. The next five rows under the theme colors are lighter and darker variations of the theme colors. The specific theme colors available might change from one document to another. The row of colors under the Standard Colors label does not change from one document to the next—this row of colors is always available.

 **ACTIVITY**

Change the color of text.

1 Select the **Education heading**.

Exhibit 10-15 Color palette in the Font button gallery

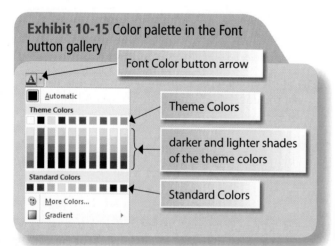

If you want to use colors in addition to the colors available in the color palette, click More Colors below the color palette.

2 On the Home tab, in the Font group, click the **Font Color button arrow** [A ▾]. The color palette appears.

3 In the Theme Colors section, in the first row, point to the **orange color** (the last color). The ScreenTip that appears identifies this as Orange, Accent 6.

4 In the Theme Colors section, in the first row, click the **Dark Blue, Text 2 color**, using the ScreenTip to identify the color name.

5 Save the document.

> **Tip:** To restore selected text to the default font, size, and color, click the Clear Formatting button [AB] in the Font group on the Home tab.

Using Text Effects

To really make text stand out, you can use formatting such as an outline, shadows, reflections, and colorful glow effects. To apply these types of formatting, click the Text Effects button in the Font group on the Home tab. When you click the button, a gallery of predesigned text effects appears. Like other galleries, point to an effect to see a

Live Preview of its effect on the selected text, and click an effect to apply that formatting. You can also use the commands below the gallery to create a customized format.

LO10.7 Formatting Paragraphs

In addition to formatting text, you can also apply formatting to entire paragraphs. For example, you can change the amount of space before or after a paragraph or between the lines within a paragraph, change the alignment of a paragraph from left-aligned to centered, or indent a paragraph.

Adjusting Paragraph Spacing

Paragraph spacing refers to the space that appears directly above and below a paragraph. Remember, in Word, any text that ends with ¶ (a paragraph mark symbol) is a paragraph. So, a paragraph can be a group of words that is many lines long, a single word, or even a blank line, in which case the only character on the line is a paragraph mark symbol. Paragraph spacing is measured in points. The default setting for paragraph spacing in Word is 0 points before each paragraph and 10 points after each paragraph.

To adjust paragraph spacing in Word, you use the Before and After boxes in the Spacing section in the Paragraph group on the Page Layout tab. You can also use the Add Space Before Paragraph or Remove Space After Paragraph commands on the Line and Paragraph Spacing button menu in the Paragraph group on the Home tab.

Understanding Spacing Between Paragraphs

When discussing the correct format for letters, many business style guides talk about single spacing and double spacing between paragraphs. In these style guides, "to single space between paragraphs" means creating paragraphs with no extra space between them. Likewise, "to double space between paragraphs" means creating paragraphs with a blank line between them. In many word processors, after you type a paragraph, you press the Enter key once for single spacing and twice for double spacing. With the default paragraph spacing in Word 2010, however, you only need to press the Enter key once to insert a double space after a paragraph. Keep this in mind if you are accustomed to pressing the Enter key twice; otherwise, you will end up with more space than you want between paragraphs.

3 In the Paragraph group, in the Spacing section, click the **After box down arrow** twice. The value in the After box changes to 0 pt and the extra space is removed after the selected paragraphs.

ACTIVITY

Adjust paragraph spacing.

1 In the Resume Final document, at the top of the résumé under *Education*, select the three lines from **University of Chicago** through **Concentration: Marketing**.

2 On the Ribbon, click the **Page Layout tab**. In the Paragraph group, in the Spacing section, 10 pt appears in the After box, indicating that there is 10 points of space after each of the selected paragraphs. See Exhibit 10-16.

Exhibit 10-16 Paragraph spacing settings on the Page Layout tab

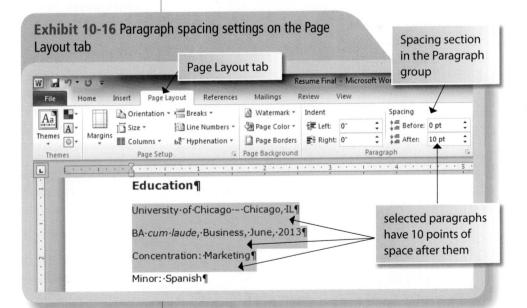

paragraph spacing The space above and below a paragraph.

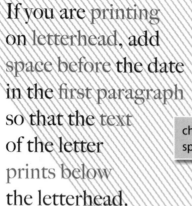

If you are printing on letterhead, add space before the date in the first paragraph so that the text of the letter prints below the letterhead.

4 Select the **Education heading**.

5 In the Paragraph group, in the Spacing section, click the **Before box up arrow** twice. The space above the selected paragraph increases to 12 points.

6 Switch to the **Cover Letter document**, and then scroll the document so that *1107 Park St.* appears at the top of the document window.

7 Select the first three lines in the inside address (from **Mabel Wong** through **132 South Canal St.**).

8 On the Home tab, in the Paragraph group, click the **Line and Paragraph Spacing button** ↕≡▾. A menu of line spacing options appears, with two paragraph spacing commands at the bottom. See Exhibit 10-17.

> **Tip:** When entering text, you can press the Shift+Enter keys to move the insertion point to a new line *without* starting a new paragraph and therefore create new lines without the paragraph spacing.

9 At the bottom of the menu, click **Remove Space After Paragraph**. The menu closes, and the 10

line spacing The amount of space between lines of text within a paragraph.

single spaced Line spacing that has no extra space between lines of text in a paragraph.

double spaced Line spacing that has a blank line of text between each line of text in a paragraph.

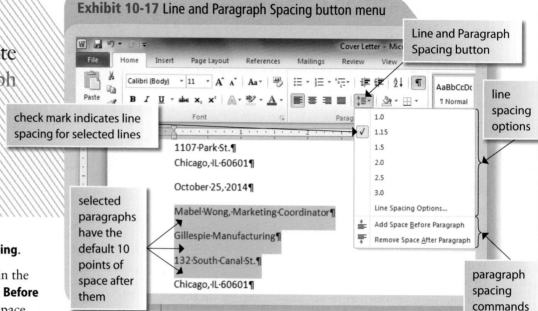

Exhibit 10-17 Line and Paragraph Spacing button menu

Line and Paragraph Spacing button

line spacing options

check mark indicates line spacing for selected lines

selected paragraphs have the default 10 points of space after them

paragraph spacing commands

points of space are removed after each of the selected paragraphs.

Adjusting Line Spacing

Line spacing is the amount of space that appears between lines of text within a paragraph. Word offers a number of preset line spacing options. Paragraphs formatted with the 1.0 setting are called **single spaced**. Single spacing allows the least amount of space between lines—essentially no extra space. Paragraphs formatted with the 2.0 setting are called **double spaced** and have a blank line of space between each line of text in the paragraph. The default line spacing setting is 1.15, which allows a little more space between lines than 1.0 spacing. The 1.15 line spacing setting is designed to make it easier to read text on a computer screen.

ACTIVITY

Adjust line spacing.

1 Select all the text in the document.

2 On the Home tab, in the Paragraph group, click the **Line and Paragraph Spacing button** ↕≡▾. The default line spacing setting for the selected text (1.15) is indicated by a check mark.

3 On the menu, click **1.0**. The spacing between lines in each paragraph is changed to single spaced.

Aligning Paragraphs

Normal paragraphs are **left-aligned**—they are flush with the left margin and **ragged**, or uneven, along the right margin. **Right-aligned** paragraphs are aligned along the right margin and ragged along the left margin. Paragraphs that are **centered** are positioned midway between the left and right margins and ragged along both margins. **Justified** paragraphs are flush with both the left and right margins. Text in newspaper columns is often justified. See Exhibit 10-18.

The Paragraph group on the Home tab includes a button for each of the four types of alignment described in Exhibit 10-18. To align a single paragraph, click anywhere in that paragraph and then click the appropriate alignment button. To align multiple paragraphs, select the paragraphs, and then click an alignment button.

Exhibit 10-18 Varieties of text alignment

> **left alignment**
> When you go to an interview, don't forget about your appearance. First impressions count, and you want to be able to spend the bulk of the interview discussing your abilities and accomplishments, not trying to overcome a negative first impression.

> **right alignment**
> When you go to an interview, don't forget about your appearance. First impressions count, and you want to be able to spend the bulk of the interview discussing your abilities and accomplishments, not trying to overcome a negative first impression.

> **center alignment**
> When you go to an interview, don't forget about your appearance. First impressions count, and you want to be able to spend the bulk of the interview discussing your abilities and accomplishments, not trying to overcome a negative first impression.

> **justified alignment**
> When you go to an interview, don't forget about your appearance. First impressions count, and you want to be able to spend the bulk of the interview discussing your abilities and accomplishments, not trying to overcome a negative first impression.

ACTIVITY

Change the alignment of paragraphs.

1. Switch to the **Resume Final document**.

2. At the top of the document, select the first two lines of text (Stephen Konoski's name and address).

3. On the Ribbon, click the **Home tab**. Note that in the Paragraph group, the Align Text Left button is selected.

4. On the Home tab, in the Paragraph group, click the **Center button**. The selected paragraphs are centered horizontally on the page.

5. Click anywhere in the **Education heading**. In the Paragraph group, click the **Align Text Right button**. The Align Text Right button toggles on, and the selected paragraph is right-aligned. See Exhibit 10-19.

left-align To align paragraph text along the left margin with ragged edges along the right margin.

ragged Uneven, such as text with an uneven appearance along a margin.

right-align To align paragraph text along the right margin with ragged edges along the left margin.

center To center paragraph text between the left and right margins with ragged edges along both margins.

justify To align paragraph text along both the left and right margins.

Exhibit 10-19 Paragraphs with different alignments

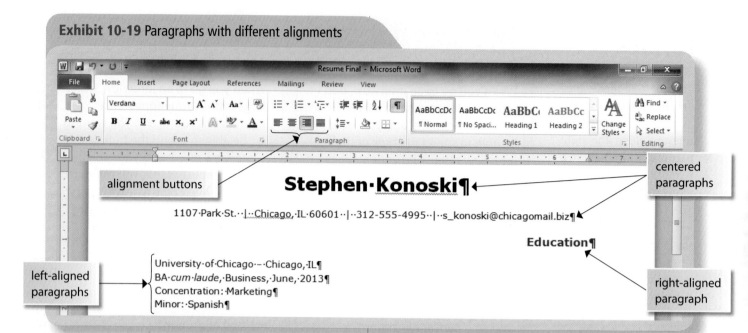

alignment buttons

centered paragraphs

Stephen·Konoski¶

1107·Park·St.··|··Chicago,·IL·60601··|··312-555-4995··|··s_konoski@chicagomail.biz¶

Education¶

right-aligned paragraph

left-aligned paragraphs

University·of·Chicago··—··Chicago,·IL¶
BA·*cum·laude*,·Business,·June,·2013¶
Concentration:·Marketing¶
Minor:·Spanish¶

6 In the Paragraph group, click the **Align Text Left button** . The Education heading is left-aligned again.

Using Tabs

A **tab stop** (often called a **tab**) is a location on the horizontal ruler where the insertion point moves when you press the Tab key. Tab stops are useful for aligning small amounts of data in columns. There are default tab stops every one-half inch on the horizontal ruler, indicated by the small tick marks that appear along the ruler's bottom edge. When you press the Tab key, the insertion point moves to the next tab stop to the right. It's important to have the Show/Hide ¶ button selected when you work with tab stops, because then you can see the nonprinting tab character (→) that is inserted when you press the Tab key. A tab is just like any other character you type; you can delete it by pressing the Backspace key or the Delete key.

You can override the default tab stops by setting custom tab stops. The four types of tab stops are Left, Center, Right, and Decimal. (The default tab stops are all Left Tab stops.) A fifth tab stop, the Bar Tab stop, is not actually a tab stop—it simply inserts a vertical bar in the document at the location of the stop placed

tab stop (tab) A location on the horizontal ruler where the insertion point moves when you press the Tab key.

leader line A line that appears between two elements, such as between tabbed text.

Tabs Dialog Box

The Tabs dialog box lets you add a leader line and set tabs at precise positions. A **leader line** is a line or row of dots or dashes that appears in the space between tabbed text. A leader line makes it easier to read a long list of tabbed material because the eye can follow the dots from one item to the next, such as in a table of contents. To use the Tabs dialog box, double-click a tab stop on the ruler or click the Dialog Box Launcher in the Paragraph group on the Home tab, and then click Tabs at the bottom of the Indents and Spacing tab in the Paragraph dialog box. To create a tab stop at a precise position, click in the Tab stop position box, and then type the location on the ruler where you want to insert the tab—for example, 4.15.

To change the alignment, click an option button in the Alignment section. To set a leader line, click an option button in the Leader section. To change a tab stop, select it in the list, and then modify it as needed. Make sure you click Set to set the tab stop or the changes; clicking OK only closes the dialog box.

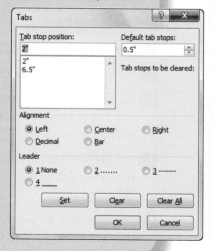

Exhibit 10-20 Tab stop alignment styles

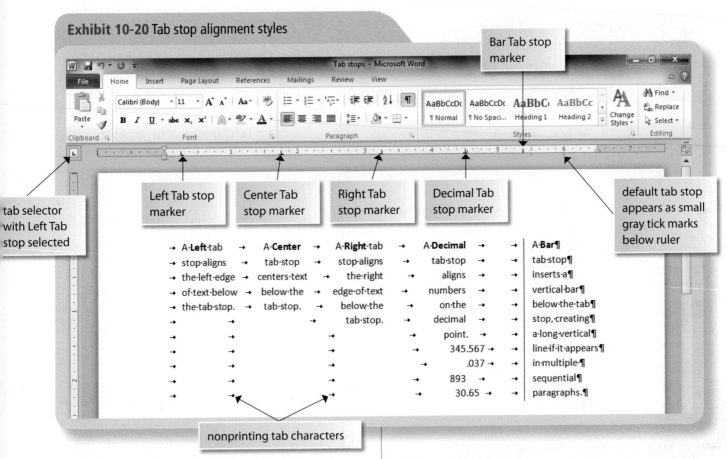

Bar Tab stop marker

tab selector with Left Tab stop selected

Left Tab stop marker

Center Tab stop marker

Right Tab stop marker

Decimal Tab stop marker

default tab stop appears as small gray tick marks below ruler

nonprinting tab characters

on the ruler. Exhibit 10-20 shows the different tab stop styles in a document.

To set a tab stop, first select a tab stop style using the tab selector, located to the left of the horizontal ruler, and then click on the horizontal ruler where you want to insert the tab stop. The default tab stop style is the Left Tab. When you click the tab selector, you cycle through the four types of tab stops, and then through two markers that can be used to set indents. To return to the Left Tab style, continue clicking the tab selector until it returns to the Left Tab style.

When you insert a tab stop (except the Bar Tab stop), all of the default tab stops to its left are removed. This means you press the Tab key only once to move the insertion point to the newly created tab stop, no matter where it is on the ruler. The Left Tab style is selected by default and is probably the tab style you will use most often.

 **ACTIVITY**

Use tabs.

1 Scroll so that the Experience heading is at the top of the document window. In the line beginning with *Internship* (below the Experience heading), click immediately before the word *Sanford*.

2 Press the **Tab key**. A tab symbol appears, and the insertion point moves to the next default tab stop at the 1-inch mark.

3 In the line beginning with *Sales Manager*, click immediately before the word *PowerPlugs*, and then press the **Tab key**.

> **Tip:** One way to align columns of text is to separate the text in each row with tabs, and then add the appropriate tab stops.

4 In the line beginning with *Sales Clerk*, insert a tab immediately before the word *PowerPlugs*.

5 Click anywhere in the line beginning with *Internship*. On the horizontal ruler, click the **2-inch mark**. Word inserts a Left Tab stop at that location and removes the default tab stops to its left. The text after the new tab stop shifts to the right and starts at the 2-inch mark. See Exhibit 10-21.

6 To the left of the horizontal ruler, click the **tab selector** ⌊. It changes to show the Center Tab style ⊥.

7 Click the **tab selector** ⊥ again. It changes to show the Right Tab style ⌋.

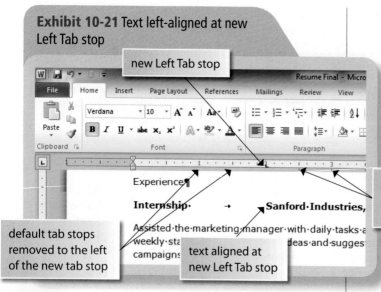

Exhibit 10-21 Text left-aligned at new Left Tab stop

- new Left Tab stop
- default tab stops removed to the left of the new tab stop
- text aligned at new Left Tab stop
- default tab stops still appear to the right of the new tab stop

8 On the horizontal ruler, click the **6-inch mark**. A Right Tab stop is added to the ruler at the 6-inch mark.

9 On the ruler, point to the **Right Tab stop**, and then press and hold the mouse button. A dotted vertical line appears. See Exhibit 10-22.

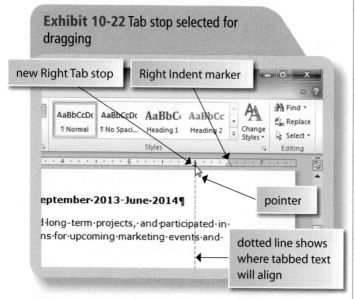

Exhibit 10-22 Tab stop selected for dragging

- new Right Tab stop
- Right Indent marker
- pointer
- dotted line shows where tabbed text will align

10 Drag the **Right Tab stop** to the right until it is on top of the Right Indent marker △, and then release the mouse button. The Right Tab stop is repositioned.

bulleted list A group of related paragraphs with a symbol to the left of each paragraph.

numbered list A group of related paragraphs that have a particular order with sequential numbers to the left of each paragraph.

11 Click immediately before the word *Sanford* in the *Internship* line, and then press the **Tab key**. The text moves to the right so that the text after the second tab in the paragraph is right-aligned at the new Right Tab stop.

12 At the 2-inch mark on the horizontal ruler, drag the **Left Tab stop** down off of the ruler. The Left Tab stop is removed from the ruler, and the text after the second tab in the current paragraph moves to the right off the page. This is because there are no default tab stops before the Right Tab stop you inserted at the right margin. So the first tab in the line moves the text after it to the right margin, and the second tab in the line moves the text after it to the next tab stop. In this case, the next tab stop is the default tab stop at the 7-inch mark on the ruler.

13 Click in the *Internship* line between the two tab symbols. The insertion point appears to the left of the second tab symbol.

14 Press the **Backspace key**. The first tab in the line is deleted and the text after the only tab symbol in the line right-aligns properly at the Right Tab stop you inserted.

Creating Bulleted and Numbered Lists

A **bulleted list** is a group of related paragraphs with a symbol, such as a dot, dash, or other character, that appears to the left of each paragraph. For a group of related paragraphs that have a particular order (such as steps in a procedure), you can use numbers instead of bullets to create a **numbered list**. If you insert a new paragraph, delete a paragraph, or reorder the paragraphs in a numbered list, Word adjusts the numbers to make sure they remain consecutive.

When you create a bulleted or numbered list, the bullet symbol or the number is placed at the beginning of the paragraph and a tab character is inserted

Use a bulleted list if the items have no particular order; use a numbered list if the items have a specific, sequential order.

between the bullet symbol or the number and the text in the paragraph.

Creating a Bulleted List

To add bullets to a series of paragraphs, use the Bullets button in the Paragraph group on the Home tab. You can change the symbol used for the bullet by clicking the Bullets button arrow to open a gallery of bullet styles.

ACTIVITY

Create bulleted lists.

1 Below the *Internship* line, select the four paragraphs beginning with **Developed relationships with . . .** through **Maintained and updated existing customer database**.

2 On the Home tab, in the Paragraph group, click the **Bullets button** . The Bullets button toggles on, black circles appear as bullets before each selected paragraph, and the bulleted list is indented.

3 In the Paragraph group, click the **Bullets button arrow** . A gallery of bullet styles opens. The Recently Used Bullets section at the top of the gallery displays the bullet styles that have been used since you started this session of Word. The Bullet Library section, which appears below the Recently Used Bullets section, offers a variety of common bullet styles. See Exhibit 10-23.

4 In the Bullet Library section, point to the bullet styles to see a Live Preview of the bullet styles in the document.

5 In the Bullet Library section, click the **four diamonds shape**. The round bullets are replaced with the four diamonds symbol.

6 Scroll down until you can see the bottom of the page. Under the Technical Skills heading, select the two paragraphs from **Proficient with . . .** through **Advanced user . . .**, and then under the Activities heading, select the two paragraphs from **American Marketing Association . . .** through **Chicago Crew Team . . . .**

7 In the Paragraph group, click the **Bullets button** . The selected paragraphs are formatted as two bulleted lists with the four diamonds symbol as the bullet character. Clicking the Bullets button applies the last symbol used during this session of Word as the bullet symbol.

> **Tip:** To find additional bullet symbols, click the Bullets button arrow , click Define New Bullet to open the Define New Bullet dialog box, and then click Symbol or Picture.

Creating a Numbered List

To create a numbered list from text already in a document, use the Numbering button in the Paragraph group on the Home tab. As with the Bullets button arrow, you can click the Numbering button arrow and then select from a gallery of numbering styles.

ACTIVITY

Create a numbered list.

1 Switch to the **Cover Letter document**. Scroll so that the salutation *Dear Ms. Wong:* appears at the top of the document window.

2 In the body of the letter, below the third paragraph, select the three paragraphs starting with **Verifying radio ad frequency . . .** through **Updating existing customer database**.

Exhibit 10-23 Bullets gallery

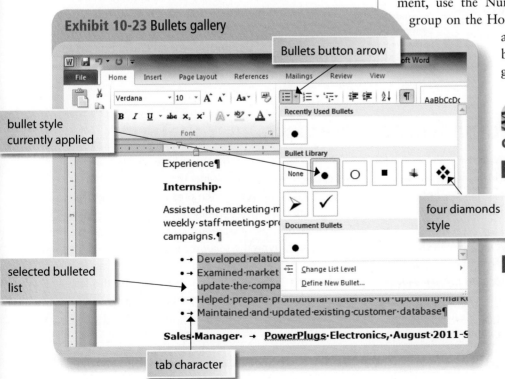

bullet style currently applied

selected bulleted list

tab character

Bullets button arrow

four diamonds style

3 On the Home tab, in the Paragraph group, click the **Numbering button** 📋. The selected paragraphs are changed to a numbered list.

4 On the Home tab, in the Paragraph group, click the **Numbering button arrow** 📋▾. A gallery of numbering formats appears. See Exhibit 10-24.

To add a colored horizontal line at the insertion point, click the Border button arrow in the Paragraph group on the Home tab, and then click Horizontal Line.

Exhibit 10-24 Numbering gallery

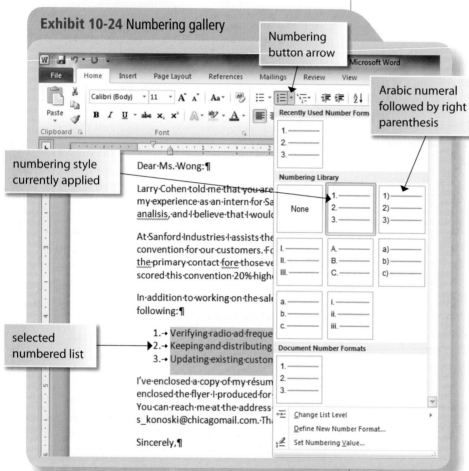

5 In the gallery, click the numbering style that shows **Arabic numeral followed by right parenthesis**. The gallery closes, and the style of numbers in the selected paragraphs is changed.

6 In the Paragraph group, click the **Bullets button** 📋. The selected numbered list is changed to a bulleted list.

7 Save the Cover Letter document.

Adding a Paragraph Border

A paragraph border is an outline that appears around one or more paragraphs in a document. You can choose to include only part of a border—for example, a bottom border that appears as an underline under the last line of text in the paragraph—or an entire box around a paragraph. You can select different

Creating Bulleted or Numbered Lists as You Type

To create a bulleted list as you type, click the Bullets button in the Paragraph group on the Home tab, type the first item in the list, and then press the Enter key. The next paragraph is formatted with the bullet symbol and the Tab character.

To create a numbered list as you type, you can click the Numbering button in the Paragraph group on the Home tab and then start typing, or you can use Auto-Correct to create the list. To do this, type the number 1 followed by a period, and then press the Tab key. AutoCorrect formats the paragraph as the first item

in a numbered list and the Numbering button in the Paragraph group on the Home tab is selected. After you type the first item and then press the Enter key, the number 2 automatically appears in the next paragraph and the insertion point appears after a Tab character, ready for you to type the second item.

To end both a bulleted and numbered list as you type, press the Enter key twice after you type the last item in the list. This creates a new blank paragraph at the left margin with no bullet or number in front of it.

colors and line weights for the border as well, making the border more or less prominent as needed. To add a paragraph border, use the Border button in the Paragraph group on the Home tab.

ACTIVITY

Add a paragraph border.

1 Switch to the **Resume Final document**. Scroll the document so *Stephen Konoski* is at the top of the document window.

2 Select the **Education paragraph**, including the **paragraph mark**.

3 On the Home tab, in the Paragraph group, click the **Border button arrow** ⊞ ▾. A menu of border options appears, as shown in Exhibit 10-25.

> **Tip:** The exact name that appears in the ScreenTip for the Border button changes depending on which border option is currently selected. In this case, the ScreenTip is *Bottom Border* because the bottom border is selected by default.

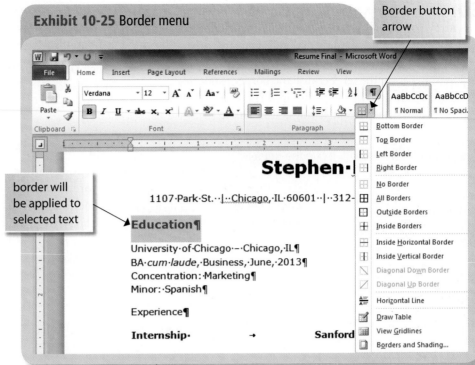

Exhibit 10-25 Border menu

border will be applied to selected text

Border button arrow

4 On the Border menu, click **Top Border**. The menu closes, a black border appears above the selected paragraph, and the Border button in the Paragraph group changes to show the Top Border option. See Exhibit 10-26.

⚠ **Problem?** If a box appears around *Education* instead of a border above the paragraph that spans the width of the page, you did not select the paragraph mark before applying the border. Undo the action, and then repeat Steps 2 through 4.

Exhibit 10-26 Top border applied

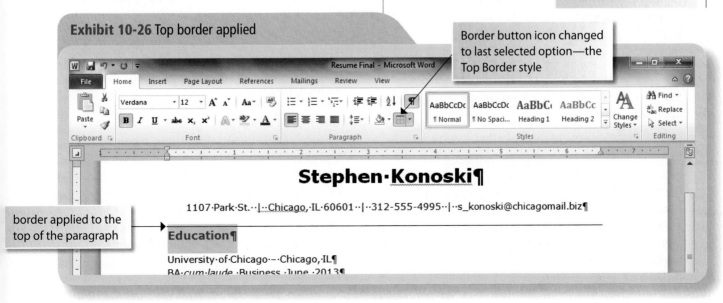

Border button icon changed to last selected option—the Top Border style

border applied to the top of the paragraph

5 In the Paragraph group, click the **Border button arrow** 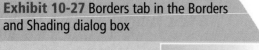, and then click **Borders and Shading**. The Borders and Shading dialog box opens with the Borders tab selected. Custom is selected in the Setting list on the left because the border is not applied to all sides of the paragraph. The Preview section shows the current settings. See Exhibit 10-27.

Exhibit 10-27 Borders tab in the Borders and Shading dialog box

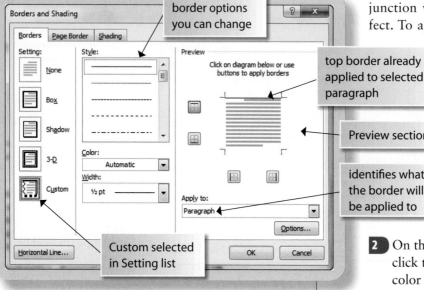

6 In the Style list, click the **down scroll arrow** four times, and then click the line style that shows a **thick line above a thin line**.

7 Click the **Color arrow**. The same color palette you used when you changed the font color appears.

8 In the color palette, under Theme Colors, click **Dark Blue, Text 2**. The selected line style in the Style box and the sample in the Width box change to the dark blue color.

9 Click the **Width arrow**, and then click **1½ pt**. Do not close the dialog box yet; you still need to apply the selected border style.

10 In the Preview section, click the **top of the paragraph**. The solid black border is replaced with the double-line blue border. Below the Preview section, the

> ⚠ **Problem?** If you clicked OK before clicking the top border in the Preview section of the dialog box, the custom border is not applied. Repeat Steps 5 through 9.

Apply to box contains Paragraph, indicating that the border will be applied to the current paragraph.

11 Click **OK**. The dialog box closes, and the border above the Education heading changes to the 1½-point, dark blue border you selected.

Adding Paragraph Shading

You can add shading as background color to one or more paragraphs. You can use shading in conjunction with a border for a more defined effect. To apply shading, use the Shading button in the Paragraph group on the Home tab.

Add shading to a paragraph.

1 At the top of the document, select **Stephen Konoski** and the **paragraph mark** at the end of the line.

2 On the Home tab, in the Paragraph group, click the **Shading button arrow**. The color palette appears.

3 In the second row under Theme Colors, click the **Dark Blue, Text 2, Lighter 80% color**. The color palette closes and light blue shading is applied to the width of the entire paragraph containing Stephen's name. See Exhibit 10-28.

> ⚠ **Problem?** If the shading was applied only behind Stephen's name rather than across the width of the page, you did not select the paragraph mark. Undo the action, and then repeat Steps 1 through 3.

Indenting a Paragraph

Word offers a number of options for indenting a paragraph. You can shift the left edge of an entire paragraph to the right—increasing the left indent—or shift the right edge to the left—increasing the right indent. You can also create specialized indents. A **first-line indent** shifts the first line of a paragraph from the left margin, and a **hanging indent** shifts all the lines of a paragraph from the left margin *except* the first line.

Exhibit 10-28 Shading applied to a paragraph

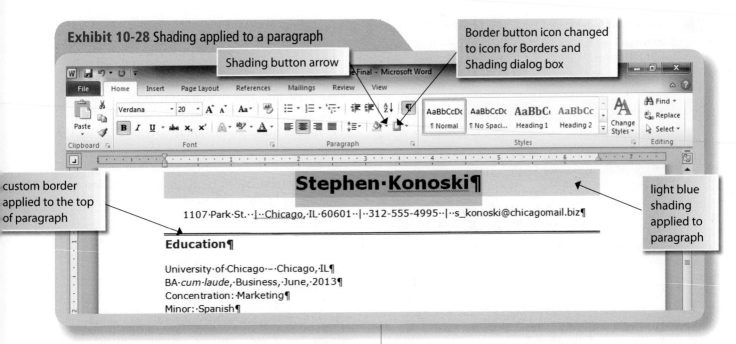

Shading button arrow

Border button icon changed to icon for Borders and Shading dialog box

custom border applied to the top of paragraph

light blue shading applied to paragraph

Stephen·Konoski¶

1107·Park·St.··|··Chicago,·IL·60601··|··312-555-4995··|··s_konoski@chicagomail.biz¶

Education¶

University·of·Chicago·–·Chicago,·IL¶
BA·*cum·laude*,·Business,·June,·2013¶
Concentration:·Marketing¶
Minor:·Spanish¶

To create indents, you can use the indent markers on the ruler. First, click in the paragraph you want to indent or select multiple paragraphs. Then, drag the appropriate indent marker to the left or right on the horizontal ruler. The marker on the left end of the ruler contains three parts: the First Line Indent marker ▽, the Hanging Indent marker △, and the Left Indent marker ▭. When the three parts are aligned, the marker looks like ⧗. The Right Indent marker △ is the only marker on the right end of the ruler. ScreenTips appear as you point to each marker so that you can drag the correct marker.

To quickly indent an entire paragraph one-half inch from the left margin, position the insertion point in the paragraph you want to indent and then click the Increase Indent button in the Paragraph group on the Home tab. You can continue to indent the paragraph in increments of half inches by repeatedly clicking the Increase Indent button. To move an indented paragraph back to the left one-half inch, click the Decrease Indent button. Note that if you use the Increase Indent button to indent a bulleted list, it will indent the list one-quarter inch at a time. When you indent an entire paragraph from the left, all three in-

dent markers move as a unit along with the paragraphs you are indenting.

ACTIVITY

Change paragraph indents.

1 Under the *Internship* line, click anywhere in the paragraph that begins with *Assisted the marketing manager.*

2 On the horizontal ruler, point to the **Left Indent marker** ▭, which is the rectangle at the bottom of the marker at the left margin on the horizontal ruler ⧗. Use the ScreenTip to make sure you are pointing to the correct section of the marker.

> **Tip:** You can also click in the paragraph you want to indent or select multiple paragraphs, click the Dialog Box Launcher in the Paragraph group, and then adjust the settings in the Indentation section.

3 While still pointing to the **Left Indent marker** ▭, press and hold the mouse button. A dotted vertical line appears over the document.

In research papers formatted using the MLA style, all the body paragraphs must have a first-line indent.

first-line indent A paragraph in which the first line is indented from the left margin.

hanging indent A paragraph in which all the lines are indented from the left margin except the first line.

4 Drag the **Left Indent marker** 🔲 right to the **.5-inch mark** on the horizontal ruler, as shown in Exhibit 10-29.

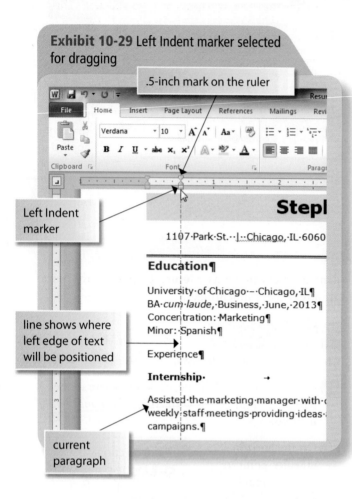

Exhibit 10-29 Left Indent marker selected for dragging

.5-inch mark on the ruler

Left Indent marker

line shows where left edge of text will be positioned

current paragraph

5 Release the mouse button. All three sections of the marker move when you drag the Left Indent marker. The entire paragraph containing the insertion point indents from the left one-half inch.

6 Scroll down so that the Experience heading is at the top of the document window.

7 Below the *Sales Manager* line, select the text in the paragraph that begins **Managed staff of five cashiers . . .**, press and hold the **Ctrl key**, and then below the *Sales Clerk* line, click to the left of the paragraph that begins **Staffed sales register . . . .** Release the **Ctrl key**. The two nonadjacent lines are selected.

8 On the Home tab, in the Paragraph group, click the **Increase Indent button** 🔲. The selected paragraphs indent one-half inch.

9 Under the *Internship* line, select the four items in the bulleted list, from **Developed relationships with . . .** through **Maintained and updated existing customer database**. On the ruler, notice that the First Line Indent marker is at the .25-inch mark. The first line of each of the selected paragraphs is indented one-quarter inch. Also on the ruler, notice that the Hanging Indent marker is at the .5-inch mark. In the second bulleted item, the only item that is more than one line long, the second line is indented one-half inch. See Exhibit 10-30.

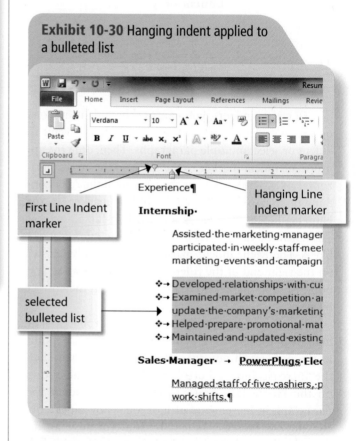

Exhibit 10-30 Hanging indent applied to a bulleted list

First Line Indent marker

Hanging Line Indent marker

selected bulleted list

10 In the Paragraph group, click the **Increase Indent button** 🔲. The selected paragraphs indent one-quarter inch from their original position, which is one-half inch from the left margin.

11 Scroll to the bottom of the document. Select the four nonadjacent bulleted items.

12 In the Paragraph group, click the **Decrease Indent button** 🔲. The indent of the selected paragraphs decreases by one-half inch and the selected bulleted items are aligned at the left margin.

13 Save the Resume Final document.

LO10.8 Copying Formats

If you are working with a document that contains a lot of formatting, it can be easier to copy the formatting rather than trying to re-create it on a different block of text. Likewise, if you are pasting text that is formatted differently from the text in the location where you are pasting it, you can control whether the formatting is pasted.

Using the Format Painter

The **Format Painter** is a tool that allows you to copy formatting from one location to another, such as from one paragraph of text to another. You can use the Format Painter to apply the copied formatting once or over and over again until you toggle it off. To use the Format Painter, select the text with the formatting you want to copy, click the Format Painter button in the Clipboard group on the Home tab to toggle it on, and then click or select the text you want to format. The Format Painter toggles off after the formatting is applied. If you want to format multiple blocks of text with the same formatting, double-click the Format Painter button. It will remain toggled on until you click the button again or press the Esc key.

ACTIVITY

Use the Format Painter.

1 In the Resume Final document, scroll to the top of the document, and then select the **Education heading**.

2 On the Home tab, in the Clipboard group, click the **Format Painter button**, and then move the pointer to the document. The Format Painter button toggles on, and the pointer changes to ▲.

3 Five lines below the Education heading, click anywhere on the **Experience heading**. The font and paragraph formatting applied to the Education heading is copied to the Experience heading, the Format Painter button toggles off, and the pointer returns to its usual shape.

4 Select the **Experience heading**. In the Clipboard group, double-click the **Format Painter button**.

5 Scroll down, and then click anywhere on the **Technical Skills heading**. The paragraph formatting is copied to the heading, but the character formatting is copied only to the word you clicked. This time, the Format Painter button remains toggled on so the pointer is still ▲.

6 Select **Technical Skills** and then **Activities** to copy the formatting to those headings.

7 In the Clipboard group, click the **Format Painter button**. The Format Painter button toggles off, and the pointer returns to its usual shape.

8 Scroll up, and then under the Experience heading, select the line beginning with **Internship**. In the Clipboard group, double-click the **Format Painter button**.

9 Click anywhere in the line beginning with **Sales Manager**. The formatting is copied, including the Right Tab stop you set in the line beginning with *Internship*.

10 Click anywhere in the line beginning with **Sales Clerk**. The Right Tab stop is applied to this paragraph.

11 Press the **Esc key**. The Format Painter button toggles off, and the pointer returns to its original shape.

12 Under the *Internship* line, select any of the paragraphs in the bulleted list. In the Clipboard group, click the **Format Painter button**.

13 Under the *Sales Manager* line, select the three paragraphs from **Created new training program . . .** through **Developed an electronic . . . .**

> **Tip:** To see the entire document at once, click the One Page button in the Zoom group on the View tab.

The paragraph formatting, including the bullet characters and the indent level, is copied to the three paragraphs you selected, and the Format Painter toggles off. The document should look similar to Exhibit 10-31.

14 Save the Resume Final document.

> **Format Painter** A tool that is used to copy formatting from one location to another, such as from one block of text to another.

Exhibit 10-31 Completed résumé

Stephen Konoski

1107 Park St. | Chicago, IL 60601 | 312-555-4995 | s_konoski@chicagomail.biz

Education

University of Chicago – Chicago, IL
BA *cum laude*, Business, June, 2013
Concentration: Marketing
Minor: Spanish

Experience

Internship   **Sanford Industries, September 2013–June 2014**

Assisted the marketing manager with daily tasks and long-term projects, and participated in weekly staff meetings providing ideas and suggestions for upcoming marketing events and campaigns.

- ❖ Developed relationships with customers, vendors, and coworkers
- ❖ Examined market competition and costs, and prepared a report that was used to update the company's marketing plan
- ❖ Helped prepare promotional materials for upcoming marketing campaign
- ❖ Maintained and updated existing customer database

Sales Manager   **PowerPlugs Electronics, August 2011–September 2013**

Managed staff of five cashiers, providing training, resolving conflicts, and scheduling work shifts.

- ❖ Created new training program to facilitate faster start up and improve customer relations
- ❖ Awarded Employee of the Month eight times
- ❖ Developed an electronic scheduling tool for creating weekly employee work hours

Sales Clerk   **PowerPlugs Electronics, August 2009–August 2011**

Staffed sales register during peak store hours.

Technical Skills

- ❖ Proficient with both PCs and Macintosh computers
- ❖ Advanced user of Microsoft Office, Adobe Dreamweaver, Adobe Flash

Activities

- ❖ American Marketing Association, collegiate member
- ❖ Chicago Crew Team, four years

Using Paste Options

When you paste text in Word, a Paste Options button appears below the lower-right corner of the pasted text. You can click this button to open a menu with buttons that control the formatting of the pasted text. The buttons you see on the menu depend on what you are pasting. The buttons that you will use most often are Keep Source Formatting and Keep Text Only. The Keep Source Formatting option allows you to retain the formatting that the copied or cut item had in its original location. The Keep Text Only option inserts the text using the formatting of the surrounding text in the new

location. Another button that commonly appears is the Merge Formatting button, which combines the formatting from the cut or copied text with the formatting of the paragraph in which it is being pasted. When other buttons are available, they will have similar descriptive names that appear in a ScreenTip when you point to them. You can also use Live Preview to see the effect clicking each button will have.

You can preview the pasted material before actually pasting it by clicking the Paste button arrow, and then pointing to each of the Paste Options buttons on the menu that opens. (This is the same menu that appears when you click the Paste Options button after pasting the text.)

ACTIVITY

Use paste options.

1 At the top of the document, select **Stephen Konoski** and the **paragraph mark** at the end of the line.

2 On the Home tab, in the Clipboard group, click the **Copy button**.

3 Switch to the **Cover Letter document**. At the bottom of the letter, click after the word *Sincerely*, and then press the **Enter key** three times.

4 In the Clipboard group, click the **Paste button**. The copied text is pasted in the letter with the same character formatting as the original text—20 point, bold Verdana—and because you copied the paragraph mark as well, the same paragraph formatting—centered with blue shading—as the

Sometimes, the formatting is not copied with pasted text, even when you select the Keep Source Formatting button.

original text. The Paste Options button [icon] (Ctrl) ▾ appears below the lower-right corner of the pasted text.

5 Click the **Paste Options button** [icon] (Ctrl) ▾. A menu with buttons appears, similar to Exhibit 10-32.

6 On the Paste Options menu, point to the **Keep Source Formatting button** [icon]. This option retains the basic formatting of the pasted text but tries to match it to the styles used in the document in which you pasted the text.

> ➤ **Tip:** To select a paste option before pasting an item, click the Paste button arrow in the Clipboard group on the Home tab, and then click the paste option that you want.

7 On the Paste Options menu, point to the **Merge Formatting button** [icon]. Live Preview changes the pasted text so it matches the formatting in the

Organizing a Résumé

The document you worked on in this chapter is only one example of a résumé. You can organize the information in a résumé in many ways. The Resume Final document is organized chronologically. If you have more relevant experience, you might place a list of accomplishments or a summary of your qualifications at the top. Some career counselors advise job seekers to include a mission or an objective statement as the first item in a résumé. Before creating your own résumé, conduct research so you can decide on the best format. Then you can use the skills you learned in this chapter to format your résumé to best highlight your abilities.

letter; that is, it changes to 11-point Calibri. This option also removes the blue shading. However, the pasted text is still bold.

8 On the Paste Options menu, click the **Keep Text Only button** [icon]. The menu closes, and all the formatting is removed from the pasted text including the paragraph mark.

9 Press the **Enter key** to insert a blank paragraph between the name and the word *Enclosures*.

10 Save the document.

Exhibit 10-32 Pasted text with formatting still applied

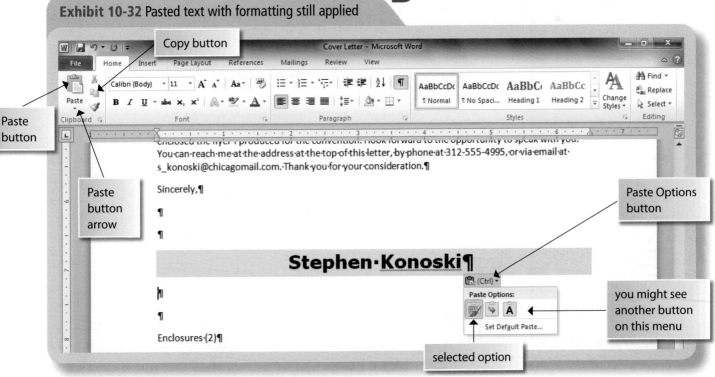

LO10.9 **Finding and Replacing Text**

When working with a longer document, you can waste a lot of time reading through the text to locate a particular word or phrase. It's more efficient to use the Navigation Pane to locate the word or phrase. If you want to replace text throughout a document, you can use the Find and Replace dialog box.

Finding Text

To find specific text in a document, first open the Navigation Pane by clicking the Find button in the Editing group on the Home tab. Then, in the Search Document box in the Navigation Pane, type the text for which you are searching. As you type, Word highlights every instance of the search text in the document, and a list of text snippets containing each instance of the search text appears in the Navigation Pane. You can click a snippet to go immediately to that location in the document.

ACTIVITY

Find text.

1 In the Cover Letter document, on the Home tab, in the Editing group, click the **Find button**. The Navigation Pane opens on the left side of the document window.

2 At the top of the Navigation Pane, click in the **Search Document box**, and then type **c**. Every letter *c* in the document is highlighted with yellow.

3 Continue typing **onvention** to complete the word *convention*. As you continue typing, the highlighting is removed from words that do not match the search text. All seven instances of the word *convention* are now highlighted in the document.

4 In the Navigation Pane, if it is not the current tab, click the **Browse the results from your current search tab** 🗎. Snippets of text surrounding each instance of the word *convention* appear on the tab. See Exhibit 10-33.

Exhibit 10-33 Navigation Pane with search results for *convention*

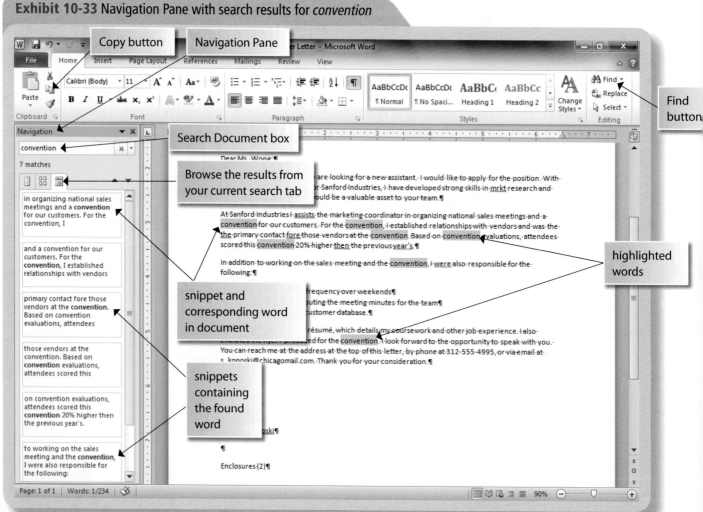

Narrowing a Search

To customize a search to narrow the results, you can click the Find Options and additional search commands arrow  to the right of the Search Document box in the Navigation Pane, and then click Options to open the Find Options dialog box (shown below). You can also click the More button on the Replace tab to expand the Find and Replace dialog box to display the Search Options section. For example, select the Find whole words only check box to search for complete words, or select the Match case check box to find text with the same case (upper or lower) as the search text.

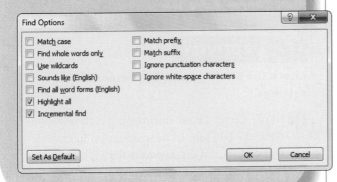

5 In the Navigation Pane, click the **first snippet**. In the document, the first instance of the word *convention* is highlighted with a blue box on top of the yellow highlight. You cannot simply type to replace this.

6 In the document, double-click the selected instance of the word **convention**, and then type **conference**. The snippets in the Navigation Pane and the highlighting in the document disappear.

7 In the Navigation Pane, click the **Next Search Result button** . The search is performed again, and the remaining six instances of *convention* are

> **Tip:** To make the search more specific, in the Navigation Pane, click the Find Options and additional search commands arrow  to the right of the Search Document box, and then click Options to open the Find Options dialog box.

highlighted in the document and listed as snippets in the Navigation Pane.

8 In the Navigation Pane title bar, click the **Close button** .

Replacing Specific Text

You can replace specific text using the Find and Replace dialog box, which you open by clicking the Replace button in the Editing group on the Home tab. This dialog box contains three tabs, with the Replace tab selected by default. Type the text you want to find in the Find what box, and the text you want to substitute in the Replace with box.

ACTIVITY

Replace specific text.

1 Press the **Ctrl+Home keys**. The insertion point moves to the beginning of the document.

2 On the Home tab, in the Editing group, click the **Replace button**. The Find and Replace dialog box opens, with the Replace tab displayed. The Find what box contains the search text you typed in the Search Document box in the Navigation Pane. See Exhibit 10-34.

3 Click in the **Replace with box**, and then type **conference**.

4 Click **Find Next**. The dialog box stays open, and in the document the next instance of the word *convention* is highlighted.

> **Tip:** To see additional options to narrow the search, click More at the bottom of the Replace tab.

5 In the dialog box, click **Replace**. The selected word in the document changes to *conference*, and the next instance of the word *convention* is selected.

Exhibit 10-34 Replace tab in the Find and Replace dialog box

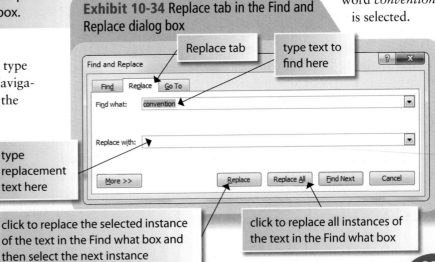

Using Replace All

Be careful when you use the Replace All command. If you search for a short word, such as *car*, and replace all instances of *car* with *auto*, and then use the Replace All command, you could end up replacing the text string *car* in words such as *careful* and *carry*, resulting in *autoeful* and *autory*, or you could end up replacing *Car* with *car*. One way to avoid this is to use the options described in the Narrowing the Search box to make the search more specific.

Mike Flippo/Shutterstock.com

6 In the dialog box, click **Replace All**. All instances of the word *convention* in the document are changed to *conference*, and another dialog box opens telling you that five replacements were made.

7 Click **OK**. The dialog box closes. The Find and Replace dialog box is still open.

8 Click **Close**. The Find and Replace dialog box closes.

9 Save the document.

LO10.10 Checking Spelling and Grammar

Before you print or send a document, you should always perform a final check of the spelling using the Spelling and Grammar Checker. This is commonly called using the spell checker or **spell checking**. The spell checker continually checks your document against the Office built-in dictionary. If it finds a word that doesn't match the correct spelling in the Office dictionary and was not fixed by AutoCorrect, or if a word, such as a

spell check To check a file for spelling and grammatical errors using the Spelling and Grammar Checker.

last name, is not in the dictionary, a red, wavy line appears beneath it. A red, wavy underline also appears if the same word appears twice in a row. The context in which words are used can also be checked, so words that are spelled correctly but might be used incorrectly are underlined with a blue, wavy line. For example, if you type *their* when you mean *there*, the word would be flagged. Of course, a computer program can't be 100 percent accurate in determining the correct context, so Word doesn't always catch every instance of this type of error. Finally, Word also checks the grammar in a document and flags potential grammatical errors with a green, wavy underline.

To make sure your document will be checked for all types of errors, you need to check the settings in the Word Options dialog box.

ACTIVITY

Check the Spelling and Grammar Checker settings.

1 In the Cover Letter document, on the Ribbon, click the **File tab**. In the navigation bar, click **Options**. The Word Options dialog box opens.

2 In the list in the left pane, click **Proofing**. The right pane of the dialog box changes to display options for proofing and correcting documents.

3 Near the bottom of the dialog box, under When correcting spelling and grammar in Word, click the **Use contextual spelling** check box to select it, if necessary. A check mark appears in the check box. The other check boxes in this section except Show readability statistics should already be checked. Compare your screen to Exhibit 10-35.

> ⚠ **Problem?** If any of the four selected check boxes in the When correcting spelling and grammar in Word section in Exhibit 10-35 are not selected on your screen, click them to select them now.

4 Click **OK**. The dialog box closes.

There are three ways to correct misspelled words. You can correct words individually by right-clicking flagged words and then using options on the shortcut menu that opens. You can check the entire document by opening the Spelling dialog box. Or, you can simply delete the misspelled word and retype it.

Exhibit 10-35 Word Options dialog box with Proofing selected

ACTIVITY

Check flagged words individually.

1 In the body of the letter, in the first paragraph, in the last sentence, right-click the flagged spelling error **analisis**. A shortcut menu opens. See Exhibit 10-36.

> **Tip:** If a flagged word is one you frequently mistype, on the shortcut menu, point to AutoCorrect, and then click the spelling you want to always replace your mistyped word.

2 On the shortcut menu, click **analysis**. The spelling of the word is corrected, and the red, wavy underline is removed.

3 In the second paragraph, in the first sentence, right-click the flagged grammar error **assists**. Only one word appears at the top of the shortcut menu as a suggested replacement, *assist*, and this is incorrect.

4 Click a blank area of the window to close the shortcut menu without selecting anything.

Checking Flagged Words Individually

You can right-click a word flagged with a colored wavy underline to open a shortcut menu containing suggestions for alternate spellings or a correction for a grammatical error as well as commands for ignoring the misspelled word or grammatical error or opening the Spelling dialog box.

Proofreading Your Document

Although the Spelling and Grammar Checker is a useful tool, there is no substitute for careful proofreading. Always take the time to read through your document to check for errors the Spelling and Grammar Checker might have missed. Keep in mind that the Spelling and Grammar Checker cannot pinpoint inaccurate phrases or poorly chosen words. You will have to find those yourself. To produce a professional document, you must read it carefully several times. It's also a good idea to ask one or two other people to read your documents as well; they might catch something you missed.

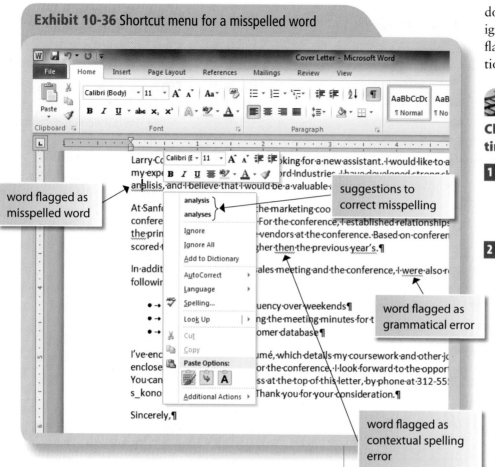

Exhibit 10-36 Shortcut menu for a misspelled word

word flagged as misspelled word

suggestions to correct misspelling

word flagged as grammatical error

word flagged as contextual spelling error

document, ignore this instance or ignore all instances, or add the flagged word to the built-in dictionary or to the AutoCorrect list.

ACTIVITY

Check the spelling in the entire document.

1 Press the **Ctrl+Home keys**. The insertion point moves to the beginning of the document.

2 On the Ribbon, click the **Review tab**. In the Proofing group, click the **Spelling & Grammar button**. The Spelling and Grammar: English (U.S.) dialog box opens. The first flagged word in the document, *mrkt*, is highlighted in the document and appears in red in the Not in Dictionary box in the dialog box. A list of correctly spelled words appears in the Suggestions box. The first word—*market*—in the Suggestions list is highlighted. This is the correct word. See Exhibit 10-37.

5 Click after the word *assists*, press the **Backspace key**, and then type **ed**. The word is changed to *assisted*, and the green, wavy underline is removed.

6 In the second paragraph, in the second sentence, right-click the flagged contextual spelling error **fore**. On the shortcut menu, click **for**. The menu closes and the spelling of the flagged word is changed to *for*.

Checking the Spelling in the Entire Document

To spell-check the entire document, click the Spelling & Grammar button in the Proofing group on the Review tab. This opens the Spelling and Grammar dialog box and highlights the first error after the insertion point. In the dialog box, the flagged word is colored with the same color as the wavy underline in the document. Options for handling the flagged error change depending on the type of error found. For example, when a duplicated word is found, you can ignore it or delete it; but when a word is flagged as a misspelled word, you can select a suggested correct spelling and then change it once, change all instances of the misspelling in the

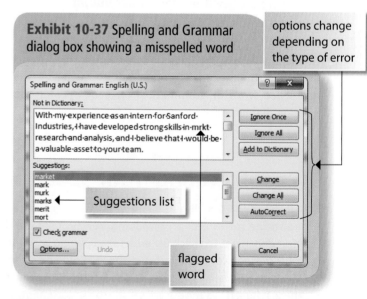

Exhibit 10-37 Spelling and Grammar dialog box showing a misspelled word

options change depending on the type of error

Suggestions list

flagged word

3 In the dialog box, click **Change**. The word is corrected in the document and the next flagged word is highlighted. In this case, the word *the* appears

Using the Research Pane

The Research pane is a feature that allows you to explore information in an encyclopedia, look up a definition, find a synonym, or translate a word. To open the Research pane, in the Proofing group on the Review tab, click the Research button. At the top of the Research pane, type the word or phrase you are looking up in the Search for box. To choose a research tool, click the arrow in the box below the Search for box at the top of the pane, and then click the tool you want to use. For example, if you want to look up a topic in the Encarta Dictionary, select that tool from the list. The research tools available are described below:

▶ **Encarta Dictionary**—look up the definition of a word

▶ **Thesaurus**—look up a synonym or antonym for a word using the U.S. English, French, or Spanish thesaurus

▶ **Translation**—look up the translation of a word; you can select the language you are translating from and the language you are translating to

▶ **Bing**—use the Bing search engine to return results for a word or phrase

▶ **Factiva iWorks**—use the Factiva iWorks business search engine to return business-related results for a word or phrase

▶ **HighBeam Research**—use the HighBeam Research periodical search engine to return links to articles in periodicals for a word or phrase

▶ **MSN Money Stock Quotes**—use the MSN Money Web site to look up stock quotes for a company

▶ **Thomson Gale Company Profiles**—look up a company profile in the Thomson Gale Company Profiles database

To open the Research pane directly to the Thesaurus to find synonyms of the currently selected word, click the Thesaurus button in the Proofing group on the Review tab; or right-click the word, point to Synonyms on the shortcut menu, and then click Thesaurus. (If you right-click a word, when you point to Synonyms, you'll see several synonyms listed above the Thesaurus command.) To open the Research pane directly to the Translation tool, click the Translate button in the Language group on the Review tab, and then click Translate Selected Text; or right-click a word, and then click Translate on the shortcut menu.

---

twice in a row. No suggested alternate spellings appear in the Suggestions box because the only choice here is to delete the repeated word or leave it as is.

4 Click **Delete**. The repeated word is deleted, and the next flagged word, *then*, is highlighted. This is a contextual spelling error.

5 Click **Change**. The word is corrected in the document and the next flagged error is highlighted. This is a grammar error.

Even with the contextual spell-checking feature, the spell checker doesn't catch every instance of a misused word.

6 Click **Explain**. The Word Help window opens with an explanation of the grammar problem. In this case, it describes subject-verb agreement.

7 In the Word Help window, click the **Close button** ☒. The dialog box closes.

8 In the Spelling and Grammar dialog box, click **Change**. The flagged word is corrected and the next flagged word is highlighted. This is a surname, so it should not be changed.

9 Click **Ignore All**. The word is not changed. This is the last flagged word in the document, so the Spelling and Grammar dialog box closes, and another dialog box

⚠ **Problem?** If another word in the presentation is flagged as misspelled, select the **correct spelling** in the Suggestions list, and then click the **Change button**.

opens telling you that the spelling and grammar check is complete.

10 In the dialog box, click **OK**. The dialog box closes.

11 Save the document.

LO10.11 Previewing and Printing Documents

To be sure the document is ready to print, and to avoid wasting paper and time, you should first review it on the Print tab in Backstage view to make sure it will appear as you want when printed. The Print tab contains options for printing the document and a preview displaying a full-page version of the document in the right pane. However, you cannot edit the document on the Print tab; it simply provides one last quick look

You can also use One Page and Two Page zoom commands to see entire pages at once.

at the document before printing. See Exhibit 10-38. The Print settings in the left pane allow you to control a variety of print options. For example, you can change the number of copies that will print. If your document consisted of more than one page, you can click the Next Page ▶ and Previous Page ◀ buttons at the bottom of the preview to scroll from page to page, or you can drag the scroll bar to the right of the preview down.

ACTIVITY

Preview the document.

1 Proof the Cover Letter document one last time and correct any remaining errors.

Exhibit 10-38 Print tab in Backstage view

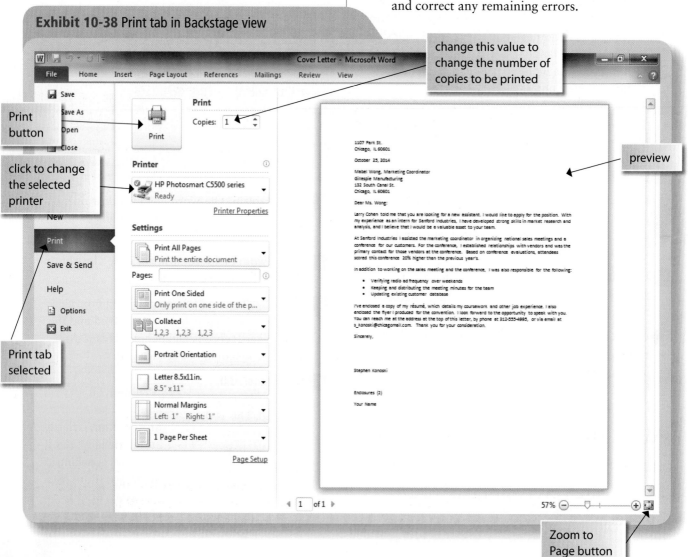

Creating an Envelope

Most printers are capable of printing envelopes. To create an envelope, you have to create a document with the address and return address sized and positioned correctly. To do this, click the Envelope button in the Create group on the Mailings tab to open the Envelopes and Labels dialog box with the Envelope tab selected. Type the recipient's name and address in the Delivery address box, type your return address in the Return address box, load an envelope in the printer, and then print it. If you click Add to Document instead of Print, the envelope will be added as a new page to the current document. Alternatively, if a letter is open in the document window, select the inside address and then open the Envelopes and Labels dialog box to have the recipient's name and address pasted in the Delivery address box. You can choose whether or not to include a return address; if you are using envelopes with a preprinted return address, you will not want to include a return address.

2 Press the **Ctrl+End keys** to move the insertion point to the end of the document, press the **Enter key**, and then type your name.

3 Save the Cover Letter document.

4 On the Ribbon, click the **File tab** to open Backstage view. In the navigation bar, click **Print**. The Print tab appears.

> ⚠ **Problem?** If the document doesn't appear to fill the preview pane, at the bottom-right corner of the window, click the **Zoom to Page button** 🔲.

5 Review your document and make sure its overall layout matches the document in Exhibit 10-38. If you notice a problem with paragraph breaks or spacing, click the **File tab** on the Ribbon, edit the document, and then repeat Step 4.

6 Make sure your printer is turned on and contains paper.

7 Click the **Print button** in the left pane of the Print tab. Backstage view closes and the letter prints.

8 On the Ribbon, click the **File tab**. In the navigation bar, click **Close**. The Cover Letter document closes, and the Resume Final document is the current document again.

9 Proof the document one last time and correct any remaining errors.

10 Replace *Stephen Konoski* at the top of the document with your name.

11 Save the document.

12 View the Resume Final document on the Print tab in Backstage view.

> ⚠ **Problem?** If the Resume Final document does not fit on one page, click the **1 Page Per Sheet button** near the bottom of the Print tab in Backstage view, point to **Scale to Paper Size**, scroll down the submenu, and then click **Letter 8.5×11in.**

13 Print the document, and then close it.

Quiz Yourself

1. What are nonprinting characters and how do you display them?

2. How do you insert symbols that are not included in the AutoCorrect list?

3. How do you undo more than one action at a time?

4. What does the New from existing command do?

5. When you use drag and drop to move text, can you next use the Paste command to paste that text somewhere else? Why or why not?

6. According to the chapter, what is a point?

7. What is the default paragraph spacing in a Word document? What is the default line spacing?

8. What is justified text?

9. Where are the default tab stops? What happens to them when you insert a new tab stop?

10. When you create a bulleted or a numbered list, what character is inserted after the bullet symbol or the number, and what type of indent is applied to the paragraph?

11. Describe two ways to indent a paragraph one-half inch from the left margin.

12. What tool will copy the format of a block of text to another block of text?

13. What happens when you type text in the Search Document box in the Navigation Pane?

14. How are possible spelling errors, contextual spelling errors, and grammatical errors flagged in a document? (Specify the colors used.)

15. What does the Print tab in Backstage view show?

Practice It

Practice It 10-1

1. Start Word. Display the rulers, show nonprinting characters, and then save the document as **Complaint Draft**.

2. Type the date **March 10, 2014** using AutoComplete for *March*.

3. Press the Enter key, and then type the following inside address, using the default paragraph spacing and allowing AutoCorrect to change *Cafe* to *Café*:

   David Lefevre, Manager

   Corner Café

   132 South Central St.

   Jacksonville, FL 32099

   Dear Mr. Lefevre:

   I am writing to express my disappointment at the service my colleagues and I received at our corporate function to celebrate the launch of our new product EasyGo.

4. After *EasyGo*, type **(tm)** allowing AutoCorrect to change it to ™.

5. Undo the AutoCorrection that changed *(tm)* to ™.

6. Press the Spacebar. Type **You can reach me at** and then type your email address followed by a period. Press the Enter key, and then type your name.

7. Remove the hyperlink formatting from your email address.

8. Remove the spacing after the first three paragraphs in the inside address.

9. Save and close the document.

10. Open the data file **Complaint** located in the Chapter 10\Practice It folder. Use the Save As command to save the file as **Complaint Letter**. Use the New from existing command to open the file **Menu** located in the Chapter 10\Practice It folder. Save this file as **Cafe Menu**.

11. In the Complaint Letter document, in the body of the letter, in the first paragraph, select *we did not enjoy the evening* and replace it with **instead of the usual delightful service**. At the end of the letter, replace *Your Name* in the closing with your name.

12. Use drag and drop to move the second paragraph (which begins with *Our main course*) after the third paragraph so it becomes the third paragraph. Then use drag and drop to copy *Corner Café* from the second sentence in the first paragraph to the end of the last sentence in the first paragraph after *from*.

13. Switch to the Cafe Menu document. In the third line, delete the *e* from *Fixe* and use the Symbol button to insert **é** so the word is *Fixé*.

14. Select all the text in the document, change the font to Copperplate Gothic Light, and change the font size to 14 points. Change the font size of the text in the second paragraph to 12 points.

15. In the first line, make *Corner Café* bold, increase the font size to 20 points, and change the font color to Red, Accent 2.

16. Center align the first two paragraphs.

17. In the third paragraph, add a Right Tab stop at the 6-inch mark on the ruler, and then drag it to the 6.5-inch mark. Insert a tab character after *Prix Fixé Meal*, and then type **$35.00**.

18. Increase the spacing above the second to last paragraph to 42 points. Increase the spacing before and after the third paragraph to 24 points.

19. Select all the text and the paragraph mark in the lines starting with *Appetizer*, *Entrée*, and *Dessert*. Format the lines as bold, and then format them as a numbered list using Arabic numerals followed by a period. Decrease the indent so they are aligned at the left margin.

20. Format the three paragraphs under *Appetizer*, the four paragraphs under *Entrée*, and the three paragraphs under *Dessert* as bulleted lists using the right pointing arrowhead in the Bullet Library.

Increase the indent so that the bullet character is at the .5-inch mark on the ruler.

21. Add a custom border to the top and bottom of the paragraph containing *Prix Fixé Meal*. Use the style that appears at the bottom of the Style list without scrolling on the Borders tab in the Borders and Shading dialog box; the Red, Accent 2 color; and a width of 3 points.

22. Add Red, Accent 2, Lighter 80% shading to the first paragraph.

23. Copy the formatting of the first paragraph to the second to last paragraph (*Make your reservation today!*). Change the spacing before this paragraph back to 42 points.

24. Copy the first paragraph to the Clipboard. Switch to the Complaint Letter document. Paste the copied text as the second line in the inside address as text only. Add a paragraph break if necessary after the pasted text.

25. Select all the text in the document, and then change the line spacing to single spacing.

26. Find all instances of the word *function* in the Complaint Letter document. Change the first instance to **party**, and then use the Replace dialog box to replace all other instances with the word **event**.

27. In the first paragraph, correct the spelling of the misspelled word *colleagues* using the shortcut menu. Then use the Spelling and Grammar dialog box to check the rest of the document. If a word is flagged but spelled correctly, ignore it.

28. Save the Complaint Letter document, examine it in the preview pane on the Print tab in Backstage view, and then print it. Close the Complaint Letter document.

29. In the Cafe Menu document, add your name in the last paragraph at the end of the document. Save the document.

30. Examine the Cafe Menu document in the preview pane on the Print tab in Backstage view, and then print it. Close the Cafe Menu document.

Practice It 10-2

1. Open a new blank document and then save the document as **Thank You Letter**.

2. Change the font to Candara, change the font size to 12 points, and change the line spacing to single spaced.

3. Type the following as the return address:
   Baltimore Community Center
   248 19th St.
   Baltimore, MD 21201

4. Press the Enter key, and then add **September 15, 2014** as the date.

5. Press the Enter key, and then type the following as the inside address:
   Susan Tyson
   Career Counseling
   12 Bayview Rd.
   Baltimore, MD 21201

6. Press the Enter key, type the salutation **Dear Ms. Tyson:** and then press the Enter key.

7. Type the following paragraph: **Thank you for agreeing to give a presentation describing job search strategies. We surveyed our members, and they were hoping that you would address the following questions as part of your presentation:**

8. Press the Enter key, and then type the following questions as separate paragraphs:
   How do I learn how to network?
   What is the best way to find job listings?
   How do I prepare for an interview?
   Do I have to dress in a business suit?

9. Insert a new paragraph after the last question, and then type **Thank you again for your time.** Press the Enter key, and then type the complimentary closing **Sincerely,** (including the comma).

10. Press the Enter key three times, and then type your name. Press the Enter key again, and type **Baltimore Community Center**.

11. Format the four questions as a numbered list, and then increase the indent so that the numbers are aligned at the .5-inch mark.

12. Format the four questions as bold.

13. Remove the extra space after the first two lines in the return address, after the first three lines in the inside address, and after your name in the closing.

14. Increase the space before the first line in the letter to 30 points.

15. Change the alignment of the return address, the date, and the closing to right-aligned.

16. Check the spelling and grammar in the document and correct any errors.

17. Save the document, preview and print it, and then close it.

On Your Own

On Your Own 10-1

1. Create a new document based on the Equity Fax template. (*Hint*: Click the Sample templates button on the New tab in Backstage view.) This template contains placeholders that you click once to select and replace with text.

2. Save the document as **Price Quote**.

3. Next to *To:*, click Type the recipient name to select the placeholder. Type your instructor's name.

4. Next to *From:*, click the name, delete it, and then type your name.

5. Next to *Fax:*, type **617–555–2098**.

6. Next to *Pages:*, type **2**.

7. Next to *Phone:*, type **617–555–2090**.

8. Next to *Re:*, type **Quote to complete remodeling project**.

9. Next to *Date:*, click the placeholder, click the arrow that appears, and then click Today below the calendar.

10. Next to *CC:*, click the placeholder, click the small tab on the left edge of the placeholder, and then press the Delete key.

11. In the line of check boxes, click the check box next to *For Review*, and then type **x**.

12. Below *Comments*, click the placeholder, and then type the following. In the paragraphs containing prices, press the Tab key instead of the Spacebar before the price.

Per your request, here is my quote for completing your remodeling project:

5 Windows $1,325.79

Skylight $399.99

Labor $900.00

Total $2,625.78
Please let me know if you have any questions.

13. Change the size of the text below *Comments* to 14 points.

14. Format the dollar amounts in bold.

15. Indent all the text under *Comments* one-half inch. Indent all the text under *Comments* from the right one inch.

16. Add shading using the Tan, Background 2 color behind all the text below *Comments*. (Note that this document uses a different color palette than the other documents you have created.)

17. Indent the four paragraphs containing prices another inch. Notice that the shading is no longer a rectangle behind all the text.

18. Decrease the indent of the four paragraphs containing prices one inch.

19. In the four paragraphs containing the prices, set a Left Tab stop at the 1-inch mark on the ruler, and set a Decimal Tab stop at the 3-inch mark on the ruler. Insert a tab before the first character in each of the four lines containing prices.

20. Save the document, examine it in the preview pane on the Print tab in Backstage view, print it, and then close the document.

ADDITIONAL STUDY TOOLS

Chapter 10

IN THE BOOK

▶ Complete end-of-chapter exercises

▶ Study tear-out Chapter Review Card

ONLINE

▶ Complete additional end-of-chapter exercises

▶ Take practice quiz to prepare for tests

▶ Review key term flash cards (online, printable, and audio)

▶ Play "Beat the Clock" and "Memory" to quiz yourself

▶ Watch the videos "Insert the Date with AutoComplete," "Use AutoCorrect," "Change Font and Font Size," "Adjust Paragraph Spacing," "Change the Alignment of Paragraphs," "Create Bulleted Lists," and other concept videos

Formatting a Long Document

Introduction

Although a shorter document is useful for providing a summary or snapshot view, longer documents are a fact of life in the business world, the government arena, and personal life. Businesspeople and government workers often create long documents for developing business plans, proposing new ideas or products, evaluating current strategies, and explaining new products or approaches. Members of the academic world commonly use long documents when applying for grants, documenting research, submitting journal articles, and even writing books.

Word provides many tools for working with longer documents and for making them easier to read. You can change the format of headings to make them stand out, add page numbers and other information at the top or bottom of pages, add notes at the bottom of a page to clarify statements in the document, and so on. When a document contains information based on other documents, you need to include the source in your document. Word provides tools to do this easily and to give your document a consistent look.

Learning Objectives

After studying the material in this chapter, you will be able to:

LO11.1 Work with styles

LO11.2 Work with themes

LO11.3 Change the style set

LO11.4 Work with the document outline

LO11.5 Change the margins

LO11.6 Control pagination

LO11.7 Add page numbers, headers, and footers

LO11.8 Create citations and a list of works cited

LO11.9 Create footnotes and endnotes

LO11.1 Working with Styles

A **style** is a named set of formatting instructions. All text has a style applied to it. Unless you change to a different style, text is formatted with the Normal style, which, as you have seen, is text formatted as 11-point Calibri in a left-aligned paragraph with line spacing set to 1.15 and 10 points of space after the paragraph.

The Normal style is part of the **Normal template**, which is the template on which all Word documents are based. In Chapter 10, you learned that a template is a file that contains formatting and usually sample content to guide you as you develop your own content. If you don't select a specific template, new blank docu-

style A named set of formatting instructions.

Normal template The template on which all Word documents are based.

In longer Word documents, applying consistent formatting, using an effective organization, and adding information helps to convey the important points in the document more successfully.

Yuri Arcurs/Shutterstock.com

ments are based on the Normal template. The Normal template does not contain any text or graphics, but it does include the Normal style and other built-in styles.

Using styles instead of direct formatting saves time and makes the elements in a document consistent. For example, if you want all the headings in a document to be bold, dark red, 14-point Cambria, and centered, you could create a style named Heading that includes all those formatting instructions, which you apply to every heading in the document. If you then change your mind and decide you want the headings to be 16-point Arial on a shaded blue background, you simply change the style definition, and then all the text that has the Heading style applied to it will update to the new style. When you change the text formatting, such as by applying bold, or the paragraph formatting, such as by changing the alignment, you are applying direct formatting. **Direct formatting** overrides the style currently applied, but it does not change the style definition.

direct formatting Formatting that overrides the style currently applied.

There are five types of styles. A **paragraph style** formats an entire paragraph, and can include both paragraph and text formatting instructions. The Heading style described in the previous paragraph would be a paragraph style. Another commonly used style type is the character style. **Character style** definitions include only text formatting instructions. A third style type, the **linked style**, behaves as a paragraph or a character style depending on what is selected when you apply the style. If you select only a character or a few words, the style is applied as a character style, and any paragraph formatting included in the style definition is ignored. If you apply a linked style to a paragraph, it is treated as a paragraph style—in other words, it applies both paragraph and text formatting. The other two style types are table and list styles, which are used to format, as the names indicate, tables and lists.

Style definitions include more than text and paragraph formatting instructions and the style type. They also specify which style the style is based on—often the Normal style. Paragraph and linked style definitions also specify which style will be applied to the next paragraph created when you press the Enter key. For paragraphs formatted with the Normal style, the next paragraph created is also formatted with the Normal style. For some styles, such as a style that is intended to format headings, the style for the next paragraph is usually the Normal style or another style created for body text. That makes sense, because you typically only want to format a single paragraph with a heading style.

Word comes with many built-in styles, and the most commonly used are listed in the Styles gallery in the Styles group on the Home tab. See Exhibit 11-1.

Understanding Linked Styles

Linked styles can help you work more efficiently. For example, you could create a heading style that formats text as bold and with a color to match the colors in a company logo, and also center the text. You might want to format the company name whenever it appears in text using the same color and bold formatting as the headings, but without changing the alignment of the paragraph containing the company name. You could create a second style using a character style type. But if the heading style was a linked style instead of a paragraph style, you could use that heading style to apply only the text formatting to the company name. If you apply a style and the results aren't what you expected—that is, if you expected paragraph formatting to be applied and only character formatting was applied or vice versa—make sure the correct elements are selected before you apply the style. For example, to be sure that the paragraph formatting in a linked style definition is applied when you want it, make sure the insertion point is positioned in the paragraph with no text selected, or that all of the text in the paragraph is selected.

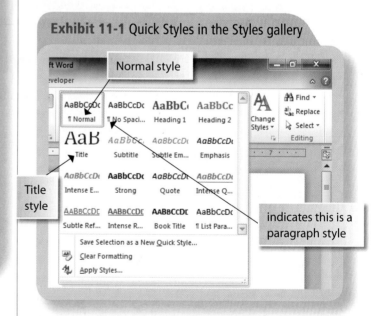

Exhibit 11-1 Quick Styles in the Styles gallery

ysfylmz/Shutterstock.com

paragraph style A style type that includes instructions for formatting text and paragraphs.

character style A style type that includes instructions only for formatting text.

linked style A style type that acts as a paragraph style if applied to a paragraph and as a character style if applied to text.

Don't worry about identifying the style type of a style. Just be sure to correctly select the text to which you want to apply the style.

Styles that appear in the Styles gallery are called **Quick Styles**. Each built-in style has a name that reflects its suggested use. For example, the Title style is intended for formatting the title at the beginning of a document, and the various Heading styles are intended to format different levels of headings. The Quick Styles are designed to complement each other and help you create a document with a cohesive look. In the Styles gallery, a paragraph symbol (¶) appears next to the names of the Quick Styles that are paragraph styles. Styles without the paragraph symbol next to their names are either character or linked styles. In the Styles gallery, the Normal, No Spacing, and List Paragraph styles are paragraph styles; the Heading, Title and Subtitle, and two Quote styles are linked styles; and the rest of the styles (the Strong style, the three Emphasis styles, and the two Reference styles) are character styles.

Heading Styles

You can choose from different levels of heading styles. The highest level, Heading 1, is used for the major headings in a document and applies the most noticeable formatting, with a larger font than all the other heading styles. (In heading styles, the highest level has the lowest number.)

Heading 1
Heading 2
Heading 3

The Heading 2 style is used for headings that are subordinate to the highest level headings; it applies slightly less prominent formatting than the Heading 1 style. There are nine built-in heading styles. When you apply a heading style, the font labeled (*Headings*) in the Font list is applied to the text.

Applying a Quick Style

To apply a Quick Style, select the text or paragraph to which you want to apply the style, and then click the Quick Style name in the Styles gallery. When you apply a style, that style is selected in the Styles gallery.

When you create a new document, only two heading styles, Heading 1 and Heading 2, appear in the Styles gallery. If you apply the Heading 2 style to text, the Heading 3 style is added to the Styles gallery. As you apply each more subordinate heading style, the next level of heading style is added to the gallery.

To apply a style that does not appear in the Styles gallery, open the Styles pane by clicking the Dialog Box Launcher in the Styles group, and then click the style in the list.

ACTIVITY

Apply Quick Styles.

1 Open the data file **Proposal** located in the Chapter 11\ Chapter folder. Save the document as **Biking Proposal**.

2 Select the first paragraph in the document (the title line).

3 On the Home tab, in the Styles group, click the **More button** ⬇. The Styles gallery opens. Refer back to Exhibit 11-1.

4 Point to several of the styles in the gallery to see the Live Preview on the selected paragraph, and then click the **Title style**. The gallery closes and the Title style is applied to the selected paragraph. The row of styles visible in the Styles group on the Home tab is scrolled to display the style you just applied—the Title style. The Title style is a linked style and changes the text to blue, 26-point Cambria, adds a blue border below the text, and changes the space after the paragraph from 10 points to 15 points. Cambria is the font labeled (*Headings*) at the top of the font list. See Exhibit 11-2.

5 Select the nonadjacent heading paragraphs **Overview** and **Program Development**.

6 In the Styles group, click the **up arrow** ⬆ to scroll the gallery up one row, and then click the **Heading 1 style**. The Heading 1 style is a linked style that formats the selected paragraphs in bold, blue, 14-point Cambria, removes all the space after each paragraph, and changes the space before each selected paragraph to 24 points.

Quick Style A style that appears in a gallery.

Exhibit 11-2 Title style applied to selected text

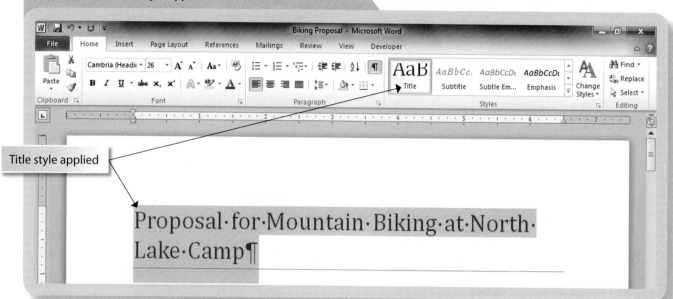

Title style applied

Proposal·for·Mountain·Biking·at·North·
Lake·Camp¶

7 Scroll down, and then select the **Budget heading paragraph**. In the Styles group, click the **More button** ⊡. Notice that only two Heading styles are in the gallery.

8 In the Styles gallery, click the **Heading 2 style**. The selected text is formatted with the Heading 2 style, which is similar to the Heading 1 style but the color is a little lighter shade of blue, the size of the text is 13 points, and the space before the paragraph is 10 points.

9 In the Styles group, click the **More button** ⊡. Notice that the Heading 3 style has been added to the gallery.

10 Use the list below to apply Heading Quick Styles to the following paragraphs:

Minimum Funding—$200	Heading 3
Moderate Funding—$3,200	Heading 3
Questions	Heading 2
Opportunity	Heading 1
Description of Program	Heading 1
Issues to Consider	Heading 2
Potential Trip Routes	Heading 2
East	Heading 3
North	Heading 3
West	Heading 3
South	Heading 3

11 At the top of the document, under the Program Development heading, in the first line, select **key**.

12 Open the Styles gallery, and then click the **Emphasis style**. The Emphasis style is a character style. The selected text is formatted with the Emphasis style, which applies italic formatting to text.

Modifying a Quick Style

If you want to change some parts of the definition of a Quick Style, you can modify it. To modify a Quick Style, first apply the Quick Style to text or a paragraph, and then modify the formatting of the text or paragraph using direct formatting. Next, right-click the Quick Style name in the Styles gallery, and then on the shortcut menu, click Update <*Quick Style Name*> to Match Selection (where <*Quick Style Name*> is replaced by the name of the style).

Modify a Quick Style.

1 Scroll down, and then select the **Budget heading paragraph**.

2 Reduce the font size of the selected text to **12 points**.

3 On the Home tab, in the Font group, click the **Bold button** B to deselect it, and then click the **Underline button** U. The bold formatting is removed and the selected text is underlined.

Exhibit 11-3 Redefined Heading 2 style

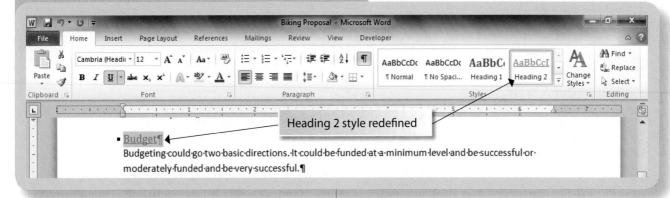

4 On the Home tab, in the Styles group, right-click the **Heading 2 style**. On the shortcut menu, click **Update Heading 2 to Match Selection**. The style is redefined to match the formatting changes you made to the Budget heading, and all the headings with the Heading 2 style applied now match this style. See Exhibit 11-3.

5 Select the **Minimum Funding—$200 heading paragraph**. Remove the bold formatting.

6 In the Styles group, right-click the **Heading 3 style**. On the shortcut menu, click **Update Heading 3 to Match Selection**. Notice that the formatting of the Moderate Funding—$3,200 heading changed to match the new style definition.

Saving a Style to the Template

The modified style is saved only with the current document. If you want to make the modified style available to all documents created based on the current template (even if it is the Normal template), right-click the Quick Style name, and then click Modify on the shortcut menu to open the Modify Style dialog box. In the Modify Style dialog box, click the New documents based on this template option button at the bottom of the dialog box, and then click OK.

Creating a New Quick Style

You might find that you need to create a new style for your document. The easiest way to create a new Quick Style is to format text in the way that you want, and then create the style based on the formatted text. To do this, select the formatted text, click the More button in the Styles group, and then click Save Selection as a New Quick Style to open the Create New Style from Formatting dialog box. You can name and save the style from this dialog box.

New Quick Styles are created as linked styles. To change this, in the Create New Style from Formatting dialog box, click Modify to open a larger version of the Create New Style from Formatting dialog box, click the Style type arrow, and then select the style type from the list.

Remember that part of a style definition is the style on which the style is based. So when you create a new style based upon the formatting of selected text, the new style retains a connection to the original style. If you modify the original style, these changes will also be applied to the new style. For example, suppose you need to create a new style that will be used exclusively for formatting the heading *Budget* in all upcoming reports. You could start by selecting text formatted with the Heading 1 style, change the font color of the selected text to purple, and then save the formatting of the selected text as a new style named *Budget*. If you then modify the Heading 1 style—perhaps by adding italics—the text in the document that is formatted with the Budget style will also have italics, because it is based on the Heading 1 style. This connection between a new style and the style on which it is based enforces a consistent look among styles, helping to create a document with a coherent design. To take full advantage of this feature, you need to think carefully about what style you want to use as the basis for a new style. For example, if you are creating a new style that will be used as a heading, you should base that new style on a heading style.

Finally, when you create a new paragraph or linked style, the style for the next paragraph created when you press the Enter key is the new style. To change this, open the larger version of the Create New Style from Formatting dialog box, as described above, click the Style for following paragraph arrow, and then select the style you want.

ACTIVITY

Create a new Quick Style.

1 At the top of the document, under the Over-view heading, in the first line, select **North Lake Camp**. In documents produced at camp, the camp name is in a different font and a dark green color.

2 Change the font of the selected text to **Candara**. Change the color to **Olive Green, Accent 3, Darker 50%**.

3 In the Styles group, click the **More button** ⊡. Below the gallery, click **Save Selection as a New Quick Style**. A small Create New Style from Formatting dialog box opens with the temporary style name selected in the Name box. See Exhibit 11-4.

Exhibit 11-5 Large Create New Style from Formatting dialog box

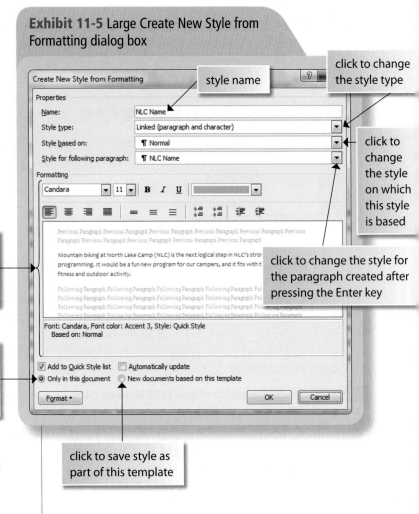

formatting applied to the text before the dialog box was opened

keep selected to save the style only with the current document

click to save style as part of this template

Exhibit 11-4 Small Create New Style from Formatting dialog box

type new style name here

4 In the Name box, type **NLC Name**.

5 Click **Modify**. The larger Create New Style from Formatting dialog box opens. See Exhibit 11-5.

6 Click the **Style type arrow**, and then click **Character**.

7 Click **OK**. The dialog box closes and the new Quick Style is added to the Styles gallery.

8 In the Styles group, if you don't see the NLC Name style, click the **up scroll arrow** ⏶. The new NLC Name style is the second style in the gallery and is selected.

9 Under the Overview heading, in the parentheses in the same line of text, select **NLC**. In the Styles group, click the **NLC Name style**. See Exhibit 11-6.

10 In the Editing group, click the **Replace button**. The Find and Replace dialog box opens with NLC in the Find what box.

11 Click in the **Replace with box**, type **NLC**, and then click **More**. The dialog box expands to show additional options.

12 At the bottom of the dialog box, click **Format**, and then click **Style**. The Replace Style dialog box opens.

13 In the list, select **NLC Name**, and then click **OK**. The dialog box closes, and Style: NLC Name appears under the Replace with box.

Exhibit 11-6 Custom style applied to text

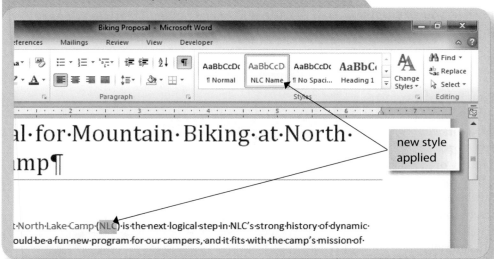

14 Click **Replace All**. Click **Yes** in the dialog box that asks if you want to continue searching from the beginning of the document.

15 Click **OK** in the dialog box that tells you that 13 replacements were made. All instances of NLC formatted with the Normal style are replaced with NLC formatted with the NLC Name style.

16 Click **Close** to close the dialog box.

17 Save the document.

Using the Styles Pane

The Styles pane displays the complete list of styles available to a document, as well as indicates the style type of each style. To open the Styles pane, click the Dialog Box Launcher in the Styles group on the Home tab. The list of styles displayed when you open the Styles pane is the list of recommended styles. For new documents, this means it lists the styles that appear in the Styles gallery. To see the complete list of styles available, click the Options link at the bottom of the Styles pane, and then in the Style Pane Options dialog box that opens, click the Select styles to show arrow, and then click All styles. If you want to add a style to the Styles gallery, point to the style name in the Styles pane, click the arrow that appears, and then click Add to Quick Style Gallery.

The symbols to the right of each style name in the Styles pane indicate the style type: Paragraph styles are labeled with ¶, character styles with **a**, and linked styles with ¶a. At the bottom of the Styles pane, you can select the Show Preview check box to see the format of each style, and select the Disable Linked Styles check box to change all linked styles to paragraph styles.

LO11.2 **Working with Themes**

After you format a document with a variety of styles, you can alter the look of the document by changing the document's theme. A **theme** is a coordinated set of colors, fonts, and effects. Created by professional designers, themes ensure that a document has a polished, coherent look. Forty-four themes are included in Office. The default theme for new documents is the Office theme.

Every theme assigns a font to headings and to body text. These two theme fonts are always listed at the top of the Fonts menu with the labels *(Headings)* and *(Body)* on the right. You have already seen this when you opened the Fonts menu to apply a different font. Some themes use one font for headings and another for body text; other themes use the same font for both elements. In the Office theme, the heading font is Cambria, and the body font is Calibri. If you change the theme, the theme fonts in the Font list change to match the fonts for the new theme.

This is the Office theme's heading font, Cambria.

This is the Office theme's body font, Calibri.

This is the Newsprint theme's heading font, Impact.

This is the Newsprint theme's body font, Times New Roman.

When you type text in a new document, the text is formatted with the body text font. If you change the theme, text formatted with the theme fonts changes to

theme A coordinated set of colors, fonts, and effects.

the format of the new theme's fonts. If you change the font of text to a non-theme font, when you change the theme, the font will not change.

You have also already seen the colors associated with a theme. When you displayed the color palette to change the font color or a paragraph border color, the colors under Theme Colors are the coordinated colors of the current theme. This set of colors changes when you change the theme. So if you apply one of these theme colors using direct formatting, or if you apply a style, such as a heading style, that formats text with color, when you apply a different theme, the color will change to match the equivalent color in the new theme. The Theme Colors are coordinated to look good together, so if you are going to use multiple colors in a document (perhaps for paragraph shading and font color), it's a good idea to stick with the Theme Colors.

Applying a New Theme

To change the theme, click the Themes button in the Themes group on the Page Layout tab, and then select the theme you want in the gallery. The new theme is applied to the entire document and all the elements within it, with the colors and fonts changing to match the colors and fonts of the new theme.

ACTIVITY

Change the document's theme.

1 Scroll the document so you can see the title at the top of the window and the Budget heading near the bottom of the window.

2 On the Ribbon, click the **Page Layout tab**. In the Themes group, point to the **Themes button**. The name of the current theme, the Office Theme, appears in a ScreenTip. See Exhibit 11-7.

Exhibit 11-7 Themes button

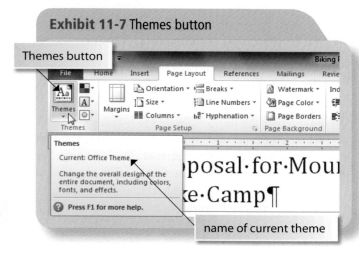

3 Click the **Themes button**. The Themes gallery opens. See Exhibit 11-8.

Exhibit 11-8 Themes gallery

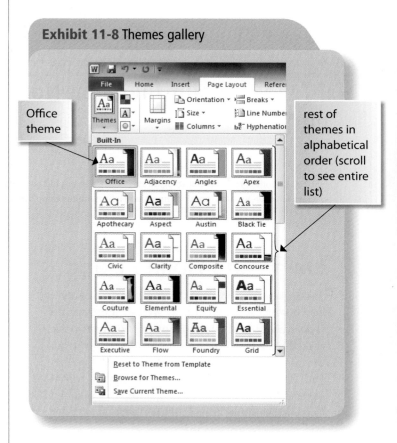

4 In the gallery, point to the **Austin theme** to see a Live Preview in the document. The fonts in the document change, and the color of the text formatted with the Title style and with the Heading styles changes. Notice that the changes you made to the Heading 2 style definition are retained.

5 Point to several other themes, and then scroll down and click the **Urban theme**. The fonts and colors in the document change to those used in the Urban theme.

6 On the Ribbon, click the **Home tab**. In the Font group, click the **Font box arrow**. The Font gallery opens. Notice that at the top, the Headings font is Trebuchet MS and the Body font is Georgia.

7 Click a blank area of the document to close the Font list, select the **title**, and then in the Font group, click the **Font Color button arrow** [A ▾]. The color palette opens. The Theme Colors in the palette are the Urban theme colors. The Theme Colors you saw previously were the Office theme colors. See Exhibit 11-9.

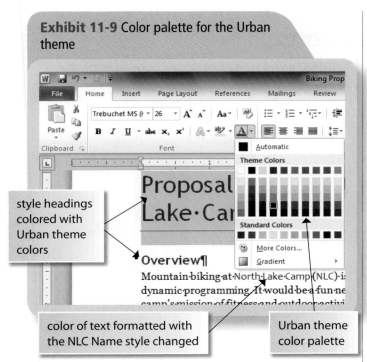

Exhibit 11-9 Color palette for the Urban theme

style headings colored with Urban theme colors

color of text formatted with the NLC Name style changed

Urban theme color palette

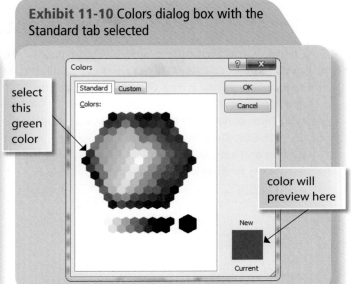

Exhibit 11-10 Colors dialog box with the Standard tab selected

select this green color

color will preview here

8 Scroll through the document to examine the differences. One unexpected change is to the NLC Name style.

9 At the top of the document, under the Overview heading, select **North Lake Camp**. In the Font group, click the **Font Color button arrow** A ▾. The selected color, as indicated by the orange box around the color in the palette, is Purple, Accent 3, Darker 50%. This color is in the same position as the theme color you selected when you created the style. There is no dark green color in the current theme color palette, and the greens in the Standard Colors are too bright. The font did not change because Candara was not one of the theme fonts.

10 Below the palette, click **More Colors**. The color palette closes and the Colors dialog box opens with the Custom tab selected.

11 Click the **Standard tab**. The Standard tab is selected, displaying a hexagon composed of small colored hexagons. See Exhibit 11-10.

12 On the left, in the row above the center row, click the **leftmost green hexagon**. The New portion of the preview box changes to the dark green color you selected.

13 Click **OK**. The dialog box closes and the selected text is reformatted with the dark green color.

14 In the Font group, click the **Font Color button arrow** A ▾. A new row named Recent Colors appears below the Standard Colors row. This row will be available in every document you work on during this session of Word.

15 Close the color palette without selecting a different color.

16 In the Styles group, right-click the **NLC Name style**, and then click **Update NLC Name to Match Selection**. The style definition is updated and all the text with that style applied changes color to match the new definition.

⚠ **Problem?** If the instances of *NLC* in the document did not change from the purple color to the new green color, right-click the **NLC Name style**, click **Select All 14 Instances** on the shortcut menu, and then click the **NLC Name style**.

Modifying a Theme

Once you have chosen a theme, you can change any of the three elements that make up the theme: the fonts, the colors, and the effects. To do this, click the Fonts, Colors, or Effects button in the Themes group on the Page Layout tab, and then select the fonts, colors, or effects from another theme. You can also change the fonts and colors by clicking the appropriate command on the Change Styles button menu in the Styles group on the Home tab.

Creating New Theme Fonts and Colors

If none of the theme font sets suits your needs, you can click the Create New Theme Fonts command on the Fonts button menu in the Themes group on the Page Layout tab, or on the Fonts submenu on the Change Styles button menu in the Styles group on the Home tab. In the Create New Theme Fonts dialog box, select a heading and a body text font, and type a name for the new theme font set in the Name box.

You can customize theme colors by clicking the Create New Theme Colors command on the Colors button menu in the Themes group on the Page Layout tab, or on the Colors submenu on the Change Styles button menu in the Styles group on the Home tab. In the Create New Theme Colors dialog box, select a color for each theme element

listed, and type a name for the new color set in the Name box. In both cases, the new, custom font set and theme color set will be listed at the top of their respective menus.

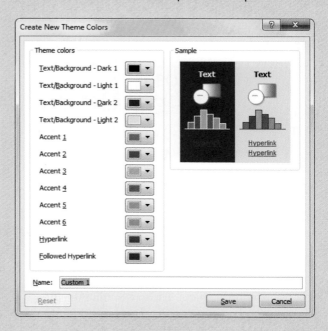

ACTIVITY

Modify the theme fonts and colors.

1. On the Ribbon, click the **Page Layout tab**. In the Themes group, click the **Theme Fonts button** [Aa]. The Theme Fonts menu opens.

2. Scroll to the bottom of the list to see that Urban is selected. See Exhibit 11-11.

3. Point to several of the themes listed to see the Live Preview, scroll up the list, and then click the **Module fonts**. The Module theme fonts (Corbel for both headings and body text) are applied to the document.

4. In the Themes group, click the **Theme Colors button** [■]. Scroll down the list to see that the Urban color palette is selected. See Exhibit 11-12.

5. Point to several of the themes listed to see the Live Preview, and then click the **Grid theme colors**. The elements in the document formatted with theme colors change to the corresponding theme colors of the Grid theme.

Exhibit 11-11 Theme Fonts menu

Exhibit 11-12 Theme Colors menu

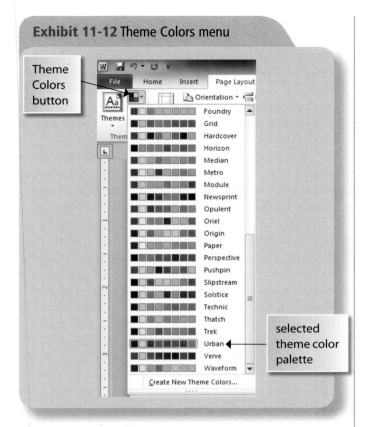

Theme Colors button

Foundry
Grid
Hardcover
Horizon
Median
Metro
Module
Newsprint
Opulent
Oriel
Origin
Paper
Perspective
Pushpin
Slipstream
Solstice
Technic
Thatch
Trek
Urban ← selected theme color palette
Verve
Waveform

Create New Theme Colors...

6 At the top of the document, under the Overview heading, select **North Lake Camp**. On the Ribbon, click the **Home tab**. Notice in the Font box that the font of the text formatted with the NLC Name style is still Candara. Also notice that all of the text formatted with the NLC Name style is still the same dark green you selected. This is because the dark green color was not a theme color, so it is unaffected by changing the theme colors.

7 Save the document.

LO11.3 **Changing the Style Set**

A **style set** is a coordinated group of Quick Styles available to each document. The default style set for new documents is the Word 2010 style set. If you change the style set, the Quick Style definitions are changed. For example, with the default Word 2010 style set selected, the Heading 1 style, as you have already seen, is formatted as 14-point Cambria with the Blue, Accent 1, Darker 25% color; the paragraph is left-aligned, and there are 24 points of space before the paragraph. If you change the style set to the Formal style set, the Heading 1 Quick Style definition changes;

it is still 14-point Cambria, but the color is Red, Accent 2, Darker 50%; the paragraph is centered; there is 20 points of space before the paragraph and 10 points of space after the paragraph; and there is a Red, Accent 2, Darker 25% double-line border under the paragraph. You can select from a total of 14 style sets to change the look of all the text in a document.

You can change the style set before or after you apply styles. Be aware that if you redefine Quick Styles before you apply a different style set, the changes might not all be retained if you change the style set after you change the style definitions.

ACTIVITY

Change the Style Set.

1 On the Home tab, in the Styles group, click the **Change Styles button**. On the menu that opens, notice the Colors and Fonts commands. Pointing to these commands opens the same menus you saw when used the Theme Colors and Theme Fonts buttons in the Themes group on the Page Layout tab.

2 On the menu, point to **Style Set**. A menu of style sets opens. See Exhibit 11-13.

Exhibit 11-13 Style Set menu

Change Styles button

AaBbCcD AaBbCcD AaBbCcD AaBbC(
¶ Normal   NLC Name ¶ No Spaci... Heading 1

Change Styles

Find
Replace
Select

list of style sets

Default (Black and White)
Distinctive
Elegant
Fancy
Formal
Manuscript
Modern
Newsprint
Perspective
Simple
Thatch
Traditional
Word 2003
Word 2010

Style Set
Colors
Fonts
Paragraph Spacing
Set as Default

Reset to Quick Styles from Template
Reset Document Quick Styles
Save as Quick Style Set...

style set A group of Quick Styles.

Customizing the Normal Template

The combination of themes and style sets provides an almost dizzying number of choices. You can select a theme; change the theme fonts, colors, or effects; and change the style set to create a document quickly formatted with a distinctive look. As you have seen, if you re-define Quick Styles and then apply a different style set, your changes might not carry through. If you come up with a combination you want to save as the default when you create new documents—in other words, if you want to save changes to the Normal template—make all the changes you want using theme fonts and colors and the Style Set command, click the Change Styles button in the Styles group on the Home tab, and then click Set as Default.

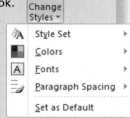

3 Point to **Modern**. Live Preview shows a preview of the Modern style set in the document. Notice that the changes to the Heading 2 definition are not retained with this style set.

4 On the submenu, click **Formal**. The style set is changed to the Formal style set. The changes to the Heading 2 style are retained with this style set. And note that the text formatted with the NLC Name style is unaffected because it was created using a non-theme font and color.

5 Save the document.

LO11.4 Working with the Document Outline

Reviewing a document's outline can help you keep track of a document's overall organization. It lets you see, at a glance, the hierarchy of the docu-

promote To move an item to a higher level in an outline.

demote To move an item to a lower level in an outline.

ment headings. Paragraphs formatted with the Heading 1 style are the highest level headings. Paragraphs formatted with the Heading 2 style are subordinate to Heading 1 paragraphs. In an outline, subordinate headings—or subheadings—are indented below the Heading 1 paragraphs. Each successive level of heading styles (Heading 3, Heading 4, and so on) is indented further to the right.

When you work with an outline, you can move topics to other locations in the outline, or you can promote or demote headings. Moving a heading to a higher level in the outline—for example, changing a Heading 2 paragraph into a Heading 1 paragraph—is called **promoting** the heading. Moving an item lower in the outline is called **demoting** the heading. If you used the built-in heading styles to format the headings in your document, when you promote or demote a heading, the next higher or lower level of heading style is applied to the heading paragraph.

When you work with multiple-page documents, there are several ways to move among the pages in the document. To see the current page number and the total number of pages, look at the page count indicator at the left end of the status bar, which lists the current page number and the total number of pages in the document. You can drag the scroll box in the vertical scroll bar to move between the pages in the document. As you drag, a ScreenTip appears identifying the current page number. If paragraphs are formatted with the built-in heading styles, the first heading on the page also appears in the ScreenTip. (Remember that pressing the Page Up and Page Down keys scrolls the document one screen at a time, not necessarily one page at a time, unless the document was displayed at One Page zoom.) You can also click the page count indicator to open the Go To tab in the Find and Replace dialog box, and then type the page number you want to go to.

ACTIVITY

View different pages in a multiple-page document.

1 In the vertical scroll bar, point to the **scroll box**, and then press and hold the mouse button. A ScreenTip appears identifying the page as page 1. The first heading on the page, Overview, also appears in the ScreenTip. See Exhibit 11-14.

Exhibit 11-14 ScreenTip identifying the current page number

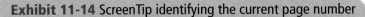

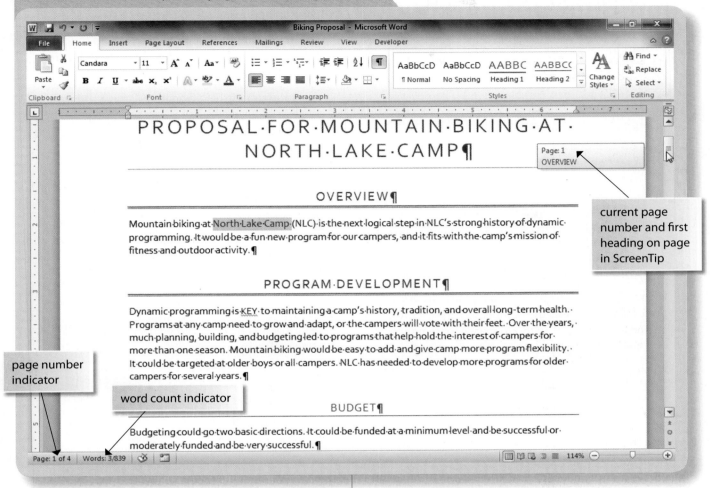

current page number and first heading on page in ScreenTip

page number indicator

word count indicator

2 Drag the **scroll box** slowly down the vertical scroll bar until the ScreenTip identifies the current page as page 3, and then release the mouse button. Page 3 appears in the document window, and the page number indicator on the status bar identifies the page as Page 3 of 4.

3 On the status bar, click the **page count indicator** 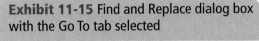. The Find and Replace dialog box opens with the Go To tab selected. In the Go to what box, Page is selected, and the insertion point is in the Enter page number box. See Exhibit 11-15.

4 In the Enter page number box, type **1**. The Next command button changes to Go To.

Exhibit 11-15 Find and Replace dialog box with the Go To tab selected

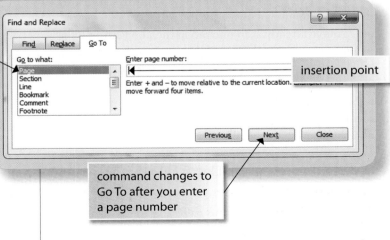

Page selected in list

insertion point

command changes to Go To after you enter a page number

5 Click **Go To**. The document scrolls to page 1.

6 In the dialog box, click **Close**.

Document Statistics

The word count indicator, which lists the number of words in the document, is located next to the page count indicator on the status bar. When text is selected, the number of words in the selection is identified before a slash and the total number of words. To see more statistics, click the word count indicator or click the Word Count button in the Proofing group on the Review tab to open the Word Count dialog box. The Word Count dialog box lists the number of pages, words, characters with and without spaces, paragraphs, and lines in the document or selected text.

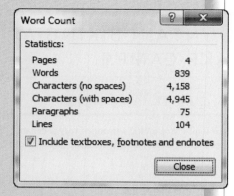

Word Count

Statistics:	
Pages	4
Words	839
Characters (no spaces)	4,158
Characters (with spaces)	4,945
Paragraphs	75
Lines	104

☑ Include textboxes, footnotes and endnotes

[Close]

There are two ways to work with a document outline: in the Navigation Pane in Normal view and in Outline view.

Using the Navigation Pane

The Navigation Pane offers two ways to view a document's structure and navigate within it. You can view and navigate the document's outline by displaying its headings in the document, or you can view and navigate the document's pages by displaying thumbnail images of the pages.

You've already seen one tab in the Navigation Pane when you used it to find search text in a document. In addition to the Browse the results from your current search tab, which is the tab you used to find and highlight search text in a document, the Navigation Pane includes the Browse the pages in your document tab and the Browse the headings in your document tab.

Browse the Pages of a Document in the Navigation Pane

To move quickly among the pages in your document, use the Browse the pages in your document tab in the Navigation Pane. This tab displays the pages of your document as thumbnails. You click a thumbnail to instantly move to that page in the document.

ACTIVITY

Browse the pages of a document.

1 On the Ribbon, click the **View tab**. In the Show group, click the **Navigation Pane check box** to select it. The Navigation Pane opens.

2 At the top of the Navigation Pane, if it is not already selected, click the **Browse the pages in your document tab** 🔲. That tab becomes the current tab and displays a thumbnail of each page in the document in the Navigation Pane. Page 1 is selected and displayed in the document window. See Exhibit 11-16.

3 In the Navigation Pane, click the **page 2 thumbnail**. The page 2 thumbnail becomes selected and page 2 appears in the document window.

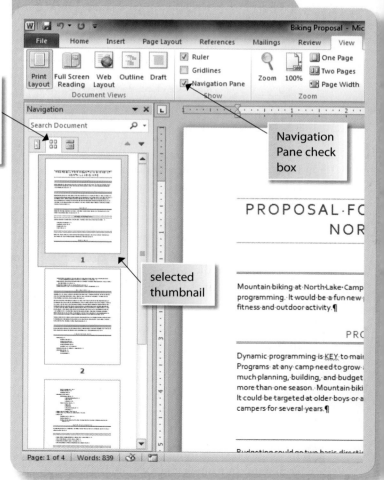

Exhibit 11-16 Browsing by pages in the Navigation Pane

Browse the Headings in a Document in the Navigation Pane

To work with a document outline, use the Browse the headings in your document tab in the Navigation Pane, which displays the document headings as an outline. You can click a heading in the Navigation Pane to display that heading at the top of the document window. You can also drag a heading up or down in the Navigation Pane to position it in a new location in the outline. When you do this, any subheadings and body text under the heading move to the new location with the heading you drag. You can also promote and demote headings in the Navigation Pane. When you change the level of a heading, subheadings are promoted or demoted one level as well. To identify headings that have subheadings, either a Collapse arrow ◢ or an Expand arrow ▷ appears next to them in the Navigation Pane.

ACTIVITY

Change the outline in the Navigation Pane.

1 At the top of the Navigation Pane, click the **Browse the headings in your document tab** 🔲. The document headings are displayed in the Navigation Pane, as shown in Exhibit 11-17. The orange highlighted heading, Questions, indicates the part of the document that contains the insertion point, which is positioned at the top of page 2.

2 In the Navigation Pane, click the **Description of Program heading**. The document scrolls to display that heading at the top of the document window with the insertion point at the beginning of the heading.

3 In the Navigation Pane, next to the Potential Trip Routes heading, click the **Collapse arrow** ◢. The headings formatted as Heading 3 headings under the Potential Trip Routes heading disappear, and the arrow next to the Potential Trip Routes heading changes to an Expand arrow ▷. See Exhibit 11-18.

4 In the Navigation Pane, drag the **Description of Program heading** up, but do not release the mouse button. As you drag the heading, the pointer changes to ▨, which is the same pointer you saw when you used the drag and drop technique, and a black line appears indicating the position of the heading when you release the mouse button. See Exhibit 11-19.

Exhibit 11-17 Headings displayed in the Navigation Pane

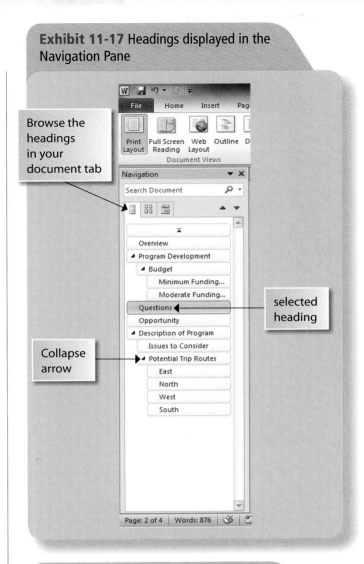

Exhibit 11-18 A collapsed heading in the Navigation Pane

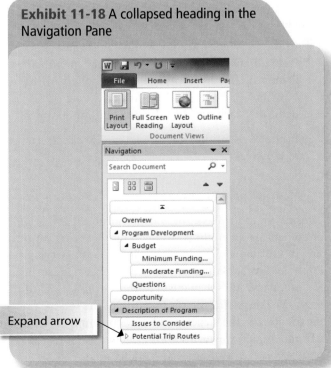

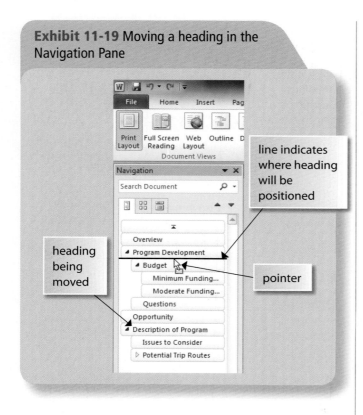

Exhibit 11-19 Moving a heading in the Navigation Pane

In Outline view, outline symbols appear to the left of each paragraph. The plus sign symbol ⊕ appears next to headings that have subheadings or body text below the heading. The minus sign symbol ⊖ appears next to headings that do not have any subordinate text. A small gray circle ◯ next to a paragraph indicates the text is body text and not a heading.

When you click the outline symbol next to a heading, you select the heading and all of its subordinate text, or a section. To move a section after you select it, you can drag it or click the Move Up or Move Down button in the Outline Tools group on the Outlining tab, which is visible only in Outline view. You can also use buttons on the Outlining tab to promote or demote headings, or to demote text from a heading to body text.

ACTIVITY

Change the outline in Outline view.

1 On the View tab, in the Document Views group, click the **Outline button**. The document switches to Outline view, and a new tab, Outlining, appears on the Ribbon and is the active tab.

▲**Tip:** If the formatting applied to the headings in your document makes it difficult to read the text in Outline view, click the Show Text Formatting check box in the Outline Tools group on the Outlining tab to deselect it and show all the text in Outline view as black text.

2 Change the zoom level to **120%** to match the figures in this section.

3 On the Outlining tab, in the Outline Tools group, click the **Show Level box arrow**, and then click **Level 3**. Now only text formatted with the Heading 1, Heading 2, or Heading 3 style appears. The horizontal line below headings indicates that the heading has body text below it. See Exhibit 11-20.

4 Next to the Budget heading, click the **plus sign symbol** ⊕. The Budget heading and its subheadings are selected. In the Outline Tools group, Level 2 appears in the Outline Level box (directly below the Outlining tab name). This is the level of the selected Budget heading.

5 In the Outline Tools group, click the **Promote button** . The selected heading is promoted so

---

5 When the black line is positioned below the Program Development heading, as shown in Exhibit 11-19, release the mouse button. The Description of Program heading and all the subheadings under it are moved to the new position in the document.

6 In the Navigation Pane, right-click the **Questions heading**. On the shortcut menu, click **Promote**. The heading moves to the left in the Navigation Pane so it aligns below the other headings formatted with the Heading 1 style.

7 In the Navigation Pane, click the **Close button** ✖ to close it.

Using Outline View

Outline view displays the various heading levels in a document as an outline. You can either create an outline in Outline view, and the built-in heading styles are applied automatically; or apply heading styles in Print Layout view, and then display the outline in Outline view. Working with the outline in Outline view is similar to viewing the structure of a document in the Navigation Pane; however, in Outline view, you can see body text below the headings.

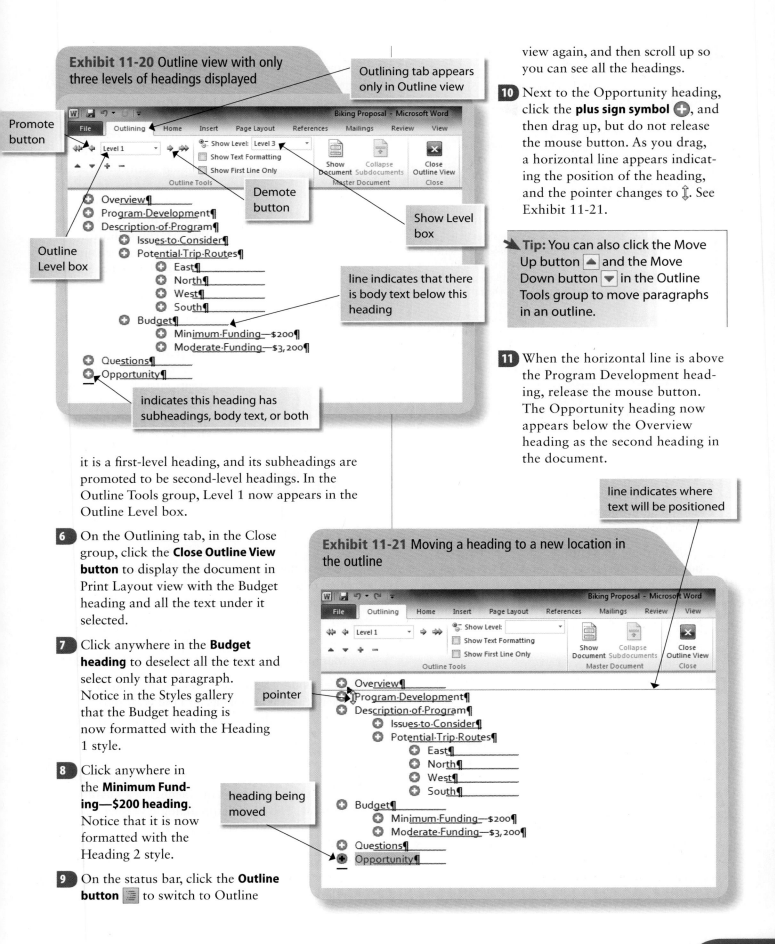

Exhibit 11-20 Outline view with only three levels of headings displayed

Outlining tab appears only in Outline view

Promote button

Demote button

Show Level box

Outline Level box

line indicates that there is body text below this heading

indicates this heading has subheadings, body text, or both

view again, and then scroll up so you can see all the headings.

10 Next to the Opportunity heading, click the **plus sign symbol**, and then drag up, but do not release the mouse button. As you drag, a horizontal line appears indicating the position of the heading, and the pointer changes to ↕. See Exhibit 11-21.

➤ Tip: You can also click the Move Up button ▲ and the Move Down button ▼ in the Outline Tools group to move paragraphs in an outline.

11 When the horizontal line is above the Program Development heading, release the mouse button. The Opportunity heading now appears below the Overview heading as the second heading in the document.

it is a first-level heading, and its subheadings are promoted to be second-level headings. In the Outline Tools group, Level 1 now appears in the Outline Level box.

6 On the Outlining tab, in the Close group, click the **Close Outline View button** to display the document in Print Layout view with the Budget heading and all the text under it selected.

7 Click anywhere in the **Budget heading** to deselect all the text and select only that paragraph. Notice in the Styles gallery that the Budget heading is now formatted with the Heading 1 style.

8 Click anywhere in the **Minimum Funding—$200 heading**. Notice that it is now formatted with the Heading 2 style.

9 On the status bar, click the **Outline button** to switch to Outline

line indicates where text will be positioned

Exhibit 11-21 Moving a heading to a new location in the outline

pointer

heading being moved

12 Next to the Questions heading, double-click the **plus sign symbol** ⊕. The heading expands to display all the body text under it. See Exhibit 11-22.

Exhibit 11-22 Body text in Outline view

double-click to display body text and any subheadings

indicates this paragraph is body text

⊕ Budget¶
    ⊕ Minimum·Funding—$200¶
    ⊕ Moderate·Funding—$3,200¶
⊕ Questions¶
   ● 1. → This·proposal·does·not·address·all·concerns·and·leads·to·additional·topics· that·would·need·further·study·and·review.·Here·is·a·partial·list·of·potential·questions:¶
   ● 2. → Do·we·need·to·obtain·permission·or·permits·from·North·Lake·Land· Management·Consortium·or·North·Meadows·State·Park?¶
   ● 3. → What·will·the·policy·be·if·a·camper's·bike·is·ruined?¶
   ● 4. → Does·the·camp's·liability·insurance·cover·excursions·off·camp·property?¶
   ● Camping·at·NLC·has·always·been·a·significant·experience.·Mountain·biking·at·NLC· is·untapped,·unlimited,·and·there·for·the·taking.·Mountain·biking·could·easily·and· economically·be·a·next·program·feature·for·camp.·2,400·acres·await.¶

position insertion point here

Page: 4 of 4 | Words: 109/876

13 In the last paragraph of body text, click before the word *Camping*, type **Conclusion**, press the **Enter key**, and then press the **Up Arrow key** to position the insertion point in the *Conclusion* line. *Conclusion* is formatted as body text.

14 In the Outline Tools group, click the **Promote button** ⇐ . *Conclusion* is promoted to a Level 1 heading.

15 On the status bar, click the **Print Layout button** 🗐. Outline view closes and you see that the Heading 1 style has been applied to the Conclusion heading.

16 Save the document.

LO11.5 **Changing the Margins**

Another aspect of document formatting is how the document fits on the printed page. The **margins** are the blank areas at the top, bottom,

> **margin** The blank area above or below text, or to the left or right of text between the text and the edge of the page.

left, and right sides of the page between the text and the edge of the page. By default, Word documents have one-inch margins on all sides of the document. See Exhibit 11-23. This is fine for most documents. Sometimes you might want to change the margins. For example, you might want to provide additional space in the margins to allow readers to take notes. To change the margins, click the Margins button in the Page Setup group on the Page Layout tab. You can choose from a number of predefined margin options, or you can click the Custom Margins command to select your own settings. After you create custom margin settings, the most recent set appears as an option at the top of the menu.

ACTIVITY

Change the page margins.

1 On the Ribbon, click the **View tab**. In the Zoom group, click the **One Page button**. The current page of the document, page 3, appears completely in the Word window and you can easily see the margins.

2 On the Ribbon, click the **Page Layout tab**. In the Page Setup group, click the **Margins button**. The Margins menu opens, as shown in Exhibit 11-24.

3 Click **Wide**. The menu closes and the margins in the document are changed to the Wide setting, which keeps the one-inch margin at the top and bottom, but changes both the left and right margins to two inches.

4 In the Page Setup group, click the **Margins button**. At the bottom of the menu, click **Custom Margins**. The Page Setup dialog box opens with the Margins tab selected. See Exhibit 11-25. The current margin settings are displayed in the boxes in the Margins section at the top of the Margins tab. The value in the Top box is selected.

Exhibit 11-23 One-inch margins in a document

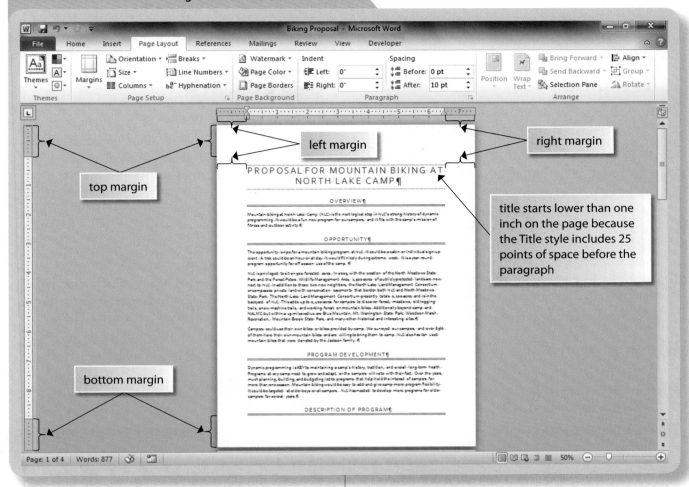

left margin

right margin

top margin

bottom margin

title starts lower than one inch on the page because the Title style includes 25 points of space before the paragraph

Exhibit 11-24 Margins menu

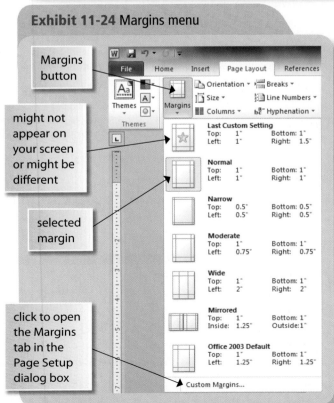

Margins button

might not appear on your screen or might be different

selected margin

click to open the Margins tab in the Page Setup dialog box

Exhibit 11-25 Page Setup dialog box with the Margins tab selected

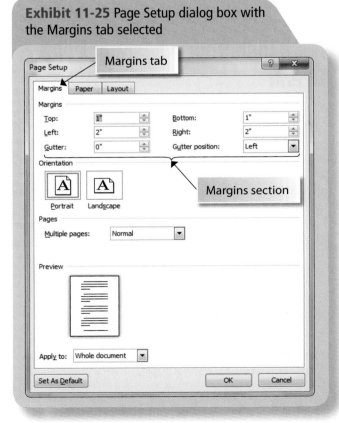

Margins tab

Margins section

Working with Custom Margins

For most documents, the Word default of one-inch margins is fine. In some professional settings, however, you might need to use a particular custom margin setting for all your documents. In that case, define the custom margins using the Margins tab of the Page Setup dialog box, and then click the Set As Default button to make the settings the default for all new documents. Keep in mind that most printers cannot print to the edge of the page. If you select custom margins that are too narrow for your printer to use, a dialog box opens telling you to change the margin settings.

5 Press the **Tab key** twice to select the value in the Left box, and then type **1.5**.

6 In the Right box, click the **down arrow** five times to change the value to 1.5".

7 Click **OK**. The margins are changed to the custom settings.

8 Change the zoom level back to **Page Width**, and then save the document.

LO₁₁.6 Inserting a Manual Page Break

As you add text to a document, **automatic page breaks** (sometimes called **soft page breaks**) are inserted as new pages are created as each page fills with text. Sometimes, you need to create a new page manually. To do this, you need to insert a **manual page break** (sometimes called a **hard page break**), which is a page break you insert at a specific location. To insert a manual page break, use the Page Break button in the Pages group on the Insert tab. When nonprinting characters

automatic page break (soft page break)
A page break that is created when content fills a page and a new page is created automatically.

manual page break (hard page break) A page break that you insert to force content after the break to appear on a new page.

are displayed, manual page breaks appear as a dotted line with the words *Page Break* in the center of the line.

 **ACTIVITY**

To insert a manual page break.

1 Scroll to the bottom of page 2, and then click before the word *Potential* in the Potential Trip Routes heading.

2 On the Ribbon, click the **Insert tab**. In the Pages group, click the **Page Break button**. A manual page break is inserted before the insertion point and the Potential Trip Routes heading moves to the top of the next page. See Exhibit 11-26.

> **Tip:** You can also press the Ctrl+Enter keys to insert a manual page break at the insertion point.

3 Save the document.

Exhibit 11-26 Manual page break inserted into the document

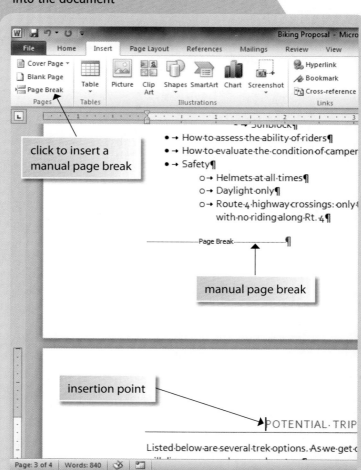

Controlling Page Breaks with Paragraph Settings

When you apply a built-in heading style to a paragraph, you also apply settings that prevent awkward page breaks. One of these settings is widow and orphan control. A **widow** is the first line of a paragraph left at the bottom of a page before the page break, and an **orphan** is the last line of a paragraph that appears by itself at the top of a page. You also apply "Keep" settings. When the Keep with next setting is applied to a paragraph, the paragraph never appears at the bottom of a page. It is connected to the next paragraph and the page will break before the paragraph with the Keep with next setting. The Keep lines together setting doesn't allow a soft page break to appear within the paragraph. And the Page break before setting inserts a soft page break before the paragraph. Unfortunately, when you change style sets, these settings are not always retained with the Heading style definitions. To adjust these settings, right-click the Quick Style in the Styles gallery, and then click Modify to open the Modify Style dialog box. At the bottom of the dialog box, click Format, and then click Paragraph to open the Paragraph dialog box. Click the Line and Page Breaks tab, and then click the desired check boxes in the Pagination section. Click OK in both open dialog boxes to redefine the style to include the settings you chose.

Line and Page Breaks tab

Pagination section

> **To see the code (instruction) for a field, right-click the field, and then on the shortcut menu, click Toggle Field Codes.**

LO11.7 Adding Page Numbers, Headers, and Footers

To insert page numbers in a document, you insert a page number field. A **field** is a placeholder for variable information that includes an instruction to insert the specific information. A page number field inserts the correct page number. Usually, page numbers appear in the top or bottom margin. You can also insert page numbers in the side margins; although for business or academic documents, it's customary to place them at the top or bottom of a document.

When you insert a page number field, the document switches to Header and Footer view. A **header** is text that appears at the top of every page in a document; a **footer** is text that appears at the bottom of every page. In this book, the chapter number and title appear in the footer. In Header and Footer view, the document is dimmed, indicating that it cannot be edited, and you can type only in the header or footer area.

When you insert a page number or a header or footer, it appears on every page in the document. If you don't want the header and footer to appear on the first page of a document, you can specify this by selecting the Different First Page check box in the Options group on the Header & Footer Tools Design tab, a contextual tab that appears in Header and Footer view.)

> **widow** The first line of a paragraph left at the bottom of a page before the page break.
>
> **orphan** The last line of a paragraph that appears by itself at the top of a page.
>
> **field** In Word, a placeholder for variable information that includes an instruction to insert the specific information.
>
> **header** Text that appears at the top of every page.
>
> **footer** Text that appears at the bottom of every page.

Inserting Page Numbers

To add page numbers to a document, click the Page Number button in the Header & Footer group on the Insert tab. You can choose to insert the page number in the header or footer area, in the left or right margin, or at the current position of the insertion point.

ACTIVITY

Add page numbers.

1 On the Insert tab, in the Header & Footer group, click the **Page Number button** to open the Page Number menu.

2 Point to **Bottom of Page**. A gallery of page number styles opens. See Exhibit 11-27.

3 Scroll down and examine the styles of page number that you can insert.

> ▲ **Tip:** To remove page numbers from a document, click the Remove Page Numbers command on the Page Number button menu.

4 Scroll back to the top of the list, and then click the **Plain Number 3 style**. The document switches to Header and Footer view, and the page number for the current page (page 3) appears right-aligned in the footer area. The page number has a gray background, indicating that it is actually a page number field and not simply a number that you typed. The Header & Footer Tools Design tab appears on the Ribbon and is the active tab. See Exhibit 11-28.

5 Scroll up so you can see the footer area on page 1, and then click to the left of the page number.

6 On the Header & Footer Tools Design tab, in the Options group, click the **Different First Page check box** to select it. The page number field is removed from the first page footer.

> ▲ **Tip:** To change the numbering style for a page number or to specify a number to use as the first page number, click the Page Number button in the Header & Footer group, and then click Format Page Numbers.

7 Scroll down to the bottom of page 2 and observe the page number at the bottom of the page.

8 On the Header & Footer Tools Design tab, in the Close group, click the **Close Header and Footer button**. The document returns to Print Layout view with the insertion point at the top of page 3, and the Header & Footer Tools Design tab no longer appears on the Ribbon.

Exhibit 11-27 Gallery of page number styles

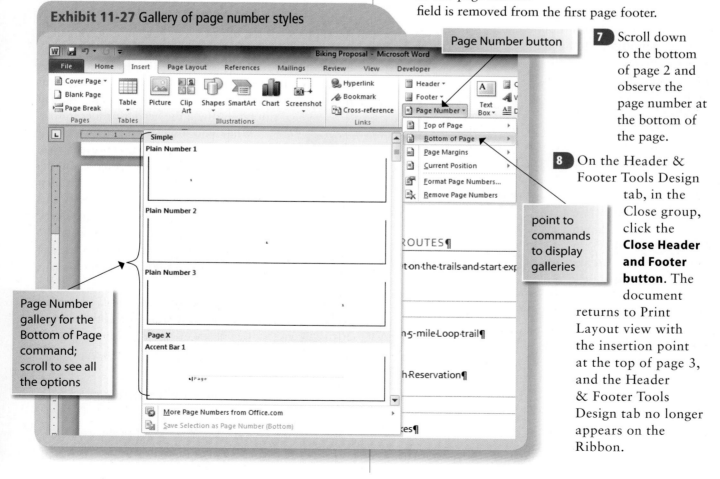

Page Number button

Page Number gallery for the Bottom of Page command; scroll to see all the options

point to commands to display galleries

Exhibit 11-28 Page number inserted in footer

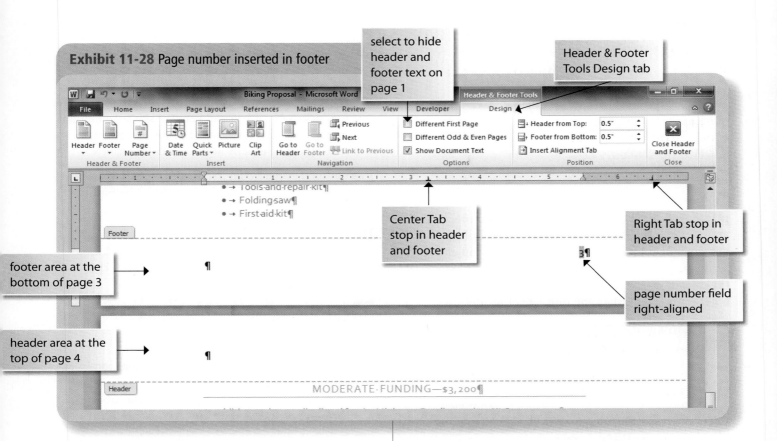

- select to hide header and footer text on page 1
- Header & Footer Tools Design tab
- Center Tab stop in header and footer
- Right Tab stop in header and footer
- footer area at the bottom of page 3
- page number field right-aligned
- header area at the top of page 4

Adding a Header and Footer

There are several ways to insert a header or footer. For a simple header or footer, first switch to Header and Footer view by double-clicking in the header or footer area or clicking the Header or Footer button in the Header & Footer group on the Insert tab, and then clicking Edit Header or Edit Footer. Then, type the header or footer text directly in the header or footer area, formatting the text as you would any other text in a document. To insert a predesigned header or footer style, use the Header and Footer buttons in the Header & Footer group on the Insert tab or on the Header & Footer Tools Design tab, and then click a style in the gallery of headers and footers that opens.

Headers and footers are preset with a Center Tab stop at the 3.25-inch mark and a Right Tab stop at the 6.5-inch mark. These tab stops center and right-align the inserted text based on the Normal margins. If you change the margin settings, then you might want to change the tab settings to better align the header or footer text with the document text.

Many of the header and footer styles in the galleries include page numbers and graphic elements such as horizontal lines or shaded boxes. Some also include

content controls. A **content control** is a placeholder for text you insert and that can store a specific type of text, such as a date or a document property. A **property** is identifying information about a file that is saved with the file, such as the author's name and the date the file was created. Information entered in a content control associated with a property will appear in any other content control that is associated with that property. For example, if you enter the company name in a Company content control in the header, and the Company content control also appears in the footer, the company name that you typed in the header will appear automatically in the footer. Some content controls are associated with properties that appear automatically in the content control. For example, the registered user's name is saved as the document author property every time you create a document, so that name will appear in a content control that displays the author name. Most of the content controls that appear in headers and footers are text

> **content control** A special field used as a placeholder for text you insert, or designed to contain a specific type of text.
>
> **property** Identifying information about a file that is saved with the file.

To change the registered user's name, click the File tab on the Ribbon, click Options, and then change the name in the User name box.

placeholders; click the text placeholder once to select it, and then type the text to replace the placeholder. Date content controls are formatted so that you can click an arrow to display a calendar and then select a date from the calendar. You can always delete a content control in a header or footer that you don't want to use.

 **ACTIVITY**

Create a footer.

1 On page 2, double-click in the **footer area**. The document switches to Header and Footer view, and the Header & Footer Tools Design tab appears on the Ribbon and is the active tab. The insertion point is positioned before the page number field in the footer area, ready for you to begin typing.

2 Type your name.

3 On the Ribbon, click the **Home tab**. In the Paragraph group, click the **Align Text Left button** 📄. The text in the footer is now left-aligned.

4 With the insertion point between your name and the page number field, press the **Tab key** twice. The page number moves to the 6.5-inch mark on the ruler, aligning the text with the Right Tab stop at the 6.5-inch mark. If you had kept the standard margins of one-inch on the left and the right, the Right Tab stop would be exactly at the right margin.

5 On the Header & Footer Tools Design tab, in the Navigation group, click the **Go to Header button**. The insertion point moves to the header on page 2.

6 On the Header & Footer Tools Design tab, in the Header & Footer group, click the **Header button**. The Header gallery opens, very similar to the Page Number gallery.

7 Scroll down, and then click the **Exposure header**. The gallery closes, and two content controls are inserted in the header area. See Exhibit 11-29.

8 Click the **Type the document title content control**. The entire content control becomes selected and the Title tab—in this case, with the label *Title*—appears.

9 Type **Proposal for Mountain Biking at North Lake Camp**. The placeholder text is replaced by the text you typed.

10 Click the **Pick the date content control**. The entire content control becomes selected, the title tab with the label *Date* appears, and an arrow appears on the right side of the control.

11 Click the **arrow**. A calendar appears.

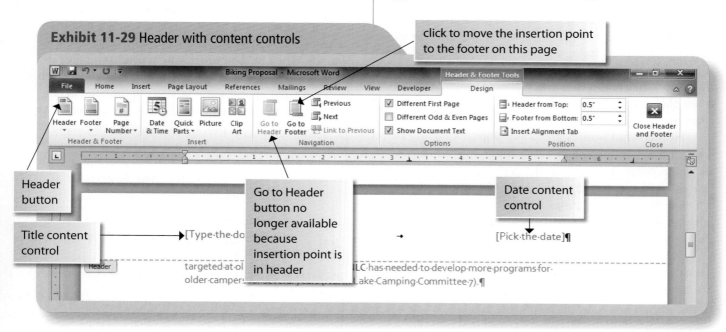

Exhibit 11-29 Header with content controls

click to move the insertion point to the footer on this page

Header button

Title content control

Go to Header button no longer available because insertion point is in header

Date content control

12 At the bottom of the calendar, click **Today**. The calendar closes and today's date replaces the placeholder text in the Date content control.

> ➤ **Tip:** You can click the arrows to the right and left of the month name to scroll to other months.

13 Click the **Date title tab**. The entire control is selected.

14 Press the **Delete key**. The Date content control is deleted.

15 On page 2, double-click in the document area. The document returns to Page Layout view with the insertion point at the top of page 3, where it was before you switched to Header and Footer view.

16 Scroll up so you can see the header area on page 1 and confirm that the header you inserted does not appear on page 1.

17 Save the document.

Preformatted Cover Pages

A document's cover page typically includes the title and the name of the author. Some people also include a summary of the report on the cover page; this is commonly referred to as an abstract. In addition, you might include the date, the name and possibly the logo of your company or organization, and a subtitle. A cover page should not include the document header or footer. You can create your own cover page, or you can use one of the preformatted cover pages included with Word. To use a preformatted cover page, click the Cover Page button in the Pages group on the Insert tab, and then click a cover page in the gallery. The cover page includes content controls in which you can enter the document title and author, the date, and so on. Many of these content controls are linked to document properties. For example, if you enter the document title in the Title content control in a header, and then insert a cover page that contains a Title content control, the title you entered will appear automatically on the cover page.

LO11.8 Creating Citations and a List of Works Cited

When you write a research paper, you should always cite your sources. A **source** is anything you use to research your topic, including books, magazines, Web sites, and movies. Every time you quote or refer to a source within the research paper itself, you need to include a **citation**, a formal reference to the work of others, usually as a parenthetical reference to the author and page number of a source. A citation should include enough information to identify the quote or referenced material so that the reader can easily locate the source in the accompanying works cited list.

Every source you cite needs to be listed in a **list of works cited**, sometimes called **references** or a **bibliography**. In common usage, the list of works cited, references, and the bibliography are the same thing: a list of the sources cited in a document. Sometimes, the list of works cited and the bibliography are different, where the list of works cited is a list only of the works cited in the document, and the bibliography is a complete list of all the sources consulted when researching a topic, even sources that are not cited in the document. Sometimes, this complete list of sources is called a complete bibliography or a complete list of works cited, and the shorter list of works actually cited is called a works consulted list or a selected bibliography.

The exact form for citations and the list of works cited varies, depending on the style guide you are using and the type of material you are referencing. A **style guide** is a set of rules that describe the preferred format and style for a certain type of writing. People in different fields use different style guides, with each style guide designed to suit the needs of a specific discipline. For example, journalists commonly use the Associated Press (AP) style, which focuses on the concise writing common in magazines and newspapers. Researchers in the social and behavioral sciences use the American Psychological Association (APA) style, which is

source Anything you use to research your topic.

citation A formal reference to the work of others.

list of works cited, **references**, or **bibliography** A list of sources cited in a document or consulted while researching a topic.

style guide A set of rules that describe the preferred format and style for a certain type of writing.

Formatting a Research Paper Using MLA Style

The *MLA Handbook for Writers of Research Papers*, published by The Modern Language Association of America, contains instructions for formatting a research document and citing the sources used in research conducted for a paper using the MLA style. The MLA guidelines were developed, in part, to simplify the process of transforming a manuscript into a journal article or a chapter of a book. The style calls for minimal formatting; the simpler the formatting in a manuscript, the easier it is to turn the text into a published document. The MLA guidelines were also designed to ensure consistency in documents, so that all research papers look alike. Therefore, there should be no special formatting applied to the text in an MLA style research paper. Headings should be formatted like the other text in the document, with no bold or heading styles.

Compared to style guides for technical fields, the MLA style is flexible about the form and location of citations, making it easy to include citations without disrupting the natural flow of the writing. In this style, citations of other writers take the form of a brief parenthetical entry, with a complete reference to each item included in the alphabetized bibliography at the end of the research paper. Typically, though, you insert an MLA citation at the end of a sentence in which you quote or refer to material from a source. For books or journals, the citation usually includes the author's last name and a page number. However, if the sentence containing the citation already includes the author's name, you only need to include the page number in the citation. For detailed guidelines, consult the current edition of the *MLA Handbook for Writers of Research Papers*, which includes many examples.

MLA STYLE CHECKLIST

✓ Font is standard and easy to read (such as Times New Roman or Calibri) and at a standard size (such as 12 points)

✓ No extra space before or after all paragraphs in the document

✓ All lines double-spaced

✓ Text is aligned left (with a ragged right), and there is only one space after periods and other punctuation marks

✓ All margins are one inch

✓ First line of each body paragraph is one-half inch from the left margin, even the first paragraph after headings

✓ A page number, preceded by your last name, appears in the upper-right corner of each page; if requested, do not include the page number on the first page

✓ List of works cited is titled *Works Cited*

✓ Works Cited list begins on a new page

✓ Paragraphs in the Works Cited list are formatted with a hanging indent

✓ Include a title page only if requested; otherwise, include your name, instructor's name, course name, and the date as the first four lines in the document, followed by the title, which is centered horizontally

✓ Title of the paper and Works Cited title do not use any special formatting except to be centered horizontally on the page

✓ Works Cited list is arranged alphabetically by author (consult the *MLA Handbook* for more detailed instructions)

---

designed to help readers scan an article quickly for key points and emphasizes the date of publication in citations. Other scientific and technical fields have their own specialized style guides. In the humanities, the Modern Language Association (MLA) style is widely used. Refer to the style guide you are using to see exactly what information you need to include in citations and the list of works cited, as well as how to format this information. Note that some style guides require both a list of works cited and a complete bibliography.

In Word documents, you can specify the style you want to use from a list of 10 styles; and then when you

insert citations and create the list of works cited, they are formatted appropriately for the selected style. You can change the style you select at any time, and if any citations already exist, or if the list of works cited is already created, they are reformatted using the new style.

 **ACTIVITY**

Select a style for the citations and list of works cited.

1 On the Ribbon, click the **References tab**.

2 In the Citations & Bibliography group, click the **Style box arrow**, and then click **MLA Sixth Edition** in the list of styles.

> ⚠ **Note:** At the time this book was published, the current edition of the *MLA Handbook for Writers of Research Papers* was the seventh edition, but the option in the Style list was still MLA Sixth Edition. The editions have some style differences for the list of works cited—for example, in the seventh edition, the titles of works are italicized instead of underlined. If you are using the seventh edition of the *MLA Handbook* as your style guide, read the green box titled "Converting a List of Works Cited to Static Text" on page 377, and then edit the style of the list of works cited in your document as needed. Note that Microsoft might update the Bibliography style list through an automatic software update.

Creating a New Source and Inserting a Citation

To create a new source and insert a citation to it, click the Insert Citation button in the Citations & Bibliography group on the References tab, and then click Add New Source to open the Create Source dialog box. In the dialog box, you choose the type of source—book, Web site, sound recording, etc.—and the dialog box changes to contain the appropriate boxes for gathering the information about the specified source type according to the style guide you selected prior to opening this dialog box. When you close the dialog box, the citation will be inserted in the style you selected in the Style box in the Citations & Bibliography

group. For example, if you chose the MLA style, the author's last name will be inserted between parentheses.

Create a new source and insert a citation.

1 On page 1, below the Opportunity heading, in the second paragraph, position the insertion point immediately before the period at the end of the third sentence (after *Park*).

2 On the References tab, in the Citations & Bibliography group, click the **Insert Citation button**, and then click **Add New Source**. The Create Source dialog box opens. In Exhibit 11-30, Book is selected in the Type of Source box, and the boxes shown in the dialog box collect the information needed to document the source when the source is a book. If a different source type is listed in the Type of Source box on your screen, the boxes in the dialog box will differ from those shown in Exhibit 11-30.

Exhibit 11-30 Create Source dialog box

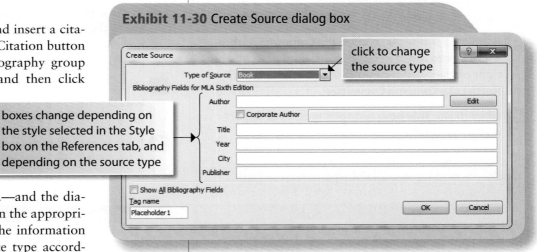

boxes change depending on the style selected in the Style box on the References tab, and depending on the source type

click to change the source type

3 Click the **Type of Source arrow**, scroll down one line, and then click **Web site**. The boxes in the dialog box change to collect the information needed when the source is a Web site.

4 Click in the **Author box**, and then type **Alan Freeman**. Click in the **Name of Web Page box**, and then type **Protected Land in the North Lake Area**.

> ➤ **Tip:** Web sites don't always provide all the information used to create a citation; include as much information as you can.

> The seventh edition of the MLA Handbook discourages including URLs in the source information for a Web site.

5 Click in the **Year box**, and then type **2005**. Click in the **Month box**, and then type **August**.

6 Click in the **Year Accessed box**, and then type **2014**. Click in the **Month Accessed box**, and then type **May**. Click in the **Day Accessed box**, and then type **5**.

7 Click in the **URL box**, and then type **http://www.northlakemag.com/freeman04-05.html**.

8 Click **OK**. The dialog box closes and the parenthetical *(Freeman)* is inserted at the insertion point.

9 At the bottom of page 1, in the last paragraph before the Program Development heading, position the insertion point before the period at the end of the paragraph.

10 On the References tab, in the Citations & Bibliography group, click the **Insert Citation button**. Notice that the source you just added is listed on the Insert Citation menu.

11 Click **Add New Source**.

12 Click the **Type of Source arrow**, and then click **Report**. The boxes in the dialog box change to collect the information needed when the source is a report.

13 Below the Author box, click the **Corporate Author check box** to select it, click in the empty box to the right of the Corporate Author label, and then type **North Lake Camping Committee**.

14 Click in the **Title box**, and then type **2013 Report on Survey Results**.

When you cite a Web site, you will not always be able to find an author name or the date the content was published.

15 Click in the **Year box**, and then type **2005**. Click in the **City box**, and then type **Elliot**.

16 Click **OK**. The dialog box closes and the citation is inserted.

Inserting a Citation to an Existing Source

If you need to insert a citation to a source you have already added to your source list, you simply select the source from the Insert Citation menu.

ACTIVITY

Insert a citation to an existing source.

1 At the top of page 2, at the end of the sentence above the Description of Program heading, position the insertion point immediately before the last period in the paragraph.

2 On the References tab, click the **Insert Citation button**. The two sources you added are listed at the top of the menu. See Exhibit 11-31.

3 Click **North Lake Camping Committee**. The citation is inserted at the insertion point.

Exhibit 11-31 Insert Citation menu with citations

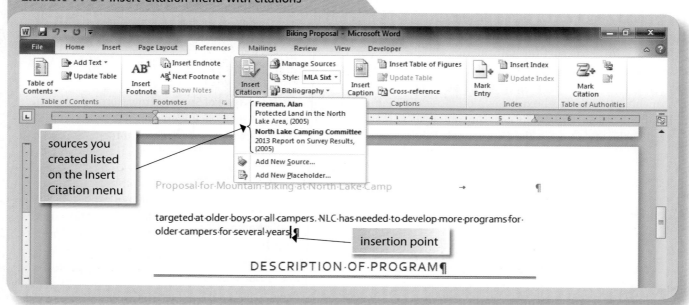

sources you created listed on the Insert Citation menu

insertion point

Acknowledging Your Sources

A research paper is a way for you to explore the available information about a subject and then present this information, along with your own understanding of the subject, in an organized and interesting way. Acknowledging all the sources of the information presented in your research paper is essential. If you fail to do this, you might be subject to charges of plagiarism, or trying to pass off someone else's thoughts as your own. Plagiarism is an extremely serious accusation, for which you could suffer academic consequences ranging from failing an assignment to being expelled from school. To ensure that you don't forget to cite a source, be careful to create citations in your document as you type it. It's very easy to forget to go back and cite all your sources correctly after you've finished typing a research paper. Forgetting to cite a source could lead to accusations of plagiarism and all of the consequences that entails.

Editing a Citation or a Source

Although a citation looks like ordinary text, it is actually contained inside a content control. As you saw when you inserted headers and footers, you can see the content control itself only when it is selected. If you need to add additional information to the citation, such as a page number, click the citation to display the content control, click the Citation Options arrow that appears, and then click Edit Citation to open the Edit Citation dialog box where you can enter the page number. If your style guide allows it, you can also use the Edit Citation dialog box to remove, or suppress, the author's name by selecting the Author check box in the Edit Citation dialog box, so that only the page number appears in the citation. Because Word will replace the suppressed author name with the title of the source, you need to suppress the title as well by selecting the Title check box in the Edit Citation dialog box.

ACTIVITY

Edit a citation to include the page number.

1 At the top of page 2, above the Description of Program heading, click the **North Lake Camping Committee citation**. The content control containing the citation appears. See Exhibit 11-32.

2 Click the **Citation Options arrow** , and then click **Edit Citation**. The Edit Citation dialog box opens with the insertion point in the Pages box.

Exhibit 11-32 Citation content control

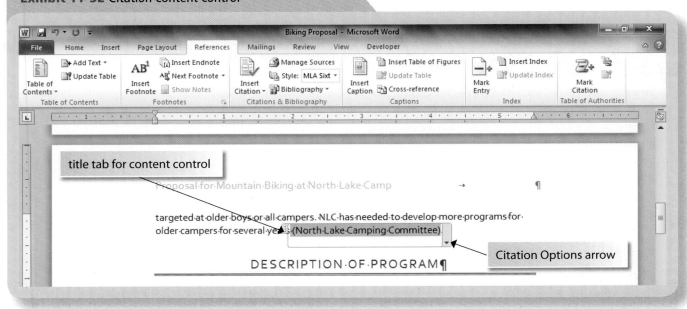

3 Type **7**, and then click **OK**. The dialog box closes and the citation changes to include the referenced page number from the report.

4 On page 1, in the paragraph above the Program Development heading, modify the North Lake Camping Committee citation to include the page reference **12**.

> ➤ **Tip:** To delete a citation, click the citation to display the content control, click the title tab (the tab with the three dots) on the left side of the content control, and then press the Delete key.

Modifying an Existing Source

To modify information about a source, you need to open the Edit Source dialog box for that source. To do this, click a citation to that source in the document to display the content control, click the Citation Options arrow on the content control, and then click Edit Source; or in the Source Manager dialog box, select the source in either the Master List or the Current List, and then click Edit. After you are finished editing the source, if the source is listed in both the Master List and the Current List, a dialog box opens prompting you to update both lists. In almost all cases, you should click Yes to ensure that the source information is correct in all places it is stored on your computer.

 **ACTIVITY**

To edit a source in the research paper.

1 Near the top of page 2, in the second paragraph under the Opportunity heading, click the **Freeman citation**.

2 On the content control, click the **Citation Options arrow**, and then click **Edit Source**. The Edit Source dialog box opens. It is identical to the Create Source dialog box, but, obviously, contains all the information you already entered for this source. Note that the name in the Author box has been altered to display the last name first, just as it would appear in a list of works cited.

3 Click the **Show All Bibliography Fields check box** to select it. The dialog box expands to show additional boxes for collecting information.

4 Click in the **Name of Web Site box**, and then type **North Lake Online Magazine**.

5 Click **OK**. A dialog box opens asking if you want to update the master source list and the current document.

6 Click **Yes**. The dialog box closes and the source is modified, although the citation remains unchanged.

Generating a List of Works Cited

To create a list of works cited for a document, click the Bibliography button in the Citations & Bibliography group on the References tab, and then click one of the options in the list. This creates a field that lists all the works in the Current List in the Source Manager dialog box. Because it is a field, you can update the list later to reflect changes to the source list. If you select the Works Cited style or the Bibliography style in the gallery, the appropriate title is inserted along with the field inside a content control. If you select Insert Bibliography, only the list of sources in the Current List in the Source Manger is inserted as a field; there is no content control, and you need to insert your own title. The format of the entries in the list of works cited matches the style selected in the Style box in the Citations & Bibliography group.

 **ACTIVITY**

Generate the bibliography.

1 Move the insertion point to the end of the document, and then insert a manual page break. A new page 5 is created.

2 On the References tab, in the Citations & Bibliography group, click the **Bibliography button**. The Bibliography menu opens, displaying two styles with preformatted headings: *Bibliography* and *Works Cited*. The command at the bottom inserts a bibliography without a preformatted heading. See Exhibit 11-33.

If there are no sources in the Current List and you create a list of works cited, a message is inserted telling you that there are no sources in the current document.

Exhibit 11-33 Bibliography menu

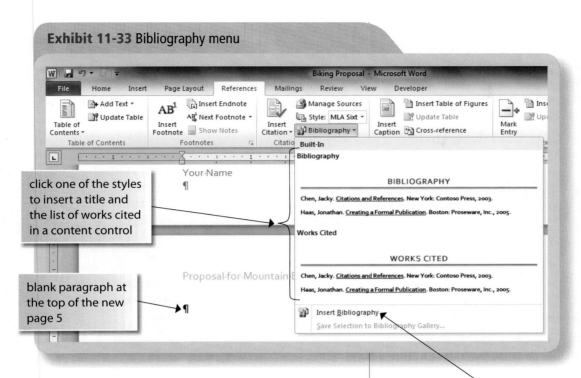

click one of the styles to insert a title and the list of works cited in a content control

blank paragraph at the top of the new page 5

click to insert the list of works cited as a field with no title and not in a content control

3 Click **Works Cited**. Word inserts the list of works cited below the Works Cited heading in the style selected in the Style box in the Citations & Bibliography group on the References tab. The text is formatted in the body font and the Works Cited heading is formatted with the Heading 1 style.

Using the Source Manager

When you create a source, it is added to both the Current List and the Master List of sources on the computer. The Current List is the list of sources associated with the current document. The Master List is available for use with any document created using the same user account on that computer. Both the Master List and the Current List are accessible via the Source Manager dialog box, which you open by clicking the Manage Sources button in the Citations & Bibliography group on the References tab. Using this dialog box, you can copy sources from the Master List to the Current List and remove sources from the Current List (and delete them from the Master List), as well as edit or create new sources. In the previous set of steps, when you confirmed that you wanted to update the master source list, you were confirming that you wanted to update the source information in both the Master List and the Current List.

If you want to add a source without inserting a citation, you can create a new source and insert the cita-

tion in the usual way; and then after the citation is inserted, click the citation to display the content control, click the title tab to select the entire control, and then press the Delete key to delete the citation. Or you can open the Source Manager dialog box, and then click New to display the Create Source dialog box. This will allow you to create the new source without inserting a citation. Sources listed in the Current List that are cited in the document have a check mark next to them. If you add a source to the Current List without adding a citation to it in the document, the source will not have a check mark next to it.

ACTIVITY

Examine the Source Manager dialog box.

1 On the References tab, in the Citations & Bibliography group, click the **Manage Sources button**. The Source Manager dialog box opens with the Master List of sources on the left and the Current List on the right. You can select a source in either list, and then click Copy, Delete, or Edit to perform those operations on that source.

2 Click **New**. The Create Source dialog box opens.

3 Click the **Type of Source arrow**, and then click **Book**.

4 Add the following information:

Author:	**Anne Santiago**
Title:	**Mountain Biking for Youth Programs**
Year:	**2013**
City:	**Boston**
Publisher:	**Holmes Press**

5 Click **OK**. The Create Source dialog box closes and the book you added appears in both the Master List and the Current List. In the Current List, there is no check mark next to it, indicating that the book is not cited in the document. See Exhibit 11-34.

6 Click **Close**. The Source Manager dialog box closes.

Updating the List of Works Cited

Because the list of works cited is a field, you can update the bibliography later to reflect any new source you add. If you created the list of works cited using the Insert Bibliography command, to update the field, you need to right-click it, and then on the shortcut menu, click Update Field. If you used one of the styles in the gallery and the list of works cited is in a content control, click the list to display the content control, and then on the title tab, click the Update Citations and Bibliography button.

Update the list of works cited.

1 On page 5, click anywhere in the **list of works cited**. The list itself is highlighted in gray, indicating that it is a field and not regular text. The content control containing the list is also visible. See Exhibit 11-35.

Exhibit 11-34 Source Manager dialog box

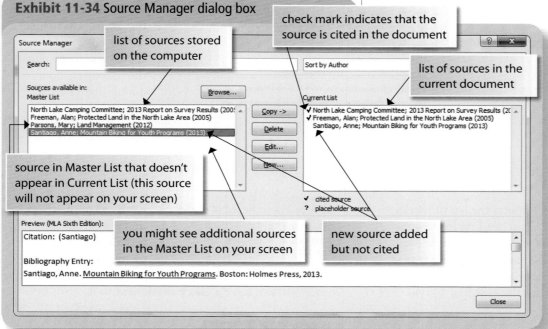

check mark indicates that the source is cited in the document

list of sources stored on the computer

list of sources in the current document

source in Master List that doesn't appear in Current List (this source will not appear on your screen)

you might see additional sources in the Master List on your screen

new source added but not cited

Exhibit 11-35 Works Cited displayed in a content control

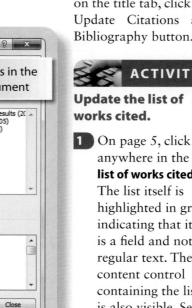

Update Citations and Bibliography button

Bibliographies button

sources inserted as fields

2 On the title tab, click the **Update Citations and Bibliography button**. The book you added in the Source Manager dialog box is added to the Works Cited list. The Web site name you added to the entry for Alan Freeman was not added because the selected style, the MLA style, does not display Web site names.

Tip: You can also click any citation in the document, click the Citation Options arrow, and then click Update Citations and Bibliography on the menu that opens.

3 Save the document.

Converting a List of Works Cited to Static Text

The Works Cited list is created using the style you select in the Style list in the Citations & Bibliography group on the References tab. Because styles get updated, or if your company or instructor wants you to use a modified style, you might need to adjust the style of the list. You can select the text and paragraphs as usual and add formatting, but if you then update the list, the formatting will revert to the selected style. When you are sure that you are finished updating the list, click the list to display the content control, click the Bibliographies button in the content control title tab, and then click Convert bibliography to static text to convert the list from a field that can be updated automatically to **static text**—that is, text that can't be updated automatically. Then you can modify the format of the list as desired; for example, change the format of titles from underlined to italics or modify the indent. Remember, after you convert a bibliography to static text, you can no longer update it to reflect changes to the sources. So don't convert it until the bibliography contains all the necessary source information.

LO11.9 Creating Footnotes and Endnotes

A **footnote** is an explanatory comment or reference that appears at the bottom of a page. When you create a footnote, Word inserts a small, superscript number called a **reference marker** in the text and in the bottom margin of the page, and positions the insertion point next to it so you can type the text of the footnote. **Endnotes** are similar, except that the text of an endnote appears at the end of a section or at the end of the document and the reference marker is a lowercase Roman numeral.

Word automatically manages the reference markers for you, keeping them sequential from the beginning of the document to the end, no matter how many times you add, delete, or move footnotes or endnotes. For example, if you move a paragraph containing footnote 4 so that it falls before the paragraph containing footnote 1, Word renumbers all the footnotes in the document to keep them sequential.

 **ACTIVITY**

Add a footnote.

1 On page 4, under the Questions heading, position the insertion point after the question mark after question number 4.

2 On the References tab, in the Footnotes group, click the **Insert Footnote button**. A superscript 1 is inserted as a reference marker at the insertion point and the same reference marker—the superscript number 1—appears in the bottom margin below a separator line (just above the footer area). The insertion point is now located next to the number in the bottom margin, ready for you to type the text of the footnote. See Exhibit 11-36.

static text Text that cannot be updated automatically.

footnote An explanatory comment or reference that appears at the bottom of a page.

reference marker A small, superscript number to the right of text that corresponds to the footnote or endnote.

endnote An explanatory comment or reference that appears at the end of a section or at the end of a document.

Exhibit 11-36 Insertion point in a new footnote

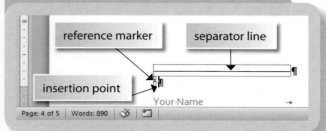

reference marker

separator line

insertion point

Your Name

Page: 4 of 5 | Words: 890

3 Type **If we need to increase our liability insurance, this will affect the budget.**

4 In the footnote, double-click directly on the reference marker (the superscript number 1). The document scrolls to the location of the reference marker in the text.

5 Scroll up to the bottom of page 2, and then in the bulleted list, position the insertion point after the last first-level item in the bulleted list, *Safety.*

6 On the References tab, in the Footnotes group, click the **Insert Footnote button**. A superscript 1 is again inserted as a reference marker, and the insertion point moves to the new footnote.

7 Type **We might want to have each participant sign a contract agreeing to these terms.**

8 On the References tab, in the Footnotes group, click the **Next Footnote button**. The document scrolls and the footnote you typed previously on page 4 appears. This footnote has been renumbered to 2 because it appears in the document after the footnote you added on page 2.

9 Save the document, and then close it.

A footnote always appears at the foot of the same page as its reference marker.

Citations in Footnotes or Endnotes

Footnotes and endnotes can contain any kind of information you think might be useful to your readers. Citations, however, are only used to list specific information about a book or other source you refer to or quote from in the document. Many style guides require citations to be inline and appear in parentheses at the end of the sentence containing information from the source you are citing. You can also display citations in footnotes or endnotes. This style is used in many nonfiction books. To insert a citation in a footnote or endnote, first click the Insert Footnote or Insert Endnote button in the Footnotes group on the References tab, and then insert the citation using the usual method.

Quiz Yourself

1. What style is applied to text if you do nothing to change it?

2. What is the template on which all Word documents are based?

3. How is a linked style different from a paragraph or character style?

4. How do you apply a Quick Style to text already in a document?

5. What is a theme?

6. What happens when you apply a different style set to a document?

7. What happens when you promote a paragraph in an outline?

8. How do you move a heading up or down in a document in both the Navigation Pane and in Outline view?

9. What is the default setting for margins in a new document?

10. Explain the difference between an automatic and a manual page break.

11. What do you actually insert when you use the Page Number command to insert page numbers in a document?

12. Define *header* and *footer*.

13. What is a content control?

14. What is a source?

15. Why do you need to cite your sources?

16. What is included in the list of works cited when you use the Bibliography command to create the list?

17. What is the difference between a footnote and an endnote?

Practice It

Practice It 11-1

1. Open the data file **Dams** located in the Chapter 11\ Practice It folder. Save the document as **Embankment Dams**.

2. Apply the Title Quick Style to the first paragraph.

3. Apply the Heading 1 Quick Style to the following paragraphs: History, Overview, Aswan Dam, Dams on the Missouri River, Largest Embankment Dam: Itaipu Dam, and Problems.

4. Apply the Heading 2 Quick Style to the following paragraphs: Types of Dams, First Dam on the Missouri River: Fort Peck, Dams That Followed the Fort Peck Dam, and Construction.

5. Apply the Heading 3 Quick Style to the following paragraphs: Slope and Permeability.

6. At the beginning of the document, select the History paragraph, change its size to 16 points, and underline it. Then update the definition of the Heading 1 Quick Style to match the formatting of the History paragraph.

7. At the beginning of the document, select the first paragraph, change the line spacing to single-spacing, and set the alignment to justified. Then create a new paragraph Quick Style based on this paragraph named **Body**, and apply this new style to all the body text in the document.

8. Change the theme to the Civic theme.

9. Change the theme colors to the Pushpin theme colors, and then change the theme fonts to the Elemental fonts.

10. Change the style set to the Distinctive style set.

11. Browse the document using the thumbnails in the Navigation Pane.

12. In the Navigation Pane, promote the Types of Dams heading to a Level 1 heading, and then move the History heading down so it follows the Types of Dams heading.

13. In Outline view, promote the Construction heading and its subheadings one level so that the Construction heading is a Level 1 heading. Then move the Construction heading and its subheadings up to precede the Dams on the Missouri River heading.

14. In Outline view, display the body text below the Problems heading. Create a new paragraph before the last paragraph in the document, type **Conclusion**, and then promote this paragraph to Level 1.

15. Change the bottom margin to 1.2 inches and the left and right margins to 1.5 inches.

16. At the end of the document, create a manual page break to create a new, blank page 5.

17. Use the Plain Number 3 style to insert a page number in the top right corner of every page. Do not show the page number on the first page.

18. Position the insertion point to the left of the page number in a header, left-align the paragraph, type your name, and then add two tab characters to move the page number back to the Right Tab stop in the header.

19. Insert the Stacks footer in the Footer gallery. In the Company content control, type your course name.

20. Change the style for citations and the list of works cited to the APA style.

21. On page 1, in the first paragraph under the History heading, delete the highlighted text *[citation]*, and then insert the following citation:

Type of Source:	Book
Author:	**R. L. Warren**
Title:	**Dam Building Deconstructed**
Year:	**2003**
City:	**Boston**
Publisher:	**Anston Press**

22. On page 2, in the first paragraph under the Aswan Dam heading, replace the highlighted text *[citation]* with the following citation:

Type of Source:	Web site
Name of Web Page:	**Modern Dams**
Name of Web Site:	**The Science of Building**
Year Accessed:	**2014**

Month Accessed: **June**
Day Accessed: **4**
URL: **http://www.scienceofbuilding.org/dams/modern.html**

23. On page 4, replace the highlighted text *[citation]* with a citation to *Dam Building Deconstructed* by R. L. Warren.

24. Add the page reference **53** to the citation on page 4, and then add the page reference **22** to the citation on page 1.

25. Modify the source Modern Dams to include **Sam Blackwater** as the author.

26. On page 5, generate a list of works cited using the built-in Bibliography style.

27. Create the following source without inserting a citation to it:

Type of Source: Book
Author: **Mark Crawford**
Title: **Dams on the Missouri**
Year: **2001**
City: **New York**
Publisher: **Messier Publishing**

28. Update the bibliography to include the new source.

29. On page 4, after the last sentence in the first paragraph at the top of the page (above the Largest Embankment Dam: Itaipu Dam heading), insert the following footnote: **Sheet piling was used as the impermeable layer in the Oahe Dam.** Then, on page 1, under the History heading, after the last sentence in the first paragraph, insert the following footnote: **This dam no longer exists, and the reservoir is now a desert.**

30. Save and close the document.

Practice It 11-2

1. Open the data file **Constitution** located in the Chapter 11\Practice It folder. Save the document as **New Constitution**.

2. Apply the Title Quick Style to the first paragraph, reduce the font size of the text in this paragraph to 22 points, and then update the Title Quick Style definition to match this change.

3. Apply the Heading 1 Quick Style to the following paragraphs: Introduction, A New Direction, Evolving Issues, Money Problems, Lack of Protection, States' Rights Concerns, and Conclusion.

4. Adjust the outline as follows:

Introduction
Evolving Issues
    States' Rights Concerns
    Money Problems
    Lack of Protection
A New Direction
Conclusion

5. Change the theme to Newsprint, and then change the theme fonts to Angles.

6. At the beginning of the document, change the line spacing in the first paragraph under the Introduction heading to 1.5, and then create a new linked Quick Style named **Extra Spacing**. Apply this style to all of the body text in the document.

7. Change the size of the text in a paragraph formatted with the Heading 1 style to 16 points, and then update the Heading 1 Quick Style definition to match this formatting. Change the size of the text in a paragraph formatted with the Heading 2 style to 12 points, and then update the Heading 2 Quick Style to match this formatting.

8. Change the top and bottom margins to 1.3 inches, and the left margin to 1.5 inches.

9. Replace the first instance of the highlighted text *[citation]* (under the States' Rights Concerns heading) with a citation to the following using the Turabian style:

Type of Source: Web site
Author: **G. S. Hardiman**
Name of Web
Page: **The Constitution: The Beginning**
Year Accessed: **2014**
Month Accessed: **February**
Day Accessed: **24**
URL: **http://www.illustratedushistory.net/constitution/beginning.html**

10. Replace the second instance of the highlighted text *[citation]* (under the Lack of Protection heading) with a citation to the following using the Turabian style:

Type of Source: Book
Author: **Mary P. Constant**
Title: **Shay's Rebellion: A Second Revolution**
Year: **2012**
City: **Sacramento**
Publisher: **Four Square Press**

11. Replace the third instance of the highlighted text *[citation]* (under the A New Direction heading) with a citation to the Web page authored by G.S. Hardiman.

12. At the end of the document, create a new page and insert a list of works cited using the built-in Bibliography style.

13. Create the following source without inserting a citation to it:

Type of Source:	Journal Article
Author:	**Devon Washington**
Title:	**Dissecting the Articles**
Journal Name:	**Journal of U.S. History**
Year:	**2011**
Pages:	**13–16**

14. Edit the journal article source by Devon Washington. Show all fields in the Edit Source dialog box, and then add the following:

Volume:	**16**

15. Update the list of works cited.

16. Add your name left-aligned in the header.

17. On page 1, after the last sentence in the first paragraph under the Introduction heading, insert the following footnote: **All amendments to the Articles of Confederation required a super majority.**

18. Save and close the document.

On Your Own

On Your Own 11-1

1. Open the data file **Lab** located in the Chapter 11\On Your Own folder. Save the document as **Lab Report**.

2. Change the style set to Manuscript.

3. Format the second paragraph (*Introduction*) so the text is 12 points. Use the Font dialog box to format the text as all uppercase letters. (*Hint*: On the Home tab, in the Font group, click the Dialog Box Launcher, and then select the All caps check box in the Font dialog box.) Center the paragraph, and then change the space before the paragraph to 36 points. Update the Heading 1 Quick Style to match this formatting.

4. Apply the redefined Heading 1 Quick Style to the following paragraphs: Purpose, Materials and Methods, Results, and Discussion.

5. Move the section titled *Purpose* so it is the first section in the document following the title.

6. Use the Cover Page button in the Pages group on the Insert tab to insert the Conservative cover page. On the cover page, type your course name in the Company content control. In the Title content control, type **Mitosis and the Cell Cycle**. In the Author content control, add your name. In the Date content control, add the current date. Click the Subtitle content control, click the Subtitle tab that appears, and then press the Delete key.

7. On the second page, cut the paragraph under the Purpose heading, and then paste it in the Abstract content control at the bottom of the cover page. On page 2, delete the Purpose heading.

8. Using the APA style, add the following sources without inserting citations. (*Hint*: Show all the fields in the Create Source dialog box.)

Type of Source:	Book
Author:	**Carolyn Davis, John Griffin, Sandra Suleki**
Title:	**Biology Basics**
Year:	**2013**
City:	**New York**
Publisher:	**Kenfield Books**
Edition:	**4**

Type of Source:	Article in a Periodical
Author:	**Jeremy Smith, M.D.**
Title:	**Mitosis Myths**
Periodical Title:	**Science for Today**
Year:	**2014**
Month:	**August**
Pages:	**35–42**
Volume:	**4**
Issue:	**5**

9. On a new page at the end of the document, create a list of works cited titled *Works Cited*.

10. Edit the Biology Basics source so the edition is **4th**, and then update the list of works cited.

11. Use the Newsprint footer to insert your name and the page number in the footer. Do not show the footer on the title page.

12. In the footer, click your name. Note the name of the content control containing your name.

13. Position the insertion point in the last paragraph in the document (after the Works Cited list). Insert an endnote that explains why your name was inserted automatically in the footer.

Enhancing a Document

Introduction

Word documents can contain much more than text. Elements such as tables, illustrations, graphical headlines, and formatted headings can be used to enhance documents. Some documents (including this book) are formatted in multiple columns. Other documents have decorative borders around the entire page. People often add these elements to documents to make the information easier to read and understand, highlight specific points, and add interest.

Word provides many tools for creating these effects. Tables allow you to easily organize information in rows and columns. Sections allow you to format different parts of a document in different ways. Clip art provides a variety of images you can add to your document and WordArt allows you to create eye-catching headlines. Building blocks allow you to create formatted text and graphical elements to reuse in many documents. This helps to give related documents a consistent look.

These enhancements are used in any kind of document, though you'll commonly see them in flyers and newsletters. Longer documents, whether a business proposal, a research report, or an employee handbook, also benefit from these kinds of enhancements.

Learning Objectives

After studying the material in this chapter, you will be able to:

LO12.1 Create and modify tables

LO12.2 Change the page orientation

LO12.3 Divide a document into sections

LO12.4 Insert and modify graphics

LO12.5 Add WordArt

LO12.6 Wrap text around graphics

LO12.7 Work with columns

LO12.8 Work with building blocks

LO12.1 Organizing Information in Tables

A **table**, a grid of horizontal rows and columns, is a useful way to present information that is organized into categories. For example, you can use a table to organize contact information for a list of clients. For each client, you could include in the following information: first name, last name, street address, city, state, and ZIP code.

Tables are organized into columns and rows. The box at the intersection of a column and a row is a **cell**. The row at the top of the table, called the **header row**,

table A grid of horizontal rows and vertical columns.

cell The intersection of a column and a row.

header row The top row in a table that contains the names.

StockLite/Shutterstock.com

Inserting tables and images in a document and using special formatting, such as columns, can help clarify main points of a document as well as enhance its appearance.

typically contains the labels for the columns so you know what type of data appears in each column.

Creating a Table

When you create a table in Word, you specify how many rows and columns to include in the table. You do this with the Table button on the Insert tab in the Tables group. When you click the Table button, you can drag across the grid that appears to select the number of columns and rows to include in the table. You can also click the Insert Table command to open the Insert Table dialog box in which you can specify the number of columns and rows. After you create a table, the Table Tools contextual tabs appear on the Ribbon.

Exhibit 12-1 Table selected on Table menu grid

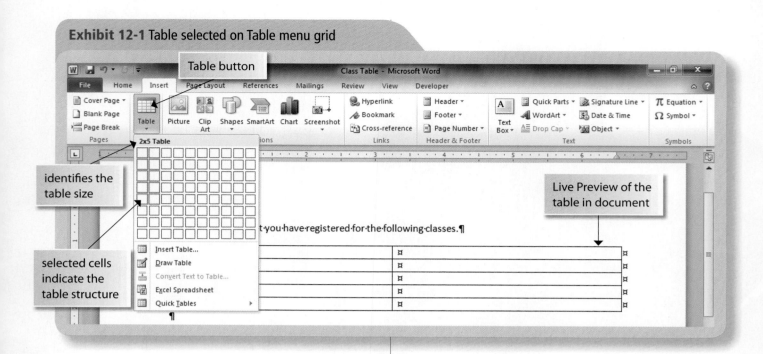

Table button

identifies the table size

selected cells indicate the table structure

Live Preview of the table in document

2x5 Table

Insert Table...
Draw Table
Convert Text to Table...
Excel Spreadsheet
Quick Tables

t·you·have·registered·for·the·following·classes.¶

ACTIVITY

Create a table.

1. Open the data file **Table** located in the Chapter 12\Chapter folder. Save the document as **Class Table**.

2. In the body of the letter, position the insertion point in the second paragraph (the blank paragraph).

3. On the Ribbon, click the **Insert tab**. In the Tables group, click the **Table button**. A table grid opens, with a menu at the bottom.

4. Point to the grid to highlight **two columns** and **five rows**. (The outline of a cell turns orange when it is highlighted.) As you move the pointer across the grid, Word indicates the size of the table (columns by rows) at the top of the grid. A Live Preview of the table structure appears in the document. See Exhibit 12-1.

5. When **2×5 Table** appears at the top of the grid, click the lower-right cell. An empty table consisting of two columns and five rows is inserted in the

document, with the insertion point in the upper-left cell. The two columns are of equal width. Because nonprinting characters are displayed in the document, each cell contains an end-of-cell mark, and each row contains an end-of-row mark. The Table Tools Design and Layout contextual tabs appear on the Ribbon, and the Design tab is now the active tab. See Exhibit 12-2.

Creating a Quick Table

A **Quick Table** is a table template that contains sample text and formatting. To insert a Quick Table, point to the Quick Tables command on the Table button menu, and then scroll through the gallery of Quick Tables that appears. You can insert a calendar, a simple list, tables with subheads, and other types of formatted tables. You can then replace the text in the Quick Table with your own text.

ITEM	NEEDED
Books	1
Magazines	3
Notebooks	1
Paper pads	1
Pens	3
Pencils	2
Highlighter	2 colors
Scissors	1 pair

Quick Table A table template with sample text and formatting.

Exhibit 12-2 Blank table with two columns and five rows

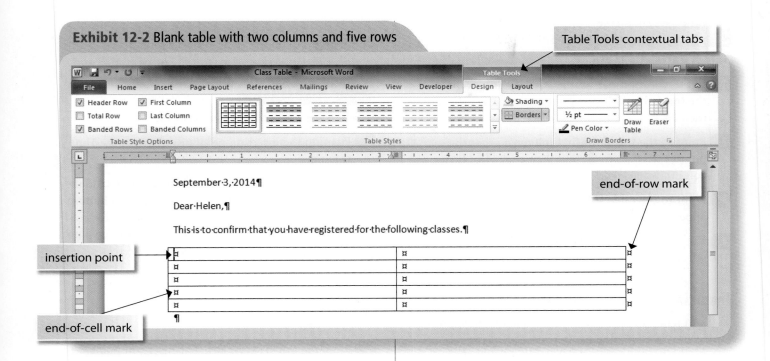

Table Tools contextual tabs

insertion point

end-of-row mark

end-of-cell mark

Entering Data in a Table

To enter data in a table, simply move the insertion point to a cell and type. You can move the insertion point to a cell by clicking in that cell. You can also use the keyboard to move the insertion point between cells. To move to the next cell to the right, press the Tab key. To move to the next cell to the left, press the Shift+Tab keys. You can also press the arrow keys. If the data takes up more than one line in the cell, Word automatically wraps the text to the next line and increases the height of that cell as well as all of the cells in that row.

 **ACTIVITY**

Enter data into a table.

1 With the insertion point in the upper-left cell in the table, type **Class**. As you type, the end-of-cell mark moves right to accommodate the text.

2 Press the **Tab key** to move the insertion point to the next cell to the right.

3 Type **Time** and then press the **Tab key**. Because the insertion point was in the last column, it moves to the first cell in the next row.

4 Type the following information in the table, pressing the **Tab key** to move from cell to cell:

Ballet	5–6
Tap	6–7
Jazz	6–7:30
Modern	6–8

Selecting Parts of a Table

As you work with tables, you need to be able to select parts of them. You can select a cell, a row or column, multiple rows or columns, or the entire cell. To select parts of a table from the Ribbon, with the insertion point positioned in a cell, click the Select button in the Table group on the Table Tools Layout tab, and then click the appropriate command—Select Cell, Select Column, Select Row, or Select Table. You can also use the pointer to select parts of a table. To select an entire row, point to the row in the left margin so that the pointer changes to ⟋, and then click to select that row; to select a column, point just above the top of a column so the pointer changes to ↓, and then click. You can drag to select adjacent rows, columns, or cells, or use the Shift or Ctrl key while clicking to select adjacent and nonadjacent cells, rows, or columns. You can also click the table move handle ⊞ in the upper-left corner of the table to select the entire table. To deselect a cell or table, click anywhere else in the document.

> ⚠ **Problem?** If a new row appears at the bottom of your table, you pressed the Tab key when the insertion point was in the last cell in the table. On the Quick Access Toolbar, click the **Undo button** ↺ to remove the extra row from the table.

Select parts of a table.

1 In the selection bar (in the left margin), point to the **top row** so that the pointer changes to ↗, and then click. The top row is selected.

2 Point to the **top of the first column** so that the pointer changes to ↓, and then click. The first column is selected.

3 Point to the table so that the **table move handle** ⊞ appears above the upper-left corner of the table.

4 Click the **table move handle** ⊞. The entire table is selected.

Inserting a Row or Column

You can modify the structure of a table by adding or removing rows and columns. If you need to insert a new row to the bottom of a table because you need to enter additional rows of data, make sure the insertion point is located in the right-most cell in the bottom row, and then press the Tab key. To insert a row anywhere else in the table, position the insertion point in a row below or above where you want to insert the new row, and then click either the Insert Above button or the Insert Below button in the Rows & Columns group on the Table Tools Layout tab. Inserting a column is similar to inserting a row. First, click anywhere in the column to the right or left of where you want to insert a new column. Then click either the

Insert Left button or Insert Right button in the Rows & Columns group on the Table Tools Layout tab.

 **ACTIVITY**

Insert rows and columns in a table.

1 Position the insertion point anywhere in the **Time column**.

2 On the Ribbon, click the **Table Tools Layout tab**. In the Rows & Columns group, click the **Insert Left button**. A new, blank column is inserted to the left of the column containing the insertion point (the Time column). The width of the original two columns decreases, and all three columns are the same width. The overall width of the table did not change. See Exhibit 12-3.

3 In the new column, click in the **top cell**, and then type **Day**.

4 Press the **Down Arrow key**. The insertion point moves down one row.

5 Type the following information in the new column, pressing the **Down Arrow key** to move from cell to cell:
Tuesday
Tuesday
Thursday
Wednesday

> **Tip:** You can use AutoComplete to enter the days of the week.

Exhibit 12-3 New column inserted

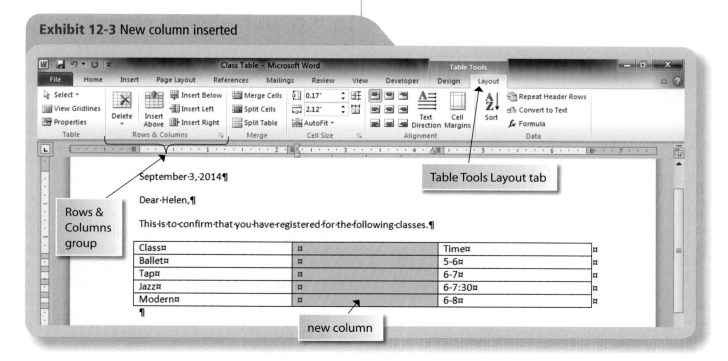

Exhibit 12-4 Table with new column and row

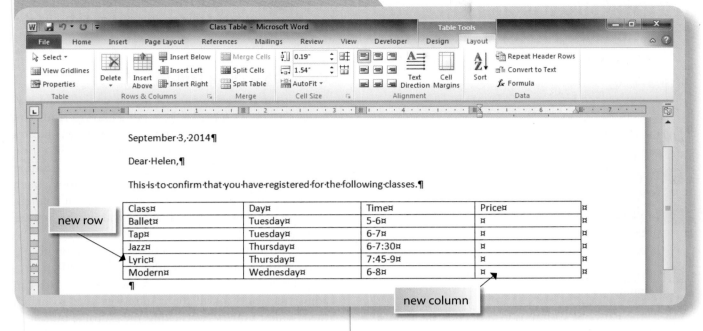

6 Make sure the insertion point is in the second cell in the last row. On the Table Tools Layout tab, in the Rows & Columns group, click the **Insert Above button**. A new row is inserted above the row containing the insertion point.

7 Click in the first cell in the new row, type **Lyric**, press the **Tab key**, type **Thursday**, press the **Tab key**, and then type **7:45–9**.

8 Position the insertion point anywhere in the **last column**. In the Rows & Columns group, click the **Insert Right button**. A new column is inserted to the right of the Time column, and all the columns are resized.

9 In the new column, click in the **top cell**, and then type **Price**. See Exhibit 12-4.

Deleting a Row, Column, or Table

You can delete content from a table without deleting the structure of the table or the table itself. To delete the *contents* of a cell, row, column, or table, select the parts of the table containing the contents you want to delete, and then press the Delete key.

You can also delete a row or column or the entire table. To delete the *structure* of a row, column, or the entire table—including its contents—you select the row (or column or the entire table) and then use the Delete button in the Rows & Columns group on the Table

Tools Layout tab. To delete multiple rows or columns, start by selecting all the rows or columns you want to delete.

ACTIVITY

Delete the table, a column, and a row.

1 Make sure the insertion point is positioned anywhere in the table.

2 On the Table Tools Layout tab, in the Rows & Columns group, click the **Delete button**. The Delete menu opens, displaying options for deleting cells, columns, rows, or the entire table. See Exhibit 12-5.

Exhibit 12-5 Delete button menu

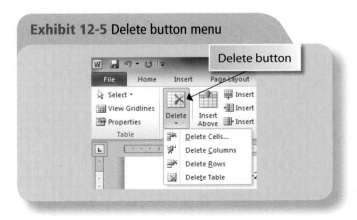

3 On the menu, click **Delete Table**. The entire table is deleted.

To create text in columns, it is often easier and faster to use a table rather than tabs.

4 On the Quick Access Toolbar, click the **Undo button** . The table is restored.

5 Position the insertion point anywhere in the **Jazz row**.

6 In the Rows & Columns group, click the **Delete button**, and then click **Delete Rows**. The Jazz row is deleted.

7 Position the insertion point anywhere in the **Price column**.

8 In the Rows & Columns group, click the **Delete button**, and then click **Delete Columns**.

9 The Price column is deleted. Notice that the width of the three remaining columns does not change and the table no longer extends to fill the width of the page.

Changing Column Widths

Columns that are too narrow or too wide for the material they contain can make a table hard to read. You can change a column's width by dragging the column's right border to a new position. When the insertion point is positioned in a table, Move Table Column markers appear on the horizontal ruler above each column border to indicate the width of each column. You can use these as a guide when you resize a border manually.

If you prefer, you can double-click a column border to make the column width adjust automatically to accommodate the widest entry in the column. You can adjust the width of all the columns at once to match their widest entries by clicking the AutoFit button in the Cell Size group on the Table Tools Layout tab, and

Sorting Rows in a Table

You can sort a table based on the contents of one of the columns in alphabetical, numerical, or chronological order. For example, you could sort the table you just created based on the contents of the Class column. When you sort, you can choose to sort either in ascending (alphabetical or lowest to highest) or descending (reverse alphabetical or highest to lowest) order.

You can also sort a table based on more than one column. For example, if a table included a list of items purchased at several stores, you could sort the table first on the store names, and then on the item names so that the list would be alphabetized by store name and then by item name within each store. To sort a table, select the table, then, on the Table Tools Layout tab, click the Sort button to open the Sort dialog box.

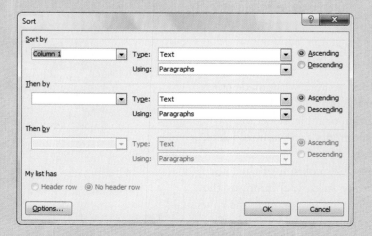

> When creating tables, be sure to adjust both the table width and column widths as needed to make the content easy to read.

then clicking AutoFit Contents. To make the entire table span the page width, click the AutoFit button in the Cell Size group on the Table Tools Layout tab, and then click AutoFit Window.

When you adjust the width of a table column, you need to be sure that nothing is selected in the table. If a cell is selected when you change the column width, only the width of the selected cell will be changed.

ACTIVITY

Change the width of the columns in the table.

1 Click anywhere in the table, if necessary. On the ruler, Move Table Column markers ▦ indicate the width of each column. See Exhibit 12-6.

2 Point to the **Time column right border** so that the pointer changes to ◂‖▸.

3 Double-click the **Time column right border**. The column border moves left so that the Time column is just wide enough to accommodate the widest entry in the column.

> **Tip:** To change the height of a row, point to the bottom row border and drag the border up or down.

4 On the Table Tools Layout tab, in the Cell Size group, click the **AutoFit button**. A menu opens.

5 On the menu, click **AutoFit Contents**. All the columns in the table adjust so that each is just wide enough to accommodate its widest entry.

6 Point to the **Class column right border** so that the pointer changes to ◂‖▸, and then press and hold the mouse button. A vertical dotted line the length of the window appears.

7 Drag the **Class column right border** to the right until the Move Table Column marker on the ruler is at the 1-inch mark. The right border of the middle column did not move, so the middle column is now too narrow.

8 Drag the **Time column right border** to the right until the Move Table Column marker on the ruler is at the **3-inch mark** on the ruler.

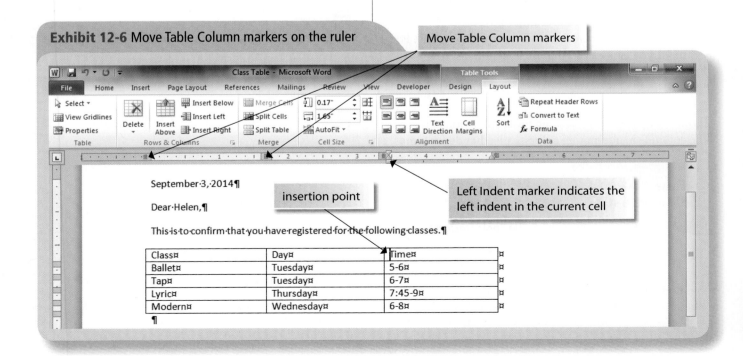

Exhibit 12-6 Move Table Column markers on the ruler

9 Drag the **Day right column border** to the right to the **2-inch mark** on the ruler. See Exhibit 12-7.

Exhibit 12-7 Table with columns one-inch wide

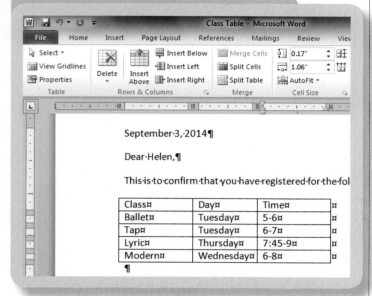

Formatting Tables with Table Styles

You have already used styles to format text and paragraphs. Word also includes a variety of built-in styles that you can use to add borders, shading, and color to tables. You select a table style from the Table Styles group on the Table Tools Design tab, which displays a selection of table styles.

When you apply a style to a table, you can select or deselect the check boxes in the Table Style Options group on the Table Tools Design tab to format the rows and columns either before or after you apply a style. For example, you can specify that the first and last rows—the header and total rows—and the first and last columns be formatted differently from the rest of the rows and columns in the table. Some styles format the rows in alternating colors, called **banded rows**, while others format the columns in alternating colors, called **banded columns**.

 **ACTIVITY**

Apply a table style.

1 On the Ribbon, click the **Table Tools Design tab**. In the Table Styles group, the plain black-and-white grid style is highlighted, indicating that it is the ta-

banded rows (banded columns) Formatting that displays alternate rows (or columns) in a table with different fill colors.

Understanding AutoFit in Tables

The default setting for tables in Word is for the table width to be the same width as the page, for text to wrap within cells, and for the columns to automatically resize as you enter text. This means that if you enter text in a cell with a natural breaking point, such as between words, the text will wrap within the cell. But if there is no natural breaking point, the column will widen to accommodate the long entry and the other columns will become narrower to keep the total width of the table the same. You can control this behavior using the commands on the AutoFit button menu in the Cell Size group on the Table Tools Layout tab. The first command, AutoFit Contents, changes the column width to just fit the contents of each cell, including shrinking the width of empty columns. The second command, AutoFit Window, returns the table to the default behavior. The third command, Fixed Column Width, causes the column widths to stay the same no matter how wide an entry is.

group, the Header Row, First Column, and Banded Rows check boxes are selected.

2 In the Table Styles group, click the **More button** . The Table Styles gallery opens. Now the plain black-and-white grid style appears at the top of the gallery, in the Plain Tables section. The rest of the Table Styles appear in the Built-In section. See Exhibit 12-8.

3 In the Built-In section, in the fifth row, click the

Like other styles, if you change the theme after applying a table style, the colors in the table change to match the colors of the new theme.

Exhibit 12-8 Table Styles gallery

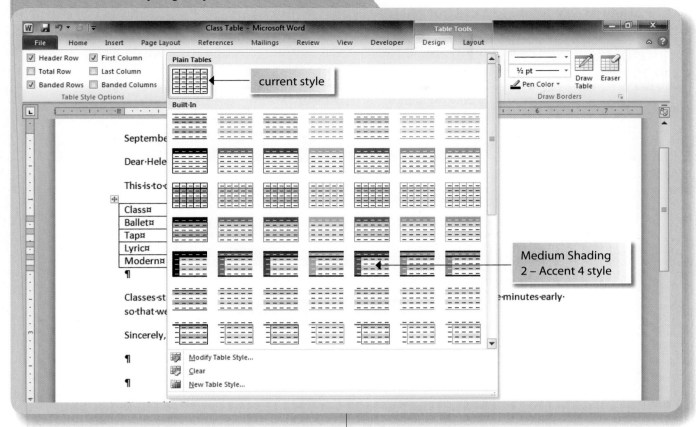

current style

Medium Shading 2 – Accent 4 style

Medium Shading 2 – Accent 4 style (the purple style). The Table Styles gallery closes and the table is formatted with the style you selected.

4 In the Table Style Options group, click the **First Column** check box to deselect it. The bold formatting and dark purple shading are removed from the first column in the table.

Fine-tuning Table Styles

After you apply a table style to a table, you might like the look of the table, but find that it no longer effectively conveys the information or is not quite as easy to read. To solve this problem, you can, of course, apply a different style to the table. You can also customize the table formatting by using the Shading and Borders buttons in the Table Styles group on the Table Tools Design tab. Remember that built-in styles and shading and border colors that you choose from the Theme Colors in the color palette will change if you change the theme.

Aligning Tables and Text in Tables

You can change the alignment of text in cells and you can change the alignment of the entire table. To change the alignment of text in cells, use the alignment buttons in the Alignment group on the Table Tools Layout tab. To change the alignment of the table, align it the same way you align a paragraph by using the paragraph alignment buttons in the Paragraph group on the Home tab.

 **ACTIVITY**

Align a table and the text in a table.

1 Click the **table move handle** to select the entire table.

2 On the Ribbon, click the **Home tab**. In the Paragraph group, click the **Center button**. The table is centered horizontally on the page.

3 Select the **Time column**.

4 On the Ribbon, click the **Table Tools Layout tab**. In the Alignment group, click the **Align Top Center button**. All the text in the Time column is centered in the cells. See Exhibit 12-9.

5 Save the document.

Exhibit 12-9 Center-aligned table and column text

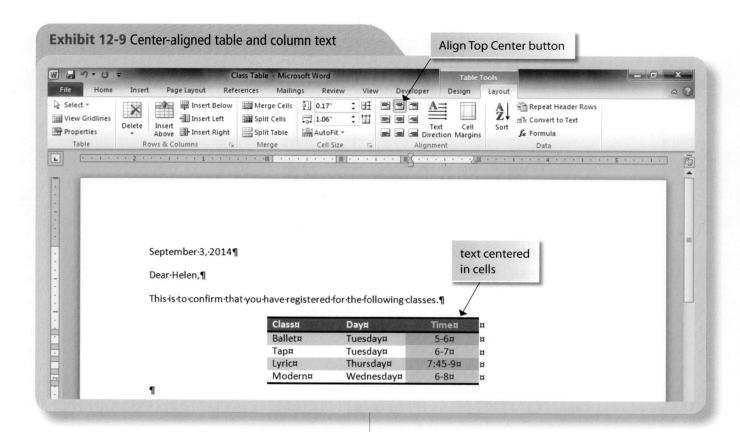

Align Top Center button

text centered in cells

September·3,·2014¶

Dear·Helen,¶

This·is·to·confirm·that·you·have·registered·for·the·following·classes.¶

Class¤	Day¤	Time¤	¤
Ballet¤	Tuesday¤	5-6¤	¤
Tap¤	Tuesday¤	6-7¤	¤
Lyric¤	Thursday¤	7:45-9¤	¤
Modern¤	Wednesday¤	6-8¤	¤

¶

LO12.2 Changing the Page Orientation

You can set the **orientation**—the way a page is turned—for the pages in a document. A page set to **portrait orientation** is taller than it is wide. This orientation, most commonly used for letters, reports, and other formal documents, is the usual orientation for most Word documents. **Landscape orientation** is a page that is wider than it is tall. You can easily change the orientation of a document using the Orientation button in the Page Setup group on the Page Layout tab.

orientation The way a page is turned.

portrait orientation The layout of a page taller than it is wide.

landscape orientation The layout of a page wider than it is tall.

section A part of a document that can have its own page-level formatting and properties.

ACTIVITY

Change the page orientation.

1 Open the data file **Flyer** located in the Chapter 12\ Chapter folder. Save the document as **Dance Flyer**. The document opens in One Page view.

2 On the Ribbon, click the **Page Layout tab**. In the Page Setup group, click the **Orientation button**. The Orientation menu opens with Portrait selected.

3 On the menu, click **Landscape**. The document changes to landscape orientation, with the page wider than it is tall. See Exhibit 12-10.

LO12.3 Working with Document Sections

A **section** is a part of a document that can have its own page-level formatting and properties. For example, you can format one section in a document with one-inch margins and portrait orientation, and the next section with two-inch margins and landscape orientation. Different sections in a document could also have

Exhibit 12-10 Document in landscape orientation

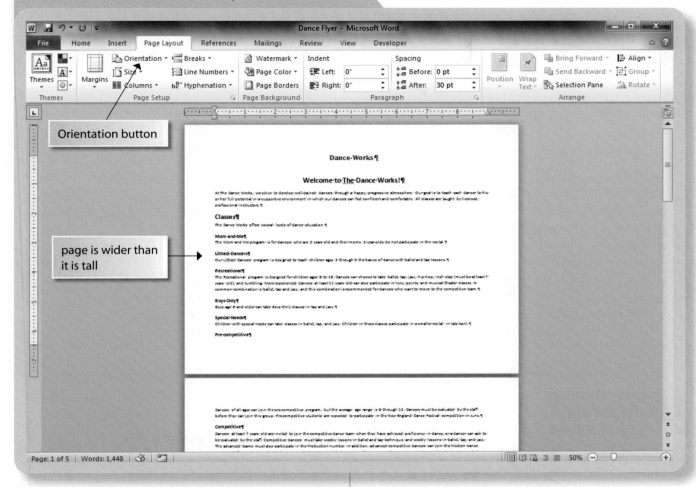

Orientation button

page is wider than
it is tall

different headers and footers, or a new section can restart the page numbering.

Every document has at least one section. To divide a document into multiple sections, you insert a **section break**, which appears as a dotted line with the words *Section Break*. The four types of section breaks are:

▶ **Next Page**—inserts a section break and forces a new page to start after the section break

▶ **Continuous**—inserts a section break without starting a new page

▶ **Even Page**—inserts a section break and forces a new page to start on the next even-numbered page

▶ **Odd Page**—inserts a section break and forces a new page to start on the next odd-numbered page

The information for the formatting of a section is contained in the section break that follows the section. This means that if you delete a section break, the formatting from the section below the deleted section break is applied to the section above the deleted

section break. The formatting information for the last section in a document, or in a document with no section breaks, is contained in the last paragraph mark in the document.

Inserting a Section Break

To insert a section break, use the Breaks button in the Page Setup group on the Page Layout tab to select the type of section break you want to insert. When non-printing characters are displayed, a section break is indicated by a double dotted line with the words *Section Break* in the center of it, followed by the type of section break. If the section break appears at the end of a line, you can see only the first part of the dotted line. To see the type of section break inserted, you can switch to Draft view, which displays the text of the document without showing its layout.

section break A formatting mark in a document that indicates the start of a new section.

Creating Odd and Even Pages

Most professionally produced books and reports are printed on both sides of the paper and then bound. When you open a bound book or report, odd-numbered pages appear on the right, and even-numbered pages appear on the left. The margin on the inside of each page, where the pages are bound together, is called the gutter. Often, the headers and footers for odd-numbered pages are different from the headers or footers for the even-numbered pages. For instance, the page numbers might appear on the outside edge of the footer. So on odd-numbered pages, page numbers appear on the right side of the footer; and on even-numbered pages, they appear on the left side of the footer.

You can set up the pages in a multiple-page document with odd and even pages. After you insert a header or footer, on the Header & Footer Tools Design tab, select the Different Odd & Even Pages check box in the Options group. To increase the width of the gutter to allow for binding, click the Margins button in the Page Setup group on the Page Layout tab, and then click Custom Margins to open the Page Setup dialog box with the Margins tab selected. Change the measurement in the Gutter box.

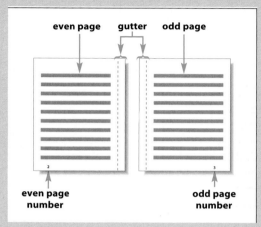

even page   gutter   odd page

even page number   odd page number

ACTIVITY

Insert a section break.

1 On the Ribbon, click the **View tab**. In the Zoom group, click the **Page Width button**.

2 Scroll down to the bottom of page 3, and then position the insertion point in front of the Faculty heading.

3 On the Ribbon, click the **Page Layout tab**. In the Page Setup group, click the **Breaks button**. The Breaks menu opens, as shown in Exhibit 12-11. The Page Breaks section of the menu includes options for controlling how the text flows from page to page. The first option, Page, inserts a page break (just like the Page Break button on the Insert tab that you used earlier). The Section Breaks section of the menu includes four types of section breaks.

> **Tip:** To delete a section break, click the line representing the break, and then press the Delete key.

4 In the Section Breaks section, click **Next Page**. A section break is inserted, and the insertion point moves to the top of the new page 4. See Exhibit 12-12.

5 On the status bar, click the **Draft button** ▤. The document switches to Draft view, and the section break appears all the way across the screen. See Exhibit 12-13.

6 Switch back to **Print Layout view**.

Exhibit 12-11 Breaks menu

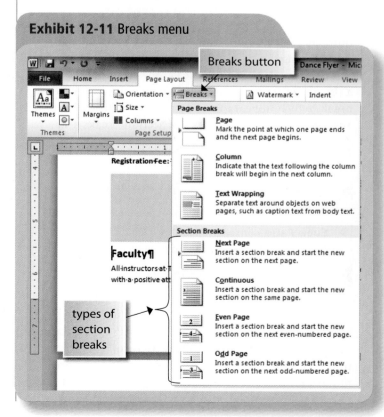

Exhibit 12-12 Next Page section break

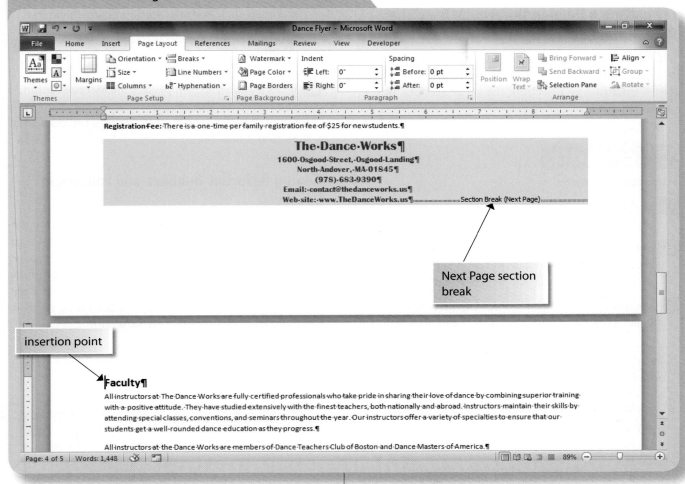

Next Page section break

insertion point

Exhibit 12-13 Next Page section break in Draft view

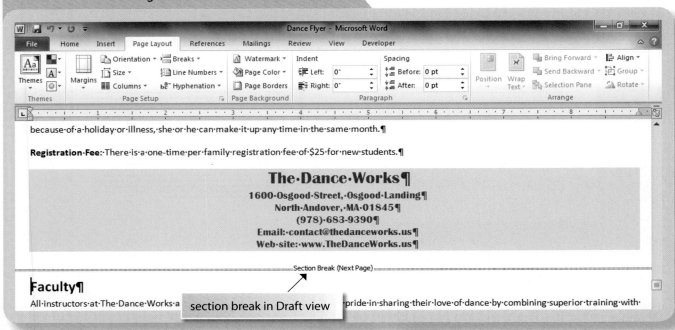

section break in Draft view

Formatting a Section Differently from the Rest of the Document

Once you have inserted a section break, you can format each section separately. When you change the page-level formatting of a section, the other sections in the document remain unchanged.

ACTIVITY

Format a section.

1 Make sure the insertion point is positioned before the Faculty heading on page 4.

2 On the Ribbon, click the **View tab**. In the Zoom group, click the **Two Pages button**. Pages 3 and 4 of the document appear side by side in the window.

3 On the Ribbon, click the **Page Layout tab**. In the Page Setup group, click the **Orientation button**,

and then click **Portrait**. Section 2, which consists of pages 4 and 5, changes to portrait orientation. Section 1, which consists of pages 1–3, remains in landscape orientation.

4 In the Page Setup group, click the **Margins button**, and then click **Narrow**. The margin settings for Section 2 change to the Narrow setting, and the text in Section 2 now fits all on page 4. See Exhibit 12-14.

Adding Different Headers and Footers in Sections

One of the advantages of dividing a document into sections is that the headers and footers in each section can differ. For example, if the document includes a cover page, and you want the page numbering to begin on the first page after the cover page, you can insert a section break after the cover page, and then have the page numbers start and appear only in Section 2.

Exhibit 12-14 Page 4 formatted in portrait orientation with narrow margins

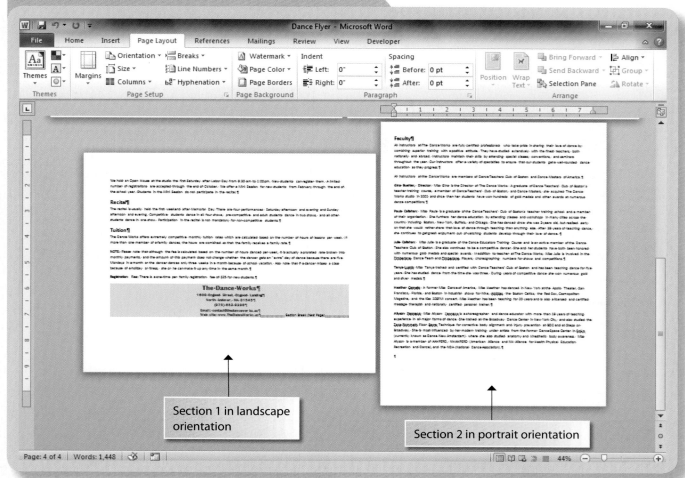

Section 1 in landscape orientation

Section 2 in portrait orientation

The Cover Page button in the Pages group on the Insert tab automatically inserts a section break after the cover page.

ACTIVITY

Add different headers and footers in sections.

1. Change the zoom back to **Page Width**, and make sure the insertion point is still before the Faculty heading on page 4.

2. On the Ribbon, click the **Insert tab**. In the Header & Footer group, click the **Footer button**, and then below the gallery, click **Edit Footer**. The insertion point moves to the footer area on page 4. The Footer area is labeled Footer -Section 2-, and on the right, a tag labels this footer the Same as Previous. See Exhibit 12-15.

3. Press the **Tab key**, and then type your name. Your name is aligned with the Center Tab stop in the footer.

4. Scroll up to see the bottom of page 3. The footer area on this page is labeled Footer -Section 1-, and your name appears here as well.

5. Scroll back down, and make sure the insertion point is still in the footer area for Section 2.

6. On the Header & Footer Tools Design tab, in the Navigation group, click the **Link to Previous button**. The button is no longer selected, and the Same as Previous tag on the footer disappears.

7. Scroll up so you can see the bottom of page 3. Notice that the Section 2 header area on page 4 still contains the Same as Previous tag.

8. On page 3, in the footer area, delete the tab character before your name so it is left-aligned, and then position the insertion point after your name.

9. Press the **Tab key** twice, and then type **DRAFT**.

Exhibit 12-15 Footer area for Section 2

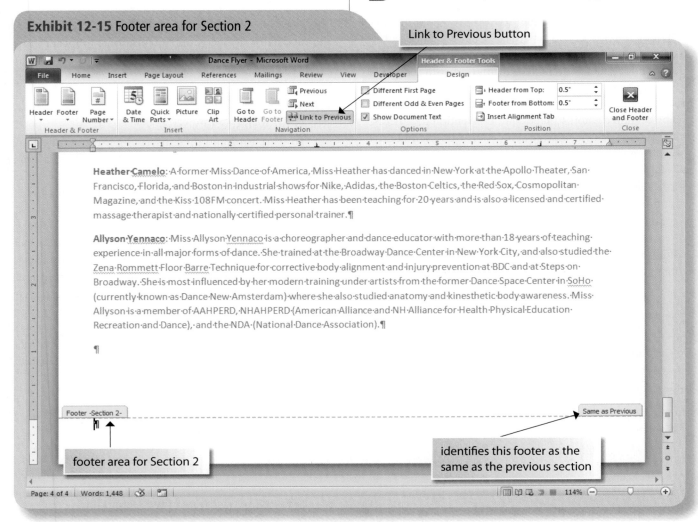

10 Scroll back down so you can see the footer at the bottom of page 4. It is unchanged and does not include the word *DRAFT*.

11 Double-click anywhere in the document outside the header or footer areas. The header and footer areas are no longer available.

12 Save the document.

LO12.4 Inserting and Modifying Graphics

A **graphic** is a picture, shape, design, graph, chart, or diagram. You can include many types of graphics in your presentation: graphics created using other programs; scanned photographs, drawings, and cartoons; and other picture files or clip art stored on your computer or network. You can also create graphics using drawing tools in Word.

A graphic is an example of an object. An **object** is anything in a document or other file that can be treated as a whole. For example, a table is an object. Objects can be added, deleted, moved, formatted, and resized.

Graphics are saved in a variety of file types. Photographs, generated by taking pictures with a digital camera or by scanning photos taken with conventional cameras, and pictures drawn using graphics software such as Microsoft Paint are a type of picture file called a bitmap. A **bitmap** is a grid (or "map") of square colored dots that form a picture. The colored dots are pixels. A **vector graphic** is composed of straight and curved lines and is stored as a mathematical formula. File types for vector graphics are often proprietary, which means they can be opened and edited only in specific graphics programs, such as Adobe Illustrator or CorelDRAW. Vector graphics are often used

for line drawings and, because they tend to be small, are widely used on the Web. **Metafiles** contain both bitmaps and vectors. Graphics are saved in several file formats, including the formats described in Exhibit 12-16.

Exhibit 12-16 Graphic file types

Format	Abbreviation	Type
Windows Bitmap	BMP	Bitmap
Tagged Image File	TIF	Bitmap
Graphics Interchange Format	GIF	Bitmap
Portable Network Graphic	PNG	Bitmap
Joint Photographic Experts Group	JPEG	Bitmap
Scalable Vector Graphic	SVG	Vector
Windows Metafile	WMF	Metafile
Enhanced Metafile	EMF	Metafile

Inserting Clip Art

Clip art can be electronic illustrations, photographs, video, and audio stored in collections so that you can easily locate and insert them into documents. A small collection of clip art is installed on your computer with Office. You can also download more clip art from the Microsoft Web site, Office.com.

To search for and then insert clip art in your document, click the Clip Art button in the Illustrations group on the Insert tab to open the Clip Art task pane. In the Search for box in the Clip Art task pane, enter keywords that describe the image, sound, or video you need. Each clip art file included with Word is associated with a set of keywords. For example, clip art of a car might be associated with the keywords *car* and *racing*. If the clip art is a car going down a road, additional keywords might be *road* and *driving*. If you search using any one of these keywords, that image will appear in your results, along with images of cars not on a road and images of cars without drivers. The more keywords you use, the narrower (more specific) the search results will be.

 **ACTIVITY**

Insert clip art.

1 Change the zoom to **Page Width**. At the top of the document, position the insertion point to the left of the word *Welcome* in the second line.

---

graphic A picture, shape, design, graph, chart, or diagram.

object Anything in a document or other file that can be treated as a whole.

bitmap A grid of pixels that form a picture.

vector graphic An image composed of straight and curved lines and stored as a mathematical formula.

metafile A graphic that contains both bitmaps and vectors.

clip art Electronic illustrations, photographs, video, and audio stored in collections so that you can easily locate and insert them into documents.

2 On the Ribbon, click the **Insert tab**. In the Illustrations group, click the **Clip Art button**. The Clip Art task pane opens to the right of the document window. See Exhibit 12-17.

Exhibit 12-17 Clip Art task pane

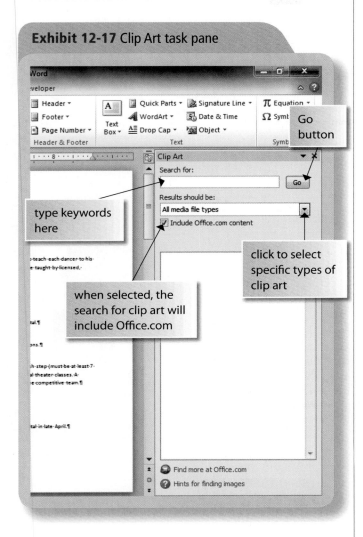

type keywords here

when selected, the search for clip art will include Office.com

click to select specific types of clip art

Go button

3 Click in the **Search for box**, delete its contents if necessary, and then type **ballet**.

4 Click the **Results should be arrow**, and then click the **All media types check box** to deselect it if it is selected. Click the **Illustrations** and **Photographs check boxes** to select them if they are not already selected, and click the **Videos** and **Audio check boxes** to deselect them if they are selected.

5 To the right of the Search for box, click the **Go button**. The Results should be list closes and after a moment, clip art related to ballet appears.

6 In the Clip Art task pane, click the **photograph of the feet of a ballerina on pointe clip art** (on her

toes). See Exhibit 12-18. (If you don't see this clip, choose another one.) The clip art is in the line at the current location of the insertion point, at the beginning of the *Welcome to The Dance Works!* paragraph. The text shifts right to make room for the clip art but does not wrap around it, because the clip art is an inline graphic.

⚠ **Problem?** If no results appear in the Clip Art task pane, make sure the **Include Office.com content check box** is selected. If you do not have access to the Internet, delete the text in the Search for box, and then click the **Go button**. Browse through the clips displayed in the task pane, and select one to use in place of the ballet clip.

The clip art is selected, as indicated by its border, and the Picture Tools Format tab is active on the Ribbon.

7 In the Clip Art task pane, click the **Close button** ✖. The Clip Art task pane closes.

Examining a Selected Object

To work with or delete any object in a document, such as clip art or a table, you first need to select that object. Once an object is selected, a contextual tab appears on the Ribbon with options for formatting, editing, moving, and resizing that object. For graphics, either the Picture Tools Format tab or the Drawing Tools Format tab appears on the Ribbon, depending on the type of graphic. For tables, the two Table Tools contextual tabs appear. Most clip art in the Illustrations and Photos categories are bitmaps or metafiles and are treated as pictures, so selecting them will cause the Picture Tools Format tab to appear. However, some pieces of clip art are vector graphics, and vector graphics are treated as drawings, so the Drawing Tools Format tab appears when they are selected.

When most objects are selected, a **selection box** surrounds the object. Small circles at each corner of selection boxes and small squares in the center of each side of selection boxes are **sizing handles** that you can drag

selection box The box that surrounds an object when it is selected.

sizing handle A small circle that appears at the corner of a selection box or a square that appears on the side of a selection box.

Exhibit 12-18 Selected clip art in the document

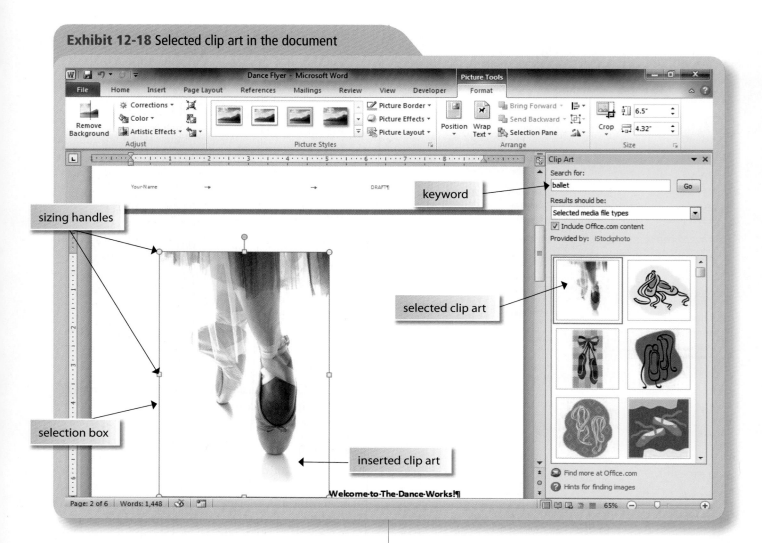

to change the size of the selected object. Refer to Exhibit 12-18.

Resizing a Graphic

You can change the size of graphics you insert. The easiest way to do this is to drag the sizing handles. To maintain the object's **aspect ratio**—the proportion of the object's height to its width—drag a corner sizing handle (a circle) to resize it. You can also change the measurements of a graphic using the Shape Height and Shape Width boxes in the Size group on the Picture Tools or Drawing Tools Format tab. If you change one of these measurements, the other will change to maintain the aspect ratio.

aspect ratio The proportion of an object's height to its width.

ACTIVITY

Resize a graphic.

1 On the selected clip art, point to the **upper-left circular sizing handle**. The pointer changes to ⬉.

2 Drag the **sizing handle** down and to the right until the top of the selection box that you are dragging is halfway down the clip art (aligned with the right middle sizing handle on the selection box around the original clip art) as shown in Exhibit 12-19. As you drag the handle, the pointer changes to +, and an outline of the photo showing the decrease in its size appears.

3 When the clip art is approximately half its original size, as shown in Exhibit 12-19, release the mouse button. The page with the photo scrolls out of view.

4 Scroll up to see the photo at the top of page 1.

Exhibit 12-19 Graphic being resized

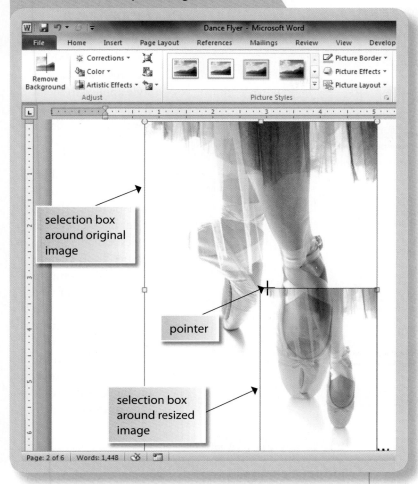

selection box around original image

pointer

selection box around resized image

Image Quality of Resized Graphics

When you increase the size of a bitmapped graphic in a document, the quality of the graphic degrades. This is because the number of pixels used to create the image doesn't change as you make the image larger; instead, each pixel increases in size. Because pixels are square, as they get larger, you start to see the corners of each pixel, resulting in jagged edges in the image. You can change the size of a vector graphic as much as you want without affecting its quality because it is stored as a mathematical formula.

More Images/Shutterstock.com

Cropping a Photo

If you want to cut off part of a photo, you can **crop** it. For example, you could crop an illustration of an ice cream cone by cropping off the cone, leaving only the ice cream itself. When you crop a photo, the cropped part, which is shaded with dark gray, stays visible until you deselect the shape to make it easier to adjust the crop borders. You can also drag the cropped portion inside the crop area to reposition it. Once you crop a graphic, the part you cropped is hidden from view. However, it remains a part of the graphic, so you can restore the cropped graphic to its original form. Just select the cropped photo, and then click the Crop button to display the entire photo and the crop handles again.

The Crop button appears only on the Picture Tools Format tab. There is no Crop button on the Drawing Tools Format tab.

 **ACTIVITY**

Crop a photo.

1 On the Picture Tools Format tab, in the Size group, click the **Crop button**. The Crop button is selected and dark black crop handles appear inside the sizing handles on the clip art's selection border.

2 Point to the **bottom-middle crop handle**. The pointer changes to **T**.

3 Press and hold down the mouse button. The pointer changes to **+**.

4 Drag up to just below the tip of the pointe shoe, and then release the mouse button. The bottom portion of the clip art that will be cropped is shaded gray.

5 Drag the **top-middle crop handle** down just below the bottom of the dark pink part of the dress.

6 Drag the **left-middle crop handle** about one-quarter inch to the right. See Exhibit 12-20.

7 On the Picture Tools Format tab, in the Size group, click the **Crop button**. The Crop button is deselected, and the crop handles and the cropped portions of the photo disappear.

crop To cut off part of a graphic.

Exhibit 12-20 Cropped clip art

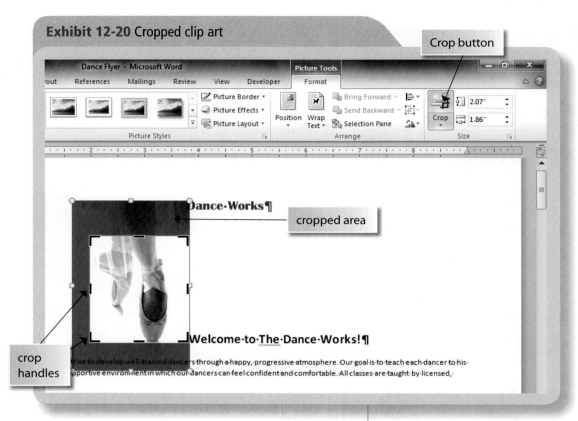

Crop button

Dance Works¶

cropped area

crop handles

Welcome·to·The·Dance·Works!¶

...rive·to·develop·well-trained·dancers·through·a·happy,·progressive·atmosphere.·Our·goal·is·to·teach·each·dancer·to·his·...pportive·environment·in·which·our·dancers·can·feel·confident·and·comfortable.·All·classes·are·taught·by·licensed,·

Formatting a Picture

Like text and tables, pictures can have a style applied to them. A picture style can consist of a border, a shape, or effects such as a shadow or a three-dimensional effect. To apply a style to a picture, select a style in the Picture Styles gallery on the Picture Tools Format tab. If you want to modify part of the style definition, you can use the Picture Border and Picture Effects buttons in the Picture Styles group on the Picture Tools Format tab.

8 In the Size group, click the **Crop button** again. The cropped portions of the image are visible again.

9 Click the **Crop button** once more to deselect it.

Specialized Crop Commands

You can use commands on the Crop button menu to crop to specific shapes or proportions. To crop a photo to a shape, which means trimming the edges of a graphic so it fits into a star, oval, arrow, or other shape, click the Crop button arrow, point to Crop to Shape, and then click a shape on the menu that appears. To crop to specific proportions, click the Crop button arrow, point to Aspect Ratio, and then select a ratio on the list.

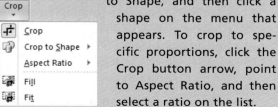

ACTIVITY

Format a picture.

1 On the Picture Tools Format tab, in the Picture Styles group, click the **More button** .

2 Point to the various styles and observe the Live Preview of the picture styles on the photo.

3 In the Picture Styles gallery, click the **Simple Frame, White style** (the first style in the first row). The gallery closes and the style you selected is applied.

4 In the Picture Styles group, click the **Picture Border button arrow**, and then in the color palette under Theme Colors, click the **Purple, Accent 4, Lighter 60% color**. The border color on the photo is changed to the purple color you selected.

5 In the Picture Styles group, click the **Picture Effects button arrow**, point to **Shadow**, and then under Perspective, click **Perspective Diagonal Upper Left**. The gallery closes and a shadow appears behind the image. See Exhibit 12-21.

6 Save the document.

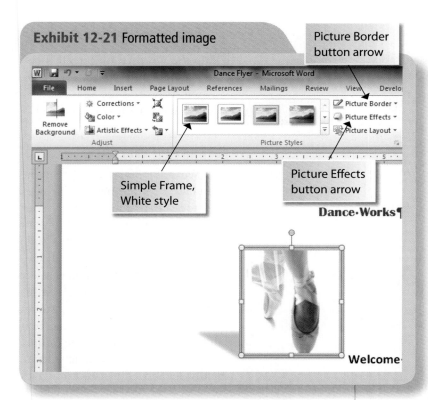

Exhibit 12-21 Formatted image

Picture Border button arrow

Simple Frame, White style

Picture Effects button arrow

Removing a Photo's Background

One specialized technique for editing photos allows you to remove the background of a photo, leaving only the foreground image. For example, you can edit a photo of a bird in the sky to remove the sky, leaving only the image of the bird. To edit a photo to remove the background, use the Remove Background button in the Adjust group on the Picture Tools Format tab. Removing a photo's background can be tricky, especially if you are working on a photo with a background that is not clearly differentiated from the foreground image. For example, you might find it difficult to remove a white, snowy background from a photo of an equally white snowman.

LO12.5 Adding WordArt

WordArt is formatted, decorative text that is treated as an object. In addition to the formatting that you can use with ordinary text, you can add beveled edges to the individual letters, format the text in 3D, and transform the text into waves, circles, and other shapes. You can also rotate WordArt text so it stretches vertically on the page. Another advantage of WordArt over regular text is that

you can edit the colors of WordArt text in two ways: by changing the fill and outline color. You can also change the style of the outline, by, for example, making it thicker, or breaking it into dashes.

WordArt is actually a text box. A **text box** is an object that contains text. You can format the text in the object just as you would format any text in a document. You can also format the entire object. When the selection border around WordArt is a dashed line, the insertion point is positioned in the text, and you can treat the text as you would ordinary text. You can edit it or select it and then apply formatting. When the selection border around WordArt is a solid line, the entire WordArt object is selected. When the WordArt object is selected, you can apply formatting to the WordArt text even though it is not specifically selected, and you can apply formatting to the text box itself, such as changing the fill or outline color.

Inserting WordArt

You can create WordArt out of existing text in a document by selecting the text, clicking the WordArt button in the Text group on the Insert tab, and then selecting a WordArt style from the gallery that opens. You can also click the WordArt button in the Text group on the Insert tab, and then click the style you want in the WordArt gallery to open a WordArt text box containing placeholder text. You can then replace the placeholder with the text you want to format as WordArt.

 **ACTIVITY**

Insert WordArt.

1 At the top of the document, select **Dance Works** without selecting the paragraph mark at the end of the line.

2 On the Ribbon, click the **Insert tab**. In the Text group, click the **WordArt button**. The WordArt gallery opens. See Exhibit 12-22.

> **WordArt** Formatted, decorative text that is treated as a graphic object.
>
> **text box** An object that contains text.

Exhibit 12-22 WordArt gallery

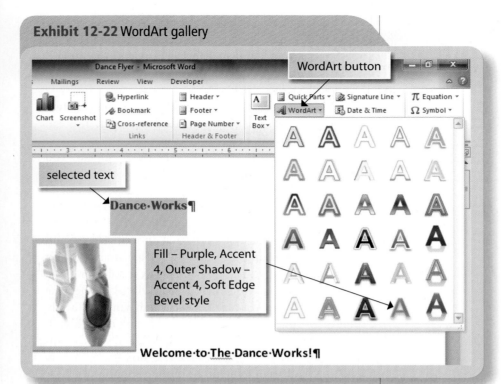

selected text → **Dance·Works¶**

Fill – Purple, Accent 4, Outer Shadow – Accent 4, Soft Edge Bevel style

Welcome·to·The·Dance·Works!¶

WordArt button

3 In the bottom row, click the **Fill – Purple, Accent 4, Outer Shadow – Accent 4, Soft Edge Bevel style**. The gallery closes, the selected text is changed to a WordArt object, and the Drawing Tools Format tab appears on the Ribbon and is the active tab. See Exhibit 12-23.

4 In the WordArt object, click before the word *Dance*. Type **The** and then press the **Spacebar**. The WordArt text is modified.

Formatting WordArt

The WordArt Styles group on the Drawing Tools Format tab includes four tools that allow you to alter the color, shape, and overall look of WordArt. If you don't like the style you selected when you originally created your WordArt, you can select a new style using the Quick Styles button in the WordArt Styles group. To change the fill color, use the Text Fill button, or, to change the outline color, use the Text Outline button. Finally, the Text Effects button gives you access to a variety of special effects, including shadows, beveling, and 3D rotation, and transforming the shape of the WordArt. If your WordArt already includes some of these features, you can use the Text Effects button to fine tune the effects, perhaps by making a shadow or bevel more noticeable, or by removing an effect entirely. In addition, you can

Exhibit 12-23 WordArt inserted in document

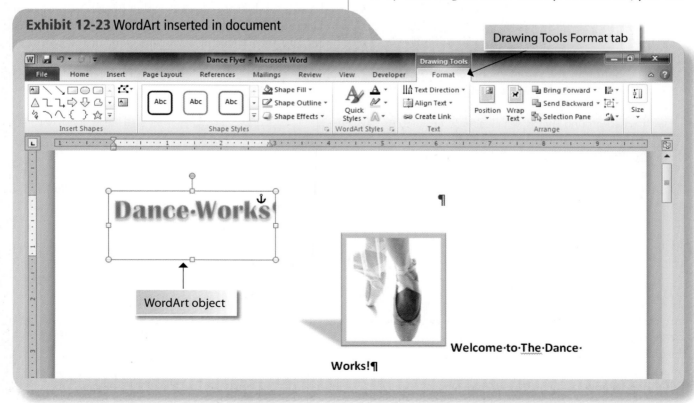

Drawing Tools Format tab

WordArt object

Welcome·to·The·Dance·Works!¶

Text Boxes

You can insert text boxes containing ordinary text—that is, text that is not WordArt. To do this, click the Text Box button in the Text group on the Insert tab. Click one of the styles in the gallery to insert a formatted text box containing placeholder text, or click Draw Text Box to insert an empty text box. You can format the text in a text box just as you would any text. You can also format the text box itself by adding or changing the fill color or the color or weight of the border. Text boxes are inserted as floating objects.

change the shape of the WordArt object by using the Transform command on the Text Effects button.

You can also change the size of WordArt. When resizing WordArt, you need to consider both the font size of the text and the size of the text box that contains the WordArt. You change the font size for WordArt text

just as you would for ordinary text, by selecting it and then choosing a new font size. If you choose an especially large font for a headline, you might also need to resize the text box to ensure that the resized text appears on a single line.

 **ACTIVITY**

Format WordArt.

1 Click the **WordArt dotted line selection border**. It becomes a solid line.

2 On the Drawing Tools Format tab, in the WordArt Styles group, click the **Text Outline button arrow**. The color palette opens.

3 In the color palette, under Theme Colors, click the **Purple, Accent 4, Lighter 80% color**.

4 In the WordArt Styles group, click the **Text Effects button**, and then point to **Transform**. A gallery of transform effects appears. See Exhibit 12-24.

Exhibit 12-24 Transform submenu on the Text Effects menu

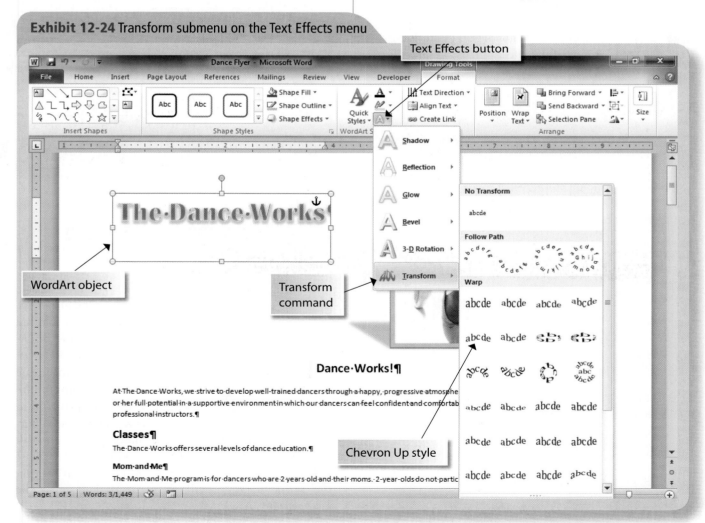

Use WordArt to quickly create eye-catching and colorful headlines, titles, or letterhead for your documents.

5 In the Warp section, click the **Chevron Up effect** (the first effect in the second row). The text is formatted in the shape you selected, and a pink diamond-shaped adjustment handle appears on the left side of the selection border. You can drag the pink diamond handle to make a transform effect more or less noticeable.

Tip: To format text with WordArt styles without changing the text to a graphic object, use the Text Effects button in the Font group on the Home tab.

6 Drag the **pink adjustment handle** down until the pointer is on top of the left-middle sizing handle. The effect is increased. See Exhibit 12-25.

Exhibit 12-25 Formatted WordArt

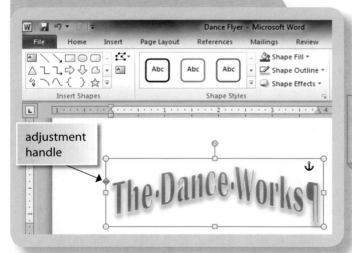

adjustment handle

7 On the Drawing Tools Format tab, in the Size group, click the **Size button**. The Size menu opens displaying the current height and width of the WordArt text box.

inline graphic A graphic that is positioned in a line of text and moves along with the text.

8 Click in the **Width box**, type **5** and then press the **Enter key**. The WordArt is resized to five inches wide.

9 Click a blank area of the document to deselect the WordArt, and then click the WordArt again to select it. The transform effect is removed temporarily while the WordArt is selected.

10 Save the document.

Translate Text

If you are connected to the Internet, you can use the Mini Translator to translate text in a document. To select the language into which you want to translate text, click the Translate button in the Language group on the Review tab, and then click Choose Translation Language. To turn the Mini Translator on, click the Translate button, and then click Mini Translator. Point to a word or selected text, and then after a moment, a pop-up box appears containing the transla-tion. The pop-up box might appear very faintly at first; to make it appear darker, move the pointer toward it.

LO12.6 **Wrapping Text Around Graphics**

Graphic objects in a document can be either in-line or floating. An **inline graphic** is located in a specific position in a line of text in the document, and the graphic moves along with the text. For example, if you type text to the left of an inline graphic, the graphic moves right to accommodate the new text. You can drag it to another position in the document, but it appears in a line of text wherever you drop it. When you format a paragraph with an inline graphic, the inline graphic is also format-ted. For example, if you right-align the paragraph, the inline graphic will be right-aligned with the paragraph.

A **floating graphic** can be positioned anywhere in the document. When you change a graphic to a floating graphic, you need to consider how the text will wrap around it. You can choose to wrap the text around the graphic on all sides or on the top and bottom of the graphic, or you can position the graphic behind the text so the words flow on top of the graphic, or in front of the text so the graphic covers the text. The wrap settings for graphics are:

- **Square**—Text flows around the straight edges of an object's border.

- **Tight**—Text flows around the contours of the object itself.

- **Through**—Text flows around the contours of the object itself and also fills any open spaces in the graphic.

- **Top and Bottom**—Text stops at the top border of an object and resumes below the bottom border.

- **Behind Text**—Text flows over the graphic.

- **In Front of Text**—Text flows behind the graphic.

Changing Text Wrap Properties

Clip art is inserted as an inline graphic. To change an inline graphic to a floating graphic, you apply one of the text wrap settings to it. To do this, select the graphic, click the Wrap Text button in the Arrange Group on the Picture Tools Format tab, and then select the wrap text option you want. (The Wrap Text button is also available in the Arrange group on the Drawing Tools Format tab.)

WordArt is inserted as a floating graphic. If you create it by selecting text and then applying the WordArt style, the wrapping is set to Square. If you create it by inserting the WordArt object and then typing the text, the wrapping is set to In Front of Text. To change a floating graphic to an inline graphic, select the In Line with Text command on the Wrap Text button menu.

ACTIVITY

Change a graphic's text wrap properties.

1 If the WordArt is not already selected, click the **WordArt**, and then click the **dashed line border** to select the entire object.

2 On the Ribbon, click the **Drawing Tools Format tab** if it is not already selected. In the Arrange group, click the **Wrap Text button**. A menu of text

Anchors

All floating graphics are attached, or anchored, to a paragraph. If you move the paragraph to which a floating graphic is anchored, the graphic will move also. If you cut the paragraph to the Clipboard, the graphic is cut as well. When nonprinting characters are displayed, an anchor icon appears next to the paragraph to which the floating graphic is anchored. If you drag a floating graphic to a new position on the page, the anchor moves as well, and the graphic is anchored to a new paragraph close to its new location.

You can anchor a floating graphic to another paragraph if you want. However, unless you lock the anchor, if you move the graphic, it will be anchored to another paragraph if you subsequently move the floating graphic. To lock a floating graphic's anchor to a specific paragraph, click More Layout Options on the Wrap Text button menu, click the Position tab, and then select the Lock anchor check box.

Stephen Coburn/Shutterstock.com

wrapping options opens, with the Square option selected. See Exhibit 12-26.

3 Click **In Line with Text**. The menu closes and the WordArt is positioned in the paragraph at the top of the page.

⚠ **Problem?** If the WordArt moved down to the first character in the first line in the document, to the left of the clip art, you selected the paragraph mark when you selected the text to create the WordArt. Click to the left of the word *Welcome*, press the **Left Arrow key** to position the insertion point just to the right of the WordArt, and then press the **Enter key** so that the WordArt is the only thing in the first paragraph.

4 Click the **clip art** to select it.

floating graphic A graphic that can be positioned anywhere in a document.

Exhibit 12-26 Wrap Text menu

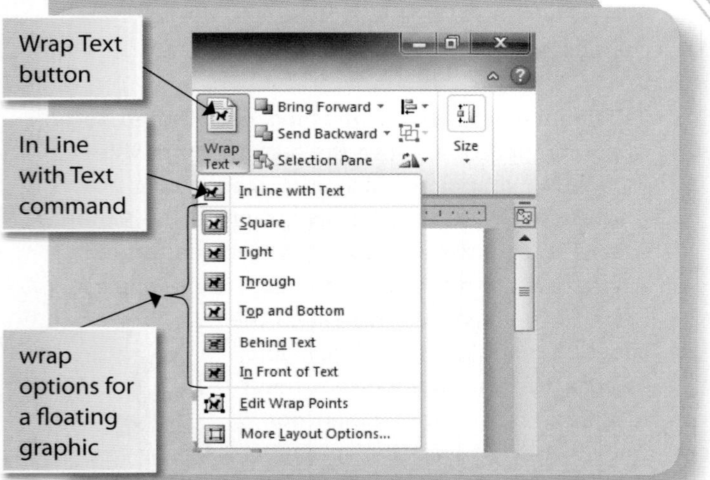

Wrap Text button

In Line with Text command

wrap options for a floating graphic

Bring Forward
Send Backward
Selection Pane

Wrap Text

Size

In Line with Text
Square
Tight
Through
Top and Bottom
Behind Text
In Front of Text
Edit Wrap Points
More Layout Options...

5 On the Ribbon, click the **Picture Tools Format tab**. In the Arrange group, click the **Wrap Text button**, and then click **Square**. The menu closes, and the text wraps around both sides of the clip art. See Exhibit 12-27.

A document containing inline graphics is hard to work with because every edit you make to the text moves the graphics to a new position.

Moving Graphics

To move a graphic, you drag it to its new position. If the graphic is an inline graphic, you can drag it to its new position in any line of text. The same pointer and vertical indicator line that you saw when you dragged selected text appears. When you drag a floating graphic, the graphic follows the pointer as you drag, and you can drop the graphic anywhere on the page. You might need to make small adjustments in the graphic's position if the text doesn't wrap as you expect.

Exhibit 12-27 Inline and floating graphics

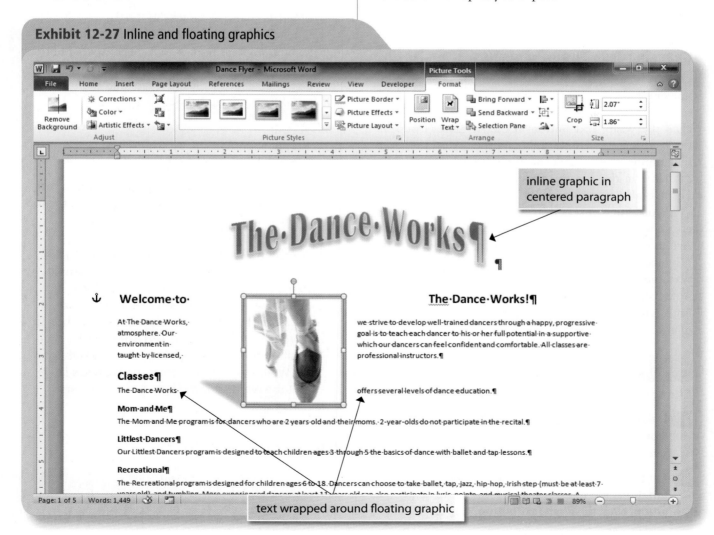

inline graphic in centered paragraph

text wrapped around floating graphic

Move graphics.

1 Click the **WordArt**, and then click the **dashed line border**.

2 Point to the **WordArt border** so that the pointer changes to ↖, and then begin dragging down. As you drag, the pointer changes to ↖, and the vertical line indicator appears to indicate where the graphic will appear when you drop it.

3 When the vertical line indicator is to the right of the Littlest Dancers heading, release the mouse button. The WordArt is positioned to the right of *Dancers* as the list "character" in that paragraph.

4 Drag the **WordArt** back up to the blank paragraph at the top of the document.

5 Drag the **clip art** to the left so the text wraps around it only on its right side.

6 Drag the **clip art** down so that the top of the clip art is aligned with the top of the first paragraph in the body of the flyer (it starts with *At the Dance Works, we strive . . .*) and the text *Welcome to The Dance Works!* is centered below the WordArt. See Exhibit 12-28.

7 Save the document.

Exhibit 12-28 Clip art repositioned

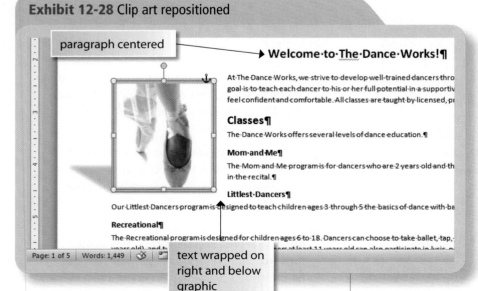

paragraph centered

→ **Welcome·to·The·Dance·Works!¶**

text wrapped on right and below graphic

Using the Position Button

The Position button in the Arrange group on the Picture Tools Format tab is a shortcut to formatting a graphic as a floating graphic with the Square wrapping option and moving the graphic to a specific position on the page (top left, top middle, top right, and so on). For example, to position a graphic in the lower right corner of the page and wrap the text around the top and left sides of the graphic, click the Position button, and then click the style in the bottom right of the gallery.

LO12.7 Working with Columns

Columns allow the eye to take in a lot of text and to scan quickly for interesting information. Formatting text in multiple columns also allows you to fit more text on a page than if the text were in only column.

Creating Columns

You can format an entire document or only a section of a document in columns. To format the current section (or an entire document if it does not contain any section breaks) in columns, click the Columns button in the Page Setup group on the Page Layout tab, and then select a command on the Columns menu. Selecting Two or Three formats the section in the corresponding number of columns of equal width. Selecting Left or Right formats the section in two columns of unequal width with the narrower column on the side identified by the command. The command One formats the section in one column (the normal setting for ordinary documents). To create columns with any other format or

You can add a drop cap, a large first letter of a paragraph, to embellish a document by using the Drop Cap button in the Text group on the Insert tab.

adjust the width between columns, add a line between columns, format the entire document in columns when it contains section breaks, or insert a continuous section break automatically and format the text after the section break in columns, click the More Columns command to open the Columns dialog box.

ACTIVITY

Format a document in columns.

1 Below the WordArt, position the insertion point before the word *Welcome*.

2 On the Ribbon, click the **Page Layout tab**. In the Page Setup group, click the **Columns button**. The Columns menu opens.

3 Click **Two**. All the text in Section 1 is formatted in two columns.

4 Scroll down so you can see the top of page 4. Page 4, which is in Section 2, is not formatted in two columns.

5 Scroll back to the beginning of the document, and then make sure the insertion point is still positioned before the word *Welcome*.

6 In the Page Setup group, click the **Columns button**, and then click **One**. The text in Section 1 is again formatted in one column.

7 Click the **Columns button** again, and then click **More Columns**. The Columns dialog box opens. In the Presets section, the One button is selected. In the Preview section, the text is formatted in one column. At the bottom of the dialog box, This section appears in the Apply to box. See Exhibit 12-29.

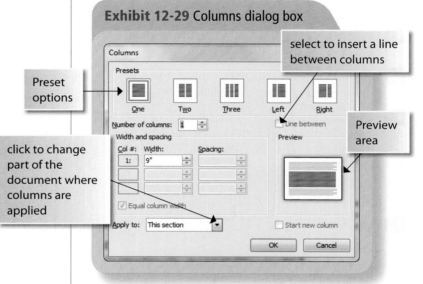

Exhibit 12-29 Columns dialog box

- select to insert a line between columns
- Preset options
- Preview area
- click to change part of the document where columns are applied

8 In the Presets section, click the **Two button**. The preview changes to show the middle part of a document formatted in two columns of equal width. This corresponds to the fact that This section is selected in the Apply to box.

9 Above the Preview section, click the **Line between check box** to select it. A vertical line appears in the Preview separating the two columns.

10 At the bottom of the dialog box, click the **Apply to arrow**, and then click **This point forward**. The preview changes again to the first part of a document formatted in a single column and the rest formatted in two columns.

Inserting a Page Border

A page border adds interest to a document by decorating/embellishing the edges/boundary of a page. On the Page Layout tab, in the Page Background group, click the Page Borders button. The Borders and Shading dialog box opens with the Page Border tab selected. Select any of the line styles in the Style list, or click the Art arrow and then select a graphic to use as the border. If you are working with a document that contains section breaks, make sure the Apply to box contains the correct setting (Whole document or This section).

11 Click **OK**. The Columns dialog box closes. The headline (the WordArt) is still centered in one column, a continuous section break appears at the end of the first paragraph (the paragraph containing the WordArt), and the rest of the document text is formatted in two columns. See Exhibit 12-30.

12 Scroll down to page 4. The text in this section is now Section 3. This time, the text in the section that includes the Faculty heading was affected because you chose This point forward in the Columns dialog box. To change this, you can either format the text in Section 3 to be one column, or undo the columns you just created, insert the continuous section break manually, and then format the new Section 2 (below the WordArt and above the Faculty heading) with two columns.

13 Position the insertion point anywhere on page 4. In the Page Setup group, click the **Columns button**, and then click **One**. The menu closes and Section 3 is formatted as one column again.

14 Save the document.

Balancing Columns

Balancing columns—that is, making the columns on pages in a section the same length—creates a professional-looking document. You can insert a continuous section break at the end of the last column to attempt to automatically balance columns. The columns then remain balanced no matter how much material you add or remove from either column. The columns also remain balanced if you add material that causes the columns to flow to a new page; the overflow will also be formatted in balanced columns.

Exhibit 12-30 Document formatted in two columns

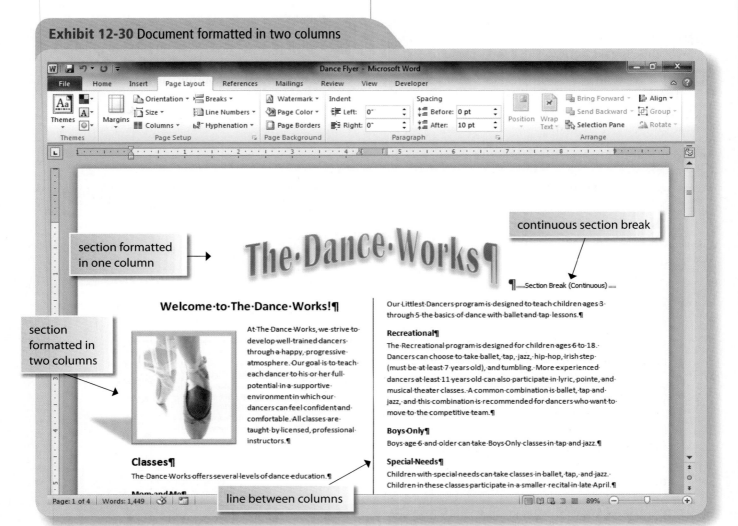

Sometimes you will want a column to end at a specific point or you might want to manually balance the columns. You can manually adjust the length of a column by inserting a column break using the Breaks button in the Page Setup group on the Page Layout tab. A column break forces all the text and graphics following it to the next column. Column breaks are useful when you have a multi-page document formatted in three or more columns, with only enough text on the last page to fill some of the columns.

ACTIVITY

Balance columns.

1. Scroll up so that you can see all of the text on page 3.

2. In the last line on the page, position the insertion point between the paragraph mark after the Web site URL and the dotted line that indicates the next page section break you inserted earlier.

3. On the Page Layout tab, in the Page Setup group, click the **Breaks button**. The Breaks menu opens.

4. In the Section Breaks section, click **Continuous**. The menu closes, a continuous section break is inserted at the insertion point, before the next page section break, and the columns on the last page are balanced. See Exhibit 12-31.

5. On the status bar, click the **Draft button** to switch to Draft view, and then scroll down so you can see both section breaks.

6. Switch back to **Print Layout view**, and then scroll so you can see page 1. At the bottom of the first column on page 1, the Littlest Dancers heading is by itself.

7. Position the insertion point before the word *Littlest*. In the Page Setup group, click the **Breaks button**, and then under Page Breaks, click **Column**. A column break is inserted at the insertion point and the Littlest Dancers heading is moved to the top of the second column.

8. Scroll down so you can see the text on page 2. At the bottom of the first column on page 2, before the Schedule heading, insert a **column break**.

9. Switch to **Two Pages zoom**, and then scroll up so you can see pages 1 and 2. Notice that the columns break at appropriate places. See Exhibit 12-32.

Exhibit 12-31 Document with balanced columns

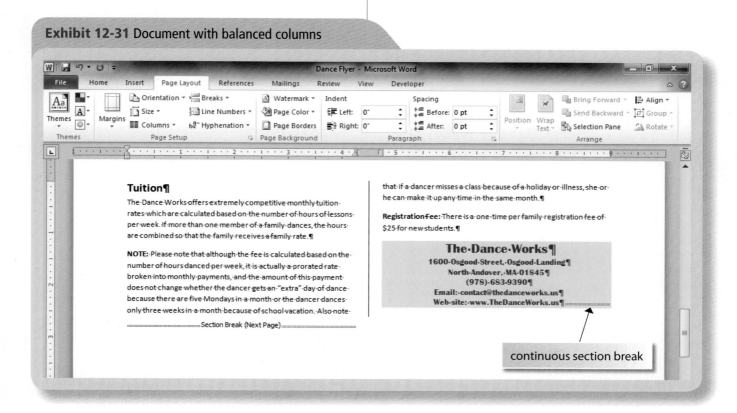

Exhibit 12-32 Manual column breaks in document

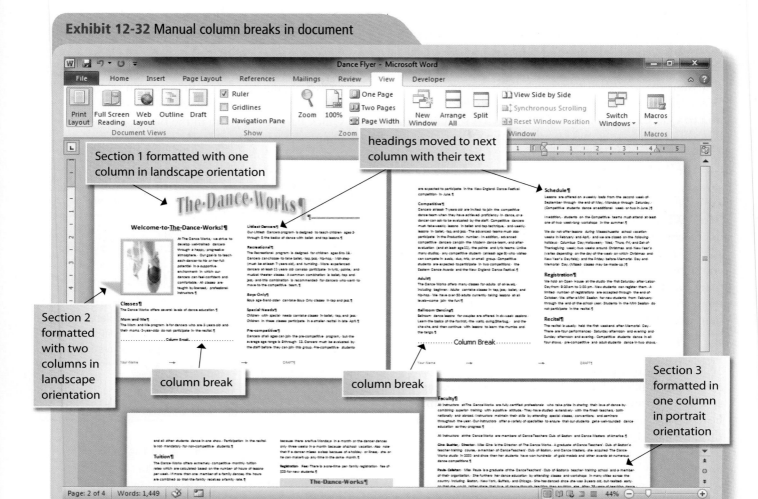

Section 1 formatted with one column in landscape orientation

headings moved to next column with their text

Section 2 formatted with two columns in landscape orientation

column break

column break

Section 3 formatted in one column in portrait orientation

LO12.8 Working with Building Blocks

HomeStudio/Shutterstock.com

Building blocks are parts of a document that are stored and reused. Word has many predesigned building blocks for a wide variety of items, including cover pages, calendars, numbering, text boxes, and more. You used building blocks when you added formatted headers and footers. You can create custom building blocks as well.

Building blocks are stored in galleries. For example, the predesigned choices listed on the Header button menu are building blocks stored in the Header gallery. If you save a custom building block to another gallery, it will be available when you access that gallery along with the built-in building blocks in that gallery. For example, if you create a custom footer and then save it to the Footers gallery, you can click the Footers button in the Header & Footer group on the Insert tab to see your custom footer in the Footers gallery.

Creating Quick Parts

Building blocks that are stored in the Quick Parts gallery in the Text group on the Insert tab are called **Quick Parts**. There are no predefined Quick Parts; you need to create these. For example, you might make your signature block for a letter ("Sincerely," several blank lines, your name, and

building block A part of a document that is stored and reused.

Quick Part A building block stored in the Quick Parts gallery.

your title) a Quick Part so you can quickly insert that text without typing it every time; or, you might create a Quick Part that is a company name and logo.

To create a Quick Part, select the formatted text you want to save, click the Quick Parts button in the Text group on the Insert tab, and then click Save Selection to Quick Part Gallery. In the Create New Building Block dialog box that opens, you can type the name of the Quick Part.

The building blocks that come with Word are stored in the global Building Blocks template, which is available to all Word documents created on the computer. When you create a custom building block in a document, it is stored in the Building Blocks template so that it can be used in all documents created on your computer. If the document was based on a custom template, or if you create the custom building block in a template, the custom building block is stored with the template so that it will be available to anyone who uses the template on any computer to which the template is copied.

You can also choose the gallery in which to save a custom building block. Unless you are creating a specialty custom building block, such as a customized header, the Quick Parts gallery is a good choice. To further organize Quick Parts, you can click the Category arrow in the Create New Building Block dialog box, and then click Create New Category.

Finally, when you save the custom building block, you can choose how the content will be inserted. The default is for only the content of the custom building block to be inserted, but you can also choose to insert the content in its own paragraph or on its own page.

 **ACTIVITY**

Create Quick Parts.

1 Change the zoom level to **Page Width**. On page 1, select the entire **WordArt object** (the selection border is a solid line).

Building blocks and Quick Parts are great time savers because you don't need to re-create elements that you use again and again.

2 On the Ribbon, click the **Insert tab**. In the Text group, click the **Quick Parts button**, and then click **Save Selection to Quick Part Gallery**. The Create New Building Block dialog box opens. An asterisk appears in the Name box because you selected an object. The building block will be saved in the Quick Parts gallery and in the Building Blocks template. See Exhibit 12-33.

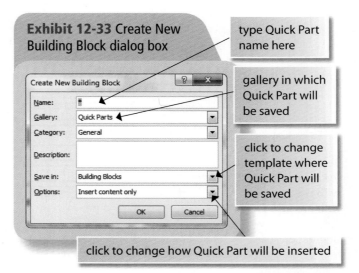

Exhibit 12-33 Create New Building Block dialog box

type Quick Part name here

gallery in which Quick Part will be saved

click to change template where Quick Part will be saved

click to change how Quick Part will be inserted

3 In the Name box, type **Logo-WordArt**.

4 Click the **Options arrow**, and then click **Insert content in its own paragraph**.

5 Click **OK**. The dialog box closes and the WordArt logo is saved as a custom building block.

> **Tip:** To make the Quick Part available to anyone using a custom template no matter what computer that person is working on, click the Save in arrow, and then click the template name.

6 Scroll so that you can see the text on page 3, and then select the **formatted business name and address** in the second column. Do not select the section break after the URL.

7 On the Insert tab, in the Text group, click the **Quick Parts button**. The Quick Parts menu opens. The Quick Part you created, Logo-WordArt, appears on the Quick Parts menu.

8 Click **Save Selection to Quick Part Gallery**. The Create New Building Block dialog box opens.

9 In the Name box, type **DW Name and Address**.

Creating AutoText Building Blocks

When you save a building block to the AutoText gallery, you can insert it by typing the first few letters of the building block name, and then pressing the Enter key when a ScreenTip with the full name appears. When you used the AutoComplete feature to insert a date, you used built-in AutoText. To save text as AutoText, click the Gallery arrow in the Create New Building Block dialog box, and then click AutoText. Or, on the Quick Parts button menu, point to AutoText, and then click Save Selection to AutoText Gallery to open the Create New Building Block dialog box with AutoText already selected in the Gallery box.

10 Click the **Options arrow**, and then click **Insert content in its own paragraph**.

11 Click **OK**. The dialog box closes and the new Quick Part is created.

12 Save the document, and then close it.

Inserting Quick Parts

Once you've created a Quick Part, you can insert it in documents. To insert a Quick Part, use the Quick Parts button in the Text group on the Insert tab. You can use the same button to access the built-in building blocks that come with Word.

 **ACTIVITY**

Insert Quick Parts.

1 Switch to the **Class Table document**, and then position the insertion point at the beginning of the document (before the word *September*).

> **Tip:** To quickly insert a Quick Part that appears on the Quick Parts menu, place the insertion point where you want to insert the Quick Part, type the Quick Part name, and then press the F3 key.

2 On the Ribbon, click the **Insert tab**. In the Text group, click the **Quick Parts button**. The two Quick Parts you created appear at the top of the Quick Parts gallery in alphabetical order. See Exhibit 12-34.

Exhibit 12-34 Quick Parts menu

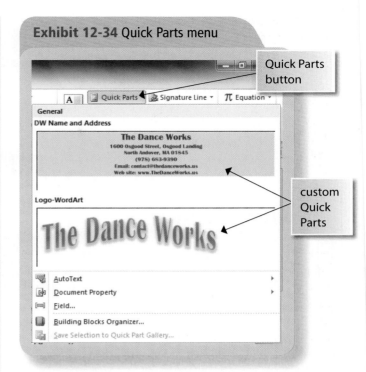

3 Click the **Logo-WordArt Quick Part**. The menu closes and the logo is inserted in its own paragraph at the insertion point. It is not centered because you saved only the WordArt object, not the centered paragraph that contained the WordArt object.

4 With the insertion point between the purple WordArt paragraph mark and the text paragraph mark, center-align the paragraph.

5 Position the insertion point before the word *September* again, and then insert the **DW Name and Address Quick Part**. This inserted text is centered because you saved paragraphs, and therefore the paragraph formatting, when you saved this Quick Part.

6 Below the WordArt, delete the paragraph containing *The Dance Works*. See Exhibit 12-35.

> **Tip:** You could select the paragraphs containing the WordArt and the contact information, and then save them as a new Quick Part named Letterhead.

7 In the closing of the letter, replace *Gina Buehler* with your name.

8 Save the document.

Exhibit 12-35 Letter with Quick Parts inserted

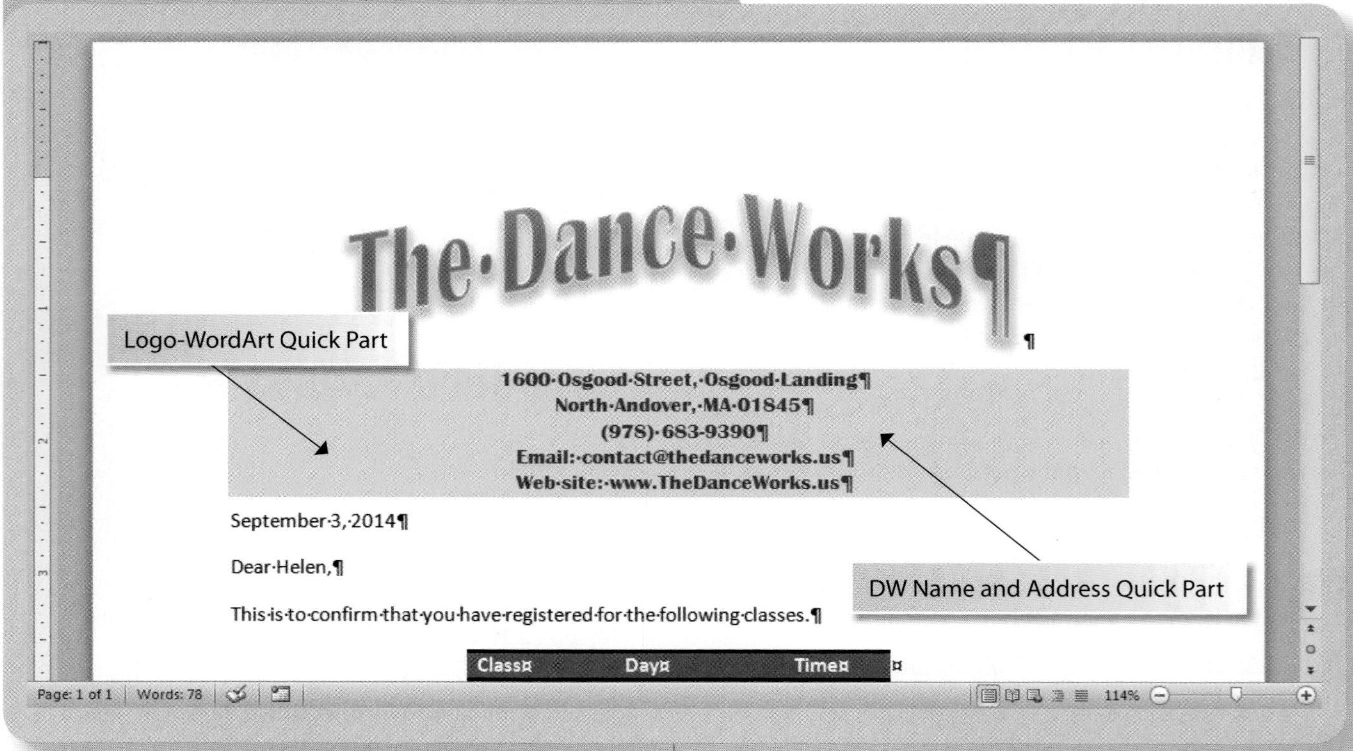

The·Dance·Works¶
¶

Logo-WordArt Quick Part

1600·Osgood·Street,·Osgood·Landing¶
North·Andover,·MA·01845¶
(978)·683-9390¶
Email:·contact@thedanceworks.us¶
Web·site:·www.TheDanceWorks.us¶

September·3,·2014¶

Dear·Helen,¶

DW Name and Address Quick Part

This·is·to·confirm·that·you·have·registered·for·the·following·classes.¶

| Class¤ | Day¤ | Time¤ | ¤ |

Page: 1 of 1   Words: 78   114%

Managing Building Blocks

The Building Blocks Organizer dialog box lists all of the building blocks in the global Building Blocks template and in the current template. If you have a template open when you open the Building Blocks Organizer, any building blocks that are part of that template will also be listed. In the Building Blocks Organizer dialog box, you can sort the building blocks by their names, gallery location, categories, or template location. You can also use the Building Blocks Organizer to insert a building block into the document, edit the properties of a building block, or delete a building block.

 **ACTIVITY**

Use the Building Blocks Organizer and delete Quick Parts.

1 On the Insert tab, in the Text group, click the **Quick Parts button**, and then click **Building Blocks Organizer**. The Building Blocks Organizer dialog box opens.

2 Click the **Name column header**. The list is sorted in alphabetical order by name.

3 Click the **Gallery column header**. The list is sorted in alphabetical order by gallery.

4 Scroll down until you see the two entries in the Quick Parts gallery.

5 In the Building blocks list, click the **DW Name and Address building block**. A preview of the selected building block appears in the preview pane. See Exhibit 12-36.

> **Tip:** To open the Building Blocks gallery with a Quick Part selected, right-click the Quick Part on the Quick Parts menu, and then on the shortcut menu, click Organize and Delete.

6 Below the Building blocks list, click **Delete**. A dialog box opens asking if you are sure you want to delete the selected building block.

7 Click **Yes**. The dialog box closes and the DW Name and Address custom building block is deleted from the computer. The Logo-WordArt building block is selected.

Exhibit 12-36 Building Blocks Organizer dialog box sorted by Gallery

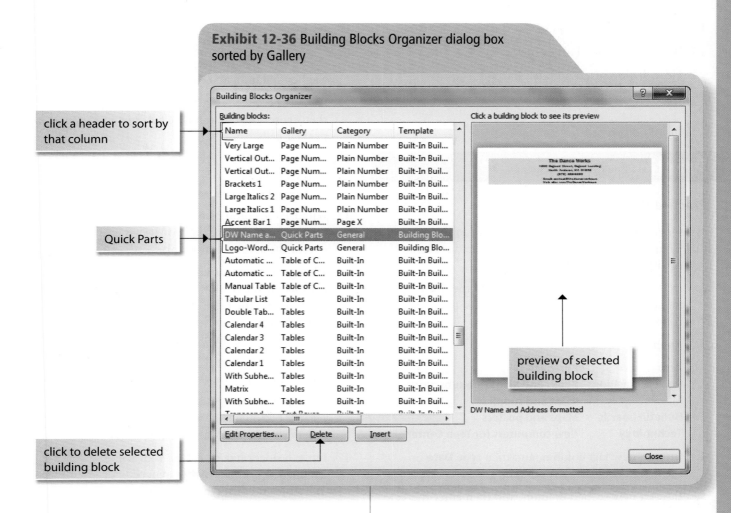

click a header to sort by that column

Quick Parts

preview of selected building block

click to delete selected building block

8 Delete the **Logo-WordArt building block**.

9 Click **Close**. The Building Blocks Organizer dialog box closes.

10 Close the Class Table document and exit Word. A dialog box opens asking if you want to save changes to Building Blocks. If you had not deleted the Quick Parts and you wanted to save them for use in the future, you would click Save. Since you deleted them, it doesn't matter if you save the changes to the Building Blocks template.

11 Click **Don't Save**. The dialog box closes and Word exits.

Quiz Yourself

1. In a table, what is the intersection of a column and a row called?

2. When a table is formatted with banded rows, what does it mean?

3. Explain the difference between portrait and landscape orientation.

4. What is a section?

5. How many sections does a document have if it does not contain a section break?

6. What is clip art?

7. What happens to a photo when you crop part of it?

8. What is WordArt?

9. Explain the difference between an inline graphic and a floating graphic.

10. When you click one of the options on the Columns button menu, what part of the document is the column formatting applied to?

11. How do you balance columns without inserting manual column breaks?

12. What is a building block?

13. Where are Quick Parts stored?

14. How do you insert a Quick Part?

15. Describe the Building Blocks Organizer.

Practice It

Practice It 12-1

1. Open the data file **Newsletter** located in the Chapter 12\Practice It folder. Save the document as **Library Newsletter**.

2. In the blank paragraph at the end of the document, insert a table with two columns and five rows.

3. Enter the following data in the table:

Area	Purchase
Book acquisitions	Books and magazine subscriptions
Murals	Paint and supplies
Bulletin boards	Maps and posters
Technology	New computers for Teen Center

4. Insert a new last column, and then type **Date** in the first row in the new column.

5. Insert a new second column, and then enter the following data:

Budget
$4500
$200
$100
$5000

6. Insert a new row above the Technology row with the following data in the first three columns:

Supplies
$300
Book rack, book plates, maps, and posters

7. Delete the row containing Bulletin boards and the column labeled Date.

8. AutoFit all of the columns.

9. Increase the width of the first column to 1.5 inches, AutoFit the Budget column, and then increase the width of the Purchase column so the right border is at the 5.25-inch mark on the ruler.

10. Format the table with the Colorful Shading – Accent 3 table style. Apply special formatting to the header row, remove special formatting from the first column, and use banded rows.

11. Center the table horizontally on the page, and then center the column labels *Area* and *Purchase* in their cells.

12. Format all the text after the date in the third line of the document in two columns. Include a line between the two columns.

13. Balance the columns by inserting a continuous section break before the Donations heading at the end of the second paragraph.

14. Change the formatting of the last section in the document (the section containing the Donations heading and the table) so that it is one column and in landscape orientation, and has its margins set to the Wide setting on the Margins menu.

15. Insert a column break before the Book Recommendations Bulletin Board heading.

16. On page 2, use the Edit Header command on the Header button menu to insert a header, and then unlink the header on page 2 from the previous section.

17. In the header on page 2, type your name so that it is left aligned, type **Newsletter** aligned under the Center Tab stop, and then type **page 2** aligned under the Right Tab stop.

18. At the top of page 1, insert clip art. Use the keywords **library building**, restrict the search to photographs, and insert clip art of a building with trees on one side.

19. Crop the photo to show just the building, and then resize the final photo so it is approximately one inch high.

20. Format the clip art using the Bevel Rectangle picture style, and then apply a 2.5 point soft edge (using the Soft Edges submenu on the Picture Effects button menu).

21. Change the clip art to a floating graphic using the Square wrapping option. Drag it so that it is positioned approximately two inches below the top edge of the document and one-quarter inch from the left edge of the document.

22. Convert the text in the first line of the document—*Friends of the Portland Public Library*—into WordArt using the Fill – Olive Green, Accent 3, Outline – Text 2 style.

23. Reduce the point size of the WordArt text to 28 points, and then change the Text Outline color of the WordArt to Tan, Background 2, Darker 50%.

24. Apply the Deflate transform effect to the Word-Art, and then increase the curve of the Deflate transform effect slightly. Reposition the clip art if necessary so it is above the Spine Label Replacement heading and below the WordArt.

25. Save the WordArt, the paragraph containing *Newsletter*, and the clip art if it is selected when you select the other two paragraphs as a Quick Part named **Logo**.

26. Create a new document, and then insert the Logo Quick Part in the new document. Save the document as a Word template named **Logo QP** by clicking the File tab, clicking Save As, clicking the Save as type arrow, and then clicking Word Template.

27. Open the Building Blocks Organizer dialog box, and then delete the Logo Quick Part.

28. Select the two paragraphs in the Logo QP template (including the clip art if it is there), and then save it as a Quick Part named **Logo Template** in the Logo QA template so that it will be inserted in its own paragraph. (*Hint*: In the Create New Building Block dialog box, make sure Logo QP is selected in the Save in box.)

29. Save the Logo QP template, and then close it. Save the Library Newsletter, and then close it.

30. Exit Word without saving changes to the Building Blocks.

Practice It 12-2

1. Open the data file **Notice** located in the Chapter 12\ Practice It folder. Save the document as **Fieldtrip Notice**.

2. Change the top margin of the document to .7 inches, and the bottom margin to .5 inches.

3. Format the paragraphs between the Driving Directions heading and the Alternate Transportation Options heading in three columns.

4. Insert a column break at the bottom of the first column before the From North/South/East heading.

5. Insert another column break at the bottom of the second column before the From the West/Southwest heading.

6. Change the right and left margins of the section formatted with three columns to one-half inch.

7. Convert the text in the first line, *First Grade Field Trip*, to WordArt, using any style.

8. Change the font size of the WordArt to 24 points.

9. Center the WordArt above the top line of text in the document.

10. Insert clip art of a bird.

11. Resize the clip art to approximately one-inch square, and change the text wrapping to Square.

12. Add the Offset Diagonal Bottom Right shadow effect to the clip art.

13. Add your name as a footer.

14. Save the document, and then close it.

On Your Own

On Your Own 12-1

1. Open the data file **Brochure** located in the Chapter 12\ On Your Own folder. Save the document as a template named **Auction Brochure**. (*Hint*: In the Save As dialog box, click the Save as type arrow, and then click Word Template.)

2. Select all the text in the document without selecting the first empty paragraph, and then convert the selected text into a table with three columns. (*Hint*: Use the Convert Text to Table command on the Table button menu. Adjust the number of columns, and make sure the Paragraphs option button is selected in the Separate text at section.)

3. Change the orientation of the document to Landscape.

4. Change the zoom level to Page Width.

5. Add a new row to the top of the table with the labels **Package**, **Value**, and **Description**.

6. Change the theme to Black Tie, and then apply the Medium List 2 table style to the table. Format the header row and the first column with special formatting and use banded rows.

7. Adjust the column widths so that the first column is two inches wide, the second column is AutoFit, and the third column is 6.25 inches wide.

8. Center all the text in the Value column using the Align Center command. Center all the text in the Package column using the Align Center Left command.

9. In the empty paragraph at the top of the document, insert WordArt using the Gradient Fill – Black, Outline – White, Outer Shadow style, and then type **AUCTION!** as the WordArt text.

10. Position the WordArt as a floating graphic above the table and approximately aligned with the left edge of the table.

11. Use the keyword **auction** to search for clip art, and insert a piece of black and white clip art.

12. Crop off part of the clip art.

13. Change the wrap properties of the clip art to Tight. Position it in the upper-right corner of the document, reducing its size as needed to fit above the table.

14. Save the WordArt as a Quick Part in the Auction Brochure template. Name the Quick Part **Auction Heading** and save it with the option to be inserted in its own paragraph.

15. Save the document, and then close it.

ADDITIONAL STUDY TOOLS

Chapter 12

IN THE BOOK

▶ Complete end-of-chapter exercises

▶ Study tear-out Chapter Review Card

ONLINE

▶ Complete additional end-of-chapter exercises

▶ Take practice quiz to prepare for tests

▶ Review key term flash cards (online, printable, and audio)

▶ Play "Beat the Clock" and "Memory" to quiz yourself

▶ Watch the videos "Work with Headings in the Navigation Pane," "Create Sections in a Document," "Crop a Graphic," "Rotate a Graphic," and more

Word: Create a Flyer

1. Plan a flyer for an upcoming event, such as a sale. Identify the content you will include on the flyer, such as at least five items for sale, a description of each item, the original cost of each item, the sale price for each item, and the location, date, and time of the sale (for this project, you can use real or fictional data). Decide how the document should be organized and formatted.

2. Create a new document for the flyer.

3. Enter the text for the flyer.

4. Use WordArt to create an attractively formatted title for the flyer. Be sure to use a descriptive title that accurately describes the content of your flyer.

5. Create a table that has at least five rows and three columns. Enter descriptive column headers for each column, and then enter appropriate data in each row.

6. Format the table with a style. Make sure it is clear and easy to read.

7. Include at least one piece of clip art to add interest to the flyer. Use an appropriate keyword to find images related to your flyer's content.

8. Position, size, and orient the clip art attractively on the flyer.

9. Change the style set of the flyer to anything other than Word 2010. Change the theme of the flyer to any theme other than the Office theme.

10. Use Quick Styles to format some of the text on the flyer, such as the date and time.

11. Modify the formatting of the text with Quick Styles applied so that the text looks better in your flyer, and then update the definitions of the Quick Styles with the new formatting.

12. Format the rest of the flyer by changing fonts, font sizes, font colors, borders, and so forth as needed to make the flyer attractive and easy to read.

13. Change the margins and page orientation as needed to fit the flyer on one page.

14. Format the flyer for your printer. Include headers and footers that display the file name, your name, and the date on which the flyer is printed.

15. Use the spell checker to check the spelling and grammar of the document, and then proofread it.

16. Preview the document in Backstage view to be sure that it will print as expected, and then print it.

17. Save the document, and then close it.

Using the Word Web App

The Office Web Apps are free versions of the Office programs that are available through Windows Live. The Web Apps do not make all of the features of the full version of the program installed on your computer available. Note that you do not need to have Microsoft Office 2010 programs installed on your computer to access and use Office Web Apps.

There are two ways to work with files using the Word Web App: You can view a file in View mode, or you can edit it in Edit mode. In View mode, you are limited to using the Find command and changing the zoom level. In Edit mode, you can enter and edit text, apply basic direct font and paragraph formatting and Quick Styles, use the spell checker, and insert tables, clip art, and pictures. Exhibit 12-37 shows a document in View mode in the Word Web App. Exhibit 12-38 shows the same document in Edit mode.

To open a document stored in a folder on your SkyDrive, go to www.windowslive.com, and then sign in to your Windows Live account. After you are signed in, point to the Office link at the top of the window, and then click Your documents. In the list of folders, click the folder containing the document you want to work with. Click a file to open it in View mode, or point to the file and then click Edit in browser in the list of links that opens to open it in Edit mode. Exhibit 12-39 shows a file in a folder on SkyDrive.

Exhibit 12-37 Document in View mode in Word Web App

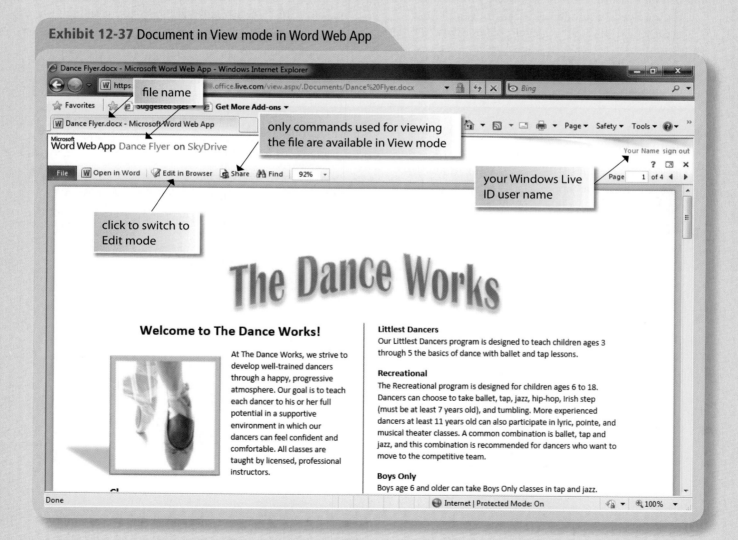

Exhibit 12-38 Document in Edit mode in Word Web App

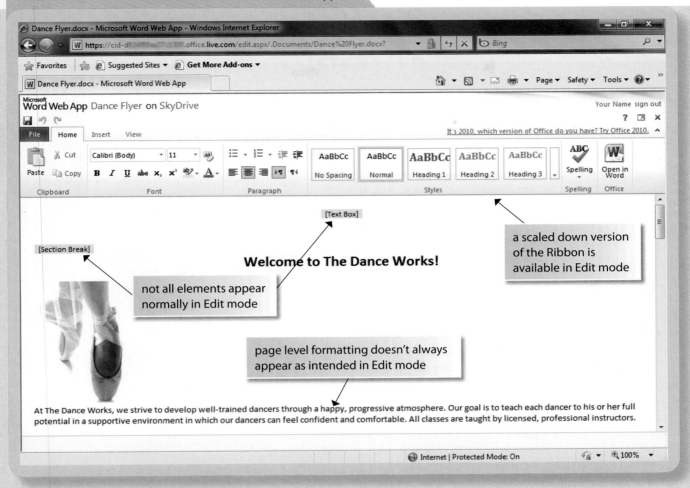

Exhibit 12-39 File in a folder on SkyDrive

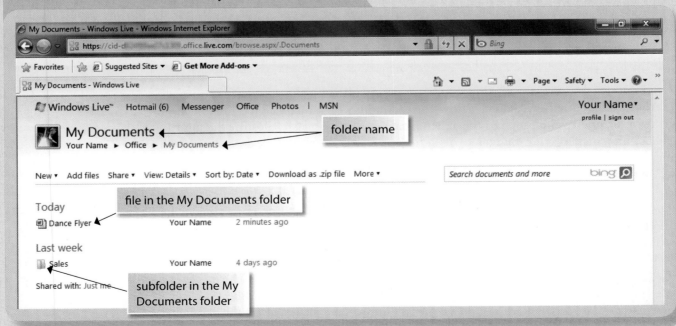

Creating a Workbook

Introduction

A spreadsheet is group of values and other data organized into rows and columns, similar to the ruled paper worksheets traditionally used by bookkeepers and accountants. Companies use spreadsheets to track budgets and inventory, and to help create a plan for future business. You can use a spreadsheet to create a personal budget or to balance a checkbook. You can create a spreadsheet using **Microsoft Excel 2010** (or just **Excel**), which is application software used to enter, analyze, and present quantitative data. By using Excel and taking advantage of the powerful calculations it can perform, you can automate tasks that would otherwise take many hours.

Learning Objectives

After studying the material in this chapter, you will be able to:

LO13.1 Understand spreadsheets and Excel

LO13.2 Enter data in cells

LO13.3 Edit cell content

LO13.4 Work with columns and rows

LO13.5 Work with cells and ranges

LO13.6 Work with formulas and functions

LO13.7 Preview and print a workbook

LO13.1 Understanding Spreadsheets and Excel

Exhibit 13-1 shows a cash flow report in a spreadsheet. The spreadsheet records the estimated and actual cash flow for the month of January. Each line, or row, displays a different value, such as the starting cash balance or cash sales for the month. Each column displays the budgeted or actual numbers or text that describes those values.

The total cash expenditures in row 12 in the spreadsheet, the net cash flow in row 13, and the closing cash balance for the month in row 14 are not entered directly, but calculated from other numbers in the spreadsheet. For example, the total cash expenditure is equal to the expenditures on advertising, wages, and supplies in rows 9 through 11. This allows you to use Excel to perform a **what-if analysis** in which you change one or more values in a spreadsheet and then assess how those changes affect the calculated values.

Microsoft Excel 2010 (Excel) Application software used to enter, analyze, and present quantitative data.

what-if analysis A process in which you change one or more values in a spreadsheet and then assess how those changes affect the calculated values.

Businesspeople and individuals use Excel to plan budgets, track inventory and assets, and create schedules. As data changes, Excel worksheets automatically update to provide current information.

Dmitriy Shironosov/Shutterstock.com

Exhibit 13-1 Spreadsheet data in Excel

values calculated by adding values in other cells

Exhibit 13-2 Parts of the Excel window

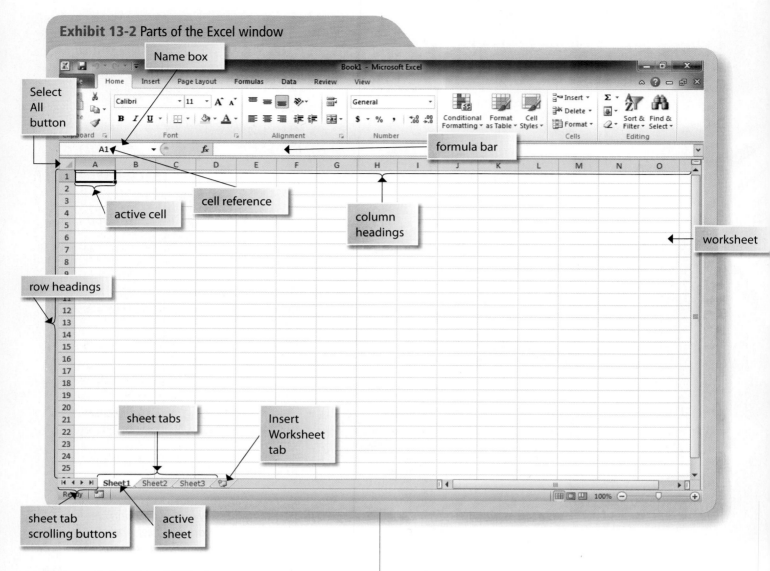

Parts of the Excel Window

In addition to the common elements found in all Office 2010 programs, including the title bar, Ribbon, scroll bars, and status bar, the Excel window contains features that are unique to Excel, as shown in Exhibit 13-2.

Excel stores spreadsheets in files called **workbooks**. The contents of a workbook are shown in a workbook

workbook An Excel file, which stores a spreadsheet.

sheet An individual page in a workbook that is either a worksheet or a chart sheet.

worksheet A sheet that contains data, laid out in a grid of rows and columns.

chart sheet A sheet that contains a visual representation of spreadsheet data.

window. The workbook that is currently being used is the active workbook and is displayed in the active workbook window. The name of the active workbook appears in the title bar of the Excel window. By default, Excel starts with a blank workbook named Book1 in the workbook window, maximized to fill the entire Excel window.

Each workbook is made up of individual **sheets**. Each sheet is identified by a sheet name, which is displayed in its sheet tab. Excel supports two kinds of sheets: worksheets and chart sheets. A **worksheet** contains data, laid out in a grid of rows and columns. A **chart sheet** contains a visual representation of spreadsheet data. Charts can also be embedded within worksheets, so you can view both the data and the charts in one sheet.

Each workbook can contain multiple worksheets and chart sheets. You can add sheets as needed to the default three worksheets that are included when you create a new workbook. This enables you to better

Each worksheet can have as many as 1,048,576 rows and 16,385 columns, creating more than 17 billion cells.

organize data and focus each worksheet on one area of data. For example, a sales report workbook might have a different worksheet for each sales region and another worksheet that summarizes the results from all the regions. A chart sheet might contain a chart that graphically compares the sales results from all of the regions.

Worksheets are laid out in rows and columns. Row headings identify each row with a number, ranging from 1 to 1,048,576. Column headings identify each column with a letter. The first 26 are columns A through Z. After Z, the next column headings are labeled AA, AB, AC, and so forth until you reach the last possible column, which is labeled XFD.

Rows and columns intersect in a single **cell**; all the data entered in a worksheet is placed in cells. Each cell is identified by a **cell reference**, which indicates its column and row location. For example, the cell reference B6 indicates the cell located where column B intersects row 6. The column letter always appears before the row number in a cell reference.

Moving the Active Cell

The cell in which you are currently working is the **active cell**. Excel distinguishes the active cell by outlining it with a thick black box. In Exhibit 13-2, cell A1 is the active cell. The cell reference for the active cell appears in the **Name box** located in the upper-left corner of the worksheet.

Both the pointer and the keyboard can change which cell is active in a worksheet. You can click a cell to make it the active cell, or you can press the arrow keys to move from one cell to another. Exhibit 13-3 identifies the keys you can use to move around a worksheet.

Exhibit 13-3 Excel navigation keys

Press	To move the active cell
Arrow keys	Up, down, left, or right one cell
Home	To column A of the current row
Ctrl+Home	To cell A1
Ctrl+End	To the last cell in the worksheet that contains data
Enter	Down one row or to the start of the next row of data
Shift+Enter	Up one row
Tab	One column to the right
Shift+Tab	One column to the left
Page Up, Page Down	Up or down one screen
Ctrl+Page Up, Ctrl+Page Down	To the previous or next sheet in the workbook

The mouse and keyboard provide quick ways to move around the parts of the worksheet you can see. For larger worksheets that span several screens, you can move directly to a specific cell by typing a cell reference in the Name box.

ACTIVITY

Move the active cell.

1 Start **Excel**. The Excel window opens displaying a blank worksheet in an untitled workbook.

2 If the Excel program window is not maximized, click the **Maximize button** 🗖.

3 On the Quick Access Toolbar, click the **Save button** 🖫. Because this is the first time you are saving the workbook, the Save As dialog box opens. Save the workbook as **ModArte Inventory**.

> **Tip:** In the Save As dialog box, notice that the file type is Excel Workbook.

cell The location in a worksheet where a row and column intersect.

cell reference The row and column location of a specific cell.

active cell The selected cell in which you are working.

Name box The location where the active cell reference is displayed.

Save Your Files

Remember to save your files to the drive and folder where you are storing the files you create as you complete the steps in this book. Also, be sure to save frequently as you go.

Scrolling the worksheet does not change the location of the active cell.

4 Point to the **worksheet area**. The pointer changes to ✛. A1 appears in the Name box because cell A1 is the active cell. The column heading for column A and the row heading for row 1 are orange to help you locate the active cell.

5 Click **cell A5**. Cell A5 now has a dark box around it to indicate that it is the active cell, the cell reference in the Name box changes to A5, and the row heading for row 5 is orange instead of the row heading for row 1.

6 Press the **Tab key**. The active cell moves one cell to the right to cell B5.

7 Press the **Page Down key**. The active cell moves down one full screen.

8 Click in the **Name box**. The active cell reference in the Name box is selected.

9 Type **D4**. The cell reference you typed replaces the selected reference.

10 Press the **Enter key**. Cell D4 is now the active cell.

11 Press the **Ctrl+Home keys**. The active cell returns to the first cell in the worksheet, cell A1.

Switching Between Sheets

New workbooks contain three worksheets named Sheet1, Sheet2, and Sheet3. The sheet currently displayed in the workbook window is the **active sheet**, and its sheet tab is white. The sheet tabs for inactive sheets are gray. You can easily move from one sheet to another, add new sheets to the workbook, remove unneeded ones, and move or copy entire sheets. You can also give sheets more descriptive and meaningful names.

As you build workbooks, data and charts are often organized on different sheets. An inactive sheet becomes

active sheet The sheet currently displayed in the workbook window.

active when you click its sheet tab. In Exhibit 13-2, the active sheet is named Sheet1.

For workbooks that contain more sheet tabs than can be displayed at the same time in the workbook window, you can scroll through the sheet tabs using the four sheet tab scrolling buttons to the left of the first sheet tab (refer back to Exhibit 13-2). Just like the scroll bars and the active cell, scrolling does not change the active sheet.

ACTIVITY

Switch the active sheet.

1 Click the **Sheet2 sheet tab**. The Sheet2 worksheet, which is also blank, becomes the active sheet. The Sheet2 sheet tab is white, indicating that this is the active sheet.

2 Change the zoom level of the worksheet to **120%**.

3 Click the **Sheet1 sheet tab** to make the first worksheet active.

> **Tip:** You can change the zoom level using the Zoom slider ⬜, the Zoom In button ⊕, or the Zoom level button 100% at the right side of the status bar.

4 Change the zoom level of the worksheet to **120%**.

Inserting and Deleting a Sheet

Although each workbook includes three worksheets to start, sometimes you will need more or fewer worksheets. You can add worksheets or delete unneeded ones. A new worksheet you add is named with the next consecutive sheet number, such as Sheet4.

ACTIVITY

Insert and delete worksheets.

1 To the right of the Sheet3 sheet tab, click the **Insert Worksheet tab** 📄. Excel inserts a new worksheet named Sheet4 to the right of the last sheet tab.

2 Right-click the **Sheet3 sheet tab**. On the shortcut menu, click **Delete**. The Sheet3 worksheet is deleted.

3 Right-click the **Sheet4 sheet tab**. On the shortcut menu, click **Delete**. The Sheet4 worksheet is deleted.

Effective Workbook Design

Effective workbooks are carefully planned and designed. An effective workbook should clearly identify its goal and present information in a well-organized format.

To develop a good workbook, you should determine the workbook's purpose, content, and organization before you start entering data. It is often helpful to use a planning analysis sheet, which includes a series of questions that help you think about the purpose of the workbook and how to achieve the desired results. You should also create a list of the sheets you plan to use in the workbook, making note of each sheet's purpose.

After you know what the workbook should include and how it should be organized, you are ready to create it. Follow this basic process to build a complete and accurate workbook that you and others can easily use:

1. Insert a documentation sheet.
Describe the workbook's purpose and organization. Include the name of the workbook author, the date the workbook was created, and any additional information that others can use to track the workbook to its source.

2. Enter all of the data (both values and labels).
Add text to indicate what the values represent and, if possible, where they originated. Other users might want to view the source of your data.

3. Enter formulas for calculated values.
Use formulas to calculate results rather than entering the results of the calculations. For more complex calculations, provide documentation explaining them.

4. Test the workbook.
Try out a variety of sample values to weed out any errors in your calculations. Edit the data and formulas to correct any errors.

Planning Analysis Sheet—Order Form

What problems do I want to solve?
- I need to have contact information for each customer.
- I need to identify the item and quantity ordered for my customers.
- I need to record the price per item.
- I need to determine how much revenue I am generating.

What data do I need?
- Each customer's name and contact information
- The date each customer order was placed
- The item and quantity each customer ordered

What calculations do I need to enter?
- The total charge for each order
- The total number of items ordered for all orders
- The total revenue generated from all orders

What form should my solution take?
- The customer orders should be placed in a grid with each row containing data on a different customer.
- Information about each customer should be placed in separate columns.
- The last column should contain the total charge for each customer.
- The last row should contain the total number of items ordered and the total revenue from all customer orders.

---

5. Distribute the final workbook.
Be sure to save the final version and create a backup copy when the project is completed. You can store and share the workbook's contents in a variety of ways—online, as a printed copy, or as a PDF file (a special file that preserves the formatting of the worksheet but does not allow it to be edited), among others.

Renaming a Sheet

The default worksheet names, Sheet1, Sheet2, and so on, are not very descriptive. You can rename sheets with more meaningful names so that you know what they contain. The width of the sheet tab will adjust to the length of the name you enter.

ACTIVITY

Rename sheets.

1 Double-click the **Sheet1 sheet tab**. The sheet name is selected in the sheet tab. Because the focus is on the sheet tab, the black border disappears from around cell A1 (the active cell).

2 Type **Inventory**. The text you type replaces the selected sheet name, the width of the sheet tab expands as you type to accommodate the longer sheet name, and the insertion point remains in the sheet tab. See Exhibit 13-4.

Exhibit 13-4 Sheet tab being renamed

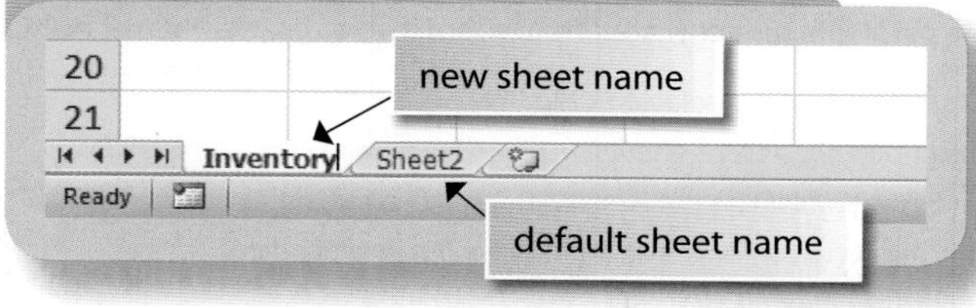

| 20 | new sheet name |
| 21 | |

Inventory   Sheet2
Ready

default sheet name

3 Press the **Enter key**. The sheet name is entered, and cell A1 again has a black box around it.

> **Tip:** Sheet names cannot exceed 31 characters in length, including blank spaces.

4 Double-click the **Sheet2 sheet tab**, type **Documentation** and then press the **Enter key**. The newly named Documentation worksheet is now the active sheet.

Moving and Copying a Sheet

You can change the placement of the sheets in a workbook. A good practice is to place the most important sheets at the beginning of the workbook (the leftmost sheet tabs) and less important sheets toward the end (the rightmost tabs).

> **formula bar** A bar used to enter, edit, or display the contents of the active cell.

ACTIVITY

Move a sheet.

1 Click the **Documentation sheet tab**, but don't release the mouse button. The pointer changes to ⬚ and a small black triangle appears in the upper-left corner of the sheet tab.

2 Drag the **Documentation sheet tab** to the left until the small black triangle is at the left edge of the Inventory sheet tab, and then release the mouse button. The Documentation worksheet is now the first sheet in the workbook.

> **Tip:** To copy rather than move a sheet, press and hold the Ctrl key as you drag and drop the sheet tab. The copy is placed where you drop the sheet tab; the original sheet remains in its initial position.

3 Save the workbook.

LO13.2 **Entering Data in Cells**

You enter data by typing it into the active cell. When you finish typing, you can press the Enter key or the Tab key to complete the data entry and move to the next cell in the worksheet. As you enter data into the worksheet, it appears in both the active cell and in the formula bar. The **formula bar** displays the contents of the active cell, which can be data or, as you'll see later, the underlying formulas used to create a calculated value.

Entering Data

Text you type is not entered into the worksheet until you accept it. The easiest way to accept data is to press the Enter key, the Tab key, or an arrow key. You can also click the Enter button ✔, which appears between the formula bar and the Name box as soon as you start typing.

ethylalkohol/Shutterstock.com

In Excel, data falls into three general categories: text, numbers, and dates and times.

Entering Text

Text data is a combination of letters, numbers, and symbols that form words and sentences. Text data is often referred to as a **text string** because it contains a string of text characters.

When creating a worksheet, you should make sure its intent and content are clear to others. One way to do this is to create a documentation sheet, which documents why you created the workbook and what it contains. It is also a good way to relay the workbook's purpose and content to others with whom you share the workbook.

 **ACTIVITY**

Enter text.

1 In the Documentation worksheet, in cell A1, type **ModArte**. As you type, the text appears in both cell A1 (the active cell) and in the formula bar.

2 Press the **Enter key**. Excel enters the text into cell A1 and moves the active cell down one cell to cell A2.

3 Press the **Enter key** to move the active cell down one cell to cell A3.

4 Type **Author** and then press the **Tab key**. The text is entered and the active cell moves one cell to the right to cell B3.

5 Type your name, and then press the **Enter key**. The text is entered and the active cell moves one cell down and to the left to cell A4.

6 Type **Date** and then press the **Tab key**. The text is entered and the active cell moves one cell to the right to cell B4, where you will later enter the date you created the workbook.

7 Click **cell A5** to make it the active cell, type **Purpose** and then press the **Tab key**. The active cell moves one cell to the right to cell B5.

8 Type **To record current inventory** and then press the **Enter key**. Exhibit 13-5 shows the text entered in the Documentation worksheet.

Exhibit 13-5 Documentation sheet with data

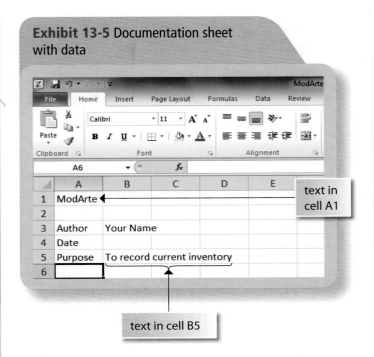

text in cell A1

text in cell B5

9 Click the **Inventory sheet tab** to make it the active sheet. Cell A1 is the active cell.

10 Type **Inventory Date** and then press the **Enter key**. The label is entered in the cell, and cell A2 is the active cell.

11 Enter the following column labels, pressing the **Tab key** after each entry:

cell A2: **Artist**

cell B2: **Title**

cell C2: **Inventory**

cell D2: **Unit Cost**

cell E2: **Inventory Value**

> **Tip:** To place text on separate lines within the same cell, press the Alt+Tab keys to create a line break within the cell.

12 Press the **Enter key**. The active cell moves to cell A3, the start of the next row where you want to begin entering the customer data.

13 Type **Dali** in cell A3, press the **Tab key** to move to the next cell, type **The Disintegration of the Persistence of Memory** in cell B3, and then press the **Enter key**. You have entered the first artist and title and moved the active cell to cell A4.

> **text data (text string)** Any combination of letters, numbers, and symbols that form words and sentences.

Including the company name, a descriptive title, and the date is part of good worksheet design. It lets others quickly see the *who*, *what*, and *when* of the data.

14 Enter the following text in **cells A4** through **B7**, and then compare your screen to Exhibit 13-6:

cell A4: **Kandinsky**   cell B4: **Merry Structure**

cell A5: **Picasso**   cell B5: **Woman with a Blue Hat**

cell A6: **Rothko**   cell B6: **Blue, Green, and Brown**

cell A7: **van Gogh**   cell B7: **Starry Night over the Rhone**

Exhibit 13-6 Text data entered in cells

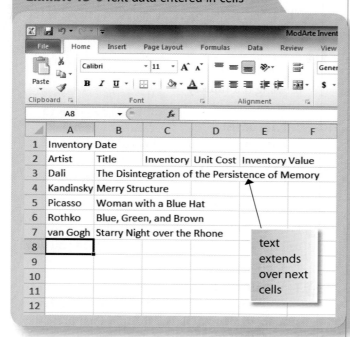

text extends over next cells

date data Text or numbers in commonly recognized formats for date values.

time data Text or numbers in commonly recognized formats for time values.

Using AutoComplete

As you enter text in a worksheet, Excel tries to anticipate what you are about to enter by displaying text that begins with the same letters as a previous entry in the same column. This feature, known as AutoComplete, helps make entering repetitive text easier. To accept the suggested text, press the Tab or Enter key. To override the suggested text, continue to type the text you want to enter in the cell. AutoComplete does not work with dates or numbers, or when a blank cell is between the previous entry and the text you are typing.

	A
1	Artist
2	Dali
3	Kandinsky
4	Picasso
5	Dali

Entering Dates and Times

Date data and **time data** are commonly recognized formats for date and time values. When you enter a date in a cell, such as April 15, 2014, Excel interprets it as a date and not as text and formats it appropriately. You can enter dates in any of the standard formats, including the following date formats (as well as many others), and Excel recognizes each format as representing the same date:

▶ **4/6/2014**   ▶ **April 6, 2014**

▶ **4/6/14**   ▶ **6-Apr-14**

▶ **4-6-2014**

In Excel, dates are actually numbers that are formatted to appear as text. This allows you to perform calculations with dates, such as determining the elapsed time between two dates.

No matter how you enter dates, Excel alters the date format to one of two default formats. If you use numbers separated by slashes or hyphens, Excel displays the date with the four-digit year value. For example, if you enter the date 4/6/14, Excel changes it to 4/6/2014. If you use text for the month, for example, April 6, 2014, Excel converts the date to the format 6-Apr-14.

 **ACTIVITY**

Enter dates.

1 Make **cell B1** the active cell.

2 Type **3/12/14** and then press the **Tab key**. The date you typed appears in cell B1, but is reformatted as 3/12/2014.

International Date Formats

As business transactions become more international in scope, you may need to adopt international standards for expressing dates, times, and currency values. For example, a cell might contain 06/05/14. This format could represent any of the following dates:

▶ The 5th of June, 2014

▶ The 6th of May, 2014

▶ The 14th of May, 2006

The date depends on which country the workbook has been designed for. You can avoid this problem by entering the full date as in the example June 5, 2014. However, this will not work with documents written in languages such as Japanese that use different character symbols.

To solve this problem, many international businesses adopt ISO (International Organization for Standardization) dates in the format *yyyy-mm-dd*, where *yyyy* is the four-digit year value, *mm* is the two-digit month value, and *dd* is the two-digit day value. So, a date such as June 5, 2014 is entered as 2014/06/05. If you use this international date format, make sure that people using your workbook understand this format so that they do not misinterpret the dates. You can include information about the date format in the documentation sheet.

Korn/Shutterstock.com

---

3 Make the **Documentation worksheet** the active sheet.

4 Click **cell B4**, type today's date, and then press the **Enter key**. The date appears in one of the two default date formats, depending on the format in which you entered the date.

5 Make the **Inventory worksheet** the active sheet.

Entering Numbers

Number data is any numerical value that can be used in a mathematical calculation. In Excel, numbers can be integers such as 378, decimals such as 1.95, or negatives such as −5.2. In the case of currency and percentages, you can include the currency symbol and percent sign when you enter the value. Excel treats a currency value such as $87.25 as the number 87.25 and a percentage such as 95% as the decimal number 0.95. Currency and percentages, like dates, are formatted in a convenient way for you to read.

If an integer is longer than its cell size, you see ###### in the cell instead of its value. Decimal values are rounded to fit the cell. You can display the entire number by increasing the column width.

ACTIVITY

Enter number data.

1 Click **cell C3**, type **25** and then press the **Tab key**. The inventory quantity for the Dali print is entered in cell C3 and the active cell is now cell D3. Because cell C3 contains data, the excess text from cell B3 cannot flow over cell C3.

2 In cell D3, type **$4.83** and then press the **Enter key**. The unit cost is entered in cell D3 as a currency value, and the active cell moves to cell C4.

3 Enter the following inventory values and unit costs into **cells C4** through **D7**, and then compare your screen to Exhibit 13-7:

cell C4: **18**	cell D4: **$5.17**	
cell C5: **22**	cell D5: **$6.24**	
cell C6: **4**	cell D6: **$8.96**	
cell C7: **36**	cell D7: **$4.12**	

4 Save the workbook.

By default, text is left-aligned in cells; other types of data—numbers, dates, and times—are right-aligned in cells.

---

number data Any numerical value that can be used in a mathematical calculation.

Exhibit 13-7 Number data entered in the worksheet

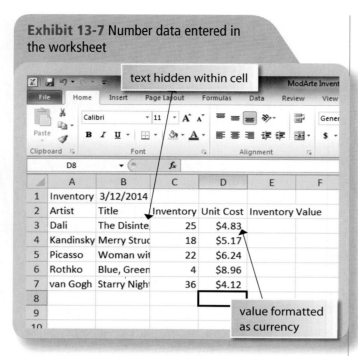

text hidden within cell

value formatted as currency

LO13.3 Editing Cell Content

As you work, you might make mistakes that you want to correct or undo, or you might need to replace a value based on more current information. You could simply make the cell active and type the new entry, or you could clear the value in the cell and then type the correct value. However, sometimes you need to edit only a portion of an entry rather than change the entire contents of a cell, especially if the cell contains a large block of text or a complex formula. You can edit the contents of a selected cell in the formula bar, or you can do one of the following to edit the cell contents directly in the cell:

▶ Double-click the cell.

▶ Select the cell, click anywhere in the formula bar, and then click in the cell.

▶ Select the cell, and then press the F2 key.

When editing content directly in a cell, some of the keyboard shortcuts work differently because now they apply only to the text within the selected cell. For example, pressing the Home key moves the insertion point to the beginning of the cell's content, and pressing the Left Arrow key or the Right Arrow key moves the insertion point backward or forward through the cell's content.

ACTIVITY

Edit cell content.

1 Double-click **cell D6**. The currency formatting disappears from the active cell. See Exhibit 13-8.

Exhibit 13-8 Cell content being edited

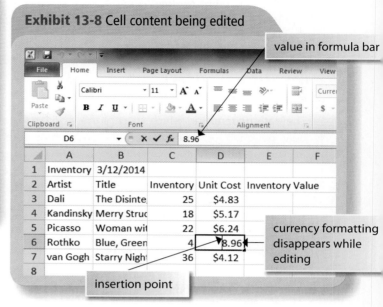

value in formula bar

currency formatting disappears while editing

insertion point

2 Press the **Right Arrow key** as many times as necessary to move the insertion point to the end of the cell, after the 6.

3 Press the **Backspace key** twice to delete 96, and then type **72**. The unit cost value in cell D6 changes to 8.72.

> ⚠ **Problem?** If you make a mistake as you edit, press the **Esc key** or click the **Cancel button** X on the formula bar to cancel all of the changes you made while editing.

4 Press the **Enter key** to accept the edit in cell D6. The value in cell D6 is displayed as $8.72.

5 Save the workbook.

LO13.4 Working with Columns and Rows

You can modify a worksheet to make it easier to read and include more data. To do this, you will need to change the column widths and row heights, insert columns and rows, and delete columns and rows.

Selecting Columns and Rows

You can select two or more columns or rows at the same time. To select an entire column, you click its column heading. Likewise, to select an entire row, you click its row heading. You can drag across multiple column headings or row headings to select adjacent columns or rows. Or, you can click the first heading, press and hold the Shift key, and then click the last heading. To select nonadjacent columns or rows, you press the Ctrl key as you click column or row headings. Finally, you can select all the columns and rows in a worksheet by clicking the Select All button in the upper-left corner of the worksheet.

Select columns and rows.

1. Click the **column A column heading**. The entire column is selected.

2. Press and hold the **Shift key**, click the **column C column heading**, and then release the **Shift key**. Columns A through C are selected.

3. Press and hold the **Ctrl key**, click the **column F column heading**, and then release the **Ctrl key**. Columns A through C and column F are selected.

4. Click the **column A column heading**, but do not release the mouse button. The entire column is selected.

5. Without releasing the mouse button, drag to the **column B column heading**, and then release the mouse button. Both columns A and B are selected.

6. Click anywhere in the worksheet to deselect the columns.

Changing Column Widths and Row Heights

The default sizes of the columns and rows in a worksheet might not always accommodate the information you need to enter. For example, on the Inventory sheet, the text in cell E2 is so long that it seems to overflow into cell F2. If the adjacent cells also contain data, Excel displays only as much text as fits into the cell, cutting off, or **truncating**, the rest of the text entry. The text itself is not affected. The complete text is still entered in the cell; it's just not displayed. For example, all of the titles in cells B3 through B4 are truncated because the adjacent cells in column C contain data. To make the cell content easier to read or fully visible, you can resize the columns and rows in the worksheet.

> When you enter more text than can fit in a cell, the additional text is visible in the adjacent cells as long as they are empty.

Column widths are expressed in terms of either the number of characters the column can contain or the size of the column in pixels. A pixel is a single point, or the smallest colorable area, on a computer monitor or printout. The default column width allows you to type about eight or nine characters in a cell before that entry is either truncated or overlaps the adjacent cell. Of course, if you decrease the font size of characters, you can fit more text within a cell. Row heights are expressed in points or pixels, where a point is 1/72 of an inch. The default row height is 15.75 points.

Setting Column Widths Properly

You should set column widths based on the maximum number of characters you want to display in the cells rather than pixel size. Pixel size is related to screen resolution, and a cell might be too narrow under a different resolution. This might come into play if you work on multiple computers or share your workbooks with others.

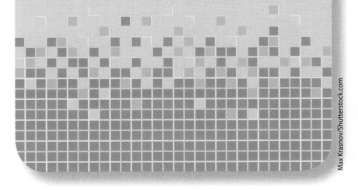

Max Krasnov/Shutterstock.com

If the default column width is too narrow, you can widen it by dragging the column border. When you drag the column border, a ScreenTip appears identifying the width of the column in characters, followed in

truncate To cut off, such as a text entry in a workbook cell.

parentheses by the width of the column in pixels. Another option is to AutoFit a column or row to its content. **AutoFitting** eliminates any empty space by matching the column to the width of its longest cell entry. If the column is blank, Excel restores the column to its default width. The simplest way to AutoFit a column is to double-click its right border. You can also use the AutoFit Column Width command on the Format button menu in the Cells group on the Home tab.

Row heights are set in the same way as column widths. You can drag the bottom border of the row. You can double-click the bottom border of a row to AutoFit the row to the height of its tallest cell entry. Or, you can use the AutoFit Row Height command on the Format button menu in the Cells group on the Home tab.

Rather than resizing each column or row separately, you can select multiple columns or rows and resize them at the same time.

ACTIVITY

Change column widths.

1 Point to the **right border** of the column B column heading. The pointer changes to ✛.

2 Drag to the right until the ScreenTip identifies the width of the column as **25 characters**, but do not release the mouse button. See Exhibit 13-9.

3 Release the mouse button. The width of column B expands to 25 characters and all of the titles in column B except the title in cell B3 fit on one line.

> ➤ **Tip:** You can also click the Format button in the Cells group on the Home tab, click Column Width, and then type the width you want in the Column Width dialog box.

AutoFit To eliminate empty space by matching a column to the width of its longest cell entry or matching a row to the height of its tallest cell entry.

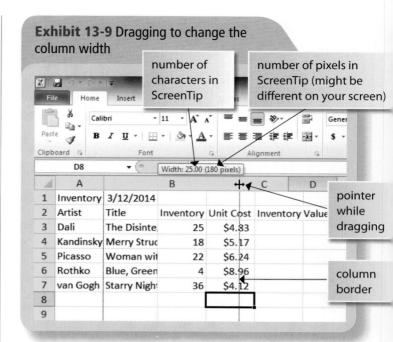

Exhibit 13-9 Dragging to change the column width

- number of characters in ScreenTip
- number of pixels in ScreenTip (might be different on your screen)
- pointer while dragging
- column border

4 Point to the **right border** of the column A column heading. When the pointer changes to ✛, double-click. The width of column A AutoFits to 13.57 characters, which displays all of the text in cell A1, the widest entry in the column, entirely within the cell.

5 Select **column C** and **column D**.

6 Drag the **right border** of the column D column heading to the right until the column width changes to **12 characters**, and then release the mouse button. Both of the selected columns are now wider. See Exhibit 13-10.

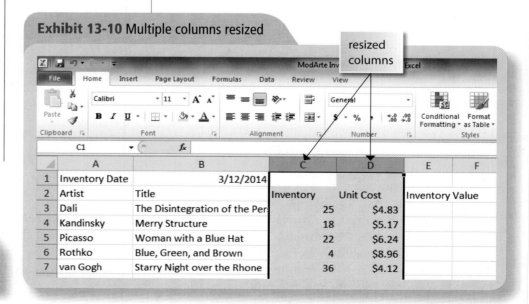

Exhibit 13-10 Multiple columns resized

- resized columns

7 Select **column E**.

8 On the Home tab, in the Cells group, click the **Format button**. A menu of commands opens. The top five, in the Cell Size section, provide options for adjusting column width and row height.

9 Click **AutoFit Column Width**. The width of the selected column—column E—AutoFits to its content.

10 Click anywhere in the worksheet to deselect the column.

Inserting a Column or Row

You can insert a new column or row anywhere within a worksheet. When you insert a new column, the existing columns shift to the right and the new column has the same width as the column directly to its left. When you insert a new row, the existing rows shift down and the new row has the same height as the row above it. You can insert a column or row using the Insert button in the Cells group on the Home tab, and then selecting the appropriate command on the menu.

ACTIVITY

Insert columns and rows.

1 Select **column C**.

2 On the Home tab, in the Cells group, click the **Insert button**. A new column C is inserted into the worksheet and the rest of the columns shift to the right. The new column has the same width as the column to its left, column B.

3 Click **cell C2**, type **Item Number** and then press the **Enter key**. The new column label is entered, and cell C3 is the active cell.

4 Enter the following data in **cells C3** through **C7**:

cell C3: **D-1287**

cell C4: **K-0283**

cell C5: **P-9273**

cell C6: **R-5392**

cell C7: **V-3028**

5 AutoFit the contents of **column C**.

6 Click the **row 2 row heading**. The entire second row is selected.

7 In the Cells group on the Home tab, click the **Insert button**. A new row 2 is inserted, and the remaining rows shift down. See Exhibit 13-11.

Exhibit 13-11 New column and new row inserted in the worksheet

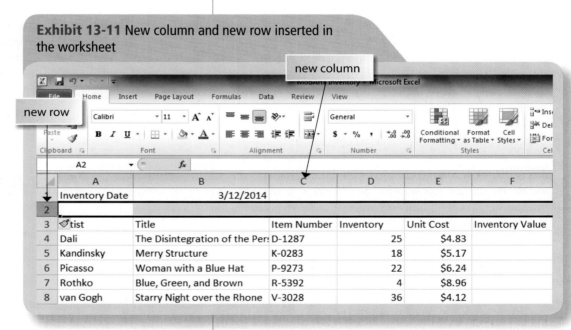

Clearing and Deleting a Row or Column

Adding new data to a workbook is common, as is removing old or erroneous data. You can remove data in two ways: clearing and deleting.

▶ **Clearing**—Removes data from a worksheet but leaves the blank cells

▶ **Deleting**—Removes both the data and the cells from the worksheet

clear To remove data from cells but leave the blank cells in the worksheet.

delete To remove both the data and the cells from a worksheet.

Pressing the Delete key only clears the contents of selected cells but does not remove the selected cells from the worksheet.

When you delete a column, the columns to the right shift left to fill the vacated space. Similarly, the rows below a deleted row shift up to fill the vacated space. Deleting a column or row has the opposite effect from inserting a column or row.

You can delete entire columns or rows by selecting them, and then clicking the Delete button in the Cells group on the Home tab. You can also right-click the selected column or row headings, and then click Delete on the shortcut menu. To clear data from a column or row without deleting the column or row itself, you can right-click the selected column or row heading, and then click Clear Contents on the shortcut menu. Another option is to select the columns or rows with data to clear, and then press the Delete key, which clears the data without deleting the selected cells.

You'll first clear data from the worksheet and then delete the row that contained the data. Usually, you would do this in one step by simply deleting the row, but this activity highlights the difference between clearing and deleting.

 **ACTIVITY**

Clear a row and delete a row.

1. Right-click the **row 7 row heading**. Row 7 is selected, and a shortcut menu appears.

2. On the shortcut menu, click **Clear Contents**. Excel clears the values in row 7.

3. With row 7 still selected, on the Home tab, in the Cells group, click the **Delete button**. Row 7 is deleted, and the rows below it shift up.

4. Save the workbook.

cell range (range) A group of cells.

adjacent range A single rectangular block of cells.

nonadjacent range Two or more distinct adjacent ranges.

range reference The location and size of a range.

LO13.5 Working with Cells and Ranges

A group of cells is called a **cell range** or **range**. Ranges can be either adjacent or nonadjacent. An **adjacent range** is a single rectangular block of cells. All of the customer order data entered in cell A1 through cell G5 is an adjacent range because it forms one rectangular block of cells. A **nonadjacent range** consists of two or more distinct adjacent ranges. All of the last names in cell A1 through cell A5 and all the numbers in cell F1 through cell G5 together are a nonadjacent range because they are two distinct blocks of cells.

Just as a cell reference indicates the location of an individual worksheet cell, a **range reference** indicates the location and size of a range. For adjacent ranges, the range reference specifies the locations of the upper-left and lower-right cells in the rectangular block separated by a colon. For example, the range reference A1:A5 refers to all the cells from cell A1 through cell A5.

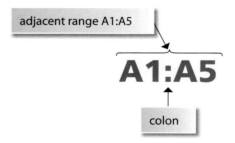

The range reference for nonadjacent ranges separates each adjacent range reference by a semicolon. For example, A1:A5;F1:G5 is the range reference for cells A1 through A5 and cells F1 through G5.

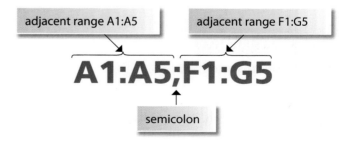

A nonadjacent range can include as many adjacent ranges as you want.

Selecting a Range

You select adjacent and nonadjacent ranges of cells with the pointer, just as you selected individual cells. Selecting a range enables you to work with all of the cells in the range as a group. This means you can do things like move the cells, delete them, or clear their contents at the same time.

 **ACTIVITY**

Select ranges.

1 Click **cell A1**, but do not release the mouse button. This cell will be the cell in the upper-left corner of the range A1:F7.

2 Drag the pointer to **cell F7**. The cells you drag over are shaded blue (except cell A1). Cell F7 is the cell in the lower-right corner of the range A1:F7.

3 Release the mouse button. All cells in the adjacent range A1:F7 are selected. The selected cells are highlighted with color and surrounded by a black box. The first cell you clicked, cell A1, remains white to indicate that it is the active cell in the worksheet.

4 Click any cell in the worksheet to deselect the range.

5 Select the adjacent **range A3:A7**.

6 Press and hold the **Ctrl key**, select the adjacent **range D3:E7**, and then release the **Ctrl key**. As shown in Exhibit 13-12, all of the cells

in the nonadjacent range A3:A7;D3:E7 are selected.

7 Click any cell in the worksheet to deselect the nonadjacent range.

Moving and Copying a Range

One way to move a cell or range is to select it, position the pointer over the bottom edge of the selection, and then drag the selection to a new location. This technique is called drag and drop because you are dragging the range and dropping it in a new location. You can also use the drag-and-drop technique to copy cells by pressing the Ctrl key as you drag the selected range to its new location. A copy of the original range is placed in the new location without removing the original range from the worksheet.

Some people find drag and drop a difficult and awkward way to move or copy a selection, particularly if the worksheet is large and complex. In those situations, it is often more efficient to cut and paste the cell contents or to copy and paste them.

When you cut or copy a range, the selected cells are surrounded by a blinking border, indicating that the selection is stored on the Clipboard. The blinking border remains until you paste the range or start entering data in another cell. After the blinking border disappears, the selection is no longer stored on the Clipboard and you cannot paste it.

When you paste, you can select only the upper-left cell of the range in the new location rather than the exact range where you want to paste. Excel will paste the entire range on the Clipboard with the same pattern of cells in the new location. Be aware that the pasted data will overwrite any data already in those cells.

Exhibit 13-12 Nonadjacent range A3:A7;D3:E7 selected

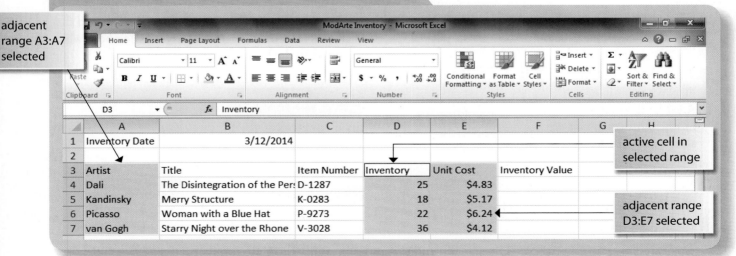

Move a range and a cell.

1 Select the **range A1:B1**.

2 Move the pointer over the **bottom border** of the selected range so that the pointer changes to ⟨pointer⟩.

3 Press and hold the **left mouse button** to change the pointer to ⟨pointer⟩.

4 Drag the selection down eight rows, but do not release the mouse button. A ScreenTip appears, indicating the new range reference for the selected cells—*A9:B9*. See Exhibit 13-13.

Exhibit 13-13 Range being moved with drag and drop

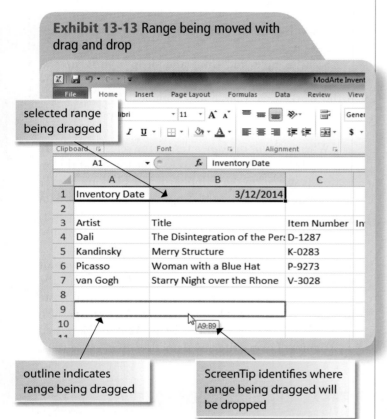

selected range being dragged

outline indicates range being dragged

ScreenTip identifies where range being dragged will be dropped

5 When the ScreenTip displays the range *A9:B9*, release the mouse button. The selected cells move to the new location.

6 Make sure the **range A9:B9** is selected.

7 On the Home tab, in the Clipboard

> **Tip:** To move a selection to a location that is not visible, drag the selection to the edge of the worksheet in the direction you want to scroll. When the new location is visible, drop the selection.

group, click the **Cut button** ⟨icon⟩. The selected range is surrounded by a blinking border, which indicates that its contents are stored on the Clipboard.

8 Click **cell A1**. This cell is the upper-left corner of the range where you want to paste the data.

9 In the Clipboard group, click the **Paste button**. Excel pastes the contents of the range A9:B9 into the new range A1:B1. The blinking border disappears and the Paste button is grayed out as visual clues that the Clipboard is now empty.

Inserting and Deleting a Range

Another use of selecting a range is to insert or delete cells within the worksheet. If you select a range and then click the Insert button in the Cells group on the Home tab, the selected range shifts down when the selected range is wider than it is long, and shifts right when the selected range is longer than it is wide, as illustrated in Exhibit 13-14.

If you click the Insert Cells button arrow, you can then use the Insert Cells command on the menu to open the Insert dialog box shown in Exhibit 13-15. This allows you to specify whether you want to shift the existing cells right or down, or whether to insert an entire row or column. The selected option is Excel's best guess of which way you want the current cells to shift.

If you no longer need a specific cell or range in a worksheet, you can delete those cells and any content they contain. To delete a range, select the range, and then click the Delete button in the Cells group on the Home tab. As with deleting a row or column, cells adjacent to the deleted range either move up or left to fill in the vacancy left by the deleted cells. To specify how the adjacent cells shift, or if you want to delete the entire row or column, click the Delete button arrow, and then click Delete Cells to open the Delete dialog box, which is similar to the Insert dialog box.

Insert and delete ranges.

1 Select the **range B3:C4**.

> **Tip:** You can select a range of a single cell.

2 On the Home tab, in the Cells group, click the **Insert button arrow** to open the Insert button menu.

Exhibit 13-14 Cells inserted within a range

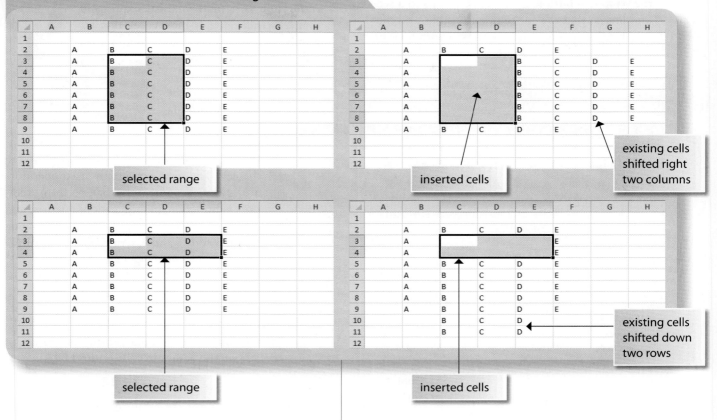

selected range

inserted cells

existing cells shifted right two columns

selected range

inserted cells

existing cells shifted down two rows

Exhibit 13-15
Insert dialog box

3 On the Insert button menu, click **Insert Cells**. The Insert dialog box opens. The Shift cells down option button is selected because this is the most likely action you will take for the selected range.

4 Click **OK**. The dialog box closes, four cells are inserted, and the selected cells move down two rows.

5 Make sure the **range B3:C4** is selected.

6 On the Home tab, in the Cells group, click the **Delete button arrow** to open the Delete button menu.

7 On the Delete button menu, click **Delete Cells**. The Delete dialog box opens. The Shift cells up option button is selected by default.

8 Click **OK**. The dialog box closes, the selected cells are deleted, and the cells below the selected cells move up two rows.

Wrapping Text Within a Cell

You can force text that extends beyond a cell's border to fit within the cell. First, make the cell with truncated text the active cell. Then, click the Wrap Text button in the Alignment group on the Home tab. The row height increases as needed to wrap all the text within the cell. You can click the Wrap Text button again to turn off the text wrapping within the active cell.

 **ACTIVITY**

Wrap text within a cell.

1 Make **cell B4** the active cell. The title of the Dali print extends past the right border of cell B4.

2 On the Home tab, in the Alignment group, click the **Wrap Text button** ⊞. The text wraps to a second line so that the entire title is visible, and the row height increases so you can see both lines of text within cell B4. See Exhibit 13-16.

Exhibit 13-16 Cell with text wrapping

Wrap Text button

	A	B	C	D
1	Inventory Date	3/12/2014		
2				
3	Artist	Title	Item Number	Inventory
4	Dali	The Disintegration of the Persistence of Memory	D-1287	25
5	Kandinsky	Merry Structure	K-0283	18
6	Picasso	Woman with a Blue Hat	P-9273	22
7	van Gogh	Starry Night over the Rhone	V-3028	36

B4 — fx The Disintegration of the Persistence of Memory

text wrapped to two lines

3 Save the workbook.

LO13.6 Entering Formulas and Functions

Up to now, you have entered only text, numbers, and dates in the worksheet. However, the main reason for using Excel is to display values calculated from data. For example, the workbook has all the data needed to determine the total inventory ModArte has in stock and the value of the current inventory. Such calculations are added to a worksheet using formulas and functions.

formula A mathematical expression that returns a value.

operator A mathematical symbol used to combine values.

order of precedence A set of predefined rules used to determine the sequence in which operators are applied in a calculation—first exponentiation (^), second multiplication (*) and division (/), and third addition (+) and subtraction (−).

Entering a Formula

A **formula** is a mathematical expression that returns a value. In most cases, this is a number. Every Excel formula begins with an equal sign (=) followed by an expression that describes the operation to be done. A formula is written using **operators** that combine different values, returning a single value that is then displayed in the cell. The most commonly used operators are arithmetic operators that perform addition, subtraction, multiplication, division, and exponentiation. For example, the following formula adds 5 and 7, returning a value of 12:

$$=5+7$$

However, most formulas in Excel contain references to cells that store numbers rather than the specific values. For example, the following formula returns the result of adding the values in cells A1 and B2:

$$=A1+B2$$

So, if the value 5 is stored in cell A1 and the value 7 is stored in cell B2, this formula would also return a value of 12. Exhibit 13-17 describes the different arithmetic operators and provides examples of formulas.

If a formula contains more than one arithmetic operator, Excel performs the calculation using the same order of precedence you might have already seen in math classes. The **order of precedence** is a set of predefined rules used to determine the sequence in which operators are applied in a calculation—first exponentiation (^), second multiplication (*) and division (/), and third addition (+) and subtraction (−). For example, the following formula returns the value 23 because multiplication—in this case, 4*5—takes precedence over addition:

$$=3+4*5$$

If a formula contains two or more operators with the same level of precedence, the operators are applied in order from left to right. The following formula first

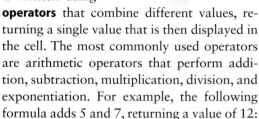

You can also create formulas in Excel that return text strings, a yes/no value, or a date.

Exhibit 13-17 Arithmetic operators

Operation	Arithmetic Operator	Example	Description
Addition	+	=10+A1 =B1+B2+B3	Adds 10 to the value in cell A1 Adds the values in cells B1, B2, and B3
Subtraction	−	=C9−B2 =1−D2	Subtracts the value in cell B2 from the value in cell C9 Subtracts the value in cell D2 from 1
Multiplication	*	=C9*B9 =E5*0.06	Multiplies the values in cells C9 and B9 Multiplies the value in cell E5 by 0.06
Division	/	=C9/B9 =D15/12	Divides the value in cell C9 by the value in cell B9 Divides the value in cell D15 by 12
Exponentiation	^	=B5^3 =3^B5	Raises the value of cell B5 to the third power Raises 3 to the value in cell B5

calculates the leftmost operation—in this case, 4*10—and then divides that result (40) by 8 to return the value 5:

$$=4*10/8$$

Order of Precedence Rules in Action

The order of precedence has a big impact on how Excel calculates the results of a formula. As you can see in the following examples, including or moving parentheses within a formula can greatly affect the results.

Formula	Result
=50+10*5	100
=(50+10)*5	300
=50/10−5	0
=50/(10−5)	10
=50/10*5	25
=50/(10*5)	1

Notice the large difference in the result for each pair of equations. Imagine if you were in charge of ordering cases of widgets based on the formula =50/(10*5), but you input the formula into the worksheet as =50/10*5, resulting in a total of 1 instead of 25. Customers might end up in a tug-of-war for the single widget.

To change the order of operations, you can enclose parts of the formula within parentheses. Any expression within a set of parentheses is calculated before the rest of the formula. The formula

$$=(3+4)*5$$

first calculates the value of the expression inside the parentheses—in this case, (3+4)—and then multiplies that total of 7 by 5 to return the value 35.

You can enter a formula by typing each cell reference. You can also enter a cell reference by clicking the cell as you enter the formula. The latter technique reduces the possibility of error caused by typing an incorrect cell reference.

 **ACTIVITY**

Enter formulas.

1 Make **cell F4** the active cell. You will enter a formula to calculate the inventory value of the Dali print.

2 In cell F4, type = to begin the formula. The equal sign indicates that you are entering a formula rather than data.

> **Tip:** Remember, formulas always begin with = (an equal sign).

Be sure to check that the parentheses are correctly placed within a formula to ensure the accuracy of the results.

3 After the equal sign, type **D** so that the formula so far is =D. A list of Excel function names starting with the letter D appears below the cell. You can ignore this for now; you'll learn more about Excel functions shortly.

4 Type **4** so that the formula so far is =D4. The function list closes because it is obvious you are entering a formula, not a function. A blue box surrounds cell D4 to show you which cell you are referencing in the formula, and the corresponding cell reference D4 in the formula you are typing is also colored blue. Cell D4 contains the current inventory of the Dali print. See Exhibit 13-18.

9 Click **cell D5**. The cell reference is inserted into the formula on the formula bar. At this point, any cell you click changes the cell reference used in the formula. The cell reference isn't "locked" until you type an operator.

> **Tip:** You can type the cell reference directly in the formula instead of clicking a cell.

10 Type * to enter the multiplication operator. The cell reference for cell D5 is "locked" in the formula, and the next cell you click will be inserted after the operator.

11 Click **cell E5** to enter its cell reference in the formula.

12 Press the **Enter key** to enter the formula. Cell F5 displays the value $93.06, which is the total value of the inventory.

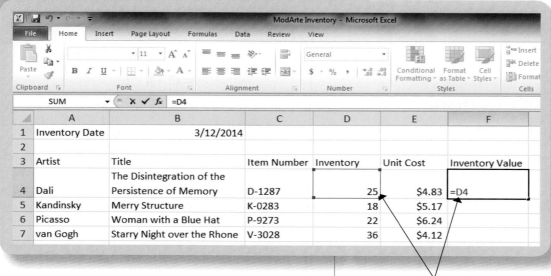

Exhibit 13-18 Formula using a cell reference

color of cell reference in formula matches cell border

5 Type * to enter the multiplication operator.

6 Type **E4**. A green border appears around cell E4 and the cell reference E4 in the formula changes to green. Cell E4 contains the unit cost for each Dali print.

7 Press the **Enter key**. The formula is entered in cell F4, which now displays the calculated value $120.75. The result is displayed as currency because cell E4, referenced in the formula, contains a currency value.

8 In cell F5, type = to begin the formula. Any cell that you click now will be inserted as the cell reference of the selected cell into the formula until you complete the formula by pressing the Enter or Tab key.

Viewing Formula Results and Formulas

After a formula has been entered into a cell, the cell displays the *results* of the formula and not the formula itself. If the results are not what you expect, you might have entered the formula incorrectly. You can view the formula by selecting the cell and reviewing the expression in the formula bar. You can also double-check that the formula references the correct cell by looking at which cells are color coded.

 **ACTIVITY**

View a formula in a cell.

1 Make **cell F4** the active cell. The formula you entered appears in the formula bar, and the value

Creating Effective Formulas

You can use formulas to quickly perform calculations on business, science, and engineering data. To use formulas effectively, keep in mind the following:

▶ **Keep formulas simple.**
Use functions in place of long, complex formulas whenever possible. For example, use the SUM function instead of entering a formula that adds individual cells. This makes it easier to confirm that the formula is accurate.

▶ **Do not place important data in formulas.**
The worksheet displays only formula results rather than the actual formulas with that important data. For example, the formula =0.05*A5 calculates a 5% sales tax on a price in cell A5, but hides the 5% tax rate. Instead, you should enter the tax rate in an-

other cell, such as cell A4, with an appropriate label and use the formula =A4*A5 to calculate the sales tax. Readers can then see the tax rate as well as the resulting sales tax.

▶ **Break up formulas to show intermediate results.**
Complex calculations should be split so that the different parts of the computation are easily distinguished and understood. For example, the formula =SUM(A1:A10)/SUM(B1:B10) calculates the ratio of two sums, but hides the two sum values. Instead, enter each SUM function in a separate cell, such as cells A11 and B11, and use the formula =A11/B11 to calculate the ratio. Readers can see both sums and the value of their ratio in the worksheet and better understand the final result.

---

returned by the formula appears in the cell. See Exhibit 13-19.

2 Click in the **formula bar**. The cell displays the formula again, the colored boxes appear around each cell referenced in the formula, and the cell references in the formula bar are colored with the same colors so that you can quickly match the cell references with their locations in the worksheet.

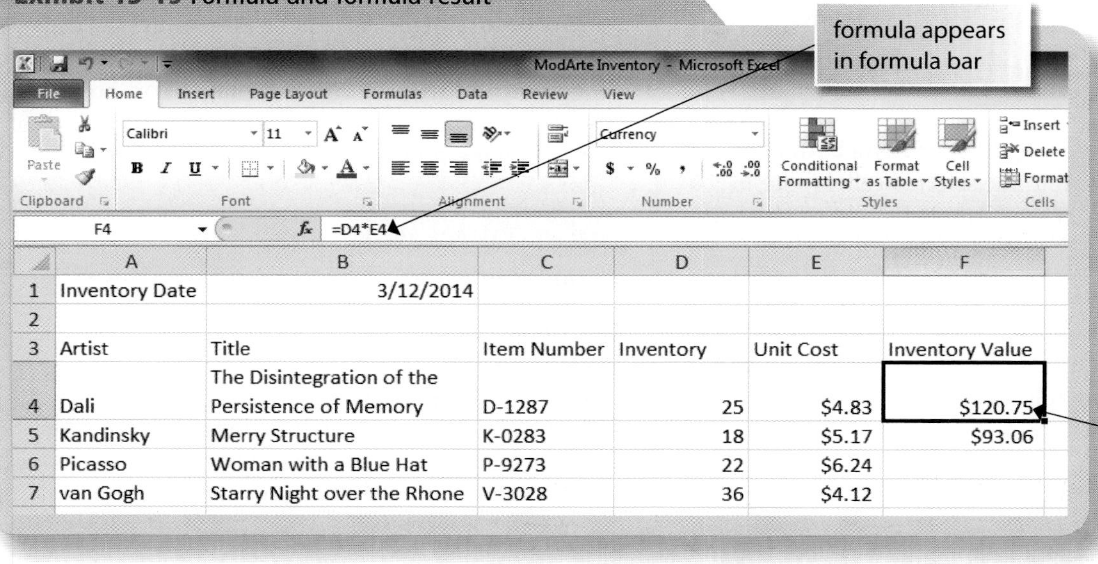

3 Press the **Esc key** to remove the focus from the formula bar and to display the calculated value in cell F4.

Copying and Pasting Formulas

Sometimes, you'll need to repeat the same formula for several rows of data. Rather than retyping the formula, you can copy the formula, and then paste it into the remaining rows.

Pasting a formula is different from pasting a value. When you paste a copied or cut formula, Excel adjusts the cell references used in the formula to reflect the new location of the formula in the worksheet. For example, if a formula in cell C3 contains a cell reference to cell B1, it contains a cell reference to

Exhibit 13-19 Formula and formula result

formula appears in formula bar

formula result appears in cell

It's a good idea to check the cell references in a copied formula to ensure the cell references changed as you expected them to.

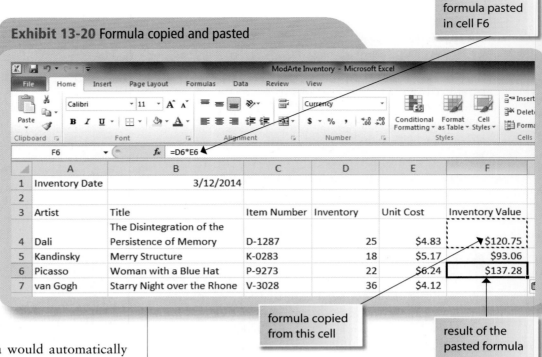

Exhibit 13-20 Formula copied and pasted

formula pasted in cell F6

	A	B	C	D	E	F
1	Inventory Date	3/12/2014				
2						
3	Artist	Title	Item Number	Inventory	Unit Cost	Inventory Value
4	Dali	The Disintegration of the Persistence of Memory	D-1287	25	$4.83	$120.75
5	Kandinsky	Merry Structure	K-0283	18	$5.17	$93.06
6	Picasso	Woman with a Blue Hat	P-9273	22	$6.24	$137.28
7	van Gogh	Starry Night over the Rhone	V-3028	36	$4.12	

formula copied from this cell

result of the pasted formula

the cell two cells above and one cell to the left of the cell containing the formula. You could copy this formula and then paste it into cell E5, and the cell reference in the formula would automatically change to cell D3, the cell that is two cells above and one cell to the left of the cell containing the formula. Excel does this automatically because you want to replicate the actions of a formula rather than duplicate the specific value the formula generates.

ACTIVITY

Copy and paste formulas.

1 Make sure **cell F4** is the active cell. This cell contains the formula you want to copy.

2 On the Home tab, in the Clipboard group, click the **Copy button** 📋. The formula is copied to the Clipboard. A blinking box surrounds the cell, indicating that you can paste the cell contents.

3 Click **cell F6**. This is the cell in which you want to paste the formula.

4 In the Clipboard group, click the **Paste button**. Excel pastes the formula into the selected cell. Notice in the formula bar that the formula has changed from =D4*E4 to =D6*E6. See Exhibit 13-20.

5 Make **cell F7** the active cell. Paste the contents of the Clipboard into the cell. You can paste the formula without recopying because the blinking box still surrounds the cell whose contents you copied to the Clipboard.

function A named operation that returns a value.

Entering a Function

In addition to cell references and operators, formulas can also contain functions. A **function** is a named operation that returns a value. Functions are used to simplify formulas, reducing what might be a long expression into a compact statement. For example, to add the values in the range A1:A9, you could enter the long formula:

$$=A1+A2+A3+A4+A5+A6+A7+A8+A9$$

Or, you could use the SUM function to accomplish the same thing:

$$=SUM(A1:A9)$$

In both cases, Excel adds the values in cells A1 through A9, but the SUM function is faster and simpler to enter and less prone to a typing error. You should always use a function, if one is available, in place of a long, complex formula.

ACTIVITY

Enter a function.

1 Make **cell D8** the active cell.

2 Type **=** to begin the formula.

3 Type **SUM** to enter the function name. As when you entered the formula, a list of functions opens listing functions that begin with the letters you typed.

Excel Functions

Excel supports over 300 different functions from the fields of finance, business, science, and engineering. For example, the PMT function calculates the amount of the loan payments based on an interest rate and a payment schedule; and the CONVERT function converts a number in one unit of measurement system to another unit of measurement.

Functions are not limited to numbers. Excel also provides functions that work with text and dates, such as LOWER, which converts all the characters in a cell to lowercase letters, or NETWORKDAYS, which calculates the number of workdays between two dates.

4 Type (. The list closes and a ScreenTip appears, showing how the SUM function should be written.

5 Select the **range D4:D7**. The function changes to include the cells you selected, and a blinking box surrounds the selected range. The values to calculate the total inventory are stored in the range D4:D7.

> **Tip:** You can also type a range reference directly in a function.

6 Type) to complete the function. The blinking box changes to solid blue, the range reference in the function changes to blue text, and the complete function, =SUM(D4:D7), appears in cell D8.

7 Press the **Tab key** to enter the function. The calculated value of the SUM function appears in cell D8, indicating that the total inventory is 101 prints.

Using AutoSum

A quick and easy way to enter commonly used function is with the AutoSum feature. **AutoSum** inserts one of five common functions and a range reference that Excel determines by examining the layout of the data and choosing the most likely range. For example, if you use AutoSum with the SUM function in a cell that is below a column of numbers, Excel assumes that you want to summarize the values in the column. Similarly,

if you use AutoSum with the SUM function in a cell to the right of a row of values, Excel assumes you want to summarize the values in that row. If the range reference is incorrect, you can change it.

To use AutoSum with the SUM function, click the Sum button Σ in the Editing group on the Home tab or click the AutoSum button in the Function Library group on the Formulas tab.

More AutoSum Functions

In addition to the SUM function, you can use AutoSum to insert all of the functions described below:

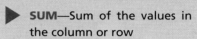

▶ **SUM**—Sum of the values in the column or row

▶ **AVERAGE**—Average value in the column or row

▶ **COUNT**—Total count of numeric values in the column or row

▶ **MIN**—Minimum value in the column or row

▶ **MAX**—Maximum value in the column or row

To use AutoSum with a function other than the SUM function, click the Sum button arrow in the Editing group on the Home tab or click the AutoSum button arrow in the Function Library group on the Formulas tab, and then select one of the functions in the list.

ACTIVITY

Use AutoSum.

1 Make **cell F8** the active cell.

2 On the Home tab, in the Editing group, click the **Sum button** Σ. The SUM function with the range reference F4:F7 is entered in cell F8. See Exhibit 13-21.

> **Tip:** To change the range reference, drag the square in any corner of the selected range, select a different range in the worksheet, or type a different range reference directly in the formula.

AutoSum A feature that inserts the SUM, AVERAGE, COUNT, MIN, or MAX function.

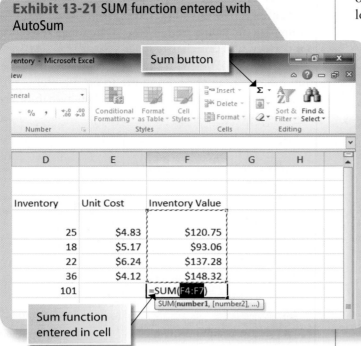

Exhibit 13-21 SUM function entered with AutoSum

Sum button

Sum function entered in cell

3 Press the **Enter key** to accept the formula. The total inventory value, $499.41, is displayed in cell F8.

4 Save the workbook.

LO13.7 **Previewing and Printing a Workbook**

When you have finished the final edit of the workbook, you might want to print a hard copy. However, before you print the workbook, you should preview it to ensure that it will print correctly.

Changing Worksheet Views

You can view a worksheet in three ways. **Normal view**, which you have been using, simply shows the contents

Normal view The Excel view that shows the contents of the current sheet.

Page Layout view The Excel view that shows how the current sheet will look when printed.

Page Break Preview The Excel view that displays the location of page breaks within the worksheet.

of the sheet. **Page Layout view** shows how the sheet will look when printed. **Page Break Preview** displays the location of page breaks within the worksheet. This is particularly useful when a worksheet will span several printed pages and you want to control what content appears on each page. The view buttons are located on the right edge of the status bar. You can also change the view by clicking the appropriate button in the Workbook Views group on the View tab.

ACTIVITY

Change worksheet views.

1 On the right end of the status bar, click the **Page Layout button** ▯. The page layout of the worksheet appears in the workspace. The data appears on two pages.

> **Tip:** To view the workbook in the full screen space, click the Full Screen button in the Workbook Views group on the View tab.

2 Change the zoom level to **60%**. See Exhibit 13-22.

3 On the status bar, click the **Page Break Preview button** ▦. The view switches to Page Break Preview, which shows only those parts of the current worksheet that will print. A dotted blue line separates one page from another.

> ⚠ **Problem?** If the Welcome to Page Break Preview dialog box opens, click **OK** to close the dialog box, and then continue with Step 4.

4 Change the zoom level to **120%** so that you can more easily read the contents of the worksheet. See Exhibit 13-23.

5 Make the **Documentation worksheet** the active sheet. The Documentation worksheet is still in Normal view.

6 Make the **Inventory worksheet** the active sheet.

7 On the status bar, click the **Normal button** ▦. The worksheet returns to Normal view. A dotted black line indicates where a page break will be placed when the worksheet is printed.

Exhibit 13-22 Worksheet displayed in Page Layout view

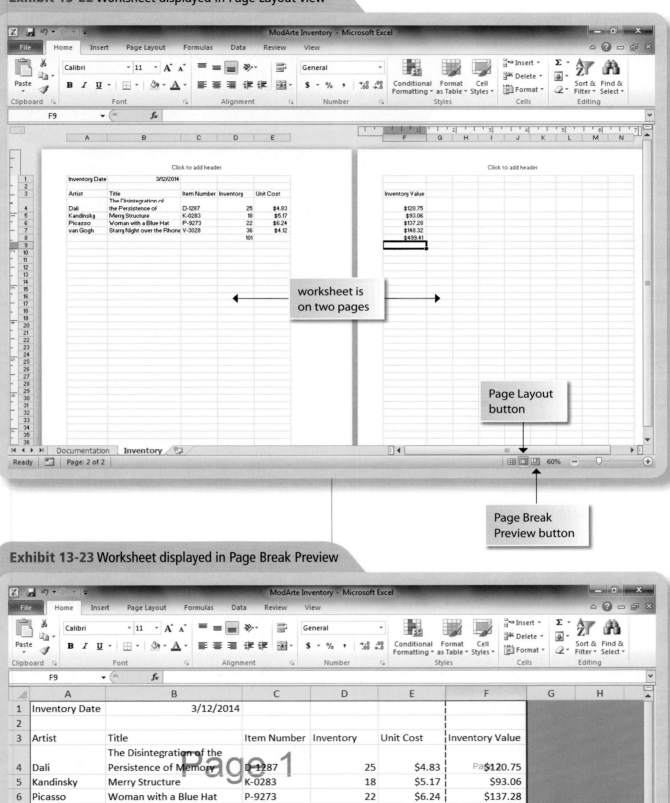

Exhibit 13-23 Worksheet displayed in Page Break Preview

Changing the Orientation

You can adjust the worksheet so that it prints on a single page. The simplest way to accomplish this is to change the page orientation. By default, Excel displays pages in portrait orientation, where the page is taller than it is wide. In many cases, however, you will want to print the page in land-scape orientation, where the page is wider than it is tall.

ACTIVITY

Change the page orientation.

1 On the Ribbon, click the **Page Layout tab**.

2 Change the zoom level to **110%**.

3 In the Page Setup group, click the **Orientation button**.

4 On the menu, click **Landscape**. The page orienta-tion changes to landscape, and the dotted line moves to between columns I and J to indicate the new page break. The Inventory worksheet content now fits on one page.

Previewing and Printing a Workbook

You can print the contents of a workbook by using the Print tab in Backstage view. The Print tab provides options for choosing what to print and how to print. For example, you can specify the number of copies to print, which printer to use, and what to print. You can choose to print only the selected cells, the active sheets, or all of the worksheets in the workbook that contain data. The printout will include only the data in the worksheet. The other elements in the worksheet, such as the row and column headings and the gridlines around the cells, will not print. You also see a preview of the workbook so you can check exactly how the printed pages will look with the settings you selected before you print.

ACTIVITY

Preview and print a workbook.

1 Click the **File tab**. In the navigation bar, click **Print**. The Print tab appears in Backstage view.

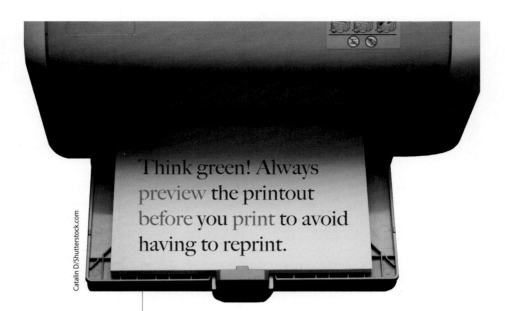

Think green! Always preview the printout before you print to avoid having to reprint.

Catalin D/Shutterstock.com

2 At the top of the left column, in the Copies box, make sure **1** appears so that only one copy of the workbook will print.

3 If the printer to which you want to print is not already listed in the Printer button, click the **Printer button**, and then click the desired printer.

4 In the Settings group, click the **Print Active Sheets button**, and then click **Print Entire Workbook**. The preview changes to show the Docu-mentation work-sheet as the first page to be printed of two pages. The Documentation worksheet is still in portrait orientation.

> **Tip:** You can also choose to print only the selected cells, the active sheet (or sheets), or all the worksheets in the workbook that contain data.

5 Below the preview, click the **Next Page button** ▶. The second page appears in the preview. The Inventory worksheet is in landscape orientation. See Exhibit 13-24.

6 At the top of the second column, click the **Print button**. The workbook is sent to the printer and Backstage view closes.

Exhibit 13-24 Print tab in Backstage view

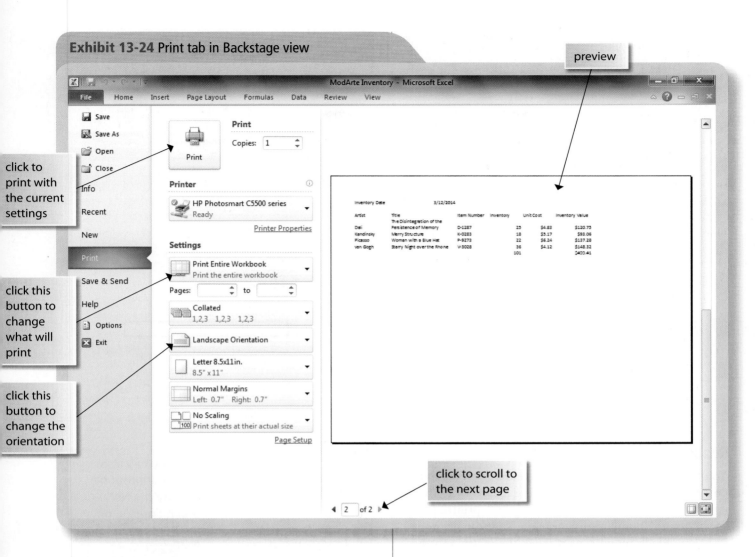

preview

click to print with the current settings

click this button to change what will print

click this button to change the orientation

click to scroll to the next page

Viewing Worksheet Formulas

Most of the time, you will be interested in only the final results of a worksheet, not the formulas used to calculate those results. In some cases, you might want to view the formulas used to develop the workbook. This is particularly useful when you encounter unexpected results and you want to examine the underlying formulas, document the formulas, or show the formulas to someone else. You can view the formulas in a workbook by switching to **formula view**, which displays the formulas used in a worksheet instead of the resulting values. In formula view, the columns containing formulas temporarily widen so that you can see the entire formulas.

 **ACTIVITY**

View the worksheet formulas.

1 On the Ribbon, click the **Formulas tab**.

2 In the Formula Auditing group, click the **Show Formulas button**. The cells containing formulas now display the formulas instead of the calculated values, and the columns widen so you can see the entire formulas.

3 Scroll the worksheet to the right to view the formulas in columns D and F. See Exhibit 13-25.

Tip: You can also view formulas by pressing the Ctrl+` keys. The ` key (grave accent symbol) is usually located above the Tab key.

formula view The Excel view that displays formulas used in a worksheet instead of the resulting values.

Exhibit 13-25 Worksheet in formula view

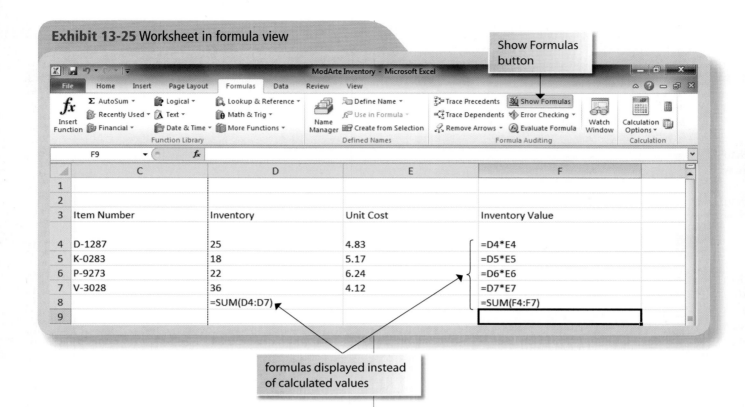

Show Formulas button

	C	D	E	F
1				
2				
3	Item Number	Inventory	Unit Cost	Inventory Value
4	D-1287	25	4.83	=D4*E4
5	K-0283	18	5.17	=D5*E5
6	P-9273	22	6.24	=D6*E6
7	V-3028	36	4.12	=D7*E7
8		=SUM(D4:D7)		=SUM(F4:F7)
9				

formulas displayed instead of calculated values

Scaling a Printout

You can scale the worksheet to force the contents to fit on a single page. To scale something means to change its size proportionately. You can scale a printout by specifying the number of pages you want the printout to fit on, which reduces, as needed, the width and the height of the printout to fit. You can also scale a printout by specifying that it print at a percentage of its actual size. You can scale a printout using the Width and Height boxes in the Scale to Fit group on the Page Layout tab.

 **ACTIVITY**

Scale a printout.

1 On the Ribbon, click the **Page Layout tab**.

When formulas are displayed, you can scale the worksheet to fit on one page with the expanded column widths.

2 In the Scale to Fit group, click the **Width arrow**, and then click **1 page**.

3 In the Scale to Fit group, click the **Height arrow**, and then click **1 page**. The worksheet in formula view now fits on a single page.

4 Switch to **Page Layout view**. Change the zoom level to **60%** if it is not already set.

5 If you cannot see all of the contents of the worksheet, scroll the worksheet as needed. As you can see, the formula view of the worksheet fits on one page. See Exhibit 13-26.

6 On the Ribbon, click the **Formulas tab**. In the Formula Auditing group, click the **Show Formulas button**. The cells containing formulas now display the calculated values, and the columns return to their previous widths.

7 Save the workbook, and then close it.

Tip: You can also scale a printout by clicking the No Scaling button on the Print tab in Backstage view, and then clicking Fit Sheet on One Page.

Exhibit 13-26 Worksheet in formula view scaled to one page

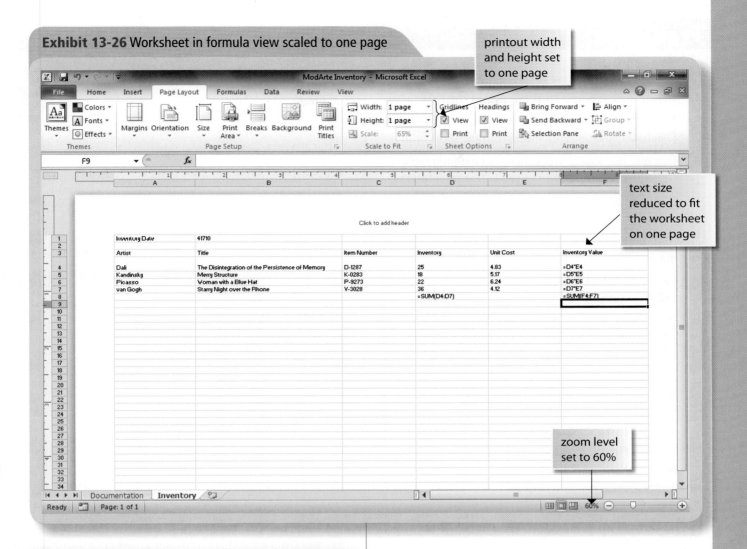

printout width and height set to one page

text size reduced to fit the worksheet on one page

zoom level set to 60%

Quiz Yourself

1. Define *what-if analysis*.

2. What is the difference between a workbook and a worksheet?

3. What is the cell reference for the cell located in the third column and fifth row of a worksheet?

4. List two ways of identifying the active cell in the worksheet.

5. List the three types of data you can enter into a worksheet.

6. In what two places can you edit cell content?

7. What does it mean when text is truncated?

8. Explain how the AutoFit feature works.

9. Describe the difference between clearing data and deleting data.

10. Describe the two types of cell ranges in Excel.

11. What is the range reference for cells A1 through A5 and cells F1 through G5?

12. How can you force text that extends beyond a cell's border to fit within the cell?

13. What is a formula?

14. What is the order of precedence?

15. Write the formula that adds the values in cells D4 and E7 and then divides the sum by the value in cell C2.

16. What is a function? Why are functions used?

17. What formula would you enter to add the values in cells B4, B5, and B6? What function would you enter to achieve the same result?

18. How do you display the formulas used in a worksheet?

Practice It

Practice It 13-1

1. Create a new, blank workbook, and then save the workbook as **Card Shoppe**.

2. Delete the Sheet3 worksheet from the workbook.

3. Rename the Sheet1 worksheet as **Customer Orders**. Rename the Sheet2 worksheet as **Documentation**.

4. Move the Documentation worksheet to be the first sheet in the workbook.

5. In the Documentation worksheet, enter the following data in the cells specified:

   cell A1: **Card Shoppe**

   cell A3: **Author:**   cell B3: your name

   cell A4: **Date:**   cell B4: the current date

   cell A5: **Purpose:**   cell B5: **To track customer orders for Card Shoppe**

6. In the Customer Orders worksheet, enter the following labels in the cells specified:

   cell A1: **Last Name**

   cell B1: **First Name**

   cell C1: **Number of Cards**

   cell D1: **Price per Card**

   cell E1: **Total Charge**

7. In the Customer Orders worksheet, enter the following customer names:

   cell A2: **Ferrara**   cell B2: **Joseph**

   cell A3: **Roberts**   cell B3: **Mildred**

   cell A4: **Klasner**   cell B4: **Floyd**

   cell A5: **Foust-Whitman**   cell B5: **Isabella**

   cell A6: **Rasnick**   cell B6: **Shirlee**

8. In the Customer Orders worksheet, enter the following order quantities and charges:

   cell C2: **22**   cell D2: **$2.99**

   cell C3: **11**   cell D3: **$3.49**

   cell C4: **2**   cell D4: **$3.99**

   cell C5: **8**   cell D5: **$3.99**

   cell C6: **35**   cell D6: **$2.49**

9. Edit the contents of cell C1 to **Cards**. Edit the contents of cell C2 to **17**.

10. Insert a new column A.

11. Enter the following data into the new column A:

    cell A1: **Order Date**

    cell A2: **9/30/2014**

    cell A3: **10/4/2014**

    cell A4: **10/8/2014**

    cell A5: **10/9/2014**

    cell A6: **10/17/2014**

12. Set the width of columns A, B, and C to 15 characters. AutoFit the contents of columns D, E, and F.

13. Clear the data from row 4, and then delete the row.

14. Select the range A1:F5. Use drag and drop or cut and paste to move the selected range to range A4:F8.

15. In cell A1, enter **Customer Orders**. In cell A2, enter **September 29 to October 17**.

16. Wrap the text in cell A2.

17. In cell F5, enter a formula that multiplies the number of cards in cell D5 by the price per card in cell E5 to calculate the total charge for the customer in row 5.

18. Copy the formula in cell F5, and then paste it into cells F6, F7, and F8.

19. In cell D9, enter the SUM function to add the total number of cards ordered.

20. In cell F9, use AutoSum to enter the SUM function to calculate the total charge for all of the customer orders.

21. View the worksheet in Page Layout view and Page Break Preview. Return to Normal view.

22. Change the page orientation of the Customer Orders worksheet to landscape.

23. Print the entire workbook.

24. Change the Customer Orders worksheet to formula view. Scale the worksheet to fit on one page.

25. View the worksheet in Page Layout view at 70% zoom.

26. Turn off formula view.

27. Save the workbook, and then close it.

Practice It 13-2

1. Open the data file **Sunderbruch** located in the Chapter 13\Practice It folder. Save the workbook as **Sunderbruch Paper**.

2. At the top of the Sheet1 worksheet, insert three new rows.

3. In cell A1, enter the text **Sunderbruch Paper Company Income Statement***. (The asterisk is a footnote reference to the note in cell A29.)

4. In cell A2, enter the text **For the years ending December 31, 2012 through December 31, 2014**.

5. In the range C6:E7, enter the following net sales and cost of sales:

   cell C6: **$20,720**

   cell C7: **$6,344**

   cell D6: **$16,829**

   cell D7: **$6,068**

   cell E6: **$13,845**

   cell E7: **$4,614**

6. In the range C11:E14, enter the following expenses:

   cell C11: **$2,020**

   cell C12: **$3,257**

   cell C13: **$644**

   cell C14: **$620**

   cell D11: **$1,833**

   cell D12: **$2,614**

   cell D13: **$507**

   cell D14: **$500**

   cell E11: **$1,723**

   cell E12: **$2,277**

   cell E13: **$464**

   cell E14: **$347**

7. In the nonadjacent range C18:E18;C20:E20; C24:E24, enter the following values for Other Income, Income Taxes, and Shares:

   cell C18: **$422**

   cell D18: **$373**

   cell E18: **$295**

   cell C20: **$1,516**

   cell D20: **$1,247**

   cell E20: **$1,016**

   cell C24: **$3,621**

   cell D24: **$3,001**

   cell E24: **$2,844**

8. Expand column A to 17 characters, and then AutoFit column B.

9. In the range C8:E8, enter a formula to calculate the gross margin for each year, where the gross margin is equal to the net sales minus the cost of sales.

10. In the range C15:E15, enter the SUM function to calculate the total operating expenses for each year, where the total operating expenses equal the sum of the four expense categories.

11. In the range C17:E17, enter a formula to calculate the operating income for each year, where operating income is equal to the gross margin minus the total operating expenses.

12. In the range C19:E19, enter a formula to calculate the pretax income for each year, where pretax income is equal to the operating income plus other income.

13. In the range C22:E22, enter a formula to calculate the company's net income for each year, where net income is equal to the pretax income minus income taxes.

14. In the range C25:E25, enter a formula to calculate the earnings per share for each year, where earnings per share is equal to the net income divided by the number of shares.

15. AutoFit columns C, D, and E.

16. Edit the contents of cell A18 to capitalize the word *income*.

17. Rename the Sheet1 worksheet as **Income Statement**.

18. Rename the Sheet2 worksheet as **Documentation** and move it to the beginning of the workbook.

19. Delete the Sheet3 worksheet.

20. In the Documentation worksheet, enter the following text and values:

   cell A1: **Sunderbruch Paper Company**

   cell A3: **Author:** cell B3: **your name**

   cell A4: **Date:** cell B4: **the current date**

   cell A5: **Purpose:** cell B5: **Income statement for Sunderbruch Paper Company for 2012 through 2014**

21. View both worksheets in Page Layout view, making sure each worksheet fits on one page in portrait orientation.

22. Print the entire workbook.

23. Save the workbook, and then close it.

On Your Own

On Your Own 13-1

1. Open the data file **Sunny** located in the Chapter 13\ On Your Own folder. Save the workbook as **Sunny Day Pizza**.

2. Rename the Sheet1 worksheet as **Sales History**.

3. Insert 12 rows at the top of the Sales History worksheet. (*Hint*: Select rows 1 through 12 before using the Insert command.)

4. Increase the width of column A to 23 characters and increase the width of columns B through F to 14 characters.

5. Copy the contents of the range B13:F13. Paste the contents of the Clipboard in the range B7:F7.

6. In the range A8:A11, enter the following data:

   cell A8:   **Total Pizzas Served**
   cell A9:   **Average per Month**
   cell A10: **Maximum**
   cell A11: **Minimum**

7. Select the range B26:F26, and then use AutoSum to calculate the sum of the pizzas served in each of the five restaurants.

8. Drag and drop the calculated values that are in the range B26:F26 to the range B8:F8. Notice that the formulas still show the original results because the cell references in the function did not change when you moved the range.

9. Select the range B26:F26, and then use AutoSum to calculate the average number of pizzas served in each of the five restaurants. (*Hint*: Click the AutoSum button arrow to access additional functions.)

10. Drag and drop the calculated values that are in the range B26:F26 to the range B9:F9.

11. Select the range B26:F26, and then use AutoSum to calculate the maximum number of pizzas served in each of the five restaurants. Move the calculated values in the range B26:F26 to the range B10:F10.

12. Select the range B26:F26, and then use AutoSum to calculate the minimum number of pizzas served in each of the five restaurants. Move the calculated values in the range B26:F26 to the range B11:F11.

13. In the Sales History worksheet, enter the following data:

   cell A1: **Sunny Day Pizza**
   cell A2: **Sales Report**
   cell A3: **Year**   cell B3: **2014**
   cell A4: **Total Pizzas Served**

14. In cell B4, use the SUM function to add the values in the range B8:F8.

15. Insert a new worksheet. Rename the worksheet as **Restaurant Directory**. Move the Restaurant Directory worksheet to be the first sheet in the workbook.

16. In the Restaurant Directory worksheet, enter the following data:

   cell A1: **Sunny Day Pizza**
   cell A2: **Restaurant Directory**

17. In the range A4:D9, enter the following data:

Restaurant	Manager	Location	Phone
1	Grace Anthony	958 Pine Drive	555–3585
2	Lanell Nunez	4514 Trainer Avenue	555–3728
3	Christina Steward	525 Simpson Street	555–4093
4	Letitia Breton	3654 Apple Lane	555–7831
5	Eileen Jones	1087 Summit Boulevard	555–6117

18. Set the widths of columns A through D so that all of the data is visible. (*Hint*: Column A should be wide enough to display the Restaurant heading, but not fit the contents in cells A1 and A2. You can AutoFit the rest of the columns to their contents.)

19. Insert a new worksheet in the workbook. Rename the inserted sheet as **Documentation**. Move the Documentation worksheet to be the first sheet in the workbook.

20. In the Documentation worksheet, enter appropriate data to record the company name, yourself as the author, the current date, and the purpose of the workbook.

21. View each sheet in the workbook in Page Layout view, and change the page orientation or scale each worksheet as needed so that it fits on a single page.

22. Print the entire workbook.

23. Save the workbook, and then close it.

ADDITIONAL STUDY TOOLS

Chapter 13

IN THE BOOK

▶ Complete end-of-chapter exercises

▶ Study tear-out Chapter Review Card

ONLINE

▶ Complete additional end-of-chapter exercises

▶ Take practice quiz to prepare for tests

▶ Review key term flash cards (online, printable, and audio)

▶ Play "Beat the Clock" and "Memory" to quiz yourself

▶ Watch the videos "Enter Text," "Enter Dates and Times," "Change Column Widths," "Insert a Columns or Rows," "Enter Formulas," "Enter a Function," "Use AutoSum," and other concept videos

Formatting a Workbook

Introduction

Formatting is the process of changing a workbook's appearance by defining the fonts, styles, colors, and decorative features. Formatting changes only the appearance of data—it does not affect the data itself. Excel organizes its formatting tools in terms of themes. As in Word, the Office theme is the default, although you can apply other themes or create your own. You can also use fonts and colors that are not part of the current theme. As you format a workbook, Live Preview shows the effects of the formats on the workbook's appearance.

A well-formatted workbook can be easier to read and establish a sense of professionalism. It can also help draw attention to the points you want to make and provide continuity between the worksheets. Too little formatting can make the data hard to understand, but too much formatting can overwhelm the data. Proper formatting is a balance between these two extremes. Always remember, the goal of formatting is not simply to make a visually attractive workbook, but more importantly to accentuate important trends and relationships in the data.

Learning Objectives

After studying the material in this chapter, you will be able to:

LO14.1 Format text, numbers, dates, and time

LO14.2 Format cells and ranges

LO14.3 Create an Excel table

LO14.4 Highlight cells with conditional formatting

LO14.5 Hide worksheet data

LO14.6 Format a worksheet for printing

LO14.1 Formatting Data in Cells

Data stored in a workbook is usually a combination of text, numbers, and dates and times. Formatting can be added to help distinguish one type of data from the other, and clarify the purpose of data entered in specific cells. For example, labels that identify columns or rows can be formatted differently than text entered in those columns and rows. Numbers can be formatted to display symbols such as $ and %, thousands separators, and decimal places to clarify what the numbers mean. Dates can be formatted to display with text and numbers, numbers only, or only part of the stored date. Times can also be displayed in a variety of formats.

45.699,32	7.959,23	12.584,85	7.
1.282,12	11.52	12,45	11.
294,35		4,32	
7.959,23		,32	
11.521,20		,12	
594,32			
45.699,32			
1.282,12			
594,32		2	
45.699,3		7.93	
1.282		1 521 2	

Whether a workbook is for personal use or to share with others, data is more quickly and easily comprehended when formatted appropriately. Symbols such as $ and %, borders, and shading help make the purpose of data apparent at a glance.

ACTIVITY

Open the workbook.

1 Open the data file **Singleton** located in the Chapter 14\Chapter folder. Save the workbook as **Singleton Rentals**.

2 In the Documentation worksheet, enter your name in **cell B3** and the date in **cell B4**.

3 Review the contents of the three worksheets. As stated on the Documentation worksheet, the purpose of this workbook is to compare vacancy rates among rental properties owned by Singleton Property Management in Los Angeles. The Yearly Rates worksheet lists the rental income and number of vacancies for each property for the past two years. The Monthly Rates worksheet will contain an analysis of the vacancy rates by month.

Formatting Text

Formatting text involves changing fonts, font sizes, font styles, and color. These text formatting options are the same as those you worked with in Word. They are available in the Font group on the Home tab. As in Word, every font can be further formatted with a font style such as *italic*, **bold**, or bold italic, and special effects such as <u>underline</u>, ~~strikethrough,~~

EXCEL 2010

Formatting Workbooks for Readability and Appeal

Designing a workbook requires the same care as designing any written document or report. A well-formatted workbook is easier to read and establishes a sense of professionalism with readers. Do the following to improve the appearance of your workbooks:

▶ **Clearly identify each worksheet's purpose.** You can do this by including descriptive column and row titles as well as labels to identify other important aspects of the worksheet. Also, use a descriptive sheet name for each worksheet.

▶ **Don't crowd a worksheet with too much information.** Each worksheet should deal with only one or two topics. Place extra topics on separate sheets. Readers should be able to interpret each worksheet with a minimal amount of horizontal and vertical scrolling.

▶ **Place the most important information first in the workbook.** Position worksheets summarizing your findings near the front of the workbook. Position worksheets with detailed and involved analysis near the end as an appendix.

▶ **Use consistent formatting throughout the workbook.** If negative values appear in red on one worksheet, format them in red on all sheets. Also, be consistent in the use of thousands separators, decimal places, and percentages.

▶ **Pay attention to the formatting of the printed workbook.** Make sure your printouts are legible with informative headers and footers. Check that the content of the printout is scaled correctly to the page size and that page breaks divide the information into logical sections.

Excel provides many formatting options. However, keep in mind that too much formatting can be intrusive, overwhelm data, and make the document difficult to read. A well-formatted workbook seamlessly conveys data to the reader. If the reader is spending time thinking about how the workbook looks, it means he or she is not thinking about the data.

and color. Finally, you can set the font size to increase or decrease the size of the text. Remember that fonts are organized into theme and non-theme fonts, so if you want to format text with a font that will not change when the theme is changed, use a non-theme font.

 **ACTIVITY**

Format fonts and font styles.

1. Make the **Documentation worksheet** the active sheet. Make sure **cell A1** is the active cell.

2. On the Home tab, in the Font group, click the **Font box arrow** to display a list of fonts available on your computer. The first two fonts are the theme fonts for headings and body text—Cambria and Calibri. See Exhibit 14-1.

3. At the top of the Font list, click **Cambria (Headings)**. The company name in cell A1 changes to the Cambria font, the default headings font in the current theme.

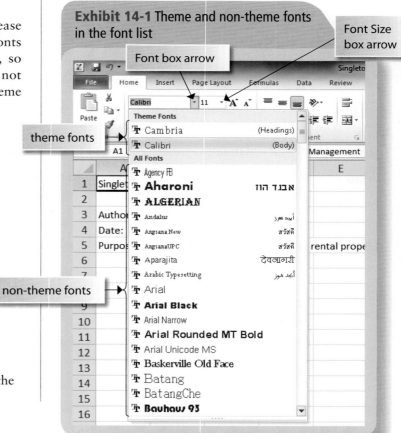

Exhibit 14-1 Theme and non-theme fonts in the font list

4 In the Font group, click the **Font Size box arrow**, and then click **24**. The company name changes to 24 points and is displayed in cell G1.

5 In the Font group, click the **Bold button B**. The company name is formatted in bold.

6 In the Font group, click the **Italic button I**. The company name is italicized.

7 Select the **range A3:A5**. In the Font group, click the **Bold button B**. The labels are formatted in bold. See Exhibit 14-2.

> **Tip:** You can also change the font size incrementally by clicking the Increase Font Size **A'** or Decrease Font Size button **A'** in the Font group on the Home tab.

Exhibit 14-2 Formatted cell text

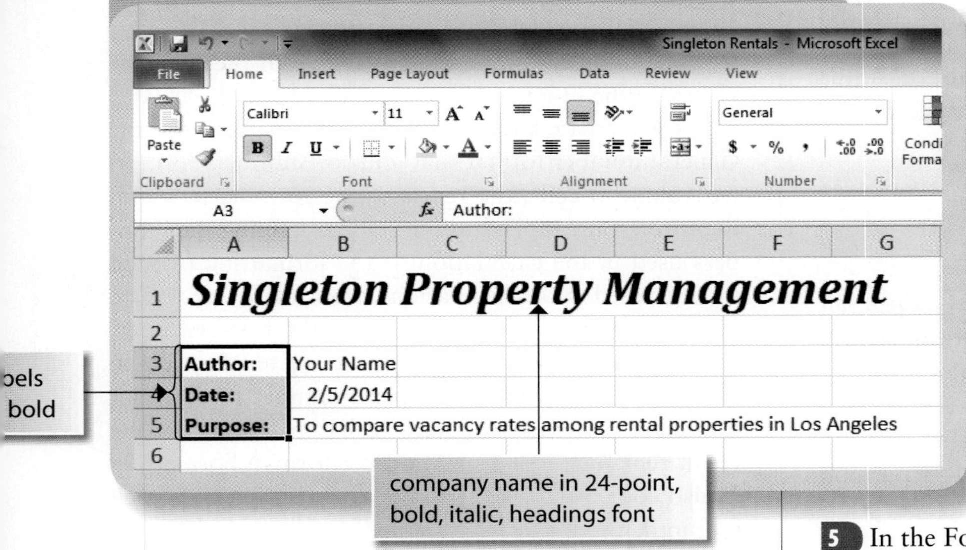

labels
bold

company name in 24-point, bold, italic, headings font

Color can transform a plain workbook filled with numbers and text into a powerful presentation that captures the user's attention and adds visual emphasis to the points you want to make. Excel displays text in a black color font unless you change it.

Like fonts, colors are organized into theme and non-theme colors. Theme colors are the 12 colors that

belong to the workbook's theme. Four colors are designated for text and backgrounds, six colors are used for accents and highlights, and two colors are used for hyperlinks (followed and not followed links). These 12 colors are designed to work well together and to remain readable in all combinations. Each theme color has five variations, or accents, in which a different tint or shading is applied to the theme color.

Ten standard colors—dark red, red, orange, yellow, light green, green, light blue, blue, dark blue, and purple—are always available regardless of the workbook's theme. You can also open an extended palette of 134 standard colors. You can specify a mixture of red, blue, and green color values, making available 16.7 million custom colors—more colors than the human eye can distinguish. Some dialog boxes have an automatic color option that uses your Windows default text and background colors, usually black text on a white background.

ACTIVITY

Change the font color.

1 Select **cell A1**.

2 On the Home tab, in the Font group, click the **Font Color button arrow A** to display the theme and standard colors.

3 In the Standard Colors section, click the **Blue color**. Remember to use the ScreenTip to identify the correct color. The company name changes to blue.

4 Select the **range B3:B5**.

5 In the Font group, click the **Font Color button A**. The text in the selected cells is formatted with the same blue font color.

6 Double-click **cell A1**. The insertion point appears in the cell.

7 Double-click **Singleton** to select it. See Exhibit 14-3.

8 On the Home tab, in the Font group, click the **Font Color button arrow A**. In the Standard Colors section, click the **Dark Blue color**.

> **Tip:** You must manually format words or selected text within a cell; Format Painter only copies and pastes formatting applied to the entire cell.

One goal of formatting is to maintain a consistent look throughout a workbook.

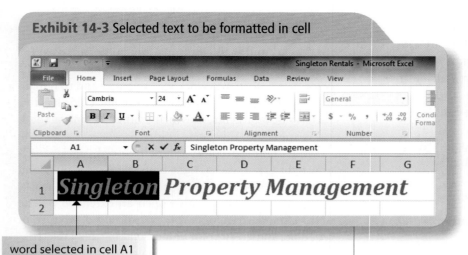

Exhibit 14-3 Selected text to be formatted in cell

word selected in cell A1

The word *Singleton* is now formatted with the dark blue color.

9 Press the **Enter** key. Cell A2 is selected, and the formatting in cell A1 is visible.

10 Use the Format Painter to copy the formatting from cell A1 on the Documentation worksheet to cell A1 on the Yearly Rates and Monthly Rates worksheets, and then format the word *Singleton* with the dark blue color.

Formatting Numbers

The numbers displayed in cells are either values entered directly in cells or values calculated with formulas. Either way, you can format the displayed value to make the workbook easier to interpret (which is the same goal of any formatting you apply to a workbook). For example, adding a comma as a thousands separator, changing the number of decimal places, and using percentage and currency symbols can make a large table of numbers simpler to read and comprehend.

You can format values using a **number format**, which displays the values in a way that makes it easy to be understood and interpreted. You can change the number format for the displayed value without affecting the underlying stored value. Excel formats numbers in the **General number format**, which, for the most part, displays values exactly as they are typed by the user. If

number format A format that displays values in a way that makes it easy for them to be understood and interpreted.

General number format The default number format, which, for the most part, displays values exactly as they are typed.

the value is calculated from a formula or function, Excel shows as many digits after the decimal point as will fit in the cell with the last displayed digit rounded. Calculated values too large to fit into the cell are displayed in scientific notation.

The General number format is good for simple calculations, but some values require additional formatting to make the numbers easier to interpret. You can format numbers to:

- Set how many digits appear to the right of the decimal point.

- Add commas to act as a thousands separator for large values.

- Include currency or accounting symbols to identify the monetary unit being used.

- Display percentages using the % symbol.

The number formats are available in the Number group on the Home tab.

If you create a formula in a cell formatted with the General number format that adds or subtracts formatted values in cells, the result of the formula picks up the formatting applied to the cells containing the numbers used in the calculation. If the formatting of each number used in the calculation differs, the result will be formatted with the same format as the first cell reference used in the formula. When you create a formula in a cell formatted with the General number format that multiplies or divides values in cells, the format of the result remains the General number format. Formatting is also copied when you copy a formula from one cell to another.

Formatting Numbers in the Accounting Format

When you use the Comma Style button to add the thousands separator, the button actually applies an accounting style used for currency to the values in the columns. This accounting style lines up the values within a column by the currency symbol and decimal point. When the values do not have a currency symbol, the values

Modifying the number format has absolutely no effect on the value that is stored in the workbook.

Accounting vs. Currency Formats

The Accounting number format places currency symbols along the left edge of the cell, inserts the thousands separator in values larger than 999, adds two decimal places to the value, and aligns values by their decimal points, shifting the entire value one character from the right edge of the cell. Both the Accounting Number Format button and the Comma Style button change the formatting of a cell to the Accounting number format. The difference is that the Comma Style button applies the Accounting number format without including the currency symbol. The Currency number format is similar to the Accounting number format, except that it adds a currency symbol directly to the left of the value and doesn't shift the values within the cell.

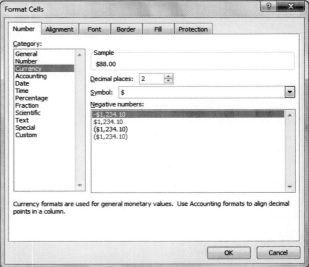

are aligned by the decimal point. The accounting style also encloses negative numbers, such as −124, within parentheses, such as (124). This is a standard accounting practice. If you prefer to display negative numbers in a different way, you can modify this format. Another standard accounting practice is to add a currency symbol to only the first and last entries within a column of values.

ACTIVITY

Format numbers.

1. Make the **Yearly Rates worksheet** the active sheet.

2. Select the **range D6:E13**. On the Home tab, in the Number group, the Number Format box identifies these numbers as having the General number format.

3. On the Home tab, in the Number group, click the **Comma Style button**. Each rental income value in the selected range now includes a thousands separator and has two digits to the right of the decimal point. Also, the Number Format box identifies the selected range as having the Accounting number format.

4. Select the **nonadjacent range D6:E6;D14:E14**. The range D6:E6 is the first row of rental income values. The range D14:E14, which will contain the total income for each year, is the last row of rental income values.

5. In the Number group, click the **Accounting Number Format button $**. $ symbols are added to the rental income values in the first and last rows.

6. Make **cell F6** the active cell. The Number Format box indicates that this cell is formatted with the General number format.

Tip: For international documents, you can select other currency symbols: In the Number group on the Home tab, click the Accounting Number Format button arrow $ ▾, and then click a currency symbol.

7 Enter the formula **=E6–D6** to calculate the increase in rental income from 2012 to 2013. The result, $13,920.00, is formatted with the same format as the cells used to calculate the result.

8 Copy the formula in **cell F6** and paste it into **cell F7**. The result in cell F7, $34,016.25, contains the dollar sign because the cell you copied had that format applied.

9 On the Quick Access Tool-bar, click the **Undo button**.

10 In **cell F7**, enter the formula **=E7–D7**. The result, 34,016.25, includes the comma formatting that was applied to the cells used to calculate the value.

> ⚠️ **Problem?** If the result in cell F7 includes a dollar sign, you deleted the value rather than undoing the paste action, and the cell retains the format that was applied when you pasted the formula. On the Home tab, in the Number group, click the **Comma Style button**.

11 Copy the formula in **cell F7** and paste it into **cell F8**. Because the rental income for 2011 N. Sheridan decreased from 2012 to 2013, the result is enclosed in parentheses, (528.00), indicating that it is a negative value.

12 Copy the formula in **cell F8** and paste it into the **range F9:F13**.

13 Select the **range C14:F14**. In the Editing group, click the **Sum button Σ** to calculate the total units per building in column C, the total income for 2012 and 2013 in columns D and E, and the total increase in rental income in column F. The values in cells C14, D14, and E14 are formatted correctly, but the value in cell F14 is not because

you did not apply the Accounting number format to that cell.

14 Make **cell F14** the active cell. Notice that the cell is formatted with the General number format.

15 In the Number group, click the **Accounting Number Format button $**. See Exhibit 14-4.

Exhibit 14-4 Currency values formatted

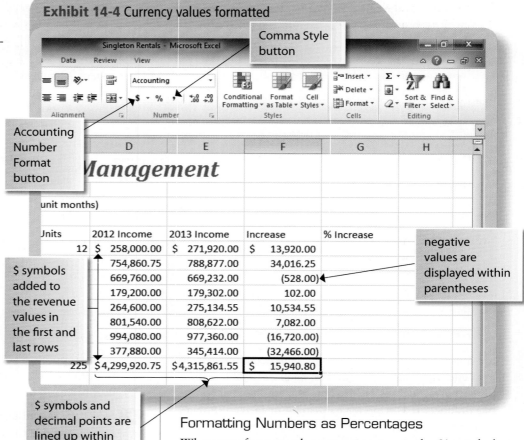

Formatting Numbers as Percentages

When you format values as percentages, the % symbol appears after the number and no digits appear to the right of the decimal point. You can change how many decimal places are displayed in the cell. When you decrease the number of decimal places shown, the values are rounded using standard rounding practices: If the number is five or higher, the value is rounded up and the number to its left is increased by one. If the number is four or lower, the value is rounded down and the number to its left remains the same.

ACTIVITY

Format numbers as percentages.

1 In **cell G6**, enter the formula **=F6/D6** to calculate the percent increase in rental income from 2012 to 2013. The result of the calculation, 0.053953488, is displayed as a decimal because the cell is formatted with the General format.

2 Make **cell G6** the active cell.

3 On the Home tab, in the Number group, click the **Percent Style button** . The result is now displayed as 5%—an integer followed by the % symbol, and the Number Format box in the Number group identifies the format as Percentage.

4 On the Home tab, in the Number group, click the **Increase Decimal button** twice to display the percentage to two decimal places. The value that is displayed changes to 5.40%.

5 In the Number group, click the **Increase Decimal button** to display the percentage to three decimal places. The displayed value changes to 5.395%.

6 In the Number group, click the **Decrease Decimal button** . One decimal place is removed, and the displayed value is again 5.40%.

7 Copy the formula in **cell G6** and paste it into the **range G7:G14**. The formatting from cell G6 is applied to the formula results displayed in the range G7:G14. See Exhibit 14-5.

8 Copy the **range F6:G14** and paste it into the **range F17:G25**. The formulas and formatting are pasted into the selected range. Column F is formatted with the Accounting number format with $ in the first and last cell of the range, even though the values in the range F17:F25 are not dollar amounts. Column G is formatted with the Percentage number style.

When calculating a percent increase, always divide the amount of increase by the starting value and not the ending value.

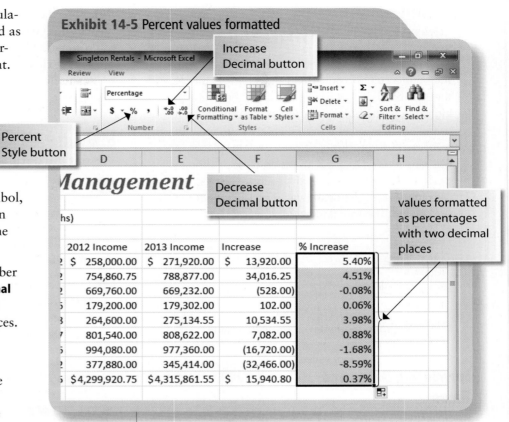

Exhibit 14-5 Percent values formatted

Increase Decimal button

Percent Style button

Decrease Decimal button

values formatted as percentages with two decimal places

	2012 Income	2013 Income	Increase	% Increase
	$ 258,000.00	$ 271,920.00	$ 13,920.00	5.40%
	754,860.75	788,877.00	34,016.25	4.51%
	669,760.00	669,232.00	(528.00)	-0.08%
	179,200.00	179,302.00	102.00	0.06%
	264,600.00	275,134.55	10,534.55	3.98%
	801,540.00	808,622.00	7,082.00	0.88%
	994,080.00	977,360.00	(16,720.00)	-1.68%
	377,880.00	345,414.00	(32,466.00)	-8.59%
	$4,299,920.75	$4,315,861.55	$ 15,940.80	0.37%

9 Select the **range F17:F25**.

10 On the Home tab, in the Number group, click the **Number Format box arrow** (which currently displays Accounting), and then click **General**. See Exhibit 14-6.

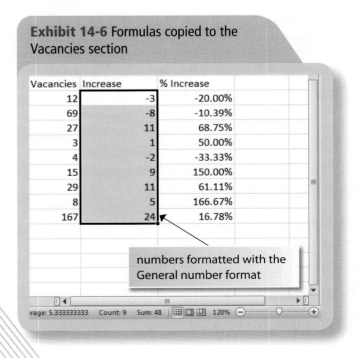

Exhibit 14-6 Formulas copied to the Vacancies section

Vacancies	Increase	% Increase
12	-3	-20.00%
69	-8	-10.39%
27	11	68.75%
3	1	50.00%
4	-2	-33.33%
15	9	150.00%
29	11	61.11%
8	5	166.67%
167	24	16.78%

numbers formatted with the General number format

Rounding Numbers

When you decrease the number of decimal places shown in a cell, the only thing that changes is how the number is displayed in the cell. The underlying value of the number stored in the cell does not change. This is because the values are rounded, not truncated. If you display fewer decimal places of the value stored in a cell and then create formulas that use the cell displaying the rounded values, the calculation uses the actual value of the number in the cell, not the rounded value.

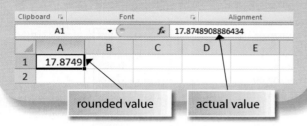

rounded value

actual value

Formatting Dates and Times

Because Excel stores dates and times as numbers and not as text, you can apply different formats without affecting the date and time value. The format that is applied when you enter a date, *mm/dd/yyyy*, is the Short Date format. You can also apply a Long Date format that displays the day of the week and the full month name in addition to the day of the month and the year. To change a date

format to the Long Date format, you click the Number Format box arrow in the Number group on the Home tab. Other built-in Excel formats include formats for displaying time values in 12- or 24-hour time, which you can select on the Number tab in the Format Cells dialog box.

ACTIVITY

Format the date.

1 Make the **Documentation worksheet** the active sheet.

2 Select **cell B4**. On the Home tab, in the Number group, the Number Format box displays Date.

3 In the Number group, click the **Number Format box arrow** to display commonly used number formats. The two date formats are in the middle of the list. See Exhibit 14-7.

Exhibit 14-7 Number Format menu

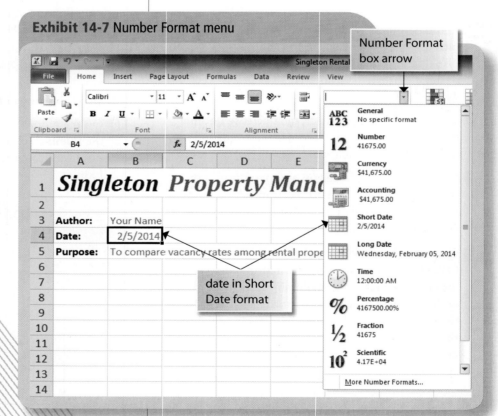

4 Click **Long Date**. The date format is changed to the Long Date number format, but because the formatted number is now too long to appear in the cell, a series of pound signs (#) appears in the cell. See Exhibit 14-8.

Text that is too long for a cell flows over the next cells, but when numbers are too long for a cell, the symbol # fills the cell instead.

Exhibit 14-8 Number too long to fit in a cell

number too long to display in cell

5 AutoFit the contents of **column B**. The date formatted with the Long Date number format now appears in cell B4, and the width of column B increased to fit the widest entry in the column, which is the Purpose statement in cell B5. You'll adjust the way this looks later. See Exhibit 14-9.

6 Save the workbook.

Excel Dates and Times as Numeric Values

Although dates and times entered into a cell usually are displayed as text, they are actually stored by Excel as numbers measuring the interval between the specified date and time and January 1, 1900 at 12:00 a.m. For example, the date May 1, 2014 is stored as 41,760, which is the number of days between January 1, 1900 and May 1, 2014.

Times are stored as fractional parts of one day. A time of 6:00 a.m. is stored as 0.25 because that represents one-fourth of a 24-hour day (starting the day from 12:00 a.m.). Similarly, the date and time of May 1, 2014 at 6:00 a.m. is stored as 41,760.25.

Excel stores dates and times as numbers to make it easier to calculate time intervals. For example, to calculate the difference between one date and another, you subtract the earlier date from the later date. If you subtract the date and time of April 30, 2014 at 12:00 a.m. from May 1, 2014 at 6:00 p.m., Excel displays 1.75—or one and three quarters of a day. You can always view the actual date and time by selecting the cell that contains the date/time entry and applying the General number format, or by switching the workbook window to Formula view.

HomeStudio/Shutterstock.com

LO14.2 Formatting Cells and Ranges

A workbook often contains several cells that store the same type of data. For example, each worksheet might have a cell displaying the sheet title, or a range of financial data might have several cells containing summary totals. A good design

Exhibit 14-9 Date formatted with the Long Date number format

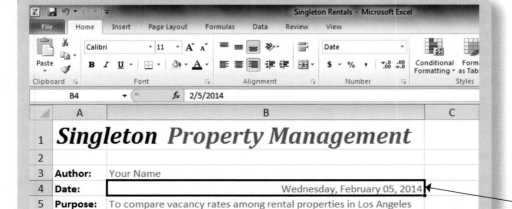

date in cell B4 shows weekday name, month name, day, and year (your date will be different) practice is to apply the same format to worksheet cells that contain the same type of data.

You can format the appearance of individual cells by modifying the alignment of text within the cell, indenting cell text, or adding borders of different styles and colors to individual cells or ranges.

Applying Cell Styles

One way to ensure that you are using consistent formats is to copy and paste the formats using the Format Painter. The Format Painter is effective, but it can also be time-consuming if you need to copy the same format to several cells scattered across the workbook. Also, if you decide to modify the format, you must copy and paste the revised format all over again. A better way to ensure that cells displaying the same type of data use the same format is with styles.

A style is a selection of formatting options using a specific font and color from the current theme. For example, you can create a style to display titles in a bold, white, 20-point Calibri font on a blue background. You can then apply that style to any cell with a title in the workbook. If you later revise the style, the appearance of any cell formatted with that style is updated automatically. This saves you the time and effort of reformatting each cell individually.

Excel has a variety of built-in styles to format worksheet titles, column and row totals, and cells with emphasis. These are available in the Cell Styles gallery, which you access by clicking the Cell Styles button in the Styles group on the Home tab. Some styles are based on the workbook's current theme and may change if the theme is changed.

ACTIVITY

Apply cell styles.

1 Make the **Yearly Rates worksheet** the active sheet. Select **cell A3**.

2 On the Home tab, in the Styles group, click the **Cell Styles button**. The Cell Styles gallery opens. See Exhibit 14-10.

Exhibit 14-10 Cell Styles gallery

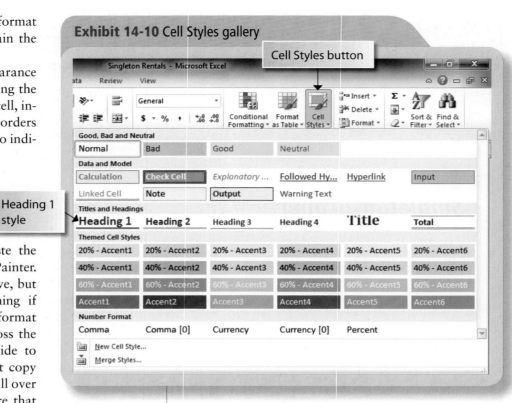

3 Point to different styles in the Cell Styles gallery to preview cell A3 with each of those styles. For each style, notice that the text that doesn't fit in cell A3 is formatted the same way as the text that fits in cell A3; any additional formatting, such as borders or shading, is visible only within the borders of cell A3.

4 In the Titles and Headings section, click the **Heading 1 style**. The gallery closes and the text in cell A3 is formatted as 15-point, blue, and bold with a solid blue border at the bottom of cell A3.

5 Select the **nonadjacent range A5:G5;A16:G16**.

6 In the Styles group, click the **Cell Styles button**. In the Themed Cell Styles section, click the **Accent1 style**. Each cell in the selected range is formatted with the selected style—white text on a blue background.

7 Select the **nonadjacent range F6:G14;F17:G25**.

8 In the Styles group, click the **Cell Styles button**. In the Themed Cell Styles section, click the **20% – Accent1 style**. The calculated values are formatted differently from the data.

9 Click any cell in the worksheet to deselect the range. See Exhibit 14-11.

Exhibit 14-11 Cells formatted with cell styles

Heading 1 style

Accent1 style

20% – Accent1 style

	Rental Income	Building	Units	2012 Income	2013 Income	Increase	% Increase
2							
3	**Analysis of Property Vacancy Rates (in unit months)**						
4							
5	Rental Income	Building	Units	2012 Income	2013 Income	Increase	% Increase
6		1431 1st Ave.	12	$ 258,000.00	$ 271,920.00	$ 13,920.00	5.40%
7		47 Park St.	52	754,860.75	788,877.00	34,016.25	4.51%
8		2011 N. Sheridan St.	32	669,760.00	669,232.00	(528.00)	-0.08%
9		153-155 Lake Rd.	6	179,200.00	179,302.00	102.00	0.06%
10		2099 Harrison Ave.	18	264,600.00	275,134.55	10,534.55	3.98%
11		415 9th Ave.	37	801,540.00	808,622.00	7,082.00	0.88%
12		1632 8th Blvd.	56	994,080.00	977,360.00	(16,720.00)	-1.68%
13		9853 O'Rourke Pl.	12	377,880.00	345,414.00	(32,466.00)	-8.59%
14		Total	225	$4,299,920.75	$4,315,861.55	$ 15,940.80	0.37%
15							
16	Vacancies	Building	Units	2012 Vacancies	2013 Vacancies	Increase	% Increase
17		1431 1st Ave.	12	15	12	(3.00)	-20.00%
18		47 Park St.	52	77	69	(8.00)	-10.39%
19		2011 N. Sheridan St.	32	16	27	11.00	68.75%

Documentation | **Yearly Rates** | Monthly Rates

Ready | 120%

Aligning Cell Content

Cell text is aligned with the left and bottom borders of a cell, and cell values are aligned with the right and bottom borders. You might want to change these alignments to make cell content more readable or visually appealing. In general, you should center column titles, left-align other cell text, and align numbers within a column by their decimal places. The buttons to set these alignment options are located in the Alignment group on the Home tab. Exhibit 14-12 describes the actions of these buttons.

Unless you make a change, the alignment for all cells of a workbook is Bottom Align.

Working with Themes

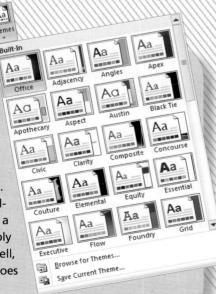

Most of the formatting you have applied so far is based on the workbook's current theme—the default Office theme. As you have seen, fonts, colors, and cell styles are organized in theme and non-theme categories. The appearance of these fonts, colors, and cell styles depends on the workbook's current theme. If you change the theme, the formatting of these elements also changes throughout the entire workbook.

Keep in mind that only elements directly tied to a theme change when you select a different theme. For example, cells formatted with the Accent1 cell style change from blue in the Office theme to orange in the Aspect theme. The Heading 1 style uses the Cambria typeface in the Office theme and the Verdana typeface in the Aspect theme. However, standard colors are not part of a theme. So if you apply standard colors to a cell, changing the theme does not affect these colors.

Exhibit 14-12 Alignment buttons

Button	Name	Description
☰	Top Align	Aligns the cell content with the cell's top edge
☰	Middle Align	Centers the cell content vertically within the cell
☰	Bottom Align	Aligns the cell content with the cell's bottom edge
☷	Align Text Left	Aligns the cell content with the cell's left edge
☰	Center	Centers the cell content horizontally within the cell
☷	Align Text Right	Aligns the cell content with the cell's right edge
⯈	Decrease Indent	Decreases the size of the indentation used in the cell
⯇	Increase Indent	Increases the size of the indentation used in the cell
✎	Orientation	Rotates the cell content to any angle within the cell
▤	Wrap Text	Forces the cell text to wrap within the cell borders
▦	Merge & Center	Merges the selected cells into a single cell and centers the content horizontally within the merged cell

 **ACTIVITY**

Align cell content.

1 Make the **Documentation worksheet** the active sheet. Select **cell B4** if it is not already the active cell.

2 On the Home tab, in the Alignment group, click the **Align Text Left button** ☷. The date shifts to the left edge of the cell.

3 Make the **Yearly Rates worksheet** the active sheet. Select the **nonadjacent range B5:G5;B16:G16**.

4 In the Alignment group, click the **Center button** ☰. The column labels in columns B through G are centered.

merge To combine two or more cells into one cell.

Tip: Although the date in the Documentation worksheet is formatted to display as text, it is right-aligned in the cell because Excel treats dates and times as numbers.

Indenting Cell Content

Sometimes you want a cell's content moved a few spaces from the cell left edge. This is particularly useful for entries that are considered subsections of a worksheet. For example, the worksheet records the total rental income and total vacancies for eight buildings. The totals can be considered a subsection, and would be easier to identify if the labels were indented a few spaces. Each time you click the Increase Indent button in the Alignment group on the Home tab, you increase the indentation by roughly one character space. To decrease or remove an indentation, click the Decrease Indent button.

 **ACTIVITY**

Indent cell content.

1 Select the **nonadjacent range B14;B25**.

2 On the Home tab, in the Alignment group, click the **Increase Indent button** ⯇ twice. Each Total label indents, or moves right, two character spaces.

3 In the Alignment group, click the **Decrease Indent button** ⯈. Each label moves left one character space. See Exhibit 14-13.

Merging Cells

Merging combines two or more cells into one cell. When you merge cells, only the content from the upper-left cell in the range is retained. The cell reference for the merged cell is the upper-left cell reference. So, if you merge cell A1 and cell A2, the merged cell reference is cell A1. For example, you can merge several cells into one cell to align text over several columns or rows.

You can quickly merge the selected cells and center the content using the Merge button in the Alignment group on the Home tab. If you click the Merge button arrow, you can choose from the following merge options:

▶ **Merge & Center**—Merges the range into one cell and horizontally centers the content

▶ **Merge Across**—Merges each of the rows in the selected range across the columns in the range

▶ **Merge Cells**—Merges the range into a single cell, but does not horizontally center the cell content

▶ **Unmerge Cells**—Reverses a merge, returning the merged cell back into a range of individual cells

After you merge a range into a single cell, you can realign its content.

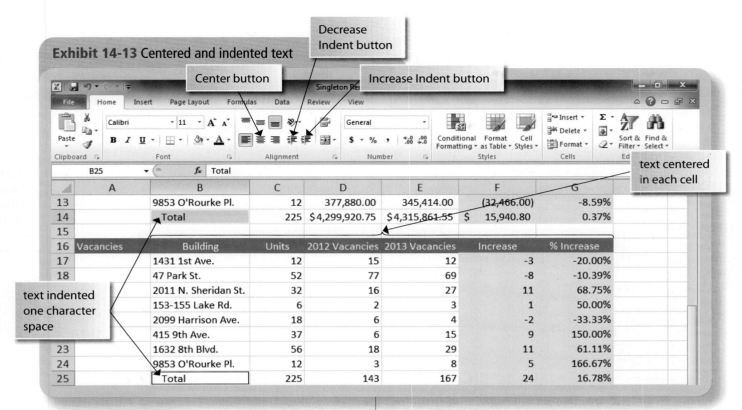

Exhibit 14-13 Centered and indented text

Decrease Indent button

Center button

Increase Indent button

text centered in each cell

text indented one character space

	A	B	C	D	E	F	G
13		9853 O'Rourke Pl.	12	377,880.00	345,414.00	(32,466.00)	-8.59%
14		Total	225	$4,299,920.75	$4,315,861.55	$ 15,940.80	0.37%
15							
16	Vacancies	Building	Units	2012 Vacancies	2013 Vacancies	Increase	% Increase
17		1431 1st Ave.	12	15	12	-3	-20.00%
18		47 Park St.	52	77	69	-8	-10.39%
		2011 N. Sheridan St.	32	16	27	11	68.75%
		153-155 Lake Rd.	6	2	3	1	50.00%
		2099 Harrison Ave.	18	6	4	-2	-33.33%
		415 9th Ave.	37	6	15	9	150.00%
23		1632 8th Blvd.	56	18	29	11	61.11%
24		9853 O'Rourke Pl.	12	3	8	5	166.67%
25		Total	225	143	167	24	16.78%

 **ACTIVITY**

Merge and center cells.

1 In the Yearly Rates worksheet, select the **range A3:G3**.

2 On the Home tab, in the Alignment group, click the **Merge & Center button** [icon]. The range A3:G3 merges into one cell with a cell reference of A3 and the text is centered within the cell.

3 Click any other cell in the worksheet to deselect the merged cell. The text is formatted with the cell style from cell A3, but the bottom blue border was lost.

4 Select **cell A3**. On the Home tab, in the Styles group, click the **Cell Styles button**, and then click

Rotating Cell Content

Text and numbers are usually displayed within cells horizontally. However, you can rotate cell text to save space or to provide visual interest to a worksheet. This is commonly used as a way to label narrow columns or identify rows in a category. For example, in the Yearly Rates worksheet in the Singleton Rentals workbook you are working on, you could rotate the labels *Rental Income* and *Vacancies* in the merged cells in column A so that they read vertically from bottom to top. You can choose from the following Orientation options:

▶ **Angle Counterclockwise**—Rotates cell content to a 45 degree angle to the upper-right corner of the merged cell

▶ **Angle Clockwise**—Rotates cell content to a 45 degree angle to the lower-right corner of the merged cell

▶ **Vertical Text**—Rotates cell content to appear stacked from the top of the cell to the bottom

▶ **Rotate Text Up**—Rotates cell content 90 degrees counterclockwise so that text is placed sideways in the cell and read from the bottom of the cell to the top

▶ **Rotate Text Down**—Rotates cell content 90 degrees clockwise so that text is placed sideways in the cell and read from the top of the cell to the bottom

After you rotate cell content, you may need to resize the column width or row height to eliminate excess space or add more space so that the cell contents are attractively and completely visible.

Exhibit 14-14 Merged cells

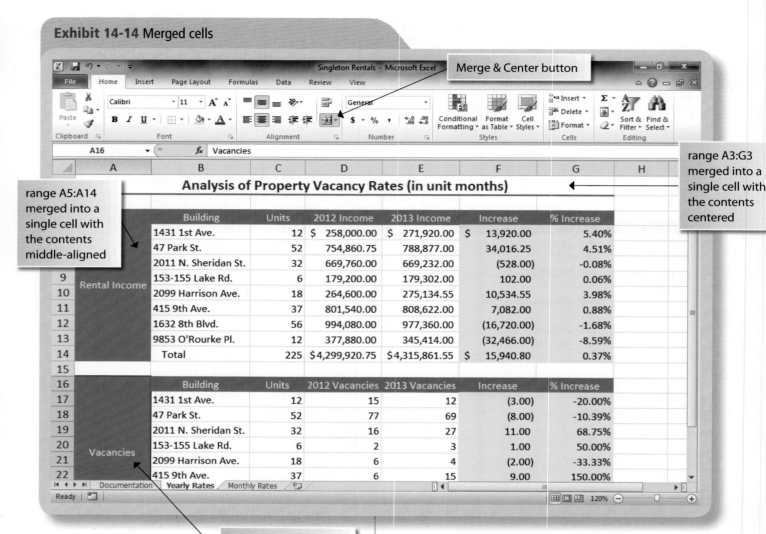

range A3:G3 merged into a single cell with the contents centered

range A5:A14 merged into a single cell with the contents middle-aligned

range A16:A25 merged into a single cell with the contents middle-aligned

Merge & Center button

the **Heading 1 style** to reapply that style to the cell.

5 Select the **range A5:A14**. In the Alignment group, click the **Merge & Center button** . The cells are merged vertically into a single cell, displaying the text *Rental Income* aligned with the bottom of the cell and formatted with the cell style from cell A5.

6 In the Alignment group, click the **Middle Align button** . The label is now vertically centered in the merged cell.

7 Merge and center the **range A16:A25**, and then middle-align the merged cell. See Exhibit 14-14.

border A line added along an edge of a cell.

Adding Cell Borders

Sometimes you want to include lines along the edges of cells to improve the readability of the rows and columns of data. One way to do this is by adding a border to a cell or range. A **border** is a line you add along an edge of a cell. You can add borders to the left, top, right, or bottom of a cell or range; around an entire cell; or around the outside edges of a range. You can also specify the thickness of and the number of lines in the border. All of these border options are

Standard accounting practice is to add a single top border and a double bottom border to the total rows to clearly differentiate them from financial data.

available from the Border button in the Font group on the Home tab.

Borders are different than the gridlines that surround the cells in each worksheet. Gridlines appear on the worksheet as a guide. When a worksheet is printed, the gridlines are not printed unless you specify that they should. Borders always print.

Add cell borders.

1 Select the **nonadjacent range B14:G14;B25:G25**. These rows show the totals.

2 On the Home tab, in the Font group, click the **Borders button arrow** to display a list of available borders and options. See Exhibit 14-15.

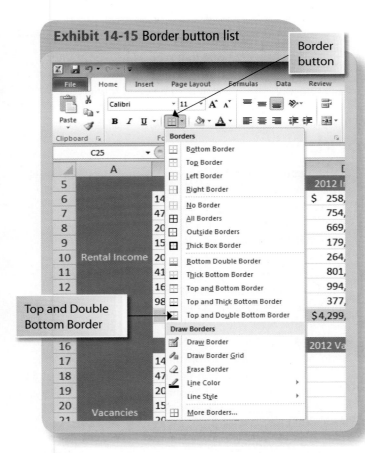

Exhibit 14-15 Border button list

3 Click **Top and Double Bottom Border**. Both Total rows now have a single top border and a double bottom border,

Tip: You can use the Total cell style to make cell text bold and add colored top and double bottom borders to selected cells.

following standard accounting practice. Notice that the Border button changed to  to match the selection you just made.

Changing Cell Background Color

Another way to distinguish sections of a worksheet is by formatting the cell background. You can add background colors, also known as **fill colors**, to cells using the theme color palette. The fill colors are useful for differentiating parts of a worksheet or highlighting data. You already added fill colors when you used the Accent styles to format the ranges B5:G5, B16:G16, F6:G14, and F17:G25. If you don't like any of the styles in the Themed Cell Styles section in the Cell Styles gallery, you can select any background color you like from the color palette on the Fill Color button. The Fill Color button is located in the Font group on the Home tab.

If you add a dark fill color to cells, black text can be harder to read than text formatted with a light or white font color. The Accent 1 cell style that you applied to the column labels in the Yearly Rates worksheet changed the font color in these cells to white as part of the style. If you change the fill color of cells using the Fill Color button, you might then need to change the font color in those cells.

Change the fill color.

1 Make the **Documentation worksheet** the active sheet. Select the **range A3:A5**.

2 On the Home tab, in the Font group, click the **Fill Color button arrow** to display the color palette.

3 In the Standard Colors section, click the **Blue color**. The background color of the selected cells is now blue.

4 In the Font group, click the **Font Color button arrow**. In the Theme Colors section, click the **White, Background 1 color**.

5 Select the **range B3:B5**.

6 In the Font group, click the **Fill Color button arrow**. In the Themes Color section, click the **White, Background 1 color**. The background color of the cells is now white, hiding the gridlines.

fill color A background color added to cells.

7 Click anywhere in the worksheet to deselect the range. See Exhibit 14-16.

Exhibit 14-16 Fill color added to cells

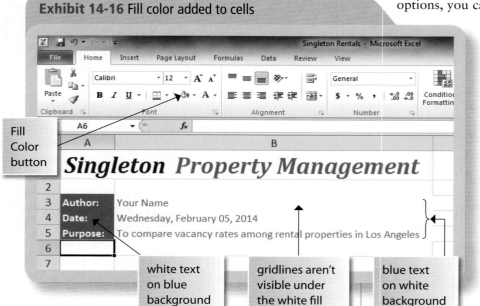

Fill Color button

white text on blue background

gridlines aren't visible under the white fill

blue text on white background

Using the Format Cells Dialog Box

The buttons on the Home tab provide quick access to the most commonly used formatting choices. For more options, you can use the Format Cells dialog box to apply formats to selected cells. The Format Cells dialog box has the following six tabs, each focusing on a different set of formatting options:

▶ **Number**—Provides options for formatting the appearance of numbers, including dates and numbers treated as text such as telephone or Social Security numbers

▶ **Alignment**—Provides options for how data is aligned within a cell

▶ **Font**—Provides options for selecting font types, sizes, styles, and other formatting attributes such as underlining and font colors

Using Color to Enhance a Workbook

When used wisely, color can enhance any workbook. However, when used improperly, color can distract the user, making the workbook more difficult to read. As you format a workbook, keep in mind the following tips:

▶ **Use colors from the same theme within a workbook.** This helps to maintain a consistent look and feel across the worksheets. If the built-in themes do not fit your needs, you can create a custom theme.

▶ **Use colors to differentiate types of cell content and to direct users where to enter data.** For example, you can format a worksheet so that formula results appear in cells without a fill color and users enter data in cells with a light gray fill color.

▶ **Use pleasing color combinations.** Although somewhat subjective, keep in mind that some color

combinations can annoy the intended readers, and others can just be difficult to read.

▶ **Print the workbook on both color and black-and-white printers.** This extra step helps to ensure that the printed copy is readable in both versions.

▶ **Understand your printer's limitations and features.** Colors that look good on your monitor might not look as good when printed.

▶ **Be sensitive to your audience.** About 8 percent of all men and 0.5 percent of all women have some type of color blindness and might not be able to see the text when certain color combinations are used. Red-green color blindness is the most common, so avoid using red text on a green background or green text on a red background.

Border—Provides options for adding and removing cell borders as well as selecting a line style and color

Fill—Provides options for creating and applying background colors and patterns to cells

Protection—Provides options for locking or hiding cells to prevent other users from modifying their contents

Although you have applied many of these formats from the Home tab, the Format Cells dialog box presents them in a different way and provides more choices.

ACTIVITY

Use the Format Cells dialog box.

1 Make the **Yearly Rates worksheet** the active sheet. Select the **range F17:F25**. These cells are formatted with the General number format.

2 On the Home tab, in the Number group, click the **Dialog Box Launcher** . The Format Cells dialog box opens with the Number tab displayed. General, indicating the General number format, is selected in the Category box.

> **Tip:** You can also open the Format Cells dialog box by right-clicking a cell or selected range, and then clicking Format Cells on the shortcut menu.

3 In the Category box, click **Number**. The Number options appear in the dialog box showing the current options for the Number format—in this case, the default options are two decimal places, no comma, and negative numbers displayed with a minus sign in black. See Exhibit 14-17.

4 Click the **Use 1000 Separator (,) check box** to select it. This has the same effect as selecting the Comma Style button in the Number group on the Home tab.

5 In the Negative numbers box, click the **black (1,234.10)**. Now the format of the negative numbers in the range F17:F25 will match the format of the other negative numbers in the worksheet.

6 Click the **Decimal places down arrow** twice to change the value in that box to 0.

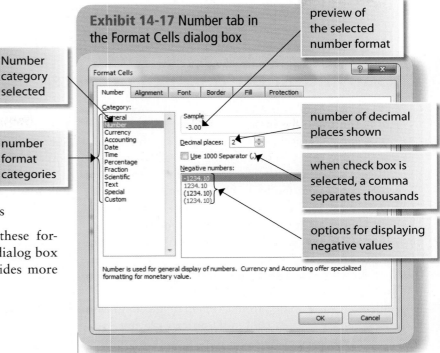

Exhibit 14-17 Number tab in the Format Cells dialog box

- preview of the selected number format
- Number category selected
- number format categories
- number of decimal places shown
- when check box is selected, a comma separates thousands
- options for displaying negative values

7 Click **OK**. The Format Cells dialog box closes and the numbers in the range F17:F25 appear with the options you chose in the dialog box.

8 Select the **no range B5:G5;B16:G16**.

9 On the Home tab, in the Font group, click the **Borders button arrow** , and then click **More Borders**. The Format Cells dialog box opens with the Border tab displayed. See Exhibit 14-18.

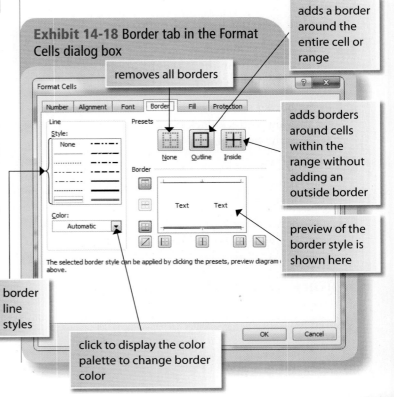

Exhibit 14-18 Border tab in the Format Cells dialog box

- adds a border around the entire cell or range
- removes all borders
- adds borders around cells within the range without adding an outside border
- preview of the border style is shown here
- border line styles
- click to display the color palette to change border color

Copying and Pasting Formats

The Format Painter is a fast and efficient way to copy formatting and maintain a consistent look and feel throughout a workbook. So, after you set the formatting in one cell, you can use the Format Painter button in the Clipboard group on the Home tab to copy that formatting to another cell or range without duplicating the data. You can double-click the Format Painter button to paste the same format multiple times. Click the Format Painter button again to turn it off.

Sometimes you want to copy and paste more than a cell's formatting. When you want to paste the format-

ting from a copied range along with its contents, you can use the Paste Options button. Each time you paste, the Paste Options button appears in the lower-right corner of the pasted cell or range. When you click the Paste Options button, you can choose from a list of pasting options, such as pasting only the values or only the formatting. These paste options also are available by clicking the Paste button arrow in the Clipboard group on the Home tab.

The Paste Special command is another way to control what you paste from the Clipboard. To use Paste Special, select and copy a range, select the range where you want to paste the Clipboard contents, click the Paste button arrow in the Clipboard group on the Home tab, and then click Paste Special to open the Paste Special dialog box. From the Paste Special dialog box, you can control exactly how to paste the copied range.

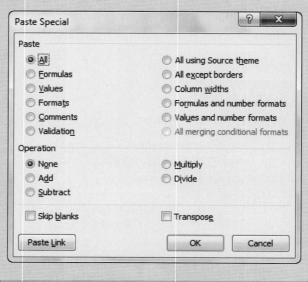

10 In the Line section, in the Style box, click the **thick line** (the sixth line in the second column).

11 In the Line section, click the **Color arrow** to display the color palette. In the Standard Colors section, click the **Dark Blue color**.

12 In the Border section, click the **bottom border** of the preview. A thick dark blue bottom border appears in the preview.

13 Click **OK**. The dialog box closes and the selected cells with column titles have a thick, dark blue bottom border.

14 Save the workbook.

Excel table A range of data that is treated as a distinct object in a worksheet.

table style A preset style that specifies the formatting for an entire table.

LO14.3 Creating an Excel Table

You can treat a range of data as a distinct object in a worksheet known as an **Excel table**. An Excel table makes it easier to identify, manage, and analyze the related data. For example, you can quickly sort the data, filter the data to show only those rows that match specified criteria, and add formulas to entire columns. In addition, the entire table is formatted using a single **table style**, which specifies formats for the entire table, such as font color, fill color, and borders. Formatting an entire table with a table style is more efficient than formatting individual cells in the table. Excel tables can include optional elements such as a header row that contains titles for the different columns in the table, and a total row that contains formulas summarizing the values in the table's data. You can create more than one Excel table in a worksheet.

When you create an Excel table, arrows appear next to each column label. You can click these arrows to change the way the data in the table is displayed

Exhibit 14-19 Table styles

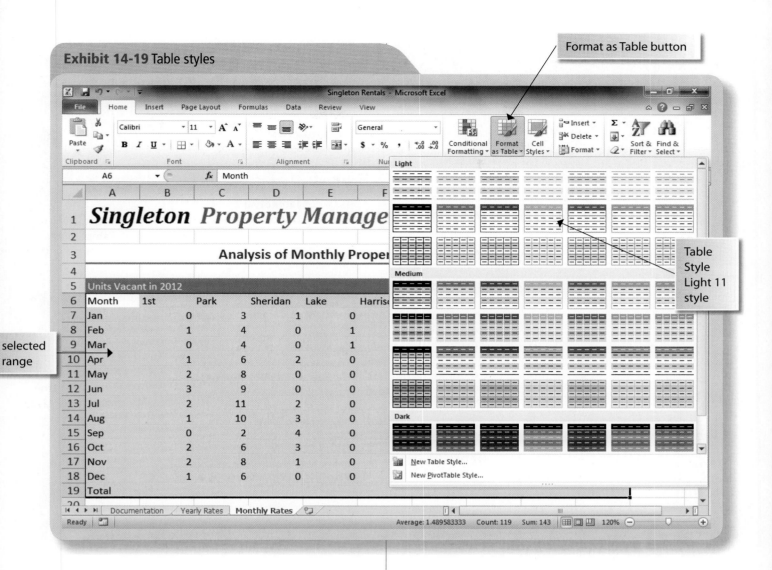

by sorting it or hiding rows that contain certain data. Finally, when you scroll the table above the column headings, the text of the header row replaces the letters in the column headings, making it easier to track which columns you are viewing.

Table dialog box opens, confirming the range you selected for the table. It also has the My table has headers check box selected, which means that the column labels in row 6 will be treated as labels and not data. See Exhibit 14-20.

ACTIVITY

Create an Excel table.

1. Make the **Monthly Rates worksheet** the active sheet. Select the **range A6:J19**.

2. On the Home tab, in the Styles group, click the **Format as Table button**. A gallery of table styles opens. See Exhibit 14-19.

3. In the Light section, click **Table Style Light 11** (the green style in the second row). The Format As

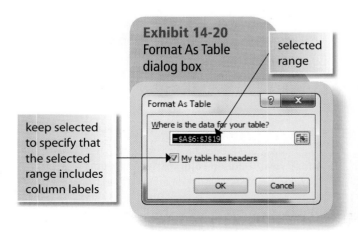

Exhibit 14-20 Format As Table dialog box

selected range

keep selected to specify that the selected range includes column labels

Format As Table

Where is the data for your table?

=$A$6:$J$19

☑ My table has headers

OK   Cancel

Exhibit 14-21 Range formatted as an Excel table

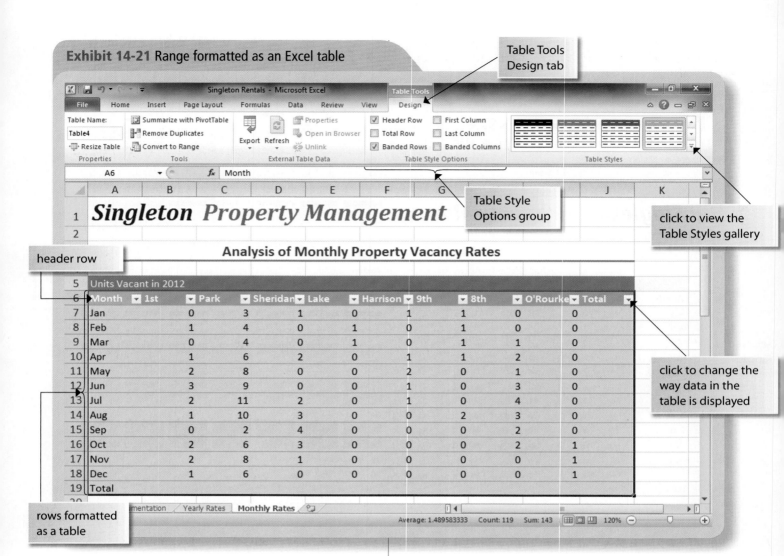

Table Tools Design tab

Table Style Options group

click to view the Table Styles gallery

header row

click to change the way data in the table is displayed

rows formatted as a table

Singleton Rentals - Microsoft Excel

Table Tools

File Home Insert Page Layout Formulas Data Review View Design

Table Name: Table4 · Resize Table | Properties

Summarize with PivotTable · Remove Duplicates · Convert to Range | Tools

Export Refresh | Properties · Open in Browser · Unlink | External Table Data

☑ Header Row ☐ First Column
☐ Total Row ☐ Last Column
☑ Banded Rows ☐ Banded Columns | Table Style Options

Table Styles

A6   fx   Month

	A	B	C	D	E	F	G		J	K
1	*Singleton Property Management*									
2										
			Analysis of Monthly Property Vacancy Rates							
5	Units Vacant in 2012									
6	Month	1st	Park	Sheridan	Lake	Harrison	9th	8th	O'Rourke	Total
7	Jan	0	3	1	0	1	1	0	0	
8	Feb	1	4	0	1	0	1	0	0	
9	Mar	0	4	0	1	0	1	1	0	
10	Apr	1	6	2	0	1	1	2	0	
11	May	2	8	0	0	2	0	1	0	
12	Jun	3	9	0	0	1	0	3	0	
13	Jul	2	11	2	0	1	0	4	0	
14	Aug	1	10	3	0	0	2	3	0	
15	Sep	0	2	4	0	0	0	2	0	
16	Oct	2	6	3	0	0	0	2	1	
17	Nov	2	8	1	0	0	0	0	1	
18	Dec	1	6	0	0	0	0	0	1	
19	Total									

...mentation / Yearly Rates / Monthly Rates

Average: 1.489583333   Count: 119   Sum: 143   120%

4 Click **OK**. The dialog box closes, the selected range is formatted as an Excel table using the table style you selected in the gallery, and the Table Tools Design tab appears on the Ribbon and is the active tab. See Exhibit 14-21.

Tip: If you insert rows and columns, the range of the Excel table automatically expands to include the new rows and columns. To add a new column to the right of the table or a new row at the bottom of the table, enter data in the next column or row.

Using Banded Rows

After you identify a range as an Excel table, you can choose a different table style at any time. Using a table style ensures that the table's formatting reflects any changes made to the table, such as adding or deleting table rows or columns. For example, many tables display alternate rows with different fill colors. This **banded rows** effect makes the data easier to read, especially in large tables with many rows. You could create the banded rows effect by applying a cell style with a background fill to every other row in the table; but if you later add or delete a row from

banded rows (banded columns) Formatting that displays alternate rows (or columns) in an Excel table with different fill colors.

You can perform the same tasks more easily in an Excel table than in a range of data.

the table, the banded rows effect might be lost. If you choose a table style that includes banded rows, on the other hand, alternating row colors are applied to the entire Excel table and if you add or delete rows, the banded rows effect is adjusted as needed. This is because a table style treats the table as a single object rather than a collection of cells. You can also create **banded columns**.

 **ACTIVITY**

Change a table style.

1 Click **cell A6** to make the table active. The Table Tools Design tab appears on the Ribbon.

> **Tip:** You can click any cell within a table to make the table active; you do not need to select all of the table cells.

2 If it is not already selected, on the Ribbon, click the **Table Tools Design tab**. In the Table Style Options group, the Header Row and Banded Rows check boxes are selected. Refer back to Exhibit 14-21.

3 In the Table Styles group, click the **More button**. The Table Styles gallery opens with the same table style options you saw earlier. Most of the styles use banded rows when the Banded Rows check box is selected.

4 In the Medium section, click **Table Style Medium 16** (the blue style in the third row). The table is reformatted with the new style. See Exhibit 14-22.

5 Format the **range A22:J34** (Units Vacant in 2013) as an Excel table using the **Table Style Medium 16 table style**. The range A38:J50 is already formatted as an Excel table.

Exhibit 14-22 Excel table formatted with banded rows

Selecting Table Style Options

After you apply a table style, you can change whether to show or hide the header row, total row, banded rows, and banded columns in the table, as well as whether to format the first column and last column of the table. These options are available in the Table Style Options group on the Table Tools Design tab and are the same check boxes you saw when you created a table in Word. You can also use cell styles and the formatting tools you have used with individual cells and ranges to format Excel tables.

ACTIVITY

Select table style options.

1 Click **cell A7** to make the Units Vacant in 2012 table active.

2 On the Table Tools Design tab, in the Table Style Options group, click the **Last Column check box** to select it. The last column—the Total column—is formatted with a Blue, Accent 1 fill.

> ➤ **Tip:** Some table styles do not include formatting for all of the options available; in those cases, selecting an option has no visible effect on the table.

3 In the Table Style Options group, click the **Total Row check box** to select it. A new row labeled *Total* is added to the bottom of the table. Because the

Total column contains no values, cell J20 displays 0. See Exhibit 14-23.

4 Delete **row 19** to delete the original Total row that had been added manually.

5 Select the **range A6:J6**. On the Ribbon, click the **Home tab**. In the Alignment group, click the **Center button** ☰. The column labels are centered.

6 Select **cell A19**. On the Home tab, in the Styles group, click the **Cell Styles button**. In the Titles and Headings section, click the **Heading 4 style**. The Total label is formatted in a bold blue font.

7 Click any cell in the table other than cell A19. See Exhibit 14-24.

8 Make the Excel table in the **range A23:J34** active.

9 On the Ribbon, click the **Table Tools Design tab**. In the Table Style Options group, select the **Last Column check box** and the **Total Row check box**.

10 Center the labels in the **nonadjacent range A22:J22;A38:J38**.

11 Apply the **Heading 4 cell style** to **nonadjacent range A35;A51**.

Adding Formulas to an Excel Table

One advantage of using an Excel table rather than a range of data is the speed with which you can add

SUBTOTAL Function

You can use the Total row in an Excel table to insert commonly used functions to summarize data in each column. Although you are inserting a common function, such as SUM, the formula that Excel enters is the SUBTOTAL function. The syntax of the SUBTOTAL function is

SUBTOTAL(*function_num,ref1[,ref2] . . .*)

where *function_num* is one of the numbers shown in the table on the right that specifies which function to use in the calculation, and *ref1, ref2, . . .* are one or more references for the table columns or ranges you want to include in the calculation. Excel table columns are referenced by their label in the header row. For example, the following function tells Excel to use the SUM function to add all of the numbers in the Total column:

=SUBTOTAL(109,[TOTAL])

Function Number (includes hidden data)	Function Number (includes all data)	Function
1	101	AVERAGE
2	102	COUNT
3	103	COUNTA
4	104	MAX
5	105	MIN
6	106	PRODUCT
7	107	STDEV
8	108	STDEVP
9	109	SUM
10	110	VAR
11	111	VARP

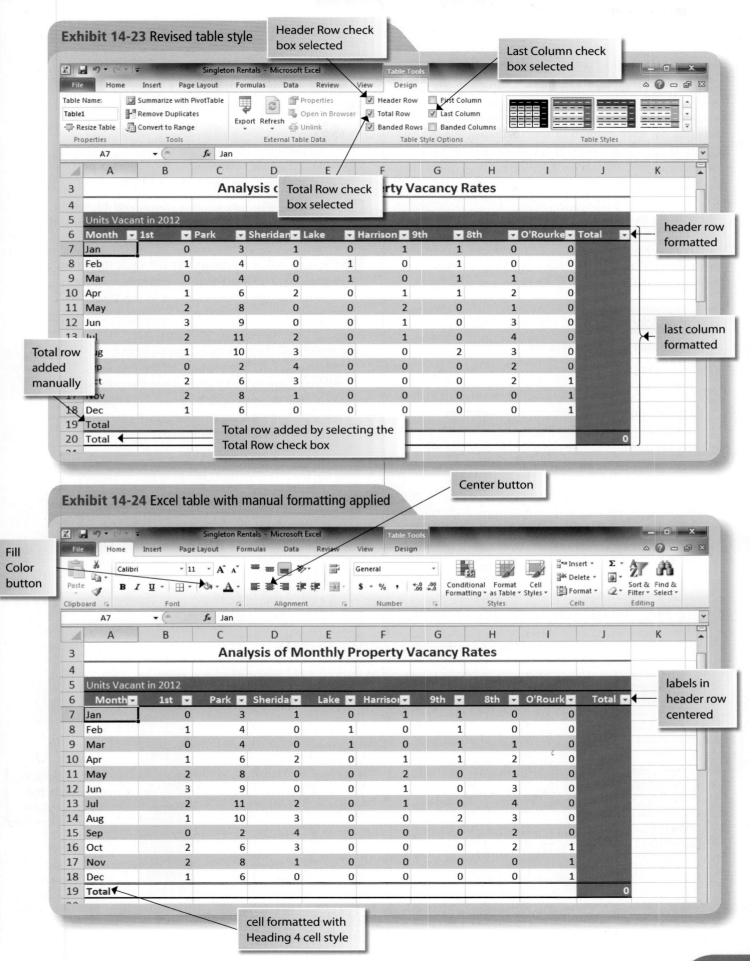

Exhibit 14-23 Revised table style

- Header Row check box selected
- Last Column check box selected
- Total Row check box selected
- header row formatted
- last column formatted
- Total row added manually
- Total row added by selecting the Total Row check box

Exhibit 14-24 Excel table with manual formatting applied

- Center button
- Fill Color button
- labels in header row centered
- cell formatted with Heading 4 cell style

formulas to the table. When you enter a formula in one cell of an Excel table, the formula is automatically copied to all other cells in that column; this is called a calculated column. You can also quickly enter a summary function for each column in the Total row. When you click in a cell in the Total row, an arrow button appears. When you click the arrow button, a list of the most commonly used functions opens, including SUM, AVERAGE, COUNT, MIN, and MAX. The function you select is applied to that column. By default, the Total row adds the numbers in the last column of the Excel table or counts the number of records if the data in the last column contains text using the COUNT function. None is the default for all of the other columns.

ACTIVITY

Add formulas to an Excel table.

1 Select **cell J7**.

2 On the Home tab, in the Editing group, click the **Sum button** Σ, and then press the **Enter key**. The SUM function is added to all of the cells in the Total column in the Excel table. Cell J19 displays 12, which is the number of rows above the cell that contain data.

3 Click **cell B19**. Because this cell is in the Total row added to the table using the table style option, an arrow button appears to the right of the cell.

4 Click the **arrow button** ▼ to display a list of the available functions. See Exhibit 14-25.

5 Click **Sum**. The function list closes, and 15, which is the number of vacancies in 2012 for the property on 1st Ave., appears in the cell.

6 For each cell in the **range C19:I19**, click the **arrow button** ▼ and select **SUM** to enter the Sum function for the remaining columns in the Total row.

⚠ **Problem?** If you copy a formula from one cell to another in the Total row, the formula will continue to add the values in the original column instead of updating to reflect the current column. Repeat Step 6 making sure you click the arrow button in each cell.

Exhibit 14-25 List of functions available in the Total row

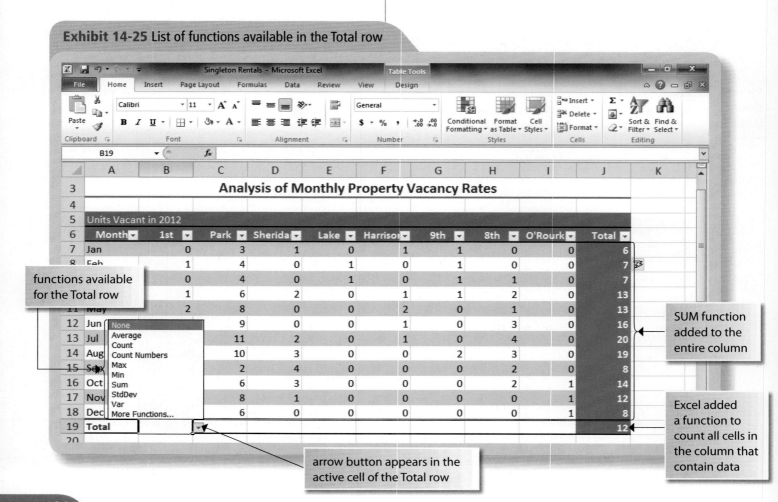

functions available for the Total row

SUM function added to the entire column

Excel added a function to count all cells in the column that contain data

arrow button appears in the active cell of the Total row

7 Click **cell J19**. Click the **arrow button** ▾ to the right of the cell. Count is selected in the list.

8 Click **Sum**. The function list closes, and the value in cell J19 is now 143, which is the total number of vacancies in 2012.

9 Select **cell J23**, and then insert the **SUM function**. The function is inserted in the range J23:J34.

10 In the **range B35:J35**, use the **arrow button** ▾ to insert the **SUM function** in each cell of the Total row.

11 Save the workbook.

Exhibit 14-26 Highlighting rules

Rule	Highlights
Greater Than	Cells that are greater than a specified number
Less Than	Cells that are less than a specified number
Between	Cells that are between two specified numbers
Equal To	Cells that are equal to a specified number
Text That Contains	Cells that contain specified text
A Date Occurring	Cells that contain a specified date
Duplicate Values	Cells that contain duplicate or unique values
Top 10%	Cells that contain the values in the top 10 percent
Bottom 10%	Cells that contain the values in the bottom 10 percent

LO14.4 Highlighting Cells with Conditional Formatting

Conditional formatting applies formatting only when a cell's value meets a specified condition. This is often used to help analyze data. For example, conditional formatting is often used to highlight important trends and values of interest.

With conditional formatting, the format applied to a cell depends upon the value or content of the cell. For example, conditional formatting can make negative numbers red and positive numbers black. Conditional formatting is dynamic—if the cell's value changes, the cell's format also changes as needed. Each type of conditional formatting has a set of rules that define how the formatting should be applied and under what conditions the format will be changed.

Each time you apply a conditional format, you are creating a **conditional formatting rule**. A rule specifies the type of condition (such as formatting cells greater than a specified value), the type of formatting when that condition occurs (such as light red fill with dark red text), and the cell or range to which the formatting is applied. You can see all of the conditional formatting rules used in the workbook in the Conditional Formatting Rules Manager dialog box.

Highlighting a Cell Based on Its Value

Cell highlighting changes a cell's font color or background fill color or both based on the cell's value.

Exhibit 14-26 describes some of the ways that cells can be highlighted with conditional formatting. You can apply more than one conditional formatting rule to the same range.

To highlight cells with conditional formatting, first select the range that you want to highlight. Click the Conditional Formatting button in the Styles group on the Home tab, point to Highlight Cells Rules or Top/Bottom Rules, and then click the type of condition you want to create for the rule. A dialog box opens so you can specify the formatting to use for that condition.

 **ACTIVITY**

Highlight cells with conditional formatting.

1 Select the **range B39:I50**.

2 On the Home tab, in the Styles group, click the **Conditional Formatting button**. See Exhibit 14-27.

3 Point to **Highlight Cells Rules**. A submenu lists the available highlighting rules.

conditional formatting Formatting that is applied to a cell only when the cell's value meets a specified condition.

conditional formatting rule A list of the condition, the type of formatting applied when the condition occurs, and the cell or range to which the formatting is applied.

Exhibit 14-27 Highlight Cells Rules submenu on the Conditional Formatting button menu

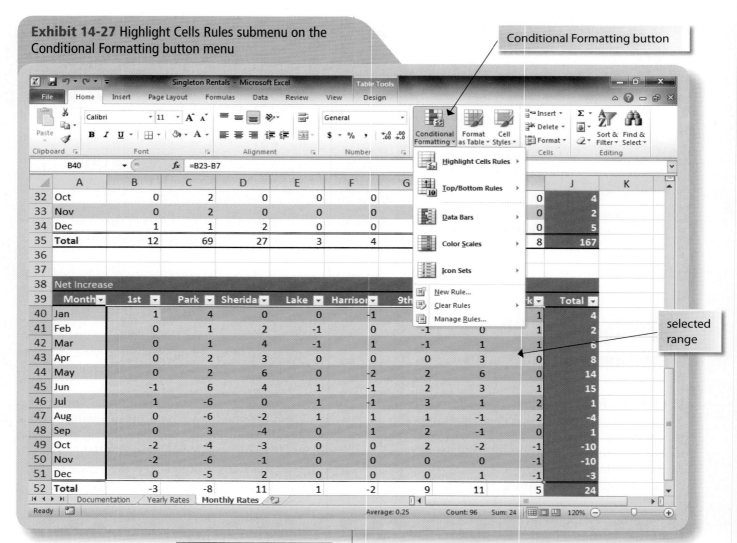

Conditional Formatting button

selected range

4 Click **Greater Than**. The Greater Than dialog box opens. The default condition specifies to highlight cells in the selected range with a value greater than zero (months and buildings in which vacancies increased) with a light red fill and dark red text. See Exhibit 14-28.

⚠ **Problem?** If 0 (a zero) doesn't appear in the Format cells that are GREATER THAN box, select the current entry and then type **0**.

5 Click the **with arrow**, and then click **Red Border**. All cells in the selected range with a value greater than zero will be highlighted with a red border.

6 Click **OK** to apply the highlighting rule.

7 In the Styles group, click the **Conditional Formatting button**, point to **Top/Bottom Rules**, and then click **Top 10 %**. The Top 10% dialog box, which is similar to the Greater Than dialog box, opens. The number 10 in the left box in the dialog box specifies the percentage to highlight.

8 Click the **with arrow**, and then click **Green Fill with Dark Green Text**.

9 Click **OK**. Cells containing the top 10 percent of vacancy increases between 2012 and 2013 are filled with light green and contain dark green text.

Exhibit 14-28 Greater Than dialog box

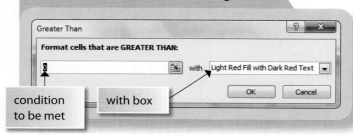

condition to be met

with box

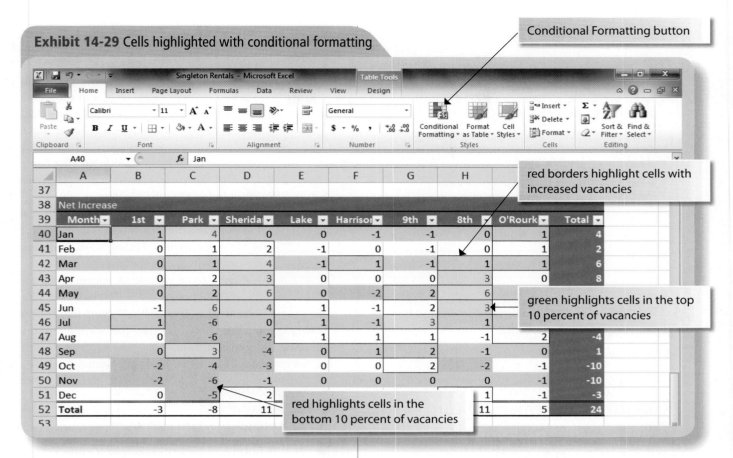

Exhibit 14-29 Cells highlighted with conditional formatting

Conditional Formatting button

red borders highlight cells with increased vacancies

green highlights cells in the top 10 percent of vacancies

red highlights cells in the bottom 10 percent of vacancies

10 In the Styles group, click the **Conditional Formatting button**, point to **Top/Bottom Rules**, and then click **Bottom 10 %**. The Bottom 10% dialog box opens with 10 in the left box and Light Red Fill with Dark Red Text selected in the with box.

11 Click **OK**. Cells containing the bottom 10 percent of vacancy increases between 2012 and 2013 are filled with light red and contain dark red text.

12 Click anywhere in the Excel table to deselect the range. See Exhibit 14-29.

Clearing a Conditional Formatting Rule

If you no longer want to highlight cells using the conditional formatting, you can remove, or clear, the current highlighting rule. Note that clearing a conditional formatting rule doesn't affect the contents of the cells. You can clear all of the rules from a selected range, an entire worksheet, or the active table. These commands are available by clicking the Conditional Formatting button, and then pointing to Clear Rules. If you only want to delete some of the conditional formatting rules, you need to use the Conditional Formatting Rules Manager dialog box. To open this dialog box, click the Conditional Formatting button, and then click Manage Rules.

ACTIVITY

Clear a conditional formatting rule.

1 On the Home tab, in the Styles group, click the **Conditional Formatting button**, and then click **Manage Rules**. The Conditional Formatting Rules Manager dialog box opens, listing the three rules you created for the active table. See Exhibit 14-30.

Tip: To clear all of the conditional formatting rules from a range, table, or worksheet, click the Conditional Formatting button in the Styles group on the Home tab, point to Clear Rules, and then click the appropriate Clear command in the submenu.

2 Click the **Cell Value > 0 rule** to select it.

3 On the toolbar at the top of the dialog box, click the **Delete Rule button**. The rule is deleted from the list.

Exhibit 14-30 Conditional Formatting Rules Manager dialog box

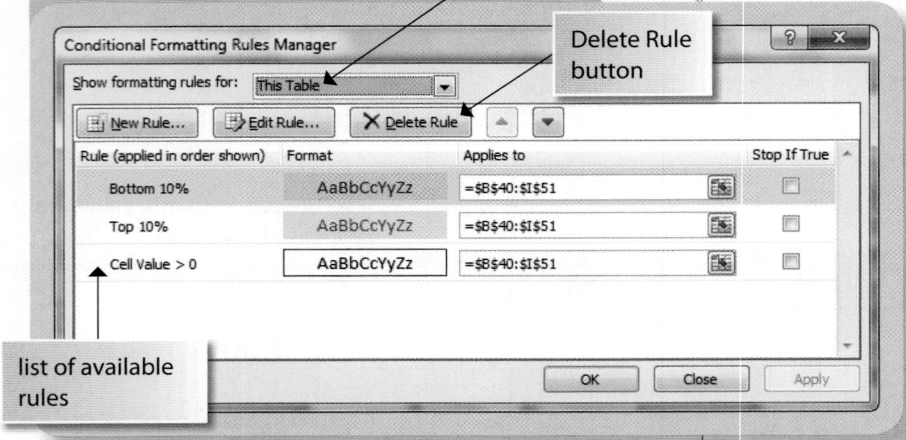

indicates that list of rules applies to the current table

Conditional Formatting Rules Manager

Show formatting rules for: This Table

New Rule... | Edit Rule... | ✕ Delete Rule

Delete Rule button

Rule (applied in order shown)	Format	Applies to		Stop If True
Bottom 10%	AaBbCcYyZz	=$B$40:$I$51		☐
Top 10%	AaBbCcYyZz	=$B$40:$I$51		☐
Cell Value > 0	AaBbCcYyZz	=$B$40:$I$51		☐

list of available rules

OK | Close | Apply

4 Click **OK**. The dialog box closes, and the red borders disappear from the table.

5 Save the workbook.

Conditional formatting can help isolate and highlight potential problems or identify trends.

LO14.5 Hiding Worksheet Data

Sometimes a worksheet will contain too much data to fit into the worksheet window without drastically reducing the zoom level, which would make the contents too small to read easily. One way to manage the contents of a large worksheet is to selectively hide (and later unhide) rows and columns containing extraneous information. This allows you to focus your attention on only a select few data points. Hiding rows, columns, and worksheets is a good way to manage a large volume of information; but it should never be used to hide data that is crucial to understanding a workbook. Note that hiding a row or column does not affect the other formulas in the workbook. Formulas still show the correct value even if they reference a cell in a hidden row or column.

ACTIVITY

Hide and unhide worksheet data.

1 In the Monthly Rates worksheet, select **row 5** through **row 36**.

Using Conditional Formatting Effectively

Conditional formatting is an excellent way to highlight important trends and data values to clients and colleagues. However, it should be used judiciously. An overuse of conditional formatting can sometimes obscure the data values you want to emphasize. You will need to make decisions about what to highlight and how it should be highlighted. Keep in mind the following tips as you consider the best ways to effectively communicate your findings to others:

▶ **Document the conditional formats you use.** If a bold, green font means that a sales number is in the top 10 percent of all sales, include that information in a legend in the worksheet. The legend should identify each color used in the worksheet and what it means, so others know why certain cells are highlighted.

▶ **Don't clutter data with too much highlighting.** Limit highlighting rules to one or two per data set. Highlights are designed to draw attention to

points of interest. If you use too many, you will end up highlighting everything—and, therefore, nothing.

▶ **Use color sparingly in worksheets with highlights.** It is difficult to tell a highlight color from a regular fill color, especially when fill colors are used in every cell.

▶ **Consider alternatives to conditional formats.** If you want to highlight the top 10 sales regions, it might be more effective to simply sort the data with the best-selling regions at the top of the list.

Remember that the goal of highlighting is to provide a strong visual clue of important data or results. Careful use of conditional formatting helps readers to focus on the important points you want to make rather than be distracted by secondary issues and facts.

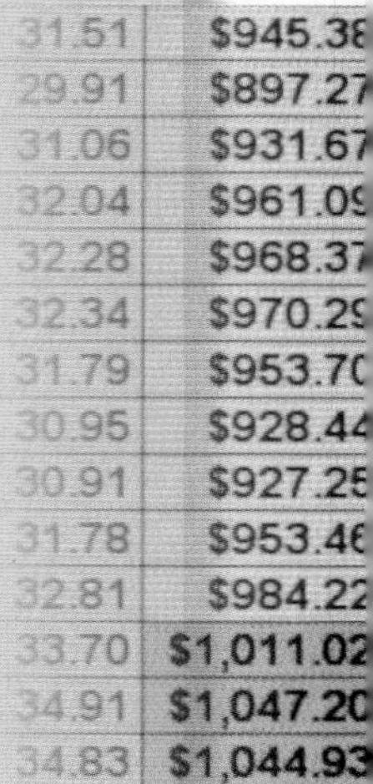

31.51	$945.38
29.91	$897.27
31.06	$931.67
32.04	$961.09
32.28	$968.37
32.34	$970.29
31.79	$953.70
30.95	$928.44
30.91	$927.25
31.78	$953.46
32.81	$984.22
33.70	$1,011.02
34.91	$1,047.20
34.83	$1,044.93

Stephen Aaron Rees/Shutterstock.com

2 On the Home tab, in the Cells group, click the **Format button**, and then point to **Hide & Unhide**. A submenu opens listing the commands for hiding and unhiding the selected rows, columns, or sheet.

Tip: You can also hide or unhide a row or column by right-clicking the row or column header and clicking Hide or Unhide on the shortcut menu.

3 On the submenu, click **Hide Rows**. Rows 5 to 36 are hidden, and the row numbers in the worksheet jump from row 4 to row 37. Notice that the data in the third table does not change even though its formulas use data from the hidden tables. See Exhibit 14-31.

Exhibit 14-31 Rows hidden in the worksheet

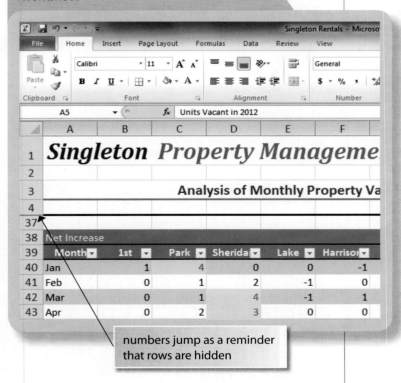

numbers jump as a reminder that rows are hidden

4 Drag to select **row 4** and **row 37**, which are the rows before and after the hidden rows.

5 In the Cells group, click the **Format button**, point to **Hide & Unhide**, and then click **Unhide Rows**. Rows 5 through 36 reappear.

6 Click any cell in the worksheet to deselect the unhidden rows.

7 Save the workbook.

LO14.6 Formatting a Worksheet for Printing

You should take as much care in formatting the printed output as you do in formatting the contents of the electronic file. Before you print, you can set the page orientation and margins, specify what area of the worksheet to print, indicate what should print on each page, and specify what information should print on each page. Print settings can be applied to an entire workbook or to individual sheets.

kolosigor/Shutterstock.com

ACTIVITY

View a worksheet in Page Layout view.

1 On the status bar, click the **Page Layout button**. The worksheet switches to Page Layout view.

Tip: You can set the gridlines or the row and column headings to print by clicking the Print check boxes on the Sheet Options group on the Page Layout tab.

2 Change the zoom level of the worksheet to **40%** to view more of the page layout. The worksheet's contents do not fit on a single page and the tables break across pages. See Exhibit 14-32.

3 On the Ribbon, click the **Page Layout tab**. In the Page Setup group, click the **Orientation button**, and then click **Landscape**. The page orientation changes to landscape, making each page wide enough to display all of the columns in each table.

Exhibit 14-32 Page Layout view of the Monthly Rates worksheet

worksheet zoomed to 40% in Page Layout view

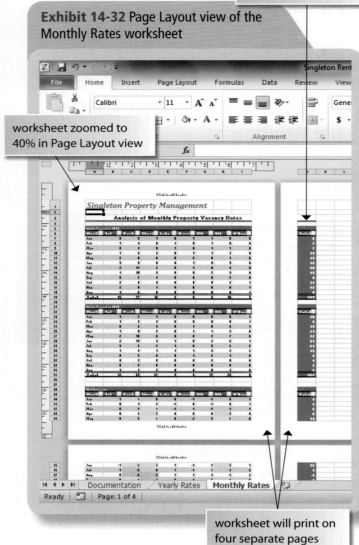

worksheet will print on four separate pages

Setting the Print Area

By default, all cells in the active worksheet containing text, formulas, or values are printed. The region that is sent to the printer from the active sheet is known as the **print area**. To print part of a worksheet, you can define the print area, overriding the default setting. A print area can cover an adjacent or non-adjacent range in the current worksheet.

The easiest way to set the print area is in Page Layout view or Page Break Preview. For example, to print only the first table in the Monthly Sales worksheet, you could set the print area to cover that range while in Page Break Preview.

print area The region that is sent to the printer from the active sheet.

ACTIVITY

Set and clear the print area.

1 On the status bar, click the **Page Break Preview button**. The worksheet switches to Page Break Preview.

> **⚠ Problem?** If the Welcome to Page Break Preview dialog box opens, click **OK**.

2 Change the zoom level of the worksheet to **60%**.

3 Select the **range A1:J19**. This range includes the worksheet title and subtitle and the first table.

4 On the Page Layout tab, in the Page Setup group, click the **Print Area button**, and then click **Set Print Area**. The print area changes to cover only the range A1:J19. The rest of the worksheet content is gray to indicate that it will not be part of the printout. See Exhibit 14-33.

Exhibit 14-33 Print area set in Page Break Preview

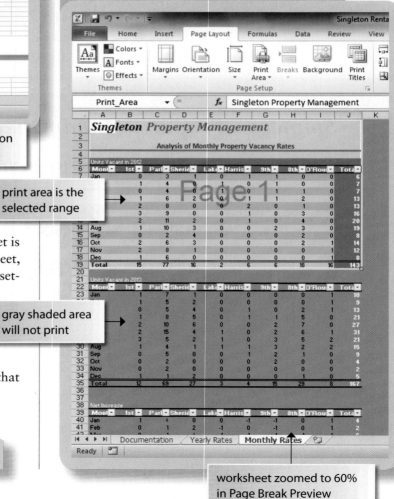

print area is the selected range

gray shaded area will not print

worksheet zoomed to 60% in Page Break Preview

5 On the Ribbon, click the **File tab**. In the navigation bar, click **Print**. On the Print tab, the preview shows that only the area you set as the print area will print.

6 On the Ribbon, click the **Page Layout tab** to close Backstage view and display the worksheet with the Page Layout tab selected on the Ribbon.

7 In the Page Setup group, click the **Print Area button**, and then click **Clear Print Area**. The print area is reset to include the entire contents of the worksheet.

Inserting and Removing Page Breaks

Often the contents of a worksheet do not fit onto a single page. By default, Excel prints as much of the content that fits on a single page without resizing the content, and then inserts **automatic page breaks** to continue printing the remaining worksheet content on successive pages. This can result in page breaks that leave a single column or row on a separate page or split worksheet content in awkward places such as within a table.

One way to fix this problem is to scale the printout by reducing the font size to fit on a single sheet of paper. However, if you have more than one or two columns or rows to fit onto the page, the resulting text is often too small to read comfortably. A better fix is usually to split the worksheet into logical segments, which you can do by inserting **manual page breaks** that specify exactly where the page breaks occur. A page break is inserted directly above and to the left of a selected cell, directly above a selected row, or to the left of a selected column. Remember that page breaks appear as dotted blue lines in Page Break Preview. Manual page breaks appear as solid blue lines.

ACTIVITY

Insert page breaks.

1 Click **cell A20**. With this cell selected, a page break will be inserted between rows 19 and 20, above the active cell.

2 On the Page Layout tab, in the Page Setup group, click the **Breaks button**, and then click **Insert Page Break**. A dark blue manual page break separates row 19 from row 20.

3 Click **cell A36**, and then insert a page break. The printout is now three pages, and each table appears on a separate page. See Exhibit 14-34.

> **Tip:** To remove a manual page break, click the cell below or to the right of the page break, click the Breaks button, and then click Remove Page Break.

Exhibit 14-34 Worksheet in Page Break Preview

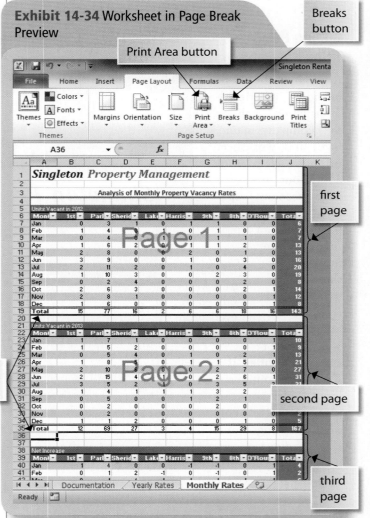

4 On the Ribbon, click the **File tab**. In the navigation bar, click **Print**. The preview shows the first page of the current worksheet.

> **automatic page break** A page break Excel inserts when no more content will fit on the page.

> **manual page break** A page break you insert to specify where a page break occurs.

5 Below the preview, click the **Next Page button** ▶. The second page of the worksheet appears. The second table is on the second page, but the worksheet title and subtitle do not appear on this page.

6 On the Ribbon, click the **File tab**. Backstage view closes.

7 View the worksheet in **Normal view** and change the zoom level to **120%**, if necessary.

Adding Print Titles

A good practice is to include descriptive information such as the company name, logo, and worksheet title on each page of a printout in case a page becomes separated from the other pages. You can repeat information in the worksheet by specifying which rows or columns in the worksheet act as **print titles**. If a worksheet contains a large table, you can print the table's column headings and row headings on every page of your printout by designating those initial columns and rows as print titles.

ACTIVITY

Create print titles.

1 On the Page Layout tab, in the Page Setup group, click the **Print Titles button**. The Page Setup dialog box opens with the Sheet tab displayed.

print title Information from a workbook that appears on every printed page.

2 In the Print titles section, click in the **Rows to repeat at top box**.

3 Click in the worksheet, and then select **rows 1 through 3**. The row reference $1:$3 appears in the Rows to repeat at top box. A blinking border appears around the first three rows of the worksheet indicating that the contents of these rows will be repeated on each page of the printout. See Exhibit 14-35.

4 Click **OK**. The dialog box closes.

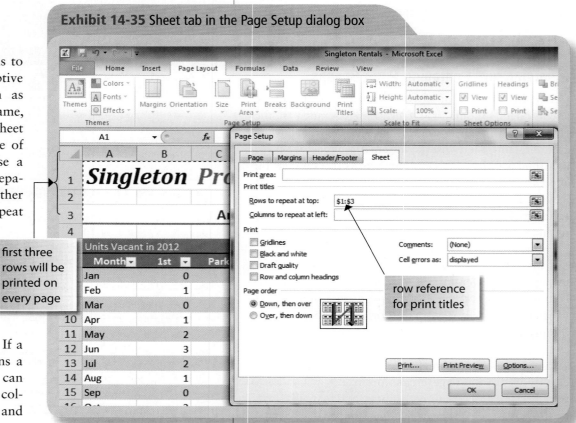

Exhibit 14-35 Sheet tab in the Page Setup dialog box

Print Options on the Sheet Tab

The Sheet tab in the Page Setup dialog box provides other print options, such as printing the gridlines or row and column headings. You can also print the worksheet in black and white or in draft quality. For a multiple page printout, you can specify whether the pages are ordered by going down the worksheet and then across, or across first and then down.

5 View the worksheet in **Page Layout view**. Notice that rows 1 through 3 are repeated at the top of each page of the printout.

Creating Headers and Footers

Another way to repeat information on each printed page is with headers and footers, as you did in Word. Recall that headers and footers contain helpful and descriptive text that is usually not found within the worksheet, such as the workbook's author, the current date, or the workbook file name. A header is information that appears in the top margin of each printed page. It often includes summary information such as the file name and the date. A footer is information that is printed in the bottom margin of each printed page. Like a header, it often includes summary information such as the current page number and the number of pages in the printout.

The header and footer each have a left section, a center section, and a right section. Within each section, you type the text you want to appear or insert elements such as the worksheet name or the current date and time. These header and footer elements are dynamic; if you rename the worksheet, for example, the name is automatically updated in the header or footer.

ACTIVITY

Insert a header and footer.

1 In Page Layout view, change the zoom level of the worksheet to **90%**.

2 At the top of the worksheet, point to **Click to add header**. A blue box highlights the middle section of the header.

> Include a header or footer with the page number and the total number of pages in a multiple page printout to help ensure you and others have all the pages.

3 Point to the **right section** of the header. Again, a blue box highlights the section.

4 Click the **left section** of the header. The blue box disappears, a black border appears around the left section, the insertion point appears in the left section, and the Header & Footer Tools Design tab appears on the Ribbon and is the active tab.

5 In the left section of the header, type **File name:** and then press the **Spacebar**.

6 On the Header & Footer Tools Design tab, in the Header & Footer Elements group, click the **File Name button**. The code &[File], which displays the file name of the current workbook, is added to the left section of the header.

7 Press the **Tab key** twice to move the insertion point to the right section of the header. In the left section, the &[File] code is replaced with the workbook file name, *Singleton Rentals*.

8 In the Header & Footer Elements group, click the **Current Date button**. The code &[Date] is added to the right section of the header. See Exhibit 14-36.

Exhibit 14-36 Header with content

buttons to insert codes into the header and footer

buttons to move between the header and footer

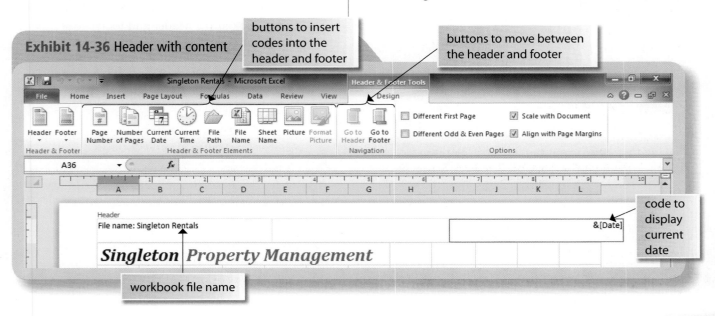

workbook file name

code to display current date

9 On the Header & Footer Tools Design tab, in the Navigation group, click the **Go to Footer button**. The footer appears at the top of the window, and the insertion point is in the right section of the footer.

10 Click in the **center section** of the footer. Type **Page** and then press the **Spacebar**.

> ➤ **Tip:** You can quickly enter commonly used header or footer text. In the Header & Footer group, click the Header button or the Footer button, and then click the text you want.

11 In the Header & Footer Elements group, click the **Page Number button**. The code &[Page] is added after the text in the center section of the footer.

12 Press the **Spacebar**, type **of** and then press the **Spacebar**.

13 In the Header & Footer Elements group, click the **Number of Pages button**. The text *Page &[Page] of &[Pages]* appears in the center section of the footer.

14 Press the **Tab key** to move to the right section of the footer. *Page 3 of 3* appears in the center section.

> ⚠ **Problem?** If the footer shows a different page number, the active cell in your worksheet is in the first or second table.

15 Type **Prepared by:**, press the **Spacebar**, and then type your name. See Exhibit 14-37.

16 Click any cell in the worksheet to make the worksheet area active.

17 Scroll through the three pages of the worksheet to verify that the same header appears for each page, and the center section of the footer displays the correct page number and total number of pages.

Setting the Page Margins

Another way to fit a large worksheet on a single page is to reduce the size of the page margins. A margin is the space between the page content and the edges of the page. In a new worksheet, the page margins are set to 0.7 inches on the left and right and 0.75 inches on the top and bottom with 0.3-inch margins around the page header and footer. You can change these margins as needed by selecting from a set of predefined margin sizes or specifying your own. For example, you might need wider margins to fit all of the columns on a page or to accommodate the page binding.

 **ACTIVITY**

Set the page margins.

1 On the Ribbon, click the **Page Layout tab**. In the Page Setup group, click the **Margins button**. A menu opens with a list of predefined margins.

2 Click **Wide** to set 1-inch margins around the printed content with 0.5-inch margins above the header and below the footer. The size of the margins around the page increases, but does not affect the content. Each of the three tables and the print titles still fit on single sheets.

3 View the worksheet in **Normal view**.

4 On the Ribbon, click the **File tab**. In the navigation bar, click **Print**. The one-inch margin is apparent on the left side of the worksheet. On the right, you need to look at the header and footer to see the one-inch margin. See Exhibit 14-38.

Exhibit 14-37 Page footer with content

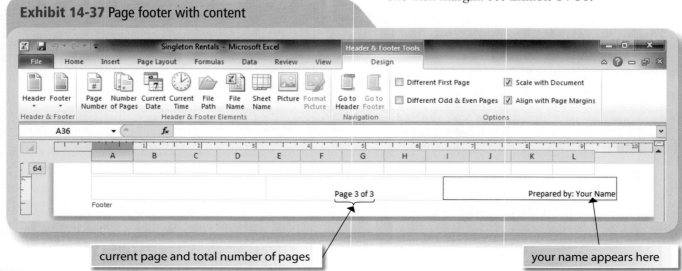

current page and total number of pages

your name appears here

Exhibit 14-38 Print tab in Backstage view showing Wide margins

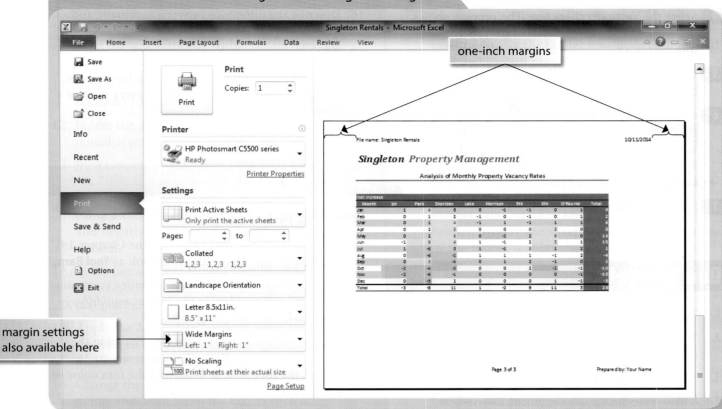

one-inch margins

margin settings also available here

Singleton Property Management

Analysis of Monthly Property Vacancy Rates

File name: Singleton Rentals 10/11/2014

Month	1st	Park	Sheridan	Lake	Harrison	9th	8th	O'Rourke	Total
Jan	1	4	0	0	-1	-1	0	1	4
Feb	0	1	2	-1	0	-1	0	1	2
Mar	0	1	4	-1	1	-1	1	1	6
Apr	0	2	3	0	0	0	0	0	5
May	0	2	8	0	-2	2	6	0	14
Jun	-1	6	4	1	-1	2	3	1	15
Jul	1	-6	0	1	-1	3	1	2	1
Aug	0	-6	-2	1	1	1	-1	1	-4
Sep	0	3	-4	0	1	2	-1	0	1
Oct	-2	-4	-4	0	0	2	-2	-1	-10
Nov	-2	-6	-1	0	0	0	0	-1	-10
Dec	0	-3	1	0	0	0	1	-1	-3
Total	-3	-8	11	1	-2	9	11	5	24

Page 3 of 3 Prepared by: Your Name

Centering Content on a Page

Worksheet content is printed on pages starting from the left and top margins. This can leave a lot of empty space on the right and top sides of the pages. To center the content on the page, open the Page Setup dialog box, display the Margins tab, and then select the Horizontally and Vertically check boxes to center the content of the current sheet on the page.

ACTIVITY

Center content on a page.

1. In the left pane of the Print tab, click the **Wide Margins button**. The same options that appeared on the Margins button menu in the Page Setup group on the Page Layout tab appear.

2. Click **Custom Margins**. The Page Setup dialog box opens with the Margins tab selected. See Exhibit 14-39.

> ➤ **Tip:** You can also click Custom Margins on the Margins button menu in the Page Setup group on the Page Layout tab to display the Margins tab in the Page Setup dialog box.

Exhibit 14-39 Margins tab in the Page Setup dialog box

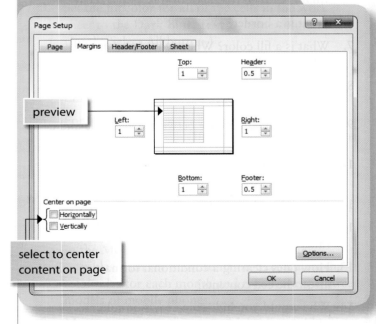

preview

select to center content on page

3. Select the **Horizontally check box**. The preview in the dialog box changes to show the worksheet centered between the left and right margins.

4 Select the **Vertically check box**. The preview shows the worksheet centered between the top and bottom margins.

5 Click **OK**. The preview on the Print tab shows the content of the worksheet centered on the page.

6 Click the **Print button**. Backstage view closes, and the Monthly Sales worksheet prints on three pages with the headers and footers displaying the file name, current date, page number and total number of pages, and your name.

7 Save and close the workbook.

Quiz Yourself

1. What is the General number format?

2. Why are dates right-aligned within a worksheet cell by default?

3. Why would you use a cell style?

4. Unless you change the alignment, how is text aligned within a cell, and how are values aligned within a cell?

5. If the range A1:C5 is merged into a single cell, what is the cell reference of this merged cell?

6. What is a border?

7. What is a fill color? When would you use fill colors?

8. Where can you access all of the formatting options for worksheet cells?

9. Describe the difference between a cell style and a table style.

10. What happens when you enter a formula in one cell of an Excel table?

11. What is conditional formatting?

12. How would you highlight the top 10 values in the range A1:C20?

13. How does clearing a conditional formatting rule affect the cell contents?

14. Why would you hide some rows or columns in a worksheet?

15. Why would you define a print area?

16. Describe the difference between automatic and manual page breaks.

17. What are print titles?

18. Describe how to add the workbook file name in the center section of the footer on every page of a printout.

Practice It

Practice It 14-1

1. Open the data file **Tool** located in the Chapter 14\Practice It folder. Save the workbook as **Tool Barn**.

2. In the Documentation worksheet, enter your name in cell B3 and the date in the format *mm/dd/yyyy* in cell B4.

3. Format the contents of cell A1 by changing the font to Times New Roman, the font size to 26 points, the font style to bold, and the font color to the Red, Accent 2 theme color.

4. In the range A3:A5, set the font color to white and boldface and set the fill color to the Red, Accent 2 theme color. In the range B3:B5, set the fill color to the Tan, Background 2 theme color.

5. In the range A3:B5, add all borders around the cells.

6. In cell B4, display the date with the Long Date format and left-align it within the cell.

7. Make the Model Comparison worksheet the active sheet. In the ranges E4:E8 and E12:E16, enter formulas that subtract the units sold in 2012 from the units sold in 2013 to calculate the increase in sales for each model.

8. In the ranges F4:F8 and F12:F16, enter formulas that divide the increase in units sold by the units sold in 2012 to calculate the percent increase in units sold for each model.

9. Select the nonadjacent range C9:E9;C17:E17, and then use the Sum button in the Editing group on the Home tab to enter formulas to calculate for each type of chainsaw the total units sold per year, the total increase in units sold, and the percent increase in total units sold. Then copy formula in cell F4 to cells F9 and F17.

10. Merge and center the range A3:A9 and middle-align the text vertically within the merged cell. Repeat for the range A11:A17.

11. Center the text in the nonadjacent range B3:F3;B11:F11.

12. Indent the model numbers one character in the nonadjacent range B4:B8;B12:B16.

13. In the nonadjacent range C4:E9;C12:E17, use the Number tab in the Format Cells dialog box to format the numbers in a Number format using a thousands separator, no decimal places, and negative numbers displayed with a minus symbol.

14. In the nonadjacent range F4:F9;F12:F17, format the numbers in a Percentage format with two decimal places.

15. Apply the Accent2 cell style to the merged cell A3, the merged cell A11, and the nonadjacent range B3:F3;B11:F11.

16. Change the font of merged cells A3 and A11 to 16 points and bold. Wrap the text in each cell.

17. Apply the Total cell style to the nonadjacent range B9:F9;B17:F17.

18. In the range E4:E8, use conditional formatting to add a Highlight Cells Rule to cells with values greater than zero with a green fill and dark green text. Repeat for the range E12:E16.

19. Make the Monthly Sales worksheet the active sheet. Merge and center the range A3:D3 and the range F3:I3. Apply the Heading 1 style to both merged cells.

20. In the nonadjacent range A4:D4;F4:I4, center the text.

21. Select the range A4:D16. Format the range as a table using the Table Style Light 10 (the red table style in the second row of the Light section). Repeat for the range F4:I16.

22. In cell D5, enter the SUM function to calculate the total units sold for all chainsaws by month. Repeat for cell I5.

23. In the nonadjacent range D5:D16;I5:I16, format the numbers to show a thousands separator (,) with no decimal places.

24. For each table, change the table style to Table Style Medium 3 (the red table style in the first row

of the Medium section) and set the table style options to display the header row, first column, total row, and banded rows.

25. In the total row of each table, use the SUM function to add the totals of each column.

26. For the Model Comparison and Monthly Sales worksheets, view the sheets in Page Layout view and set the page orientation to landscape.

27. For the Model Comparison and Monthly Sales worksheets, create headers and footers that display your name in the center section of the header, display the sheet name in the left section of the footer, display the workbook file name in the center section of the footer, and display the current date in the right section of the footer.

28. Save the workbook, and then close it.

Practice It 14-2

1. Open the data file **TalkWell** located in the Chapter 14\Practice It folder. Save the workbook as **TalkWell Mobile Phones**.

2. In the Documentation worksheet, enter your name in cell B3 and the date in cell B4.

3. Set the fill color for all of the cells in the worksheet to the Dark Blue, Text 2 theme color. (*Hint*: Use the Select All button.)

4. For the range B3:B5, set the background color to white and add all borders around each cell in the range.

5. For cell A1, change the font to Cambria, the Headings font of the Office theme, change the font size to 28 points, change the font color to white, and then bold the text.

6. For the range A3:A5, change the font size to 14 points, change the font color to white, and then bold the text.

7. In the Mobile Phone Sales worksheet, enter formulas with the SUM function to calculate the total sales for each month and region for the three models of mobile phones.

8. Merge and center the range A1:H1, apply the Title cell style to the merged cell, and then increase the font size to 26 points.

9. Merge and center the range A2:H2, apply the Heading 4 cell style to the merged cell, and then increase the font size to 16 points.

10. Merge and center the range A3:A16, set the alignment to Middle Align, apply the Accent1 cell style, increase the font size to 16 points, bold the text, and then wrap the text in the cell.

11. Use the Format Painter to copy the format of merged cell A3 to the ranges A18:A31 and A33:A46.

12. Center the text in the range B3:H3.

13. Increase the indent of the text in the range B4:B15 by one character.

14. Format the range C4:H16 to include thousands separators (,) and no decimal places.

15. Format the range B3:H16 as a table with the Table Style Medium 2 table style. Display the header row, first column, and last column.

16. In the range B16:H16, change the fill color to standard yellow.

17. Use the Format Painter to copy the formats in the range B3:H16 to the range B18:H31 and the range B33:H46 to format the other two tables in the worksheet.

18. Use conditional formatting to highlight the top 10 items in the nonadjacent range C4:G15;C19:G30;C34:G45 with a red border. (*Hint*: Select the nonadjacent range, and then apply the conditional formatting.)

19. View the Mobile Phone Sales worksheet in Page Layout view. Set the margins to Wide and set the page orientation to landscape.

20. View the Mobile Phone Sales worksheet in Page Break Preview. Insert manual page breaks at cells A18 and A33.

21. Repeat rows 1 and 2 of the worksheet on every printed page.

22. Display your name in the center header, display the file name in the left footer, display **Page** *page number* **of** *number of pages* in the center footer, and then display the current date in the right footer.

23. Save the workbook, and then close it.

On Your Own

On Your Own 14-1

1. Open the data file **Getaway** located in the Chapter 14\On Your Own folder. Save the workbook as **Getaway Travel**.

2. In the Documentation worksheet, enter your name in cell B3 and the date in cell B4.

3. Format the Documentation worksheet attractively, changing fonts, font sizes, font colors, fill colors, text wrapping, alignments, and cell styles as needed.

4. In the Trip Comparison worksheet, in the Total column, enter formulas to calculate the total cost of plane tickets and hotel accommodations for each destination.

5. Insert a new column to calculate the difference between the total for purchasing plane tickets and hotel accommodations separately, and the package price.

6. In the % Savings column, enter formulas to calculate the percentage saved for each destination when purchasing a package rather than purchasing separate plane tickets and hotel accommodations.

7. Format all of the numbers appropriately, using symbols such as $ and %, including the thousands separator, and displaying or hiding decimal places as needed.

8. Format the rest of the Trip Comparison worksheet attractively, including at least one example of each of the following design elements:
   - A range merged into a single cell
   - Cell content aligned and indented
   - Cell styles
   - Borders applied to one or more elements

9. Format the Trip Comparison data as a table, using the table style and table style options of your choice.

10. Use conditional formatting to highlight percent savings that are greater than 15 percent with the format of your choice.

11. Add descriptive headers and footers to the printed document, being sure to include your name, the current date, and the file name.

12. View the worksheet in Page Layout view, and then change the margins, orientation, page scale, and/or page breaks as needed to ensure that the printout is easily read and interpreted.

13. Save the workbook, and then close it.

ADDITIONAL STUDY TOOLS

Chapter 14

IN THE BOOK

▶ Complete end-of-chapter exercises

▶ Study tear-out Chapter Review Card

ONLINE

▶ Complete additional end-of-chapter exercises

▶ Take practice quiz to prepare for tests

▶ Review key term flash cards (online, printable, and audio)

▶ Play "Beat the Clock" and "Memory" to quiz yourself

▶ Watch the videos "Format Fonts and Font Styles," "Apply Cell Styles," "Align Cell Content," "Merge and Center Cells," "Change a Table Style," and more

Working with Formulas and Functions

Introduction

Most Excel workbooks are created to record and analyze data. To do this effectively, you enter data in cells in a worksheet, and then reference the cells with data in formulas that perform calculations on that data, such as adding the total of a column of numbers as part of a budget. By referencing cells instead of retyping data, you avoid errors in transcription. This also allows you to change data in one place and automatically have the new data used in calculations. This ability to change data and see the effect on calculations is what allows you to easily perform what-if analyses.

Some functions provide a shorter way to enter common formulas, such as the SUM function for adding numbers, the AVERAGE function for calculating the average value of a group of numbers, and so forth. Other functions perform complex calculations based on the data you enter. For example, Excel has a function that lets you display one of two results based on criteria you specify, and it has another function you can use to determine loan payments based on the parameters you enter.

Learning Objectives

After studying the material in this chapter, you will be able to:

LO15.1 Use relative, absolute, and mixed cell references in formulas

LO15.2 Enter functions

LO15.3 Use AutoFill

LO15.4 Work with the IF logical function

LO15.5 Work with date functions

LO15.6 Work with the PMT financial function

LO15.1 Using Relative, Absolute, and Mixed Cell References in Formulas

One of the most powerful aspects of Excel is being able to copy formulas between cells. This allows you to enter a formula—simple or complex—one time and then use that same formula throughout a workbook. When you paste the formula, sometimes you will want the cell references in the formula to change according to the new location in the spreadsheet. Other times, you will want the cell references to stay the same as they were in the original formula. You can control whether cell references change by how you enter them.

Monkey Business Images/Shutterstock.com

Whether a spreadsheet is used to track and analyze personal or business finances, formulas and functions make it simpler and more accurate to track assets, evaluate budgets, or plan for upcoming expenses.

ACTIVITY

Use cell references in a formula.

1 Open the data file **Turner** located in the Chapter 15\Chapter folder. Save the workbook as **Turner Budget**.

2 In the Documentation worksheet, enter your name in **cell B3** and the date in **cell B4**.

3 Make the **Budget worksheet** the active sheet, and then review its contents.

4 Select the **range D8:E8**.

5 On the Home tab, in the Editing group, click the **Sum button** Σ. The SUM function is inserted in both cells, and the estimated income calculated for the school and summer months. is See Exhibit 15-1.

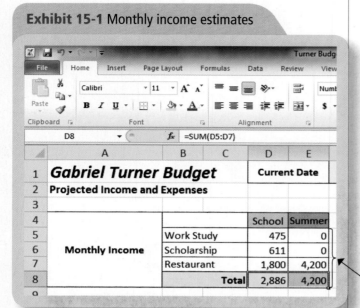

Exhibit 15-1 Monthly income estimates

estimated income during school and summer months

Using Relative References

So far, you have used relative cell references in formulas. A **relative reference** is always interpreted in relation, or relative, to the location of the cell containing the formula. For example, when you entered the formula in cell D8 to sum the income for the school months, Excel interprets the cell references in that formula relative to the location of cell D8. In other words, Excel interprets the formula =SUM(D5:D7) as adding the values entered in the three cells directly above cell D8.

Excel will use this same interpretation of the cell references if the formula is moved or copied into other cells. For example, if you paste the formula into cell D31, the formula changes to =SUM(D28:D30), which has different cell references but the same meaning: adding the values of the three cells directly above the cell with the formula.

relative reference A cell reference that is interpreted in relation to the location of the cell containing the formula.

Exhibit 15-2 illustrates how a relative reference in a formula changes when the formula is copied to another group of cells. In this figure, the formula =A2 entered in cell D5 displays 10, which is the value entered in cell A2. When pasted to a new location, each of the pasted formulas contains a reference to a cell that is three rows up and three rows to the left of the current cell's location. One of the great advantages of relative references is that you can quickly generate row and column totals without having to worry about revising the formulas as you copy them to new locations.

ACTIVITY

Use relative references in formulas.

1 Scroll down to view the **range A24:M32**. This range lists the estimated monthly expenses by category for the coming year.

2 In **cell B32**, enter the formula **=SUM(B24:B31)**. Cell B32 displays 9,000, indicating estimated expenses of $9,000 in January.

3 Copy the formula in **cell B32** and paste it into the **range C32:M32** to calculate the estimated monthly expenses for the rest of the year. See Exhibit 15-3.

4 Review the total expenses for each month. Notice that January and August are particularly expensive months because the expenses include both tuition and the purchase of books for the upcoming semester.

5 Click each cell in the **range B32:M32** and review the formula entered in the cell. The formulas all calculate the sums of values in different cell references. For example, the formula =SUM(C24:C31) was inserted in cell C32, the formula =SUM(D24:D31) was inserted in cell D32, and so forth.

If formula results are not what you expected, you may need to switch relative references to absolute references.

Exhibit 15-2 Formulas using relative references

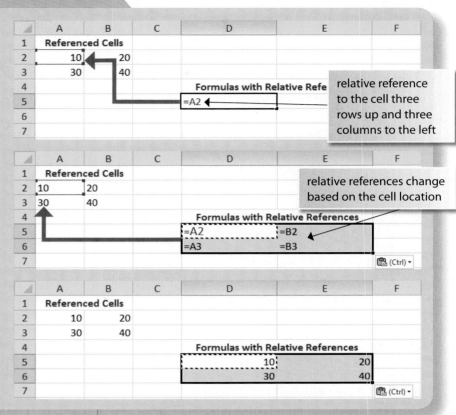

formula containing a
relative reference to cell A2

relative reference
to the cell three
rows up and three
columns to the left

each copied formula still references a cell
three rows up and three columns to the left

relative references change
based on the cell location

values returned by formulas

Exhibit 15-3 Total monthly expenses

formula to calculate the sum
of values in the range C24:C31

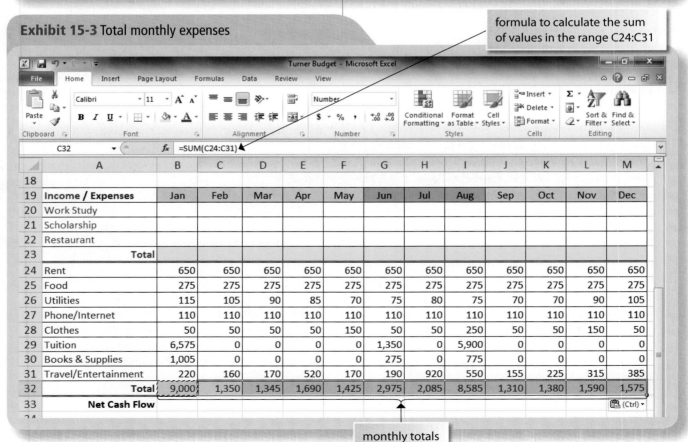

C32   =SUM(C24:C31)

Income / Expenses	Jan	Feb	Mar	Apr	May	Jun	Jul	Aug	Sep	Oct	Nov	Dec
Work Study												
Scholarship												
Restaurant												
Total												
Rent	650	650	650	650	650	650	650	650	650	650	650	650
Food	275	275	275	275	275	275	275	275	275	275	275	275
Utilities	115	105	90	85	70	75	80	75	70	70	90	105
Phone/Internet	110	110	110	110	110	110	110	110	110	110	110	110
Clothes	50	50	50	50	150	50	50	250	50	50	150	50
Tuition	6,575	0	0	0	0	1,350	0	5,900	0	0	0	0
Books & Supplies	1,005	0	0	0	0	275	0	775	0	0	0	0
Travel/Entertainment	220	160	170	520	170	190	920	550	155	225	315	385
Total	9,000	1,350	1,345	1,690	1,425	2,975	2,085	8,585	1,310	1,380	1,590	1,575
Net Cash Flow												

monthly totals

Exhibit 15-4 Formulas using absolute references

formula containing an absolute reference to the sales tax rate in cell A2

	A	B	C	D	E	F
1	Sales Tax Rate		Purchase	Sales Tax	Total	
2	0.05		$24.95	=C2*$A$2	=C2+D2	
3			$122.35			
4			$199.81			
5			$45.40			
6						
7						

relative references to cells C2 and D2

absolute reference to cell A2

relative reference to cell C2

each copied formula still references the same cell (cell A2)

	A	B	C	D	E	F
1	Sales Tax Rate		Purchase	Sales Tax	Total	
2	0.05		$24.95	=C2*$A$2	=C2+D2	
3			$122.35	=C3*$A$2	=C3+D3	
4			$199.81	=C4*$A$2	=C4+D4	
5			$45.40	=C5*$A$2	=C5+D5	
6						(Ctrl) ▾
7						

relative references change based on the cell location

relative reference changes based on cell location

$A$2 remains referenced in the formula

values returned by the formulas

	A	B	C	D	E	F
1	Sales Tax Rate		Purchase	Sales Tax	Total	
2	5%		$24.95	$1.25	$26.20	
3			$122.35	$6.12	$128.47	
4			$199.81	$9.99	$209.80	
5			$45.40	$2.27	$47.67	
6						(Ctrl) ▾

Using Absolute References

Cell references that remain fixed when a formula is copied to a new location are called **absolute references**. In Excel, absolute references have a $ (dollar sign) before each column and row designation. For example, B8 is a relative reference to cell B8, but $B$8 is an absolute reference to cell B8. When you copy a formula that contains an absolute reference to a new location, the reference does not change.

Exhibit 15-4 shows an example of how copying a formula with an absolute reference results in the same cell reference being pasted in different cells regardless of their location. In this figure, the sales tax of different purchases is calculated and displayed. All items have the same 5 percent tax rate, which is stored in cell A2,

applied to the purchase. The sales tax and the total cost of the first item are calculated in cells D2 and E2, respectively. When those formulas are copied and pasted to the remaining purchases, the relative references in

absolute reference A cell reference that remains fixed when copied to a new location; includes $ in front of both the column letter and row number.

Reduce Data Entry

A good practice when designing a workbook is to enter values in separate cells in one location of the worksheet, and then reference the appropriate cells in formulas throughout the worksheets. This reduces the amount of data entry when you need to use the same data in more than one location. It also makes it faster and more accurate when you need to change a data value, as all the formulas based on that cell are updated to reflect the new value.

wrangler/Shutterstock.com

the formulas change to point to the new location of the purchase cost; the sales tax rate continues to point to cell A2, regardless of the cell in which the formula is pasted.

ACTIVITY

Use absolute references in formulas.

1 In **cell B20**, enter **=$D$5**. This formula contains an absolute reference to cell D5, which contains the monthly work study income for the school months.

2 In **cell B21**, enter **=$D$6**. This formula contains an absolute reference to cell D6, which contains the monthly scholarship income for the school months.

3 In **cell B22**, enter **=$D$7**. This formula contains an absolute reference to cell D7, which contains the monthly restaurant income for the school months.

4 In **cell B23**, enter **=SUM(B20:B22)**. This formula adds the monthly work study, scholarship, and restaurant income during the school months.

5 Copy the formulas in the **range B20:B23** and paste them into the **range C20:F23;J20:M23**. February through May and September through December show the estimated income for the school months. See Exhibit 15-5.

6 Click each cell in the **range C20:F23;J20:M23** and verify that the formulas with absolute cell references =$D$5, =$D$6, and =$D$7 were copied into the appropriate cells.

Changing the Reference Type

You can quickly switch a cell reference between relative and absolute and mixed references. First, select or click in the cell reference and then press the F4 key. As you press the function key, Excel cycles through the different reference types, starting by changing a relative reference to an absolute reference, then to a mixed reference with the row absolute, then to a mixed reference with the column absolute, and then finally back to a relative reference.

7 Enter the following formulas with absolute references to the income sources for the summer months:

cell G20: =$E$5
cell G21: =$E$6
cell G22: =$E$7

> **Tip:** You can also type =E5 to enter the formula with a relative reference, press the F4 key to change the cell reference in the formula to $E$5, and then press the Enter key.

8 In **cell G23**, enter the formula **=SUM(G20:G22)**. This formula adds the work study, scholarship, and restaurant income during the summer months.

9 Copy the **range G20:G23** and paste the copied formulas into the **range H20:I23**. The total income is summed for the months of June through August.

Exhibit 15-5 Results of formulas with absolute references

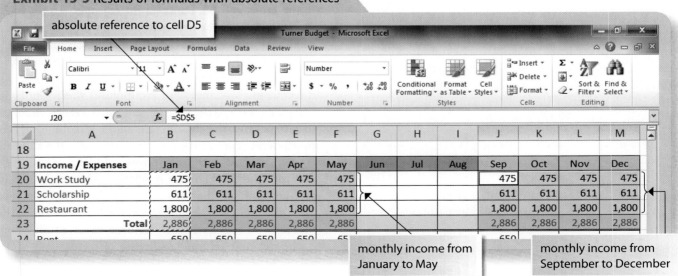

absolute reference to cell D5

monthly income from January to May

monthly income from September to December

Exhibit 15-6 Multiplication table using mixed references

	A	B	C	D	E	F	G
1				Multiplication Table			
2		1	2	3	4	5	
3	1	=$A3*B$2					
4	2						
5	3						
6	4						
7	5						
8							
9							

formula with mixed cell references multiplies the first row by the first column

	A	B	C	D	E	F	G
1				Multiplication Table			
2		1	2	3	4	5	
3	1	=$A3*B$2	=$A3*C$2	=$A3*D$2	=$A3*E$2	=$A3*F$2	
4	2	=$A4*B$2	=$A4*C$2	=$A4*D$2	=$A4*E$2	=$A4*F$2	
5	3	=$A5*B$2	=$A5*C$2	=$A5*D$2	=$A5*E$2	=$A5*F$2	
6	4	=$A6*B$2	=$A6*C$2	=$A6*D$2	=$A6*E$2	=$A6*F$2	
7	5	=$A7*B$2	=$A7*C$2	=$A7*D$2	=$A7*E$2	=$A7*F$2	
8							(Ctrl) ▾
9							

each copied formula multiplies the first row entries by the first column entries

	A	B	C	D	E	F	G
1				Multiplication Table			
2		1	2	3	4	5	
3	1	1	2	3	4	5	
4	2	2	4	6	8	10	
5	3	3	6	9	12	15	
6	4	4	8	12	16	20	
7	5	5	10	15	20	25	
8							(Ctrl) ▾
9							

values returned by each formula

Using Mixed References

A formula can also include cell references that are mixed. A **mixed reference** contains both relative and absolute references. For example, a mixed reference for cell A2 can be either $A2 or A$2. In the mixed reference $A2, the reference to column A is absolute and the reference to row 2 is relative. In the mixed reference A$2, the column reference is relative and the row reference is absolute. As you can see, a mixed reference "locks" one part of the cell reference while the other part can change. When you copy and paste a formula with a mixed reference to a new location, the absolute portion of the cell reference remains fixed and the relative portion shifts.

Exhibit 15-6 shows an example of using mixed references to complete a multiplication table. The first cell in the table, cell B3, contains the formula =$A3*B$2, which multiplies the first column entry (A3) by the first row entry (B2), returning 1. When this formula is copied to another cell, the absolute portions of the cell references remain unchanged and the relative portions of the references change. For example, if the formula is copied to cell E6, the first mixed cell reference changes to $A6 because the column reference is absolute and the row reference is relative, and the second cell reference changes to E$2 because the row reference is absolute and the column reference is relative. The result is that cell E6 contains the formula =$A6*E$2 and returns 16. Other cells in the multiplication table are similarly modified so that each entry returns the multiplication of the row and column headings.

mixed reference A cell reference that contains an absolute row reference or an absolute column reference, such as $A2 or A$2.

When to Use Relative, Absolute, and Mixed References

An important part of effective formula writing is using the correct type of cell reference. Keep in mind the following when choosing whether to use relative, absolute, or mixed cell references:

▶ **Relative references**—Use relative references when you want to repeat the same formula with cells in different locations on your worksheet. Relative references are commonly used when copying a formula that sums a column of numbers or that calculates the cost of several items by multiplying the item cost by the quantity being purchased.

▶ **Absolute references**—Use absolute references when you want different formulas to refer to the same cell. This usually occurs when a cell contains a constant value, such as a tax rate, that will be used in formulas throughout the worksheet.

▶ **Mixed references**—Mixed references are seldom used other than when creating tables of calculated values such as a multiplication table in which the values of the formula or function can be found in the initial rows and columns of the table.

ACTIVITY

Enter formulas with mixed references.

1 Make the **Car Savings Plan worksheet** the active sheet.

2 In **cell B5**, enter =$A5*B$4. This formula uses mixed references to calculate the amount of savings generated by saving $50 per month for 12 months. The calculated value 600 is displayed.

3 Copy the formula in **cell B5** and paste it in the **range B5:G7** to calculate total savings over 12, 24, and 36 months for deposits ranging from $50 to $200 per month.

4 Press the **Esc key** to deselect the range. See Exhibit 15-7.

5 Make the **Budget worksheet** the active sheet.

6 Save the workbook.

LO15.2 Entering Functions

Every function follows a set of rules, or **syntax**, which specifies how the function should be written. The general syntax of all Excel functions is

FUNCTION(argument1,argument2, . . .)

where *FUNCTION* is the name of the function, and *argument1*, *argument2*, and so forth are **arguments**, which are the numbers, text, or cell references used by the function to return a value. Arguments are always separated by a comma.

Not all functions have arguments. Some functions have **optional arguments**, which are not required for the

syntax A set of rules.

argument The numbers, text, or cell references used by a function to return a value.

optional argument An argument that is not required for the function to return a value, but provides more control over how the returned value is calculated.

Exhibit 15-7 Mixed references create a savings plan table

	A	B	C	D			
					B5	fx	=$A5*B$4

formula uses mixed cell references to multiply each column value by each row value

Car Savings Projections

Months	$50	$75	$100	$125	$150	$200
12	$600	$900	$1,200	$1,500	$1,800	$2,400
24	$1,200	$1,800	$2,400	$3,000	$3,600	$4,800
36	$1,800	$2,700	$3,600	$4,500	$5,400	$7,200

Savings Deposit per Month

total amount saved over 12, 24, and 36 months

function to return a value, but can be included to provide more control over how Excel calculates the returned value. If an optional argument is not included, Excel assumes a default value for it. This chapter shows optional arguments within square brackets along with the argument's default value:

FUNCTION(argument1[,argument2=value2, . . .])

In this function, *argument1* is required, *argument2* is an optional argument, and *value2* is the default value used for *argument2*. Optional arguments are always placed last in the argument list.

The hundreds of available Excel functions are organized into the 11 categories described in Exhibit 15-8.

You have already worked with the SUM function, which is one of the most commonly used Math & Trig functions. Exhibit 15-9 describes the SUM function as well as some of the other common Math, Trig, and Statistical functions

Exhibit 15-8 Excel function categories

Category	Description
Cube	Functions that retrieve data from multidimensional databases involving online analytical processing (OLAP)
Database	Functions that retrieve and analyze data stored in databases
Date & Time	Functions that analyze or create date and time values and time intervals
Engineering	Functions that analyze engineering problems
Financial	Functions that have financial applications
Information	Functions that return information about the format, location, or contents of worksheet cells
Logical	Functions that return logical (true-false) values
Lookup & Reference	Functions that look up and return data matching a set of specified conditions from a range
Math & Trig	Functions that have math and trigonometry applications
Statistical	Functions that provide statistical analyses of a set of data
Text	Functions that return text values or evaluate text

Exhibit 15-9 Common Math, Trig, and Statistical functions

Function	Category	Description
AVERAGE(*number1*[,*number2*, *number3*,...])	Statistical	Calculates the average of a collection of numbers, where *number1*, *number2*, and so forth are either numbers or cell references. Only *number1* is required. For more than one cell reference or to enter numbers directly into the function, use the optional arguments *number2*, *number3*, and so forth.
COUNT(*value1*[,*value2*, *value3*,...])	Statistical	Counts how many cells in a range contain numbers, where *value1*, *value2*, and so forth are text, numbers, or cell references. Only *value1* is required. For more than one cell reference or to enter numbers directly into the function, use the optional arguments *value2*, *value3*, and so forth.
COUNTA(*value1*[,*value2*, *value3*,...])	Statistical	Counts how many cells are not empty in ranges *value1*, *value2*, and so forth, or how many numbers are listed within *value1*, *value2*, and so forth.
INT(*number*)	Math & Trig	Displays the integer portion of a number, *number*.
MAX(*number1*[,*number2*, *number3*,...])	Statistical	Calculates the maximum value of a collection of numbers, where *number1*, *number2*, and so forth are either numbers or cell references.
MEDIAN(*number1*[,*number2*, *number3*,...])	Statistical	Calculates the median, or middle, value of a collection of numbers, where *number1*, *number2*, and so forth are either numbers or cell references.
MIN(*number1*[,*number2*, *number3*,...])	Statistical	Calculates the minimum value of a collection of numbers, where *number1*, *number2*, and so forth are either numbers or cell references.
RAND()	Math & Trig	Returns a random number between 0 and 1.
ROUND(*number*,*num_digits*)	Math & Trig	Rounds a number to a specified number of digits, where *number* is the number you want to round and *num_digits* specifies the number of digits to round the number.
SUM(*number1*[,*number2*, *number3*,...])	Math & Trig	Adds a collection of numbers, where *number1*, *number2*, and so forth are either numbers or cell references.

used in workbooks. You can learn about any function using the Help system.

For example, the AVERAGE function calculates the average value from a collection of numbers. The syntax of the AVERAGE function is

AVERAGE(*number1*[,*number2*,*number3*, . . .])

where *number1*, *number2*, *number3*, and so forth are either numbers or cell references to numbers. The following formula uses the AVERAGE function to calculate the average of 1, 2, 5, and 8, returning the value 4:

=AVERAGE(1,2,5,8)

However, functions usually reference values entered in the worksheet. So, if the range A1:A4 contains the values 1, 2, 5, and 8, the following formula also returns 4:

=AVERAGE(A1:A4)

The advantage of using cell references in the function is that the values used for the calculation can be easily changed. The values are also readily apparent to anyone reviewing the worksheet.

Functions can be included as part of larger formulas. For example, the following formula, which includes the MAX function, returns the maximum value from the range A1:A100, and then divides that value by 100:

=MAX(A1:A100)/100

Parentheses Pairs

One challenge of nested functions is to make sure that you include all of the parentheses. You can check this by counting the number of left parentheses, and making sure that number matches the number of right parentheses. Excel will also display each level of nested parentheses in a different color to make it easier to match the opening and closing parentheses in the formula. If the number of parentheses doesn't match, Excel will not accept the formula and will offer a suggestion for rewriting the formula so the number of left and right parentheses does match.

	A	B	C	D	E
1	=INT(SUM(A3:A12)-(SUM(B3:B12)/SUM(C3:C12)))				
2					
3	765	681	215		
4	186	184	275		
5	760	465	721		
6	657	419	194		
7	620	130	486		
8	152	412	481		
9	617	274	202		
10	113	607	243		
11	696	541	271		
12	672	116	554		

Functions provide a quick way to calculate summary data such as the total, average, minimum, and maximum in a collection of values.

Functions can also be placed inside another function, or **nested**. If a formula contains several functions, Excel starts with the innermost function and then moves outward. For example, the following formula first calculates the average of the values in the range A1:A100 using the AVERAGE function, and then extracts the integer portion of that value using the INT function:

=INT(AVERAGE(A1:A100))

Inserting a Function Using the Insert Function Dialog Box

The Insert Function dialog box organizes all of the functions by category and includes a search feature for locating a function that performs a particular calculation. This is helpful when you don't know the category or name of a function. You can open the Insert Function dialog box by clicking the Insert Function button to the left of the formula bar or in the Function Library group on the Formulas tab. If you know the function's category and name, you can select that function by clicking the appropriate category button in the Function Library group on the Formulas tab, and then clicking the function you want.

After you select a function, the Function Arguments dialog box opens, listing all of the arguments associated with that function. Required arguments are in bold type; optional arguments are in normal type. You can click between the Function Arguments dialog box and the worksheet to select ranges to use in the function arguments. As you select a range, the dialog box collapses to show only the selected argument box.

nest To place one item inside another, such as a function.

Searching for a Function in the Insert Function Dialog Box

A simple way to insert a function when you know what you want to do but don't know the function's name is to use the search function in the Insert Function dialog box.

Insert functions using the Insert Function dialog box.

1 Select **cell E10**.

2 To the left of the formula bar, click the **Insert Function button** f_x. The Insert Function dialog box opens with the text in the Search for a function box selected. See Exhibit 15-10.

> **Tip:** To learn more about the function selected in the Select a function box in the Insert Function dialog box, click the Help on this function link.

Exhibit 15-10 Insert Function dialog box

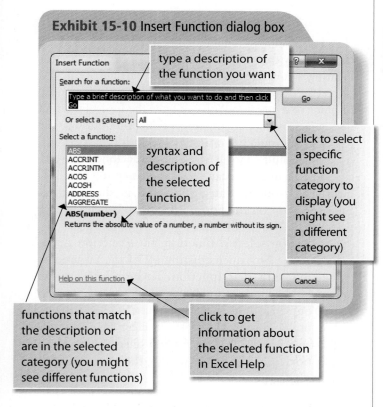

type a description of the function you want

syntax and description of the selected function

click to select a specific function category to display (you might see a different category)

functions that match the description or are in the selected category (you might see different functions)

click to get information about the selected function in Excel Help

3 In the Search for a function box, type **Add numbers** and then click **Go**. A list of the functions used to add numbers appears in the Select a function box.

4 In the Select a function box, click **SUM**. The syntax and a description of the SUM function appear below the Select a function box. See Exhibit 15-11.

Exhibit 15-11 SUM function selected in the Insert Function dialog box

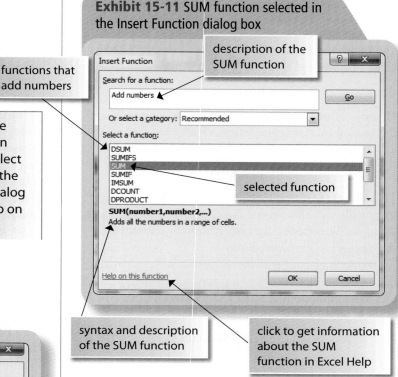

description of the SUM function

functions that add numbers

selected function

syntax and description of the SUM function

click to get information about the SUM function in Excel Help

5 Click **OK**. The Function Arguments dialog box opens, listing all of the arguments associated with the SUM function. The Number1 box shows Excel's best guess of the range you want to sum.

6 Click any cell in the worksheet. The selected cell has a blinking border to indicate it is selected for the formula, and the cell reference appears in the Number1 box in the Function Arguments dialog box.

7 Select the **range B23:M23**. The dialog box collapses to its title bar and the Number1 box as you drag and expands to its full size when you release the mouse button. The range reference, which includes all the monthly income amounts, appears as the value of the Number1 argument. See Exhibit 15-12.

8 Click **OK**. The formula =SUM(B23:M23) is entered in cell E10, which displays 38,574, the estimated total annual income.

9 Select **cell E11**.

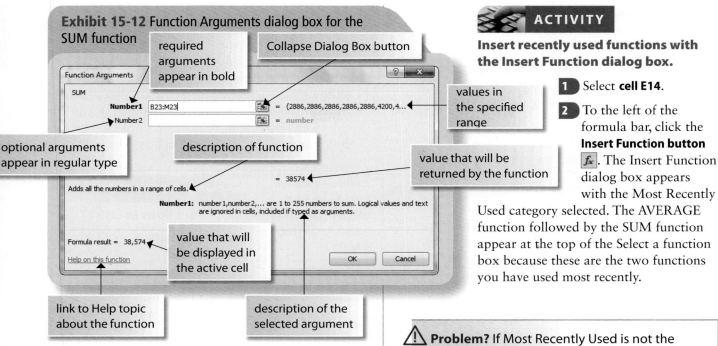

Exhibit 15-12 Function Arguments dialog box for the SUM function

- required arguments appear in bold
- Collapse Dialog Box button
- optional arguments appear in regular type
- description of function
- values in the specified range
- value that will be returned by the function
- value that will be displayed in the active cell
- link to Help topic about the function
- description of the selected argument

Function Arguments

SUM

Number1   B23:M23   = {2886,2886,2886,2886,2886,4200,4...

Number2   = number

    = 38574

Adds all the numbers in a range of cells.

Number1: number1,number2,... are 1 to 255 numbers to sum. Logical values and text are ignored in cells, included if typed as arguments.

Formula result = 38,574

Help on this function   OK   Cancel

10 To the left of the formula bar, click the **Insert Function button** f_x. The Insert Function dialog box opens.

11 In the Search for a function box, type **Calculate an average value** and then click **Go**. Functions for calculating an average appear in the Select a function box.

12 In the Select a function box, click **AVERAGE** if it is not already selected, and then click **OK**. The Function Arguments dialog box appears with the arguments for the AVERAGE function. A range reference for a cell directly above this cell is selected in the Number1 box.

13 Make sure the range reference in the Number1 box is selected, and then select the **range B23:M23** in the worksheet.

14 Click **OK**. The dialog box closes, and the formula =AVERAGE(B23:M23) is entered in cell E11, which displays 3,215—the average monthly income.

Inserting Recently Used Functions

One of the categories available in the Insert Functions dialog box is the Most Recently Used category. This category lists the most recently used functions, sorted in order of recent use, in the Select a function box.

ACTIVITY

Insert recently used functions with the Insert Function dialog box.

1 Select **cell E14**.

2 To the left of the formula bar, click the **Insert Function button** f_x. The Insert Function dialog box appears with the Most Recently Used category selected. The AVERAGE function followed by the SUM function appear at the top of the Select a function box because these are the two functions you have used most recently.

> ⚠ **Problem?** If Most Recently Used is not the current category, click the **Or select a category arrow**, and then click **Most Recently Used**.

3 In the Select a function box, click **SUM**. The Function Arguments dialog box for the SUM function appears.

4 Click **OK**, and then scroll the worksheet to display the **range B32:M32**.

5 In the worksheet, select the **range B32:M32**. The range with the estimated monthly expenses appears in the Number1 box.

> **Tip:** You can also click the Collapse Dialog Box button to shrink the Function Arguments dialog box to see more of the worksheet, select the range, and then click the Expand Dialog Box button to restore the dialog box.

6 In the Function Arguments dialog box, click **OK**. The formula =SUM(B32:M32) is inserted in cell E14, which displays 34,310—total projected expenses for the upcoming year.

7 Select **cell E15**.

8 Open the **Insert Function dialog box**. Make sure **Most Recently Used** is the selected category.

9 In the Select a function box, click **AVERAGE**, and then click **OK**.

10 Select the **range B32:M32** in the worksheet to insert the range reference B32:M32 in the Number1 box.

11 Click **OK**. The formula =AVERAGE(B32:M32) is entered in cell E15, displaying 2,859—estimated average expenses per month. See Exhibit 15-13.

Exhibit 15-13 Total annual and average monthly income and expenses

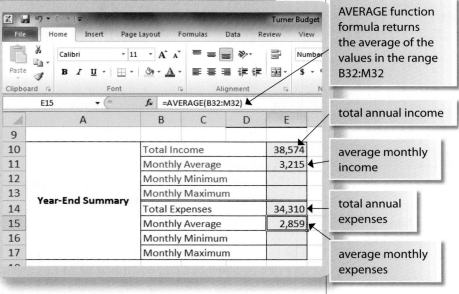

the function name does not need to be selected; you can double-click any function name to insert that function in the cell without typing the rest of its name.

The active cell includes a formula with the selected function name and the opening parenthesis. A Screen-Tip shows the function's syntax with the first argument in bold. You can either select a cell or range, or type the appropriate reference or argument. When the function is complete, you enter it into the cell as usual.

ACTIVITY

Type functions in cells.

1 Select **cell E12**.

2 Type **=M**. As you type a formula, a list with function names starting with the letter M opens.

3 Type **I**. The list shows only those functions starting with the letters MI.

4 Click **MIN** to select the name of the function you want to use. A ScreenTip appears, describing the selected function. See Exhibit 15-14.

Typing a Function in a Cell

After you become familiar with a function, it can be faster to type the function directly in a cell rather than using the Insert Function dialog box. As with any formula, first type = (an equal sign). Then start typing the function name. As you type, a list of functions that begin with the letters you typed appears. For example, when you type S, the list shows all of the functions starting with the letter *S*; when you type SU, the list shows only those functions starting with the letters *SU*, and so forth. This helps to ensure that you are entering a legitimate Excel function name. If you don't know what a specific function does, you can select the function to display a ScreenTip with a description of that function. To insert a function in the active cell, double-click its function name. Note that

Exhibit 15-14 Function names list

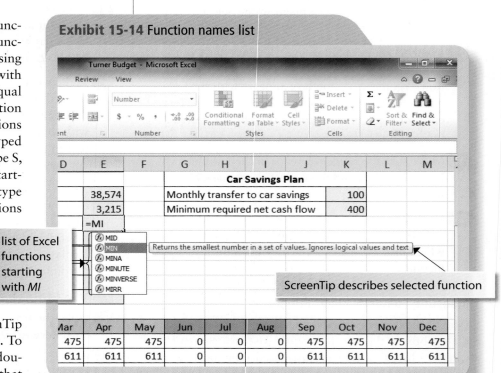

5 Double-click **MIN**. The MIN function with its opening parenthesis is inserted into cell E12 and a Screen-Tip shows the syntax for the function. At this point, you can either type in the range reference or select the range with your mouse. See Exhibit 15-15.

Exhibit 15-15 ScreenTip with the function syntax

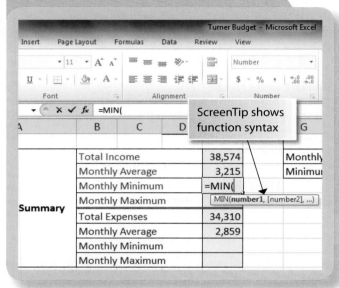

6 Select the **range B23:M23**. The range reference is added to the formula.

> **Tip:** To avoid typing errors, it's often better to use your mouse to enter range references.

7 Type **)** (the closing parenthesis), and then press the **Enter key**. The formula =MIN(B23:M23) is entered in cell E12, which displays 2,886—the lowest estimated income for any month of the year.

8 In **cell E16**, enter the formula **=MIN(B32:M32)**. Cell E16 displays 1,310—the lowest estimated expenses for any month of the year.

9 In **cell E13**, enter the formula **=MAX(B23:M23)**. Cell E13 displays 4,200—the highest estimated income for any month.

> ⚠ **Problem?** If #NAME? appears in the cell, you probably mistyped the function name. Edit the formula to correct the misspelling.

10 In **cell E17**, enter the formula **=MAX(B32:M32)**. Cell E17 displays 9,000—the highest estimated expenses for any month. See Exhibit 15-16.

Exhibit 15-16 Year-end summary values

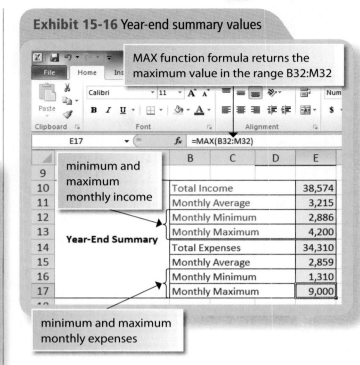

minimum and maximum monthly income

minimum and maximum monthly expenses

Editing Data Used in Formulas

Formulas provide the greatest flexibility for working with data that changes. By entering data values in cells and then referencing those cells in formulas, you can quickly change a value and immediately see the new formula results.

 **ACTIVITY**

Edit data used in a formula.

1 In **cell D5**, enter **655**.

2 Confirm that the monthly income for work study in January through May and September through December has been updated.

3 Review how the year-end summary data has changed. See Exhibit 15-17.

4 Save the workbook.

Be sure to end all of the functions with a closing parenthesis) to ensure that Excel interprets the formula correctly.

Exhibit 15-17 Revised income projection

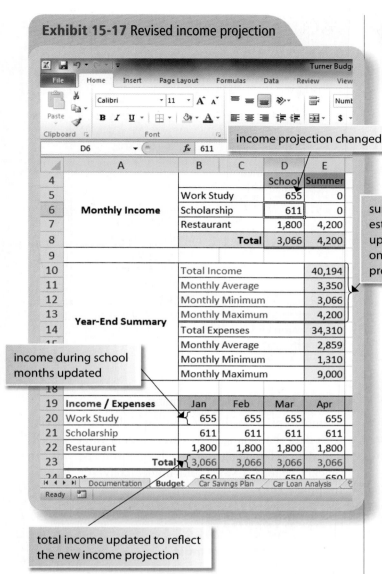

income projection changed

income during school months updated

summary estimates updated based on new income projection

total income updated to reflect the new income projection

	A	B	C	D	E
4				School	Summer
5		Work Study		655	0
6	**Monthly Income**	Scholarship		611	0
7		Restaurant		1,800	4,200
8			Total	3,066	4,200
9					
10		Total Income			40,194
11		Monthly Average			3,350
12		Monthly Minimum			3,066
13	**Year-End Summary**	Monthly Maximum			4,200
14		Total Expenses			34,310
15		Monthly Average			2,859
16		Monthly Minimum			1,310
17		Monthly Maximum			9,000
18					
19	**Income / Expenses**	Jan	Feb	Mar	Apr
20	Work Study	655	655	655	655
21	Scholarship	611	611	611	611
22	Restaurant	1,800	1,800	1,800	1,800
23	Total	3,066	3,066	3,066	3,066
24	Rent	650	650	650	650

LO15.3 Using AutoFill

AutoFill copies content and formats from a cell or range into an adjacent cell or range. The cell contents can be text, values, or formulas. AutoFill can also extend a series of numbers, patterned text, and dates into the adjacent selection.

AutoFill An Excel feature that copies content and formats from a cell or range into an adjacent cell or range.

fill handle A box in the lower-right corner of a selected cell or range that you drag over an adjacent cell or range to copy the content and formatting from the original cells into the adjacent range.

Enter a formula to calculate net cash flow.

1 In **cell B33**, enter **=B23–B32**. This formula subtracts total expenses from total income for January. The resulting −5,934 indicates a projected shortfall of $5,934 for January, due to the cost of tuition and books that occur in that month.

> **Tip:** Net cash flow is equal to the amount of money earned after paying expenses.

2 Apply conditional formatting to **cell B33** to highlight the cell with a **yellow fill with dark yellow text** if the value in the cell is **less than 0**. When you copy the formula and formatting to the rest of the budget, months with negative cash flow will be highlighted on the worksheet. See Exhibit 15-18.

Exhibit 15-18 January net cash flow

January net cash flow equals income (cell B23) minus expenses (cell B32)

	A	B	C	
18				
19	**Income / Expenses**	Jan	Feb	Mar	Apr
20	Work Study	655	655	655	6
21	Scholarship	611	611	611	6
22	Restaurant	1,800	1,800	1,800	1,8
23	Total	3,066	3,066	3,066	3,0
24	Rent	650	650	650	6
25	Food	275	275	275	2
26	Utilities	115	105	90	
27	Phone/Internet	110	110	110	1
28	Clothes	50	50	50	
29	Tuition	6,575	0	0	
30	Books & Supplies	1,005	0	0	
31	Travel/Entertainment	220	160		
32	Total	9,000	1,350		
33	Net Cash Flow	-5,934			

conditional formatting highlights the negative cash flow (less than 0) for January

Using the Fill Handle

After you select a cell or range, the **fill handle** appears in the lower-right corner of the selection. When you drag the fill handle over an adjacent range, AutoFill copies

Although you could copy and paste the formula and formatting from one cell into another cell or range, as you have done before, AutoFill is faster.

the content and formats from the original cell into the adjacent range. This process is often more efficient than the two-step process of copying and pasting.

 **ACTIVITY**

Use the fill handle.

1 Make sure **cell B33** is the active cell. The fill handle appears in the lower-right corner of the cell.

2 Point to the **fill handle** in the lower-right corner of the cell. The pointer changes to ✚.

3 Click the **fill handle** and drag over the **range C33:M33**. A dotted outline appears around the selected range.

4 Release the mouse button. The selected range is filled with the formula and conditional formatting from cell B33, and the Auto Fill Options button 🔳 appears in the lower-right corner of the selected cells. See Exhibit 15-19.

5 Review the monthly net cash flows to confirm that AutoFill correctly copied the formula and conditional formatting into the selected range. These calculations provide a picture of how the net cash flow varies from month to month. Only in January and August, when tuition payments are due, do expenses exceed income.

> ⚠ **Problem?** If the formula and formatting are copied into the wrong range, click the **Undo button** ↩ on the Quick Access Toolbar and try again.

6 In **cell B36**, enter **=J5** to retrieve the balance in the main savings account at the beginning of the year.

7 In **cell B37**, enter **=B23** to retrieve the January income. The relative reference will change when you copy the formula to other months.

Exhibit 15-19 Formulas and formatting pasted with AutoFill

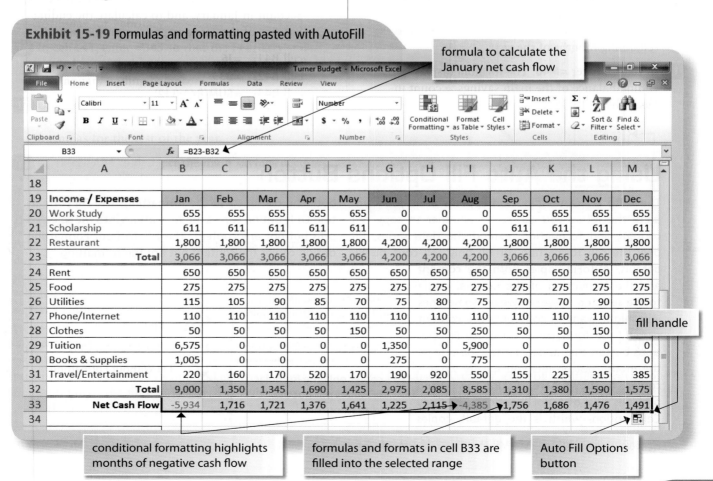

formula to calculate the January net cash flow

B33   =B23-B32

	A	B	C	D	E	F	G	H	I	J	K	L	M
18													
19	**Income / Expenses**	**Jan**	**Feb**	**Mar**	**Apr**	**May**	**Jun**	**Jul**	**Aug**	**Sep**	**Oct**	**Nov**	**Dec**
20	Work Study	655	655	655	655	655	0	0	0	655	655	655	655
21	Scholarship	611	611	611	611	611	0	0	0	611	611	611	611
22	Restaurant	1,800	1,800	1,800	1,800	1,800	4,200	4,200	4,200	1,800	1,800	1,800	1,800
23	**Total**	3,066	3,066	3,066	3,066	3,066	4,200	4,200	4,200	3,066	3,066	3,066	3,066
24	Rent	650	650	650	650	650	650	650	650	650	650	650	650
25	Food	275	275	275	275	275	275	275	275	275	275	275	275
26	Utilities	115	105	90	85	70	75	80	75	70	70	90	105
27	Phone/Internet	110	110	110	110	110	110	110	110	110	110	110	110
28	Clothes	50	50	50	50	150	50	50	250	50	50	150	
29	Tuition	6,575	0	0	0	0	1,350	0	5,900	0	0	0	0
30	Books & Supplies	1,005	0	0	0	0	275	0	775	0	0	0	0
31	Travel/Entertainment	220	160	170	520	170	190	920	550	155	225	315	385
32	**Total**	9,000	1,350	1,345	1,690	1,425	2,975	2,085	8,585	1,310	1,380	1,590	1,575
33	**Net Cash Flow**	-5,934	1,716	1,721	1,376	1,641	1,225	2,115	-4,385	1,756	1,686	1,476	1,491
34													

fill handle

conditional formatting highlights months of negative cash flow

formulas and formats in cell B33 are filled into the selected range

Auto Fill Options button

Exhibit 15-23 AutoFill applied to values, dates and times, and patterned text

Type	Initial pattern	Extended series
Values	1, 2, 3	4, 5, 6, …
	2, 4, 6	8, 10, 12, …
Dates and times	Jan	Feb, Mar, Apr, …
	January	February, March, April, …
	15-Jan, 15-Feb	15-Mar, 15-Apr, 15-May, …
	12/30/2013	12/31/2013, 1/1/2014, 1/2/2014, …
	12/31/2013, 1/31/2014	2/28/2014, 3/31/2014, 4/30/2014, …
	Mon	Tue, Wed, Thu, …
	Monday	Tuesday, Wednesday, Thursday, …
	11:00AM	12:00PM, 1:00PM, 2:00PM, …
Patterned text	1st period	2nd period, 3rd period, 4th period, …
	Region 1	Region 2, Region 3, Region 4, …
	Quarter 3	Quarter 4, Quarter 1, Quarter 2, …
	Qtr3	Qtr4, Qtr1, Qtr2, …

ACTIVITY

Use AutoFill to enter a series.

1 In **cell B35**, enter **Jan**. This is the first value in the series. Because "Jan" is a common abbreviation for January, Excel recognizes it as a month and you don't need to type "Feb" for the next month in the series.

2 Select **cell B35** if it is not the active cell.

Creating a Series with a Complex Pattern

For more complex patterns, you can use the Series dialog box. To do so, enter the first value of the series in a worksheet cell, select the entire range that will contain the series, click the Fill button in the Editing group on the Home tab, and then click Series. The Series dialog box opens. You can use the Series dialog box to specify a linear or growth series for numeric values; a Date series for dates that increase by day, weekday, month, or year; or an AutoFill series for patterned text. With numeric values, you can also specify the step value (indicating how much each numeric value increases over the previous entry) and a stop value (to specify the endpoint for the entire series).

3 Drag the **fill handle** over the **range C35:M35**. As you drag the fill handle, ScreenTips show the month abbreviations for the selected cell.

4 Release the mouse button. AutoFill enters the three-letter abbreviations for each remaining month of the year.

5 Use the Format Painter to copy the formatting from the **range B19:M19** to the **range B35:M35**.

Tip: You can click cell B35 to apply the copied formatting to all cells in the range B35:M35.

6 Deselect the range. See Exhibit 15-24.

7 Save the workbook.

Exhibit 15-24 Month series completed with AutoFill

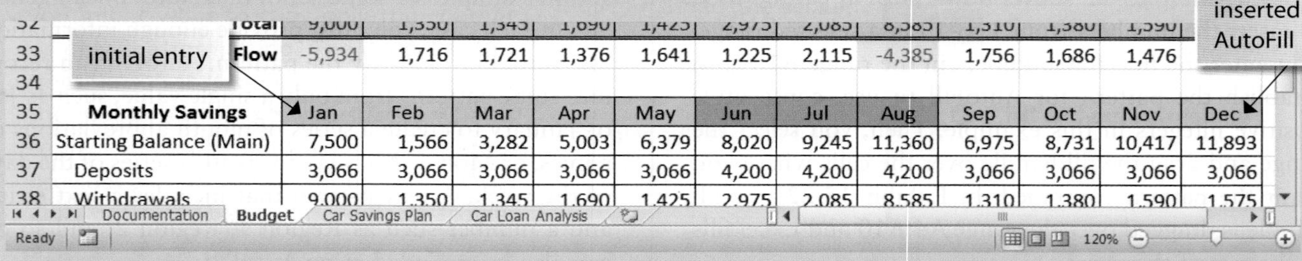

month abbreviations inserted with AutoFill

		Total	9,000	1,350	1,345	1,690	1,425	2,975	2,085	8,585	1,310	1,380	1,590
33	initial entry	Flow	-5,934	1,716	1,721	1,376	1,641	1,225	2,115	-4,385	1,756	1,686	1,476
34													
35	**Monthly Savings**		Jan	Feb	Mar	Apr	May	Jun	Jul	Aug	Sep	Oct	Nov	Dec
36	Starting Balance (Main)		7,500	1,566	3,282	5,003	6,379	8,020	9,245	11,360	6,975	8,731	10,417	11,893
37	Deposits		3,066	3,066	3,066	3,066	3,066	4,200	4,200	4,200	3,066	3,066	3,066	3,066
38	Withdrawals		9,000	1,350	1,345	1,690	1,425	2,975	2,085	8,585	1,310	1,380	1,590	1,575

Documentation | Budget | Car Savings Plan | Car Loan Analysis

Ready   120%

Although you could copy and paste the formula and formatting from one cell into another cell or range, as you have done before, AutoFill is faster.

the content and formats from the original cell into the adjacent range. This process is often more efficient than the two-step process of copying and pasting.

ACTIVITY

Use the fill handle.

1 Make sure **cell B33** is the active cell. The fill handle appears in the lower-right corner of the cell.

2 Point to the **fill handle** in the lower-right corner of the cell. The pointer changes to **✚**.

3 Click the **fill handle** and drag over the **range C33:M33**. A dotted outline appears around the selected range.

4 Release the mouse button. The selected range is filled with the formula and conditional formatting from cell B33, and the Auto Fill Options button 🔡 appears in the lower-right corner of the selected cells. See Exhibit 15-19.

5 Review the monthly net cash flows to confirm that AutoFill correctly copied the formula and conditional formatting into the selected range. These calculations provide a picture of how the net cash flow varies from month to month. Only in January and August, when tuition payments are due, do expenses exceed income.

⚠ **Problem?** If the formula and formatting are copied into the wrong range, click the **Undo button** 🔄 on the Quick Access Toolbar and try again.

6 In **cell B36**, enter **=J5** to retrieve the balance in the main savings account at the beginning of the year.

7 In **cell B37**, enter **=B23** to retrieve the January income. The relative reference will change when you copy the formula to other months.

Exhibit 15-19 Formulas and formatting pasted with AutoFill

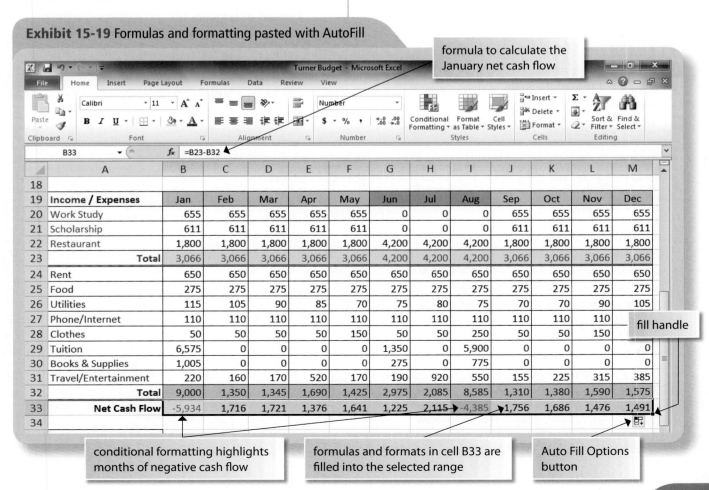

formula to calculate the January net cash flow

conditional formatting highlights months of negative cash flow

formulas and formats in cell B33 are filled into the selected range

Auto Fill Options button

8 In **cell B38**, enter **=B32** to retrieve the January expenses. The relative reference will change when you copy the formula to other months. You'll leave cell B39 blank because, at this point, you won't assume that any money will be transferred from the main savings account to the car savings account.

9 In **cell B40**, enter **=B36+B37−B38−B39**. This formula calculates the ending balance for the main savings account, which is equal to the starting balance plus any deposits minus the withdrawals and transfers. Cell B40 displays 1,566, which is the projected balance in the main savings account at the end of January. See Exhibit 15-20.

10 Select the **range B36:B40**, and then drag the fill handle over the **range C36:C40** to calculate the February savings.

11 Change the formula in **cell C36** to **=B40** so that the February starting balance for the main savings account is based on the January ending balance.

12 Select the **range C36:C40**, and then drag the fill handle over the **range D36:M40**. The formulas and formatting from February are copied into the remaining months of the year.

13 In **cell K5**, enter **=M40**. The formula displays the ending balance of the main savings account in December—13,384.

Exhibit 15-20 January savings

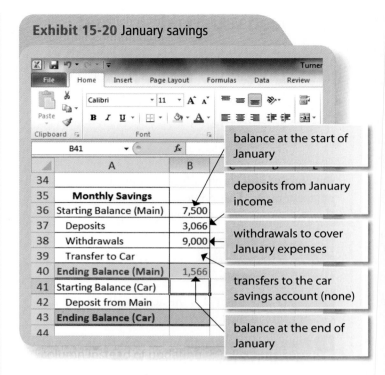

14 Enter the following formulas to retrieve the starting balance for the car savings account (0) and the amount that will be transferred to the car savings account in January, and to calculate the ending balance of the car savings account for January:

cell B41: **=J6**

cell B42: **=B39**

cell B43: **=SUM(B41:B42)**

Using the Auto Fill Options Button

The Auto Fill Options button appears after you complete the fill so you can select whether to copy cell content and formatting, extend the data series, fill only the cell formatting, or fill only cell content. By default, AutoFill copies both the content and the formatting of the original range to the selected range. However, sometimes you might want to copy only the content or only the formatting. The Auto Fill Options button that appears after you release the mouse button lets you specify what is copied. As shown here, clicking this button provides a list of AutoFill options. The Copy Cells option, which is the default, copies both the content and the formatting. The Fill Formatting Only option copies the formatting into the selected cells but not any content. The Fill Without Formatting option copies the content but not the formatting.

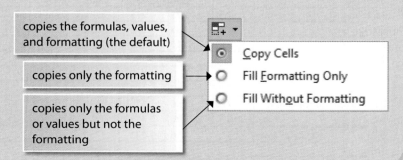

Exhibit 15-21 January through December savings

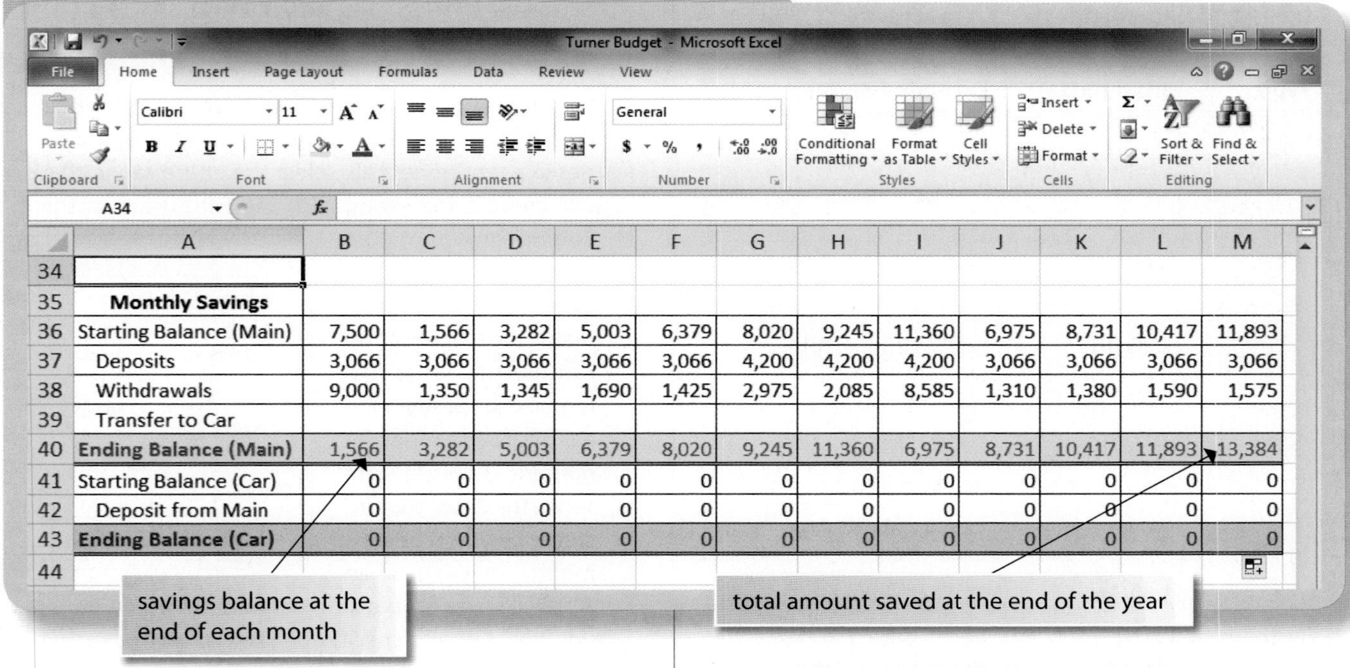

	A	B	C	D	E	F	G	H	I	J	K	L	M
34													
35	**Monthly Savings**												
36	Starting Balance (Main)	7,500	1,566	3,282	5,003	6,379	8,020	9,245	11,360	6,975	8,731	10,417	11,893
37	Deposits	3,066	3,066	3,066	3,066	3,066	4,200	4,200	4,200	3,066	3,066	3,066	3,066
38	Withdrawals	9,000	1,350	1,345	1,690	1,425	2,975	2,085	8,585	1,310	1,380	1,590	1,575
39	Transfer to Car												
40	**Ending Balance (Main)**	1,566	3,282	5,003	6,379	8,020	9,245	11,360	6,975	8,731	10,417	11,893	13,384
41	Starting Balance (Car)	0	0	0	0	0	0	0	0	0	0	0	0
42	Deposit from Main	0	0	0	0	0	0	0	0	0	0	0	0
43	**Ending Balance (Car)**	0	0	0	0	0	0	0	0	0	0	0	0
44													

savings balance at the end of each month

total amount saved at the end of the year

15 Use the fill handle to copy the formulas from the **range B41:B43** into the **range C41:C43** to enter the formulas for February.

16 In **cell C41**, enter **=B43** so that the February starting balance for the car savings account is equal to the January ending balance.

17 Use the fill handle to copy the formulas from the **range C41:C43** into the **range D41:M43** to enter the formulas for the rest of the year.

18 Click **cell A34** to deselect the main savings account data. See Exhibit 15-21.

Creating a Series

AutoFill can also be used to create a series of numbers, dates, or text based on a pattern. To create a series of numbers, you enter the initial values in the series in a selected range and then use AutoFill to complete the series. Exhibit 15-22 shows how AutoFill can be used to insert the numbers from 1 to 10 in a selected range. You enter the first few numbers in the range A1:A3 to establish the pattern for AutoFill to use, consecutive positive integers in this example. Then, you select the range and drag the fill handle over the cells where you want the pattern continued. In Exhibit 15-22, the fill handle is dragged over the range A4:A10 and Excel fills in the rest of the series.

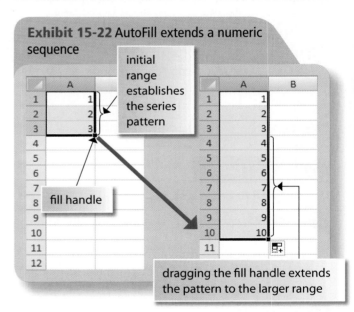

Exhibit 15-22 AutoFill extends a numeric sequence

initial range establishes the series pattern

fill handle

dragging the fill handle extends the pattern to the larger range

AutoFill can extend a wide variety of series, including dates and times and patterned text. Exhibit 15-23 shows examples of some series that AutoFill can generate. In each case, you must provide enough information for AutoFill to identify the pattern. AutoFill can recognize some patterns from only a single value, such as Jan or January to create a series of month abbreviations or names, or Mon or Monday to create a series of the days of the week. A text pattern that includes a text string and a number such as Region 1, Region 2, and so on can also be extended using AutoFill.

Exhibit 15-23 AutoFill applied to values, dates and times, and patterned text

Type	Initial pattern	Extended series
Values	1, 2, 3	4, 5, 6, ...
	2, 4, 6	8, 10, 12, ...
Dates and times	Jan	Feb, Mar, Apr, ...
	January	February, March, April, ...
	15-Jan, 15-Feb	15-Mar, 15-Apr, 15-May, ...
	12/30/2013	12/31/2013, 1/1/2014, 1/2/2014, ...
	12/31/2013, 1/31/2014	2/28/2014, 3/31/2014, 4/30/2014, ...
	Mon	Tue, Wed, Thu, ...
	Monday	Tuesday, Wednesday, Thursday, ...
	11:00AM	12:00PM, 1:00PM, 2:00PM, ...
Patterned text	1st period	2nd period, 3rd period, 4th period, ...
	Region 1	Region 2, Region 3, Region 4, ...
	Quarter 3	Quarter 4, Quarter 1, Quarter 2, ...
	Qtr3	Qtr4, Qtr1, Qtr2, ...

Creating a Series with a Complex Pattern

For more complex patterns, you can use the Series dialog box. To do so, enter the first value of the series in a worksheet cell, select the entire range that will contain the series, click the Fill button in the Editing group on the Home tab, and then click Series. The Series dialog box opens. You can use the Series dialog box to specify a linear or growth series for numeric values; a Date series for dates that increase by day, weekday, month, or year; or an AutoFill series for patterned text. With numeric values, you can also specify the step value (indicating how much each numeric value increases over the previous entry) and a stop value (to specify the endpoint for the entire series).

ACTIVITY

Use AutoFill to enter a series.

1 In **cell B35**, enter **Jan**. This is the first value in the series. Because "Jan" is a common abbreviation for January, Excel recognizes it as a month and you don't need to type "Feb" for the next month in the series.

2 Select **cell B35** if it is not the active cell.

3 Drag the **fill handle** over the **range C35:M35**. As you drag the fill handle, ScreenTips show the month abbreviations for the selected cell.

4 Release the mouse button. AutoFill enters the three-letter abbreviations for each remaining month of the year.

5 Use the Format Painter to copy the formatting from the **range B19:M19** to the **range B35:M35**.

> **Tip:** You can click cell B35 to apply the copied formatting to all cells in the range B35:M35.

6 Deselect the range. See Exhibit 15-24.

7 Save the workbook.

Exhibit 15-24 Month series completed with AutoFill

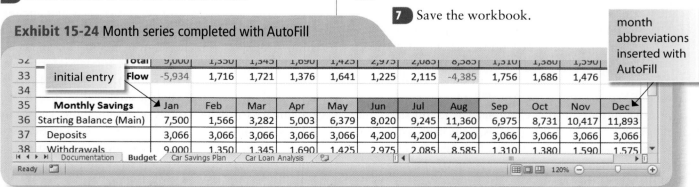

LO15.4 Working with the IF Logical Function

A **logical function** is a function that works with statements that are either true or false. Consider a statement such as *cell A5=3*. If cell A5 is equal to 3, this statement is true; if cell A5 is not equal to 3, this statement is false. Excel supports many different logical functions, one of which is the IF function.

The **IF function** is a logical function that returns one value if a statement is true and returns a different value if that statement is false. The syntax of the IF function is

IF(*logical_test*[,*value_if_true*]
[,*value_if_false*])

where *logical_test* is a statement that is either true or false, *value_if_true* is the value returned by the IF function if the statement is true, and *value_if_false* is the value returned by the function if the statement is false. For example, the following formula tests whether the value in cell A1 is equal to the value in cell B1. If it is, the formula returns 100; otherwise, it returns 50.

=IF(A1=B1,100,50)

In many cases, however, you will not use values directly in the IF function. The following formula uses cell references, returning the value of cell C1 if A1 equals B1; otherwise, it returns the value of cell C2:

=IF(A1=B1,C1,C2)

The = symbol in these formulas is a comparison operator. A **comparison operator** is a symbol that indicates the relationship between two values. Exhibit 15-25 describes the comparison operators that can be used within a logical function.

The IF function also works with text. For example, the following formula tests whether the value of cell A1 is equal to YES. If the value of cell A1 is equal to YES, the formula returns the text DONE; otherwise, it returns the text RESTART.

=IF(A1="YES","DONE","RESTART")

In addition, you can nest other functions inside an IF statement. The following formula first tests whether cell A5 is equal to the maximum of values within the range

Exhibit 15-25 Comparison operators

Operator	Relationship	Example	Description
=	Equal to	A1=B1	Tests whether the value in cell A1 *is equal to* the value in cell B1
>	Greater than	A1>B1	Tests whether the value in cell A1 *is greater than* the value in cell B1
<	Less than	A1<B1	Tests whether the value in cell A1 *is less than* the value in cell B1
>=	Greater than or equal to	A1>=B1	Tests whether the value in cell A1 *is greater than or equal to* the value in cell B1
<=	Less than or equal to	A1<=B1	Tests whether the value in cell A1 *is less than or equal to* the value in cell B1
<>	Not equal to	A1<>B1	Tests whether the value in cell A1 *is not equal to* the value in cell B1

A1:A100. If it is, the formula returns the text "Maximum"; otherwise, it returns no text.

=IF(A5=MAX(A1:A100),"Maximum","")

The following formula determines how much to transfer for the month of January, if cell B33 contains the net cash flow for January, cell K11 contains the minimum net cash flow needed to transfer the money between accounts, and cell K10 contains the amount of money to transfer when the net cash flow meets or exceeds the minimum:

=IF(B33>=$K$11,$K$10,0)

This function tests whether the net cash flow for the month of January (cell B33) is greater than or equal to 400 (cell K11). If it is, the formula returns 100 (in cell K10) as the amount to transfer into the savings account. Otherwise, it returns 0 and no money will be transferred that month.

This logical test uses both relative and absolute references. The B33 reference is relative so you can copy this formula into cells for the remaining months of the

logical function A function that works with statements that are either true or false.

IF function A logical function that tests a condition and then returns one value if the condition is true and another value if the condition is false.

comparison operator A symbol that indicates the relationship between two values.

year. The $K$11 and $K$10 references are absolute so that they always reference the minimum net cash flow specified in cell K11 and the amount to transfer specified in cell K10.

Insert the IF function.

1 Select **cell B39**.

2 On the Ribbon, click the **Formulas tab**. In the Function Library group, click the **Logical button**, and then click **IF** in the list of logical functions. The Function Arguments dialog box for the IF function opens.

3 In the Logical_test box, enter **B33>=$K$11**. This tests whether the net cash flow for January is greater than or equal to the value in cell K11 (400).

4 In the Value_if_true box, enter **$K$10**. If the value in cell B33 is greater than or equal to the value in cell K11, the formula returns the value in cell K10 (100).

> **Tip:** When you type the IF function directly in a cell, remember that the *value_if_true* argument comes before the *value_if_false* argument.

5 In the Value_if_false box, enter **0**. If the value in cell B33 is less than the value in cell K11, the formula returns 0 and no money will be transferred from the main savings account into the car savings account that month. See Exhibit 15-26.

Using Logical Functions to Make Decisions

When creating a budget, it is common to want to transfer money into a savings account when the net cash flow is greater than a predetermined amount. With Excel, you need a formula that can "choose" whether to transfer the funds. You can build this kind of decision-making capability into a formula through the use of a logical function. For example, you can use an IF function for each month to test whether the net cash flow for that month is greater than a certain amount, such as $400. If it is, the IF function can indicate to transfer some of the extra money into a savings account. On the other hand, if the net cash flow is less than the specified amount, no money is transferred.

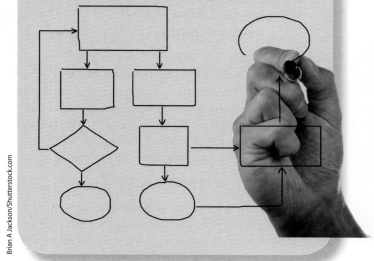

Brian A Jackson/Shutterstock.com

Exhibit 15-26 Function Arguments dialog box for the IF function

test condition that is either true or false → Logical_test B33>=$K$11 = FALSE

value returned if the condition is true → Value_if_true $K$10 = 100 ← amount to transfer to the home account if the value is true

value returned if the condition is false → Value_if_false 0 = 0 ← no money is transferred if the value is false

Checks whether a condition is met, and returns one value if TRUE, and another value if FALSE.

Value_if_false is the value that is returned if Logical_test is FALSE. If omitted, FALSE is returned.

Formula result = 0

Help on this function   OK   Cancel

Using the IF Function to Explore Financial Options

With financial decisions, you will often explore the impact of alternative scenarios on a projected outcome. Budget planning should not be limited to a single budget projection, but instead include several possible budgets. Your decision is then based on the evaluation of these different budgets. The budget you choose should prepare you to deal with shortages in future revenue or ways to take advantage of better-than-expected revenue.

Using Excel to manage your finances allows you to quickly explore these multiple scenarios. You can quickly examine how changing one or more values will affect such outcomes as income, expenses, and cash flow. You can use logical functions such as the IF function to help you explore these what-if scenarios because you can set the outcome of one value only if certain conditions

are met. Different scenarios can be coded with names such as Option1, Option2, and Option3. By using these scenario names as input values to an IF function, you can set up the worksheet to display the results specific to each scenario. In a well-designed workbook, you can quickly switch between scenarios simply by changing a few values in the worksheet.

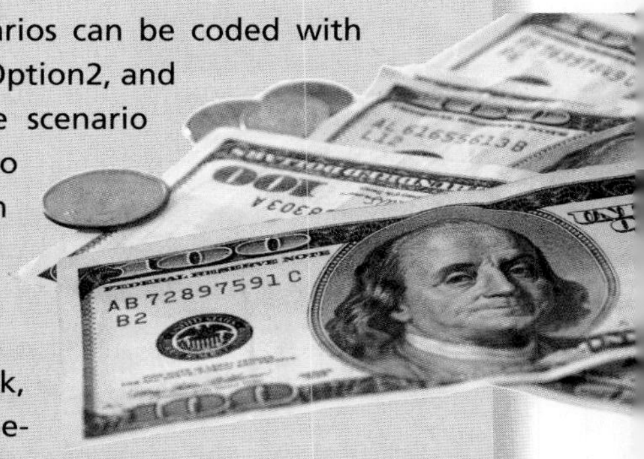

Logical functions help you more easily plan for different outcomes, and avoid the problems associated with unexpected occurrences.

6 Click **OK**. A value of 0 is displayed in cell B39. Because the net cash flow for January is –5,934, no money will be transferred from the main savings account into the car savings account that month.

7 Use the **fill handle** to copy the IF function formula from **cell B39** into the **range C39:M39**. The amounts to transfer are calculated for the remaining

months of the budget, and the car savings account balances are updated based on the results.

8 Click **cell M39** to deselect the range. See Exhibit 15-27.

Changing the Conditions of an IF Function

By using a formula that references the underlying values stored in other cells of the worksheet, it is simple to change a value and quickly see the results of

Exhibit 15-27 Monthly savings account balances

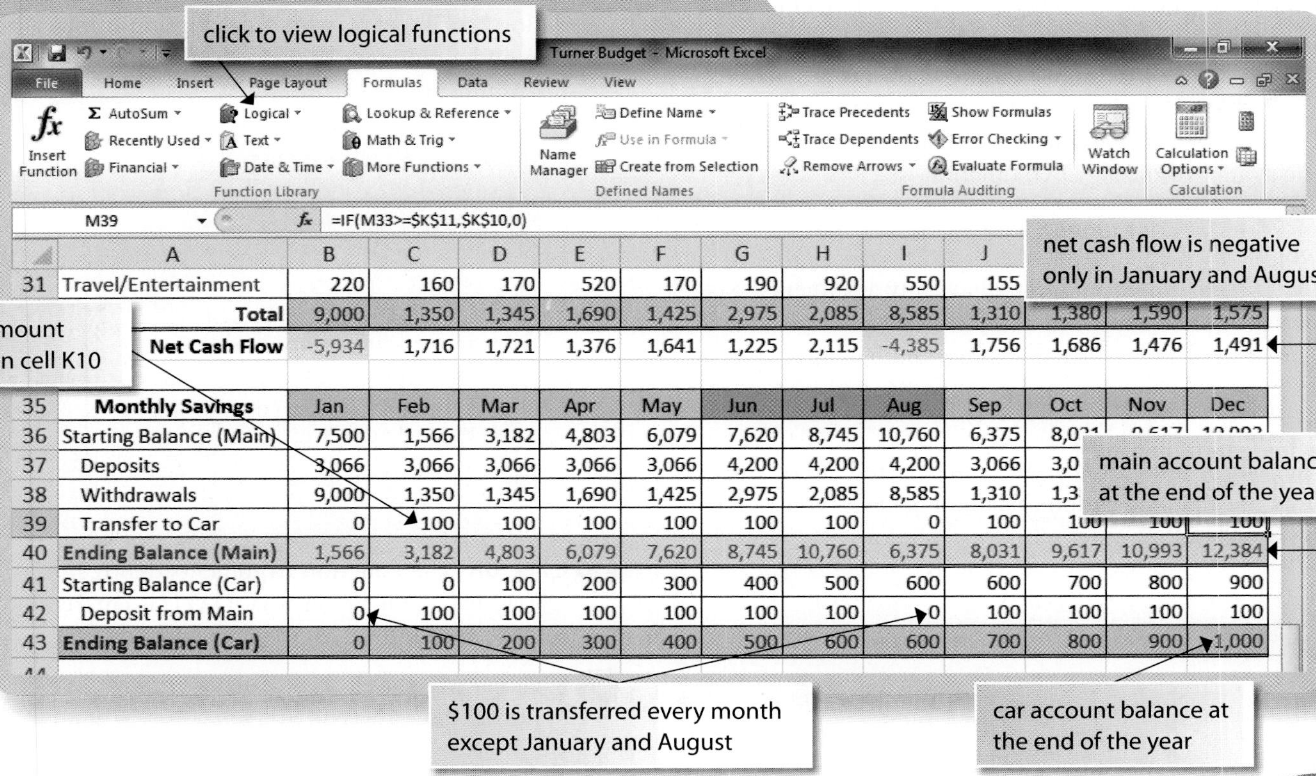

click to view logical functions

Turner Budget - Microsoft Excel

M39 =IF(M33>=$K$11,$K$10,0)

net cash flow is negative only in January and August

transfer amount specified in cell K10

main account balance at the end of the year

	A	B	C	D	E	F	G	H	I	J	K	L	M
31	Travel/Entertainment	220	160	170	520	170	190	920	550	155			
	Total	9,000	1,350	1,345	1,690	1,425	2,975	2,085	8,585	1,310	1,380	1,590	1,575
	Net Cash Flow	-5,934	1,716	1,721	1,376	1,641	1,225	2,115	-4,385	1,756	1,686	1,476	1,491
35	**Monthly Savings**	Jan	Feb	Mar	Apr	May	Jun	Jul	Aug	Sep	Oct	Nov	Dec
36	Starting Balance (Main)	7,500	1,566	3,182	4,803	6,079	7,620	8,745	10,760	6,375	8,031	9,617	10,993
37	Deposits	3,066	3,066	3,066	3,066	3,066	4,200	4,200	4,200	3,066	3,0		
38	Withdrawals	9,000	1,350	1,345	1,690	1,425	2,975	2,085	8,585	1,310	1,3		
39	Transfer to Car	0	100	100	100	100	100	100	0	100	100	100	100
40	**Ending Balance (Main)**	1,566	3,182	4,803	6,079	7,620	8,745	10,760	6,375	8,031	9,617	10,993	12,384
41	Starting Balance (Car)	0	0	100	200	300	400	500	600	600	700	800	900
42	Deposit from Main	0	100	100	100	100	100	100	0	100	100	100	100
43	**Ending Balance (Car)**	0	100	200	300	400	500	600	600	700	800	900	1,000

$100 is transferred every month except January and August

car account balance at the end of the year

that change. This allows you to quickly analyze data and explore other options.

 **ACTIVITY**

Change the conditions of an IF function.

1 In **cell K10**, enter **300**. The end-of-year balance in the car savings account increases to $3,000 (cell K6) while the main savings account balance decreases to $10,384 (cell K5).

2 Scroll down the worksheet and examine how the monthly balance in the main savings account changes throughout the year.

3 In **cell K10**, change the value to **375**. This plan saves $3,750 toward a car.

4 Save the workbook.

LO15.5 Working with Date Functions

A date function is a function that inserts or calculates dates and times. Exhibit 15-28 describes seven date functions supported by Excel. You can use these functions to help with scheduling or to determine on what days of the week certain dates occur.

Perhaps the most commonly used date function is the TODAY function, which returns the current date. The syntax of the TODAY function is:

=TODAY()

The TODAY function doesn't have any arguments. Neither does the NOW function, which returns both the current date and the current time, and has the syntax:

=NOW()

The values returned by the TODAY and NOW functions are updated automatically whenever you reopen the workbook or enter a new calculation.

---

date function A function that inserts or calculates dates and times.

Exhibit 15-28 Date and time functions

Function	Description
DATE(*year,month,day*)	Creates a date value for the date represented by the *year, month,* and *day* arguments
DAY(*date*)	Extracts the day of the month from the *date* value
MONTH(*date*)	Extracts the month number from the *date* value where 1=January, 2=February, and so forth
YEAR(*date*)	Extracts the year number from the *date* value
WEEKDAY(*date*[,*return_type*])	Calculates the day of the week from the *date* value, where 1=Sunday, 2=Monday, and so forth; to choose a different numbering scheme, set the optional *return_type* value to "1" (1=Sunday, 2=Monday, ...), "2" (1=Monday, 2=Tuesday, ...), or "3" (0=Monday, 1=Tuesday, ...)
NOW( )	Displays the current date and time
TODAY( )	Displays the current date

 **ACTIVITY**

Enter a date function.

1 Select **cell F1**.

2 On the Formulas tab, in the Function Library group, click the **Date & Time button**, and then click **TODAY** in the date functions list. The Function Arguments dialog box appears, with a description of the function and a reminder that the TODAY function has no arguments. See Exhibit 15-29.

Tip: If you don't want the date and time to change, you must enter the date and time value directly in the cell.

Exhibit 15-29 Function Arguments dialog box for the TODAY function

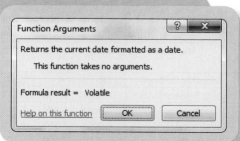

3 Click **OK**. The Function Arguments dialog box closes, and the formula =TODAY() is entered into cell F1. See Exhibit 15-30.

4 Save the workbook.

Exhibit 15-30 TODAY function displays the current date

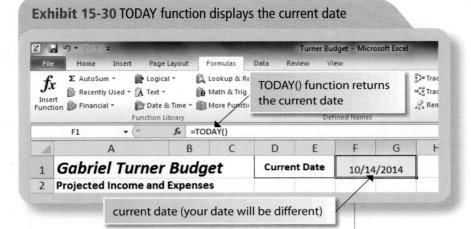

TODAY() function returns the current date

F1 | =TODAY()

	A	B	C	D	E	F	G	H
1	**Gabriel Turner Budget**			Current Date		10/14/2014		
2	Projected Income and Expenses							

current date (your date will be different)

LO15.6 Working with the PMT Financial Function

A **financial function** is a function related to monetary calculations, such as loans and payments. Excel provides a wide range of financial functions. One of these is the **PMT function**, which can be used to calculate a payment schedule required to completely pay back a mortgage or loan. Exhibit 15-31 describes the PMT function and some of the other financial functions often used to develop budgets. These financial functions are the same as those widely used in business and accounting to perform various financial calculations, such as depreciation of an asset, the amount of interest paid on an investment, and the present value of an investment. Payments are expressed as negative numbers because they are treated as expenses.

The cost of a loan to the borrower is largely based on three factors: the principal, the interest, and the time required to pay back the loan. **Principal** is the amount of money being loaned, and **interest** is the amount added to the principal by the lender. You can think of interest as a kind of "user fee" because the borrower is paying for the right to use the lender's money for a period of time. For example, if the bank loans you money to buy a car, you repay the bank for the principal and interest on that loan until the entire amount is repaid. On the other hand, you usually receive interest payments from a bank in return for money deposited in a savings account.

Interest is calculated either as simple interest or as compound interest. In **simple interest**, the interest is equal to a percentage of principal for each period that the money has been lent. For

Exhibit 15-31 Financial functions for loans and investments

Function	Description
FV(*rate,nper,pmt*[*,pv*=0][*,type*=0])	Calculates the future value of an investment, where *rate* is the interest rate per period, *nper* is the total number of periods, *pmt* is the payment in each period, *pv* is the present value of the investment, and *type* indicates whether payments should be made at the end of the period (0) or the beginning of the period (1)
PMT(*rate,nper,pv*[*,fv*=0][*,type*=0])	Calculates the payments required each period on a loan or investment, where *fv* is the future value of the investment
IPMT(*rate,per,nper,pv*[*,fv*=0] [*,type*=0])	Calculates the amount of a loan payment devoted to paying the loan interest, where *per* is the number of the payment period
PPMT(*rate,per,nper,pv*[*,fv*=0] [*,type*=0])	Calculates the amount of a loan payment devoted to paying off the principal of a loan
PV(*rate,nper pmt*[*,fv*=0][*,type*=0])	Calculates the present value of a loan or investment based on periodic, constant payments
NPER(*rate,pmt,pv*[*,fv*=0][*,type*=0])	Calculates the number of periods required to pay off a loan or investment
RATE(*nper,pmt,pv*[*,fv*=0][*,type*=0])	Calculates the interest rate of a loan or investment based on periodic, constant payments

financial function A function related to monetary calculations, such as loans and payments.

PMT function A financial function that calculates the monthly payment required to pay back a loan.

principal The amount of money being loaned.

interest The amount added to the principal by the lender.

simple interest Interest that is equal to a percentage of principal for each period that the money has been lent.

Using Functions to Manage Personal Finances

Excel has many financial functions to manage personal finances. The following list can help you determine which function to use for the most common personal finance problems:

▶ To determine how much an investment will be worth after a series of monthly payments at some future time, use the FV (future value) function.

▶ To determine how much you need to spend each month to repay a loan or mortgage within a set period of time, use the PMT (payment) function.

▶ To determine how much of your monthly loan payment is used to pay the interest, use the IPMT (interest payment) function.

▶ To determine how much of your monthly loan payment is used for repaying the principal, use the PPMT (principal payment) function.

▶ To determine the largest loan or mortgage you can afford given a set monthly payment, use the PV (present value) function.

▶ To determine how long it will take to pay off a loan with constant monthly payments, use the NPER (number of periods) function.

wacpan/Shutterstock.com

example, if you deposit $1,000 at a simple interest rate of 5 percent, you will receive $50 in interest payments each year. After one year, your investment will be worth $1,050; after two years, it will be worth $1,100; and so forth.

With **compound interest**, the interest is applied not only to the principal but also to any accrued interest. For example, if you deposit $1,000 in a bank at 5 percent annual interest compounded every year, you will earn $50 in the first year, raising the value of the account to $1,050. If you leave that money in the bank for another year, the interest payment in the second year rises to 5 percent of $1,050 or $52.50, resulting in a total value of $1,102.50. So you earn more money the second year because you are receiving interest on the interest earned in previous years.

Compound interest payments are divided into the period of time in which the interest is applied. For example, an 8 percent annual interest rate compounded monthly results in 12 interest payments per year with

the interest each month equal to $\frac{1}{12}$ of 8 percent, or about 0.67 percent per month.

Another factor in calculating the cost of a loan is the length of time required to pay it back. The longer it takes to pay back a loan, the more the loan costs because the borrower is paying interest over a longer period of time. To save money, loans should be repaid quickly and in full.

To calculate the costs associated with a loan or mortgage, you need the following information:

• The amount being borrowed

• The annual interest rate

• The number of payment periods per year

• When loan payments are due

• The length of the loan in terms of the number of payment periods

You can use the PMT function to determine the monthly loan payments for a specific amount, such as $10,000 for a car payment. The syntax of the PMT function is

PMT(*rate,nper,pv*[,*fv=0*][,*type=0*])

---

compound interest Interest that is applied not only to the principal but also to any accrued interest.

The PMT function calculates the amount of a monthly loan payment, based on *rate* (the interest rate per month), *nper* (the total number of months to repay the loan), and *pv* (the present value of the loan).

where *rate* is the interest rate for each payment period, *nper* is the total number of payment periods required to pay off the loan, and *pv* is the present value of the loan or the amount that needs to be borrowed.

The PMT function has two optional arguments: *fv* and *type*. The *fv* argument is the future value of the loan. Because the intent with most loans is to pay them off completely, the future value is equal to 0 by default. The *type* argument specifies when the interest is charged on the loan, either at the end of the payment period (*type*=0), which is the default, or at the beginning of the payment period (*type*=1).

For most mortgages and loans, the payment period is one month. This means that the borrower must make a payment on the loan every month, and interest on the loan is compounded every month. Interest

rates are usually presented as an annual interest rate. To determine the interest rate per month, you divide the annual interest rate by 12. For example, if the annual interest rate is 6 percent, the interest rate each month is 6 percent divided by 12, or about 0.5 percent per month.

For example, if a car loan is $20,000, the annual interest rate is 6 percent, and the borrower wants to repay the loan in five years or 60 months (5 years multiplied by 12 months per year), the following formula calculates the monthly payment for the loan:

$$=PMT(0.06/12,5*12,20000)$$

This formula returns a value of −$386.66. The value is negative because the payment is considered an expense, which Excel treats as a negative value. If you want to display this value as a positive number in a worksheet, you must enter a minus sign directly before the PMT function:

$$=-PMT(0.06/12,5*12,20000)$$

Based on these calculations, the borrower would have to pay the bank $386.66 every month for five years before the loan and the interest are completely repaid.

ACTIVITY

Use the PMT function to calculate a monthly payment.

1 Make the **Car Loan Analysis worksheet** the active sheet.

2 In **cell B3**, enter **6**. This is the annual interest rate for the loan.

3 In **cell B4**, enter **12** for the number of payments per year.

4 In **cell B5**, enter the formula **=B3/B4** to calculate the interest per period, which is 0.50 percent per month.

> **Tip:** Be sure to enter the interest rate per month for the Rate argument and not the annual interest rate for any loan or investment that has monthly payments.

5 In **cell B6**, enter **5** for the length of the car loan in years.

6 In **cell B7**, enter the formula **=B4*B6** to calculate the total number of monthly payments, which is 60.

7 In **cell B8**, enter **20000** for the amount of the loan.

Interest Rates

For most loan and investment calculations, you need to enter the annual interest rate divided by the number of times the interest is compounded during the year. If interest is compounded monthly, divide the annual interest rate by 12. If interest is compounded quarterly, divide the annual rate by 4. You must also convert the length of the loan or investment to the number of interest payments per year. If you will make payments monthly, multiply the number of years of the loan or investment by 12.

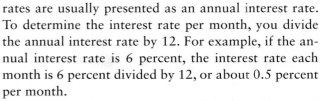

Presenting a Budget

In business, government, and personal lives, budgets play a key role in making sound financial decisions. However, a well-organized budget is only the first step. The budget must also convey information that is easily grasped by your audience or clients. Keep in mind the following guidelines as you work on budget spreadsheets:

▶ **Plan the budget around a few essential goals.**
What is your budget trying to achieve? Be specific and focused.

▶ **Select a few important measures or "bottom lines."**
These items should convey whether the proposed budget will meet your goals. Are you trying to pay off a debt, raise money, or achieve a specific level of savings?

▶ **Create budget projections based on your financial history.**
Search for important trends and take into account other factors such as inflation in your projections.

▶ **Explain the budget results in terms of everyday examples.**
Avoid the temptation of overwhelming your audience with raw facts and figures. Instead, interpret what those facts and figures mean in terms of your bottom line measures.

You want your budget spreadsheet to remain current as new data and projections become available. This means continually updating the budget. But, do not just over-write or delete the old budget spreadsheets. Keep earlier budgets easily accessible so you can access the original assumptions and goals when preparing the next budget. By keeping an audit trail of your past work, you can make your future budgets more accurate and reliable.

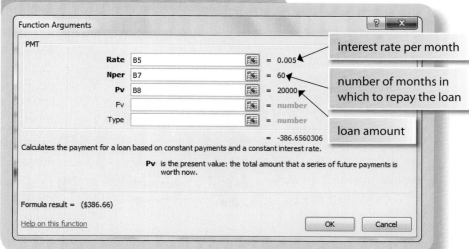

Yuri Arcurs/Shutterstock.com

8. Select **cell B10**.

9. Open the Function Arguments dialog box for the **PMT** function.

10. In the Rate box, enter **B5** to reference the cell with the interest rate per month.

11. In the Nper box, enter **B7** to reference the cell with the total number of monthly payments required to repay the loan.

12. In the Pv box, enter **B8** to reference the cell with the present value of the loan. See Exhibit 15-32.

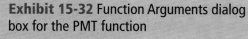

Exhibit 15-32 Function Arguments dialog box for the PMT function

interest rate per month

number of months in which to repay the loan

loan amount

13 Click **OK**. The value $386.66 is displayed in parentheses in cell B10 to indicate a negative currency value. See Exhibit 15-33.

Exhibit 15-33 PMT function used to calculate loan payments

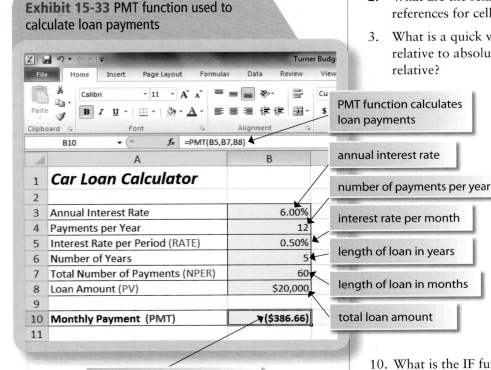

PMT function calculates loan payments

annual interest rate

number of payments per year

interest rate per month

length of loan in years

length of loan in months

total loan amount

monthly payment is negative because it is an expense

Analyze Other Loan Options

Often, when determining loan payments, you will want to consider multiple possibilities. Because you already set up the worksheet, you can quickly try other scenarios without having to reenter any formulas.

ACTIVITY

Analyze other loan options.

1 In **cell B6**, change the value to **3**. The amount of the monthly payment increases to $608.44.

2 In **cell B8**, change the value to **18,000**. For this smaller loan, the monthly payment drops to $547.59 per month.

3 Save the workbook, and then close it.

Quiz Yourself

1. Explain the difference between a relative reference, an absolute reference, and a mixed reference.

2. What are the relative, absolute, and mixed cell references for cell H9?

3. What is a quick way to cycle a cell reference from relative to absolute to mixed and then back to relative?

4. What is the general syntax of all Excel functions?

5. In a function, what is an argument?

6. Describe how to type a function directly in a cell.

7. What is AutoFill?

8. How do you use the fill handle?

9. Describe how to use AutoFill to create a series of numbers.

10. What is the IF function?

11. Write the formula that tests whether the value in cell S2 is equal to the value in cell P7, and then, returns 75 if it is, but returns 150 otherwise.

12. What is a date function?

13. Which date function returns the current date?

14. What is the PMT function?

15. What is the syntax of the PMT function?

16. Most interest rates are presented as an annual interest rate. How do you determine the interest rate per month?

17. Write the formula to determine the monthly payment for a $50,000 loan with an annual interest rate of 4 percent that will be repaid in three years.

18. Why does the PMT function return a negative value? How would you display the value as a positive number in the worksheet?

Practice It

Practice It 15-1

1. Open the data file **Car** located in the Chapter 15\ Practice It folder. Save the workbook as **Car Loan**.

2. In the Documentation worksheet, enter your name in cell B3. Enter the TODAY function in cell B4 to display the current date.

3. Make the Budget worksheet the active sheet. In cell B12, enter **Jan**.

4. In the range B12:M12, use AutoFill to replace the month numbers with the abbreviations Jan through Dec.

5. In cell B19, enter **=SUM(B14:B18)** to use the SUM function to calculate total January expenses in the range B14:B18.

6. In cell B20, enter the formula **=B13−B19** (the total income minus the total expenses) to calculate the net cash flow for January.

7. Use the fill handle to copy the formulas in the range B19:B20 to the range C19:M20.

8. In cell B3, enter **=SUM(B13:M13)** to calculate the total monthly income for the entire year.

9. In cell C3, enter **=AVERAGE(B13:M13)** to calculate the average monthly income for the year.

10. In cell D3, enter **=MAX(B13:M13)** to calculate the maximum monthly income for the year.

11. In cell E3, enter **=MIN(B13:M13)** to calculate minimum monthly income for the year.

12. Select the range B3:E3, and then use AutoFill to copy the formulas in the selected range to the range B4:E10 to complete the Year-End Summary table.

13. Click the Auto Fill Options button, and then click the Fill Without Formatting option button to copy only the formulas and not the formatting into the selected range. Note that cell C8 will show the value #DIV/0!, indicating that Excel cannot calculate the average car payment, because you haven't yet entered any payment values.

14. In the range J3:J8, enter the following data:

cell J3	**6.45%**
cell J4	**12**
cell J5	**=J3/J4**

cell J6   **4**
cell J7   **=J6*12**
cell J8   **15,000**

15. In cell J9, enter **=PMT(J5,J7,J8)** to use the PMT function to calculate the monthly payment required to repay the loan.

16. In cell J9, edit the formula to add a minus sign between the equal sign and the PMT function to make the value returned by the formula positive rather than negative.

17. In the range N3:N8, enter the following data:

cell N3	**5.75%**
cell N4	**12**
cell N5	**=N3/N4**
cell N6	**3**
cell N7	**=N6*12**
cell N8	**15,000**

18. In cell N9, enter the PMT function to calculate the monthly payment to repay this loan. Edit the formula to make the value displayed in the cell positive.

19. In cell L1, enter **1**. The car loan being applied to the budget will be determined by whether 1 or 2 is entered into cell L1.

20. In cell B18, enter **=IF($L$1=1,$J$9,$N$9)** to use the IF function to test whether cell L1 equals 1, and then return the value of cell J9 if it does and the value of cell N9 if it doesn't.

21. Use AutoFill to copy the formula in cell B18 into the range C18:M18. Verify that the values in the range B18:M18 match the monthly payment for car loan 1. (Note that the worksheet will display the monthly payment amount to the nearest dollar.)

22. In cell L1, change the value from 1 to **2**. Verify that the monthly payment for car loan 2 appears in the range B18:M18.

23. Save the workbook, and then close it.

Practice It 15-2

1. Open the data file **Online** located in the Chapter 15\ Practice It folder. Save the workbook as **Online Backup Services**.

2. In the Documentation worksheet, enter your name in cell B3 and enter the TODAY function in cell B4.

3. In the Price Comparison worksheet, use Auto-Fill to enter the labels Month 1, Month 2, and so forth in the range B14:M14 and the range B19:M19.

4. In cell B12, enter a formula that first multiplies the monthly timeframe (cell B5) by the monthly cost (cell B10), and then adds that product to the GB to back up (cell B3) multiplied by the yearly timeframe (cell B4) multiplied by the yearly cost per GB (cell B11), and then adds the setup cost (cell B9). Be sure to use absolute references to cells B3, B4, and B5 so you can copy the formula.

5. Copy the formula in cell B12 to cell F12 and cell J12 to calculate the total cost for vendors 2 and 3. Use the Paste Options button to paste only the formula without any formatting.

6. In cell B15, enter a formula to add the setup cost, the monthly cost, and the GB to back up located in cell B3 multiplied by the Yearly cost per GB for the first vendor. Enter similar formulas in cells B16 and B17 to calculate the Month 1 cost for the first year for the second and third vendors.

7. In the range C15:C17, enter formulas to retrieve the monthly cost for the corresponding vendor. Be sure to use an absolute reference to the cell in each formula so you can copy the formulas.

8. Use AutoFill to copy the formulas in the range C15:C17 to the range D15:M17.

9. In the range B20:B22, enter formulas to add the monthly cost to the GB to back up each year multiplied by yearly cost per GB for the corresponding vendor.

10. In the range C20:C22, enter formulas to retrieve the monthly cost for the corresponding vendor. Be sure to use an absolute reference to the cell in each formula so you can copy the formulas.

11. Use AutoFill to copy the formulas in the range C20:C22 to the range D20:M22.

12. In the range N15:N17;N20:N22, use the SUM function to total the first year and additional year costs for each vendor.

13. In cell F3, calculate the average total cost for the first year. In cell G3, calculate the average total cost for the second year.

14. In cell F4, calculate the maximum total cost for the first year. In cell G4, calculate the maximum total cost for the second year.

15. In cell F5, calculate the minimum total cost for the first year. In cell G5, calculate the minimum total cost for the second year.

16. In cell J3, write an IF function to test whether the total first year cost of vendor 1 (cell N15) is greater than the average first year cost (cell F3); if it is, return the text **"HIGH"**; otherwise, return the text **"LOW"** (use quotation marks around the text you want the formula to return). Be sure to use absolute references as needed so you can copy the formula.

17. In cell K3, write a similar IF function formula for the additional year cost of vendor 1.

18. Use AutoFill to copy the formulas in the range J3:K3 to the range J4:K5. Use the Auto Fill Options button to fill the formulas without formatting.

19. Save the workbook, and then close it.

On Your Own

On Your Own 15-1

1. Open the data file **Clear** located in the Chapter 15\ On Your Own folder. Save the workbook as **Clear Lake Jazz**.

2. In the Documentation worksheet, enter your name in cell B3 and enter the NOW function in cell B4.

3. In the Fundraising worksheet, use AutoFill to enter the three-letter month abbreviations (Jan, Feb, and so on) for each year. For example, for 2013, enter the month abbreviations in the range C12:N12.

4. In the range E3:G9, enter the loan conditions and then use the PMT function to calculate the monthly payment required to repay a $1,000,000 loan (principal) in 30 years at an annual rate of 3.26% that is compounded monthly.

5. Make the value returned by the function positive rather than negative. Format the labels and data appropriately.

6. In cell C16, enter a formula with an absolute reference that retrieves the loan amount you used in the PMT function.

7. For each year, enter a formula with an absolute reference that retrieves the loan payment returned by the PMT function. (*Hint*: Enter the formula for the Loan Payment expense in January 2013, use AutoFill to copy the formula to the remaining months of the year, and then copy that range of formulas to the Loan Payment expense cells for the other two years, being sure to paste only the formula.)

8. For each year, use the SUM function to calculate total income per month and total expenses per month. Use AutoFill and copy and paste as appropriate.

9. In column O, use the SUM function to calculate the total annual income and expense for each entry (individual donations, major donors, grants, loan, total income, construction expenses, loan payments, and total expenses).

10. For each year, enter a formula to calculate the net cash flow per month (monthly total income minus monthly total expenses). Use AutoFill and copy and paste as appropriate.

11. In cell C24, enter a formula that adds the starting cash available (cell C4) and the January net cash flow (cell C23) to calculate the January 2013 cash available.

12. In cell D24, enter a formula that adds the cash available from the previous month and the net cash flow for the current month.

13. Copy the formula in cell D24 to the remaining months of the current year and then copy the 2013 cash available formulas to the other two years. Use AutoFill and copy and paste as appropriate.

14. For 2014 and 2015, edit the January cash available formulas to add the cash available from the previous year to the cash available for the current month.

15. Save the workbook, and then close it.

ADDITIONAL STUDY TOOLS

Chapter 15

IN THE BOOK

▶ Complete end-of-chapter exercises

▶ Study tear-out Chapter Review Card

ONLINE

▶ Complete additional end-of-chapter exercises

▶ Take practice quiz to prepare for tests

▶ Review key term flash cards (online, printable, and audio)

▶ Play "Beat the Clock" and "Memory" to quiz yourself

▶ Watch the videos "Use Relative References in a Formula," "Use Absolute References in a Formula," "Insert Functions Using the Insert Function Dialog Box," "Use AutoFill to Enter a Series" "Insert the IF Function," "Use the PMT Financial Function to Calculate a Monthly Payment," and other concept videos

Inserting and Formatting Charts

Introduction

Charts provide a way to illustrate numbers and demonstrate trends. They are often used in financial reports or numerical analyses to summarize data. Because many people are overwhelmed by tables of numbers, including charts and graphs in reports provides a way to visually demonstrate the numerical data, highlight trends, and show comparisons. Charts are frequently used in financial reports on investments, comparisons of current and past performances, summaries of holdings, and performance records.

In Excel, you can choose from a variety of charts to create the type of chart that best illustrates the data. Each chart can be formatted to highlight specific data and to include chart elements that help others understand the data. Charts can be included on a worksheet or in a chart sheet devoted to that chart. You can also create mini charts that appear near or within cells with data. With all of these options, you can easily develop workbooks and reports that are effectively illustrated with attractive and helpful charts.

Learning Objectives

After studying the material in this chapter, you will be able to:

LO16.1 Create a chart

LO16.2 Work with chart elements

LO16.3 Modify a chart

LO16.4 Create an exploded pie chart

LO16.5 Create a column chart

LO16.6 Create a line chart

LO16.7 Edit chart data

LO16.8 Insert and format sparklines

LO16.9 Insert and modify data bars

LO16.1 Creating a Chart

A **chart**, or **graph**, is a visual representation of a set of data values. Charts show trends or relationships that may not be readily apparent from numbers alone. Charts show trends or relationships in data that are more difficult to see by simply looking at numbers, such as the range of months in which a mutual fund performed exceptionally well.

ACTIVITY

Review chart data.

chart (graph) A visual representation of a set of data values.

1 Open the data file **Minneapolis** located in the Chapter 16\Chapter folder. Save the workbook as **Minneapolis Real Estate**.

When presenting budgets, inventories, invest-ments, or other numerical data to others, charts help the audience to quickly see the trend, distribution, or comparison being demonstrated by the values.

2 In the Documentation worksheet, enter your name in **cell B3** and the date in **cell B4**.

3 Review the contents of each worksheet. The Summary Report worksheet will summa-rize data and facts about Minneapolis real estate. The Historical Prices worksheet lists real estate prices from 2009 through 2013. The Metro Population worksheet lists the populations of Minnesota cities. The Structure Types worksheet shows the breakout of Minneapolis structure types compared to the entire United States. The Population His-tory worksheet shows population changes in Minnesota cities between 1980 and 2010. Much of this numerical data would be easier to understand as charts.

Selecting a Data Source

Each chart has a **data source**, which is the range that contains the data to display in the chart. A data source is a collection of one or more **data series**, which is a range of values that is plotted as a single unit on the chart. After you select a range to use as the chart's data source, Excel uses the first row of the selected range as the series name, the first column as the category values, and the remaining columns as the series values. The **series name**, the first row of the data range, identifies the data series. The first column of the data range contains the **category values**, which are the groups or categories to which the series values belong. The **series values** are the data displayed in the chart. If the data source is organized in rows rather than in columns, the first row contains the category values, the remaining rows contain the data values for each data series, and the first column of each series row contains the series names.

Select the data source for a chart.

1 Make the **Metro Population worksheet** the active sheet.

2 Select the **range A3:B8**. The data source in this range has one data series, named Population. Its category values in the range A4:A8 list the different cities. Its series values in the range B4:B8 contain the data to be charted. See Exhibit 16-1.

Selecting a Chart Type

You can apply a wide variety of chart types to the selected data source. Excel supports 73 built-in charts organized into 11 categories, which are described in Exhibit 16-2. You can also create custom chart types based on the

data source The range that contains the data to display in a chart.

data series A range of values that is plotted as a single unit on a chart.

series name The first row of the data range, which identifies the data series.

category values The first column of the data range, which contains the groups or categories to which the series values belong.

series values The data displayed in the chart.

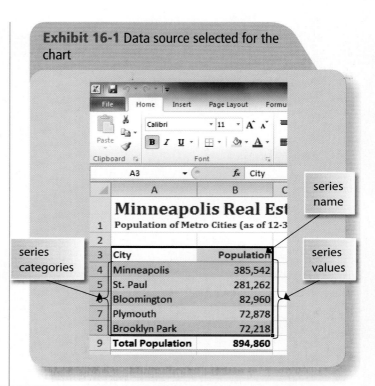

Exhibit 16-1 Data source selected for the chart

Exhibit 16-2 Excel chart types

Chart type	Description
Column	Compares values from different categories. Values are indicated by the height of the columns.
Line	Compares values from different categories. Values are indicated by the height of the line. Often used to show trends and changes over time.
Pie	Compares relative values of different categories to the whole. Values are indicated by the areas of the pie slices.
Bar	Compares values from different categories. Values are indicated by the length of the bars.
Area	Compares values from different categories. Similar to the line chart except that areas under the lines contain a fill color.
Scatter	Shows the patterns or relationship between two or more sets of values. Often used in scientific studies and statistical analyses.
Stock	Displays stock market data, including the high, low, opening, and closing prices of a stock.
Surface	Compares three sets of values in a three-dimensional chart.
Doughnut	Compares relative values of different categories to the whole. Similar to the pie chart except that it can display multiple sets of data.
Bubble	Shows the patterns or relationship between two or more sets of values. Similar to the XY (Scatter) chart except the size of the data marker is determined by a third value.
Radar	Compares a collection of values from several different data sets.

Choosing the Right Chart Type

Excel supports a wide variety of charts. Deciding which type of chart to use requires evaluating the data and determining the ultimate purpose or goal of the chart. Consider how the data will appear with each type of chart before making a final decision.

▶ Pie charts are generally most effective when there are six or fewer slices, when each slice is large enough to view, and when the relative sizes of the different slices can be easily distinguished.

▶ Column or bar charts work well for data that includes more than six categories or whose values are close together.

▶ Line charts are best for categories that follow a sequential order. Be aware, however, that the time intervals must be a constant length if used in a line chart. Line charts will distort data that occurs in irregular time intervals, making it appear that the data values occurred at regular intervals when they did not.

▶ Pie, column, bar, and line charts assume that numbers are plotted against categories. In science and engineering applications, you will often want to plot two numeric values against one another. For that data, use XY scatter charts, which show the patterns or relationship between two or more sets of values. XY scatter charts are also useful for data recorded at irregular time intervals.

▶ If you still can't find the right chart to meet your needs, you can create a custom chart based on the built-in chart types. Third-party vendors also sell software to allow Excel to create charts not built into the software.

cubens 3d/Shutterstock.com

built-in charts. The chart types are available on the Insert tab. After you create a chart, the chart types are available on the Chart Tools Design tab, so you can switch the chart to another chart type at any point.

You should select the type of chart that best represents the data. For example, a pie chart provides the best way to show the breakout of the asset data you selected. A **pie chart** is a chart in the shape of a circle (like a pie) that shows data values as a percentage of the whole. Each value in the data series represents a slice of the pie. The larger the value, the larger the pie slice. When you chart the population data, each slice will represent the percentage of the total population from each of the five metro cities in Minnesota. The data source for a pie chart should include only the category labels and data values, and not row or column totals, because Excel will treat those totals as another category to be graphed. In this case, you will not include the Total Population row as part of the data source, because it is not a population category and should not be included in a pie chart.

When you create or select a chart, three Chart Tools tabs appear on the Ribbon. The Design, Layout, and Format tabs provide additional commands for working with the chart's content and appearance. On the Design tab, you set the chart's overall design. On the Layout tab, you work with individual elements of the chart, such as the chart's title. On the Format tab, you can change the appearance of graphic shapes found in the chart, such as the chart's border or markers placed in the chart. When you select a cell or another object that is not a chart, the Chart Tools tabs disappear until you reselect the chart.

ACTIVITY

Insert a pie chart.

1 On the Ribbon, click the **Insert tab**.

2 In the Charts group, click the **Pie button**. The Pie charts gallery opens. See Exhibit 16-3.

> Each slice in a pie chart is a different size based on its value in the data series.

pie chart A chart in the shape of a circle (like a pie) that shows data values as a percentage of the whole.

Exhibit 16-3 Pie charts gallery

Pie button

data source

3 In the 2-D Pie section, click **Pie** (the first pie chart). The pie chart is inserted in the Metro Population worksheet, and the three Chart Tools tabs appear on the Ribbon. See Exhibit 16-4.

LO16.2 Working with Chart Elements

After you create a chart, you can change the appearance of each element of the chart. In order to format an element, you need to select it. You can also work with the entire chart, moving it to another sheet, repositioning it on a sheet, or resizing the chart.

Selecting Chart Elements

Charts include individual elements that can be formatted, including the chart area, the chart title, the plot area, data markers, and a legend. See Exhibit 16-5. The **chart area** contains the chart and all of the other chart ele-

Exhibit 16-4 Pie chart inserted into worksheet

Chart Tools tabs appear when chart is selected

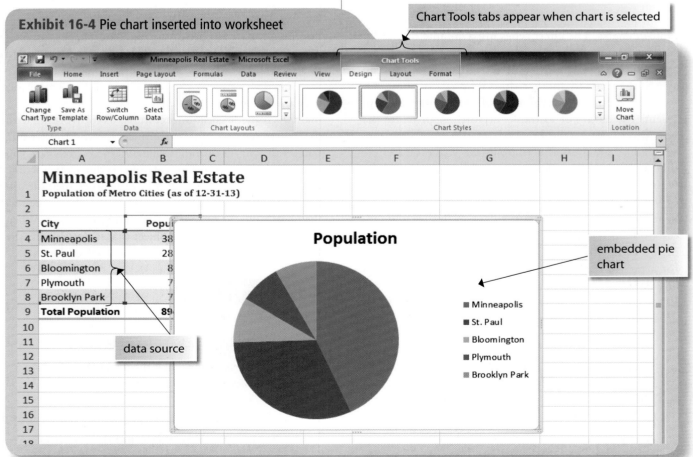

data source

embedded pie chart

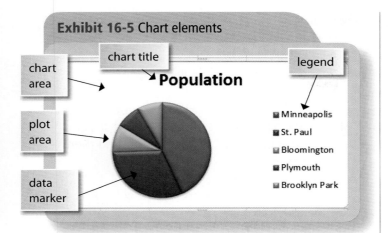

Exhibit 16-5 Chart elements

chart area

chart title

Population

legend

plot area

data marker

- Minneapolis
- St. Paul
- Bloomington
- Plymouth
- Brooklyn Park

ments. The **chart title** is a descriptive label or name for the chart. The **plot area** is the part of the chart that contains the graphical representation of the data series. Each value in a data series is represented by a **data marker** such as a pie slice. A **legend** is a rectangular area that indicates the data markers associated with the data series. You can choose which of these elements to include in the chart as well as where each element is placed and how each element looks. You'll work with these elements as you create and format charts in this chapter.

Before you can work with a chart element, you must select it. The simplest way to select a chart element is to click it. To ensure that you are clicking the right element, first point to the element and check that the correct element name appears in the ScreenTip. The name of the selected element also appears in the Chart Elements box located in the Current Selection group on both the Chart Tools Layout tab and the Chart Tools Format tab. You can also use this box to select chart elements. Click the Chart Elements box arrow, and then select the appropriate chart element in the list. The corresponding element is then selected in the chart. A selection box with sizing handles, which you use to reposition or resize the element, surrounds the selected element.

ACTIVITY

Select chart elements.

1 Point to an empty area of the selected chart. The pointer changes to 🕂 and the ScreenTip *Chart Area* appears, indicating that the pointer is over the chart area.

2 In the chart area above the pie chart, point to **Population**. The ScreenTip *Chart Title* appears, indicating that the pointer is over the chart title.

3 Click **Population**. A selection box appears around the chart title, indicating that it is selected.

4 On the Ribbon, click the **Chart Tools Layout tab**. In the Current Selection group, notice that *Chart Title* appears in the Current Selection box.

⚠ **Problem?** If you don't see the Chart Tools Layout tab, the chart is not selected. In the Metro Population worksheet, click any part of the **chart** to select it, and then repeat Step 4.

5 Click the **Current Selection box arrow** to display a list of elements in the current chart. See Exhibit 16-6.

6 In the Current Selection list, click **Plot Area**. The selection box surrounds the pie chart.

Exhibit 16-6 Current Selection list

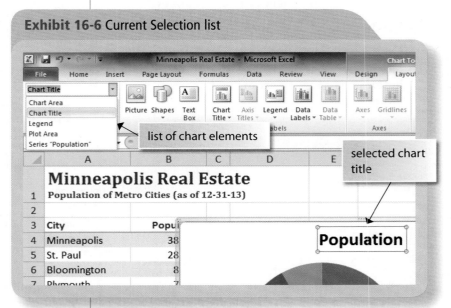

list of chart elements

selected chart title

chart area The area that contains the chart and all of the other chart elements.

chart title A descriptive label or name for the chart.

plot area The part of the chart that contains the graphical representation of the data series.

data marker An object in a chart that represents a value in a data series, such as a pie slice or column.

legend A rectangular area that indicates the data markers associated with the data series.

Moving a Chart to a Different Sheet

Each chart you create is inserted as an **embedded chart**, which is an object in a worksheet. The advantage of an embedded chart is that you can display the chart alongside any text or graphics that can explain the chart's meaning and purpose. However, an embedded chart covers worksheet cells, which might contain data and formulas. To prevent this, you can move an embedded chart to a different worksheet in the workbook or you can move it into a **chart sheet** (a sheet that contains only the chart and no worksheet cells). Likewise, you can move a chart from a chart sheet and embed it in any worksheet you select. The Move Chart dialog box provides options for moving charts between worksheets and chart sheets. You can also cut and paste a chart to a new location in the workbook.

 **ACTIVITY**

Move an embedded chart to another sheet.

1 Select the **chart area**.

2 On the Ribbon, click the **Chart Tools Design tab**. In the Location group, click the **Move Chart button**. The Move Chart dialog box opens. See Exhibit 16-7.

Exhibit 16-7 Move Chart dialog box

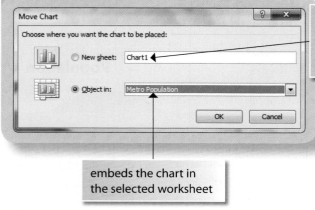

moves the chart to the Chart1 chart sheet

embeds the chart in the selected worksheet

> **embedded chart** A chart that is an object in a worksheet.
>
> **chart sheet** A sheet in a workbook that contains only a chart and no worksheet cells.

3 Click the **Object in box arrow** to display a list of worksheets in the active workbook, and then click **Summary Report**.

4 Click **OK**. The embedded pie chart moves from the Metro Population worksheet to the Summary Report worksheet and remains selected.

> **Tip:** To move a chart to a chart sheet, in the Move Chart dialog box, click the New sheet option button, type a name for the chart sheet in the box, and then click OK.

Repositioning and Resizing a Chart

An embedded chart might cover other data in the worksheet or be placed in an awkward location. You can reposition and resize the embedded chart to better fit on the worksheet. To do so, first select the chart. A selection box, which you use to reposition or resize the object, surrounds the chart. To reposition chart, drag the selection box to a new location in the worksheet. To resize the chart, drag a sizing handle on the selection box to change the object's width and height.

 **ACTIVITY**

Reposition and resize a chart.

1 Point to an empty part of the chart area until the pointer changes to and the ScreenTip *Chart Area* appears.

2 Click the **chart area**, drag up and to the left until the chart's upper-left corner is in cell A3, and then release the mouse button. The chart moves to a new location.

3 Point to the **sizing handle** in the lower-right corner of the chart until the pointer changes to .

> ⚠ **Problem?** If the chart resizes or other chart elements move, undo your last action, and then repeat Steps 1 and 2, being sure to drag the pie chart from the chart area.

> **Tip:** To retain the chart's proportions, hold down the Shift key as you drag the sizing handle.

Creating a Chart Sheet

Chart sheets are helpful for detailed charts that need more space to be seen clearly or when you want to show a chart without any worksheet text or data. Some reports require large expansive charts rather than compact graphs to provide more detail and make them easier to view and share. In those situations, you may want to devote an entire sheet to a graph rather than embed it within a worksheet. To create a larger version of a chart that covers an entire sheet, you move the chart to a chart sheet. Chart sheets are used for graphic elements like charts and images, and do not contain worksheet cells for calculating numeric values.

To move an embedded chart to a chart sheet, first select the chart in the worksheet. On the Chart Tools Design tab, in the Location group, click the Move Chart button. In the Move Chart dialog box that opens, click the New sheet option button, type a name for the chart sheet in the box, and then click OK. The chart is moved to a new chart sheet with the name you specified. You can format the chart in the chart sheet using the same tools and commands as you use to format a chart embedded in a worksheet. You can rename and move the chart sheet the same way as you rename and move a worksheet.

4 Drag the **sizing handle** up to cell F12. The chart resizes to cover the range A3:F12 and remains selected. See Exhibit 16-8.

5 Save the workbook.

Exhibit 16-8 Pie chart repositioned and resized

selection box

sizing handle

LO16.3 Modifying a Chart

After you create a chart, you can change its style and layout. You can also choose chart elements to include with the chart and how each element is formatted. This flexibility enables you to create a chart that best conveys its data. It also lets you create a chart with a look and feel that best suits your intended readers.

Changing the Chart Style

You can modify the appearance of a chart by applying a **chart style** that formats the entire chart. A chart style is similar to a cell style or a table style in that it applies several formats to the chart at one time. When you create a chart, Excel applies the default chart style for that chart type. For example, the default pie chart style applies a solid color to each slice. You can quickly change the appearance of the entire chart by selecting a different chart style in the Chart Styles gallery. There are both two-dimensional and three-dimensional chart styles. The 3-D chart styles provide the illusion of depth and distance, which makes the charts appear to stand out on the page and add visual interest. Live Preview shows how each the selected chart will look with the different chart styles.

For even more control over how a chart looks, you can select and format individual elements. To apply formatting to an individual chart element, double-click

chart style A style that modifies the appearance of or formats an entire chart.

Exhibit 16-9 Chart Styles gallery for pie charts

Exhibit 16-9 Chart Styles gallery for pie charts

that chart element to open a dialog box with format options specific to the selected element. You can also open the dialog box by clicking the appropriate element button on the Chart Tools Layout tab.

 **ACTIVITY**

Change the chart style.

1 On the Chart Tools Design tab, in the Chart Styles group, click the **More button** ⬇. The Chart Styles gallery opens. See Exhibit 16-9.

2 In the fourth row, click **Style 26** (the second style). Each pie slice now has a rounded, raised look.

Changing a Chart Layout

Chart layouts provide different options for displaying and arranging chart elements. The built-in chart layouts specify which chart elements are displayed and how they are formatted. The chart layouts include some of the most common ways of displaying different charts. Each chart type has its own collection of layouts. For a pie chart, the chart layout you choose may hide or display the chart title, display a chart legend or place legend labels in the pie slices, and add percentages to the pie slices. The chart layouts are available on the Chart Tools Design tab in the Chart Layouts group.

chart layout An option for displaying and arranging chart elements.

ACTIVITY

Change the chart layout.

1 On the Chart Tools Design tab, in the Chart Layouts group, click the **More button** ⬇ to open the Chart Layouts gallery. See Exhibit 16-10.

Exhibit 16-10 Chart Layouts gallery for pie charts

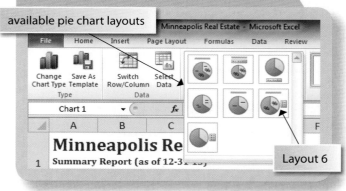

2 In the second row, click **Layout 6** (the third layout). Percentages appear on or next to the slices in the pie chart, and the chart title and legend remain in their original locations. To fit the percentages, Excel reduced the size of the pie chart in the plot area. See Exhibit 16-11.

With the percentages displayed on the pie chart, clients can quickly see how the values are allocated among the categories.

Exhibit 16-11 Pie chart with new chart style and layout

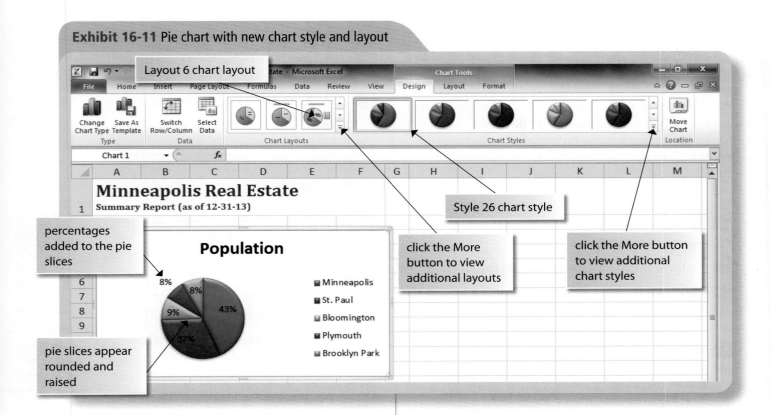

Layout 6 chart layout

Style 26 chart style

click the More button to view additional layouts

click the More button to view additional chart styles

percentages added to the pie slices

pie slices appear rounded and raised

Minneapolis Real Estate
Summary Report (as of 12-31-13)

Population

Positioning and Formatting a Chart Title

The chart title provides a description of a chart or an overview of its purpose. When you create a chart, Excel uses the series name for the chart title. You can edit or replace this default chart title. You can also format the text of the chart title just like you can format text in a cell.

ACTIVITY

Replace and position a chart title.

1 Click the **chart title** to select it. A selection box appears around the chart title.

2 Type **Population of Metro Cities**. The new chart title appears in the formula bar, but no changes are made to the title in the chart.

3 Press the **Enter key**. The chart title is updated with the entry and remains selected.

4 Change the font size to **12 points**. The chart title reduces in size, and the pie chart increases in size to fill the extra space. See Exhibit 16-12.

Tip: You can revise the title text rather than replacing it by double-clicking the chart title to place the insertion point in the text, and then editing the text.

Exhibit 16-12 Chart title updated and formatted

Minneapolis Real Estate
Summary Report (as of 12-31-13)

plot area increases in response to the smaller chart title

Population of Metro Cities

revised chart title

Positioning the Chart Legend

The chart legend identifies each of the data series in the chart. With a pie chart, the legend shows the color used for each slice and its corresponding category value. In this case, the category values are the different cities. As with the other elements, you can choose where to position the legend with options on the Legend button, which is on the Chart Tools Layout tab in the Labels group. You can also use the Format Legend dialog box for additional options for formatting the element's appearance, including the legend fill, border color, border styles, shadow, glow, and soft edges.

ACTIVITY

Position the chart legend.

1 On the Ribbon, click the **Chart Tools Layout tab**.

2 In the Labels group, click the **Legend button**, and then click **Show Legend at Left**. The legend moves to the left side of the chart.

3 In the Labels group, click the **Legend button**, and then click **More Legend Options**. The Format Legend dialog box opens.

> **Tip:** You can also double-click the legend to open the Format Legend dialog box.

4 On the left side of the dialog box, click **Border Color**. The Border Color options appear on the right side of the dialog box.

5 Click the **Solid line option button**. Two options related to border colors appear in the dialog box.

6 Click the **Color button** 🎨▼ to display the color palette, and then select the **Dark Blue, Text 2 theme color**. See Exhibit 16-13.

7 Click **Close**. The legend now has a dark blue border.

8 Click the **chart area** to deselect the legend. See Exhibit 16-14.

Exhibit 16-14 Chart legend positioned and formatted

click to access formatting options for the legend

positioned and formatted legend

Working with Data Labels

A **data label** is text for an individual data marker, such as pie slices. A data label can show a value or other descriptive text. When you use a chart layout that shows data labels, each label is placed where it best fits—either on the pie slice or along its side. You can use this placement to specify that all data labels appear next to their pie slices. Labels placed outside of the pie might appear far from their slices. In those cases, you can use leader lines to connect each data label to its corresponding data marker. Note that a leader line disappears when enough space exists in the chart area to place a label next to its slice. The label options are available on the Data Labels button in the Labels group on the Chart Tools Layout tab and in the Format Data Labels dialog box.

Exhibit 16-13 Border Color options in the Format Legend dialog box

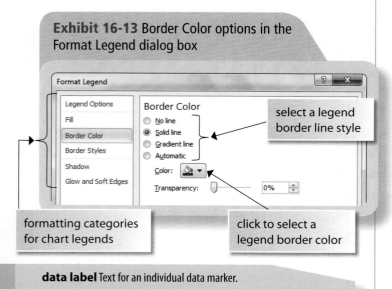

select a legend border line style

formatting categories for chart legends

click to select a legend border color

data label Text for an individual data marker.

Format data labels.

1 On the Chart Tools Layout tab, in the Labels group, click the **Data Labels button**, and then click **More Data Label Options**. The Format Data Labels dialog box opens with the Label Options displayed. See Exhibit 16-15. In the Label Contains section, the Percentage and the Show Leader Lines check boxes are already checked because these were included in the chart layout you applied earlier. These options set the data labels to display as percentages and use leader lines when needed to connect the labels with their corresponding pie slices.

Exhibit 16-15 Label Options in the Format Data Labels dialog box

options to define the number format of the data label

options to define the fill and border styles of the data label

displays the data values as percentages

shows leader lines next to the labels if necessary

places labels at the outer edge of each slice

options to define the alignment of the label text

2 In the Label Position section, click the **Outside End option button**. This option sets the data labels outside the pie chart.

3 On the left side of the dialog box, click **Number**. The options related to number formats appear in the dialog box.

4 In the Category box, click **Percentage**. The Decimal places box shows 2, which means that the percentage values for each slice will show two decimal places.

5 Click **Close**. The data labels appear as percentages on the outer edges of the slices. Leader lines don't appear in the pie chart because the chart area has enough space to place the labels close to their slices. See Exhibit 16-16.

Exhibit 16-16 Formatted data labels

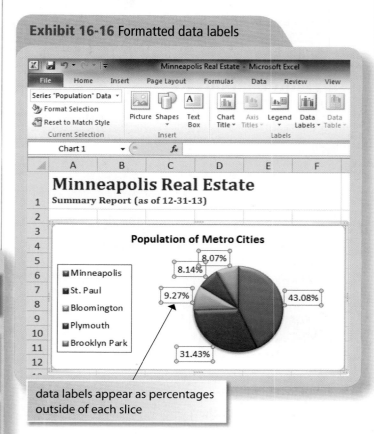

data labels appear as percentages outside of each slice

Changing the Color of a Data Series

The data series is the range of values plotted on the chart. The values in each data series are plotted as a single unit on a chart. Usually, you use one color for an entire data series. However, in a pie chart, you want each slice to have a different color so that the slices are easy to distinguish. Because of this, you must format individual slices rather than the entire data series.

You can change the color of each slice in a pie chart. Pie slice colors should be as distinct as possible to avoid confusion. Using distinct colors is especially important for adjacent slices. Depending on the printer quality or the monitor resolution, similarly colored slices might be difficult to distinguish. You can use the Fill Color button in the Font group on the Home tab to change the fill color. Or, you can double-click the slide to open the Format Data Point dialog box, select Fill on the right side of the dialog box, and then select the type of fill you want to use for the selected slice.

Exhibit 16-17 Pie slices with new colors

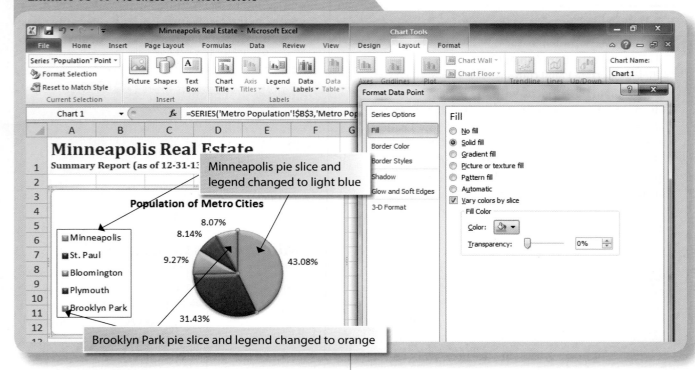

ACTIVITY

Change the color of a data series.

1 Click the **pie chart** to select the entire data series (you will see the ScreenTip *Series "Population"* . . . followed by whichever point you clicked on the pie chart).

2 Click the light blue **Brooklyn Park slice**, which represents 8.07 percent of the pie. Only that value, or slice, is selected.

3 Double-click the light blue **Brooklyn Park slice**. The Format Data Point dialog box appears.

4 On the left side of the dialog box, click **Fill**. The Fill options appear on the right side of the dialog box.

> **Tip:** You can also use the Fill Color button in the Font group on the Home tab to change the font color of a selected data series.

5 Click the **Solid fill option button**. Click the **Color button** to display the color palette, and then select the **Orange,**

> **exploded pie chart** A pie chart where one slice is moved away from the pie.

Accent 6 theme color. The Brooklyn Park slice and legend marker change to orange.

6 In the pie chart, click the dark blue **Minneapolis slice**, which covers 43.08 percent of the pie. The Format Data Point dialog box changes to reflect the current selection.

> ⚠ **Problem?** If you cannot see the pie chart, drag the Format Data Point dialog box out of the way.

7 On the left side of the dialog box, click **Fill**. Change the fill color for the selected slice to a **solid fill** using the **Light Blue standard color**. The Minneapolis slice and legend marker change to light blue. Each slice of the pie now has a distinct color. See Exhibit 16-17.

8 Click **Close**.

LO16.4 Creating an Exploded Pie Chart

Pie slices do not need to be fixed within the pie. An **exploded pie chart** moves one slice away from the others as if someone were taking the piece away from the pie. Exploded pie charts are useful for emphasizing one category above all of the others. For example, to emphasize how much of a mutual fund is allocated toward U.S. stocks, you could explode that single slice, moving it away from the other slices in the pie.

To explode a pie slice, select that slice from the pie chart and then drag the slice away from the pie. You can also explode multiple slices by selecting each slice and dragging them away. To explode all of the slices, select the entire pie and drag the pointer away from the pie's center. Each slice will be exploded and separated from the others. Although you can explode more than one slice, the resulting pie chart is rarely effective as a visual aid to the reader.

 **ACTIVITY**

Create an exploded pie chart.

1 Click the **pie chart** to select the entire data series (you will see the ScreenTip *Series "Population"* . . . followed by whichever point you clicked when you point to the pie chart).

2 Click the light blue **Minneapolis slice** to select that slice.

3 Drag the selected **Minneapolis slice** away from the center of the pie chart. The slide is separated from the rest of the pie chart. See Exhibit 16-18.

Exhibit 16-18 Exploded pie chart

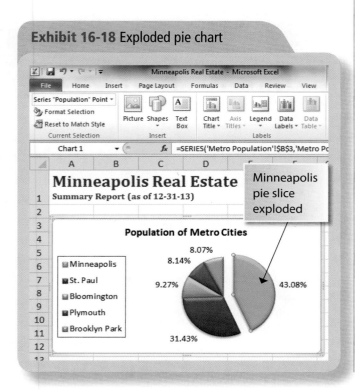

LO16.5 **Creating a Column Chart**

A **column chart** displays values in different categories as columns; the height of each column is based on its value. Related to the column chart is the **bar chart**, which is a column chart turned on its side so that the length of each bar is based on its value. Each data series is represented by the columns or bars of the same color.

Column and bar charts can also be applied to a wider range of data than pie charts. For example, you can demonstrate how a set of values changes over time, such as housing prices over several years. You can also include several data series in a column or bar chart, such as the populations of five cities over several years. The values from different data series are displayed in columns side by side. Pie charts usually show only one data series.

The process for creating a column chart is the same as for creating any other chart. First, you select the data source. Then, you select the type of chart you want to create. After the chart is embedded in the worksheet, you can move and resize the chart as well as change the chart's design, layout, and format.

 **ACTIVITY**

Create a column chart.

1 Make the **Structures Types worksheet** the active sheet. Select the **range A3:C12**.

2 On the Ribbon, click the **Insert tab**. In the Charts group, click the **Column button**, and then in the 2-D Column section, click the **Clustered Column chart** (the first chart). The column chart is inserted in the active worksheet, and the Chart Tools Design tab is selected on the Ribbon.

3 On the Chart Tools Design tab, in the Location group, click the **Move Chart button**. The Move Chart dialog box opens.

4 Click the **Object in box arrow**, and then click **Summary Report**.

5 Click **OK**. The column chart moves to the Summary Report worksheet and is still selected.

column chart A chart that displays values in different categories as columns so that the height of each column is based on its value.

bar chart A column chart that is turned on its side so that the length of each bar is based on its value.

Pie Chart or Column Chart?

Column and bar charts are better than pie charts when the number of categories is large or the categories are close in value. It is easier to compare height or length than area. When data includes more than six categories, a pie chart cannot display the categories effectively. Instead, you should create a column chart to display the data. Below, the same data is shown as a pie chart and as a column chart. As you can see, it is more difficult to determine which pie slice has the largest area and by how much. This is much simpler to determine with the column chart.

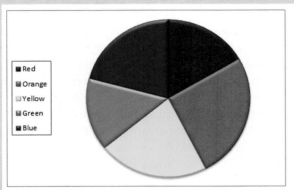
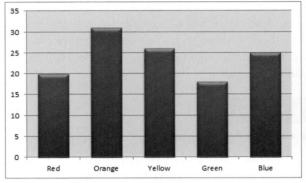

6 In the Summary Report worksheet, drag the selected column chart down so its upper-left corner is in **cell A14**.

7 Drag the lower-right **sizing handle** until the chart covers the **range A14:F27**. The chart is resized smaller. See Exhibit 16-19.

Exhibit 16-19 Column chart of structure types

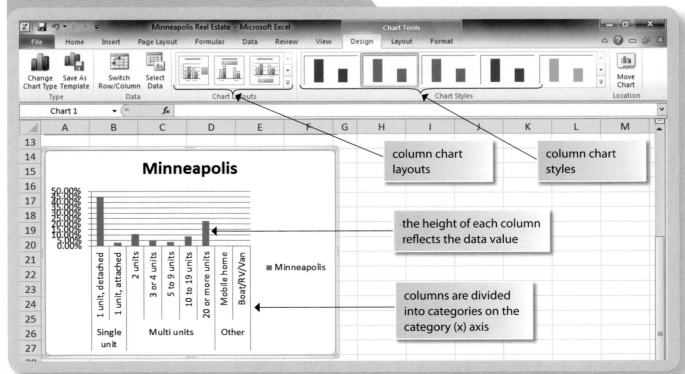

> When a chart has only one data series, the chart title and legend are redundant.

Formatting a Column Chart

The process for formatting a chart is the same for each type of chart, although the specific formats and options available reflect the current chart type. The Chart Tools Design tab provides a gallery of column chart layouts and a gallery of column chart styles. The Chart Tools Layout tab provides access to the individual chart elements you can include on the column chart. You can change the appearance of a column chart by formatting these chart elements.

Formatting Data Series

In a pie chart, each slice or data marker has a different format. In a column chart, all of the columns usually have the same format because the columns are distinguished by height, not color. However, you can format individual columns in a data series to highlight a particular column value. You can also modify the appearance of the data markers in a column chart using a variety of formatting options.

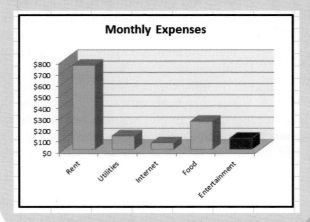

Format a column chart.

1 On the Ribbon, click the **Chart Tools Layout tab**. In the Current Selection group, click the **Chart Elements box arrow**. The list includes each element you can select in the column chart.

2 Click **Series "Minneapolis"**. All of the columns for the data series in the chart are selected.

> **Tip:** You can also select a data series by clicking any of its columns in the column chart.

3 On the Chart Tools Layout tab, in the Current Selection group, click the **Format Selection button**. The Format Data Series dialog box opens with the Series Options displayed.

4 Drag the **Gap Width slider** to **50%** to reduce the gap between adjacent columns. The columns become wider to fill the space.

> ⚠ **Problem?** If you cannot drag the Gap width slider to exactly 50%, select the value in the Gap Width box below the slider, and then type **50**.

5 On the left side of the dialog box, click **Fill**. On the right side of the dialog box, click the **Gradient fill option button** to fill the columns with a gradually changing mix of colors.

6 Click the **Direction button** [▣ ▾] to display a gallery of fill directions. In the first row, click **Linear Right** (the fourth fill direction). The columns will have a gradient fill that blends to the right. See Exhibit 16-20.

Exhibit 16-20 Fill options in the Format Data Series dialog box

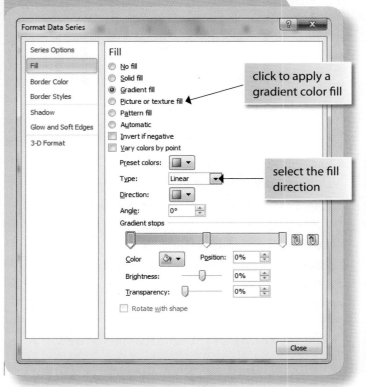

7 Click **Close**. The columns show the new width and fill.

8 On the Chart Tools Layout tab, in the Labels group, click the **Legend button**, and then click **None**. The chart legend is removed, and the column chart resizes to fill the available space.

9 Click the **chart title** to select it.

10 Change the font size of the chart title to **12 points**. The chart title is smaller, and remains selected.

11 Type **Structure Types** as the new chart title, and then press the **Enter key**. See Exhibit 16-21.

Exhibit 16-21 Formatted column chart

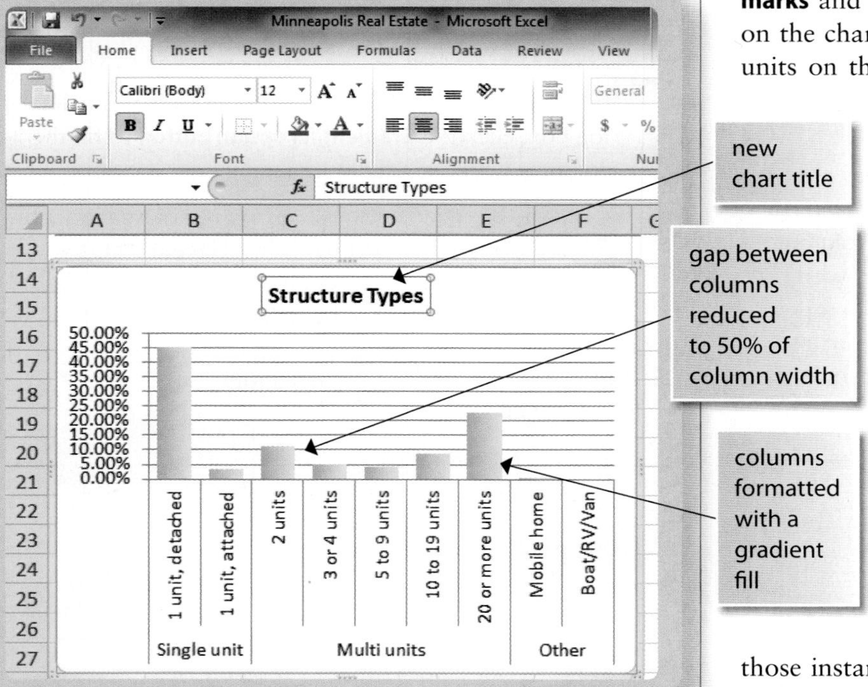

new chart title

gap between columns reduced to 50% of column width

columns formatted with a gradient fill

value axis The vertical axis that shows the range of series values from all of the data series plotted on the chart.

category axis The horizontal axis that shows the category values from each data series.

scale The range of values along an axis.

tick mark A line that identifies the unit on a chart axis at regular intervals.

primary axis The axis that usually appears along the left side of a chart.

secondary axis An axis that is usually placed on the right side of a chart.

Changing the Axis Scale for a Column Chart

Chart data is plotted along axes. The vertical **value axis** shows the range of series values from all of the data series plotted on the chart. The horizontal **category axis** shows the category values from each data series. The range of values, or **scale**, of an axis is based on the values in the data source. The scale usually ranges from 0 (if the data source has no negative values) through the maximum value. If the scale includes negative values, it ranges from the minimum value through the maximum value. You can modify the scale of the value axis to make it easier to read. You do this in the Format Axis dialog box.

Excel divides the scale into regular intervals, which are marked on the axis with tick marks and labels. **Tick marks** and labels identify the units at regular intervals on the chart axes. Major tick marks identify the main units on the chart axis. You can also add minor tick marks to identify smaller intervals between the major tick marks. Keep in mind that more tick marks at smaller intervals could make a chart difficult to read when the tick mark labels overlap, but fewer tick marks at larger intervals could make the chart less informative.

By default, no titles appear next to the value and category axes. This is fine when the axis labels are self-explanatory. Otherwise, you can add descriptive axis titles. In general, you should avoid adding extra chart elements such as axis titles when that information is easily understood from other parts of the chart.

Some charts involve multiple data series that have vastly different values. In those instances, you can plot one data series against a **primary axis**, which usually appears along the left side of the chart, and the other against a **secondary axis**, which is usually placed on the right side of the chart. The two axes can use different scales and labels.

The axis options are available on the Chart Tools Layout tab, in the Axes group, on the Axes button.

 **ACTIVITY**

Change the axis scale and title.

1 On the Ribbon, click the **Chart Tools Layout tab**.

2 In the Axes group, click the **Axes button**, point to **Primary Vertical Axis**, and then click **More Primary**

ON THE JOB

Communicating Effectively with Charts

Studies show that people interpret information more easily in a graphic form than in a tabular format. As a result, charts can help communicate the real story underlying the facts and figures you present to colleagues and clients. A well-designed chart can illuminate the bigger picture that might be hidden by viewing only the numbers. However, poorly designed charts can mislead readers and make it more difficult to interpret data.

To create effective and useful charts, keep in mind the following tips as you design charts:

▶ **Keep it simple.** Do not clutter a chart with too many graphic elements. Focus attention on the data rather than on decorative elements that do not inform.

▶ **Focus on the message.** Design the chart to highlight the points you want to convey to readers.

▶ **Limit the number of data series used in the chart.** Line charts and column charts should display no more than three or four data series. Pie charts should have no more than six slices.

▶ **Use gridlines in moderation.** Gridlines should be used to provide only approximate values for the data markers. Having too many gridlines can obscure the data being graphed.

▶ **Choose colors carefully.** Display different data series in contrasting colors to make it easier to distinguish one series from another. Modify the default colors as needed to make them distinct on the screen and in the printed copy.

▶ **Limit the chart to a few text styles.** Use a maximum of two or three different text styles in the same chart. Having too many text styles in one chart can distract attention from the data.

OtnaYdur/Shutterstock.com

Vertical Axis Options. The Format Axis dialog box opens with the Axis Options displayed. The value axis options are set to Auto, meaning that Excel will set the values. The minimum value is set to 0 and the maximum value is set to 0.5, or 50 percent. See Exhibit 16-22.

3 Next to Major unit, click the **Fixed option button**, and then type **0.10** in the box. The major tick marks will appear at 10 percent intervals.

4 On the left side of the dialog box, click **Number**. In the Category box, make sure **Percentage** is selected. In the Decimal places box, type **0**. The percentages will show only integers.

click to set the number format of the tick mark values

click to define the appearance of the tick mark values

click to set the alignment of the tick mark values

Exhibit 16-22 Axis options in the Format Axis dialog box

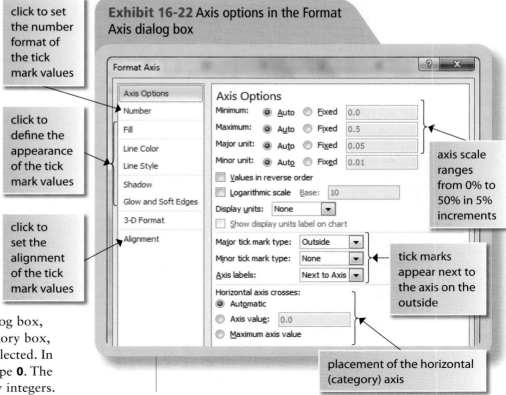

axis scale ranges from 0% to 50% in 5% increments

tick marks appear next to the axis on the outside

placement of the horizontal (category) axis

Everything in a workbook, including worksheets and charts, should inform the reader in the simplest, most accurate, and most direct way possible.

5 Click **Close**. The percentages on the value axis range from 0 percent to 50 percent in 10 percent intervals with no decimal places.

6 With the vertical axis still selected, change the font size to **8 points**. The values displayed in the vertical axis are smaller, leaving more room for the data series.

7 Click anywhere within the **category axis** to select it.

8 Change the font size of the horizontal axis to **8 points**. See Exhibit 16-23.

9 Save the workbook.

Exhibit 16-23 Formatted chart axes

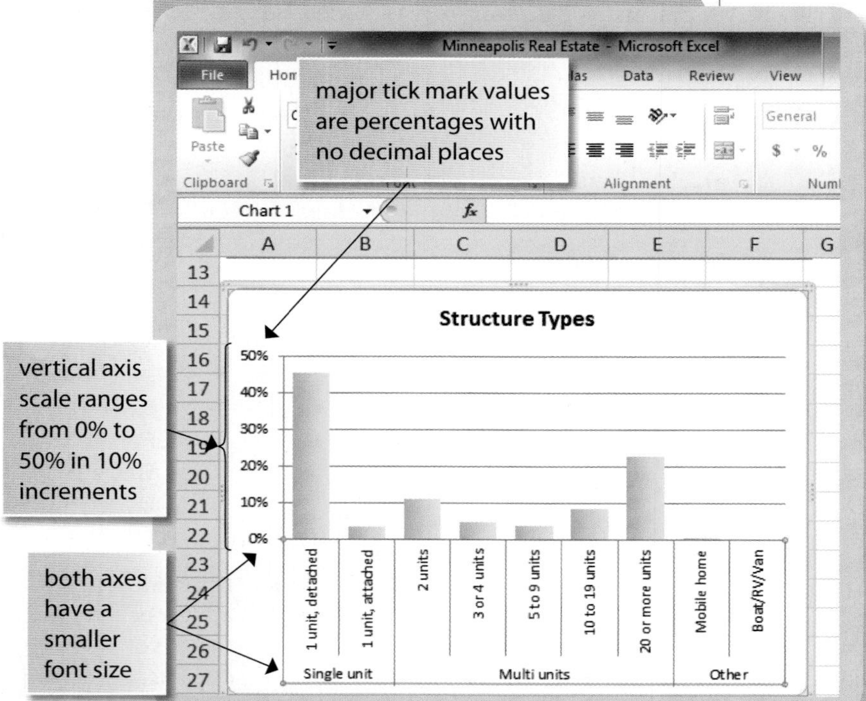

major tick mark values are percentages with no decimal places

vertical axis scale ranges from 0% to 50% in 10% increments

Structure Types

both axes have a smaller font size

line chart A chart that displays data values using a connected line rather than columns or bars.

LO16.6 Creating a Line Chart

A **line chart** displays data values using a connected line rather than columns or bars. Line charts are typically used when the data consists of values drawn from categories that follow a sequential order at evenly spaced intervals, as with historical data in which the data values are recorded periodically such as monthly, quarterly, or yearly. Each series has a different line color. Line charts are also commonly used instead of column charts when there are many data points across several data series. For example, when there are 40 data points across three data series, a column chart of this data would be difficult to read and interpret. The process for creating a line chart is the same as for creating pie charts and column charts, though the specific options available differ a bit. A data marker for a line chart can appear with or without the connecting line.

ACTIVITY

Create and format a line chart.

1 Make the **Historical Prices worksheet** the active sheet. Select the **range A3:D56**.

2 On the Ribbon, click the **Insert tab**. In the Charts group, click **Line button**. In the 2-D Line section, click the **Line chart**. A line chart is embedded in the Historical Prices worksheet.

3 Move the line chart to the **Summary Report worksheet**. Reposition and resize the chart to cover the **range H3:M12**.

4 On the Ribbon, click the **Chart Tools Layout tab**. In the Labels group, click the **Chart Title button**, and then click **Above Chart**. The chart title appears above the line chart and is selected.

5 Type **Price History** as the chart title, and then press the **Enter key**. Change the font size of the chart title to **12 points**.

6 Click the **value axis** to select it, and then set its font size to **8 points**.

7 Select the **category axis**, and then set its font size to **8 points**.

Creating a Combination Chart

A **combination chart** combines two or more chart types in a single graph, such as a column chart and a line chart. To create a combination chart, first select the data series in an existing chart that you want to appear as another chart type. Then, on the Chart Tools Design tab, in the Type group, click the Change Chart Type button, click the chart type you want to apply to the selected series, and then click OK. The selected series changes to the new chart type on the chart, leaving the other data series in its original format.

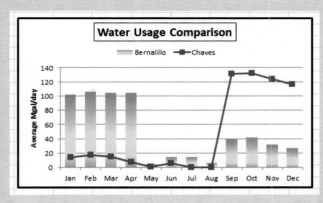

8 Click the **chart legend**, and then set its font size to **8 points**. The line chart resizes to fill the space left by the smaller chart title, axes, and chart legend.

9 Double-click the **value axis** to open the Format Axis dialog box with the Axis Options displayed.

10 Next to Minimum, click the **Fixed option button**, and then type **100000** in the box.

11 Click **Close**. The scale of the vertical axis now ranges from $100,000 to $400,000 in $50,000 increments. See Exhibit 16-24.

Exhibit 16-24 Formatted line chart

Editing the Axis Scale and Labels in a Line Chart

In addition to numbers, a scale can be based on dates, as the category axis is in the Fund History line chart. As with numerical scales, you can set the minimum and maximum dates to use in the scale's range. You can also set the major and minor units as days, months, or years to use for the scale's interval. This is helpful when the data source includes exact dates, but the chart trends only need to show years.

Sometimes you will want a chart to show the labels at specific intervals to save space or make the chart more attractive. You can do this by setting the major and minor tick marks. For example, to show labels every other year, you would set the major tick marks to appear at two-year intervals, and then set the minor tick marks to appear at one-year intervals.

When a chart involves large numbers, the axis labels can take up a lot of the available chart area and be difficult to read. You can simplify the chart's appearance by displaying units of measure more appropriate to the data values. For example, you can display the value 20 to represent 20,000 or 20,000,000. This is particularly useful when space is at a premium, such as in an embedded chart confined to a small area of the worksheet. When you select the display units, such as Thousands, you can choose to show the display unit in the axis title.

The axis options are available in the Format Axis dialog box.

> **combination chart** A chart that combines two or more chart types in a single graph, such as a column chart and a line chart.

Custom Number and Date Formats

You can create custom formats for all types of numbers. One application of a custom format is to add text to a number, which is often used to include the units of measure alongside the value, such as 10k to indicate 10,000, 20k to indicate 20,000, and so forth. To add text to a value, you use the custom format

value"text"

where *value* is the number format applied to the value, and *text* is the text to include next to the value. The text must be placed within quotation marks. For example, the format to display integers with a comma as a thousands separator is

#,##0

The # sign is a placeholder for a number; the 0 indicates that a 0 will appear if there is not a number in that position. To change this to a format that displays the letter *k* at the end of the value, the custom format would be

#,##0"k"

Custom date formats use combinations of the letters *m*, *d*, and *y* for months, days, and years, respectively. The number of letters controls how Excel displays the date, as follows:

▶ With months, *m* or *mm* displays the one- or two-digit month number, *mmm* displays the month's three-letter abbreviation, and *mmmm* displays the month's full name.

▶ With days, *d* or *dd* displays the one- or two-digit day value and *dddd* displays the day's full name.

▶ With years, *yy* displays the year with two-digits, and *yyyy* displays the year with four digits.

For example, the date format *m/d/yyyy* displays April 5, 2014 as 4/5/2014. The custom format *mmm-dd*, which displays a three-letter month abbreviation followed by a hyphen and a two-digit day number, would display the same date as Apr-05.

To create a custom number format, open the Number tab in the Format Cells dialog box and then click Custom in the Category list, or open the Format Axis dialog box with Number selected in the Axis Options list. In the Type box in the Format Cells dialog box or in the Format Code box in the Format Axis dialog box, type the code for the format you want to use, or select a built-in format, and then modify its code to suit your needs. In the Format Axis dialog box, you need to then click Add to add the format code to the list of custom formats in the Type box.

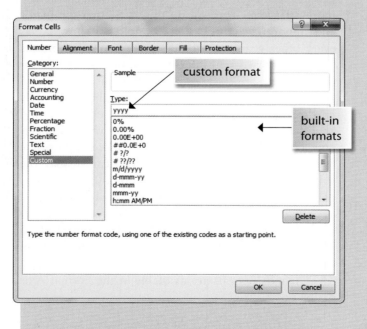

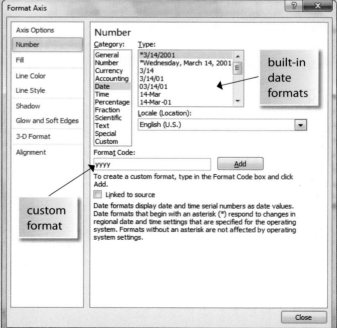

Edit axis scale and labels.

1 Double-click the **category axis** to open the Format Axis dialog box with the Axis Options displayed.

2 Next to Major unit, click the **Fixed option button**, type **2** in the box, and then select **Years** in the list. The major tick marks are set to every two years.

3 Next to Minor unit, click the **Fixed option button**, type **1** in the box, if necessary, and then select **Years** in the list. The minor tick marks are set to every year. See Exhibit 16-25.

Exhibit 16-25 Major and minor tick mark intervals

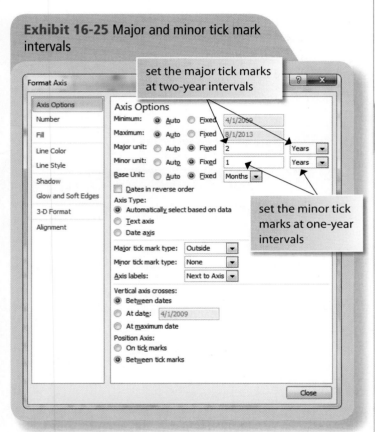

4 On the left side of the dialog box, click **Number**. In the Number pane, the Date category is selected.

5 In the Format Code dialog box, select the text, and then type **yyyy**. Click **Add**. The custom number format is added to the Custom number category, and will display only the year.

6 Click the **value axis** to open the Format Axis dialog box for the vertical axis with the Axis Options displayed. Note that you don't have to close the Format Axis dialog box before clicking another

chart element to format. The dialog box changes to show the options available for the new selection.

Problem? If you cannot see the line chart's value axis, drag the dialog box by its title bar to another location.

7 Click the **Display units box arrow**, and then click **Thousands**. The scale of the value axis changed from $100,000 to $400,000 in intervals of $50,000 to $100 through $400 in intervals of $50. The axis title *Thousands* indicates that the values are expressed in units of 1,000.

8 Click the **Show display units label on chart check box** to deselect it. The axis title is removed from the chart.

9 Click **Close**. See Exhibit 16-26.

Exhibit 16-26 Rescaled vertical and horizontal axes

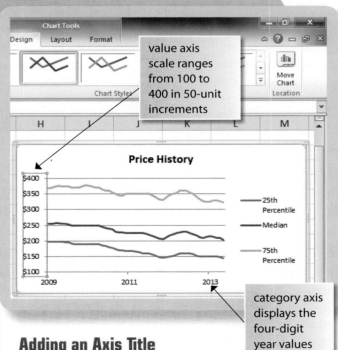

Adding an Axis Title

An axis title is descriptive text that appears next to the axis values. An axis title can provide additional information that is not covered in the chart title. It can include information about the source of the data and the units in which the data is measured. You can choose how the axis title appears on the chart by selecting an option from the Axis Titles button in the Labels group on the Chart Tools Layout tab.

ACTIVITY

Add an axis title.

1 Click the **Chart Tools Layout tab**. In the Labels group, click the **Axis Titles button**, point to **Primary Vertical Axis Title**, and then click **Rotated Title**. A title rotated 90° is added to the axis.

2 Type **Prices in Thousands**, and then press the **Enter key**. The descriptive title is entered.

3 Change the font size of the axis title to **8 points**.

4 Remove the boldface from the axis title.

Overlaying Chart Titles and Legends

You can overlay chart titles and legends in the chart area, which means they are placed on top of the chart. Overlaying these elements makes more space for the plot area because the chart does not resize to make room for that element. An overlaid chart element floats in the chart area and is not fixed to a particular position. This means that you can drag the chart element to a new location. This is helpful because when you overlay a chart element, it might overlap some of the chart contents. After you overlay an element, you might want to format it to make it easier to read. To overlay a chart title or legend, on the Chart Tools Layout tab, in the Labels group, click the Chart Title or Legend button, and then click the overlay option on the menu.

Adding Gridlines

Gridlines extend the values of the major or minor tick marks across the plot area. By default, horizontal gridlines appear on line charts and column charts. Each gridline is aligned with a major tick mark on the value axis. You can change the gridlines so that they appear for only the minor units, appear for both the major and minor units, or do not appear at all. The category axis has these same gridline options. The Gridlines button is in the Axes group on the Chart Tools Layout tab.

gridlines Lines that extend the values of the major or minor tick marks across the plot area of a chart.

Gridlines are similar to borders in that you can change their color and design style as well as add drop shadows or glowing color effects.

ACTIVITY

Add gridlines to a chart.

1 Click the **Chart Tools Layout tab** on the Ribbon.

2 In the Axes group, click the **Gridlines button**.

3 Point to **Primary Vertical Gridlines**, and then click **Minor Gridlines**. Vertical gridlines appear on the chart at each minor tick mark (in this case, every year). See Exhibit 16-27.

4 Save the workbook.

Exhibit 16-27 Line chart with gridlines

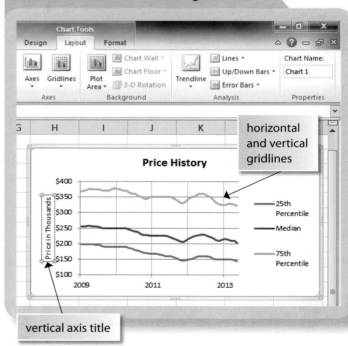

LO16.7 Editing Chart Data

Chart data can be edited and revised at any time. You do this by modifying the data range that the chart is based on, not by directly modifying the data in the chart. The change can be as simple as updating

Understanding the Series Function

If you select a chart's series, the formula displayed in the formula bar uses the SERIES function. The SERIES function describes the content of a chart data series, and has the syntax

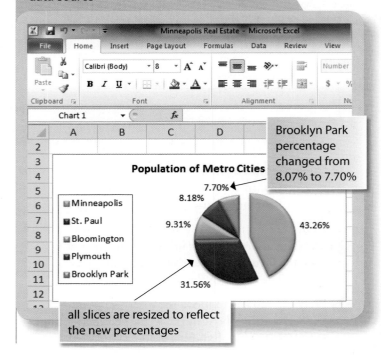

=SERIES(*name, categories, values, order*)

where *name* is the name that appears in the chart, *categories* are the labels that appear on the category axis of the chart, *values* are the values that Excel plots for the data series, and *order* is the order in which the series appears in the chart. For example, a data series might be represented by the following SERIES function:

=SERIES(Sheet1!$D$1,Sheet1!$A$2:$A$9, Sheet1!$D$2:$D$9,3)

In this function, the name of the series is in cell D1 in the Sheet1 worksheet, the labels are in the range A2:A9 in the Sheet1 worksheet, the data values are in the range D2:D9 in the Sheet1 worksheet, and the series is the third data series in the chart.

Although you can edit the SERIES function within the formula bar to make quick changes to your chart, the function is tied to an existing chart. It cannot be used within a worksheet cell or referenced from another Excel formula.

a specific value within the data source. Or it can be as involved as adding another data series to the chart.

Changing a Data Value or Label

Charts remain linked or connected to their data sources, even if they appear in different worksheets. If you change any value or label in the data source, the chart is automatically updated to show the new content. One advantage of creating charts in Excel is that you can quickly see how changing one or more values affects the chart.

ACTIVITY

Change a chart's data source.

1 Make the **Metro Population worksheet** the active sheet.

2 In **cell B8**, change the value to **68610**.

3 Make the **Summary Report worksheet** the active sheet. The pie chart was updated with the new data value. Note that the percentage values for each category were recalculated based on the new data. See Exhibit 16-28.

Exhibit 16-28 Pie chart updated to match data source

Adding a Data Series to an Existing Chart

You can modify a chart by adding a new data series. The new data series appears in the chart with a different set of data markers in the same way that the line chart you created had different data markers for each of the three different series. You modify a chart from the Select Data Source dialog box.

Add a data series to an existing chart.

1 In the Summary Report worksheet, click the **Structure Types column chart** to select it.

2 On the Ribbon, click the **Chart Tools Design tab**. In the Data group, click the **Select Data button**. The Select Data Source dialog box opens. The left side lists the data series displayed in the chart. The right side lists the category axis labels associated with each data series. You can add, edit, or remove any of these data series from the chart. See Exhibit 16-29.

Exhibit 16-29 Select Data Source dialog box

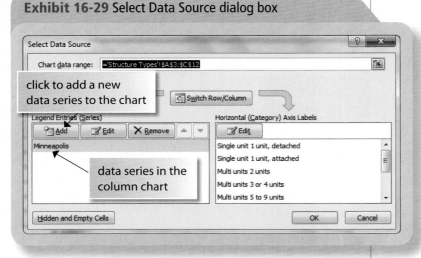

3 Click the **Add button**. The Edit Series dialog box opens. In this dialog box, you specify the name of the new data series and its range of data values.

4 With the insertion point in the Series name box, click the **Structure Types sheet tab**, and then click **cell D3**. The cell with the series name is entered.

5 Press the **Tab key** to move the insertion point to the Series values box. In the worksheet, select the **range D4:D12**. See Exhibit 16-30.

Exhibit 16-30 Edit Series dialog box

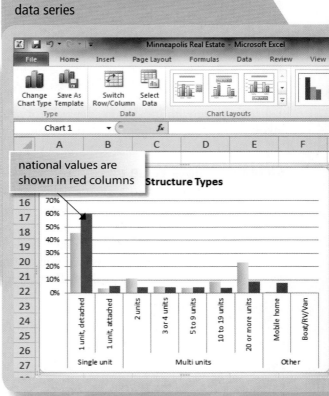

6 Click **OK**. The Select Data Source dialog box reappears with the national data added to the list of data series in the chart.

7 Click **OK**. The national structure type values appear as red columns in the chart. See Exhibit 16-31.

Exhibit 16-31 Column chart with added data series

Modifying Lines and Data Markers

You can change the appearance of the lines and data markers in a line chart. You do this with the Marker Options in the Format Data Series dialog box. For example, you can remove the lines connecting categories when they have no meaning. You can also change the shape and size of the marker itself, such as changing square markers to horizontal line markers at each data point.

ACTIVITY

Modify lines and data markers.

1 In the Summary Report worksheet, select the **Price History chart**. Select the line for the **Median data series** to select it.

2 On the Ribbon, click the **Chart Tools Layout tab**. In the Current Selection group, click the **Format Selection button**. The Format Data Series dialog box opens.

3 On the left side of the dialog box, click **Line Color**. On the right side of the dialog box, click the **No line option button** to remove the line from the chart.

4 On the left side of the dialog box, click **Marker Options**. On the right side of the dialog box, click the **Built-in option button**. You can now select the type and size of the marker.

5 Click the **Type box arrow**, and then click the **short horizontal line** (the sixth marker in the list).

6 Click the **Size down arrow** so 4 appears in the box. See Exhibit 16-32.

Exhibit 16-32 Marker Options in the Format Data Series dialog box

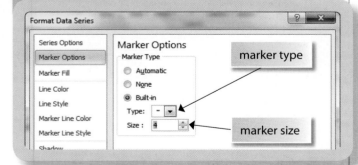

7 Click **Close**. The Median values appear on the chart as data markers without a line.

8 In the chart, deselect the **Median data series**. See Exhibit 16-33.

9 Save the workbook.

Exhibit 16-33 Line chart with lines and data markers

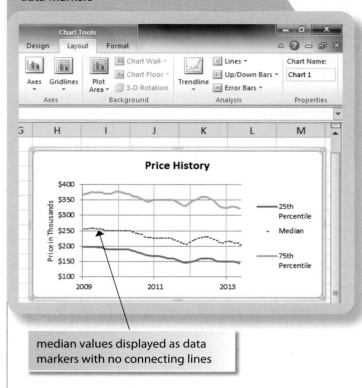

median values displayed as data markers with no connecting lines

LO16.8 **Inserting and Formatting Sparklines**

A **sparkline** is a graph that is displayed within a cell. The goal of a sparkline is to convey a large amount of graphical information within a very small space. They don't include chart elements such as legends, titles, gridlines, or axes. You can create three types of sparklines:

- A line sparkline, used to highlight trends

- A column sparkline, used for column charts

- A win/loss sparkline, used to highlight positive and negative values

Exhibit 16-34 shows examples of each type of sparkline. The line sparklines show the sales history of each department and all four departments for a computer manufacturer. The sparklines show the recent

sparkline A graph that is displayed within a cell.

Exhibit 16-34 Examples of sparklines

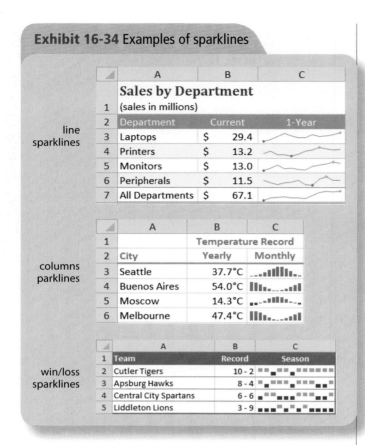

line sparklines

	A	B	C
	Sales by Department		
1	(sales in millions)		
2	Department	Current	1-Year
3	Laptops	$ 29.4	
4	Printers	$ 13.2	
5	Monitors	$ 13.0	
6	Peripherals	$ 11.5	
7	All Departments	$ 67.1	

columns parklines

	A	B	C
1		Temperature Record	
2	City	Yearly	Monthly
3	Seattle	37.7°C	
4	Buenos Aires	54.0°C	
5	Moscow	14.3°C	
6	Melbourne	47.4°C	

win/loss sparklines

	A	B	C
1	Team	Record	Season
2	Cutler Tigers	10 - 2	
3	Apsburg Hawks	8 - 4	
4	Central City Spartans	6 - 6	
5	Liddleton Lions	3 - 9	

temperature averages for four cities. Temperatures above 0°C are in blue columns; temperatures below 0°C are in red columns that extend downward. Finally, the win/loss sparklines reveal a snapshot of the season results for four sports teams. Wins are displayed in blue; losses are in red.

Sparklines can be inserted anywhere within the workbook and can represent data from several rows or columns. To create a set of sparklines, you first select a data range containing the data you want to graph, and then you select a location range where you want the sparklines to appear. Note that the cells in which you insert the sparklines need not be blank. Sparklines are added as part of the cell background and do not replace any cell content.

The Sparkline Tools Design tab provides options for formatting the appearance of sparklines. Sparklines can show data markers to identify the high and low points, negative points, first and last point, and all points. Just select the check boxes for the markers you want to display in the Show group. As with other charts, the Style gallery in the Style group provides built-in styles for sparklines. In addition, you can specify the sparkline color and the marker color,

which are also available in the Style group. The only other feature you can add to a sparkline is an axis, which for sparklines is simply a horizontal line that separates positive values from negative values. Click the Axis button in the Group group, and then click Show Axis.

To remove sparklines from the worksheet, select the sparkline or sparklines to delete. On the Sparkline Tools Design tab, in the Group group, click the Clear button.

ACTIVITY

Insert and format sparklines.

1 Make the **Metro Population worksheet** the active sheet. Select the **range D4:D8**.

2 On the Ribbon, click the **Insert tab**. In the Sparklines group, click the **Line button**. The Create Sparklines dialog box opens with the insertion point in the Data Range box. The location range is already entered because you selected it before opening the dialog box. See Exhibit 16-35.

Exhibit 16-35 Create Sparklines dialog box

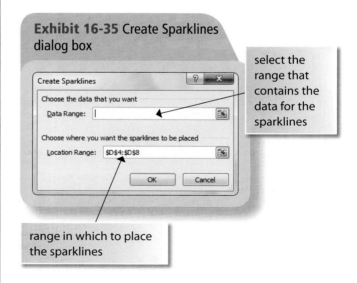

select the range that contains the data for the sparklines

range in which to place the sparklines

3 With the insertion point in the Data Range box, click the **Population History sheet tab**, and then select the **range B4:E8** to enter the range that contains the data to chart.

4 Click **OK**. Sparklines are inserted into each cell in the selected location range. The Sparkline Tools Design tab appears on the Ribbon.

Sparkline Groups

Sparklines can be grouped or ungrouped. Grouped sparklines share a common format. Ungrouped sparklines can be formatted individually. When you create sparklines, all of the sparklines in the location range are part of a single group. Clicking any cell in the location range selects all of the sparklines in the group. Similarly, any formatting you apply affects all the sparklines in the group. This ensures that all the sparklines for related data are formatted consistently.

You can differentiate one sparkline in a group by formatting that sparkline differently. First, select the individual sparkline you want to format. Then, on the Sparkline Tools Design tab, in the Group group, click the Ungroup button. The selected sparkline is split from the rest of the sparklines in the group. Finally, apply a unique format to the selected sparkline. To regroup the sparklines, select all of the cells in the location range containing sparklines, and then click the Group button in the Group group.

5 On the Sparkline Tools Design tab, in the Show group, click the **High Point check box** and the **Low Point check box** to display markers for the high and low points within each sparkline.

> **Tip:** On the Sparkline Tools Design tab, in the Style group, click the Sparkline Color button to change the sparkline color and click the Marker Color button to change the data marker color.

6 On the Sparkline Tools Design tab, in the Style group, click the **More button** ⯆. In the Style gallery, in the second row, click **Sparkline Style Accent 5, Darker 25%**. The line changes to dark blue and the markers change to orange. See Exhibit 16-36.

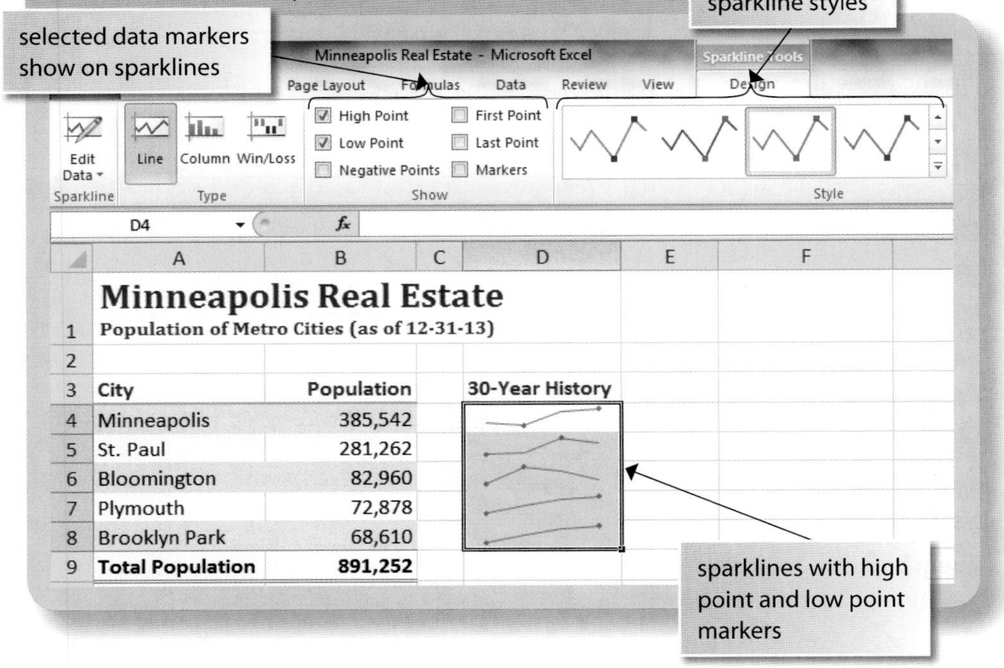

> Charts that can be viewed and comprehended at a glance have a greater impact than large and cluttered graphs.

LO16.9 Inserting and Modifying Data Bars

A **data bar** is conditional formatting that adds a horizontal bar to the background of a cell containing a number. When applied to a range of cells, the data bars have the same appearance as a bar chart with each cell containing one bar. The lengths of data bars are based on the values in the selected range. Cells with larger values have longer bars; cells with smaller values have shorter bars. Data

data bar Conditional formatting that adds a horizontal bar to a cell's background that is proportional in length to the cell's value.

Exhibit 16-36 Line sparklines with data markers

selected data markers show on sparklines

sparkline styles

sparklines with high point and low point markers

bars are dynamic, which means that if one cell's value changes, the lengths of the data bars in the selected range are automatically updated. When data bars are used with negative values, the data bars originate from the center of the cell with negative bars extending to the left and positive bars extending to the right.

The lengths of the data bars are determined based on the values in the selected range. The cell with the largest value contains a data bar that extends across the entire width of the cell, and the lengths of the other bars in the selected range are determined relative to that bar. In some cases, this means that the longest data bar overlaps the cell's data value, making it difficult to read. You can modify the length of the data bars by altering the conditional formatting rule.

Data bars are always placed in the cells containing the value they represent, and each cell represents only a single bar.

ACTIVITY

Add data bars.

1 Make the **Structure Types worksheet** the active sheet. Select the **range C4:D12**.

2 On the Home tab, in the Styles group, click the **Conditional Formatting button**, and then point to **Data Bars** to display the Data Bars gallery.

3 In the Gradient Fill group, click **Orange Data Bar**. The data bars are added to the selected cells. See Exhibit 16-37. The data bars in Exhibit 16-37 present essentially the same information as the column chart you created earlier. However, the data bars have the advantage of being compact and integrated with the values in the Structure Types data.

4 On the Home tab, in the Styles group, click the **Conditional Formatting button**, and then click **Manage Rules**. The Conditional Formatting Rules Manager dialog box opens. Current Selection appears in the Show formatting rules for box.

5 Click the **Edit Rule button**. The Edit Formatting Rule dialog box opens. You want to modify the data bar rule to proportionally reduce the lengths of the data bars.

6 In the Type row, click the **Maximum box arrow**, and then click **Number**.

Exhibit 16-37 Data bars added to the Structure Types worksheet

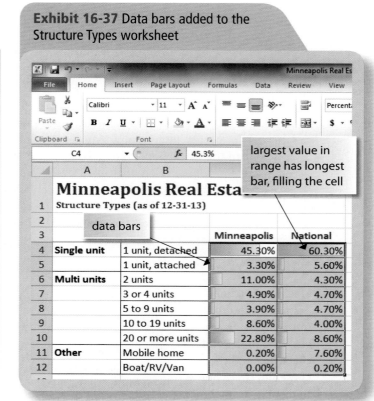

largest value in range has longest bar, filling the cell

data bars

7 In the Value row, in the Maximum box, type **0.75**. The rule now sets the maximum value for the data bar to 0.75, or 75 percent. All data bar lengths will then be determined relative to this value. See Exhibit 16-38.

Exhibit 16-38 Edit Formatting Rule dialog box

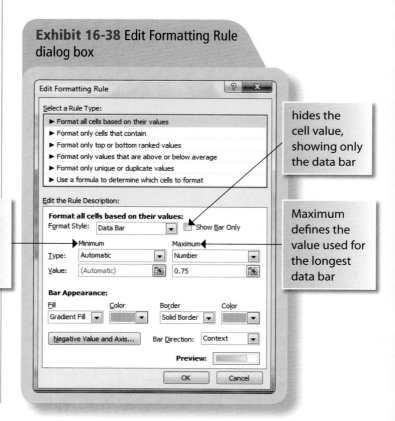

hides the cell value, showing only the data bar

Minimum defines the value used for the shortest data bar

Maximum defines the value used for the longest data bar

8 Click **OK** in each dialog box. The longest data bar now spans three-fourths of the cell width. See Exhibit 16-39.

9 Save the workbook, and then close it.

Exhibit 16-39 Edited data bars

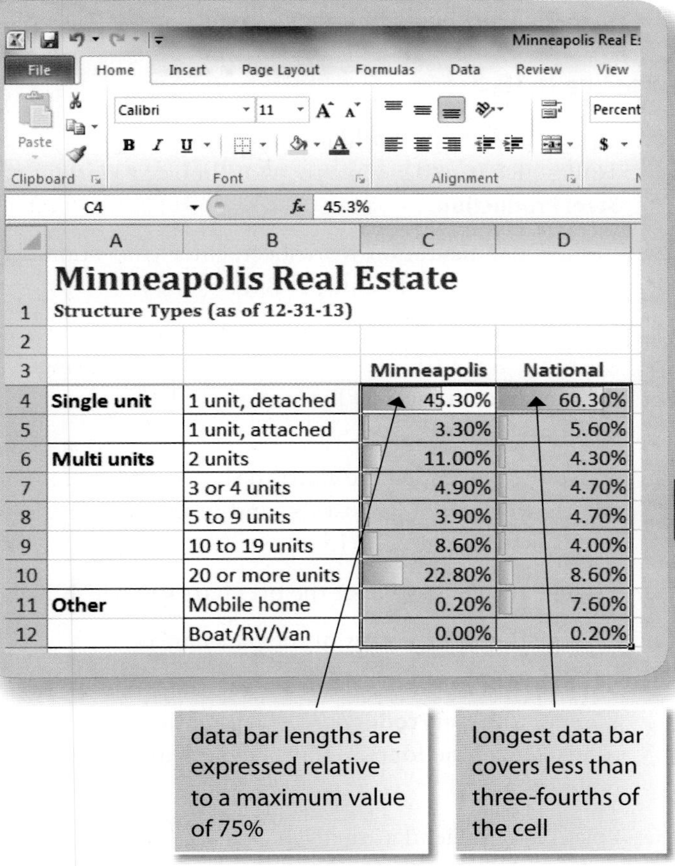

data bar lengths are expressed relative to a maximum value of 75%

longest data bar covers less than three-fourths of the cell

Quiz Yourself

1. What is the difference between a data source and a data series?

2. What is the difference between the chart area and the plot area?

3. In what two locations can you place a chart?

4. If a data series contains values divided into 10 categories, would this data be better displayed as a pie chart or a column chart? Why?

5. What is a column chart, and how is a bar chart different?

6. Why would you change the scale of a chart axis?

7. What are major tick marks and minor tick marks?

8. When should you use a line chart instead of a column chart?

9. What is a combination chart? Describe how to create a combination chart.

10. What does it mean to overlay a chart title or legend?

11. How do you update a chart after editing the chart data?

12. How do you add a data series to an already existing chart?

13. What are sparklines? Describe the three types of sparklines.

14. What are data bars?

15. How do data bars differ from sparklines?

Practice It

Practice It 16-1

1. Open the data file **Hot** located in the Chapter 16\Practice It folder. Save the workbook as **Hot Springs Resorts**.

2. In the Documentation worksheet, enter your name in cell B3 and the date in cell B4.

3. In the Usage Data worksheet, select the range B4:E4;B17:E17. Insert a pie chart using the Pie chart type in the 2-D Pie section in the Charts gallery.

4. Move the embedded pie chart to the Summary Charts worksheet. Reposition and resize the chart to cover the range A3:F14.

5. Change the chart style of the pie chart to Style 31.

6. Change the chart layout of the pie chart to Layout 6.

7. Change the chart title to **Total Annual Usage**. Change the font size of the chart title to 12 points.

8. Position the legend to the left of the pie chart. Change the border color of the legend to a solid line using the Black, Text 1 theme color.

9. Change the data labels to appear on the outside end of the pie chart.

10. In the Usage Data worksheet, select the range A4:E16. Insert a column chart using the 3-D Clustered Column chart type in the 3-D Column section in the Charts gallery.

11. Move the embedded column chart to the Summary Charts worksheet. Reposition and resize the embedded column chart to cover the range A16:M32.

12. Change the chart style of the column chart to Style 31.

13. Change the chart layout of the column chart to Layout 3.

14. Change the chart title to **Amenities Usage By Month**. Set the font size of the chart title to 12 points.

15. Add a primary vertical axis title to the column chart as a rotated title. Enter **Attendance** as the vertical axis title.

16. Change the axis scale of the column chart so that the maximum is 900.

17. In the Usage Data worksheet, change the month labels in the range A5:A16 to the full month names. Change the value in cell E5 to 96. In the Summary Charts worksheets, make sure the charts updated to reflect the new totals.

18. In the Usage Data worksheet, select the range A4:A16;F4:F16. Insert a line chart using the Line chart type in the 2-D Line section in the Charts gallery.

19. Move the embedded line chart to the Summary Charts worksheet. Reposition and resize the embedded column chart to cover the range G3:M14.

20. Remove the legend from the line chart.

21. Add a chart title above the chart. Change the chart title to **Total Monthly Usage**. Set the font size of the chart title to 12 points.

22. Change the axis scale of the line chart to a minimum of 750 and a maximum of 2,150 with a major unit of 250.

23. In the Usage Data worksheet, in the range G5:G16, insert line sparklines based on the data range B5:E16.

24. On the sparklines, show the high point and low point markers.

25. Change the sparkline style to Sparkline Style Accent 5, Darker 25%.

26. Select the range F5:F16, and then insert data bars using the Orange Data Bar option in the Gradient Fill section of the gallery.

27. Save the workbook, and then close it.

Practice It 16-2

1. Open the data file **World** located in the Chapter 16\Practice It folder. Save the workbook as **World Steel Production**.

2. In the Documentation worksheet, enter your name in cell B3 and the date in cell B4.

3. In the Production by Country worksheet, select the range A5:A10;N5:N10. Insert a pie chart using the Pie chart in the 2-D Pie section in the Charts gallery.

4. Move the embedded pie chart to the Summary Charts worksheet. Reposition and resize the chart to cover the range A4:F15.

5. Change the chart style of the pie chart to Style 42.

6. Change the chart layout of the pie chart to Layout 6.

7. Enter **Total Steel Production by Country** as the chart title. Change the font size of the chart title to 12 points.

8. Position the legend at the left of the pie chart. Change the border color of the legend to a solid line in the White, Background 1 theme color.

9. In the Production by Country worksheet, select the range A4:M10. Insert a column chart using the Clustered Column chart in the 2-D Column section in the Charts gallery.

10. Move the embedded column chart to the Summary Charts worksheet. Reposition and resize the embedded column chart to cover the range A17:K33.

11. Change the chart style of the column chart to Style 42.

12. Insert a chart title using the Centered Overlay Title option. Change the chart title to **Steel Production by Country and Month**. Set the font size of the chart title to 12 points.

13. Change the border color of the legend to a solid line in the White, Background 1 theme color.

14. Change the fill color of the plot area to a gradient fill. Change the fill direction to Linear Down.

15. In the column chart, change the Asia data series to a line. (*Hint*: Select the Asia data series. On the Chart Tools Design tab, in the Type group, click the Change Chart Type button. In the Change Chart Type dialog box, in the Line group, click Line, and then click OK.)

16. In the Summary Charts worksheet, in the merged cell H6, insert a line sparkline based on the data range B11:M11 in the Production by Country worksheet.

17. On the sparkline, show the high point and low point markers.

18. Change the sparkline style to Sparkline Style Colorful #1.

19. Change the sparkline type to Column. (*Hint*: On the Sparkline Tools Design tab, in the Type group, click the Column button.)

20. Save the workbook, and then close it.

On Your Own

On Your Own 16-1

1. Open the data file **Portlandia** located in the Chapter 16\On Your Own folder. Save the workbook as **Portlandia Skies**.

2. In the Documentation worksheet, enter your name in cell B3 and the date in cell B4.

3. In the Weather worksheet, based on the data in the range A4:M8, insert an appropriate chart (such as a column chart, line chart, or bar chart). Move the embedded chart to a chart sheet named **Average Days Chart**.

4. Format the chart using an appropriate chart layout and chart style.

5. Insert an appropriate chart title for the chart, and then change the font size as needed.

6. Add appropriate axis titles, and change the font sizes as needed.

7. Position the legend appropriately, and change its font size, border color, fill color, and so forth as desired.

8. Change the axis scale as needed to eliminate blank areas of the chart.

9. Add vertical gridlines to the major tick marks in the chart.

10. Format the plot area to use an attractive fill.

11. Change the data series as needed so that each data series uses a distinct data marker fill and line color.

12. In the Weather worksheet, edit the text in cell A6 to **Partly Cloudy**.

13. In the Weather worksheet, based on the data in the range A5:A8;N5:N8, insert a pie chart. Reposition and resize the chart attractively on the Weather worksheet.

14. Format the pie chart attractively, using the chart layout, chart style, chart title, legend, and data labels of your choice.

15. In the Weather worksheet, in the cells of your choice, insert a line or column sparkline for each of the following data: Clear (range B5:M5), Partly Cloudy (range B6:M6), Cloudy (range B7:M7), and Rainy (range B8:M8). Format the sparklines appropriately and enter labels to identify each sparkline.

16. In the Weather worksheet, insert data bars in the range N5:N8.

17. Save the workbook, and then close it.

ADDITIONAL STUDY TOOLS

Chapter 16

IN THE BOOK

▶ Complete end-of-chapter exercises

▶ Study tear-out Chapter Review Card

ONLINE

▶ Complete additional end-of-chapter exercises

▶ Take practice quiz to prepare for tests

▶ Review key term flash cards (online, printable, and audio)

▶ Play "Beat the Clock" and "Memory" to quiz yourself

▶ Watch the videos "Select Chart Elements," "Move an Embedded Chart to Another Sheet," "Change the Color of a Data Series," "Format a Column Chart," "Change the Axis Scale and Title," "Add a Data Series to an Exisiting Chart," "Insert and Format Sparklines," and more

CAPSTONE

Excel: Create a Budget

1. Plan a budget workbook. Identify the workbook's purpose or goal. Figure out the data you need to collect and enter in the workbook (for this project, you can use real or fictional data). Determine what calculations you need to enter in the workbook. Decide how the workbook should be organized and formatted.

2. Create a new workbook for the financial data. Use the first worksheet as a documentation sheet that includes your name, the date on which you start creating the workbook, and a brief description of the workbook's purpose. Format the worksheet appropriately.

3. Use a second worksheet to create the budget. Enter appropriate labels to identify the data the budget will include. Include a section to enter values that remain consistent from month to month, such as monthly income and expenses. You can then reference these cells in formulas.

4. In the budget worksheet, enter the data on which the budget will be based. Be sure to enter realistic earnings for each month of the year and realistic expenses for each month. Apply appropriate number formats and styles to the values.

5. In the budget worksheet, enter formulas and functions to calculate the total earnings each month, the average monthly earnings, and the total earnings for the entire year. Also, calculate the total expenses for each month, the average monthly expenses, and the total expenses for the year.

6. Calculate the monthly net cash flow (the value of total income minus total expenses).

7. Use the cash flow values to track the savings throughout the year. Use a realistic amount for savings at the beginning of the year. Use the monthly net cash flow values to add or subtract from this value. Project the end-of-year balance in savings under your proposed budget.

8. Format the budget worksheet by changing fonts, font sizes, font colors, borders, cell styles, fill colors, and so forth as needed to make the worksheet attractive, ensure it is easy to read and interpret, and have a uniform appearance.

9. Use conditional formatting to automatically highlight negative net cash flow months.

10. Insert a pie chart that compares the monthly expenses for the categories.

11. Insert a column chart that charts all of the monthly expenses regardless of the category.

12. Insert a line chart or sparkline that shows the change in the savings balance throughout the 12 months of the year.

13. Insert new rows at the top of the worksheet and enter titles that describe the worksheet's contents.

14. Use a third worksheet to plan for a major purchase, such as a car or a computer. Determine the amount of the purchase and the current annual interest rate charged by your local bank. Provide a reasonable length of time to repay the loan, such as five years for a car loan or 20 to 30 years for a home loan. Use the PMT function to determine how much you would have to spend each month on the payments for your purchase. You can do these calculations in a separate worksheet.

15. Add the loan information to the monthly budget and evaluate the impact of the purchase of this item on the budget. Examine other possible loans and evaluate their impact on the budget. If the payment exceeds the budget, reduce the estimated price of the item being purchased until you determine an affordable monthly payment.

16. Format the worksheets for your printer. Include headers and footers that display the workbook file name, the workbook's author, and the date on which the report is printed. If the report extends across several pages, repeat appropriate print titles on all of the pages, set page breaks and orientation as needed, and include page numbers and the total number of pages on every printed page.

17. Save the workbook, and then close it.

Working with the Excel Web App

Similar to the Word Web App, you can use the Excel Web App to view or edit Excel workbooks on SkyDrive. When you edit a workbook in the Excel Web App, you can apply basic formatting, perform calculations, and create charts. You can use functions; however, you need to know the function you want to insert as the Formulas tab and the Insert Function dialog box are not available.

The Excel Web App, however, does contain a valuable feature not available in the Word or PowerPoint Web Apps. The Excel Web App allows co-authoring, a feature that allows you to edit a workbook stored in a SkyDrive folder at the same time as a colleague. To allow someone to co-author a workbook, you must share the file with that person. To do this, store the file in a shared folder to which the person has access, or, if you create a file in the Web App, edit the permissions of the file to make it a shared file. To do this, click the Share link in the list of commands at the top of the window (see Exhibit 16-40); or when you point to the file, click the Share link that appears, and then click Edit permissions on the menu. On the Edit permissions page (shown in Exhibit 16-41), you can use the slider bar to allow everyone to view the file or to allow just your friends as listed on your Windows Live ID account and their friends to view the file. Or you can give permission to all your friends or only to specific friends to edit the file. Finally, you can give permission to specific people not in your friends list to view or edit a file. To send the link to the shared file to the people with whom you are sharing, click the Share link, and then click Send a link.

After you have given someone editing privileges for an Excel workbook, you and that person can each log in to your own SkyDrive accounts and then open the file in the Excel Web App. When you co-author a workbook, the number of people currently co-authoring appears at the bottom of the window, and you can click this to see a list of their names or email addresses. See Exhibit 16-42. If either of you edits the workbook, the other will see the edit moments later.

Exhibit 16-40 Share link for a folder

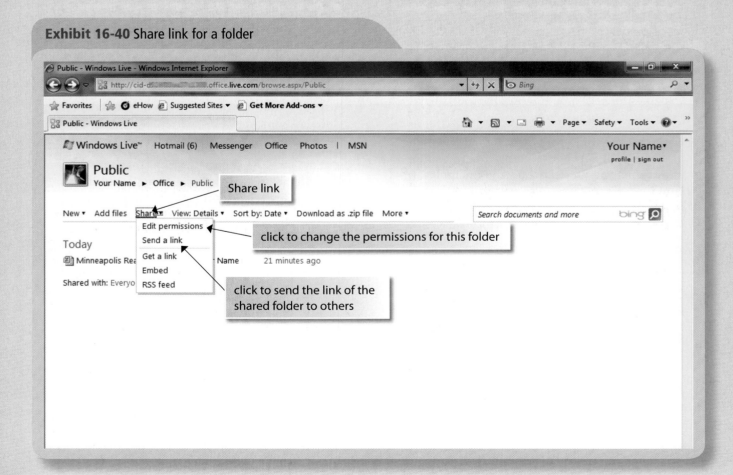

Exhibit 16-41 Edit permissions page for a folder

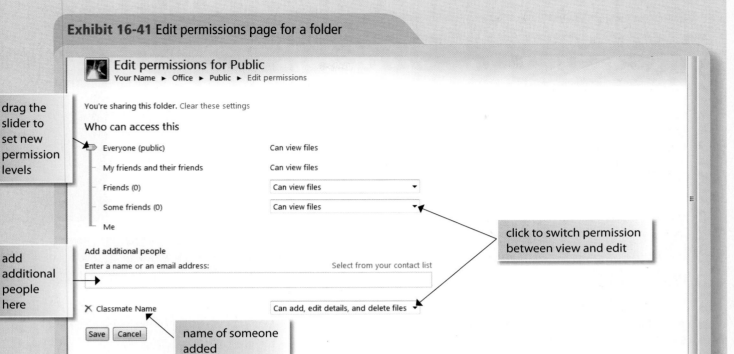

Exhibit 16-42 Excel workbook in Excel Web App with two co-authors

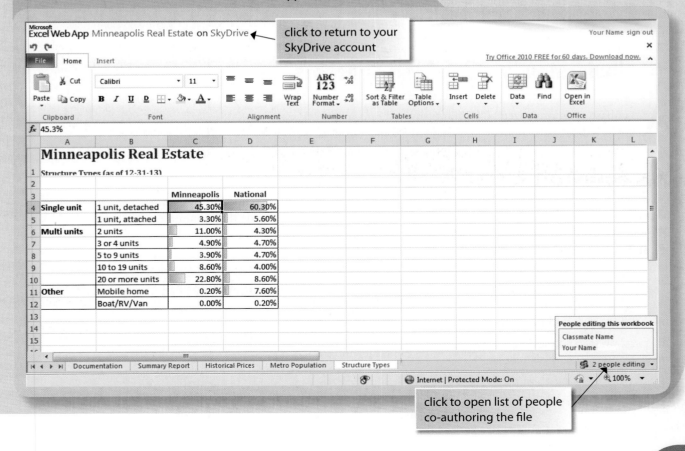

Creating a Database

Introduction

Data is a valuable resource to any business. Important data for many businesses includes customers' names and addresses and contract amounts and dates. Organizing, storing, maintaining, retrieving, and sorting this type of data are critical activities that enable a business to find and use information effectively.

Microsoft Access 2010 (or simply **Access**) is used to enter, maintain, and retrieve related data. Businesses often use Access to maintain such data as information about customers, contracts, and invoices, as well as information about assets and inventory.

LO17.1 Understanding Database Concepts

A database is an organized collection of related information. For example, a database containing information about a business might be called BusinessInfo and a database containing information about personal finances, such as stock portfolio information, might be called MyFinances.

Each piece of data in a database—that is, a single characteristic or attribute of a person, place, object, event, or idea—is stored in a **field**. For example, a database named BusinessInfo that contains information about a business's customers might include fields that contain the following customer data: ID number, first name, last name, company name, street address, city, state, ZIP code, and phone number.

Related fields are grouped into tables. A **table** is a collection of related fields. Exhibit 17-1 shows a table with the following fields that contain information about customers: CustomerID, LastName, FirstName, and Phone.

The content of a field is the **field value**. In Exhibit 17-1, the field values in the first row for CustomerID, LastName, FirstName,

Learning Objectives

After studying the material in this chapter, you will be able to:

LO17.1 Understand database concepts

LO17.2 Create a database

LO17.3 Work in Datasheet view

LO17.4 Work with fields and properties in Design view

LO17.5 Modify a table's structure

LO17.6 Close and open objects and databases

LO17.7 Create simple queries, forms, and reports

LO17.8 Compact and repair a database

Microsoft Access 2010 (Access) A computer application used to enter, maintain, and retrieve related data in a format known as a database.

field A part of a database that contains a single characteristic or attribute of a person, place, object, event, or idea.

table In Access, a collection of related fields.

field value The content of a field.

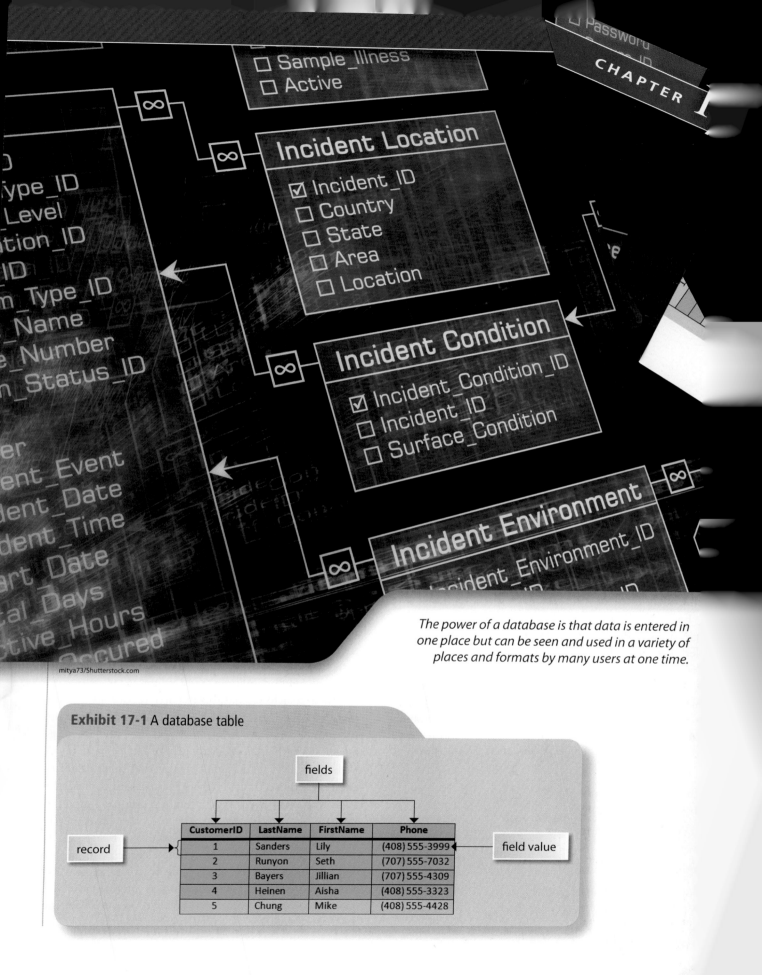

Sample_Illness
Active

CHAPTER

Incident Location

☑ Incident_ID
☐ Country
☐ State
☐ Area
☐ Location

Incident Condition

☑ Incident_Condition_ID
☐ Incident_ID
☐ Surface_Condition

Incident Environment

Incident_Environment_ID

The power of a database is that data is entered in one place but can be seen and used in a variety of places and formats by many users at one time.

mitya73/Shutterstock.com

Exhibit 17-1 A database table

fields

CustomerID	LastName	FirstName	Phone
1	Sanders	Lily	(408) 555-3999
2	Runyon	Seth	(707) 555-7032
3	Bayers	Jillian	(707) 555-4309
4	Heinen	Aisha	(408) 555-3323
5	Chung	Mike	(408) 555-4428

record

field value

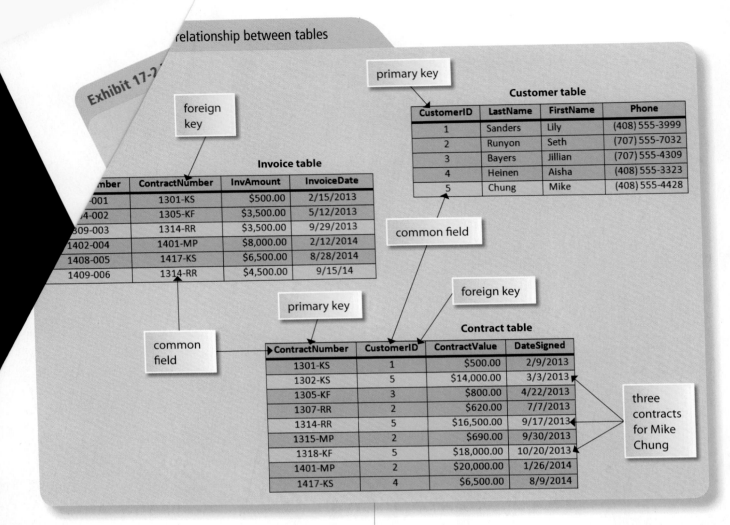

Exhibit 17-2 relationship between tables

foreign key

primary key

Customer table

CustomerID	LastName	FirstName	Phone
1	Sanders	Lily	(408) 555-3999
2	Runyon	Seth	(707) 555-7032
3	Bayers	Jillian	(707) 555-4309
4	Heinen	Aisha	(408) 555-3323
5	Chung	Mike	(408) 555-4428

Invoice table

...mber	ContractNumber	InvAmount	InvoiceDate
...-001	1301-KS	$500.00	2/15/2013
...4-002	1305-KF	$3,500.00	5/12/2013
...309-003	1314-RR	$3,500.00	9/29/2013
...1402-004	1401-MP	$8,000.00	2/12/2014
1408-005	1417-KS	$6,500.00	8/28/2014
1409-006	1314-RR	$4,500.00	9/15/14

common field

primary key

common field

foreign key

Contract table

ContractNumber	CustomerID	ContractValue	DateSigned
1301-KS	1	$500.00	2/9/2013
1302-KS	5	$14,000.00	3/3/2013
1305-KF	3	$800.00	4/22/2013
1307-RR	2	$620.00	7/7/2013
1314-RR	5	$16,500.00	9/17/2013
1315-MP	2	$690.00	9/30/2013
1318-KF	5	$18,000.00	10/20/2013
1401-MP	2	$20,000.00	1/26/2014
1417-KS	4	$6,500.00	8/9/2014

three contracts for Mike Chung

and Phone are, respectively: 1; Sanders; Lily; and (408) 555-3999.

Each row in a table contains all the fields about a single person, place, object, event, or idea, and this is called a **record**. The table shown in Exhibit 17-1 contains five records.

A database that contains more than one related table is a **relational database**. In a relational database, the tables are related to each other using a **common field**, which is simply a field that appears in more than one table. For example, a relational database that in-

cluded the table of customer information shown in Exhibit 17-1 might also contain a table named Contract that stores data about customer contracts, and a table named Invoice that stores data that is used to create customer invoices. To track the information for each customer, each of the three tables needs to have at least one field in common. See Exhibit 17-2.

In a relational database, each record in a table must be unique. To ensure that each record in a table is unique, one or more fields in each table is designated as the primary key. A **primary key** is a field, or a collection of fields, whose values uniquely identify each record in a table. No two records can contain the same value for the primary key field. For example, in the Customer table in Exhibit 17-2, the CustomerID field is the primary key field. Usually a field such as the CustomerID field is designated as the primary key because no two customers will have the same Customer ID number. Two customers might, however, have the same last name, so you would not select the LastName field as the table's primary key because th...

record All the fields in a table about a single person, place, object, event, or idea; that is, a row in a table.

relational database A database that contains a collection of related tables.

common field A field that appears in more than one table.

primary key A field, or a collection of fields, whose values uniquely identify each record in a table.

Database Management Systems

A **database management system (DBMS)** is software used to create and maintain a database, control the storage of databases on disk, and facilitate the creation, manipulation, and reporting of data. A **relational database management system (relational DBMS)** is a DBMS that is used to create and maintain relational databases. Most database management systems, including Access, are relational database management systems. Specifically, a relational DBMS:

- Allows you to create database structures containing fields, tables, and table relationships

- Lets you easily add new records, change field values in existing records, and delete records

- Contains a built-in query language, which lets you obtain immediate answers to the questions you ask about your data

- Contains a built-in report generator, which lets you produce professional-looking, formatted reports from your data

- Protects databases through security, control, and recovery facilities

A relational DBMS allows multiple users to share the same data. For example, the BusinessInfo database in the earlier example contains only one copy of the Customer, Contract, and Invoice tables, and all users can access those tables when they need information.

Finally, a DBMS can handle massive amounts of data and can be used to create relationships among multiple tables.

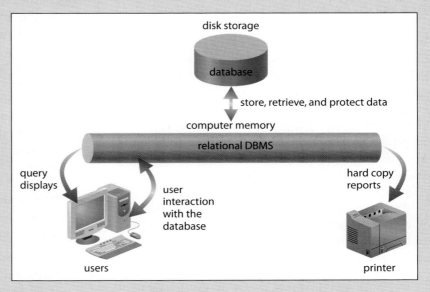

last name alone might not uniquely identify each record in the table.

To form a relationship between two tables—that is, to connect two tables—the two tables must contain one common field, and the common field must be the primary key in at least one of the tables being related. This is how the database knows which record in one table is related to which record or records in the other table or tables. In Exhibit 17-2, the common field CustomerID, the primary key in the Customer table, is included in the Contract table so that we can identify the contracts for each customer. The CustomerID field is not the primary key in the Contract table because a customer might have signed more than one contract.

When the primary key from one table is included in another table, it is called a **foreign key**. In the Contract table, the CustomerID field is a foreign key. Although a table may have only one primary key, it can have many foreign keys.

An Access database can be two gigabytes in size, can contain up to 32,768 objects (tables, queries, forms, and so on), and can have as many as 255 people using the same database at the same time.

database management system (DBMS)
Software used to create databases and manipulate the data in them.

relational database management system (relational DBMS) A database management system in which data is organized as a collection of related tables.

foreign key A field in a table that is a primary key in another table and that is included to form a relationship between the two tables.

LO17.2 **Creating a Database**

When you start Access, the program opens in Backstage view. From Backstage view, you can get information about the current database, create a new database, or open an existing database. To create a new database that does not contain any data or objects, you use the Blank database option. If you need to create a database that contains objects matching those found in common databases, such as databases that store data about contacts or events, you can click Sample templates and use a template provided with Access.

After you create or open a database, the **Navigation Pane** appears along the left side of the Access window and displays all of the tables, reports, and other objects in the database. It is the main control center for opening and working with database objects. Some people prefer to work with the Navigation Pane closed. You can click the Shutter Bar Open/Close Button « in the upper-right corner of the Navigation Pane to hide the pane, making more room on the screen for the right pane; click the Shutter Bar Open/Close Button » to redisplay the hidden pane.

Any open table, report, or other object appears in the right pane with a tab that displays its name. You can open more than one object at a time, and click the tabs to switch between them. The selected tab is orange.

Understanding the Database File Type

Access 2010 uses the .accdb file extension, which is the same file extension used for databases created with Microsoft Access 2007. To ensure compatibility between databases created with Access 2007 and Access 2010, new databases created using Access 2010 have the same file extension and file format as Access 2007 databases. This is why the File New Database dialog box provides the Microsoft Access 2007 Databases option in the Save as type box. In addition, *(Access 2007)* appears in the title bar next to the name of an open database in Access 2010.

Navigation Pane In Access, the main control center for opening and working with database objects.

ACTIVITY

Create a new, blank database.

1 Start Access. The program starts, and opens in Backstage view with the New tab displayed and Blank database selected in the Available Templates pane.

2 If the Access program window is not maximized, click the **Maximize button** ▫. See Exhibit 17-3.

3 In the right pane, to the right of the File Name box, click the **Browse button** 📂. The File New Database dialog box, which is the same as the Save As dialog box in other programs, opens. The Save as type box displays Microsoft Access 2007 Databases (or Microsoft Access 2007 Databases (*.accdb) if your computer is set up to show file extensions).

> **Tip:** To save the database in the location specified in the right pane, select the text in the File Name box, type a new file name, and then click the Create button.

4 Navigate to the **Chapter 17\Chapter folder** or the drive and folder in which you will store the files you create in this book.

5 In the File name box, change the file name to **Solar**.

6 Click **OK**. The dialog box closes, and Solar.accdb appears in the File Name box. Access added the file extension .accdb to identify the file as an Access 2007 database.

7 Click the **Create button**. Access creates the new database, saves it to the specified drive, and then opens an empty table named Table1 in Datasheet view. The Table1 table is listed in the Navigation Pane. See Exhibit 17-4.

Save Your Files

Remember to save your files to the drive and folder where you are storing the files you create as you complete the steps in this book.

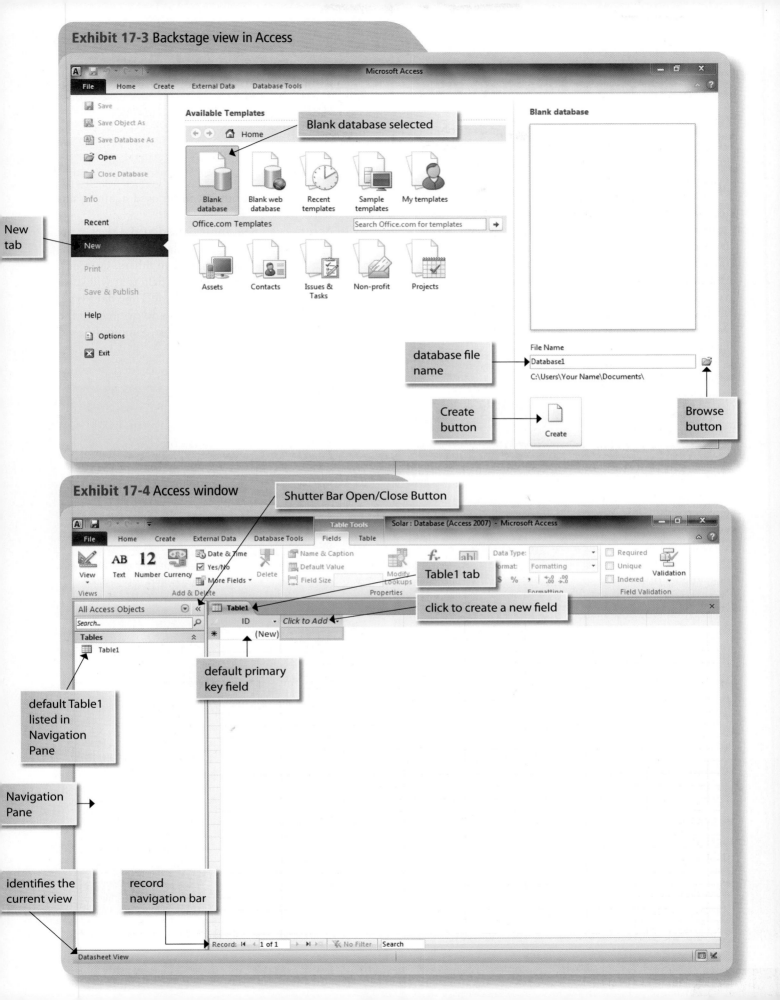

Exhibit 17-3 Backstage view in Access

Exhibit 17-4 Access window

Working in Datasheet View

All objects and fields in an Access database must have a name.

Just as in Word and Excel, a table is a grid of columns and rows that contains data. The data in a database is stored in tables. To create your database, you need to design a table and enter data into it.

One way to create and work with tables is to work in Datasheet view. **Datasheet view** shows the table's contents as a datasheet. A **datasheet** displays the table's contents in rows and columns, similar to a Word table or an Excel worksheet. In Access, each column is a field, and each row is a record. In Datasheet view, you can create fields and enter records, much like you enter data in a Word table or an Excel worksheet. When you first create a new database, an empty table opens in Datasheet view.

When you create a table, keep in mind that you should divide all information into its smallest useful part. For example, instead of including a person's full name in one field, separate the first name and the last name into separate fields. When you name a field, you should choose a name that describes the purpose or contents of the field so you and other users can quickly tell what the field stores. For example, you might use CustomerID, FirstName, LastName, and Phone as field names. A field name must be

unique within a table, but it can be used again in another table.

In Access, each field must be assigned a data type. A **data type** specifies the type of data that may be entered for that field—such as text, numbers, currency, and dates and times. For example, a field that will store invoice dates will be assigned the Date/Time data type, limiting users to entering only dates and/or times in the field. Exhibit 17-5 describes the most commonly used data types.

Datasheet view
The Access view that shows a table's contents as a datasheet.

datasheet Rows and columns in which a table's contents are displayed.

data type The type of data that can be entered for a field.

Exhibit 17-5 Common data types

Data type	Description	Field size	Use for
Text	Letters, digits, spaces, and special characters	0 to 255 characters; default is 255	Names, addresses, descriptions, and numbers not used in calculations
Memo	Letters, digits, spaces, and special characters	1 to 65,535 characters; exact size is determined by entry	Long comments and explanations
Number	Positive and negative numbers that can contain digits, a decimal point, commas, and a plus or minus sign	1 to 15 digits	Fields that will be used in calculations, except those involving money
Date/Time	Dates and times from January 1, 100 to December 31, 9999	8 bytes	
Currency	Monetary values	Accurate to 15 digits on the left side of the decimal point and to 4 digits on the right side	
AutoNumber	Unique integer created by Access for every record; can be sequential or random numbering	9 digits	The primary key in any table
Yes/No	Values that are yes or no, on or off, and true or false	1 character	Fields that indicate the presence or absence of a condition, such as whether an invoice has been paid
Hyperlink	Text used as a hyperlink address	Up to 65,535 characters total	A link to a file or Web page, a location within a file or Web page, another field

Planning a Table

Before creating a table, you should plan what data it will store and how that data will be organized. For example, a table to track information about a company's contracts might be organized based on the plan shown here. As shown in the plan, data about contracts will be stored in four fields, including fields to contain the contract ID, customer ID, contract value, and date signed. The ContractID field

Field	Purpose
ContractID	Unique number assigned to each contract; will serve as the table's primary key
CustomerID	Unique number assigned to each customer; common field that will be a foreign key to connect the Customer table
ContractValue	Dollar amount for the contract
DateSigned	Date on which the contract was signed

will be the primary key for the table because each contract is assigned a unique contract number. The CustomerID field is a foreign key that connects the information about contracts to customers. The data about customers and contracts will be stored in separate tables.

In a table, the column headers across the top of the datasheet list the field names, and each row contains a unique record.

Creating a Table in Datasheet View

When you create a table in Datasheet view, you first need to create the empty table structure. A blank table is created automatically when you start Access and create a new database. If you need to create a new, blank table in Datasheet view, click the Table button in the Tables group on the Create tab.

After creating a blank table, you use the Click to Add column in the datasheet to add fields. You can also use the options in the Add & Delete group on the Table Tools Fields tab on the Ribbon to add fields to your table. To define a new field, you assign a data type and enter a field name. To rename a field, you can right-click the field name in the column heading, click Rename Field on the shortcut menu that opens, type the new field name, and then press the Enter or Tab key.

If a field name is not completely visible in a datasheet because the column is too narrow, you can resize the column using the same techniques you used for

Naming Tables and Fields

Each table in a database and each field in a single table must have a unique name. Be sure to use descriptive names that indicate what the field or table stores. For

example, you might use Customer as a table name and CustomerID, FirstName, and LastName as field names because these names describe their contents.

In addition, when naming fields, keep in mind the following guidelines:

- A field name can have up to 64 characters, including letters, numbers, spaces, and special characters, except for a period (.), exclamation mark (!), accent grave ('), and square brackets ([ ]).

- A field name cannot begin with a space.

- Capitalize the first letter of each word in a field name that combines multiple words (for example, InvoiceDate).

- Use concise field names that are easy to remember and reference, and that won't take up a lot of space in the table datasheet.

- Use standard abbreviations, such as Num for Number, Amt for Amount, and Qty for Quantity.

- Give fields descriptive names so that you can easily identify them when you view or edit records.

- Avoid using spaces in field names (even though Access allows them) because they can cause errors when you perform other tasks.

Use a descriptive name for each field to make it easier for you and others to enter, view, or edit records.

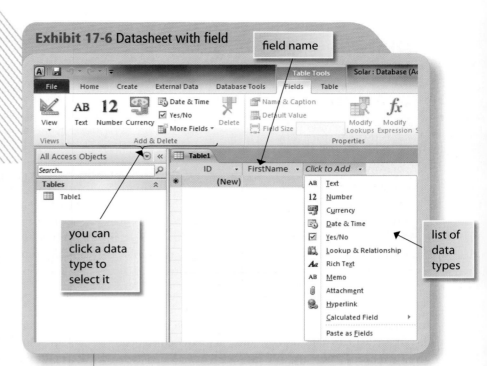

Exhibit 17-6 Datasheet with field

field name

you can click a data type to select it

list of data types

columns in Word tables and Excel worksheets: you can double-click the column border to AutoFit the contents or drag a column border to change the column width to any size you want.

When you first create a table in Datasheet view, the first field in the datasheet is named *ID* and is identified as the primary key for the table. This field is assigned the AutoNumber data type, which will add a unique number, beginning with 1, to the ID field as you enter each record in the table. If you want, you can rename the primary key field, change its data type, and then type your own values for the primary key.

 **ACTIVITY**

Create a table in Datasheet view.

1 In the datasheet, click the **Click to Add column heading**. The list of available data types appears.

2 Click **Text** to select the type of data to store in the field. A new field is added to the table and its placeholder name *Field1* is selected in the column heading.

> **Tip:** You can also add a field by clicking the appropriate data type button in the Add & Delete group on the Table Tools Fields tab, and then typing the field name.

3 Type **FirstName** as the field name, and then press the **Enter key**. The list of available data types appears for the next field so you can quickly add another field. See Exhibit 17-6.

4 Select **Text** as the data type, type **LastName** as the field name, and then press the **Tab key**. The list of available data types appears for the next field.

5 Select **Date & Time** as the data type, type **Since** as the field name, and then press the **Tab key**. The list of available data types appears for the next field.

6 Right-click the field name **Since**. On the shortcut menu, click **Rename Field**. The Since field name is selected.

> **Tip:** To change a data type in Datasheet view, click the field whose data type you want to change, click the Data Type arrow in the Formatting group on the Table Tools Fields tab, and then click the new data type.

7 Type **CustomerSince** and then press the **Tab key**. The list of available data types appears for the next field.

8 Right-click the field name **ID**. On the shortcut menu, click **Rename Field**, type **CustomerID** and then press the **Tab key**.

9 Double-click the **CustomerSince column heading right border** to widen the column to fit the contents.

> ⚠ **Problem?** If a menu opens, you clicked the arrow on the CustomerSince column heading. Click the arrow again to close the menu, and then repeat Step 9.

Saving a Table

A table is not stored in the database until you save it. The first time you save a table, you should give it a descriptive name that identifies the information it contains. Like a field name, a table name can have 64 characters, including spaces. To save the table, you click the Save button on the Quick Access Toolbar. When you save a table, you are saving its structure—the number of fields, the field names, the column widths in the datasheet, and so on.

2 In the Table Name box, type **Customer** and then click **OK**. The Customer table is saved in the database and the table name is updated in the Navigation Pane and on the table's tab. See Exhibit 17-7.

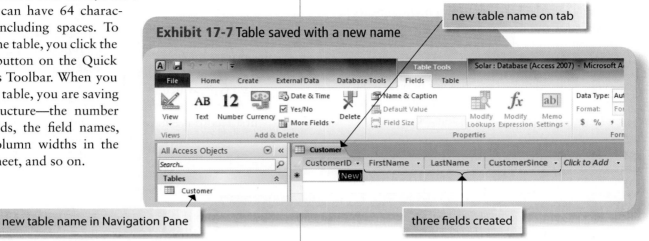

Exhibit 17-7 Table saved with a new name

new table name on tab

new table name in Navigation Pane

three fields created

Saving a Database

Unlike other Office programs, you do not need to save the database after you add or delete records. Access automatically saves changes to the active database when you change or add a record or close the database. Instead, clicking the Save button saves the design and format of an Access object, such as a table. For example, if you add or delete fields, or change the width of a column in a datasheet, you need to save these changes.

If you store your database on a removable drive, such as a USB drive, you should never remove the drive while the database file is open. If you do, Access will encounter problems when it tries to save the database, which might damage the database.

ACTIVITY

Save and name a table.

1 On the Quick Access Toolbar, click the **Save button** 🔲. The Save As dialog box opens with the default table name *Table1* selected in the Table Name box.

> **Tip:** You can also use the Save and Save As commands in the navigation bar in Backstage view.

Entering Records

After you create the structure of a table by naming fields and assigning data types, you can enter records. To enter records in a table datasheet, you type the field values below the column headings for the fields. When you start typing a value in a field, a pencil symbol appears in the row selector at the beginning of the row for the new record. The pencil symbol indicates that the record is being edited.

One way a datasheet differs from Word tables and Excel worksheets is that when you add a record to a table, you may enter it only in the next available row. You cannot insert a row between existing records for the new record. A star symbol ✳ appears at the beginning of the next available row for a new record. When the table contains many records and you cannot see the next available row, you can click the New (blank) record button ▶✳ on the record navigation bar to scroll the datasheet to the next available row.

If you mistype a field value or need to change it, you can correct it. Click in the field to position the insertion point, use the Backspace key or Delete key to delete incorrect text, type the correct text, and then press the Tab key or the Enter key. Note that you cannot edit the values in a field that has the Auto-Number data type.

Remember that data is stored in the database as soon as you enter it. You do not need to click the Save button to save records.

ACTIVITY

Enter records in a table.

1 In the first row of the datasheet, click in the **FirstName column**. The FirstName column header is highlighted and the insertion point appears in the FirstName column for the first record, ready for you to enter the field value.

2 Type **Lily** and then press the **Tab key**. The field value is entered and the insertion point moves to the LastName column for the first record. Access assigns the first primary key value. See Exhibit 17-8.

Exhibit 17-8 First field value entered

pencil symbol

star symbol

primary key value for first record

first field value entered

insertion point

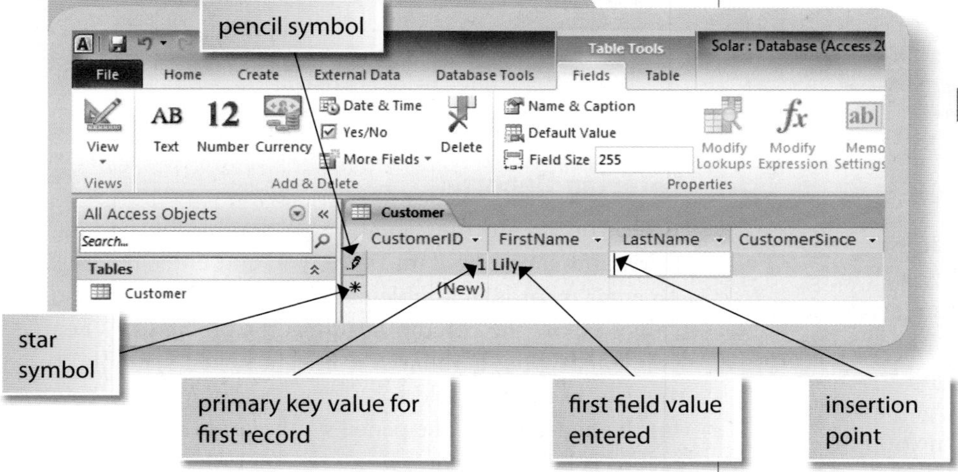

3 Type **Sanders** and then press the **Tab** key. Access enters the field value and moves the insertion point to the CustomerSince column.

4 Type **3/17/14** and then press the **Tab** key. The year changes to 2014 even though you entered only the final two digits of the year because the CustomerSince field has the Date/Time data type, which by default formats dates with four-digit years. The first record is entered into the table, and the insertion point appears in the CustomerID field for the second record. The pencil symbol is removed from the first row because the record in that row is no longer being edited.

⚠ **Problem?** If you see another date format for the CustomerSince field, your Windows date setting is different. Continue with Step 5; this difference will not cause any problems.

5 Press the **Enter key** to move to the FirstName field in the second row, type **Seth**, press the **Enter key** to move to the LastName field, type **Runyon**, press the **Enter key** to move to the CustomerSince field, type **2-2-14**, and then press the **Enter key**. The second record is entered, the number 2 was assigned automatically to the CustomerID field in the second row, and the third row is active, ready for a new record. Again, notice that the CustomerSince date you entered was changed to match the Date/Time format.

Copying Records from Another Access Database

After you created the Customer table, you entered records directly into the table's datasheet. You can also enter records in a table by copying and pasting records from a table in the same database or in a different database. To use this method, however, the tables must have the same structure—that is, the tables must contain the same fields, with the same design and characteristics, in the same order.

To insert records from another table, first select the records you want to copy. If the records are in a second database, you need to open the second database

file. Next, copy the records to the Clipboard. Then, with the table where you want to paste the data open in Datasheet view, select the next available row for a new record, making sure the entire row is selected. Finally, paste the records into the table by clicking the Paste button arrow in the Clipboard group on the Home tab, and then clicking Paste Append. When a dialog box opens asking you to confirm that you want to paste all the records, click Yes. The dialog box closes, and the pasted records are highlighted.

6 In the third row, enter **Jillian** as the first name, **Connor** as the last name, and **6/15/2014** as the CustomerSince date.

7 Click the field containing **Connor**. The insertion point appears in the field.

8 Use the same editing techniques you've used in Word and Excel to change the name to **Bayers**.

9 Enter the following data for the fourth and fifth records:

FirstName	LastName	CustomerSince
Aisha	**Heinen**	**10-5-13**
Mike	**Chung**	**6/13/2014**

> ⚠ **Problem?** If you enter a value in the wrong field, a menu might open with options for addressing the problem. If this happens, click the **Enter new value option** to highlight the field with the incorrect value, and then type the correct value.

LO17.4 Working with Fields and Properties in Design View

Each field in a table is defined by a variety of attributes, or characteristics, called properties. A **property** describes one characteristic of a field. A field name and its data type are field properties. Properties are listed in the **Field Properties pane**.

The properties for a field depend on the field's data type. In addition to the field name and the data type, the following are some common additional properties for different fields:

▸ **Description**—an optional property for describing a field; usually used only when the field name is not descriptive enough or the field has a special function such as a primary key.

▸ **Field Size**—the maximum storage size for Text, Number, and AutoNumber fields. The default field size of a Text field is 255 characters.

▸ **Format**—describes how the value is displayed; for example, with the Date/Time data type, you can choose an existing format or enter a custom format using the same custom codes as you used in Excel.

Analyze the values that will be stored in a Number field to determine the best Field Size property and ensure the most efficient user experience.

▸ **Decimal Places**—the number of decimal places that are displayed to the right of the decimal point in a field defined with the Number or Currency data type.

▸ **Caption**—an alternate way of displaying the field name in database objects. For example, you might use the field name *CustNum* in the table's design, but set the Caption property to display *Customer Number* as the field's caption to enhance readability in datasheets and forms.

▸ **Default Value**—the value automatically entered in a field. For example, if all customers in a Customer table live in a certain state, you might set the Default Value property for the State field to the state's abbreviation.

The field name and data type properties are available on the Ribbon on the Table Tools Fields tab in Datasheet view, but more properties are available in Design view. **Design view** shows a listing of a table's fields and field properties. In Design view, you can create and modify fields, but you cannot enter records. A table design grid in the top portion of the window lists the field names and data types. The table design grid can also include a description of each field. At the bottom of the window in Design view, the Field Properties pane lists the additional properties available for the field currently selected in the table design grid, and the Help box displays information about the currently selected property.

> **property** One characteristic or aspect of a field, such as its name or data type.
>
> **Field Properties pane** The list of properties for a field.
>
> **Design view** The Access view that shows the underlying structure of a database object and allows you to modify that structure.

If no predefined format matches the layout you want for date values, you can type a custom date format such as *mm/dd/yyyy* to create the exact date format you want.

To switch between Datasheet view and Design view, you can use the View button on the Ribbon. This button appears in the Views group on the Home tab; in Datasheet view, it also appears in the Views group on the Table Tools Fields tab; and in Design view, it also appears in the Views group on the Table Tools Design tab. The icon on the View button on the Ribbon changes to reflect the view that you will switch to; that is, in Datasheet view, the icon shows that clicking it will switch you to Design view, and vice versa in Design view. You can also use buttons on the status bar to switch among views, similar to the view buttons on the status bars in Word and Excel.

Changing Field Properties in Design View

When you first create a field, most properties are assigned default values. You can change these values to match the field's content or purpose. To do this, you change the values in the Field Properties pane in Design

view. Often you can change a property by typing the new value in the property's box. For some properties, when you click the box in the Field Properties pane, an arrow appears at the right end of the box. This indicates that in addition to typing the new value, you can click the arrow, and then choose from a list of predesigned formats or values for that property.

Change field properties in Design view.

1 On the status bar, click the **Design View button** 📉. The table switches to Design view. See Exhibit 17-9. The table design grid lists the fields you entered in Datasheet view. The Field Properties pane lists the available properties for the selected CustomerID field, and a description of the selected property (field name) appears in the Help box.

2 In the table design grid, in the Field Name column, click **FirstName**. The field is selected in the table design grid, and its properties appear in the Field Properties pane.

3 In the Field Properties pane, select the value in the **Field Size box**, and then type **20**. This is the maximum number of characters allowed for a customer's first name. Notice

> **Tip:** To change a field property in Datasheet view, use the buttons in the Formatting group on the Table Tools Fields tab.

Field Size Property for Number Fields

When you use the Number data type to define a field, you should set the Field Size property based on the largest value you expect to store in that field. Access processes smaller data sizes faster, using less memory, so you can optimize the database's performance and its storage space by selecting the correct field size for each field. Number fields have the following Field Size property settings:

▶ **Byte**—stores whole numbers (numbers with no fractions) from 0 to 255 in one byte
▶ **Integer**—stores whole numbers from –32,768 to 32,767 in two bytes
▶ **Long Integer** (default)—stores whole numbers from –2,147,483,648 to 2,147,483,647 in four bytes
▶ **Single**—stores positive and negative numbers to precisely seven decimal places and uses four bytes

▶ **Double**—stores positive and negative numbers to precisely 15 decimal places and uses eight bytes
▶ **Replication ID**—establishes a unique identifier for replication of tables, records, and other objects in databases created using Access 2003 and earlier versions and uses 16 bytes
▶ **Decimal**—stores positive and negative numbers to precisely 28 decimal places and uses 12 bytes

Choosing appropriate field sizes creates the best database efficiency. For example, it would be wasteful to use the Long Integer field size for a Number field that will store only whole numbers ranging from 0 to 255 because the Long Integer field size uses four bytes of storage space. A better choice would be the Byte field size, which uses one byte of storage space to store the same values.

Exhibit 17-9 Table in Design view

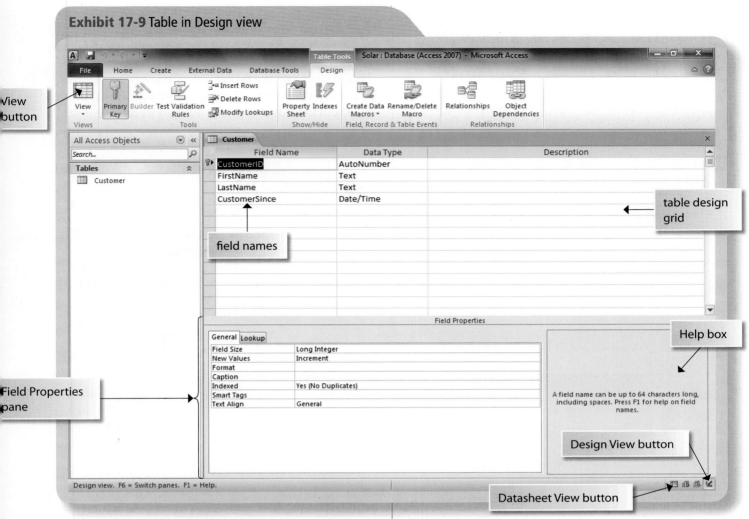

that the description in the Help box changed to describe the currently selected property.

4 In the table design grid, in the Field Name column, click **CustomerSince**. The properties for the CustomerSince field appear in the Field Properties pane. A Date/Time field does not have a Field Size property, so that property is not listed.

5 In the Field Properties pane, click in the **Format box**. An arrow appears at the right end of the Format box.

6 Click the **Format box arrow**. A list of date formats opens. These are similar to the data formats you used in Excel.

7 In the list, click **Long Date**. The format is changed.

8 On the Quick Access Toolbar, click the **Save button** 🖫 to save the changes to the design of the Customer table. Because you reduced the Field Size property of the FirstName field from

255 characters to 20 characters, a dialog box appears, indicating that some data may be lost because the field size was decreased. If you click Yes and any value in the FirstName field contains more than 20 characters, any characters after the twentieth will be deleted. None of the values in the FirstName field in your table have more than 20 characters.

Generally, it's a good idea to create the structure of a table and change field properties before you enter any data so you can avoid values already entered changing unexpectedly if a property changes.

9 Click **Yes**. The table is saved.

10 On the Table Tools Design tab, in the Views group, click the **View button**. The table returns to Datasheet view. The date no longer fits in the CustomerSince column because the Long Date format that you chose as the field's Format property displays many more characters than the default Short Date format.

11 Double-click the **CustomerSince column header right border** to widen the column to fit the contents. The dates in that field now appear in the Long Date format. See Exhibit 17-10. Note that the property change to the FirstName field is not apparent because none of the names entered have more than 20 characters.

12 Save the Customer table.

Exhibit 17-10 Records with Long Date format

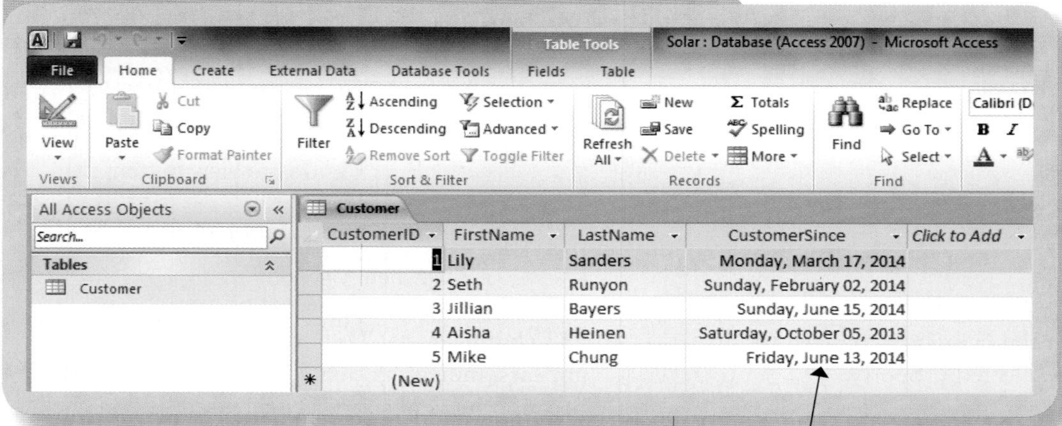

dates in Long Date format

Creating a Table and Setting Properties in Design View

Because you can set additional properties for fields in Design view, it can be a good idea to create a table in Design view. Then, after you have named all the fields and modified the field properties, you can switch to Datasheet view to enter records. To create a new, blank table in Design view, switch to Design view immediately after creating a new database, or, if a table already exists and you need to create a new one, click the Table Design button in the Tables group on the Create tab. You can also create a table in Datasheet view and then switch to Design view, but you must save the table before switching views.

When you first create a table in Design view, the insertion point appears in the table design grid in the first row's Field Name box, ready for you to begin defining the first field in the table. To name a field, type it in the Field Name box. To assign a data type to a field, click in the Data Type box, click the arrow that appears, and then select the data type. If you need to rename a field in Design view, click its name in the table design grid, and then edit it.

ACTIVITY

Create a table in Design view.

1 On the Ribbon, click the **Create tab**. In the Tables group, click the **Table Design button**. The view switches to Design view and a new, blank table named Table1 is created. This table will contain contract data, and its first field will contain the unique number that identifies each contract.

2 In the table design grid, in the Field Name column, in the first row, type **ContractID** and then press the **Tab key** to select the Data Type box. The default data type, Text, appears highlighted in the Data Type box, which now also contains an arrow, and the field properties for a Text field appear in the Field Properties pane. See Exhibit 17-11. The Help box provides an explanation for the current property, Data Type. Contract ID numbers at this company are always two digits that identify the year, followed by two numbers that identify the actual contract number, a hyphen, and the initials of the sales person at the company who completed the contract. Therefore, the default Text data type is appropriate.

Design view lists all of the fields in a table, but none of its records.

Exhibit 17-11 New table in Design view after entering the first field name

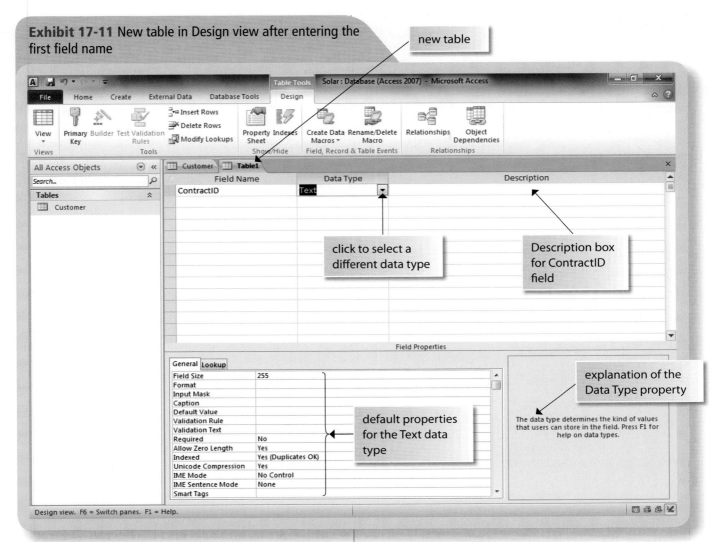

new table

click to select a different data type

Description box for ContractID field

explanation of the Data Type property

The data type determines the kind of values that users can store in the field. Press F1 for help on data types.

default properties for the Text data type

---

3 Press the **Tab key** to accept Text as the data type and to move the insertion point to the Description box.

4 In the Description box, type **Primary key**. The description you entered will appear on the status bar when you view the table in Datasheet view. (Note that specifying *Primary key* as the Description property does not set the current field as the primary key; you will set the primary key shortly.)

5 In the Field Properties pane, change the **Field Size property** to **7**.

6 In the Field Properties pane, click in the **Caption box**, and then type **Contract Number**. This value is what will appear in Access objects, including tables. So when

> **Tip:** You can press the F6 key to move the insertion point from the table design grid to the Field Properties pane.

you look at a table in Datasheet view, you will see this caption as the field name for this field instead of ContractID. See Exhibit 17-12.

7 In the table design grid, in the **second row**, enter **CustomerID** as the field name, **Number** as the data type, **Foreign key** as the description, and then **Customer ID** as the Caption property. The CustomerID field is the field that will connect (relate) the Contract table to the Customer table you already created. The related field in the Customer table is also named CustomerID, and it has the AutoNumber data type. The data type of a foreign key must be compatible with the data type of the primary key in the original table.

8 In the table design grid, in the **third row**, enter **ContractValue** as the field name, **Currency** as the data type, **Total value of the contract** as the description, and **Contract Value** as the Caption property.

Exhibit 17-12 ContractID field defined

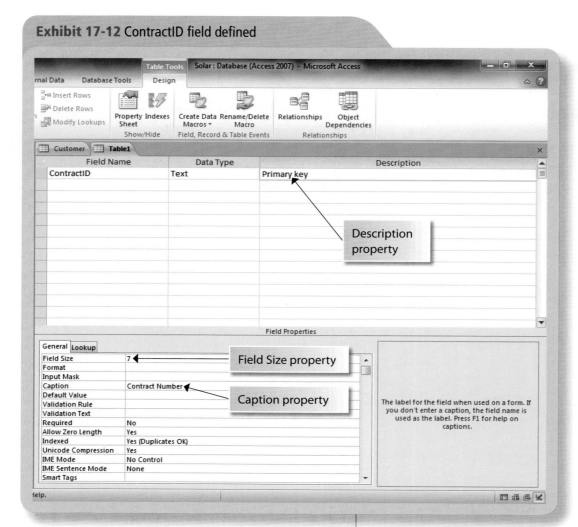

Signed as the Caption property.

10 In the table design grid, in the **fifth row**, enter **Signed** as the field name, **Yes/No** as the data type, and **Signed?** as the Caption property. This field can have only two values: Yes (the contract was signed) or No (it hasn't been signed yet).

11 In the Field Properties pane, click in the **Format box**, click the **arrow** that appears, and then click **Yes/No**.

9 In the table design grid, in the **fourth row**, enter **DateSigned** as the field name, **Date/Time** as the data type, **Date contract was signed** as the description, **Short Date** as the Format property, and **Date**

12 Click in the **Default Value box**, delete the **0**, and then type **No**. Until the contract is signed, No will be entered as the default value in the Signed field

Input Mask Property

The Input Mask property can be used to display data in a specific format, without requiring any additional effort by the user. For example, you might use the Input Mask property to format a field that stores phone numbers with parentheses and a dash to separate the digits. In this case, the user would enter the digits in the phone number, and the input mask would format the field value using the input mask. If you decide at a later time to change the display of the phone numbers, you only need to change the Input Mask property for the field, and all of the phone numbers would immediately use the new formatting.

Input masks can help ensure that data is formatted correctly. However, if you add an input mask to a field, you need to keep the big picture in mind. For instance, if the customer list for a company includes international customers, an input mask that restricts a phone number field to the format (000) 000-0000 would cause problems because other countries use different formats to display their phone numbers and some use a different number of digits.

Exhibit 17-13 New table in Design view

you have actually given the field a **null value**. You cannot give a null value to the primary key field because entity integrity prevents Access from accepting and processing that record.

- Organizes records by that field value and provides a meaningful way to work with records regardless of the order in which the records were entered.

- Creates a faster response to requests for specific records based on the primary key.

in all new records. Because the default appearance for the Yes/No data type is a check box, this means the check box will be unchecked for new records. See Exhibit 17-13.

Specifying the Primary Key

Although not required, including a primary key in a table:

- Uniquely identifies each record in a table.

- Prevents duplicate values in the primary key field. For example, if a record already exists in the Contract table with a ContractID value of 1402-TB, you cannot add another record with this same value in the ContractID field.

- Forces users to enter a value for the primary key field in every record in the table (known as **entity integrity**). If you do not enter a value for a field,

You can choose which field to use as the primary key when the table is in Design view. The Primary Key button in the Tools group on the Table Tools Design tab is a toggle. You can click the button to remove the key symbol if you want to specify a different field as the primary key.

Specify a primary key.

1 In the table design grid, click in the **ContractID row** to make it the current field.

> **entity integrity** A setting that forces users to enter a value for the primary key field in every record in the table.
>
> **null value** A field with no value.

2 On the Table Tools Design tab, in the Tools group, click the **Primary Key button**. A key symbol 🔑 appears in the row selector for the ContractID row, indicating that the ContractID field is the table's primary key. See Exhibit 17-14.

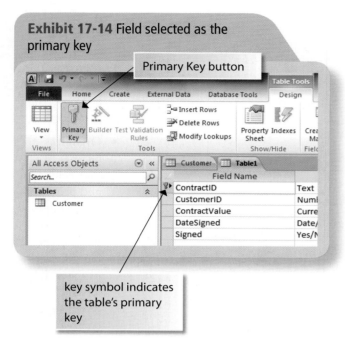

Exhibit 17-14 Field selected as the primary key

Primary Key button

key symbol indicates the table's primary key

Changing the Default Primary Key Field

When you create a new table in Datasheet view, Access creates the ID field as the table's default primary key. You can rename the ID field to better reflect the contents of the field you want to use for the primary key. Right-click the ID field, click Rename Field on the shortcut menu, type a new name, and then click in the next row.

The renamed primary key field still retains the properties of the default field, including its data type. The default ID primary key field is assigned the AutoNumber data type. For primary keys that contain a mix of letters and numbers, such as contract numbers, select the Text data type. However, you can also change the data type. In Datasheet view, you use the Data Type box for changing the data type. On the Fields tab, in the Formatting group, click the column, click the Data Type box arrow, and then click the new data type.

Saving the Table Design and Entering Records

After you design a table, you need to save it. To enter records into the new table, you need to switch to Datasheet view. You can use the Save button, or let Access remind you to save the table when you switch to Datasheet view.

ACTIVITY

Save the table design and enter records.

1 On the Table Tools Design tab, in the Views group, click the **View button**. A dialog box opens telling you that you must first save the table.

2 Click **Yes**. The Save As dialog box opens with Table1 selected in the Table Name box.

3 Type **Contract** and then click **OK**. The Contract table is added to the Tables list in the Navigation Pane, and the Contract table is displayed in Datasheet view.

4 Double-click the right borders of each column to AutoFit the widths.

5 In the first row of the datasheet, type **1401-RR** as the contract number, and then press the **Tab key**.

6 Type **5** as the customer ID, press the **Tab key**, type **620** as the contract value, and then press the **Tab key**. The contract value amount is displayed with a dollar sign and two decimal places to match the default format for the Currency data type even though you didn't type them. To the right of the Date Signed field, a calendar icon appears.

7 In the Date Signed field, type **1/26/14** and then press the **Tab key**. The Signed? field is selected.

> **Tip:** To use the mouse to enter the date, click the calendar icon and then select the date. To use the mouse to select the check box, click it.

8 Press the **Spacebar**. A check mark appears in the check box.

9 Press the **Tab key** to move to the second record. See Exhibit 17-15.

10 Save the Contract table.

> **Tip:** You can press the Tab key to leave a Yes/No check box unchecked, and press the Spacebar or click the check box to select and deselect it..

Guidelines for Designing Databases

Database design involves determining the fields, tables, and relationships needed to satisfy the data and processing requirements for an organization. When you design a database, keep in mind the following guidelines:

▶ **Identify the fields needed to produce the required information.** Be sure to consider and include both the obvious and not so obvious data.

▶ **Divide each piece of data into its smallest useful part.** Individual units make the data more useful and flexible. For example, a person's complete name should be stored in two fields rather than one field.

▶ **Group related fields into tables.** Each table should have one focus. For example, fields related to invoices could be grouped into an Invoice table, and the fields related to customers could be grouped into a Customer table.

▶ **Determine each table's primary key.** Often, one of the fields in the table naturally serves the function of a primary key. For some tables, two or more fields might be needed to function as the primary key. In these cases, the primary key is called a **composite key**. For example, a school grade table would use a combination of student number and course code to serve as the primary key. For other tables, no single field or combination of fields can uniquely identify a record in a table. In these cases, you need to add a field whose sole purpose is to serve as the table's primary key.

▶ **Include a common field in related tables.** You use the common field to connect one table logically with another table. For example, Contract and Customer tables both include the CustomerID field as a common field; the CustomerID field is a foreign key in the Contract table. With this common field, you can find all contracts for a particular customer; use the CustomerID value for a customer and search the Contract table for all records with that CustomerID value. Likewise, you can determine which customer has a particular contract by searching the Customer table to find the record with the same CustomerID value as the corresponding value in the Contract table.

▶ **Avoid data redundancy and inconsistent data.** When you store the same data in more than one place, **data redundancy** occurs. With the exception of using common fields to connect tables, data redundancy wastes storage space and can cause inconsistencies. An inconsistency exists when you type a field value such as a company name one way in one table and a different way in another table.

▶ **Determine the properties of each field.** You need to identify the properties, or characteristics, of each field so that the DBMS knows how to store, display, and process the field values. These properties include the field's name, maximum number of characters or digits, description, valid values, and other field characteristics.

Cybrain/Shutterstock.com

Exhibit 17-15 Record entered in the Contract table

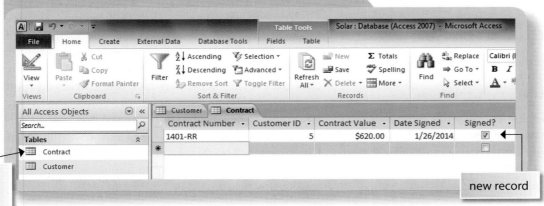

composite key
A primary key that requires two or more fields to uniquely identify each record in a table.

data redundancy Data stored in more than one place.

new record

Contract table in Navigation Pane

LO17.5
Modifying a Table's Structure

Exhibit 17-16 Field being moved in the table structure

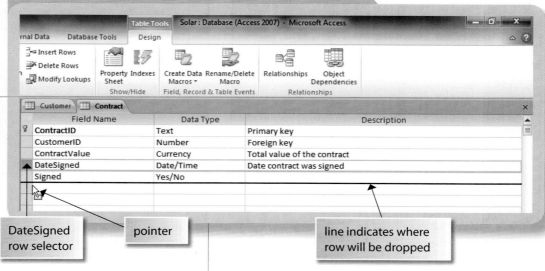

Exhibit 17-16 Field being moved in the table structure

DateSigned row selector

pointer

line indicates where row will be dropped

Even a well-designed table might need to be modified. Some changes you can make to a table's structure in Design view are changing the order of fields, adding and deleting fields, and changing field properties. After you modify the table's structure, be sure to save the table.

To select a field, click the corresponding column header (sometimes referred to as a field selector or column selector). To select a record, click the box to the left of the row (sometimes called a record selector or row selector). To select all the records, click the datasheet selector, which is the box to the left of the first field name in the datasheet.

Moving a Field

To move a field, you use the mouse to drag it to a new location in the table design grid. Although you can move fields in Datasheet view by dragging a field's column heading to a new location, doing so rearranges only the *display* of the table's fields; the table structure is not changed. To move a field permanently, you must display the table in Design view.

 **ACTIVITY**

Move a field in a table.

1 Display the Contract table in **Design view**.

2 In the table design grid, point to the **DateSigned row selector**. The pointer changes to ➡. Click the **DateSigned row selector** to select the row.

3 Press and hold the mouse button while pointing to the **DateSigned row selector**. The pointer changes to ⬚. Drag down until the dark line indicating the drop location for the field appears below the Signed field. See Exhibit 17-16.

4 Release the mouse button. The DateSigned field now appears below the Signed field in the table.

5 Save the Contract table, and then click the **Customer tab** to display the Customer table.

6 Display the Customer table in **Design view**.

7 Move the **LastName Field** above the FirstName field.

8 Save the Customer table, and then switch to **Datasheet view** to confirm that the LastName field appears to the left of the FirstName field.

Adding a Field

You can add a new field to a table at any time. If the field will be the last field in the table, you can add the field the same way as when you added fields to a new table. If you decide the field belongs in a different location, you can always move it to its proper position.

You can also insert a new field between existing fields. In Datasheet view, select the field to the left of where you want the new field to be inserted. Then, in the Add & Delete group on the Table Tools Fields tab, click the button for the data type of the field you want to insert. In Design view, select the row below where you want the new field to be inserted. Then, in the Tools group on the Table Tools Design tab, click the Insert Rows button. You then enter the field name, data type, optional description, and any additional field properties for the new field as usual.

Keep in mind that the new field does not contain data for any existing records. If you want to add data to the new field in existing records, you need to go back to each existing record, click in the column for that record, and type the new data.

![ACTIVITY]

Add a field to a table.

1. In Datasheet view for the Customer table, click the **FirstName column header** to select the field.

2. On the Ribbon, click the **Table Tools Fields tab**. In the Add & Delete group, click the **Text button**. A new field is inserted between the FirstName and CustomerSince fields with the temporary field name *Field1* selected. See Exhibit 17-17.

appears between the FirstName and Email fields. The insertion point is in the Field Name box, ready for you to type the name for the new field. See Exhibit 17-18.

Exhibit 17-18 Table with new field in Design view

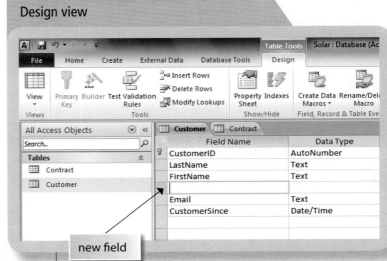

new field

Exhibit 17-17 Table with new field in Datasheet view

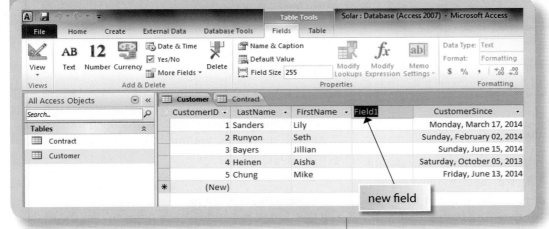

new field

3. Type **Email** as the field name, and then press the **Enter key**. The CustomerID field value for the first record is selected.

4. In the first record, click in the **Email column**, type **lsanders@onecalweb.com** as the email address, and then press the **Tab key**. Resize the column to fit the widest value.

5. Switch the table to **Design view**. In the table design grid, in the Field Name column, click **Email**.

6. On the Table Tools Design tab, in the Tools group, click the **Insert Rows button**. A new, blank row

7. Type **InvoiceItem** as the field name, set the data type to **Text**, change the Field Size property to **40**, and set the Caption property to **Invoice Item**.

8. Save the table.

Deleting a Field

After you've created a table, you might need to delete a field. When you delete a field, you also delete all the values for that field from the table. So, *before* you delete a field, make sure that you really want to do so and that you choose the correct field to delete. You can delete one field at a time, or you can select and delete a group of fields at the same time.

You can delete fields from either Datasheet view or Design view. In Datasheet view, select the field to delete, and then click the Delete button in the Add & Delete group on the Table Tools Fields tab. In Design view, click the Field Name box for the field to delete, and then click the Delete Rows button in the Tools group on the Table Tools Design tab.

Delete a field from a table.

1 In the table design grid, in the Field Name column, click **InvoiceItem** to make it the current field.

2 On the Table Tools Design tab, in the Tools group, click the **Delete Rows button**. A dialog box appears confirming that you want to permanently delete the selected field and all of the data in that field.

> **Tip:** You can also select the column header in Datasheet view, and then click the Delete button in the Add & Delete group on the Table Tools Fields tab.

3 Click **Yes**. The selected InvoiceItem field is removed from the Customer table.

4 Save the Customer table.

LO17.6 Closing and Opening Objects and Databases

Unlike other programs, you need to open and close the tables and other objects in a database. A database can be open but have all its objects closed.

Closing a Table

When you are done working with a table, you should close it. You close the selected table by clicking the Close button ☒ in the upper-right corner of the pane. Note that the ScreenTip for the Close button shows the name of the tab that will close as part of the button name, such as *Close 'Table1'*. If you changed the table structure but didn't save it, a dialog box opens reminding you to save. It is a good idea to work in an object and then save and close it as you go.

Close a table.

1 If it is not already selected, click the **Customer tab**.

2 In the gray bar to the right of the tabs, click the **Close 'Customer' button** ☒. The Customer table closes, and the Contract table is displayed.

3 Right-click the **Contract tab**. On the shortcut menu, click **Close**. The Contract table closes, and the main portion of the Access window is now blank because no table or other database object is open.

> **⚠ Problem?** If a dialog box opens asking if you want to save the changes to the layout of the Contract table, click **Yes**.

Closing a Database

When you are done working with a database, you should close it. To close an open database without exiting the Access program, click the File tab to display Backstage view, and then click Close Database. You can also exit Access to close the database as you exit the program.

Close an existing database.

1 On the Ribbon, click the **File tab**. In Backstage view, in the navigation bar, click **Close Database**. The Solar database closes, leaving Access in Backstage view with the New tab displayed.

Opening a Database

You open an existing database from Backstage view by clicking Open in the navigation bar, and then using the Open dialog box to navigate to and open the database. As with other files, you might need to enable the content to remove the Security Warning.

Open an existing database.

1 Open the data file **Solar17** located in the Chapter 17\ Chapter folder. The Solar17 database opens. This database contains three objects: the Contract, Customer, and Invoice tables.

> **⚠ Problem?** If the Security Warning bar appears, click the **Enable Content button** to close it. If the Security Warning dialog box opens asking if you want to make this file a Trusted Document, click **Yes** to prevent the Security Warning bar from appearing again, or click **No** to have the Security Warning bar appears the next time you open the database.

In the Navigation Pane, icons identify the different types of database objects, making it simpler to distinguish between them.

2 Open Backstage view, and then in the navigation bar, click **Save Database As** to open the Save As dialog box. Save the database as **SolarPower17**.

Opening a Table

All of the tables (as well as any query, form, or report) in a database are listed in the Navigation Pane. You open a table or other object by double-clicking its name in the Navigation Pane. To see more of the table, you can hide the Navigation Pane. The Shutter Bar Open/Close Button « at the top of the Navigation Pane hides the pane.

ACTIVITY

Open a table.

1 In the Navigation Pane, double-click **Customer** to open the Customer table in Datasheet view. Drag the scroll box on the horizontal scroll bar to the right to examine all the fields in the table.

▸ **Tip:** You can click the Shutter Bar Open/ Close Button « to hide the pane and display more of the datasheet.

2 In the Navigation Pane, double-click **Contract** to open the Contract table in Datasheet view. Examine the fields in the Contract table.

3 Open the **Invoice table** and then examine the fields in the Invoice table. See Exhibit 17-19.

4 Close the Customer and Contract tables.

Exhibit 17-19 Three open tables

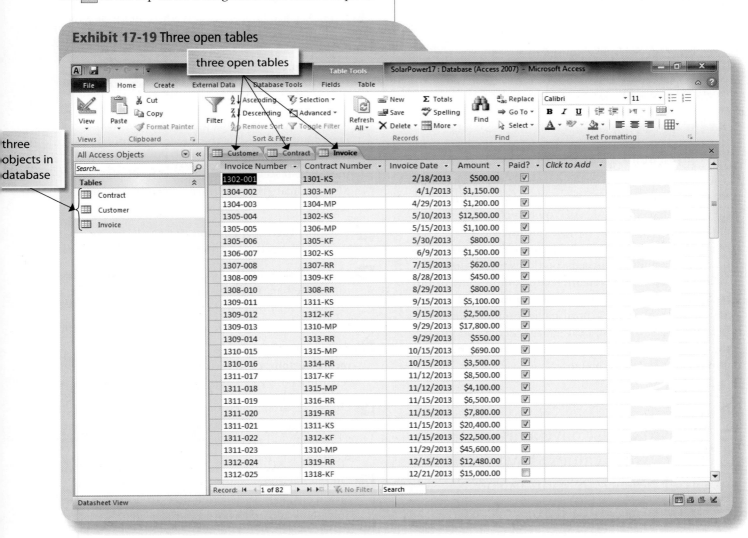

Navigation Pane

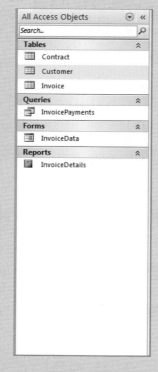

The Navigation Pane lists all of the objects in the open database in separate groups. You can click the arrow on the title bar of the Navigation Pane to display a menu with options for various ways to group and display objects in the Navigation Pane. In addition, you can use the Search box to enter text to find in the listed objects. For example, you could search for all objects that contain the word *Invoice* in their names. Note that Access searches for objects only in the categories and groups currently displayed in the Navigation Pane.

Moving Around a Datasheet

You move around a datasheet using many of the same techniques you learned when you worked with Word tables and Excel worksheets. You can click in a field to make it the active field or you can use the Tab key or the arrow keys to move to a different field. Access databases can contain hundreds or thousands of records. When a table contains many records, only some of the records are visible on the screen. You can use the navigation buttons on the record navigation bar, shown in Exhibit 17-20, to move through the records and to see the number of the current record as well as the total number of records in the table.

> Records must have a unique primary key value. However, other fields can contain the same value in multiple records.

Exhibit 17-20 Navigation buttons on the record navigation bar

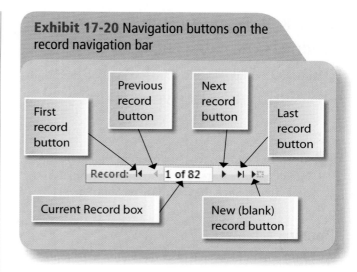

ACTIVITY

Move around a datasheet.

1. In the Invoice table, click anywhere in the **second record** except in the Paid field (this would change the value of the check box). On the record navigation bar, the Current Record box shows that record 2 is the current record and there are 82 records in the table.

2. On the record navigation bar, click the **Next record button** ▶. The third record is now highlighted, identifying it as the current record, and the Current Record box changed to display *3 of 82* to indicate that the third record is the current record.

3. Click the **Last record button** ▶❙. The last record in the table, record 82, is now the current record.

4. In the vertical scroll bar, drag the **scroll box** to the top of the bar. Although the first records are now visible, record 82 is still the current record, as indicated in the Current Record box.

5. On the record navigation bar, click the **Previous record button** ◀. Record 81 is now the current record.

6. On the record navigation bar, click in the **Current Record box**, press the **Backspace key** twice to delete 81, type **1**, and then press the **Enter key**. The first record is selected.

7. On the record navigation bar, click the **New (blank) record button** ▶❊. The first field in the next available blank record (record 83) is selected.

Scrolling changes the datasheet's display, but does not change the current record.

8 On the record navigation bar, click the **First record button** ◄. The first record is now the current record and is visible on the screen.

LO17.7 Creating Simple Queries, Forms, and Reports

The data in a database becomes even more useful when you can extract specific information and display it in a format that is easy to read and understand. You can do this by creating simple queries, forms, and reports based on the tables and other queries in a database.

Creating a Simple Query

A **query** is a question about the data stored in a database. When you create a query, you specify which fields to use to answer the question. Then Access displays only the records that fit, so you don't have to navigate through the entire database. In the Invoice table, for example, you might create a query to display only the invoice numbers and the invoice dates. Even though a query can display information in a different way, the information still exists in the table in its original form.

You can use the Simple Query Wizard to create a query based on the records and fields in a table. (A wizard is a series of dialog boxes that take you step by step through a process.) First, you select the table or another query on which to base the new query. Then you select which fields to include in the query. If values in one of the selected fields can be used in calculations, such as the Amount field, a second Simple Query Wizard dialog box appears, asking whether you want a detail or summary query. A detail query shows every field of every record. A summary query allows you to choose to calculate the sum or average of the values for the field that can be used in calculations, find its minimum or maximum value, and count the total

records in the table. Access then returns the query results in a datasheet. The datasheet shows fields in columns and records in rows, but only for those fields and records that answer the query.

Query results are not stored in the database. However, the query design is stored in the database with the name you specified. You can re-create the query results at any time by opening the query again.

ACTIVITY

Create a query using the Simple Query Wizard.

1 On the Ribbon, click the **Create tab**. In the Queries group, click the **Query Wizard button**. The New Query dialog box opens with Simple Query Wizard selected in the list.

2 Click **OK**. The first Simple Query Wizard dialog box opens. Table: Invoice is selected in the Tables/Queries box, and the fields in the Invoice table are listed in the Available Fields box. The first field in the list is selected. See Exhibit 17-21.

Exhibit 17-21 First Simple Query Wizard dialog box

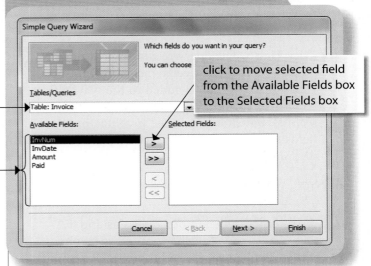

default source for the query

fields in the selected table

click to move selected field from the Available Fields box to the Selected Fields box

3 Click the **Tables/Queries box arrow**. Notice that all three objects in the database are listed. The Invoice table was selected because it was the selected table in the Navigation Pane before you started the Simple Query Wizard.

query A question about the data stored in a database.

4 Click **Table: Invoice**.

5 With InvNum selected in the Available Fields box, click the `>` button. The InvNum field moves to the Selected Fields box.

> **Tip:** You can also double-click a field to move it from the Available Fields box to the Selected Fields box.

6 In the Available Fields box, click the **Paid field**, and then click the `>` button to move the Paid field to the Selected Fields box.

7 Click **Next**. The second Simple Query Wizard dialog box appears, asking whether you want a detail or summary query. The Detail option button is selected.

8 Click **Next**. The final Simple Query Wizard dialog box appears, asking what title you want to use for the query. The suggested query title is based on the name of the table you are using.

9 In the What title do you want for your query box, change the suggested name to **InvoicePayments**. Near the bottom of the dialog box, the Open the query to view information option button is selected.

10 Click **Finish**. The query results appear on a new tab named InvoicePayments in Datasheet view, and the query is added to the Navigation Pane. See Exhibit 17-22. The query lists all the records, but shows only the InvNum and Paid fields as you specified in the first dialog box in the Simple Query Wizard.

11 Close the InvoicePayments query.

> ⚠ **Problem?** If a dialog box opens asking if you want to save the changes to the layout of the query, you changed the query layout in some way, such as by resizing a column. If the change is intentional, click **Yes**; otherwise, click **No**.

form A database object used to enter, edit, and view records in a database.

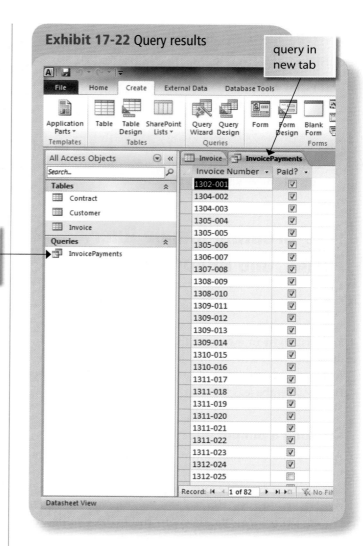

Exhibit 17-22 Query results

Creating and Using a Simple Form

You use a **form** to enter, edit, and view records in a database. Although you can perform these same functions with tables and queries, forms can present data in customized and helpful ways. In a simple form, the fields from the table or query on which the form is based are displayed one record at a time, allowing you to focus on the values for one record. Each field name appears on a separate line with its field value for the current record displayed in a box to the right. You use the navigation buttons at the bottom of the form to move between records.

Create a Simple Form

The Form tool quickly creates a form containing all of the fields in a table (or query) on which the form is based. The table or other database object on which you are basing the form must be selected in the Navigation Pane when you use the Form tool.

Exhibit 17-23 Form created by the Form tool

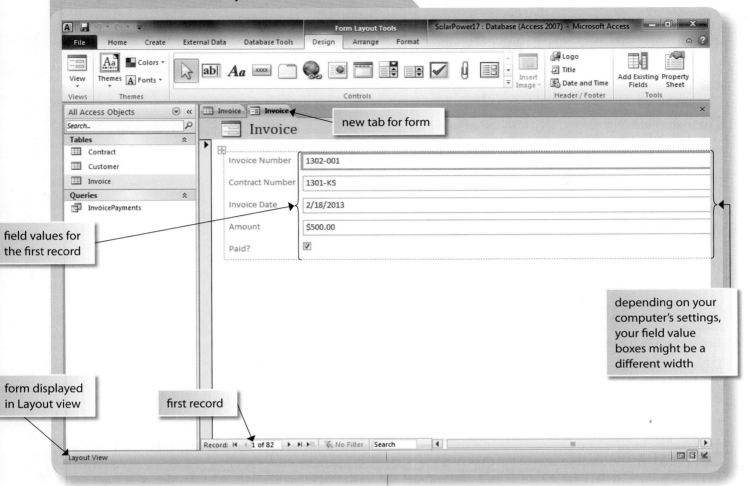

new tab for form

field values for the first record

Invoice

Invoice Number	1302-001
Contract Number	1301-KS
Invoice Date	2/18/2013
Amount	$500.00
Paid?	☑

depending on your computer's settings, your field value boxes might be a different width

form displayed in Layout view

first record

Record: ◄ ◄ 1 of 82 ► ►► ►✱ ✻ No Filter Search

Layout View

When you first create a form, it opens in Layout view. If necessary, you can use **Layout view** to make design changes to the form and see the effects of those changes immediately.

Create a simple form.

1 In the Navigation Pane, select the **Invoice table**.

2 On the Create tab, in the Forms group, click the **Form button**. Because the Invoice table is open and nothing else is selected in the Navigation Pane, a simple form showing every field in the Invoice table is created. See Exhibit 17-23. The name on

> ► **Tip:** You can also select a query in the Navigation Pane to create the form based on the query you select.

the tab is the same as the table name on which the form is based, and the fields in the form display the Caption properties set for the fields. The field values for the first record appear in the form, and a border appears around the value for the first field in the form, Invoice Number, indicating that it is selected. The form is in Layout view.

3 On the record navigation bar, click the **Next record button** ►. The values for the second record in the Invoice table appear in the form.

4 On the record navigation bar, click the **New (blank) record button** ►✱. A blank form is created, and 83 of 83 appears in the Current Record box on the record navigation bar.

> **Layout view** The Access view in which you can make design changes to database objects such as forms and reports, and see the effects of those changes immediately.

5 Next to the Invoice Number field name, click the **empty field box**. It is highlighted with an orange border.

6 Type any character. Nothing happens because the form is in Layout view.

7 On the Quick Access Toolbar, click the **Save button** 💾. The Save As dialog box opens.

8 In the Form Name box, type **InvoiceData** and then click **OK**. The form's tab now displays the name *InvoiceData*, and the form is added to the Navigation Pane.

Enter Data in a Form

After you create a form, you can use it to enter data in the table. To do this, you need to switch from Layout view to Form view.

 **ACTIVITY**

Enter data in a form and refresh a table.

1 On the Form Layout Tools Design tab, in the Views group, click the **View button**. The form appears in Form view. The insertion point is blinking in the first field, Invoice Number.

2 Type **1412-056** and then press the **Tab key**. The insertion point moves to the next field.

3 Enter the following data, pressing the **Tab key** after entering each field value:

Contract Number	**1414-KS**
Invoice Date	**12/12/14**
Amount	**6000**
Paid	**No**

4 Compare your screen to Exhibit 17-24.

5 Close the **InvoiceData form**. The Invoice table is displayed in Datasheet view.

6 On the record navigation bar, click the **Last record button** ▶️. There are still only 82 records in the datasheet, and the record you entered using the form isn't included.

> **report** A database object that shows a formatted printout or screen display of the contents of the table or query objects on which the report is based.

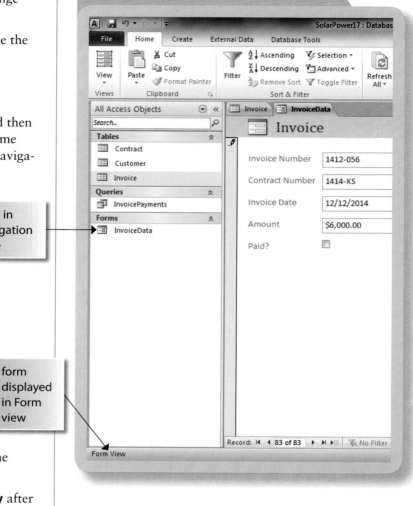

Exhibit 17-24 Form with new data

form in Navigation Pane

form displayed in Form view

7 On the Home tab, in the Records group, click the **Refresh All button**. The datasheet is refreshed, and the first record is selected.

8 Display the **last record** in the datasheet. The datasheet now contains 83 records and the record you added using the form is the last record.

9 Close the Invoice table.

Creating a Simple Report

A **report** is a formatted printout or screen display of the contents of one or more tables or queries. You can use the Report tool to quickly create a report based on all of the fields from a selected table or query. The Report tool also generates summaries and totals in the report automatically.

A report shows each field in a column with the field values for each record in a row, similar to a datasheet.

However, the report has a more visually appealing format for the data—column headings are in a different color, borders appear around each field value, a graphic of a report is included in the upper-left corner of the report, and the current day, date, and time appear in the upper-right corner. Dotted horizontal and vertical lines mark the edges of the page and show where text will be printed on the page.

ACTIVITY

Create a simple report using the Report tool.

1 In the Navigation Pane, click the **Invoice table**.

2 On the Ribbon, click the **Create tab**. In the Reports group, click the **Report button**. A simple report showing every field in the Invoice table is created. See Exhibit 17-25. The name on the tab is *Invoice*, because the report is based on the Invoice table. The report opens in Layout view. On the Rib-

bon, the Report Layout Tools tabs appear and the Design tab is selected.

Formatting a Report

The report is displayed in Layout view. In Layout view, you can change the format of the report. One way is to resize columns to better fit the data and ensure that all values will be printed. Also note that the page area, the area that will print, is defined by the dotted lines. Anything outside of the page area will not be printed.

ACTIVITY

Format a report.

1 In the Contract Number column, click **any field value**. All of the field values in the Contract Number column are highlighted with an orange box.

2 In the Contract Number column, point to the **right border** of any field value. The pointer changes to ↔.

Exhibit 17-25 Report created by the Report tool

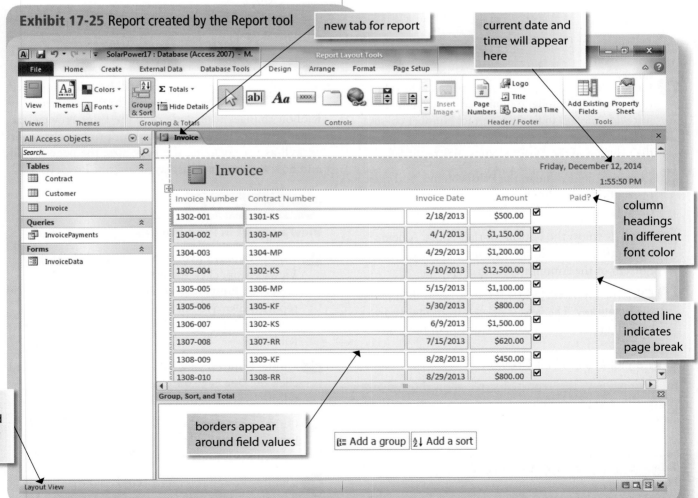

report displayed in Layout view

new tab for report

current date and time will appear here

column headings in different font color

dotted line indicates page break

borders appear around field values

Exhibit 17-26 Report after resizing columns

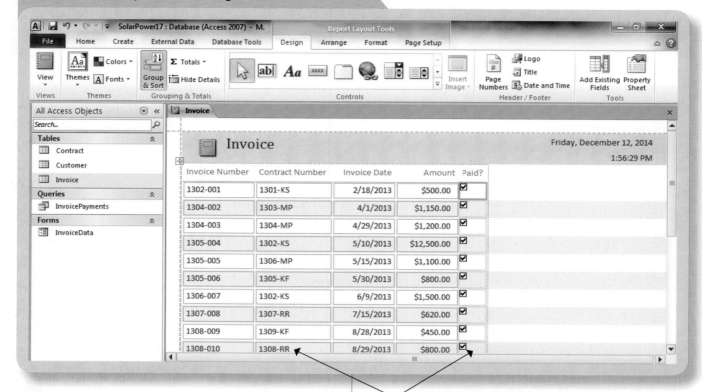

columns resized

3 If necessary, drag the right border of any field value in the **Contract Number column** until the column is just wide enough to fit the Contract Number column heading. The column is now narrower, better fitting the values, and the other columns shift to the left.

4 Click any field value in the **Paid? column**, and then resize the **Paid? column** until it is slighter wider than its field name. See Exhibit 17-26.

5 Scroll down to the bottom of the report. A field containing a total dollar amount was added at the bottom of the Amount column.

6 Click the **total field** ($1,052,510.00), and then press the **Delete key**. The field is deleted from the report, and the report scrolls back to the top of the page.

View a Report in Print Preview

In Layout view, the report doesn't show how many pages the report includes. To see this, you need to switch to Print Preview. **Print Preview** shows exactly how the report will look when printed.

When you switch to Print Preview, the Ribbon changes to include only the Print Preview tab, which includes tools and options for printing the report as well as for changing the page size, the page layout, and how the report is displayed in Print Preview.

ACTIVITY

View a report in Print Preview.

1 On the Report Layout Tools Design tab, in the Views group, click the **View button arrow**, and then click **Print Preview**. The first page of the report is displayed in Print Preview, and the Print Preview tab replaces all of the other tabs on the Ribbon.

2 On the Print Preview tab, in the Zoom group, click the **One Page button** (even if it is already selected). See Exhibit 17-27.

3 On the page navigation bar, click the **Next Page button** ▶ twice. The second and then the third page of the report are displayed in Print Preview.

4 Change the zoom level to **100%**, and then scroll down to see the bottom of the third page of the

Print Preview The Access view that shows exactly how a report will look when printed.

Exhibit 17-27 First page of the report in Print Preview

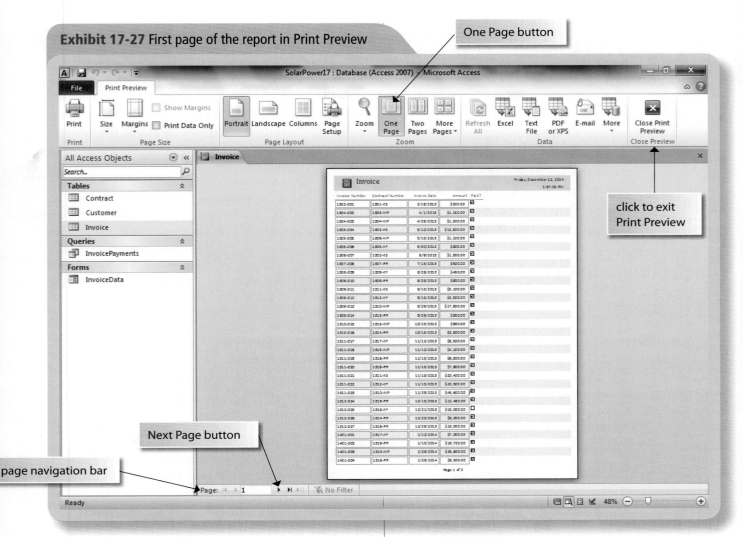

One Page button

click to exit Print Preview

Next Page button

page navigation bar

report. "Page 3 of 3" appears at the bottom of the page.

5 On the Quick Access Toolbar, click the **Save button** . The Save As dialog box opens.

6 Save the report as **InvoiceDetails**. The tab displays the new report name, and the report appears in the Navigation Pane.

Although table and query datasheets can be printed, they are usually used for viewing and entering data; reports are generally used for printing the data in a database.

Printing a Report

A report is often printed and then distributed to others to review. You can change the print settings in the Print dialog box, which you open by clicking the Print button in the Print group on the Print Preview tab or by clicking Print on the Print tab in Backstage view. You can also print a report without changing any print settings using the Quick Print option in Backstage view.

ACTIVITY

Print a report.

1 On the Ribbon, click the **File tab**. In the navigation bar, click **Print**. Three print options appear on the Print tab.

2 On the Print tab, click **Quick Print**. Backstage view closes and the report prints with the default print settings.

3 Close the report.

When to Save Database Objects

In general, it is best to save a database object—query, form, or report—only if you anticipate using the object frequently or if it is time-consuming to create because all objects use storage space on your disk. For example, you most likely would not save a form created with the Form tool because you can re-create it easily with one mouse click.

LO17.8 Compacting and Repairing a Database

Each time you open and work in a database, the size of the database increases. In addition, when you delete records or when you delete or replace database objects—such as queries, forms, and reports—the space they occupied does not become available for other records or objects until you compact the database. As illustrated in Exhibit 17-28, **compacting** a database rearranges the data and objects in a database to decrease its file size, making more space available and letting you open and close the database more quickly.

When you compact a database, Access repairs the database at the same time. In many cases, Access detects that a database is damaged when you try to open it and gives you the option to compact and repair it at that time. For example, the data in a database might become damaged, or corrupted, if you exit the Access program suddenly by turning off your computer. If you think your database might be damaged because it is behaving unpredictably, you can use the Compact & Repair Database option to fix it.

You can also set an option to compact and repair a database automatically every time you close the file. The Compact on Close option is available in the Current Database section of the Access Options dialog box, which you open from Backstage view by clicking the Options command in the navigation bar. By default, the Compact on Close option is turned off.

ACTIVITY

Compact and repair a database.

1 On the Ribbon, click the **File tab**. Backstage view opens with the Info tab selected.

2 On the Info tab, click the **Compact & Repair Database button**. Backstage view closes and the database is compacted and repaired.

3 Close the database.

Exhibit 17-28 Compacting a database

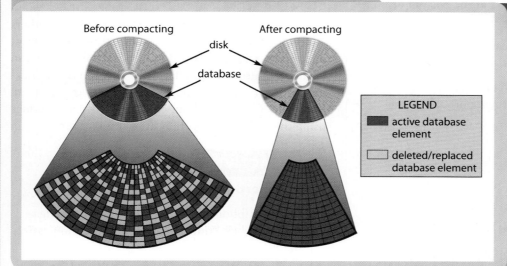

Before compacting — disk — database — After compacting

LEGEND
- active database element
- deleted/replaced database element

compact To rearrange data and objects in a database to decrease its file size.

Quiz Yourself

1. What is a field?

2. What is a record?

3. How are tables related in a relational database?

4. Explain the difference between a primary and a foreign key.

5. What does the Data Type property do?

6. Describe how the data in a table is displayed in Datasheet view.

7. Describe how a table's contents appear in Design view.

8. When you create a new table in Datasheet view, which field does Access create, by default, as the primary key field for the new table and what are its default field name and data type?

9. In Datasheet view, what do the pencil symbol and the star symbol at the beginning of a record represent?

10. What is a property?

11. What does the Caption property do?

12. What is a query?

13. What is a form?

14. What is a report?

15. When you create a form using the Form tool, in which view does the form open?

16. What happens when you compact a database?

Practice It

Practice It 17-1

1. Start Access, and create a new, blank database named **Clients**.

2. Add the following fields to the table in the order shown, leaving the first field named *ID*:

Text	**Company**
Text	**FirstName**
Text	**LastName**
Text	**Phone**
Date/Time	**CustomerSince**

3. Resize the CustomerSince column width so it fits the column name.

4. Save the table as **Customer**.

5. Enter the following records in the Customer table:

	Record 1	Record 2
Company	**Bangor Lighting**	**High Estate Realtors**
FirstName	**Scott**	*your first name*
LastName	**Woodman**	*your last name*
Phone	**207-555-6869**	**207-555-3132**
CustomerSince	**1/15/2013**	**11/23/2014**

6. Resize columns in the datasheet so that all the field values are completely displayed, and then save the table.

7. Switch to Design view, and then for each field set the following field sizes and captions:

	Field Size	Caption
Company	**150**	
FirstName	**20**	**First Name**
LastName	**25**	**Last Name**
CustomerSince	**Long Date**	**Customer Since**

8. Add a new field as the last field in the Customer table with the field name **CallPM**, the Yes/No data type, a Format property of Yes/No, and a Caption property of **Call after 8?**. Set the Default Value property to **No**.

9. Add the following descriptions to the Description property for each of the fields listed below:

ID	**Primary key**
CallPM	**Indicates whether client has given permission for us to call after 8:00 pm**

10. Save the table and switch the table to Datasheet view. Resize the Customer Since column to its best fit.

11. In the Call after 8? column, click the check boxes for both records.

12. Save the table, and then close the database.

13. Open the data file **Snow17** located in the Chapter 17\Practice It folder. Save the database as **SnowRemoval17**.

14. In the ServiceAgreement table, set the Agreement-Num field to be the primary key, and then save and close the table.

15. In Design view for the Invoice table, move the Paid field so it follows the InvAmt field, and then save and close the table.

16. In Design view for the Client table, add a new Text field named **Email** between the Phone and Street fields, and then save and close the table.

17. Create a query named **AllAmounts** that includes the AgreementNum and Amount fields from the ServiceAgreement table. Save and close the query.

18. Create a form based on the ServiceAgreement table, and then enter the following as a new record in the form:

Agreement #	**1424**
Client ID	**22**
Amount	**1700**
Date Signed	**12/20/14**

19. Display the ServiceAgreement table to see the new record, and then close the table. Save the form as **AgreementForm**, and then close it.

20. Create a report based on the ServiceAgreement table. Resize each field so it is slightly wider than the longest entry (either the field name itself or an entry in the field).

21. At the bottom of the report, delete the box that contains the total in the Amount column.

22. Display the report in Print Preview, and then print it.

23. Save the report as **AgreementReport**, and then close it.

24. Compact and repair the database.

25. Close the database.

Practice It 17-2

1. Start Access, and create a new, blank database named **Classes**.

2. Add the following fields to the table in the order shown, leaving the first field named *ID*:

Text	**ClassName**
Yes/No	**Juniors**
Currency	**Cost**
Number	**Length**

3. Save the table as **Class**.

4. Enter the following records in the Class table:

	Record 1	Record 2
Class	**Clay Discovery**	*your first and last names*
Juniors	**Yes**	**No**
Cost	**100**	**150**
Length	**45**	**60**

5. Resize columns in the datasheet so that all the field values are completely displayed, and then save the table.

6. Switch to Design view, and then for the ClassName field, change the Field Size property to **45** and the Caption property to **Class Name**.

7. For the Juniors field, change the Format property to Yes/No.

8. Add a new field as the last field in the Class table with the field name **Level**, the Text data type, a Field Size property of **20**, and a Caption property of **Class Level**. Set the Default Value property to **Beginning**.

9. Add the following descriptions to the Description property for each of the fields listed below:

ID	**Primary key**
Juniors	**Does the class allow teen participation?**
Length	**Class duration in minutes**

10. Save the table and switch the table to Datasheet view, and then resize all columns to their best fit.

11. Save the table, and then close the database.

12. Open the data file **Art17** located in the Chapter 17\Practice It folder. Save the database as **ArtClasses17**.

13. In the Class table, specify that the following classes accept juniors: CL-293, CL-295, DR-105, DR-106, PA-024, and PH-311.

14. In Design view, move the Cost field so it follows the Length field. Delete the Level field. Save and close the table.

15. Create a query named **ClassCost** that includes the ClassName, Length, and Cost fields (in that order) from the Class table. Close the query.

16. Create a form based on the Class table, and then enter the following as a new record in the Class table using the form.

Class ID	**PH-315**
Class Name	**Darkroom III**
Juniors	**No**
Length	**120**
Cost	**400**

17. After entering the record, save the form as **ClassInfo** and then close it.

18. Open the Class table in Datasheet view to see the new record.

19. Create a report based on the Class table. Resize each field so it is slightly wider than the longest entry (either the field name itself or an entry in the field).

20. Delete the total field that was added at the bottom, display the report in Print Preview, and then print the report.

21. Save the report as **ClassList**, and then close it.

22. Close all open objects, and then compact and repair the database.

23. Close the database.

On Your Own

On Your Own 17-1

1. Open the data file **DonationTable17** located in the Chapter 17\On Your Own folder. Save the database as **DonationTable17Edited**.

2. Open the Donation table, and then switch to Design view.

3. Rename the ID field as **AgencyID**.

4. Set the DonationID field as the primary key.

5. Set appropriate values for the DonationID field's Description, Field Size, and Caption properties. (*Hint*: To determine the field size of the DonationID field, look at the records in the datasheet.)

6. Change the Field Size and Caption properties for each of the remaining fields, as appropriate (use the Medium Date format for the DonationDate field, leave the Description field size at 255, and set the default value for Pickup to **No**). Save the table.

7. In Datasheet view, resize the columns as needed so that all of the field values are displayed. Save the table, and then close it.

8. In the Navigation Pane, select the Donation table. Copy the Donation table to the Clipboard.

9. Open the data file **Donations17** located in the Chapter 17\On Your Own folder. Save the database as **DonationsList17**.

10. In DonationsList17, paste the contents of the Clipboard. In the Paste Table As dialog box that opens, change the table name to Donation, make sure the Structure and Data option button is selected, and then click OK.

11. Open the Donor table, and then edit the first record to use your title, first name, and last name in the corresponding fields. Close the table.

12. Open the Agency table, and then delete the Fax and Notes fields from the table. Save and close the table.

13. Use the Simple Query Wizard to create a query that includes all the fields in the Donor table *except* the Title field. (*Hint*: Use the >> and < buttons to select the necessary fields.) Save the query as **DonorPhoneList**.

14. Sort the query results by the Last Name column. (*Hint*: Make the Last Name column the current field, and then click the appropriate button on the Home tab in the Sort & Filter group.)

15. Rearrange the fields in the query design so the Last Name field is to the left of the First Name field in the datasheet.

16. Widen columns widths as needed in the datasheet, and then save and close the query.

17. Create a form based on the Donor table.

18. In the new form, navigate to record 8, and then print the form *for the current record only*. (*Hint*: Use the Print button in Backstage view instead of the Quick Print button.) Save the form as **DonorInfo**, and then close it.

19. Create a report based on the Donor table.

20. In Layout view, resize each field so it is slightly wider than the longest entry (either the field name itself or an entry in the field).

21. Delete the summary field at the bottom of the report.

22. Move the page number at the bottom of the report so it appears completely on the page. (*Hint*: Select the field, and then drag it to the left.)

23. Save the report as **DonorList**.

24. Display the report in Print Preview and verify that the fields and page number fit within the page area. Print the report, and then close it.

25. Compact and repair the database, and then close it.

26. Open the **DonationTable17Edited** database, compact and repair it, and then close it.

Maintaining and Querying a Database

Introduction

Creating/designing a database is just the beginning. Once the database structure is developed, the ongoing work of recordkeeping begins. Data is constantly changing. People regularly get new phone numbers and email addresses. Invoices are sent and then paid. Customer activity is ongoing, and tracking this accurately leads to developing new strategies for promoting services. So, no matter what kind of information the database contains—customer, contract, invoice, or asset data, to name just a few—the information must be accurate and up to date to be of value. This requires continual and diligent entering and updating of records.

Entering and updating data is just one aspect of databases. The records can also be used to monitor and analyze other aspects of the business. This is accomplished by creating and using queries that retrieve information from the database. Queries can also be saved so anyone can run the queries at any time, modify them as needed, or use them as the basis for designing new queries to meet additional information requirements.

Learning Objectives

After studying the material in this chapter, you will be able to:

LO18.1 Maintain database records

LO18.2 Work with queries in Design view

LO18.3 Sort and filter data

LO18.4 Define table relationships

LO18.5 Create a multitable query

LO18.6 Add criteria to a query

LO18.7 Add multiple criteria to queries

LO18.8 Create a calculated field

LO18.9 Use functions in a query

LO18.1 Maintaining Database Records

A database is only as useful and accurate as the data it contains. Maintaining a database involves adding new records, updating the field values of existing records, and deleting outdated records to keep the database current and accurate.

Editing Field Values

Records often need to be edited to update or correct a field value. For example, information, such as a phone number or email address, might have changed or the original record might have been entered inaccurately and as a result, it contains an error. To replace a field value,

Whether a database is used by one person or many, the information in the database must be updated continually to ensure currency as well as to retrieve relevant and accurate information from the database with queries.

you select it in the table datasheet, and then type the new entry. To edit a field value, position the insertion point in the field value and use the standard editing techniques to delete and insert text as needed.

You can use the navigation buttons, keystroke combinations, or the F2 key to navigate a datasheet and select field values.

Navigate and Edit Fields

...oggle that you use to switch be-
...on mode and editing mode. In
The F... ode, Access selects an entire
...t...w The entry you type while in
... mode replaces the high-
...ield value. In editing mode, you
...ert or delete characters in a field
... You can use the mouse or the keyboard to
...ve the location of the insertion point, as you
...ave done in Word and Excel.

ACTIVITY

Modify records.

1 Open the data file **Solar18** located in the Chapter 18\Chapter folder. Save the database as **SolarPower18**.

2 In the Navigation Pane, double-click the **Customer table**. The table opens in Datasheet view. In the first record, the field value for the first field—the Customer ID field—is selected.

3 Press the **Ctrl+End keys**. The records from the end of the Customer table are displayed, and the field value for the last field—the Email field—in the last record (record 35) is selected.

4 Press the **Up Arrow key**. The Email field value for record 34, the second to last record, is now selected.

5 Press the **Shift+Tab keys**. The Phone field value for record 34 is selected.

6 Click at the end of the field value to position the inser-tion point to the right of the phone number. Press the **Backspace key** to de-lete the 0, type **1** as the new final digit

> **Tip:** Remember that changes to field values are saved when you move to a new field or another record, or when you close the table.

of the phone number, and then press the **Enter key**. The Phone field value is updated.

7 Press the **Home key**. The Customer ID field value for record 34 is now selected.

8 Press the **Ctrl+Home keys**. The Customer ID field value for the first record is selected.

9 Press the **Tab key** to select the Last Name field value for the first record, and then type your last name.

10 Press the **Tab key** to select the First Name field value for the first record, and then type your first name.

11 Press the **Tab key** to move to the next field.

Finding and Replacing Data

As a database grows, the number of records becomes numerous—too numerous to scroll and search for a specific record that you need to update or delete. In-stead of scrolling the table datasheet to find the field value you need to change or delete, you can use the Find and Replace dialog box to locate a specific field value in a table, query datasheet, or form. In the Find and Replace dialog box, you specify the value you want to find, where to search for that value, and whether to locate all or part of a field value. You also can choose to search up or down from the currently selected record. If you want to substitute a different field value, you can enter that value on the Replace tab.

ACTIVITY

Find data.

1 Open the **Invoice table** in Datasheet view. The in-sertion point is positioned in the Invoice Number field, which is the field you want to search.

2 On the Home tab, in the Find group, click the **Find button**. The Find and Replace dialog box opens with the value in the Find What box selected. Th... value is the Invoice Number field value for the ... record in the Invoice table. See Exhibit 18-1.

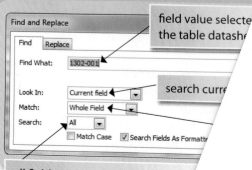

Exhibit 18-1 Find and Replace dialog box

3 In the Find What box, type **1406-033** to replace the selected value. You want to find the record for invoice number 1406-033.

4 Click **Find Next**. The datasheet scrolls to the record for invoice number 1406-033 and selects the Invoice Number field value.

5 In the Find and Replace dialog box, click **Cancel**. The Find and Replace dialog box closes.

6 For invoice number 1406-033, click in the **Amount box**, and then edit the value to **$13,750.00**.

7 Close the Invoice table.

Deleting a Record

Deleting a record removes all of the field values for that record from the database. Before you delete a record, you must select the entire row for the record in the datasheet. Then, you can delete the selected record using the Delete button in the Records group on the Home tab or the Delete Record command on the shortcut menu. Keep in mind that the deletion of a record is *permanent* and cannot be undone.

AutoNumbered Field Values

Each value generated by a field is unique. When you use the AutoNumber data type to define the primary key field, the AutoNumber data type ensures that all primary key field values are unique. When you delete a record that has an AutoNumber field, the corresponding value is also deleted and cannot be reused. After deleting a record with an AutoNumber field, you might see gaps in the numbers used for the field values.

ACTIVITY

Delete a record.

1 In the Customer table, find the record for the customer with the last name **Chappelle**.

2 Click the **row selector** to select the entire record for the customer with the last name Chappelle.

3 On the Home tab, in the Records group, click the **Delete button**. A dialog box appears, confirming that you want to delete the record and reminding you that you cannot undo this deletion.

4 Click **Yes**. The dialog box closes, and the record is removed from the table.

5 Close the Customer table.

LO18.2 Working with Queries in Design View

In Chapter 17, you used the Simple Query Wizard to create a query based on one table. You can base a query on one table, on multiple tables, on other queries, or on a combination of tables and queries. For example, you might use a query to find records in the Customer table for only those customers located in a specific city who have unpaid invoices. When you design a query, you specify which fields you need and what criteria to use to select the records. You can use queries to:

- Display selected fields and records from a table.
- Sort records.
- Perform calculations.
- Generate data for forms, reports, and other queries.
- Update data in the tables in a database.
- Find and display data from two or more tables.

You work with a query in the Query window. In Design view, specify the data you want to view by constructing a query by example. **Query by example (QBE)**

With queries, you can retrieve specific data from a database to meet various requests for information.

query by example (QBE) A query that retrieves the information that precisely matches the example you provide of the information being requested.

Designing Queries vs. Using a Query Wizard

More specialized, technical queries, such as finding duplicate records in a table, are best created using a Query Wizard. A Query Wizard prompts you for information by asking a series of questions and then creates the appropriate query based on your answers. You used the Simple Query Wizard to display only some of the fields in the Invoice table. The other Query Wizards can create more complex queries. For common, informational queries, it is often easier to design the query yourself than to use a Query Wizard.

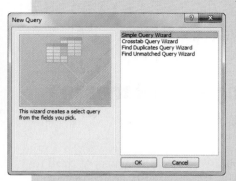

retrieves the information that precisely matches the example you provide of the information being requested. The top portion of the Query window in Design view contains the field list for each table or query used in the query. A **field list** contains the fields in the table or query used to create the query. The fields are listed in the same order as they appear in the table or query, and the primary key for a table is identified by 🔑. Scroll or resize the field list to see all of the fields in the field list. The bottom portion of the Query window contains the **design grid**, which shows the fields and record selection criteria for the information you want to see in the query results. Each column in the design grid contains specifications about a field being used in the query.

field list A box that contains the fields for the table or query used in a query.

design grid The bottom portion of the Query window in Design view that shows the fields and record selection criteria for a query.

recordset The result of a query, which is a set of records that answers the question.

select query A query in which you specify the fields and records you want Access to select.

As you are constructing a query, you can see the query results at any time by clicking the View button or the Run button in the Results group on the Query Tools Design tab. The results appear in the query datasheet. The result of a query is also referred to as a **recordset** because the query produces a set of records that answers your question.

Designing a Select Query

Most questions about data are general queries in which you specify the fields and records you want to select. These common requests for information, such as "Which customers are located in Berkeley?" or "How many invoices have been paid?", are select queries. A **select query** is a query in which you specify the fields and records you want Access to select. The answer to a select query is returned in a query datasheet.

When you design a query, you specify which fields to include in the query. First, add the table or query whose fields you want to include in the query to the Query window. Then move fields from the field lists to the design grid in the order you want them to appear in the query results. After you view or run the query, the results appear in a datasheet. You can save a query to use it again.

Although a query datasheet looks like a table datasheet, a query datasheet is temporary and its contents are based on the criteria set in the query design grid. In contrast, a table datasheet shows the permanent data in a table. However, data is not duplicated in a query datasheet; it is the same data displayed in a different way.

Unlike a table datasheet, which displays all of the fields in the table in the same order as they appear in the table, a query datasheet can display selected fields from a table in the order you specify, which can be different from the table order. With this flexibility, the query results display only the information you need and in the order you want.

You can update the data in a table using a query datasheet just as you can when working in a table datasheet. When you make changes in a query datasheet, the underlying table will be updated with those changes.

 **ACTIVITY**

Design a select query.

1 On the Ribbon, click the **Create tab**. In the Queries group, click the **Query Design button**. The Query window opens in Design view, and the Show Table dialog box, as shown in Exhibit 18-2, opens listing the three tables in the database.

Exhibit 18-2 Show Table dialog box

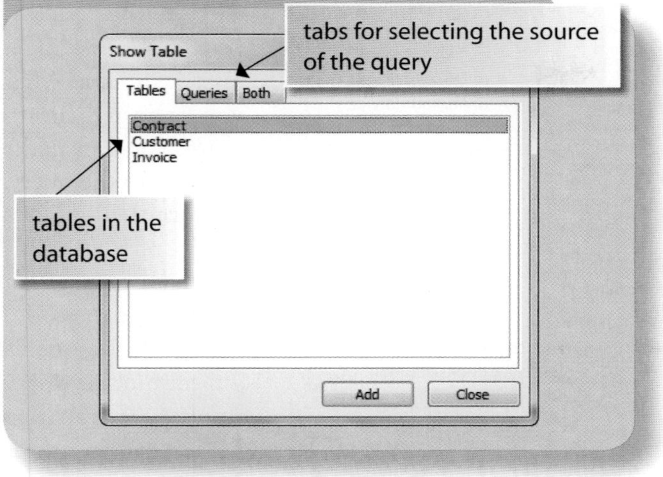

tabs for selecting the source of the query

Show Table

Tables | Queries | Both

Contract
Customer
Invoice

tables in the database

Add | Close

Exhibit 18-3 Field added to the design grid

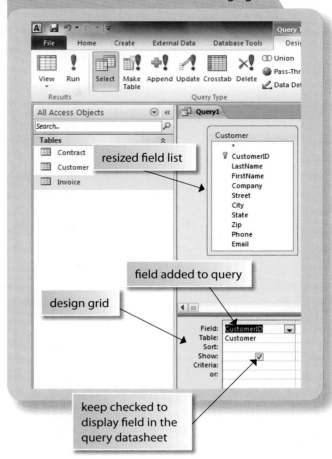

resized field list

field added to query

design grid

keep checked to display field in the query datasheet

2 In the Tables list, click **Customer**, and then click **Add**. The field list for the Customer table is added to the Query window.

3 In the Show Table dialog box, click **Close**. The Show Table dialog box closes.

4 Point to the **bottom border** of the Customer field list to change the pointer to ↕, and then drag the **bottom border** of the Customer field list down until the vertical scroll bar in the field list disappears and all of the fields are visible.

5 In the Customer field list, double-click **CustomerID**. The field is placed in the Field box in the first column of the design grid. The field name CustomerID appears in the Field box, the table name Customer appears in the Table box, and the selected Show check box indicates that the field will be displayed in the datasheet after you run the query. See Exhibit 18-3.

> ⚠ **Problem?** If the wrong table is added to the Query window, right-click the table name in the field list, and then click **Remove Table**. To add the correct table to the Query window, click the **Show Table button** in the Query Setup group on the Query Tools Design tab to redisplay the Show Table dialog box, and then repeat Steps 2 and 3.

> ➤ **Tip:** You can also drag a field from the field list to a column in the design grid to add the field to the query.

6 In the Customer field list, double-click **Company**, **FirstName**, **LastName**, **City**, **Email**, and **Phone** to add these fields to the design grid in the order specified.

7 On the Ribbon, on the Query Tools Design tab, in the Results group, click the **Run button**. The query runs and the results are displayed in Datasheet view. The fields you added to the design grid appear in the datasheet in the same order as they appear in the design grid. The records are displayed in order based on the values in the primary key field, Customer ID. A total of 34 records are displayed in the datasheet. See Exhibit 18-4.

> ⚠ **Problem?** If a wrong field is added to the design grid, select that field's column by clicking the field selector (the thin bar above the Field box), and then press the **Delete key** (or click the **Delete Columns button** in the Query Setup group on the Query Tools Design tab).

Exhibit 18-4 Query datasheet with query results

Modifying a Query

If the results of a query are not what you expected or require, you can make changes to the query. You can add fields to or remove fields from the query. You can change the order in which the fields appear in the query results. You can also hide a field's values in the query results. You might do this when all the records in the query results will have the same field value, such as a query that lists all customers located in San Francisco. Keep in mind that hiding a field's values does

Customer ID	Company	First Name	Last Name	City	Em
1		Your	Name	Palo Alto	dtam@onecalweb.
2		Barbara	Derrick	Oakland	bderrick@interoakl
3		Sumiko	Sharma	Redwood City	ssharma@redwood
4	Brisbane Engineering Dept.	Misti	Stanwood	Brisbane	mstanwood@brisb.
5		Leopold	Faries	Dublin	lfaries@onecalweb
6		Bradley	Schumer	San Francisco	bschumer@onecal
7	San Rafael Medical Partners	Yvette	Grady	San Rafael	ygrady@sanrafmed
8		Chung	Colberg	Oakland	ccolberg@onecalw
9	Jack's Café	Xenia	Selin	Oakland	xselin@onecalweb
10	Pleasanton Waldorf School	Pamela	Kennison	Pleasanton	pkennison@pleasa
11		Khali	Christofferson	San Francisco	kchristofferson@or
12	M. Doufay Financial	Anthony	Tedeschi	Concord	itedeschi@doufayf
13	Oak Roots Development	Manda	Miga	Oakland	mmiga@oakrootsd
14		Frank	Walker	Fremont	dwelker@onecalwe
15	Prentice College	Tamara	Stille	Oakland	tstille@prentice.ed
16	Oakland Neighborhood Development	Julianne	Ferebee	Oakland	jferebee@interoak
17		Alexa	Lemaire	Oakland	alemaire@interoak
18		Emerita	Borgmeyer	Rohnert Park	eborgmeyer@onec
19		Al	Doten	San Carlos	adoten@onecalwel
20	Sauerbrook & Mars Fashions	Cecille	Hartt	San Francisco	chartt@sauerbrook
21	Prancing Pony Grill	Kathleen	Arter	San Francisco	karter@prancingpo
22	Swan Senior Living Center	Jennifer	Wilcox	Oakland	jwilcox@swansenic
23	Bay Area Communities United	Juanita	Fry	San Francisco	jfry@onecalweb.co
24		Raymond	Hearns	Oakland	rhearns@interoakl
25	LKW Construction	Krystle	Frevert	Palo Alto	kfrevert@lkwdcons

number of records that match the query

Record: 1 of 34   No Filter   Search

8 Save the query as **CustomerContact**. The query name appears on the tab for the query object, and also in the Queries group in the Navigation Pane.

not remove the field from the query design; the field must remain in the query design to be included as a condition for the query.

Adding All Fields to the Design Grid

If the query you are creating requires every field listed in a field list, you can use one of the following methods to transfer all the fields from the field list to the design grid:

▶ **Click and drag each field individually from the field list to the design grid.** Use this method if you want the fields to appear in a different order in the query than they do in the field list.

▶ **Double-click the asterisk at the top of the field list.** The table name followed by a period and an asterisk (as in "Customer.*") appears in the

field list title bar

asterisk

fields

Field box of the first column in the design grid, signifying that the order of the fields is the same in the query as it is in the field list. Use this method if you don't need to sort the query or specify conditions for the records you want to select. The advantage of this method is that you do not need to change the query if you add or delete fields from the underlying table structure.

▶ **Double-click the field list title bar to highlight all of the fields, and then drag the highlighted fields to the first column in the design grid.** Each field is placed in a separate column and the fields appear in the order in which they appear in the field list. Use this method when you need to sort your query or include record selection criteria.

To move or delete a field, you need to select the entire field. In the design grid, the thin bar above a column is the field selector. Click the field selector to select the entire column in the design grid. You can drag across the field selector to highlight more fields. To move a field, drag the selected field to the new location and drop it when the vertical line is in the location where you want the field to be inserted. To delete a field, click in its column and then click the Delete Columns button in the Query Setup group on the Query Tools Design tab. You can also select the field to delete, and then press the Delete key.

![Activity icon] **ACTIVITY**

Modify a query.

1 On the Home tab, in the Views group, click the **View button**. The CustomerContact query switches to Design view.

2 In the design grid, in the Show row for the City column, click the **Show check box**. The Show check box is no longer selected, indicating that the City field will still be included in the query but will not appear in the results.

3 Click the **LastName field selector** to select the field, and then drag the selected field to the left until the vertical line to the left of the FirstName field is highlighted. See Exhibit 18-5.

field, and then press the **Delete key**. The Email field is removed from the query design.

6 On the Query Tools Design tab, in the Results group, click the **Run button**. The results of the modified query are displayed in the query datasheet. Notice that the City field is hidden, the Last Name field values appear before the First Name field values, and the Email field is no longer included in the query results.

LO18.3 Sorting and Filtering Data

The records in the query datasheet are listed in order by the field values in the primary key field for the table. Sometimes, however, you will want to display the records in a specific order, such as in alphabetical order by city. Other times, you will want to display a subset of the records, such as only the records for a certain city. To make these changes, you can sort and filter the data.

Sorting Data

Sorting is the process of rearranging records in a specified order or sequence. When you sort data in a query, only the records in the query datasheet are rearranged. The records in the underlying tables remain in their original order. For example, you might sort customer information by the Last Name field to more easily find specific customers, or you might sort contracts by the Contract Value field to monitor the financial aspects of a business.

To sort records, you must select the **sort field**, which is

Exhibit 18-5 Selected field being moved in the design grid

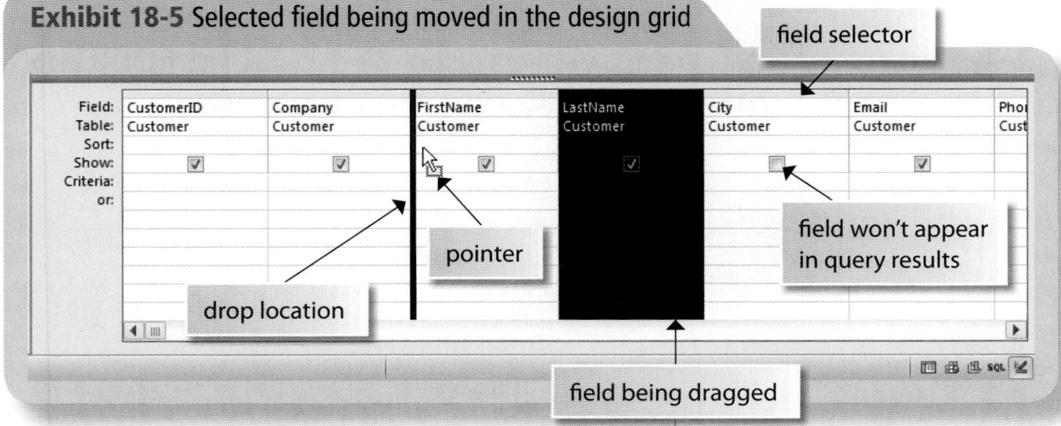

4 Release the mouse button. The LastName field moves to the left of the FirstName field.

5 Click the **Email field selector** to select the

Tip: You can select and move multiple fields at once; simply select adjacent fields, and then drag the selected fields to their new location.

sort The process of rearranging records in a specified order or sequence.

sort field The field used to determine the order of records in the datasheet.

the field used to determine the order of records in the datasheet. For example, to sort data by city, you would specify City as the sort field. Sort fields can be Text, Number, Date/Time, Currency, AutoNumber, or Yes/No fields, but not Memo, OLE object, Hyperlink, or Attachment fields. You sort records in either ascending (increasing) or descending (decreasing) order, as described in Exhibit 18-6.

Exhibit 18-6 Sort results for different data types

Data type	Ascending sort results	Descending sort results
Text	A to Z	Z to A
Number	Lowest to highest numeric value	Highest to lowest numeric value
Date/Time	Oldest to most recent date	Most recent to oldest date
Currency	Lowest to highest numeric value	Highest to lowest numeric value
AutoNumber	Lowest to highest numeric value	Highest to lowest numeric value
Yes/No	Yes (check mark in check box) then no values	No then yes values

Using AutoFilter to Sort Data

One of the easiest ways to sort data is to use **AutoFilter**. In Datasheet view, each column heading in the table or query datasheet displays an arrow to the right of its field name. When you click this arrow, the AutoFilter menu opens with options for sorting and displaying field values. The first two commands sort the values in the current field in ascending or descending order. When records are sorted, an arrow appears on the right side of the column heading, indicating the sort order. If you sort in ascending order, the arrow points up. If you sort in descending order, the arrow points

AutoFilter A feature used to quickly sort a column of data or find a matching value.

down. Note that AutoFilter only works for sorting a single field.

A sort is temporary unless you save the datasheet or form after sorting the records.

ACTIVITY

Use AutoFilter to sort data.

1 In the Last Name column heading, click the **arrow** to display the AutoFilter menu. See Exhibit 18-7.

2 On the AutoFilter menu, click **Sort A to Z**. The records are rearranged in ascending alphabetical order by last name, as indicated by the up arrow on the right side of the Last Name column heading.

Tip: You can also use the Ascending and Descending buttons in the Sort & Filter group on the Home tab to quickly sort records based on the selected field in a datasheet.

Exhibit 18-7 AutoFilter menu

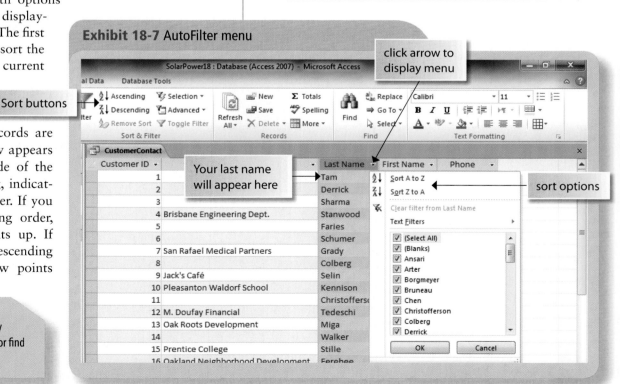

You can sort data in a table datasheet, in a query datasheet, in a form, and in a report.

Sorting Multiple Fields in Design View

Sometimes, you need to sort using more than one field. Sort fields can be unique or nonunique. A sort field is unique if the value in the sort field for each record is different, as is the case with a primary key field. A sort field is nonunique if more than one record can have the same value for the sort field, as is the case for a City field where more than one record can have the same city.

When you use a nonunique sort field, records with the same sort field value are grouped together, but are not sorted in a specific order within the group. To sort each group of records in a specific order, you specify a secondary sort field, which determines the order of records that are already sorted by the primary sort field (the first sort field specified).

You can select as many as 10 different sort fields. Each additional sort field organizes the records within the higher level sort. For example, you might sort invoices based on whether they are paid or unpaid. Then you could sort each group of invoices by the invoice date. Then you could sort the invoices for each date by the invoice amount. Each additional sort affects more but smaller groups of records.

In Datasheet view, the sort fields must be in adjacent columns in the datasheet and you can specify only one type of sort—either ascending or descending—for the selected columns. The records are sorted by the leftmost selected column and then by each remaining selected column in order from left to right.

To sort fields in nonadjacent columns or with different sort orders, you must specify the sort fields in Design view. As in Datasheet view, the leftmost sort field is the primary sort field and each remaining sort field is applied from left to right in the design grid. However, in Design view,

sort fields do not have to be adjacent, although they must be in the correct left-to-right order. As a result, fields that are not being sorted can appear between the sort fields. You can also specify the appropriate sort order—ascending or descending—for each sort field.

ACTIVITY

Sort multiple fields in Design view.

1 On the Home tab, in the Views group, click the **View button**. The CustomerContact query switches to Design view.

2 In the design grid, in the City field, click the **Show check box**. The field will be displayed in the query results.

3 Move the **City field** to the left of the Company field. The fields are in the correct left-to-right order in the design grid.

4 In the design grid, in the Sort row for the City column, click the **Sort box** to display the arrow button. Click the **arrow button** to display the sort options, and then click **Descending**. The City field, which will be the primary sort field, now has a descending sort order. Because the City field is a Text field, the field values will be displayed in reverse alphabetical order.

5 In the Sort row for the LastName field, click the **Sort box**, click the **arrow button**, and then click **Ascending**. The LastName field, which will be the secondary sort field because it appears to the right of the primary sort field (City) in the design grid, now has an ascending sort order. See Exhibit 18-8.

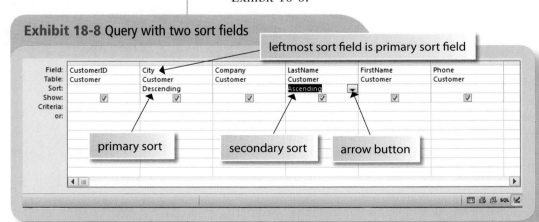

Exhibit 18-8 Query with two sort fields

leftmost sort field is primary sort field

primary sort

secondary sort

arrow button

6 On the Query Tools Design tab, in the Results group, click the **Run button**. In the query datasheet, the records appear in descending order based on the values in the City field. Records with the same City field value appear in ascending order by the values in the Last Name field. See Exhibit 18-9.

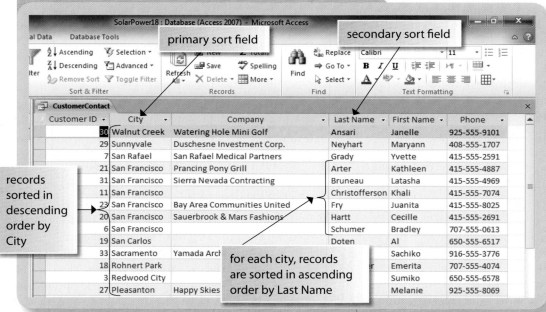

Exhibit 18-9 Query datasheet sorted on two fields

7 Save the CustomerContact query. All the design changes—including the selection of the sort fields—are saved with the query.

Filtering Data

A **filter** is a set of restrictions you place on the records in a datasheet or form to *temporarily* isolate a subset of the records. A filter lets you view different subsets of displayed records so that you can focus on only the data you need. Unless you save the object with a filter applied, the filter is not available the next time you open the object. There are several methods for filtering records:

- Filter By Selection lets you select all or part of a field value in a datasheet or form, and then display only those records that contain the selected value in the field.

- AutoFilter provides options for filtering the datasheet based on a field value or the selected part

---

of a field value; just select the check boxes for the fields you want to include in the filter.

- Filter By Form changes the datasheet to display blank fields so that you can choose a value for any blank field to apply a filter that selects only those records containing that value.

After you filter records, the column heading for the filtered field includes a filter icon, which you can click to display additional options for filtering the field.

You can tell that a datasheet has been filtered because *Filtered* appears on the status bar and a Filtered button appears to the right of the navigation buttons. You can redisplay all of the query records by clicking the Toggle Filter button in the Sort & Filter group on the Home tab, which switches between the filtered and unfiltered datasheet.

Filter records by selection.

1 In the query datasheet, locate the first occurrence of a City field containing the value **San Francisco**, and then click anywhere within that field value.

The primary sort field is not the same as a table's primary key field. A table has only one primary key, which must be unique, whereas any field in a table can serve as a primary sort field.

---

filter A set of restrictions placed on records in a datasheet or form to *temporarily* isolate a subset of the records.

2 On the Home tab, in the Sort & Filter group, click the **Selection button**. A menu opens with options for the type of filter to apply. See Exhibit 18-10. You can choose to display only those records with a City field value that equals the selected value (in this case, San Francisco); does not equal the value; contains the value somewhere within the field; or does not contain the value somewhere within the field. You want to display all the records whose City field value equals San Francisco.

5 Close the CustomerContact query. A dialog box appears, asking if you want to save changes to the design of the query which now includes the filter you just created.

6 Click **No** to close the query without saving the changes.

LO18.4 Defining Table Relationships

Exhibit 18-10 Filter By Selection

3 In the Selection menu, click **Equals "San Francisco"**. The filtered results appear in the datasheet, and the filter icon appears in the column heading for the City field. Only six records have a City field value of San Francisco. See Exhibit 18-11.

One of the most powerful features of a relational database management system is its ability to define relationships between tables. You use a common field to relate one table to another. The process of relating tables is often called joining tables. When you join tables that have a common field, you can use data from them as if they were one larger table. For example, you can join the Customer and Contracts tables by using the CustomerID field in both tables as the common field. Then you can use a query, a form, or a report to display selected data from each table, even though the data is contained in two separate tables, as shown in Exhibit 18-12.

A **one-to-many relationship** exists between two tables when one record in the first table matches zero, one, or many records in the second table, and when each record in the second table matches at most one record in the first table. For example, as shown in Exhibit 18-12, customer 16 has two contracts in the Contract table. Every con-

Exhibit 18-11 Query datasheet with filter

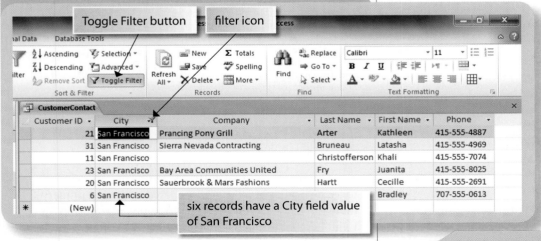

4 On the Home tab, in the Sort & Filter group, click the **Toggle Filter button**. The filter is removed, and all 34 records are redisplayed in the query datasheet.

one-to-many relationship A connection between two tables when one record in the primary table matches zero, one, or many records in the related table, and when each record in the related table matches at most one record in the primary table.

Exhibit 18-12 One-to-many relationship and query

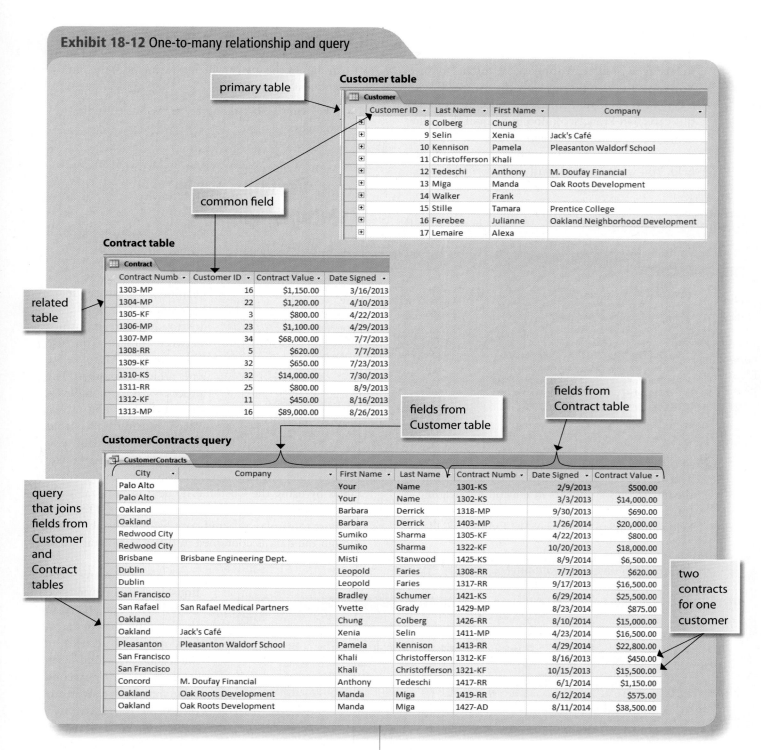

primary table

Customer table

common field

Contract table

related table

CustomerContracts query

query that joins fields from Customer and Contract tables

fields from Customer table

fields from Contract table

two contracts for one customer

tract has a single matching customer (the "one" side of the relationship) and a customer can have zero, one, or many contracts (the "many" side of the relationship).

primary table The "one" table in a one-to-many relationship.

related table The "many" table in a one-to-many relationship.

The two tables that form a relationship are referred to as the primary table and the related table. The **primary table** is the "one" table in a one-to-many relationship. In Exhibit 18-12, the Customer table is the primary table because there is only one customer for each contract. The **related table** is the "many" table. In Exhibit 18-12, the Contract table is the related table because a customer can have zero, one, or many contracts.

Referential integrity is a set of rules to maintain consistency between related tables when data in a database is updated. The referential integrity rules are:

- You cannot add a record to a related table unless a matching record already exists in the primary table, preventing the possibility of **orphaned records**.

- You cannot change the value of the primary key in the primary table if matching records exist in a related table. However, you can select the Cascade Update Related Fields option, which updates the corresponding foreign keys when you change the primary key field value, eliminating the possibility of inconsistent data.

- You cannot delete a record in the primary table if matching records exist in the related table. However, you can select the Cascade Delete Related Records option to delete the record in the primary table as well as all records in the related table that have matching foreign key field values. This option is rarely used because it often leads to related records being unintentionally deleted from the database.

Defining a One-to-Many Relationship Between Tables

When two tables have a common field, you can define a relationship between them in the Relationships window. To create a relationship, you need to add the field list for each table in the relationship to the Relationships window. To form the relationship between the tables, you drag the common field from the primary table to the related table. The Edit Relationships dialog box then opens so you can select the relationship options for the two tables.

ACTIVITY

Define a one-to-many relationship between tables.

1. On the Ribbon, click the **Database Tools tab**. In the Relationships group, click the **Relationships button**. The Relationships window opens.

2. On the Relationship Tools Design tab, in the Relationships group, click the **Show Table button**. The Show Table dialog box opens, listing the three tables in the database on the Tables tab.

3. In the Show Table dialog box, double-click **Customer**. The Customer table's field list is added to the Relationships window.

4. Double-click **Contract**. The Contract table's field list is added to the Relationships window.

5. Click **Close**. The Show Table dialog box closes.

6. In the Customer field list, click **CustomerID** and then drag it to **CustomerID** in the Contract field list. The Edit Relationships dialog box opens. The primary table, related table, common field, and relationship type (one-to-many) appear in the dialog box. See Exhibit 18-13.

> **Tip:** If fields are hidden in a table field list, you can drag the bottom of the field list down until the vertical scroll bar disappears and all of the fields are visible.

Exhibit 18-13 Edit Relationships dialog box

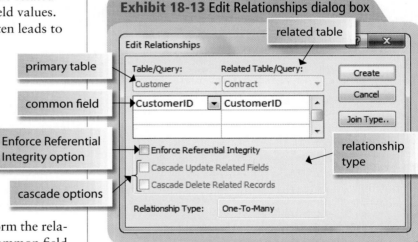

7. Click the **Enforce Referential Integrity check box** to select it. The two cascade options become available.

8. Click the **Cascade Update Related Fields check box** to select it. The appropriate foreign key field values in the related table will be updated if a primary key field value in the primary table changes. You will not select the Cascade Delete Related Records option to prevent deleting records unintentionally; remember, this option is rarely selected.

> **referential integrity** A set of rules to maintain consistency between related tables when data in a database is updated.
>
> **orphaned record** A record in a related table that has no matching record in the primary table.

9 Click **Create**. The Edit Relationships dialog box closes, and the one-to-many relationship between the two tables is defined. See Exhibit 18-14. In this relationship, Customer is the primary ("one") table because there is at most one customer for each contract. Contract is the related ("many") table because each customer can have zero, one, or many contracts. The completed relationship appears in the Relationships window, with the join line connecting the common field of CustomerID in each table.

Exhibit 18-14 Defined relationship in the Relationships window

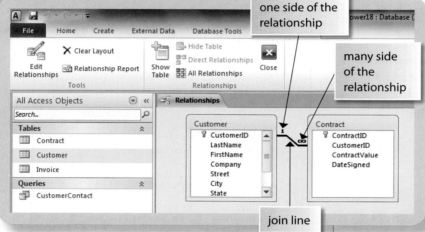

10 On the Quick Access Toolbar, click the **Save button** 💾 to save the layout in the Relationships window.

11 Close the Relationships window.

Working with Related Data in a Subdatasheet

After defining a relationship between tables with a common field, the primary table in the one-to-many relationship contains a **subdatasheet**, that displays the records from the related table. When you open the primary table, the subdatasheet for each record in the primary table is collapsed until you expand it. You navigate and update an open subdatasheet the same way as a table datasheet.

> **subdatasheet** A datasheet that displays the records from a related table in the primary table's datasheet.

If you did not select the option to cascade deletions to related records when you created a relationship between two tables, you cannot delete a record in a primary table that has matching records in a related table. Before you can delete a record from the primary table, you first must delete the related records in the related table. Although you could open the related table and then find and delete the related records, a simpler way is to delete the related records from the subdatasheet, which deletes the records from the related table. For example, you must delete the records from the Contract table that are related to a customer before you can delete the customer record from the Contract table.

ACTIVITY

Work with related data in a subdatasheet.

1 Open the **Customer table** in Datasheet view. To the left of each record is an expand button ⊞, indicating that the Customer table is related to another table—in this case, the Contract table.

2 To the left of Customer ID 2, click the **expand button** ⊞. The subdatasheet appears for this customer listing the related records from the Contract table, the contracts signed with that customer. The expand icon changes to a collapse icon ⊟ because the related records are displayed. See Exhibit 18-15.

3 Select the entire row for **Customer ID 2**. On the Home tab, in the Records group, click the **Delete button**. A dialog box opens indicating that you cannot delete the record because the Contract table contains records that are related to the current customer. This occurs because you enforced referential integrity and did not select the option to cascade deletions to related records. To delete the record for the customer, you would first need to delete the related records in the Contract table.

4 Click **OK** to close the dialog box.

5 If necessary, to the left of Customer ID 2, click the **collapse button** ⊟. The subdatasheet for that record collapses.

Exhibit 18-15 Subdatasheet with related records

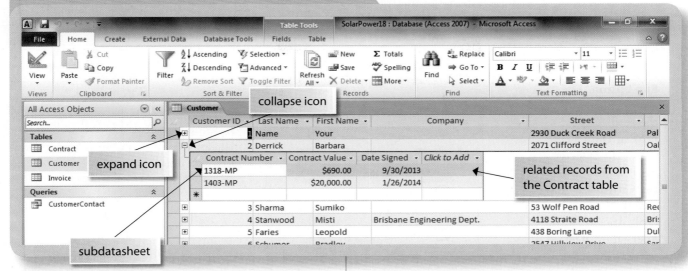

6 Display the subdatasheet for **Customer ID 3**. Two related records from the Contract table for this customer appear in the subdatasheet.

7 In the subdatasheet, for Contract Number 1305-KF, edit the Contract Value field value to **$800.00**.

8 Collapse the subdatasheet for Customer ID 3.

9 Open the Contract table, find the record for Contract Number 1305-KF, and then verify that the contract value is now $800.00.

10 Close the Contract and Customer tables.

LO18.5 Creating a Multitable Query

A **multitable query** is a query based on more than one table. To create a query that retrieves data from multiple tables, the tables must have a common field. Because you established a relationship between the Customer (primary) and Contract (related) tables based on the common CustomerID field that exists in both tables, you can now create a query to display data from both tables at the same time. The process for creating a multitable query is similar to creating a query with one table. The only differences are that you add more than one table's field list to the Query window and you can add fields from any of the tables to the query design.

The one-to-many relationship between two tables is shown in the Query window with a join line, which is the same way the relationship is indicated in the Relationships window. When the join line has thick ends, this indicates that the relationship is set to enforce referential integrity. If it wasn't, the join line would be thin at both ends and neither the "1" nor the infinity symbol would appear, even though the tables have a one-to-many relationship.

Create and run a multitable query.

1 On the Ribbon, click the **Create tab**. In the Queries group, click the **Query Design** button. The Show Table dialog box appears.

2 In the Tables box, double-click **Customer**, and then double-click **Contract**. The field lists for the Customer and Contract tables appear in the Query window with a join line indicating the one-to-many relationship between the tables.

3 Click **Close** to close the Show Table dialog box.

4 Resize the Customer field list so that all the fields in the table are displayed.

5 In the Customer field list, double-click **City** to place this field in the first column of the design grid.

6 Add the following fields from the Customer field list to the design grid: **Company**, **FirstName**, and **LastName**.

7 Add the following fields from the Contract field list to the design grid: **ContractID**, **DateSigned**, and

ContractValue. See Exhibit 18-16.

8 On the Query Tools Design tab, in the Results group, click the **Run button**. The query runs, and the results appear in Datasheet view. The selected fields from both the Customer table and the Contract table appear in the query datasheet. See Exhibit 18-17. The records are displayed in order according to the values in the CustomerID field because it is the primary key field in the primary table, even though this field is not included in the query datasheet.

9 Save the query as **CustomerContracts**.

10 In the query datasheet, click in the **Date Signed field** for any record.

11 On the Home tab, in the Sort & Filter group, click the **Selection button**. In the Selection menu, click **Between**. The Between Dates dialog box opens.

12 In the Oldest box, type **1/1/2014**. In the Newest box, type **12/31/2014**.

Exhibit 18-16 Multitable query

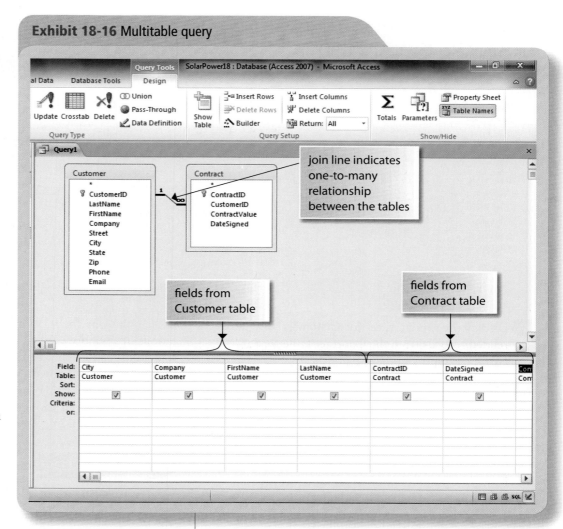

Exhibit 18-17 Results of a multitable query

13 Click **OK**. The filter is applied to the query datasheet, which now shows the 31 records for customers who signed contracts in 2014.

14 In the query datasheet, click in the first occurrence of a City field that contains the value **Oakland**.

15 On the Home tab, in the Sort & Filter group, click the **Selection button**. In the Selection menu, click **Equals "Oakland"**. The second filter is applied to the query datasheet, which now shows only eight records—customers located in Oakland who signed contracts during 2014.

16 Close the CustomerContracts query without saving the changes to the design.

LO18.6 Adding a Condition to a Query

You can refine a query to display only selected records by specifying a condition as part of the query. A **condition** is a criterion, or rule, that determines which records are selected. You enter a condition in a field's Criteria box in the design grid. For example, you could create a query that displays customer names and invoice numbers for all customers, and use a condition to select only those records with unpaid invoices.

Specifying an Exact Match

An **exact match** is when the value in the specified field must match the condition exactly in order for the record to be included in the query results. The query results then include only the records that meet the specified condition. For example, you could use an exact match query to display only those records in the Customer table with the value *San*

Francisco in the City field. When specifying a condition for a field that has the Text data type, the condition must be encosed in quotation marks. If you don't type the quotation marks, Access adds them automatically.

ACTIVITY

Create a query with an exact match.

1 Create a new query in Design view.

2 Add the **Invoice table** to the Query window, and then close the Show Table dialog box.

3 Add the following fields from the Invoice table to the design grid: **InvNum**, **Amount**, and **Paid**.

4 In the design grid, in the Criteria row for the Paid field, type **No** to enter the condition for this Yes/No field. This tells Access to retrieve only the records for unpaid invoices. As soon as you type the letter *N*, a menu appears with options for entering various functions for the criteria. You don't need to enter a function, so you can close this menu.

5 Press the **Esc key** to close the menu. You must close the menu so that you don't enter a function, which would cause an error. The query results will now show only customers with unpaid invoices. See Exhibit 18-18.

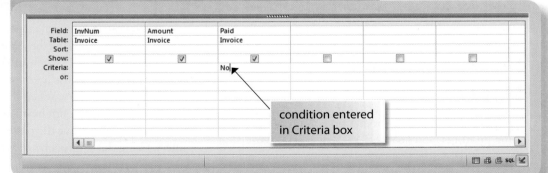

Exhibit 18-18 Criteria added to the design grid

Field:	InvNum	Amount	Paid			
Table:	Invoice	Invoice	Invoice			
Sort:						
Show:	☑	☑	☑	☐	☐	☐
Criteria:			No			
or:						

condition entered in Criteria box

condition A criterion, or rule, that determines which records are selected in a query.

exact match A query in which the value of a specified field must match the condition exactly for a record to be included in the query results.

6 Save the query as **InvoicesUnpaid**.

7 Run the query. The query datasheet displays the field values for only the 15 records that have a Paid field value of No. See Exhibit 18-19.

8 Close the InvoicesUnpaid query.

Exhibit 18-19 Exact match query results show unpaid invoices

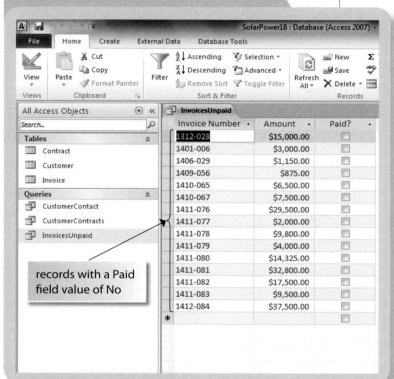

records with a Paid field value of No

Formatting a Datasheet

You can format a datasheet using many of the same features you learned in Word and Excel. For example, you can change the font, font size, and font color using the buttons in the Text Formatting group on the Home tab. You can also change the alternate row color in a datasheet by using the Alternate Row Color button in the Text Formatting group on the Home tab.

Using a Comparison Operator to Match a Range of Values

A condition can include one of the comparison operators shown in Exhibit 18-20 and a value. Access uses the comparison operator to compare a field value to the condition value and then selects all of the records for which that condition is true. The query results then include only the records that meet the specified criteria.

Exhibit 18-20 Access comparison operators

Operator	Description	Example
=	Equal to (optional; default operator)	="Hall"
<>	Not equal to	<>"Hall"
<	Less than	<#1/1/99#
<=	Less than or equal to	<=100
>	Greater than	>"C400"
>=	Greater than or equal to	>=18.75
Between … And …	Between two values (inclusive)	Between 50 And 325
In ()	In a list of values	In ("Hall", "Seeger")
Like	Matches a pattern that includes wildcards	Like "706*"

After you create and save a query, you can double-click the query name in the Navigation Pane to run the query again. You can switch to Design view to change its design. You can also use an existing query as the basis for creating another query. When the design of the query you need to create next is similar to an existing query, you can copy, paste, and rename the pasted query to create the new query. Using this approach keeps the original query intact.

 **ACTIVITY**

Create a query with a comparison operator.

1 In the Navigation Pane, in the Queries group, right-click **CustomerContracts**, and then on the shortcut menu, click **Copy**.

2 At the bottom of the Navigation Pane, right-click an empty area, and then on the shortcut menu, click **Paste**. The Paste As dialog box opens with Copy Of CustomerContracts selected in the Query Name box.

3 In the Query Name box, type **TopContractValues** as the name for the new query, and then press the **Enter key**. The query appears in the Queries section of the Navigation Pane.

4 In the Navigation Pane, in the Queries section, double-click the **TopContractValues query** to open, or run, the query.

5 Switch the query to **Design view**.

6 In the design grid, delete the **City field**.

7 In the design grid, in the Contract-Value column, click in the **Criteria box**, and then type **>=25000**. The condition specifies that a record will be selected only if its ContractValue field value is $25,000 or greater. See Exhibit 18-21.

⚠️ **Problem?** If a dialog box opens indicating that you entered an expression containing invalid syntax, you might have typed a comma in the amount. Commas are not allowed in selection criteria for Currency fields. Click **OK** to close the dialog box, and then delete the comma from the ContractValue Criteria box.

Exhibit 18-21 Criteria entered for the ContractValue field

Field:	Company	FirstName	LastName	ContractID	DateSigned	ContractValue	
Table:	Customer	Customer	Customer	Contract	Contract	Contract	
Sort:							
Show:	☑	☑	☑	☑	☑	☑	
Criteria:						>=25000	
or:							

new condition entered

8 Run the query. The query datasheet displays the selected fields for only those 20 records with a ContractValue field value that is greater than or equal to $25,000. See Exhibit 18-22. Notice that the City field values are not included in the query datasheet.

9 Save the TopContractValues query, and then close the query.

records with a contract value greater than or equal to $25,000

Exhibit 18-22 Modified query results

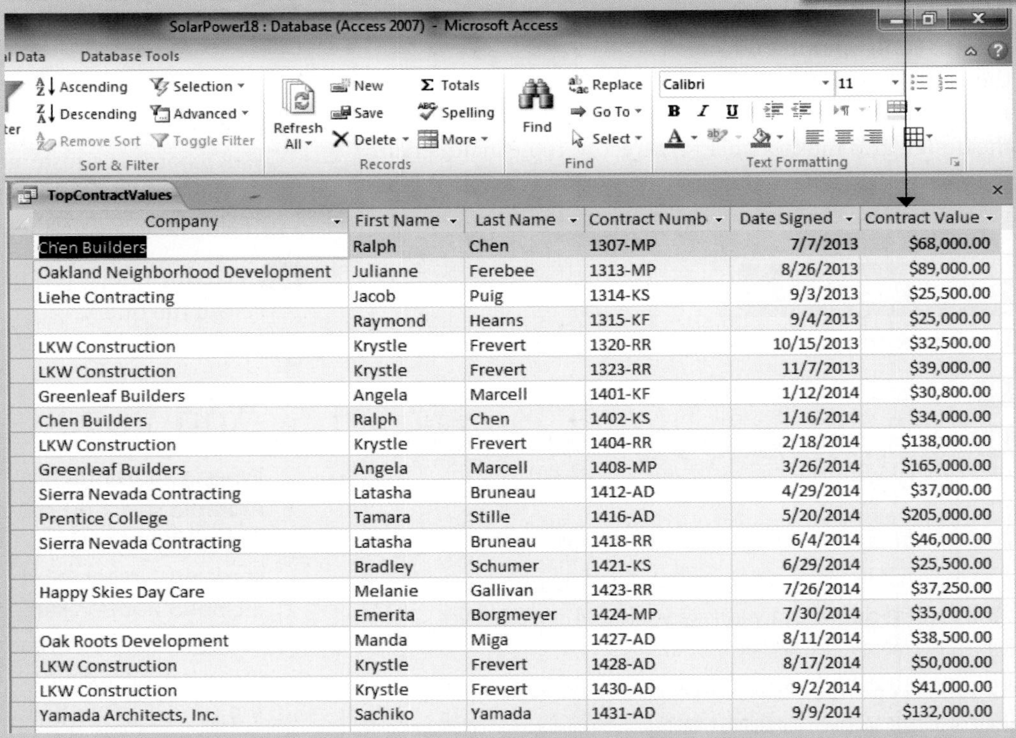

SolarPower18 : Database (Access 2007) - Microsoft Access

Database Tools

	Ascending	Selection ▾		New	Σ Totals		Replace	Calibri	▾ 11 ▾
	Descending	Advanced ▾	Refresh All ▾	Save	Spelling	Find	Go To ▾	**B** *I* U
ter	Remove Sort	Toggle Filter		Delete ▾	More ▾		Select ▾	A ▾
	Sort & Filter			Records		Find		Text Formatting

TopContractValues

Company ▾	First Name ▾	Last Name ▾	Contract Numb ▾	Date Signed ▾	Contract Value ▾
Chen Builders	Ralph	Chen	1307-MP	7/7/2013	$68,000.00
Oakland Neighborhood Development	Julianne	Ferebee	1313-MP	8/26/2013	$89,000.00
Liehe Contracting	Jacob	Puig	1314-KS	9/3/2013	$25,500.00
	Raymond	Hearns	1315-KF	9/4/2013	$25,000.00
LKW Construction	Krystle	Frevert	1320-RR	10/15/2013	$32,500.00
LKW Construction	Krystle	Frevert	1323-RR	11/7/2013	$39,000.00
Greenleaf Builders	Angela	Marcell	1401-KF	1/12/2014	$30,800.00
Chen Builders	Ralph	Chen	1402-KS	1/16/2014	$34,000.00
LKW Construction	Krystle	Frevert	1404-RR	2/18/2014	$138,000.00
Greenleaf Builders	Angela	Marcell	1408-MP	3/26/2014	$165,000.00
Sierra Nevada Contracting	Latasha	Bruneau	1412-AD	4/29/2014	$37,000.00
Prentice College	Tamara	Stille	1416-AD	5/20/2014	$205,000.00
Sierra Nevada Contracting	Latasha	Bruneau	1418-RR	6/4/2014	$46,000.00
	Bradley	Schumer	1421-KS	6/29/2014	$25,500.00
Happy Skies Day Care	Melanie	Gallivan	1423-RR	7/26/2014	$37,250.00
	Emerita	Borgmeyer	1424-MP	7/30/2014	$35,000.00
Oak Roots Development	Manda	Miga	1427-AD	8/11/2014	$38,500.00
LKW Construction	Krystle	Frevert	1428-AD	8/17/2014	$50,000.00
LKW Construction	Krystle	Frevert	1430-AD	9/2/2014	$41,000.00
Yamada Architects, Inc.	Sachiko	Yamada	1431-AD	9/9/2014	$132,000.00

LO18.7 Adding Multiple Conditions to Queries

Some queries require more than one condition. To create these more complex queries that have multiple conditions (also called criteria), you need to use **logical operators** to combine two or more conditions. Use the **And logical operator** when you want a record selected only if *all* of the specified conditions are met, such as a City field value of Oakland *and* a ContractValue field value greater than $25,000. Use the **Or logical operator** when you want a record selected if *at least one* of the specified conditions is met, such as a City field value of Oakland *or* a ContractValue field value greater than $25,000. Note that Access automatically places pound signs around date values in the condition to distinguish them from the operators.

Using the And Logical Operator

To create a query with the And logical operator, you specify all of the conditions in the same Criteria row of the design grid. The query will then display records only if all of the conditions are met.

In other words, all conditions in the *same* Criteria row of the design grid must be met for a record to be included in the query results. If at least one condition is not met, the record is not included in the query results.

ACTIVITY

Use the And logical operator in a query.

1. Create a new query in Design view.

2. Add the **Customer table** and **Contract table** to the Query window.

> **logical operator** An operator used to combine two or more conditions.
>
> **And logical operator** The logical operator used to select records only if *all* of the specified conditions are met.
>
> **Or logical operator** The logical operator used to select records if *at least one* of the specified conditions is met.

3. Add the following fields from the Customer field list to the design grid: **Company**, **FirstName**, **LastName**, and **City**.

4. Add the following fields from the Contract field list to the design grid: **ContractValue** and **DateSigned**.

5. In the design grid, in the City column, click in the **Criteria box**, type **Oakland** and then press the **Tab key**. The first condition is entered. Notice that quotation marks were added around the condition because the City field is a Text field.

6. In the Criteria box for the ContractValue field, type **>25000** and then press the **Tab key**. The second condition is entered. See Exhibit 18-23. Because both conditions appear in the same Criteria row, both conditions must be met for a record to appear in the query results.

Exhibit 18-23 Query with And logical operator

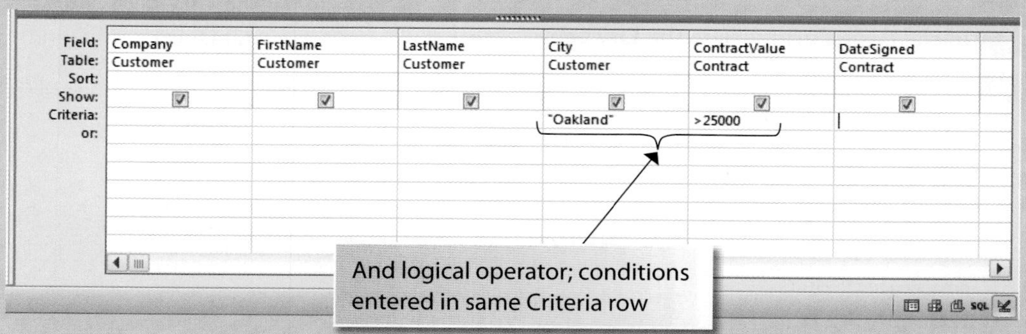

And logical operator; conditions entered in same Criteria row

7. Run the query. The query datasheet includes only the six records for customers who meet both conditions: a City field value of Oakland and a ContractValue field value greater than $25,000. See Exhibit 18-24.

8. Save the query as **TopOaklandCustomers** and then close the query.

And versus Or

When you use the And logical operator to define multiple selection criteria in a query, you *narrow* the results produced by the query because a record must meet more than one condition to be included in the results. When you use the Or logical operator, you *broaden* the results produced by the query because a record must meet only one of the conditions to be included in the results.

Exhibit 18-24 Results of query using the And logical operator

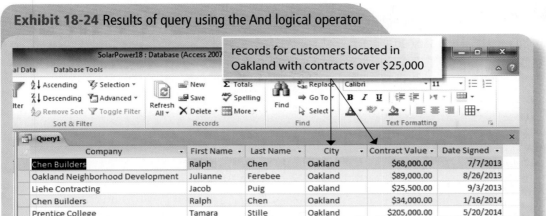

records for customers located in Oakland with contracts over $25,000

Company	First Name	Last Name	City	Contract Value	Date Signed
Chen Builders	Ralph	Chen	Oakland	$68,000.00	7/7/2013
Oakland Neighborhood Development	Julianne	Ferebee	Oakland	$89,000.00	8/26/2013
Liehe Contracting	Jacob	Puig	Oakland	$25,500.00	9/3/2013
Chen Builders	Ralph	Chen	Oakland	$34,000.00	1/16/2014
Prentice College	Tamara	Stille	Oakland	$205,000.00	5/20/2014
Oak Roots Development	Manda	Miga	Oakland	$38,500.00	8/11/2014

Using the Or Logical Operator

To create a query with the Or logical operator, you specify each relevant condition in a different Criteria row. The query will then display records if at least one of the conditions is met or if all of the conditions are met. If none of the conditions are met, the record is not displayed. In other words, at least one condition in *any* Criteria row of the design grid must be met for a record to be included in the query results. If at least one condition is not met, the record is not included in the query results.

Use the Or logical operator in a query.

1. Create a new query in Design view.

2. Add the **Customer table** and the **Contract table** to the Query window.

3. Add the following fields from the Customer field list to the design grid: **FirstName**, **LastName**, **Company**, and **City**.

4. Add the following fields from the Contract field list to the design grid: **ContractValue** and **DateSigned**.

5. In the ContractValue column, click in the **Criteria box**, type **<10000** and then press the **Tab key**. The first condition—to select contracts with amounts less than $10,000—is specified and the Criteria box for the DateSigned field is selected.

6. Press the **Down Arrow key** to select the or box for the DateSigned field. Entering a condition in the or box creates a query with the Or logical operator.

7. In the or box for the DateSigned field, type **Between 1/1/2014 And 3/31/2014** and then press the **Tab key**. The second condition—to select contracts when the DateSigned field value is between 1/1/2014 and 3/31/2014—is specified.

8. In the design grid, resize the DateSigned column so that the entire condition is visible. Notice that pound signs (#) surround the date values in the condition to distinguish them from the operators. See Exhibit 18-25.

Exhibit 18-25 Query window with the Or logical operator

Field:	LastName	Company	City	ContractValue	DateSigned
Table:	Customer	Customer	Customer	Contract	Contract
Sort:					
Show:	✓	✓	✓	✓	✓
Criteria:				<10000	
or:					Between #1/1/2014# And #3/31/2014#

Or logical operator; conditions entered in different rows

pound signs surround date values

9. In the design grid, in the DateSigned column, click in the **Sort box**, click the **arrow button**, and then click **Descending**. The query results will appear in descending order by DateSigned to create a logical order in which to analyze the data.

10. Run the query. The query results include the selected fields for the 27 records that meet one or both of the following conditions: a ContractValue field value of less than $10,000 or a DateSigned field value between 1/1/2014 and 3/31/2014. The records in the query datasheet appear in

Exhibit 18-26 Results of query using the Or logical operator

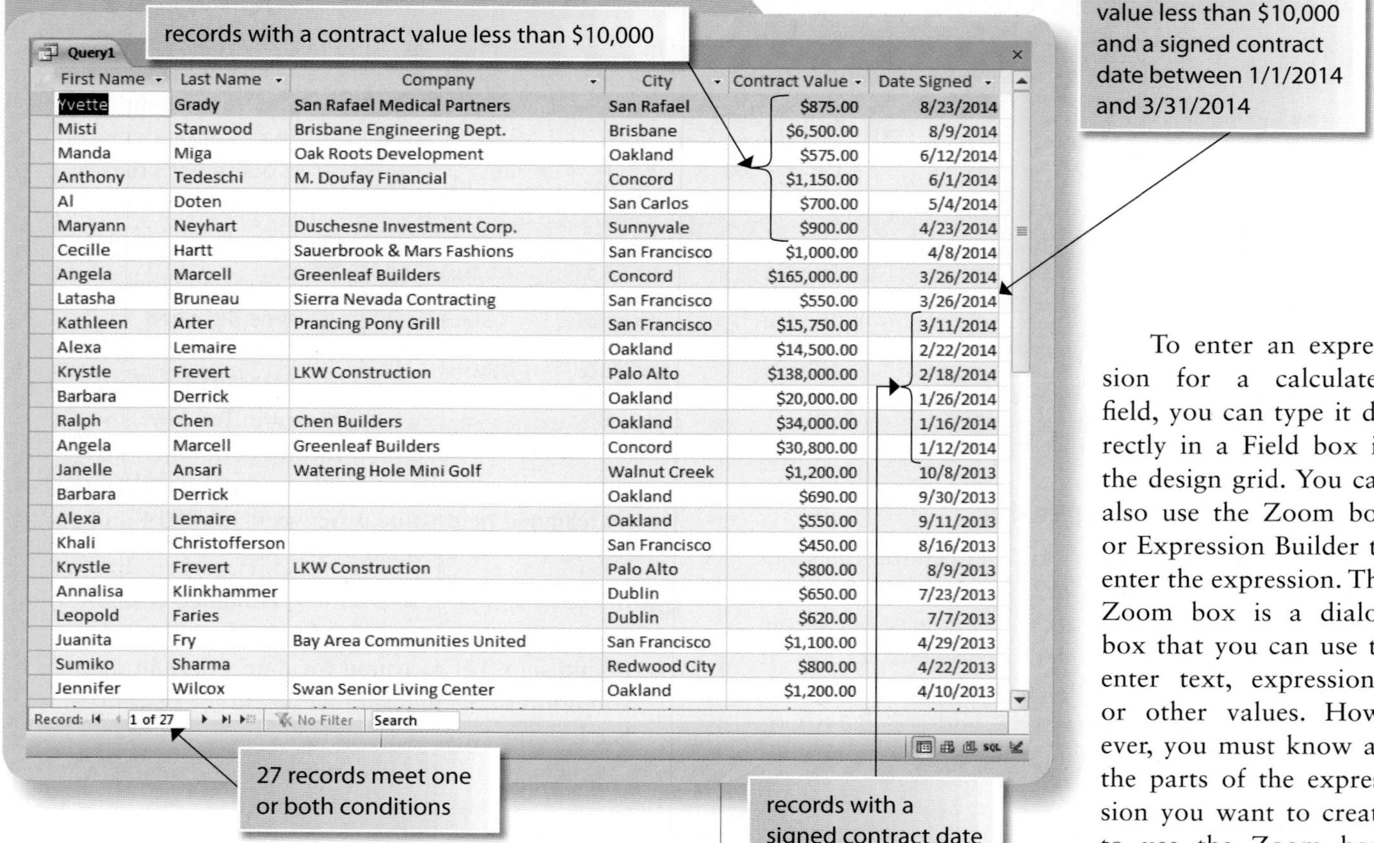

records with a contract value less than $10,000

record with a contract value less than $10,000 and a signed contract date between 1/1/2014 and 3/31/2014

First Name	Last Name	Company	City	Contract Value	Date Signed
Yvette	Grady	San Rafael Medical Partners	San Rafael	$875.00	8/23/2014
Misti	Stanwood	Brisbane Engineering Dept.	Brisbane	$6,500.00	8/9/2014
Manda	Miga	Oak Roots Development	Oakland	$575.00	6/12/2014
Anthony	Tedeschi	M. Doufay Financial	Concord	$1,150.00	6/1/2014
Al	Doten		San Carlos	$700.00	5/4/2014
Maryann	Neyhart	Duschesne Investment Corp.	Sunnyvale	$900.00	4/23/2014
Cecille	Hartt	Sauerbrook & Mars Fashions	San Francisco	$1,000.00	4/8/2014
Angela	Marcell	Greenleaf Builders	Concord	$165,000.00	3/26/2014
Latasha	Bruneau	Sierra Nevada Contracting	San Francisco	$550.00	3/26/2014
Kathleen	Arter	Prancing Pony Grill	San Francisco	$15,750.00	3/11/2014
Alexa	Lemaire		Oakland	$14,500.00	2/22/2014
Krystle	Frevert	LKW Construction	Palo Alto	$138,000.00	2/18/2014
Barbara	Derrick		Oakland	$20,000.00	1/26/2014
Ralph	Chen	Chen Builders	Oakland	$34,000.00	1/16/2014
Angela	Marcell	Greenleaf Builders	Concord	$30,800.00	1/12/2014
Janelle	Ansari	Watering Hole Mini Golf	Walnut Creek	$1,200.00	10/8/2013
Barbara	Derrick		Oakland	$690.00	9/30/2013
Alexa	Lemaire		Oakland	$550.00	9/11/2013
Khali	Christofferson		San Francisco	$450.00	8/16/2013
Krystle	Frevert	LKW Construction	Palo Alto	$800.00	8/9/2013
Annalisa	Klinkhammer		Dublin	$650.00	7/23/2013
Leopold	Faries		Dublin	$620.00	7/7/2013
Juanita	Fry	Bay Area Communities United	San Francisco	$1,100.00	4/29/2013
Sumiko	Sharma		Redwood City	$800.00	4/22/2013
Jennifer	Wilcox	Swan Senior Living Center	Oakland	$1,200.00	4/10/2013

Record: 1 of 27

27 records meet one or both conditions

records with a signed contract date between 1/1/2014 and 3/31/2014

descending order based on the values in the DateSigned field. See Exhibit 18-26.

11 Save the query as **SmallOrQ1Contracts** and then close the query.

LO18.8 Creating a Calculated Field

To perform a calculation in a query, you add a calculated field to the query. A **calculated field** displays the results of an expression (a combination of database fields, constants, and operators). A calculated field appears in a query datasheet or in a form or report; however, it does not exist in a database. When you run a query that contains a calculated field, Access evaluates the expression in the calculated field and displays the resulting value in the query datasheet, form, or report.

calculated field A field that displays the results of an expression (a combination of database fields, constants, and operators).

To enter an expression for a calculated field, you can type it directly in a Field box in the design grid. You can also use the Zoom box or Expression Builder to enter the expression. The Zoom box is a dialog box that you can use to enter text, expressions, or other values. However, you must know all the parts of the expression you want to create to use the Zoom box. Expression Builder is an Access tool that makes it easy for you to create an expression; it contains a box for entering the expression, an option for displaying and choosing common operators, and one or more lists of expression elements, such as table and field names. Unlike a Field box, which is too narrow to show an entire expression at one time, the Zoom box and Expression Builder are large enough to display longer expressions. In most cases, Expression Builder provides the easiest way to enter expressions because you don't have to know all the parts of the expression; you can choose the necessary elements from the Expression Builder dialog box.

You can specify a particular format for a calculated field, just as you can for any field, by modifying its properties.

In Access, calculations are performed using the standard order of precedence.

Calculated Fields

The Calculated Field data type, which is available only for tables in Datasheet view, lets you store the result of an expression as a field in a table. However, database experts caution against storing calculations in a table for the following reasons:

1. Storing calculated data in a table consumes space and increases the size of the database.

The preferred approach is to use a calculated field in a query; with this approach, the result of the calculation is not stored in the database—it is produced only when you run the query—and it is always current.

2. Using the Calculated Field data type provides limited options for creating a calculation.

A calculated field in a query provides more functions and options for creating expressions.

3. Including a field in a table whose value is dependent on other fields in the table violates database design principles.

To avoid problems, create a query that includes a calculated field to perform the calculation you want, instead of creating a field in a table that uses the Calculated Field data type.

Mike Flippo/Shutterstock.com

ACTIVITY

Create a query with a calculated field.

1 In the Navigation Pane, copy and paste the **InvoicesUnpaid query** and then save the query with the name **InvoicesUnpaidFees**.

2 Open the **InvoicesUnpaidFees query**, and then switch to Design view.

3 Add the **ContractID field** from the Invoice table field list to the fourth column in the design grid.

4 In the Show row for the Paid column, click the **Show check box** to remove the check mark. The query name indicates that the data is for unpaid invoices, so you don't need to include the Paid field values in the query results.

5 Save the Invoices-UnpaidFees query.

> **Tip:** A query must be saved and named in order for its fields to be listed in the Expression Categories box of the Expression Builder.

6 Click the blank Field box to the right of the ContractID field. This field will contain the calculated expression.

7 On the Query Tools Design tab, in the Query Setup group, click the **Builder button**. The Expression Builder dialog box opens. The insertion point is in the large box at the top of the dialog box, ready for you to enter the expression. The Expression Categories box lists the fields from the query so you can include them in the expression. The

Expression Elements box contains other elements you can use in the expression, including functions, constants, and operators.

8 In the Expression Categories box, double-click **Amount**. The field name is added to the expression box and placed within brackets and followed by a space.

9 Type ***** (an asterisk) to enter the multiplication operator, and then type **.05** for the constant. The expression you entered for the calculated field will multiply the Amount field values by .05 (which represents a 5 percent late fee). See Exhibit 18-27.

Exhibit 18-27 Expression Builder dialog box

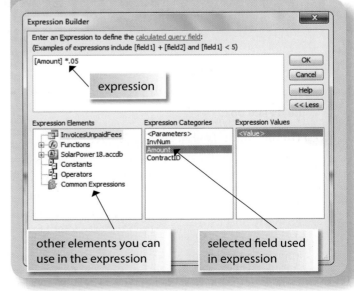

10 Click **OK**. The Expression Builder dialog box closes, and the expression is added to the design grid in the Field box for the calculated field.

11 At the beginning of the expression, select **Expr1** and then type **Late Fee** to specify a more descriptive name for the field. *Be sure to leave the colon after the field name*; it is needed to separate the calculated field name from the expression. The complete expression is *Late Fee: [Amount]*0.05*.

12 Run the query. The query datasheet contains the specified fields and the calculated field with the column heading *Late Fee*. See Exhibit 18-28.

Exhibit 18-29 Property Sheet for the calculated field

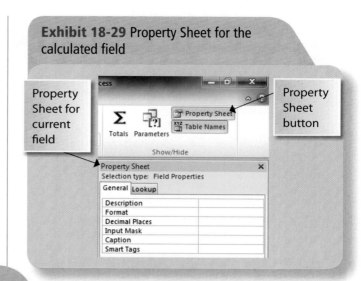

Exhibit 18-28 Datasheet displaying the calculated field

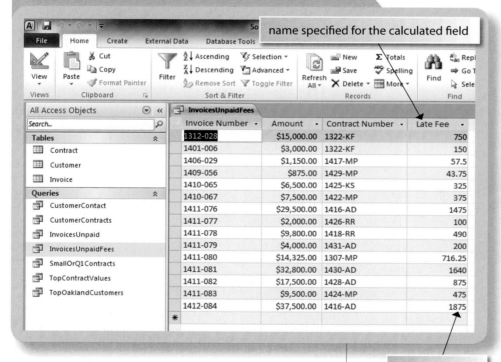

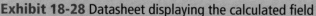

13 Switch to **Design view**.

14 In the design grid, select the **Late Fee calculated field Field box**.

15 On the Query Tools Design tab, in the Show/Hide group, click the **Property Sheet button**. The Property Sheet for the calculated field appears on the right side of the Query window. See Exhibit 18-29.

▲ **Tip:** You can also right-click a field in the design grid, and then click Properties on the shortcut menu to open the Property Sheet for that field.

16 In the Property Sheet, click the **Format box**, click the **arrow button** ▼ to display a list of available formats, and then click **Currency**. The Format property is set to Currency, which displays values with a dollar sign and two decimal places.

17 On the Ribbon, click the **Property Sheet button** to close the Property Sheet for the calculated field.

18 Run the query. The amounts in the Late Fee calculated field are now displayed with dollar signs and two decimal places.

19 Save the Invoices-UnpaidFees query, and then close it.

LO18.9 **Using Functions in a Query**

You can use a table or query datasheet to perform calculations, such as sums, averages, minimums, and maximums, on the displayed records. To do this, you use functions to perform arithmetic operations on selected records in a database. These are the same functions that are available in Excel.

Using the Total Row

To quickly perform a calculation using a function in a table or query datasheet, you can add a Total row at the bottom of the datasheet. In the Total row, you can then choose one of the functions for a field in the datasheet, and the results of the calculation will be displayed in the Total row for that field. You can add or remove the Total row from the datasheet by clicking the Totals button in the Records group on the Home tab; this button works as a toggle to switch between the display of the Total row and the results of any calculations in the row, and the display of the datasheet without this row.

Use the Total row.

1 Open the **Contract table** in Datasheet view.

2 On the Home tab, in the Records group, click the **Totals button**. A Total row appears at the bottom of the datasheet.

3 Scroll to the bottom of the datasheet to view the last records in the datasheet and the Total row.

4 In the Total row, click in the **Contract Value column**, and then click the **arrow button** that appears on the left side of the field to display a menu of functions. See Exhibit 18-30. The available functions depend on the data type of the current field. In this case, the menu provides functions for a Currency field.

5 On the menu, click **Sum**. Access adds all the values in the Contract Value column and displays the total $1,555,310.00 in the Total row for the column.

6 On the Home tab, in the Records group, click the **Totals button**. The Total row disappears from the datasheet.

7 Close the Contract table without saving the changes to the table's layout.

Creating Queries That Use Functions

Functions can also operate on the records that meet a query's selection criteria. You specify a function for a specific field, and the appropriate operation applies to that field's values for the selected records. For example, you can use the Minimum, Average, and Maximum functions for the ContractValue field to display the minimum, average, and maximum of all the contract amounts in the Contract table. For each calculation you want to perform on the same field, you need to add the field to the design grid.

After you run the query, the query datasheet uses a default column name that includes the function and the field name, such as *MinOfContractValue*, for the field. You can change the datasheet column name to a more descriptive or readable name by entering that name in the Field box followed by a colon and the field name, such as *Minimum Contract Value: ContractValue*. You must also keep the field name in the Field box because it identifies the field to use in the calculation.

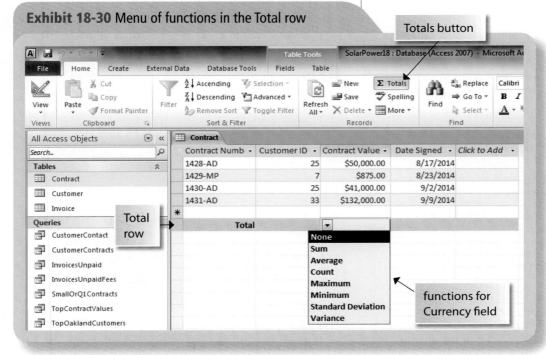

Exhibit 18-30 Menu of functions in the Total row

Create a query with functions.

1 Create a new query in Design view.

2 Add the **Contract table** to the Query window.

3 Double-click **ContractValue** in the Contract field list three times to add three copies of the field to the design grid.

4 On the Query Tools Design tab, in the Show/Hide group, click the **Totals button**. The Total row appears between the Table and Sort rows in the design grid.

Exhibit 18-32   Result of query using functions

5 In the design grid, in the first ContractValue column, click in the **Total box**, click the **arrow button** ⬇, and then click **Min** to specify the function to use for the field. This function will calculate the minimum amount of all the ContractValue field values.

6 In the first column, in the **Field box**, click to the left of ContractValue, type **Minimum Contract Value:** (including the colon), and then press the **Spacebar**. The Field box now contains the descriptive datasheet column name you specified (Minimum Contract Value) followed by the field name (ContractValue) with a colon separating the two names—*Minimum Contract Value: ContractValue*.

> ▲ **Tip:** Be sure to type the colon following the name or the query will not work correctly.

7 In the design grid, resize the first column so you can see all of the text in the Field box. See Exhibit 18-31.

8 In the second column, click in the **Total box**, click the **arrow button** ⬇, and then click **Max**. This function will calculate the maximum amount of all the ContractValue field values.

9 In the Field row in the second column, click to the left of ContractValue in the Field box, and then add **Maximum Contract Value:**.

10 In the third column, click in the **Total box**, click the **arrow button** ⬇, and then click **Avg**. This function will calculate the average of all the ContractValue field values.

11 In the Field row in the third column, click to the left of ContractValue in the Field box, and then add **Average Contract Value:**.

12 Run the query. The query datasheet includes one record with the results of the three calculations. These calculations are based on all of the records selected for the query—in this case, all 54 records in the Contract table.

13 Resize all of the columns to their best fit so that the column names are fully displayed. See Exhibit 18-32.

14 Save the query as **Contract-ValueStats**.

Creating Calculations for Groups of Records

In addition to calculating statistical information on all or

Exhibit 18-31   Total row inserted in the design grid

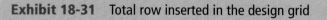

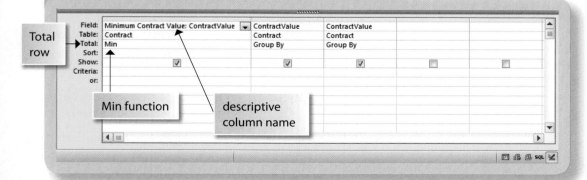

selected records in se-
lected tables, you can
calculate statistics for
groups of records. For
example, you can de-
termine the number of
customers in each city
or the average con-
tract amount by city.
The **Group By operator**
divides the selected
records into groups
based on the values
in the specified field.
Those records with
the same value for
the field are grouped
together, and the
datasheet displays
one record for each
group. Functions, which appear in the other columns
of the design grid, provide statistical information for
each group.

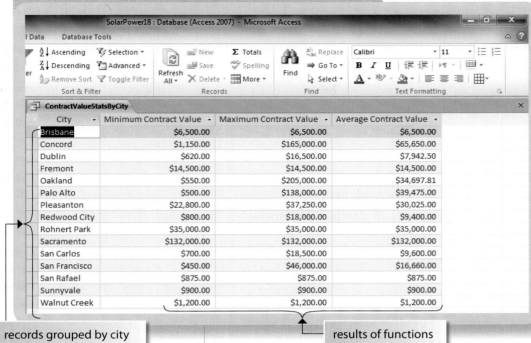

Exhibit 18-34 Functions grouped by City

City	Minimum Contract Value	Maximum Contract Value	Average Contract Value
Brisbane	$6,500.00	$6,500.00	$6,500.00
Concord	$1,150.00	$165,000.00	$65,650.00
Dublin	$620.00	$16,500.00	$7,942.50
Fremont	$14,500.00	$14,500.00	$14,500.00
Oakland	$550.00	$205,000.00	$34,697.81
Palo Alto	$500.00	$138,000.00	$39,475.00
Pleasanton	$22,800.00	$37,250.00	$30,025.00
Redwood City	$800.00	$18,000.00	$9,400.00
Rohnert Park	$35,000.00	$35,000.00	$35,000.00
Sacramento	$132,000.00	$132,000.00	$132,000.00
San Carlos	$700.00	$18,500.00	$9,600.00
San Francisco	$450.00	$46,000.00	$16,660.00
San Rafael	$875.00	$875.00	$875.00
Sunnyvale	$900.00	$900.00	$900.00
Walnut Creek	$1,200.00	$1,200.00	$1,200.00

records grouped by city

results of functions

![ACTIVITY]

Create a query with the Group By operator.

1 Display the ContractValueStats query in **Design view**.

2 On the Ribbon, click the **File tab**. In the navigation
bar, click **Save Object As**. The Save As dialog box
opens, indicating that you are saving a copy of
the ContractValueStats query as a new query. See
Exhibit 18-33.

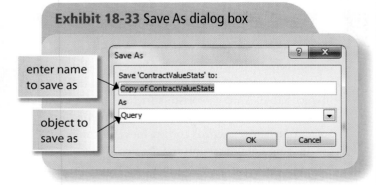

Exhibit 18-33 Save As dialog box

enter name
to save as

object to
save as

3 In the Save 'ContractValueStats' to box, type
ContractValueStatsByCity as the new query name.

4 Click **OK**. The new query is saved with the name
you specified.

5 On the Ribbon, click the **Query Tools Design tab** to
return to the Query window in Design view.

6 On the Query Tools Design tab, in the Query
Setup group, click the **Show Table button**. The
Show Table dialog box appears.

7 Add the **Customer table** to the Query window, and
then close the Show Table dialog box.

8 Drag the **City field** from the Customer field list to
the first column in the design grid. The City field
appears in the first column, and the existing fields
shift to the right. Group By, the default option in
the Total row, appears for the City field.

9 Run the query. The query results include 15
records—one for each City group. Each record
contains the City field value for the group and the
results of each calculation using the Min, Max,
and Avg functions. The summary statistics represent calculations based on the 54 records in the
Contract table. See Exhibit 18-34.

10 Save the ContractValuesStatsByCity query, and
then close it.

11 Compact and repair the SolarPower18 database,
and then close the database. Do not save the contents of the Clipboard.

Group By operator An operator that divides selected
records into groups based on the values in the specified field.

Quiz Yourself

1. In Datasheet view, what is the difference between navigation mode and editing mode?

2. Describe the field list and the design grid in the Query window in Design view.

3. What is a select query?

4. How are a table datasheet and a query datasheet similar? How are they different?

5. Describe how records are organized when you select multiple sort fields.

6. What is a filter?

7. When does a one-to-many relationship exist between tables?

8. What is referential integrity?

9. How do you create a multitable query?

10. What is a condition, and when do you use it?

11. What happens when you specify an exact match in a query?

12. In the design grid, where do you place the conditions for two different fields when you use the And logical operator?

13. In the design grid, where do you place the conditions for two different fields when you use the Or logical operator?

14. How do you perform a calculation in a query?

15. How do you calculate statistical information, such as sums, averages, minimums, and maximums, on the records displayed in a table datasheet or selected by a query?

16. Explain what the Group By operator does.

Practice It

Practice It 18-1

1. Open the data file **Snow18** located in the Chapter 18\Practice It folder. Save the database as **SnowRemoval18**.

2. Open the **Client table** in Datasheet view. For Client ID 1, change the field values in the First Name and Last Name columns to your first and last names.

3. Find the record with the Company field value of **Hanford Fashion**. Change the Phone field value to **207-555-4968**. Close the Client table.

4. Open the **ServiceAgreement** table, find the record for Agreement # 1436, and then delete the record. Close the ServiceAgreement table.

5. Create a query in Design view based on the Client table. Include the following fields in the query: Company, FirstName, LastName, and Phone. Save the query as **ClientPhoneList**, and then run the query.

6. Modify the ClientPhoneList query in Design view to sort the query results in ascending order by the Company field, and then in ascending order by the LastName field. Save the modified query, run the query, and then close it.

7. Create a one-to-many relationship between the primary Client table and the related ServiceAgreement table based on the ClientID field. Enforce referential integrity and select the Cascade Update Related Fields check box.

8. Create a one-to-many relationship between the primary ServiceAgreement table and the related Invoice table based on the AgreementNum field. Enforce referential integrity and select the Cascade Update Related Fields check box. Save the layout in the Relationships window, and then close the window.

9. Open the **ServiceAgreement table** in Datasheet view, find the record for Agreement # 1416, display the subdatasheet, change the record for invoice number 1411-071 to unpaid by clicking the Paid? check box, and then close the table.

10. Create a query in Design view based on the ServiceAgreement and Invoice tables. Select the AgreementNum, AgreementAmt, and ServiceType fields from the ServiceAgreement table, and then select the InvNum and InvAmt fields from the Invoice table. Apply a sort to sort the query results in descending order based on the AgreementAmt. Select only those records for business customers by entering **Commercial** in the ServiceType Criteria box. Do not display the ServiceType field values in the query results. Save the query as **BusinessAgreements**, run the query, and then close it.

11. Create a query in Design view that lists all unpaid invoices that are dated between 1/1/2014 and 12/31/2014. Include the following fields from the Invoice table in the query: InvNum, InvAmt, InvDate, and Paid. Sort the InvDate field in ascending order. Do not show the Paid field in the query results. Save the query as **UnpaidInvoices**, run the query, and then close it.

12. Create a query in Design view that lists clients located in Veazie or service agreements for less than $1,000. Include the Company, City, FirstName, and LastName fields from the Client table; and the AgreementNum and AgreementAmt fields from the ServiceAgreement table. Sort the query in ascending order by the City field and then in descending order by the AgreementAmt field. Save the query as **VeazieOrSmallAgreements**, run the query, and then close it.

13. In the Navigation Pane, copy and paste the UnpaidInvoices query using the query name **UnpaidInvoicesCashDiscount**. Open the UnpaidInvoicesCashDiscount query in Design view, and then add a calculated field to the fifth column in the design grid that calculates a seven percent discount based on the InvAmt field values. Change the field's column name to **Cash Discount**. Save the query, and then run it.

14. In Design view for the UnpaidInvoicesCashDiscount query, modify the format of the Cash Discount field so that it uses the Standard format and two decimal places. Run the query, resize all columns in the datasheet to best fit, and then save and close the query.

15. Create a query in Design view that calculates the minimum, maximum, and average agreement amounts for all service agreements using the field names **Lowest**, **Highest**, and **Average**, respectively. Save the query as **AgreementStats**. Run the query.

16. Use the Save As command to save the AgreementStats query as **AgreementStatsByCity**. Modify the AgreementStatsByCity query so that the records are grouped by the City field in the Client table. Sort the query in ascending order by the City field. The City field should appear first in the query datasheet. Save the query, run the query, and then close it.

17. Compact and repair the SnowRemoval18 database, and then close it. (Do not save the contents of the Clipboard.)

Practice It 18-2

1. Open the data file **Art18** located in the Chapter 18\Practice It folder. Save the database as **ArtClasses18**.

2. In the Instructor table, for Instructor ID 15-9384, change the value in the First Name and Last Name columns to your first and last names.

3. In the Instructor table, find the record with the last name of Weigel, and then change the value in the Hire Date column to **5/12/2012**. Close the Instructor table.

4. Create one-to-many relationships between the primary Instructor table and the related Class table using the InstructorID field, and between the primary Class table and the related Student table using the ClassID field. In each relationship, enforce referential integrity and select the option to cascade updates to related fields. Save and close the Relationships window.

5. In the Instructor table, find the record with the Instructor ID 98-9123, delete the related record in the subdatasheet for this instructor, and then delete the record for this instructor. Close the Instructor table.

6. Create a query in Design view based on the Student table that includes the LastName, FirstName, and Phone fields. Sort the query in ascending order by LastName. Save the query as **StudentPhoneNumbers**, and then run the query.

7. In the StudentPhoneNumbers query results, change the phone number for Christa Harris to **740-555-2920**. Close the query.

8. Create a query in Design view based on the Instructor and Class tables. Add the LastName and InstructorID fields from the Instructor table. Add the ClassID, ClassName, Juniors, Length, and Cost fields from the Class table. Sort in ascending order on the LastName field, and then sort in ascending order by the ClassID field. Save the query as **ClassesByInstructor**, and then run it.

9. Save the ClassesByInstructor query as **JuniorsClasses**. Modify the JuniorsClasses query to display all classes taught by instructors who allow teens (juniors) to participate. Do not include the Juniors field in the query results. Save the query, and then run it.

10. Save the JuniorsClasses query as **JuniorsClassesLowCost**. Modify the JuniorsClassesLowCost query to display only those classes taught by instructors who allow teens (juniors) to participate and that cost $100 or less. Do not include the Juniors field values in the query results. Save the query, and then run it.

11. In the JuniorsClassessLowCost query datasheet, calculate the total cost of the classes selected by the query. Save and close the query.

12. Compact and repair the ArtClasses18 database, and then close it.

On Your Own

On Your Own 18-1

1. Open the data file **Donations18** located in the Chapter 18\On Your Own folder. Save the database as **DonationsList18**.

2. In the Donor table, for Donor ID 36001, change the Title field to an appropriate title, change the First Name field value to your first name, and change the Last Name field value to your last name.

3. Create one-to-many relationships between the primary Agency table and the related Donation table, and between the primary Donor table and the related Donation table. For each relationship, enforce referential integrity and cascade updates to related fields. Save and close the Relationships window.

4. In the Donor table, delete the record for Donor ID 36028. (Be sure to delete the related record first.)

5. Create a query based on the Agency table that includes the Agency, FirstName, LastName, and City fields. Save the query as **AgenciesByCity**, and then run it.

6. Modify the AgenciesByCity query design so that it sorts records in ascending order first by City and then in ascending order by Agency. Save and run the query.

7. In the AgenciesByCity query datasheet, change the contact for the Carpenter After-School Center to **Valerie Jackson**. Close the query.

8. Create a query in Design view that displays the DonorID, FirstName, and LastName fields from the Donor table, and the Description and DonationValue fields from the Donation table for all donations over $100. Sort the query in descending order by DonationValue. Save the query as **BigDonors**, and then run the query.

9. Save the BigDonors query as **BigCashDonors**. Modify the BigCashDonors query to display only records with cash donations of more than $100. Do not include the Description field values in the query results. In the query datasheet, calculate the sum of the cash donations. Save and close the query.

10. Create a query in Design view that displays the Agency from the Agency table, and the DonationID, DonationDate, and Description fields from the Donation table. Save the query as **TrailsDonations**, and then run the query.

11. Use the Selection button in the Sort & Filter group on the Home tab to filter the TrailsDonations query datasheet to display only the records for donations to Eastern Wyoming Trails.

12. Format the TrailsDonations query datasheet to use an alternate row color of the Purple, Accent 4, Lighter 80% theme color. (*Hint*: Use the Alternate Row Color button in the Text Formatting group on the Home tab to select the row color.) Resize the columns to best fit the complete field names and values. Save the TrailsDonations query.

13. Save the TrailsDonations query as **FurnitureOrHousewares**. Modify the FurnitureOrHousewares query to display donations of furniture or housewares and to list the Agency ID instead of the Agency name. Sort the records in ascending order first by Description and then in ascending order by AgencyID. Run the query, adjust the column widths, save the query, and then close it.

14. Create a query in Design view that displays the DonorID, Agency, Description, and DonationValue fields for all donations that require a pickup. Do not display the Pickup field in the query results. Save the query as **PickupCharge**. Create a calculated field named **Net Donation** that displays the results of subtracting $9.25 from the DonationValue field values. Display the results in ascending order by DonationValue. Format the calculated field with the Currency format. Run the query,

resize the columns in the query datasheet to their best fit, save the query, and then close it.

15. Create a query in Design view based on the Donation table that displays the sum, average, and count of the DonationValue field for all donations. (*Hint*: Use the Count function to count the number of rows.) Enter appropriate column names for each field. Format the sum and average values using the Standard format and two decimal places. Save the query as **DonationStats**, and then run the query. In the query datasheet, resize the columns to their best fit, save the query, and then close it.

16. Create a copy of the DonationStats query named **DonationStatsByAgency**. Modify the DonationStatsByAgency query to display the sum, average, and count of the DonationValue field for all donations grouped by Agency, with Agency appearing as the first field. Sort the records in descending order by the donation total. Save the query, run the query, and then close it.

17. Compact and repair the DonationsList18 database, and then close it. (Do not save the contents of the Clipboard.)

ADDITIONAL STUDY TOOLS

Chapter 18

IN THE BOOK

▶ Complete end-of-chapter exercises

▶ Study tear-out Chapter Review Card

ONLINE

▶ Complete additional end-of-chapter exercises

▶ Take practice quiz to prepare for tests

▶ Review key term flash cards (online, printable, and audio)

▶ Play "Beat the Clock" and "Memory" to quiz yourself

▶ Watch the videos "Design a Select Query," "Sort Multiple Fields in Design View," "Filter Records by Selection," "Define a One-to-Many Relationship Between Tables," "Use the Total Row," and more

Creating Forms and Reports

Introduction

Forms can be based on a table or query, providing a simpler, more intuitive layout for displaying, entering and changing data. Forms can also display data from two or more tables at the same time, providing a more complete picture of the information in the database. For example, a form might show data about customers and their associated contracts, which are stored in separate tables.

Reports provide a formatted printout or screen display of the data in a database. For example, a database might include a formatted report of customer and contract data that staff can use for market analyses and strategic planning for selling services to customers. With reports, information can be formatted in a professional manner, making the report appealing and easy to use.

LO19.1 Creating a Form Using the Form Wizard

You have already used the Form tool to create a simple form to enter, edit, and view records in a database. The Form tool creates a form automatically, using all the fields in the selected table or query. You can also create a form using the **Form Wizard**, which guides you through the process of creating a form. In the Form Wizard dialog boxes, you select the tables or queries on which to base the form, choose which fields to include in the form, and specify the order in which the selected fields should appear in the form. You then select a form layout, which can be Columnar, Tabular, Datasheet, and Justified. The Tabular and Datasheet layouts display the fields from multiple records at one time. The Columnar and Justified layouts display the fields from one record at a time. Finally, you enter a title for the form and choose whether to open the form in Form view so you can work with data, or in Design view so you can modify the form's design.

Form Wizard The Access feature that guides you through the process of creating a form; you choose which fields to display from tables and, queries and the order in which they appear.

Forms make it easier to enter, view, and update data in a database. Reports are used to display data in an attractive and professional format.

Dmitriy Shironosov/Shutterstock.com

ACTIVITY

Create a form using the Form Wizard.

1 Open the data file **Solar19** located in the Chapter 19\Chapter folder. Save the database as **SolarPower19**.

2 In the Navigation Pane, select the **Customer table**.

3 On the Ribbon, click the **Create tab**. In the Forms group, click the **Form Wizard button**. The first Form Wizard dialog box opens. The Customer table is selected in the Tables/Queries box, and the fields from the Customer table are listed in the Available Fields box. See Exhibit 19-1.

4 Click  to move all the fields to the Selected Fields box.

Exhibit 19-1 First Form Wizard dialog box

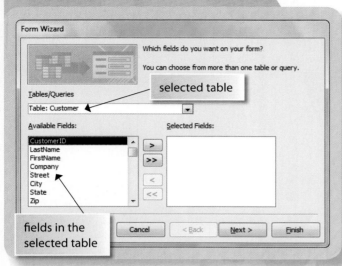

selected table

fields in the selected table

5 In the Selected Fields box, click **Phone**, and then click < to move the Phone field back to the Available Fields box. In the Selected Fields box, the Email field is selected. The next field you add will be added below the selected Email field.

6 With the Phone field selected in the Available Fields box, click >. The Phone field is added back to the Selected Fields box below the Email field.

7 Click **Next** to display the second Form Wizard dialog box, which provides the available layouts for the form: Columnar, Tabular, Datasheet, and Justified. A sample of the selected layout appears on the left side of the dialog box. See Exhibit 19-2.

Exhibit 19-2 Second Form Wizard dialog box

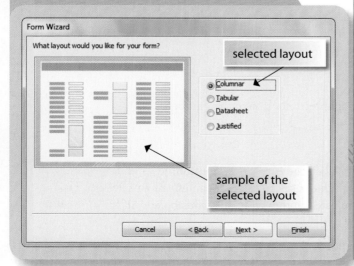

selected layout

sample of the selected layout

8 Click the **Tabular option button** and review the corresponding sample layout. Review the **Datasheet** and **Justified** layouts.

9 Click the **Columnar option button** to select that layout for the form.

10 Click **Next**. The third and final Form Wizard dialog box shows the Customer table's name as the default form title. *Customer* is also the default name that will be used for the form object. See Exhibit 19-3.

Exhibit 19-3 Third Form Wizard dialog box

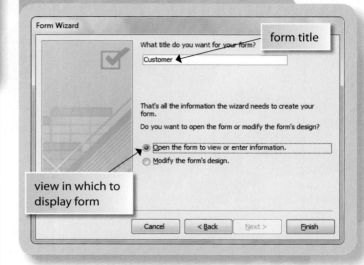

form title

view in which to display form

11 In the What title do you want for your form box, edit the form name to **CustomerInfo**.

12 Click **Finish**. The CustomerInfo form opens in Form view, displaying the field values for the first record in the Customer

> **Tip:** You can close the Navigation Pane to display more of the Form window.

table. The form title appears on the object tab, as the object name in the Navigation Pane, and as a title on the form itself. The Columnar layout places the captions for each field on the left and the field values in boxes on the right. The width of the field value boxes is based on the size of the field. See Exhibit 19-4.

The Columnar form layout is good for displaying and updating data in the table because it lets users focus on one record at a time.

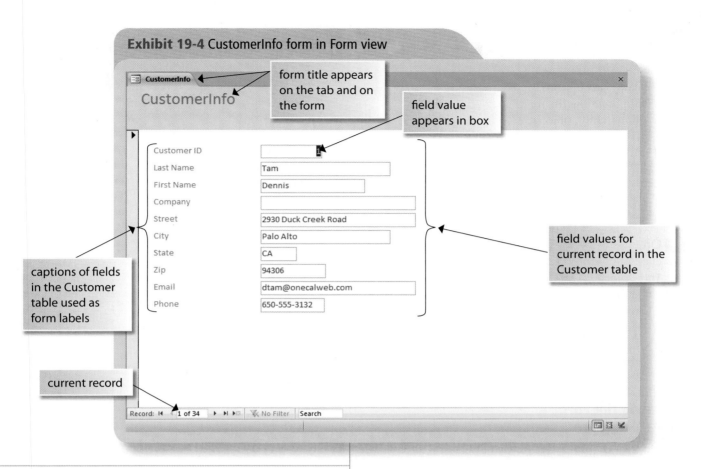

Exhibit 19-4 CustomerInfo form in Form view

form title appears on the tab and on the form

field value appears in box

field values for current record in the Customer table

captions of fields in the Customer table used as form labels

current record

CustomerInfo

Customer ID

Last Name — Tam

First Name — Dennis

Company

Street — 2930 Duck Creek Road

City — Palo Alto

State — CA

Zip — 94306

Email — dtam@onecalweb.com

Phone — 650-555-3132

Record: 1 of 34 | No Filter | Search

LO19.2 Modifying a Form's Design in Layout View

After you create a form, it opens in Form view. If you need to improve its appearance or to make the form easier to use, you need to switch to Layout view. In Layout view, you can see a record in the form and change its layout at the same time, which lets you easily see the results of any design changes you make. You can continue to make changes, undo modifications, and rework the design in Layout view to achieve the look you want for the form. For example, you might change the font, font size, or font color of the labels; add a picture; or modify other form elements such as the type of line used for the field value boxes. You can make all of these changes in Layout view. To make one of these changes, you must select an object. In Layout view, a solid orange outline identifies the currently selected object on the form.

Keep in mind that some changes to the form design must be done in Design view, which gives you a more detailed view of the form's structure.

Applying a Theme to a Form

You can quickly change the look of a form by applying a different theme, which determines the design scheme for the colors and fonts used in the form. Forms are originally formatted with the Office theme, but you can apply a different theme in Layout view. The theme you select is applied to all of the objects in the database unless you specify to apply the theme to the current object only or to all matching objects, such as all forms.

 **ACTIVITY**

Apply a theme to a form.

1 Display the form in **Layout view**. The Form Layout Tools tabs appear on the Ribbon. The field value box for the Customer ID field, is selected, as indicated by the orange border. See Exhibit 19-5.

2 On the Form Layout Tools Design tab, in the Themes group, click the **Themes button**. The Themes gallery appears, showing the available themes for the form.

3 Point to several themes to see their effects on the form's appearance.

4 In the Themes gallery, right-click the **Elemental theme**. A shortcut menu appears with options for applying the theme to all matching objects, applying the theme to this object only (the CustomerInfo form), or making the theme the default for all objects in the database.

5 On the shortcut menu, click **Apply Theme to This Object Only**. The gallery closes, and the CustomerInfo form is formatted with the Elemental theme. See Exhibit 19-6.

Changing the Form Title's Text and Appearance

A form's title should be descriptive and indicate the form's purpose. To make the form's purpose clearer, you can edit or replace the form's current title. You can also format it to change its appearance. For example, you can bold, italicize, and underline text; change the font, font color, and font size; and change the alignment of text. These options are located in the Font group on the Form Layout Tools Format tab.

Change the appearance of a form title.

1 Click the **CustomerInfo form title**. An orange box surrounds the title, indicating it is selected.

Exhibit 19-5 Form displayed in Layout view

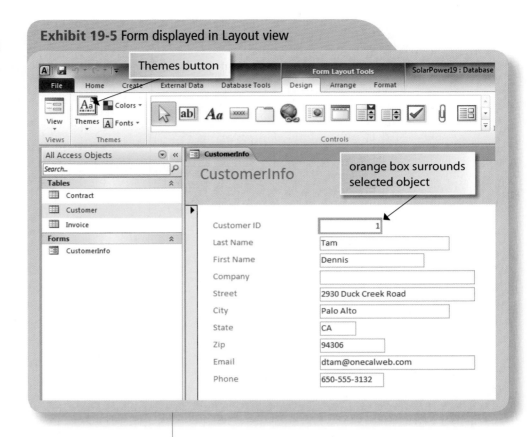

Exhibit 19-6 Form with theme applied

Working with Themes

Themes provide a quick way to format the objects in a database consistently. When you apply a theme to an object, you can choose whether to apply a theme to the current object or to all matching objects, such as all forms in the database. You can also choose to make a theme the default theme for the database, which means any existing objects and any new objects you create in the database will be formatted with the selected theme. Instead of clicking a theme in the Themes gallery, you right-click the theme and then click the option you want on the shortcut menu.

When you choose to apply a theme to all matching objects in the database or to make the theme the default for the database, Access applies that theme to all the *existing* forms and reports in the database as well as to any new forms and reports you create. Although this approach ensures design consistency, it can also introduce problems with existing objects. For example, applying a theme that uses a larger font size could cause the text in labels and field value boxes to be cut off or to overlap with other objects on an existing form or report. The colors applied by the theme could also interfere with any colors that you specified on existing forms and reports. You would then have to spend time checking the existing forms and reports for any unintended results and fixing the problems introduced by applying the theme.

A better approach is to select the Apply Theme to This Object Only option on the shortcut menu for a theme in the Themes gallery, for each existing form and report. If the new theme causes problems for that form or report, you can simply reapply the previous theme to return the object to its original design.

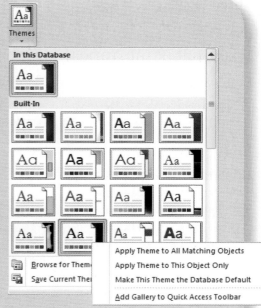

> Apply Theme to All Matching Objects
> Apply Theme to This Object Only
> Make This Theme the Database Default
> Add Gallery to Quick Access Toolbar

---

2 Click between the letters *r* and *I* to position the insertion point in the title text, and then press the **Spacebar**. The form title is now *Customer Info*.

3 Press the **End key** to move the insertion point to the end of the title, and then type **rmation**. The form title is now *Customer Information*, and the title appears on two lines.

4 Click in the **main form area** to deselect the title. Click **Customer Information** to reselect the title. The orange outline appears around the title.

5 On the Ribbon, click the **Form Layout Tools Format tab**. In the Font group, click the **Font Color button arrow** A·, and then click the **Dark Purple, Text 2 theme color**. The color is applied to the form title. See Exhibit 19-7.

> **Tip:** The theme colors change based on the theme applied to the object. The standard colors are always the same.

Exhibit 19-7 Form title with new color applied

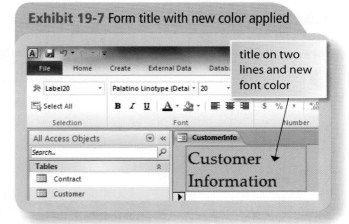

title on two lines and new font color

Adding a Logo to a Form

A logo can be used to provide color and visual interest in a form. A logo is one of many controls you can use in a form. A **control** is an item in a form,

> **control** An item in a form, report, or other database object that you can manipulate to modify the object's appearance.

Changing the title of a form has no effect on the form object name; its original name appears on the object tab and in the Navigation Pane.

report, or other database object that you can manipulate to modify the object's appearance. The controls you add and modify in Layout view are available on the Form Layout Tools Design tab in the Controls group and the Header/Footer group.

When you add a logo or other control to a form, it is placed in a **control layout**, which is a set of controls grouped together in a form or report so that you can manipulate the set as a single control. The dotted outline indicates the control layout is selected. You can remove a control from the control layout so you can move the control independently of the control layout.

ACTIVITY

Add a picture to a form.

1 On the Ribbon, click the **Form Layout Tools Design tab**. In the Header/Footer group, click the **Logo button**. The Insert Picture dialog box opens.

2 Click the data file **Panels** located in the Chapter 19\Chapter folder, and then click **OK**. A picture of solar

control layout A set of controls grouped together in a form or report so that you can manipulate the set as a single control.

panels appears on top of the form title. A solid orange outline surrounds the picture, indicating it is selected, and a dotted outline surrounds the control layout. See Exhibit 19-8.

Exhibit 19-8 Form with picture

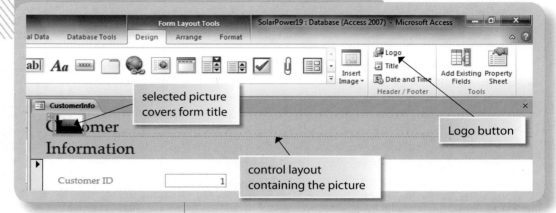

3 Right-click the selected picture to display the shortcut menu, point to **Layout**, and then click **Remove Layout**. The picture is removed from the control layout.

4 Drag the **picture** to the right of the title so that it does not block any part of the form title.

5 Drag a corner of the orange box to enlarge the picture to fit within the shaded title area. See Exhibit 19-9.

Exhibit 19-9 Form with repositioned and resized picture

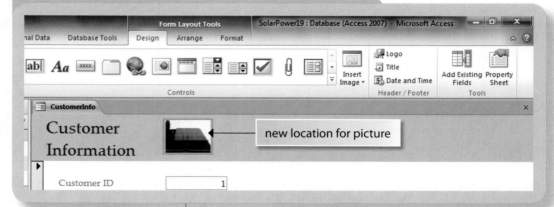

Changing the Lines in a Form

Each field value in the form is displayed in a field value box. The field value boxes are made up of solid lines, which, depending on the theme, might overshadow the field values and make them difficult to read. Fortunately, the lines are another type of control that you can modify in Layout view. The Control Formatting group on the Form Layout Tools Format tab provides options for changing the thickness, type, and color of any line in a form. You can change the line type for each field value box in the form one at a time. Or, you can select all of the field value boxes and apply a new line type to all of them at the same time.

ACTIVITY

Change the lines in a form.

1. Click the **Customer ID field value box**, which contains the field value 1. An orange outline appears around the field value box to indicate it is selected.

2. On the Ribbon, click the **Form Layout Tools Format tab**. In the Control Formatting group, click the **Shape Outline button**. The Shape Outline gallery opens with options for changing the line color, line thickness, and line type.

3. Point to **Line Type** to display a submenu with various line formats, and then click the **Dots line type**.

> You navigate a form in the same way as you navigate a table or query datasheet.

4. Click a blank area of the main form to deselect the field value box. The Customer ID field value box is now a dotted line.

5. Click the **Last Name field value box**, press and hold the **Shift key**, click each remaining field value box below the Last Name field value box, and then release the **Shift key**. All of the field value boxes except the Customer ID field value box are selected.

6. On the Form Layout Tools Format tab, in the Control Formatting group, click the **Shape Outline button**, and then point to **Line Type**. See Exhibit 19-10.

7. Click the **Dots line type**, and then click a blank area of the main form. The line type for each box is now dotted.

8. Save the form.

Exhibit 19-10 Form with multiple field value boxes selected

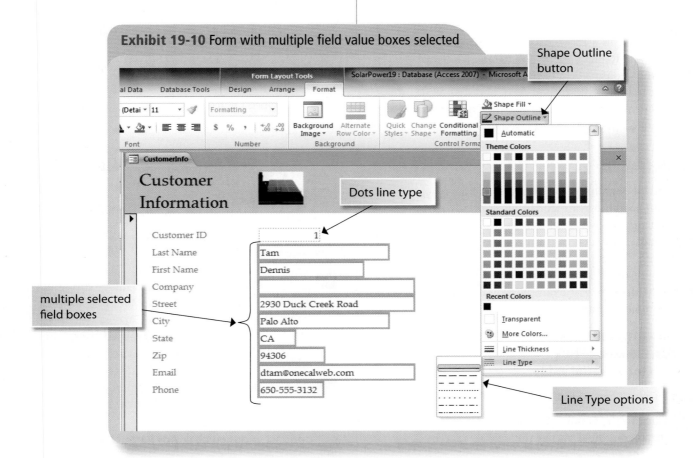

Use an Effective Form Design

A form, like any written document, should convey information clearly and effectively. By producing a well-designed and well-written form, you can ensure that other people will be able to work productively and efficiently. As you create a form:

▶ **Consider how the form will be used.** The form's design should accommodate the needs of the people who will use the form to view, enter, and maintain data. For example, if a database form matches an existing paper form, use the same fields in the same order as those on the paper form so users can use the Tab key to move from one field to the next in the database form to enter the necessary information from the paper form.

▶ **Include a meaningful title.** The form should clearly identify its purpose, and a descriptive title ensures that users immediately know what the form is intended for.

▶ **Use correct spelling and grammar.** The text in a form should not contain any spelling or grammatical errors. This not only creates a professional image, but also keeps users focused on the task at hand—entering or reviewing data.

▶ **Enhance the form's appearance.** A visually appealing form is user-friendly and can improve the form's readability, helping to prevent data entry errors.

▶ **Use a consistent design.** Use similar elements—titles, pictures, fonts, and so on—in each form in a database to provide a cohesive appearance. A mix of styles and elements in a database could lead to problems when working with the forms.

LO19.3 Finding Data Using a Form

You can use the Find and Replace dialog box to search for data in a form. As you did when using the Find and Replace dialog box to search a datasheet, you choose a field to base the search on by making that field the current field, and then you enter the value you want to match. The record you want to view is then displayed in the form.

Searching for a Partial Value

Instead of searching for an entire field value, you can search for a record that contains part of the value anywhere in that field. Performing a partial search such as this is often easier than matching the entire field value and is useful when you don't know or can't remember the entire field value. For example, you can search for part of a company's name.

ACTIVITY

Search for a partial value.

1 Display the form in **Form view**.

2 Click in the **Email field value box** to select Email as the current field and as the field to search.

3 On the Home tab, in the Find group, click the **Find button**. The Find and Replace dialog box opens. The Look In box shows that the current field (in this case, Email) will be searched. See Exhibit 19-11.

Exhibit 19-11 Find and Replace dialog box

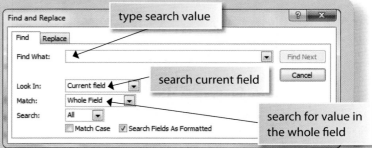

4 In the Find What box, type **welker** to search for records that contain the text *welker* in the email address.

5 Click the **Match arrow** to display the list of matching options, and then click **Any Part of Field** to find

Tip: Unless you select the Match Case check box, Access will find any record containing the search text with any combination of uppercase and lowercase letters.

Exhibit 19-12 Wildcard characters

Wildcard character	Purpose	Example
*	Match any number of characters. It can be used as the first and/or last character in the character string.	th* finds the, that, this, therefore, and so on
?	Match any single alphabetic character.	a?t finds act, aft, ant, apt, and art
[]	Match any single character within the brackets.	a[fr]t finds aft and art but not act, ant, and apt
!	Match any character not within brackets.	a[!fr]t finds act, ant, and apt but not aft and art
-	Match any one of a range of characters. The range must be in ascending order (a to z, not z to a).	a[d-p]t finds aft, ant, and apt but not act and art
#	Match any single numeric character.	#72 finds 072, 172, 272, 372, and so on

records that contain the text *welker* in any part of the Email field.

6 Click **Find Next**, and then drag the Find and Replace dialog box by its title bar so you can see the field value boxes in the form. The CustomerInfo form now displays record 14, which is the record for Frank Walker. The text *welker* is selected in the Email field value box because you searched for this word.

7 Click in the **form area** to make the form active. The Find and Replace dialog box remains open.

8 Type **walker** to replace the selected text in the Email field. The contact's email address is now correct.

Searching with Wildcards

Instead of entering an exact value to find when you search for text with the Find and Replace dialog box, you can use wildcards. A **wildcard character** is a placeholder you use when you know only part of a value or when you want to start or end with a specific character or match a certain pattern. Exhibit 19-12 lists wildcard characters.

For example, you might want to view the records for customers with phone numbers beginning with the area code 707. You could search for any field containing the digits 707 in any part of the field, but this search would also find records with the digits 707 in other parts of the phone number. To find only those records with the 707 area code, you can use the * wildcard character.

 **ACTIVITY**

Search with a wildcard character.

1 In the CustomerInfo form, click in the **Phone field value box**. This is the field you want to search.

2 Click the **Find and Replace dialog box** to make it active. The Look In box setting is still Current field, which is now the Phone field; this is the field that will be searched.

3 Click in the Find What box to select **welker**, and then type **707***.

4 Click the **Match arrow**, and then click **Whole Field**. Because you are using a wildcard character in the search value, you want to search the whole field.

5 Click **Find Next**. The search process starts from the point of the previously displayed record in the form, which was record 14, and then finds records in which any field value in the Phone field begins with 707. Record 18 is the first record found for a customer with the area code 707.

6 Click **Find Next**. Record 6 is the next record found for a customer with the area code 707. The search process cycled back through the beginning of the records in the underlying table.

7 Continue to click **Find Next** to find each record for a customer with the area code 707 until a dialog box appears, indicating that the search is finished.

8 Click **OK** to close the dialog box.

9 Click **Cancel** to close the Find and Replace dialog box.

> **wildcard character** A placeholder you use when you know only part of a value, or when you want to start or end with a specific character or match a certain pattern.

Maintaining Table Data Using a Form

You can use a form to update the data in a table. Maintaining data using a form is often easier than using a datasheet because you can focus on all the changes for one record at one time. In Form view, you can edit the field values for a record, delete a record from the underlying table, or add a new record to the table. If you know the number of the record you want to view, you can enter the number in the Current Record box to move to that record.

Exhibit 19-13 Form for a new record

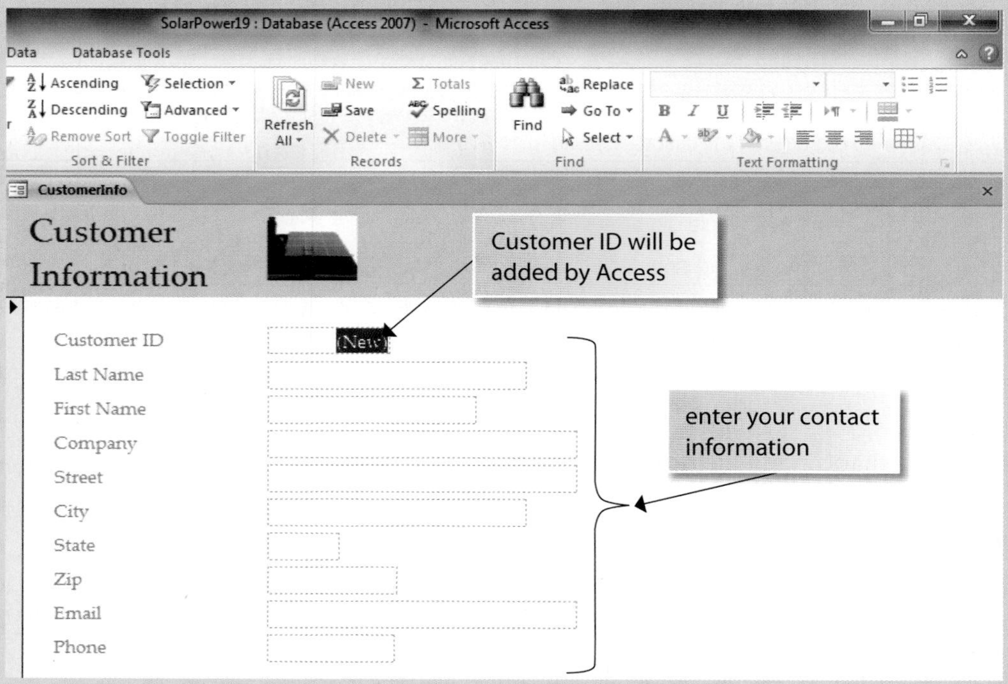

ACTIVITY

Maintain table data using a form.

1 At the bottom of the form, in the Current Record box, select **14**, type **25** and then press the **Enter key**. Record 25 (LKW Construction) is now current.

2 In the Street field value box, double-click **4457** to select the entry, and then type **8274**. The address is updated.

3 On the Home tab, in the Records group, click the **New button**. Record 35, the next available new record, becomes the current record. All field value boxes are empty, and the insertion point is positioned in the Customer ID field value box. See Exhibit 19-13.

4 Press the **Tab key**, and then enter your name and contact information in the appropriate fields, pressing the **Tab key** to move from field to field.

5 After entering the Phone field value, press the **Tab key**. Record 36, the next available new record, becomes the current record, and the record for Customer ID 35 is saved in the Customer table.

6 Close the CustomerInfo form.

main form The part of a form that displays data from the primary table in a defined relationship.

subform The part of a form that displays data from a related table in a defined relationship.

LO19.4 Creating a Form Based on Related Tables

You can create a form that displays the data from two tables at the same time, such as when you want to review the data for each customer and the customer's contracts at the same time. A form based on two tables requires the tables to have a defined relationship. For example, defining a relationship between a Customer (primary) table and a Contract (related) table enables you to create a form based on both tables. When you use related tables in a form, the form includes a main form and a subform. A **main form** displays the data from the primary table. A **subform** displays the data from the related table.

You use Layout view to modify the appearance of a form.

You use Form view to view, navigate, and change data using a form.

Access uses the defined relationship between the tables to join them automatically through the common field that exists in both tables.

You can also create a linked form in which only the main form fields are displayed. A button with the subform's name on it appears on the main form. You can click this button to display the associated subform records. You can use the Form Wizard to create either type of form.

Creating a Form with a Main Form and a Subform

When creating a form based on two tables, first you choose the primary table and select the fields to include in the main form. Then you choose the related table and select the fields to include in the subform.

Create a form with a main form and a subform.

1 On the Ribbon, click the **Create tab**. In the Forms group, click the **Form Wizard button**. The first Form Wizard dialog box opens.

2 If necessary, click the **Tables/Queries arrow**, and then click **Table: Customer**.

3 Move each of the following fields from the Available Fields box to the Selected Fields box: **CustomerID**, **Company**, **FirstName**, **LastName**, and **Phone**.

> **Tip:** You can double-click a field to move it between the Available Fields box and Selected Fields box.

4 Click the **Tables/Queries arrow**, and then click **Table: Contract**. The fields from the Contract table appear in the Available Fields box.

5 Move all the fields in the Contract table to the Selected Fields box. The table name (Contract) is included in the CustomerID field name to distinguish it from the same field (CustomerID) in the Customer table.

6 Move the **Contract.CustomerID** field back to the Available Fields box.

7 Click **Next**. The second Form Wizard dialog box appears. The Form with subform(s) option button is selected. The left box shows the order in which the data will be displayed—first data from the primary Customer table, and then data from the related Contract table. The preview on the right shows how the form will appear—fields from the Customer table at the top in the main form and fields from the Contract table at the bottom in the subform. See Exhibit 19-14.

Exhibit 19-14 Formats for the main form and subform

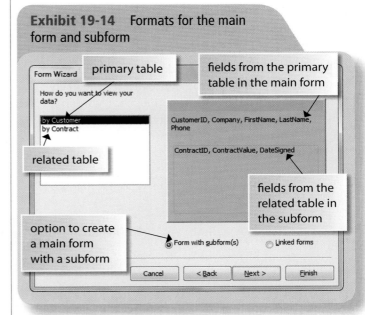

Main Form and Subform Names

The main form name (*CustomerContracts*, in this case) appears on the object tab and as the form title. The subform name (*Contract*, in this case) appears to the left of the subform. Access displays only the table name for the subform, but uses the complete object name, *ContractSubform*, in the Navigation Pane. The subform designation is necessary in a list of database objects, so that you can distinguish the Contract subform from other objects, such as the Contract table. The subform designation is not needed in the CustomerContracts form; only the table name is required to identify the table containing the records in the subform.

8 Click **Next**. The third Form Wizard dialog box opens, in which you choose the subform layout. The Tabular layout displays subform fields as a table. The Datasheet layout displays subform fields as a table datasheet.

9 Click the **Datasheet option button** if it is not already selected, and then click **Next**. The fourth Form Wizard dialog box opens, in which you choose titles for the main form and the subform.

10 In the **Form box**, click to the right of the last letter, and then type **Contracts**. The main form name is now *CustomerContracts*.

11 In the **Subform box**, delete the space between the two words so that the subform name is *ContractSubform*.

12 Click **Finish**. The completed form opens in Form view formatted with the Office theme. The main form displays the fields from the first record in the Customer table in a columnar format. The records in the main form appear in primary key order by Customer ID. Customer ID 1 has two related records in the Contract table, which appear in the subform in the datasheet format. See Exhibit 19-15.

Modifying a Main Form and Subform in Layout View

You can modify a form with a main form and a subform, just as you can a form based on one table. For example, you can edit the form title, resize the subform, and resize columns to fully display their field values. You can make these types of changes in Layout view or Design view.

ACTIVITY

Modify a main form and subform in Layout view.

1 Display the CustomerContracts form in **Layout view**.

2 In the shaded title area at the top of the form, select and then edit the **CustomerContracts form title** so that the title in the form is **Customer Contracts**.

3 Click a blank area of the main form to deselect the title.

4 Click the **subform** to select it. An orange outline surrounds the subform.

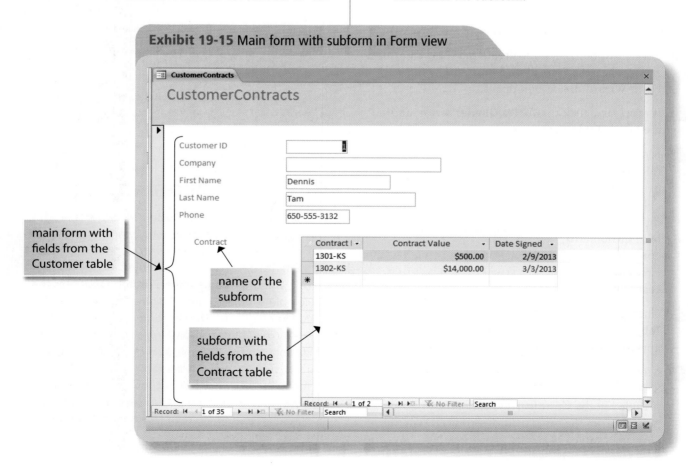

Exhibit 19-15 Main form with subform in Form view

main form with fields from the Customer table

name of the subform

subform with fields from the Contract table

5 Resize each column in the subform datasheet to its best fit.

6 Drag the left edge of the subform to the left to align it with the left edge of the field value boxes, and then drag its right edge to the left until it is just to the right of the Date Signed column. See Exhibit 19-16.

Exhibit 19-16 Modified form in Layout view

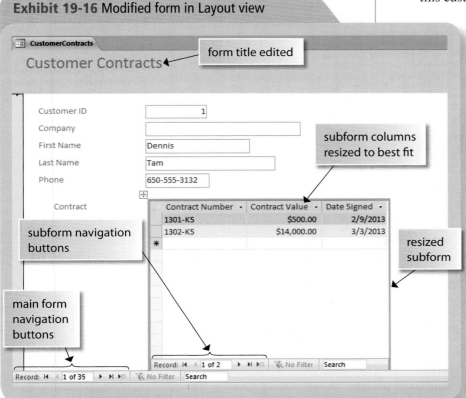

7 Save the CustomerContracts form.

8 Display the CustomerContracts form in **Form view**.

Displaying Records in a Main Form and a Subform

A form with a main form and subform includes two sets of navigation buttons. The navigation buttons at the bottom of the Form window select records from the primary table in the main form. The navigation buttons at the bottom of the subform select records from the related table in the subform. The subform navigation buttons may not be visible until you scroll to the bottom of the main form. If you enter data in the main form, the primary table is updated. If you enter data in the subform, the related table is updated.

Navigate main form and subform records.

1 At the bottom of the Form window, click the **Last record button**. Record 35 in the Customer table (your contact information) becomes the current record in the main form. The subform shows that this customer currently has no contracts.

2 At the bottom of the Form window, click the **Previous record button**. Record 34 in the Customer table (for Chen Builders) becomes the current record in the main form. The subform shows that this customer has two contracts.

3 At the bottom of the Form window, in the Current Record box, select **34**, type **25** and then press the **Enter key**. Record 25 in the Customer table (for LKW Construction) becomes the current record in the main form. The subform shows that this customer has six contracts.

4 In the subform, click the **Next record button**. Contract Number 1320-RR in the Contract table becomes the current record in the subform.

5 In the subform, click the **Last record button**. Contract Number 1430-AD in the Contract table becomes the current record in the subform.

LO19.5 Previewing and Printing Selected Form Records

When you print a form, Access prints as many form records as can fit on a printed page. If only part of a form record fits on the bottom of a page, the remainder of the record prints on the next page. You can choose to print all pages or a range of pages. In addition, you can print the currently selected form record. You do this from the Print dialog box. Before printing, you should always preview the form to see how it will look when printed. Both the Print dialog box and Print Preview are available on the Print tab in Backstage view.

Preview and print form data.

1 On the Ribbon, click the **File tab**. In the navigation bar, click **Print**. The Print tab has three options: Quick Print, Print, and Print Preview.

2 On the Print tab, click **Print Preview**. The Print Preview window opens, showing the records for the CustomerContracts form. Each record appears in its own form, and shading distinguishes one record from the next. See Exhibit 19-17.

3 On the Ribbon, on the Print Preview tab, in the Close Preview group, click the **Close Print Preview button**. Print Preview closes, and you return to the CustomerContracts form in Form view with the record for LKW Construction still displayed in the main form.

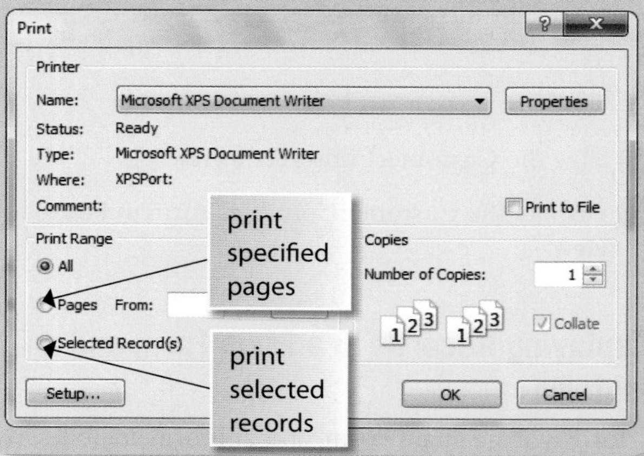

4 On the Ribbon, click the **File tab**. In the navigation bar, click **Print**. On the Print tab, click **Print**. The Print dialog box appears. See Exhibit 19-18.

5 Click the **Selected Record(s) option button**. Now only the current form record (record 25) will print.

6 Click **OK** to close the dialog box and print the selected record, or click **Cancel** to close the dialog box without printing.

7 Close the CustomerContracts form.

> **Tip:** You can also click the Print button in the Print group on the Print Preview tab to open the Print dialog box. However, to print only the current record, you must open the Print dialog box from the Print tab in Backstage view.

Exhibit 19-17 Form records displayed in Print Preview

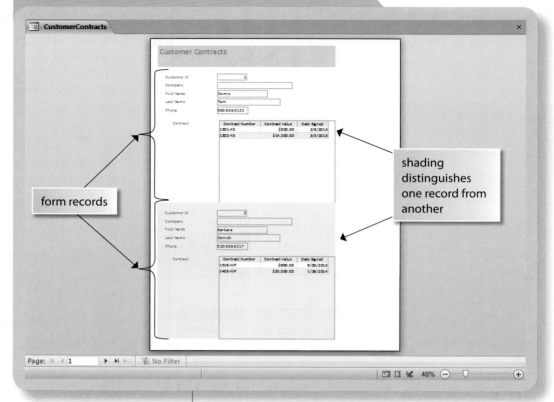

form records

shading distinguishes one record from another

Exhibit 19-18 Print dialog box

print specified pages

print selected records

LO19.6 Creating a Report Using the Report Wizard

A report is a formatted printout of the contents of one or more tables or queries in a database. You can design your own reports or you can use the Report

Wizard to create them. The **Report Wizard** guides you through the process of creating a report. You choose which fields to display from tables and queries as well as how to group and sort the records in the report, the page orientation, and the report's title. As with a form, you can change the report's design after you create it.

Creating a Report

When you create a report with the Report Wizard, you choose the table or query on which to base the report, and then select the fields you want to include in the report. You can select fields from more than one table as long as the tables are related, such as the Customer and Contract tables.

The selected data can be grouped in the report by table or ungrouped. A grouped report places the data from the first table in one group followed by the related records. For example, each customer record will appear in its own group followed by the related contract records for that customer. An example of an ungrouped report would be a report of records from the Customer and Contract tables in order by ContractID. Each contract and its associated customer data would appear together on one or more lines of the report, not grouped by table.

Whether the report is grouped or ungrouped, you can select grouping levels to add to the report. Grouping levels are useful for reports with multiple levels, such as those containing monthly, quarterly, and annual totals, or for those containing city and country groups. You can sort the detail records for the report by up to four fields, choosing ascending or descending order for each field. As the last steps, you select a layout, select the page orientation, and enter a report title.

Create a Report Based on a Query

You can create a report based on one or more tables or queries. When you base a report on a query, you can use criteria and other query features to retrieve only the information you want to display in the report. Experienced Access users often create a query just so they can create a report based on that query. When planning a report, consider creating a query first and then basing the report on that query to produce the exact results you want to see in the report.

ACTIVITY

Create a report using the Report Wizard.

1 On the Ribbon, click the **Create tab**. In the Reports group, click the **Report Wizard button**. The first Report Wizard dialog box opens. As with the first Form Wizard dialog box, you select the table or query, and then add fields to use in the report.

2 If necessary, click the **Tables/Queries arrow**, and then click **Table: Customer**.

3 Move the following fields from the Available Fields box to the Selected Fields box: **CustomerID**, **Company**, **FirstName**, **LastName**, **City**, and **Phone**. The fields will appear in the report in the order you select them.

4 Click the **Tables/Queries arrow**, and then click **Table: Contract**. The fields from the Contract table appear in the Available Fields box.

5 Move all of the fields from the Available Fields box to the Selected Fields box.

> **Tip:** Remember, you can click [>>] to move all the fields in the Available Fields box to the Selected Fields box.

6 Move the **Contract.CustomerID** field from the Selected Fields box back to the Available Fields box. The CustomerID field will appear on the report with the customer data, so you do not need to include it in the detail records for each contract.

7 Click **Next**. The second Report Wizard dialog box appears, in which you select whether the report is grouped by table or ungrouped. You will leave the report grouped by the Customer table. See Exhibit 19-19.

> **Tip:** You can display tips for creating reports and examples of reports by clicking the Show me more information button.

8 Click **Next**. The third Report Wizard dialog box opens, in which you can choose additional grouping levels. Two grouping levels are shown: one for

Report Wizard The Access feature that creates a report based on the fields you choose to display from tables and queries as well as options such as the grouping, sort order, page orientation, and title you specify.

Exhibit 19-19 Second Report Wizard dialog box

data grouped by table

how fields will appear in the report

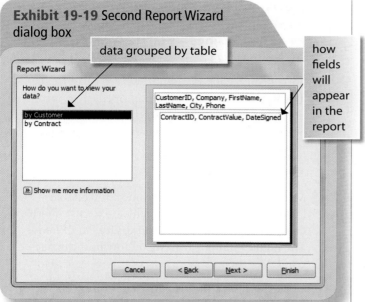

11 Click **Next**. The fifth Report Wizard dialog box opens, in which you choose a layout and page orientation for the report. See Exhibit 19-21.

Exhibit 19-21 Fifth Report Wizard dialog box

layout options

page orientation options

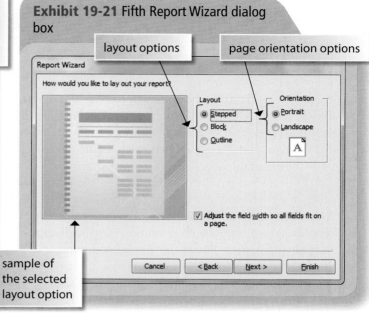

sample of the selected layout option

a customer's data, and the other for a customer's contracts.

9 Click **Next**. The fourth Report Wizard dialog box opens, in which you can choose the sort order for the detail records. The records from the Contract table for a customer represent the detail records for the report. See Exhibit 19-20.

12 In the Layout section, click the **Outline option button** to select the Outline layout.

13 In the Orientation section, click the **Landscape option button**. This page orientation provides more space across the page to display longer field values.

14 Click **Next**. The sixth and final Report Wizard dialog box opens, in which you enter a report title, which also serves as the name for the report object in the database.

Exhibit 19-20 Fourth Report Wizard dialog box

click to select a field in the related table

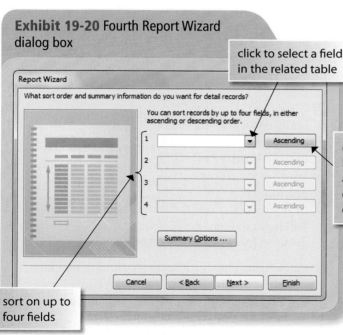

click to toggle between ascending and descending order

sort on up to four fields

15 In the box for the title, enter **CustomersAndContracts**. You entered the report name as one word so that the report object is named appropriately. You will edit the title in the report later.

16 Click **Finish**. The Report Wizard creates the report, saves the report as an object in the database, and opens the report in Print Preview.

Previewing a Report

In Print Preview, you can check the overall layout of the report, as well as zoom in to read the text. This enables you to find any formatting problems or other issues and make the necessary corrections.

10 Click the **1 arrow**, and then click **DateSigned**. The Ascending option is selected, so the contracts will be shown in chronological order.

In Print Preview, you can use the pointer to toggle between a full-page display and a close-up display of the report.

ACTIVITY

Preview a report.

1 On the Ribbon, on the Print Preview tab, in the Zoom group, click the **Zoom button arrow**, and then click **Fit to Window**. The entire first page of the report is displayed in Print Preview.

2 Click the center of the report. The display changes to show a close-up view of the report. See Exhibit 19-22. Shading distinguishes one customer's record from the next, as well as one contract record from the next within a group of each customer's contract records. The detail records for the Contract table fields appear in ascending order based on the values in the DateSigned field. Because the

DateSigned field is used as the sort field for the contracts, it appears as the first field in this section, even though you used the Report Wizard to select the fields in a different order.

3 Scroll to the bottom left of the first page, reading the report as you scroll. Notice the current date at the left edge of the bottom of the first page of the report; the Report Wizard included this as part of the report's design.

4 Scroll to the right and view the page number at the right edge of the footer.

5 Click the report to zoom back out, and then use the navigation buttons to review the 12 pages of the report.

6 On the Print Preview tab, in the Close Preview group, click the **Close Print Preview button**. The report is displayed in Design view.

⚠️ **Problem?** If you see blank pages every other page as you navigate the report, the text of the page number might not be completely within the page border. You'll fix this problem shortly.

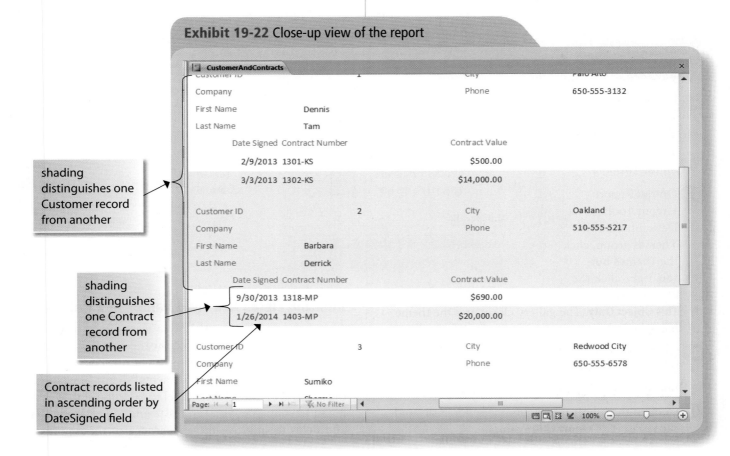

Exhibit 19-22 Close-up view of the report

shading distinguishes one Customer record from another

shading distinguishes one Contract record from another

Contract records listed in ascending order by DateSigned field

LO19.7 Modifying a Report's Design in Layout View

You modify a report's design in Layout view or in Design view. Many of the same options that are available for forms are also provided for reports.

Changing a Report's Appearance

You can change the text of the report title as well as the color of text in a report to enhance its appearance. The same themes available for forms are also available for reports. You can choose to apply a theme to the current report object only, or to all reports in the database. When you point to a theme in the Theme gallery, a ScreenTip displays the names of the database objects that use the theme. You can also add a picture to a report for visual interest or to identify a particular section of the report.

Change a report's appearance.

1 Display the report in **Layout view**. The Report Layout Tools tabs appear on the Ribbon.

2 On the Report Layout Tools Design tab, in the Themes group, click the **Themes button**, right-click the **Elemental theme**, and then click **Apply Theme to This Object Only**. The gallery closes and the theme is applied to the report.

3 At the top of the report, select the report title **CustomersAndContracts**, and then edit the text to **Customers and Contracts**.

4 Click in the **report** to deselect the report title, and then select the **report title** again.

5 On the Ribbon, click the **Report Layout Tools Format tab**. In the Font group, click the **Font Color button arrow** **A ·**, and then click the **Dark Purple, Text 2 theme color**. The color is applied to the report title.

6 On the Ribbon, click the **Report Layout Tools Design tab**. In the Header/Footer group, click the **Logo button**.

7 Double-click the data file **Panels** located in the Chapter 19\Chapter folder. The picture is inserted in the upper-left corner of the report, partially covering the report title.

8 Drag the selected **picture** to the right of the report title within the shaded title area. See Exhibit 19-23.

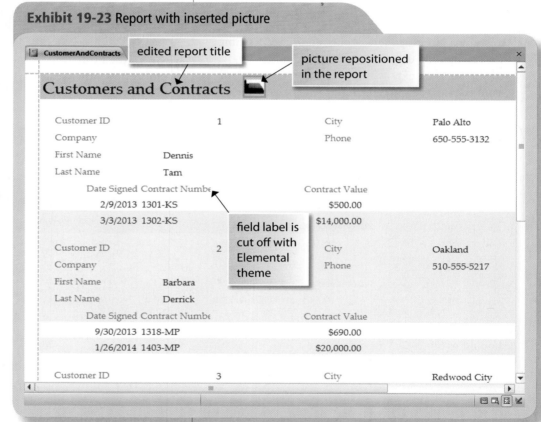

Exhibit 19-23 Report with inserted picture

Resizing Fields and Field Values in a Report

After you apply a new theme to a report, you should check the report to be sure that the theme's design didn't cause spacing issues or text to be cut off. For example, the larger font used by the Elemental theme has caused the Contract Number field label to be truncated. Working in Layout view, you can resize and reposition labels and fields to improve the appearance of the report or to address the problem of some field values not being completely displayed. To select and re-size multiple fields, you press the Shift key as you select the different fields. You should also check the page number in the footer to make sure it fits completely on the page.

 **ACTIVITY**

Resize field labels and field value boxes.

1. In the report, click the first **Contract Number field label** to select it. When you select a field label in Layout view, all of the labels for that field are selected in the report, Any changes you make to a single selected field will also be made to the other labels for that field.

2. Resize the **Contract Number field label** until the entire field label is visible. The change is made throughout the report.

3. Find the record for **Customer ID 16**, Oakland Neighborhood Development. The right part of the company name is cut off because the field value box is not wide enough.

4. In the record for Customer ID 16, click the **City field label**, press and hold the **Shift key**, and then click the **Phone field label**. Both field labels are selected and can be resized. See Exhibit 19-24.

5. Drag the **left edge** of either selected field label to the right until the left edge of the City field label aligns vertically with the *e* in the Contract Value label above it. As you drag, black outlines indicate the size of the labels. The City and Phone field labels for the entire report are now smaller, moving them closer to their values, and there is now more space available on the report to expand the Company field value box.

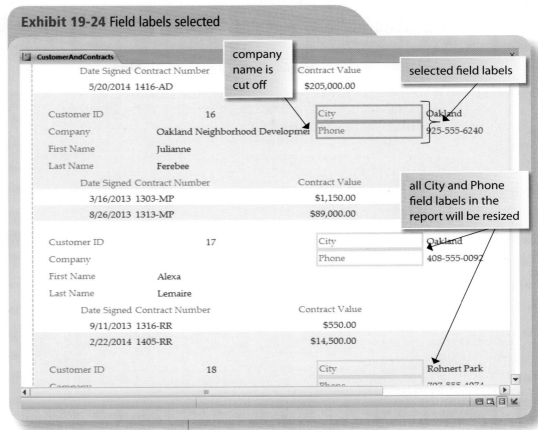

Exhibit 19-24 Field labels selected

6. In the record for Customer ID 16, click the **Company field value box** to select it.

7. Drag the **right edge** of the selected field value box to the right until the complete company name is visible. All of the Company field value boxes in the report are longer, ensuring that no company name is cut off. See Exhibit 19-25.

8. Scroll the report to the bottom and to the right and view the page number text. If the page number in the footer is not completely within the page border, select the footer text, and then drag the orange box to the left until the page number text is within the page border.

Using Conditional Formatting in a Report

You can add conditional formatting to a report or form. As when you used conditional formatting in Excel, special formatting is applied to field values that meet the condition or conditions you set. For example, you might use conditional formatting in a report to format contract amounts that are greater than or equal to $20,000 in a bold, red font.

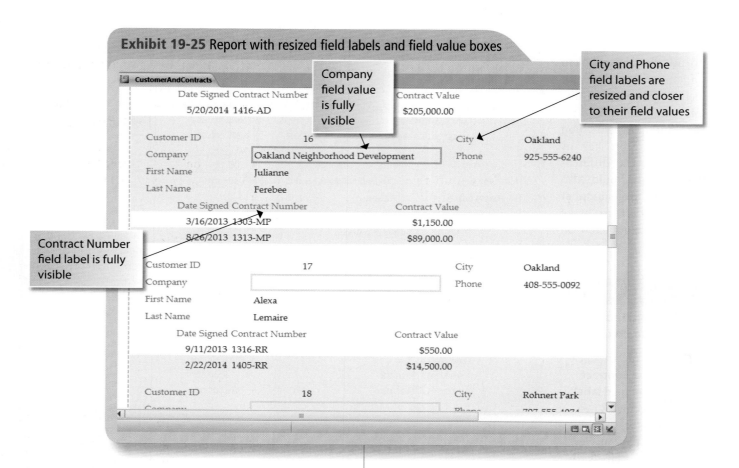

Exhibit 19-25 Report with resized field labels and field value boxes

Company field value is fully visible

City and Phone field labels are resized and closer to their field values

Contract Number field label is fully visible

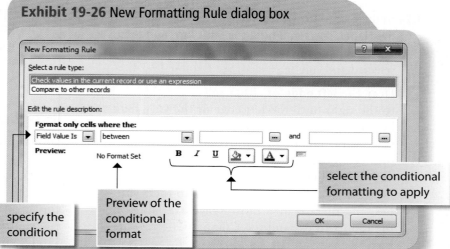

ACTIVITY

Use conditional formatting in a report.

1 In the record for Customer ID 33, click the **Contract Value field value**. An orange outline appears around the field value box, and a lighter orange outline appears around the other Contract Value field value boxes in the report. The conditional formatting you specify will affect all the values for the field.

Tip: You must select a field *value box*, and not the field *label*, before applying a conditional format.

2 On the Ribbon, click the **Report Layout Tools Format tab**. In the Control Formatting group, click the **Conditional Formatting button**. The Conditional Formatting Rules Manager dialog box opens. The field selected in the report, Contract Value, appears in the Show formatting rules for box. No conditional formatting rules are set for the selected field.

3 In the dialog box, click the **New Rule button**. The New Formatting Rule dialog box opens. The selected rule type specifies that Access will check field values in the selected field to determine if they meet the condition. You enter the condition in the Edit the rule description box. The Field Value Is setting means that the conditional format you specify will be applied only when the value for the selected ContractValue field meets the condition. See Exhibit 19-26.

Exhibit 19-26 New Formatting Rule dialog box

specify the condition

Preview of the conditional format

select the conditional formatting to apply

4 On the box that contains the word *between*, click the **arrow**, and then click **greater than or equal to**.

5 Press the **Tab key** to move to the next box, and then type **20000**. The condition is set to format cells where the field value is greater than or equal to 20,000.

6 In the Preview section, click the **Font color button arrow** 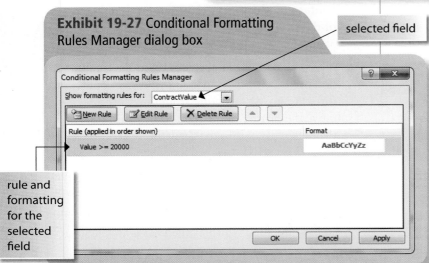, and then click the **Red standard color**.

7 In the Preview section, click the **Bold button** **B**. Any field value that meets the condition will be formatted in bold, red text.

8 Click **OK**. The new rule you specified appears in the Rule section of the Conditional Formatting Rules Manager dialog box as *Value >= 20000*. The Format section on the right shows the conditional formatting (red, bold font) that will be applied based on this rule. See Exhibit 19-27.

9 Click **OK**. The conditional formatting is applied to the Contract Value field values.

10 Display the report in **Print Preview**. Change the zoom level of the report to **Fit to Window**.

11 Go to **page 5** of the report. The conditional formatting is applied only to Contract Value field values greater than or equal to $20,000. See Exhibit 19-28.

Exhibit 19-28 Print Preview of report with conditional formatting

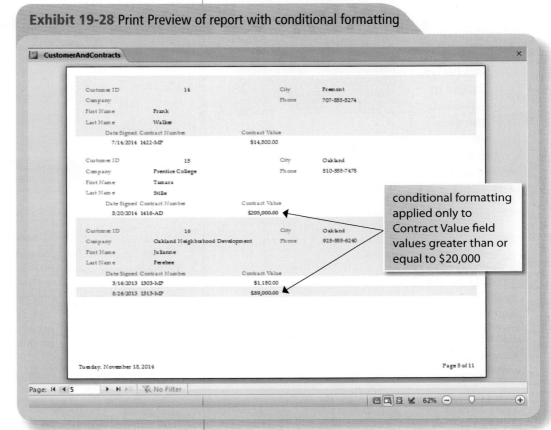

conditional formatting applied only to Contract Value field values greater than or equal to $20,000

Exhibit 19-27 Conditional Formatting Rules Manager dialog box

selected field

rule and formatting for the selected field

Printing a Report

When you print a report, you can specify whether to print the entire report or select pages to print. You do this from the Print dialog box.

ACTIVITY

Print a report.

1 On the Print Preview tab, in the Print group, click the **Print button**. The Print dialog box opens.

2 In the Print Range section, click the **Pages option button**. The insertion point is in

Preview Reports Before Printing

Before printing a report, be sure to review the report in Print Preview so you can find and correct any formatting problems or other issues. You can also determine where the pages will break and make adjustments as needed. It is particularly important to preview a report after you have changed its design to ensure new problems have not occurred in the report. This approach ensures that the final printed report looks exactly the way you want it to, and also saves time and resources because you won't need to reprint the report.

the From box so that you can specify the range of pages to print.

3 In the From box, type **1**, press the **Tab key** to move to the To box, and then type **1**. These settings specify that only page 1 of the report will be printed.

4 Click **OK** to print the first page of the report, or click **Cancel** to close the Print dialog box without printing.

5 Save the CustomersAndContracts report, and then close it.

6 Compact and repair the SolarPower19 database, and then close the database.

Quiz Yourself

1. Describe the difference between creating a form using the Form tool and creating a form using the Form Wizard.

2. How do you apply a theme to an existing form?

3. What is a control?

4. What is a wildcard character?

5. Which wildcard character matches any single alphabetic character?

6. In a form that contains a main form and a sub-form, what data is displayed in the main form and what data is displayed in the subform?

7. Describe the navigation buttons used to move through a form containing a main form and a subform.

8. Describe how to print only the current record displayed in a form.

9. What are detail records?

10. Describe how to resize a field in a report.

11. When working in Layout view for a report, how do you select multiple fields in the report?

12. How do you apply conditional formatting to a report?

Practice It

Practice It 19-1

1. Open the data file **Snow19** located in the Chapter 19\Practice It folder. Save the database as **SnowRemoval19**.

2. Use the Form Wizard to create a form based on the Client table. Select all fields for the form, use the Columnar layout, and specify the title **ClientContactInfo** for the form.

3. Display the form in Layout view, and then apply the Waveform theme to the ClientContactInfo form *only*.

4. Edit the form title so that it appears as **Client Contact Info** (three words). Change the font color of the form title to the Blue, Accent 2, Darker 50% theme color.

5. Insert the data file **Shovel** located in the Chapter 19\Practice It folder as a logo in the ClientContactInfo form. Remove the picture from the control layout, move the picture to the right of the form title, and then resize it to fit in the shaded title area.

6. Change the line type for all of the field value boxes, except for the Client ID field value box, to Dots.

7. Resize the field value box for the First Name field so it is the same width as the Last Name field value box.

8. Switch to Form view, use the Client Contact Info form to update the Client table as follows, and then save and close the form:

    a. Use the Find command to search for **pony** anywhere in the Company field to display the record for the Pony Grill (Client ID 21). Change the Street field value in this record to **8930 Saddle Brook Way**.

    b. Add a new record with your contact information.

9. Use the Form Wizard to create a form containing a main form and a subform based on the Client and ServiceAgreement tables. Select all fields from the Client table for the main form, and select AgreementNum, AgreementDate, and AgreementAmt from the ServiceAgreement table for the subform. Use the Datasheet layout. Specify the title **ClientAndServiceAgreement** for the main form and **ServiceAgreementSubform** for the subform.

10. Change the form title text to **Client Service Agreements**.

11. Resize all columns in the subform to their best fit. Navigate through each record in the main form to make sure all of the field values in the subform are completely displayed, resizing subform columns as necessary. Save and close the ClientAndServiceAgreement form.

12. Use the Report Wizard to create a report based on the primary ServiceAgreement table and the related Invoice table. Select all the fields from the ServiceAgreement table, and select the InvNum, InvDate, InvAmt, and Paid fields from the Invoice table. Do not specify any additional grouping levels, and sort the detail records by the Paid field in descending order. Choose the Outline layout and Landscape orientation. Specify the title **InvoicesByAgreement** for the report.

13. Display the report in Layout view. Change the report title text to **Invoices by Agreement**.

14. Apply the Waveform theme to the InvoicesByAgreement report *only*.

15. Resize the report title so that the text of the title is fully visible. Change the color of the report title text to the Blue, Accent 2, Darker 50% theme color.

16. Scroll through the report to make sure all field values are fully displayed, resizing field label and

field value boxes as needed, and moving the page number field as needed.

17. Apply conditional formatting so that the Invoice Date field values greater than 12/31/2013 are bold with a background color of Light Green.

18. Preview each page of the report, verifying that all the fields fit on the page. If necessary, return to Layout view and make changes so the report prints within the margins of the page and so that all field names and values are completely displayed.

19. Save the InvoicesByAgreement report, print only page 3 of the report, and then close the report.

20. Compact and repair the SnowRemoval19 database, and then close it.

Practice It 19-2

1. Open the data file **Art19** located in the Chapter 19\Practice It folder. Save the database as **ArtClasses19**.

2. Use the Form Wizard to create a form based on the Student table. Select all the fields for the form and the Columnar layout. Specify the title **StudentData** for the form.

3. Apply the Clarity theme to the StudentData form *only*.

4. Edit the form title so that it appears as **Student Data** (two words), and change the font color of the form title to the Blue-Gray, Accent 4, Lighter 40% theme color.

5. Use the Find command to display the record for Marcus Elam, and then change the Address field value for this record to **304 Forest Avenue**.

6. Use the StudentData form to add a new record to the Student table using the Student ID **NEL7584**, the Class ID **CL-296**, and your contact information.

7. Save and close the StudentData form.

8. Use the Form Wizard to create a form containing a main form and a subform. Select all the fields from the Instructor table for the main form, and select the ClassID, ClassName, and Juniors fields from the Class table for the subform. Use the Datasheet layout. Specify the title **ContractsByInstructor** for the main form and the title **ClassSubform** for the subform.

9. Change the form title text for the main form to **Contracts by Instructor**.

10. Change the line type for the field value boxes—except for the Full Time? check box—to Dots.

11. Resize columns in the subform to their best fit, and then move through all the records in the main form and check to make sure that all subform field values are fully displayed, resizing the columns as necessary.

12. Save and close the ContractsByInstructor form.

13. Use the Report Wizard to create a report based on the primary Class table and the related Student table. Select all fields from the Class table, and select the FirstName, LastName, and Birth-Date fields from the Student table. Do not select any additional grouping levels, and sort the detail records in ascending order by LastName. Choose the Outline layout and Landscape orientation. Specify the title **StudentClasses** for the report.

14. Apply the Clarity theme to the StudentClasses report *only*.

15. Resize the report title so that the text is fully displayed; edit the report title so that it appears as **Student Classes** (two words); and change the font color of the title to the Blue-Gray, Accent 4, Lighter 40% theme color.

16. In Layout view, scroll through the report to make sure all of the field labels and field values are fully displayed, resizing the controls as needed. Make sure the page number is completely within the page border, moving the control as needed.

17. Insert the data file **Paint** located in the Chapter 19\ Practice It folder in the report. Move the picture to the right of the report title and resize it larger to fit the space.

18. Apply conditional formatting so that any Cost field value greater than 200 appears as bold and with the text color as Maroon 5.

19. Preview the entire report to confirm that it is formatted correctly. If necessary, return to Layout view and make changes so that all field labels and field values are completely displayed. When you are finished, save the report, print the first page, and then close the report.

20. Compact and repair the ArtClasses19 database, and then close it.

On Your Own

On Your Own 19-1

1. Open the data file **Donations19** located in the Chapter 19\On Your Own folder. Save the database as **DonationsList19**.

2. Use the Form Wizard to create a form based on the Donation table. Select all the fields for the form and the Columnar layout. Specify an appropriate title for the form.

3. Apply a different theme to the form *only*.

4. Edit the form title as needed so that spaces separate each word. Change the font color of the form title to a color that is easy to read with the theme you applied to the form.

5. Use the appropriate buttons in the Font group on the Form Layout Tools Format tab to bold and underline the form title. Resize the title, as necessary, so that all of the title text appears on the same line.

6. Use the form to update the Donation table. Search for records that contain the word **small** anywhere in the Description field. Find the record with the field value *Small appliances* (and the Donation ID 2126) and then change the Donation Value for this record to **120.00**. Save and close the form.

7. Use the Form Wizard to create a form containing a main form based on the Donor table and a subform based on the Donation table. Select appropriate fields from each table for the main form and the subform. Use the Datasheet layout. Specify appropriate titles for the main form and the subform.

8. Apply the same theme you applied in Step 3 to this form *only*.

9. Edit the form title so that each word is separated by a space and uses correct capitalization. Resize the form title as needed so that the text fits on one line. Change the font color of the title to the same color you used in Step 4.

10. Use the appropriate button in the Font group on the Form Layout Tools Format tab to apply a background color of your choice to all the field value boxes in the main form. (*Hint*: Select all the field value boxes before making this change.)

11. Use the appropriate button in the Control Formatting group on the Form Layout Tools Format tab

to change the outline of all the main form field value boxes to a different line thickness.

12. Resize the subform so that the entire subform is visible, and then resize each column in the subform to its best fit. Navigate through each record in the main form to make sure all the field values in the subform are completely displayed, resizing subform columns as necessary. Save the form.

13. Use the appropriate wildcard character to find all records with a Phone field value that begins with the area code 208. Change the record with the Phone field value of 208-555-9033 (Donor ID 36032) to **970-555-9033**. Close the form.

14. Use the Report Wizard to create a report based on the primary Agency table and the related Donation table. Select the Agency and Phone fields from the Agency table, and select all fields except AgencyID and Pickup from the Donation table. In the third Report Wizard dialog box, add DonorID as an additional grouping level. Sort the detail records in descending order by DonationValue. Choose the Outline layout and Portrait orientation. Specify the name **AgencyDonations** for the report.

15. Apply the same theme you applied in Step 3 to this report *only*.

16. Edit the report title appropriately, resize the report title so that the text is fully visible, and then change the font color of the report title to the same color you used in Step 4.

17. Resize field labels and field value boxes as needed to fully display their values, being sure that all the boxes remain within the page boundaries.

18. Insert the data file **CharityLogo** located in the Chapter 19\On Your Own folder in the report. Place the picture appropriately in the report. Resize it larger to fill the space.

19. Apply conditional formatting to the Donation Value field using an appropriate condition and formatting.

20. Preview the report to confirm that it is formatted correctly and all field labels and field values are fully visible. Save the report, print one page that shows the conditional formatting you applied, and then close the report.

21. Compact and repair the DonationsList19 database, and then close it.

ADDITIONAL STUDY TOOLS

Chapter 19

IN THE BOOK

▶ Complete end-of-chapter exercises

▶ Study tear-out Chapter Review Card

ONLINE

▶ Complete additional end-of-chapter exercises

▶ Take practice quiz to prepare for tests

▶ Review key term flash cards (online, printable, and audio)

▶ Play "Beat the Clock" and "Memory" to quiz yourself

▶ Watch the videos "Create a Form Using the Form Wizard," "Apply a Theme to a Form," "Add a Picture to a Form," "Create a Form with a Main Form and a Subform," "Create a Report Using the Report Wizard," and more

Access: Create a Database

1. Plan a database to track data for an organization, an event, or a project (either real or fictional). Determine how many tables you need and what data will go into each table. Identify the layout of the columns (fields) and rows (records) for each table. Determine the field properties you need for each field.

2. Create a new database to contain the data you want to track.

3. Create at least two tables in the database that can be joined through one-to-many relationships.

4. Define the properties for each field in each table. Include a mix of data types for the fields (for example, do not include only Text fields in each table).

5. Specify a primary key for each table.

6. Define the necessary one-to-many relationships between the tables in the database with referential integrity enforced.

7. Enter at least 10 records in each table.

8. Create 3 to 4 queries based on single tables and multiple tables. The queries should include some or all of the following: exact match conditions, comparison operators, and logical operators.

9. For some of the queries, use sorting and filtering techniques to display the query results in various ways. Save these queries with the sort and/or filter applied.

10. Create at least one calculated field in one of the queries.

11. Use at least one function to produce a summary statistic based on the data in at least one of the tables.

12. Create at least one form for each table in the database. Enhance each form's appearance with pictures, themes, line colors, and so on.

13. Create at least one form with a main form and subform based on related tables in the database. Enhance the form's appearance appropriately.

14. Create at least one report based on each table in the database. Enhance each report's appearance with pictures, themes, color, and so on.

15. Apply conditional formatting to the values in at least one of the reports.

16. Compact and repair the database, and then close it.

Creating a Presentation

Introduction

People give presentations to groups of all sizes for many purposes. For example, business professionals give presentations in company meetings; government officials give presentations at press conferences; instructors give presentations during class lectures; and individuals give presentations at parties or reunions. A PowerPoint presentation might be used one time, such as at a stockholder meeting, or repeated for different groups of people, such as a seminar that is offered several times or a sales pitch to potential clients. It can be used to supplement a live presentation, such as a company retrospective for an organization's milestone anniversary or personal achievements for a retirement dinner. Or, it can be used to provide information, such as services a vendor offers, at a kiosk that runs during a conference or fair.

  Microsoft PowerPoint 2010 (or simply **PowerPoint**) is a powerful presentation graphics program used to create slides that can contain text, charts, pictures, sound, movies, and so on. Files created in PowerPoint are called **presentations**, which consist of slides. You can show these presentations as slide shows on a computer monitor, project them onto a screen, share them over the Internet, or publish them to a Web site. You can also create documents from the presentation by printing the slides, outlines, or speakers' notes.

Learning Objectives

After studying the material in this chapter, you will be able to:

LO20.1 Create a presentation

LO20.2 Rearrange and delete text and slides

LO20.3 Run a slide show

LO20.4 Add animations

LO20.5 Add transitions

LO20.6 Add speaker notes

LO20.7 Add footers and headers to slides and handouts

LO20.8 Preview and print a presentation

LO20.1 Creating a Presentation

Microsoft PowerPoint 2010 (PowerPoint) A presentation graphics program used to create a collection of slides that can contain text, charts, pictures, sound, movies, multimedia, and so on.

presentation A file created in PowerPoint.

Normal view The PowerPoint view that displays slides one at a time in the Slide pane and thumbnails of all the slides in the Slides tab or all the text of the presentation in the Outline tab.

When PowerPoint starts, it displays a blank presentation in Normal view. See Exhibit 20-1. **Normal view** displays slides one at a time in the Slide pane, and displays thumbnails of all the slides in the Slides tab or an outline of the text of the presentation in

Clara/Shutterstock.com

Business professionals are often called upon to give presentations to small groups of people in company meetings or to larger audiences at conferences. A well-designed slide show can help grab the audience's attention and emphasize main topics.

the Outline tab. The **Slide pane** shows how the text and graphics on the current slide will look during a slide show. The **Slides tab** shows a column of numbered slide thumbnails. The **Outline tab** shows an outline of the titles and text of each slide in the presentation. The pane below the Slide pane is the **Notes pane**, which contains notes for the presenter to refer to when delivering the presentation.

As you create presentations, you will work extensively with these different panes and tabs. This provides you the flexibility to work with and view the presentation in a variety of ways, enabling you to create the most effective presentation for conveying the slide show's purpose and goals to the intended audience.

Slide pane The area of the PowerPoint window that displays the currently selected slide as it will look during the slide show.

Slides tab The area of the PowerPoint window that shows a column of numbered slide thumbnails so you can see a visual representation of several slides at once.

Outline tab The area of the PowerPoint window that shows an outline of the titles and text of each slide in the presentation.

Notes pane The area of the PowerPoint window that contains notes for the presenter to refer to when delivering the presentation.

Exhibit 20-1 Blank presentation in the PowerPoint window in Normal view

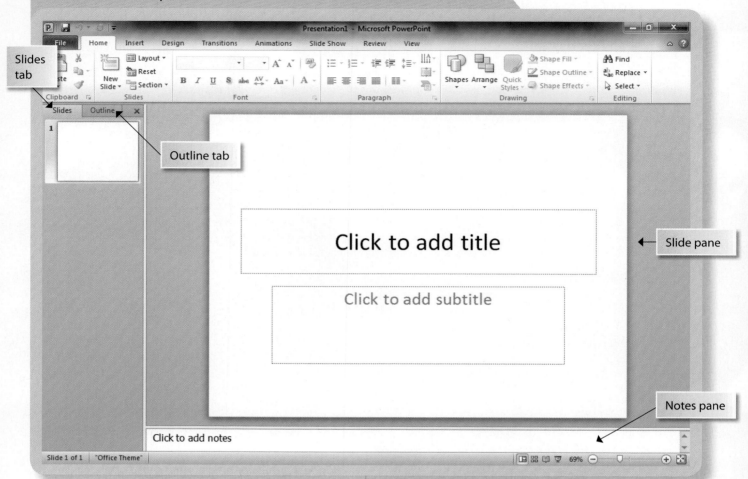

Slides tab

Outline tab

Click to add title

Slide pane

Click to add subtitle

Notes pane

Click to add notes

 **ACTIVITY**

Start PowerPoint.

1 Start **PowerPoint**. PowerPoint starts and displays a blank presentation.

2 If the PowerPoint program window is not maximized, click the **Maximize button** ▢. Refer back to Exhibit 20-1.

Tip: To create a new, blank presentation when PowerPoint is already running, click the File tab, click New in the navigation bar, and then, with Blank presentation selected on the New tab, click the Create button.

3 On the Quick Access Toolbar, click the **Save button** 🖫. Because this is the first time this presentation has been saved, the Save As dialog box opens. Save the presentation as **Business Expansion**.

Creating a Title Slide

The first slide in a PowerPoint presentation is usually the **title slide**, which typically contains the title of the presentation and a subtitle, often the presenter's name.

title slide The first slide in a presentation; typically contains the presentation title and a subtitle.

Planning a Presentation

As you prepare a presentation, consider a few key questions to help you plan what to say. Being able to answer these questions will help you create a presentation that successfully delivers its message or motivates the audience to take an action.

▶ **What is the purpose of the presentation?**

Goal !?!

In other words, what action or response do you want the audience to have? If you are making a sales pitch, you want the audience to buy what you are selling. If you are delivering good or bad news, you want the audience to hear the message clearly and take action based on the facts you provide.

▶ **Who is the audience?**

Think about the needs and interests of the audience, as well as any decisions they will make as a result of what you have to say. Make sure what you choose to say to the audience is relevant to their needs, interests, and decisions, or it will be forgotten.

▶ **How much time do you have for the presentation?**

Consider the amount of time available. Make sure you pace yourself as you speak. You don't want to spend too much time on the introduction and end up having to eliminate some of your closing remarks because you run out of time. This diminishes the effectiveness of the entire presentation and weakens its impact on the audience.

▶ **Will the audience benefit from printed output?**

Some presentations are effectively delivered with on-screen visuals. Others require printed support materials because there is too much information to be displayed on the screen. In other cases, you want the audience to have something to take with them to help remember what you said.

Monkey Business Images/Shutterstock.com

The blank title slide contains two text placeholders. A **placeholder** is a region of a slide reserved for inserting text or graphics. A **text placeholder** is a placeholder designed to contain text. The larger text placeholder on the title slide is the **title text placeholder** and is designed to hold the presentation title. The smaller text placeholder below the title text placeholder is the **subtitle text placeholder**; it is designed to contain a subtitle for the presentation. After you enter text into a text placeholder, it becomes a **text box**, which is simply a container that holds text.

ACTIVITY

Add text to text placeholders.

1 Click anywhere in **Click to add title box**, which is the title text placeholder. The title text placeholder text disappears, a dashed line appears on top of the dotted line indicating the placeholder border, and the insertion point blinks in the placeholder. See Exhibit 20-2. This means the placeholder is active, and any text you type will appear in the placeholder.

> **placeholder** A region of a slide reserved for inserting text or graphics.
>
> **text placeholder** A placeholder designed to contain text.
>
> **title text placeholder** A placeholder designed to contain the presentation title or slide title.
>
> **subtitle text placeholder** A placeholder designed to contain the presentation subtitle.
>
> **text box** A container that holds text.

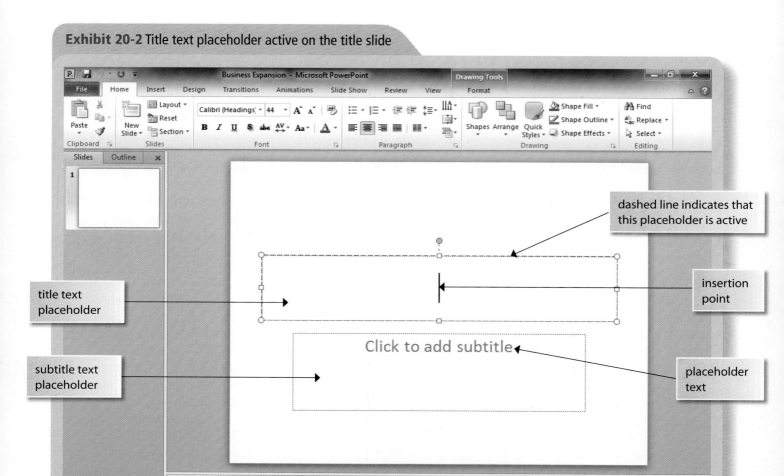

Exhibit 20-2 Title text placeholder active on the title slide

title text placeholder

subtitle text placeholder

dashed line indicates that this placeholder is active

insertion point

Click to add subtitle

placeholder text

2 Type **Gourmet on Call** as the title, and then click a blank area of the slide. The border of the title text placeholder disappears and the text you typed appears in place of the placeholder text. The thumbnail in the Slides tab also contains the text you typed.

3 Click in the **Click to add subtitle box**, which is the subtitle text placeholder, type your first and last name, and then click anywhere else on the slide except in the title text box.

layout A predetermined way of organizing the objects on a slide.

content placeholder A placeholder designed to hold the slide content, which can be text or a graphic object.

Adding a New Slide and Choosing a Layout

After the title slide, you need to add additional slides to the presentation. When you add a new slide, the slide is formatted with a **layout**, which is a predetermined way of organizing the objects on a slide, including title text and other content (bulleted lists, photographs, charts, and so forth). PowerPoint provides nine built-in layouts, as described in Exhibit 20-3. All layouts, except the Blank layout, include placeholders to help you create a presentation. Slides can include several types of placeholders, but the most common are text and content placeholders. You have already seen text placeholders on the title slide. Most layouts include a title text placeholder to contain the slide title. A **content placeholder** is intended to contain the slide content, which can be text or a graphic object, such as a table, a chart, a diagram, a picture, clip art, or a video. If you click in a content placeholder and then add text,

Exhibit 20-3 Built-in layouts in PowerPoint

Layout	Description
Title Slide	Contains the presentation title and a subtitle; is usually used as the first slide in a presentation
Title and Content	Contains either a bulleted list or a graphic in addition to the slide title
Section Header	Contains a section title and text that describes the presentation section
Two Content	The same as the Title and Content layout, but with two side-by-side content placeholders, each of which can contain a bulleted list or a graphic
Comparison	The same as the Two Content layout, but includes text placeholders above the content placeholders to label the content
Title Only	Includes only a title text placeholder for the slide title
Blank	Does not contain any placeholders
Content with Caption	Contains a content placeholder, a title text placeholder to identify the slide or the content, and a text placeholder to describe the content; suitable for photographs or other graphics that need an explanation
Picture with Caption	Similar to the Content with Caption layout, but with a picture placeholder instead of a content placeholder

the content placeholder is no longer a placeholder and becomes a text box.

To insert a new slide, you use the New Slide button in the Slides group on the Home tab. If you are inserting a new slide after the title slide and you click the New Slide button, the new slide is created using the Title and Content layout. Otherwise, the new slide is created using the same layout as the current slide. If you want to choose a different layout, click the New Slide button arrow, and then select the layout you want to use from the menu that opens.

You can also change the layout of a slide after it is created. To do this, click the Layout button in the Slides group on the Home tab, and then select the layout you want to use.

ACTIVITY

Create new slides and change the layout.

1. On the Home tab, in the Slides group, click the **New Slide button**. A new Slide 2 appears in the Slide pane and in the Slides tab with the Title and Content layout applied. See Exhibit 20-4. The

Exhibit 20-4 New slide with the Title and Content layout

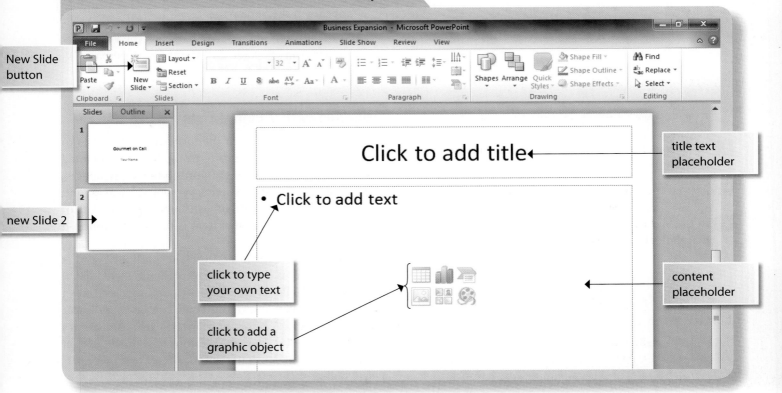

content placeholder contains placeholder text that you can click to insert your own text and six icons that you can click to insert the specific item identified by each icon.

2 In the Slide pane, click anywhere in the **title text placeholder**, and then type **About Our Company**.

3 On the Home tab, in the Slides group, click the **New Slide button arrow**. The New Slide gallery opens displaying the nine layouts available. See Exhibit 20-5.

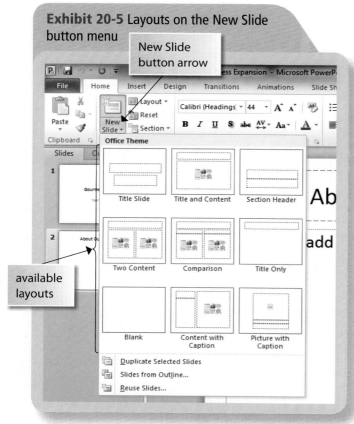

Exhibit 20-5 Layouts on the New Slide button menu

4 In the gallery, click the **Two Content layout**. Slide 3 is created with the Two Content layout, which consists of three placeholders: the title text placeholder and two content placeholders side by side.

5 In the Slide pane, click anywhere in the **title text placeholder**, and then type **Contact Us**.

bulleted list A list of paragraphs with a special symbol to the left of each paragraph.

bulleted item One paragraph in a bulleted list.

subbullet A sub paragraph in a bulleted list, positioned below and indented from a higher-level bullet.

6 On the Home tab, in the Slides group, click the **Layout button**. The same gallery of layouts you saw on the New Slide gallery appears.

7 In the gallery, click the **Title and Content layout**. The layout of Slide 3 changes to the layout you selected.

Moving Between Slides in Normal View

As you work on a presentation, you'll need to move from one slide to another. In Normal view, you can click a slide thumbnail in the Slides tab to display that slide in the Slide pane. You can also use the scroll bar in the Slide pane to scroll from slide to slide, or click the Next Slide ⬇ or Previous Slide ⬆ buttons at the bottom of the vertical scroll bar in the Slide pane.

ACTIVITY

Move from one slide to another.

1 In the Slides tab, click the **Slide 1 thumbnail**. The title slide appears in the Slide pane.

2 In the Slide pane, drag the **scroll box** to the bottom of the scroll bar. As you drag, a ScreenTip appears identifying the slide that will appear when you release the mouse button.

3 Release the mouse button. Slide 3 ("Contact Us") appears in the Slide pane.

4 At the bottom of the scroll bar, click the **Previous Slide button** ⬆. Slide 2 ("About Our Company") appears in the Slide pane.

Working with Bulleted Lists

Often, text on a slide is in the form of bulleted lists to emphasize important points to the audience. A **bulleted list** is a list of "paragraphs" (words, phrases, sentences, or paragraphs) with a special symbol such as a dot, dash, circle, box, star, or other character to the left of each paragraph. A **bulleted item** is one paragraph in a bulleted list.

Bullets can appear at different outline levels. A first-level bullet is a main paragraph in a bulleted list; a second-level bullet is a bullet below and indented from a first-level bullet; and so on. There can be many lower levels of bullets. A bullet at a lower level is sometimes called a **subbullet**. Usually, the font size of the text in subbullets is smaller than the font size of text in higher-level bullets.

Creating a Bulleted List

To add a bulleted list to a slide, click in a content place-holder and start typing. When you press the Enter key, the insertion point moves to the next line and a new bullet is created. If you don't type anything next to a bullet, the bullet will not appear on the slide.

Create a bulleted list.

1 In Slide 2, in the Slide pane, click to the right of the bullet in the content placeholder. The place-holder text ("Click to add text") disappears, and the insertion point appears to the right of the bullet. In the Font group, notice that the font size in the Font Size box of this first-level bullet is 32 points. See Exhibit 20-6.

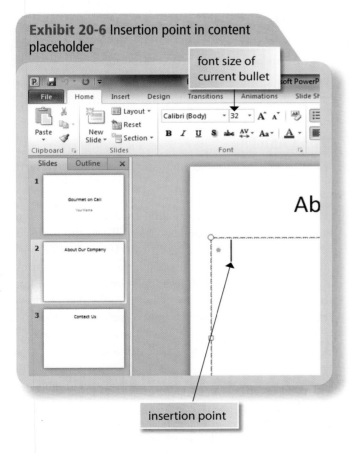

Exhibit 20-6 Insertion point in content placeholder

font size of current bullet

insertion point

2 Type **We prepare gourmet meals** and then press the **Enter key**. A new bullet that is lighter than the first bullet appears. It will darken as soon as you start typing text.

3 Type **Ready for you to** and then press the **Enter key**. A third bullet is added to the slide.

4 Press the **Tab key**. The new bullet is in-dented and becomes a subbullet. The subbullet is a very faint dash. The font size of the subbullet is 28 points, which is smaller than the font size used in the first-level bullets on the slide. See Exhibit 20-7.

Tip: You can also use the Increase List Level or Decrease List Level buttons in the Paragraph group on the Home tab to change the level of a bullet.

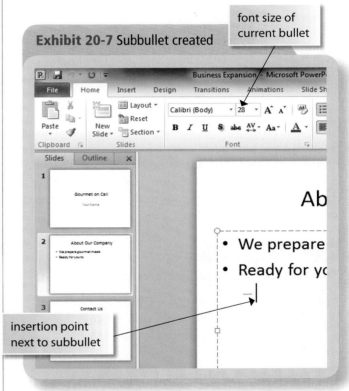

Exhibit 20-7 Subbullet created

font size of current bullet

insertion point next to subbullet

5 Type **Serve** and then press the **Enter key**. A second subbullet is created.

6 Type **Heat** and then press the **Enter key** to create a third subbullet.

7 Type **Freeze** and then press the **Enter key** to create a fourth subbullet.

8 Press the **Shift+Tab keys**. The subbullet changes to a first-level bullet.

9 Type **Select from a variety of menus** as the bullet text.

10 Click a blank area of the slide outside the content text box. The dashed line border of the text box disappears.

Contact Information in a Presentation

A presentation should usually include contact information so that audience members know how to contact the presenter. In a sales presentation, the contact information might be more general, describing how to contact the company. The information should include all possible methods to contact the presenter, including the presenter's name, office phone number, cell phone number, email address, mailing address, and company Web site. If the presenter is not the only contact person at the company, or not the best contact person, include information about other people—sales representatives, marketing personnel, accountants, or other employees.

Creating a New Line without Creating a New Bullet

Sometimes, you will want to create a new line within a bulleted item without creating a new bullet. This is helpful when you include an address as a bullet item and want to split the address on two lines of the same bullet. To create a new line, press the Shift+Enter keys. This moves the insertion point to the next line without creating a new paragraph.

 ACTIVITY

Create a new line without creating a new bullet.

1. Display **Slide 3** ("Contact Us") in the Slide pane. Click to the right of the bullet in the content placeholder, and then type **Phone:** as the bullet text.

2. Press the **Shift+Enter keys**. The insertion point moves to the next line without creating a new bullet.

3. Type **912–555–3800** and then press the **Enter key**. A new bullet is created.

4. Type **Address:** and then press the **Shift+Enter keys**.

> **Tip:** To change a bulleted list into a list without any bullets, select the bulleted items, and then click the Bullets button in the Paragraph group on the Home tab to deselect it.

AutoFit A PowerPoint feature that automatically changes the line spacing and the font size of text if you add more text than will fit in a placeholder.

5. Type **101 West Bayside Ave.** and then press the **Shift+Enter keys**. Type **Savannah, GA 31401**. The address is entered on two lines under the Address bullet without creating new bullets.

6. On the Quick Access Toolbar, click the **Save button** 🖫 to save the presentation.

7. On the Ribbon, click the **File tab**. In the navigation bar, click **Close**. The file closes.

Using AutoFit

As you add text to a content placeholder, the **AutoFit** feature changes the line spacing and the font size of the text if you add more text than will fit in the placeholder. The AutoFit feature is turned on by default. When you start typing the next bullet, you will see the AutoFit feature adjust the text to make it fit. If the AutoFit feature adjusts the text in a text box, the AutoFit Options button appears in the Slide pane below and to the left of the placeholder. You can click the AutoFit Options button and select an option on the menu to control the way AutoFit works. If you select the option to turn off AutoFit for a text box, you can turn it back on later.

 ACTIVITY

Use the AutoFit feature.

1. Open the data file **Expansion** located in the Chapter 20\Chapter folder. Save the file as **Expansion Goals**.

2. Select the subtitle text **Your Name**, and then type your name.

3. Display **Slide 2** ("About Our Company") in the Slide pane.

Tiut Lucian/Shutterstock.com

4 In the last bulleted item, click after the word *menus*, and then press the **Enter key**. A new first-level bullet is created.

5 Type **V**. After you type the first character in this new bullet, the line spacing in the text box tightens up slightly and the AutoFit Options button ÷ appears next to the lower-left corner of the text box.

6 Point to the **AutoFit Options button** ÷ so that it changes to ÷ ▾, and then click the **AutoFit Options button** ÷ ▾. The AutoFit Options button menu appears. The default option, AutoFit Text to Placeholder, is selected. See Exhibit 20-8.

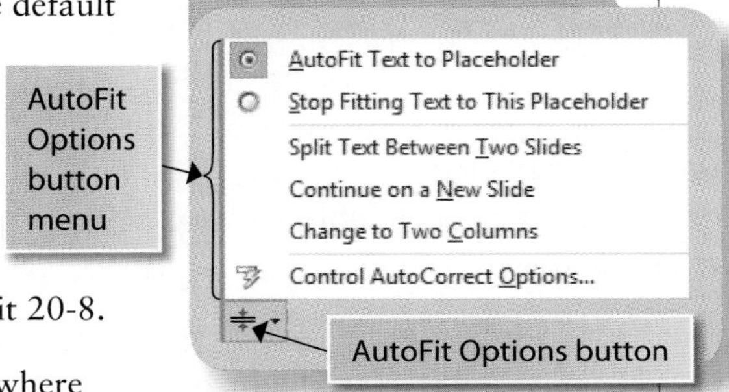

7 Click anywhere on the slide to close the AutoFit Options button menu without changing the selected default option.

> **Exhibit 20-8** AutoFit Options button menu
>
> AutoFit Options button menu →
>
> ⦿ AutoFit Text to Placeholder
> ○ Stop Fitting Text to This Placeholder
> — Split Text Between Two Slides
> — Continue on a New Slide
> — Change to Two Columns
> ⌨ Control AutoCorrect Options...
>
> ÷ ▾ ← AutoFit Options button

> ▲ **Tip:** You can also press the Esc key to close a menu without selecting a command or option.

8 In the last bulleted item, click immediately after *V*, and then type **egetarian and vegan options available** to complete the bulleted item.

9 On the Home tab, in the Paragraph group, click the **Increase List Level button** ⧉. The item changes to a subbullet under the previous bulleted item.

> ▲ **Tip:** If you position the insertion point in front of the first character in the bulleted item or select the entire bulleted item, you can press the Tab key to increase the list level.

10 Press the **Enter key**, and then type **M**. AutoFit adjusts the text again, this time by decreasing the point size of both levels of bullets by two points. The first-level bulleted items are now 30 points, and the subbullets are now 26 points.

11 Type **enus change seasonally**.

> **Many themes arrange background graphics differently on the title slide than on the content slides.**

Changing Themes

Plain white slides with a common font (such as black Times New Roman or Calibri) often fail to hold an audience's attention. Today's audiences expect more interesting color schemes, fonts, graphics, and other effects. You can easily change the fonts and color used for the background, title text, body text, accents, and graphics in a presentation as well as the style used in your presentation by changing the theme. In a presentation, the headings theme font is used for the slide titles and the body theme font is used for text in content placeholders. Some PowerPoint themes include graphics as part of the slide background. By default, new, blank presentations have the Office theme applied.

The theme you choose for a presentation should reflect the content and the intended audience. For example, if you are presenting a new curriculum to a group of elementary school teachers, you might choose a theme that uses bright, primary colors. If you are presenting a marketing plan to a mutual fund company, you might choose a theme that uses dark colors formatted in a way that conveys sophistication.

■ ACTIVITY

Change the theme.

1 On the Ribbon, click the **Design tab**. In the Themes group, the first theme displayed in the group is always the currently applied theme.

2 In the Themes group, point to the first theme, which has an orange highlight around it, but do not click the mouse button. A ScreenTip appears identifying the theme, which, in this case, is the Office Theme. The name of the current theme also appears in the status bar. See Exhibit 20-9. After the currently applied theme, all the available themes are listed in alphabetical order, except the Office Theme, which is listed as the first available theme. (In this case, it appears twice because it is also the current theme.)

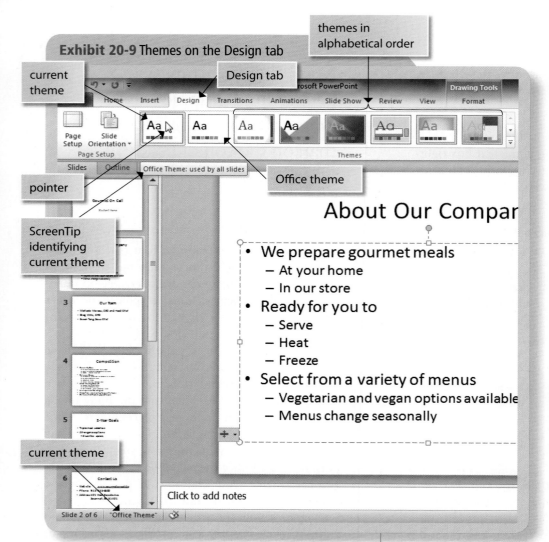

Exhibit 20-9 Themes on the Design tab

themes in alphabetical order

current theme

Design tab

pointer

Office theme

ScreenTip identifying current theme

current theme

About Our Compar

- We prepare gourmet meals
  - At your home
  - In our store
- Ready for you to
  - Serve
  - Heat
  - Freeze
- Select from a variety of menus
  - Vegetarian and vegan options available
  - Menus change seasonally

Click to add notes

Slide 2 of 6   "Office Theme"

⚠ **Problem?** If your screen is set at a different resolution than the screens shown in the figures in this book, the Pushpin theme will be in a different position in the gallery. Point to each theme and use the ScreenTips to identify the Pushpin theme.

applied theme appears in the status bar.

Modifying Text and Changing Bullet Levels in the Outline Tab

The Outline tab displays the outline of the entire presentation. Slide titles appear at the top level in the outline and the slide content—that is, the bulleted lists—are indented below the slide titles. When you view the outline in the Outline tab, you see only the text of the slide titles and the text in content placeholders; you do not see any graphics on the slides or any text that is not in a content placeholder. The Slide pane still displays the currently selected slide as usual.

You can modify the text of a slide in the Outline tab as well as in the Slide pane. You can also use the Outline tab or the Slide pane to move text. For example, you can move a bulleted item from one position to another on a slide, or you can change a subbullet into a first-level bullet or a first-level bullet into a subbullet. However, in the Outline tab, you can also easily move a bulleted item from one slide to another, and you can change a bulleted item into a slide title, creating a new slide.

Moving an item to a higher level in the outline, such as changing a second-level bullet to a first-level bullet or changing a first-level bulleted item to a slide title, is called **promoting** the item. Moving an item lower in the outline, such as changing a slide title to a bulleted item on the previous slide or changing a first-level bullet to a second-level bullet, is called **demoting** the item.

3 In the Themes group, point to the second-to-last theme. The ScreenTip that appears identifies this as the Aspect theme, and the Live Preview feature changes the design and colors on the slide in the Slide pane, as well as the layout of the text boxes, to those of the Aspect theme.

4 In the Themes group, click the **More button** ⏷ to open the Themes gallery.

5 Scroll down to the end of the gallery list. Point to the last theme in the second-to-last row of the Built-In section (two rows above the From Office. com section header). The ScreenTip identifies this as the Pushpin theme.

6 Click the **Pushpin theme**. The design and colors of the slides in the presentation change to those of the Pushpin theme, and the name of the newly

promote To move an item to a higher level in an outline.

demote To move an item to a lower level in an outline.

If you need to move a bulleted item from one slide to another, it is usually easier to work in the Outline tab.

You promote and demote items in the Outline tab using the same techniques you use in the Slide pane: You can click the Increase List Level ⊞ or Decrease List Level ⊞ button in the Paragraph group on the Home tab; or, when the insertion point is positioned at the beginning of an item or when the entire item is selected, you can press the Tab key to increase the indent or the Shift+Tab keys to decrease the indent. Any changes you make in the Outline tab appear on the slide in the Slide pane.

Modify text in the Outline tab.

1 In the left pane, click the **Outline tab**. The outline of the presentation appears.

2 In the Outline tab, scroll down until Slide 4 ("Competition") is at the top of the Outline tab. Slide 2 ("About Our Company") still appears in the Slide pane.

3 In the Outline tab, click anywhere on the text in **Slide 4** ("Competition"). Slide 4 appears in the Slide pane. See Exhibit 20-10.

⚠ **Problem?** If the slide in the Slide pane is too large to fit in the window, click the **Fit slide to current window button** ⊞ on the right end of the status bar.

Exhibit 20-10 Presentation outline in the Outline tab

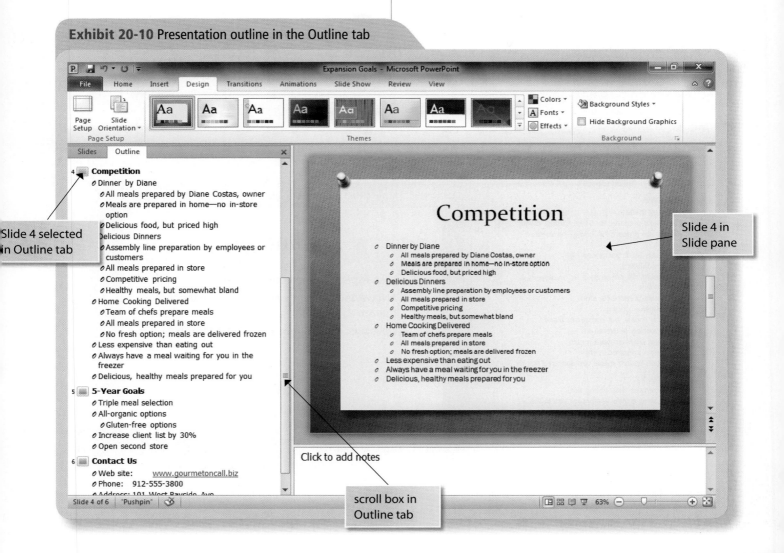

4 In the Outline tab, in the fourth bullet in Slide 4 ("Competition"), click immediately before the word *Less*, and then press the **Enter key**. A new line is created above the current bulleted item in both the Outline tab and the Slide pane, and the last three bulleted items are moved down.

5 Press the **Up Arrow key**. The insertion point moves up to the new line, and the bullet appears in the new line.

6 Type **Advantages**.

7 In the Outline tab, in Slide 5 ("5-Year Goals"), point to the bullet to the left of *All-organic options* so that the pointer changes to ✛, and then click. The All-organic options bulleted item and its subbullet are selected.

8 On the Ribbon, click the **Home tab**. In the Paragraph group, click the **Increase List Level button**. The selected first-level bulleted item is demoted—it

indents and becomes a second-level bulleted item—and its subbullet becomes a third-level bulleted item.

9 In the Outline tab, in Slide 5 ("5-Year Goals"), click the **Gluten-free options bullet** to select the entire bulleted item.

10 On the Home tab, in the Paragraph group, click the **Decrease List Level button**. The selected third-level bulleted item is promoted to the second level.

11 In the Outline tab, in Slide 4 ("Competition"), click the **Advantages bullet**.

12 On the Home tab, in the Paragraph group, click the **Decrease List Level button**. The selected first-level bulleted item is promoted to a slide title for a new Slide 5, and the three bulleted items below it are now on the new Slide 5. See Exhibit 20-11.

13 Save the presentation.

Exhibit 20-11 New slide created by promoting text

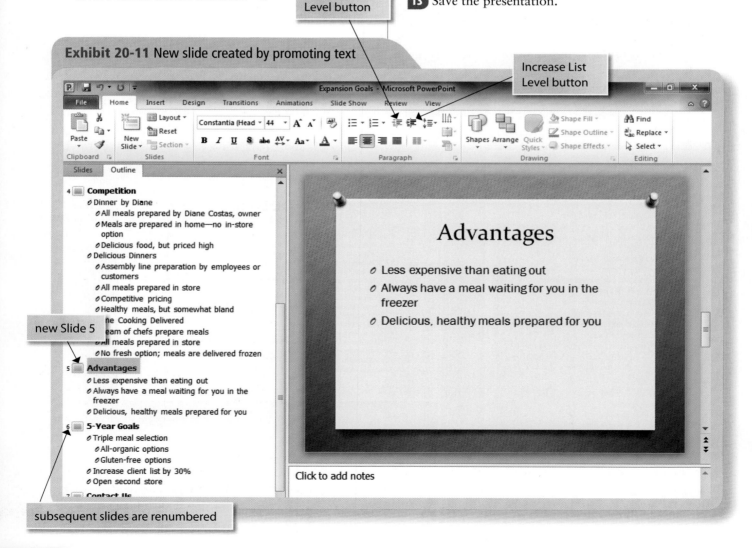

Increasing and Decreasing List Levels

In an outline, the top-level items are called first-level headings, the items indented below the first-level headings are second-level headings, the items indented below those items are third-level headings, and so on. When you change a bulleted item from a higher-level heading to a lower-level heading, such as from level 2 to level 3, you indent and demote it, but you are increasing its level number from 2 to 3. When you change a bulleted item from a lower-level heading to a higher-level heading, such as from 3 to 2, you promote it, but you are decreasing its level number from 3 to 2. This is why when you *demote* a bulleted item, you use the *Increase* List Level button in the Paragraph group, and when you *promote* a bulleted item, you use the *Decrease* List Level button.

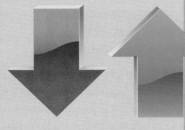

Valentina Rusinova/Shutterstock.com

You can also use the Cut, Copy, and Paste commands to move text or slides.

TRINACRIA PHOTO/Shutterstock.com

LO20.2 Rearranging Text and Slides, and Deleting Slides

In addition to changing the level of bulleted items on slides, you can move bulleted items to new positions on slides or from one slide to another, and you can rearrange the slides themselves. To move bulleted items from one position to another, you must work in the Outline tab or in the Slide pane. To move slides from one position to another, you can work in the Slides or Outline tab in Normal view or in Slide Sorter view. **Slide Sorter view** displays all the slides in the presentation as thumbnails to provide you with a visual overview of the presentation.

Moving Bulleted Items

Bulleted items should be placed in a logical order, such as most to least important, alphabetical order, or chronologically. You can move a bulleted item to a new position in the outline by using drag and drop. You drag the bulleted item by its bullet. As you drag, a horizontal line follows the pointer to show you where the bulleted item will be positioned after you release the pointer.

ACTIVITY

Move bulleted items.

1. If Slide 5 is not the current slide, in the Outline tab, click the **Slide 5 slide icon** ▣. Slide 5 appears in the Slide pane.

2. In the Outline tab, in the Slide 5 text, point to the **Less expensive than eating out bullet** so that the pointer changes to ✥.

3. Drag the bulleted item down until the horizontal line indicating the position of the item you are dragging appears below the Delicious, healthy meals prepared for you bullet on Slide 5, as shown in Exhibit 20-12.

> **Slide Sorter view** The PowerPoint view that displays all the slides in a presentation as thumbnails to provide a visual overview of the presentation.

Exhibit 20-12 Bulleted item being dragged in the Outline tab

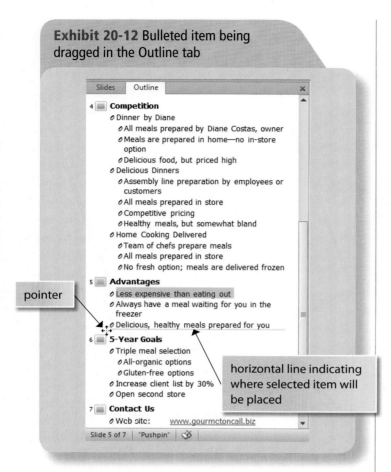

pointer

horizontal line indicating where selected item will be placed

Rearranging Slides

As you develop a presentation, you might want to change the order in which the slides appear. You can drag slides to reposition them. If you are working in the Outline tab, you can move a slide to a new position in the outline by dragging it by its slide icon. In the Slides tab and in Slide Sorter view, you move a slide by dragging its thumbnail.

Rearrange slides.

1 In the Outline tab, drag the **Slide 4 slide icon** (the slide titled "Competition") down until the horizontal line indicating the new position of the slide appears just above the slide title for Slide 7 ("Contact Us"). The slide titled "Competition" is now Slide 6.

2 In the left pane, click the **Slides tab**. The slide thumbnails appear in the Slides tab.

3 In the Slides tab, scroll up until you can see the Slides 2–7 thumbnails in the Slides tab.

> ⚠ **Problem?** If you cannot see Slides 2 through 7 in the Slides tab at the same time, drag the **splitter bar** between the Slides tab and the Slide pane to the left to decrease the size of each thumbnail and increase the number of thumbnails you can see at one time.

4 Drag the **Slide 5 thumbnail** (the "5-Year Goals" slide) up until the horizontal line indicating the new position of the slide is between Slides 2 and 3. The slide titled "5-Year Goals" is now Slide 3.

4 With the horizontal line positioned below the Delicious, healthy meals prepared for you bullet, release the mouse button. The bulleted item you dragged is now the last bulleted item on Slide 5 both in the Outline tab and on Slide 5 ("Advantages") in the Slide pane.

5 In the Slide pane, point to the **Delicious, healthy meals prepared for you bullet** so that the pointer changes to ⊕.

6 Drag the bulleted item up until the horizontal line indicating the new position of the bullet is above the first bulleted item on the slide, and then release the mouse button.

> ⚠ **Problem?** If you cannot see the line because the Mini Toolbar is in the way, move the pointer to the right side of the Outline tab while you are dragging.

The Delicious, healthy meals prepared for you bullet is now the first bulleted item on Slide 5 ("Advantages") in both the Slide pane and the Outline tab.

5 On the status bar, click the **Slide Sorter button** ▦. The presentation appears in Slide Sorter view. A thick colored frame appears around the Slide 3 thumbnail indicating that the slide is selected.

6 If necessary, change the zoom level to **90%** so you can see four slides in the first row and three slides in the second row. See Exhibit 20-13.

7 Drag the **Slide 4 thumbnail** (the "Our Team" slide) down until the vertical line indicating the new position of the slide is between the Slide 6 and Slide 7 thumbnails. The slide titled "Our Team" is now Slide 6.

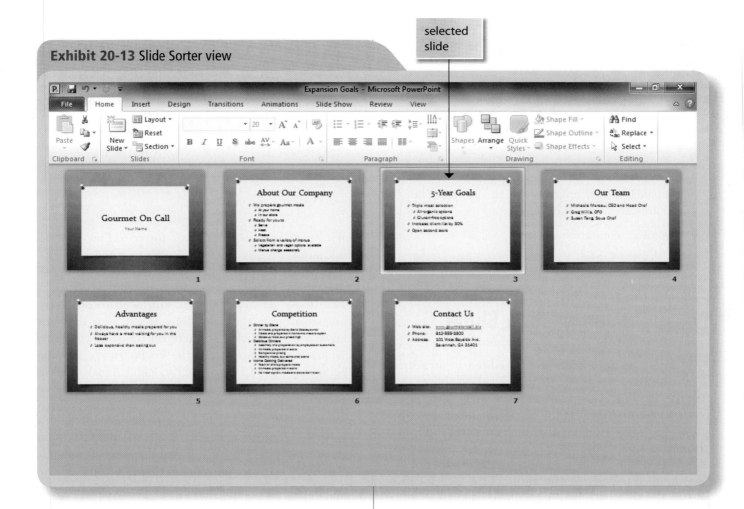

Exhibit 20-13 Slide Sorter view

selected slide

---

8 On the status bar, click the **Normal button** ⊞ to return to Normal view. Slide 6 ("Our Team") appears in the Slide pane because it was the selected slide in Slide Sorter view.

> ➤ **Tip:** You can also double-click any slide thumbnail in Slide Sorter view to return to the previous view with the slide you double-clicked as the current slide.

Deleting Slides

As you develop a presentation, you will sometimes need to delete slides. You can delete slides in the Slides and Outline tabs in Normal view and in Slide Sorter view. To delete a slide, right-click the thumbnail in the Slides tab or Slide Sorter view, and then click Delete Slide on the shortcut menu. You can also click its thumbnail in the Slides tab or Slide Sorter view or click the slide icon in the Outline tab, and then press the Delete key. It's a good idea to verify that you are deleting the correct slide by first displaying it in the Slide pane.

Duplicating Slides

As you create a presentation, you might want to create a slide that is similar to another slide. Starting with a copy of a slide that already exists can save time. To duplicate a slide, right-click the slide thumbnail in the Slides tab in Normal view, and then click Duplicate Slide on the shortcut menu. You can also use the Ribbon to duplicate one or multiple slides. In the Slides group on the Home tab, click the New Slide button arrow, and then click Duplicate Selected Slides. If you select more than one slide before you use the Duplicate Selected Slides command, all of the selected slides will be duplicated.

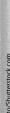

ACTIVITY

Delete a slide.

1 In the Slides tab, click the **Slide 5 thumbnail**. Slide 5 ("Competition") appears in the Slide pane.

2 In the Slides tab, right-click the **Slide 5 thumbnail**. On the shortcut menu, click **Delete Slide**. Slide 5 is deleted. The slide titled "Our Team" is now Slide 5 and appears in the Slide pane.

3 Save the presentation.

LO20.3 Running a Slide Show

After you have created and edited a presentation, you are ready to run the slide show. You can run the slide show in Slide Show view, Mini Slide Show view, and Reading view. **Slide Show view** displays one slide after another so that each slide fills the entire screen with no toolbars or other Windows elements visible on the screen, and displays special effects applied to the text and graphics on each slide or to the slide itself. **Mini Slide Show view** displays the slide show in a small window that opens on top of the PowerPoint program window. **Reading view**, which is very similar to Slide Show view, displays each slide so that it almost fills the entire screen, but it also displays the title bar and status bar, and provides navigation buttons on the status bar for moving from slide to slide as you review the presentation, as well as a

Slide Show view The PowerPoint view that displays one slide after another so that each slide fills the entire screen with no toolbars or other Windows elements visible on the screen, and displays special effects applied to the text and graphics on each slide or to the slide itself.

Mini Slide Show view The PowerPoint view that displays one slide after another in a small window on top of the PowerPoint program window.

Reading view The PowerPoint view that displays each slide so that it almost fills the entire screen, but also displays the title bar and status bar, and provides navigation buttons on the status bar for moving from slide to slide and a menu button with commands for working with the slide show.

To quickly start a slide show from the first slide, press the F5 key. To start a slide show from the current slide, press the Shift+F5 keys.

menu button with commands for working with the slide show.

As the presenter, when you switch to Slide Show, Mini Slide Show, or Reading view, you need to *advance* the slide show; that is, you need to do something to display the next slide. To advance the slide show, you can click anywhere on the slide currently displayed, or you can use the keyboard by pressing the Spacebar, the Enter key, the Right Arrow key, or the Page Down key. You can also use the keyboard to move to the previous slide by pressing the Left Arrow key, the Page Up key, or the Backspace key. If you right-click the currently displayed slide during a slide show, a shortcut menu that contains commands to jump to specific slides opens. Finally, you can also use buttons on a toolbar that appears in the lower-left corner of the currently displayed slide in Slide Show and Mini Slide Show views or on the toolbar that appears on the status bar in Reading view to navigate to a specific slide.

After you display the last slide in a slide show, the screen changes to black with a small note at the top that tells you that you have reached the end of the slide show. To end the slide show—that is, remove the black screen and return to the view from which you started—advance the slide show once more. You can also end a slide show at any time by pressing the Esc key or by right-clicking the slide, and then clicking End Show on the shortcut menu.

Using Slide Show View

To start a slide show from the current slide in Slide Show view, click the Slide Show button on the status bar to start the slide show from the current slide, or click the From Current Slide button in the Start Slide Show group on the Slide Show tab. You can also start the slide show from the first slide by clicking the From Beginning button in the Start Slide Show group on the Slide tab.

ACTIVITY

Run a slide show in Slide Show view.

1 Display **Slide 1** (the title slide) in the Slide pane.

2 On the status bar, click the **Slide Show button** 🖳. The slide show starts from the current slide, and Slide 1 fills the screen in Slide Show view.

> ➤ **Tip:** To use the Ribbon to start the slide show, click the Slide Show tab, and then click the From Beginning or From Current Slide button in the Start Slide Show group.

3 Click anywhere on the screen to advance the slide show. Slide 2 appears on the screen.

4 Press the **Spacebar** to display the next slide. Slide 3 ("5-Year Goals") appears on the screen.

5 Press the **Enter key** to display the next slide. Slide 4 ("Advantages") appears on the screen.

6 Press the **Left Arrow key** to redisplay the previous slide. Slide 3 ("5-Year Goals") reappears.

7 Right-click anywhere on the screen. On the shortcut menu, point to **Go to Slide** to display a submenu with a list of all the slides in the presentation. Click **6 Contact Us**. Slide 6 ("Contact Us") appears on the screen.

8 Right-click anywhere on the screen. On the shortcut menu, click **Last Viewed**. The most recently viewed slide prior to the current slide—Slide 3 ("5-Year Goals")—reappears.

9 Move the pointer without clicking. A very faint toolbar appears in the lower-left corner. See Exhibit 20-14.

10 On the toolbar, click the **Next Slide button** ➡. Slide 4 ("Advantages") appears.

11 Press the **Right Arrow key** twice to advance two slides. The next two slides, Slide 5 ("Our Team") followed by Slide 6 ("Contact Us"), appear.

12 Click anywhere on the screen. A black screen with a message that this is the end of the slide show appears.

13 Use any method to advance the slide show. Slide Show view closes, and the presentation appears in Normal view with Slide 1 in the Slide pane.

Using Mini Slide Show View

You can also run the slide show in Mini Slide Show view. In this view, a mini slide show window opens as a small window on top of the program window. You use the same techniques to advance the slide show in Mini Slide Show view as you do in Slide Show view. To open Mini Slide Show View, press and hold the Ctrl key, and then click the Slide Show button on the status bar. If you start a slide show in Mini Slide Show view, you must end the slide show in this window. If you don't, the next time you open Slide Show view, the mini slide show window will open instead.

ACTIVITY

Run a slide show in Mini Slide Show view.

1 Display **Slide 2** ("About Our Company") in the Slide pane.

2 Press and hold the **Ctrl key**. On the status bar, click the **Slide Show button** 🖳, and then release the **Ctrl key**. The current slide—Slide 2—appears in a small window on top of the program window. See Exhibit 20-15.

3 Advance the slide show in the mini slide show window to view each slide in the presentation. When the black slide indicating the end of the slide show appears, end the slide show. The mini slide show window closes.

> ⚠ **Problem?** If the mini slide show window disappears when you advance the slide show, you clicked in the PowerPoint program window instead of in the mini slide show window. Point to the **PowerPoint button** on the taskbar, click the **PowerPoint Slide Show thumbnail**, and then continue advancing the slide show.

Exhibit 20-14 Toolbar in Slide Show view

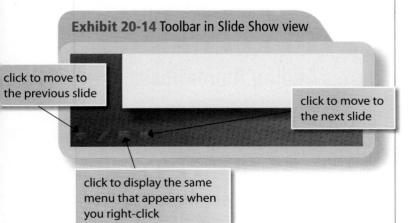

click to move to the previous slide

click to move to the next slide

click to display the same menu that appears when you right-click

Exhibit 20-15 Slide 2 in Mini Slide Show view

Using Reading View

Reading view is very similar to Slide Show view. To run a slide show in Reading view, click the Reading View button 📖 on the status bar or in the Presentation Views group on the View tab on the Ribbon. Exhibit 20-16 shows Slide 2 of the Expansion Goals presentation in Reading view with the Menu button menu open. A toolbar similar to the one that appears when you move the pointer in Slide Show view appears on the status bar in Reading view. The Menu button 📑 on this toolbar is similar to the button on the toolbar in Slide Show view, but it contains commands to copy and print the slide in addition to the navigation commands. The Menu button menu also contains the Edit Slides command, which

animation A special effect applied to an object that makes the object move or change.

you can click to return to the previous view so you can edit the presentation. The Reading view status bar also contains the same view buttons that appear on the status bar in Normal and Slide Sorter views.

In Reading view, you use the same techniques for advancing through a slide show as you do in Slide Show view. You cannot edit the presentation in Reading view.

LO20.4 Adding Animations

Animations are special effects applied to an object, such as a graphic or a bulleted list, that make the object move or change. Animations add interest to a slide show and draw attention to the text or object being animated. For example, you can animate a slide title to fly in from the side or spin around like a pinwheel to draw the audience's attention to that title.

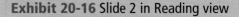

Exhibit 20-16 Slide 2 in Reading view

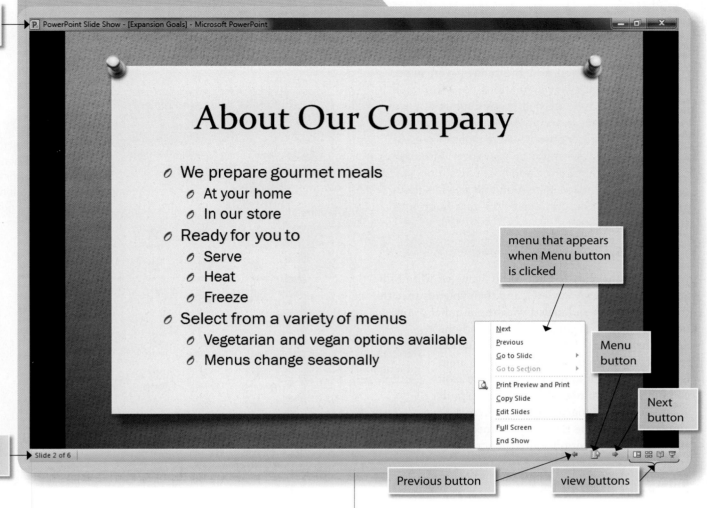

When you apply an animation to text, you are applying it to all the text in the text box. If you animate a bulleted list, the default for first-level bulleted items is to appear using **progressive disclosure**, an animation process in which bulleted items appear one at a time. This type of animation focuses the audience's attention on each item without the distractions of items that have not been discussed yet. By default, subbullets animate at the same time as their first-level bullets.

Animation effects are grouped into four types:

▶ **Entrance**—Text and objects animate as they appear on the slide; one of the most commonly used animation types.

▶ **Emphasis**—The appearance of text and objects already visible on the slide changes or the text or objects move in place.

▶ **Exit**—Text and objects leave the screen before the slide show advances to the next slide.

▶ **Motion Paths**—Text and objects move following a path on a slide.

Unless you change the behavior, animations occur when you advance the slide show—that is, when you click the screen, or press the Spacebar, the Enter key, or the Right Arrow key. After you apply an animation to an object on a slide, an animation sequence icon appears near the upper-left corner of the object. The number in the icon indicates the order of the animation when you advance the slide show. This means that when

> **progressive disclosure** An animation process in which bulleted items appear one at a time on a slide during a slide show.

Selecting Appropriate Animations

When you choose an animation, keep the purpose of the presentation and the audience in mind. Flashy or flamboyant animations are acceptable for informal, fun-oriented presentations but are not appropriate in formal business, technical, or educational presentations. These types of presentations should be more conservative. Although you want to capture the audience's attention, you should not select an animation that appears frivolous, such as one that makes the text bounce or spin onto the screen.

you display the slide in Slide Show view (or Mini Slide Show view or Reading view), and then you advance the slide show, the item labeled with the number 1 animation sequence icon animates first, and the item labeled with the number 2 animation sequence icon animates second. If an item is labeled with an animation sequence icon containing the number 0 (zero), the default behavior was changed, and that item will animate at the same time as or immediately after the slide transitions onto the screen.

Animating Slide Titles

If you animate a slide title, make sure you consider how it will appear to the audience. You don't want to leave them wondering what type of information the next slide will contain.

 **ACTIVITY**

Animate the slide titles.

1 On the Ribbon, click the **Animations tab**. The animations in the Animation group are grayed out, indicating they are not available. This is because nothing is selected on the slide.

2 In the Slide pane, click anywhere on the **title text** in Slide 2 ("About Our Company"). A dotted line appears around the border of the title text box, and the animations in the Animation group are now available. All of the animations currently visible in the Animation group are entrance animations.

3 In the Animation group, point to the **Fly In button**. Live Preview shows the slide title flying in from the bottom of the slide.

4 In the Animation group, click the **More button** ⊡. The Animation gallery opens. See Exhibit 20-17.

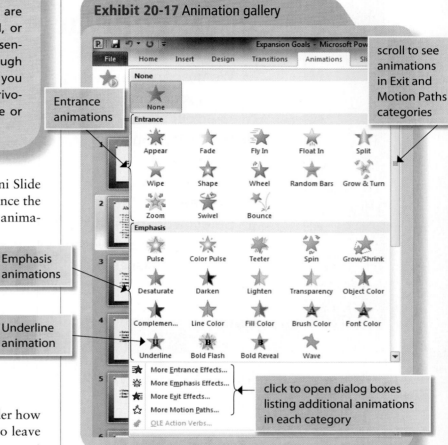

Exhibit 20-17 Animation gallery

5 In the Emphasis section, click the **Underline animation**. The gallery closes and the animation previews in the Slide pane by underlining the slide title from left to right. An animation sequence icon with the number 1 in it appears next to the upper-left corner of the title text box. See Exhibit 20-18.

Tip: You can also click the Add Animation button in the Advanced Animation group to open the Animation gallery.

6 On the Animations tab, in the Preview group, click the **Preview button**. The slide title animates on the slide again.

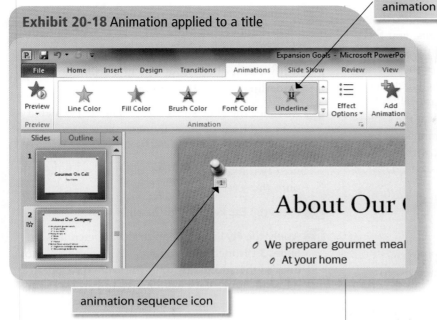

Exhibit 20-18 Animation applied to a title

selected animation

animation sequence icon

---

box, animated with the Underline animation, is active.

2 In the Advanced Animation group, click the **Animation Painter button**. The button changes to orange to indicate that it is selected.

3 Move the pointer onto the slide. The pointer changes to ⌖ indicating that the Animation Painter is active.

4 In the Slides tab, click the **Slide 3 thumbnail**. Slide 3 ("5-Year Goals") appears in the Slide pane.

5 In the Slide pane, click anywhere on the **title text**. The Underline animation copied from the title text on Slide 2 is applied to the title text on Slide 3, and the animation previews in the Slide pane. The Animation Painter button is no longer selected, and the pointer returns to its default shape. The border still appears around the title text indicating that it is selected.

6 On the Animations tab, in the Advanced Animation group, double-click the **Animation Painter button**.

7 Display **Slide 4** ("Advantages") in the Slide pane. In the Slide pane, click the **title text**. The Underline animation is applied to the title text on Slide 4, the Animation Painter button remains selected, and the pointer is still ⌖.

8 Apply the copied animation to the title text on Slide 5.

9 Display **Slide 1** in the Slide pane, and then click the **title text** to apply the Underline animation to the slide title.

10 On the Animations tab, in the Advanced Animation group, click the **Animation Painter button**. The button is deselected, and the pointer returns to its usual shape.

> **Tip:** You can also press the Esc key to turn off the Animation Painter button.

---

7 On the status bar, click the **Slide Show button** 🖵. Slide 2 appears in Slide Show view.

8 Advance the slide show. The animation you applied, the emphasis Underline animation, occurs and the slide title is underlined.

9 Right-click a blank area of the slide. On the shortcut menu, click **End Show**.

Using the Animation Painter

For consistency, you will usually want to apply the same animation to all the slide titles in the presentation. You can display each slide in the Slide pane and repeat the same procedure to apply the same animation to each slide title. You can also use the **Animation Painter** to copy an animation from one object to another. To do so, you click the animated object, click the Animation Painter button in the Advanced Animation group on the Animations tab, click the slide containing the object you want to animate, and then click that object. If you want to copy the animation to multiple objects, double-click the Animation Painter button. You can then click as many objects as you want and the Animation Painter will remain selected and active until you click it again or press the Esc key to turn it off.

 **ACTIVITY**

Use the Animation Painter.

1 In the Slide pane, click anywhere on the **title text** on Slide 2 ("About Our Company"). The title text

---

> **Animation Painter** A tool in PowerPoint that you can use to copy an animation from one object to another.

Animating Bulleted Lists

You can also animate bulleted lists. To do this, you follow the same process as animating the slide titles. When you apply an animation to text, it affects all of the text in the text box. If you animate a bulleted list, each first-level bulleted item appears one at a time. If a first-level bullet has any subbullets, the subbullets will appear at the same time as the first-level bullets. This type of animation focuses the audience's attention on each item, without the distractions of items that haven't been discussed yet.

ACTIVITY

Animate bulleted lists.

1. Display **Slide 2** ("About Our Company") in the Slide pane. Click anywhere in the bulleted list to make the text box active.

2. On the Animations tab, in the Animation group, click the **Fly In animation**. Each first-level bulleted item flies in from the bottom along with its subbullets. The numbered animation sequence icons next to each item indicate the order of the animations. See Exhibit 20-19.

3. On the status bar, click the **Slide Show button** 🖵. Slide 2 appears in Slide Show view with only the slide title visible.

4. Advance the slide show. The first animation—the Underline animation—occurs.

5. Advance the slide show again. The first bulleted item and its subbullets fly onto the screen.

6. Advance the slide show twice more to make the next two first-level bullets and their subbullets fly onto the screen.

7. Press the **Esc key** to end the slide show.

8. Apply the **Fly In animation** to the bulleted lists on **Slides 3** through **6**. On Slide 6 ("Contact Us"), both lines of the address fly in at the same time because the Shift+Enter keys were pressed to create the second line of the address, so it is only one paragraph.

Removing an Animation

As you create a presentation, you might decide to remove an animation. For example, too many animations on a slide can distract an audience rather than enhance your message. If you change your mind and decide that you don't want an object to be animated, you can remove the animation.

Exhibit 20-19 Animation sequence icons for a bulleted list with subbullets

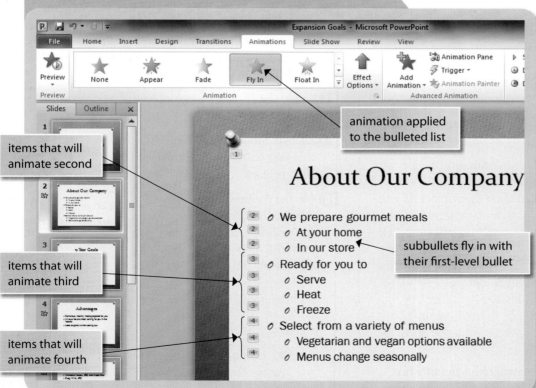

ACTIVITY

Remove an animation.

1. Display **Slide 1** (the title slide) in the Slide pane. In the Slide pane, click the **title text**.

2. On the Animations tab, in the Animation group, click the **More button** ⊡.

3. At the top of the gallery, click the **None animation**. The gallery closes and the Underline animation is removed from the title text on Slide 1.

Modifying the Start Timing of an Animation

When you apply an animation to a bulleted list that contains subbullets, as is the case with Slide 2, the subbullets animate at the same time as their first-level bullet. In some cases, you might want to animate the subbullets individually to emphasize those items as well. You can do this by changing the start timing. First, select the animated bulleted item or object whose start timing you want to change, and then click the Start arrow in the Timing group on the Animations tab to change whether an animation starts when you advance the slide show (On Click), at the same time as when the previous item animates (With Previous), or automatically after the previous item animates (After Previous). The numbers in the animation sequence icons increase by one for each item that is set to animate On Click. When an animation is set to start With Previous or After Previous, the animation sequence number does not increase.

As you have seen, when you preview an animation, it plays automatically on the slide in the Slide pane, even if the timing setting for the animation is On Click. To make sure the timing settings are correct, you should watch the animation in Slide Show or Reading view.

ACTIVITY

Modify the start timing of an animation.

1 Display **Slide 2** ("About Our Company") in the Slide pane.

2 In the first bulleted item, double-click any word to select it. See Exhibit 20-20. On the Animations tab, in the Timing group, On Click appears in the Start box indicating that this item—the first-level

Problem? If you do not see anything in the Start box, you simply clicked in the text of the bulleted item. Be sure to *double-click* a word in the bulleted item to select it.

You cannot use the Animation Painter to copy modified start timings.

Exhibit 20-20 Start timing for the first bullet

first bullet will animate when you advance the slide show

selected text in first bullet

bullet—will animate when you advance through the slide show.

3 Click directly on the first **subbullet icon**. The first subbullet is selected. On the Animations tab, in the Timing group, With Previous appears in the Start box. This means that the selected item will animate with—at the same time as—the previous item.

4 Press and hold the **Ctrl key**, click each of the remaining six **subbullet icons**, and then release the **Ctrl key**. The seven subbullets on Slide 2 are selected, and With Previous appears in the Start box. See Exhibit 20-21.

Problem? If you accidentally click a first-level bullet, keep the Ctrl key pressed, and then click the bullet again to deselect it.

5 On the Animations tab, in the Timing group, click the **Start arrow**. The three choices for starting an animation appear.

Exhibit 20-21 Subbullets set to appear using progressive disclosure

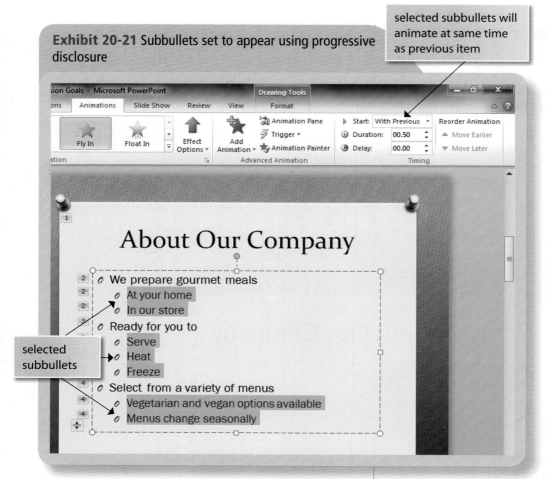

selected subbullets will animate at same time as previous item

selected subbullets

click the Animations tab, and then examine the numbers in the animation sequence icons. Items labeled with lower number animation sequence icons animate before items labeled with higher number animation sequence icons.

To change the animation order, click the animation sequence icon associated with the item whose animation order you want to change. In the Timing group on the Animations tab, click the Move Earlier or Move Later button under the Reorder Animation label. Usually, clicking one of these buttons shifts the animated item one position in the list of animated items. However, in an animated bulleted list, the text box is treated as a single item in the animation order sequence. This helps to ensure that the list animates in a logical sequence. It would be odd, for example, to have a slide appear, then have one bulleted item animate, followed by the slide title, the second bulleted item, and so forth.

6 Click **On Click**. Each subbullet now has a different animation sequence number next to it. This means that each subbullet will animate individually when you advance the slide show.

7 On the status bar, click the **Slide Show button**, and then advance the slide show twice. The Underline animation occurs, and the first first-level bulleted item flies onto the screen.

8 Advance the slide show twice more to animate the two subbullets for the first bulleted item onto the screen.

9 Advance the slide show seven more times to animate the rest of the items from Slide 2 onto the screen.

10 Press the **Esc key** to end the slide show.

Modifying the Order of Animations

If objects on a slide do not animate in the order you expected, you can change the order of the animations. To see the current order, display the slide in the Slide pane,

ACTIVITY

Change the order of animations.

1 Display **Slide 6** ("Contact Us") in the Slide pane. The bulleted list on this slide is animated, but the slide title is not.

2 Click anywhere in the **title text**, and then apply the **Underline animation** (located in the Emphasis section). An animation sequence icon containing the number 4 appears near the left edge of the slide. This means the animation applied to the title is the fourth animation on the slide.

3 On the status bar, click the **Slide Show button**. Slide 6 appears in Slide Show view, and the title is the only object on the slide.

4 Advance the slide show three times. The three bulleted items appear on the slide.

5 Advance the slide show once more. The slide title is underlined. This should be the first animation that occurs on Slide 6.

6 Press the **Esc key** to end the slide show.

7 In the Slide pane, click the **title text animation sequence icon** (which contains the number 4) to select it.

8 On the Animations tab, in the Timing group, click the **Move Earlier button**. The number in the title text animation sequence icon changes to a 1 to indicate that it will animate first.

9 Display **Slide 6** in Slide Show view, and then advance the slide show twice. The slide title is underlined, and then the first bulleted item appears on the slide.

10 End the slide show.

11 Save the presentation.

LO20.5 Adding Transitions

When you move from one slide to another in PowerPoint, the next slide simply appears on the screen in place of the previous slide. To make the slide show more interesting, you can add transitions between slides. A **transition** is a special effect that changes the way a slide appears on the screen in Slide Show or Reading view. You apply transitions in Normal or Slide Sorter view.

As with animations, make sure the transitions you choose are appropriate for the audience and the presentation. In presentations with a formal tone, it's a good idea to apply one type of transition to all of the slides in the presentation. In a presentation designed to really grab the audience, such as a sales presentation, or to entertain them, such as a slide show displaying photos in a photo album, you can use a variety of transitions. Sometimes, presenters apply a different, more interest-

The Dynamic Content transitions in the Transitions Gallery make it appear as if the slide background remains stationary while only the text on the slide transitions.

ing, transition to the last slide in a presentation to signal the audience that the presentation is almost finished.

 **ACTIVITY**

Add transitions to the slides.

1 On the Ribbon, click the **Transitions tab**. In the Transition to This Slide group, click the **Push transition**. The Push transition is applied to the current slide, and you see a preview of the Push transition in the Slide pane.

2 On the Transitions tab, in the Preview group, click the **Preview button**. The transition is again previewed in the Slide pane.

> **Tip:** Clicking the Play Animations button 🌟 below the slide number in the Slides tab displays a preview of both the transition and any animations on the slide.

3 In the Transition to This Slide group, click the **More button** ⊽ to display the gallery of transitions.

4 In the second row in the Exciting section, click the **Switch transition** to apply the Switch transition to the current slide and see a preview.

5 In the Transition to This Slide group, click the **Gallery transition**. The Gallery transition replaces the Switch transition for the current slide, and the new transition previews.

6 On the Transitions tab, in the Timing group, click the **Apply To All button**. The Gallery transition is applied to all of the slides in the presentation.

7 Display **Slide 6** ("Contact Us") in the Slide pane, if it is not already displayed.

8 In the Transition to This Slide group, click the **Flip transition**. The Flip transition is applied only to the current slide, Slide 6, and a preview of the Flip transition appears.

9 Display **Slide 4** ("Advantages") in the Slide pane. On the status bar, click the **Slide Show button** 🖵. Slide 4 transitions onto the screen with the Gallery transition.

> **transition** A special effect that changes the way a slide appears on the screen in Slide Show or Reading view.

10 Advance the slide show five times to animate and display all of the content on Slide 4 and transition to Slide 5 ("Our Team") with the Gallery transition.

11 Advance the slide show five more times to animate and display all of the content on Slide 5 and transition to Slide 6 ("Contact Us") with the Flip transition.

12 End the slide show.

13 Save the presentation.

LO20.6 Adding Speaker Notes

Speaker notes help the speaker remember what to say when a particular slide appears during the presentation. They appear in the Notes pane below the Slide pane in Normal view; they do not appear during the slide show. You can switch to **Notes Page view** to display each slide in the top half of the presentation window and display the speaker notes for that slide in the bottom half. You can also print notes pages with a picture of and notes about each slide.

ACTIVITY

Create a note and view slides in Notes Page view.

1 Display **Slide 3** ("5-Year Goals") in the Slide pane. The placeholder text "Click to add notes" appears in the Notes pane below the Slide pane.

speaker notes Notes that appear in the Notes pane to remind the speaker of points to make when the particular slide appears during the slide show.

Notes Page view The PowerPoint view that displays each slide in the top half of the presentation window and the speaker notes for that slide in the bottom half.

2 Click in the **Notes pane,** and then type **Pass out marketing plan handouts** as the note. See Exhibit 20-22.

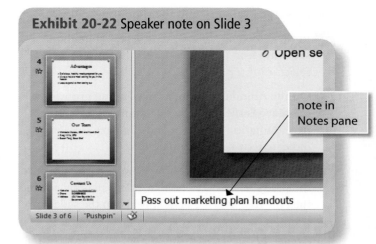

Exhibit 20-22 Speaker note on Slide 3

3 On the Ribbon, click the **View tab.** In the Presentation Views group, click the **Notes Page button.** Slide 3 is displayed in Notes Page view. See Exhibit 20-23.

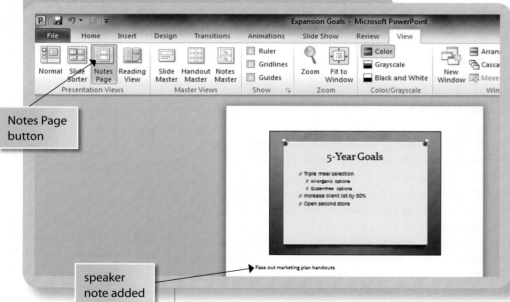

Exhibit 20-23 Slide 3 in Notes Page view

4 At the bottom of the vertical scroll bar, click the **Next Slide button**. Slide 4 ("Advantages") appears in Notes Page view. The notes placeholder appears below the slide

Tip: In Normal view and in Notes Page view, you can also press the Page Up key to move to the previous slide or the Page Down key to move to the next slide.

because this slide does not contain any speaker notes.

5 At the bottom of the vertical scroll bar, click the **Next Slide button** twice to display Slide 6 ("Contact Us"). This slide has a speaker note as well.

6 On the View tab, in the Presentation Views group, click the **Normal button**. Slide 6 appears in the Slide pane in Normal view.

7 Save the presentation.

LO20.7 **Adding Footers and Headers**

In PowerPoint, a **footer** is text that appears on every slide or at the bottom of handouts and notes pages, and a **header** is text that appears at the top of handouts and notes pages in a document. **Handouts** are print-outs of the slides.

When you add a footer to a slide, the same footer is not automatically applied to handouts and notes pages. You must add the footer to notes and handouts separately. Also, depending on the theme applied, the footer on slides might appear somewhere other than the bottom of the slides.

When you insert headers and footers, you can also choose to display the slide or page number and the date. To display the various elements, you select those elements in the Header and Footer dialog box.

Inserting Footers, Slide Numbers, and the Date on Slides

To add a footer, the slide number, and the date to slides, you need to open the Slide tab on the Header and Footer dialog box by clicking the Header & Footer button in the Text group on the Insert tab. When you add this information, you can choose to add it only to the current slide or to all the slides. Because title slides don't usually have footers on them, you can select an option to hide the footer on the title slide. There is also a Preview area in the dialog box that shows where the footer, slide number, and date will appear on the slide.

ACTIVITY

Insert footers, slide numbers, and the date on slides.

1 On the Ribbon, click the **Insert tab**. In the Text group, click the **Header & Footer button**. The Header and Footer dialog box opens with the Slide tab on top. In the lower-right corner of the dialog box, the Preview box shows a preview slide with rectangles that identify where the footer, date, and slide number will appear. Their exact positions change depending on the current theme. See Exhibit 20-24.

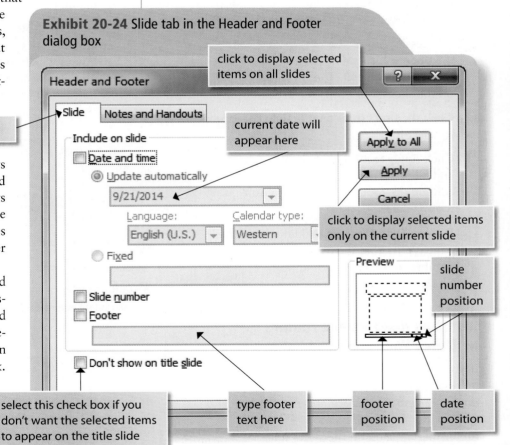

Exhibit 20-24 Slide tab in the Header and Footer dialog box

footer **In PowerPoint, text that appears at the bottom of every slide or at the bottom of handouts and notes pages.**

header **In PowerPoint, text that appears at the top of handouts and notes pages in a document.**

handout **A printout of the slides in a presentation.**

2 Click the **Footer check box** to select it. In the Preview box, the left rectangle turns black to indicate that the footer will appear on the slides. The insertion point is blinking in the Footer box.

3 In the Footer box, type **Gourmet On Call**.

4 Click the **Slide number check box** to select it. The right rectangle in the Preview box turns black to indicate that the slide number will appear in this location on each slide.

5 Click the **Date and time check box**. The center rectangle in the Preview box turns black, and the options under this check box darken so you can choose one of them.

> **Tip:** To have a specific date always appear on the slides, select the Fixed option button on the Slide tab in the Header and Footer dialog box, and then type a date in the Fixed box.

6 If necessary, click the **Update automatically option button**. The current date will appear on the slides every time the presentation is opened.

7 Click the **Don't show on title slide check box** to select it.

8 Click **Apply to All**. The dialog box closes and all the slides except the title slide contain the footer, slide number, and today's date.

9 Display **Slide 1** (the title slide) in the Slide pane. Verify that the footer, slide number, and date do not appear on the slide.

Inserting Headers and Footers on Notes Pages and Handouts

If you plan to print notes for your reference or distribute handouts to the audience, you might want to add information to the header and footer in these printouts. The footer that appears on the slides does not appear on the notes pages or the handouts. You need to open the Notes and Handouts tab in the Header and Footer dialog box to set the options for both headers and footers on notes and handouts. The page number appears in the footer of notes and handouts by default.

To insert footers or headers on all slides except the title slide, any slide other than Slide 1 must be displayed in the Slide pane.

ACTIVITY

Add a header and footer to the notes pages and handouts.

1 Display **Slide 2** ("About Our Company") in the Slide pane.

2 On the Insert tab, in the Text group, click the **Header & Footer button**. The Header and Footer dialog box opens with the Slide tab on top.

3 Click the **Notes and Handouts tab**. Unlike the Slide tab, this tab contains a Header check box and a box in which to type a header as well as a Page number check box that is selected by default. See Exhibit 20-25.

Exhibit 20-25 Notes and Handouts tab in the Header and Footer dialog box

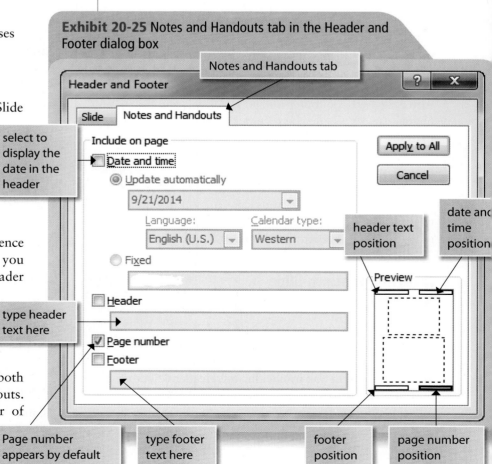

4 Click the **Header check box** to select it. A thick border appears around the placeholder in the upper-left corner of the Preview. That is where the header will appear.

5 In the Header box, type **Business Expansion Plans**.

6 Click the **Footer check box**, and then in the Footer box, type **Presentation to Investors**.

7 Click **Apply to All**. The dialog box closes, and all notes pages and handouts that you print will now contain the header and footer you typed, as well as the page number in the footer.

8 Save the presentation.

LO20.8 Reviewing, Previewing, and Printing a Presentation

After you complete your presentation, you should always check the spelling in your presentation, proofread it, and view it in Slide Show or Reading view to make sure everything works as expected.

Checking and Reviewing a Presentation

You should always check the spelling in a presentation and proofread it for errors. Using the spell checker in PowerPoint is similar to using the spell checker in Word—click the Spelling button, examine any flagged words, and decide whether to change the word or ignore the suggested correction.

After you check the spelling, you should run the slide show to verify that all of your animations and transitions work as you expect, and to review the contents of each slide.

ACTIVITY

Check and review the presentation.

1 On the Ribbon, click the **Review tab**. In the Proofing group, click the **Spelling button**.

2 If there are spelling errors, the Spelling dialog box opens. In that case, decide how to handle each word that is flagged because it was not found in the PowerPoint dictionary, just as you would in a Word document. If there aren't any spelling errors, or after you correct all the spelling errors, a dialog box opens telling you that the spelling check is complete.

3 Click **OK**.

4 Display **Slide 1** (the title slide) in the Slide pane. On the status bar, click the **Slide Show button**. The slide show starts in Slide Show view.

5 Advance through the slide show. If you see any problems while you are watching the slide show, press the **Esc key** to exit the slide show and return to Normal view, make the necessary corrections, and then return to Slide Show view.

Are Handouts Necessary?

Before taking the time to create handouts for a presentation, consider when to provide the audience with handouts and whether the audience will find value in having them. Many speakers provide printed copies of their presentation slides to the audience at the beginning of their presentation. This usually reduces the need for the audience to take notes on each slide as it's presented. However, sometimes the audience starts to read the handouts as soon as they are distributed, getting ahead of the speaker. The audience may also stop listening to the speaker because they are focused more intently on the printed text. And as they turn the pages, the rustle of paper can be distracting to the speaker and other audience members. To avoid this problem, first decide if handouts are truly necessary. If they are, consider providing handouts at the end of your presentation instead of before your presentation. If you need to provide a hand- out designed to support a specific part of your presentation, wait and distribute this handout when you get to that point.

Exhibit 20-26 Completed presentation in Slide Sorter view

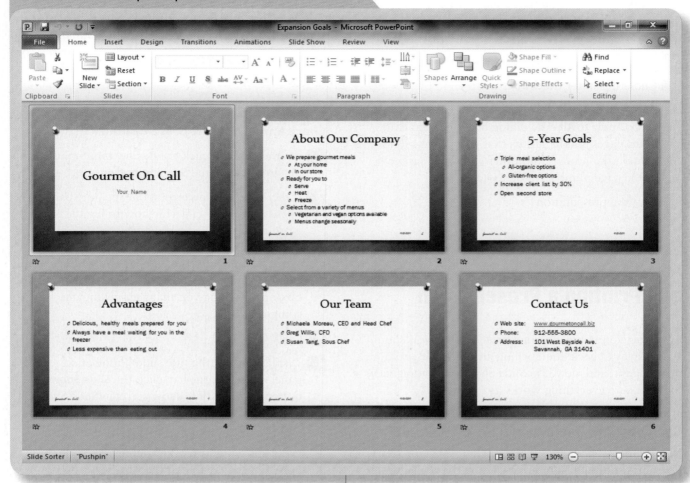

6 Switch to **Slide Sorter view**. Change the zoom level to **130% zoom** so that the slide thumbnails are as large as possible but still all appear within the Slide Sorter window. Compare your presentation to Exhibit 20-26.

7 Save the presentation.

Opening the Print Tab

PowerPoint provides several ways to print the slides in your presentation. You access the print options from the Print tab in Backstage view. See Exhibit 20-27. In the Settings section, you can click the Full Page Slides button to choose from the following options for printing the presentation:

▶ **Full Page Slides**—Prints each slide full size on a separate piece of paper; speaker notes are not printed.

▶ **Notes Pages**—Prints each slide as a notes page, with the slide at the top of the page and speaker notes below the slide, similar to how a slide appears in Notes Page view.

▶ **Outline**—Prints the text of the presentation as an outline.

▶ **Handouts**—Prints the presentation with one, two, three, four, six, or nine slides on each piece of paper. When printing three slides per page, the slides appear down the left side of the page and lines for notes appear to the right of each slide. When printing four, six, or nine slides, you can choose whether to order the slides from left to right in rows (horizontally) or from top to bottom in columns (vertically).

You can also click the Print All Slides button to specify whether you will print all the slides, selected slides, the current slide, or a custom range. Custom

Exhibit 20-27 Print tab in Backstage view

Print button

click to change which slides print

type slide numbers of specific slides to print

click to change what is printed

click to print slides in grayscale or black and white

change this value to number of copies to print

Print

Copies: 1

Print

Printer

HP Photosmart C5500 series
Error: 1 document waiting

Printer Properties

Settings

Print All Slides
Print entire presentation

Slides:

Full Page Slides
Print 1 slide per page

Collated
1,2,3 1,2,3 1,2,3

Color

Edit Header & Footer

Gourmet On Call

Your Name

preview

1 of 6   53%

current slide

Next Page button

Range is selected automatically if you click in the Slides box and type the slide numbers of the slides you want to print. If the slides you want to print are sequential, type the first and last slide numbers separated by a hyphen. If the slides you want to print are not sequential, type the slide numbers separated by commas.

A preview of the presentation using the print options you select appears on the right side of the Print tab. You can click the Next Page ▶ and Previous Page ◀ buttons at the bottom of the preview to scroll from page to page, or you can drag the scroll bar.

ACTIVITY

Open the Print tab in Backstage view.

1 On the Ribbon, click the **File tab**. Backstage view appears.

2 In the navigation bar, click **Print**. The Print tab appears in Backstage view. The Print tab contains options for printing the presentation, and a preview of the first slide or page as it will print with the currently selected options. Refer to Exhibit 20-27.

Printing Full Page Slides

The default option for printing a presentation is to print all the slides as full page slides, one slide per page.

ACTIVITY

Print the title slide as a full page slide.

1 If the second button in the Settings section is not labeled "Full Page Slides," click it, and then click **Full Page Slides**.

Choosing Color Options

You can choose whether to print a presentation in color, grayscale, or black and white. Obviously, if your computer is connected to a black and white printer, the presentation will print in black and white or grayscale even if Color is selected in the bottom button in the Settings section. If you plan to print in black and white or grayscale, you should change this setting so you can see what the slides will look like without color and to make sure they are legible. You can do this using the View tab on the Ribbon or the Print tab in Backstage view. To do this from the View tab on the Ribbon, in the Color/Grayscale group, click the Grayscale or Black and White button. To do this from the Print tab in Backstage view, click the Color button, and then click Grayscale or Pure Black and White. The preview will change to show the presentation in grayscale or black and white.

2 In the Settings section, click the **Print All Slides button**. You can print all the slides, selected slides, the current slide, or a custom range. In this case, you want to print just the title slide as a full page slide, not all six slides.

3 Click **Custom Range**. The menu closes and the insertion point is blinking in the Slides box. The preview now is blank and the page number information at the bottom shows 0 of 0.

4 In the Slides box, type **1**.

5 In the preview pane, click anywhere. Slide 1 (the title slide) appears in the preview pane, and the page number information indicates that you are viewing a preview of page 1 of a total of 1 page to print.

6 At the top of the Print section, click the **Print button**. Backstage view closes and Slide 1 prints.

Printing Handouts

If you print a presentation as handouts, you can fit multiple slides on a page. When you choose 1 Slide in the Handouts section, the slide prints in the middle of the page with space around it for note taking.

 **ACTIVITY**

Print handouts.

1 On the Ribbon, click the **File tab**. In the navigation bar, click **Print**.

2 In the Settings section, click the **Full Page Slides button**. A menu opens with choices for printing the presentation. At the bottom of the menu, Frame Slides does not have a check mark next to it because the default for Full Page Slides, the currently selected option, is to not frame the slides on the page. See Exhibit 20-28.

> **Tip:** To print full page slides with a border around them, click the Full Page Slides button in the Settings section, and then click Frame Slides.

click to print presentation as notes pages

Exhibit 20-28 Print options menu on the Print tab

click to print presentation as full page slides

options for printing handouts

click to print presentation as an outline

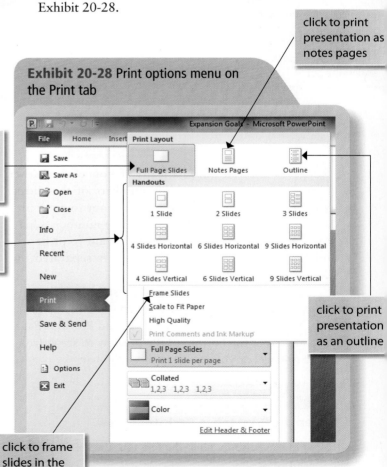

click to frame slides in the printout

3 In the Handouts section, click **6 Slides Horizontal**. The preview changes to show Slide 1 smaller and in the upper-left corner of the page.

4 In the Settings section, click the **6 Slides Horizontal button**. The Frame Slides command now has a check mark next to it because the default for handouts is to frame the slides. You can click this command at any time to toggle it on or off.

5 Click a blank area of the screen to close the open menu.

6 Below the Custom Range button, click in the **Slides box**, and then press the **Delete** or **Backspace key** to delete the 1. The button above the Slides box changes from Custom Range to Print All Slides, and all six slides appear on the page in the preview, arranged in order in three rows from left to right.

7 At the top of the Print section, click the **Print button**. Backstage view closes and the handout prints.

Printing Notes Pages

You can print the slides as notes pages to include any speaker notes. Click the second button under Settings, and then click Notes Pages. Then you can scroll through the preview to see which slides contain notes. If you want to print only the slides that contain notes, click in the Slides box, and then type the slide numbers.

ACTIVITY

Print slides containing speaker notes.

1 Open the **Print tab** in Backstage view.

2 In the Settings section, click the **6 Slides Horizontal button**. The button is labeled "6 Slides Horizontal," one of the options for printing handouts, because that was the last printing option selected.

> **Tip:** If you select 3 Slides to print handouts as three slides per page, the slides print with horizontal lines to the right of each slide to make it easier for someone to take notes.

3 In the Print Layout section of the menu, click **Notes Pages**. The menu closes and the preview shows Slide 1 as a notes page. You will verify that Slides 3 and 6 contain speaker notes.

4 Below the preview, click the **Next Page button** ▶ twice to display Slide 3 ("5-Year Goals") in the preview, and then click the **Next Page button** ▶ three more times to display Slide 6 ("Contact Us"). These slides contain speaker notes.

5 In the Settings section, click in the **Slides box**, type **3,6** to specify the slides to print, and then click a blank area of the Print tab. Only the two specified pages will print.

6 Scroll through the preview to confirm that Slides 3 and 6 will print.

7 Click the **Print button**. Slides 3 and 6 print as notes pages.

Printing the Presentation as an Outline

You can also print the presentation as an outline. The printout matches the text you see in the Outline tab in Normal view.

ACTIVITY

Print the presentation as an outline.

1 Open the **Print tab** in Backstage view.

2 In the Settings section, click the **Notes Pages button**, and then click **Outline**. Slides 3 and 6 appear as an outline in the preview pane.

3 Click the **Custom Range button**, and then click **Print All Slides**. The entire outline appears in the preview.

> **Tip:** If an outline is a bit longer than one page, you can click the Outline button, and then click Scale to Fit Paper to try to force the outline to fit on one page.

4 At the top of the Print section, click the **Print button**. Backstage view closes and the outline prints.

5 Close the presentation.

1. What is the name of the view that displays the slide thumbnails or presentation outline in a tab on the left, the slides in a Slide pane, and speaker notes below the Slide pane?

2. What is a placeholder?

3. What is a text box?

4. What is a layout?

5. What does AutoFit do?

6. What happens when you demote a slide title one level?

7. Describe Reading view.

8. Describe Mini Slide Show view.

9. What is a transition?

10. Define progressive disclosure.

11. When you add a footer and slide number to slides, how do you prevent them from appearing on the title slide?

12. How do you create speaker notes?

13. What are the four ways you can print the content of a presentation?

Practice It

Practice It 20-1

1. Start PowerPoint, and then save the new, blank presentation as **Bookstore Plan**.

2. In Slide 1, add the title **Best Books**, and add your name as the subtitle.

3. Add a new Slide 2 using the Title and Content layout.

4. Add the slide title **A Bookstore for Booklovers** and then add the following first-level bulleted items:

   Independent bookseller
   Skilled staff
   Events

5. Below the Events bullet item, add the following second-level bulleted items:

   Book clubs
   Author signings
   Book launch parties

6. Add a new Slide 3 using the Comparison layout, and then add the slide title **Contact Us**.

7. Change the layout of Slide 3 ("Contact Us") to Title and Content.

8. In the content placeholder on Slide 3, add the first-level bulleted item **Address**, add a second-level bulleted item **3891 Elm St.**, and then add **Philadelphia, PA 19107** on a new line without creating a new subbullet.

9. Save the presentation, and then close it. Open the data file **Bookstore** located in the Chapter 20\Practice It folder. Save the presentation as **Bookstore Growth**.

10. Display Slide 6 ("A Bookstore for Booklovers"). Below "Skilled staff," add the following second-level bulleted items, allowing the text to AutoFit in the text box:

    Genre specialists
    Invested in the community

11. Change the theme of the presentation to the Paper theme.

12. Display the Outline tab. In the Outline tab on Slide 6, add **New Ideas** as a new, first-level bulleted item as the fourth first-level bulleted item on the slide.

13. On Slide 6, drag the last bulleted item, "Staff Picks" lists, up so it appears above the Add pastries to coffee shop bulleted item.

14. In the Outline tab, on Slide 6, promote the New Ideas bulleted item so it becomes a new Slide 7.

15. In the Outline tab, on Slide 4 ("Time for a New Store"), under the Sales have risen steadily first-level bulleted item, demote the At least 10% increase each quarter bulleted item to a subbullet. If necessary, promote the Marked increase after coffee shop opened bulleted item to a second-level bulleted item.

16. Rearrange the slides so that Slide 2 ("About Us") becomes Slide 6, Slide 5 ("A Bookstore for Booklovers") becomes Slide 2, Slide 3 ("Contact Us") becomes Slide 6, and Slide 7 ("New Ideas") becomes Slide 5.

17. Delete Slide 4 ("Celebrate with Us!").

18. On Slide 2 ("A Bookstore for Booklovers"), animate the slide title using the Bold Reveal animation in the Emphasis category.

19. Use the Animation Painter to apply the animation applied to the title text on Slide 2 to the titles on Slides 3 through 6 and then to the title text on Slide 1.

20. On Slides 2 through 6, apply the Wipe animation in the Entrance category to the bulleted lists.

21. On Slide 2 ("A Bookstore for Booklovers") and Slide 3 ("Time for a New Store"), modify the start timing of the subbullets animation to start On Click.

22. Apply the Pan transition in the Dynamic Content category to all of the slides. Apply the Zoom transition in the Exciting category to only Slide 6 ("Contact Us").

23. On Slide 4 ("New Ideas"), add **Explain that we solicited ideas from both staff and customers.** as a speaker note. On Slide 6 ("Contact Us"), add **Mention that the Web site is being redesigned.** as a speaker note.

24. Add the footer **Best Books New Store Proposal** to all the slides except the title slide, and then display the current date and the slide number on all the slides except the title slide.

25. On the notes and handouts, add **Best Books** as a header and **New Store Presentation** as a footer.

26. Check the spelling in the presentation, making any corrections necessary. Review each slide in the presentation.

27. View the entire slide show in Slide Show, Mini Slide Show, or Reading view. Make sure the animations and transitions work as you expect, and look carefully at each slide and check the content. If you see any errors or formatting problems, press the Esc key to end the slide show, fix the error, and then start the slide show again from the current slide.

28. Save the presentation. Print the title slide as a full page slide. Print the entire presentation as handouts, 6 slides per page, and as an outline. Print Slides 4 and 6 as notes pages.

29. Close the presentation.

Practice It 20-2

1. Open the data file **Customer** located in the Chapter 20\Practice It folder. Save the presentation as **Customer Presentation**.

2. In the title slide, add **OfficePro** as the title, press the Enter key, and then type **Cleaning Specialists**. The title text AutoFits to the title text box. Add your name as the subtitle.

3. Delete Slide 3 ("Our Cleaning Staff").

4. Move Slide 6 ("Weekly Services") so it becomes Slide 3.

5. On Slide 3 ("Weekly Services"), at the end of the bulleted list, add **Stair and elevator cleaning** as a new first-level bulleted item.

6. On Slide 3, add **Remember to pause for questions from the audience.** as the speaker note.

7. On Slide 2 ("Daily Services"), at the end of the bulleted list, add **Restroom cleaning and disinfecting** as a new first-level bulleted item.

8. In Outline view, on Slide 4 ("Specialized Services"), move the "Pressure washing" and "Carpet cleaning" bulleted items so that they appear below "Stripping and refinishing" and above "Air condition vent cleaning."

9. On Slide 2 ("Daily Services"), in the second first-level bulleted item, make the word *Sinks* a new first-level bullet.

10. On Slide 2 ("Daily Services"), demote the bulleted items "Sinks" and "Toasters" to second-level bullets so that four second-level bulleted items now appear under "Kitchen and lounge area cleaning including."

11. Animate the slide titles for all the slides with the Darken animation in the Emphasis category.

12. Remove the animation from the title on the title slide.

13. Animate all of the bulleted lists with the Shape animation in the Entrance category using progressive disclosure for all bullet levels. Do not animate the text in the content text box on Slide 6 ("For More Information").

14. On Slide 6 ("For More Information"), animate the content text box using the Fly In animation in the Entrance category.

15. Add the Push transition to all of the slides, and then remove it from the title slide.

16. Display the footer text **Presentation for New Clients** as well as the slide number and the current date on all of the slides except the title slide.

17. Check the spelling throughout the presentation. Change misspelled words to the correct spelling, and ignore any words (such as proper names) that are spelled correctly but are not in the built-in dictionary.

18. View the slide show. If you see any errors, press the Esc key to end the slide show, correct the error, and then start the slide show again from the current slide. Save your changes.

19. Preview the presentation in grayscale, and then in pure black and white. If you have a color printer, switch back to color so the presentation will print in color.

20. Print the title slide as a full page slide, print Slides 2 through 6 as a handout with six slides per page arranged vertically, and then print Slide 3 as a notes page.

21. Close the presentation.

On Your Own

On Your Own 20-1

1. Open the data file **Sales** located in the Chapter 20\On Your Own folder. Save the presentation as **Sales Presentation**.

2. In the title slide, add **Mike's Mini Golf and More** as the presentation title, and then add your name as the subtitle.

3. Change the theme to the Elemental theme. Change the theme fonts to the Angles theme fonts. (*Hint*: The Fonts button is on the Design tab.)

4. On Slide 2 ("Price Packages"), add **Mention that these packages can be customized.** as the speaker note.

5. On Slide 3 ("Mini Golf"), add **Variety of pitch speeds** as the fourth subbulleted item under "Batting Cages."

6. On Slide 2 ("Price Packages"), move the Birthday Basics bulleted item and its subbullets to be the first bulleted item.

7. On Slide 2, change the last three bulleted items into subbulleted items under The Fundraiser bulleted item.

8. On Slide 3 ("Mini Golf"), promote the Batting Cages bulleted item so it becomes a new Slide 4 and its four subbullets become first-level bullets.

9. On Slide 6 ("Arcade"), promote the Current Classics subbulleted item so it becomes a first-level bulleted item with three subbulleted items.

10. Move Slide 5 ("Customer Comments") so that it becomes Slide 6.

11. Add a new Slide 6 using the Title and Content layout with the slide title **Go Carts** and the following three first-level bulleted items:

    Two tracks
    Helmets provided
    Minimum age: 13

12. Under the Two tracks bulleted item, add the following subbullets:

    Twist and Turn—lots of curves
    Slick—go really fast

13. Animate the bulleted lists on Slides 2 through 7 using the Zoom animation. Do not use progressive disclosure for subbullets.

14. Add the Dissolve transition to Slide 1 (the title slide), add the Vortex transition to Slide 8 ("Contact Us"), and add the Gallery transition to the rest of the slides (Slides 2 through 7).

15. Apply a sound of your choice to the transitions on Slides 2 through 7. (*Hint*: Use the Sound button in the Timing group on the Transitions tab.)

16. Display the slide number and current date on all slides, including the title slide. Add your name as a header on the notes and handouts.

17. Check the spelling in the presentation. Correct any spelling errors and ignore any words that are spelled correctly.

18. View the slide show. If you see any errors, press the Esc key to end the slide show, correct the error, and then start the slide show again from the current slide. Save the presentation.

19. Preview the presentation in grayscale, and then in pure black and white. If you have a color printer, switch back so the presentation will print in color.

20. Print the presentation as handouts with four slides per page arranged horizontally. Print Slide 2 ("Price Packages") as a notes page. Print the presentation outline on one page. (If the outline does not fit on one page even after selecting Scale to Fit Paper, print it on two pages.)

21. Close the presentation.

ADDITIONAL STUDY TOOLS

Chapter 20

IN THE BOOK

▶ Complete end-of-chapter exercises

▶ Study tear-out Chapter Review Card

ONLINE

▶ Complete additional end-of-chapter exercises

▶ Take practice quiz to prepare for tests

▶ Review key term flash cards (online, printable, and audio)

▶ Play "Beat the Clock" and "Memory" to quiz yourself

▶ Watch the videos "Add Text to Text Placeholders," "Create New Slides and Change the Layout," "Change the Theme," "Modify Text in the Outline Tab," "Animate the Slide Titles," "Add Transitions to the Slides," and more

Enhancing a Presentation

Introduction

We live in a highly visual society. Most people are exposed to multi-media daily and expect to have information conveyed visually as well as verbally. In many cases, a graphic is more effective than words for communicating an important point. For example, if a sales force has reached its sales goals for the year, a graphic of a person summiting a mountain can convey a sense of exhilaration.

PowerPoint allows you to incorporate many types of graphics and multimedia in slide shows. You can insert tables and charts, clip art and pictures stored on a computer or network, and video and music. You can use animation to make the slides come alive with movement. Judicious use of graphics and multimedia elements can clarify a point for audience members and help them remember it later. Of course, the audience needs to see a slide show to appreciate the graphic content. The Broadcast feature in PowerPoint allows you to deliver a slide show live over the Internet to anyone with a browser.

Learning Objectives

After studying the material in this chapter, you will be able to:

LO21.1 Work with slide masters

LO21.2 Insert graphics

LO21.3 Create SmartArt diagrams

LO21.4 Customize animations by changing options

LO21.5 Add video to a slide

LO21.6 Add sound to a presentation

LO21.7 Broadcast a presentation

LO21.1 Working with Slide Masters

The **slide master** stores theme fonts, colors, elements, and styles, as well as text and other objects that appear on all the slides in the presentation. Slide masters ensure that all the slides in the presentation have a similar appearance and contain the same elements. A slide master is associated with a theme. The **theme Slide Master** is the primary slide master, and text, graphics, and formatting on the theme Slide Master appear on all slides in the presentation. Changes made to the theme Slide Master affect all of the slides in the presentation. Each theme Slide Master has an associated **layout master** for each layout in the presentation. If you modify a layout master, the changes affect only slides that

slide master A slide that contains theme elements and styles, as well as text and other objects that appear on the slides in the presentation.

theme Slide Master The primary slide master for a presentation.

layout master A slide master for a specific layout in a presentation.

iofoto/Shutterstock.com

A well-designed slide show is only part of the presentation; an enthusiastic, knowledgeable, well-rehearsed speaker will engage an audience and bring the slides to life.

have that layout applied. For example, the Title Slide Layout master is used by slides with the Title Slide Layout applied, and the Title and Content Layout master is used by slides with the Title and Content Layout applied.

You can modify slide masters by changing the size and design of text in the content placeholders, adding or deleting graphics, changing the background, and making other modifications.

Rehearsing Your Presentation

Unless you create a presentation for a kiosk that is intended for a user to watch without a presenter, the content of a slide show is only one part of a presentation. The other part is you—the presenter. Presenters who try to stand up and "wing it" in front of a crowd usually reveal this amateur approach the moment they start speaking—by looking down at their notes, rambling off topic, or turning their back on the audience to read from the slides displayed on the screen.

To avoid being seen as an amateur, you need to rehearse your presentation. Even the most knowledgeable speakers rehearse to ensure they know how the topic flows, what the main points are, how much time to spend on each slide, and where to place emphasis. Experienced presenters understand that while practice may not make them perfect, it will certainly make them better.

Where you practice isn't that important. You can talk to a mirror, your family, or a group of friends. If you have a video camera, you can record yourself and then review the video. Watching video evidence of your performance often reveals the weaknesses you don't want the audience to see and that your friends or family may be unwilling or unable to identify. Whatever you choose to do, the bottom line is this: If you practice, you will improve.

As you rehearse, you should remember to focus on the following steps:

▶ **Practice speaking fluently.** Be sure to speak in an easy, smooth manner, and avoid using nonwords and fillers. Nonwords consist of *ums*, *ahs*, *hms*, and other such breaks in speech. Fillers are phrases that don't add any value yet add length to sentences, such as *like* or *you know*. Both can dilute a speaker's message because they are not essential to the meaning of what's being spoken. At best, they can make you sound unprofessional. At worst, they can distract the audience and make your message incomprehensible.

▶ **Work on your tone of voice.** When delivering a presentation, you usually want to speak passionately, with authority, and with a smile. If you aren't excited about your presentation, how will your audience feel? By using your voice to project energy, passion, and confidence, your audience will automatically pay more attention to you. Smile and look directly at audience members and make eye contact. If your message is getting across, they will instinctively affirm what you are saying by returning your gaze, nodding

their heads, or smiling. There is something compelling about a confident speaker whose presence commands attention. However, be careful not to overdo it. Speaking too loudly or using an overly confident or arrogant tone will quickly turn off an audience and make them stop listening altogether.

▶ **Decide how to involve the audience.** If you involve audience members in your presentation, they will pay closer attention to what you have to say. When an audience member asks a question, be sure to affirm him or her before answering. For example, you could respond with "That's a great question. What do the rest of you think?" or "Thanks for asking. Here's what my research revealed." An easy way to get the audience to participate is to start with a question and invite responses, or to stop partway through to discuss a particularly important point. Also, remember to repeat the question to the audience in case other audience members were not able to hear the original question.

▶ **Be aware of your body language.** Although the content of your presentation plays a role in your message delivery, it is your voice and body language during the presentation that make or break it. Maintain eye contact to send the message that you want to connect and that you can be trusted. Stand up straight to signal confidence. Conversely, avoid slouching (which can convey laziness, lack of energy, or disinterest) and fidgeting or touching your hair (which can signal nervousness.) Resist the temptation to glance at your watch; you don't want to send a signal that you'd rather be someplace else. Finally, be aware of your hand movements. The best position for your hands is to place them comfortably by your side, in a relaxed position. As you talk, it's fine to use hand gestures to help make a point, but be careful not to overdo it.

▶ **Check your appearance.** Just as a professional appearance makes a good impression during a job interview, an audience's first impression of a speaker is also based on appearance. Before a single word is spoken, the audience sizes up the way the presenter looks. You want to make sure you look professional and competent. Make sure your appearance is neat, clean, and well coordinated, and that you dress in appropriate clothing.

Exhibit 21-1 Title and Content layout applied to Slide 2

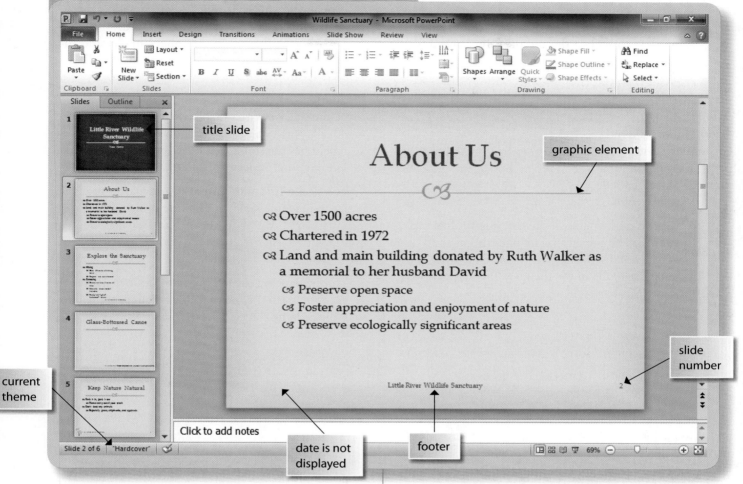

Working in Slide Master View

To view the slide masters, you need to switch to **Slide Master view**. In Slide Master view, the largest thumbnail in the pane on the left is the slide master associated with the current theme.

 **ACTIVITY**

Work in Slide Master view.

1. Open the data file **Wildlife** located in the Chapter 21\ Chapter folder. Add your name as the subtitle. Save the file as **Wildlife Sanctuary**. The theme applied to this presentation is the Hardcover theme. Notice the various elements on the title slide.

2. Display **Slide 2** ("About Us") in the Slide pane. This slide has the Title and Content layout applied. A graphic appears below the title placeholder. At the bottom of the slide, the footer is displayed in the center and the slide number is displayed on the right. The date is not displayed. See Exhibit 21-1.

Handouts and Notes Masters

In addition to the slide masters, each presentation has a **handouts master** that contains the elements that appear on all the printed handouts, and a **notes master** that contains the elements that appear on the notes pages. To display these masters, click the appropriate buttons in the Master Views group on the View tab.

> **Slide Master view** The PowerPoint view that displays the slide masters.
>
> **handouts master** A master that contains the elements that appear on printed handouts.
>
> **notes master** A master that contains the elements that appear on the notes pages.

3 Display **Slide 3** ("Explore the Sanctuary") in the Slide pane. This slide has the Two Content layout applied. The same graphic that appeared in Slide 2 appears below the title, and the footer and slide number appear on this slide as well.

4 On the Ribbon, click the **View tab**. In the Master Views group, click the **Slide Master button**. The presentation is displayed in Slide Master view.

> ➤ **Tip:** You can also press and hold the Shift key and click the Normal button on the status bar to switch to Slide Master view.

5 At the top of the pane on the left, point to the **top thumbnail**. The ScreenTip identifies this as the Hardcover Slide Master. The theme Slide Master includes the name of the theme as the first part of the Slide Master name.

6 Click the **Hardcover Slide Master**. The Hardcover Slide Master appears in the Slide pane. The Hardcover Slide Master contains a title text placeholder, a content placeholder, and the Date, Footer, and Slide Number placeholders. See Exhibit 21-2.

7 In the pane on the left, point to the **Title and Content Layout master**. The ScreenTip not only displays the name of the layout master, it also identifies the slides that have this layout applied—in this case, Slides 2, 5, and 6.

8 Click the **Title and Content Layout master** to display it in the Slide pane. In addition to the elements on the Hardcover Slide Master, the Title and Content Layout master includes the graphic you saw in Normal view below the title placeholder.

9 In the pane on the left, point to the **Two Content Layout master**. Note that this layout is applied to Slides 3 and 4.

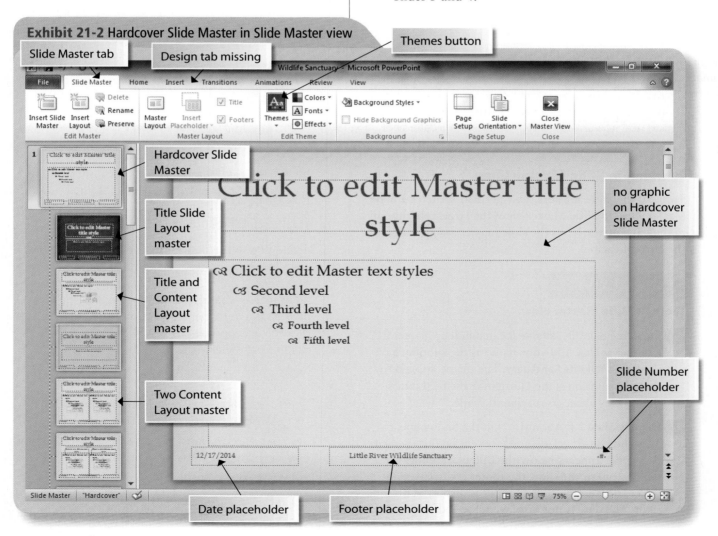

Exhibit 21-2 Hardcover Slide Master in Slide Master view

Adding Placeholders and Creating a Custom Layout

Insert Placeholder

- Content
- Text
- Picture
- Chart
- Table
- SmartArt
- Media
- Clip Art

Although each theme comes with nine layouts, you might find that none of them meets your needs. You already know how to customize an existing layout by resizing, moving, and deleting the placeholders. In addition, you can add placeholders to an existing layout master or you can create a completely new layout master.

To insert a new placeholder, switch to Slide Master view. Click the Insert Placeholder button arrow in the Master Layout group on the Slide Master tab, select a placeholder type, and then click or drag on the slide, similar to creating a text box.

To create a new layout master, click the Insert Layout button in the Edit Master group on the Slide Master tab. A new layout identical to the Title Only Layout master is created. To create a custom layout that doesn't include any of the elements of the current slide master, click the Insert Slide Master button instead of the Insert Layout button. When you create a new layout, the default name is *Custom Layout Layout*. To change the name of the new layout, right-click it, and then click Rename Layout on the shortcut menu. In Normal view, the new layout will be available on the New Slide button menu and on the Layout button menu.

10 Click the **Two Content Layout master**. This layout master includes the same graphic between the title and content placeholders that is on the Title and Content Layout master.

11 In the pane on the left, click the **Title Slide Layout master**. The Title Slide Layout master appears in the Slide pane. On the Title Slide Layout master, the title is in a different position than on the other layout masters, and the font color is different. Also, the slide background is different and a border graphic appears around the edge of the slide in addition to the graphic in the middle of the slide.

Modifying Elements in the Slide Master

You already know how to modify the look of documents, worksheets, database forms and reports, and presentations by applying a different theme and changing the theme colors and fonts. If you want to make additional changes to the overall look of slides, it is a good idea to make this type of change in the slide masters rather than on the individual slides. For example, if you want to change the color of bullets in bulleted lists or add a graphic to every slide in a presentation, you should do this in the slide master to keep the look of the slides in the presentation consistent.

Modifying Text Placeholders in the Slide Master

You can adjust the size and position of text placeholders on slides, just as you would an ordinary text box. You can also delete placeholders if you want. Again, to keep the look of your slides consistent, you should make this type of adjustment in the slide master.

ACTIVITY

Modify text placeholders in the Slide Master.

1 In the pane on the left, click the **Hardcover Slide Master**.

2 At the bottom of the Slide pane, click the **Date placeholder border**, and then position the pointer on the selected border. The pointer changes to ⁺↕⁺.

3 Drag the **Date placeholder** to position it above the Footer placeholder.

4 Select the **Footer placeholder**, and then drag it to the left until the left edge is aligned with the left edge of the content placeholder.

5 Select the **Date placeholder**, and then drag it to position it between the Footer and the Slide Number placeholders. See Exhibit 21-3.

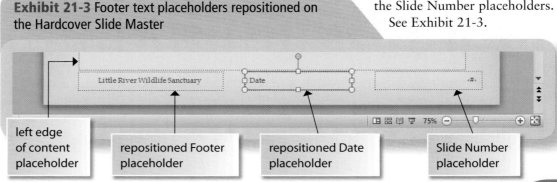

Exhibit 21-3 Footer text placeholders repositioned on the Hardcover Slide Master

Little River Wildlife Sanctuary | Date | ‹#›

75%

- left edge of content placeholder
- repositioned Footer placeholder
- repositioned Date placeholder
- Slide Number placeholder

6 Click the **Footer placeholder border**, and then position the pointer on the selected border. The pointer changes to ⊹⧉.

7 Display the **Title and Content placeholder** in the Slide pane. The Footer and Date placeholders are repositioned on this layout master.

Deleting a Graphic from the Slide Master

Many themes contain graphics in the Slide Master or on individual layout masters. Often the graphics are attractive elements of the slide design. However, sometimes you might want to delete a graphic because it doesn't fit well with your content or you would rather use something else. You can do this in Slide Master view.

 **ACTIVITY**

Delete a graphic from the Slide Master.

1 In the Slide pane, click the **graphic** below the title placeholder to select it. See Exhibit 21-4.

2 Press the **Delete key**. The graphic is deleted.

3 Display the **Two Content Layout master** in the Slide pane, and then delete the **graphic** below the title placeholder.

Inserting Clip Art in the Slide Master

You can also add graphics to the slide master. For instance, you might want a company logo to appear on every slide, or you might want a colored line to appear below the slide titles. To add clip art or a picture to the theme Slide Master or to specific layout masters, you must use the Clip Art or Picture button in the Images group on the Insert tab. You cannot use the Clip Art or Insert Picture from File buttons in the content placeholder on the theme Slide Master because doing so will replace the content placeholder in the master, making it unavailable on the slides.

ACTIVITY

Insert clip art in the Slide Master.

1 On the Ribbon, click the **Insert tab**. In the Images group, click the **Clip Art button**. The same Clip Art task pane that you saw when you inserted clip art in a Word document opens.

2 In the **Search for box**, type **tree** and then click **Go**.

3 In the list of results, click a drawing of a tree to insert it in the slide. (Refer to Exhibit 21-5.)

4 On the Picture Tools Format tab, in the Size group, delete the value in the **Shape Height box**, type **1** and then press the **Enter key**. The clip art is resized to one-inch square.

5 Drag the **clip art** to the lower-left corner of the layout master. See Exhibit 21-5.

Exhibit 21-4 Graphic selected on the Title and Content Layout master

[Screenshot of PowerPoint window showing the Slide Master view with "Wildlife Sanctuary - Microsoft PowerPoint" title bar, Drawing Tools, and the slide showing "Click to edit Master title style" with labels "Title and Content Layout master" and "selected graphic"]

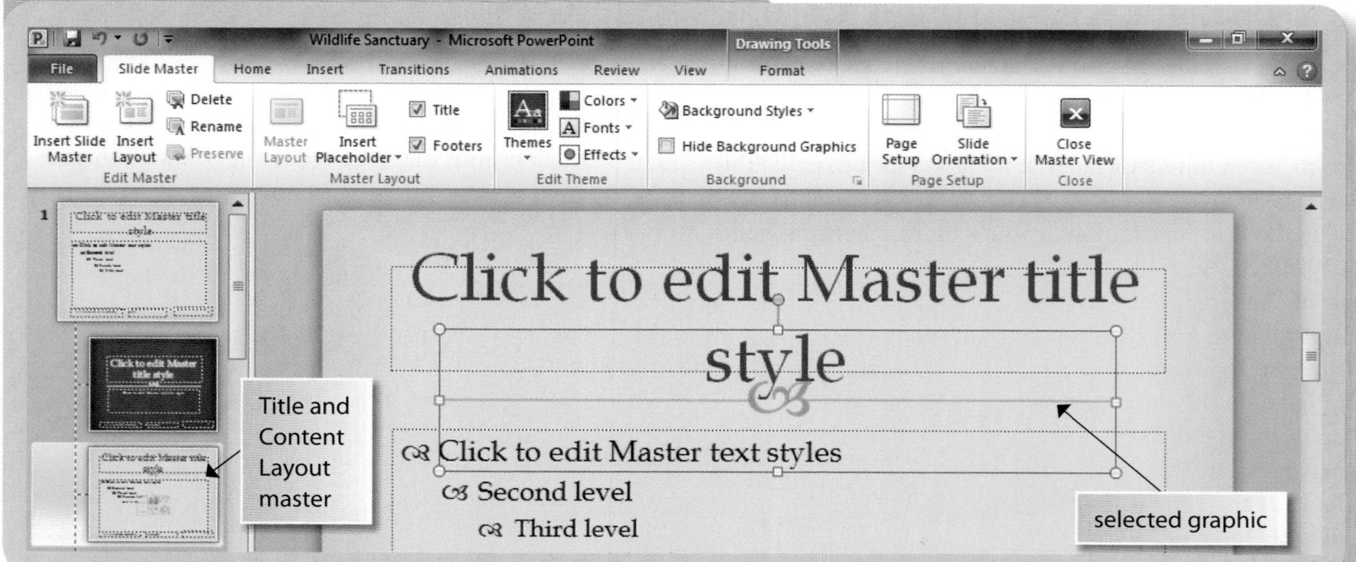

Exhibit 21-5 Clip art resized and positioned on the Two Content Layout master

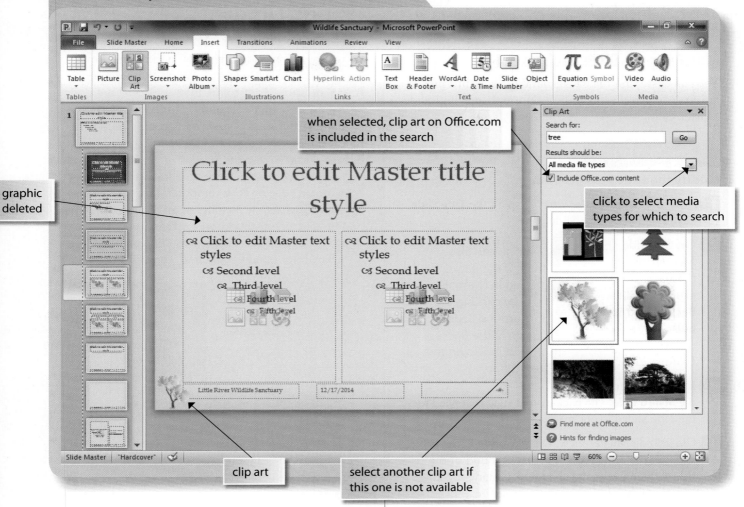

graphic deleted

when selected, clip art on Office.com is included in the search

click to select media types for which to search

clip art

select another clip art if this one is not available

6. Close the Clip Art task pane.

7. Select the **clip art**, and then copy it to the Clipboard.

8. Display the **Title and Content Layout master** in the Slide pane, and then paste the **clip art** from the Clipboard. The clip art appears in the lower-left corner of the slide.

Closing Slide Master View

When you are finished modifying the slide master, you need to close Slide Master view and return to Normal view. You should always examine the slides in Normal view after you make changes to the slide master to make sure they look as you expected them to.

ACTIVITY

Close Slide Master view and examine the results of the changes.

1. On the Ribbon, click the **Slide Master tab**. In the Close group, click the **Close Master View button**. Slide Master view closes, and the presentation appears in Normal view with Slide 3 in the Slide pane. The changes you made to the Hardcover Slide Master and to the Two Content Layout master are visible on the slide.

> **Tip:** You can also click the Normal button on the status bar to close Slide Master view.

2 Display **Slide 5** ("Keep Nature Natural") in the Slide pane. This slide has the Title and Content layout applied. The changes made in Slide Master view are visible on this slide as well.

Modifying the Slide Background

You can customize the background of slides in a presentation. You can do this in both Normal view and Slide Master view.

ACTIVITY

Modify the slide background.

1 Switch to **Slide Master view**. Display the **Title Slide Layout master** in the Slide pane.

2 On the Slide Master tab, in the Background group, click the **Background Styles button**. A gallery of styles opens. See Exhibit 21-6.

> **Tip:** You can also change the background in Normal view by clicking the Background Styles button in the Background group on the Design tab.

3 In the gallery, click the **Style 6 style**. The background style is applied to the Title Slide Layout master.

4 Close Slide Master view. Display **Slide 1** (the title slide) in the Slide pane. The background of the title slide matches the change you made in Slide Master view.

5 Save the presentation.

Selecting Appropriate Font Colors

When you select font colors for use on slides or when you modify the slide background, make sure your text is easy to read on the slide during a slide show. Font colors that work well are dark colors on a light background, or light colors on a dark background. Avoid red text on a blue background or blue text on a green background (and vice versa) unless the shades of those colors are in strong contrast. These combinations might look good up close on your computer monitor, but they are almost totally illegible to an audience watching your presentation on a screen in a darkened room. Also avoid using red/green combinations, which color-blind people find illegible.

Exhibit 21-6 Background Styles gallery

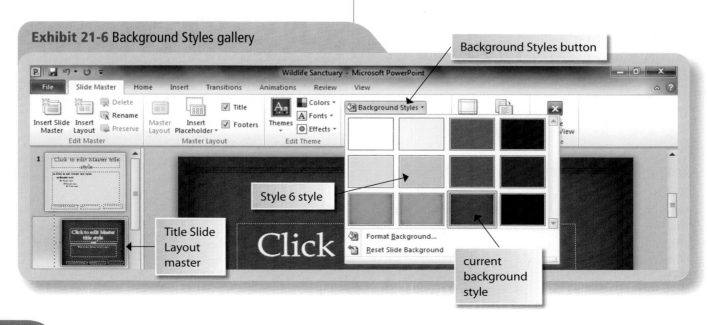

LO21.2 **Inserting Graphics**

Graphics can add information, clarification, emphasis, variety, and pizzazz to a PowerPoint presentation. Remember that a graphic is a picture, shape, design, graph, chart, or diagram. You can include many types of graphics in your presentation: clip art; graphics created using other programs; scanned photographs, drawings, and cartoons; other picture files stored on your computer or network; or graphics you create using drawing tools in PowerPoint.

There are many ways to add graphics to a slide. On slides with a content placeholder, you can click the icon in the content placeholder that corresponds to the type of graphic you want to insert. In PowerPoint, you can also click the Clip Art button in a content placeholder to open the Clip Art task pane. You can also add a picture from a file.

When you insert a graphic in a PowerPoint slide (or an Excel worksheet), you do not have to set text wrapping options; graphics are always floating graphics in PowerPoint slides and Excel worksheets. To reposition a floating graphic, drag it to its new position. In PowerPoint, objects "snap to" or align with an invisible grid when they are moved. This usually helps you align objects on a slide. If a graphic jumps from one location to another as you drag it and you can't position it exactly where you want it, press and hold the Alt key as you drag it. The Alt key temporarily disables the feature that forces objects to snap to the grid.

Inserting a Picture from a File

You can insert graphics stored on your computer on a slide using the Insert Picture from File button in a content placeholder or the Picture button in the Images group on the Insert tab. Either method opens the Insert Picture dialog box. Once you insert a graphic from a file, you can resize it using the sizing handles as you did when you worked with clip art.

Insert clip art in Excel and PowerPoint using the same process as in Word; in PowerPoint, you can also click the Insert Clip Art button in a content placeholder.

Inserting Tables on a Slide

To insert a table on a slide, click the Insert Table button in a content placeholder to open a dialog box in which you specify the number of columns and rows you want to insert. You can also click the Table button in the Tables group on the Insert tab to insert a table using the same grid you used in Word. After you insert a table, the steps for working with the table are the same as working with a table in a Word document.

 **ACTIVITY**

Add a graphic from a file.

1 Display **Slide 2** ("About Us") in the Slide pane.

2 On the Home tab, in the Slides group, click the **Layout button**, and then click the **Two Content layout**. The bulleted list moves to the left side of the slide in the Slide pane, and a second content placeholder appears on the right side of the slide. See Exhibit 21-7.

3 On the right side of the slide, in the content placeholder, click the **Insert Picture from File button**. The Insert Picture dialog box opens. This dialog box is similar to the Open and New from existing dialog boxes.

4 Click the picture data file **Landscape** located in the Chapter 21\Chapter folder, and then click **Insert**. The dialog box closes, and the picture replaces the content placeholder on the slide. The Picture Tools Format tab appears on the Ribbon and is the active tab.

5 Display **Slide 6** ("Directions") in the Slide pane.

6 On the Ribbon, click the **Insert tab**. In the Images group, click the **Picture button**. The Insert Picture dialog box opens.

7 Click the picture data file **Goose** located in the Chapter 21\Chapter folder, and then click **Insert**. The dialog box closes, and the picture of the goose appears in the center of Slide 6.

8 Drag the **goose picture** to the left of the slide number. See Exhibit 21-8.

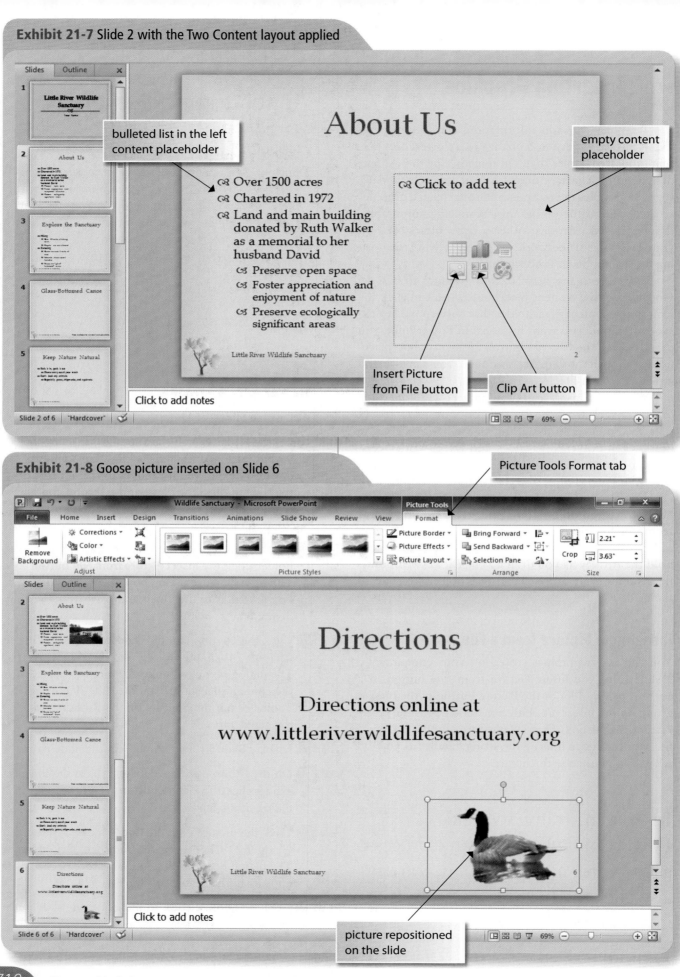

Exhibit 21-7 Slide 2 with the Two Content layout applied

bulleted list in the left content placeholder

empty content placeholder

Insert Picture from File button

Clip Art button

Exhibit 21-8 Goose picture inserted on Slide 6

Picture Tools Format tab

picture repositioned on the slide

9 Display **Slide 3** ("Explore the Sanctuary") in the Slide pane, and then insert the picture data file **Hikers**, located in the Chapter 21\ Chapter folder, in place of the content placeholder.

10 Display **Slide 4** ("Glass-Bottomed Canoe"), and then insert the picture data file **Canoe** located in the Chapter 21\ Chapter folder, in place of the content placeholder on the left.

Drawing a Shape

Another way to add a graphic to a slide is to draw it using tools available in PowerPoint. You can add many shapes to a slide, including lines, rectangles, stars, and many more. Shapes you draw using a selection from the Shapes gallery are vector graphics, so the Drawing Tools Format tab appears on the Ribbon when a drawn shape is selected. After you insert a shape, you can add text to it. You can also resize a shape in the same manner as you resize other objects, and format it.

To draw a shape, click the Shapes button in the Illustrations group on the Insert tab or in the Drawing group on the Home tab, and then click a shape in the gallery. (There is no icon in the content placeholders to insert a shape.) To insert the shape on the slide at the default size, simply click in the slide. If you want to create a shape of a specific size, click and drag to draw the shape until it is the size you want.

ACTIVITY

Draw a shape on a slide.

1 With Slide 6 ("Directions") displayed in the Slide pane, on the Ribbon, click the **Insert tab**.

2 In the Illustrations group, click the **Shapes button**. The Shapes gallery opens. See Exhibit 21-9. The gallery is organized into nine categories of shapes, plus the Recently Used Shapes group at the top.

The Picture and Shapes buttons are also available in Word and Excel.

Exhibit 21-9 Shapes gallery

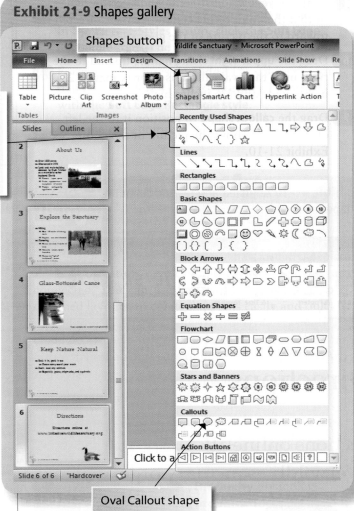

Recently Used Shapes section (shapes in this section on your screen might differ)

Shapes button

Oval Callout shape

3 In the Callouts section, click the **Oval Callout shape**. The gallery closes and the pointer changes to $+$.

4 Click a blank area of the slide to the left of the picture of the goose. An oval callout shape approximately one-inch wide appears on the slide, and the Drawing Tools Format tab appears on the Ribbon. A selection box and sizing handles appear around the shape, and a yellow diamond-shaped adjustment handle appears on the bottom point of the shape that you can drag to change the way a shape looks without changing its size.

Tip: To draw a circle, square, or equilateral triangle, hold the Shift key while you drag the pointer after selecting the Oval, Rectangle, or Isosceles Triangle shape, respectively.

Exhibit 21-22 Video playback options

Video option	Function
Volume	Change the volume of the video from high to medium or low, or mute it.
Start	Change how the video starts, either when the presenter advances the slide show (On Click) or automatically when the slide appears during the slide show.
Play Full Screen	When selected, the video fills the screen during the slide show.
Hide While Not Playing	When selected, the video does not appear on the slide when it is not playing; make sure the video is set to play automatically if this option is selected.
Loop Until Stopped	When selected, the video will play continuously until the next slide appears during the slide show.
Rewind After Playing	When selected, the video will rewind after it plays so that the first frame or the poster frame appears again.

Exhibit 21-23 Video Options group on the Video Tools Playback tab

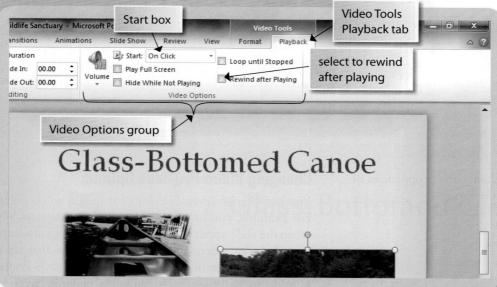

Changing the Video Volume

You can also set the volume options for video. To do this, click the Volume button in the Video Options group on the Video Tools Playback tab to select from Low, Medium, High, or Mute. You can make more precise adjustments using the Volume control on the right end of the video's play bar.

2 In the Video Options group, click the **Rewind after Playing check box** to select it. Now the video will rewind to the beginning after playing in the slide show.

Trimming a Video

If a video is too long, or if it contains parts you don't want to show during the slide show, you can trim the clip from within PowerPoint. To do this, click the Trim Video button in the Editing group on the Video Tools Playback tab, and then in the Trim Video dialog box, drag sliders to indicate where you want the video to start and stop.

ACTIVITY

Trim a video.

1 On the Video Tools Playback tab, in the Editing group, click the **Trim Video button**. The Trim Video dialog box opens. See Exhibit 21-24.

2 On the bar below the video, drag the green **Start Time slider** to the right to approximately the **8-second mark**. The time in the Start Time box changes to match the time point where you dragged the slider. The video will now start playing at this point.

9 Display **Slide 3** ("Explore the Sanctuary") in the Slide pane, and then insert the picture data file **Hikers**, located in the Chapter 21\Chapter folder, in place of the content placeholder.

10 Display **Slide 4** ("Glass-Bottomed Canoe"), and then insert the picture data file **Canoe** located in the Chapter 21\Chapter folder, in place of the content placeholder on the left.

Drawing a Shape

Another way to add a graphic to a slide is to draw it using tools available in PowerPoint. You can add many shapes to a slide, including lines, rectangles, stars, and many more. Shapes you draw using a selection from the Shapes gallery are vector graphics, so the Drawing Tools Format tab appears on the Ribbon when a drawn shape is selected. After you insert a shape, you can add text to it. You can also resize a shape in the same manner as you resize other objects, and format it.

To draw a shape, click the Shapes button in the Illustrations group on the Insert tab or in the Drawing group on the Home tab, and then click a shape in the gallery. (There is no icon in the content placeholders to insert a shape.) To insert the shape on the slide at the default size, simply click in the slide. If you want to create a shape of a specific size, click and drag to draw the shape until it is the size you want.

ACTIVITY

Draw a shape on a slide.

1 With Slide 6 ("Directions") displayed in the Slide pane, on the Ribbon, click the **Insert tab**.

2 In the Illustrations group, click the **Shapes button**. The Shapes gallery opens. See Exhibit 21-9. The gallery is organized into nine categories of shapes, plus the Recently Used Shapes group at the top.

The Picture and Shapes buttons are also available in Word and Excel.

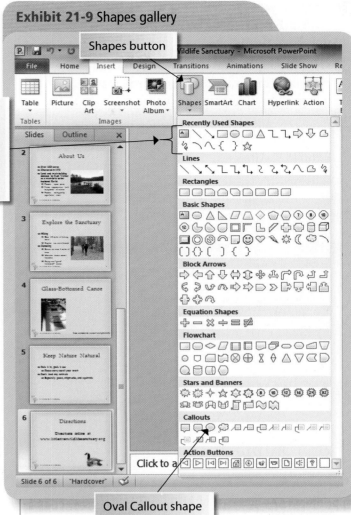

Exhibit 21-9 Shapes gallery

Shapes button

Recently Used Shapes section (shapes in this section on your screen might differ)

Oval Callout shape

3 In the Callouts section, click the **Oval Callout shape**. The gallery closes and the pointer changes to $+$.

4 Click a blank area of the slide to the left of the picture of the goose. An oval callout shape approximately one-inch wide appears on the slide, and the Drawing Tools Format tab appears on the Ribbon. A selection box and sizing handles appear around the shape, and a yellow diamond-shaped adjustment handle appears on the bottom point of the shape that you can drag to change the way a shape looks without changing its size.

Tip: To draw a circle, square, or equilateral triangle, hold the Shift key while you drag the pointer after selecting the Oval, Rectangle, or Isosceles Triangle shape, respectively.

5 Drag the **yellow adjustment handle** to the right so that the point of the callout shape is directed toward to the picture of the goose.

6 Drag the **upper-right sizing handle** up and to the right until the oval callout is approximately 2¼ inches wide and 1½ inches high.

7 Drag the **callout shape** to position it to the left of and a little above the picture of the goose. See Exhibit 21-10.

Exhibit 21-10 Adjusted and resized callout shape

adjustment handle

fill and border color is the default fill color for shapes in the Hardcover theme

Adding Text to a Shape

To add text to a shape, select it, and then type. The text will be inserted at 18 points in the Body font of the selected theme. The text will wrap in the shape automatically. If you type more text than the shape can hold, you can resize the shape or change the font size to make it fit. The color of the text is black or white, depending on the fill color of the shape.

> When a text or content placeholder on a slide is selected, the Drawing Tools Format tab is available.

ACTIVITY

Add text to a shape.

1 With the shape still selected, type **Come visit us!**. The text is white so that it is readable on the dark background.

2 Click the **callout shape dashed line border** to select the entire shape, and then change the font size to **28 points**.

> ⚠ **Problem?** If the callout shape is not large enough to fit the text, resize it.

Inserting and Formatting Text Boxes

Sometimes, you need to add text to a slide in a location other than in one of the text box placeholders included in the slide layout. You can insert a rectangle shape and add text to it, or you can add a text box, an object designed to hold text. To insert a text box, click the Text Box button in the Text group on the Insert tab, or use the Text Box shape in the Shapes gallery. When you enter text in a text box, the text box will keep widening to accommodate the text you type. If you want the text to wrap to additional lines, drag a sizing handle to change the height of the text box object.

A Text Box

Formatting Graphics

You can apply formatting to any object on a slide. For example, after you insert a picture from a file, you can format it in the same manner that you formatted clip art. You can crop it, apply a style using one of the styles in the Picture Styles group, or apply a border or effects using the Picture Border or Picture Effects buttons.

When a drawn object is selected on a slide, the Drawing Tools Format tab appears instead of the Picture Tools Format tab. The commands on the Drawing

Tools Format tab are very similar to those on the Picture Tools Format tab. You can change the style of a drawn shape, change the color and width of a shape's border, and add special effects to a shape.

ACTIVITY

Format drawings and pictures on slides.

1 If necessary, on Slide 6, select the **callout shape**. On the Ribbon, click the **Drawing Tools Format tab**. In the Shape Styles group, an orange border appears around one of the styles. When you draw a shape, this default style is applied.

2 In the Shape Styles group, click the **More button** ⬇. The Shape Styles gallery opens.

3 In the gallery, click the **Subtle Effect – Gold, Accent 3 style**. The style is applied to the callout shape.

4 In the Shape Styles group, click the **Shape Outline button arrow**. On the menu, point to **Weight**, and then click **2¼ pt**. The weight of the shape border increases to 2¼ points. See Exhibit 21-11.

5 Display **Slide 2** ("About Us") in the Slide pane. On Slide 2, select the **picture**. The Picture Tools Format tab appears on the Ribbon.

6 On the Ribbon, click the **Picture Tools Format tab**. In the Picture Styles group, click the **Soft Edge Rectangle style**. The style is applied to the picture.

7 Format the pictures on **Slide 3** ("Explore the Sanctuary") and **Slide 4** ("Glass-Bottomed Canoe") with the **Soft Edge Rectangle style**.

8 Save the presentation.

LO21.3 Creating SmartArt Diagrams

A **diagram** is an illustration that visually depicts information or ideas and shows how they are connected. You can use **SmartArt**, diagrams with pre-designed layouts, to create diagrams easily and quickly. In addition to shapes, SmartArt diagrams usually include text to help describe or label the shapes. You can create the following types of diagrams using SmartArt:

▶ **List**—Shows a list of items in a graphical representation

▶ **Process**—Shows a sequence of steps in a process

▶ **Cycle**—Shows a process that has a continuous cycle

▶ **Hierarchy** (including **organization charts**)—Shows the relationship between individuals or units within an organization

▶ **Relationship** (including **Venn diagrams, radial diagrams**, and **target diagrams**)—Shows the relationship between two or more elements

▶ **Matrix**—Shows information in a grid

diagram An illustration that visually depicts information or ideas and shows how they are connected.

SmartArt A diagram with a predesigned layout.

Exhibit 21-11 Drawn shape with style applied and border modified

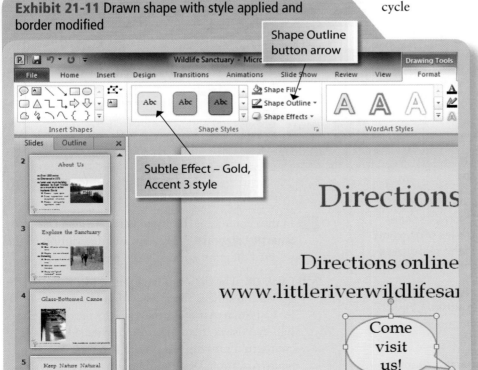

▶ **Pyramid**—Shows foundation-based relationships

▶ **Picture**—Provides a location for a picture or pictures

There is also an Office.com category, which, if you are connected to the Internet, displays additional SmartArt diagrams available on Office.com. You also might see an Other category, which contains SmartArt diagrams previously downloaded from Office.com.

Creating a SmartArt Diagram

To create a SmartArt diagram, you can click the Insert SmartArt Graphic button in a content placeholder, or you can click the SmartArt button in the Illustrations group on the Insert tab to open the Choose a SmartArt Graphic dialog box. You can also convert an existing bulleted list into a SmartArt diagram by using the Convert to SmartArt Graphic button in the Paragraph group on the Home tab.

Create a SmartArt diagram.

1 Display **Slide 5** ("Keep Nature Natural") in the Slide pane, and then click the **bulleted list**.

> ➤ **Tip:** If there is no text on a slide, you can click the Insert SmartArt button ▧ in the content placeholder on a slide, or you can click the SmartArt button in the Illustrations group on the Insert tab.

2 On the Home tab, in the Paragraph group, click the **Convert to SmartArt Graphic button** ▧▾. A gallery of SmartArt diagram types opens. See Exhibit 21-12.

3 Below the gallery, click **More SmartArt Graphics**. The gallery closes, and the Choose a SmartArt Graphic dialog box opens. See Exhibit 21-13.

Exhibit 21-12 Convert to SmartArt Graphic gallery

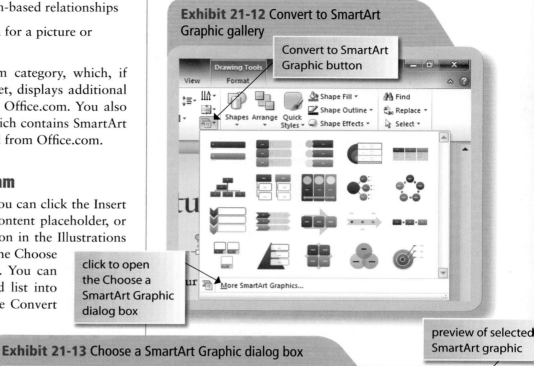

Convert to SmartArt Graphic button

click to open the Choose a SmartArt Graphic dialog box

preview of selected SmartArt graphic

Exhibit 21-13 Choose a SmartArt Graphic dialog box

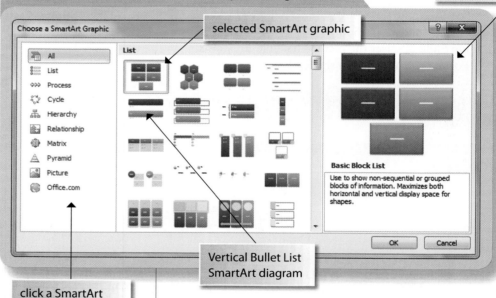

selected SmartArt graphic

Vertical Bullet List SmartArt diagram

click a SmartArt category to filter the list of diagrams in the center pane

4 In the center pane, click the **Vertical Bullet List SmartArt diagram**. A preview and description of the selected diagram appear in the pane on the right.

5 Click **OK**. The dialog box closes, and the bulleted list on the slide is replaced with a Vertical Bullet List SmartArt diagram with the text from the bulleted list in the diagram. The SmartArt Tools contextual tabs appear on the Ribbon, and the SmartArt Tools Design tab is the active tab. You might see a Text pane labeled *Type your text here* to the left of the diagram.

Exhibit 21-14 Vertical Bullet List SmartArt diagram on a slide

SmartArt Tools contextual tabs

Text Pane button

Text pane Close button

Text pane

shape containing a first-level bullet in original bulleted list

shape containing a second-level bullet in original bulleted list

Name of the SmartArt diagram

6 If the Text pane is not visible, on the SmartArt Tools Design tab, in the Create Graphic group, click the **Text Pane button**. The button is selected and the Text pane appears to the left of the Smart-Art diagram. See Exhibit 21-14. The SmartArt diagram consists of colored rectangles that contain the text from the first-level bullets in the original list with the second-level bullets from the original list below each one. The border around the diagram defines the borders of the entire SmartArt diagram object.

Modifying a SmartArt Diagram

A SmartArt diagram is a larger object composed of smaller objects. You can modify the diagram by adding or deleting shapes, modifying the text by changing the font attributes, and changing the way the shapes look. You can also modify the diagram as a whole.

ACTIVITY

Modify a SmartArt diagram.

1 In the SmartArt diagram, click the **Don't feed any animals shape**. The shape is selected and the corresponding bulleted item in the Text pane is selected as well.

2 On the SmartArt Tools Design tab, in the Create Graphic group, click the **Add Shape button arrow**. The top command on the menu is the default command that would be executed if you clicked the icon on the Add Shape button. The commands in gray on the menu are available when different SmartArt diagrams are on the slide.

3 Click **Add Shape After**. The menu closes and a new shape is added to the diagram below the selected shape. The new shape is selected, and a corresponding bullet appears in the Text pane. See Exhibit 21-15.

> ➤ **Tip:** You can work in the Text pane using the same skills you use to work with a bulleted list on a slide.

4 Type **Leave only footprints**. The text appears in the new shape and next to the corresponding bullet in the Text pane.

5 On the SmartArt Tools Design tab, in the Create Graphic group, click the **Add Shape button arrow**, and then click **Add Shape Before**. A new shape appears above the selected shape and a new bullet appears above the last bullet in the Text pane.

6 Type **Take only pictures**.

7 Click in the **Leave only footprints shape**.

8 On the SmartArt Tools Design tab, in the Create Graphic group, click the **Demote button**. The shape is changed to a bulleted item at the same level as the second-level bulleted items in the Text pane.

9 In the diagram, click the **last shape border** ("Leave only footprints") to select the last shape, and then press the **Delete key**. The shape is removed.

10 Point to the text **Take only pictures** so that the pointer changes to Ⅰ, click to position the insertion point, and then press the **Right Arrow key** as many times as needed to move the insertion point after the *s* in *pictures*.

11 Type **;** (a semicolon), press the **Spacebar**, and then type **leave only footprints**.

12 In the upper-right corner of the Text pane, click the **Close button** ⊠. The Text pane closes.

Exhibit 21-15 New shape added to the SmartArt diagram

13 Click inside the Smart-Art diagram border without clicking a shape. The new shape is deselected, but the border still appears around the diagram to indicate that the diagram is still selected.

Formatting a SmartArt Diagram

As with any object, you can add formatting to a Smart-Art diagram using the commands on the Smart-Art Tools Format tab. You can also use options on the SmartArt Tools Design tab to apply special effects to the diagram.

 **ACTIVITY**

Format a SmartArt diagram.

1 On the SmartArt Tools Design tab, in the SmartArt Styles group, click the **More button**. A gallery of styles available for the diagram opens. See Exhibit 21-16.

Exhibit 21-16 SmartArt diagram Styles gallery

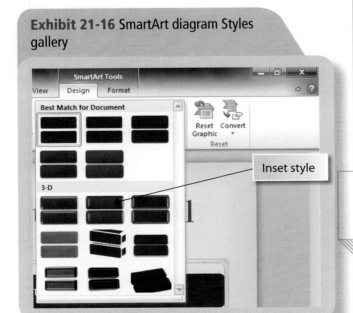

Exhibit 21-17 SmartArt diagram with new colors

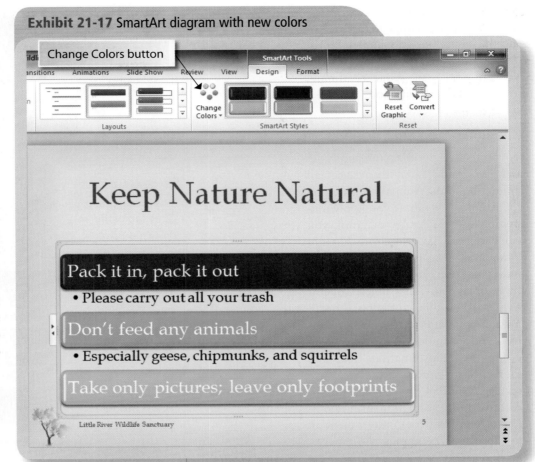

2 In the gallery, in the 3-D section, click the **Inset style**. The style of the graphic changes to the one you chose.

3 In the SmartArt Styles group, click the **Change Colors button**. A gallery of color options opens.

4 In the gallery, in the Colorful section, click the **Colorful Range – Accent Colors 5 to 6 style**. The gallery closes and the colors in the SmartArt diagram change to the style you selected. See Exhibit 21-17.

5 Save the presentation.

LO21.4 Changing Animation Options

When you animated text in Chapter 20, you actually animated the text boxes, which are objects. You can animate any object on a slide, including photos and clip art. Even SmartArt diagrams can be enhanced by applying animations. You also learned how to change the start timing of animations in Chapter 20. In addition to changing the start timing, you can modify the sequence, timing, and speed of an animation.

Changing the Effect Options

To animate a graphic, you simply select the graphic, and then select an animation in the Animation group on the Animations tab. If you apply animation to a SmartArt diagram, you can choose to have the entire diagram animate at once as a single object, as individual objects but all at the same time, or as individual objects one at a time. To do this, you apply the animation you want to use, click the Effect Options button in the Animation group on the Animations tab, and then click an option in the Sequence section. You can also change the direction of an animation using commands on the Effect Options menu in the Direction section.

 **ACTIVITY**

Change animation effect options.

1 Make sure **Slide 5** ("Keep Nature Natural") is displayed in the Slide pane, and the SmartArt graphic is selected.

2 On the Ribbon, click the **Animations tab**. In the Animation group, click the **Fly In animation**. The animation previews and the entire diagram flies up from the bottom. The single animation sequence icon indicates that the diagram will animate all at once.

3 In the Animation group, click the **Effect Options button**. The Effect Options menu appears. See Exhibit 21-18. The options on this menu change depending on the selected animation and on the object being animated. The options in the Sequence section reflect that you are animating an object composed of multiple objects.

4 At the bottom of the menu, in the Sequence section, click **One by One**. The animation previews again and each shape flies in individually. Instead

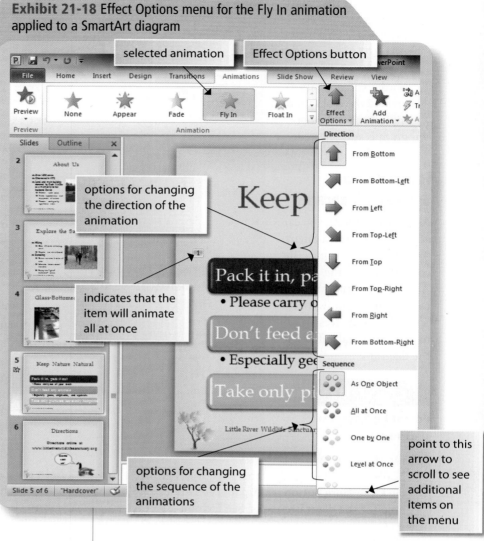

Exhibit 21-18 Effect Options menu for the Fly In animation applied to a SmartArt diagram

selected animation

Effect Options button

options for changing the direction of the animation

indicates that the item will animate all at once

options for changing the sequence of the animations

point to this arrow to scroll to see additional items on the menu

of one animation sequence icon at the upper-left corner of the diagram, there are now five, indicating that each of the five objects in the diagram will animate one at a time.

5 On the Animations tab, in the Animation group, click the **Effect Options button**. The Effect Options menu appears.

The Effect Options menu for an animated bulleted list includes Sequence options similar to those for SmartArt, except the last option is By Paragraph.

6 In the Direction section, click **From Right**. The animation previews and each object in the diagram flies in from the right.

Changing the Speed of Animations

You can adjust the speed of animations. To change the speed of an animation, you change the time in the Duration box in the Timing group on the Animations tab. To make an animation go faster, decrease the time in the Duration box; to make it go slower, increase the time.

ACTIVITY

Change the speed of animations.

1 If necessary, on Slide 5, click the **animated Smart-Art diagram** to select it.

2 On the Animations tab, in the Timing group, click the **Duration up arrow** four times. See Exhibit 21-19. Each animation will now take 1½ seconds to complete instead of one-half second.

Exhibit 21-19 Speed of the Fly In animation modified

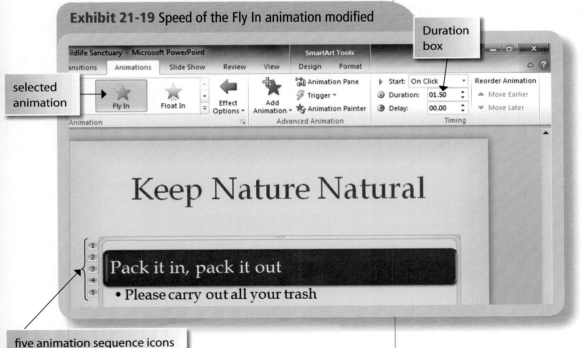

selected animation

five animation sequence icons

Duration box

3 Click the **2 animation sequence icon**, press and hold the **Ctrl key**, and then click the **4 animation sequence icon**. The two icons are selected. These two icons are the animation sequence icons associated with the two subbullet shapes in the diagram.

Effect Options for Transitions

Most transitions also have options you can change by clicking the Effect Options button on the Transitions tab. To change a transition effect option, select a transition in the Transition to This Slide group on the Transitions tab, and then click the Effect Options button in the same group. Like animation effect options, the exact options on the menu change depending on the transition selected.

4 In the Timing group, click the **Duration down arrow** twice to change the Duration for the two selected objects to one second.

5 On the Animations tab, in the Preview group, click the **Preview button**. The diagram animates in the Slide pane.

6 On the status bar, click the **Slide Show button**. Slide 5 appears in Slide Show view.

7 Advance the slide show. The first object in the SmartArt diagram flies in somewhat slowly from the right.

8 Advance the slide show. The subordinate object to the first object in the SmartArt diagram flies in more quickly from the right.

9 Advance the slide show three more times to display the other three objects in the diagram.

10 Press the **Esc key** to end the slide show.

11 Save the presentation.

LO21.5 Adding Video

Y ou can insert digital video in slides or in slide masters. PowerPoint supports various file formats, but the most commonly used are the Audio Visual Interleave format (listed in Explorer windows as the Video Clip file type), which uses the file name extension .avi, and the Windows Media Video format, which uses the file name extension .wmv. After you insert a video, you can modify it by changing the length of time the video plays, changing playback options, and applying formats and styles.

Inserting a Video on a Slide

You can insert a video clip in two different ways. You can change the layout to one of the content layouts, click the Insert Media Clip button, and then use the Insert Video dialog box. You can also use the Video button in the Media Clips group on the Insert tab.

ACTIVITY

Insert a video on a slide.

1 Display **Slide 4** ("Glass-Bottomed Canoe") in the Slide pane.

2 In the content placeholder on the right, click the **Insert Media Clip button** . The Insert Video dialog box opens.

> ▸ **Tip:** You can also click the Video button arrow in the Media group on the Insert tab, and then click Video from File to open the Insert Video dialog box.

3 Click the movie data file **Canoe Video** located in the Chapter 21\Chapter folder, and then click **Insert**. The movie is inserted in place of the content placeholder. The Video Tools contextual tabs appear on the Ribbon, and the Video Tools Format tab is the active tab. See Exhibit 21-20.

Exhibit 21-20 Video inserted on Slide 4

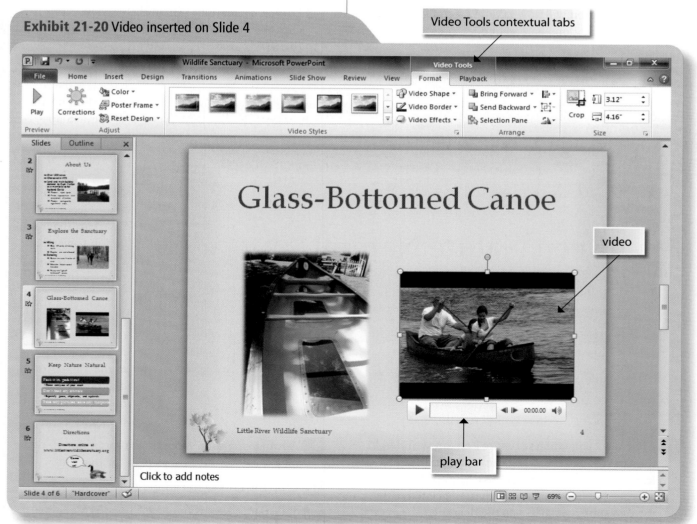

4 On the play bar below the movie, click the **Play button** ▶, and then watch the video, which is approximately 23 seconds long. Note that this video has no sound.

Formatting a Video

Videos can be formatted just like pictures. For example, you can apply a style, apply special effects, crop the sides of a video, or resize it by dragging the sizing handles. However, be very careful if you resize a video. Normally, you don't want to change the proportions of a video because it will distort the image.

ACTIVITY

Format a video.

1 On the Video Tools Format tab, in the Size group, click the **Crop button**.

2 Crop the black area from the top and bottom of the video, and then in the Size group, click the **Crop button** to deselect it.

3 In the Video Styles group, click the **Video Effects button**. On the menu, point to **Reflection**, and then in the Reflection Variations section, click the **Half Reflection, touching style**. A reflection appears below the video. See Exhibit 21-21.

4 On the play bar below the movie, click the **Play button** ▶. The video plays in the reflection as well as in the main video window.

Exhibit 21-21 Cropped video with a reflection style applied

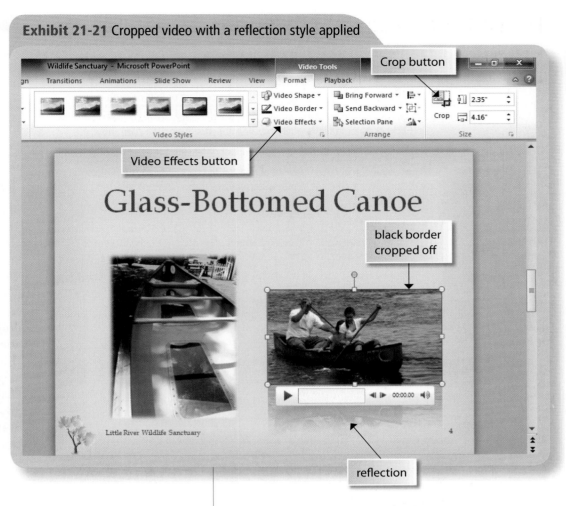

Changing Video Playback Options

You can change several options for how a video plays. For example, you can set a video to play automatically when the slide appears during a slide show or wait until you click the video's play button. You can also set a video to loop continuously until the next slide is displayed or to fill the screen while it is playing, covering the other objects on the slide. Video playback options are described in Exhibit 21-22.

ACTIVITY

Change video playback options.

1 On the Ribbon, click the **Video Tools Playback tab**. The options for changing how the video plays are in the Video Options group. See Exhibit 21-23.

> **Tip:** To play the movie so that it fills the entire screen, select the Play Full Screen check box in the Video Options group on the Video Tools Playback tab.

Exhibit 21-22 Video playback options

Video option	Function
Volume	Change the volume of the video from high to medium or low, or mute it.
Start	Change how the video starts, either when the presenter advances the slide show (On Click) or automatically when the slide appears during the slide show.
Play Full Screen	When selected, the video fills the screen during the slide show.
Hide While Not Playing	When selected, the video does not appear on the slide when it is not playing; make sure the video is set to play automatically if this option is selected.
Loop Until Stopped	When selected, the video will play continuously until the next slide appears during the slide show.
Rewind After Playing	When selected, the video will rewind after it plays so that the first frame or the poster frame appears again.

Exhibit 21-23 Video Options group on the Video Tools Playback tab

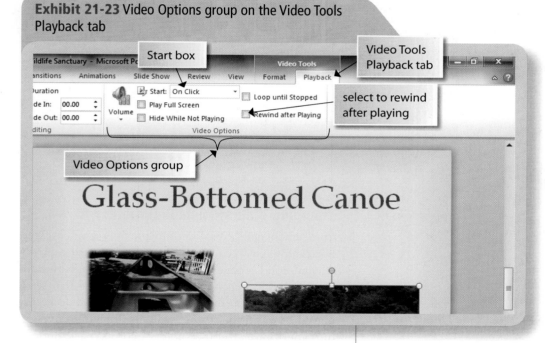

Changing the Video Volume

You can also set the volume options for video. To do this, click the Volume button in the Video Options group on the Video Tools Playback tab to select from Low, Medium, High, or Mute. You can make more precise adjustments using the Volume control on the right end of the video's play bar.

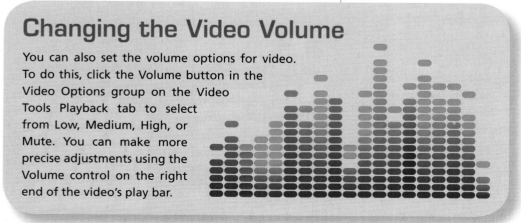

2 In the Video Options group, click the **Rewind after Playing check box** to select it. Now the video will rewind to the beginning after playing in the slide show.

Trimming a Video

If a video is too long, or if it contains parts you don't want to show during the slide show, you can trim the clip from within PowerPoint. To do this, click the Trim Video button in the Editing group on the Video Tools Playback tab, and then in the Trim Video dialog box, drag sliders to indicate where you want the video to start and stop.

ACTIVITY

Trim a video.

1 On the Video Tools Playback tab, in the Editing group, click the **Trim Video button**. The Trim Video dialog box opens. See Exhibit 21-24.

2 On the bar below the video, drag the green **Start Time slider** to the right to approximately the **8-second mark**. The time in the Start Time box changes to match the time point where you dragged the slider. The video will now start playing at this point.

Exhibit 21-24 Trim Video dialog box

Drag the green Start Time slider to specify the point at which the video will start playing

drag the red End Time slider to specify the point at which the video will stop playing

3 Drag the red **End Time slider** to the left to approximately the **19.5-second mark**. The time in the End Time box changes to match the time point where you dragged the slider. The video will stop playing at this point.

4 Click **OK**. You can watch the trimmed video in Normal view.

5 On the play bar, click the **Play button** ▶. The trimmed video—now about 11.5 seconds long—plays.

Setting a Poster Frame

A **poster frame**, sometimes called a **preview frame**, is the image that appears before the video starts playing. The default poster frame for a video is the first frame of the video. You can change this so that any frame from the video or any image stored in a file is the poster frame.

Set the poster frame for a video.

1 In the Slide pane, point to the play bar so that you see a ScreenTip identifying the time at the point where the pointer is positioned.

2 Move the pointer until it is at approximately the 4-second mark, and then click. The gray indicator in the play bar moves back to the 4-second mark.

3 On the Ribbon, click the **Video Tools Format tab**, and then in the Adjust group, click the **Poster Frame** button. A menu opens.

4 On the menu, click **Current Frame**. The menu closes and a note appears in the play bar indicating that this will be the poster frame. See Exhibit 21-25. This frame will now be the poster frame for this video clip.

5 On the status bar, click the **Slide Show button** 🖵. Slide 4 appears in Slide Show view. The poster frame for the video appears in the video object.

6 Point to the **video**. The play bar appears on top of the video.

7 On the play bar, click the **Play button** ▶, and then move the pointer off the video to make the play bar disappear. The trimmed video plays. When the video is finished, it rewinds and displays the poster frame again.

8 Press the **Esc key** to end the slide show.

9 Save the presentation.

Video should clearly convey, illustrate, or support your message to enhance rather than distract from your presentation.

Tatiana Popova/Shutterstock.com

poster frame (preview frame) In a video object, the image that appears before the video starts playing.

Exhibit 21-25 Video after the poster frame is set

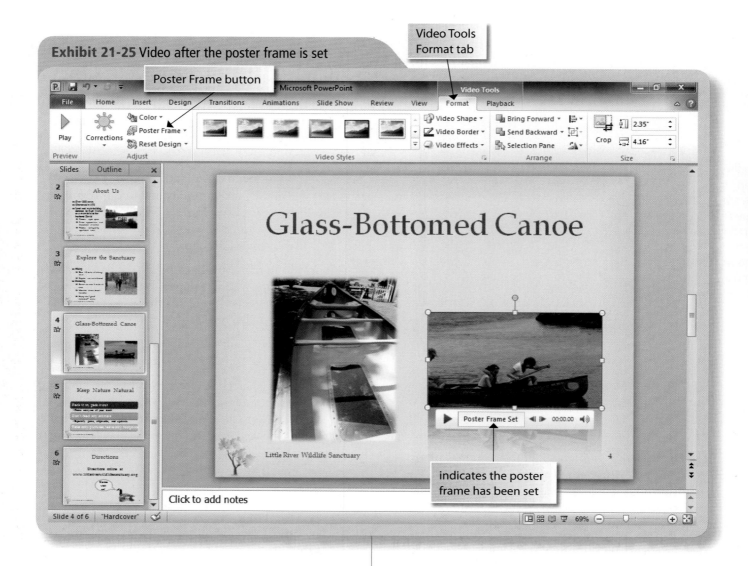

Video Tools Format tab

Poster Frame button

indicates the poster frame has been set

LO21.6 Adding Sound

Music clips can add interest to a presentation and help create a mood that reaches the audience on an emotional level. PowerPoint supports most digital music file formats; but to ensure it works seamlessly, try using Wave or MP3 files.

Inserting a Sound Clip

To add a sound clip to a slide, use the Audio button in the Media group on the Insert tab. If you click the Audio button arrow, you can choose to add audio from a file, open the Clip Art task pane with Audio as the only selected media file type, or open a dialog box to record audio to accompany a slide.

mikeledray/Shutterstock.com

ACTIVITY

Insert a sound clip on a slide.

1. If necessary, display **Slide 4** ("Glass-Bottomed Canoe") in the Slide pane.

2. On the Ribbon, click the **Insert tab**. In the Media group, click the **Audio button**. The Insert Audio dialog box opens.

3. Navigate to the **Music Library**, and then double-click the Sample Music folder. The songs included as sample music with Windows 7 appear.

4 Click **Sleep Away**, and then click **Insert**. A sound icon appears in the middle of the slide with a play bar below it. The Audio Tools contextual tabs appear on the Ribbon, and the Audio Tools Format tab is the active tab.

⚠️ **Problem?** If the Sleep Away song is not in the Sample Music folder, use any digital song stored on your computer.

5 On the Ribbon, click the **Audio Tools Playback tab**. See Exhibit 21-26.

6 Drag the **sound icon** to the blank area above the video.

Changing Playback Options for a Sound

Similar to videos, the options for changing how the sound plays during the slide show appear on the Audio Tools Playback tab. They are the same options that appear on the Video Tools Playback tab, except there is no option to play full screen. Sound clips can start playing when you click the Play button on the play bar in the slide show (On Click); they can start Automatically when the slide appears on the screen during the slide show; or they can be set to play throughout the rest of the slide show (Play Across Slides).

ACTIVITY

Change the playback options for a sound clip.

1 On the Audio Tools Playback tab, in the Audio Options group, click the **Start box arrow**. A menu opens listing the three ways a sound can play.

2 On the menu, click **Automatically**.

> **Tip:** You can also trim a song in the same way you trimmed the video. Click the Trim Audio button in the Editing group on the Audio Tools Playback tab, and then drag the green and red sliders.

3 In the Audio Options group, click the **Hide During Show check box** to select it.

Exhibit 21-26 Sound icon on Slide 4

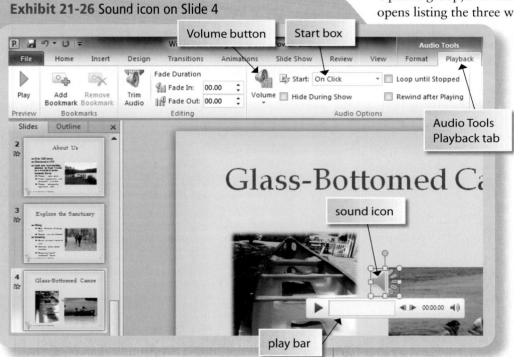

Understanding Video and Audio Animation Effects

When you insert video and audio clips, media animation effects are applied to the clip automatically, and the Start setting of these animation effects (shown on the Animations tab) is tied to the Start setting of the media clip (shown on the Video Tools or Audio Tools Playback tab). When you insert a media clip, the default Start setting is On Click. A Play animation is also automatically applied to the clip and it too is set to start On Click.

If you insert audio or video on a slide that contains other animations, and the animations and media do not play as you expect during a slide show, remember to check the Animations tab to see if the Play animation settings are in conflict with the settings on the Playback tab. One thing to keep in mind is if you want an animation to play at the same time as the previous animation or when the slide transitions, you need to change the Play animation start setting to With Previous.

4 In the Audio Options group, click the **Volume button**, and then on the menu, click **Low**.

5 On the status bar, click the **Slide Show button** 🖵. Slide 4 appears in Slide Show view. After the slide transitions onto the screen, the music starts. You don't see the sound icon because you set it to hide during the slide show.

6 Play the **video**.

7 Advance the slide show. The music stops and the next slide appears on the screen.

8 End the slide show.

9 Save the presentation.

LO21.7 Broadcasting a Presentation

You can broadcast a presentation over the Internet, and anyone with the URL for the presentation and a browser can watch it. When you **broadcast** a presentation, you send the presentation to a special Microsoft server that is made available for this purpose. (If you have access to a SharePoint server, you can send the presentation to that server instead.) A unique Web address is created, and you can send this Web address to anyone you choose. Then, while you run your presentation on your computer in Slide Show view, remote audience members can view it on their computers in a Web browser at the same time. In order to use the broadcast feature, you need a Windows Live ID (or access to a SharePoint server) and you need to be connected to the Internet.

Note: You must have a Windows Live ID to complete the Activities in this section.

To obtain a Windows Live ID, go to www.windowslive.com, and then click Sign up.

broadcast To send a presentation to a special Microsoft server so that other people can watch the slide show in real time using a browser.

Starting a Broadcast

To start a broadcast, you connect to the broadcast service from within the PowerPoint presentation. A unique Web address will be created and the broadcast will start.

Start a broadcast.

1 On the Ribbon, click the **Slide Show tab**. In the Start Slide Show group, click the **Broadcast Slide Show button**. The Broadcast Slide Show dialog box opens. See Exhibit 21-27.

> **Tip:** The Broadcast Slide Show command is also available on the Save & Send tab in Backstage view.

Exhibit 21-27 Broadcast Slide Show dialog box

click to start the broadcast

2 Click the **Start Broadcast** button. The dialog box changes to show that you are connecting to the PowerPoint Broadcast Service, and then another dialog box opens asking for your Windows Live ID credentials. See Exhibit 21-28.

Saving a Presentation for Distribution

PowerPoint lets you save presentations in several formats that allow others to view the presentation, but does not allow them to make any changes to it. Each method produces a different type of file for you to distribute. Before distributing a presentation, you should consider checking it for hidden or private information. To do this, click the Check for Issues button on the Info tab in Backstage view, and then click Inspect Document.

▶ **Video**—You can save a presentation as a Windows Media Video file (with a .wmv file extension). After you have created the video, you can play it in Windows Media Player or any other video player. To save the presentation as a video, display the Save & Send tab in Backstage view, and then in the File Types section, click Create a Video. Options for customizing the video appear in the right pane.

▶ **Picture Presentation**—You can save a presentation as a picture presentation, which saves each slide as an image file in the JPEG format, and then places that image on a slide in a new presentation so that it fills the entire slide. This prevents other people from modifying it or copying complex animations, backgrounds, or other features. To save a presentation as a picture presentation, click Change File Type in the File Types section on the Save & Send tab in Backstage view, and then click PowerPoint Picture Presentation in the right pane.

▶ **PowerPoint Show**—A PowerPoint Show file causes the presentation to open only in Slide Show view.

To save a presentation as a PowerPoint Show, click Change File Type on the Save & Send tab in Backstage view, and then click PowerPoint Show.

▶ **Individual Image Files**—Another way to save the slides as individual image files is to select one of the file types under Image File Types in the right pane on the Save & Send tab in Backstage view. Doing this saves each slide as a separate graphic file stored in a folder named for the presentation.

▶ **Portable Document Format (PDF)**—You can also save a presentation as a PDF file, and then open it using Adobe's free Reader software. When you save a presentation as a PDF file, each slide becomes a page in the PDF file. To publish the presentation in PDF format, select Create PDF/XPS Document in the File Types list on the Save & Send tab in Backstage view.

▶ **Package Presentation for CD**—The Package Presentation for CD command, on the Save & Send tab in Backstage view, saves all the files needed to run the presentation in a folder or on removable media, such as a CD or a USB drive. If you package a presentation to a CD, when the CD is inserted in the computer and starts running, the user is offered the opportunity to download PowerPoint Viewer, a program that allows you to run a slide show, but not edit it. You can also search the Microsoft Web site for this program and install it on any computer that does not already have PowerPoint installed on it.

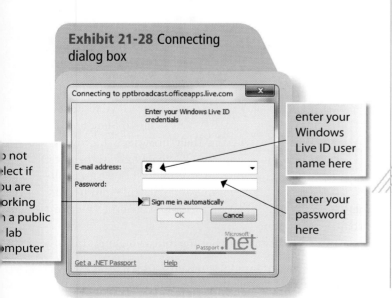

Exhibit 21-28 Connecting dialog box

You can check PowerPoint, Word, and Excel files for hidden or private information using the Check for Issues button on the Info tab in Backstage view.

3 In the **E-mail address box**, type your Windows Live ID username. Click in the **Password box**, and then type your Windows Live ID password.

4 Click **OK**. The dialog box closes, and the Broadcast Slide Show dialog box displays the progress of the connection. After a few moments, the Broadcast Slide Show dialog box changes to display the custom URL as a link to your presentation on the PowerPoint Broadcast server. See Exhibit 21-29. In the presentation window behind the dialog box, the Ribbon includes only the File and Broadcast tabs, and a yellow Broadcast View bar appears below the Ribbon indicating that you are broadcasting the presentation and you cannot make changes.

Exhibit 21-29 Broadcast Slide Show dialog box and presentation after broadcast has started

Inviting People to a Broadcast

Once you have the unique URL for the broadcast, you can send it to people to invite them to watch the broadcast. To do this, you can use the options in the Broadcast Slide Show dialog box to send the link using email, or to copy the link to the Clipboard so that you can paste it in an email message, a Facebook post, a blog post, or any other way of communicating electronically with your audience.

ACTIVITY

Invite people to the broadcast.

1 In the dialog box, make sure the link is still selected in the white box, and then click **Copy Link**. The link is copied to the Clipboard.

Tip: If you need to invite people after this dialog box is closed, click the Send Invitations button in the Broadcast group on the Broadcast tab to reopen it.

2 Send the link to a friend, if possible, or send it to yourself, by pasting it into the body of an email message, a Facebook post, or another method of communicating over the Internet.

Broadcasting a Slide Show

After you start the broadcast and invite people to it, you can start the slide show. You can start a slide show even if no one is watching it. On your computer, the slide show will look like an ordinary slide show. Anyone watching the slide show will see a view similar to Slide Show view in their browser window. If people go to the Web site before you start the slide show, they will see a message in the middle of the window telling them that the site is waiting for the broadcast to begin.

The Broadcast feature has the following limitations:

• There is no audio, but you can set up a conference call as many people do with Webinars.

- There is a slight lag from when you advance the slide show and when your audience sees the next animation or transition.

- Broadcast doesn't support any transitions except the Fade transition, so no matter what transitions are applied, the audience sees the Fade effect.

- Not all fonts and animations are supported. If a font or animation in the slide show is not supported, another one will be substituted.

- Movies are not supported. So if the presentation includes a video, the audience will see only a static image.

These limitations do not prevent a broadcast, but you should be aware of them so you know what the audience will see when you play the broadcast.

ACTIVITY

Broadcast a slide show.

1 In the dialog box, click **Start Slide Show**. The slide show starts from Slide 1 in Slide Show view. Anyone watching the broadcast in a browser sees the screen shown in Exhibit 21-30.

2 Advance to Slide 2. You see the Gallery transition, but anyone watching the broadcast sees the Fade transition.

3 Continue advancing through the slide show until you see Slide 6. You hear the music playing, but anyone watching the broadcast does not. Also, the sound icon is not hidden in the broadcast slide show.

4 Play the **video**. The video plays on your computer, but anyone watching the broadcast sees the poster frame.

Exhibit 21-30 Title slide in Internet Explorer during a broadcast

Address bar with copied URL

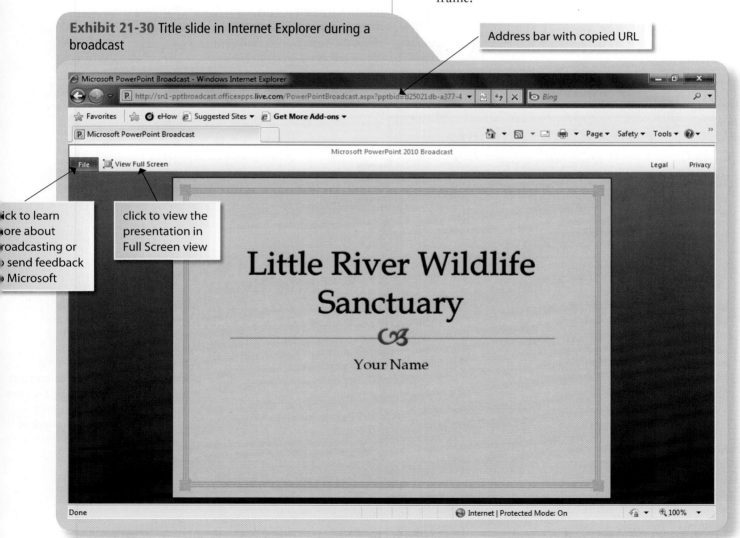

click to learn more about broadcasting or to send feedback to Microsoft

click to view the presentation in Full Screen view

Little River Wildlife Sanctuary

Your Name

5 Advance the slide show until the black slide that indicates the end of the show appears, and then advance the slide show once more to exit Slide Show view on your computer. Anyone watching the slide show continues to see the black slide that indicates the end of the slide show. Now you need to end the broadcast.

6 In the yellow Broadcast View bar below the Ribbon, click **End Broadcast**. A dialog box opens warning you that remote viewers will be disconnected.

Viewing a Broadcast and a Slide Show on the Same Computer

If you want to test a broadcast to see exactly what remote viewers will see, you can preview the broadcast using Mini Slide Show view. Make sure the PowerPoint window containing the presentation you want to broadcast is the only window maximized on your computer. Copy the broadcast link from the Broadcast Slide Show dialog box, and then start your browser. Right-click the address in the Address bar, click Paste on the shortcut menu, and then press the Enter key to go to the broadcast Web site. Next, you need to display the two windows side by side with the PowerPoint window on the left. To do this, first click the PowerPoint button on the taskbar to make the PowerPoint window the active window. Right-click the Windows taskbar, and then on the shortcut menu, click Show windows side by side. Finally, in the PowerPoint window, start the slide show in Mini Slide Show view by pressing and holding the Ctrl key, and then clicking the Slide Show button on the status bar. You'll see the broadcast start in the browser window a few seconds later. Advance through the slide show as usual. When you are done, make sure you end the slide show in the mini slide show window.

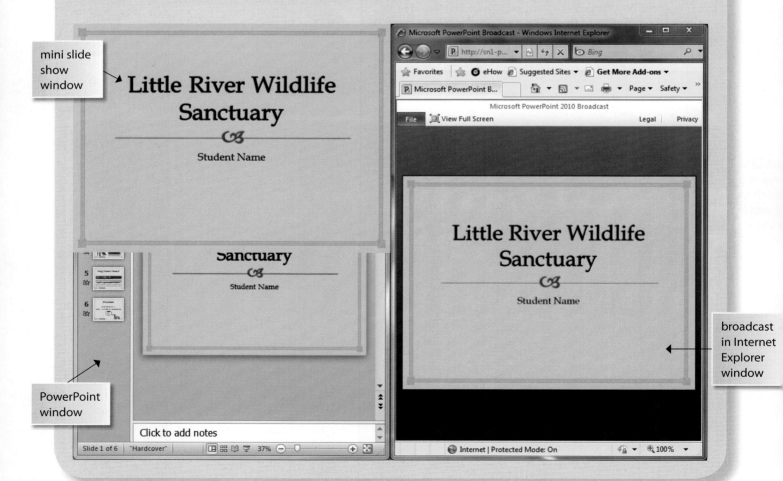

Tip: You can also click the End Broadcast button in the Broadcast group on the Broadcast tab on the Ribbon to end the broadcast.

7 In the dialog box, click **End Broadcast** to confirm that you want to end the broadcast. The dialog box closes, the yellow Broadcast View bar below the Ribbon disappears, and the ordinary tabs replace the Broadcast tab on the Ribbon. The last slide displayed during the broadcast disappears from the browser window of anyone still watching the broadcast, and a message explaining that the broadcast is over appears in its place.

8 Close the presentation.

Quiz Yourself

1. What is the difference between the theme Slide Master and a layout master?

2. If you want to add clip art or a picture from a file to a layout master that includes a content placeholder, can you use the Clip Art or Insert Picture from File icon in the content placeholder? Why or why not?

3. How do you add a shape in the default size to a slide?

4. How do you add text to a shape?

5. What is a diagram?

6. Describe how to create a SmartArt diagram with no text and how to convert a bulleted list into a SmartArt diagram.

7. How do you change the direction of an animation?

8. How do you change the speed of an animation?

9. What happens during playback when you add a reflection effect to a video?

10. How do you shorten a video's playback?

11. What is a poster frame?

12. Describe the three ways you can set an audio clip to start playing.

13. What happens when you broadcast a presentation?

14. If a slide includes a video, can a broadcast audience see the video during the broadcast?

15. When your slide show ends during a broadcast, is the broadcast ended?

Practice It

Practice It 21-1

1. Open the data file **Geese** located in the Chapter 21\Practice It folder. Save the presentation as **Geese Problem**.

2. Switch to Slide Master view. On the Thatch Slide Master, insert clip art of a drawing of a house. Resize the clip art to approximately 1-inch square, and then position it in the upper-right corner of the Thatch Slide Master.

3. Insert a drawing of a rectangle.

4. Type Macon Road Neighborhood Association in the rectangle. Change the font size of the text to 12 points, and then resize the rectangle so the text just fits on three lines. Change the shape style to the Colored Fill – Black, Dark 1 style.

5. Position the rectangle below the clip art.

6. On the Thatch Slide Master, switch the positions of the Footer and Date placeholders, and then change the alignment of the text in the Footer placeholder so it is left-aligned.

7. Verify that the changes you made to the Thatch Slide Master appear on the Title and Content Layout master and on the Two Content Layout master. Close Slide Master view.

8. Display Slide 5 ("Possible Solutions") in the Slide pane, and then in place of the content placeholder on the right, insert the picture data file **Barrier** located in the Chapter 21\Practice It folder. Apply the Reflected Rounded Rectangle style to the picture.

9. Display Slide 6 ("West Bend River: Alternative Nesting Site"), and then in place of the content placeholder on the right, insert the picture data file **Geese** located in the Chapter 21\Practice It folder. Apply the Reflected Rounded Rectangle style to the picture.

10. Display Slide 4 ("Causes") in the Slide pane. Convert the bulleted list on the slide to the Converging Radial SmartArt diagram (located in the Relationship category).

11. Add a new shape after the People feed shape in the SmartArt diagram, and then add the words **Cut grass** to the shape.

12. Change the style of the SmartArt diagram to the Cartoon style. Change the colors of the diagram to the Colored Fill – Accent 4 style (in the Accent 4 section on the Change Colors menu).

13. Animate the SmartArt diagram with the Wipe entrance animation. Change the direction of the animation to From Top. Change the sequence of the animation to One by One.

14. Change the speed of the second through fifth animated objects to 1.25 seconds.

15. Display Slide 3 ("Listen!") in the Slide pane, and then insert the video data file **GeeseVideo** located in the Chapter 21\Practice It folder.

16. Use the Shape Height box in the Size box on the Video Tools Format tab to reduce the height of the video to 4.5 inches. Apply the Half Reflection, 4 pt offset reflection style to the video.

17. Set the video to rewind after playing.

18. Trim the video so it ends at approximately the 8.5-second mark.

19. Use the frame at approximately the 4.5-second mark as the poster frame.

20. On Slide 1, insert the Smooth Jazzy clip art sound. Set the sound to start automatically, loop until stopped, and hide during the slide show.

21. On Slide 1, add your name in the line below the word *by* in the subtitle. Save the presentation.

22. Broadcast the presentation.

23. Close the presentation.

Practice It 21-2

1. Open the data file **Round Lake** located in the Chapter 21\Practice It folder. Save the file as **Round Lake Resort**.

2. Modify the title text on the Title Slide Layout master so the font used is Arial Narrow, bold, and 54 points. Widen the title text placeholder by

dragging the left, middle sizing handle to the left until the placeholder is 7.5 inches wide.

3. Modify the content placeholder on the Title and Content Layout master so that the text is 24 points, and then modify both content placeholders on the Two Content Layout master the same way.

4. In the Title and Content Layout master, resize the content placeholder so it is 4.8 inches high. In the Two Content Layout master, resize the content placeholders so they are 4.4 inches high.

5. In the Tradeshow Slide Master, change the title text font to 24 points, and then change the height of the title text placeholder to 2.2 inches, and change the width to 2.85 inches. (*Hint*: Use the Size group on the Drawing Tools Format tab.)

6. In Normal view, add your name as the subtitle on Slide 1.

7. On Slide 2 ("Why Build at Round Lake?"), insert the video data file **Lake** located in the Chapter 21\Practice It folder.

8. Change the volume of the video to Low. Set the video to loop until stopped and to rewind after playing.

9. Trim the video so that it starts at approximately the 25-second mark and ends at the 1 minute, 25-second mark (01:25.000).

10. Set the poster frame to the frame at approximately the 8-second mark.

11. Apply the Beveled Rounded Rectangle video style to the video.

12. On Slide 2, insert a rectangle shape below the video, the same width as the video, and about ¼ inch high.

13. Add the text **Property Today** to the rectangle.

14. Format the rectangle using the Subtle Effect – Blue-Gray, Accent 1 shape style.

15. On Slide 4 ("Benefits"), insert clip art showing a photo of an attractive lake and trees. Apply the Circle Bevel effect to the picture.

16. On Slide 5 ("Plan"), convert the bulleted list to a Basic Bending Process SmartArt diagram.

17. After the Submit proposal to council shape, add a new shape containing the text **Begin lake cleanup**.

18. Change the color of the SmartArt diagram to Colored Fill – Accent 2 (in the Accent 2 section).

19. Change the style to the Subtle Effect SmartArt style.

20. Animate the SmartArt diagram with the Darken emphasis animation.

21. Modify the SmartArt animation so that the shapes darken one by one.

22. Change the speed of all the SmartArt animations to 1 second.

23. On Slide 6 ("Round Lake Resort"), insert the picture data file **Logo** located in the Chapter 21\Practice It folder.

24. Proportionately resize the logo so it is 3.5 inches high.

25. Insert the sound clip **Maid with the Flaxen Hair**, located in the Sample Music folder installed with Windows 7.

26. Set the volume to Low.

27. Change the sound clip so it starts automatically, hides during the show, and loops until stopped.

28. Save the presentation.

29. Broadcast the presentation.

30. Close the presentation.

On Your Own

On Your Own 21-1

1. Open the data file **Landmarks** located in the Chapter 21\On Your Own folder. Save the file as **Landmarks Quiz**.

2. On Slide 2 ("Question 1"), in the content placeholder, insert clip art of a photo of a single statue on Easter Island.

3. On Slide 3 ("Question 2"), in the content placeholder, insert clip art of a photo of the Arc de Triomphe.

4. On Slide 4 ("Question 3"), in the content placeholder, insert clip art of a photo of the Parthenon.

5. On Slides 2, 3, and 4, change the second, third, and fourth bullet symbols to a lettered list from A to C.

6. On Slide 2 ("Question 2"), draw a rectangle, and then resize it to .5 inches high and 1.3 inches wide. Position this rectangle about 1.5 inches to the right of *Stonehenge*.

7. Copy the rectangle. Paste a copy of the rectangle to the right of *Black Hills Native American Standing Stone*, and then paste another copy to the right of *Easter Island*. The three rectangles should align vertically in the space between the text and the photo.

8. Select all three rectangles and then copy them to Slides 3 and 4. On Slide 3, proportionately reduce the size of the photo so that the rectangles will fit, and then adjust the position of each rectangle as needed to position a rectangle to the right of each lettered list item. On Slide 4, move the photo to the right, and reduce its size so that the rectangles will fit, and then adjust the position of the rectangles as needed.

9. On Slide 2, add the text **Incorrect** to the first two rectangles, and then add the text **Correct** to the third rectangle. Make the text in all three rectangles bold.

10. On Slide 3, add the text **Correct** to the middle rectangle, and then add the text **Incorrect** to the top and bottom rectangles. Make the text in all three rectangles bold.

11. On Slide 4, add the text **Correct** to the bottom rectangle, and then add the text **Incorrect** to the top two rectangles. Make the text in all three rectangles bold.

12. On Slide 4, draw another rectangle, and then resize it so it is the same size as the other rectangles (.5 inches high and 1.3 inches wide). Change its fill to black, and then copy the rectangle to the Clipboard.

13. Position the rectangle so it is directly on top of one of the blue rectangles. Paste the copied rectangle twice, and then position the copied rectangles on top of the other two rectangles on the slide.

14. Display Slide 3 in the Slide pane, paste the rectangle three times, and then position the pasted rectangles on top of the three blue rectangles. Do the same on Slide 2.

15. On Slide 2, insert the photo data file **SmallBlue1** located in the Chapter 21\On Your Own folder. Position the small blue rectangle you inserted to the left of the letter *A*. Then insert the photo data file **SmallBlue2** and position this rectangle to the left of the letter *B*. Finally, insert the photo data file **SmallBlue3** and position this rectangle to the left of the letter *C*.

16. Select the three rectangles, copy them, and then paste them on Slides 3 and 4. Reposition them to the left of the letters, keeping them in the same order.

17. Add the following as a footer on all slides except the title slide: **Click the blue box next to the correct answer.**

18. On Slide 2, select the three black rectangles, and then apply the exit animation Wipe. Change the direction of the animation to From Top. Repeat this on Slides 3 and 4.

19. On Slide 2, select the top black rectangle. On the Animations tab, set the small blue box to the left of the letter *A* as the trigger for this animation. (*Hint*: Use the Trigger button in the Advanced Animation group on the Animations tab. Select the Picture with the lowest number at the bottom of the list.)

20. On Slide 2, set the small blue box to the left of the letter *B* as the trigger for the middle black box, and then set the small blue box to the left of the letter *C* as the trigger for the bottom black box.

21. Display Slide 2 in Slide Show view, and then click each of the small blue boxes to watch the animations. End the slide show.

22. On Slides 3 and 4, set the small blue boxes to the left of the letters as triggers for their respective black boxes.

23. In the Title Slide Layout master, delete the subtitle placeholder, the box around it, and the blue rectangle at the left end of the box.

24. In the Origin Slide Master, swap the position of the Footer and Slide Number placeholders. Change the alignment of the text in the Footer placeholder to left-aligned, change the font size to 20 points, and then widen the Footer placeholder so it the right edge aligns with the right edge of the Slide Number placeholder.

25. Select the blue triangle at the bottom of the Origin Slide Master and the Footer placeholder, and position them at the top of the slide above the title placeholder.

26. Close Slide Master view, and then examine the slides. Reset any slides that did not pick up all of the changes made in Slide Master view.

27. On Slide 5, add your name as a bulleted item.

28. Run the presentation in Slide Show view, and check the animation on each slide.

29. Save the presentation. Close the presentation.

ADDITIONAL STUDY TOOLS

Chapter 21

IN THE BOOK

▶ Complete end-of-chapter exercises

▶ Study tear-out Chapter Review Card

ONLINE

▶ Complete additional end-of-chapter exercises

▶ Take practice quiz to prepare for tests

▶ Review key term flash cards (online, printable, and audio)

▶ Play "Beat the Clock" and "Memory" to quiz yourself

▶ Watch the videos "Add a Graphic from a File," "Draw a Shape on a Slide," "Format Drawings and Pictures on Slides," "Create a SmartArt Diagram," "Broadcast a Presentation," and more

PowerPoint: Prepare a Presentation

1. Plan a presentation about a topic of your choosing. For example, you can create a presentation to train others how to do a job; convey information about a person, place, or thing; influence others to buy or do something; or create a slide show of photographs around a specific topic, event, or person. Develop the basic outline of the presentation and decide what content will go on each slide.

2. Create a new PowerPoint presentation and apply an appropriate theme. Make sure you choose a theme that is relevant to your presentation and intended audience.

3. On Slide 1, add an appropriate title for the presentation. Add your name as a subtitle.

4. On the theme Slide Master, add a digital image that is related or relevant to the presentation you are creating.

5. Look at each layout master, and make sure the digital image is appropriately placed on it. If not, remove the digital image from the theme Slide Master and then add it and position it appropriately on each layout master.

6. Create a presentation based on your plan.

7. Where needed, create bulleted lists to provide details or information about the topic.

8. Add clip art or graphics to illustrate your points. Use at least one SmartArt diagram. (*Hint*: Examine the diagrams in the Picture category.)

9. On at least one slide, insert a shape, such as a rectangle, triangle, circle, arrow, or star.

10. If appropriate, add video and audio clips. Trim the clips as needed and set appropriate playback and formatting options.

11. On at least one slide, do not use a bulleted list; use only an image, clip art, a video, SmartArt, or another graphic element, with animation if appropriate. Make sure the effect during the slide show conveys your planned spoken message.

12. Examine the presentation outline. Are you using too many words? Can any of your bulleted lists be replaced with a graphic?

13. Re-evaluate the theme you chose. Do you think it is still appropriate? Does it fit the content of the presentation? If not, apply a different theme or modify the colors or fonts.

14. Add appropriate transitions and animations. Remember that the goal is to keep audience members engaged without distracting them.

15. Check the spelling, including contextual spelling, of the presentation, and then proofread it.

16. Rehearse the presentation. Consider your appearance, and decide on appropriate clothing to wear. Practice in front of a mirror and friends or family. If possible, create a video of yourself giving the presentation. Notice and fine tune your body language, tone of voice, and fluency to fully engage your audience.

Working with the PowerPoint Web App

As with the Word and Excel Web Apps, you can use the PowerPoint Web App to view or edit PowerPoint presentations stored on a SkyDrive account. When you open a presentation in the PowerPoint Web App in View mode, it appears in the browser window similar to the way it looks in Reading view. See Exhibit 21-31. If you use the buttons on the navigation bar, when you scroll through the presentation, you will see the presentation as it appears in Slide Show view with a few exceptions. First, as when you broadcast a slide show, no matter what transitions are applied, you will see the Fade transition. Second, animations most likely will not work as expected. Third, you will not see a video clip play; you will see only the poster frame. And finally, if your presentation contains audio clips, it might not display in View mode.

If you open a presentation in the PowerPoint Web App in Edit mode, you can add and delete slides; format text; insert pictures, clip art, and SmartArt; and create hyperlinks. See Exhibit 21-32. You can only insert objects on slides that contain an empty content placeholder.

From both View mode and Edit mode, you can switch to Slide Show view. (Note that if your pop-up blocker is set to block most pop-ups, you might need to allow pop-ups from the Windows Live Web site.) See Exhibit 21-33. As you can see, Slide Show view in the PowerPoint Web App looks very similar to the way a presentation looks in a browser window during a broadcast. The same limitations apply in this view as for a broadcast. However, as with Edit mode, if your presentation contains audio clips, the presentation might not display at all in Slide Show view. Note that in Slide Show view in the PowerPoint Web App, you can click the mouse button or press the appropriate keys to advance the slide show, but you cannot right-click to access the shortcut menu. Also, the Slide Show toolbar contains only the Next Slide and Previous Slide buttons.

Exhibit 21-31 Presentation in View mode in PowerPoint Web App

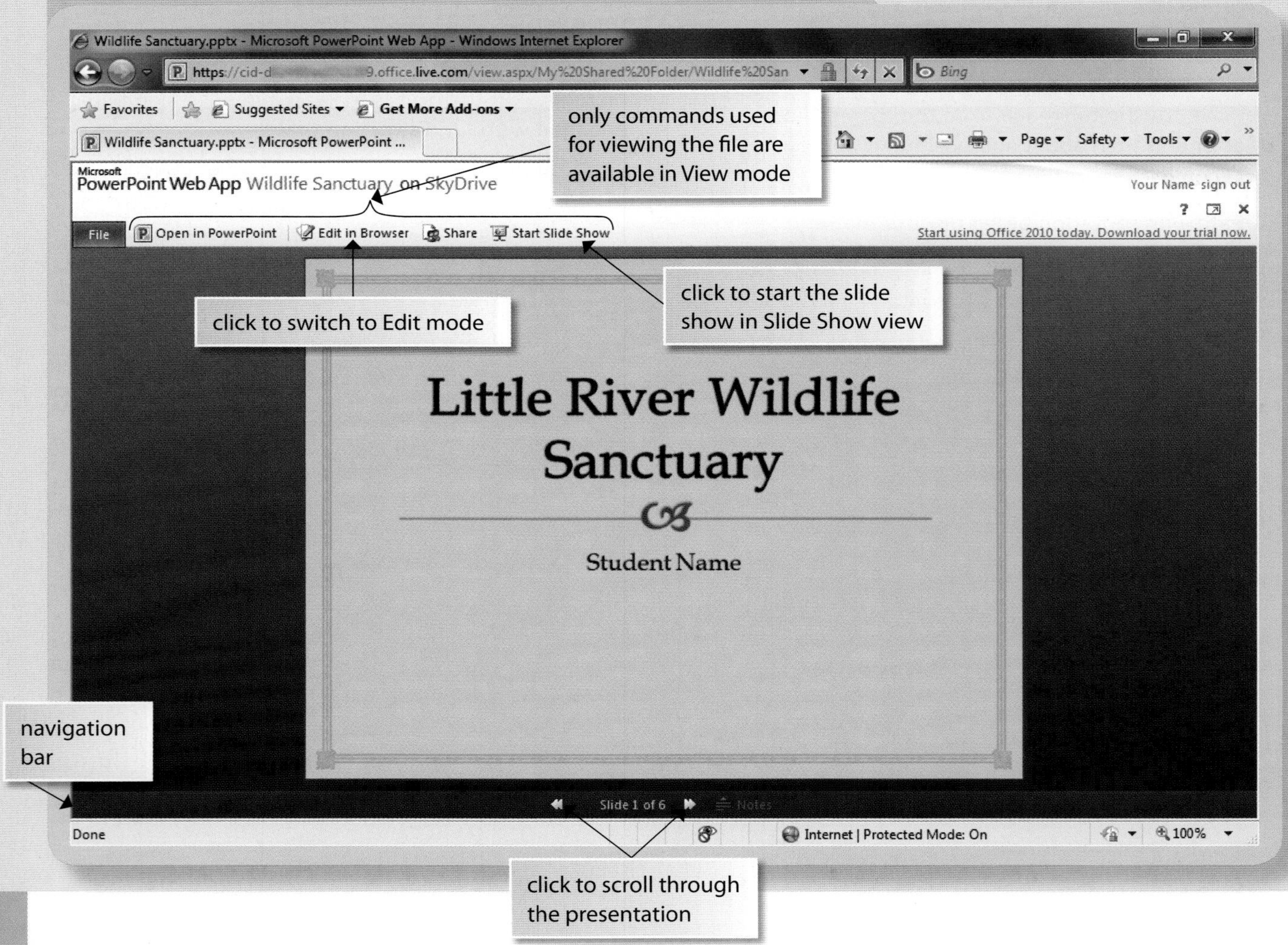

only commands used for viewing the file are available in View mode

click to switch to Edit mode

click to start the slide show in Slide Show view

navigation bar

click to scroll through the presentation

Exhibit 21-32 Presentation in Edit mode in PowerPoint Web App

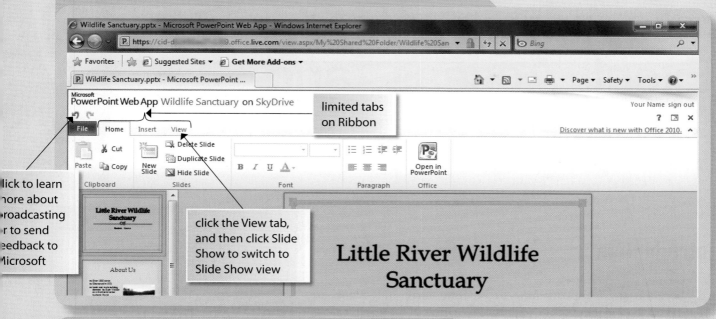

click to learn more about broadcasting or to send feedback to Microsoft

limited tabs on Ribbon

click the View tab, and then click Slide Show to switch to Slide Show view

Exhibit 21-33 Presentation in Slide Show view in PowerPoint Web App

navigation buttons

Integrating Word, Excel, Access, and PowerPoint

Introduction

Collaboration and teamwork have become the norm. Individuals are often asked to prepare or focus on a specific aspect of a project, report, or event. They research, create, and analyze the information, and then develop the related files needed for the final product. In many cases, they use one type of application to create the documents. The different files are then integrated to create an in-depth and complete product, with each part of the file having been created in the program that best fits that data. This process allows each person to use his or her expertise and as a team create a stronger, better final product.

The integration capabilities of Microsoft Office allow team members to share files and data easily. In addition to copying and pasting among different programs, you can embed a file of one type in a file of another type; link files so that when the original file changes, the changes appear in the file linked to it; and import and export data from one file format to another.

Learning Objectives

After studying the material in this chapter, you will be able to:

LO22.1 Understand object linking and embedding (OLE)

LO22.2 Import and export data

LO22.3 Use the Object command to insert text from a file

LO22.4 Copy and paste among Office programs

LO22.5 Create PowerPoint slides from a Word outline

LO22.6 Create form letters with mail merge

LO22.1 Object Linking and Embedding

Office 2010 supports **object linking and embedding** (**OLE**, pronounced O-L-E or oh-lay), a way of transferring and sharing objects between programs. Remember that an object is anything that can be manipulated as a whole; in other words, it is the specific information that you want to share between programs and can be anything from a chart or a table to a picture, video, sound clip, or almost anything else you can create on a computer. The program used to create the object you want to integrate into another program is the **source program**; the file that initially contains the object is the **source file**. The program used to create the file where you want to insert the object is called

object linking and embedding (**OLE**) A way of transferring and sharing objects between programs.

source program The program used to create an object.

source file The file that contains an object that you want to integrate into another file.

EDHAR/Shutterstock.com

The ability to integrate Microsoft Office documents allows people to share info and create complex docs even if they're not in the same location, an important consideration in our global society.

the **destination program**; the file where you want to insert the object is called the **destination file**.

When you **embed** an object, a copy of the object along with a link to the source program become part of the destination file, and you can edit the object using the source program's commands. There is no connection between an embedded object and its source file; therefore, changes made to the object in the source file do not appear in the destination file. You must have access to the source program to edit an embedded object; however, you do not need access to the source file.

destination program The program used to create the file where you want to insert an object created in a different file.

destination file The file into which you want to insert an object created in another file.

embed To copy an object along with a link to the source program in a destination file.

Exhibit 22-1 Embedding contrasted with linking

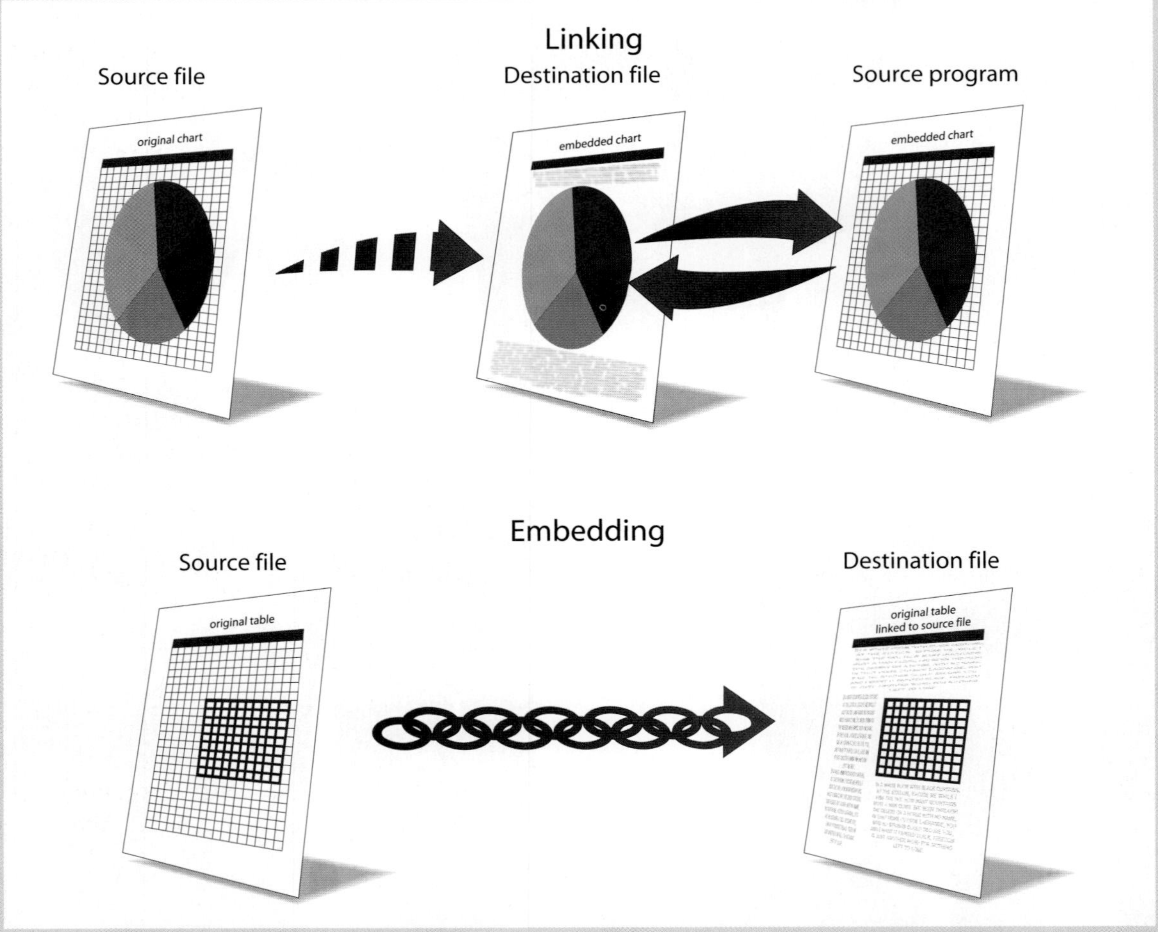

When you **link** an object, a direct connection is created between the source and destination files. The object exists in only one place—the source file—but the link displays the object in the destination file as well. You must have access to the source file if you want to make changes to the linked source object. If you edit a linked object in the source file, the link ensures that the changes appear in the destination file. If you edit a linked object in the destination file, the changes do not appear in the source file. The next time the link is updated, the changes made in the destination file will be overwritten with the linked data from the source file.

Both linking and embedding involve inserting an object into a destination file; the difference lies in where their respective objects are stored. The advantage of embedding an object instead of linking it is that the source file and the destination file can be stored separately. You can use the source program commands to make changes to the object in the destination file, and the source file will be unaffected. The disadvantage is that the destination file size is somewhat larger than it would be if the object was simply pasted as a picture or text, or if it was linked. The advantage of linking an object instead of embedding it is that the object remains identical in the source and destination files, and the destination file size does not increase as much as if the object were embedded. The disadvantage is that the source and destination files must be stored together. When you need to copy information from one program to another, consider which option is the best choice for your needs.

Exhibit 22-1 compares linking and embedding, and Exhibit 22-2 summarizes embedding and linking and compares their advantages and disadvantages.

link To establish a direct connection between a source and a destination file.

Exhibit 22-2 Comparing integration methods

	Embedding	Linking
Description	Displays and stores an object in the destination file.	Displays an object in the destination file along with the source file's location; stores the object in the source file.
Use if you want to	Include the object in the destination file, and edit the object using the source program without affecting the source file.	Edit the object in the source file and have the changes appear in the destination file.
Advantages	The source file and destination file can be stored separately. You can use source program commands to make changes to the object in the destination file.	The destination file size remains fairly small. The source file and the object in the destination file remain identical.
Disadvantages	The destination file size increases to reflect the addition of the object from the source file.	The source and destination files must be stored together.

To do this, in either program, click the Chart button in the Illustrations group on the Insert tab to open the Chart dialog box. After you select the type of chart you want to create, the Word or PowerPoint window resizes to half the screen width, an Excel window with sample data opens on the other half of the screen, and a chart based on the sample data and the chart style you selected appears in the document or slide. Modify the sample data in the worksheet so that it contains your data, and the chart will adjust as you edit the worksheet.

When you create a chart using this method, you don't need to save the Excel workbook before closing it because it is part of the Word file and will be saved when you save the Word file.

Creating an Embedded Excel Chart in Word or PowerPoint

If you want to embed a chart in a Word document or PowerPoint slide, and the chart or the data to create it does not already exist in a separate Excel file, you can create the chart from within the Word or PowerPoint file.

 **ACTIVITY**

Create an embedded Excel chart in a Word document.

1 Open the Word data file **EcoBrochure** located in the Chapter22\Chapter folder. At the bottom of

Sharing Information

Most organizations rely heavily on teams to complete work tasks, and, consequently, team members rely on each other to complete their assigned projects successfully. For example, you might be responsible for providing data for others to analyze, or for collecting other team members' data and creating a report. When a team works together to complete a project, it is vital that each member of the team complete his or her piece of the project. If even one person fails to do this, the entire project is affected. Learning the different roles team members play, how they complement each other for efficient task completion, and how to lead and motivate a team toward goal achievement can mean the difference between professional success and failure. As you work in different Microsoft Office programs, keep in mind that you might need to share your work with others on your team, at school, or in a professional environment. Take the time to make sure your work is complete and ready to be shared with others, and that it can be imported or exported, as needed, for use in other programs.

page 1, after *Prepared by:*, type your name, and then save the document as **EcoFlooring Brochure**.

2 On page 2, in the paragraph above the *What installation options can I choose from?* heading, delete the **yellow highlighted text**. The insertion point is in the now empty paragraph.

3 On the Ribbon, click the **Insert tab**. In the Illustrations group, click the **Chart button**. The Insert Chart dialog box opens. Column is selected in the list of chart types.

> **Tip:** You can also create an embedded chart in a PowerPoint slide using the Chart button in the Illustrations group on the Insert tab, or by clicking the Insert Chart button in a Content placeholder.

4 Click **OK**. The dialog box closes, the Word window shrinks to half its width, and an Excel window opens to the right of the Word win-

If the data on which a chart will be based exists in an Excel worksheet, you can copy the data to the Excel worksheet that opens when you click the Chart button in the Word or PowerPoint file.

dow. The worksheet in the Excel window contains sample data, and a column chart of the Excel data is inserted in the Word document. Chart Tools contextual tabs appear on the Ribbon.

5 In the Word window, change the Zoom level so that you can see all of the columns in the chart and read the labels. See Exhibit 22-3.

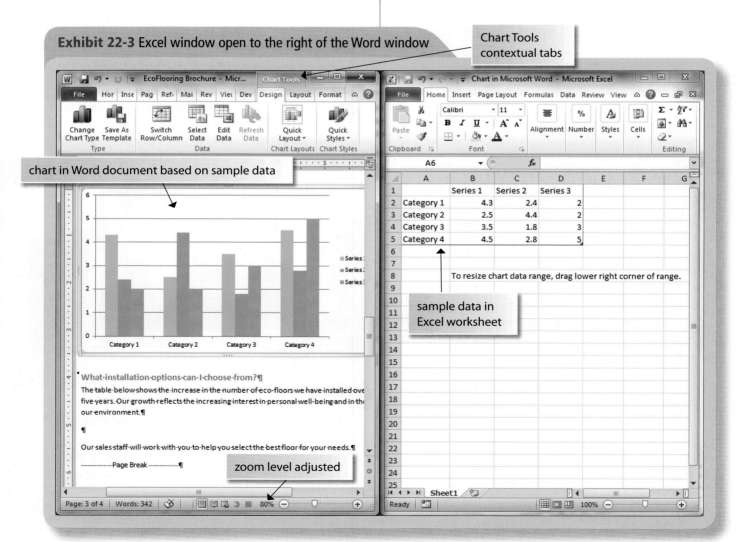

Exhibit 22-3 Excel window open to the right of the Word window

Chart Tools contextual tabs

chart in Word document based on sample data

To resize chart data range, drag lower right corner of range.

sample data in Excel worksheet

zoom level adjusted

6 In the Excel worksheet, click **cell A2**, type **Ash** and then press the **Down Arrow key**. The text you type replaces the placeholder text in the cell and below the first set of columns in the chart in the Word window.

7 In the Excel worksheet, in the **range A3:A10**, enter the following labels:

Bamboo
Beech
Cherry birch
Hevea
Kempas
Maple
Oak
Walnut

8 Examine the chart in the Word window. Notice that the three labels outside of the blue border in the Excel worksheet are not included in the chart.

9 Click in the Excel window, and then drag the **lower-right blue border sizing handle** down to below row 10 so that the blue border surrounds the range A1:D10. The chart in the Word window adjusts to include columns for all the labels that you typed. See Exhibit 22-4.

10 In the Excel window, click **cell B2**, type **3.8** and then press the **Enter key**. The first green column in the chart shortens to the 3.8 mark.

11 In the **range B3:B10**, enter the following values:

6.1
3.1
3.1
4.3
5.6
2.9
4.2
3.6

12 In the Excel window, drag the **lower-right blue border corner** to the left two columns so that the blue border surrounds the range A1:B10. The blue and yellow columns in the chart in the Word window disappear.

13 In the Excel window, make **cell B2** the current cell. On the Excel Ribbon, click the **Data tab**, and then in the Sort & Filter group, click the **Sort Smallest to Largest button**. The rows in the table are sorted by the values in column B from the smallest to the largest. The columns in the chart in the Word window are rearranged to match the Excel worksheet.

14 In the Excel window, click the **Close button**. The Excel window closes and the Word window resizes to its original size. The chart is selected, and the Chart Tools Design tab is selected.

15 Change the zoom level to **Page Width**.

16 On the Ribbon, click the **Chart Tools Layout tab**. In the Labels group, click the **Legend button**, and then click **None**. The legend is removed from the chart.

17 In the chart, click the **Series 1 title** to select the title text box, and then click **Series 1** again. The insertion point blinks in the title.

18 Edit the title to **Janka Rating for Common Woods**. See Exhibit 22-5.

19 Save the document.

Exhibit 22-4 Additional columns added to the chart

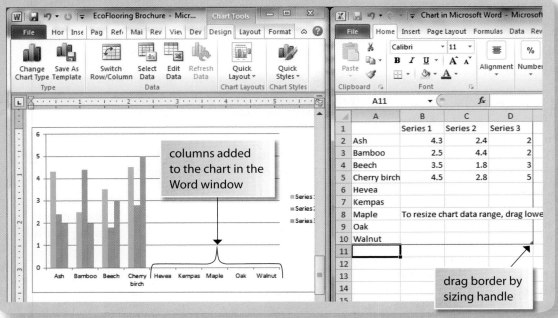

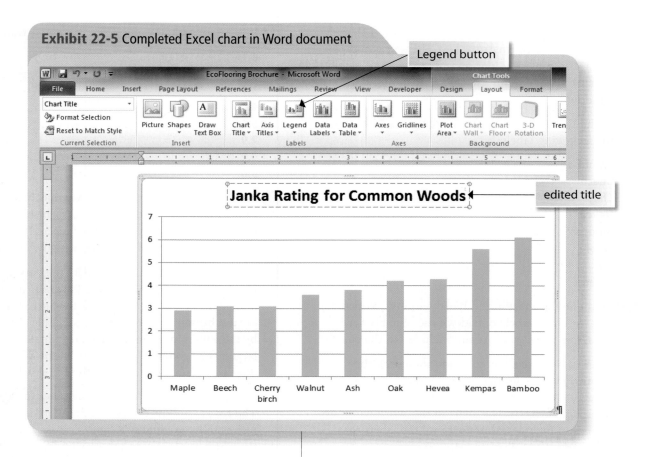

Exhibit 22-5 Completed Excel chart in Word document

Legend button

edited title

Embedding a Chart Created in an Excel Worksheet in Word or PowerPoint

If a chart already exists in an Excel worksheet, you can copy it from there and then embed it in the document or slide. You can then use Excel commands to modify the chart from within the document or slide. Your changes, however, will not appear in the original file.

Remember that when you use the Paste command, you have access to several options to paste the object in different ways. If you click the Paste button arrow instead of clicking the Paste button, a menu with Paste Options buttons appears. You can point to each button to see a Live Preview of the pasted object. For most objects, you can choose whether to keep the source file formatting or use the destination file formatting. For some objects, such as pasting an Excel chart into a Word document, you can also choose whether to embed or link the object or paste it as a picture. If you click the Paste button, you can still change the way an object is pasted by clicking the Paste Options button that appears just below and to the right of the pasted object to access the same menu of options.

 **ACTIVITY**

Embed a chart created in an Excel worksheet in a Word document.

1 Open the Excel data file **EcoMaterials** located in the Chapter 22\Chapter folder. Save the document as **EcoFlooring Materials**. On the taskbar, a Microsoft Excel button appears next to the Microsoft Word button.

2 In the Excel worksheet, click the **chart** to select it. On the Home tab, in the Clipboard group, click the **Copy button**. The chart is copied to the Clipboard.

3 On the taskbar, click the **Microsoft Word button** to return to the EcoFlooring Brochure document.

4 On page 2, under the *How do I know which eco-friendly flooring is right for me?* heading, delete the **green highlighted text**. The insertion point is in the now empty paragraph.

5 On the Home tab, in the Clipboard group, click the **Paste button arrow**. A menu of Paste options appears.

> **Tip:** The same options appear on the Paste button arrow in the PowerPoint window when an Excel chart has been copied to the Clipboard.

6 In the Paste button menu, point to the **Use Destination Theme & Embed Workbook button** (the first button). The chart appears in the document at the insertion point using the Composite theme colors and fonts in the Word document file. See Exhibit 22-6. This is the default option.

Exhibit 22-6 Paste button menu with Paste Options

Paste button arrow

ScreenTip

7 In the Paste button menu, point to the **Keep Source Formatting & Embed Workbook button** (the second button). The chart changes to use the Concourse theme colors and fonts from the source file.

> **Tip:** To change the default paste option, click Set Default Paste on the Paste menu, and then make your selections in the Cut, copy, and paste section of the Advanced page of the Word Options dialog box that opens.

8 In the Paste button menu, point to the other three buttons, noting the change in the chart in the document and reading their ScreenTips, and then click the first button, the **Use Destination Theme & Embed Workbook button**. The chart is pasted in the document as an inline object using the document theme colors and fonts.

Editing an Embedded Excel Chart in Word or PowerPoint

When you edit an embedded object within the destination program, the changes affect only the embedded object; the original object in the source program remains unchanged. To edit the embedded object, click it to display tabs and commands on from the embedded object's source program on the Ribbon. You can then use these to modify the embedded object.

ACTIVITY

Edit an embedded chart in a Word document.

1 In the Word document, click the **embedded pie chart**. The selection frame and handles appear around the chart object, and the Excel Chart Tools contextual tabs appear on the Word Ribbon.

2 On the Home tab, in the Paragraph group, click the **Center button**. The paragraph containing the inline chart object is formatted so it is centered horizontally.

3 On the Ribbon, click the **Chart Tools Design tab**. In the Chart Styles group, click the **Style 11 style** (the green style in the group). The colors used in the pie chart are changed to shades of green instead of shades of yellow.

> **Tip:** The Chart Tools contextual tabs also appear in the PowerPoint window when an embedded chart is selected.

4 On the Chart Tools Design tab, in the Data group, click the **Edit Data button**. An Excel window opens to the right of the Word window. In the title bar

The buttons on the Chart Tools contextual tabs in the Word window are very similar to the buttons on these tabs in the Excel window, but they are not all identical.

of the Excel window, the file name is *Chart in Microsoft Word*. On the taskbar, the Excel button changes to indicate that more than one workbook is open.

5 On the taskbar, point to the **Excel button** . The pop-up windows indicate that there are two Excel workbooks open: the EcoFlooring Materials workbook from which you copied the pie chart, and the Chart in Microsoft Word workbook. See Exhibit 22-7.

6 In the Excel window, in **cell B5**, change the value to **31** and then in **cell B6**, change the value to **30**. The chart in the Excel worksheet and the chart in the Word document change to reflect the new data.

7 In the Excel window, click the **Close button** . The Excel window for the embedded chart closes and the EcoFlooring Brochure document in the Word window maximizes. The Excel window with the EcoFlooring Materials workbook is the same size and in the same position as the embedded workbook window was.

8 Maximize the Excel window. Notice in this file that the values in cells B5 and B6 in the EcoFlooring Materials workbook are unchanged.

9 Close the **EcoFlooring Materials workbook**.

10 Save the **EcoFlooring Brochure document**, and then close it.

Exhibit 22-7 Embedded workbook to the right of the Word document

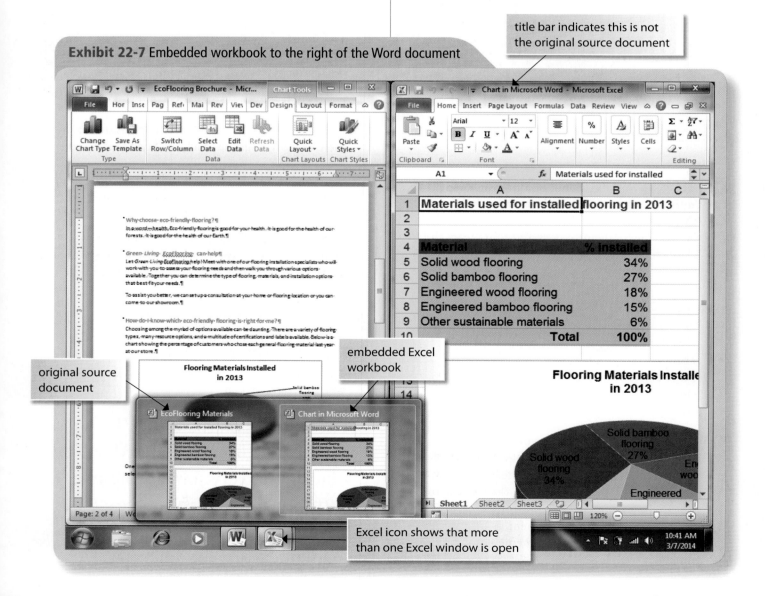

title bar indicates this is not the original source document

original source document

embedded Excel workbook

Excel icon shows that more than one Excel window is open

Embedding Excel Worksheet Data in Word and PowerPoint

When you copy worksheet data, the first two buttons on the Paste button menu are Keep Source Formatting and Use Destination Styles. Selecting either of these two buttons pastes the data as an ordinary table. The table is not embedded; it was converted to a Word or PowerPoint table. You can then format the table using the usual methods. If you want to embed worksheet data in either a Word document or a PowerPoint slide instead of pasting it as a table or linking it to the Excel worksheet, you need to use the Paste Special command. To do this, click the Paste button arrow, and then click Paste Special to open the Paste Special dialog box. With the Paste option button selected, click Microsoft Excel Worksheet Object in the As list, and then click OK. The table is placed into the document or the slide with a selection box and sizing handles around it. You cannot edit the data in an embedded table as you do an ordinary Word or PowerPoint table. Instead, you double-click the embedded table to access Excel editing commands. When you double-click the embedded table, instead of the worksheet appearing in a separate Excel window, a copy of the entire workbook from which you copied the table appears within a dashed line border and the Excel Ribbon tabs completely replace the Word or PowerPoint Ribbon tabs.

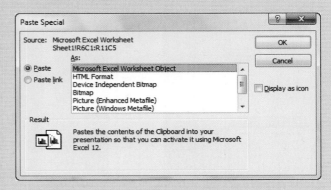

Linking an Excel Chart to a Word Document or PowerPoint Presentation

If a chart exists in an Excel worksheet and you think you might update it in the future, you can link it to a Word document or PowerPoint slide instead of embedding it. Then when you modify the Excel file, the changes will appear in the destination file. To link an Excel chart to a Word document or PowerPoint presentation, copy it in the Excel file, and then use one of the Link buttons on the Paste button menu. You must leave the Excel workbook open while you paste, or the Paste button menu will offer only options to embed the chart or paste it as an image.

 **ACTIVITY**

Link an Excel worksheet to a PowerPoint presentation.

1. Open the PowerPoint data file **EcoPresentation**, located in the Chapter 22\Chapter folder. Save the presentation as **EcoFlooring Presentation**.

2. On the title slide, add your name as the subtitle.

3. Open the Excel workbook **EcoGrowth**. Save the workbook as **EcoFlooring Growth**.

4. Select the **chart**, and then copy it to the Clipboard.

5. Switch to the PowerPoint presentation **EcoFlooring Presentation**, and then display **Slide 2** ("Growth Chart") in the Slide pane.

6. In the Clipboard group, click the **Paste button arrow**. The same buttons that appeared when you embedded the Excel chart in the Word document appear.

7. Click the **Use Destination Theme & Link Data button**. The chart object is pasted into the slide and is linked to the Excel workbook.

8. Resize the chart to fill the space below the slide title. See Exhibit 22-8.

Do not close the Excel workbook, or you will have only the option to paste the chart instead of linking it.

Exhibit 22-8 Linked Excel chart in PowerPoint slide

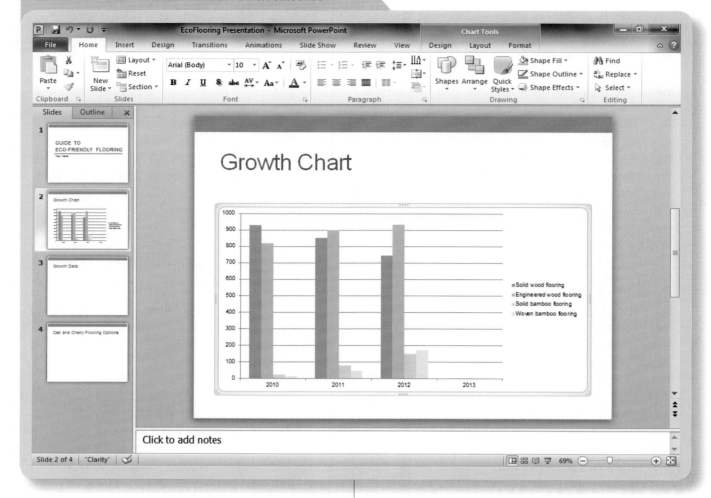

Linking Excel Worksheet Data to Word or PowerPoint

When you copy Excel worksheet data and then click the Paste button arrow in a Word document, two of the buttons on the menu are Link commands. However, if you use these buttons to link data from cells in an Excel worksheet to a Word document, the link will not always be maintained after you close the Word document. When you copy Excel worksheet data and then click the Paste button arrow in a PowerPoint presentation, none of the buttons on the menu are Link commands. To create a stable link in a Word document or to create a link in a PowerPoint slide, you need to use the Paste Special command. Then, just like with a linked chart, you can edit the source file, and the edits will appear in the destination file.

 **ACTIVITY**

Link Excel worksheet data to a PowerPoint slide.

1 Switch to the Excel workbook **EcoFlooring Growth**.

2 Select the **range A6:E11**, and then copy it to the Clipboard.

3 Switch to the PowerPoint presentation **EcoFlooring Presentation**, and then display **Slide 3** ("Growth Data") in the Slide pane.

4 On the Home tab, in the Clipboard group, click the **Paste button arrow**. Point to each of the Paste Options buttons, watching the worksheet change on the slide and reading the ScreenTips. The set of buttons on the Paste button menu are different than the sets of Paste buttons you have seen until now. None of the buttons on the Paste button menu allow you to link the worksheet data.

5 On the menu, click **Paste Special**. The Paste Special dialog box opens. The Paste option but-

> **Tip:** With the Paste option button selected, keep Microsoft Excel Worksheet Object selected in the As list to embed the worksheet in the slide.

ton is selected, and a list of format options for the copied worksheet data appears.

6 Click the **Paste link option button**. The As list changes to include link options including Microsoft Excel Worksheet Object. See Exhibit 22-9.

7 Click **OK**. The dialog box closes and the worksheet data appears on the slide.

8 Resize the chart object to fill the space below the slide title. See Exhibit 22-10.

Updating Linked Objects When the Destination File Is Open

When an object is linked from a source file to a destination file, you can edit the information in the source file, and the changes will appear in the destination file. If both files are open, sometimes the changes appear instantaneously. Sometimes linked data does not automatically update, even if both files are open. If the linked object is a chart, you can click the Refresh Data button in the Data group on the Chart Tools Design tab. If the linked object is a worksheet, right-click the linked object in the destination file, and then click Update Link on the shortcut menu.

Exhibit 22-9 Paste Special dialog box with Paste link options

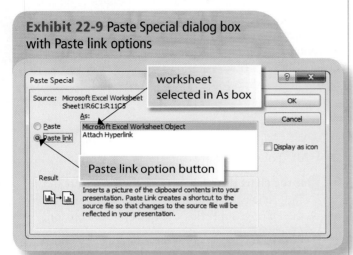

Exhibit 22-10 Linked Excel worksheet data on a PowerPoint slide

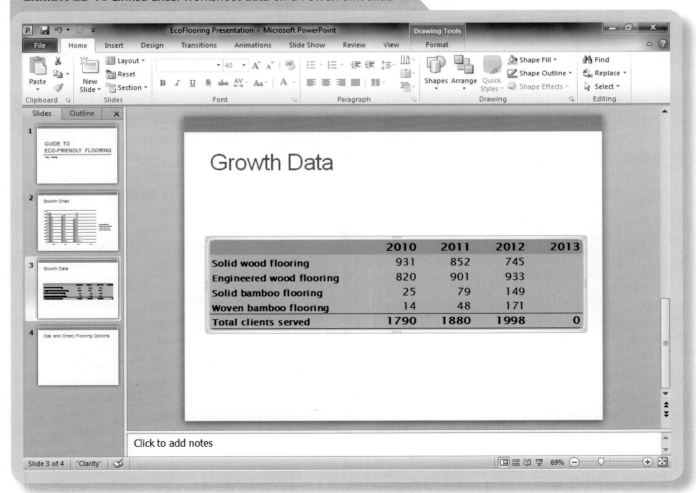

Paste Button Options vs. the Paste Special Dialog Box

Using one of the buttons on the Paste button menu (or on the Paste Options button that appears after you paste an object) allows you to choose to keep the source file theme and formatting or apply the theme and formatting in the destination file, in addition to letting you choose between pasting, embedding, and linking. Using the commands in the Paste Special dialog box offers additional choices for pasting. For example, if you want to paste an Excel table as text, you can choose to paste it as formatted or unfor- matted text; and if you want to paste a table or chart as an image, you can choose from a few additional file types. You cannot, however, choose to use the source or destination theme formatting. If you choose a formatted option, the copied object will be pasted with the source file formatting; if you choose an unformatted option, the copied object will be pasted as unformatted text or data. Ultimately, the method you use will be determined by exactly what you want to appear in your destination document.

ACTIVITY

Update linked objects.

1 In the PowerPoint presentation, display **Slide 2** ("Growth Chart") in the Slide pane, and then select the **linked chart**.

2 Click the **Chart Tools Design tab**. In the Data group, click the **Edit Data button**. The original worksheet from which you copied the worksheet data, EcoFlooring Growth, appears to the right of the PowerPoint presentation.

3 In the Excel window, click **cell E7**, type **613** and then press the **Enter key**. A bar is added to the

chart in the Excel worksheet and in the chart in the PowerPoint presentation. See Exhibit 22-11.

4 If the chart did not update, click the **chart** in the slide, click the **Chart Tools Design tab**, and then in the Data group, click the **Refresh Data button**.

5 In the PowerPoint presentation, display **Slide 3** ("Growth Data") in the Slide pane.

6 Right-click the **table**. A shortcut menu opens. See Exhibit 22-12.

7 On the shortcut menu, click **Update Link**. If the table in the slide had not updated with the new data when you entered it, it updates now. If the table was already updated, nothing changes.

Exhibit 22-11 Updated linked Excel chart in PowerPoint slide

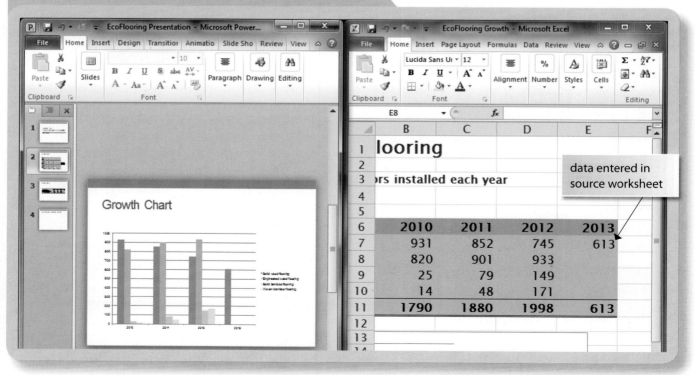

Exhibit 22-12 Shortcut menu for linked worksheet data

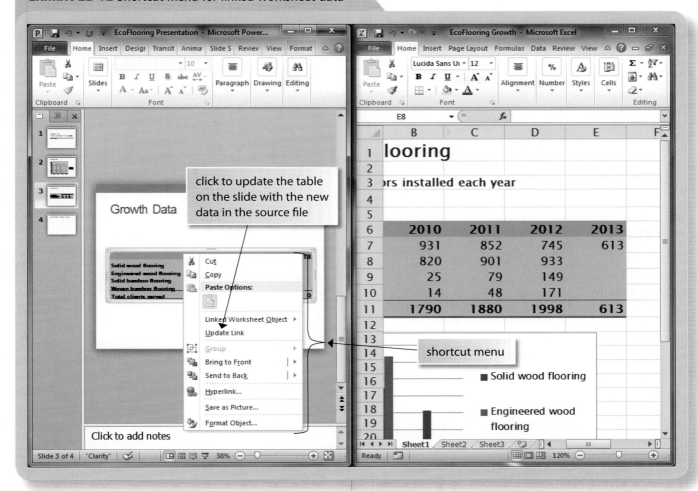

Updating Linked Objects When the Destination File Is Closed

When you link objects to a file, they are set to update automatically or manually. When you open a destination file that contains a linked object that is set to update automatically, a dialog box opens asking if you want to update the linked data. If the linked object is set to be updated manually, no dialog box appears when you open the file, but you can refresh the data or update the link.

Edit the linked object when the destination files are closed.

1 Save the PowerPoint file **EcoFlooring Presentation**, and then close it.

2 Maximize the Excel workbook window containing **EcoFlooring Growth**.

3 In **cell E8**, type **974** and then press the **Enter key**.

4 Save the Excel file.

5 Open the PowerPoint file **EcoFlooring Presentation**. A dialog box opens telling you that the presentation contains links to other files. See Exhibit 22-13.

6 Click **Update Links**. The dialog box closes and the links are updated.

Exhibit 22-13 Microsoft PowerPoint Security Notice dialog box

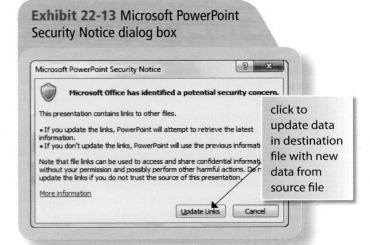

7 Display **Slide 3** ("Growth Data") in the Slide pane. The worksheet data is updated with the new value.

> ⚠ **Problem?** If the table did not update, right-click the **table**, and then on the shortcut menu, click **Update Link**.

8 Display **Slide 2** ("Growth Chart") in the Slide pane. Although you clicked Update Links, a second column of data does not appear above the 2013 label in the chart.

9 Select the **chart**, click the **Chart Tools Design tab**, and then in the Data group, click the **Refresh Data button**. A second bar is added to the 2013 data. See Exhibit 22-14.

10 In the Excel worksheet, in **cell E9**, enter **279** and then in **cell E10**, enter **387**.

11 In the PowerPoint window, refresh the data.

12 Save the **EcoFlooring Presentation** file, and then maximize it.

Exhibit 22-14 Updated link in the PowerPoint presentation

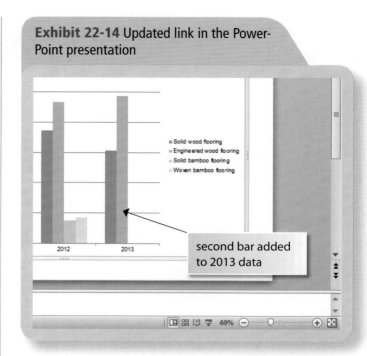

second bar added to 2013 data

13 Switch to the Excel workbook **EcoFlooring Growth**, save it, and then close it.

Using the Links Dialog Box

By default, linked objects are supposed to update automatically; however, sometimes this is not the case. To see if a link is set to update automatically or manually, you can open the Links dialog box. To do this, click the File tab in the destination file to display the Info tab in Backstage view. At the bottom of the pane on the right, click the Edit Links to Files link. The Links dialog box lists all the links in the file with the update setting on the right. To change the update setting for a link, click it, and then click the appropriate option button at the bottom of the dialog box.

You can also use the Links dialog box to change the location of a linked object's source file. For example, if you send a file containing a linked object to a colleague, you need to send the source file as well if you want your colleague to have the ability to edit the linked object and have changes appear in both the destination and the source files. Your colleague likely will not have the same folder structure as you do and, therefore, will need to identify the new location (that is, the file path) of the source file. To do this, in the list of links in the Links dialog box, click the link whose location has changed, click the Change Source button, and then navigate to the new location of the source file.

Finally, you can break a link in the Links dialog box. This is a good idea if you plan to send the file to someone who will not have access to the linked object's source file. After you break a link, users who open the destination file will not get a message asking if they want to update the links—an impossible task if the users do not have access to the source file. To break a link, select the link in the list in the dialog box, and then click Break Link.

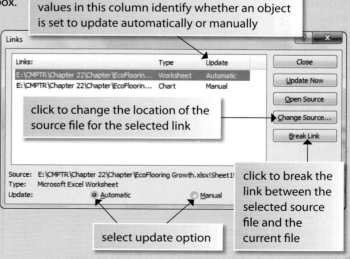

values in this column identify whether an object is set to update automatically or manually

click to change the location of the source file for the selected link

click to break the link between the selected source file and the current file

select update option

LO22.2 Importing and Exporting Data

You might want to use Access commands to analyze data stored in a list in a text file or an Excel worksheet. You cannot embed or link data in an Access datasheet. Instead, you can import data from these files to build a table in Access. Then, you can create forms, reports, queries, and other Access objects based on the tables. You cannot import data directly from a Word file, only from a plain text file, so if data already exists in a Word file, save the file as a plain text file using the Save as type arrow in the Save As dialog box.

If you need to use Access data in other Office programs, you can export it to a file format these programs can use.

Importing an Excel List into an Access Table

You can only import data that is in the form of a list—a series of paragraphs or worksheet rows that contain related data, such as product names and prices or client names and phone numbers. Before you import the list, you should check the format of the data. The first row of data will become the field names in the new table, so it is important that every column have a heading. Each row of data becomes a record in the database, so there should not be any rows above the column heads and there should not be any blank rows.

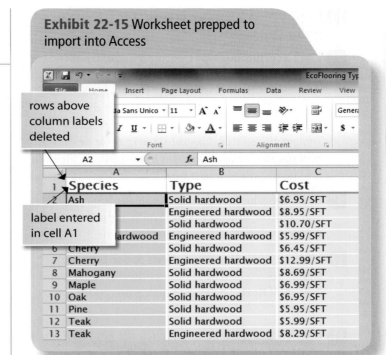

Exhibit 22-15 Worksheet prepped to import into Access

rows above column labels deleted

label entered in cell A1

6 On the Ribbon, click the **External Data tab**. In the Import & Link group, click the **Excel button**. The Get External Data – Excel Spreadsheet dialog box opens. See Exhibit 22-16.

ACTIVITY

Import an Excel list to a table in a new database.

1 Open the Excel data file **EcoTypes**, located in the Chapter 22\Chapter folder. Save the file as **EcoFlooring Types**.

2 Delete **rows 1–4**.

3 In **cell A1**, enter **Species**. See Exhibit 22-15.

4 Save and close the file.

5 Create a new Access database named **EcoFlooringTypes**.

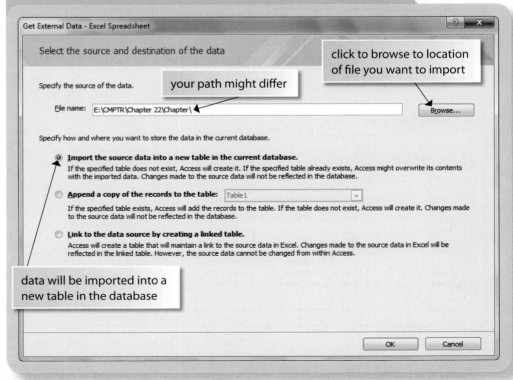

Exhibit 22-16 Get External Data – Excel Spreadsheet dialog box

your path might differ

click to browse to location of file you want to import

data will be imported into a new table in the database

7 In the dialog box, click **Browse**. The File Open dialog box opens.

8 Click **EcoFlooring Types**, located in the Chapter 22\Chapter folder included with your data files, and then click **Open**. EcoFlooring Types.xlsx and its path are listed in the File name box in the Get External Data – Excel Spreadsheet dialog box. The *Import the source data into a new table in the current database option button* is selected, so the data will be imported into a new table in the database.

9 Click **OK**. The first dialog box in the Import Spreadsheet Wizard opens. You want to import the first worksheet from the workbook.

10 Make sure the **Show Worksheets option button** and **Sheet1** are selected at the top of the dialog box, and then click **Next**. The second dialog box of the wizard opens.

11 If it is not already selected, click the **First Row Contains Column Headings check box**. A row number does not appear next to the column headings from the worksheet, which indicates that they will become the field names in the new Access table. Below the headings, the Excel data is organized into records and fields. See Exhibit 22-17.

12 Click **Next**. In the third dialog box in the wizard, you could specify information about the fields you are importing, including the data type of each field.

13 Click **Next** to accept the default field names and other information. The next dialog box in the wizard lets you assign a primary key to the data. The Let Access add primary key option button is selected. Because the worksheet you are importing does not contain information you can convert to a primary key, you will let Access add one to the table.

14 Click **Next** to let Access add a primary key. The final dialog box in the Import Spreadsheet Wizard opens. The text in the Import to Table box is selected, and the *I would like a wizard to analyze my table after importing the data* check box is deselected.

15 In the Import to Table box, type **Types** and then click **Finish**. The Get External Data – Excel Spreadsheet dialog box appears again, displaying the Save Import Steps screen. If you were going to import this table again, you could save the choices you made when you went through the wizard. You don't need to do that in this case, so you'll leave the Save import steps check box unchecked.

16 In the dialog box, click **Close**. The table appears in the Navigation Pane.

17 In the Navigation Pane, double-click **Types** to open the Types table. The Excel data has been imported into the new Access table, and the column headings are converted to field names and the row data to records. See Exhibit 22-18.

18 Close both tables.

Exhibit 22-17 Second dialog box in the Import Spreadsheet Wizard

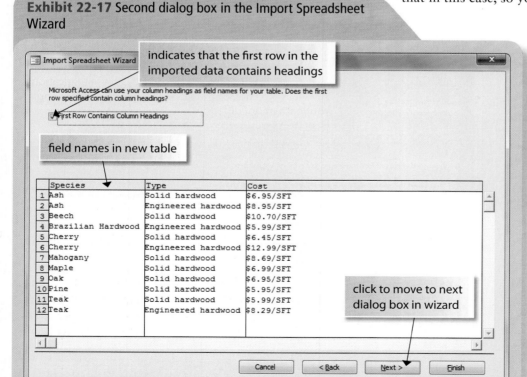

Exhibit 22-18 Excel data imported into an Access table

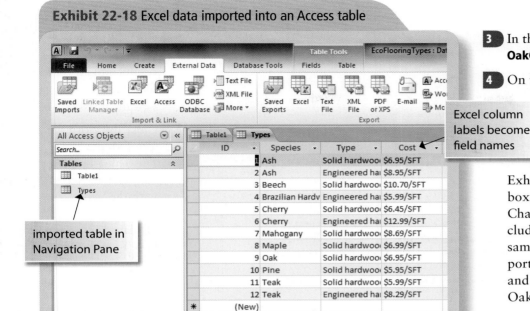

imported table in Navigation Pane

Excel column labels become field names

3 In the Navigation Pane, click the **OakCherry query** to select it.

4 On the Ribbon, click the **External Data tab**. In the Export group, click the **More** button, and then click **Word**. The Export – RTF File dialog box opens. See Exhibit 22-20. In the File name box, the path is the path to the Chapter 22\Chapter folder included with your Data Files—the same path you used when you imported the Excel file into Access, and the file name of the new file is OakCherry.rtf.

Exporting Access Data to a Word File

As you recall from your work with Access, you use a query to extract information from a database. The query results are stored in a datasheet. You can export the datasheet to a new text document or Excel worksheet. If you want to export to a text file, you can choose the Text file type, which creates a document with unformatted text, or **Rich Text Format** (**RTF**), a text format that preserves the layout of data.

ACTIVITY

Export the Access data to a Word file.

1 Create a query named **OakCherry** that lists only the records with a species of oak or cherry, and shows the Species, Type, and Cost fields for those records.

2 Run the query, and then widen the Type column to fit the widest entry. See Exhibit 22-19.

Tip: If you don't need to preserve the layout of your data, export the table or query to a plain text file by clicking the Text File button in the Export group on the External Data tab.

5 In the File name box, change the file name OakCherry.rtf to **Oak Cherry Table. rtf** (leave the rest of the file path as is). Under Specify export options, the first check box is selected and you cannot click it to remove the check mark. With this check box selected, the formatting and layout of the data in the query datasheet will be preserved. You cannot change it because you are exporting to an RTF document, so the layout and formatting will remain as originally designed.

Problem? If you can't see the last character because the path is too long, click anywhere in the File name box, and then press and hold the **Right Arrow key** until the insertion point moves to the end of the file name.

6 Click the **Open the destination file after the export operation is complete check box** to select it. Now the new file will open automatically after you close this dialog box.

Rich Text Format (**RTF**) A text format that preserves the formatting and layout of data.

Exhibit 22-19 Results of the OakCherry query

query in Navigation Pane

only oak and cherry species are listed

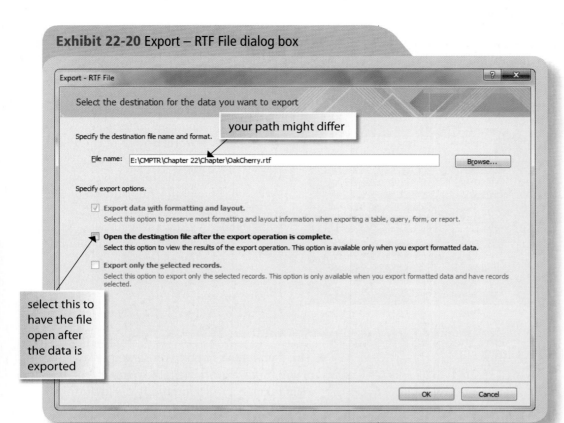

Exhibit 22-20 Export – RTF File dialog box

Export - RTF File

Select the destination for the data you want to export

Specify the destination file name and format.

your path might differ

File name: E:\CMPTR\Chapter 22\Chapter\OakCherry.rtf   Browse...

Specify export options.

☑ **Export data <u>w</u>ith formatting and layout.**
Select this option to preserve most formatting and layout information when exporting a table, query, form, or report.

☐ **Open the destination file after the export operation is complete.**
Select this option to view the results of the export operation. This option is available only when you export formatted data.

select this to have the file open after the data is exported

☐ **Export only the <u>s</u>elected records.**
Select this option to export only the selected records. This option is only available when you export formatted data and have records selected.

OK   Cancel

---

7 Click **OK**. Access converts the query results into an RTF file and opens the new file in Word.

8 Close the Word file. The Export – RTF File dialog box is still open in Access with the Save Export Steps screen displayed. As in the Save Import Steps screen you saw earlier, you can click the Save export steps check box, and then save the steps you took to export the query. You don't need to do this.

9 Click **Close**. The dialog box closes.

Saving Import and Export Steps in Access

If you know you will be importing data to or exporting data from a database more than once, it is a good idea to save the steps you took using the Import or Export Wizard. To do this, click the Save import steps or Save export steps check box in the corresponding screen in the Get External Data or Export dialog boxes. When you select this check box, the dialog box changes to display boxes that allow you to name the saved operation and add a description to remind you of the details of the operation. After you have saved a set of import or export steps, you can access them by clicking the External Data tab, and then clicking the Saved Imports button in the Import group or the Saved Exports button in the Export group. When you do, the Manage Data Tasks dialog box opens. You can then click the Saved Imports or Saved Exports tab to see each list of saved operations. To run the selected operation, click the Run button in the dialog box.

LO22.3 Using the Object Command in Word, Excel, and PowerPoint

The Object button in the Text group on the Insert tab in Word, Excel, and PowerPoint allows you to insert the contents of one file into another file. If you use the Object command and then click the Create from File tab, you can select a file and then choose to embed or link that file. If you do this, the entire file is inserted as an object in the destination file.

In Word, however, you can also use the Text from File command on the Object button menu to insert only the text of another text file into the destination document.

 **ACTIVITY**

Insert the text of a file into a different Word file.

1 Open the Word data file **EcoLetter**, located in the Chapter 22\Chapter folder. Save it as **EcoFlooring Letter**.

2 In the body of the letter, delete the **yellow highlighted text**.

3 On the Ribbon, click the **Insert tab**. In the Text group, click the **Object button arrow**, and then click **Text from File**. The Insert File dialog box opens.

> ➤ **Tip:** You could also open the RTF file in a Word window, copy the table, and then paste it into the destination document.

4 Navigate to the folder where you are storing the files you create, click **Oak Cherry Table**, and then click **Insert**. The Query results are inserted into the document as a table. See Exhibit 22-21.

5 Click anywhere in the **table**.

6 On the Ribbon, click the **Table Tools Design tab**. In the Table Style Options group, select the **Header Row check box**, and deselect the **Banded Rows** and **Banded Columns check boxes**.

7 Apply the **Medium Shading 2 – Accent 1 table style** (the green style in the fifth row under Built-In in the Table Styles gallery).

8 Select the **table**, and then center the table horizontally.

Remember that you can use the Office Clipboard to collect text and objects from various files so that you can paste them later.

9 Delete one of the blank paragraphs below the table.

10 In the closing at the end of the letter, replace *Aaron Greenburg* with your name.

11 Save the document.

LO22.4 **Copying and Pasting Among Office Programs**

If you want to use Access data in a PowerPoint slide, you cannot export it directly to a slide. You can, however, use Copy and Paste commands to copy data from a datasheet, and then paste it to a PowerPoint slide as a table.

Exhibit 22-21 Query results inserted as a table in the brochure

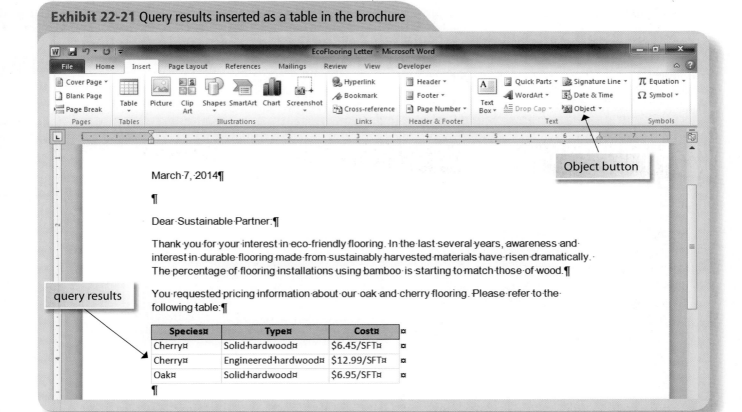

March 7, 2014¶

¶

Dear Sustainable Partner:¶

Thank you for your interest in eco-friendly flooring. In the last several years, awareness and interest in durable flooring made from sustainably harvested materials have risen dramatically. The percentage of flooring installations using bamboo is starting to match those of wood.¶

You requested pricing information about our oak and cherry flooring. Please refer to the following table:¶

query results

Species¤	Type¤	Cost¤	¤
Cherry¤	Solid hardwood¤	$6.45/SFT¤	¤
Cherry¤	Engineered hardwood¤	$12.99/SFT¤	¤
Oak¤	Solid hardwood¤	$6.95/SFT¤	¤

¶

Object button

Copy and paste Access data to a PowerPoint slide.

1 Switch to the Access database **EcoFlooringTypes**. The OakCherry query is still open.

2 To the left of the Species column heading, click the **selector box**. All the records in the query results datasheet are selected.

3 On the Home tab, in the Clipboard group, click the **Copy button**. The selected query results are copied to the Clipboard.

4 Switch to the PowerPoint file **EcoFlooring Presentation**. Display **Slide 4** ("Oak and Cherry Flooring Options") in the Slide pane.

5 Click in the Slide pane in the blank area below the title. On the Home tab, in the Clipboard group, click the **Paste button arrow**, point to each button to see its effect, and then click the **Use Destination**

Theme button 🗊. PowerPoint inserts the query results in a table on the slide.

6 Click in the **first row** in the table, and then click the **Table Tools Layout tab**.

7 In the Rows & Columns group, click the **Delete button**, and then click **Delete Rows**. The first row in the table is deleted.

8 Click the **table border** to select the entire table, and then change the font size of the table text to **28 points**.

9 Specify that the **Header row** is to be treated differently, and then apply the **Themed Style 1 – Accent 1 table style**.

10 AutoFit each column in the table, and then center the table in the area under the slide title. See Exhibit 22-22.

11 Save the presentation.

12 Switch to the Access database **EcoFlooring Types**, close the OakCherry query, saving changes if prompted, and then exit Access.

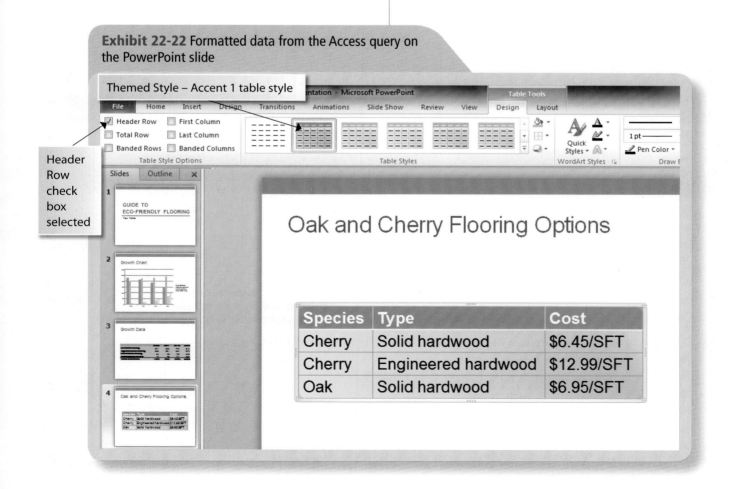

Exhibit 22-22 Formatted data from the Access query on the PowerPoint slide

LO22.5 Creating PowerPoint Slides from a Word Outline

If you have an outline in a Word document, you can use that outline to create PowerPoint slides. When you create slides from a Word outline, PowerPoint uses the heading styles in the Word document to determine how to format the text. Each paragraph formatted with the Heading 1 style becomes the title of a new slide, each paragraph formatted with the Heading 2 style becomes a first level bulleted item on a slide, and so on.

When you create slides from an outline, PowerPoint inserts them after the current slide. If the document containing the outline is formatted with a theme different from the theme applied to the presentation, you might need to reset the slides to force them to use the theme formatting in the presentation. When you reset slides, you reset the position, size, and formatting of the slide placeholders to match the settings in the slide masters.

 **ACTIVITY**

Create PowerPoint slides from a Word outline.

1 Open the Word data file **EcoOutline**, located in the Chapter 22\Chapter folder. Switch to **Outline view**. Examine the structure of the document.

2 Close the **EcoOutline document**, and then switch to the PowerPoint file **EcoFlooring Presentation**. Display **Slide 1** (the title slide) in the Slide pane.

3 On the Home tab, in the Slides group, click the **New Slide button arrow**, and then click **Slides from Outline**. The Insert Outline dialog box opens.

4 Navigate to the folder **Chapter 22\Chapter folder**, click **EcoOutline**, and then click **Insert**. PowerPoint inserts and formats the text of the Word outline to create Slides 2 through 9.

5 Display **Slide 9** in the Slide pane. Slide 9 does not contain any text because there was a blank paragraph at the end of the Word outline. See Exhibit 22-23.

Exhibit 22-23 Slides inserted from the outline

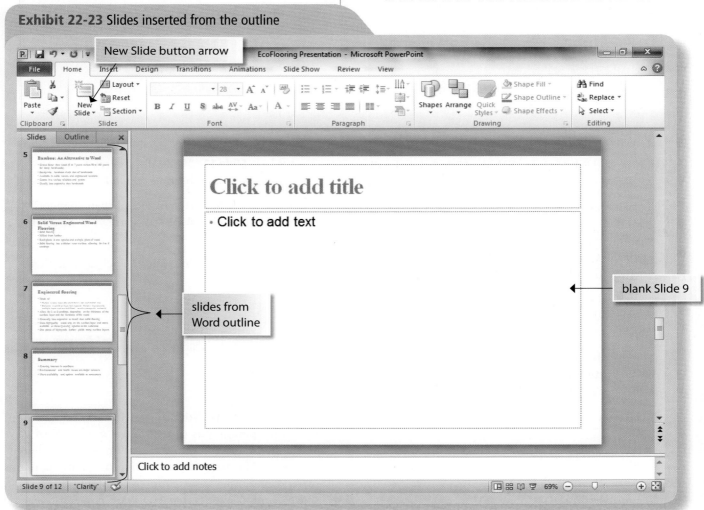

Exhibit 22-24 Final presentation in Slide Sorter view

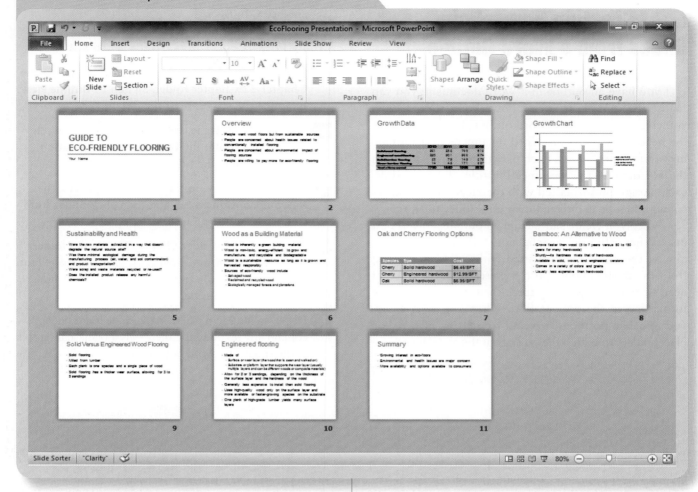

6   In the Slides tab, right-click the **Slide 9 thumbnail**, and then click **Delete Slide**. Slide 9 is deleted.

7   Display **Slide 8** ("Summary") in the Slide pane. The slide text is hard to read. This is because the document containing the outline was formatted with the Composite theme and the presentation is formatted with the Clarity theme.

8   Press and hold the **Shift key**, and then scroll up in the Slides tab and click the **Slide 2 thumbnail**. Slides 2–8 are selected.

9   On the Home tab, in the Slides group, click the **Reset button**. The slides are reformatted with the Clarity theme used in the presentation.

10   Rearrange the slides in the presentation as follows:
- Move **Slide 10** ("Growth Data") so it becomes **Slide 3**.
- Move the new **Slide 10** ("Growth Chart") so it becomes **Slide 4**.

- Move **Slide 11** ("Oak and Cherry Flooring Options") so it becomes **Slide 7**.

11   Switch to **Slide Sorter view**, and then change the zoom level to **80%**. Compare your screen to Exhibit 22-24.

12   Save the presentation, and then close it and exit PowerPoint.

LO22.6 Creating Form Letters with Mail Merge

A **form letter** is a Word document that contains standard paragraphs of text and a minimum of variable text, such as the names and addresses of the letter's recipients. The **main document** of a form letter contains the text and other information (including punctuation, spaces, and graphics) that you want to keep the same

Exhibit 22-25 Plan for the form letter

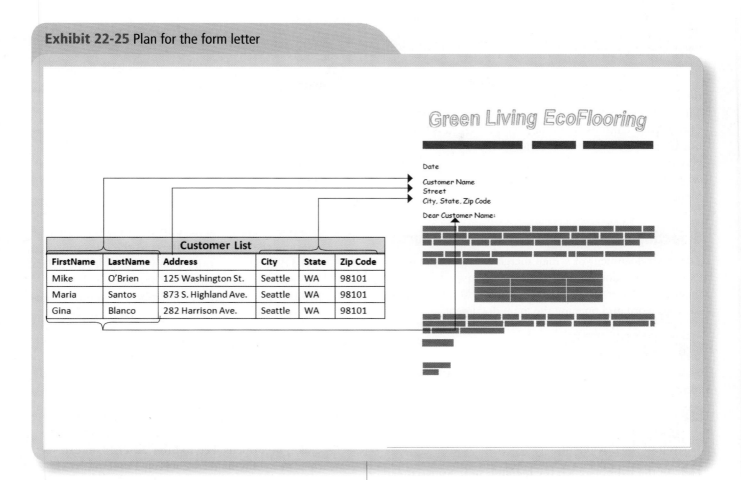

in each letter. It also includes **merge fields**, which contain instructions for replacing the field placeholder with the variable information that changes from one letter to another. The variable information is contained in a **data source**, which can be a Word table, an Access database, or some other source. When you merge the main document with the data source, Word replaces the merge fields with the appropriate information from the data source. See Exhibit 22-25. The process of combining the main document with the data source is called a **merge**. The term **mail merge** is used when you are merging a main document with a list of addresses from a data source.

The first step in completing the mail merge is to specify the type of document you want to create, such as a form letter, mailing labels, or envelopes. Next, you select the main document, which Word also calls the **starting document**. Then, you select recipients from the data source. When you use an Access database as the data source for a mail merge, you select a table or query defined in the database as the actual data source.

After you have identified the main document and the data source, you insert the merge fields into the main document. Finally, you preview the main document,

form letter A Word document that contains standard paragraphs of text and a minimum of variable text.

main document A document that contains the text and other information that you want to keep the same in each form letter.

merge field A field that contains instructions to be replaced with the variable information that changes from one letter to another.

data source A file that contains the variable information for form letters.

merge To combine a main document with a data source.

mail merge To merge a main document with a list of addresses from a data source.

starting document The main document in a Word mail merge.

make any needed changes, and merge the main document and the data source to produce customized form letters.

To perform a mail merge, you can use buttons on the Mailings tab on the Ribbon or you can use the Mail Merge Wizard, which appears in a task pane to the right of the Word window. The Mail Merge wizard is helpful; but if you work from left to right on the Mailings tab, you should have no trouble creating a main document with the correct merge fields, and then performing the merge.

Selecting a Main Document and Data Source

The main document of a mail merge can be a new or an existing Word document. In this case, the starting document is the letter to potential customers. You'll begin by starting Word and opening the main document.

Select the main document and data source for the mail merge.

1 If necessary, on the taskbar, click the **Word button** to display the **EcoFlooring Letter**. Scroll to the top of the document.

2 On the Ribbon, click the **Mailings tab**. Notice that only a few buttons on the Mailings tab are available. The other buttons will become available as you set up the mail merge.

3 In the Start Mail Merge group, click the **Start Mail Merge button**. A menu of choices opens. Normal Word Document is selected in the menu. You want to merge a letter, but you can also create email messages, envelopes, labels, or a directory of all the names in the data source.

> **Tip:** To be guided step-by-step through the mail merge process, click the Start Mail Merge button in the Start Mail Merge group on the Mailings tab, and then click Step by Step Mail Merge Wizard.

4 Click **Letters** to specify that you want to merge a letter. The next step is to select the recipients of the letter. You

want to select recipients from an existing list in an Access database.

5 In the Start Mail Merge group, click the **Select Recipients button**, and then click **Use Existing List**. The Select Data Source dialog box opens, displaying a list of possible data sources.

6 Navigate to the **Chapter 22\Chapter folder**, click the Access file **Contacts**, and then click **Open**. Because the data source is an Access database, the Select Table dialog box opens listing all the tables in the selected database (this database contains one table and one query). You need to choose a table or query in the selected database as the data source. If the database contained only one table, the Select Table dialog box would not open; instead, the Mail Merge Recipients dialog box would open immediately after you selected the database.

7 Click the **Customer table** to select it, and then click **OK**. The dialog box closes and the Edit Recipient List button, as well as several others, is now available on the Ribbon.

8 In the Start Mail Merge group, click the **Edit Recipient List button**. The Mail Merge Recipients dialog box opens. See Exhibit 22-26. You can sort this list by any field by clicking a column heading. You can also narrow the list by deselecting records individually or filtering the list to include only records that meet specific criteria.

Exhibit 22-26 Mail Merge Recipients dialog box

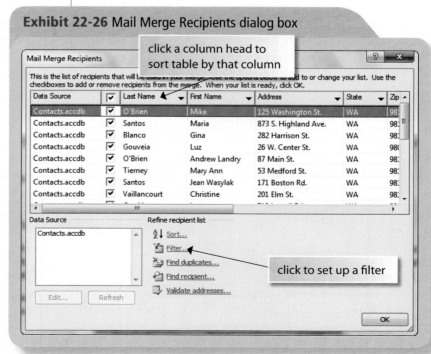

9 At the bottom of the dialog box, click the **Filter link**. The Filter and Sort dialog box opens with the Filter Records tab selected.

10 Click the **Field arrow**, and then click **City/Town**. The Comparison and Compare to boxes in the first row are now available. Equal to appears in the Comparison box, and the insertion point is blinking in the Compare to text box.

11 In the Compare to text box, type **Seattle**. See Exhibit 22-27.

Exhibit 22-27 Filter Records tab in the Filter and Sort dialog box

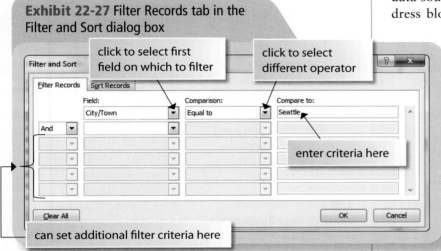

12 Click **OK**. The Filter and Sort dialog box closes and only the addresses for customers in Seattle are displayed in the Mail Merge Recipients dialog box.

Exhibit 22-28 Insert Address Block dialog box

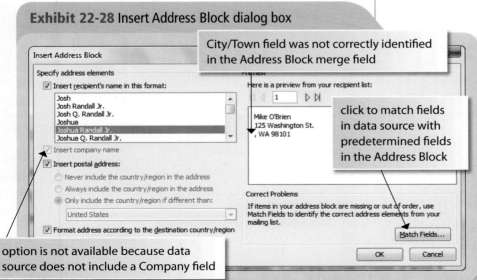

13 Click **OK** to close the Mail Merge Recipients dialog box.

Inserting the Merge Fields

As noted earlier, a merge field is a special instruction that tells Word where to insert the variable information from the data source into the main document. For example, right now the letter does not have an inside address (the address for the recipient) at the top, as business letters usually do, so you'll insert a merge field to tell Word what information to pull from the data source. For Caitlin's letter, you will insert the Address block and Greeting line merge fields. You then will check the merge fields to make sure they correspond with the fields in the Hospital Social Work Contacts table.

ACTIVITY

Insert merge fields into a main document.

1 Click in the blank paragraph below the date in the letter. This is where the recipient's name and address will appear.

2 In the Write & Insert Fields group on the Mailings tab, click the **Address Block button**. The Insert Address Block dialog box opens, as shown in Exhibit 22-28. You use this dialog box to choose the format of the recipient's name and to specify whether to include the company name and country in the address. The Preview box on the right shows you a preview of how the address block will look with data from your recipient list. The default format of first and last name is selected in the list on the left. In the Preview box, notice that the city is missing from the address. Word tries to match fields in a recipient list with predetermined fields in the Address Block, but sometimes you need to explicitly identify a field. In this case, Word did not find a match for the City field in the Address Block.

3 In the Correct Problems section of the dialog box, click **Match Fields**. The Match Fields dialog box opens, as shown in Exhibit 22-29. On the left are the fields Word expects in the Address Block. On the right are the fields in the data source. You want Word to match the City field in the Address Block with the City/Town field in the Access table.

Exhibit 22-29 Match Fields dialog box

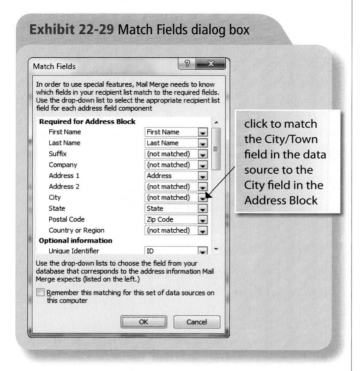

click to match the City/Town field in the data source to the City field in the Address Block

4 Click the **City arrow**, and then click **City/Town**.

5 Click **OK**. A dialog box opens warning that if you match a field in your data source with the built-in Unique Identifier field, that field might be available to people who read your document. The Unique Identifier field picks up the primary key field in the table. If the primary key field in your Access database contained confidential data such as Social Security numbers, you would click the No button, change the Unique Identifier field to "(not matched)," and then close the Match Fields dialog

Click the Insert Merge Field button to insert merge fields individually instead of a block of fields, as with the Address Block, or formatted fields, as with the Greeting Line field.

box. However, you are not using the ID field in your letter, so it's fine to click the Yes button.

6 Click **Yes**. The warning dialog box and the Match Fields dialog box close. The Preview area in the Insert Address Block dialog box now displays the city as part of the address.

7 Click **OK** to close the Insert Address Block dialog box. The Address block merge field appears in the main document between double chevrons (<< >>). Now that there is a merge field in the letter, a few more buttons on the Mailings tab are available. Now you need to insert a greeting line to personalize the salutation.

⚠ **Problem?** If the Address block merge field appears between curly braces and includes additional text, such as {ADDRESSBLOCK \f}, Word is displaying field codes. Click the **File tab**, click **Options** in the navigation bar, click **Advanced** in the list on the left, scroll down the list on the right, and then, in the Show document content section on the right, deselect the **Show field codes instead of their values check box**.

8 In the salutation, delete **Dear Sustainable Partner:** (including the colon).

9 On the Mailings tab, in the Write & Insert Fields group, click the **Greeting Line button**. The Insert Greeting Line dialog box opens, as shown in Exhibit 22-30. The Greeting line format and

Exhibit 22-30 Insert Greeting Line dialog box

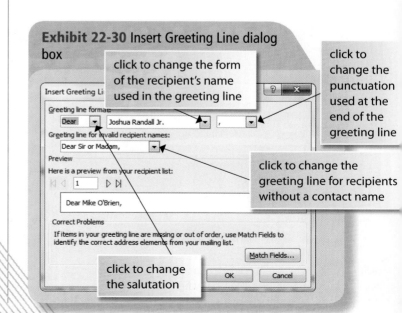

click to change the form of the recipient's name used in the greeting line

click to change the punctuation used at the end of the greeting line

click to change the greeting line for recipients without a contact name

click to change the salutation

the Preview at the bottom of the dialog box show that Word will insert as the salutation *Dear* followed by the recipient's entire name, and then a comma.

10 In the Greeting line format section (next to *Joshua Randall Jr.*), click the **third arrow**, and then click **:** (the colon). The change is reflected in the Preview section. You can accept the other options in the Greeting Line dialog box—to begin the salutation with *Dear* and to use *Dear Sir or Madam* for records in the Contacts table that do not include a contact name.

11 Click **OK**. Word inserts the Greeting Line merge field in the main document.

12 Save the document.

Previewing the Mail Merge and Checking for Errors

With the starting document and merge fields in place, you're ready to perform the mail merge. You can choose to merge the data to a new Word document or directly to a printer. It's a good idea to proofread the final document before printing all of the merged documents.

It is also a good idea to use the Auto Check for Errors command to check the main document for errors. When you select this command, you can choose to simulate the merge and list the errors in a new document or to complete the merge, reporting each error as it is found in a new document after the merge is completed. The option that simulates the merge is the safest as it allows you to easily modify the main document to correct the errors.

ACTIVITY

Preview the merged document and check for errors.

1 On the Mailings tab, in the Preview Results group, click the **Preview Results button**. The first merged form letter appears with Mike O'Brien as the first recipient. This is the first letter, as indicated by the "1" in the Preview Results group. See Exhibit 22-31. Notice, however, that each line in the inside address has a space after it. To fix this, you'll turn off the preview and then format the Address Block merge field.

2 In the Preview Results group, click the **Preview Results button**. The preview turns off and you see the merge fields again.

Exhibit 22-31 Preview of mail merge

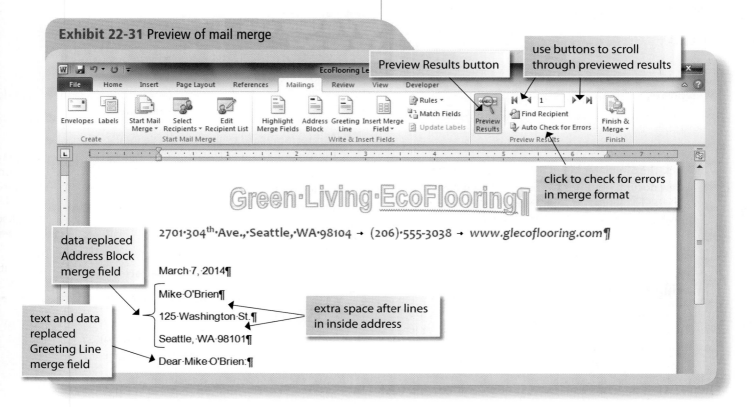

3 Click the **Address Block merge field**. On the Ribbon, click the **Home tab**.

4 In the Paragraph group, click the **Line and Paragraph Spacing button** $\boxed{\downarrow\equiv\cdot}$, and then click **Remove Space After Paragraph**. The extra space after the paragraph is removed.

5 Position the insertion point at the end of the Address Block line, and then press the **Enter key**. This inserts a single blank line (a paragraph formatted with no extra space after it) between the last line of the inside address and the salutation.

6 On the Ribbon, click the **Mailings tab**. In the Preview Results group, click the **Preview Results button**. Mike O'Brien's information appears in the letter properly formatted.

7 In the Preview Results group, click the **Next Record button** ▶ to preview the next recipient. The letter to Maria Santos appears. Now, you will use the Auto Check for Errors command to have Word check the merged document for errors.

8 In the Preview Results group, click the **Auto Check for Errors button**. The Checking and Reporting Errors dialog box opens. See Exhibit 22-32.

Exhibit 22-32 Checking and Reporting Errors dialog box

click to generate a report of errors in a new document

9 Click the **Simulate the merge and report errors in a new document option button**, and then click **OK**. After a moment, another dialog box opens reporting that no mail merge errors were found.

10 Click **OK** to close the dialog box.

Finishing the Mail Merge

After you have inserted all of the merge fields, previewed the merge, and checked the document for errors, you can finish the merge and either print the form letters or save the completed letters to a new document so that you can print them later.

ACTIVITY

Finish the mail merge.

1 On the Mailings tab, in the Finish group, click the **Finish & Merge button**, and then click **Print Documents**. The Merge to Printer dialog box opens in which you can specify the records you want to print.

> **Tip:** Before continuing, make sure you are connected to a printer and that it is loaded with paper and ready to print.

2 Click the **Current record option button**, and then click **OK**. The Print dialog box opens.

3 Click **OK**. The dialog box closes and the current letter—the letter to Maria Santos—prints.

4 In the Finish group, click the **Finish & Merge button**, and then click **Edit Individual Documents**. The Merge to New Document dialog box opens. See Exhibit 22-33.

Exhibit 22-33 Merge to New Document dialog box

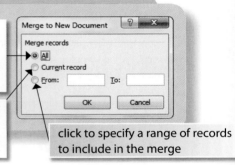

select to create a document containing merged data from all the filtered records in the data source

select to create only one merged document using data from the current record

click to specify a range of records to include in the merge

5 If it is not already selected, click the **All option button**, and then click **OK**. A new document opens with the temporary name "Letters" followed by a number. This 12-page document contains one letter for each of the contacts who live in Seattle.

6 Scroll through the merged document to see the merged addresses and salutations.

7 Save the document as **Merged Letters**.

8 Close the document. The Main Letter document is the current document again.

9 On the Mailings tab, in the Preview Results group, click the **Preview Results button** to toggle it off.

10 Save the document, and then close it.

Performing a Mail Merge with an Email Message

You can make the most of your email correspondence by merging your Outlook Contacts with an email message. To do this, you click E-Mail Messages on the Start Mail Merge button, and then click Select from Outlook Contacts from the Select Recipients button. Using the Mail Merge Recipients dialog box, you can filter the contacts to include only those people to whom you want to send your message. After you compose your message, click the Finish & Merge button, and then click Send E-mail Messages. This opens the Merge to E-mail dialog box in which you can type the subject for your email message. After you click the OK button, Word creates new email messages addressed to each person in your recipients list and places them in your Outlook Outbox, ready to send the next time you send email messages.

U.P.images_vector/Shutterstock.com

Quiz Yourself

1. What is OLE?

2. What is the difference between embedding an object and linking an object?

3. When an object is embedded, how many copies of the object exist?

4. If an Excel chart is linked to a Word document, which is the source program?

5. What happens if you make changes to a linked object in the destination file?

6. How do you use Excel data in an Access table without using the Copy and Paste commands?

7. What does RTF stand for?

8. How do you insert text from a text file into another Word file without using the Copy and Paste commands?

9. How can you use data from an Access datasheet in a PowerPoint slide without first exporting it to another file format?

10. Describe the slide or slides that PowerPoint would create from a Word outline that has one Level 1 paragraph and three Level 2 paragraphs.

11. After importing a Word outline, how do you change the format of a slide so that it matches the theme used in the presentation?

12. In a mail merge, what is a merge field?

13. What is the file that contains the variable information to be used in a mail merge called?

Practice It

Practice It 22-1

1. Open the Word data file **SandbarFlyer** located in the Chapter 22\Practice It folder. Save the document as **Sandbar CC Flyer**.

2. In the fourth paragraph, replace the yellow highlighted text with an Excel pie chart that you create from within the Word document. Use the following as data for the chart:

Biology	**1145**
Business	**359**
Chemistry	**471**
English	**1612**
Hospitality & Tourism	**549**

3. In the chart object in the Word document, change the chart title to **Distribution of Majors 2011–2013**. Add data labels to the center of the pie slices that identify the percentage of each slice.

4. Open the Excel data file **SandbarNumber** located in the Chapter 22\Practice It folder. Save the document as **Sandbar CC Number**.

5. In the worksheet, copy the column chart to the Clipboard.

6. In the Word document Sandbar CC Flyer, delete the green highlighted text, and then insert the chart as an embedded object using the destination theme.

7. Edit the data in the embedded worksheet that contains the column chart so that Business in 2013 is **610** and Hospitality and Tourism in 2013 is **250**.

8. Resize both charts so they are as wide as the paragraphs in the document, and then change their height to approximately 2.6 inches. Make more adjustments as needed so that all the text and the two charts fit on one page.

9. Open the PowerPoint data file **SandbarPresentation** located in the Chapter22\Practice It folder. Add your name as the subtitle, and then save the document as **Sandbar CC Presentation**.

10. Link the column chart in the Excel file Sandbar CC Number to Slide 2 ("Number of Students Chart") in the PowerPoint file Sandbar CC Presentation using the destination theme. Resize the chart to fill the space on the slide.

11. Link the worksheet in the Excel file Sandbar CC Number to Slide 3 ("Number of Students") in the PowerPoint file Sandbar CC Presentation.

12. Edit the data in the Excel file Sandbar CC Number so that Business in 2013 is **610**. Update the chart and datasheet in the PowerPoint presentation if necessary.

13. Save the PowerPoint file, and then close it.

14. Edit data in the Excel file so that Hospitality and Tourism in 2013 is **250**.

15. Re-open the PowerPoint file Sandbar CC Presentation, and then update the links. Examine both Slides 2 and 3, and manually update the links if necessary.

16. Open the Excel data file **SandbarCourses** located in the Chapter22\Practice It folder. Save the document as **Sandbar CC Courses**.

17. Prepare the worksheet to be imported into Access by deleting the rows above the column labels and adding the label **Dept.** above the data in column A.

18. Save the workbook, and then close it.

19. Open the Access database named **Sandbar**, located in the Chapter22\Practice It folder. Save it as **Sandbar CC**.

20. Import the Excel file Sandbar CC Courses into it to create a new table named **Course**. Make sure you indicate that the first row contains headers, and let Access set the primary key.

21. Create a query named **Business** that lists only classes in the Business department. Resize columns as needed.

22. Export the query results to a Word Rich Text File named **Business Courses**.

23. Open the Word data file **SandbarLetter** located in the Chapter22\Practice It folder. Save the document as **Sandbar CC Letter**.

24. Insert the text of the Word file Business Courses in the Word document Sandbar CC Letter. Format the table with the Medium Shading 2 – Accent 6 table style with the Header Row treated differently and the Banded Rows option set. Center the table horizontally, and delete one of the empty paragraphs below the table.

25. Copy the query results to the Clipboard, and then paste them using the destination theme to Slide 4 ("Business Courses") in the PowerPoint file Sandbar CC Presentation. Remove the first row in the pasted table, and then change the font size of the text in the table to 24 points. Apply the table style Medium Style 1 – Accent 1 with the Header Row treated differently, AutoFit the columns, and then center the table in the blank area on the slide.

26. Import the Word outline stored in the file **SandbarOutline** in the Chapter22\Practice It folder so that the slides created from the outline appear after Slide 4 ("Business Courses") in the Power-Point file Sandbar CC Presentation.

27. Reset the new Slides 5–10, and then delete the blank Slide 10.

28. In the PowerPoint file Sandbar CC Presentation, move Slide 5 ("Student Population") so that it becomes Slide 2.

29. In the Word file Sandbar CC Letter, select the Letters main document type.

30. Select the Access file Sandbar CC as the data source. Select the Student table.

31. Edit the recipient list by filtering it so that only students with an interest in Business are included in the mail merge.

32. Insert the Address Block and Greeting Line merge fields at the beginning of the document below the date. Match fields as needed. In the Greeting Line merge field, use *Dear* as the salutation, choose just the first name as the name to be used in the greeting line, and choose a comma at the end of the line.

33. Preview the document. Adjust the spacing after the Address Block merge field as needed.

34. Use Auto Check to check the document for errors by simulating the merge.

35. Complete the merge by merging all the records to a new file. (There should be six letters.) Save the file as **Sandbar CC Merged Letters**.

36. Close the merged document Sandbar CC Merged Letters. Turn the Preview off in the document Sandbar CC Letter, and then save and close the Sandbar CC Letter document.

37. Close all open files, saving if prompted.

Practice It 22-2

1. Open the Excel data file **SpaServices**, located in the Chapter22\Practice It folder. Save the document as **Salon Isle Services**.

2. Open the PowerPoint data file **SpaPresentation** located in the Chapter22\Practice It folder. Enter your name as the subtitle. Save the document as **Salon Isle Presentation**.

3. Embed the chart in the Excel file Salon Isle Services in Slide 2 ("Comparison of Prices") of the PowerPoint file Salon Isle Presentation. Apply the Shape Style Subtle Effect – Black, Dark 1 (on the Chart Tools Format tab) to the embedded chart object.

4. In the embedded chart, change the price in cell C5 to **$55** and change the price in cell C7 to **$50**.

5. In the Excel file Salon Isle Services, copy Sheet1 to a new worksheet. In the new worksheet, delete the chart, and then prepare the data on Sheet1 (2) to be exported to an Access table. (*Hint*: Make sure a label appears in every cell in column A for all rows that contain data.) Label column B **Service** and column C **Price**.

6. Save and close the Excel file Salon Isle Services.

7. Create a new Access database named **Salon Isle**.

8. In the Access database Salon Isle, import the data from Sheet1 (2) in the Excel file Salon Isle Services to a new table named **Services**. Make sure you indicate that the first row contains headers, and let Access set the primary key. (*Hint*: Make sure you select Sheet1 (2) in the first dialog box in the Import Spreadsheet Wizard.)

9. Create a query named **Hair** that lists the service and price for all services of the type *Hair*, but do not show the Type field. Resize columns as needed in the query results.

10. Export the results of the query to a Rich Text File named **Hair Services**.

11. In the PowerPoint file Salon Isle Presentation, create new slides after Slide 2 by importing the outline in the Word data file **SpaOutline**, located in the Chapter22\Practice It folder. Reset the slides. Move Slide 2 ("Comparison of Prices") so it becomes Slide 4, and then move Slide 7 (a blank slide) so it becomes Slide 5.

12. Change the title of the new Slide 5 to **Hair Services** and then change the layout to Title Only.

13. Use the Object button in the Text group on the Insert tab to embed the Hair Services file into Slide 5.

14. Double-click the embedded table to open a Word window in the Slide, select all the text and data in the table, and then increase the font size of all the text in the table to 28 points. Format the table with the Medium Grid 3 – Accent 2 table style. In the table, AutoFit each column.

15. Close all open files, saving when prompted.

On Your Own

On Your Own 22-1

1. Open the Excel data file **ZooNumbers**, located in the Chapter22\On Your Own folder. Save the document as **Zoo Visitor Numbers**.

2. Open the PowerPoint data file **ZooPresentation**, located in the Chapter22\On Your Own folder. Save the document as **Zoo Slide Show**.

3. In the Excel file Zoo Visitor Numbers, copy the column chart to the Clipboard.

4. Link the copied chart to Slide 2 ("Number of Visitors") using the destination theme. Resize the chart object to fill the slide.

5. In the Excel file Zoo Visitor Numbers, add the following data as the number of visitors in 2013: **648**, **1411**, **173**, and **80**.

6. Save the changes to the Excel file Zoo Visitor Numbers, and then update the chart in the Power-Point file Zoo Slide Show if needed.

7. Open the Word data file **ZooLetter**, located in the Chapter22\On Your Own folder. Save the document as **Zoo Customer Letter**.

8. In the PowerPoint file Zoo Slide Show, copy the chart on Slide 2 ("Number of Visitors") to the Clipboard.

9. In the Word document Zoo Customer Letter, delete the yellow highlighted text, and then link the copied chart to the document using the destination theme. Resize the chart so that it is approximately 2.5 inches high and the same width as the paragraphs.

10. In the Excel file Zoo Visitor Numbers, change the number of Adult visitors in 2013 to **710** and then change the number of Children who visited in 2013 to **1500**. Save the file.

11. Open the Excel data file **ZooAnimals**, located in the Chapter22\On Your Own folder. Save the file as **Zoo Animals by Type**.

12. Prepare the Excel file Zoo Animals by Type file for importing into Access. Use **Species** as the column A label.

13. Create a new Access database named **ZooData**. Import the Excel file **Zoo Animals by Type** to a new table named **Animals**.

14. Create four queries, each listing all the animals in one species. Do not show the Species field. Save each query with the name of the species included. Resize columns as needed in the query results.

15. Open the Office Clipboard, and then copy the query results for each of the four queries to the Office Clipboard.

16. Paste each query into the appropriate slide in the PowerPoint file Zoo Slide Show using the Text Only paste option. Select the content placeholder before you paste the objects, and then select the Keep Text Only option after you paste the objects. On each slide, delete the Type bulleted item.

17. Use the Word file Zoo Customer Letter to create a form letter using the Access file ZooVisitors as the data source.

18. Edit the recipient list by sorting the customers alphabetically by last name.

19. Insert the Address Block and Greeting Line merge fields, matching fields if necessary. In the Greeting Line merge field, change the form of the name to the first name, and change the form of greeting line for records with an invalid recipient name to **Dear Guest,**.

20. In the body of the letter, replace the green highlighted text with the Date_Visited merge field.

21. Preview the merged document, and then correct any spacing issues.

22. In the closing, replace Karl Croston with your name.

23. Turn the preview off, merge only the first and second letter of the mail merge to a new document, and then save the new document as **Zoo Letters**.

24. Close all open documents, saving when prompted.

ADDITIONAL STUDY TOOLS

Chapter 22

IN THE BOOK

▶ Complete end-of-chapter exercises

▶ Study tear-out Chapter Review Card

ONLINE

▶ Complete additional end-of-chapter exercises

▶ Take practice quiz to prepare for tests

▶ Review key term flash cards (online, printable, and audio)

▶ Play "Beat the Clock" and "Memory" to quiz yourself

▶ Watch the videos "Create an Embedded Excel Chart in a Word Document," "Link Excel Worksheet Data to a PowerPoint Slide," "Edit the Linked Object When the Destination Files are Closed," "Import an Excel List to a Table in a New Database," and more

Index

banking and e-commerce, 149
bar charts, 543
barcode printers, 73
barcode readers, 60
barcodes, 60
batteries, nonremovable, 33
BD-R DL discs, 49
Berners-Lee, Tim, 142
bibliography
    creating, 374–375
    described, 369
    MLA style, 371
Bing search engine, 337
biometric readers, 63–64
BIOS (basic input/output system), 38
bitmap images, 100
bitmaps, 398
bits, 31
BlackBerry OS, 89
block style, business letters, 301
blogs, blogging, 148, 150
Bluetooth wireless standard, 131–132
body text, 314, 362
bold, formatting text, 459, 461
Bold button, 280, 315
Bookmarks browser feature, 19
boot process, 77, 79
borders
    adding cell, 472–473, 475–476
    adding paragraph, 324–326
    inserting page, 410
botnets, 192
bots (zombie computers), 192
Box.net (online storage), 53
bps (bits per second), 117
bridges, 136
broadband over fiber (BoF), 156
broadband over Powerline (BPL), 127
broadcast networks, 119
broadcasting
    described, 119
    presentations, 726–731
    slide shows, 728–731
Brown, Michelle, 198
budgets, presenting, 525
buffers, 82
building blocks
    creating AutoText, 415
    creating Quick Parts, 413–415
    described, 413
    inserting, managing Quick Parts,
       415–417
Building Blocks Organizer, 416–417
bulleted items, 668
bulleted lists
    animating, 684, 718
    changing outline levels, 672–674
    creating as you type, 324
    described, 322, 668
    moving on slides, 675–677
    using on slides, 668–670
bullets
    defining new, 323
    types of, 281
Bullets button, Paragraph group, 280
bus interface unit, 41, 42

bus networks, 111
buses, 38–39
business continuity plans, 208, 209
business ethics, 24
business letters, block style of, 301
button arrows, 280
buttons
    alignment (table), 470
    described, 228
    on Ribbon, 279
    using, 280
bytes, 31, 32

C

cable, data transmission, 119–120
cable Internet access, 155–156
cache memory, 38
    described, 35
    internal, 39, 41
    level numbers, 36
CAD (computer-aided design), 104
calculated fields (database), 623–624
calculating
    loan payments, 522–525
    net cash flow, 512–513
Calculator program, 232, 235–236
CAN-SPAM Act, 216, 222
captions, slide, 667
Carbonite, 264
carpal tunnel syndrome (CTS), 25
category axis (charts), 546–547
category values, 532
CD/DVD drives, 43
CDMA (Code Division Multiple
       Access), 130
CD-R discs, 49
CDs, recordable, 49
cell (table)
    active, 427
    adding borders, 472–473
    aligning content, 469–470
    applying styles, 468–469
    changing background colors,
       473–474
    described, 427
    editing content, 434
    entering data in, 430–434
    formatting data in, 458–467
    highlighting those with conditional
       formatting, 483–486
    indenting content, 470–471
    merging, 470–472
    moving, 440
    and ranges, formatting, 467–476
    rotating content, 471
    truncating content, 435
    typing functions in, 510–511
    working with, 438–442
    wrapping text within, 441–442
cell ranges, 438, 467–476
cell references, 427
    changing types, 503
    formulas using, 444
    using in formulas, 498–500
cell styles, 468–469, 471–472, 478–479
cells, table, 382

cellular (cell) phones
    See also mobile phones
    described, 110, 122
cellular radio transmission, 122
cellular standards, 130
centering
    cells, 471
    content on pages, 493–494
    text, 319–320
changing
    cell reference types, 503
    charts, 537–542
    desktop themes, 229
    fonts, 282
    fonts, font size, 314–316
    line spacing, 318–319
    margins, 362–364
    outlines, 358–362
    page orientation, 392, 450
    slide themes, 671–674
    sources, 374
    style sets, 355–356
    text colors, 316
    themes, 352–353, 353–354
    worksheet views, 448–449
character styles, 346
characters
    common, inserted with AutoCorrect
       (table), 303
    inserting symbols, 305–306
    nonprinting, 296
    selecting, 310
chart area, 534–535
chart layouts, 538–539
chart sheets, 536, 537
chart styles, 537
chart title, 535
charts
    changing layouts, 538–539
    choosing the right, 533
    combination, 548
    communicating effectively with, 547
    creating, 530–534
    creating column, 543–548
    creating exploded pie, 542–543
    creating line, 548–555
    data labels, working with, 540–541
    data series, adding, 554
    described, 530
    editing data in, 552–555
    embedded, 536
    embedding Excel, in Word document,
       741–747
    Excel types (table), 532
    gridlines, using, 547, 552
    introduction to, 530
    legends, 535, 552 modifying, 537–
       542
    moving, resizing, 536–537
    sparklines, 555–559
    titles, 552
    working with chart elements, 534–537
chartsheets, 426
chief privacy officer (CPO), 219
Child Online Protection Act (COPA),
       222

exact match (query), 619
Excel
  See also workbooks, worksheets
  charts. *See* charts
  common Office program elements,
    273–286
  described, 424
  embedding chart in Word document,
    741–747
  function categories (table), 506
  Help, getting, 291–292
  integrating with other Office
    programs, 270, 738–741
  introduction to, 268
  linking chart to Word document, 747
  lists, importing into Access tables,
    753–755
  Object command, using, 756–757
  starting, 271
  task panes, using, 283–284
  window described, 426–427
  zooming, 275
Excel tables
  adding formulas to, 480–483
  changing styles, 479–480
  creating, 476–479
exiting Office programs, 293
expansion buses, 39
expansion cards, 33, 38
expansion slots, 33, 38
exploded pie charts, creating, 542–543
exporting
  Access data to Word files, 755–756
  Excel lists into Access tables,
    753–755
  saving steps in Access, 756
ExpressCard hard drives, 46
ExpressCard modules, 38
Extended Validation Secure Sockets
    Layer (EV SSL), 210
external hard drives, 46
extracting compressed files, 263–264
extranets, 116
Eye-Fi Share, Eye-Fi Pro cards, 129
eyeglasses, built-in displays for, 70

F

Facebook, 53, 147–148, 216
Factiva iWorks search engine, 337
fair use, 22
fans, 35
favorites (Web page shortcuts), 166
Favorites browser feature, 19, 166–167
FDE (full disk encryption), 204
feeds (RSS), 168
fiber-optic cable, 120
fiber-to-the-premises (FTTP), 156–157
field lists, 606
Field Properties pane, 577
field value, 566–567
fields, database
  adding, moving, 586–588
  adding to design grid, 608
  calculated, using in queries, 624–626
  changing properties, 578–580
  described, 566

editing values, 602–605
field size properties for number fields,
    580–582
naming, 573
and records, 590
sort fields, 609–610
sorting multiple, 611–612
fields, merge, 761, 763–765
fields in Word, 365
fifth-generation computers, 8
file compression programs, 90
file extensions
  See also specific extension
  Office files, 287, 288
  Web page files, 17
file management, 79, 90, 90–91
file names, 287
file sending applications, 105
file sending software, 105
file system, 250–252
File tab, Ribbon, 273, 277
File Transfer Protocol (ftp://), 17
file types of graphics (table), 398
filenames, 261
files
  closing, 288–289
  copying, 259–261
  deleting, 242–243, 262
  described, 31
  moving, 257–258
  naming, 261
  navigating to, 254–255
  opening, 289–290
  organizing, 250–255
  saving, 287–288, 296, 427, 664
  switching between open Office,
    272–274
  uploading, downloading via FTP, 143
  working with, 286–287
fill colors, changing, 473–474
fill handles
  described, 512–513
  using, 513–515
fills, using AutoFill, 513–515
filters
  database data, 610–613
  described, 612
  email, 218–219
  spam, 218
finance, and e-commerce, 149
financial functions
  described, 521
  exploring options using IF function,
    519
  working with PMT function,
    521–525
Find and Replace dialog box, 357
finding
  See also searching
  data using database forms, 642–644
  and replacing text, 332–333
fingerprint readers, 64
Firefox browser, 19
firewalls, 208, 209–210
FireWire (IEEE 1394), 39
FireWire ports, 40

firmware, updating, 134
first-generation computers, 8
first-line indents, 326, 327
fixed wireless Internet access, 156
flash memory, 37–38, 50–52
  cards, 50, 51
  disk cache, 47
  hard drives, 46
  readers, 50, 33
flat-panel displays, 66–67, 68
flexible OLED, 67
Flickr photo sharing service, 53
Flip 3D, 236
floating graphics, 407, 408
floating point unit (FPU), 41
folders
  compressed, 262
  copying, 259–261
  creating, 256–257
  deleting, 262
  described, 238
  moving, 257–258
  organic light emitting diode (OLED),
    250–255
  Recycle Bin, 242–243
  sharing on networks, 115
font size, changing, 314–316
font styles, changing, 315–316
fonts
  changing, 282, 314–316
  colors, 461–462, 708
  creating new theme, 354–355
  described, 314
footers
  adding, 367–369
  adding to slides, 688–690
  creating, 491–492
  described, 365
  handouts, 690–691
footnotes
  adding, 377–378
  citations in, 378
foreign key (database), 569
form letters, creating, 760–767
Form view (Access), 645
Form Wizard (Access), 634–637,
    645–646
Format Cells dialog box, 474–476
Format Painter, copying formats using,
    328–331
formats
  See also specific format
  copying, 328–331
  copying and pasting, 476
  copying using AutoFill, 512–516
  international date, 433
  number, 462
formatting
  cells and ranges, 467–476
  chart axes, 547–548
  conditional, 483–486
  data in cells, 458–467
  data series, 544
  database reports, 595–596
  datasheets, 620
  dates and times, 466–467

Learning Objectives

LO1.1	Explain what computers do
LO1.2	Identify types of computers
LO1.3	Describe computer networks and the Internet
LO1.4	Understand how computers impact society

Digital Backpack

Practice It: Practice It 1-3—Discuss the pros and cons of using technology in our daily lives.

On Your Own: On Your Own 1-2—Discuss your opinion about campus gossip sites.

Quiz: Take the practice quiz to prepare for tests.

Key Terms: Review the key term flash cards (online, printable, and audio).

Games: Play *Beat the Clock* and *Memory* to quiz yourself.

Videos: Watch *Searching the Web on Your iPhone* and *Climate Savers Computing Initiative*.

Infographic

URL for a Web page

tp://
eb page URLs
ually begin with
e standard protocol
entifier http://.

twitter.com
This part of the URL identifies the Web server hosting the Web page.

jobs/
Next comes the folder(s) in which the Web page is stored, if necessary.

index.html
This is the Web page document that is to be retrieved and displayed.

How email works

sender's computer
The sender composes an email message and sends it to the recipient via his or her email address.

recipient's mail server
The email message travels from the recipient's mail server to the recipient's computer.

sender's mail server
The email message travels from the sender's computer to his or her ISP's mail server.

tjones@state.edu

The Internet
The email message travels over the Internet through the sender's mail server to the recipient's mail server.

recipient's computer
The recipient requests his or her messages from the mail server and the message is displayed.

Quick Reference Tools

Primary Operations of a Computer

- Input—entering data into the computer
- Processing—performing operations on the data
- Output—presenting the results
- Storage—saving data, programs, or output

Data vs. Information

- Data are unorganized facts input into a computer.
- Information is data that has been processed into a meaningful form.
- The computer processes data into information.

Types of Computers

- An embedded computer is a tiny computer designed to perform specific tasks for a product.
- A mobile device is a small communications device that has built-in computing or Internet capability.
- A personal computer (PC) is a small computer designed for use by one person at a time.
- A midrange server is a computer used to host programs and data for a small network.
- A mainframe computer is a powerful computer many large organizations use to manage large amounts of centralized data.
- A supercomputer is the most powerful and most expensive type of computer available.

Computers and Societal Issues

- Intellectual property rights include three main types: copyrights, trademarks and patents.
- Common physical conditions from computer use include eyestrain, blurred vision, fatigue, headaches, backaches, and wrist and finger pain. Repetitive stress injuries (RSIs) include carpal tunnel syndrome and DeQuervain's tendonitis.
- Ergonomics is the science of fitting a work environment to the people who work there.
- Green computing refers to using computers in an environmentally friendly manner, including reducing the use of energy and paper ,and proper disposal of e-trash.

Computer Networks

- A network is a collection of computers and other devices that are connected to enable users to share hardware, software, and data, as well as to communicate electronically.
- Networks are used in the home, small offices, schools, large corporations, and public locations such as coffeehouses, bookstores, and libraries.
- The Internet is the largest and most well-known computer network in the world; it is technically a network of networks.

The Internet and the World Wide Web

- The Internet refers to the physical structure of that network.
- The World Wide Web (Web or WWW) refers to one resource that is available through the Internet.
- A group of Web pages belonging to one person or organization is called a Web site.
- Web pages are stored on computers called Web servers that are continually connected to the Web.
- Web servers can be accessed by anyone with a Web-enabled device and an Internet connection.

Key Definitions

Go to your CMPTR CourseMate site for a full list of key terms and definitions.

cloud computing To use data, applications, and resources stored on computers accessed over the Internet rather than on users' computers.

domain name A text-based Internet address used to uniquely identify a computer on the Internet.

input The process of entering data into a computer; can also refer to the data itself.

Internet The largest and most well-known computer network, linking millions of computers all over the world.

network Computers and other devices that are connected to share hardware, software, and data.

output The process of presenting results of processing; can also refer to the results themselves.

processing Performing operations on data that has been input into a computer to convert that input to output.

storage The operation of saving data, programs or output for future use.

Web server A computer continually connected to the Internet that stores Web pages accessible through the Internet.

Learning Objectives

LO2.1	Understand how data is represented to a computer
LO2.2	Identify the parts inside the system unit
LO2.3	Explain how the CPU works
LO2.4	Describe different types of storage systems
LO2.5	Identify and describe common input devices
LO2.6	Identify and describe common output devices

Digital Backpack

Practice It: Practice It 2-3—Research and recommend a new personal printer to purchase.

On Your Own: On Your Own 2-2—Discuss the benefits and drawbacks of online/cloud storage services.

Quiz: Take the practice quiz to prepare for tests.

Key Terms: Review the key term flash cards (online, printable, and audio).

Games: Play *Beat the Clock* and *Memory* to quiz yourself.

Videos: Watch *How to Deal with the Blue Screen of Death, The Impact of Moore's Law, A Look at Network Storage,* and *What Is a 3D Mouse?*

Infographic

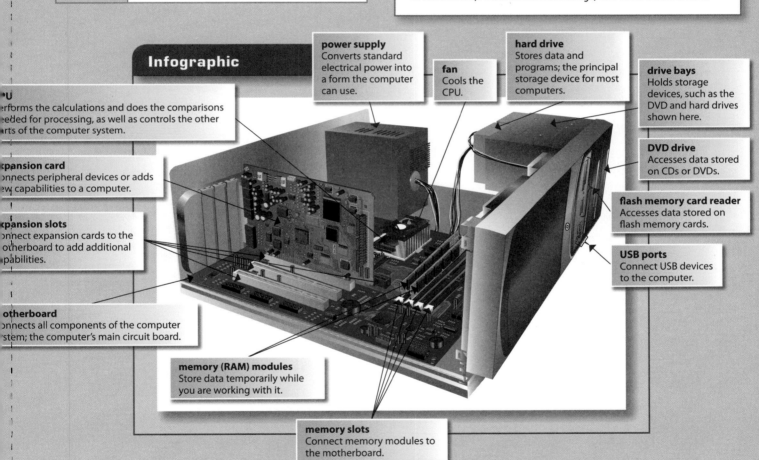

power supply
Converts standard electrical power into a form the computer can use.

fan
Cools the CPU.

hard drive
Stores data and programs; the principal storage device for most computers.

drive bays
Holds storage devices, such as the DVD and hard drives shown here.

DVD drive
Accesses data stored on CDs or DVDs.

flash memory card reader
Accesses data stored on flash memory cards.

USB ports
Connect USB devices to the computer.

CPU
Performs the calculations and does the comparisons needed for processing, as well as controls the other parts of the computer system.

expansion card
Connects peripheral devices or adds new capabilities to a computer.

expansion slots
Connect expansion cards to the motherboard to add additional capabilities.

motherboard
Connects all components of the computer system; the computer's main circuit board.

memory (RAM) modules
Store data temporarily while you are working with it.

memory slots
Connect memory modules to the motherboard.

Quick Reference Tools

Bits and Bytes

- Digital computers are binary, understanding two states represented by 0 and 1 (on and off).
- A bit is the smallest unit of data a binary computer can recognize, represented by a 0 or a 1.
- Eight bits are referred to as a byte.
- A file is a named collection of bytes that represent virtually any type of data.

The CPU

- A typical CPU includes an arithmetic/logic unit (ALU), a floating point unit (FPU), a control unit, a prefetch unit, a decode unit, a bus interface unit, registers, and an internal cache memory.
- A system clock, located on the motherboard, synchronizes all of a computer's operations.
- The machine cycle: (1) Fetch the instruction from cache or RAM; (2) Decode the instructions into a form the ALU or FPU can understand; (3) Execute the instructions; and (4) Store the data or results in registers or RAM.

Input Devices

- An input device is any piece of equipment used to enter data into the computer.
- Common input devices are keyboards, pointing devices, touch devices, scanners, and readers.
- Images, video, and audio input are becoming more common and accessible.

The System Unit

- The system unit houses the processing hardware for the computer, as well as other devices.
- The system unit includes the motherboard, power supply, central processing unit, memory, expansion slots and cards, buses, ports and connectors.
- Most computers support Plug and Play, meaning the computer automatically configures new devices upon installation and computer boot up.

Storage Systems

- Storage systems provide nonvolatile storage, making it possible to save programs, data, and processing results for later use.
- Storage systems include a storage medium (the hardware where data is stored) and a storage device (the hardware where a storage medium is inserted to be read from or written to).
- Storage devices include hard drives, optical discs, flash memory, remote storage (network or online/cloud storage), smart cards, and storage servers.

Output Devices

- An output device presents the results of processed data from the computer to the user.
- The most common output devices are computer screens, data projectors, printers, and audio speakers.

Key Definitions

Go to your CMPTR CourseMate site for a full list of key terms and definitions.

bit The smallest unit of data that a binary computer can recognize.

byte Eight bits grouped together.

central processing unit (CPU or **processor)** The chip located on the motherboard of a computer that performs the processing for a computer.

circuit board A thin board containing computer chips and other electronic components.

flash memory Nonvolatile chips that can be used for storage by the computer or the user.

memory Chips located inside the system unit used to store data and instructions while it is working with them.

monitor A display device for a desktop computer.

mouse A common pointing device that the user slides along a flat surface to move the pointer on the screen.

port A connector on the exterior of the system unit case that is used to connect an external hardware device.

ROM (read-only memory) Nonvolatile chips on the motherboard that permanently store data or programs.

universal serial bus (USB) A versatile bus architecture widely used for connecting peripherals.

USB flash drive Flash memory media integrated into a self-contained unit that plugs into a USB port.

Learning Objectives

LO3.1	Explain system software and operating systems
LO3.2	Identify operating systems for desktop PCs
LO3.3	Identify operating systems for handheld PCs and larger computers
LO3.4	Describe common types of application software
LO3.5	Describe application software used for business
LO3.6	Describe application software used for working with multimedia
LO3.7	Describe other types of application software

Digital Backpack

Practice It: Practice It 3-3—Consider the advantages and disadvantages of installed versus Web-based applications.

On Your Own: On Your Own 3-2—Discuss the impact of open source software on commercial software companies and software quality.

Quiz: Take the practice quiz to prepare for tests.

Key Terms: Review the key term flash cards (online, printable, and audio).

Games: Play *Beat the Clock* and *Memory* to quiz yourself.

Videos: Watch *How to Back Up Your Files Automatically, How to Find Out What's Running on Your PC,* and *How to Use Free Web App Alternatives to Expensive Software?*

Infographic

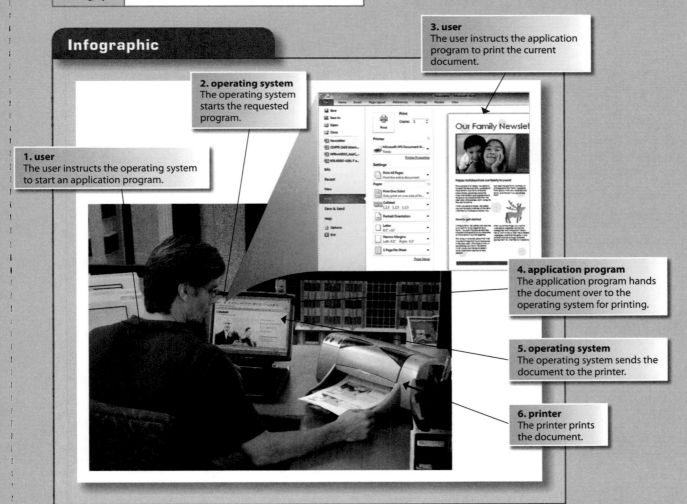

3. user
The user instructs the application program to print the current document.

2. operating system
The operating system starts the requested program.

1. user
The user instructs the operating system to start an application program.

4. application program
The application program hands the document over to the operating system for printing.

5. operating system
The operating system sends the document to the printer.

6. printer
The printer prints the document.

Quick Reference Tools

System Software and Operating Systems

- System software includes the operating system and utility programs that control a computer system and enable application software to run.
- The operating system is loaded into memory during the boot process and serves as the intermediary between the user and the computer and between application programs and the hardware.
- Most operating systems today use a graphical user interface (GUI).

Operating Systems for Desktop PCs

- Many operating systems are designed for personal computers or for network servers.
- The most widely used operating systems are DOS, Windows, Windows Server, Windows Home Server, Mac OS, Mac OS Server, UNIX, and Linux.

Operating Systems for Handheld PCs

- Notebook, netbook, UMPCs, and other portable personal computers typically use the same operating systems as desktop computers.
- Common operating systems for mobile devices include Windows Mobile, Windows Embedded, Android, iPhone OS, BlackBerry OS, Palm OS, Palm webOS, Symbian OS, and Embedded Linux.

Other Application Software

- Multimedia application software includes graphics software, audio capture and editing software, video editing and DVD authoring software, and audio and video media players.
- Special purpose software includes desktop publishing software; educational, entertainment, and reference software; note-taking software, CAD and design software; accounting and personal finance software; and project management, collaboration and remote access software.

Application Software

- Application software can be open source, commercial, shareware, freeware, or public domain.
- Mobile devices usually require mobile software.
- Software can be installed on a computer or run directly from the Internet as Web-based software.

Business Application Software

- Related software programs can be sold bundled as a software suite.
- Office suites include word processing, spreadsheet, database, and presentation software.
- Common office software suites include Microsoft Office ,Corel WordPerfect Office, Apple iWork, and OpenOffice.org.

Key Definitions

Go to your CMPTR CourseMate site for a full list of key terms and definitions.

application software The programs that allow you to perform specific tasks on a computer.

boot process The actions taken by programs built into the computer's hardware to start the operating system.

device driver (driver) A small program used to communicate with a peripheral device, such as a monitor, printer, or keyboard.

multiprocessing A processing technique in which multiple processors or multiple processing cores in a single computer each work on a different job.

operating system A collection of programs that manage and coordinate the activities taking place within the computer.

parallel processing A processing technique that uses multiple processors or multiple processing cores simultaneously, usually to process a single job as fast as possible.

shareware program A software program that is distributed on the honor system; typically available free of charge but may require a small registration fee.

software license A permit that specifies the conditions under which a buyer can use the software.

software suite Related software programs, such as a group of graphics programs, utility programs, or office-related software, that are sold bundled together.

system software Programs such as the operating system and utility programs that control a computer and its devices, and enable application software to run on the computer.

virtual memory A memory management technique frequently used by operating systems that uses a portion of the computer's hard drive as additional RAM.

Windows The operating system created by Microsoft in 1985 with a graphical user interface.

Learning Objectives

LO4.1	Explain what networks are
LO4.2	Identify network characteristics
LO4.3	Understand how data is transmitted over a network
LO4.4	Describe common types of network media
LO4.5	Identify protocols and networking standards
LO4.6	Describe networking hardware

Digital Backpack

Practice It: Practice It 4-3—Create a wired home network scenario.

On Your Own: On Your Own 4-2—Discuss possible solutions to and who should be responsible for fixing the problem of interference with wireless devices.

Quiz: Take the practice quiz to prepare for tests.

Key Terms: Review the key term flash cards (online, printable, and audio).

Games: Play *Beat the Clock* and *Memory* to quiz yourself.

Videos: Watch *How to Select a Wireless Router, How to Set Up a Wireless Network, How to Share a Printer over a Network,* and *WiMAX vs. Wi-Fi.*

Infographic

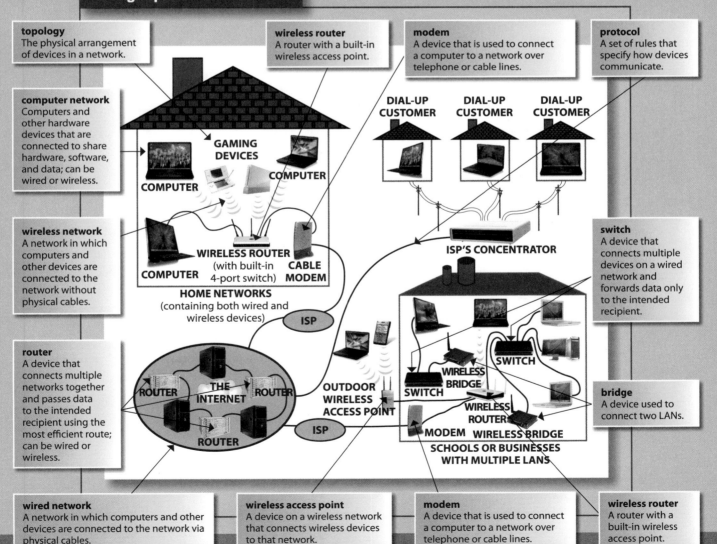

topology
The physical arrangement of devices in a network.

wireless router
A router with a built-in wireless access point.

modem
A device that is used to connect a computer to a network over telephone or cable lines.

protocol
A set of rules that specify how devices communicate.

computer network
Computers and other hardware devices that are connected to share hardware, software, and data; can be wired or wireless.

wireless network
A network in which computers and other devices are connected to the network without physical cables.

switch
A device that connects multiple devices on a wired network and forwards data only to the intended recipient.

router
A device that connects multiple networks together and passes data to the intended recipient using the most efficient route; can be wired or wireless.

bridge
A device used to connect two LANs.

wired network
A network in which computers and other devices are connected to the network via physical cables.

wireless access point
A device on a wireless network that connects wireless devices to that network.

modem
A device that is used to connect a computer to a network over telephone or cable lines.

wireless router
A router with a built-in wireless access point.

GAMING DEVICES
COMPUTER
COMPUTER
COMPUTER
WIRELESS ROUTER (with built-in 4-port switch)
CABLE MODEM
HOME NETWORKS (containing both wired and wireless devices)
ISP

DIAL-UP CUSTOMER
DIAL-UP CUSTOMER
DIAL-UP CUSTOMER
ISP'S CONCENTRATOR

ROUTER
THE INTERNET
ROUTER
ROUTER
ISP

OUTDOOR WIRELESS ACCESS POINT
MODEM
SWITCH
WIRELESS BRIDGE
SWITCH
WIRELESS ROUTER
WIRELESS BRIDGE
SCHOOLS OR BUSINESSES WITH MULTIPLE LANS

Quick Reference Tools

Common Network Topologies

- **Star network** is a network in which all networked devices connect to a central device through which all network transmissions are sent.
- **Bus network** is a network that uses a central cable to which all network devices connect.
- **Mesh network** is a network that uses a number of different connections between network devices so that data can take any of several possible paths from source to destination.

Common Network Architectures

- **Client-server networks** include both clients (computers and other devices on the network that request and use network resources) and servers (computers that are dedicated to processing client requests)
- **Peer-to-peer (P2P) networks** include computers that work at the same functional level and provide users direct access to the networks devices

Connecting to a Wi-Fi Hotspot

- To connect to a Wi-Fi hotspot, click the icon representing your wireless network connection in the system tray, click the network to which you want to connect in the list that appears, and then click **Connect**.

Sharing Folders

- Do not enable sharing for folders you want to keep private.

Serial Transmission Types

- **Synchronous transmission** organizes data into groups or blocks of data, which are transferred at regular, specified intervals.
- **Asynchronous transmission** sends data when it is ready to be sent, without being synchronized.
- **Isochronous transmission** sends data at the same time as other related data with the different types of data delivered at the proper speed for their applications.

Common Protocols for Internet Applications

- **TCP/IP (Transmission Control Protocol/Internet Protocol)** is used to transfer data over the Internet.
- **HTTP (Hypertext Transfer Protocol)** and **HTTPS (Secure Hypertext Transfer Protocol)** are used to display Web pages.
- **FTP (File Transfer Protocol)** is used to transfer files over the Internet.
- **SMTP (Simple Mail Transfer Protocol)** and **POP3 (Post Office Protocol)** are used to deliver email over the Internet.

Key Definitions

Go to your CMPTR CourseMate site for a full list of key terms and definitions.

bandwidth (throughput) The amount of data that can be transferred in a given time period.

Bluetooth A networking standard for very short-range wireless connections.

client A computer or other device on a network that requests and uses network resources.

client-server network A network that includes both clients and servers.

download To retrieve files from a server to a client.

Ethernet The most widely used standard for wired networks.

network interface card (NIC) A network adapter in the form of an expansion card.

protocol A set of rules to be followed in a specific situation.

server A computer that is dedicated to processing client requests.

TCP/IP A networking protocol that uses packet switching to facilitate the transmission of messages; the protocol used with the Internet.

upload To transfer files from a client to a server.

wide area network (WAN) A network that connects devices located in a large geographical area.

Wi-Fi (802.11) A widely used networking standard for medium-range wireless networks.

Wi-Fi hotspot A location that provides wireless Internet access to the public.

WiMAX (802.16a) An emerging wireless networking standard that is faster and has a greater range than Wi-Fi

Visit **login.CengageBrain.com** for additional study tools!

CHAPTER 5
reviewcard
Introducing the Internet and Email
Networks and the Internet

Learning Objectives

LO5.1	Understand how the Internet evolved
LO5.2	Describe common Internet communication methods and activities
LO5.3	Set up your computer to use the Internet
LO5.4	Use Microsoft Internet Explorer
LO5.5	Use Windows Mail

Digital Backpack

Practice It: Practice It 5-3—Use Internet Explorer to locate travel quotes, and then use Windows Live Mail to share your findings.

On Your Own: On Your Own 5-2—Use Internet Explorer and Google to search for information on the Web, and then use Windows Live Mail to share your findings.

Quiz: Take the practice quiz to prepare for tests.

Key Terms: Review the key term flash cards (online, printable, and audio).

Games: Play *Beat the Clock* and *Memory* to quiz yourself.

Videos: Watch *Google 15-Second Search Tips* and *Google Search Plain and Simple*.

Infographic

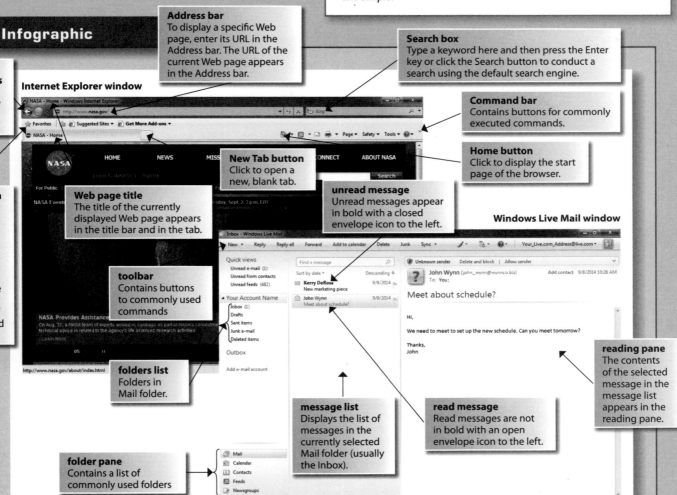

Address bar
To display a specific Web page, enter its URL in the Address bar. The URL of the current Web page appears in the Address bar.

Search box
Type a keyword here and then press the Enter key or click the Search button to conduct a search using the default search engine.

Back and Forward buttons
Use to move to the most recently viewed Web pages.

Internet Explorer window

Command bar
Contains buttons for commonly executed commands.

New Tab button
Click to open a new, blank tab.

Home button
Click to display the start page of the browser.

Favorites button
Click to open the Favorites center, which displays a list of favorites shortcuts to Web pages, feeds (frequently updated Web site content), and the History list (list of Web pages visited recently).

Web page title
The title of the currently displayed Web page appears in the title bar and in the tab.

unread message
Unread messages appear in bold with a closed envelope icon to the left.

Windows Live Mail window

toolbar
Contains buttons to commonly used commands

folders list
Folders in Mail folder.

message list
Displays the list of messages in the currently selected Mail folder (usually the Inbox).

read message
Read messages are not in bold with an open envelope icon to the left.

reading pane
The contents of the selected message in the message list appears in the reading pane.

folder pane
Contains a list of commonly used folders

Quick Reference Tools

Evolution of the Internet

- ARPANET was created in 1969 and provided the exchange of written information.
- Over the next decade, hundreds of college and university networks were connected to ARPANET.
- In 1989, Tim Berners-Lee proposed the World Wide Web as a way to organize information.
- The Mosaic Web browser, released in 1993, provided a graphical user interface, allowing users to display images.
- The Web is the most widely used part of the Internet today.
- Internet2 is a research and development tool to help create revolutionary Internet technologies.

Today's Internet Community

- The Internet community includes: users, Internet service providers (ISPs), Internet content providers, application service providers (ASPs), infrastructure companies, hardware and software companies, governments, and Internet organizations.
- Each network connected to the Internet is privately owned and individually managed.

Connecting to the Internet

- First, select the type of device to access the Internet, such as a personal computer, a mobile phone, or a television.
- Second, choose the type of connection and Internet access, such as dial-up, cable, DSL, satellite, fixed wireless, broadband over fiber, mobile wireless, or Wi-Fi hotspot.
- Third, select an ISP.

Using Windows Live Mail

- To send a message, click the New button, enter email address(es), enter a subject title, type a message, and then click the Send button.
- To receive and read a message, click the Inbox folder, click the Sync button, click the message, and then read its contents in the reading pane.
- To reply to or forward a message, click the message, click the Reply or Forward button, type an email address for a forwarded message, type a message, and then click the Send button.
- To delete a message, click the message and then click the Delete button on the toolbar.
- To attach a file to a message, click the Attach button, click the file to attach, and then click Open.

Common Internet Activities

- The most common Internet activities are browsing and email.
- Online communication includes instant messaging (IM), text messaging, tweeting, Voice over Internet Protocol (VoIP), Web conferences, Webinars, and social networking sites.
- Online writing includes blogs, wikis, and e-portfolios.

Using Internet Explorer

- To connect to a Web page, type the URL in the Address bar, and then press the Enter key.
- To move between previously viewed pages, click the Back or Forward button.
- To use tabs, click the New Tab button next to the current tab. Click a tab to make it active.
- To search the Internet, type keywords into the Search box, and then press the Enter key.

Key Definitions

Go to your CMPTR CourseMate site for a full list of key terms and definitions.

ARPANET The predecessor of the Internet, named after the Advanced Research Projects Agency (ARPA), which sponsored its development.

DSL (digital subscriber line) Fast, direct Internet access via standard telephone lines.

favorite A shortcut to a Web page saved in a list.

feed Frequently updated Web site content, such as news or blogs, delivered directly to your browser.

History list A list that tracks the Web pages you visit over a certain time period.

load To copy a Web page from a server to a computer.

search engine A software program used by a search site to retrieve matching Web pages from a search database.

Wi-Fi hotspot A location that provides wireless Internet access to the public.

wiki A collaborative Web page that is designed to be edited and republished by a variety of individuals.

Visit **login.CengageBrain.com** for additional study tools!

reviewcard

CHAPTER 6
Network and Internet Security and Privacy
Networks and the Internet

Learning Objectives

LO6.1	Explain network and Internet security concerns
LO6.2	Identify online threats
LO6.3	Describe cyberstalking and other personal safety concerns
LO6.4	Assess personal computer security
LO6.5	Identify privacy concerns
LO6.6	Discuss current network and Internet security legislation

Digital Backpack

Practice It: Practice It 6-3—Research a current virus or worm.

On Your Own: On Your Own 6-2—Research two recent virus hoaxes.

Quiz: Take the practice quiz to prepare for tests.

Key Terms: Review the key term flash cards (online, printable, and audio).

Games: Play *Beat the Clock* and *Memory* to quiz yourself.

Videos: Watch *How to Create an Encrypted Partition on Your Hard Drive, How to Protect Yourself Against Malware, How Worms Spread Using AutoPlay, Securing Your Wireless Router, Google Search Privacy – Personalized Search,* and *Proper Hardware Disposal.*

Infographic

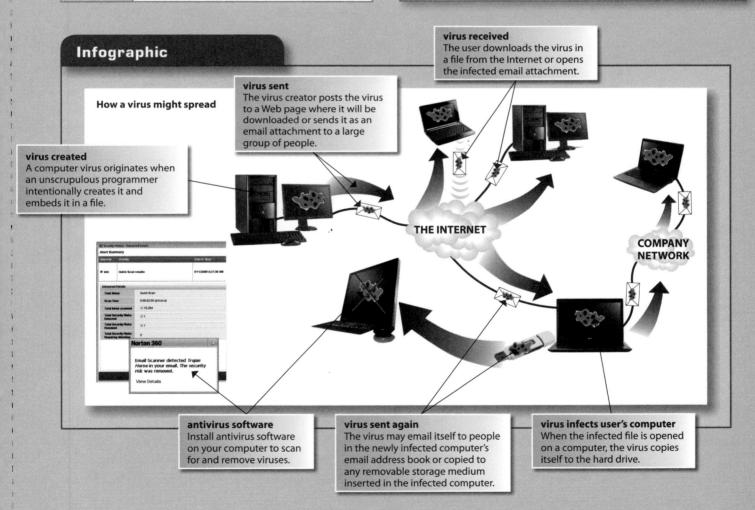

How a virus might spread

virus created
A computer virus originates when an unscrupulous programmer intentionally creates it and embeds it in a file.

virus sent
The virus creator posts the virus to a Web page where it will be downloaded or sends it as an email attachment to a large group of people.

virus received
The user downloads the virus in a file from the Internet or opens the infected email attachment.

THE INTERNET

COMPANY NETWORK

antivirus software
Install antivirus software on your computer to scan for and remove viruses.

virus sent again
The virus may email itself to people in the newly infected computer's email address book or copied to any removable storage medium inserted in the infected computer.

virus infects user's computer
When the infected file is opened on a computer, the virus copies itself to the hard drive.

Quick Reference Tools

Network and Internet Security

- Computer crime (or cybercrime) includes unauthorized access to and use of a computer, network, file, or other resource.
- Hacking is a threat to individuals and businesses, and to governments as cyberterrorism.
- Unauthorized use of a Wi-Fi network occurs with war driving and Wi-Fi piggybacking.
- Some criminals intercept communications to gain access to data, files, email, and other content.

Online Threats

- Computer sabotage leads to lost productivity, lost sales, and higher labor costs.
- Computer sabotage occurs via botnets; computer viruses and malware; denial of service (DoS) attacks; alteration of data, programs, or Web sites; dot cons; data, information, or identity theft; phishing and pharming; and other Internet scams.

Personal Computer Security

- Common security concerns are hardware theft, loss, or damage; system failures due to hardware or software problems; computer virus, natural disaster, sabotage, or terrorist attack.
- To protect against hardware loss or damage and system failures, you can lock doors and equipment, encrypt files, install security software, and use firewalls, encryption, and VPNs.

Privacy Concerns

- Personal information can be located in many different databases, leading to electronic profiling.
- Most businesses and Web sites that collect personal information have a privacy policy.
- Spam can be countered with spam or junk mail filters, and opting in or out of marketing lists.
- Legal electronic surveillance uses computer monitoring software, video surveillance, employee monitoring, and presence technology.

Personal Safety Concerns

- Cybercrime can be physically dangerous, especially for children.
- Common online harassment includes cyberbullying and cyberstalking.
- Online pornography involving minors is illegal; many believe that the Internet is making it easier for sexual predators to meet and target children.

Security Legislation

- New legislation is passed periodically to address the latest computer crimes, but it is difficult for the legal system to keep pace with the rate at which technology changes.
- Domestic and international jurisdictional issues arise because many computer crimes affect businesses and people located in areas other than the one in which the criminal is located.

Key Definitions

Go to your CMPTR CourseMate site for a full list of key terms and definitions.

antivirus software Software used to detect and eliminate computer viruses and other types of malware.

cyberbullying Children or teenagers bullying other children or teenagers via the Internet.

cyberstalking Repeated threats or harassing behavior between adults carried out via email or another Internet communications method.

cyberterrorism An attack launched by terrorists via the Internet.

encryption A method of scrambling the contents of an email message or a file to make it unreadable if an unauthorized user intercepts it.

firewall A collection of hardware and/or software that protects a computer or computer network from unauthorized access.

phishing The use of spoofed email message to gain credit card numbers and other personal data to be used for fraudulent purposes.

surge suppressor A device that protects a computer system from damage due to electrical fluctuations.

uninterruptable power supply (UPS) A device containing a built-in battery that provides continuous power to a computer and other connected components when the electricity goes out.

virus A software program installed without the user's knowledge and designed to alter the way a computer operates or to cause harm to the computer system.

Visit **login.CengageBrain.com** for additional study tools!

Learning Objectives

LO7.1	Identify the parts of the Windows 7 desktop
LO7.2	Use common Windows elements
LO7.3	Navigate Windows
LO7.4	Work with the Recycle Bin
LO7.5	Get Help
LO7.6	Shut down Windows

Digital Backpack

Practice It: Practice It 7-3—Use Windows 7 to explore the Pictures folder and change views.

On Your Own: On Your Own 7-2—Explore the Start menu and use Windows Help and Support to research a program in the Accessories folder.

Quiz: Take the practice quiz to prepare for tests.

Key Terms: Review the key term flash cards (online, printable, and audio).

Games: Play *Beat the Clock* and *Memory* to quiz yourself.

Videos: Watch *Use the Start Menu, Switch Between Menus, Touring the Windows 7 Desktop, Exploring Your Computer, Navigate in Explorer Windows, Change the View of Folders,* and *Use the Navigation Pane.*

Infographic

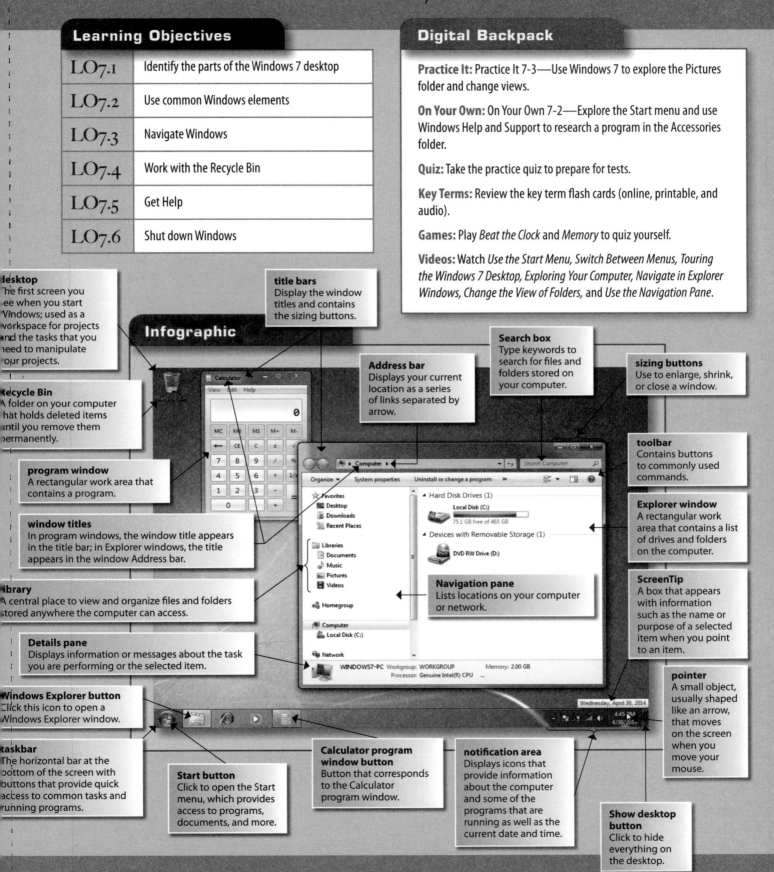

desktop
The first screen you see when you start Windows; used as a workspace for projects and the tasks that you need to manipulate your projects.

Recycle Bin
A folder on your computer that holds deleted items until you remove them permanently.

program window
A rectangular work area that contains a program.

window titles
In program windows, the window title appears in the title bar; in Explorer windows, the title appears in the window Address bar.

Library
A central place to view and organize files and folders stored anywhere the computer can access.

Details pane
Displays information or messages about the task you are performing or the selected item.

Windows Explorer button
Click this icon to open a Windows Explorer window.

taskbar
The horizontal bar at the bottom of the screen with buttons that provide quick access to common tasks and running programs.

title bars
Display the window titles and contains the sizing buttons.

Address bar
Displays your current location as a series of links separated by arrow.

Search box
Type keywords to search for files and folders stored on your computer.

sizing buttons
Use to enlarge, shrink, or close a window.

toolbar
Contains buttons to commonly used commands.

Explorer window
A rectangular work area that contains a list of drives and folders on the computer.

ScreenTip
A box that appears with information such as the name or purpose of a selected item when you point to an item.

Navigation pane
Lists locations on your computer or network.

pointer
A small object, usually shaped like an arrow, that moves on the screen when you move your mouse.

Start button
Click to open the Start menu, which provides access to programs, documents, and more.

Calculator program window button
Button that corresponds to the Calculator program window.

notification area
Displays icons that provide information about the computer and some of the programs that are running as well as the current date and time.

Show desktop button
Click to hide everything on the desktop.

Quick Reference Tools

Starting Windows 7

- Turn on your computer.
- On the Welcome screen, click your account name.
- If necessary, type your password, and then click the Go button.

Using the Mouse

- Point—position the pointer directly on top of an item.
- Click—press the left mouse button and immediately release it.
- Right-click—press the right mouse button and immediately release it.
- Double-click—press the left mouse button twice in quick succession.
- Drag—position the pointer on top of an item, and then press and hold the left mouse button while moving the pointer.

Navigating Windows

- To use Aero Flip 3D, press and hold the Windows key and press and release the Tab key to flip between open windows.
- To use the task switcher, press and hold the Alt key and press and release the Tab key to select a thumbnail in the task switcher window.
- To access a folder or file, click a folder in the Navigation pane. Double-click a folder or file in the right pane.

Common Window Elements

- All windows have a title bar, sizing buttons, window title, and Details pane/status bar.
- To resize windows, use the sizing buttons.

Using Windows Help and Support

- On the taskbar, click the Start button. In the right pane of the Start menu, click Help and Support.
- In the Help window, click a link to get basic information or find more information on the Microsoft Web site.
- On the toolbar, click the Browse Help button. In the Contents list, click a category, click a subcategory if needed, and then click a topic.
- In the Search Help box, type a word or phrase about the topic you want to find, and then click the Search Help button.

Ending a Windows Session

- Log off to close all programs, log off Windows 7, and leave the computer running.
- Sleep to keep the current session in memory and put the computer in a low-power state.
- Shut down to close all open programs, shut down Windows, and turn off your computer.

Key Definitions

Go to your CMPTR CourseMate site for a full list of key terms and definitions.

active window The window to which the next keystroke or command is applied.

button A graphical icon you click to start a program or perform a command.

Control Panel A window that contains specialized tools to change the way Windows 7 looks and behaves.

double-click To click the left mouse button twice in quick succession.

drag To position the pointer on top of an item, and then press and hold the left mouse button while moving the pointer.

point To position the pointer directly on top of an item.

right-click To click the right mouse button and immediately release it.

shortcut A very small file that points to the location of the actual folder or file.

shortcut menu A menu that lists actions you can take with the item you right-clicked.

Start menu A menu that provides access to programs, documents, and much more.

status bar A banner at the bottom of a window that displays information or messages about the task you are performing or the selected item.

theme A set of desktop backgrounds, window colors, sounds, and screen savers.

window A rectangular work area that contains a program, text, files, or other data.

Learning Objectives

LO8.1	Organize files and folders
LO8.2	Manage files and folders
LO8.3	Work with compressed files

Digital Backpack

Practice It: Practice It 8-3—Create a compressed copy of your files for this course on a removable media.

On Your Own: On Your Own 8-2—Build a logical folder structure for your course work and organize your files into folders and subfolders.

Quiz: Take the practice quiz to prepare for tests.

Key Terms: Review the key term flash cards (online, printable, and audio).

Games: Play *Beat the Clock* and *Memory* to quiz yourself.

Videos: Watch *Organizing Files and Folders, Navigate to a library and a folder, Navigate to a File, Working with Folders and Files, Create folders, Move files or folders,* and *Extract Compressed Files.*

Infographic

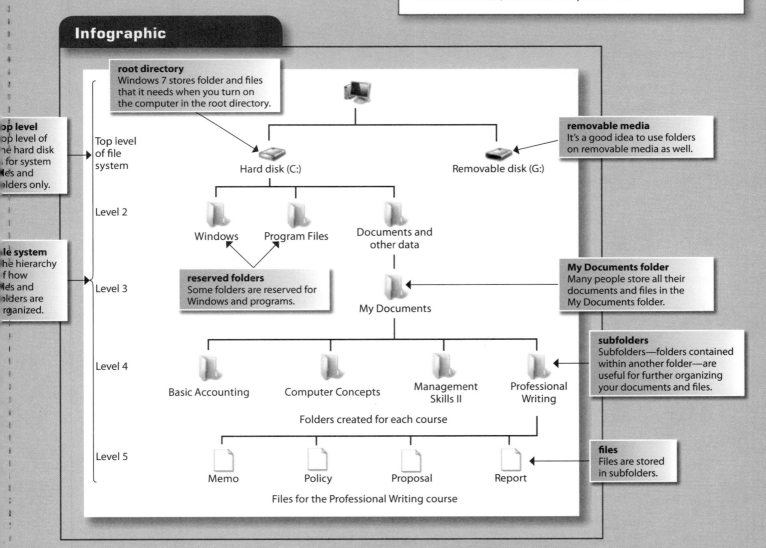

root directory
Windows 7 stores folder and files that it needs when you turn on the computer in the root directory.

op level
op level of
he hard disk
for system
les and
olders only.

Top level of file system

le system
he hierarchy
f how
les and
olders are
rganized.

removable media
It's a good idea to use folders on removable media as well.

Level 2

Hard disk (C:)   Removable disk (G:)

Windows   Program Files   Documents and other data

reserved folders
Some folders are reserved for Windows and programs.

My Documents folder
Many people store all their documents and files in the My Documents folder.

Level 3

My Documents

subfolders
Subfolders—folders contained within another folder—are useful for further organizing your documents and files.

Level 4

Basic Accounting   Computer Concepts   Management Skills II   Professional Writing

Folders created for each course

files
Files are stored in subfolders.

Level 5

Memo   Policy   Proposal   Report

Files for the Professional Writing course

Quick Reference Tools

Windows 7 File System

- Windows 7 organizes folders and files in a file system.
- At the top of the hierarchy is the root directory, which usually is drive C.
- Folders can contain subfolders.
- A well developed and effective organizational strategy makes it simpler to locate files.

File Paths

- The path sleads you through the file and folder organization to the file on a computer.
- The file path includes the drive name, the top-level folder and subfolders, and the full file name, including the file extension.
- Each part of the file path is separated by a back-slash: G:\Chapter 8\Chapter\Customer List.accdb.

Creating and Using Folders

- To create a folder, click the New folder button or right-click a blank area of the window, point to New on the shortcut menu, and then click Folder.
- To move a file or folder into a folder, drag the file or folder on top of another folder.
- To copy a file or folder, press and hold the Ctrl key as you drag the file or folder on top of another folder.
- To delete a file or folder, right-click the file or folder, and then click Delete.

File Names

- A file name includes a descriptive title for the file that you provide when you create a file, a dot or period that separates the main part of the file name from the file extension, and the file extension that identifies the program used to create the file.
- The main part of the file name can have 255 characters including spaces and punctuation, but cannot contain the symbols \ / ? : * " < > | because these have special meanings in Windows 7.

Guidelines for Creating Folders

- Keep folder names short and familiar.
- Develop standards for naming folders.
- Create subfolders to organize files.

Guidelines for Naming Files

- Use common but descriptive names.
- Don't change the file extension.
- Use file names that are long enough to be meaningful but short enough to read easily on the screen.

Compressing and Extracting Files

- To create a compressed folder, right-click one or more selected folders, point to Send to, and then click Compressed (zipped) folder. Type a file name, and then press the Enter key.

- To extract a compressed folder, right-click the compressed folder, and then click Extract All. Select the file path and file name for the extracted folder. Click Extract.

Key Definitions

Go to your CMPTR CourseMate site for a full list of key terms and definitions.

Clipboard A temporary storage area in Windows on which objects are stored when you copy or move them.

compressed (zipped) folder A folder that stores files in a compact format.

extract To create an uncompressed copy of a compressed file.

file system The hierarchy of how files and folders are organized.

path A notation that indicates a file's location on your computer.

root directory The top of the file system where Windows 7 stores folders and files that it needs when you turn on the computer.

subfolder A folder contained within another folder.

synchronize (sync) To copy the most updated version from one computer to another.

Learning Objectives

LO9.1	Start Office programs and explore common elements
LO9.2	Use the Ribbon
LO9.3	Work with Files
LO9.4	Use the Clipboard
LO9.5	Get Help
LO9.6	Exit Office programs

Digital Backpack

Practice It: Practice It 9-3—Complete a presentation with a checklist of camping supplies.

On Your Own: On Your Own 9-2—Identify the programs used to complete event planning tasks.

Quiz: Take the practice quiz to prepare for tests.

Key Terms: Review the key term flash cards (online, printable, and audio).

Games: Play *Beat the Clock* and *Memory* to quiz yourself.

Videos: Watch *Exploring Common Windows Elements, Using Contextual Tools,* and *Getting Help*.

Infographic

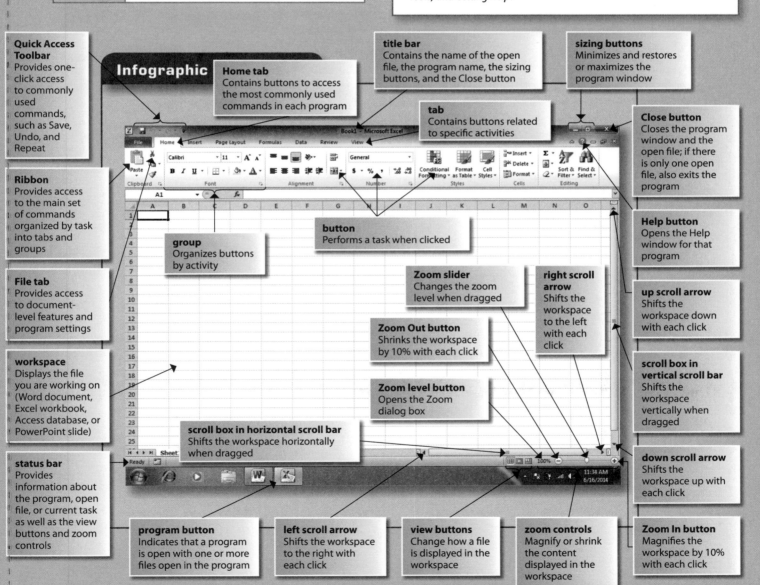

Quick Access Toolbar Provides one-click access to commonly used commands, such as Save, Undo, and Repeat

Home tab Contains buttons to access the most commonly used commands in each program

title bar Contains the name of the open file, the program name, the sizing buttons, and the Close button

sizing buttons Minimizes and restores or maximizes the program window

tab Contains buttons related to specific activities

Close button Closes the program window and the open file; if there is only one open file, also exits the program

Ribbon Provides access to the main set of commands organized by task into tabs and groups

group Organizes buttons by activity

button Performs a task when clicked

Help button Opens the Help window for that program

File tab Provides access to document-level features and program settings

Zoom slider Changes the zoom level when dragged

right scroll arrow Shifts the workspace to the left with each click

up scroll arrow Shifts the workspace down with each click

Zoom Out button Shrinks the workspace by 10% with each click

workspace Displays the file you are working on (Word document, Excel workbook, Access database, or PowerPoint slide)

Zoom level button Opens the Zoom dialog box

scroll box in vertical scroll bar Shifts the workspace vertically when dragged

scroll box in horizontal scroll bar Shifts the workspace horizontally when dragged

down scroll arrow Shifts the workspace up with each click

status bar Provides information about the program, open file, or current task as well as the view buttons and zoom controls

program button Indicates that a program is open with one or more files open in the program

left scroll arrow Shifts the workspace to the right with each click

view buttons Change how a file is displayed in the workspace

zoom controls Magnify or shrink the content displayed in the workspace

Zoom In button Magnifies the workspace by 10% with each click

Quick Reference Tools

Identify buttons

- Position the pointer on top of a button to see a ScreenTip with its name and keyboard shortcut (if it has one).

Use the Mini toolbar

- The Mini toolbar appears when you select an item using the mouse or when you right-click on the screen.
- Click buttons on it just as you click buttons on the Ribbon.
- If it disappears, move the mouse toward it or right-click on the screen.

Save vs. Save As

- The Save command saves the file using the same file name and in the same location.
- The Save As command saves a copy of the file; you can type a new name and choose a new location.

Cut vs. Delete

- The Cut command removes text or an object from the document and places it on the Clipboard.
- The Delete or Backspace key deletes text or an object from a document, but does not place it on the Clipboard

Contextual tabs

- Remember that contextual tabs appear only when an object is selected.

Use Live Preview

- Select text that you want to format.
- Point to an option in a gallery to see a live preview of the option.
- Click the option to apply it to the selected text.

Key Definitions

Go to your CMPTR CourseMate site for a full list of key terms and definitions.

Backstage view The view in Office programs that provides access to file-level features.

contextual tab A tab on the Ribbon that contains commands related to a specific type of object or activity.

dialog box A window in which you enter or choose settings for performing a task.

file name A title that describes the content of the file and a file extension assigned by Office.

gallery A menu or grid that shows visual representations of the options available for a button.

integration The ability to share information between programs.

Live Preview Shows the results that would occur if you clicked the option to which you are pointing in a gallery.

Microsoft Office 2010 (Office) A collection of Microsoft programs.

Mini toolbar A toolbar with buttons for commonly used formatting commands that appears next to the pointer when text is selected using the mouse or when you right-click.

navigation bar The left pane in Backstage view.

object Anything in a document that can be manipulated as a whole.

Protected View A view of a file in an Office program in which you can see the file contents, but you cannot edit, save, or print them until you enable editing.

ScreenTip A box that appears with descriptive text about an element on the screen when you point to it.

task pane A narrow window that appears to the left or right of the document window to help you accomplish a set of tasks.

thumbnail A small picture of an object.

toggle button A button that you click once to turn a feature on and click again to turn it off.

Learning Objectives

LO10.1	Enter text
LO10.2	Undo and redo actions
LO10.3	Create documents based on existing documents
LO10.4	Select text
LO10.5	Edit text
LO10.6	Format text
LO10.7	Format paragraphs
LO10.8	Copy formats
LO10.9	Find and replace text
LO10.10	Check spelling and grammar
LO10.11	Preview and print documents

Digital Backpack

Practice It: Practice It 10-3—Create and format a Word document using an existing document.

On Your Own: On Your Own 10-2—Modify text, review page layout, and print a Word document.

Quiz: Take the practice quiz to prepare for tests.

Key Terms: Review the key term flash cards (online, printable, and audio).

Games: Play *Beat the Clock* and *Memory* to quiz yourself.

Videos: Watch *Correcting Errors as You Type, Insert the Current Date with AutoComplete, Use AutoCorrect, Change Fonts and Font Size, Adjusting Paragraph and Line Spacing* (concept and step-by-step), *Indenting a Paragraph, Adjusting Margins, Change the Alignment of Paragraphs,* and *Create Bulleted Lists.*

Infographic

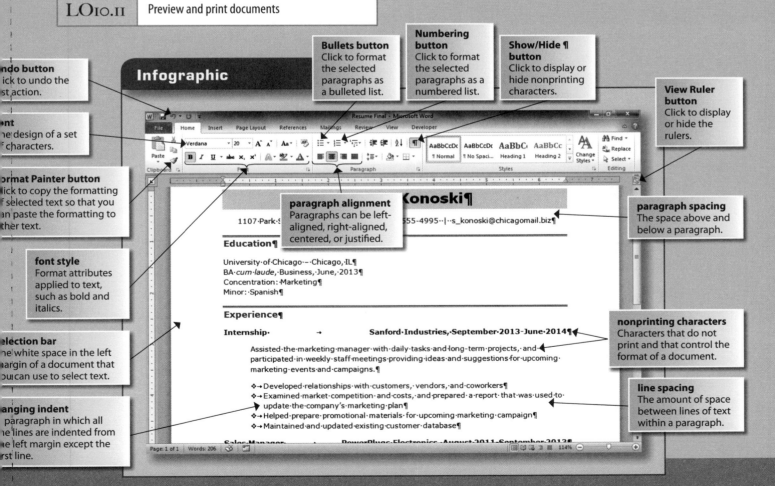

Bullets button
Click to format the selected paragraphs as a bulleted list.

Numbering button
Click to format the selected paragraphs as a numbered list.

Show/Hide ¶ button
Click to display or hide nonprinting characters.

View Ruler button
Click to display or hide the rulers.

Undo button
Click to undo the last action.

Font
The design of a set of characters.

Format Painter button
Click to copy the formatting of selected text so that you can paste the formatting to other text.

font style
Format attributes applied to text, such as bold and italics.

Selection bar
The white space in the left margin of a document that you can use to select text.

Hanging indent
A paragraph in which all the lines are indented from the left margin except the first line.

paragraph alignment
Paragraphs can be left-aligned, right-aligned, centered, or justified.

paragraph spacing
The space above and below a paragraph.

nonprinting characters
Characters that do not print and that control the format of a document.

line spacing
The amount of space between lines of text within a paragraph.

Quick Reference Tools

Create a Document

- To enter text, type in a document, pressing the Enter key only to start a new paragraph.
- To insert a symbol, click the Symbol button. Click a symbol, click Insert, and then click Close.
- To save a document with a new name, click Save As. In the Save As dialog box, change the save location, type a new file name, click Save.
- To create a document based on another document, click New. In the Available Templates pane, click the New from existing button, click the file you want to use, click Create New. Save the new document.

Format Text and Paragraphs

- You can format text by changing the font; font size, style, and color; and text effects.
- You can format paragraphs by changing the line spacing; paragraph spacing, alignment, borders, and shading; and by creating bulleted and numbered lists.
- To create a tab stop, click the tab selector to select a tab style, and then click on the horizontal ruler to add a tab stop.
- To create first-line, hanging, right, and left paragraph indents, use the indent markers on the horizontal ruler.

Select and Edit Text

- To replace text, select it and type.
- To move text, drag selected text to a new location.
- To find text, on the Home tab, in the Editing group, click the Find button, and type the search text in the Search Document box.
- To replace text, on the Home tab, in the Editing group, click the Replace button, type the search text in the Find what box, type the new text in the Replace with box, click Replace or Replace All.

Check Spelling and Grammar

- Misspelled words have a red wavy underline. Contextual spelling errors have a blue wavy underline. Grammar errors have a green wavy underline.
- Right-click a flagged word, and then click the correction on the shortcut menu.
- To check spelling in the entire document, on the Review tab, in the Proofing group, click the Spelling & Grammar button.

Undo and Redo Actions

- To undo and redo one action, on the Quick Access Toolbar, click the Undo button or the Redo button.
- To undo or redo multiple actions, click the Undo button arrow or the Redo button arrow, and then click an action to undo or redo that action and all the actions above it in the list.

Preview and Print a Document

- On the File tab, in the navigation bar, click Print.
- In the right pane, review the preview.
- In the left pane, set the number of copies to print and select a printer.
- Click the Print button.

Key Definitions

Go to your CMPTR CourseMate site for a full list of key terms and definitions.

AutoCorrect A feature that automatically corrects certain misspelled words and typing errors.

first-line indent A paragraph in which the first-line is indented from the left margin.

format To change the appearance of a file and its content.

leader line A line that appears between two elements, such as between tabbed text.

line spacing The amount of space between lines of text within a paragraph.

single spaced Line spacing that has no extra space between lines of text in a paragraph.

spell check To check a file for spelling and grammatical errors using the Spelling and Grammar Checker.

tab stop (tab) A location on the horizontal ruler where the insertion point moves when you press the Tab key.

template A file that contains formatting and sometimes sample content.

Learning Objectives

LO11.1	Work with styles
LO11.2	Work with themes
LO11.3	Change the style set
LO11.4	Work with the document outline
LO11.5	Change margins
LO11.6	Control pagination
LO11.7	Add page numbers, headers, and footers
LO11.8	Create citations and a list of works cited
LO11.9	Create footnotes or endnotes

Digital Backpack

Practice It: Practice It 11-3—Create a Word document using styles and themes and work with the document outline.

On Your Own: On Your Own 11-2—Modify the style set, insert page numbers, and create citations.

Quiz: Take the practice quiz to prepare for tests.

Key Terms: Review the key term flash cards (online, printable, and audio).

Games: Play *Beat the Clock* and *Memory* to quiz yourself.

Videos: Watch *Working with Styles; Apply Quick Styles; Modify a Quick Style; Working with Themes; Change the Document's Theme; Applying Text Effects, Font Colors, and Font Styles; Modify the Theme Fonts and Colors; Creating Citations and a Bibliography; Create a New Source and Insert a Citation;* and *Adding Headers and Footers.*

Infographic

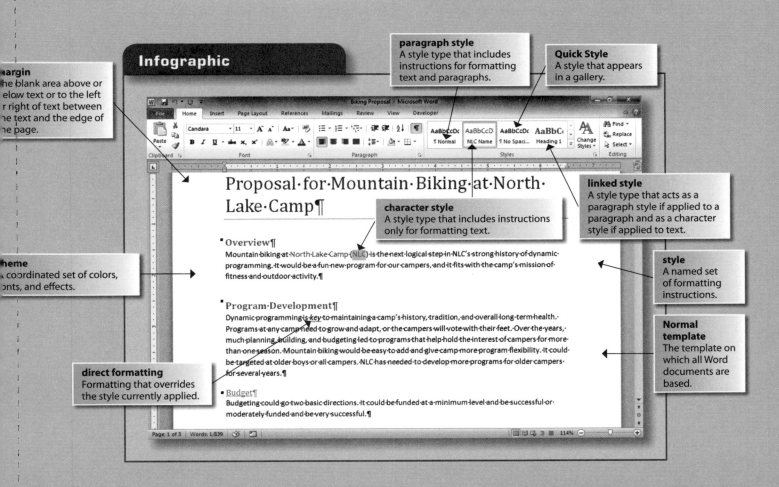

paragraph style
A style type that includes instructions for formatting text and paragraphs.

Quick Style
A style that appears in a gallery.

margin
The blank area above or below text or to the left or right of text between the text and the edge of the page.

character style
A style type that includes instructions only for formatting text.

linked style
A style type that acts as a paragraph style if applied to a paragraph and as a character style if applied to text.

theme
A coordinated set of colors, fonts, and effects.

style
A named set of formatting instructions.

direct formatting
Formatting that overrides the style currently applied.

Normal template
The template on which all Word documents are based.

Quick Reference Tools

Use Styles

- The five types of styles are paragraph, character, linked, table, and list.
- To apply a Quick Style, on the Home tab, in the Styles group, click the More button, and then click a style in the Quick Styles gallery.
- To create a new Quick Style, select the text with the formats you want, in the Quick Styles gallery, click Save Selection as a New Quick Style, type a style name, and then click OK.

Apply a Theme

- To change the theme, on the Page Layout tab, in the Themes group, click the Themes button, and then click a theme.
- You can modify the theme fonts and colors using the corresponding buttons in the Themes group on the Page Layout tab.

Set Margins, Page Breaks, Headers, and Footers

- You can set how much blank space appears around the edges of the page by changing the page margins.
- To start a new page, you can insert a manual page break.
- To add page numbers to a document, on the Insert tab, in the Header & Footer group, click the Page Number button, and then click a page number style.
- To add text as a header or footer, double-click in the header or footer area, type text and format it as needed, and then click in the document area.

Review the Document Outline

- You can view a document's structure in the Navigation Pane and then browse by the document's headings or by thumbnails of the pages.
- In the Navigation Pane, when browsing by heading, you can collapse or expand, promote or demote, and move headings.
- Outline view shows the document's heading levels as an outline. You can promote or demote and move headings to reorganize the document.

Create Footnotes or Endnotes

- On the References tab, in the Footnotes group, click the Insert Footnote button or the Insert Endnote button, and then type the note text.

Create Lists of Citations

- On the References tab, in the Citations & Bibliography group, click the Style box arrow, and then click a style, such as MLA Sixth Edition.
- To enter a new source, in the Citations & Bibliography group, click the Insert Citation button, click Add New Source, enter source information, and then click OK.
- To insert a citation to an existing source, click the Insert Citation button, and then click the source.
- To generate a bibliography, click the Bibliography button, and then select a format.

Key Definitions

Go to your CMPTR CourseMate site for a full list of key terms and definitions.

automatic page break (soft page break) A page break that is created when content fills a page and a new page is created automatically.

content control A special field used as a placeholder for text you insert or designed to contain specific type of text.

demote To move an item to a lower level in an outline.

endnote An explanatory comment or reference that appears at the end of a section or at the end of a document.

field In Word, a placeholder for variable information that includes an instruction to insert the specific information.

footer Text that appears at the bottom of every page.

footnote An explanatory comment or reference that appears at the bottom of a page.

header Text that appears at the top of every page.

manual page break (hard page break) A page break that you insert to force content after the break to appear on a new page.

promote To move an item to a higher level in an outline.

style set A group of Quick Styles.

Learning Objectives

LO12.1	Create and modify tables
LO12.2	Change the page orientation
LO12.3	Divide a document into sections
LO12.4	Insert and modify graphics
LO12.5	Add WordArt
LO12.6	Learn about wrapping text around graphics
LO12.7	Work with columns
LO12.8	Work with building blocks

Digital Backpack

Practice It: Practice It 12-3—Add a table and graphics to enhance a Word document.

On Your Own: On Your Own 12-2—Modify the formatting, page orientation, and layout and then print the document.

Quiz: Take the practice quiz to prepare for tests.

Key Terms: Review the key term flash cards (online, printable, and audio).

Games: Play *Beat the Clock* and *Memory* to quiz yourself.

Videos: Watch *Working with Headings in the Navigation Pane, Create a Table, Formatting a Document in Sections, Insert a Section Break, Inserting Clip Art, Crop a Photo, Format a Picture,* and *Insert WordArt.*

Infographic

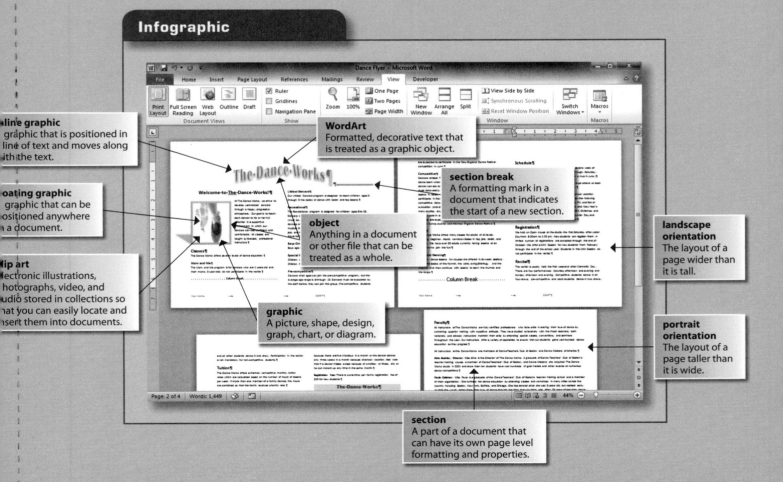

inline graphic
A graphic that is positioned in line of text and moves along with the text.

floating graphic
A graphic that can be positioned anywhere in a document.

clip art
Electronic illustrations, photographs, video, and audio stored in collections so that you can easily locate and insert them into documents.

WordArt
Formatted, decorative text that is treated as a graphic object.

object
Anything in a document or other file that can be treated as a whole.

graphic
A picture, shape, design, graph, chart, or diagram.

section break
A formatting mark in a document that indicates the start of a new section.

landscape orientation
The layout of a page wider than it is tall.

portrait orientation
The layout of a page taller than it is wide.

section
A part of a document that can have its own page level formatting and properties.

Quick Reference Tools

Organize Information in Tables

- To create a table, on the Insert tab, in the Tables group, click the Tables button, and then click the box in the grid that represents the lower-right corner of the table.
- To insert or delete rows and columns, click in the appropriate row or column, and then on the Table Tools Layout tab, in the Rows & Columns group, click the corresponding button.
- To format a table, on the Table Tools Design tag, in the Table Styles group, click the More button, and then click a table style.

Add Graphics

- To insert clip art, on the Insert tab, in the Illustrations group, click the Clip Art button. In the Clip Art task pane, type a keyword in the Search for box, and then click the Go button. Click the clip art to insert.
- To resize a graphic, drag a sizing handle on the selection box.
- To crop a photo, on the Picture Tools Format tab, in the Size group, click the Crop button, drag a crop handle, and then click the Crop button again.
- To format a picture, on the Picture Tools Format tab, in the Picture Styles group, use the appropriate buttons.

Add Section Breaks and Columns

- The four types of section breaks are Next Page, Continuous, Even Page, and Odd Page.
- You can format each section separately.
- To insert a section break, on the Page Layout tab, in the Setup group, click the Breaks button, and then click a section break.
- To format a document in columns, on the Page Layout tab, in the Page Setup group, click the Columns button, and then click a column option.
- To balance text in columns, insert a continuous section break.

Add WordArt

- To insert WordArt, on the Insert tab, in the Text group, click the WordArt button, select a style, modify or enter text as needed.
- To format WordArt, on the Drawing Tools Format tab, click the appropriate buttons to change the styles, size, etc.
- To change the text wrap option, on the Drawing Tools Format tab, in the Arrange group, click the Wrap Text button, and then select a wrap option.

Change Page Orientation

- On the Page Layout tab, in the Page Setup group, click the Orientation button, and then click an orientation.

Create Building Blocks

- To create a building block, select the text. On the Insert tab, in the Text group, click the Quick Parts button, and then click Save Selection to Quick Part gallery.

Key Definitions

Go to your CMPTR CourseMate site for a full list of key terms and definitions.

aspect ratio The proportion of an object's height to its width.

bitmap A grid of pixels that form a picture.

building block A part of a document that is stored and reused.

cell The intersection of a column and a row.

crop To cut off part of a graphic.

metafile A graphic that contains both bitmaps and vectors.

orientation The way a page is turned.

Quick Part A building block stored in the Quick Parts gallery.

selection box The box that surrounds an object when it is selected.

sizing handle A small circle that appears at the corner of a selection box or a square that appears on the side of a selection box.

text box An object that contains text.

vector graphic An image composed of straight and curved lines and stored as a mathematical formula.

reviewcard

Learning Objectives

LO13.1	Understand spreadsheets and Excel
LO13.2	Enter data in cells
LO13.3	Edit cell content
LO13.4	Work with columns and rows
LO13.5	Work with cells and ranges
LO13.6	Work with formulas and functions
LO13.7	Preview and print a workbook

Digital Backpack

Practice It: Practice It 13-3—Enter data in cells and format an Excel worksheet, working with columns, rows, and cells.

On Your Own: On Your Own 13-2—Work with formulas and functions and print an Excel worksheet.

Quiz: Take the practice quiz to prepare for tests.

Key Terms: Review the key term flash cards (online, printable, and audio).

Games: Play *Beat the Clock* and *Memory* to quiz yourself.

Videos: Watch *Enter Text; Entering Text, Numbers, and Dates; Enter Dates and Times; Working with Columns and Rows; Change Column Widths; Insert Columns and Rows; Working with Formulas; Enter Formulas; Introducing Functions; Enter a Function,* and *Use AutoSum.*

Infographic

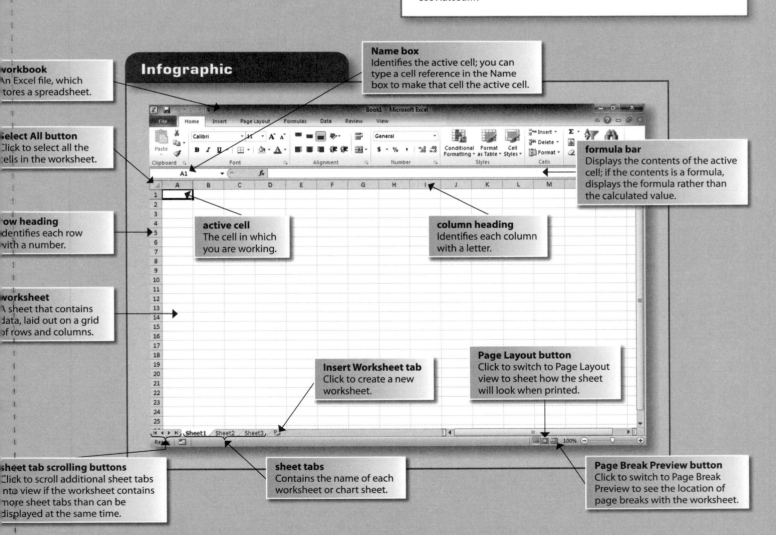

Name box
Identifies the active cell; you can type a cell reference in the Name box to make that cell the active cell.

workbook
An Excel file, which stores a spreadsheet.

Select All button
Click to select all the cells in the worksheet.

row heading
Identifies each row with a number.

worksheet
A sheet that contains data, laid out on a grid of rows and columns.

formula bar
Displays the contents of the active cell; if the contents is a formula, displays the formula rather than the calculated value.

active cell
The cell in which you are working.

column heading
Identifies each column with a letter.

Insert Worksheet tab
Click to create a new worksheet.

Page Layout button
Click to switch to Page Layout view to sheet how the sheet will look when printed.

sheet tab scrolling buttons
Click to scroll additional sheet tabs into view if the worksheet contains more sheet tabs than can be displayed at the same time.

sheet tabs
Contains the name of each worksheet or chart sheet.

Page Break Preview button
Click to switch to Page Break Preview to see the location of page breaks with the worksheet.

Quick Reference Tools

Create a Workbook

- To enter text or data in a cell, click the cell, type, and then press the Enter key or the Tab key, or click the Enter button on the formula bar.
- To move the active cell, click a new cell, use a keyboard shortcut, or type the cell reference in the Name box, and then press the Enter key.
- To switch between sheets, click the sheet tab.
- To delete a sheet, right-click the sheet tab, and then on the shortcut menu, click Delete.
- To rename a sheet, double-click the sheet tab, and then type the new name.
- To move a sheet, drag its sheet tab. To copy a sheet, press and hold the Ctrl key while dragging the sheet tab.

Work with Columns and Rows

- To select a column or row, click its column or row heading.
- To select adjacent columns or rows, drag across multiple columns or rows.
- To select nonadjacent columns or rows, press and hold the Ctrl key while clicking column or row headings.
- To insert a column or row, on the Home tab, in the Cells group, click the Insert button, and then click the item you want to insert.
- To delete a column or row, select it, and then on the Home tab, in the Cells group, click the Delete button.

Work with Ranges

- To move a range, drag it by its border.
- To insert a range, select the size of the range you want to insert, and then on the Home tab, in the Cells group, click the Insert button. Click Insert Cells.
- To delete a range, select it, and then on the Home tab, in the Cells group, click the Delete button arrow, and then click Delete Cells.

Preview and Print a Workbook

- To preview the printed workbook, click the File tab, and then in the navigation bar, click Print.
- To view formulas in a worksheet, on the Formulas tab, in the Formula Auditing group, click the Show Formulas button.
- To scale a printout, on the Page Layout tab, in the Scale to Fit group, click the Width arrow, and then click the scale you want to use.

Use the SUM Function and the AutoSum Feature

- To use the SUM function, type an equal sign, type the function name, and then type the range between parentheses.
- To use the AutoSum feature, on the Home tab, in the Editing group, click the Sum button.

Enter Formulas

- Type an equal sign, and then type the formula.
- Use parentheses to change the order of precedence.

Key Definitions

Go to your CMPTR CourseMate site for a full list of key terms and definitions.

adjacent range A single rectangular block of cells.

AutoSum A feature that inserts the SUM, AVERAGE, COUNT, MIN, or MAX function.

cell range (range) A group of cells.

cell reference The row and column location of a specific cell.

formula A mathematical expression that returns a value.

function A named operation that returns a value.

Microsoft Excel 2010 (Excel) Application software used to enter, analyze, and present quantitative data.

nonadjacent range Two or more distinct adjacent ranges.

Normal view The Excel view that shows the contents of the current sheet.

operator A mathematical symbol used to combine values.

order of precedence A set of predefined rules used to determine the sequence in which operators are applied in a calculation—first exponentiation ($\wedge$), second multiplication ($*$) and division ($/$), and third addition ($+$) and subtraction ($-$).

range reference The location and size of a range.

what-if analysis A process in which you change one or more values in a spreadsheet and then assess how those changes affect the calculated values.

Learning Objectives

LO14.1	Format text, numbers, dates, and time
LO14.2	Format cells and ranges
LO14.3	Create an Excel table
LO14.4	Highlight cells with conditional formatting
LO14.5	Hide worksheet data
LO14.6	Format a worksheet for printing

Digital Backpack

Practice It: Practice It 14-3— Format Excel data in cells and ranges and create a table.

On Your Own: On Your Own 14-2—Create an Excel worksheet with conditional formatting and hidden worksheet data.

Quiz: Take the practice quiz to prepare for tests.

Key Terms: Review the key term flash cards (online, printable, and audio).

Games: Play *Beat the Clock* and *Memory* to quiz yourself.

Videos: Watch *Formatting Worksheet Cells, Format Fonts and Font Styles, Apply Cell Styles, Align Cell Content, Merge and Center Cells, Working with Table Styles, Change a Table Style,* and *Highlighting Cells with Conditional Formatting* (concept and step-by-step).

Infographic

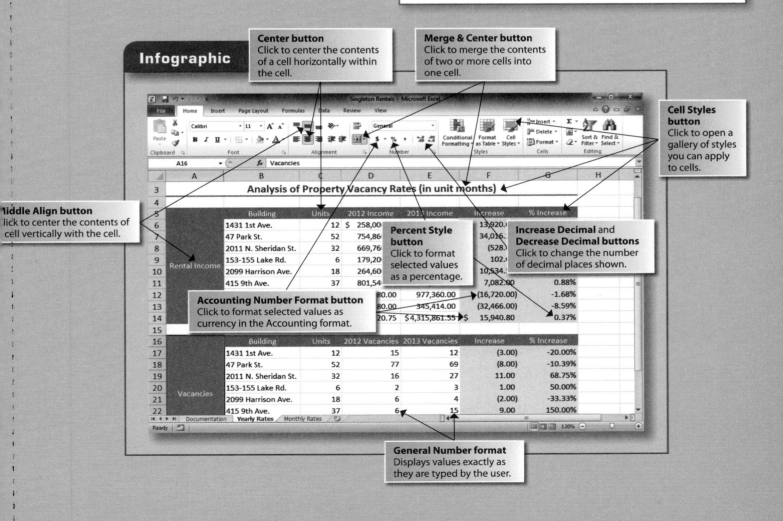

Center button
Click to center the contents of a cell horizontally within the cell.

Merge & Center button
Click to merge the contents of two or more cells into one cell.

Cell Styles button
Click to open a gallery of styles you can apply to cells.

Middle Align button
Click to center the contents of a cell vertically with the cell.

Percent Style button
Click to format selected values as a percentage.

Increase Decimal and Decrease Decimal buttons
Click to change the number of decimal places shown.

Accounting Number Format button
Click to format selected values as currency in the Accounting format.

General Number format
Displays values exactly as they are typed by the user.

Quick Reference Tools

Format Numbers

- The default number format is the General Number format, which displays values exactly as you type them.
- The Comma Style format adds a comma to separate thousands.
- The Accounting Number format adds a dollar sign and two decimal places, formats negative numbers in parentheses, and aligns values in a column on the dollar sign and on the decimal point.
- The Percent Style format changes the value to a percentage and adds the percent sign.

Hide Worksheet Data

- To hide worksheet data, select the row or column to hide, on the Home tab, in the Cells group, click the Format button, point to Hide & Unhide, and then click Hide Rows or Hide Columns.
- To unhide worksheet data, select the rows or column on either side of the hidden rows and columns, on the Home tab, in the Cells group, click the Format button, point to Hide & Unhide, and then click Unhide Rows or Unhide Columns.

Format Dates

- To change the date format, on the Home tab, in the Number group, click the Number Format box arrow, and then click the date or time format you want to use.

Apply Cell Styles or Create an Excel Table

- To apply a cell style, on the Home tab, in the Styles group, click the Cell Styles button, and then select a style in the gallery.
- To create an Excel table, select the range, and then on the Home tab, in the Styles group, click the Format as Table button. Click a style in the gallery.

Aligning Data in Cells

- To horizontally align data in cells, on the Home tab, in the Alignment group, click the Align Text Left, Center, or Align Text Right button.
- To vertically align data in cells, on the Home tab, in the Alignment group, click the Top Align, Middle Align, or Bottom Align button.
- To merge and center data in cells, select the cells to merge, and then on the Home tab, in the Alignment group, click the Merge & Center button.

Use Conditional Formatting

- To apply conditional formatting, select a range, on the Home tab, in the Styles group, click the Conditional Formatting button, select a rule, and then refine the rule in the dialog box that opens.
- To clear a conditional formatting rule, on the Home tab, in the Styles group, click the Conditional Formatting button, click Manage Rules, select the rule, and then click the Delete Rule button.

Key Definitions

Go to your CMPTR CourseMate site for a full list of key terms and definitions.

automatic page break A page break Excel inserts when no more content will fit on the page.

border A line added along an edge of a cell.

conditional formatting Formatting that is applied to a cell only when the cell's value meets a specified condition.

conditional formatting rule A list of the condition, the type of formatting applied when the condition occurs, and the cell or range to which the formatting is applied.

Excel table A range of data that is treated as a distinct object in a worksheet.

fill color A background color added to cells.

manual page break A page break you insert to specify where a page break occurs.

number format A format that displays values in a way that makes it easy for them to be understood and interpreted.

print area The region that is sent to the printer from the active sheet.

print title Information from a workbook that appears on every printed page.

table style A preset style that specifies the formatting of an entire table.

Learning Objectives

LO15.1	Use relative, absolute, and mixed cell references in formulas
LO15.2	Enter functions
LO15.3	Use AutoFill
LO15.4	Work with the IF logical function
LO15.5	Work with date functions
LO15.6	Work with the PMT financial function

Digital Backpack

Practice It: Practice It 15-3—Create an Excel worksheet that includes absolute, relative, and mixed formulas.

On Your Own: On Your Own 15-2—Modify worksheet data to include formulas and functions and prepare a worksheet for printing.

Quiz: Take the practice quiz to prepare for tests.

Key Terms: Review the key term flash cards (online, printable, and audio).

Games: Play *Beat the Clock* and *Memory* to quiz yourself.

Videos: Watch *Understanding Cell References, Use Relative References in a Formula, Use Absolute References in a Formula, Understanding Function Syntax, Insert Functions Using the Insert Function Dialog Box, Entering Data and Formulas with AutoFill, Use AutoFill to Enter a Series, Working with Logical Functions, Insert the IF Function, Working with Financial Functions,* and *Use the PMT Function to Calculate a Monthly Payment.*

Infographic

Insert Function button
Click to open the Insert Function dialog box, which organizes all of the functions by category and includes a search feature for location a specific function.

financial function
A function related to monetary calculations, such as loans and payments.

date function
A function that inserts or calculates dates and times.

logical button
A function that works with statements that are either true or false.

syntax
A set of rules that shows how to write the function.

argument
The numbers, text, or cell references used by a function to return a value.

optional argument
An argument that is not required for the function to return its value, but provides more control over how the returned value is calculated.

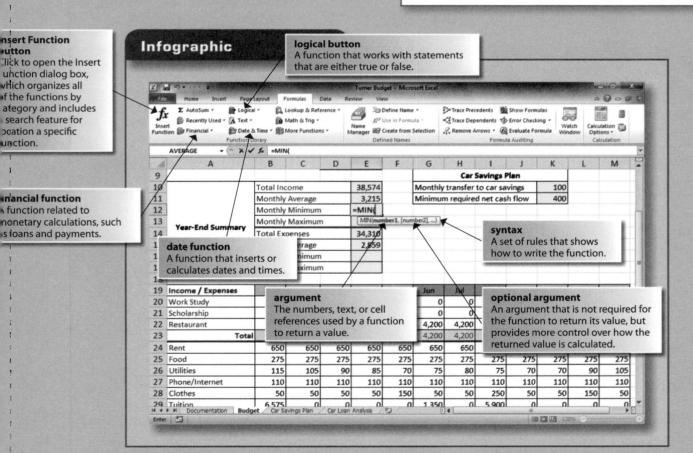

Quick Reference Tools

Enter a Function Using the Insert Function Dialog Box

- To open the Insert Function dialog box, on the Formulas tab, in the Function Library group, click the Insert Function button.
- To enter a function by searching for it using the Insert Function dialog box, in the Insert Function dialog box, in the Search box, type keywords, and then click Go.
- To enter a function by using the list of recently used functions in the Insert Function dialog box, click the Or select a category arrow, click Most Recently Used, and then in the Select a function list, click the function name.

Use Date Functions

- To return the current date, type =TODAY().
- To return the current date and time, type =NOW().
- To insert a date function using the Date & Time button, on the Formulas tab, in the Function Library group, click the Date & Time button, and then click TODAY or NOW in the date functions list.

Enter a Function by Typing It in a Cell

- Type = (an equal sign), type the first letter or two of the function you want to insert, click the function name in the list that appears, double-click the function name, select the range, and then type) (closing parenthesis).

Use AutoFill

- Select a cell or range, and then drag the fill handle to the right or down.

Use the IF Function

- IF(*logical_test*[,*value_if_true*][,*value_if_false*])

Use the PMT Function

- PMT(*rate*,*nper*,*pv*[,*fv=0*][,*type=0*])

Key Definitions

Go to your CMPTR CourseMate site for a full list of key terms and definitions.

absolute reference A cell reference that remains fixed when copied to a new location; includes $ in front of both the column letter and row number.

argument The numbers, text, or cell references used by a function to return a value.

AutoFill An Excel feature that copies content and formats from a cell or range into an adjacent cell or range.

comparison operator A symbol that indicates the relationship between two values.

compound interest Interest that is applied not only to the principal but also to any accrued interest.

date function A function that inserts or calculates dates and times.

fill handle A box in the lower-right corner of a selected cell or range that you drag over an adjacent cell or range to copy the content and formatting from the original cells into the adjacent range.

financial function A function related to monetary calculations, such as loans and payments.

IF function A logical function that tests a condition and then returns one value if the condition is true and another value if the condition is false.

interest The amount added to the principal by the lender.

mixed reference A cell reference that contains an absolute row reference or an absolute column reference, such as $A2 or A$2.

nest To place one item inside another, such as a function.

optional argument An argument that is not required for the function to return a value, but provides more control over how the returned value is calculated.

PMT function A financial function that calculates the monthly payment required to pay back a loan.

principal The amount of money being loaned.

relative reference A cell reference that is interpreted in relation to the location of the cell containing the formula.

simple interest Interest that is equal to a percentage of principal for each period that the money has been lent.

syntax A set of rules.

Learning Objectives

LO16.1	Create a chart
LO16.2	Work with chart elements
LO16.3	Modify a chart
LO16.4	Create an exploded pie chart
LO16.5	Create a column chart
LO16.6	Create a line chart
LO16.7	Edit chart data
LO16.8	Insert and format sparklines
LO16.9	Insert and modify data bars

Digital Backpack

Practice It: Practice It 16-3—Create and modify different charts and edit chart data.

On Your Own: On Your Own 16-2—Edit chart data and insert and modify sparklines and data bars.

Quiz: Take the practice quiz to prepare for tests.

Key Terms: Review the key term flash cards (online, printable, and audio).

Games: Play *Beat the Clock* and *Memory* to quiz yourself.

Videos: Watch *Creating an Excel Chart, Select Chart Elements, Move an Embedded Chart to Another Sheet, Designing a Pie Chart, Position the Chart Legend, Change the Color of a Data Series, Creating a Column Chart, Format a Column Chart, Change the Axis Scale and Title, Add a Data Series to an Existing Chart, Adding Sparklines and Data Bars,* and *Insert and Format Sparklines*.

Infographic

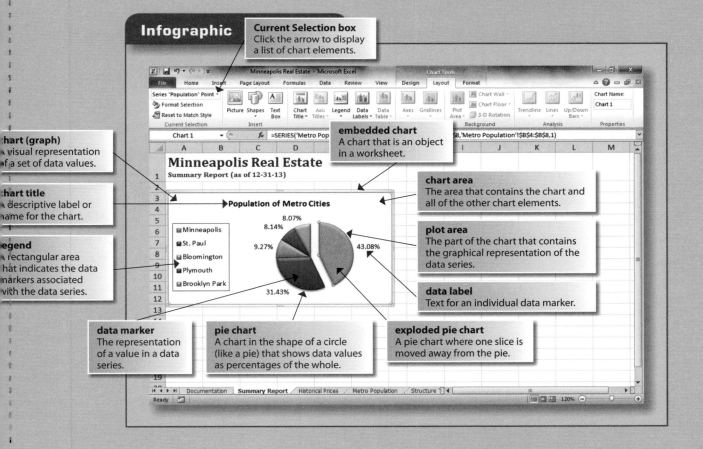

Current Selection box
Click the arrow to display a list of chart elements.

chart (graph)
A visual representation of a set of data values.

chart title
A descriptive label or name for the chart.

legend
A rectangular area that indicates the data markers associated with the data series.

data marker
The representation of a value in a data series.

pie chart
A chart in the shape of a circle (like a pie) that shows data values as percentages of the whole.

embedded chart
A chart that is an object in a worksheet.

chart area
The area that contains the chart and all of the other chart elements.

plot area
The part of the chart that contains the graphical representation of the data series.

data label
Text for an individual data marker.

exploded pie chart
A pie chart where one slice is moved away from the pie.

Quick Reference Tools

Create a Chart

- To create a chart, select the data source range, and then on the Insert tab, in the Charts group, click the chart type.

Change a Chart's Location

- To move a chart to another sheet, select the chart area, on the Chart Tools Design tab, in the Location group, click the Move Chart button; in the Move Chart dialog box, click the Object in box arrow, click the worksheet to move the chart to, and then click OK.
- To move a chart on a sheet, drag it to a new location.

Formatting a Chart

- To change the chart style, on the Chart Tools Design tab, in the Chart Styles group, select a style.
- To change the chart layout, on the Chart Tools Design tab, in the Chart Layouts group, select a layout.
- To add data labels, on the Chart Tools Layout tab, in the Labels group, click the Data Labels button, and then select an option.
- To change the color of a data series, select the data series, double-click a data marker, in the Format Data Point dialog box click Fill, click the Solid fill option button, click the Color button, click a color, and then click Close.

Create an Exploded Pie Chart

- To create an exploded pie chart, select the pie chart, click a pie slice, and then drag the slice away from the chart.

Modify an Axis

- To change the axis scale, on the Chart Tools Layout tab, in the Axes group, click the Axes button, point to the axis whose scale you want to change, click More <axis name> Options, or double-click the axis whose scale you want to change; in the Format Axis dialog box, make changes as needed, and then click Close.
- To add an axis title, on the Chart Tools Layout tab, in the Labels group, click the Axis Titles button.
- To add gridlines, on the Chart Tools Layout tab, in the Axes group, click the Gridlines button.

Insert Sparklines

- To insert sparklines, select the range, on the Insert tab, in the Sparklines group, click the Line button, in the Create Sparklines dialog box, in the Data Range box, select the range to chart, and then click OK.

Insert Data Bars

- To insert data bars, select the range, on the Home tab, in the Styles group, click the Conditional Formatting button, point to Data Bars, and then select a style in the gallery.

Key Definitions

Go to your CMPTR CourseMate site for a full list of key terms and definitions.

category axis The horizontal axis that shows the category values from each data series.

category values The first column of the data range, which are the groups or categories to which the series values belong.

combination chart A chart that combines two or more chart types in a single graph, such as a column chart and a line chart.

data bar Conditional formatting that adds a horizontal bar to a cell's background that is proportional in length to the cell's value.

data source The range that contains the data to display in a chart.

primary axis The axis that usually appears along the left side of a chart.

scale The range of values along an axis.

secondary axis An axis that is usually placed on the right side of a chart.

series name The first row of the data range, which identifies the data series.

series values The data displayed in the chart.

sparkline A graph that is displayed within a cell.

value axis The vertical axis that shows the range of series values from all of the data series plotted on the chart.

Learning Objectives

LO17.1	Understand database concepts
LO17.2	Create a database
LO17.3	Work in Datasheet view
LO17.4	Work with fields and properties in Design view
LO17.5	Modify a table's structure
LO17.6	Close and open objects and databases
LO17.7	Create simple queries, forms, and reports
LO17.8	Compact and repair a database

Digital Backpack

Practice It: Practice It 17-3—Create an Access database and modify a table's structure.

On Your Own: On Your Own 17-2—Work in Datasheet view and Design view, and compact and repair a database.

Quiz: Take the practice quiz to prepare for tests.

Key Terms: Review the key term flash cards (online, printable, and audio).

Games: Play *Beat the Clock* and *Memory* to quiz yourself.

Videos: Watch *Introduction to Database Concepts, Creating a Table in Datasheet View, Enter Records, Guidelines for Setting Field Properties, Change Field Properties in Design View, Create a Table in Design View* (concept and step-by-step), *Specifying the Primary Key, Defining Table Relationships, Move a Field in a Table,* and *Add a Field to a Table.*

Infographic

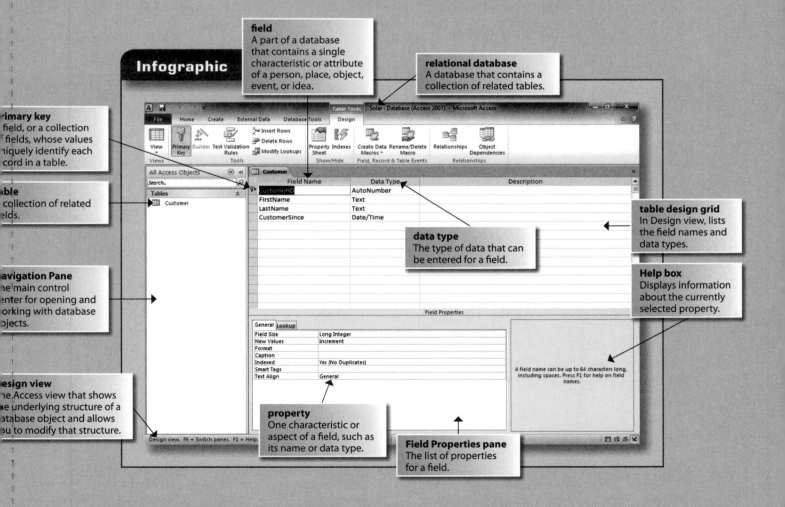

field
A part of a database that contains a single characteristic or attribute of a person, place, object, event, or idea.

relational database
A database that contains a collection of related tables.

primary key
A field, or a collection of fields, whose values uniquely identify each record in a table.

table
A collection of related fields.

Navigation Pane
The main control center for opening and working with database objects.

Design view
The Access view that shows the underlying structure of a database object and allows you to modify that structure.

data type
The type of data that can be entered for a field.

table design grid
In Design view, lists the field names and data types.

Help box
Displays information about the currently selected property.

property
One characteristic or aspect of a field, such as its name or data type.

Field Properties pane
The list of properties for a field.

Quick Reference Tools

Create a Table

- To create a table in Datasheet view, on the Create tab, in the Tables group, click the Table button; in the table, click Click to Add, click a data type, and then type a field name; click in the row below the field name, and then type data.
- To create a table in Design view, on the Create tab, in the Tables group, click the Table Design button; in the table design grid, type a field name, and then press the Enter key; click the arrow that appears in the Data Type column, and then click a data type.

Change Field Properties in Design View

- In the table design grid, click a field name, in the Field Properties pane, click in the box to the right of the property, type a new property, or click the arrow that appears, and then select the new property.

Create and Use a Simple Form

- To select a table on which to base the form, select it in the Navigation Pane.
- To create the form, on the Create tab, in the Forms group, click the Form button.
- To insert data using the form, on the Form Tools Layout tab, in the Views group, click the View button, and then enter data in the form.

Create a Simple Query

- To start the Simple Query Wizard, on the Create tab, in the Queries group, click the Query Wizard button, select Simple Query Wizard, and click OK.
- To select an object, click the Tables/Queries arrow, and then click the object.
- To select a field, click it in the Available Fields list, and then click the > button to move the selected field to the Selected Fields box.
- To name and finish the wizard, click Next, in the What title do you want for your query box, type the query name, and then click Finish.

Specify the Primary Key

- In Design view, click a field name, and then on the Table Tools Design tab, in the Tools group, click the Primary Key button.

Create a Simple Report

- To select an object on which to base the report, select it in the Navigation Pane.
- To create the report, on the Create tab, in the Reports group, click the Report button.
- To change column widths in the report, drag a column border.
- To view a report in Print Preview, on the Report Layout Tools Design tab, in the Views group, click the View button arrow, and then click Print Preview.
- To print a report, click the File tab, in the navigation bar, click Print, and then on the Print tab, click Quick Print.

Key Definitions

Go to your CMPTR CourseMate site for a full list of key terms and definitions.

common field A field that appears in more than one table.

composite key A primary key that requires two or more fields to uniquely identify each record in a table.

data redundancy Data stored in more than one place.

database management system (DBMS) Software used to create databases and manipulate the data in them..

Datasheet view The Access view that shows a table's contents as datasheet.

foreign key A field in a table that is a primary key in another table and that is included to form a relationship between the two tables.

form A database object used to enter, edit, and view records in a database.

Layout view The Access view in which you can make design changes to database objects such as forms and reports, and see the effects of those changes immediately.

query A question about the data stored in a database.

record All the fields in a table about a single person, place, object, event, or idea; that is, a row in a table.

report A database object that shows a formatted printout or screen display of the contents of the table or query objects on which the report is based.

Learning Objectives

LO18.1	Maintain database records
LO18.2	Create and run a query
LO18.3	Modify a query
LO18.4	Sort and filter data in a query
LO18.5	Define table relationships
LO18.6	Create a multitable query
LO18.7	Define record selection criteria for queries
LO18.8	Create a calculated field
LO18.9	Use functions in a query

Digital Backpack

Practice It: Practice It 18-3—Create, run, and modify a query for an Access database and then sort and filter data in a query.

On Your Own: On Your Own 18-2—Define record selection criteria for queries and use functions in a query.

Quiz: Take the practice quiz to prepare for tests.

Key Terms: Review the key term flash cards (online, printable, and audio).

Games: Play *Beat the Clock* and *Memory* to quiz yourself.

Videos: Watch *Introduction to Queries, Design a Select Query, Defining Record Selection Criteria for Queries, Sort Multiple Fields in Design View, Filter Records by Selection, Creating a Calculated Field, Defining a One-to-Many Relationship Between Tables, Create a Query with a Comparison Operator,* and *Use the Total Row.*

Infographic

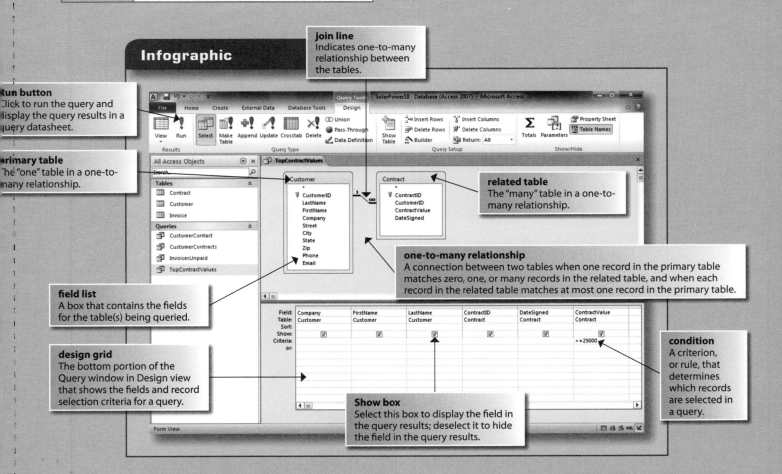

join line
Indicates one-to-many relationship between the tables.

Run button
Click to run the query and display the query results in a query datasheet.

primary table
The "one" table in a one-to-many relationship.

related table
The "many" table in a one-to-many relationship.

field list
A box that contains the fields for the table(s) being queried.

one-to-many relationship
A connection between two tables when one record in the primary table matches zero, one, or many records in the related table, and when each record in the related table matches at most one record in the primary table.

design grid
The bottom portion of the Query window in Design view that shows the fields and record selection criteria for a query.

Show box
Select this box to display the field in the query results; deselect it to hide the field in the query results.

condition
A criterion, or rule, that determines which records are selected in a query.

Quick Reference Tools

Design a Select Query

- To open a new Query window in Design view, on the Create tab, in the Queries group, click the Query Design button.
- To select tables to include in the query, in the Show Table dialog box, in the Tables list, click the table name, and then click Add.
- To add a field to the design grid, in the field list, double-click it.

Sort Multiple Fields in Design View

- To choose the first field on which to sort, in Query Design view, in the design grid, in the field column of the field you want to sort on, click in the Sort row, click the arrow button, and then click the sort order.
- To choose the second field on which to sort, in the field column to the right of the first sort field, click in the Sort row, click the arrow button, and then click the sort order.

Run a Query

- To run a query, in Design view, on the Query Tools Design tab, in the Results group, click the Run button.

Define a One-to-Many Relationship

- To open the Relationships window, on the Database Tools tab, in the Relationships group, click the Relationships button.
- To add tables to the Relationships window, on the Relationship Tools Design tab, in the Relationships group, click the Show Table button, and then in the Show Table dialog box, double-click the table name.
- To establish a relationship in the Relationship window, in the table field list on the left, click the common field, and then drag it to the table field list on the right.
- To enforce referential integrity, in the Edit Relationship dialog box, select the Enforce Referential Integrity check box.
- To update foreign key values in the related table whenever a primary key value in the primary table changes, select the Cascade Update Related Fields check box to select it.
- To create the relationship, in the Relationship window, click Create.

Create a Query with a Calculated Field

- To open the Expression Builder dialog box, in Query Design view, in the design grid, click in the Field box in which you want to create an expression, and then on the Query Tools Design grid, in the Query Setup group, click the Builder button.
- To build the expression, use the expression elements and common operators, or type the expression directly in the expression box.

Key Definitions

Go to your CMPTR CourseMate site for a full list of key terms and definitions.

And logical operator The logical operator used to select records only if *all* of the specified conditions are met.

calculated field A field that displays the results of an expression (a combination of database fields, constants, and operators).

exact match A query in which the value of a specified field must match the condition exactly for that record to be included in the query results.

Group By operator An operator that divides selected records into groups based on the values in the specified field.

Or logical operator The logical operator used to select records if *at least one* of the specified conditions is met.

orphaned record A record in a related table that has no matching record in the primary table.

query by example (QBE) A query that retrieves the information that precisely matches the example you provide of the information being requested.

referential integrity A set of rules to maintain consistency between related tables when data in a database is updated.

select query A query in which you specify the fields and records you want Access to select.

subdatasheet A datasheet in which records from a related table are displayed in the primary table.

Learning Objectives

LO19.1	Create a form using the Form Wizard
LO19.2	Modify a form's design in Layout view
LO19.3	Find data using a form
LO19.4	Create a form with a main form and a subform
LO19.5	Preview and print selected form records
LO19.6	Create a report using the Report Wizard
LO19.7	Modify a report's design in Layout view

Digital Backpack

Practice It: Practice It 19-3—Create a report using the Report Wizard and modify report design in Layout view.

On Your Own: On Your Own 19-2—Create a form with a main form and a subform and then print form records.

Quiz: Take the practice quiz to prepare for tests.

Key Terms: Review the key term flash cards (online, printable, and audio).

Games: Play *Beat the Clock* and *Memory* to quiz yourself.

Videos: Watch *Creating a Form Using the Form Wizard* (concept and step-by-step), *Applying a Theme to a Form* (concept and step-by-step), *Add a Picture to a Form*, *Creating a Form with a Main Form and a Subform* (concept and step-by-step), and *Creating a Report Using the Report Wizard* (concept and step-by-step).

Infographic

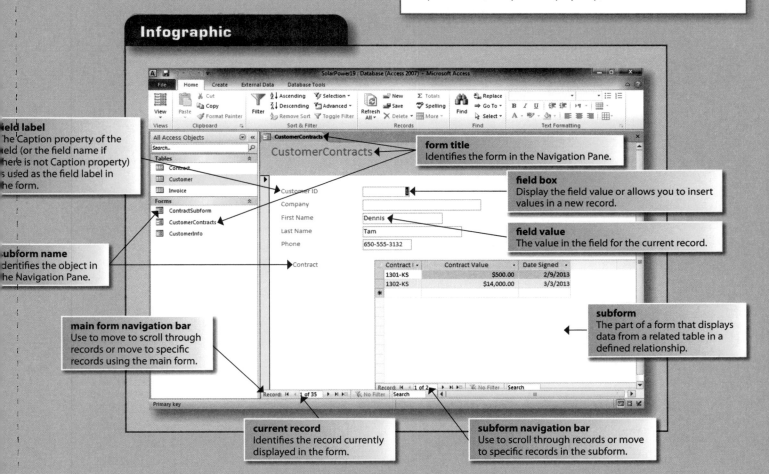

field label
The Caption property of the field (or the field name if there is not Caption property) is used as the field label in the form.

form title
Identifies the form in the Navigation Pane.

field box
Display the field value or allows you to insert values in a new record.

subform name
Identifies the object in the Navigation Pane.

field value
The value in the field for the current record.

subform
The part of a form that displays data from a related table in a defined relationship.

main form navigation bar
Use to move to scroll through records or move to specific records using the main form.

current record
Identifies the record currently displayed in the form.

subform navigation bar
Use to scroll through records or move to specific records in the subform.

Quick Reference Tools

Create a Form Using the Form Wizard

- To start the Form Wizard, on the Create tab, in the Forms group, click the Form Wizard button.
- To select the object on which to base the form, click the Tables/Queries arrow, and then click the object.
- To move fields from the Available Fields box to the Selected Fields box, click the fields, and then click the > button.
- To complete the wizard, click Next three times, in the fourth Form Wizard dialog box, in the Form box, type the form name, and then click Finish.

Find Data in a Form or Datasheet

- To open the Find and Replace dialog box, in Form view, select the field you want to search, and then on the Home tab, in the Find group, click the Find button.
- To specify the field value you want to find, in the Find and Replace dialog box, in the Find What box, type the field value.
- To specify the matching options, in the Find and replace dialog box, click the Match arrow, and then click the option you want.
- To search for the next match to the value in the Find What box, click Find Next.

Apply a Theme to a Form

- To open the Themes gallery, in Layout view, on the Design tab, in the Themes group, click the Themes button.
- To apply a theme to all objects, in the Themes gallery, click the theme you want to apply.
- To apply a theme to current object only, right-click the theme you want to apply, and then on the shortcut menu, click Apply Theme to This Object Only
- To apply a theme to all matching objects, right-click the theme you want to apply, and then on the shortcut menu, click Apply Theme to All Matching Objects

Create a Main Form and a Subform

- To start the Form Wizard, on the Create tab, in the Forms group, click the Form Wizard button.
- To select the object on which to base the main form, click the Tables/Queries arrow, and then click the object.
- To move fields from the Available Fields box to the Selected Fields box, click the fields, and then click the > button.
- To select the related object, click the Tables/Queries arrow again, click the related object, and then move the appropriate fields to the Selected Fields box.
- To complete the wizard, click Next three times, in the fourth Form Wizard dialog box, in the Form box, type the form name, in the Subform box, type the subform name, and then click Finish.

Key Definitions

Go to your CMPTR CourseMate site for a full list of key terms and definitions.

control An item on a form, report, or other database object that you can manipulate to modify the object's appearance.

control layout A set of controls grouped together in a form or report so that you can manipulate the set as a single control.

Form Wizard The Access feature that guides you through the process of creating a form; you choose which fields to display from tables and queries and the order in which they appear.

main form The part of a form that displays data from the primary table in a defined relationship.

Report Wizard The Access feature that creates a report based on the fields you choose to display from tables and queries as well as options such as the grouping, sort order, page orientation, and title you specify.

subform The part of a form that displays data from a related table in a defined relationship.

wildcard character A placeholder you use when you know only part of a value or when you want to start or end with a specific character or match a certain pattern.

Learning Objectives

LO20.1	Create a presentation
LO20.2	Rearrange and delete text and slides
LO20.3	Run a slide show
LO20.4	Add animations
LO20.5	Add transitions
LO20.6	Add speaker notes
LO20.7	Add footers and headers to slides and handouts
LO20.8	Preview and print a presentation

Digital Backpack

Practice It: Practice It 20-3—Create a PowerPoint presentation that includes animations and transitions.

On Your Own: On Your Own 20-2—Modify a PowerPoint presentation, prepare speaker notes and handouts, and print a presentation.

Quiz: Take the practice quiz to prepare for tests.

Key Terms: Review the key term flash cards (online, printable, and audio).

Games: Play *Beat the Clock* and *Memory* to quiz yourself.

Videos: Watch *Add Text to Text Placeholders, Adding a New Slide and Choosing a Layout, Create New Slides and Change the Layout, Change the Theme, Editing Text in the Outline Tab, Modify Text in the Outline Tab, Animating Text, Animate the Slide Titles, Adding Transitions,* and *Add Transitions to the Slides.*

Infographic

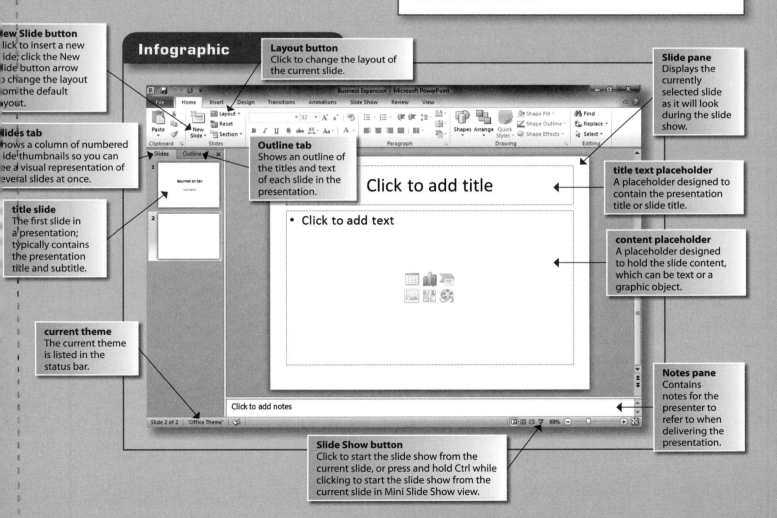

New Slide button
Click to insert a new slide; click the New Slide button arrow to change the layout from the default layout.

Slides tab
Shows a column of numbered slide thumbnails so you can see a visual representation of several slides at once.

title slide
The first slide in a presentation; typically contains the presentation title and subtitle.

current theme
The current theme is listed in the status bar.

Layout button
Click to change the layout of the current slide.

Outline tab
Shows an outline of the titles and text of each slide in the presentation.

Slide pane
Displays the currently selected slide as it will look during the slide show.

title text placeholder
A placeholder designed to contain the presentation title or slide title.

content placeholder
A placeholder designed to hold the slide content, which can be text or a graphic object.

Notes pane
Contains notes for the presenter to refer to when delivering the presentation.

Slide Show button
Click to start the slide show from the current slide, or press and hold Ctrl while clicking to start the slide show from the current slide in Mini Slide Show view.

Quick Reference Tools

Run a Slide Show

- To start a slide show from the current slide, click the Slide Show button on the status bar or on the Slide Show tab, in the Start Slide Show group, click the From Current Slide button.
- To start a slide show from the first slide, on the Slide Show tab, in the Start Slide Show group, click the From Beginning button.
- To move forward in a slide show, click the left mouse button; or press the Spacebar, the Enter key, the Left Arrow key, or the Page Down key; to move backward in a slide show, press the Right Arrow key or the Page Up key.

Print the Presentation

- To display options for printing the presentation, click the File tab, and then in the navigation bar, click Print.
- To select the type of printout, click the Full Page Slides button, and then click Full Page Slides, Notes Pages, Outline, or one of the options under Handouts.

Add Transitions

- To apply a transition, on the Transitions tab, in the Transition to This Slide group, click the transition you want to use.
- To apply a transition to all the slides, on the Transitions tab, in the Timing group, click the Apply to All button.

Animate Bulleted Lists

- Click the bulleted list, and then on the Animations tab, in the Animation group, click an animation.
- To animate subbullets with progressive disclosure, select the subbullets, and then on the Animations tab, in the Timing group, click the Start box arrow and click On Click.

Add Footers to Slides

- To add a footer to the slides, on the Insert tab, in the Text group, click the Header & Footer button.
- To remove the footer from the title slide, select the Don't show on title slide check box on the Slide tab in the Header and Footer dialog box.

Add Speaker Notes

- To add speaker notes, click in the Notes pane, and then type the note.

Key Definitions

Go to your CMPTR CourseMate site for a full list of key terms and definitions.

animation A special effect applied to an object that makes the object move or change.

bulleted item One paragraph in a bulleted list.

bulleted list A list of paragraphs with a special symbol to the left of each paragraph.

demote To move an item to a lower level in an outline.

handout A printout of the slides in a presentation.

layout A predetermined way of organizing the objects on a slide.

Microsoft PowerPoint 2010 (PowerPoint) A presentation graphics program used to create a collection of slides that can contain text, charts, pictures, sound, movies, multimedia, and so on.

placeholder A region of a slide reserved for inserting text or graphics.

presentation A file created in PowerPoint.

progressive disclosure An animation process in which bulleted items appear one at a time on a slide during a slide show.

promote To move an item to a higher level in an outline.

speaker notes Notes that appear in the Notes pane to remind the speaker of points to make when the particular slide appears during the slide show.

subbullet A sub paragraph in a bulleted list, positioned below and indented from a higher-level bullet.

text box A container that holds text.

transition A special effect that changes the way a slide appears on the screen in Slide Show or Reading view.

Learning Objectives

LO21.1	Work with slide masters
LO21.2	Insert graphics
LO21.3	Create SmartArt diagrams
LO21.4	Customize animations by changing options
LO21.5	Add video to a slide
LO21.6	Add sound to a presentation
LO21.7	Broadcast a presentation

Digital Backpack

Practice It: Practice It 21-3—Enhance a PowerPoint presentation using graphics, media, and animations.

On Your Own: On Your Own 21-2—Create a slide master and broadcast a PowerPoint presentation.

Quiz: Take the practice quiz to prepare for tests.

Key Terms: Review the key term flash cards (online, printable, and audio).

Games: Play *Beat the Clock* and *Memory* to quiz yourself.

Videos: Watch *Understanding Graphics, Add a Graphic from a File, Draw a Shape on a Slide, Formatting Objects, Format Drawings and Pictures on Slides, Creating a SmartArt Diagram* (concept and step-by-step), *Broadcasting a Presentation,* and *Broadcast a Slide Show.*

Infographic

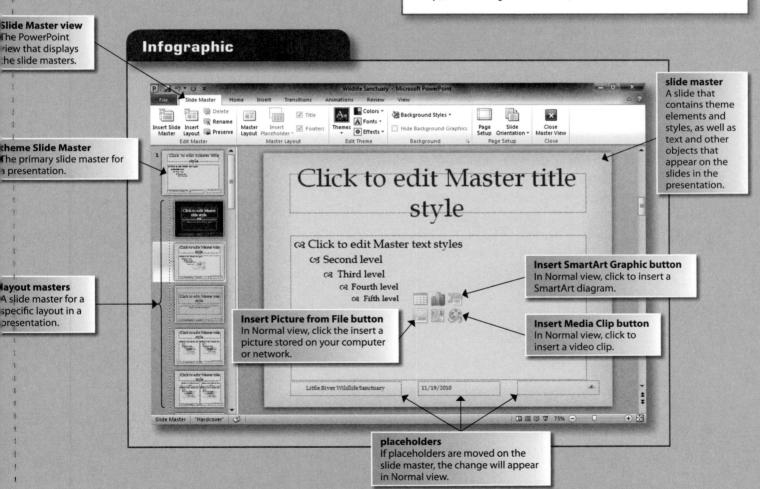

Slide Master view
The PowerPoint view that displays the slide masters.

theme Slide Master
The primary slide master for a presentation.

layout masters
A slide master for a specific layout in a presentation.

slide master
A slide that contains theme elements and styles, as well as text and other objects that appear on the slides in the presentation.

Insert SmartArt Graphic button
In Normal view, click to insert a SmartArt diagram.

Insert Picture from File button
In Normal view, click the insert a picture stored on your computer or network.

Insert Media Clip button
In Normal view, click to insert a video clip.

placeholders
If placeholders are moved on the slide master, the change will appear in Normal view.

Quick Reference Tools

Word with Slide Masters

- For each theme in a presentation, the slide master includes the theme Slide Master and a layout master for each layout.
- To modify the slide master, switch to Slide Master view.
- In Slide Master view, you can modify the placeholders, fonts, colors, and slide background, and you can insert and remove graphics.

Customize Animations

- The Effect Options button in the Animation group on the Animations tab allows you to customize animations by changing their direction or shape and by changing how objects composed of more than one single object appear.
- To change the speed of an animation, change the time in the Duration box in the Timing group on the Animations tab.

Insert Graphics and SmartArt Diagrams

- To insert a picture, use the Insert Picture from File button in a content placeholder or use the Picture button in the Illustrations group on the Insert tab.
- To insert a shape, use the Shapes button in the Illustrations group on the Insert tab.
- SmartArt can be created from scratch using the Insert SmartArt Graphic button in a content placeholder or the SmartArt button in the Illustrations group on the Home tab; or you can convert a bulleted list into a SmartArt diagram by clicking the Convert to SmartArt button in the Paragraph group on the Home tab.

Add Video and Sound to a Slide

- Insert a video by using the Insert Media Clip button in a content placeholder or by using the Video button in the Media group on the Insert tab.
- Insert audio by using the Audio button in the Media group on the Insert tab.
- Format the media clips by changing options such as changing the way a clip starts and its volume. You can also trim an audio or video clip, and set a poster frame for a video clip.

Broadcast a Presentation

- Use the Broadcast feature to deliver a presentation over the Internet.
- You can invite audience members to the broadcast by sending them the custom link to the presentation.

Key Definitions

Go to your CMPTR CourseMate site for a full list of key terms and definitions.

broadcast To send a presentation to a special Microsoft server so that other people can watch the slide show in real time using a browser.

diagram An illustration that visually depicts information or ideas and shows how they are connected.

handouts master A handout that contains the elements that appear on printed handouts.

layout master A slide master for a specific layout in a presentation.

notes master A note that contains the elements that appear on the notes pages.

poster frame (preview frame) In a video object, the image that appears before the video starts playing.

slide master A slide that contains theme elements and styles, as well as text and other objects that appear on the slides in the presentation.

Slide Master view The PowerPoint view that displays the slide masters.

SmartArt A diagram with a predesigned layout.

theme Slide Master The primary slide master for a presentation.

Visit **login.CengageBrain.com** for additional study tools!

Learning Objectives

LO22.1	Understand object linking and embedding (OLE)
LO22.2	Import and export data
LO22.3	Use the Object command to insert text from a file
LO22.4	Copy and paste among Office programs
LO22.5	Create PowerPoint slides from a Word outline
LO22.6	Create Form Letters with Mail Merge

Digital Backpack

Practice It: Practice It 22-3—Create an embedded Excel chart in a Word document and PowerPoint presentation and import Excel data into an Access table.

On Your Own: On Your Own 22-2—Use a Word outline to create a PowerPoint presentation and link Excel data to a slide.

Quiz: Take the practice quiz to prepare for tests.

Key Terms: Review the key term flash cards (online, printable, and audio).

Games: Play *Beat the Clock* and *Memory* to quiz yourself.

Videos: Watch *Create an Embedded Excel Chart in a Word Document, Object Linking and Embedding, Link Excel Worksheet Data to a PowerPoint Slide, Update Linked Objects, Edit the Linked Object When the Destination Files are Closed, Using Excel Data in Access, Import an Excel List to a Table in a New Database, Linking an Excel Chart to a PowerPoint Presentation,* and *Select the Main Document and Data Source for the Mail Merge.*

Infographic

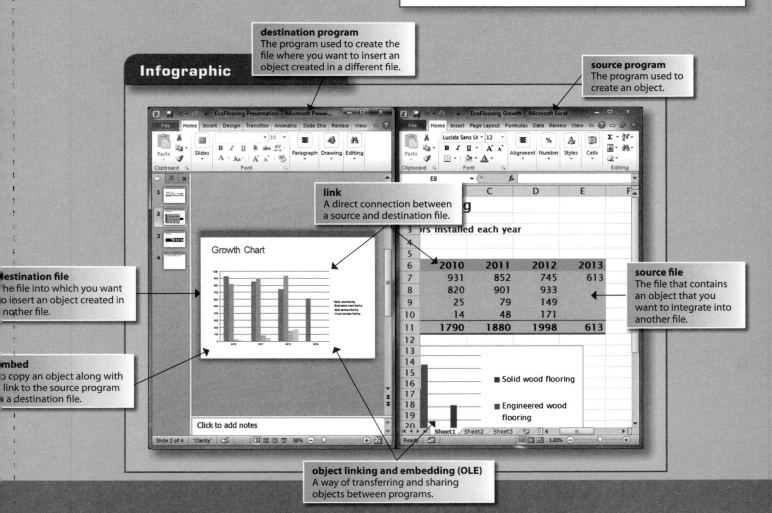

destination program
The program used to create the file where you want to insert an object created in a different file.

source program
The program used to create an object.

link
A direct connection between a source and destination file.

destination file
The file into which you want to insert an object created in another file.

source file
The file that contains an object that you want to integrate into another file.

embed
To copy an object along with a link to the source program in a destination file.

object linking and embedding (OLE)
A way of transferring and sharing objects between programs.

Quick Reference Tools

Object Linking and Embedding

- The program used to create the object you want to integrate into another file is the source program and the file that contains the object is the source file.
- The program used to create the file where you want to insert the object is the destination program and the file in which you will insert the object is the destination file.
- To embed an object means to paste it along with a link to the source program.
- To link an object means to create a connection between the source and destination file.

Import to and Export from Access

- You can import data into an Access table from another program as long as the data is in the form of a list.
- You can export data from an Access table to an Excel file, a Rich Text file, or a plain text file, and others.

Insert Objects

- Use the Object command to insert the contents of one file into another file.

Create PowerPoint Slides from a Word Outline

- When you create a PowerPoint presentation from a Word outline, paragraphs formatted with the Heading 1 style become slide titles, paragraphs formatted with the Heading 2 style become first-level bullets, and so on.
- Slides created from a Word outline are inserted after the current slide.
- You might need to reset slides created from a Word outline to apply the theme and slide master formatting correctly.

Create Form Letters with Mail Merge

- Use mail merge to merge data from a data source with a letter to create personalized form letters.
- If the column labels in the data source don't match the Word field names, you can use the Match Fields command to manually match the fields.
- Preview the merge before printing to make sure the correct data is inserted and that paragraph spacing is correct.

Copy and Paste Between Programs

- Use the Copy and Paste commands to copy an object from one file to another. Use the Office Clipboard.

Key Definitions

Go to your CMPTR CourseMate site for a full list of key terms and definitions.

data source A file that contains the variable information for form letters.

destination file The file into which you want to insert an object created in another file.

destination program The program used to create the file where you want to insert an object created in a different file.

embed To copy an object along with a link to the source program in a destination file.

form letter A Word document that contains standard paragraphs of text and a minimum of variable text.

link To establish a direct connection between a source and destination file.

mail merge To merge a main document with a list of addresses from a data source.

main document A document that contains the text and other information that you want to keep the same in each form letter.

merge field A field that contains instructions to be replaced with the variable information that changes from one letter to another.

merge To combine a main document with a data source.

object linking and embedding (OLE) A way of transferring and sharing objects between programs.

Rich Text Format (RTF) A text format that preserves the formatting and layout of data.

source file The file that contains an object that you want to integrate into another file.

source program The program used to create an object.

starting document The main document in a Word mail merge.

reviewcard

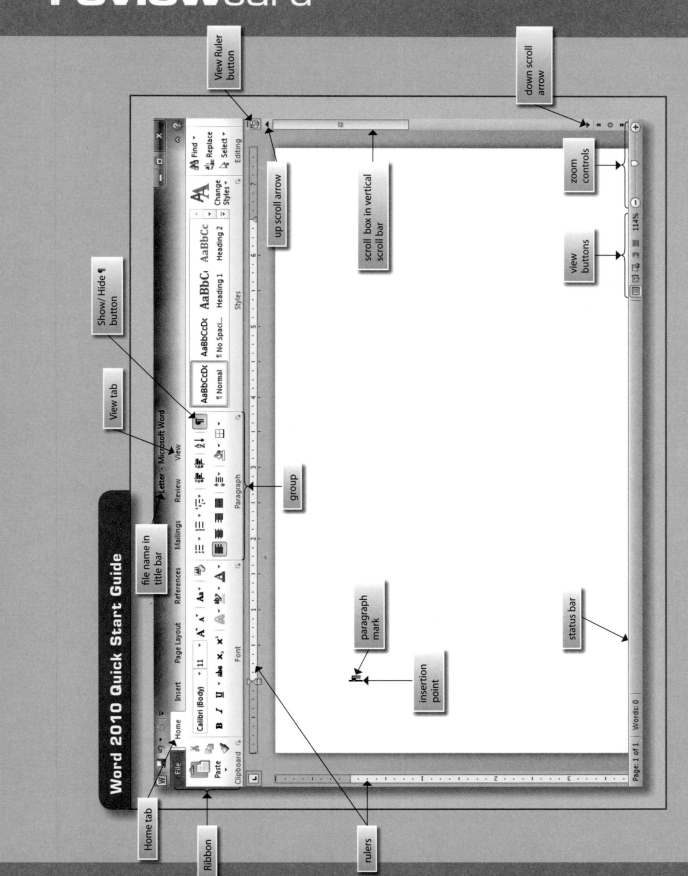

View Ruler button

down scroll arrow

up scroll arrow

scroll box in vertical scroll bar

zoom controls

view buttons

Show/Hide ¶ button

View tab

file name in title bar

group

paragraph mark

status bar

insertion point

Word 2010 Quick Start Guide

Home tab

Ribbon

rulers

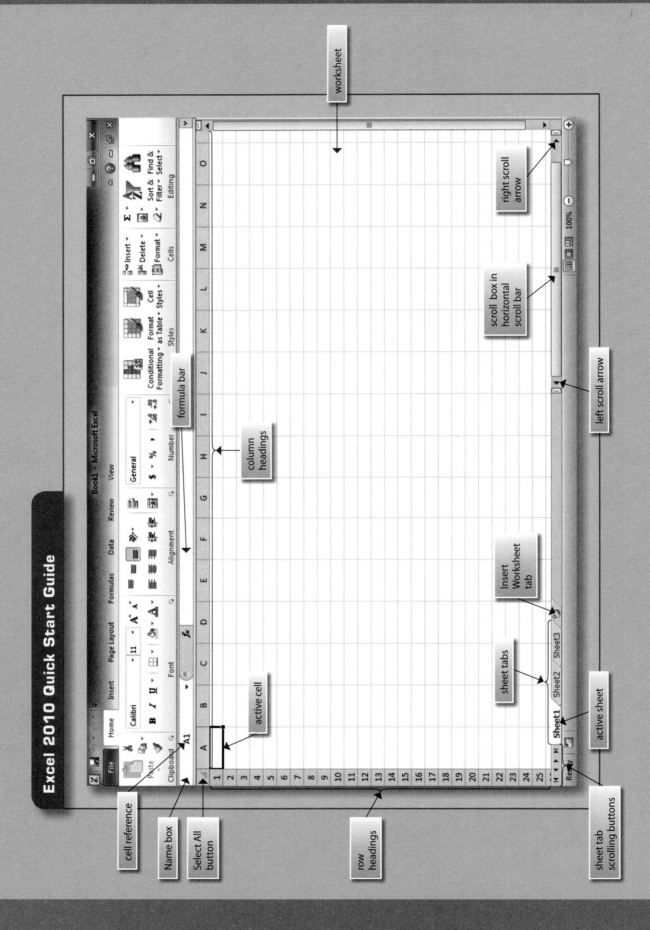

Excel 2010 Quick Start Guide

Book1 - Microsoft Excel

worksheet

right scroll arrow

scroll box in horizontal scroll bar

left scroll arrow

formula bar

column headings

Insert Worksheet tab

sheet tabs

active sheet

sheet tab scrolling buttons

row headings

cell reference

Name box

Select All button

active cell

reviewcard

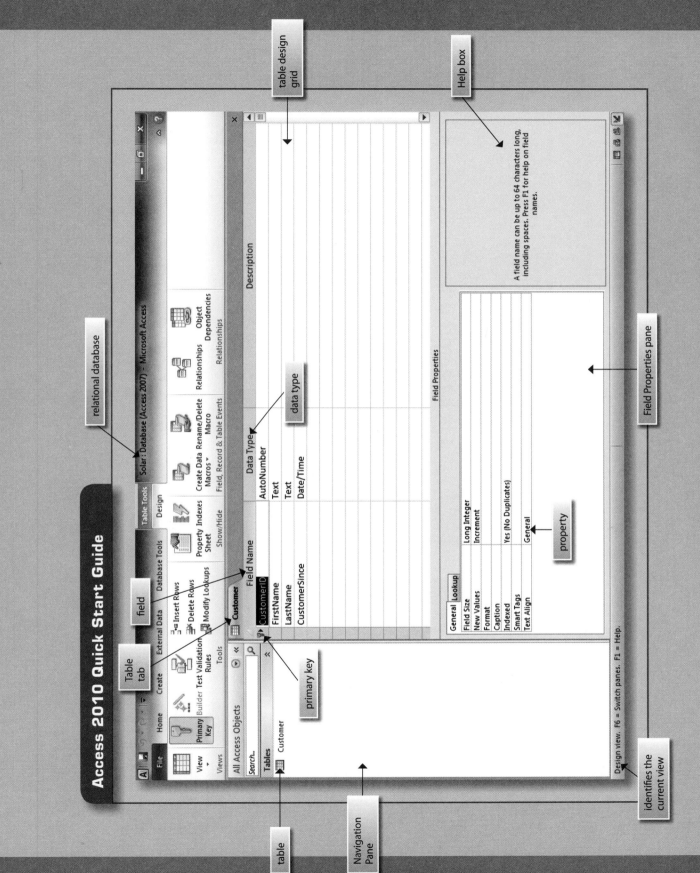

Access 2010 Quick Start Guide

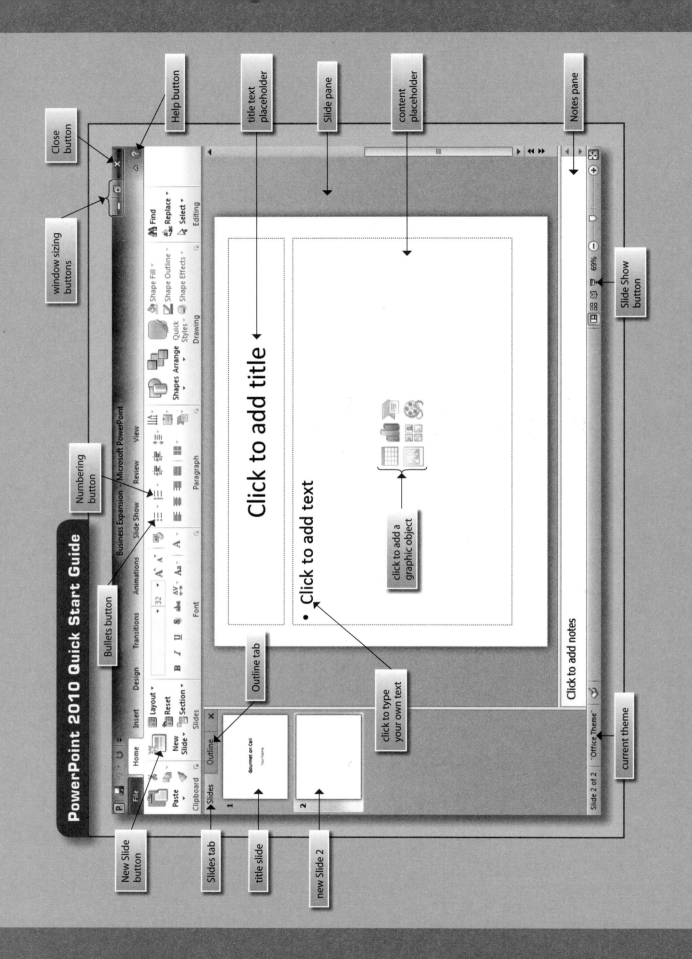

PowerPoint 2010 Quick Start Guide